D1546809

FABERGÉ

A CATALOG OF THE LILLIAN THOMAS PRATT COLLECTION OF RUSSIAN IMPERIAL JEWELS

by Parker Lesley

VIRGINIA MUSEUM/RICHMOND, VIRGINIA

Library of Congress Cataloging in Publication Data
Lesley, Parker.
Fabergé: a catalog of the Lillian Thomas Pratt Collection of Russian imperial jewels.
Published in 1960 under title: Handbook of the Lillian Thomas Pratt Collection.
1. Faberzhe, Karl Gustavovich, 1846-1920.
2. Crown jewels—Russia—Catalogs. 3. Pratt, Lillian Thomas—Art collections. I. Virginia Museum of Fine Arts, Richmond.
NK7417.F3L47 1976 739.2'092'4 76-16557
ISBN 0-917046-00-5

Printed in the United States of America

Since 1960, when the original version was published, this catalog has been the consistent bestseller on the Museum's book listings. In the *Handbook of the Lillian Thomas Pratt Collection, Russian Imperial Jewels,* Parker Lesley not only documented one of the most extraordinary collections of Fabergé in the world, but also provided a valuable introduction to a man, his style, and his period. And he did so with remarkable expressiveness. As my predecessor, Leslie Cheek, Jr., wrote in the original foreword, Mr. Lesley "has presented his great knowledge in a manner as eloquent, rich, and highly styled as the jewels themselves."

At the time of the original printing, however, it was possible to reproduce only a small portion of the works themselves, and these in black-and-white illustrations. Now, through the great generosity of a friend of the Museum, who expressed his wish to remain anonymous, a new publication is made possible, one that depicts every object in the catalog. Moreover, each of these illustrations is in color, which, suffice it to say, greatly enhances the book's usefulness to scholars and students, as well as to the devotee to whom the work of Peter Carl Fabergé is something very special.

I would like to offer several acknowledgments involving the publication of the 1976 version. Pinkney Near, Curator, George Cruger, Publications Director, and Monica Hamm, Editorial Assistant, collaborated on the review of the original manuscript and general editorial production. In charge of evolving the total visual character of the new book was the Museum's own Graphic Designer, Raymond Geary, who has produced a rich and tasteful publication that is most befitting to both the subject and the text. Chief photographer Ronald Jennings and photographers Katherine Wetzel and Dennis McWaters were responsible for producing the illustrations, fine technical achievements which clearly demonstrate the brilliance of Fabergé's art.

Finally, once again I would like to express the Museum's thanks and appreciation to Parker Lesley, whose text is as readable, informative, and instructive today as it was sixteen years ago.

JAMES M. BROWN, Director
March, 1976

In preparing the text of this handbook the author has, of course, been to a major extent dependent upon the two biographies of Fabergé, H.C. Bainbridge's *Peter Carl Fabergé*, London, 1949, and A. Kenneth Snowman's *The Art of Carl Fabergé*, London, 1953. Supplementary historical information was gathered with the guidance of the staff of the Russian Section of the New York Public Library and the staff of the New York Society Library. To Mr. and Mrs. Alexander Schaffer and Mr. Léon Grinberg, thanks are due for innumerable kindnesses and critical help; and to Mr. Armand Hammer and the personnel of the Hammer Galleries for technical assistance.

Dr. Zuhair E. Jwaideh of the Library of Congress was kind enough to identify the quotation from the Koran on check list No. 292, and Dr. George S. Switzer of the Department of Geology, The Smithsonian Institution, identified many of the minerals and semi-precious stones. The check list was prepared with the indefatigable cooperation of Miss Ellen Johnston. The entire staff of the Virginia Museum, and especially the Director, Mr. Leslie Cheek, Jr., and Associate Director, Mrs. Muriel B. Christison, gave unstinted support. *P.L., 1960.*

Scope of the Collection

The collection of Russian *objets d'art* formed between 1933 and 1946 by Lillian Thomas Pratt comprises what is, numerically, one of the three or four largest collections outside Russia of works from the atelier of the court jeweler and goldsmith Peter Carl Fabergé, as well as other masters.

Mrs. Pratt had made some tentative excursions into the collection of English and American furniture, 18th-century silver, laces, needlepoints, and modern silver, glass, and jewelry, customary interests, indeed, for one of her position and background. There must have been in her character an extreme sensitivity to craftsmanship, especially to precious materials cunningly wrought.

The collection falls into eight categories: (1) carvings of animals; (2) Easter eggs, both the imperial presentation type and many miniatures; (3) flowers; (4) picture frames, largely with photographs of the imperial family; (5) handles for parasols and umbrellas; (6) icons; (7) jewelry; and (8) miscellaneous objects—cigarette cases, seals, snuff boxes, and so forth. These correspond, in the main, to the principal output of the Fabergé workshop, so that the collection, aside from being extraordinarily intimate, is also extraordinarily representative.

In 1947, Mrs. Pratt willed the entirety to the Virginia Museum. The Lillian Thomas Pratt Collection memorializes not only the artistic forces at work in an exceptional person, but a period of craftsmanship and an imperial culture which are now a part of history.

Peter Carl Fabergé and His Atelier

The antecedents of Peter Carl Fabergé were French Huguenots who, on the Revocation of the Edict of Nantes in 1685, left Picardy and next emerged in Pernau on the Gulf of Riga, in Russian-governed Livonia. Here, on February 20, 1814, there was born to Peter, the grandfather of Peter Carl Fabergé, a son, Gustav.

PETER CARL FABERGÉ

Gustav married the daughter of Carl Jungstedt, a painter of Scandinavian origin, and came to St. Petersburg, where he was apprenticed to Andreas Ferdinand Spiegel. In 1842 he opened his own goldsmith's and jeweler's shop in a small basement on Morskaya Street, and on May 30, 1846, his son Peter Carl was born and baptized in the Protestant Church.

Gustav Fabergé continued his business in the basement shop until 1860, when he left Russia for Dresden, turning over management to a Russian, Zainontchkovsky. Peter Carl was educated in the Gymnasium Svetaya Anna, in the Handelschule at Dresden, and served an apprenticeship with the goldsmith Friedmann in Frankfurt. He traveled in Italy, spent some months in England learning the language, and finally ended his Grand Tour in Paris during the last years of the Second Empire. Returning to St. Petersburg, he took control of the shop in 1870, at the age of twenty-four.

Peter Carl Fabergé's career spanned the reigns of three Czars: Alexander II, Alexander III, and Nicholas II. Alexander II reigned from 1855 to 1881. He married the daughter of Grand Duke Louis II of Hesse in 1841, who, upon their coronation, was known as the Czarina Maria Alexandrovna.

Alexander III reigned from 1881 to 1894. His consort was the Czarina Marie Feodorovna, the daughter of King Christian IX of Denmark. Her sister was Queen Alexandra, wife of King Edward VII of England.

Nicholas II reigned from 1894 to 1917. He married a granddaughter of Queen Victoria, the Princess Alix of Hesse. She became the Czarina Alexandra Feodorovna. They had five children, the Grand Duchess Olga, Tatiana, Marie, and Anastasia, and the Czarevitch Alexis.

COURT PATRONAGE

No art can sustain itself without patronage, and the decorative arts have always seemed to flourish most auspiciously when furnished for a court. The institution of a court, with its monarch, ranks of nobles, ministers, and functionaries, with its palaces, villas, its protocol and ceremonies, provides not only the requisite concentration of wealth, but a uniformity of demand and style as well.

The last years of Czarist Russia provided the setting that fostered and supported Fabergé's art. Religious feast days, birthdays, and saint's days of the Czar, the Czarina, and the Czarevitch were occasions for the presentation of gifts and tokens. Christenings, anniversaries, engagements and marriages called for more presents: snuff boxes, cigarette cases, fancy paperweights, clocks, card cases, caskets, music boxes, and extravagant knick-knacks of all description.

After Alexander III came to the throne, the house of Fabergé was appointed goldsmiths and jewelers to the imperial court, about 1884. In contrast to the English royal warrant, which is issued by the Lord Chamberlain and may be awarded to anyone, a Russian court appointment was a very different and more personal article.

Besides being a bestowal of favor, it was actually an undertaking on the part of the Czar to promote and protect the welfare of the recipient. It carried with it an annual commission, by which there was to be purveyed to the Czar's person one object a year, with no restrictions as to subject or price, irrespective of any other commissions that might be granted. In the case of both Alexander III and Nicholas II, these annual consignments were the Easter eggs, which are dealt with in a separate section of this book.

The fame and size of the house of Fabergé had been growing rapidly even before imperial patronage. In 1882, the gold medal at the Pan-Russian Exhibition at Moscow was awarded the house, which exhibited for the first time the *objets d'art,* rather than jewelry, for which it was to become famed. The public reaction was so favorable that henceforth Fabergé's regime was settled.

At Nuremberg, in 1885, another gold medal was awarded for reproductions of Greek jewelry from Kertch, the ancient Panticapaeum, in the Crimea, collected in the Hermitage. Still another gold medal was conferred by the Pan-Russian Exhibition at Nizhni-Novgorod in 1896.

In 1900, at the *Exposition Internationale Universelle* in Paris, Fabergé achieved a momentous international success. It was necessary for him to exhibit *hors de concours,* for his eldest son Eugène was a member of the jury. The Empress Alexandra Feodorovna and the Dowager Empress Marie Feodorovna lent their Easter eggs; Fabergé was made a Chevalier of the Legion of Honor, Eugène became an Officer of the Academy, and various workmasters received special gold and silver medals.

ST. PETERSBURG HEADQUARTERS

The original basement shop had been closed and a new one opened on the opposite side of the street. In 1890 this was enlarged to twice its size, but the popularity of the firm's products compelled still further enlargement, and in 1898 a whole building of four stories was purchased, number 24 Morskaya, which was to remain the headquarters of the firm until the Revolution.

No show windows, no displays of any kind told the pedestrian that here was the most select firm of its kind in Europe. Two plaques on either side of the main entrance, one in Latin capitals and one in Russian, set forth a single word, FABERGÉ. A uniformed doorman stood between the inner and outer doors; it was he who escorted the clients from their sleighs and carriages to the showroom on the ground floor. The right side of the showroom was devoted to jewelry, the left to "fantasies": automata, miniature furniture, flowers, figurines. The atmosphere was urbane and ingratiating, with no hint of servility or strenuous salesmanship. Most of the wares were kept in their boxes, which were made of holly wood, lined with satin, and covered with morocco leather. The jewels emerged only at the request of the customer, to be turned slowly and daintily under the light. Of loud showmanship, of flaunting temptation there were none. The shop of Fabergé was as reticent, as sedate, as outwardly placid as a great London tailor's.

BRANCHES OF THE FIRM

The firm became so successful that branches were opened forthwith. The first was established in Moscow in 1887, in partnership with an Englishman, Allan Bowe, who had as his assistants his two brothers, Arthur and Charles. This section of the firm concentrated on silver work of all kinds, including table silver and the elaborate garnitures without which no aristocratic dining table was complete.

The Odessa branch, founded in 1890, was managed by two Englishmen from Moscow, Allan Gibson and George Piggott, among other people. In 1905 a third branch opened in Kiev, but it was closed down in 1910 in order to consolidate all the provincial South Russian business in Odessa. This city, being so near the Crimea and in size the fourth city of the empire, would naturally claim the patronage of not only the aristocrats in their holiday milieu, but also the merchants and wealthy commercial figures of the port.

Lastly, a full-fledged branch of the firm was set up in London in 1906, three years after Arthur Bowe had been sent there with a selection of wares. The London house, under the joint management of Nicholas Fabergé, the fourth son, and H.C. Bainbridge, continued business until shortly after the outbreak of the First World War.

For the house of Fabergé, especially between the years 1906 and 1910, during the reign of Edward VII, London was a commercial portal to a second storehouse of fabulous riches. From here were sent forth emissaries to the Maharajas of India; to the Kingdom of Siam, to which Fabergé was invited in 1904; to China, Egypt and Persia. This connection effected a fresh development in Fabergé's style and products, a basically Edwardian fashion.

ORGANIZATION OF THE WORKSHOP

The decorative arts, such as Fabergé created —although one man could carry through all their operations to the end—were usually fabricated in a workshop, where specialized contributions could be made by assorted skills. The workshop mixed its components, had them constantly adjacent to each other, and brought about its final product through the interplay of the company's total energies. There were designers, master craftsmen, journeymen, apprentices, and adepts at various media and their treatments. Out of their collective discipline emerged the finished article—often impersonal when compared to a work of the fine arts, but closer to the public, to national inclinations, and to the artistic idioms of the times.

At the top of the hierarchy was Peter Carl Fabergé himself, who worked in a kind of relaxed partnership with his younger brother Agathon, and confined himself entirely to designing. All four of Peter Carl's sons were executive assistants in various capacities.

Eugène (1874-1960), the eldest, was occupied as a designer of first drafts and initial ideas in conjunction with his father. Agathon (1876-1951), the second son, was by training a craftsman; until 1917 he was in charge of the imperial regalia and crown jewels. Alexander (1878-1952), the third son, was also a designer, and manager of the Moscow branch; from 1921 until his death he was associated with Eugène in Paris as a goldsmith and restorer of Fabergé pieces. Nicholas (1884-1939), the fourth son, was joint manager, with H.C. Bainbridge, of the London branch.

Immediately under this family group came the professional designers. Of these perhaps the most important was François Birbaum, a Swiss, chief designer of the finest objects. To him was entrusted the delicate task of refining, improving, and materializing Peter Carl's sometimes meagre outlines. Save for the head of the house, no one possessed more authority than Birbaum in ordaining the ultimate shape, color, and substance of an article. The next category was that of the "workmasters," or senior artisans, in charge of their own workshops.

SENIOR ARTISANS

These men had passed through all gradations of proficiency and were capable of working in and controlling any medium. For "objects of fantasy," the most prominent were: Erik August Kollin (1836-1901), a Swedish Finn, who worked largely in gold; Michael Perchin (1860-1903), who made all the imperial Easter eggs from 1886 to 1903; and Henrik Wigström (1862-ca. 1930), another Swedish Finn, who succeeded Perchin and made the later imperial Easter eggs. August Hollming (1854-1915) was a Finnish specialist in gold and jewelry.

For jewelry proper, there were: August Holmström (1857-1903), who also made Easter eggs, and Alfred Thielemann, a German born in St. Petersburg who specialized in brooches and pendants. In St. Petersburg the principal enamellers were Alexander Petroff and his son, Nicholas, and W. Boitzoff. In Moscow the silver department of the house was managed by Michel Tchepournoff. There were also goldsmiths, designers, and modellers at Moscow and Kiev; the London branch had one designer, R.A. Pinks, an Irishman, and two modellers, Frank Lutiger, a Swiss, and Alfred Pocock, an Englishman.

Each senior workmaster, such as Kollin, Perchin, Wigström, Hollming and Holmström, had his own largely autonomous workshop in which the object assigned was carried to completion. Within limits, all operations were performed in these independent sections.

Where enamelling was called for, one of the chief enamellers was sent for to perform his work under the direction of the workmaster concerned. Underneath the workmasters proper were the minor artisans and apprentices, with the organization ending with the *artellchik,* whose duty it was to polish the floors.

In the establishment at 24 Morskaya after 1900, Hollming's workshop occupied the first floor, Perchin's (later Wigström's) the second, Holmström's the third, and Thielemann's the top. Thus there was, rather than a single plant constantly under the supervision of one man, a federation of largely self-governing shops over which, it might almost be said, Fabergé himself reigned but did not rule.

SYSTEM OF OPERATION

Prior to starting on any important new piece, a round-table discussion (literally, there was a large round table in Fabergé's office) between the designer and all the specialists who might be affected was called. The designer made known his particular ideas and the general way in which he thought they should be carried out. The enamellers, goldsmiths, gilders, and lapidaries would then draw up schedules of the steps to be taken, and investigate in just what order they should be accomplished.

Especially trying would be the order in which the object would be subject to various degrees of heat for soldering, enamelling, and gilding. No precious stones can be subjected to intense heat for long without grave risks (the diamond, for example, burns in oxygen or air at about 850 degrees; emeralds will lose their color). Each specialist could plan to finish his work with due regard for the requirements of the others, to avoid any possibility of revision, retracing omitted steps, or conflict.

It is told that in his office on the ground floor of 24 Morskaya Street Peter Carl Fabergé kept on his desk a sheet of rolled steel. When a finished piece was brought to him, the workmaster placed it there. From all sides, it was examined. If one flaw caught the master's eye, a hammer rose and fell. There was no parley, no revision. The offending thing was smashed.

The tercentenary of the Romanoff dynasty (1913) brought about the zenith of a patriotic Russian style, which may be accurately termed "Muscovite chauvinisic," but it was in demand several decades before the anniversary. It was an expression of the political and literary ideas of the 19th-century Slavophils and the mystical, nationalistic symbolists, and of the exploitation of "Old Russian" sources.

Peter Carl Fabergé had developed, from various stylistic sources and an intrinsic taste, a personal yet official style ideally suited to his patrons. He was, above all things, a businessman, who was quite willing to adapt his wares to, if not compromise with, the inclinations of his clients and the usages of the Russian court.

FABERGÉ'S STYLE

The Age of Diamonds had passed. Dazzling though they were, they had become commonplace. Fabergé, instead, used native stones and materials, often themselves not especially precious but transfigured by unsurpassable craftsmanship. From the Urals came sapphires, emeralds, beryls, chrysoberyls, tourmalines, aquamarines, topazes, amethysts, rock crystals, garnets, malachites, and many kinds of jade. From Siberia came nephrite, rhodonite, carnelian. From the Caucasus came turquoise, lapis lazuli, and porphyry. These he worked and combined with an elegance that took captive every nature.

It is evident that this style was voluntarily absorbed by his craftsmen—Finns, Swedes, Russians, Germans, and Frenchmen alike—as soon as they became subject to his individuality. He represents, in this respect, a rare example of "benevolent paternalism" at work in a field where pride of authorship among his subordinates was certainly intense, but where each was willing, nonetheless, to play a secondary role because of the humanity and talent of the master.

END OF THE FABERGÉ REGIME

When Nicholas II abdicated in 1917, the house of Fabergé continued under the Provisional Government until September, 1918, when, on being closed down by the Bolsheviks, Peter Carl escaped to Riga, then Berlin, Frankfurt, Hamburg, and Wiesbaden. Madame Fabergé left St. Petersburg with Eugène in December, 1918, finally residing in Lausanne. Eugène, after sojourning in Stockholm, settled in Paris. Peter Carl, ill and seventy-four, went to Lausanne in June, 1920, and died there on September 24. Madame Fabergé died in Cannes on January 27, 1925; her husband's ashes were brought from Lausanne by Eugène in 1930 and were buried under a stone of black Swedish porphyry bearing the inscription: "Charles Fabergé, joaillier de la Cour de Russie."

Objects in the Collection

The catalog has been compiled to furnish all necessary data on each object in the Pratt Collection. Included are all items usually on display, plus the remaining works by Fabergé and other court jewelers. Some miscellaneous objects in the Collection—which are neither Russian, nor "imperial," nor within the provinces of the goldsmith or the decorative arts—have been omitted. In order to circumvent a typographical problem, Russian hallmarks have been transliterated. The catalog is arranged in the same categories dealt with in the text. Measurements are in inches.

Animals

Catalog entry 22.

By the time of the appearance of the house of Fabergé upon the scene of the decorative arts, two wide and originally separate currents of interest converged to create a social demand for animal figurines: on one hand, the desire for costly mementoes of aristocratic pursuits and, on the other, for naturalistic renderings of scientifically observed and classified fact.

Adaptations of Russian peasant carvings and toys *(khozyaistva)* and what were known as "Chinese trifles" *(Kitaiskaya meloch)*, inspired by statuettes from the Popov porcelain factory, were standard articles of the firm. But it was the English royal intervention that really sharpened the taste of society for animal figurines.

In 1907, the English King's horse, Persimmon, had won the Derby by a neck from Leopold Rothschild's Saint Frusquin. The King desired a portrait figurine of his winner. Persimmon, Caesar, his favorite terrier, and several of the Queen's dogs were to be done; in addition, "the whole farmyard"—cows, bullocks, geese, turkeys, hens, cocks, draft horses, and the comeliest pigs. A staff of modellers, including Boris Froedman-Cluzel and Frank Lutiger, set to work. On December 8, 1907, the finished waxes were put on view.

A craze was loosed. Everybody who was anybody must have Fabergé models of his pets. How many of these figurines were turned out before the dissolution of the firm will doubtless remain forever uncomputed. There must have been thousands. They are very seldom marked. The principal lapidaries, Kremlev, Derbyshev and Svetchnikov, were not workmasters in the strict sense. Their products were issued by the firm as a whole; hence, when a mark does occur, it is usually in the form of an engraved signature.

The rock-crystal goose (No. 29) bears "C. Fabergé" on the bottom of its left foot. This signature, because of its indifferent technique, may well be a forgery added to a genuine piece. Being for the most part unsigned and unstamped, the genuine Fabergé figurine can be distinguished from a spurious one only by making a careful appraisal of its technique and character. A stance, a look, the extraction from the stone of a typical yet peculiar pose—the tilt of a wing, the cock of an ear—may be subjective evidence of authenticity. The special attribute of Fabergé's animal figurines is not so much their execution as it is that mysterious yet appreciable quality which can only be called "charm."

This charm is disclosed most suggestively by the eyes. The basic stone is chosen either for its conformity to the model, such as white marble for a polar bear or a nacreous obsidian for an owl, or for its fantasy, as in a chalcedony hummingbird. In each case, however, the eyes are of contrasting, and not necessarily naturalistic, stones: a bear's are emerald, an owl's are of diamonds and cat's-eyes, a hummingbird's are of diamonds. The tiny, faceted stones gleam as if with intelligence, and light up an otherwise lifeless lump with almost rational spirit.

To be fully aware of these pieces one must appreciate three things: the variety of material, the use of the material, and the particular character of each item. They vary in size from diminutive pendants to life-size figures. Where the animals and birds serve the purpose of jewelry, semi-precious stones (chalcedony, opal, amethyst) or precious metals (gold) are preferred. Where they are free-standing objects they may be of a stone which almost duplicates the natural coat, such as an obsidian bulldog, a crouching cat of banded alabaster, or a dachshund of Ural agate. Or, as if to be as unnaturalistic and exotic as possible they may be of something quite the opposite, as in a lapis-lazuli pig, an amethyst rabbit, or a hornbill of smoky quartz. Some of these stones are, of course, more difficult to carve than others. Contrary to expectation, from the lapidary's point of view the hardest will cause the least trouble.

The "personality" of the piece, since the animal cannot talk or make for itself an informative environment, depends upon postures and activities caught by a meticulous and impressionable eye. Under the furry coat or the feathers lie a musculature and skeletal structure that impart the questioning perplexity of a bull pup or the helpless fragility of a chick. There is nothing symbolic about these little creatures. They are neither generalized nor emblematic. Instead, they are literal enough to win over the most critical zoologist, and engaging enough to satisfy the fussiest or handsomest of Edwardian hostesses.

5

6

8

9

BEASTS

1. Bear on trapeze, pendant.
   Chalcedony. Silver trapeze with ruby ends suspended from silver diamond-set link. Green stone eyes.
   1 high by 1/2 wide
   Marks: *P.* (?) *L.*
   Acc. No. 47-20-129

2. Polar bear, pendant.
   Gold. Standing on pearl, gold ring in back. Suspended from gold ring.
   5/8 high by 5/8 wide
   Marks: illegible
   Acc. No. 47-20-132

3. Bear, pendant.
   Opal, ruby eyes, suspended from gold ring.
   1/2 high by 3/4 long
   Marks: none
   Acc. No. 47-20-133

4. Bear, pendant.
   Amethyst, ruby eyes. Suspended from gold ring.
   1 1/8 high by 1/2 wide
   Marks: *56.*
   Acc. No. 47-20-134

5. Polar bear.
   Marble. Faceted emerald eyes.
   2 3/4 high by 1 3/4 wide by 5 3/4 long
   Marks: none
   Acc. No. 47-20-239

6. Bloodhound.
   Carnelian. Faceted diamond eyes.
   2 1/2 high by 1 wide by 2 3/4 long
   Marks: *C.F.*
   Acc. No. 47-20-240

7. Bulldog, pendant.
   Gold and silver. Set with diamonds, ruby eyes. Gold ring.
   1/2 high by 1 long
   Marks: none
   Acc. No. 47-20-131

8. Bulldog.
   Smoky quartz. Cabochon sapphire eyes. Faceted sapphire collar with sapphire pendant.
   3 1/8 high by 1 1/2 wide by 2 long
   Marks: none
   Acc. No. 47-20-241

9. Bulldog.
   Citrine quartz. Cabochon sapphire eyes. Gold collar with sapphire pendant.
   1 5/8 high by 1 1/4 wide by 2 3/4 long
   Marks: none
   Acc. No. 47-20-242

Catalog entries 1-4, 7 are illustrated on page 136 with entry 284.

10

11

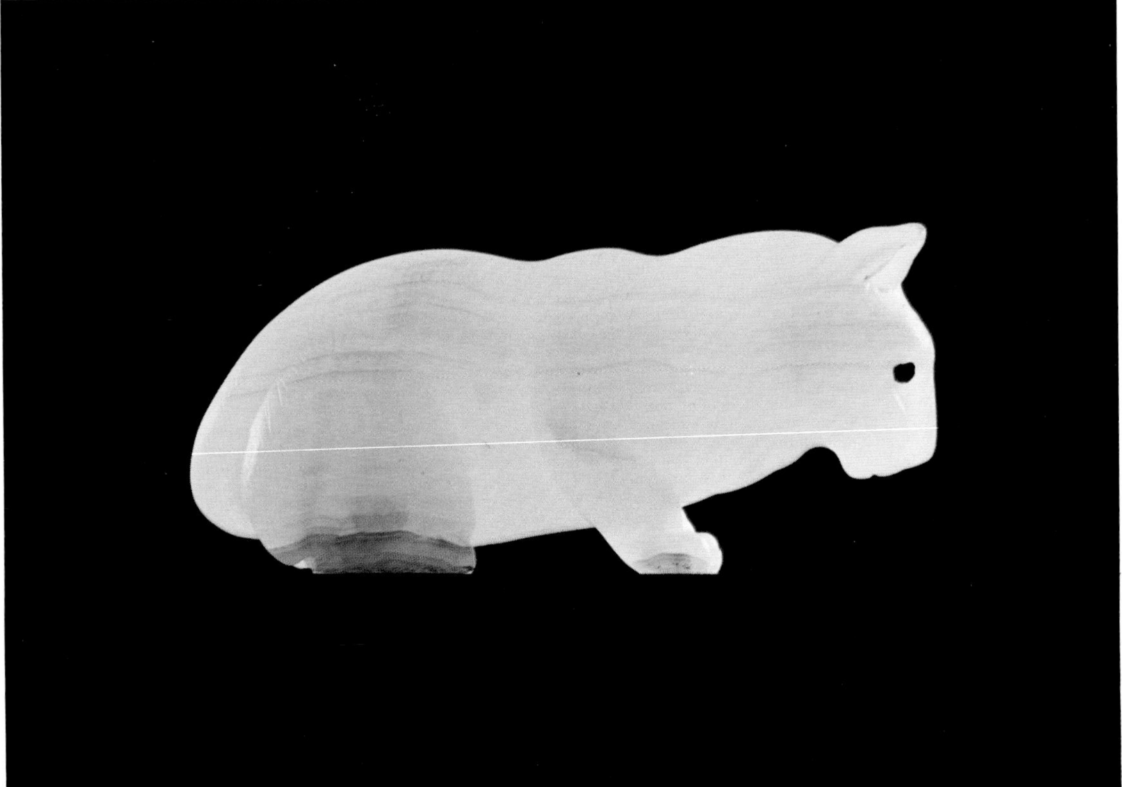
12

13

14

10. Bulldog.
Smoky quartz. Faceted ruby eyes. Gold collar with pearl pendant.
1⅝ high by ¾ wide by 1¼ long
Marks: none
Acc. No. 47-20-243

11. Bulldog.
Obsidian. Faceted diamond eyes. Gold and white enamel collar with bell.
2 high by ¾ wide by 3 long
Marks: *H.W./56*/illegible
Acc. No. 47-20-246

12. Cat.
Banded alabaster. Faceted sapphire eyes.
1¾ high by 1½ wide by 4 long
Marks: none
Acc. No. 47-20-247

13. Dachshund.
Ural agate. Diamond eyes.
2 high by 1⅛ wide by 2½ long
Marks: none
Acc. No. 47-20-244

14. Dachshund.
Carnelian. Cabochon ruby eyes.
1¼ high by ¾ wide by 3 long
Marks: none
Acc. No. 47-20-245

15. Elephant.
Silver.
1½ high by 1 wide by 2 long
Marks: *K.F./84*
Acc. No. 47-20-248

16. Elephant.
Gold.
1½ high by 1 wide by 2 long
Marks: none
Acc. No. 47-20-249

17. Elephant.
Gold. Diamond eyes, ivory tusks.
¾ high by 9/16 wide by 1⅜ long
Marks: none
Acc. No. 47-20-250

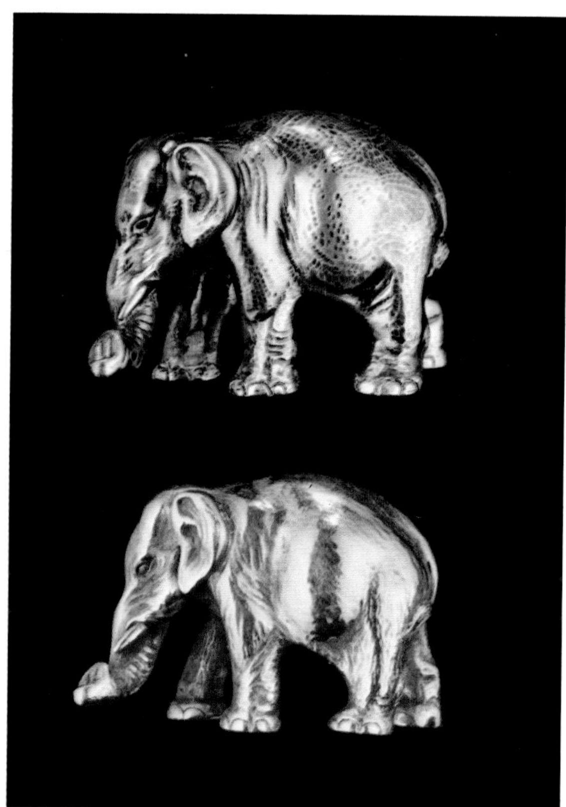
15, 16

17

18

21

18. Elephant.
    Nephrite. Diamond eyes.
    3 high by 2 wide by 3½ long
    Marks: none
    Acc. No. 47-20-251

19. Pig.
    Lapis lazuli. Diamond eyes.
    1½ high by 1 wide by 3⅛ long
    Marks: none
    Acc. No. 47-20-252

20. Rabbit, pendant.
    Amethyst. Seated on gold ovate loop suspended from small gold loop. Emerald eyes, gold collar with emerald pendant.
    1 high by ⅝ wide
    Marks: *K.F.*/anchors and sceptre/*56*
    Acc. No. 47-20-136

21. Rabbit.
    Silver. Garnet eyes which act as buttons for making electric contact when pressed.
    5¼ high by 2½ wide by 3¾ long
    Marks: *K. Fabergé*/double eagle/profile/*88*/*21240*
    Acc. No. 47-20-213

22. Rabbit, pitcher.
    Silver. Ruby eyes. Head hinged at back of neck, gilded interior.
    10 high by 4¾ wide by 6 long
    Marks: *K. Fabergé*/*LO*/double eagle/St. George and dragon/*1894*/*4639*/illegible.
    Acc. No. 47-20-214

23. Rabbit.
    Serpentine. Ruby eyes.
    1⅛ high by 1 wide by 1¾ long
    Marks: none
    Acc. No. 47-20-253

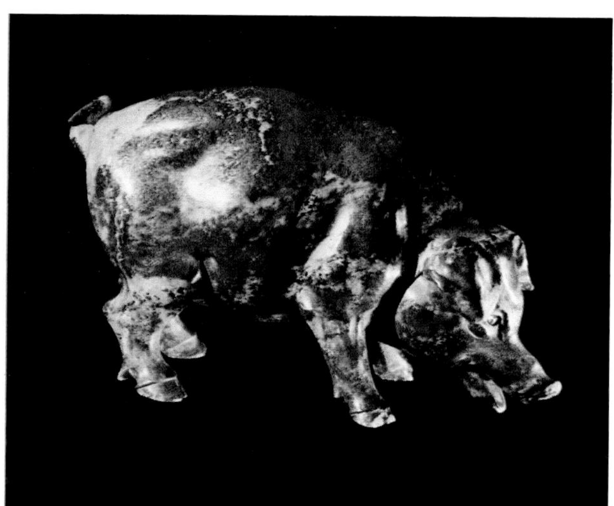

19

23

Catalog entry 20 is illustrated on page 136 with entry 284.

24

25

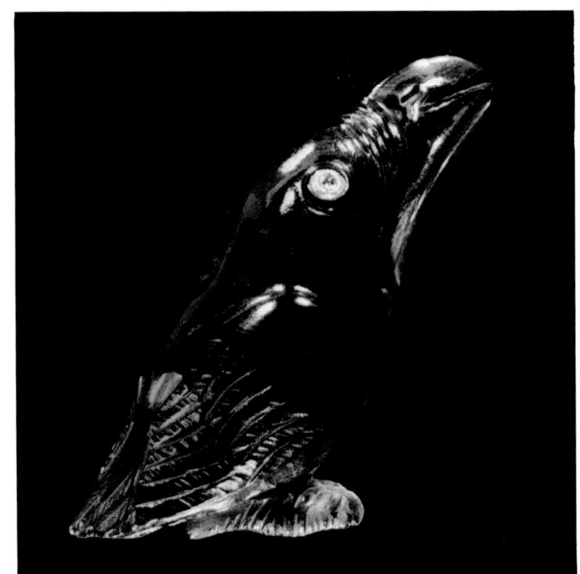

26

27

28

BIRDS

24. Bird in cage.
Fluorite. Gold cage set with pearls on upper rim with nephrite base.
4¼ high by 2⅜ diameter
Marks: *Fabergé/H. W.*
Acc. No. 47-20-207

25. Chick.
Rose jasper. Ruby eyes, gold feet and legs.
2½ high by 1½ wide by 2 long
Marks: profile/72
Acc. No. 47-20-254

26. Condor.
Obsidian. Diamond eyes.
3 high by 1¼ wide by 1¼ long
Marks: C. *Fabergé*/17760
Acc. No. 47-20-255

27. Eagle.
Agate. Diamond eyes, gold feet.
1¾ high by 1 wide by 2¾ long
Marks: *H.W.*/profile/72
Acc. No. 47-20-257

28. Goose.
Quartz. Obsidian head, neck and breast, tail and wing tips. Gold feet and beak.
1¾ high by ¾ wide by 1½ long
Marks: none
Acc. No. 47-20-258

29. Goose.
Rock crystal. Diamond eyes.
4½ high by 1½ wide by 2¾ long
Marks: C. *Fabergé* (probably false)
Acc. No. 47-20-259

29

30

32

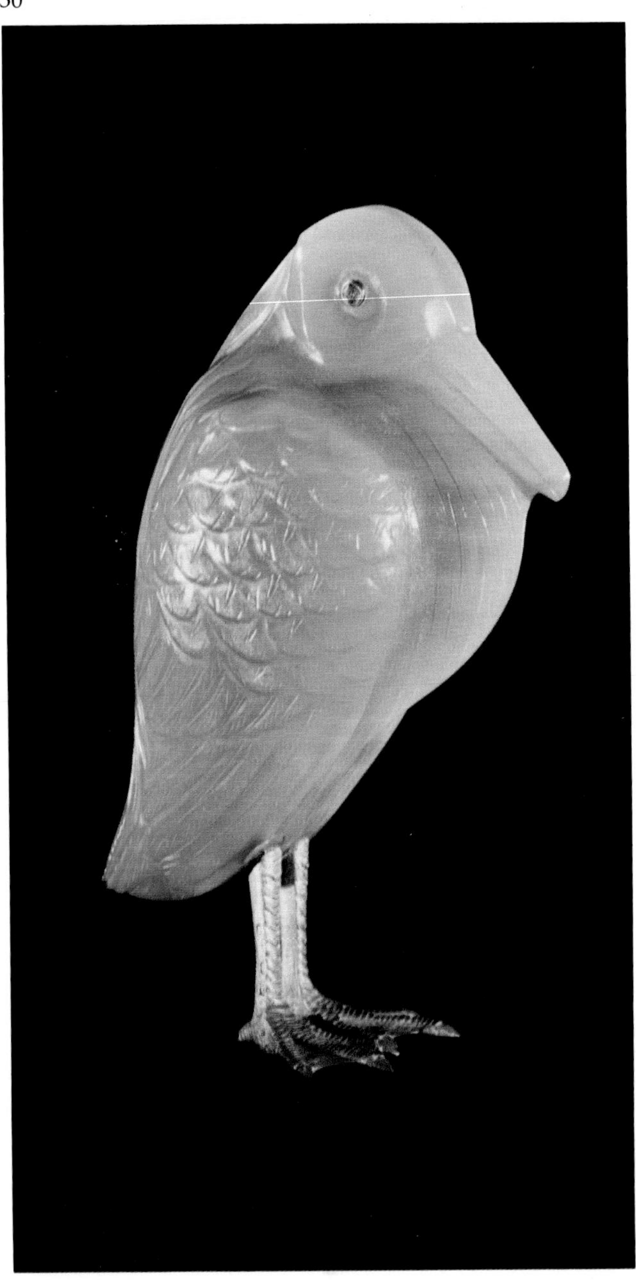

31

30. Grouse.
Obsidian. Diamond eyes, red-gold feet and legs.
3⅞ high by 2½ wide by 3¾ long
Marks: *Fabergé/H.W./72*
Acc. No. 47-20-260

31. Heron.
Blue-gray smoky agate. Diamond eyes, gold legs and feet.
4½ high by 1½ wide by 2 long
Marks: *Fabergé/H.W./72*
Acc. No. 47-20-261

32. Hornbill.
Smoky quartz. Diamond eyes.
1¾ high by ¾ wide by 2 long
Marks: none
Acc. No. 47-20-256

33. Hummingbird.
Chalcedony. Gold perch set with cabochon sapphires and diamonds. White and orange enamel base upon cup of purpurine with fascine rim and four ball feet.
7 high by 2½ wide; base, 3 diameter
Marks: *Fabergé* (partly obliterated)/72
Acc. No. 47-20-212

33

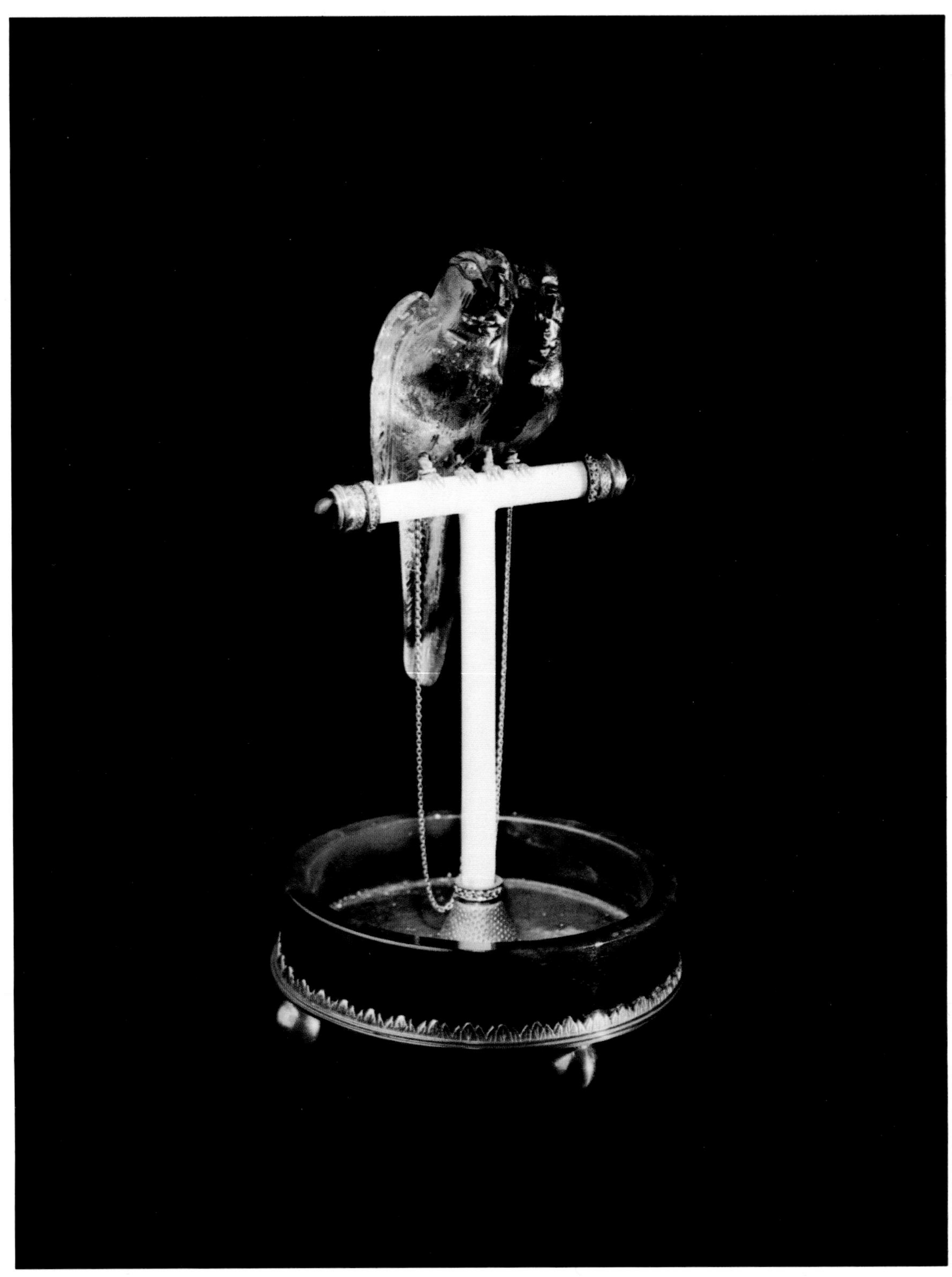

34

35

36

37

38

39

34. Lovebirds.
Amethyst. Ivory perch, gold chain. Ends of crossbar of cabochon topazes, carnelian enamel, and diamonds. Upright has enamel and diamond base, nephrite and gold tray.
4½ high by 2½ diameter
Marks: *Fabergé/H.W./72*
Acc. No. 47-20-211

35. Ostrich.
Banded agate. Diamond eyes, red-gold legs and feet. Quartzite base.
4⅝ high by 1½ wide by 2½ long
Marks: none
Acc. No. 47-20-262

36. Owl.
Opal. Ruby eyes. Gold perch on agate base.
1½ high by ⅝ wide
Marks: *C.F.*
Acc. No. 47-20-215

37. Owl.
Quartz. Demantoid garnet eyes. Ivory crossbar with lapis lazuli knobs. Ivory upright joins lapis lazuli base with rose and white enamel ring.
3⅜ high by 1⅜ wide by 1¼ diameter
Marks: *K. Fabergé*
Acc. No. 47-20-216

38. Owl.
Agate. Topaz eyes, gold feet.
3¾ high by 1¾ wide
Marks: *585*/illegible.
Acc. No. 47-20-264

39. Owl.
Obsidian. Eyes of diamonds and cat's-eyes.
3½ high by 2½ wide
Marks: none
Acc. No. 47-20-265

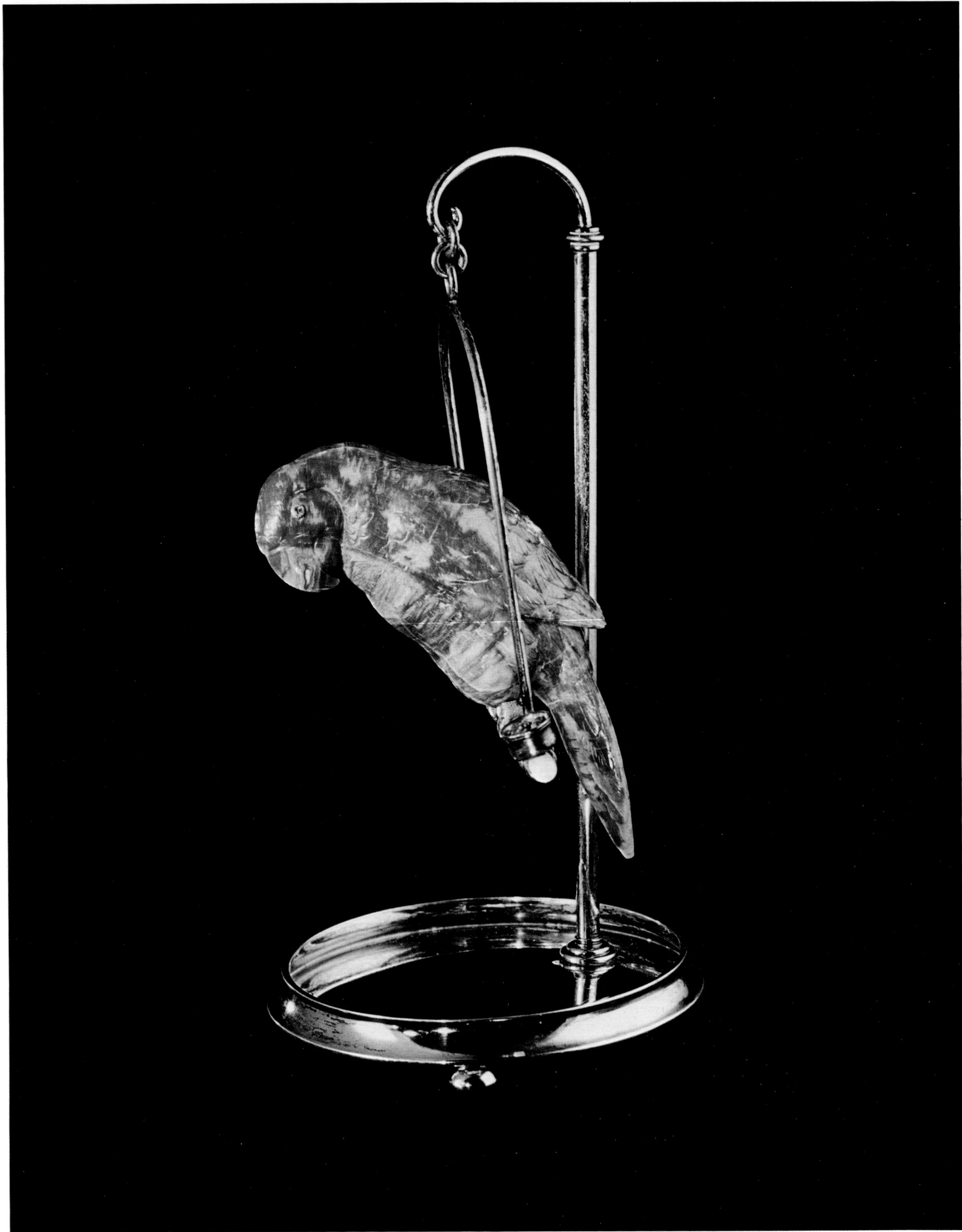

41

42

44

45

40. Parakeet.
    Agate. Silver-gilt and ivory perch with two feeding cups containing silver-gilt seeds. Emerald eyes.
    7¾ high by 3½ diameter
    Marks: *Fabergé*/*H.W.*/*11966* (99611?)/illegible.
    Acc. No. 47-20-208

41. Parrot.
    Rose and green tourmaline. Emerald eyes, diamond-set collar. Ivory and silver-gilt perch, two feeding cups with silver-gilt seeds.
    5¾ high by 3¼ diameter
    Marks: *K. Fabergé*/*A.N.*/double eagle/profile/*88*
    Acc. No. 47-20-209

42. Parrot.
    Rose quartz. Gold cage upon quartzite base.
    4½ high by 2 diameter
    Marks: *Fabergé*/*M.P.*/double eagle/*56*
    Acc. No. 47-20-210

43. Rooster, pendant.
    Gold. Standing on pearl. Gold ring.
    ½ high by ¼ diameter
    Marks: illegible
    Acc. No. 47-20-130

44. Rooster.
    Veined gray and brown agate. Diamond eyes, gold feet.
    1¼ high by ½ wide by 1⅜ long
    Marks: none
    Acc. No. 47-20-266

45. Rooster.
    Transparent carnelian. Diamond eyes, gold feet.
    1½ high by ½ wide by 1¼ long
    Marks: none
    Acc. No. 47-20-267

Catalog entry 43 is illustrated on page 136 with entry 284.

Easter Eggs

Catalog entry 46.

By the 18th century, the presentation of elaborately decorated and contrived eggs had become a regular ceremony at the court of Versailles. Boucher, Lancret, and Watteau, together with other painters less renowned, painted eggshells for Easter presents.

Just how Fabergé began his incredible series of imperial Easter eggs is a topic still subject to speculation and review. His early visits to the Green Vaults in Dresden surely acquainted him with the fantasy pieces created by Melchior Dinglinger (1664-1731) for Kurfürst August the Strong of Saxony. In the Hermitage was a peacock clock by the 18th-century English horologer James Cox—a magnificent jewelled tree in which a peacock spread its tail, a conceit copied by Fabergé.

The usual story of the Easter eggs is that about 1884, and coincident with his receiving the Imperial Warrant, Fabergé obtained an interview with Alexander III. He proposed that for Easter the Czarina Marie Feodorovna should receive a special egg, containing a "surprise"; the suggestion was accepted, and the work was commissioned, with no further details known until the finished piece was delivered. This so entranced the Czar that an annual commission was granted.

The Royal Collection at Rosenborg Castle in Copenhagen possesses an early 18th-century French ivory egg, two and one-half inches long, containing a gold egg which, when opened, discloses a gold hen containing, in turn, a jewelled crown. The tradition of the Danish royal family is that the egg was given by Duchess Charlotte of Orleans to Queen Caroline of England, wife of George II, who gave it to her daughter Mary, wife of Landgrave Frederick of Hesse, grandfather of Queen Marie of Denmark. Queen Marie passed it on to her daughter, Princess Wilhelmine Marie; after her death, it became the property of King Christian IX, the father of Queen Alexandra and Empress Marie Feodorovna. In 1879, five years before Fabergé's first effort, it had been publicly exhibited at the Industrial Exhibition at Copenhagen. There is, then, a very positive prototype for the first imperial Russian egg, the property of the Danish royal family and doubtless known to Czarina Marie Feodorovna herself.

Counting from the first egg of 1884, with one a year made for the Czarina Marie Feodorovna until the death of Alexander III in November, 1894, eleven would have been produced. Nicholas II, who vowed "to follow my father in everything," continued the commission for both the Czarina Alexandra Feodorovna and the Dowager Empress; from 1895 to 1917 forty-six were added, plus one of 1913, commissioned by the Czarina, amounting to a total of fifty-eight imperial Easter eggs.

Of the fifty-eight eggs fashioned by Fabergé, ten have disappeared without a trace; three are known but not located. The Pratt Collection contains five of the forty-five definitely extant. All five date from the reign of Nicholas II; three were presented to the Czarina, and two to the Dowager Empress. Their dates, from 1896 to 1915, cover all but two years and five months of the rule of the last of the Romanoffs.

Though cunning in their execution, a number of the eggs are not "original" in the sense of being the fruit of an unaided imagination. Reminiscences of the treasures in the Green Vaults in Dresden are not infrequent. Copies and adaptations presuppose a retentive and happily opportunistic memory on Fabergé's part and an extensive repertory of historic goldsmith's designs accessible to his designers and workmasters.

The splendor of Fabergé's imperial creations is likely to obscure the antiquarian interest of the other Easter eggs in the Pratt Collection. Many of these are Fabergé productions; some are "imperial" in the sense that they were made in factories owned and operated exclusively by the royal family, for example, the porcelain eggs done in the *Imperitorskii Farfor Zavod,* the Imperial Porcelain Factory in St. Petersburg.

This establishment was founded in 1744, when a contract was signed with Christopher Konrad Hunger, a German from Stockholm who had been trained as a gilder and enameller in Dresden. The factory remained experimental until 1758, when another German, Johann Gottfried Müller from Meissen, was put in charge. From this time forward its wares were fully comparable in quality, if not originality, to those of Sèvres, Meissen, and Vincennes. Two of these porcelain eggs are marked with the initials of Alexandra Feodorovna, one with the monogram of the Czarevitch, and another with the monogram of Marie Feodorovna, with a red cross and "1916" on one side.

Other eggs form large pendants of aventurine rhodonite, and blue-dyed agate. Still others are perfectly plain polished stones from the lapidary works at Peterhof, caskets, or lockets of gold and enamel.

Another category of Easter egg in the Pratt Collection is composed of some seventy-five miniature eggs in the form of pendants, charms or, in some cases, small lockets (Nos. 62 to 136).

These are of such varied material and color (the size is fairly uniform, about ¾ inch high by ½ inch wide) that they cannot be singled out for detailed notice. Of the group, twenty are definitely marked with either the "K. F." of the St. Petersburg house or the initials of well-known Fabergé workmasters, including Michael Perchin, Eric Kollin, August Holmström, Feodor Afanassiev, Hjalmar Armfelt, and August Hollming. The quality of gold used is almost exclusively fourteen carat, with the Russian equivalent notation "56." Enamels may be monochrome or varicolored, champlevé, cloisonné, *plique à jour*, or over guilloche grounds.

The polished natural substances used include nephrite, sapphire, natural and dyed agate, lapis lazuli, garnet, quartz, rhodonite, jadeite, dyed chalcedony, opal, topaz, serpentine, amethyst, and rock crystal. Several examples of the deep-red artificial purpurine are present. Enamel and natural substances are often combined, the enamel being used in the upper half of the pendant as a container for the polished stone beneath. Elsewhere, small precious stones—diamonds, rubies and sapphires, rose-cut and cabochon—are inserted as embellishments in gold filigree or plain surfaces.

It is, of course, impossible to tell for whom these miniature pendant eggs were made; they belong to Fabergé's commercial open stock production. Yet, though they may be infinitely less spectacular than the imperial Easter eggs, they are, in their way, more evocative of the native Russian Easter customs and usages.

During all of Easter Day, and for several days thereafter, all Russians exchanged Easter eggs, ranging in character from the simplest red-dyed egg of the poorest peasant to the extravaganzas of Fabergé. The gift was offered with the salutation "Christ is risen"; and, having been accepted, another was given in its place, "Christ is risen indeed." An embrace followed, and then some ritual exchange of toasts and food. It was not considered at all improper for the eggs received from guests to be passed on to other guests in turn. Hence, among the wealthy these brilliant miniatures would have served not as specific gifts to individuals, but rather as party favors to be handed about back and forth throughout the day.

46. Presented to Czarina Alexandra Feodorovna by Nicholas II in 1896, the year of the coronation of Nicholas II. It is the earliest of the five imperial eggs in the Pratt Collection and was the work of Michael Perchin.

Rock-crystal globe encircled with vertical diamond-set band; gold shaft, champlevé enamel, and gold base worked with Russian and German monograms of the Empress set with diamonds; top set with Siberian cabochon emerald. Rock-crystal and gold pedestal.

The hollow egg contains miniatures of Neue Palais at Darmstadt; Kranichstein in Hesse; Wolfsgarten in Hesse; Rosenau in Coburg; Balmoral, Windsor Castle, and Osborne House in England; the Winter Palace, Anitchkov Palace, and Alexander Palace in Russia; and two other royal residences, painted by Zehngraf. These revolve around the gold axis of the egg. The emerald serves as the apex of the axis, which, when depressed, lowers a hook engaging the top of a miniature to revolve on the axis.

All the edifices represented are connected with the life of the Czarina up to the time of the presentation. In the Neue Palais, Darmstadt, Princess Alix of Hesse lived. At Kranichstein and Wolfsgarten she spent her summers, and she journeyed every year to Great Britain to visit "Grandmama" at Windsor, Balmoral, or Osborne House on the Isle of Wight. In April, 1894, her brother the Grand Duke of Hesse married Victoria Melita of Saxe-Coburg. The Czarevitch attended, and it was at Rosenau, the birthplace of Queen Victoria's Prince Consort, that he and the Princess Alix became engaged. After their marriage on November 26, 1894, in the Winter Palace in St. Petersburg, they lived in a suite of six small rooms, an extension of the Czar's bachelor quarters, in the Dowager Empress's Anitchkov Palace.

The studied conception of the egg must have entailed a great deal of administrative organization. The Danish painter Johannes Zehngraf (born Copenhagen, April 18, 1857; died Berlin, February 7(?), 1908) had painted portraits of Marie Feodorovna and Alexander III, which are in the collection at Rosenborg. Zehngraf lived in Berlin from 1889 until his death.

The dozen pictures were doubtless ordered by Fabergé immediately after Easter, 1895, in consultation with the Czar. They were probably painted from photographs either collected in St. Petersburg and forwarded to the artist, or gathered in Berlin; it is quite unlikely that the miniatures were painted at sites as disparate as Balmoral and the Nevski Prospekt. Zehngraf may have come to St. Petersburg to work in conjunction with Fabergé, since he also painted the miniatures in the Dowager Empress's egg of the following year. Another possibility is that several sets of miniatures were ordered to be used as occasion and fitness warranted.

10 high by 4 diameter
Marks: *Fabergé*/*M.P.*/crossed anchors/*56*
Acc. No. 47-20-32

47. Presented to Czarina Alexandra Feodorovna by Nicholas II, 1903.

Red, green, and yellow gold and platinum, set with diamonds and rubies. Miniatures on the sides, by the court miniaturist Vassily Zuiev, comprise two portraits, of Peter and Nicholas II, and two views, one of the wooden hut traditionally said to have been built by Peter himself and one of the Winter Palace as it stood in 1903.

The inside, enamelled translucent yellow on a guilloche ground, contains the "surprise." Upon raising the top, a platform within the egg also rises bearing a removable bronze miniature replica by G. Malychev of the statue of Peter the Great, commissioned by Catherine the Great in 1766 from the French sculptor Etienne Maurice Falconet (1716-1791) and unveiled in 1782. The monument itself, on the Nevsky Prospekt, represents the Czar on horseback, charging up a boulder of Finland granite toward the Neva, his right hand extended in blessing and the horse trampling the serpent of evil. On the base is the terse inscription "Petro Primo Catharina Secunda," with a Russian translation on the other side—evidence enough of Catherine's contempt for the intervening six sovereigns. The tiny bronze of the "surprise," modelled by G. Malychev, stands upon a block of sapphire, which in turn is fastened to an engraved gold pavement surrounded by a railing and chains.

The exterior of the egg is unusually baroque in design, though full of Russian symbolism. The body is covered with an interwoven medley of laurel leaves (triumph and eternity), roses (victory, pride, and heavenly joy), and bulrushes. These plants symbolize the faithful multitude by the source of the living waters. To the inhabitants of St. Petersburg, the Neva was a counterpart of the Jordan. Every year, in the first week in January, the waters of the river were blessed; hence, the bulrushes also denote the source of salvation.

The granite boulder of Falconet's monument is a reference to the words ". . . thou art Peter, and upon this rock I will build my church" (Matt.16:18); in 1721 Peter the Great had founded the Holy Synod "because simple folks cannot distinguish the spiritual power from the sovereign power," and thus became the spiritual as well as temporal head of Orthodoxy.

4¼ high by 3⅛ diameter
Marks: *K.Fabergé*/*M.P.*/profile/*56*/*72*/*1903*/illegible
Acc. No. 47-20-33

1903

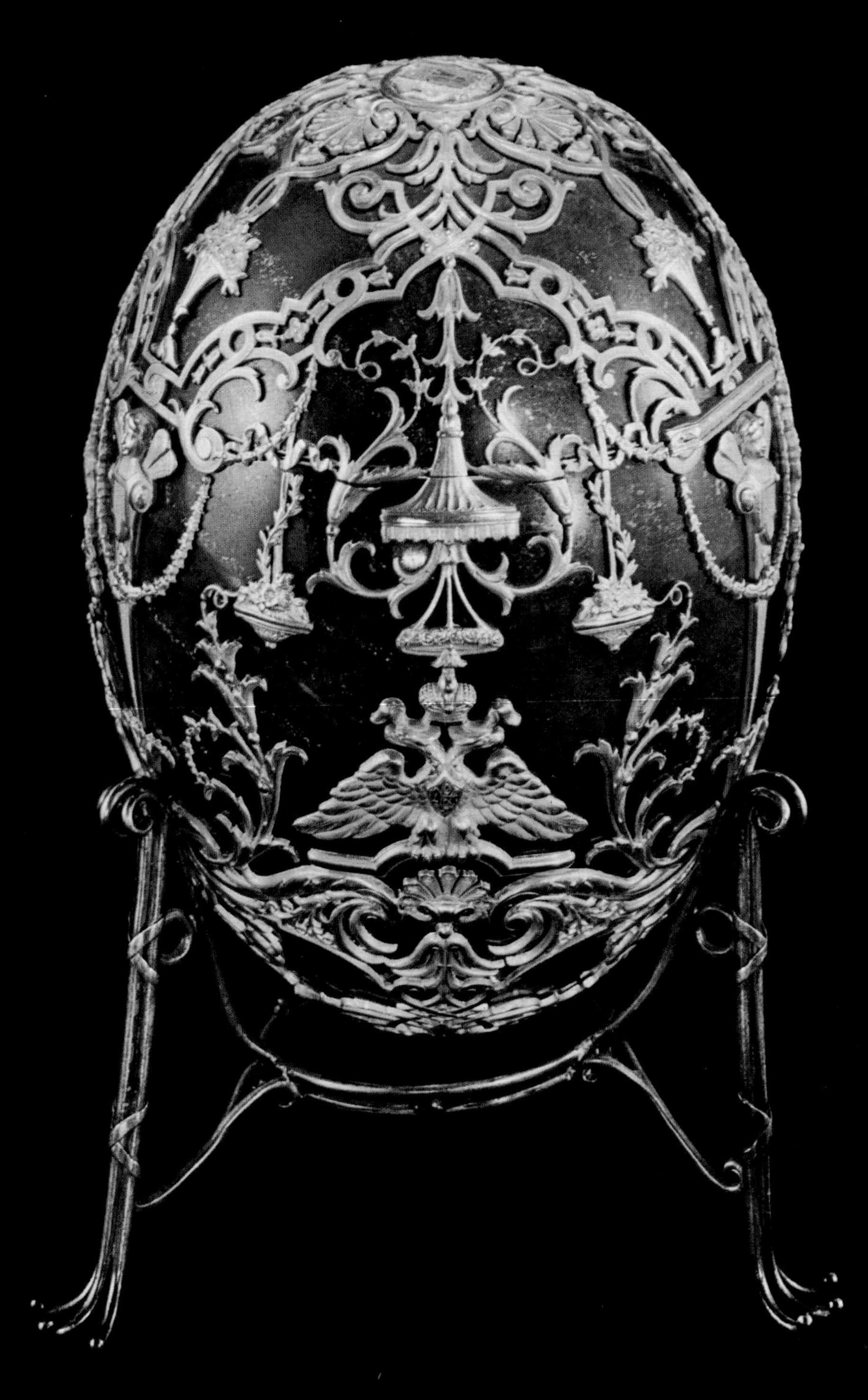

48. Presented to Czarina Alexandra Feodorovna by Nicholas II, 1912.

Lapis lazuli in six sections overlaid with gold tracery in the style of a Louis XV cagework of shells, scrolls, baskets of flowers, and cupids. On top of egg, square, flat diamond with monogram "AF," crown, and "1912." Bottom of egg set with diamond. Top opens, disclosing removable platinum Russian double eagle, set with rose diamonds on lapis lazuli base which serves as frame for a three-dimensional miniature of the Czarevitch Alexis in a simple sailor suit, both front and back views.

The Czarina gave birth to a son on August 12, 1904. The rejoicings were frantic: amnesties were granted, sentences were remitted. The child assuaged for a while the calamities of the Russo-Japanese War. As if to exorcise disaster, the child was named Alexis, from the Greek *alexein,* "to ward off, to protect." By Easter, 1912 the Czarevitch was well into his seventh year. He was handsome, but to all accounts moody, disdainful, precociously pompous, and shockingly unschooled.

The egg is by Henrik Wigström; the miniature, unsigned, is an inferior piece of work. Silver-gilt stand.

5 high by 3⅝ diameter
Marks: *Fabergé*
Acc. No. 47-20-34

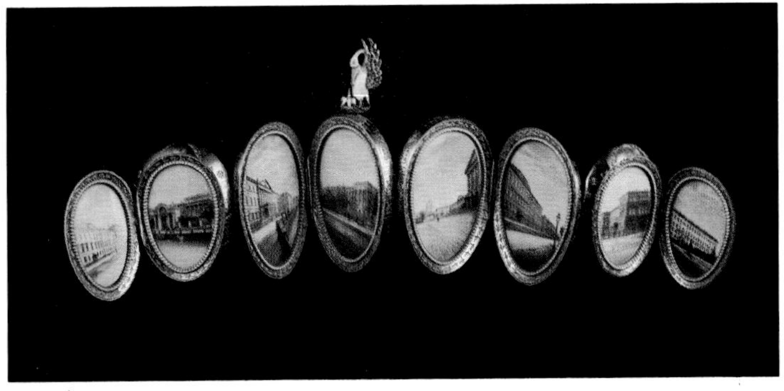

49. Presented to Dowager Empress Marie Feodorovna by Nicholas II, 1897.

Red gold, surmounted with gray, pink, and blue enamel pelican feeding its young. Engraved with commemorative dates "1797-1897," with the inscription "Visit our vineyards, O Lord, and we will live in Thee," and motifs of the arts and sciences.

Egg unfolds into eight oval panels rimmed with pearls containing miniatures of the institutions of which the Dowager Empress was patroness: the Zenia Institute, Nicholai Orphanage, Patriotic Institute, Smolny Institute, Ekaterina Institute, Pavlov Institute, St. Petersburg Orphanage of Nicholai, and Elizabeth Institute. Painted by Zehngraf on ovals of ivory, carefully graded in size to match the diminishing size of the panels.

In the center between the fourth and fifth panels a gold leaf acts as an easel and supports the pelican; it is decorated with engraved symbols of science and the arts. On the back of the second to seventh panels are listed the institutions portrayed, the second and seventh listing two, the remainder one each. The enamel pelican is not an integral part of the egg but has been attached to its support as an afterthought, to reinforce the engraved symbolism and the text.

Varicolored gold stand with claw feet, each topped with an eagle's head bearing a crown.

4 high by 2⅛ diameter
Marks: *Fabergé*/*M. P.*/anchors and scepter/*56*
Acc. No. 47-20-35

50. Presented to Dowager Empress Marie Feodorovna by Nicholas II, 1915.

White opalescent enamel on chased silver ground. Two opposing red enamel crosses bear dates "1914" and "1915." Russian inscription in band around center: "Greater love hath no man than this, that a man lay down his life for his friends." Crown and monogram of Dowager Empress Marie in silver at top, sexpartite rosette at bottom. The Dowager Empress was president of the Red Cross from the beginning of her reign until 1917. Inside is a hinged folding screen with miniatures by Vassily Zuiev of Grand Duchess Olga Alexandrovna, the Czar's sister; Grand Duchess Olga Nicholaevna, his eldest daughter; Czarina Alexandra Feodorovna; Grand Duchess Tatiana, his second daughter; Grand Duchess Maria Pavlovna, his cousin. Framed in gold and enamel, each surmounted with a red cross; all wear the Red Cross uniform. Respective monograms mounted in gold on mother-of-pearl on back.

3½ high by 2⅜ diameter
Marks: *Fabergé/H. W./65/1915*/illegible
Acc. No. 47-20-36

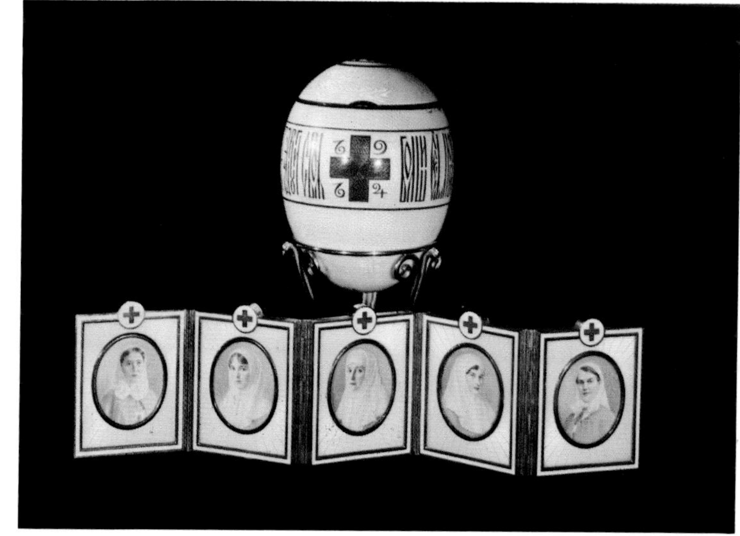

51

52

53

54

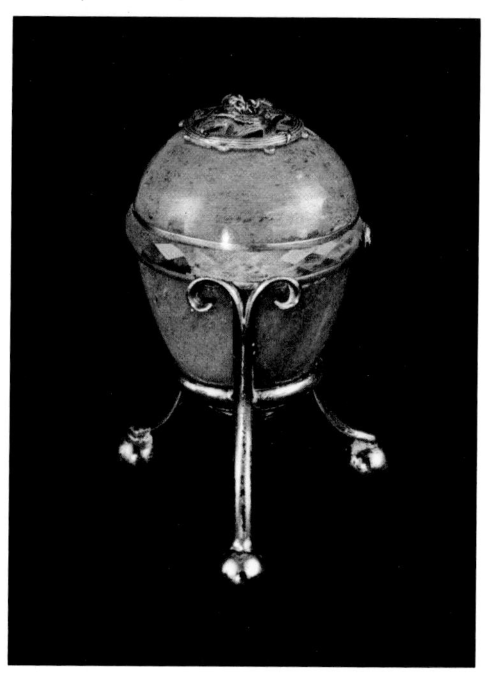
55

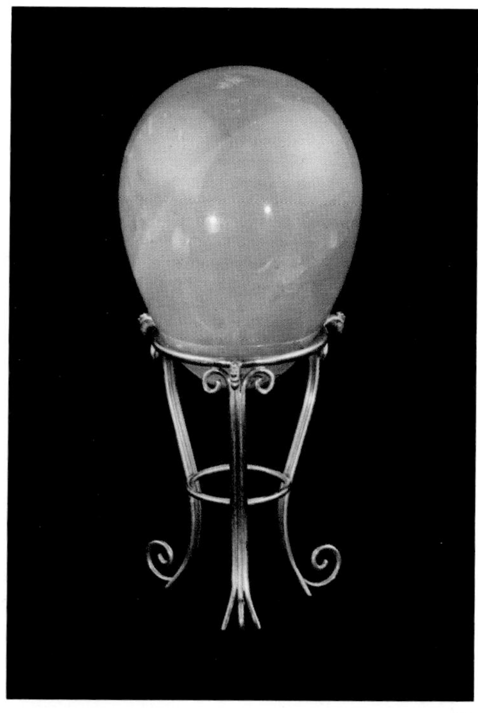
56

57

MISCELLANEOUS EGGS

51. White porcelain. Hollow, holes at either end bordered with gold. Gold monogram "AF" within gold oval on one side. Wreath of roses bound at intervals with painted blue ribbon encircling egg.
3½ high by 2¾ diameter
Marks: none
Acc. No. 47-20-37

52. White porcelain. Hollow, holes at either end. Reticulated surface formed by spiraling gold lines. Monogram "MF" and crown on one side, red cross over "1916" on other side.
2½ high by 2 diameter
Marks: none
Acc. No. 47-20-38

53. White porcelain. Hollow, holes at either end. Gold and bronze monogram "AF," surmounted by gold crown on one side, red cross on other.
2½ high by 2 diameter
Marks: none
Acc. No. 47-20-39

54. White porcelain. Hollow, holes at either end. Gold monogram of Czarevitch, surmounted by crown.
2½ high by 2 diameter
Marks: none
Acc. No. 47-20-40

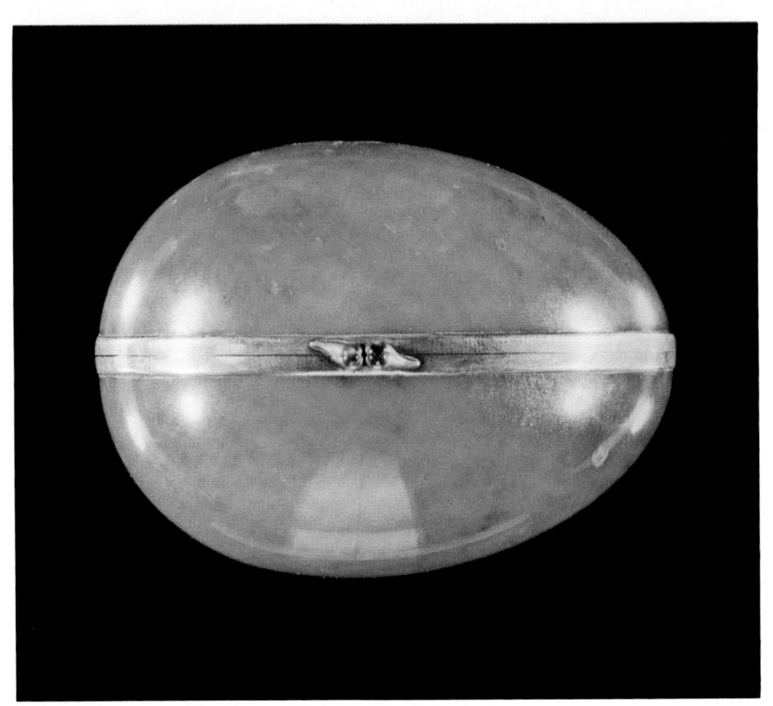

58

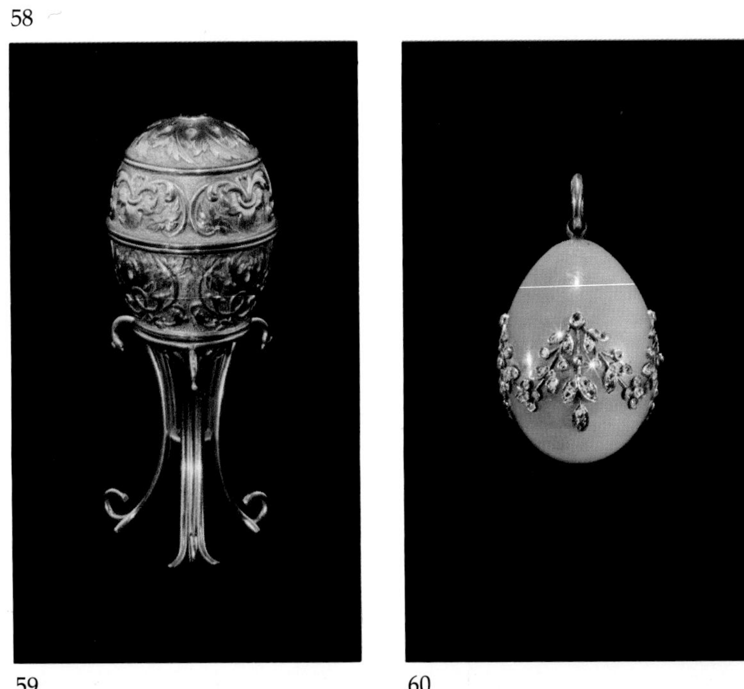

59

60

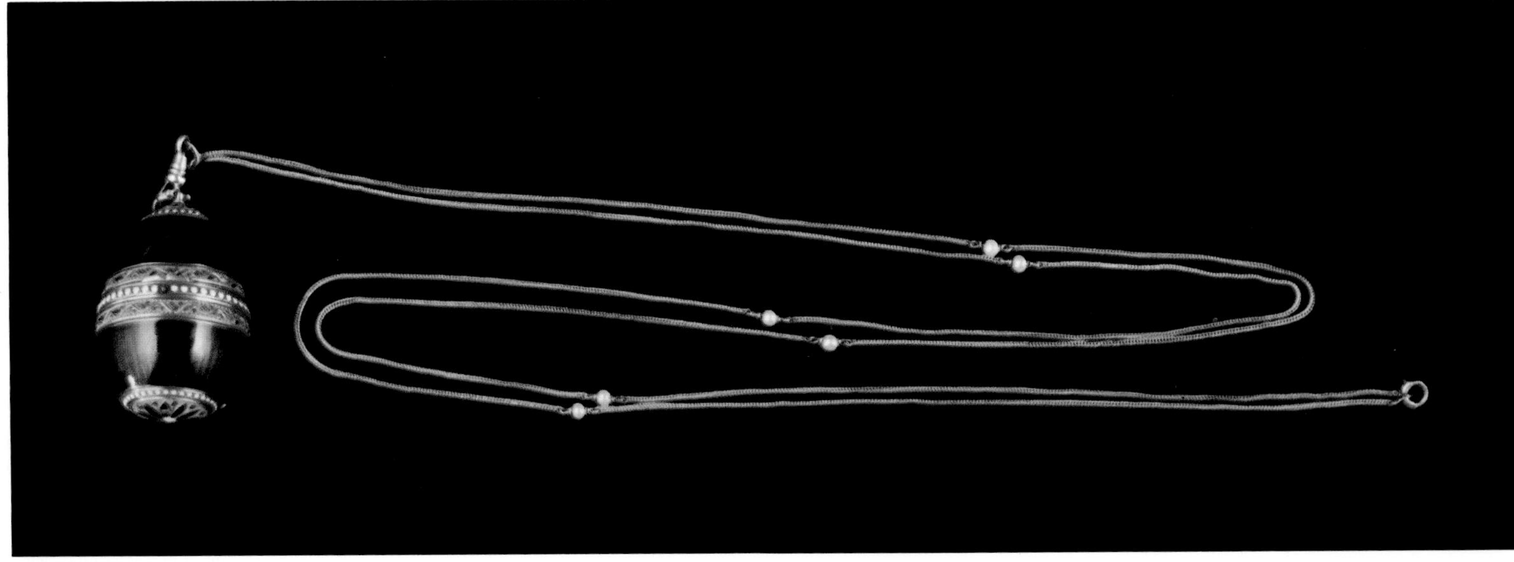

61

55. Aventurine. Two pieces separated by a disk of rock crystal faceted on circumference. Gold band on either side of crystal disk. Cap and bottom of egg in chased varicolored gold. Silver-gilt tripod stand with ball feet.
2½ high by 1½ diameter
Marks: none
Acc. No. 47-20-41

56. Rose quartz. Gold stand.
2½ high by 1½ diameter
Marks: none
Acc. No. 47-20-43

57. Rhodonite. Topped with modelled silver-gilt ribbon, suspended by loop with fluted outer edge. Gold monogram "MF" inlaid on one side of egg, surmounted with crown, encircled by chased silver-gilt leaf garland. Ribbed disk on bottom.
2 high by 1½ diameter
Marks: none
Acc. No. 47-20-44

58. Nephrite. Silver-gilt rims, ruby clasp.
3½ high by 2½ diameter
Marks: none
Acc. No. 47-20-45

59. Gold. Divided into four horizontal panels chased with interweaving foliations on stippled ground. Top set with faceted ruby.
1¾ high by 1 diameter
Marks: *Fabergé/M.P./72/*star
Acc. No. 47-20-46

60. Gold loop suspends blue-dyed agate egg decorated with applied silver and diamond flowers and leaves.
1¼ high by ⅞ diameter
Marks: *M.P./56*
Acc. No. 47-20-126

61. Gold and enamel egg, diamond catch. Center of egg ringed with small disks of white enamel edged with broad band of gold, with floral design accented with red and green enamel. Broad band of blue enamel over chased gold ground on either side. Cap and bottom of gold ringed with white enamel disks. Attached to gold chain having nine pearls. Inscription on inside rim of top: "Christ is risen."
1⅝ high by 1⅜ diameter
Marks: none
Acc. No. 47-20-128

62-68

69-75

76-82

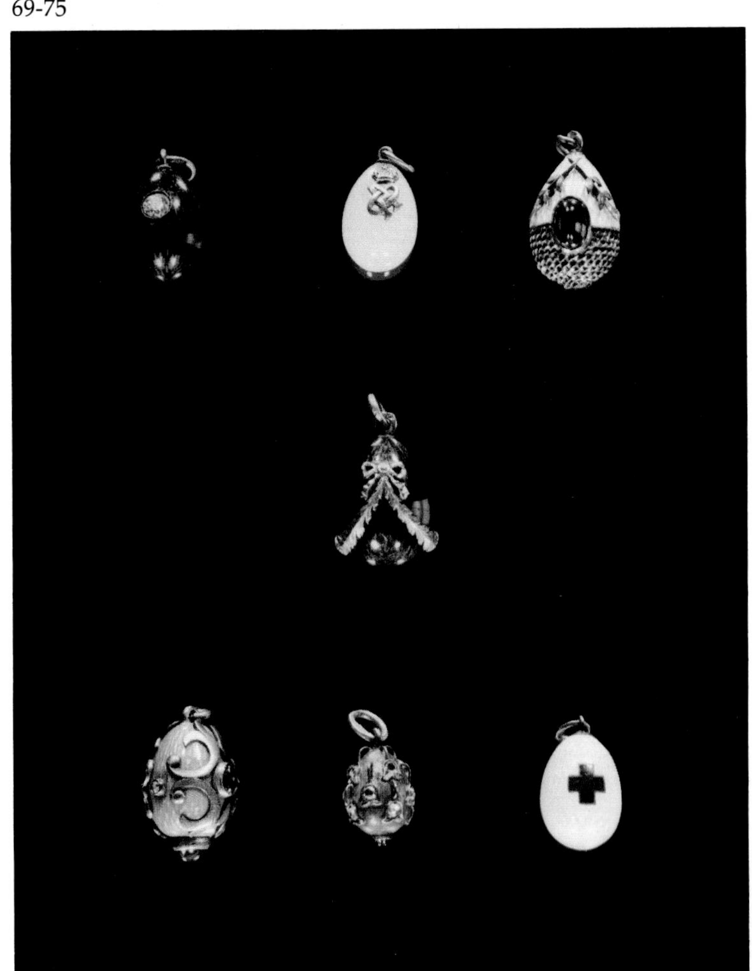
83-89

MINIATURE EGGS

62. Nephrite, gold equator set with diamonds, gold ring.
¾ high by ⅝ diameter
Marks: none
Acc. No. 47-20-47

63. Gold. Sapphire set in crescent-shaped opening in side, raised five-pointed star holds diamond, parallel chased lines on surface.
¾ high by ½ diameter
Marks: *56*/illegible
Acc. No. 47-20-48

64. Lower part of purpurine, upper part above diamond band of alternate white and green enamel. On each segment is a gold numeral, the whole forming the number "1900."
¾ high by ⅝ diameter
Marks: illegible
Acc. No. 47-20-49

65. Gold. Low relief of elephant with diamond on side surrounded by palm fronds.
¾ high by ½ diameter
Marks: [?] *K.*/*56*
Acc. No. 47-20-50

66. Bright green enamel set with ruby encircled with gold ring.
¾ high by ½ diameter
Marks: *K.F.*/*56*
Acc. No. 47-20-51

67. Dyed agate surrounded by gold band.
¾ high by ½ diameter
Marks: *56*/illegible.
Acc. No. 47-20-52

68. Crimson, blue, and white enamel with indented surface, set with horizontal band of rubies alternating with gold garlands.
¾ high by ½ diameter
Marks: *56*/illegible
Acc. No. 47-20-53

69. Crimson enamel. Two horizontal white bands enclose band of alternate green and yellow rectangles.
¾ high by ½ diameter
Marks: *72*/illegible.
Acc. No. 47-20-54

70. Gold top and purpurine lower part.
⅝ high by ⅜ diameter
Marks: *E.K.*/anchors and scepter/*56*
Acc. No. 47-20-55

71. Silver-gilt wire set with green glass.
⅝ high by ½ diameter
Marks: *A.H.*/*84*
Acc. No. 47-20-56

72. Cloisonné enamel, divided spirally with longitudinal divisions alternating crimson and opaque white. Leafy twig in each white segment.
¾ high by ½ diameter
Marks: *56*/illegible
Acc. No. 47-20-57

73. Green, vermilion, deep blue and rose enamel separated by *cloisons* of twisted silver-gilt wire.
¾ high by ⅝ diameter
Marks: none
Acc. No. 47-20-58

74. Lapis lazuli suspended from gold ring.
¾ high by ½ diameter
Marks: none
Acc. No. 47-20-59

75. Gold, opens horizontally. Diamonds set on bottom in the points of six-pointed star which holds ruby.
¾ high by ⅝ diameter
Marks: none
Acc. No. 47-20-60

76. Silver-gilt, blue-green enamel, *plique à jour*. Walls formed by branches, stems, leaves, and blossoms of plant.
¾ high by ½ diameter
Marks: *84*/illegible
Acc. No. 47-20-61

77. Garnet held in receptacle of gold wire attached to three gold chains.
⅝ high by ½ diameter
Marks: profile/*56*
Acc. No. 47-20-62

78. Red, white, and green enamel with indented surface. Overlaid gold garlands. Set with ruby.
⅝ high by ½ diameter
Marks: illegible
Acc. No. 47-20-63

79. Gold. Wire appliqué floral design with two diamonds.
⅝ high by 7/16 diameter
Marks: *56*/Greek "a"/illegible
Acc. No. 47-20-64

80. Pierced; fluted gold; diamond band extending halfway around center, larger diamond set above, sapphire set below.
¾ high by ½ diameter
Marks: *56*/illegible
Acc. No. 47-20-65

81. Gold. Champlevé enamel in green and light blue with small transparent circles of amber-colored enamel. Geometric design with *pâtée* crosses. Monogram "XB" placed on opposite sides.
¾ high by ⅝ diameter
Marks: *B★F*
Acc. No. 47-20-66

82. Gold twisted wire in linear design containing unidentified pink substance; broad band around center of three plaited, double wires.
⅝ high by ½ diameter
Marks: *A.V.* superimposed
Acc. No. 47-20-67

83. Deep blue enamel over tooled surface, diamond in silver setting.
⅝ high by ⅜ diameter
Marks: *56*/illegible
Acc. No. 47-20-68

90-96

97-99, 101-104

84. Quartz, gold chased monogram and crown on side.
5/8 high by 3/8 diameter
Marks: *A.A./56*
Acc. No. 47-20-69

85. Gold. Pearl enamel overlaid with two crossed branches of gold leaves. Lower half is basket constructed of twisted gold wire. Sapphire set at junction of two halves.
3/4 high by 1/2 diameter
Marks: *56*/illegible
Acc. No. 47-20-70

86. Deep blue enamel, encircled with green- and red-gold pendant branches held at tops with bow knots.
3/4 high by 5/8 diameter
Marks: *56*/illegible
Acc. No. 47-20-71

87. Pearl-pink transparent enamel over chased gold ground with rococo designs, set with sapphires and diamonds.
3/4 high by 1/2 diameter
Marks: none
Acc. No. 47-20-72

88. Gold. Applied diamond-set leaves, the stems of which form projecting loop. Sapphire set in bottom.
9/16 high by 7/16 diameter
Marks: *Y L/56*/illegible
Acc. No. 47-20-73

89. Pearl enamel over chased gold ground; red cross on one side.
3/4 high by 7/16 diameter
Marks: illegible
Acc. No. 47-20-74

90. Rhodonite suspended from gold ring.
5/8 high by 1/2 diameter
Marks: *F.A./56*
Acc. No. 47-20-75

91. Quartz. Diagonal gold ring holds sapphire and diamond floral design.
5/8 high by 5/8 diameter
Marks: *K.P.*/profile
Acc. No. 47-20-76

92. Gold. Horizontally ribbed. Diagonal band of sapphires.
5/8 high by 3/8 diameter
Marks: illegible
Acc. No. 47-20-77

93. Quartz. Repoussé calyx. Pointed crimson stone at bottom.
5/8 high by 1/2 diameter
Marks: *A.H./Y L/56*
Acc. No. 47-20-78

94. Pearl enamel over gold, set with two yellow and white diamonds.
5/8 high by 3/8 diameter
Marks: profile/*56*/illegible
Acc. No. 47-20-80

95. Jadeite encircled by decoration of spray of leaves with three flowers, one set with diamonds, the others with sapphires and rubies.
$5/8$ high by $3/8$ diameter
Marks: *M.L./56*/illegible
Acc. No. 47-20-81

96. Agate held by lattice of red and yellow chased leaf-design bands.
$5/8$ high by $3/8$ diameter
Marks: *A.H./Y L/56*
Acc. No. 47-20-82

97. Quartz, held by red- and yellow-gold lattice set with four rubies.
$5/8$ high by $3/8$ diameter
Marks: *56*/illegible
Acc. No. 47-20-84

98. Dyed and natural agate in three longitudinal segments separated by deep segments of gold spanned by design of ruby-set blossom in relief and scroll-like gold wires.
$9/16$ high by $5/16$ diameter
Marks: *56*/illegible
Acc. No. 47-20-85

99. Pearl enamel over tooled gold ground. Chased gold band below center. Two rubies and a diamond set above band.
$5/8$ high by $3/8$ diameter
Marks: *A.H./56*
Acc. No. 47-20-86

101. Turquoise enamel over chased ground. Diagonal band of white and dark-green champlevé enamel leaf design in silver.
$5/8$ high by $3/8$ diameter
Marks: *56*/illegible
Acc. No. 47-20-88

102. Dyed chalcedony in red- and yellow-gold framework of leaf and flower motif.
$5/8$ high by $3/8$ diameter
Marks: *A.K./Y L/56*
Acc. No. 47-20-89

103. Quartz. Ruby- and diamond-set gold design in shape of reversed S on side.
$3/4$ high by $5/8$ diameter
Marks: *Y L/56*/illegible
Acc. No. 47-20-90

104. Nephrite inlaid with gold floral spray set with rubies and diamonds.
$5/8$ high by $3/8$ diameter
Marks: none
Acc. No. 47-20-91

105. Quartz and garnet divided into four longitudinal sections with diamond-set bands. Horizontal diamond-set band around center.
$1/2$ high by $3/8$ diameter
Marks: *K.F.*
Acc. No. 47-20-92

106. Gold. Four vertical segments filled with small pearls and turquoises.
$1/2$ high by $3/8$ diameter
Marks: anchors and scepter/*56*/illegible
Acc. No. 47-20-93

105-111

107. Twisted gold wire, pointed dyed agate set at bottom.
$5/8$ high by $3/8$ diameter
Marks: *56*/illegible
Acc. No. 47-20-94

108. Lapis lazuli.
$5/8$ high by $3/8$ diameter
Marks: illegible
Acc. No. 47-20-95

109. Green enamel upper part set with diamonds, blue-dyed agate lower part.
$5/8$ high by $3/8$ diameter
Marks: *A.T./Y L/56*
Acc. No. 47-20-96

110. Opal.
$5/8$ high by $3/8$ diameter
Marks: *K.F.*
Acc. No. 47-20-97

111. Topaz. Top of white and clear crimson enamel lozenge shapes radiating from ring-bolt, set with diamonds.
$5/8$ high by $3/8$ diameter
Marks: none
Acc. No. 47-20-98

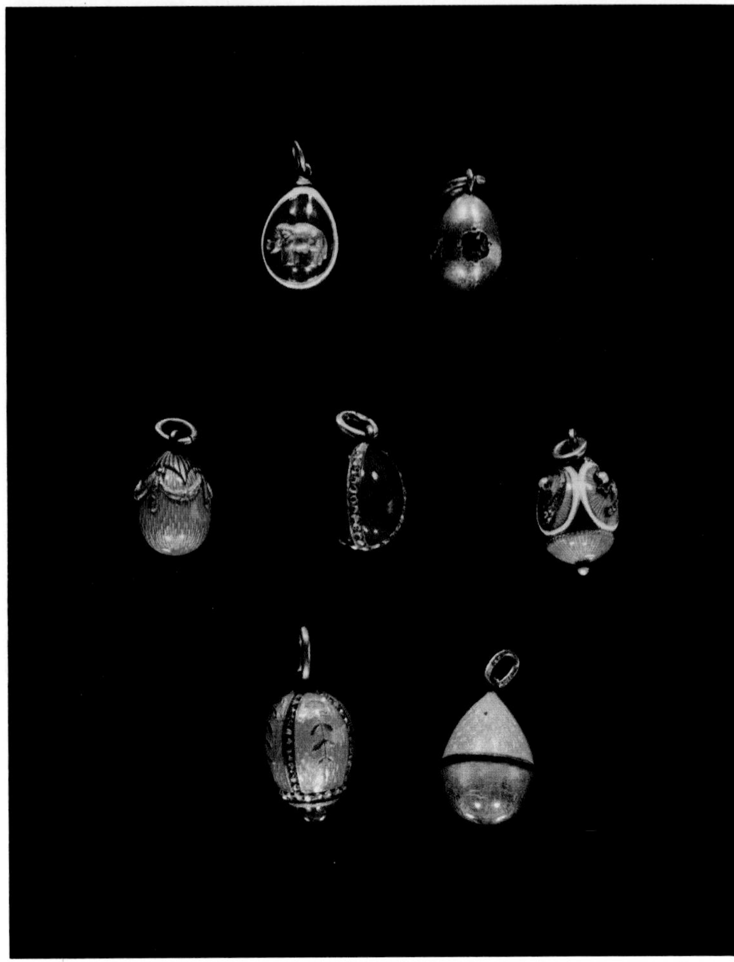

112-118

112. Raspberry-red enamel over gold chased ground. Applied gold bas-relief elephant surrounded with opaque white enamel band on side.
5/8 high by 3/8 diameter
Marks: *56*/illegible
Acc. No. 47-20-100

113. Gold. Faceted emerald, ruby, and two sapphires.
9/16 high by 7/16 diameter
Marks: anchors and scepter/*56*
Acc. No. 47-20-101

114. Green enamel over chased gold ground. Top decorated with classical fluted mounting and with chased gold garlands crossed at intervals with ribbons and festoons.
5/8 high by 3/8 diameter
Marks: *H.W./A.P./56*
Acc. No. 47-20-102

115. Alternating ruby and ultramarine translucent enamel in four longitudinal sections. Each section chased to represent veinings of leaf and separated by four gold diamond-set bands. Diamond set at intersections of bands at bottom.
5/8 high by 1/2 diameter
Marks: *B.F.*/anchors and scepter/*56*
Acc. No. 47-20-103

116. Six medallions of green enamel on chased ground, four with pearl and diamond flower on each. Medallions bordered with opaque white enamel and triangles of deep red. Pearl set in bottom.
5/8 high by 1/2 diameter
Marks: *K.F./I.* [?]./*56*
Acc. No. 47-20-104

117. Gold. Orchid-pink champlevé enamel in four panels separated by gold diamond-set bands. Horizontal base with diamonds framing cabochon emerald.
3/4 high by 1/2 diameter
Marks: none
Acc. No. 47-20-105

118. Gold. Upper part of sky-blue enamel over chased ground. Lower part of rose quartz cut *en cabochon.*
5/8 high by 9/16 diameter
Marks: *F.A./56*/illegible
Acc. No. 47-20-107

119. Serpentine. Five gold traceries in floral form set with diamonds and rubies.
5/8 high by 1/2 diameter
Marks: *M.P./56*
Acc. No. 47-20-108

120. Pink rhodonite, bent gold loops.
1/2 high by 3/8 diameter
Marks: *A.P./56*/illegible
Acc. No. 47-20-109

121. Gold. Four ultramarine enamel panels set with ruby; above and below each stone is six-pointed star. Panels separated by gold-ribbed sections.
5/8 high by 1/2 diameter
Marks: *56*/illegible
Acc. No. 47-20-110

122. Two halves of Siberian amethyst separated by a disk of rock crystal with faceted circumference.
7/8 high by 5/8 diameter
Marks: [?] *K./E.T./56*
Acc. No. 47-20-111

123. Gold. Alternating panels of ruby and white enamel. White panels contain overlaid flowers of blue and light green.
5/8 high by 1/2 diameter
Marks: *F.A./56*
Acc. No. 47-20-113

124. Ruby enamel over chased gold ground circled by gold band.
7/16 high by 5/16 diameter
Marks: illegible
Acc. No. 47-20-114

125. Gold. Eight ruby enamel panels separated by transparent white enamel bands. Each panel bears silver floral spray.
5/8 high by 3/8 diameter
Marks: illegible
Acc. No. 47-20-115

126. Silver-gilt. Repoussé swan medallion.
5/8 high by 3/8 diameter
Marks: illegible
Acc. No. 47-20-116

127. Gold. Ruby enamel set with pearl. Gold monogram "XB" on one side.
5/8 high by 3/8 diameter
Marks: *56*
Acc. No. 47-20-117

128. Rock crystal. Engraved band of blossoms around center set with rubies and emeralds.
3/4 high by 1/2 diameter
Marks: *K.F.*/anchors and scepter/*56*
Acc. No. 47-20-119

129. Light-green enamel over chased gold ground. Opaque white enamel floral design with applied gold outlines on one side. Stamens and pistils in yellow and black.
5/8 high by 3/8 diameter
Marks: *Y.* [?]./*56*/illegible.
Acc. No. 47-20-120

130. Deep-green nephrite. Chased leaf bands set with rubies at junctions. Bands joined in three places by hinges.
5/8 high by 3/8 diameter
Marks: *K.F.*/anchors and scepter/*56*
Acc. No. 47-20-121

131. Agate, held in coils of gold serpent with faceted emerald set in forehead.
3/4 high by 1/2 diameter
Marks: illegible
Acc. No. 47-20-122

132. Gold. Raised design of three sapphire-set triangles and three diamonds.
3/4 high by 5/8 diameter
Marks: illegible
Acc. No. 47-20-123

133. Deep-blue enamel over tooled-gold ground, set with faceted diamond.
5/8 high by 3/8 diameter
Marks: illegible
Acc. No. 47-20-124

134. Gold. Blue enamel calyx at top.
5/8 high by 3/8 diameter
Marks: *56*/illegible
Acc. No. 47-20-125

135. Silver-gilt with heavy raised designs. Lower half ribbed with raised bands set with cabochon ruby and diamonds. Gold link chain.
1 1/8 high by 5/8 diameter
Marks: *K.F.*/anchors and scepter/*56*
Acc. No. 47-20-127

136. Gold. Set with seven rubies.
3/4 high by 1/2 diameter
Marks: none
Acc. No. 47-20-493

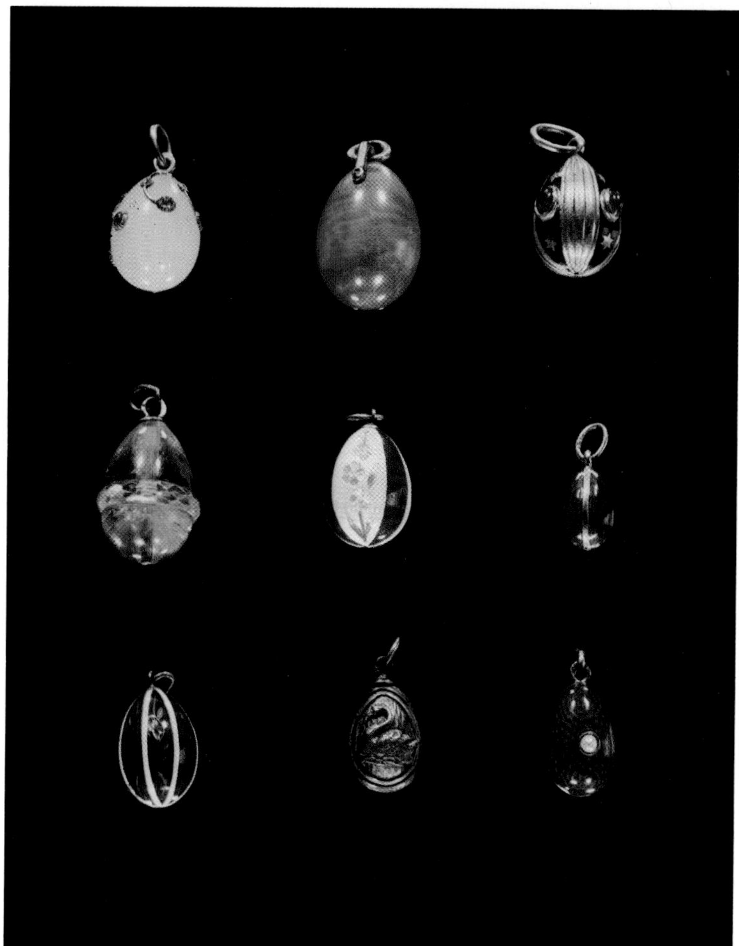

119-127

128-136

Catalog entry 152.

To cultivate a garden in which the shift of the seasons played no part, where no winter could freeze the roots and no summer's drought could scorch the blossoms; to fashion golden stems and leaves of veined nephrite, petals of chalcedony, enamel, agate, and amethyst, with stamens of gold set with sapphires and topaz, imperishable in their vases of rock crystal or pots of bloodstone with golden soil—this was Fabergé's gift to the frostbitten land of Russia. Of all his fancies, the flowers are the daintiest, the most felicitous, and the most universal.

No one can look at them without feeling a kind of intoxication: at the uncanny aptness with which stones, metals, and gems have been chosen and manipulated to repeat the structure of the model; at the admixture of extravagance which sets cornflowers with diamonds and makes lilies of the valley of pearls; at the poise of each spray, which has a prescribed and proportioned equilibrium. They are infused with a property that makes the nerves tingle and the eyes water with delight.

The idea had existed in Russia before being elaborated by Fabergé. Floral compositions of decorative and semi-precious stones had been produced in the lapidary works at Ekaterinburg from the middle of the 18th century, shortly after the foundation of the town by Peter the Great. The original workers and designers were mostly French and German, trained in Paris or Waldkirch in Breisgau; under Catherine the Great, production was increased and designs, largely the work of Dutch flower-painters employed by the Jardin des Plantes, were used.

Chinese and Japanese flower pieces, of lacquer, mother-of-pearl, jade, and silver or tinted bronze, of the later Ch'ing Dynasty and the later Edo (Tokyo) Period, made their way to St. Petersburg and the imperial collections either as diplomatic gifts or curiosities. Indeed, the Japanese influence on Fabergé's flower pieces was not only historical but direct.

How the fabrication of the flower pieces was carried out we do not know precisely. The workmaster (in the case of the Pratt Collection, predominantly Henrik Wigström) may have proceeded from detailed colored plates, from the flowers themselves—preserved, perhaps, in blocks of ice, as early botanical engravers were wont to keep their models—or from wax models made in the botanical gardens on the Apothecaries' Island in the Neva. The very fact that—save during the short, intense summer—flowers of any kind were hard to come by in Russia (for the court balls at the Winter Palace, special trains were run from Nice and Grasse, with refrigerated boxcars full of roses, orange blossoms, camellias, and daphne) was reason enough for the firm to act as a sort of magic florist's shop.

The materials selected are an excellent clue to Fabergé's sensitivity to three demands, each of which had to be met impartially. There was the need for verisimilitude. There were the limitations set by the properties of the stones, metals, and gems. And there was also the subjective requirement of originality.

For the leaves, nephrite is used. Shades of green, varying from celadon to myrtle, can be matched exactly. When carved to sufficient thinness, nephrite will reproduce their shadowed translucency, and the mottling is close to some leaves' natural maculation. Flowers, the petals of which are distinguished by a fairly opaque consistency, are rendered in chalcedony (the aster, hyacinth, two lilies of the valley, orange blossom, one poppy, verbena, and water lily). Instead of occurring as distinct crystals, like ordinary quartz, chalcedony has a fine splintery fracture and delicate fibrous structure which permit it to be worked without undue breakage or the interposition of troublesome cleavages. When polished, or left slightly clouded, it acquires a flower-like, waxy lustre.

For the buttercup, hawthorn, yellow pansies, and primrose, agate has been employed because of its denser structure, the variety of coloration, and its porosity, which makes possible the use of dyes and stains. Where the form of the perianth is too complicated to be cut in stone or the color is too special to be approximated (for example, the cornflowers, globeflower, and violet), enamel is the medium. Imitation is not, however, an inflexible rule. Amethyst, the natural hue of which is white or a bluish-purple, has been used for one group of pansies, the tulips, and an opium poppy; a cloudy white quartz is the basis of two rose buds, which are thereby made more diaphanous.

As might be expected, the materials used (as with the majority of animal figurines) are those which intrinsically coincide in color and texture with the blossoms of the flowers reproduced. But there remains just enough contrast between the substance and the subject to stir our sense of novelty, to register the quality of innovation. Thus the stems are always gold, not because stems are yellow but because gold is ductile and, when combined with baser materials, supplies both complement and luxuriance. The plain yet subtle device of turning rock crystal to form a glass half-filled with water in which the gold stem is set, is a stratagem at once so modest and so elegant that it results in surprise.

There is, thus, within these pieces a calculated and unexpected aesthetic tension: between their naturalism and their artifice, between the fitness of material and its native character, and between spontaneity and the control exercised over the composition. To the degree that this tension is perfected within the objects, and transmitted to the onlooker, that he may at once assent and learn, this craftsmanship stands rightfully within the realm of art.

137

138

139

140

137. Aster.
Blossoms of chalcedony; gold, emerald-set centers. Calyxes of green chalcedony. Siberian nephrite leaves. Gold soil in pot of jasper which shows grains of platinum. Pot banded with gold hoops. Made by Henrik Wigström.

6 high
Marks: *Fabergé/H.W./72*
Acc. No. 47-20-230

138. Buttercup.
Blossoms of translucent yellow agate, diamond-set stamens. Gold stems, nephrite leaves. Pot of lapis lazuli set on serpentine; gold soil. Made by Henrik Wigström.

6 high
Marks: *Fabergé/H.W./72*
Acc. No. 47-20-223

139. Cornflowers.
Blue enameled blossoms, gold stamens, and pistils set with diamonds, gold stems and leaves; rock-crystal vase.

5¾ high
Marks: none
Acc. No. 47-20-222

140. Dandelion seed ball.
Ball of many gold wires ending in diamonds; around each set is a tuft of asbestos filaments. Gold stem. Nephrite leaves. Rock-crystal vase. Made by Henrik Wigström.

6½ high
Marks: *Fabergé/H.W./72*
Acc. No. 47-20-235

141. Globeflower.
Blossoms of gold enameled with clear translucent yellow. Chased petals. Gold stem is grooved and lightly colored pale green. Dark-green nephrite leaves. Rock-crystal pot.

5 high
Marks: K. *Fabergé*/double eagle
Acc. No. 47-20-233

142. Hawthorn.
Haws of red and white agate. Gold stem, nephrite leaves. Agate pot on serpentine base with gold soil. Made by Henrik Wigström.

5½ high
Marks: *Fabergé/H.W./72*
Acc. No. 47-20-228

143. Hyacinth.
Blossoms of blue chalcedony, gold stamens, set with emeralds. Gold stem, Siberian nephrite leaves. Serpentine tub, gold soil. Made by Henrik Wigström.

6½ high
Marks: *Fabergé/H.W./72*
Acc. No. 47-20-224

144. Lilies of the valley.
Blossoms of translucent white chalcedony with gold centers. Gold stems, Siberian nephrite leaves. Rock-crystal container. Made by Henrik Wigström.

6¼ high
Marks: *Fabergé/H.W./72*
Acc. No. 47-20-220

141

142

143

144

145

146

147

148

149

145. Lilies of the valley.
Blossoms of white chalcedony, gold centers. Gold stems, Siberian nephrite leaves. Brown-veined agate tub with gold hoops, gold soil. Made by Henrik Wigström.

6⅛ high
Marks: *Fabergé/H.W./72*
Acc. No. 47-20-221

146. Lilies of the valley.
Pearl blossoms set with diamonds. Nephrite leaves, gold stems, bloodstone vase.

8 high
Marks: *Fabergé* (engraved on bottom of vase)
Acc. No. 47-20-237

147. Orange blossom.
Blossom with emerald center and buds of chalcedony. Gold stem, Siberian nephrite leaves. Rock-crystal vase. Made by Henrik Wigström.

7 high
Marks: *Fabergé/H.W./72*
Acc. No. 47-20-232

148. Pansies.
Blossoms of amethyst set with diamond centers. Nephrite calyxes. Gold stems, nephrite leaves. Rock-crystal vase.

5¼ high
Marks: none visible (covered by leaves?)
Acc. No. 47-20-227

149. Pansies.
Blossoms of golden-hued and carnelian agate on gold stems. Gold calyxes, centers of flowers set with diamonds. Nephrite leaves. Made by Henrik Wigström.

5 high
Marks: *Fabergé/H.W./72*
Acc. No. 47-20-234

150. Poppy.
Blossoms and bud of peach-toned chalcedony. Gold stamens set with sapphires, centers set with topaz. Gold sepals, gold stems. Siberian nephrite leaves. Tub of grayish-brown veined agate with diamond rivets, gold hoops, gold soil.

10¼ high
Marks: *Fabergé/H.W./72*
Acc. No. 47-20-217

151. Poppy.
Amethyst blossom. Cabochon Siberian amethyst set in gold and platinum forms heart of blossom. Diamond-pointed stamens. Gold stem, Siberian nephrite leaves. Tub of brown-toned striped agate. Silver-gilt hoops with diamond rivets. Gold soil. Made by Henrik Wigström.

8¾ high
Marks: *Fabergé/H.W./72*
Acc. No. 47-20-218

151

153

154

155

156

157

158

152. Primrose.
Blossoms of carnelian, gold stamens, diamond-set centers. Siberian nephrite leaves, gold stems. Rock-crystal vase. Made by Henrik Wigström.

8¾ high
Marks: *Fabergé/H.W./72*
Acc. No. 47-20-219

153. Roses.
Buds of quartz with gold stems bearing gold thorns. Nephrite leaves. Pot of gray-brown agate with gold hoops, gold soil. Made by Henrik Wigström.

5¾ high
Marks: *Fabergé/H.W./72*
Acc. No. 47-20-229

154. Tulip.
Blossoms of amethyst with diamond-set gold stamens. Gold stem, nephrite leaves. Gray-brown agate container; silver-gilt hoops with diamond rivets; gold soil. Made by Henrik Wigström.

8½ high
Marks: *Fabergé/H.W./72*
Acc. No. 47-20-231

155. Verbena.
Blossoms of blue and white chalcedony, centers pointed with diamonds. Gold pedicles and stem. Siberian nephrite leaves. Brown-veined agate tub with gold soil. Made by Henrik Wigström.

5¾ high
Marks: *Fabergé/H.W./72*
Acc. No. 47-20-226

156. Violet.
Four petals of blue stone, fifth petal of gold and yellow enamel set with diamonds, each petal edged with gold band. Leaves of nephrite. Gold stems. Rock-crystal container.

3⅞ high
Marks: none
Acc. No. 47-20-236

157. Violet.
Blossom of gold enameled in purple, diamond center. Gold stem, nephrite leaf.

3½ high
Marks: *S*/gothic *N/5/O*/illegible
Acc. No. 47-20-238

158. Water lily.
Blossoms and buds of chalcedony, stamens set with rubies. Gold stems, Siberian nephrite leaves. Rock-crystal container. Made by Henrik Wigström.

6¾ high
Marks: *Fabergé/H.W./72*
Acc. No. 47-20-225

Picture Frames

Catalog entry 172.

It is impossible to comprehend the importance of picture frames in Fabergé's output without some appreciation of several characteristics of European nobility and royalty. The first is the consanguinity, in various degrees, of practically every ruling house, major or minor. The second is the almost idolatrous attitude toward souvenirs. The third is the status of the photograph and the miniature.

A portrait was much more than a pleasant reminder. It was indispensable evidence of contact, of favor. To members of noble and royal families, a profusion of photographs (preferably autographed) was a confirmation of their alliances, a demonstration of solidarity. The highest distinction which could be conferred on a woman of the Russian court was for her to be made *dame à portrait.* The award carried no emoluments. The recipient was allowed to wear a small miniature of the Empress, set with brilliants. That was all.

Photography for the amateur was still a great novelty: it was not until the mid 1890s that cameras with roll film came into general use. But the Czar with the Czarina could employ professional photographers to record their wholesome family moments. These went not into black cardboard albums, but into frames of rock crystal, silver, and gold. Four generations of the imperial family are thus depicted and enshrined.

159

160

161

162

163

164

165

ENAMEL

159. Gold. Pale-blue translucent enamel over chased gold ground surmounted with ribbon bowknot in red gold, from which hang two green-gold laurel festoons held at upper corners of frame by red-gold bowknots set with diamonds. Two diamond-set rosettes in lower corners. Ivory back. Photograph of Grand Duchess Marie and Grand Duchess Anastasia.

 5½ high by 3⅝ wide
 Marks: *K. Fabergé*/double eagle/profile/*56*/*54522*
 Acc. No. 47-20-311

160. Gold. Gun-metal blue enamel over chasing. Outer border of egg-and-dart design, inner border of bead-and-dash design. Two borders connected by intricate motifs. Photograph of pastel drawing of Grand Duchess Olga by Frederick August Von Kaulbach.

 3½ high by 2⅞ wide
 Marks: *Fabergé*/*M.P.*/crossed anchors/*56*/*45243*
 Acc. No. 47-20-318

161. Gold. Ultramarine-blue enamel over sunburst chasing. Outer moulding of continuous leaf design, pearl-set inner moulding. Ivory back. Photograph of the Czarevitch.

 3⅜ high by 3 wide
 Marks: *Fabergé*/anchors and scepter/*11930*/*SA*/*D*/–
 Acc. No. 47-20-321

162. Silver. Sky-blue enamel over horizontal chasing. Ribbed border. Plain silver inner moulding. White wood back. Photograph of Grand Duchess Tatiana.

 3⅝ high by 3⅝ wide
 Marks: *K. Fabergé*/double eagle/profile/*84*
 Acc. No. 47-20-332

163. Gold and silver. Iridescent blue enamel. Diamond-set X at top. Outer and inner moulding of leaf-and-dart design. Ivory back. Photograph of Czarina Alexandra Feodorovna in court dress. She wears the *kokochnik,* a slightly triangular diadem of solid rows of pearls.

 3½ high by 3½ wide
 Marks: *Fabergé*/*H.W.*/profile/*88*/*91*/*16167*
 Acc. No. 47-20-333

164. Gold. Surmounted with ribbon enhancement. Two lines of white enamel enclose field of sky-blue enamel over chasing. Circular opening. Ivory back. Miniature of Grand Duchess Tatiana.

 1⅞ diameter
 Marks: *K.F.*/*M.P.*/profile/*56*/*84*/*25203*
 Acc. No. 47-20-340

165. Silver-gilt. Plain outer border surmounted with ribbon enhancement. Field of cobalt-blue enamel with wreath decoration over chasing. Russian-birch back in simulated ivory. Miniature of Empress Marie Alexandrovna, wife of Alexander II, grandmother of Nicholas II, the daughter of Grand Duke Ludwig II of Hesse.

 4 high by 2¾ wide
 Marks: *A.N.*/illegible
 Acc. No. 47-20-346

166

167

169

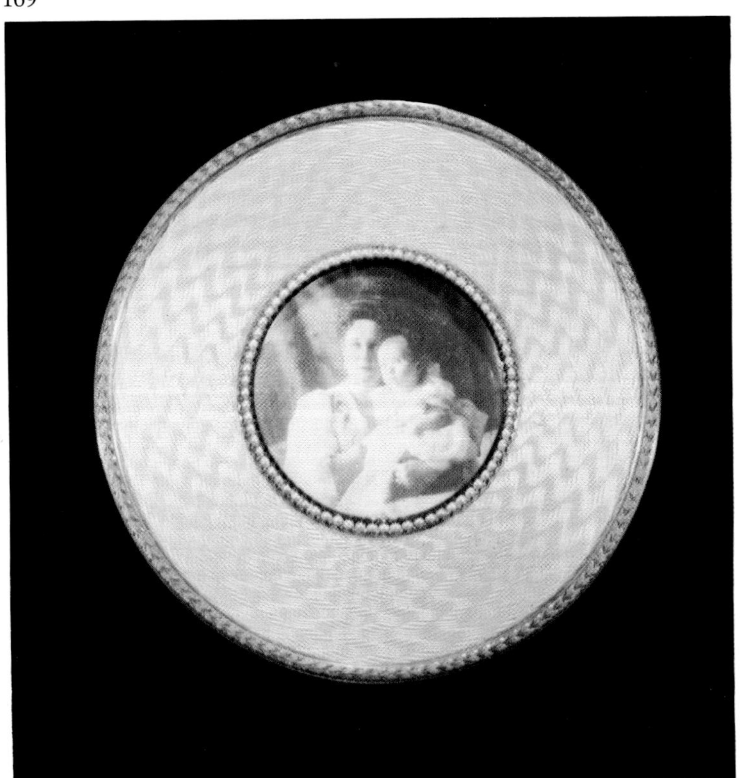

170

171

166. Silver. Deep-blue enamel over chasing. Beaded outer border, circular opening set with pearls. Ivory back. Photograph of unidentified woman.

3 1/8 high by 3 1/2 wide
Marks: *Fabergé*/*V.A.*/anchors and scepter/*88*/*59687*
Acc. No. 47-20-348

167. Red and green gold. Triangle, convex sides. Light-blue enamel over radiating chasing. Circular opening surmounted with bowknot, both set with diamonds. Outer border of leaf design. Photograph of Grand Duchess Tatiana.

2 5/8 high by 2 3/4 wide
Marks: *Fabergé*/*M.P.*/anchors and scepter/*56*
Acc. No. 47-20-349

168. Silver-gilt. Sky-blue enamel over chased ground. Outer border of double leaves. Inner border of bead design. At top, laurel-leaf festoons, rosettes, and ribbon-and-bow enhancement. Holly-wood back. Photograph of King George V of England and the Prince of Wales standing together with Nicholas II and the Czarevitch, all in yachting costume, probably taken just prior to World War I.

12 3/4 high by 9 3/16 wide
Marks: *K. Fabergé*/*A.N.*/profile/*88*
Acc. No. 47-20-413

169. Silver-gilt. Green enamel over machine-chased ground. Ovolo outer border surmounted by two griffins and an urn. Inner borders of ivory with bead fillets. Above openings is double eagle in silver set with three rubies and a diamond; below are four rosettes and three joined swags with festoons. Ivory back. Photographs of Czar Nicholas II and Czarina Alexandra Feodorovna.

4 1/4 high by 6 wide
Marks: *K. Hann*/double eagle/*88*/illegible
Acc. No. 47-20-330

170. Red and green gold. Light green enamel over chasing. Border of leaf design, pearl-set opening. Photograph of Czarina Alexandra Feodorovna and a baby.

3 diameter
Marks: *Fabergé*/*H.W.*/profile/*56*/illegible
Acc. No. 47-20-338

171. Green and yellow gold. Moss-green enamel over radiating chased lines. Outer border of leaf design. Pearl-set inner border. Ivory back. Photograph of Grand Duchess Marie.

3 high by 2 5/8 wide
Marks: *Fabergé*/*56*/illegible
Acc. No. 47-20-343

172. Silver-gilt. Cinquefoil design formed by swags fastened to rosettes-and-ribbon bows. Emerald green enamel over radiating chased lines. Circular opening in center, five oval openings around perimeter. Ivory back. Photographs of Czar Nicholas II and his family.

5 3/4 high by 5 3/4 wide
Marks: *Fabergé*/*M.P.*/anchors and scepter/*88*
Acc. No. 47-20-350

173

174

175

176

173. Silver-gilt. Mauve translucent enamel over chased ground. Outer moulding of chased acanthus-leaf motif, inner moulding set with pearls. Rock-crystal cover. Photograph of Czar Nicholas II and the Czarevitch.

4⅝ high by 3⅜ wide
Marks: *Fabergé/M.P./*crossed anchors*/88/57700*
Acc. No. 47-20-309

174. Silver-gilt. Mauve enamel over machine chasing. Rosette and two festoons in each corner. Ball-and-dash design on outer border, inner border of fascine design. Wood back with easel bearing the name "Victoria" in openwork. Rock-crystal cover. Photograph of Czarina Alexandra Feodorovna.

4½ high by 3⅜ wide
Marks: *Fabergé/84*
Acc. No. 47-20-314

175. Gold. Mauve enamel over chasing. Outer border of green- and red-gold leaf design with rosettes at corners. Small oval opening designed to simulate a pendant, which is held by a red-gold ribbon attached to a rosette. A rosette on either side of this; the three hold the ends of two swags and festoons. Ivory back. Photograph of Grand Duchess Olga.

3¾ high by 2¼ wide
Marks: *Fabergé/M.P./*profile*/56/2845/*illegible
Acc. No. 47-20-319

176. Yellow gold. Deep mauve enamel over chased ground. Leaf-design border, pearl-set opening. Ivory back. Photograph of unidentified child.

3¼ diameter
Marks: *Fabergé/H.W./*profile*/56/*illegible.
Acc. No. 47-20-337

177. Silver-gilt. Orange enamel over machine chasing. Applied garlands and crossed arrows and two running sprays of leaves which cross and recross parallel to sides. Outer border of fascine design, inner border of leaf design with square pearl in each corner. Ivory back. Photograph of Grand Duchess Tatiana.

3½ high by 2½ wide
Marks: *Fabergé/M.P./*anchors and scepter*/88/54687*
Acc. No. 47-20-315

178. Silver. Ruby enamel over chasing, applied silver-gilt openwork design of leafy sprays connected by running wavy border. Green- and white-enamel moulding. Photograph of Czar Alexander III in his study besieged by portraits on the walls and on his desk.

5½ high by 4¾ wide
Marks: *Fabergé/V.A./*profile*/88*
Acc. No. 47-20-308

179. Silver. Rose enamel over chased ground. Outer border of chased leaf motif, inner border of bead motif. Ivory and metal back. Photograph of Grand Duchess Marie.

4⅝ high by 3⅛ wide
Marks: *Fabergé/H.W./*profile*/88/22334*
Acc. No. 47-20-310

177

178

179

180

181

182

180. Silver-gilt. Rose translucent enamel over machine chasing. Outer border chased in leaf design with small rosettes at joints. Pearl-bordered oval opening designed to simulate pendant suspended by a loop through which runs a swag. Ivory back. Photograph of Czar Nicholas II.

4 high by 2½ wide
Marks: *M.P.*/profile/*88*/*S*/*8918*/illegible
Acc. No. 47-20-313

181. Silver-gilt. Ruby enamel over chased ground, applied red- and green-gold rosettes and sprays, surmounted by crown and ribbon. Outer border of green-gold leaf design with red-gold ribbons, inner border of dot-and-dash motif. Ivory back. Photograph of Grand Duchess Anastasia.

4½ high by 2¾ wide
Marks: *K. Fabergé*/double eagle/profile/*YL*/*88*/*30075*
Acc. No. 47-20-317

182. Silver-gilt. Red iridescent enamel over chased silver. Rectangle with three low concave depressions and convex semicircle on top. Outer moulding of leaf design, inner moulding of beaded design. Above opening are three bowknots with swags and festoons; below is coiled monster and sword design. Photograph of Czarina Alexandra Feodorovna in court dress.

3 11/16 high by 3 1/16 wide
Marks: profile/*88*/illegible
Acc. No. 47-20-323

183. Silver-gilt. Rose enamel over machine-chased ground. Outer moulding of leaf design surmounted with ribbon in a bowknot. Inner moulding of bead design. Above opening is double eagle with crown set with diamonds and sapphire. Swag and festoon design below. Photograph of Czarina Alexandra Feodorovna.

6 high by 3¼ wide
Marks: *K. Hann*/double eagle/*88*/illegible
Acc. No. 47-20-326

184. Yellow and green gold. Twisted-leaf design over translucent, pale-pink enamel on chased ground. In center is disk of green jade which contains small gold fillet. Frame surrounded with ruby-set bowknot. Photograph of a daughter of Nicholas II.

2½ high by 1¾ wide
Marks: *56*/illegible
Acc. No. 47-20-339

185. Gilt bronze. Yellow enamel over chased ground. Inner border set with diamonds, encircled with floral spray of diamonds and three sapphires. Diamond-and-sapphire crown surmounts opening. Two sapphires placed near upper corners. Applied gold bands over enamel form circular design of carved leaf motif. Easel bears monogram of Nicholas II. Miniature of Czar Nicholas II in uniform, a rather coarser work than some miniatures, indicative of the quality of workmanship in St. Petersburg outside the Fabergé atelier.

4¾ high by 3½ wide
Marks: *F★K*/profile/*56*/illegible
Acc. No. 47-20-307

183

184

185

186

187

188

189

190

186. Red and green gold. White enamel over chased-gold ground. Moss agate sprays radiating from circular opening set with pearls. Outer border of leaf design. Ivory back. Photograph of the Czarevitch.

3¼ diameter
Marks: *H. W.* /profile/illegible
Acc. No. 47-20-336

187. Gold. Border of leaf design set at intervals with eight rubies; surmounted with bowknot. Field of white enamel over chased ground. Oval opening set with pearls. Ivory back. Steel engraving of Catherine the Great.

3⅛ high by 2¼ wide
Marks: *Fabergé* (engraved)/*H. W.* /profile/*56*
Acc. No. 47-20-344

188. Red, yellow, and green gold. Triangle-shaped. White enamel over sunburst chasing. Sides extend and terminate in pineapples. Diamond-set rosettes in angles and along sides. From rosette in base extend two leafy stems up to rosettes on either side; third stem extends vertically, reaching the apex, and is interrupted by one of three gold openings. Openings have small hinged covers of orchid-pink enamel set with diamond. Ivory back. Photographs of the daughters of Czar Nicholas II.

2½ high by 2⅛ wide
Marks: *K.F.* /*A.N.* /profile/*56*
Acc. No. 47-20-347

189. Silver-gilt. White enamel over cross-hatch chasing. Blue ribbon placed over field forms a cross representing the Royal Order of St. Andrew. Circular, chased opening intercepts the cross. Outer moulding of fascine design. Wood back. Photograph of Grand Duchess Olga, Grand Duchess Marie, their governess, and Grand Duchess Tatiana.

5¾ high by 8¼ wide
Marks: *Fabergé*/*A.N.* /profile/*91*
Acc. No. 47-20-357

190. Silver. Triptych. White iridescent enamel over chasing. Outer border of leaf design. Ribbon-decorated baton applied over enamel with swags and festoons interrupted by opening of central panel. Opening enclosed within leaf design and a square with chamfered corners. Left and right panels of white enamel decorated with encircled rosettes. Photograph of the Czarevitch, Czar Nicholas II, Czarina Alexandra Feodorovna.

4½ high by 3⅜ wide
Marks: *Fabergé*/*YL*/profile/*88*
Acc. No. 47-20-358

191. Green-, red-, and yellow-gold and platinum. White enamel over chasing. Outer moulding of cisele. Inner moulding of bead-and-dash design. Surmounted with ribbon in bowknot. Floral swags on upper part of field, double spray of laurel on lower part. Ivory back. Photograph of Queen Alexandra of England.

2¼ diameter
Marks: none
Acc. No. 47-20-359

191

192

193

194

195

196

197

198

192. Silver-gilt. Double frame with reversible support. One face enameled in mauve over sunburst chasing, other side in white enamel. Both have opening bordered with silver moulding in fascine design with ribbon ties at intervals. Photographs of Grand Duke Michael and Grand Duchess Elizabeth.

4½ high by 2¾ wide
Marks: *Fabergé/YL/*profile/*88/18194*
Acc. No. 47-20-312

193. Gold. Cartouche with *plique à jour* enamel floral design in ruby, emerald, light blue, and dark blue. By either Alexander Tillander, a worker for the court jeweler K. Hann, or A. Tobinkov, of the firm of Nichols and Plincke. Oval opening. Ivory back. Photograph of Czar Nicholas II.

3⅛ high by 2⅝ wide
Marks: *A.T./*anchors and scepter/*86*
Acc. No. 47-20-329

194. Gold. Red, white, and blue enamel, colors of the imperial standard. Beaded moulding on outer edge, square opening bounded with narrow, ribbed moulding. Ivory and metal back. Photograph of Czar Nicholas II in uniform.

2 7/16 by 2 7/16 wide
Marks: *Fabergé/H.W./*profile/*56/91/19762*
Acc. No. 47-20-334

195. Gold. Shaped as two superimposed triangles to form a six-pointed star. The border of one triangle has a bead design and a field of white enamel over wavy chasing. Other has a pointed scallop design with field of yellow enamel over sunburst chasing. Ivory back. Photograph of unidentified young woman.

3 high by 2⅝ wide
Marks: *Fabergé/M.P./*anchors and scepter/*56/55135*
Acc. No. 47-20-352

METAL

196. Gold. Border of large diamonds, surmounted with diamond-set crown. Loop on back attaches frame to gold fluted column decorated with chased green-gold acanthus leaves and surmounted with chased, ribbon-tied wreath. Column rests on square base having four ball feet. Miniature of Czar Nicholas II. The work of Henrik Wigström, it was a birthday gift of the Czarina to her husband in 1907. Were it not for the brilliants surrounding the miniature itself, the piece might be taken for a French First Empire creation: the image of the Czar caps what is essentially a triumphal column, a painful conceit considering that the defeats of Mukden and Tsushima were only two years past.

6 high by 1½ diameter; base, 2 wide
Marks: *Fabergé/H.W./*profile/*56*
Acc. No. 47-20-303

197. Silver. Octagon, engraved crown and name "Serge" on left; crown and name "Elizaveta" on right. Below are the dates "1891-1904." At top a crown in relief and enamel plaque of St. George Slaying the Dragon. Border of fascine design with ties at angles. Ivory back. Photograph of the Grand Duke Serge Alexandrovitch and the Grand Duchess Elizaveta Feodorovna, brother and sister-in-law of Alexander III.

7½ diameter
Marks: *K.F./*profile/*84*
Acc. No. 47-20-355

198. Silver-gilt. Surmounted with crown. Edged with bead design. Miniature of Grand Duchess Olga.

3½ high by 2⅝ wide
Marks: none
Acc. No. 47-20-341

199

200

201

NATURAL SUBSTANCES

199. Gold. Face of polished ivory. Oval opening with red-gold concentric ribbing tied with running design of leaf and blossom. Outer border of acanthus leaf design. Glass held in narrow oval with bead design. Ivory back. Photograph of unidentified young girl.

3⅜ high by 2⅞ wide
Marks: *M.P.*/anchors and scepter/*56*
Acc. No. 47-20-316

200. Gold. Lapis lazuli field. Outer border of leaf design, pearl-set fillet around oval opening. Ivory back. Photograph of Grand Duchess Marie.

3⅜ high by 2½ wide
Marks: *Fabergé*/profile/*56*/*88*/*26318*
Acc. No. 47-20-342

201. Lapis lazuli. Pearl-set inner border. Applied green- and yellow-gold and silver floral sprays set with diamond at bottom. Diamond set in each lower corner. Mother-of-pearl back. Photograph of unidentified woman.

2½ high by 2 5/16 wide
Marks: none
Acc. No. 47-20-353

202. Nephrite. Three rosettes hold two red- and green-gold swags and two festoons at top. Bordered with gold leaf design and topped with gold ribbon. Inner border of fascine design. Ivory back. Photograph of the Czar's children.

5½ high by 2¾ wide
Marks: *Fabergé* (incomplete)/profile/illegible
Acc. No. 47-20-320

203. Nephrite. Two oval openings bounded with silver fillets in design of ruby, black, and white enamel. Ivory back. Photographs of Peter Carl Fabergé and his wife.

3 high by 4½ wide
Marks: *Fabergé*/*H.W.*/*88*
Acc. No. 47-20-324

204. Nephrite. Silver-gilt garland around oval opening surmounted with bowknot and two rosettes from which hang two swags and two festoons. Two rosettes below. Photograph of Czarina Alexandra Feodorovna.

2¾ high by 2 wide
Marks: *I.* [?]/profile/*88*/*E 754*/*No. 170*
Acc. No. 47-20-328

205. Nephrite. A-shaped frame. Two pearl-set rectangular openings. At top, ruby holding ribbon in place suspends a basket of flowers in three tones of gold. Four other rubies support swags of blossoms. Below, a rod ending in pineapples extends through ruby in ribbon knot. Mother-of-pearl back. Photographs of paintings of Czar Nicholas II and Czarina Alexandra Feodorovna.

3½ high by 4¾ wide
Marks: *Fabergé*/*YL*/profile/*88*
Acc. No. 47-20-354

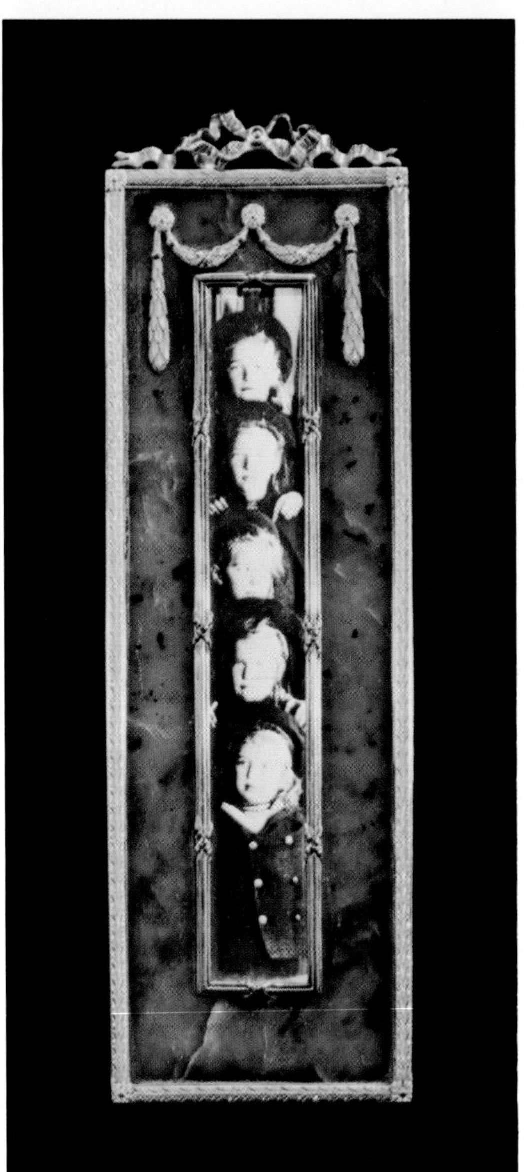

202

203

204

205

206

207

208

206. Silver-gilt. Rose quartzite field. Outer border overlaps the edge of the field at four points, which are ribbed radiations. Rounded top and lower corners. Two feet, metal back. Photograph of unidentified young girl.

3¼ high by 2¼ wide
Marks: *M.P.*/anchors and scepter/*84*/*45196*
Acc. No. 47-20-327

207. Heart-shaped, rock-crystal frame on nephrite stand. Curved wire rack of gold. Photograph of Grand Duke Boris Vladimirovitch.

3⅜ high by 3 wide
Marks: *H.W.*/*56*
Acc. No. 47-20-305

208. Yellow and green gold. Diamond shape. Gold lily spray; ruby-set stamens fastened to rock crystal with gold pinions. Outer border of gold fascine design. Circular opening bordered with emeralds. Ivory back. Photograph of Grand Duchess Tatiana.

4 high by 2¾ wide
Marks: *K.F.*/*56*/illegible
Acc. No. 47-20-351

209. Gold. Carved garland surmounted with ribbon-knot which has two rubies and is surmounted with pearl. Carved base holds frame upright upon serpentine column. Carved leaf fillet of gold at junction of column and base. Fillet near top of column with four square rubies, two swags, and two festoons. Oval openings covered with convex rock crystal. Photographs of pastels of Grand Duchess Olga and Grand Duchess Tatiana, as children, by Frederick August Von Kaulbach.

4½ high by 1½ diameter
Marks: *H.W.*/*56*/illegible
Acc. No. 47-20-304

209

210

211

212

210. Serpentine held by two fillets of leaf design. Opened, the egg becomes a double frame with two easels attached to the fillets, allowing it to stand. On outside of egg are two gold oval frames. Photographs of Grand Duchess Anastasia and Grand Duchess Tatiana.

2¼ high by 1¾ wide
Marks: *M.P.*/anchors and scepter/*56*
Acc. No. 47-20-306

211. Serpentine. Fluted gold bands radiate from circular opening which is bound with gold fillet in bead-and-dash design. Outer border is twisted gold design. Ivory and gold back. Photograph of unidentified young girl.

3 high by 3 wide
Marks: *M.P.*/anchors and scepter/*56*
Acc. No. 47-20-335

212. Wood with silver-gilt mountings. Doors have *botonée* cross catch. Central panel has field of white enamel over chasing. Pearl-set oval opening. Cherub heads and wings in high relief in corners. Pencil drawing of dead woman.

7⅜ high by 9¼ wide
Marks: *Fabergé*/*V. A.*/profile/*88*
Acc. No. 47-20-356

Handles

Catalog entries 213, 214.

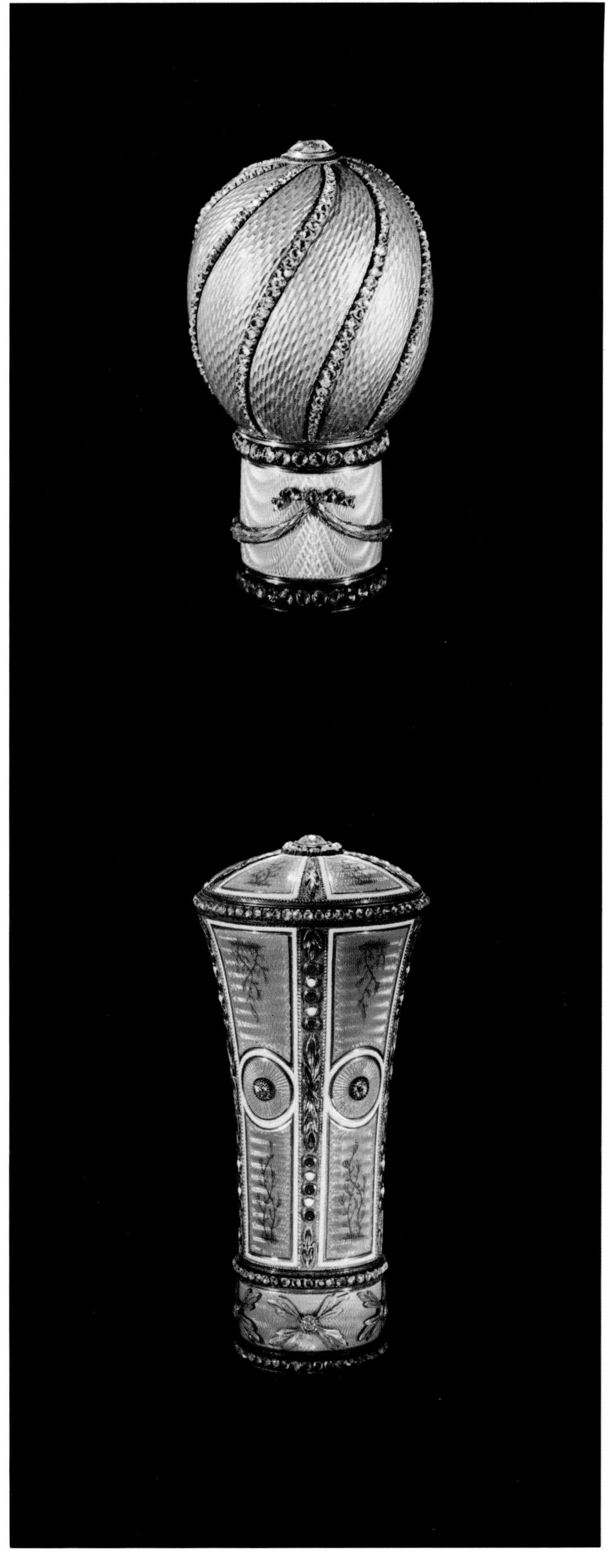

Of the thirty-eight handles in the Pratt Collection, eighteen are definitely stamped with Fabergé hallmarks. The remainder, with few exceptions, are certainly from his workshops. The handles supplied fantasy without undue expenditure of labor. The three classes of material closest to Fabergé's heart—enamel, precious metals, and semi-precious stones—could be freely adapted in a multiplicity of shapes and finishes and wrought with his wonted deference to character. The enamel handles are mauve, translucent rose, or metallic blue, the panels set between carved gold bands or rows of small rose-cut diamonds. The decorative stones are, for both practical and aesthetic reasons, preferred. Since they did not require jewelry work or repeated firings, they were more tractable in the workshop.

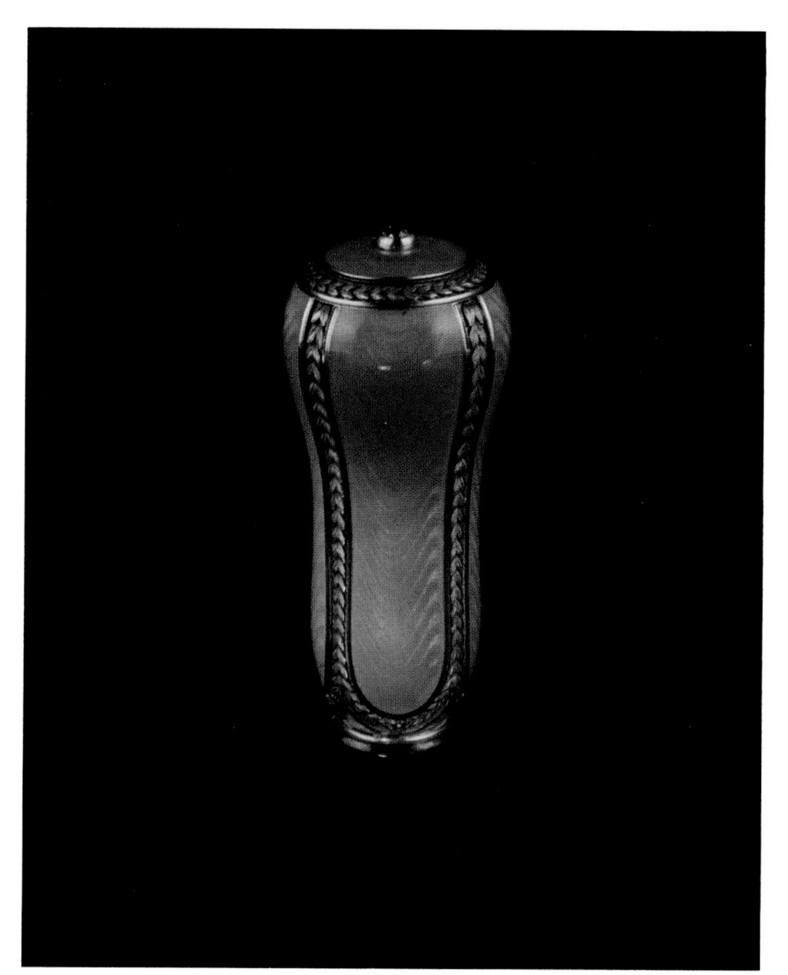

215

216

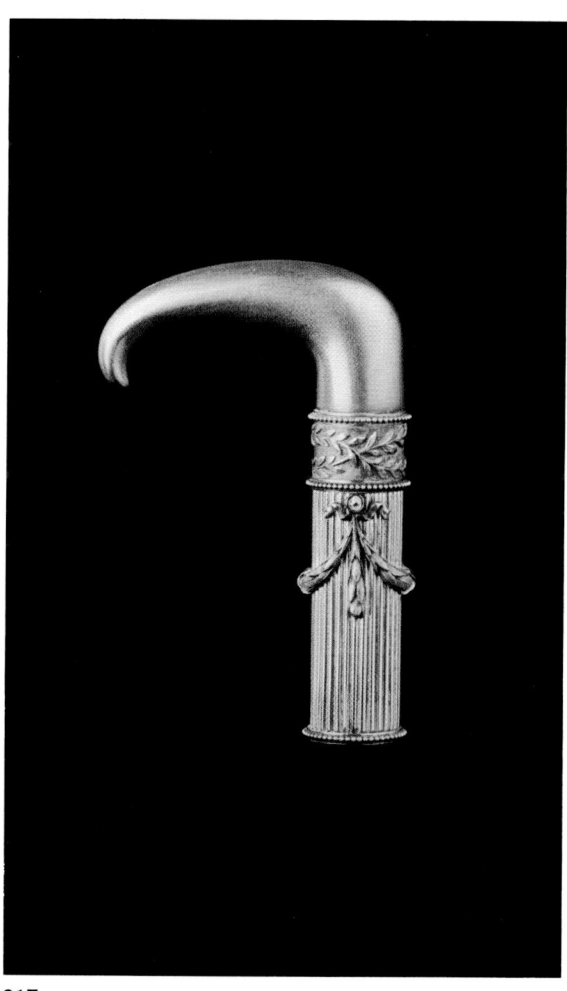

217

218

219

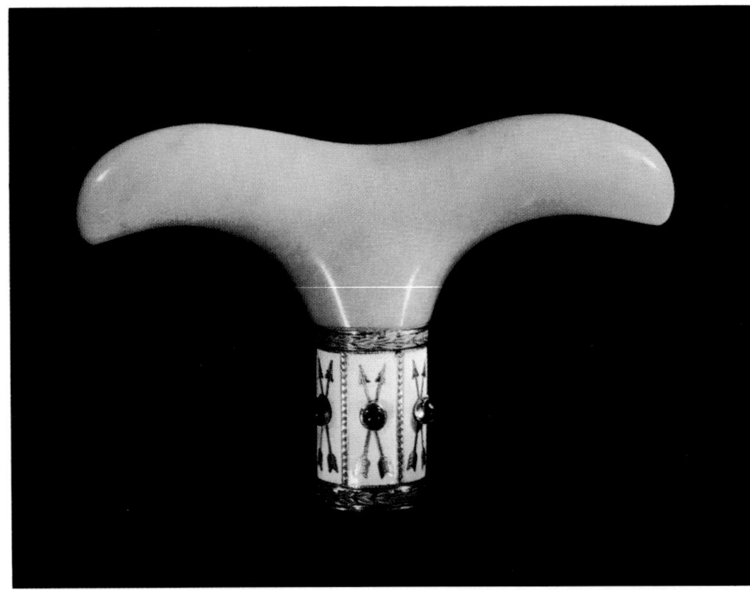
220

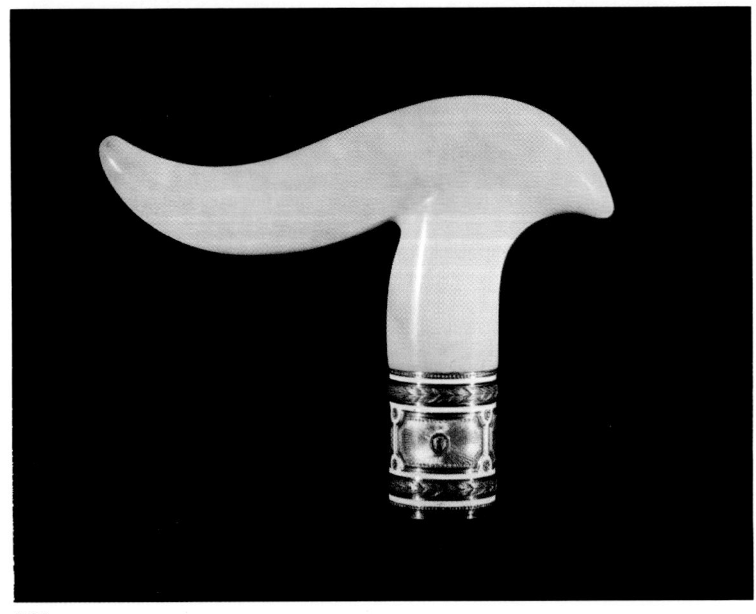
221

ENAMEL

213. Gold. Mauve enamel and diamond top. Narrow diamond-set bands spiral downward to meet diamond and yellow enamel ferrule. Two red- and green-gold swags in leaf design are suspended from two oppositely placed diamonds on ferrule.

3 high by 1½ diameter
Marks: *M.P.*/anchors and scepter/*56*
Acc. No. 47-20-172

214. Gold. Rose translucent enamel with moss agate effects in five panels with diamonds set in centers. Diamond, ringed with small diamonds, set in top; diamond-set rim. Bounded with enamel fillets with diamond-set leaf forms.

3¼ high by 1½ diameter
Marks: *M.P.*/anchors and scepter/*56*
Acc. No. 47-20-186.

215. Gold. Rose enamel over chased gold ground in four panels separated by chased gold walls. Neck of deep blue enamel fillet. Top is rounded and set with yellow diamond.

2⅝ high by 1 diameter
Marks: anchors and scepter/*56*/illegible
Acc. No. 47-20-195

216. Gold. Metallic-blue enamel panels over chased ground, chamfered corners bound with opaque white enamel. Panels separated by stiles of stippled gold bearing floral designs in ruby and green enamel. Metallic-blue enamel top set with diamond.

3 high by 1 diameter
Marks: *Fabergé*/*H.W.*/profile/*YL*/*72*/owl
Acc. No. 47-20-199

METAL

217. Gold. Neck with carved running leaf motif in green gold, bounded with beaded fillets. Below, two diamonds and red- and green-gold swags and festoons; fluted red-gold column. Is of First Empire inspiration.

2½ high by 1½ wide
Marks: *K.F.*/profile/*56*/illegible
Acc. No. 47-20-185

NATURAL SUBSTANCES

218. Amethyst of irregular shape held in five flat, irregular silver-gilt bands. Silver-gilt neck with two ribbed fillets.

2½ high by 1½ wide
Marks: *G.S.*/profile/*84*
Acc. No. 47-20-189

219. Amethyst. Two shells on a frond capital. Neck of pearl enamel over chased ground, interlaced trefoils set with diamonds at interstices. Diamond-set fillets.

2 high by 1 wide
Marks: none
Acc. No. 47-20-193

220. Aventurine. Red- and green-gold neck with six opaque-white enamel panels, each containing two crossed arrows and a cabochon red Ural stone.

2½ high by 3⅝ wide
Marks: none
Acc. No. 47-20-173

221. Aventurine. Green enamel panels bordered with white enamel and set with diamond in center on gold neck. Chased gold bands.

2¾ high by 3 wide
Marks: profile/*72*/*10886*/illegible
Acc. No. 47-20-174

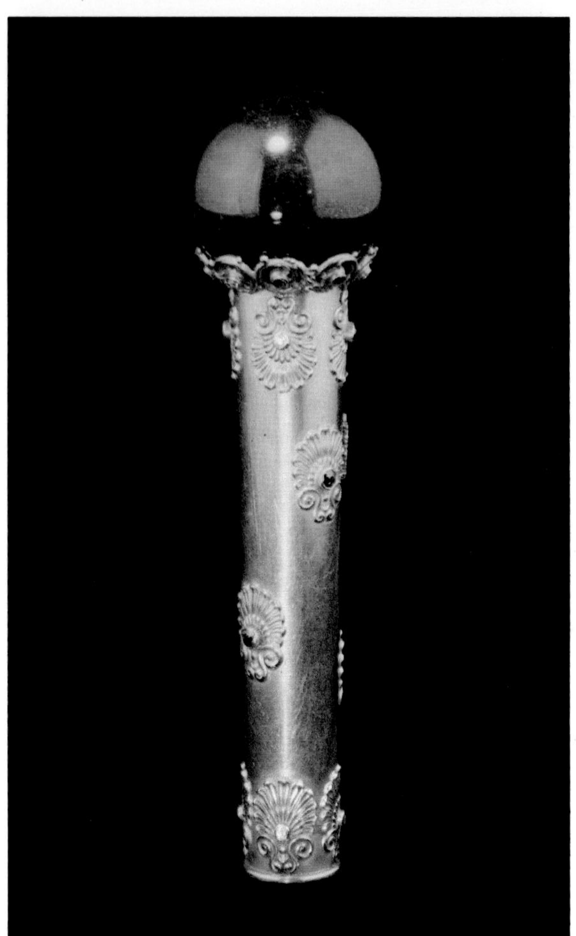
222

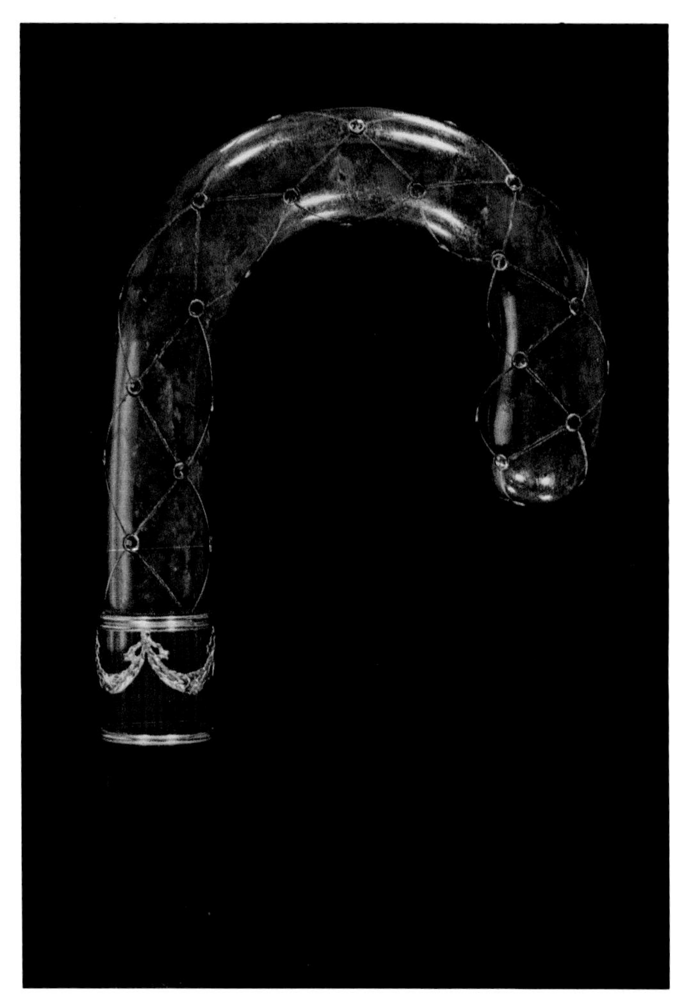
223

224

225

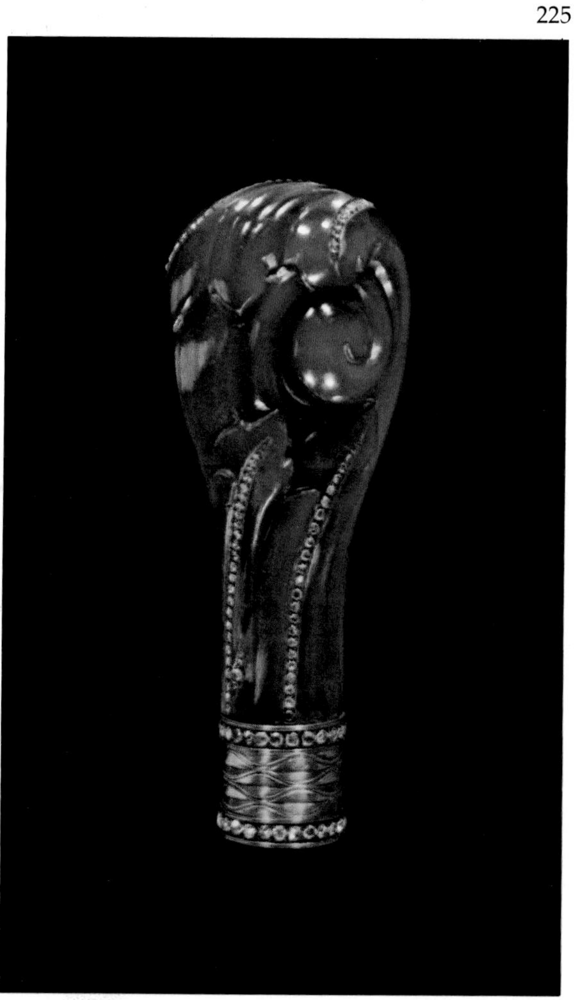

226

222. Lapis lazuli. Gold column with sphere, supported by scroll design set with diamonds, rubies, and emeralds. Column decorated with shell motifs mounted with varicolored stones. Double eagle with St. George Slaying the Dragon and numerous escutcheons applied to one side of column.

4⅞ high by 1⅜ diameter
Marks: none
Acc. No. 47-20-179

223. Nephrite. Chased lozenges set with rubies at intersections. Red-gold neck, red enamel, four swags. Attached to tortoise-shell shaft.

12¾ high by 2¾ wide
Marks: none
Acc. No. 47-20-166

224. Nephrite. Silver-gilt bands at top and bottom with fret chasing. Top encrusted with faceted light sapphire-blue stones. Tortoise-shell shaft.

12 high by 1 wide
Marks: none
Acc. No. 47-20-167

225. Nephrite, inlaid with ribbon and bowknot design of two rubies and small diamonds. Red-gold ferrule set with diamonds.

3⅞ high by ¾ diameter
Marks: none
Acc. No. 47-20-170

226. Nephrite. Diamond-set bands simulate veins of leaves. Red-gold neck with diamond-set fillets.

3¼ high by 1¼ wide
Marks: *Fabergé/M.P./1225*
Acc. No. 47-20-178

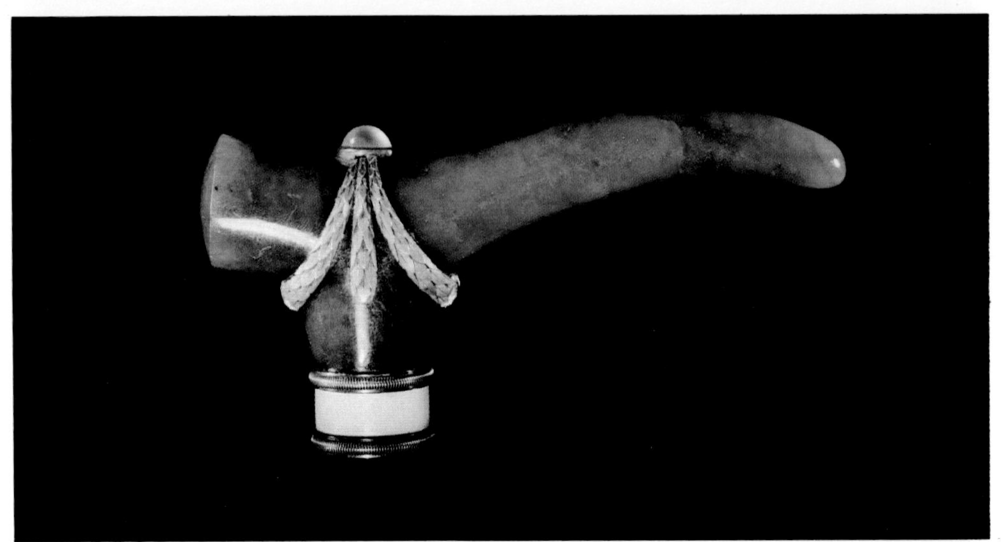
227

228

230

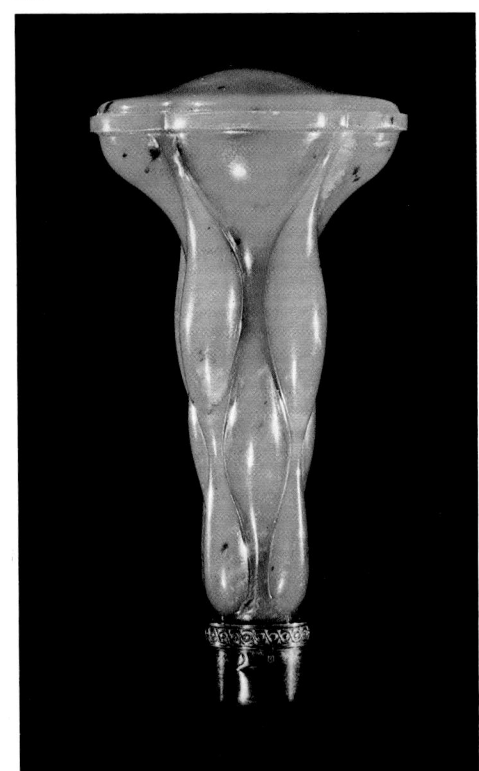
229

231

227. Nephrite. Top setting of orchid-pink quartz cut *en cabochon*. Green-gold chased garlands and festoons. White iridescent enamel over swag-cut chasing and ribbed-fillet neck.

1¾ high by 3½ wide
Marks: *72*
Acc. No. 47-20-180

228. Nephrite. Segmented sphere; diamond-encircled ruby set in top. Gold, filleted neck set with pink and white stones in chased surface resembling woven cloth.

2¾ high by 1½ diameter
Marks: *E.K.*/anchors and scepter/*56*
Acc. No. 47-20-190

229. Nephrite. Entwined bulbous shapes rise to quatrefoil convex top. Silver-gilt neck with guilloche band.

4 high by 2¼ wide
Marks: profile/*84*/illegible
Acc. No. 47-20-191

230. Nephrite. Sphere with eight panels outlined with inlaid gold set alternately with rubies and diamonds. Rose quartz set in top of sphere. Neck of ribbed gold with diamond and ruby-set fillet at lower end.

2⅝ high by 1¾ diameter
Marks: none
Acc. No. 47-20-192

231. Nephrite. Gold neck; white enamel over diagonal chasing set with four rubies, green- and red-gold swags and festoons. Fillets of carved leaf motif.

3¾ high by ⅝ diameter
Marks: none
Acc. No. 47-20-194

232. Nephrite. Lavender champlevé enamel over chasing bound with white enamel fillets.

2¼ high by 1⅜ diameter
Marks: none
Acc. No. 47-20-197

233. Nephrite. Gold neck bounded with carved fillets; enamelled in opaque white; ruby panels.

4¼ high by ¾ wide
Marks: *M.P.*/anchors and scepter/*56*
Acc. No. 47-20-198

232

233

235

234

236

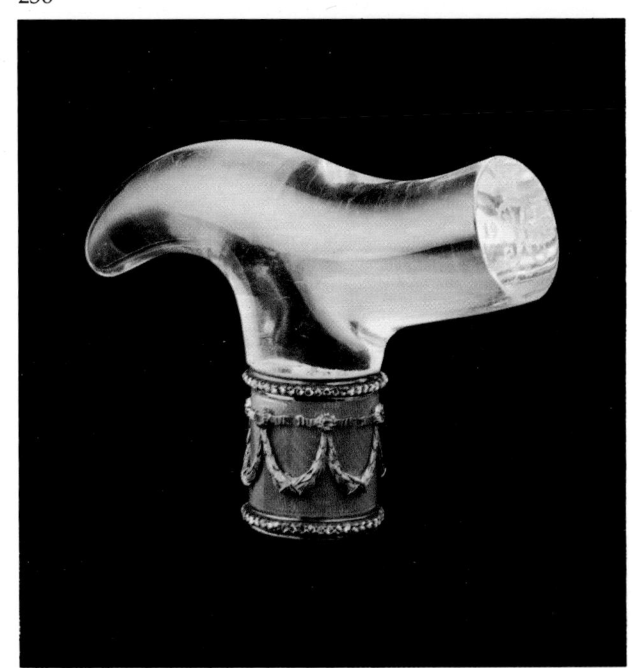

237

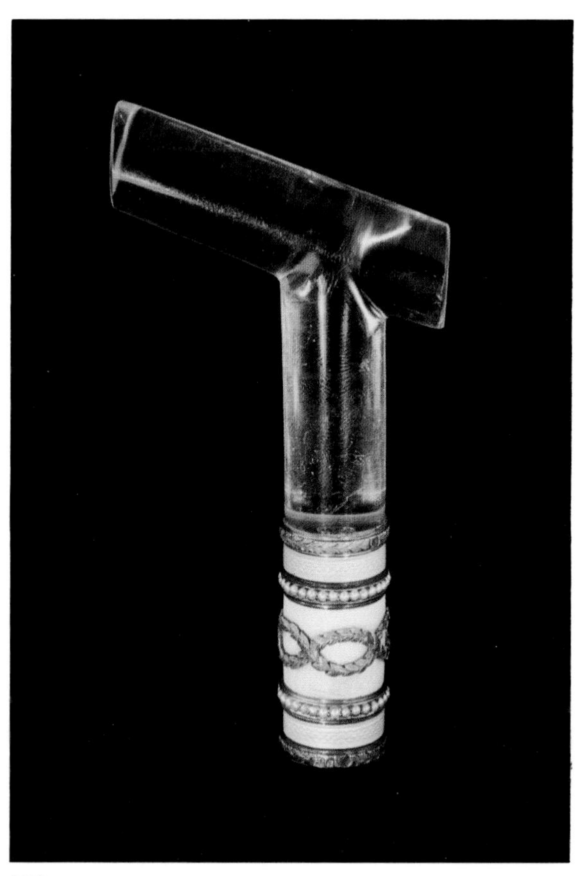

238

234. Rock-crystal duck's head. Sapphire eyes. Gold collar set with faceted tourmalines. Shaft of dark-red wood.

12¾ high by 2¾ wide
Marks: [?]. *A.*/profile
Acc. No. 47-20-165

235. Rock crystal. Two joined hemispheres containing painted intaglio dog's head. Joint masked by gold band. Gold neck set with varicolored stones.

2½ high by 1¾ diameter
Marks: none
Acc. No. 47-20-176

236. Rock crystal. Gold neck with blue enamel and three rows of diamonds. Gold beaded fillets.

1¾ high by 1 diameter
Marks: *K.F.*/profile/*56*
Acc. No. 47-20-177

237. Rock crystal. Rose enamel over chasing; two-toned gold swags and emeralds. Neck bound with diamond-set fillets. End of crystal with engraved monogram of Nicholas II and date, 1912.

2¾ high by 1¾ wide
Marks: *M.P.*/anchors and scepter/*56*
Acc. No. 47-20-188

238. Rock crystal. Gold neck of alternating leaf-carved fillets and blue enamel bands. Central band of lighter blue enamel bound by two pearl-set bands. Two carved intertwined green-gold garlands encircle center.

3½ high by 1⅞ wide
Marks: *R.*/profile/*56*/*17148*
Acc. No. 47-20-196

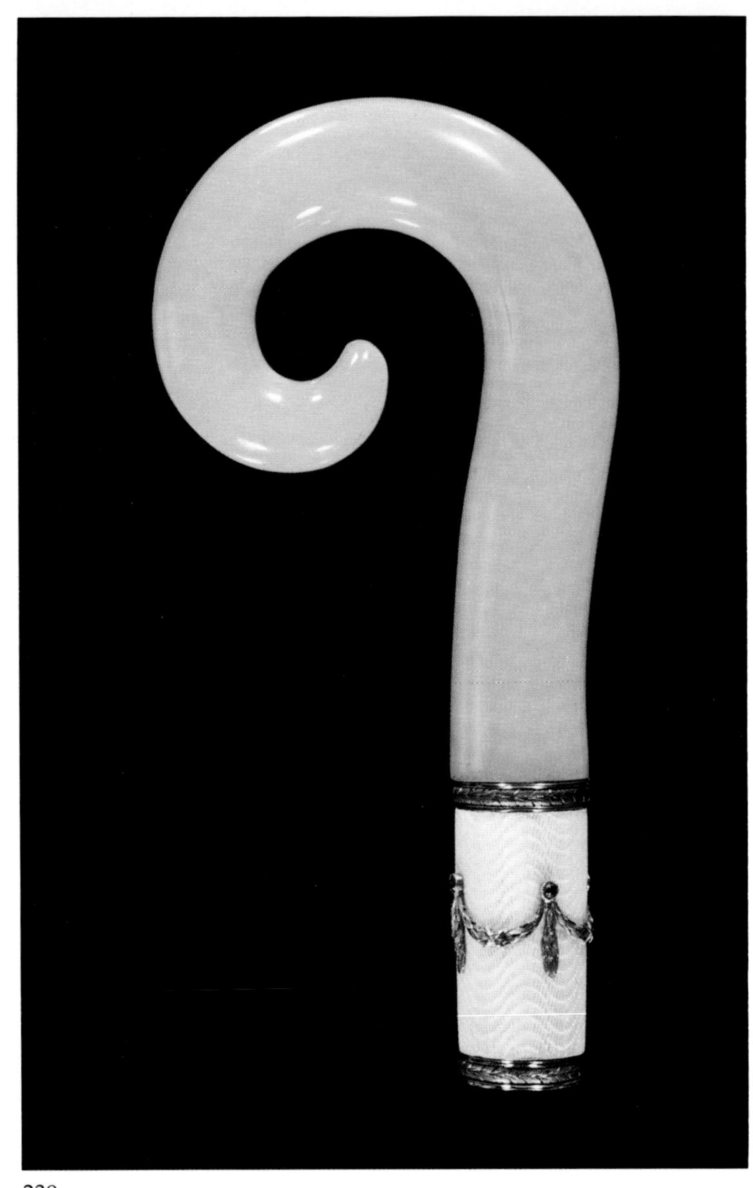
239

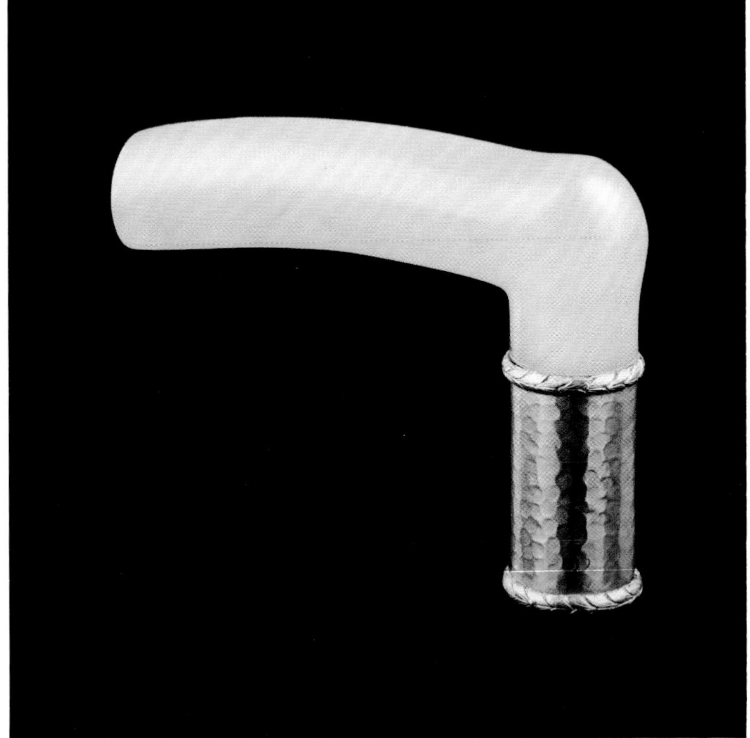
241

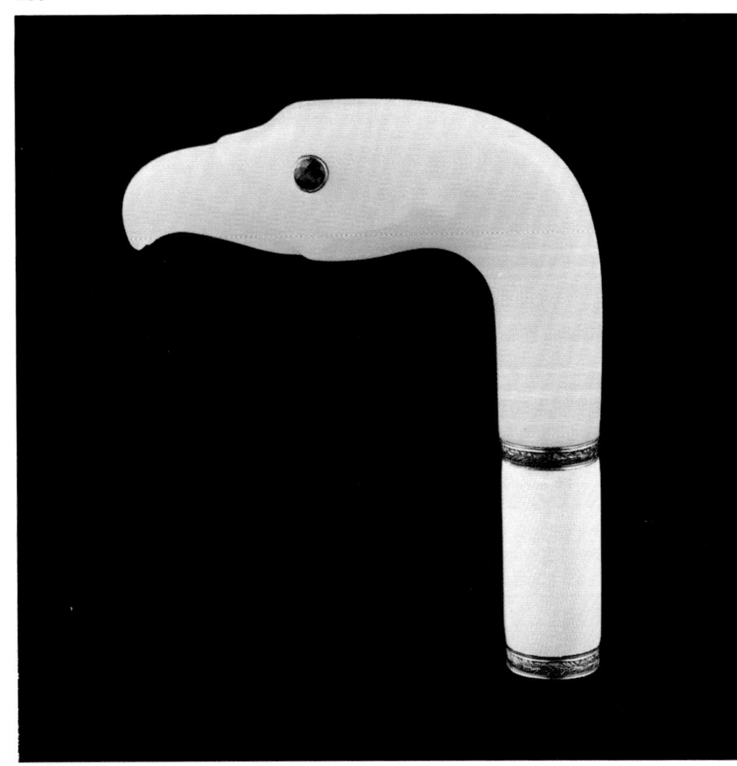
240

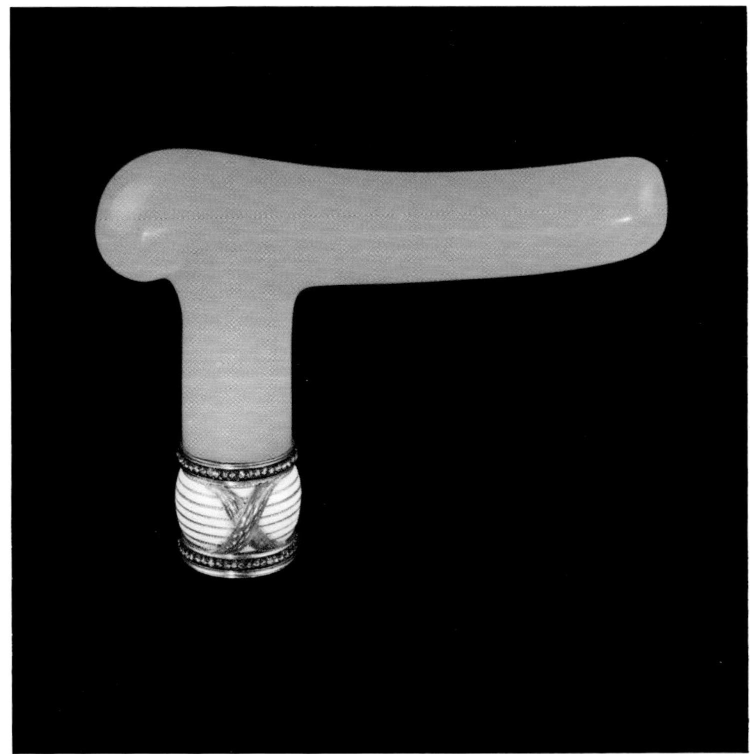
242

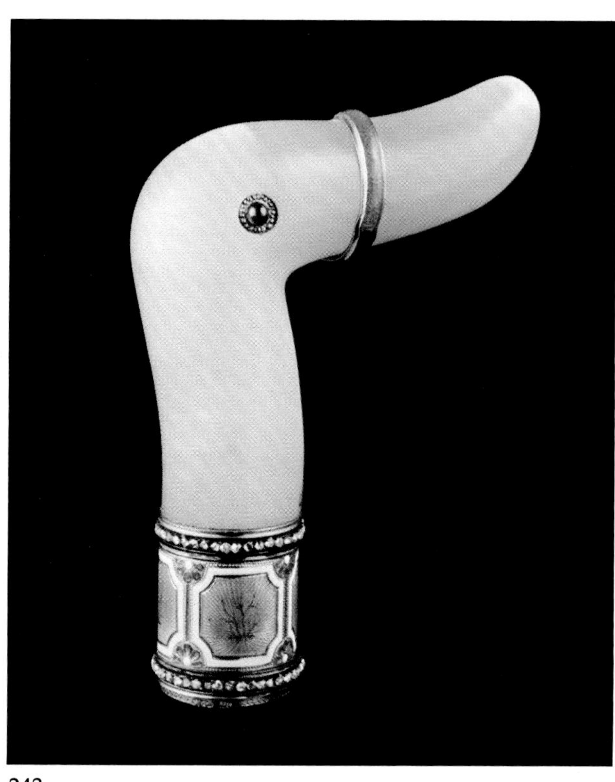

243

239. Serpentine. Iridescent white enamel over chasing; set with four rubies connected by swags, festoon hanging from each ruby. Gold ferrule rimmed with bands chased in leaf design.

5½ high by 2½ wide
Marks: profile/*56*/illegible
Acc. No. 47-20-162

240. Serpentine eagle's head. Faceted red Ural stone eyes. Ferrule of white iridescent enamel rimmed with gold bands of chased leaf form.

3¾ high by 3¼ wide
Marks: none
Acc. No. 47-20-163

241. Serpentine. Hammer-marked ferrule of gold edged with carved acanthus leaf bands.

2½ high by 3 wide
Marks: *M.P.*/*R.*/profile/*56*
Acc. No. 47-20-164

242. Serpentine. Diamond-set ferrule with opaque-white champlevé enamel. Two applied crossed ribbons of orange enamel over chasing.

2¼ high by 2¾ wide
Marks: *M.P.*
Acc. No. 47-20-168

243. Serpentine duck's head. Ruby eyes, green enamel around bill. Red-gold ferrule edged with diamond-set bands. White and orchid-pink enamel panels divided by gold walls and green lunettes; panels bear moss-like sprays.

3¼ high by 2 wide
Marks: *M.P.*/anchors and scepter/*56*
Acc. No. 47-20-169

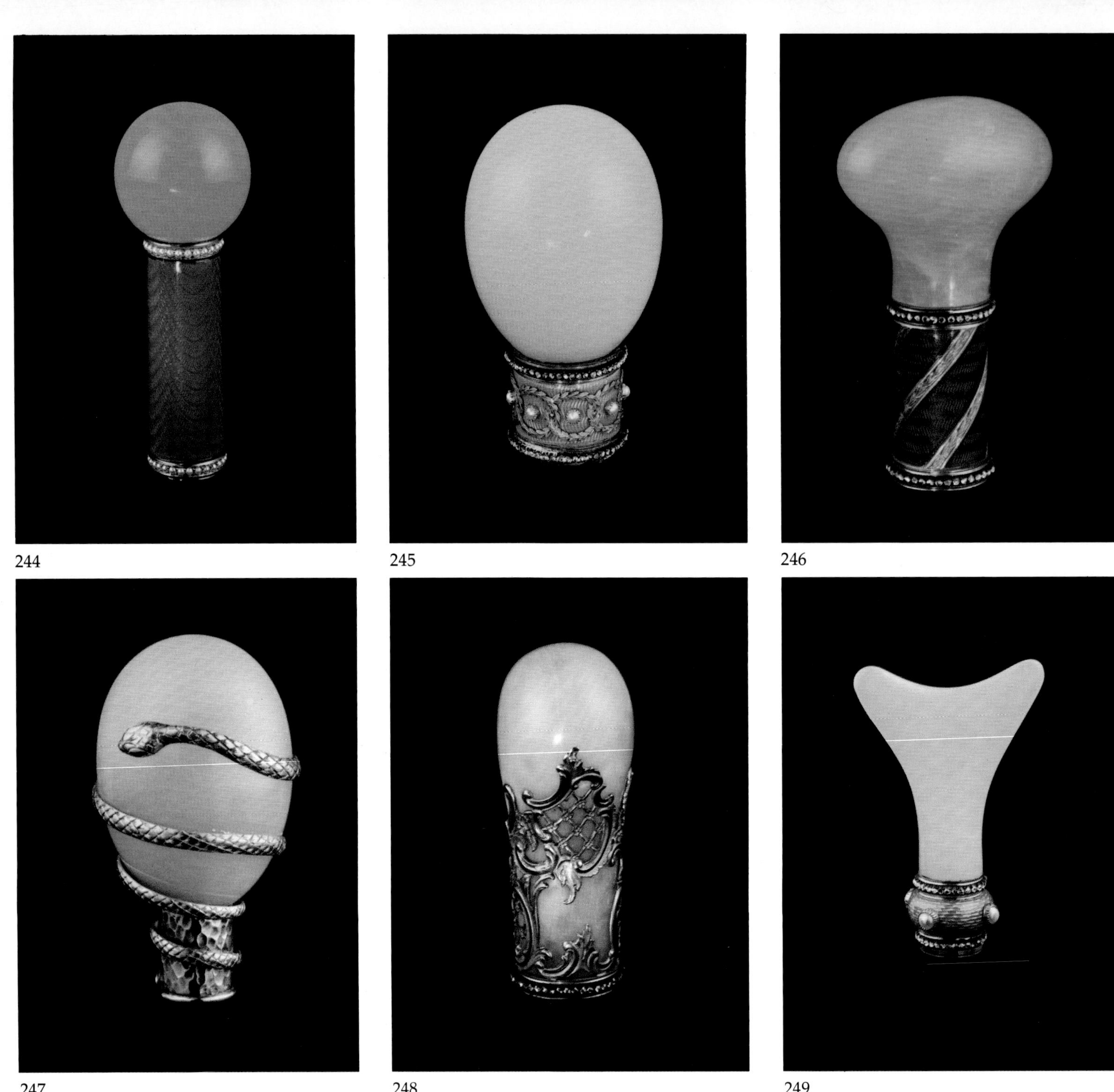

244 245 246

247 248 249

244. Serpentine. Orchid-pink enamel over chased gold column with two pearl-set bands.

2⅝ high by 1 diameter
Marks: *M.P.*/profile/*56*
Acc. No. 47-20-171

245. Serpentine. Orchid-pink enamel over chasing on neck with entwined gold garlands centered with pearls. Diamond fillets.

2½ high by 1½ diameter
Marks: *M.P.*/anchors and scepter/*56*
Acc. No. 47-30-175

246. Serpentine. Crimson enamel diagonal panels on red-gold neck separated by chased green- and red-gold bands. Bounded by diamond-set fillets.

2¾ high by 2 diameter
Marks: *M.P.*/anchors and scepter/*56*/*45.643*
Acc. No. 47-20-181

247. Serpentine. Gold hammer-marked neck. Finely chased gold serpent spirals around neck and handle.

2½ high by 1½ diameter
Marks: none
Acc. No. 47-20-182

248. Serpentine. Set in rococo gold lattice motif. Rosettes and leaves in two shades of gold. Diamond-set fillet. A design by Agathon Fabergé.

2½ high by 1½ wide
Marks: *M.P.*/anchors and scepter/*56*/*46856*
Acc. No. 47-20-183

249. Serpentine. Salmon-colored enamel neck set with pearls and bounded with diamond-set fillets.

2⅛ high by 1½ wide
Marks: *M.P.*/*56*
Acc. No. 47-20-184

250. Serpentine enfolded in coils of gold serpent whose head, set with rose cabochon stone, rests on circular top. Red-gold ferrule.

4 high by 2 wide
Marks: *H.W.*/*A.R.*/*56*/*14939*
Acc. No. 47-20-187

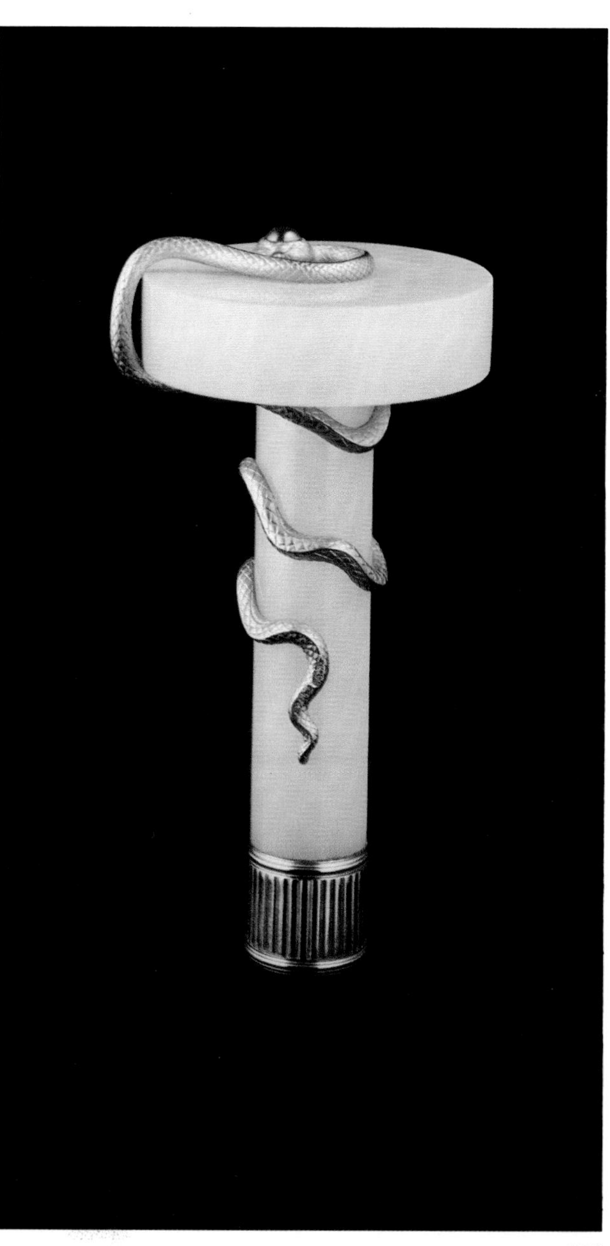

250

Icons

Catalog entry 257.

Something must also be said of the position of icon-frames in the range of Fabergé's production, and the work of other court goldsmiths in St. Petersburg and Moscow. Of the icon-frames in the Pratt Collection, seven come from the Fabergé workshops in both these cities; others were made by Khlebnikov, Ovchinnichov, and K. Hann. They are shop works based on traditional models and are distinguished, overall, only by their fidelity to Fabergé's standards of craftsmanship.

The models were on the whole typically Muscovite, representing a fusion of the 16th- and 17th-century stylistic elements: in part, indigenous East Slavic, Graeco-Byzantine, Italian Renaissance, and Oriental. The result is something usually coherent and conspicuously Russian—a decorative manner at once sumptuous, semi-barbaric, flamboyant, and sophisticated.

251

252

253

254

251. Saint Savior.

Silver-gilt. Filigreed, set with Ural stones, seed pearls, diamonds. From the Moscow branch of the firm, and evidently made for the same client at the same time as catalog no. 252, since they bear identical order numbers. Shows the frontal bust of Christ, his right hand raised in benediction, his left holding the book of the Word. The *nimbus,* or halo, of the figure is raised, and bears an abbreviated *indicium*: "IC XC" (Jesus Christ).

11⅞ high by 10⅛ wide
Marks: *K. Fabergé*/*K.F.*/double eagle/delta profile/*88*/*42563*
Acc. No. 47-20-1

255

252. Our Lady of Iberia.

Silver-gilt. Filigreed, set with Ural stones, seed pearls, diamonds. From the Moscow branch of the firm; bears an order number identical with catalog no. 251. Shows the Virgin, in a brown mantle over a green robe, holding the seated Child in her left arm; the Child, in a light mantle and green robe, raises his right hand in benediction. This iconographic type, the "Lady of Iberia," is not connected in any way with the Iberians or Spaniards, but with another race of the same name, ancient inhabitants of the Caucasus, the ancestors of the modern Kartvelians or Georgians. Iverón, their monastery on Mount Athos, contained the original icon of Our Lady of Iberia, which was brought to Moscow and installed in its own special chapel in the Red Square of the Kremlin. The *nimbus* or halo of the figure is raised, and bears an abbreviated *indicium*: "MP OY" (Mother of God).

11⅞ high by 10⅛ wide
Marks: *K. Fabergé*/*K.F.*/double eagle/delta profile/*88*/*42563*
Acc. No. 47-20-2

253. Saint Savior.

Silver. Continuous design of seed pearls over flat enamelling.

9 high by 7⅛ wide
Marks: *K. Fabergé*/double eagle/profile/*YL*/*88*
Acc. No. 47-20-3

254. Holy Virgin of Iversaya with the Child.

Silver. Repoussé and perforated to show faces and hands. Background and border chased and gilded. Enamelled halos. Presented to the Grand Duchess Tatiana Nicholaievna by the nobility of Moscow.

10½ high by 8¾ wide
Marks: *S.K.*/profile/*84*
Acc. No. 47-20-4

255. Saint Nicholas, Saint Alexander and Saint Alexis.

Silver. Repoussé and chased angels holding crown and halo above three leaf- and ribbon-bordered openings. Swags with green stones below openings, cherub at bottom.

6⅛ high by 5⅞ wide
Marks: *Klebnikov, N.X.* (or reverse)/double eagle/profile/*84*
Acc. No. 47-20-10

256

258

256. Transfiguration.

Pale gray enamel. Eight hammered- and gilded-metal leaf designs set with blue, green, and rose stones.

9¾ high by 6¾ wide
Marks: *Fabergé/Y.A./*profile/*Y L/88/14938*
Acc. No. 47-20-12

257. Virgin and Child with Saint Alexander Nevsky and Saint Maria Magdalene.

Chased silver-gilt in relief, perforated to show painted faces and hands. The robes, crowns, and haloes are in chased repoussé relief, embellished with pearls, diamonds, and rubies. The background is enamelled and set with varicolored stones in sky blue (contrasting with the gold of the Virgin's robes) and overlaid with filigree tendrils and rosette stars. The borders alternate panels of enamel with filigree and cabochon-cut stones, while above is a pierced foliage border surmounted by a *botonée* cross. The colors and designs of the enamel panels are very similar to those employed in 17th- and 18th-century Persian tiles: soft shades of blue, red, and green mat enamel with white. Greek Catholic cross spans the join of the panels. Inscribed: "To Their Imperial Majesties from the Nobility of Kharkoff, 1866-1891, October 28."

From the decorative point of view, this is perhaps the most striking icon in the Pratt Collection. It was a gift to Czar Alexander III and Marie Feodorovna on the twenty-fifth anniversary of their marriage. Being commissioned by residents of one of the greatest (though hardly the oldest) Russian provincial capitals, and executed in Moscow, it embodies practically every feature of the 19th-century Russian nationalistic, ecclesiastical style. When closed, the form is that of a square surmounted by the bulbous serpentine curve.

Closed: 12 high by 6⅝ wide
Marks: *Ovchinnichov/A.A./*double eagle/St. George/ *84/1891*
Acc. No. 47-20-16

258. Transfiguration with St. Elizabeth and St. Sergius of Randanezh.

Silver and silver gilt. This icon in the international but still Russian style shows Christ between Elijah and Moses, and Sts. John, James, and Peter below. The side panels frame St. Elizabeth and St. Sergius of Randanezh. It was a gift of the Preobrajensky Regiment, the oldest in Russia (founded by Peter the Great in 1698), and is etched with the names of the donors over the sides; two of them, Prince Obolensky, the commander, and Prince Troubetskoy, are still well-known today. When closed, a Greek Catholic cross covers the join. Decorated with carved silver-gilt wreath simulating embroidery. Names of donors engraved on sides. Russian inscription on back: "Blessing of the Preobrajensky Regiment. June 3rd, 1884. A new commandment I give unto you that ye love one another as I loved you" (*John* 13:34).

Closed: 7¼ high by 4¾ wide
Marks: *K.A./*anchors and scepter/*84/*illegible
Acc. No. 47-20-17

259

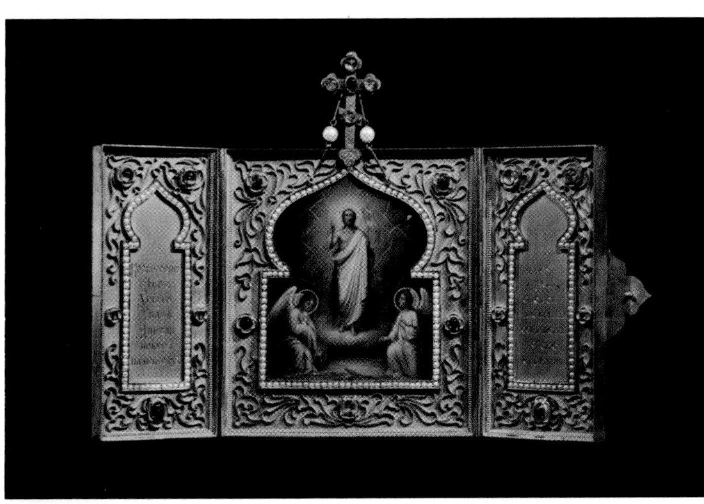

260

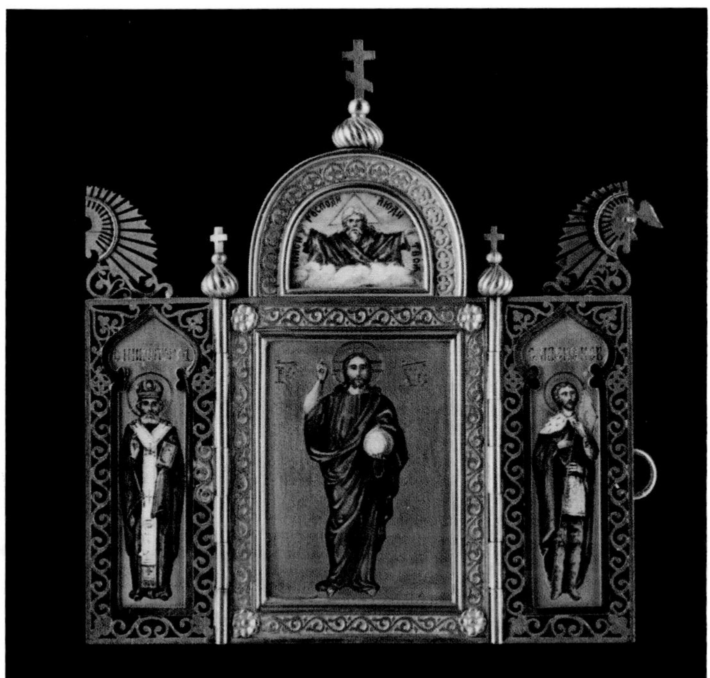

261

259. Saint Savior, Saint Nicholas, and the Guardian Angel.

Silver-gilt. In the traditional Muscovite style, this frame encloses the Saint Savior in the center with the figures of Saint Nicholas and a guardian angel, to the left and right, respectively. The figures in the side panels, in rectangular openings, are surrounded with chased filigree, with the remainder of the panel in chased design. The central figure, also enclosed in chased filigree, has an enamelled filigree halo set with stones. Blue-, red-, and green-enamel motifs at corners and at top center. Sides of panel have applied decoration set with translucent and green stones. The serpentine curve of the top, which has a border of raised filigree, is set with a large green stone. The somewhat squat proportions give to the whole its distinctly Oriental-Byzantine cast.

Closed: $7\frac{5}{8}$ high by $5\frac{1}{2}$ wide
Marks: *I. BO O.C. E*/*O.C. A*/profile/*84*
Acc. No. 47-20-18

260. Resurrection.

Gold. Set with varicolored stones and seed pearls. Two side panels bear inscriptions framed with pearls. Wood cover has gold quatrefoil set with a green stone and surmounted with a Greek Catholic cross of gold set with varicolored stones and pearls. This somewhat naturalistic presentation of the Resurrection is contained within a typically Muscovite opening, consisting of a square surmounted by a bulbous onion-shaped arch. This arcuated form, a flattened ogee extended at the end with two cusps (may be seen also in catalog Nos. 259 and 262), is perhaps the most insistently Oriental motif in Russian art.

4 high by $2\frac{3}{4}$ wide
Marks: *Fabergé*/*B. A.*/profile/*56*/*15124*
Acc. No. 47-20-19

261. Christ Blessing the Universe.

Gold. St. Nicholas at left; St. Alexander Nevsky (second only to St. Nicholas in popularity) at the right; and God the Father in the semicircular lunette above. Pierced design on doors, surmounted by sunburst with dove in center. Small ring handle at join of panels. In center of each door is enamel seraph. Two hinges and top of central panel surmounted by fluted Russian dome and Greek Catholic cross. Chased and pierced filigree decorations around the depictions. Russian inscription: "Save O Lord Thy People."

While Russo-Byzantine in its hieratic composition and brilliance of color, the substitution of the semicircular lunette for the indigenous serpentine curve indicates an Italianate eclectic tendency. Muscovite style, a more international but still Russian type, and a 19th-century adaptation of Italian Renaissance prototypes may be seen in comparing catalog Nos. 259, 258 and 261.

Closed: 3 high by $1\frac{1}{2}$ wide
Marks: *K. Hann*/*A.I.*/anchors and scepter/*56*
Acc. No. 47-20-20

262

264

263

262. Saint Nicholas the Wonder Worker and St. Princess Alexandra.

Silver-gilt. Serpentine top surmounted with cross and "XP" symbol in ring. Front panel decorated with carved scrolls and set with Ural stones, turquoises, and pearls. Back panel engraved with names of donors. St. Nicholas of Myra, the patron saint of Russia, was Bishop of Myra during the reigns of the Emperors Diocletian and Constantine, and was present at the Council of Nicaea.

The accounts of his life are entirely legendary: on the first day of his life he stood with clasped hands in his bath, giving thanks to God for having been brought into the world; he is also especially revered for his having raised from the dead some dismembered children who had been cut up and salted for food during a famine. In eastern art, he is represented as a bishop, without a mitre, bearing the cross instead of the crosier. Besides being the patron saint of Russia, he was also the patron of the serfs, children, travelers and merchants, sailors, and poor maidens.

4⅜ high by 3¼ wide
Marks: *Fabergé/E.* [?] *K./84*
Acc. No. 47-20-21

263. Saint Nicholas Crowned.

Gold. Front of case bears Russian double eagle in relief. Back has engraved Greek Catholic cross and inscription. Inside of front panel of icon is bordered with small faceted diamonds. Surmounted with ring.

1½ high by 1⅛ wide
Marks: none
Acc. No. 47-20-23

264. Saint George Slaying the Dragon.

Silver-gilt. Set with rubies in enamel, mounted on holly wood.

3⅞ high by 3⅜ wide
Marks: *Fabergé*/double eagle/profile/*88*
Acc. No. 47-20-30

Jewelry

Catalog entries 265, 266, 272.

267

268

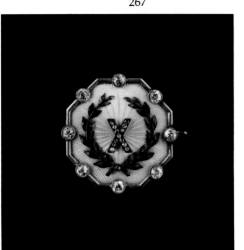

269

270

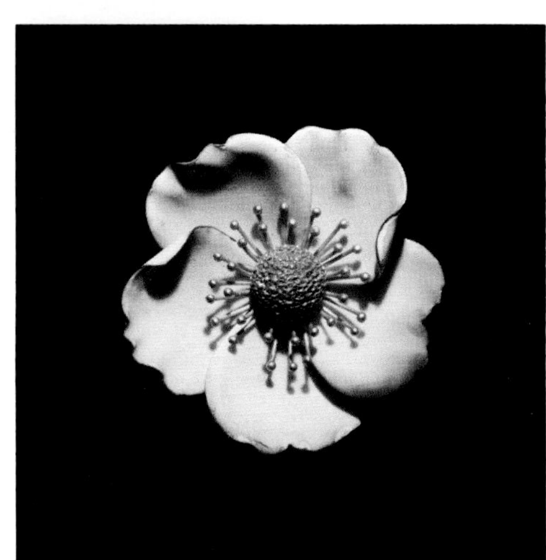

271

As a jeweler in the strict sense, that is, a producer of objects of personal adornment in precious stones and metals, Fabergé is not renowned. This is not to say that the firm (especially the frankly commercial Moscow branch) did not manufacture jewelry in quantity. It did, for items of this kind, made for the wealthy merchant class, were a tidy source of revenue.

The jewelry in the Pratt Collection (five items of which may be definitely given to Fabergé) has been divided, for the sake of discussion, into these categories: brooches; lockets; pendants; and rings, bracelets and crosses.

BROOCHES

265. Crown.
Silver-gilt. Openwork leaves and flowers set with cabochon rubies, sapphires and faceted diamonds. Surmounted by Greek cross set with diamonds and a diamond-encircled cabochon sapphire. Said to be from the personal belongings of Czarina Alexandra Feodorovna, this must date from before the infancy of the Czarevitch. After the discovery of his affliction, rubies were rarely used in pieces presented to the imperial house, because of the dire symbolism of their color.

3 long by 2½ wide
Marks: none
Acc. No. 47-20-138

266. Lion's face.
Topaz. Mounted in chased and engraved yellow- and red-gold wreath. Ruby eyes. Holds in mouth diamond and gold ring containing seven small diamonds. Designed as brooch, also has loop for suspension. Hinged back, transparent door of rock crystal. May be a Fabergé product.

2¾ high by 2 wide by 1¼ diameter
Marks: *11624*
Acc. No. 47-20-139

267. Double eagle and crown.
Gold. Lozenge, orchid-colored enamel over a guilloche ground with radiating chased lines. Applied carved double eagle and crown encrusted with small diamonds and with large diamond in center.

1 long by 1½ wide
Marks: *N. CH./56/*illegible.
Acc. No. 47-20-140

268. Wreath.
Green and red gold with diamond studding. Encloses diamond-set "M" surmounted with diamond and ruby crown.

1¼ diameter
Marks: none
Acc. No. 47-20-141

269. Octagon.
Gold. White translucent enamel over radiating chasing, typical of Fabergé. Gold wreath encircling diamond-set "X." Diamonds set in each side.

1⅛ diameter
Marks: *N.* [?]/*11*–[?]
Acc. No. 47-20-142

270. Scarab and lotus.
Deep red stone in gold mounting. From diamond at bottom rise diamond-set stems of two ultramarine and clear enamel lotus flowers set with rubies in eclectic manner of the Moscow shop.

1⅛ long by 1½ wide
Marks: *K.F./56/17925*
Acc. No. 47-20-143

271. Wild rose.
Gold. Pink enamel. Gold sponge-like forms with small ball-tipped gold wires represent the pistils and stamens.

1½ diameter
Marks: none
Acc. No. 47-20-144

272. Bird and snake.
Red, green, and yellow gold, and platinum. Bird on tree trunk, snake coiled beneath.

2⅝ long by 1 wide
Marks: none
Acc. No. 47-20-145

273-275

282

283

284

285

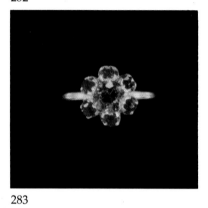

LOCKETS

273. Gold-, green-, and white-enamel rosebud which opens vertically; diamond catch. By Michael Perchin.

 1 high by 1/2 diameter
 Marks: *M.P./56*
 Acc. No. 47-20-106

274. White translucent enamel; flower of gold set with three diamonds and three rubies by Michael Perchin. Heavy gold chain.

 1 1/2 long by 1 1/8 wide
 Marks: *M.P.*/[?]*H.*/profile/*56*/*85*/illegible
 Acc. No. 47-20-155

275. Lapis lazuli. Hollow hemispheres contained in basket-work frame of twisted gold wire having gold bead at intersections. Hinged. Glass cover on inside also hinged.

 7/8 diameter
 Marks: none
 Acc. No. 47-20-156

PENDANTS

276. Gold. Rough-textured vase with hinged top set with amethyst cut *en cabochon.*

 5/8 high by 3/8 diameter
 Marks: *A.P./G.L./56*
 Acc. No. 47-20-79

277. Gold and dyed agate.

 1 high by 3/8 wide
 Marks: anchors and scepter
 Acc. No. 47-20-83

278. Gold loop with bar which holds three cabochon rose tourmalines and two seed pearls. Suspended from each tourmaline setting is an egg, one of chrysoprase, one agate, and one reconstructed turquoise.

 1 high by 7/8 wide
 Marks: *56*
 Acc. No. 47-20-99

279. Gold. Ovate loop setting holding an ovate faceted aquamarine. Setting rests upright upon the lower inside curve of another gold loop.

 3/4 high by 1/2 wide
 Marks: *K.F.*/anchors and scepter/*56*
 Acc. No. 47-20-112

280. Gold. White iridescent enamel over chased ground loop forms frame for suspended, faceted ovate ruby bound with gold strap.

 5/8 high by 3/8 diameter
 Marks: *56*/illegible
 Acc. No. 47-20-118

281. Gold- and red-enamel lobster claw holding diamond.

 1 1/8 long by 3/8 wide
 Marks: none
 Acc. No. 47-20-135

282. Insignia of the Order of St. Andrew. Framed with diamonds. Transparent amber enamel ground overlaid with double eagle and crown. Cross with saint in relief upon eagle. Suspended from diamond-set ring with two other rings attached, one split, the other telescoping. Back framed with turquoise enamel, bears double eagle. The Order of St. Andrew, the chief order of knighthood of the Russian Empire, was founded by Peter the Great in 1678, though the statutes were not promulgated until 1720. According to legend, Andrew, the brother of Simon Peter, preached in Asia Minor, Scythia, and along the Black Sea to the mouths of the Volga; hence, he is one of the patron saints of Russia. He is said to have suffered martyrdom at Patras in Graecian Achaea, on an X-shaped cross, the *crux decussata,* commonly known as St. Andrew's cross. His relics were removed to Constantinople from Patras, and on the fall of Constantinople in 1453 were dispersed throughout Christendom. The work bears no marks but may be assigned on technical grounds to the first half of the 18th century.

 2 high by 1 1/2 wide
 Marks: none
 Acc. No. 47-20-137

RINGS, BRACELETS, CROSSES

283. Finger ring.
 Gold. Central diamond surrounded with faceted rubies.

 Setting: 3/8 diameter. Ring: 5/8 diameter
 Marks: none
 Acc. No. 47-20-148

284. Bracelet.
 Yellow and red gold. Links held by rectangular catch and small safety chain.

 6 1/2 long
 Marks: *A.E.*/profile/*56*/illegible
 Acc. No. 47-20-161

285. Cross.
 Lapis lazuli. At intersection of arms is pearl surrounded with small diamonds set in leaf forms. Suspension loop of gold set with pearl, and surmounted with leaf design set with diamonds.

 3 high by 1 1/2 wide
 Marks: illegible
 Acc. No. 47-20-151

Catalog entries 276-81 are illustrated with catalog entry 284. (Illustrated, clockwise from top, are catalog entry numbers 1, 2, 3, 4, 7, 20, 43, 276, 277, 278, 279, 280, 281.)

Miscellaneous Objects

Catalog entry 302.

In the category of "miscellaneous objects" fall forty-three pieces—thirty-one of them bearing definite Fabergé hallmarks—which cannot well be called anything else. These are items which are neither strictly decorative, such as the flower compositions, nor of a special symbolic class of their own, such as the imperial Easter eggs. They are mainly functional in that they do have a use which supplements their ornamental aspect.

To supply manners with accouterments was Fabergé's whole business, a business which looked with no less favor on its mass-production side than on the side of singularity. The output was stupendous: cigarette cases, vases, powder-patch and stamp boxes, ashtrays, seals, bell-pushes, calendars, lorgnettes, barometers, thermometers, ink pots, clocks, opera glasses, scent bottles, stamp dampeners, pen holders, cigar cutters, tea glasses of rock crystal, letter openers, fans, pill vials, and an occasional dog whistle.

The Fabergé "company style" can be best appraised in these pieces. It is a style with many origins and at least two outlets for its different phases. The origins, which remain visible even though translated into Fabergé's terms, are both alien and native.

Taken in chronological order, these stylistic sources are those of: (1) the Italian Renaissance, especially Florentine; (2) the German Renaissance, as exemplified in the 16th-century Nuremberg goldsmiths, whose work Fabergé studied in the *Grünes Gewölbe* in Dresden; (3) Russian decorative art of the 17th century; (4) French style of the periods of Louis XIV, Louis XV, and Louis XVI, and the First Empire; (5) Chinese and Japanese art of the later Ch'ing and Edo periods; and, finally, (6) the Art Nouveau, or *Jugendstil,* of approximately 1890-1910. While many pieces are thoroughly eclectic, imitative, and conventional within their stylistic frameworks, others combine two or more of these sources, so that it is not at all easy to say which predominates.

286

287

288

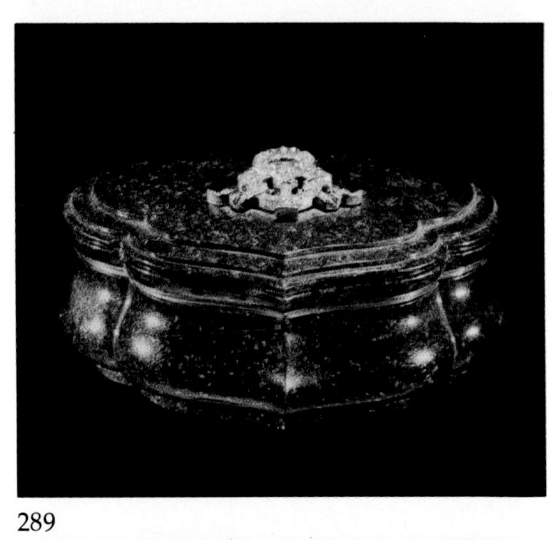
289

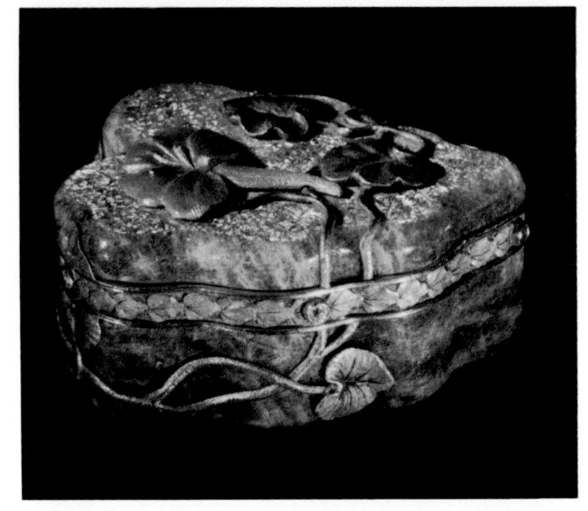
290

291

292

293

BOXES

286. Double eagle and crown presentation box.
Gold. Top enamelled in cobalt blue over chased ground. Raised oval on top frames double eagle set with diamonds and surmounted with crown containing two rubies. Other designs on top of gold containing diamonds and pearls. Interior bottom of blue enamel contains escutcheon. The influence of French classic sources is reflected in the restraint of Louis XIV style in the form.

3⅝ diameter
Marks: *K. Fabergé*/*M.P.*/double eagle/anchors and scepter/*72*
Acc. No. 47-20-270

287. Monogrammed box.
Nephrite. Top bears "N" and "II" in silver monogram, which also contains a crown, two crossed floral sprays of green gold, and diamonds. Entire monogram is set with diamonds. Box rimmed with green and red gold. The influence of French classic sources is reflected in the restraint of Louis XIV style in the form.

1½ high by 3 diameter
Marks: *Fabergé*/*M.P.*/profile/*YL*/*56*
Acc. No. 47-20-271

288. Hinged chest snuffbox.
Gold. Blue enamel, design of oak leaf and acorn.

1¼ high by 3½ wide by 2 long
Marks: profile/*56*/*2073*/*P 150*/illegible
Acc. No. 47-20-272

289. Cartouche snuffbox.
Lapis lazuli. Diamond-encrusted monogram "MF" surmounted with crown. Two hinged rims of gold join top and bottom.

1 high by 2½ wide
Marks: none
Acc. No. 47-20-273

290. Leaf-shaped box.
Aventurine feldspar. Rim of lid is chased gold with diamond, ruby, emerald, sapphire, and pearl setting. Gold-modelled forms of tendrils, leaves, and blossoms are overlaid on sides. Rose-enamelled blossom on top.

1 high by 1¾ wide by 2½ long
Marks: *K.F.*/profile/*56*/*16795*
Acc. No. 47-20-274

291. Repoussé box.
Nephrite bottom, gold top. Octagonal, tapering at bottom. On top, cast and chased design of three cupids supporting an oval shield; each edge rimmed with rubies and diamonds, alternately. The chased gold lid is Louis XV.

1½ high by 1½ wide
Marks: *Fabergé*/*M.P.*/anchors and scepter/*56*
Acc. No. 47-20-275

292. Inscribed snuffbox.
Gold. Sides enamelled in panels of emerald green over chased ground separated by blue bands. Inclines toward the First Empire in style. Top edged with rim of diamonds which encloses carnelian bearing an incised inscription in Arabic script. Intended either as a gift to the Czar from a Moslem ruler, or vice versa; despite its small size, the stone contains an entire verse from the Koran: "God, there is no God but He; the Living, the Self-subsisting. Neither slumber seizeth Him, nor sleep; His, whatsoever is in the Heavens and whatsoever is in the earth! Who is he that can intercede with Him but by His own permission? He knoweth what is present with His creatures, and what is yet to befall them; yet nought of His knowledge do they comprehend, save what He willeth. His Throne reacheth over the Heavens and the Earth, and the upholding of both burdeneth Him not; and He is the High, the Great!" (*The Koran*, Sura 2, Verse 256, translation Rodwell, London, 1896).

1 high by 1⅜ wide
Marks: *Fabergé*/*M.P.* (or *H.W.?*)/profile/*YL*/*56*
Acc. No. 47-20-276

293. Powder box.
Nephrite. Circular with curved sides rimmed with gold. Lid has handle of ivory elephant standing on a fringed drum of gold banded with alternating rubies and diamonds.

3¾ high by 4 diameter
Marks: *Fabergé*/*M.P.*/anchors and scepter/*56*
Acc. No. 47-20-277

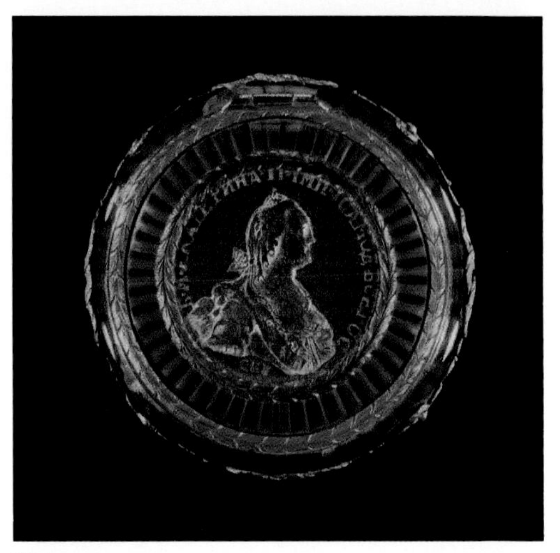
294

295

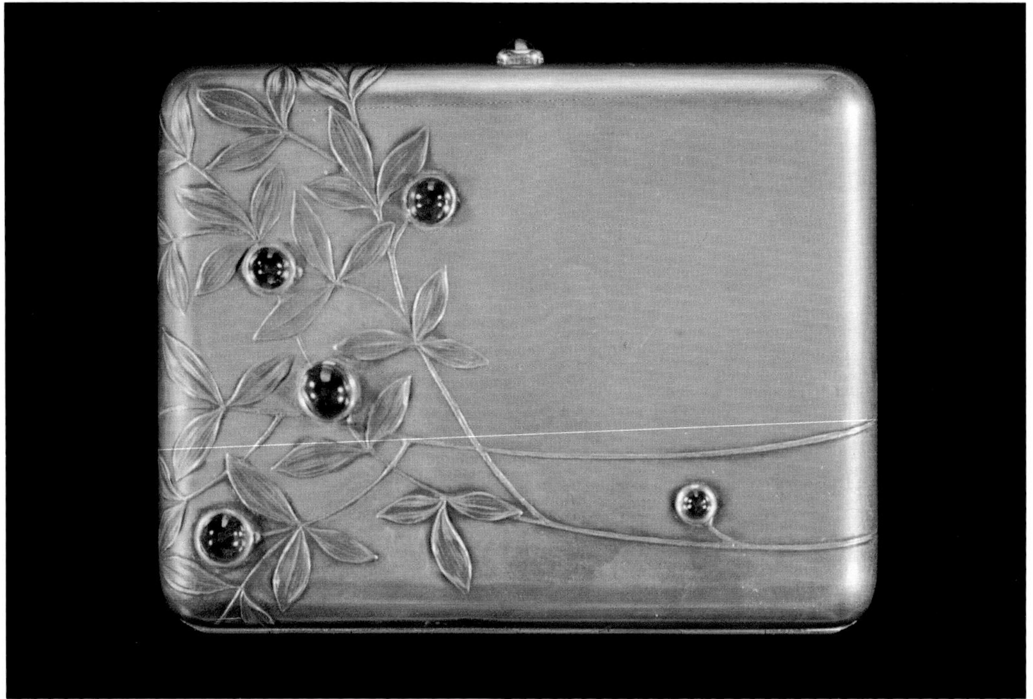
296

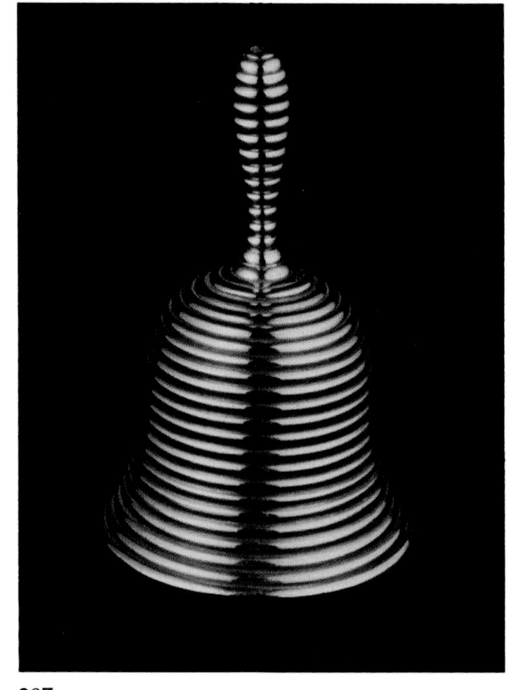
297

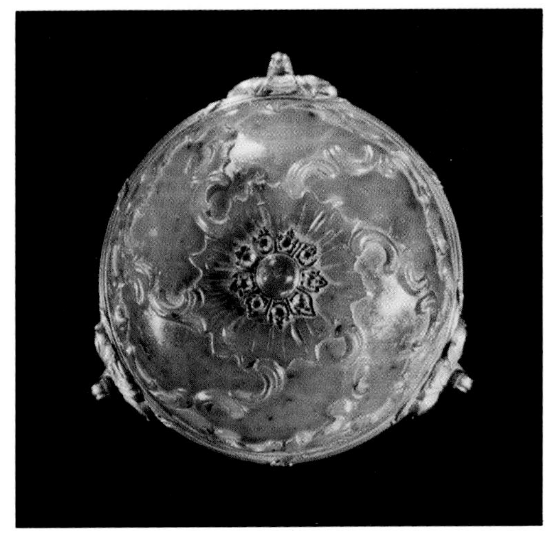

298

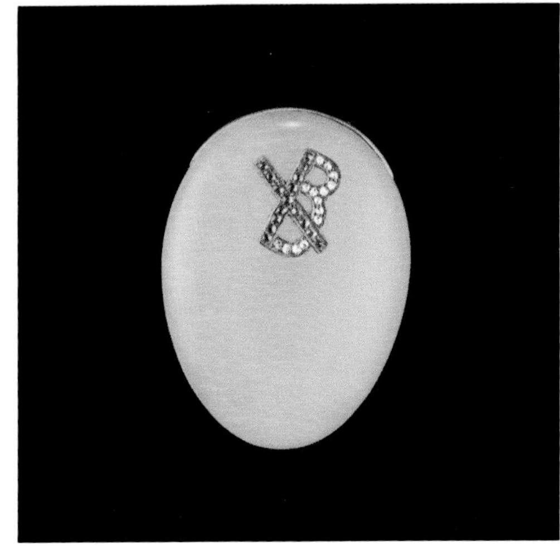

299

300

301

303

294. Circular box.
Gold. Ruby enamel over chased line ground.
Gold mounts of interlaced wreaths separated with diamond-set rosettes. Rim chased in leaf design. On top, a leaf-chased wreath borders gold relief of Catherine the Great, above gold coin visible when top is opened, dated 1773.

7/8 high by 2 diameter
Marks: *Fabergé*/profile/*YL*/*56*/illegible
Acc. No. 47-20-278

295. Floral box.
Silver-gilt. Canary-yellow enamel over chased ground. Lid bears flower set with six diamonds for petals, and ruby center. Pearl border, ruby catch. An adaptation of a Louis XVI *bonbonnière*.

7/8 high by 1 5/8 diameter
Marks: *Fabergé*/profile/*88*/illegible
Acc. No. 47-20-279

296. Flowered cigarette case.
Gold. Repoussé design of slender plants, five cabochon red stones forming flowers. Ruby catch.

3 7/8 long by 3 wide
Marks: *Fabergé*/double eagle/profile/*YL*/*56*/*1823*/*274*/*140*
Acc. No. 47-20-281

DOMESTIC ACCESSORIES

297. Bell.
Red gold. Ribbed horizontally; clapper in shape of elongated teardrop.

3 high by 1 3/4 wide
Marks: *S.A.*/anchors and scepter/*56*
Acc. No. 47-20-375

298. Bell contact.
Nephrite. Hemisphere with bas-relief of traceries carved on upper surface. Cabochon rose quartz button encircled with diamonds set in leaf forms. Gold rim with three curved feet.

2 1/2 diameter
Marks: *50056*
Acc. No. 47-20-282

299. Bookmark.
Serpentine. Gold monogram "XB" set with rubies and diamonds; gold spring catch.

1 1/2 long
Marks: *M.P.*/anchors and scepter/*56*
Acc. No. 47-20-154

300. Calendar.
Nephrite. At top, gold ribbon bows from which hang swags and festoons. Four moonstones set at corners, two lower corners contain laurel sprays. In center, two small oval apertures reveal numerals on red enamel dials which are revolved by means of knobbed lever on either side of frame. Beneath these ovals, an enamel rack set with moonstones holds six red-gold leaves which bear the names of the months. Silver back.

3 1/2 high by 3 3/4 wide
Marks: *Fabergé*/*H.W.*/profile/*88*/*23033*
Acc. No. 47-20-286

301. Figurine of sailor.
White opaque stone. Face and hands of aventurine; ribbons of cap and tie, lapis lazuli; shoes, shiny black onyx; eyes, sapphires.

4 5/8 high by 2 1/2 wide
Marks: none
Acc. No. 47-20-268

302. Globe.
Rock crystal. Engraved map of world. Red-gold frame and tripod which holds compass. Frame bears degree markings, months of year, and signs of the zodiac.

5 1/2 high by 3 1/4 diameter
Marks: *E.K.*/anchors and scepter/*56*
Acc. No. 47-20-285

303. Inkwell.
Nephrite. Red- and yellow-gold swags hang from neck over top part of bowl. Neck bound with pearl enamel field and gold fillets. Gold top, mauve and pearl enamel bound with carved gold fillet. Rock-crystal vial.

4 high by 2 3/4 diameter
Marks: *Fabergé*/*F.A.*/profile/*YL*/*56*/*88*
Acc. No. 47-20-301

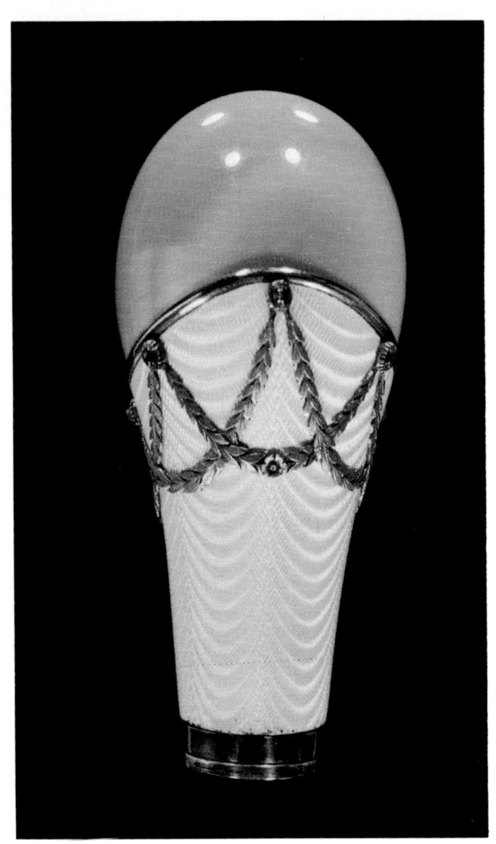

304

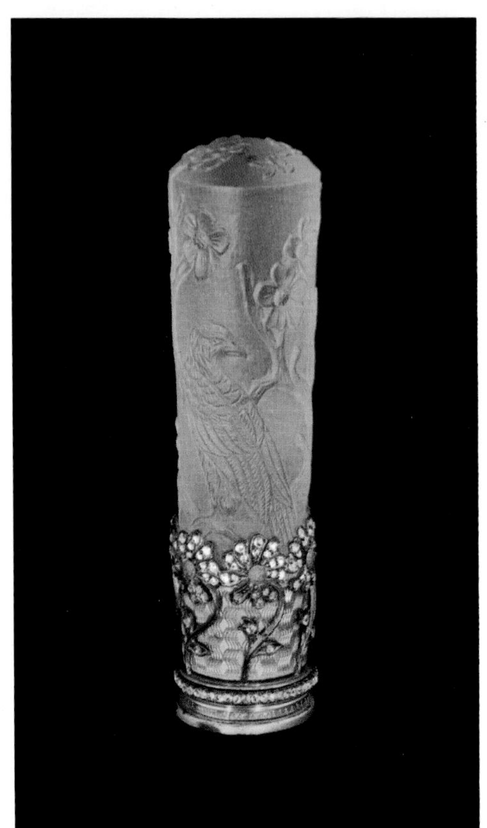

305

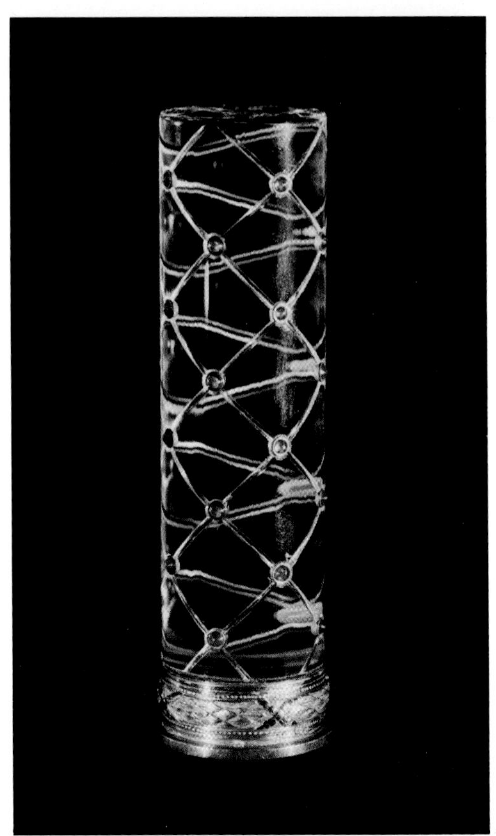

306

307

308

309

SEALS

304. Agate. Iridescent white enamel cup with gold band lip. Flat gold base. Upper edge set with six rubies with gold swags.

3¾ high by 1½ wide
Marks: none
Acc. No. 47-20-200

305. Rock-crystal shaft, rounded top. Bas-relief carving of two birds on branches of flowering plants. Neck of mauve enamel over chasing. Around top of neck, applied blossoms with gold centers, silver and diamond-set petals and leaves. Diamond-set fillet.

3 high by ¾ diameter
Marks: *Fabergé*/*M. P.*/*56*/illegible
Acc. No. 47-20-201

306. Rock crystal. Column with engraved lozenge shapes set with rubies at intersections. Red- and yellow-gold collar encircled by laurel wreath tied with ribbons. Originally designed as parasol or cane handle, base had been soldered on, changing it into a seal handle.

3½ high by 1 diameter
Marks: *M. P.*/profile/*56*/illegible
Acc. No. 47-20-202

307. Lapis lazuli. Convex top. Rim of top and corners of sides bound with gold bands fastening stone to gold neck. Neck has scroll design on upper part: two gold wires encircle the face of the neck; gold lozenges alternating with lozenge-shaped settings for diamonds are placed over these wires.

2½ high by 1¼ diameter
Marks: *A. K.*/illegible
Acc. No. 47-20-203

308. Serpentine. Gold lattice with applied lily-of-the-valley sprays, pearl blossoms.

3 high by 1 diameter
Marks: *M. P.*/anchors and scepter/*56*
Acc. No. 47-20-204

309. Aventurine. Swags of flowers in red and yellow gold and silver. Gold beads attach handle to neck of column, which has yellow-gold fillet of chased leaf form. Double-eagle seal.

3¼ high by 2 wide
Marks: *E. K.*
Acc. No. 47-20-205

310

TABLE SILVER

310. Beaker.
Silver-gilt. Dates "1894-1904," in blue enamel surmounted by applied diamond-set crown.

2½ high by 2⅛ diameter
Marks: *K. Fabergé*/double eagle/delta/profile/*88*/swan
Acc. No. 47-20-284

313

314

315

VESSELS

312. Coupe
Nephrite. Top rimmed with silver-gilt, pierced with design of dolphins, set with cabochon rubies and sapphires. Domed nephrite cover surmounted with gold trident rising from grotesque, two-faced head, which holds a ruby and a sapphire in his mouths. Silver-gilt tripod base formed by three hippocamps. Italian Renaissance influences may be seen in the dolphin border, the three hippocamps, and the mask of Neptune on the cover.

11 high by 3¾ diameter
Marks: *Fabergé/M.P./*anchors and scepter*/56/88/20-5-4* (deleted)*/20-1-7*
Acc. No. 47-20-300

313. Cup.
Gold. Lower portion repoussé, to represent water. Set in side are four sapphires, carved in form of fish heads and tails. Trefoil openwork handle.

1⅜ high by 2 diameter
Marks: *B.F./*anchors and scepter*/56/36643*
Acc. No. 47-20-292

314. Cup.
Rock crystal. Gold base and rim with square-set rubies. Handle set with diamonds.

1½ high by 3¼ long by 2½ diameter
Marks: *Fabergé/E.K./*anchors and scepter*/56/40312/*gothic K/illegible
Acc. No. 47-20-293

315. Cup.
Nephrite. Gold rim chased in ribbing with ribbon design. Nephrite cover with handle of rose quartz stone. Silver-gilt base and pedestal. As to shape and proportions, the covered cup is Italianate, but its silver-gilt mountings are strict First Empire.

5¼ high by 2¼ diameter
Marks: *Fabergé/M.P./88/*illegible
Acc. No. 47-20-294

316

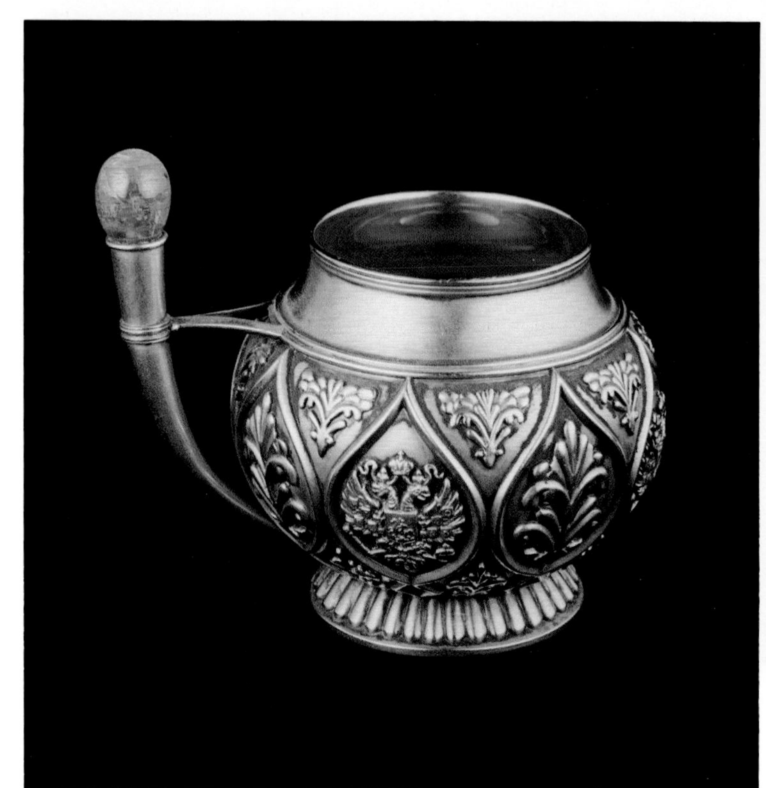
317

318

319

316. Cup.
Nephrite. Silver rosettes connected with bands form mesh over nephrite body. Rim of alternating rubies and sapphires. Carved whorls and rubies and sapphires on silver-gilt pedestal. The shape and proportions of the nephrite cup show Italian influence, with First Empire influence in the meshed bands around the body; but the insertion of large rubies and sapphires gives it a decidedly Slavic cast.

3½ high by 4 diameter
Marks: *Fabergé*/*H. W.*/profile/*88*/*24782*/*2880*/*nmj-j* [?]
Acc. No. 47-20-295

317. Embossed cup.
Yellow-gold exterior, red-gold interior. Four applied double eagles alternating with leaf patterns. Handle in form of curved horn with mouth upright holding green cabochon quartz. The embossed gold cup is remotely Scythian in inspiration, with its four applied double eagles.

2⅝ high by 2¼ diameter
Marks: *A. T.*/anchors and scepter/*56*
Acc. No. 47-20-273

318. Trefoil cup.
Red gold. Underside ribbed in shell design. Three handles, each holding gold coin with likeness of Catherine the Great and dates, respectively, 1766, 1773, 1783.

1¼ high by 4¾ wide
Marks: *Fabergé*/*E. K.*/*E. T.*/anchors and scepter/*56*/*1.24*
Acc. No. 47-20-374

319. Kovsh.
Silver-gilt. Underside enamelled in canary yellow over chased ground. Rosette and cabochon moonstone on front. Cabochon moonstone in handle. Three ball feet.

1¾ high by 4 long by 2¾ diameter
Marks: *K. Fabergé*/*A. M.*/double eagle/profile/*84*
Acc. No. 47-20-296

320. Kovsh.
Rock crystal. Etched floral design. Gold rim set with pear-shaped pearl. Broad openwork handle with carving of woman's head with diamond necklace; rubies and diamonds also in handle. Gold base with four leaf feet. The Art Nouveau tendency may be seen in the mountings of the *kovsh*. The feet are spreading, sinuous leaf forms; a paraboloid calyx holds a pear-shaped pearl; and the handle consists of jewel-set tendrils and fronds surrounding a female head.

2½ high by 5½ long by 3 diameter
Marks: *K. F.*/profile/*YL*/*56*
Acc. No. 47-20-297

321. Kovsh.
Red gold. Diamond-set double eagle on prow mounted on gold ball. Five-ruble coin, bearing the likeness of Catherine the Great, encircled by carved laurel wreath set in base. Coin dated 1776.

3½ high by 2⅜ wide
Marks: *E. K.*/anchors and scepter/*56*/*40297*
Acc. No. 47-20-298

322. Vase.
Silver-gilt. Deep green enamel over chased ground overlaid with gold scroll designs in enamel and set with varicolored stones and pearls.

6 high by 5½ diameter
Marks: *Fabergé*/double eagle/anchors and scepter/*88*/*478*/*IR*
Acc. No. 47-20-287

320

321

322

323

324

325

327

326

328

323. Vase.
Rock crystal. Surface carved with basket design. Gold rim set alternately with diamonds and rubies.

1½ high by 1½ diameter
Marks: *E.K.*/profile/*56*/*5388*
Acc. No. 47-20-288

324. Vase.
Brown- and white-veined Ural agate. Two bands of carved gold around neck with four rows of turquoises set between. This is closer to certain shapes preferred by German artists rather than Italian.

2 high by 2¼ wide by 3 long
Marks: none
Acc. No. 47-20-289

325. Vase.
Nephrite. Silver-gilt rim.

1⅛ high by 1⅞ diameter
Marks: [?]. *P.*/anchors and scepter/*88*
Acc. No. 47-20-290

326. Vase.
Silver-gilt. Red enamel over chasing. Upper part embellished with swags and festoons. Top and bottom fillets in fascine design. This red-enamel vase is wholly First Empire.

3¾ high by 2½ diameter
Marks: *K. Fabergé*/*N.V.*/double eagle/profile/*88*/*18258*/*2*, profile, *W*/*2*/owl's head (?).
Acc. No. 47-20-291

327. Vase.
Silver. Three coins set in sides. Flaring rim edged with acanthus leaf design above band with twisted motif. Three claw feet.

4 high by 4¾ diameter
Marks: *K. Fabergé*/profile/*88*/*24066*
Acc. No. 47-20-385

328. Vial.
Rock crystal. Chased gold rim with fretwork. Gold top covered with iridescent enamel over chasing. Set with small sapphires in top and crystal.

3 high by 1 diameter
Marks: [?]. *P.*/*56*
Acc. No. 47-20-299

Fabergé's Materials and Techniques

Presented below are descriptions of both the principal materials and techniques used by Fabergé, since his choice of metals and stones and his skilled working of them largely constitute the basis of his position as a great craftsman.

METALS

The basis of every Fabergé article is a metal. To determine what metal would be appropriate to the design and how it would be manipulated were thus the first considerations.

BRASS—Brass was used for *kovshi* (a *kovsh* is a uniquely Russian form of ladle, used for ladling beer, or *kvass*) and bowls.

GOLD—Of gold there was no lack. Since pure gold (24 carat) is much too ductile to be used for anything but trinkets, the weight most used by Fabergé was a 14-carat alloy, or ten parts of another metal to ninety parts of gold. In this proportion, the addition of pure copper produces red gold; the addition of pure silver produces green gold. Other metals may be introduced according to circumstances. Very often four different tints—yellow, red, green, and white golds—were combined in one piece, an elaboration of the French *quatre-couleur* technique of the 18th century.

Mat gold, or gold with a dull surface, was often combined for contrast with the highly polished metal. Still another technique affected the appearance of a gold nugget, or *samorodok*.

PLATINUM—Platinum, which when pure is exceedingly ductile and malleable, was used both as the basis of jewelry and as an adjunct to gold in fantasy pieces, automata, the Easter eggs, and so forth, where a very durable metal was required. It is typical of Fabergé's meticulous luxuriousness that in many pieces the interior, invisible mechanisms, which might just as well have been fabricated from steel, are made of platinum instead!

SILVER—Silver, in the standard Russian alloy of 84 or 88 parts of pure metal out of 96, or in the English sterling standard of 925 to 1000, was employed particularly for table services, garnitures, and samovar sets. Silver-gilt was used in the manufacture of relatively inexpensive articles such as parasol handles. The gold was most usually applied by the method of wash-gilding.

ENAMEL

The products of Fabergé's workshops are renowned especially for two peculiarities: the variety and excellence of their enamel, and the novel use of semi-precious and ornamental stones. Enamel is a pulverized compound of silica, borates, and alkalis, pigmented by various metallic oxides and fused by heat into a solid vitreous substance. It may be transparent, translucent, or opaque. As a decorative medium, enamel has exceptional advantages. The raw materials of which it is made are common and cheap. When handled by an accomplished craftsman, it is, both to the touch and to the eye, a substance of inimitable elegance: bright, sumptuous, and splendid. To be of the finest grade, enamel requires the exercise of skill and judgment equivalent to the most exacting surgery; it is an almost unalterable demonstration of an artisan's ability. The following terms are used to differentiate the techniques.

BASSE-TAILLE—This process is a combination of enamelling, carving, and engraving. The metal is engraved with a design and then carved into a bas-relief *below* the general surface. The enamel is laid over this and, when fused, is level with the uncarved parts, the design being visible beneath the surface.

CHAMPLEVÉ—Made by cutting or etching troughs in the metal plate, leaving a metal line raised between them, which forms the outline of the design. The pulverized enamel is laid in these hollows and then fused, the surface afterward being filed and polished.

CLOISONNÉ—Thin metal strips *(cloisons)* are bent and shaped to the design, and then fixed to the plate with silver solder or by the enamel itself. The unfused enamel is placed between the strips, in exactly the same way as with champlevé enamel, and then fused.

EN PLEIN—Though Fabergé used all these techniques, his work is marked by a preference for enamel *en plein*, in which the entire surface of the piece, or the larger part, is covered with translucent enamel of high finish. *En plein* enamel requires a very hard mixture: the pieces issuing from the Fabergé workshops were commonly fired in temperatures varying from 1250 to 1450 degrees Fahrenheit. When one considers that silver melts at 1800 degrees Fahrenheit, the extreme delicacy of the process is understood. After firing, the translucent enamel is polished with a wooden wheel to erase any irregularities, and is finally finished with a buff.

PAINTED ENAMEL—This type of enamel differs in both technique and effect from the foregoing. A metal plate, slightly domed, is covered both front and back with a preliminary coat of enamel, and fired. Upon this, using pigments of pure metallic oxides, the artist paints his design just as if he were using oils or tempera. This is then fired a second time.

PLIQUE À JOUR—This has no metal backing. The enamel is placed between the *cloisons*, which are fastened to themselves only, and not to the ground, which may be mica or some nonfusable, expendable material. After firing, the ground is removed. The effect is that of a stained-glass window.

METAL GROUNDS

The metal grounds used by Fabergé are extensively engraved, either by hand or by machine, with patterns of undulating, striated, interwoven, or trigonal lines, known generically as a guilloche surface. In the possession of M. Eugène Fabergé was a metal color-and-guilloche pattern chart consisting of 144 small silver squares of different colors and patterns, each numbered on the back. These models were used for the ordinary commercial productions of the St. Petersburg workshops; they by no means exhausted either the color range or the variations of patterns used.

STONES

In elevating the use of ornamental polished stones to the same prominence as enamel, Fabergé was only continuing an imperial tradition.

AGATE—An aggregate of various forms of silica. The variety characterized by a succession of parallel lines is called banded agate.

AVENTURINE—A variety of quartz containing spangles of mica or scales of iron oxide. Mostly reddish-brown or yellow, a green variety is known. It came chiefly from the Urals.

BOWENITE—A green serpentine of exceptional hardness, formerly regarded as jade.

CARNELIAN—Red chalcedony. This stone may also be brown, yellow, or even white. It is translucent, and can thus be distinguished from jasper, which is opaque. The color is due to the presence of ferric oxide.

CHALCEDONY—A variety of native silica. It is translucent and of a rather waxy lustre. The variety of colors is great, though it is usually white, gray, yellow, or brown. A rare blue variety is called sapphirine.

CROCIDOLITE—Also blue ironstone. A blue fibrous mineral, an iron sodium silicate. When polished, it develops a beautiful lustre like that of watered silk.

JADEITE—An aluminum sodium silicate, commonly very pale, often termed camphor jade. It can contain bright patches of emerald or apple green, due to the presence of chromium.

JASPER—Opaque, compact quartz, usually red, brown, yellow, or green. Ribbon jasper came not from the Urals but from Siberia.

LABRADORITE—A lime-soda felspar. Dull gray, and of a greasy lustre. When polished and held to the light in certain directions, it displays a magnificent play of colors: blue, green, orange, purple, or red. Russian labradorite comes from Finland and from near Kiev.

LAPIS LAZULI—Extensively used and highly prized for its intense, deep blue. Occurs in crystalline limestone. The best varieties came from Badakshan, on the northeastern frontier of Afghanistan adjoining Russian territory, and from Siberia, near the western end of Lake Baikal.

MALACHITE—Copper ore of fine green color. The principal sources were the Medno-Rudiansk mine near Nizhni-Tagilsk, on the Siberian side of the Urals, and Bogoskovsk and Gumishev in the same region.

NEPHRITE (or JADE)—Calcium-magnesium silicate. Most often occurring in shades of green or white, it may be also yellow or gray. The colors are due to compounds of iron, manganese, and chromium. The compact dark-green nephrite employed by Fabergé came largely from Batugol, in the vicinity of Lake Baikal. Red jade, occurring in conjunction with laterite, which is rich in iron, is found as boulders in alluvial deposits in Upper Burma, and is peculiarly precious.

OBSIDIAN—Glassy volcanic rock. Gray, very dark green, brown, or black, it was obtained principally from the vicinity of Okhotsk.

QUARTZ—Silica, one of the commonest of minerals. When violet, it is called amethyst; when brown, smoky quartz; and when yellow, citrine. The perfectly clear variety is known as rock crystal.

RHODONITE—Manganese metasilicate, of a rose-red color, often marked by black veins and patches. Russian rhodonite came from Syedelnikova.

PURPURINE—A deep crimson vitreous material, the discovery of one Petouchov, a worker in the Imperial Glass Factory. It apparently was produced by crystallizing lead chromate in a glass matrix. Fabergé seems to have had a monopoly on this material and used it often.

PRECIOUS STONES—Precious stones were not Fabergé's forte. Designs for jewelry employing rubies, diamonds, emeralds, and sapphires (in brooches, pendants, and corsage ornaments) exist, chiefly from Holmström's workshop. But he preferred to use precious stones as points of emphasis in conjunction with less costly materials. Rubies, sapphires, and emeralds were most frequently cut *en cabochon,* that is, in convex form, and were highly polished but not faceted. Diamonds were preferably rose-cut (with a flat, circular base and facets in two ranges rising to a point) so that their reduced brilliance would not overwhelm the enamel on which they were so often mounted.

only, and not to the ground, which may be mica or some non-fusable, expendable material. After firing, the ground is removed. The effect is that of a stained-glass window.

METAL GROUNDS

The metal grounds used by Fabergé are extensively engraved, either by hand or by machine, with patterns of undulating, striated, interwoven, or trigonal lines, known generically as a guilloche surface. In the possession of M. Eugène Fabergé was a metal color-and-guilloche pattern chart consisting of 144 small silver squares of different colors and patterns, each numbered on the back. These models were used for the ordinary commercial productions of the St. Petersburg workshops; they by no means exhausted either the color range or the variations of patterns used.

STONES

In elevating the use of ornamental polished stones to the same prominence as enamel, Fabergé was only continuing an imperial tradition.

AGATE—An aggregate of various forms of silica. The variety characterized by a succession of parallel lines is called banded agate.

AVENTURINE—A variety of quartz containing spangles of mica or scales of iron oxide. Mostly reddish-brown or yellow, a green variety is known. It came chiefly from the Urals.

BOWENITE—A green serpentine of exceptional hardness, formerly regarded as jade.

CARNELIAN—Red chalcedony. This stone may also be brown, yellow, or even white. It is translucent, and can thus be distinguished from jasper, which is opaque. The color is due to the presence of ferric oxide.

CHALCEDONY—A variety of native silica. It is translucent and of a rather waxy lustre. The variety of colors is great, though it is usually white, gray, yellow, or brown. A rare blue variety is called sapphirine.

CROCIDOLITE—Also blue ironstone. A blue fibrous mineral, an iron sodium silicate. When polished, it develops a beautiful lustre like that of watered silk.

JADEITE—An aluminum sodium silicate, commonly very pale, often termed camphor jade. It can contain bright patches of emerald or apple green, due to the presence of chromium.

JASPER—Opaque, compact quartz, usually red, brown, yellow, or green. Ribbon jasper came not from the Urals but from Siberia.

LABRADORITE—A lime-soda felspar. Dull gray, and of a greasy lustre. When polished and held to the light in certain directions, it displays a magnificent play of colors: blue, green, orange, purple, or red. Russian labradorite comes from Finland and from near Kiev.

LAPIS LAZULI—Extensively used and highly prized for its intense, deep blue. Occurs in crystalline limestone. The best varieties came from Badakshan, on the northeastern frontier of Afghanistan adjoining Russian territory, and from Siberia, near the western end of Lake Baikal.

MALACHITE—Copper ore of fine green color. The principal sources were the Medno-Rudiansk mine near Nizhni-Tagilsk, on the Siberian side of the Urals, and Bogoskovsk and Gumishev in the same region.

NEPHRITE (or JADE)—Calcium-magnesium silicate. Most often occurring in shades of green or white, it may be also yellow or gray. The colors are due to compounds of iron, manganese, and chromium. The compact dark-green nephrite employed by Fabergé came largely from Batugol, in the vicinity of Lake Baikal. Red jade, occurring in conjunction with laterite, which is rich in iron, is found as boulders in alluvial deposits in Upper Burma, and is peculiarly precious.

OBSIDIAN—Glassy volcanic rock. Gray, very dark green, brown, or black, it was obtained principally from the vicinity of Okhotsk.

QUARTZ—Silica, one of the commonest of minerals. When violet, it is called amethyst; when brown, smoky quartz; and when yellow, citrine. The perfectly clear variety is known as rock crystal.

RHODONITE—Manganese metasilicate, of a rose-red color, often marked by black veins and patches. Russian rhodonite came from Syedelnikova.

PURPURINE—A deep crimson vitreous material, the discovery of one Petouchov, a worker in the Imperial Glass Factory. It apparently was produced by crystallizing lead chromate in a glass matrix. Fabergé seems to have had a monopoly on this material and used it often.

PRECIOUS STONES—Precious stones were not Fabergé's forte. Designs for jewelry employing rubies, diamonds, emeralds, and sapphires (in brooches, pendants, and corsage ornaments) exist, chiefly from Holmström's workshop. But he preferred to use precious stones as points of emphasis in conjunction with less costly materials. Rubies, sapphires, and emeralds were most frequently cut *en cabochon,* that is, in convex form, and were highly polished but not faceted. Diamonds were preferably rose-cut (with a flat, circular base and facets in two ranges rising to a point) so that their reduced brilliance would not overwhelm the enamel on which they were so often mounted.

Designed by Raymond Geary. Color separations and lithography by W.M. Brown & Son, Inc., Richmond. The text was set in 11 and 9 point Palatino by Ad Type, Inc., Richmond. Paper is Champion Wedgwood Coated Offset, gloss, 100 lb. text. Bound by Optic Bindery, Baltimore.

APPLICATIONS

47. QUALITY CONTROL A box contains 35 machine parts, 8 of which are defective. A quality control inspector randomly selects 5 of the 35 parts for testing. What is the probability that at least one part is defective?

PRODUCTION A shipment of 20 sets of skateboard wheels contains 7 sets that have a new type of wheel surface.

48. What is the probability that if 5 sets are chosen, at least 1 set will have the new surface?

49. What is the probability that if 5 sets are chosen, at least 2 sets will have the new surface?

Look Back

Graph each inequality in a coordinate plane. *(LESSON 3.4)*

50. $8 > x > 3$

51. $-6 \leq x \leq -2$

52. $3 > y > -1$

Factor each quadratic trinomial. *(LESSON 5.3)*

53. $x^2 - x - 42$

54. $3x^2 - 16x - 12$

55. $81x^2 + 18x + 1$

Solve each equation. Check your solutions. *(LESSON 8.5)*

56. $\frac{x+2}{x} + 3 = \frac{x+6}{x}$

57. $\frac{3}{x-2} + x = \frac{17}{2}$

58. $\frac{2y+5}{3y-2} = \frac{4y+3}{6y-1}$

Look Beyond

59. If a card is drawn at random from a standard 52-card deck, what is the probability that the card is an ace? If a card is drawn at random from a standard deck and you are told that the card is a spade, does the probability that it is an ace change? Explain.

Let the sum of two random integers from 1 to 6 inclusive represent the sum of the roll of two number cubes.

1. Generate two random integers from 1 to 6 for a total of 40 trials. (Refer to the Keystroke Guide for Example 3 on page 687.) Record the outcomes.
2. Use your outcomes to estimate the probability of rolling "a sum of 7" *or* "a sum of 11." Describe how your results compare with the theoretical probability of rolling "a sum of 7" *or* "a sum of 11."
3. Perform another 40 trials for this experiment. Record the outcomes.
4. Use the outcomes of all 80 trials to estimate the probability of rolling "a sum of 7" *or* "a sum of 11." Compare your results with the theoretical probability of rolling "a sum of 7" *or* "a sum of 11." Describe what happens to your estimated probability as the number of trials increases.

WORKING ON THE CHAPTER PROJECT

You should now be able to complete the Chapter Project.

LESSON 10.5

EXAMPLE 3 Evaluate $\frac{365}{365} \times \frac{364}{365} \times \frac{363}{365} \times \ldots \times \frac{361}{365}$.

Page 661

(365 MATH PRB 2:nPr ENTER 35)
÷ (365 ^ 35) ENTER

LESSON 10.7

EXAMPLE 1 Generate 5 random integers from 1 to 200 inclusive.

Page 672

MATH PRB 5:randInt ENTER 1 , 200
) ENTER ENTER ENTER ENTER ENTER

For TI-82: MATH NUM 4:int ENTER (MATH PRB 1:rand
ENTER X 200 + 1) ENTER ENTER ENTER ENTER ENTER

EXAMPLE 2 Generate 10 random integers from 1 to 1000 inclusive.

Page 673

MATH PRB 5:randInt ENTER 1 , 1000)

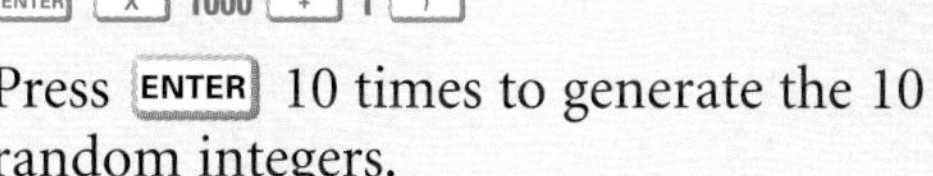
For TI-82: MATH NUM 4:int ENTER (MATH PRB 1:rand
ENTER X 1000 + 1)

Press ENTER 10 times to generate the 10 random integers.

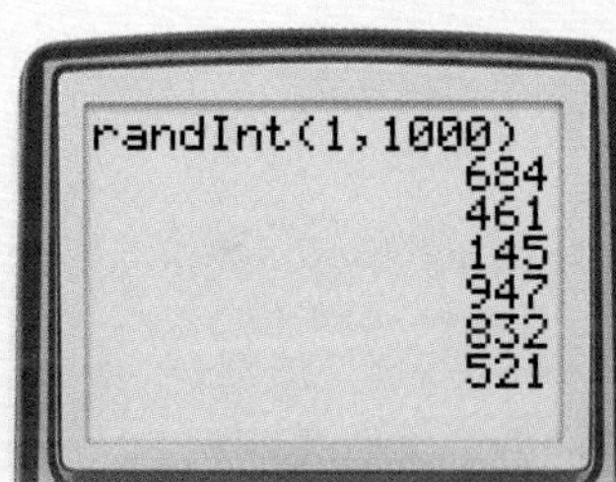

EXAMPLE 3 Generate 3 random integers from 1 to 9 for each of 10 trials.

Page 674

1st trial:

MATH PRB 5:randInt ENTER 1 , 9)
ENTER ENTER ENTER

For TI-82: MATH NUM 4:int ENTER (MATH PRB 1:rand
ENTER X 9 + 1) ENTER ENTER ENTER

2nd trial:

2nd ENTRY ENTER ENTER ENTER ENTER

Simulate additional trials by continuing to use the entry command followed by ENTER.

DISCRETE MATHEMATICS

Series and Patterns

DISCOVERING PATTERNS AND REPRESENTING them in sequences of numbers is an important mathematical skill. In this chapter, you will investigate different types of sequences, including the Fibonacci sequence. The Fibonacci sequence is used to describe a wide variety of structures in nature. For example, the spiral formed by a nautilus shell and the spiral pattern of sunflower seeds are both related to the Fibonacci sequence.

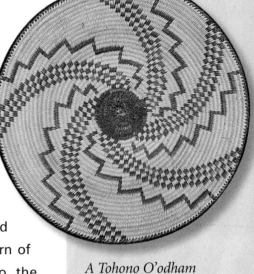

A Tohono O'odham basket from Arizona echoes the spiral pattern seen in nature.

Lessons

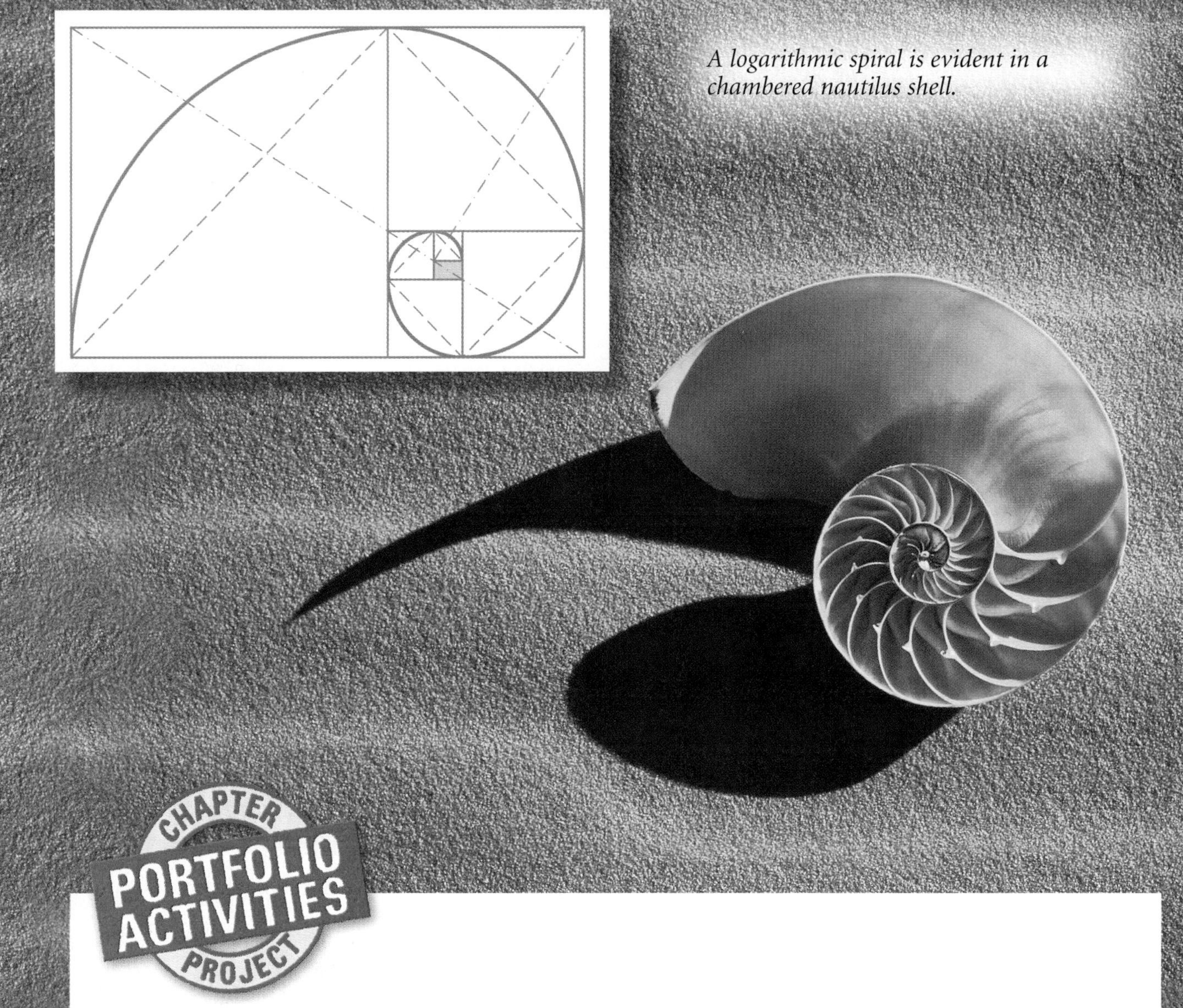

A logarithmic spiral is evident in a chambered nautilus shell.

CHAPTER PORTFOLIO ACTIVITIES PROJECT

About the Chapter Project

In this chapter, you will use series and sequences to model real-world situations.

In the Chapter Project, *Over the Edge*, you will investigate centers of gravity and perform experiments to develop a model involving sequences and series that you will use to determine whether a stack of objects will remain balanced.

After completing the Chapter Project, you will be able to do the following:

- Experimentally determine the center of gravity of an object.
- Model data from your experiments with a sequence or series.
- Determine whether your model gives predictions that are consistent with observations.

About the Portfolio Activities

Throughout the chapter, you will be given opportunities to complete Portfolio Activities that are designed to support your work on the Chapter Project.

- Finding the center of gravity of an object is included in the Portfolio Activity on page 706.
- Experimenting to determine some relationships that govern center of gravity is included inthe Portfolio Activity on page 727.
- Experimenting to determine the limits involved in keeping an object balanced is included in the Portfolio Activity on page 734.

11.1

Sequences and Series

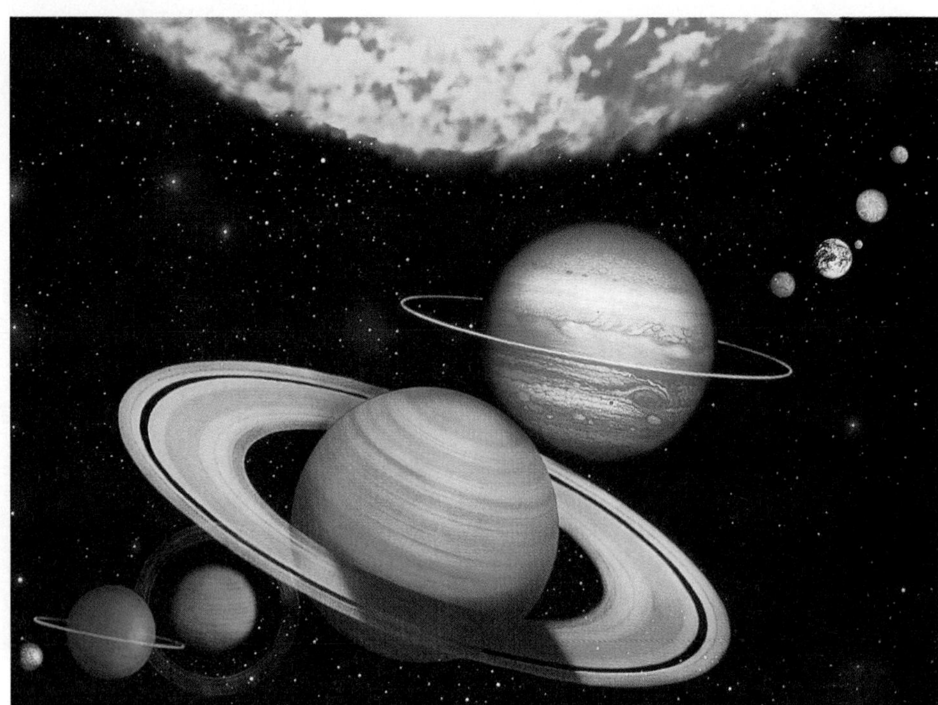

Objectives

- Find the terms of a sequence.
- Evaluate the sum of a series expressed in sigma notation.

Why *Sequences and series can be used to describe many patterns observed in the real world, such as the distances between the Sun and the planets.*

APPLICATION
ASTRONOMY

CULTURAL CONNECTION: EUROPE In the eighteenth century, German astronomers Johann Daniel Titius and Johann Elert Bode wrote a sequence of numbers to model the distances between the Sun and the planets.

They began with the number sequence below, in which each number (except 3) is double the preceding number.

$$0, 3, 6, 12, 24, 48, \ldots$$

From this sequence of numbers, Titius and Bode wrote a new sequence, called *Bode's sequence,* defined by adding 4 to each number in the original sequence and then dividing the result by 10.

Planet	Original number	Bode number
1st: Mercury	0	$\frac{0+4}{10} = 0.4$
2nd: Venus	3	$\frac{3+4}{10} = 0.7$
3rd: Earth	6	$\frac{6+4}{10} = 1.0$
4th: Mars	12	$\frac{12+4}{10} = 1.6$

Bode's law gives the distance from Earth to the Sun as 1 unit; each number in Bode's sequence represents the distance from a planet to the Sun in relation to that unit. Based on Bode's sequence, astronomers looked for a planet at the distance corresponding to the fifth Bode number, between Mars and Jupiter. The astronomers discovered Ceres, which turned out to be the largest member of the asteroid belt between Mars and Jupiter.

Sequences

In mathematics, a **sequence** is an ordered list of numbers, called **terms.** The terms of a sequence are often arranged in a pattern. Some examples are shown below.

$$2, 4, 6, 8, 10, \ldots \qquad 2, 4, 8, 16, 32, \ldots$$
$$5, 2, -1, -4, -7, \ldots \qquad 3, -9, 27, -81, 243, \ldots$$

The three dots, called an ellipsis, indicate that a sequence is an **infinite sequence,** which continues without end. A **finite sequence** has a last term.

An infinite sequence can be defined by a function whose domain is the set of all natural numbers $\{1, 2, 3, \ldots, n, \ldots\}$ and a finite sequence can be defined by a function whose domain is the first n natural numbers $\{1, 2, 3, \ldots, n\}$. The range for both functions is the set of all real numbers. For example, the sequence 2, 4, 6, 8, 10, 12, . . . can be defined by the function t, shown below.

$$t(n) = 2n, \text{ where } n = 1, 2, 3, \ldots$$

n	1	2	3	4	5	6	←*domain*
$t(n)$	2	4	6	8	10	12	←*range*

Each member of the range of a sequence is a term of the sequence. The terms of a sequence are often represented by the letter t with a subscript, as shown below.

$$t_1, t_2, t_3, \ldots, t_{n-1}, t_n$$

A formula that defines the nth term, or general term, of a sequence is called an **explicit formula.** With an explicit formula, each term of the sequence can be found by substituting the number of the term for n. This is shown in Example 1 below.

EXAMPLE 1 **Write the first six terms of the sequence defined by the explicit formula $t_n = -2n + 3$.**

SOLUTION

Evaluate $t_n = -2n + 3$ for n-values of 1, 2, 3, 4, 5, and 6.

n	1	2	3	4	5	6
t_n	1	−1	−3	−5	−7	−9

The first six terms of this sequence are 1, −1, −3, −5, −7, and −9.

TRY THIS Write the first six terms of the sequence defined by the explicit formula $t_n = 2n^2 - 1$.

A sequence can also be defined by a *recursive formula*. With a **recursive formula,** one or more previous terms are used to generate the next term. For example, the recursive formula for Example 1 is $t_1 = 1$ and $t_n = t_{n-1} - 2$, where $n \geq 2$.

$$t_n = t_{n-1} - 2 \text{ and } t_1 = 1$$
$$t_2 = t_1 - 2 = 1 - 2 = -1$$
$$t_3 = t_2 - 2 = -1 - 2 = -3$$
$$t_4 = t_3 - 2 = -3 - 2 = -5$$

EXAMPLE 2 **Write the first six terms of the sequence defined by the recursive formula $t_1 = 4$ and $t_n = 3t_{n-1} + 5$, where $n \geq 2$.**

SOLUTION

$$t_n = 3t_{n-1} + 5 \text{ and } t_1 = 4$$
$$t_2 = 3t_1 + 5 = 3(4) + 5 = 17$$
$$t_3 = 3t_2 + 5 = 3(17) + 5 = 56$$
$$t_4 = 3t_3 + 5 = 3(56) + 5 = 173$$
$$t_5 = 3t_4 + 5 = 3(173) + 5 = 524$$
$$t_6 = 3t_5 + 5 = 3(524) + 5 = 1577$$

The first six terms of this sequence are 4, 17, 56, 173, 524, and 1577.

TRY THIS Write the first six terms of the sequence defined by the recursive formula $t_1 = 1$ and $t_n = 3t_{n-1} - 1$, where $n \geq 2$.

EXAMPLE 3 **Refer to Bode's law, described at the beginning of the lesson.**

APPLICATION
ASTRONOMY

a. Find the next four terms of Bode's sequence, given the next four terms of the original sequence.

5th: Ceres	24
6th: Jupiter	48
7th: Saturn	96
8th: Uranus	192

b. Using Bode's law and 1.495×10^8 kilometers as the distance between Earth and the Sun, write the approximate distances in kilometers between the Sun and Ceres, Jupiter, Saturn, and Uranus.

SOLUTION

a.

Planet	Original number	Bode number
5th: Ceres	24	$\frac{24+4}{10} = 2.8$
6th: Jupiter	48	$\frac{48+4}{10} = 5.2$
7th: Saturn	96	$\frac{96+4}{10} = 10.0$
8th: Uranus	192	$\frac{192+4}{10} = 19.6$

b.

Planet	Bode number	Distance from planet to Sun
5th: Ceres	2.8	$2.8(1.495 \times 10^8) = 4.186 \times 10^8$
6th: Jupiter	5.2	$5.2(1.495 \times 10^8) = 7.774 \times 10^8$
7th: Saturn	10.0	$10.0(1.495 \times 10^8) = 1.495 \times 10^9$
8th: Uranus	19.6	$19.6(1.495 \times 10^8) = 2.9302 \times 10^9$

CRITICAL THINKING Write a recursive formula for the sequence of Bode numbers, beginning with the second term.

Another famous sequence is the *Fibonacci sequence.* It is defined recursively as $a_1 = 1$, $a_2 = 1$, and $a_n = a_{n-2} + a_{n-1}$, where $n \geq 3$. The sequence is

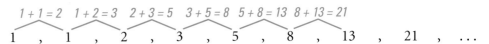

$1 + 1 = 2 \quad 1 + 2 = 3 \quad 2 + 3 = 5 \quad 3 + 5 = 8 \quad 5 + 8 = 13 \quad 8 + 13 = 21$

$1, \ 1, \ 2, \ 3, \ 5, \ 8, \ 13, \ 21, \ \ldots$

CHECKPOINT ✔ Write the next four terms of the Fibonacci sequence.

The Fibonacci sequence, also called the *golden spiral,* has been used to study animal populations, relationships between elements in works of art, and various patterns in plants, such as the sunflower.

The seeds of a sunflower are arranged in spiral curves. The number of clockwise spirals and the number of counterclockwise spirals are always successive terms in the Fibonacci sequence.

Series

A **series** is an expression that indicates the sum of terms of a sequence. For example, if you add the terms of the sequence 2, 4, 6, 8, and 10, the resulting expression is the series 2 + 4 + 6 + 8 + 10.

Summation notation, which uses the Greek letter **sigma, Σ,** is a way to express a series in abbreviated form. For example, the series 2 + 4 + 6 + 8 + 10 can be represented as $\sum_{n=1}^{5} 2n$, which is read "the sum of $2n$ for values of n from 1 to 5."

$$\sum_{n=1}^{5} 2n$$

Values of n from 1 to 5 are called the index.

Explicit formula for the general term of the related sequence

EXAMPLE 4 **Write the terms of each series. Then evaluate.**

a. $\sum_{k=1}^{4} 5k$ **b.** $5\sum_{k=1}^{4} k$

SOLUTION

a. $\sum_{k=1}^{4} 5k = 5(1) + 5(2) + 5(3) + 5(4)$
$= 5 + 10 + 15 + 20$
$= 50$

b. $5\sum_{k=1}^{4} k = 5(1 + 2 + 3 + 4)$
$= 5(10)$
$= 50$

TRY THIS Write the terms of each series. Then evaluate.

a. $\sum_{k=1}^{5} 4k$ **b.** $\frac{1}{2}\sum_{k=1}^{4} k$

Exploring Summation Properties

You will need: no special materials

1. Evaluate $\sum_{k=1}^{4}(2k + k^2)$ and $\sum_{k=1}^{4} 2k + \sum_{k=1}^{4} k^2$.

CHECKPOINT ✔ 2. Are the two results from Step 1 the same? Explain.

3. Evaluate $\sum_{k=1}^{5} 2$, $\sum_{k=1}^{5} 3$, and $\sum_{k=1}^{5} 4$. (Hint: $\sum_{k=1}^{5} 1 = 1 + 1 + 1 + 1 + 1 = 5$)

CHECKPOINT ✔ 4. Find the pattern in the results from Step 3, and write a formula for $\sum_{k=1}^{n} c$.

Two summation properties are illustrated below.

$$\sum_{n=1}^{3} 4n^2 = 4 \cdot 1^2 + 4 \cdot 2^2 + 4 \cdot 3^2 = 4(1^2 + 2^2 + 3^2) = 4\sum_{n=1}^{3} n^2$$

$$\sum_{n=1}^{3}(n + n^2) = (1 + 1^2) + (2 + 2^2) + (3 + 3^2) = (1 + 2 + 3) + (1^2 + 2^2 + 3^2) = \sum_{n=1}^{3} + \sum_{n=1}^{3} n^2$$

These summation properties do not have names. Notice, however, the properties of real-number operations that are used in the illustrations. In the first case, the Distributive Property is used. In the second case, both the Associative and Commutative Properties are used.

Summation Properties

For sequences a_k and b_k and positive integer n:

1. $\sum_{k=1}^{n} ca_k = c\sum_{k=1}^{n} a_k$
2. $\sum_{k=1}^{n}(a_k + b_k) = \sum_{k=1}^{n} a_k + \sum_{k=1}^{n} b_k$

Series such as $\sum_{k=1}^{5} 2$ and $\sum_{k=1}^{5} 3$ are called *constant series.* The general term of a series may be defined by a constant, linear, or quadratic expression. The formulas below are used to find the sums of these series.

Summation Formulas

For all positive integers n:

Constant Series	Linear Series	Quadratic Series
$\sum_{k=1}^{n} c = nc$	$\sum_{k=1}^{n} k = \frac{n(n+1)}{2}$	$\sum_{k=1}^{n} k^2 = \frac{n(n+1)(2n+1)}{6}$

CHECKPOINT ✔ Verify the formulas for the sums of constant, linear, and quadratic series by using the series 2 + 2 + 2, 1 + 2 + 3, and 1 + 4 + 9, respectively.

EXAMPLE 5 Evaluate $\sum_{m=1}^{5}(2m^2 + 3m + 2)$.

SOLUTION

$$\begin{aligned}\sum_{m=1}^{5}(2m^2 + 3m + 2) &= \sum_{m=1}^{5}2m^2 + \sum_{m=1}^{5}3m + \sum_{m=1}^{5}2 \\ &= 2\sum_{m=1}^{5}m^2 + 3\sum_{m=1}^{5}m + \sum_{m=1}^{5}2 \\ &= 2\left[\frac{5(6)(11)}{6}\right] + 3\left[\frac{5(6)}{2}\right] + 5 \cdot 2 \\ &= 110 + 45 + 10 \\ &= 165\end{aligned}$$

TRY THIS Evaluate $\sum_{j=1}^{5}(-j^2 + 2j + 5)$.

Exercises

Communicate

1. Explain the difference between a sequence and a series. Include examples in your response.

2. Explain the differences between the explicit formula $t_n = 2n + 1$ and the recursive formula $t_n = 2t_{n-1} + 1$.

3. Explain the difference between $\sum_{i=1}^{3}(i + 10)$ and $\sum_{i=1}^{3}i + 10$.

Guided Skills Practice

4. Write the first six terms of the sequence defined by the explicit formula $t_n = 3n - 2$. ***(EXAMPLE 1)***

5. Write the first six terms of the sequence defined by the recursive formula below. ***(EXAMPLE 2)***

$$t_1 = 1 \text{ and } t_n = 3t_{n-1} + 1, \text{ where } n \geq 2$$

6. The first five terms of a sequence are 3, 5, 7, 9, and 11. ***(EXAMPLE 3)***

a. Write the next five terms.

b. Write a recursive formula for the sequence.

Write the terms of each series. Then evaluate. ***(EXAMPLE 4)***

7. $\sum_{k=1}^{3}4k$

8. $5\sum_{k=1}^{4}k$

9. Evaluate $\sum_{k=1}^{4}(3k^2 + 2k + 4)$. ***(EXAMPLE 5)***

Practice and Apply

Write the first four terms of each sequence defined by the given explicit formula.

10. $t_n = 2n + 3$

11. $t_n = 4n + 1$

12. $t_n = -2n + 1$

13. $t_n = -4n - 1$

14. $t_n = 6n + 2$

15. $t_n = 5n - 1$

16. $t_n = -7n + 3$

17. $t_n = -4n + 8$

18. $t_n = 4n + 2$

19. $t_n = \frac{1}{2}n + 1$

20. $t_n = \frac{1}{4}n + 2$

21. $t_n = 8.75n + 3.67$

22. $t_n = 3.76n + 2.5$

23. $t_n = n^3$

24. $t_n = (-1)^n$

25. $t_n = -2n^2$

Write the first six terms of each sequence defined by the given recursive formula.

26. $t_1 = 1$
$t_n = t_{n-1} + 3$

27. $t_1 = 2$
$t_n = t_{n-1} + 2$

28. $t_1 = 0$
$t_n = t_{n-1} - 4$

29. $t_1 = -6$
$t_n = -2t_{n-1} + 3$

30. $t_1 = 7$
$t_n = 4t_{n-1} + 1$

31. $t_1 = 10$
$t_n = 5t_{n-1} + 1$

32. $t_1 = 10$
$t_n = 3t_{n-1} + 1$

33. $t_1 = 8$
$t_n = 3t_{n-1} - 2$

34. $t_1 = -2.24$
$t_n = 1.2t_{n-1} + 2.2$

35. $t_1 = 3.34$
$t_n = 2.2t_{n-1} - 1$

36. $t_1 = \frac{1}{3}$
$t_n = \frac{1}{2}t_{n-1} + 2$

37. $t_1 = \frac{5}{7}$
$t_n = \frac{1}{5}t_{n-1} + \frac{1}{3}$

For each sequence below, write a recursive formula and find the next three terms.

38. 1, 5, 9, 13, . . .

39. 3, 9, 15, 21, . . .

40. 5, 9, 17, 33, . . .

41. 3, 7, 15, 31, . . .

Write the terms of each series. Then evaluate.

42. $\sum_{k=1}^{3} 4$

43. $\sum_{k=1}^{4} 10$

44. $\sum_{j=1}^{4} 3j$

45. $\sum_{k=1}^{3} 4k$

46. $\sum_{k=1}^{5} -2k$

47. $\sum_{k=1}^{4} -5k$

48. $\sum_{k=1}^{3} \frac{1}{2}k^2$

49. $\sum_{k=1}^{5} \frac{1}{3}k^2$

50. $\sum_{m=1}^{5} -\frac{1}{3}m^2 - m$

51. $\sum_{n=1}^{3} -\frac{1}{4}n^2 + n$

52. $\sum_{j=1}^{4} (2j + 3)$

53. $\sum_{k=1}^{3} (-3k + 1)$

54. $\sum_{m=1}^{4} (5m^2 + 1)$

55. $\sum_{k=1}^{3} (k^2 + k + 1)$

56. $\sum_{k=1}^{3} (2k^2 + 3k + 2)$

Evaluate the sum.

57. $\sum_{k=1}^{4} 3$

58. $\sum_{k=1}^{4} 2$

59. $\sum_{j=1}^{6} 4j$

60. $\sum_{k=1}^{7} 3k$

61. $\sum_{m=1}^{3} (5m + 4)$

62. $\sum_{n=1}^{4} (2n + 3)$

63. $\sum_{k=1}^{3} (4k + 5)$

64. $\sum_{m=1}^{5} (2m^2 + 3m + 2)$

65. $\sum_{j=1}^{4} (4j^2 + 4j + 1)$

66. $\sum_{m=1}^{4} (-5m^2 + 2m + 4)$

67. $\sum_{n=1}^{4} (3 - n)^2$

68. $\sum_{k=1}^{6} (k + 2)^2$

69. $\sum_{n=1}^{3} \left(-\frac{2}{3}n^2 + \frac{1}{2}n + \frac{5}{7}\right)$

70. $\sum_{j=1}^{6} \left(\frac{1}{3}j^2 + \frac{1}{5}j + 2\right)$

71. $\sum_{m=1}^{4} (\pi m^2 + 2\pi m + 2)$

72. $\sum_{n=1}^{6} (\pi n^2 + \pi n + 4)$

73. $\sum_{k=1}^{5} (0.7k^2 + 1.3k + 2)$

74. $\sum_{j=1}^{5} (8.7j^2 + 8.6j + 7.5)$

CHALLENGES

75. Find an explicit formula for the *n*th term of Bode's sequence.

76. A certain sequence is defined recursively by $t_1 = 1$, $t_2 = 2$, $t_{2n} = 2t_{2n-2}$, and $t_{2n+1} = 3t_{2n-1}$. Find the first eight terms of the sequence.

CONNECTION

GEOMETRY The measure of each interior angle of a regular n-sided polygon is $\frac{180(n-2)}{n}$ degrees. For example, the interior angle measure of a regular (equilateral) triangle is $\frac{180(3-2)}{3} = 60°$.

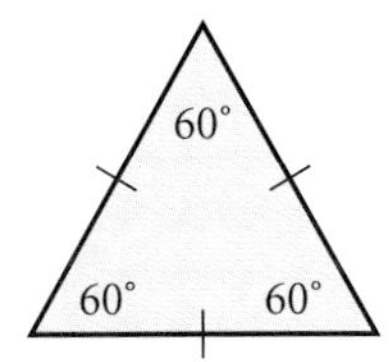

77. Find the interior angle measure of a square.

78. Find the interior angle measure of a regular pentagon.

79. Find the interior angle measure of a regular hexagon.

80. Does the interior angle measure of a regular n-sided polygon increase or decrease as n increases?

APPLICATIONS

81. INCOME Alan, a first-semester freshman, tutors in an afterschool program and earns $7.00 an hour. Each semester, Alan gets a $0.30 per hour raise. If he continues tutoring through his senior year, how much will he earn per hour in each semester of high school? Write an explicit formula to solve this problem.

82. BIOLOGY A single bacterium divides into 2 bacteria every 10 minutes. Assume that the same rate of division continues for 3 hours. Write a sequence that gives the number of bacteria after each 10-minute period.

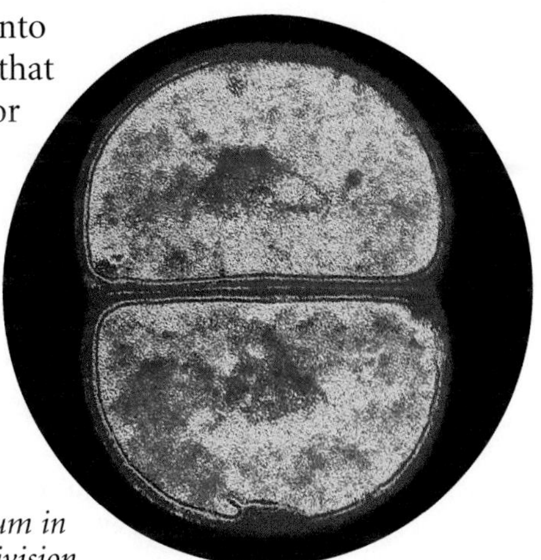

A spherical bacterium in the process of cell division

APPLICATION

83. RECREATION Anya is making paper flowers for the school prom. As she works, her speed increases. The first hour, she makes 12 flowers. During each additional hour that she works, she is able to make 4 more flowers than the hour before. If she works for 7 hours, how many flowers will she have made in total? Use sigma notation to model and solve this problem. (Hint: Start the index at 0.)

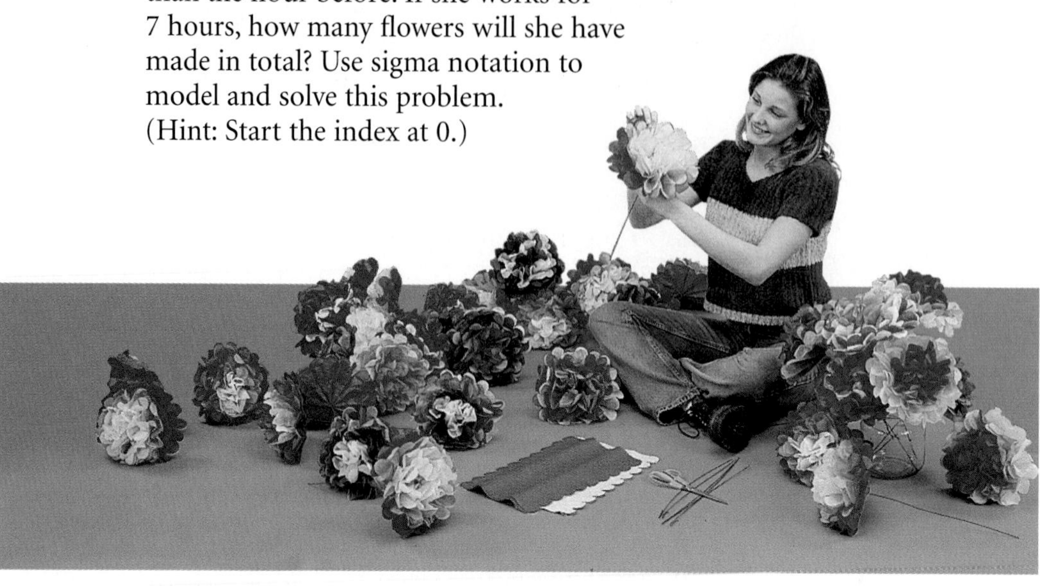

Look Back

Write an equation in slope-intercept form for the line that contains the given point and is parallel to the given line. ***(LESSON 1.3)***

84. $(-2, 5), y = \frac{3}{4}x - 1$

85. $(-4, 2), 2x - 3y = 1$

Find the discriminant, and determine the number of real solutions. Then solve. ***(LESSON 5.6)***

86. $x^2 - 6x + 12 = 0$

87. $4x^2 - 4x + 1 = 0$

88. $x^2 - 6x + 8 = 0$

Solve each nonlinear system of equations and check your answers. ***(LESSON 9.6)***

89. $\begin{cases} 2x + y = 1 \\ 4x^2 + 9y^2 = 1 \end{cases}$

90. $\begin{cases} 2y^2 = x \\ x - 2y = 12 \end{cases}$

91. $\begin{cases} y^2 + 2x = 17 \\ x + 4y = -8 \end{cases}$

Calculate each permutation and combination below. ***(LESSONS 10.2 AND 10.3)***

92. ${}_8P_3$

93. ${}_9P_2$

94. ${}_{10}C_3$

95. ${}_8C_4$

Look Beyond

96. Find the next three terms of the sequence 5, 8, 11, 14, 17, . . . Then find an explicit formula for t_n, the nth term of the sequence.

Graph each sequence below. What pattern do you see in the graphs?

97.

n	1	2	3	4	5
t_n	−4	−1	2	5	8

98.

n	1	2	3	4	5
t_n	8	4	0	−4	−8

Arithmetic Sequences

11.2

Objectives

- Recognize arithmetic sequences, and find the indicated term of an arithmetic sequence.
- Find arithmetic means between two numbers.

Why *Arithmetic sequences can be used to model real-world events such as the depreciation of a watering system.*

APPLICATION
DEPRECIATION

A new garden-watering system costs \$389.95. As time goes on, the value of the watering system depreciates. Its value decreases by \$42.50 per year. What is the value of the system after 9 years? To answer this question, you can use an arithmetic sequence. *You will answer this question in Example 2.*

Two examples of arithmetic sequences are shown below.

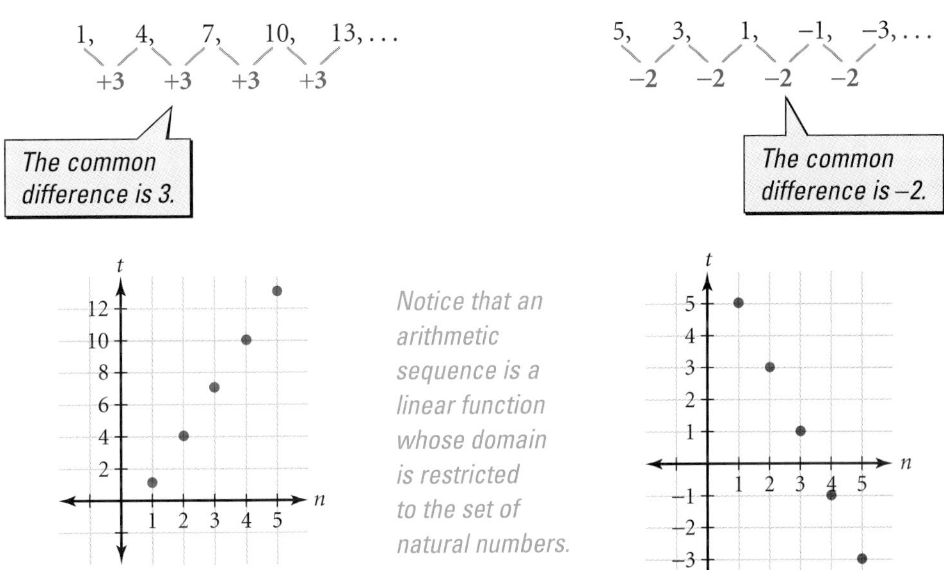
1, 4, 7, 10, 13, . . .
+3 +3 +3 +3
The common difference is 3.
5, 3, 1, −1, −3, . . .
−2 −2 −2 −2
The common difference is −2.
t
12
10
8
6
4
2
1 2 3 4 5
n
t
5
4
3
2
1
−1
−2
−3
1 2 3 4 5
n
Notice that an arithmetic sequence is a linear function whose domain is restricted to the set of natural numbers.

CHECKPOINT ✔ How does the common difference of an arithmetic sequence compare with the slope of the corresponding linear function?

An **arithmetic sequence** is a sequence whose successive terms differ by the same number, d, called the **common difference.** That is, if t_n, where $n \geq 2$, is any term in an arithmetic sequence, then the statement below is true.

$$t_n - t_{n-1} = d \quad \text{or} \quad t_n = t_{n-1} + d$$

The formula $t_n = t_{n-1} + d$, where $n \geq 2$, is a recursive formula because it gives the nth term of a sequence in relation to the previous term and d.

PROBLEM SOLVING

Look for a pattern. A pattern can be seen in the recursive formula for the arithmetic sequence defined by $t_1 = 3$ and $t_n = t_{n-1} + 4$, where $n \geq 2$.

Recursive formula	Pattern
$t_1 = 3$	$t_1 = 3 + (0)4$
$t_2 = 3 + 4$	$t_2 = 3 + (1)4$
$t_3 = (3 + 4) + 4$	$t_3 = 3 + (2)4$
$t_4 = [(3 + 4) + 4] + 4$	$t_4 = 3 + (3)4$

The pattern formed by the recursive formula gives the information needed to write an explicit formula for the same sequence.

$$t_n = 3 + (n - 1)4, \text{ where } n \geq 1$$

*n*th Term of an Arithmetic Sequence

The general term, t_n, of an arithmetic sequence whose first term is t_1 and whose common difference is d is given by the explicit formula $t_n = t_1 + (n - 1)d$.

If you know the first term of an arithmetic sequence and its common difference, you can use the explicit formula to find any term of the sequence. This is shown in Example 1.

EXAMPLE 1 **Find the fifth term of the sequence defined by the recursive formula $t_1 = -4$ and $t_n = t_{n-1} + 3$.**

SOLUTION

The sequence is arithmetic, in which $t_1 = -4$ and $d = 3$. Use the explicit formula for the general term of an arithmetic sequence.

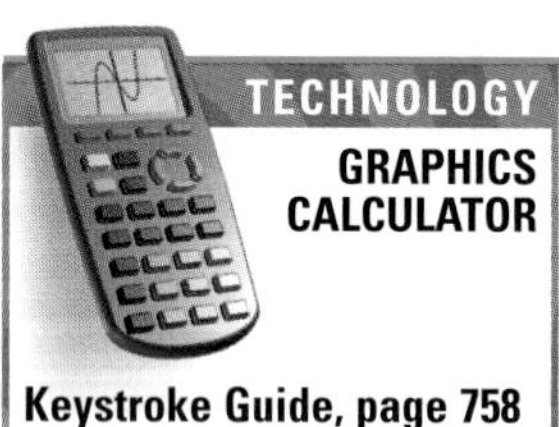

Keystroke Guide, page 758

$$t_n = t_1 + (n - 1)d$$
$$t_5 = -4 + (5 - 1)3$$
$$t_5 = 8$$

Thus, the fifth term of the sequence is 8.

CHECK

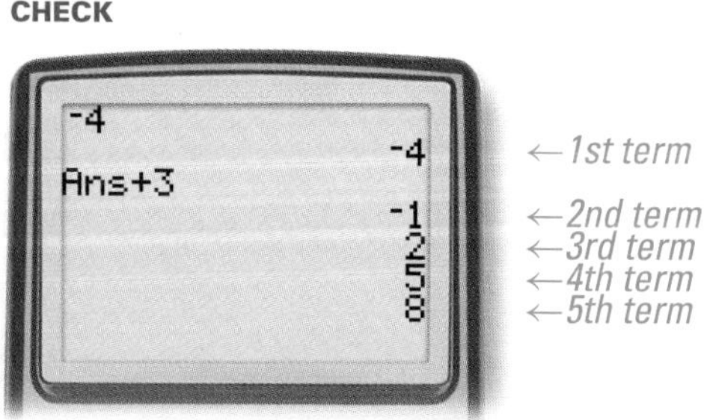

TRY THIS Find the seventh term of the sequence defined by the recursive formula $t_1 = 2.5$ and $t_n = t_{n-1} - 3$.

EXAMPLE 2 **Refer to the watering system described at the beginning of the lesson.**

APPLICATION
DEPRECIATION

a. Use a recursive formula to find the value of the system after 4 years.
b. Use the explicit formula for the nth term of an arithmetic sequence to find the value of the watering system after 9 years.

TECHNOLOGY
GRAPHICS CALCULATOR

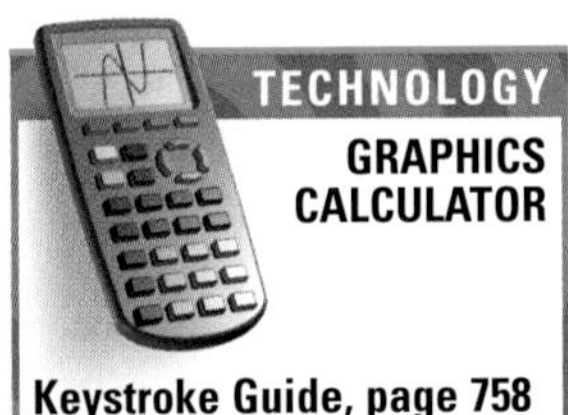

Keystroke Guide, page 758

SOLUTION

a. Initial value (year 0): 389.95
year 1: $389.95 - 42.5 = 347.45$
year 2: $347.45 - 42.5 = 304.95$
year 3: $304.95 - 42.5 = 262.45$
year 4: $262.45 - 42.5 = 219.95$

The value of the system after 4 years of use is \$219.95.

CHECK

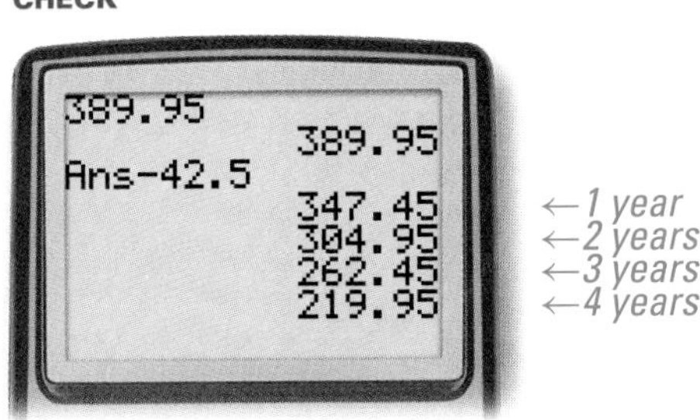

b. At year 9, $n = 10$. Find t_{10}.

$t_n = t_1 + (n - 1)d$
$t_{10} = 389.95 + (10 - 1)(-42.5)$
$t_{10} = 7.45$

The value of the system after 9 years of use is \$7.45.

CHECKPOINT ✔ Explain why you need to find the 10th term of the arithmetic sequence in Example 2 in order to find the value after 9 years.

TRY THIS A new washing machine costs \$352.65. It depreciates \$48.60 each year. Find the value of the washing machine after 7 years.

EXAMPLE 3 **Find the 10th term of the arithmetic sequence in which $t_3 = -5$ and $t_6 = 16$.**

SOLUTION

1. Find the common difference, d.

n	3	4	5	6
t_n	−5	?	?	16

d d d

$\rightarrow -5 + 3d = 16$
$d = 7$

2. Find t_1. Use $d = 7$ and either $t_3 = -5$ or $t_6 = 16$.

$t_n = t_1 + (n - 1)d$
$-5 = t_1 + (3 - 1)7$ *Use $t_3 = -5$.*
$-19 = t_1$

$t_n = t_1 + (n - 1)d$
$16 = t_1 + (6 - 1)7$ *Use $t_6 = 16$.*
$-19 = t_1$

TECHNOLOGY
GRAPHICS CALCULATOR

Keystroke Guide, page 758

3. Find the 10th term.

$t_n = t_1 + (n - 1)d$
$t_{10} = -19 + (10 - 1)(7)$
$t_{10} = 44$

Thus, the 10th term of this arithmetic sequence is 44.

CHECK

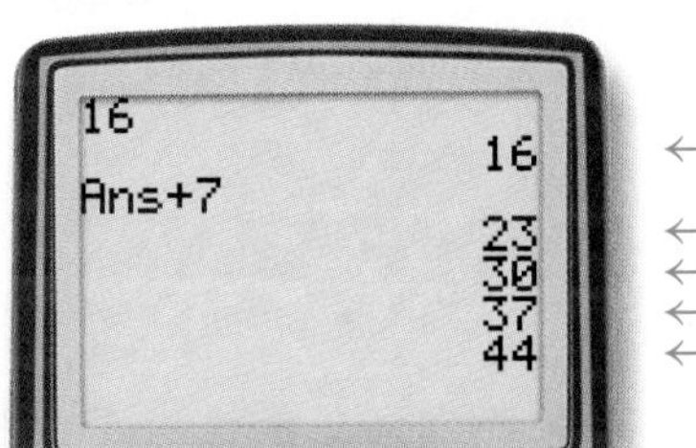

TRY THIS Find the 12th term of the arithmetic sequence in which $t_3 = 8$ and $t_7 = 20$.

CRITICAL THINKING In an arithmetic sequence, you are given consecutive terms t_i and t_j. Explain how to find d, and write an explicit formula for t_n, where n is any positive integer. Assume that $i < j$.

Investigating Sequences

TECHNOLOGY GRAPHICS CALCULATOR
Keystroke Guide, page 758

You will need: a graphics calculator or graph paper

1. Graph each sequence for n-values from 1 to 6.

   a. $t_n = 5 + 2n$ **b.** $t_n = 8 - 0.5n$ **c.** $t_n = 2^n$

   d. $t_n = \frac{1}{n}$ **e.** $t_n = 3(0.1)^n$ **f.** $t_n = n^2$

2. Which of the sequences in Step 1 are arithmetic?

CHECKPOINT ✓

3. Classify the graph of each sequence in Step 1 as linear, quadratic, exponential, or reciprocal (restricted to the domain of natural numbers).

The terms between any two nonconsecutive terms of an arithmetic sequence are called the **arithmetic means** between the two nonconsecutive terms. For example, in the sequence 5, 11, 17, 23, 29, 35, . . . , the three arithmetic means between 5 and 29 are 11, 17, and 23. In the past, you have learned that an arithmetic mean is the average of two numbers. That definition still holds because each number in the sequence is the average of the numbers on each side.

EXAMPLE 4 **Find the four arithmetic means between 10 and −30.**

SOLUTION

PROBLEM SOLVING

Draw a diagram. Let $t_1 = 10$ and $t_6 = -30$.

$$\overset{t_1}{10}, \underline{?}, \underline{?}, \underline{?}, \underline{?}, \overset{t_6}{-30}$$

Find the common difference, d.

$$t_n = t_1 + (n-1)d$$
$$-30 = 10 + (6-1)d \quad \textit{Because } t_6 = -30,\ n = 6 \textit{ and } t_n = -30.$$
$$-40 = 5d$$
$$\frac{-40}{5} = d$$
$$-8 = d$$

Use $d = -8$ to find the arithmetic means.

$$10 - 8 = 2$$
$$2 - 8 = -6$$
$$-6 - 8 = -14$$
$$-14 - 8 = -22$$

The four arithmetic means are 2, −6, −14, and −22.

TRY THIS Find the four arithmetic means between 24 and 39.

Exercises

Communicate

1. Explain how to write an explicit formula for the general term of the sequence $-4, 2, 8, 14, \ldots$

2. Explain why $(n-1)d$ instead of nd is used to find the nth term of an arithmetic sequence.

3. Describe how the arithmetic mean of 4 and 20 and the three arithmetic means between 4 and 20 are related.

Guided Skills Practice

4. Find the fourth term of the sequence defined by $t_1 = -4$ and $t_n = t_{n-1} + 2$. ***(EXAMPLE 1)***

APPLICATION

5. DEPRECIATION Sheryl purchased a sewing machine for her tailoring service. If the machine cost \$1425.65 and depreciates at the rate of \$85 per year, what will its value be after 10 years? ***(EXAMPLE 2)***

6. Find the eighth term of the arithmetic sequence in which $t_4 = 2$ and $t_7 = 6$. ***(EXAMPLE 3)***

7. Find the four arithmetic means between 6 and 26. ***(EXAMPLE 4)***

Practice and Apply

Based on the terms given, state whether or not each sequence is arithmetic. If it is, identify the common difference, *d*.

8. $6, 10, 14, 18, 22, \ldots$

9. $2, 4, 6, 8, 10, \ldots$

10. $8, 5, 2, -1, -4, \ldots$

11. $-3, 0, 3, 6, 9, \ldots$

12. $5, -5, 5, -5, 5, \ldots$

13. $1, 2, 4, 8, \ldots$

14. $9, 7, 5, 3, 1, \ldots$

15. $0, -6, -12, -18, -24, \ldots$

16. $3, 6, 12, 24, \ldots$

17. $3, 7, 12, 18, 25, \ldots$

18. $-1, 1, -1, 1, \ldots$

19. $1, -3, 5, -7, \ldots$

20. $0, \frac{1}{2}, 1, \frac{3}{2}, 2, \ldots$

21. $\frac{1}{3}, \frac{2}{3}, 1, \frac{4}{3}, \frac{5}{3}, \ldots$

22. $\frac{2}{7}, \frac{4}{7}, 1\ \frac{11}{7}, \frac{16}{7}, \ldots$

23. $\frac{2}{5}, \frac{5}{6}, \frac{6}{7}, \frac{7}{8}, \frac{8}{9}, \ldots$

24. $-2.8, 3.9, 5.0, 6.1, 12.2, \ldots$

25. $4.23, 5.67, 6.01, \ldots$

26. $\frac{\sqrt{2}}{\sqrt{3}}, \frac{2}{3}, \frac{4}{9}, \frac{16}{81}, \ldots$

27. $0.1, 0.01, 0.001, 0.0001, \ldots$

28. $\pi, 2\pi, 3\pi, 4\pi, 5\pi, \ldots$

29. $\pi, \pi^2, \pi^3, \pi^4, \pi^5, \ldots$

Use the recursive formula given to find the first four terms of each arithmetic sequence.

30. $t_1 = 5$
$t_n = t_{n-1} + 2$

31. $t_1 = 18$
$t_n = t_{n-1} - 3$

32. $t_1 = 0$
$t_n = t_{n-1} + 0.1$

33. $t_1 = 1$
$t_n = t_{n-1} + 2$

34. $t_1 = -5$
$t_n = t_{n-1} + 4$

35. $t_1 = -4$
$t_n = t_{n-1} + 3$

36. $t_1 = 3$
$t_n = t_{n-1} + 3$

37. $t_1 = 7$
$t_n = t_{n-1} + 1$

38. $t_1 = 6$
$t_n = t_{n-1} + 4$

List the first four terms of each arithmetic sequence.

39. $t_n = 4 + (n - 1)(3)$

40. $t_n = -2 + (n - 1)(4)$

41. $t_n = 3n - 4$

42. $t_n = -2n + 5$

43. $t_n = -5n + 2$

44. $t_n = 4n - 2$

45. $t_n = -3 + (n - 1)(5)$

46. $t_n = 4 + (n - 1)(-2)$

47. $t_n = \frac{1}{3} + \frac{1}{3}n$

48. $t_n = \frac{1}{5}n + \frac{4}{5}$

49. $t_n = \pi n + 4$

50. $t_n = \pi n + 5$

Find the indicated term given two other terms.

51. 5th term; $t_3 = 10$ and $t_7 = 26$

52. 5th term; $t_2 = -5$ and $t_6 = 7$

53. 10th term; $t_1 = 2.1$ and $t_4 = 1.83$

54. 10th term; $t_1 = 2.1$ and $t_6 = -2.85$

55. 1st term; $t_6 = -\frac{5}{6}$ and $t_8 = -\frac{3}{2}$

56. 1st term; $t_2 = -\frac{13}{12}$ and $t_6 = -\frac{7}{4}$

Write an explicit formula for the *n*th term of each arithmetic sequence.

57. 6, 8, 10, 12, 14, . . .

58. 11, 15, 19, 23, 27, . . .

59. 1, –6, –13, –20, –27, . . .

60. 14, 9, 4, –1, –6, . . .

61. 23, 31, 39, 47, 55, . . .

62. 17, 22, 27, 32, 37, . . .

63. 20, 15, 10, 5, 0, . . .

64. 33, 24, 15, 6, –3, . . .

65. 100, 105, 110, 115, 120, . . .

66. 500, 520, 540, 560, 580, . . .

67. –50, –45, –40, –35, –30, . . .

68. –80, –76, –72, –68, –64, . . .

Find the indicated arithmetic means.

69. Find the three arithmetic means between 5 and 17.

70. Find the four arithmetic means between 40 and 10.

71. Find the three arithmetic means between 18 and –10.

72. Find the five arithmetic means between –40 and –10.

73. Find the two arithmetic means between 5.26 and 6.34.

74. Find the three arithmetic means between 8.24 and 2.8.

75. Find the five arithmetic means between 12 and –6.

76. Find the six arithmetic means between –23 and 5.

77. Examine the pattern of dots below. How many dots will there be in the 14th figure?

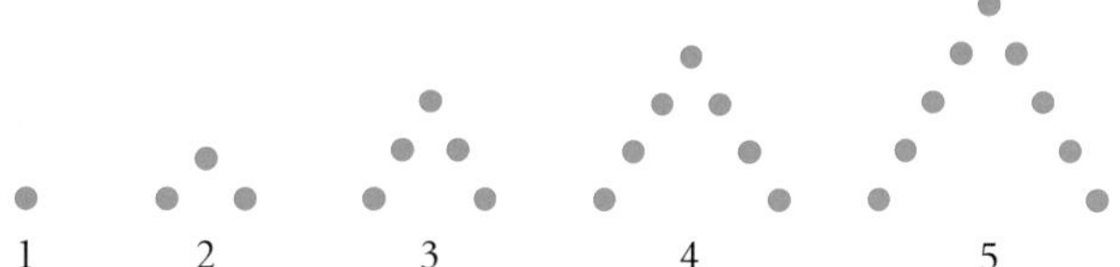

CHALLENGE

78. In a parking lot, each row has 3 more parking spaces than the previous row. If the 1st row has 20 spaces, how many spaces will the 15th row have?

CONNECTION

79. **GEOMETRY** The lengths of the sides of a certain right triangle form an arithmetic sequence. Show that the triangle is similar to a right triangle with side lengths of 3, 4 and 5.

APPLICATIONS

80. **DEPRECIATION** A machine that puts labels on bottles is bought by a small company for $10,000. The machine depreciates at a rate of $1429 per year beginning the instant that the machine is bought.

a. Write a formula for an arithmetic sequence that gives the value of the machine after n years.

b. Find the value of the machine after 1, 2, 5, and 6 years.

81. **INCOME** The starting salary for a teacher in one school district is $30,000. The salary increases by $800 each year.

a. Write a formula for an arithmetic sequence that gives the salary in the nth year.

b. Find the salary for the 10th year.

82. **HEALTH** Amanda is beginning a fitness program. During the first week, she will do 25 abdominal exercises each day. Each week she will increase the number of daily exercises by 3.

a. Write a formula for an arithmetic sequence that gives the number of daily exercises done in the nth week.

b. How many daily exercises will Amanda do after 20 weeks?

Look Back

Complete the square for each quadratic expression to form a perfect square trinomial. Then write the new expression as a binomial squared. ***(LESSON 5.4)***

83. $x^2 + 6x$ **84.** $x^2 + 20x$ **85.** $x^2 + 14x$

Solve each inequality. Check your solution. ***(LESSON 8.5)***

86. $\frac{-4}{2x+5} > 0$

87. $\frac{x-1}{x-4} \geq 2$

88 $x^3 - 2x^2 - 5x + 6 < 0$

89 $\frac{x^2-3}{x^2+3} < -\frac{1}{2}$

Write the standard equation for each circle. Then state the coordinates for its center and give its radius. ***(LESSON 9.3)***

90. $x^2 - 2x + y^2 = 0$

91. $x^2 + 4x + y^2 - 10y + 13 = 0$

Write the standard equation for each ellipse. ***(LESSON 9.4)***

92. foci: $(0, 6), (0, -6)$
vertices: $(0, 8), (0, -8)$

93. foci: $(4, 2), (-4, 2)$
co-vertices: $(0, 5), (0, 1)$

Representing a male child with *M* and a female child with *F*, a sample space for families with 2 children can be written as {*MM, MF, FM, FF*}. Assume that each family below has 2 children. List each event below with the same notation as above. Then find the theoretical probability of each event. ***(LESSON 10.1)***

94. A family has exactly two girls.

95. A family has at least one girl.

96. A family has at most one girl.

97. A family has exactly one girl.

Look Beyond

98. Find the sum of the first eight terms of the given arithmetic sequence.

$$\begin{cases} t_1 = 5 \\ t_n = t_{n-1} + 2 \end{cases}$$

Place a wooden 12-inch ruler on a desk so that one end of the ruler is aligned with the edge of the desk. Slowly slide the ruler over the edge of the desk as far as possible without the ruler falling off. The location on the ruler that is at the edge of the desk at this time is the ruler's center of gravity. Record the ruler's center of gravity.

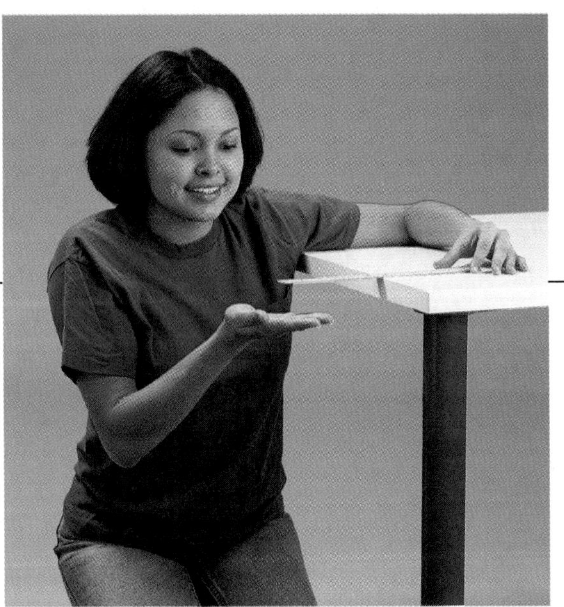

All of the weight of an object can be considered to be concentrated at a single point called the center of gravity. Balancing an object is one way to locate an object's center of gravity.

WORKING ON THE CHAPTER PROJECT

You should now be able to complete Activity 1 of the Chapter Project.

Arithmetic Series

Why *Arithmetic series can be used to solve real-world problems such as finding the total number of cans needed to set up a certain triangular display.*

Objective

- Find the sum of the first n terms of an arithmetic series.

A pattern for stacking cans is shown above. To find the number of cans in a triangular display of 15 rows stacked in this pattern, you can use the sum of an *arithmetic series.* *You will solve this problem in Example 1.*

Activity
Exploring Arithmetic Series

You will need: graph paper

The sum 1 + 2 + 3 can be represented on graph paper as shown in Figure 1. Twice the sum can be represented as shown in Figure 2.

1. Explain how Figure 1 suggests the following:

$$1 + 2 + 3 = \frac{3(4)}{2} = \frac{3(1+3)}{2}$$

2. Draw a similar figure to represent twice the sum 1 + 2 + 3 + 4 + 5 + 6, and write a similar equation for it.
3. Repeat Step 2 for twice the sum $1 + 2 + 3 + 4 + 5 + \cdots + 10$.

Figure 1

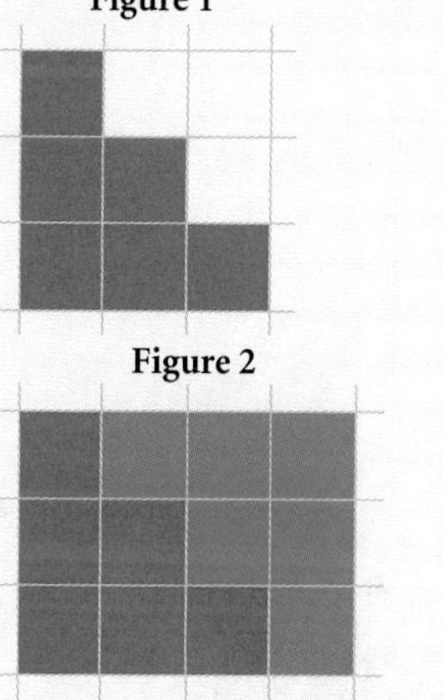

Figure 2

An **arithmetic series** is the indicated sum of the terms of an arithmetic sequence. Consider the sequence 1, 2, 3, . . . The sum of the first six terms of this sequence is denoted by S_6.

$$S_6 = 1 + 2 + 3 + 4 + 5 + 6 = 21$$

You can derive a formula for the sum of the first n terms of an arithmetic series by using the Addition Property of Equality, as shown below.

$$S_n = t_1 + (t_1 + d) + (t_1 + 2d) + \cdots + (t_n - d) + t_n$$

Because $t_n - t_{n-1} = d$, $t_{n-1} = t_{n-d}$.

$$\underline{S_n = t_n + (t_n - d) + (t_n - 2d) + \cdots + (t_1 + d) + t_1}$$

$$2S_n = \underbrace{(t_1 + t_n) + (t_1 + t_n) + (t_1 + t_n) + \cdots + (t_1 + t_n) + (t_1 + t_n)}_{(t_1 + t_n) \text{ is added } n \text{ times}}$$

$$2S_n = n(t_1 + t_n)$$

$$S_n = \frac{n(t_1 + t_n)}{2}$$

Sum of the First n Terms of an Arithmetic Series

The sum, S_n, of the first n terms of an arithmetic series with first term t_1 and nth term t_n is given by $S_n = n\left(\frac{t_1 + t_n}{2}\right)$.

CHECKPOINT ✔ Using the sequence 1, 2, 3, . . . , find S_6 by following the procedure used in the derivation of S_n.

EXAMPLE 1 Refer to the pattern for stacking cans described at the beginning of the lesson.

How many cans are in a 15-row display of cans stacked in this pattern?

CONNECTION
PATTERNS IN DATA

SOLUTION

1. Begin with the formula for the sum of the first n terms of an arithmetic series.

$$S_n = n\left(\frac{t_1 + t_n}{2}\right)$$

$$S_{15} = 15\left(\frac{1 + t_{15}}{2}\right) \qquad \textit{Substitute 1 for } t_1 \textit{ and 15 for } n.$$

2. Find t_{15}, using the recursive formula.

$$t_n = t_1 + (n - 1)d$$

$$t_{15} = 1 + (15 - 1)3 \qquad \textit{Notice from the pattern that } d = 3.$$

$$t_{15} = 43$$

3. Substitute 43 for t_{15} in the formula.

$$S_{15} = 15\left(\frac{1 + t_{15}}{2}\right)$$

$$S_{15} = 15\left(\frac{1 + 43}{2}\right)$$

$$S_{15} = 330$$

TECHNOLOGY
GRAPHICS CALCULATOR
Keystroke Guide, page 759

CHECK

Use the summation and the sequence commands of a graphics calculator. On this calculator, the summation command tells the calculator to add the items in parentheses, and the sequence command inside the parentheses describes the related sequence.

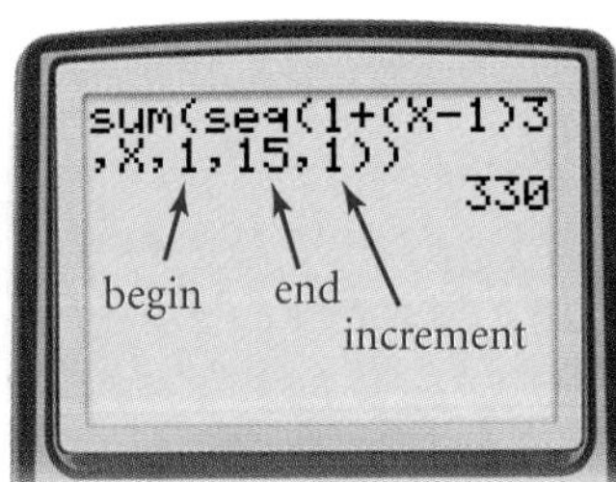

Thus, the 15-row display contains 330 cans.

The formula $S_n = n\left(\frac{t_1 + t_n}{2}\right)$ gives S_n in terms of n, t_1, and t_n. Notice that the sum is the number of terms, n, times the average term, $\frac{t_1 + t_n}{2}$. By substituting $t_1 + (n - 1)d$ for t_n in the formula for S_n, you can write a formula that can be used when the last term of the series is not known.

$$S_n = n\left(\frac{t_1 + t_n}{2}\right)$$

$$S_n = n\left[\frac{t_1 + t_1 + (n - 1)d}{2}\right]$$

$$S_n = n\left[\frac{2t_1 + (n - 1)d}{2}\right]$$

EXAMPLE 2 Given $3 + 12 + 21 + 30 + \cdots$, find S_{25}.

SOLUTION

Substitute 3 for t_1, 9 for d, and 25 for n.

Method 1 Use $S_n = n\left(\frac{t_1 + t_n}{2}\right)$.

First find t_{25}.

$$t_n = t_1 + (n - 1)d$$
$$t_{25} = 3 + (25 - 1)9$$
$$t_{25} = 219$$

Then find S_{25}.

$$S_{25} = 25\left(\frac{3 + 219}{2}\right) = 2775$$

Method 2 Use $S_n = n\left[\frac{2t_1 + (n - 1)d}{2}\right]$.

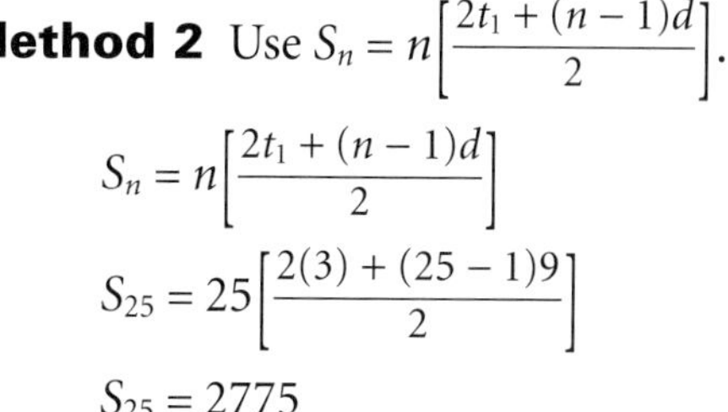

$$S_n = n\left[\frac{2t_1 + (n - 1)d}{2}\right]$$
$$S_{25} = 25\left[\frac{2(3) + (25 - 1)9}{2}\right]$$
$$S_{25} = 2775$$

TECHNOLOGY GRAPHICS CALCULATOR

Keystroke Guide, page 759

CHECK

Use the summation and the sequence commands on a graphics calculator.

Thus, $S_{25} = 2775$.

TRY THIS Given $(-16) + (-12) + (-8) + (-4) + \cdots$, find S_{20}.

EXAMPLE 3 Evaluate $\sum_{k=1}^{12}(6 - 2k)$.

SOLUTION

Method 1

This summation notation describes the summation of the first 12 terms of the arithmetic series that begins $4 + 2 + 0 + (-2) + \cdots$, in which $t_1 = 4$ and $d = -2$.

First find t_{12}.

$$t_{12} = 4 + (12 - 1)(-2) = -18$$

Then find S_{12}.

$$S_{12} = 12\left[\frac{4 + (-18)}{2}\right] = -84$$

Method 2

You can use the properties of series and the formulas for constant and linear series to find the sum.

$$\sum_{k=1}^{12}(6 - 2k) = \sum_{k=1}^{12}6 + \sum_{k=1}^{12}-2k$$
$$= 12 \cdot 6 - 2\sum_{k=1}^{12}k$$
$$= 72 - 2\left[\frac{12(1 + 12)}{2}\right]$$
$$= 72 - 156$$
$$= -84$$

TECHNOLOGY GRAPHICS CALCULATOR

Keystroke Guide, page 759

CHECK

Use the sum and sequence commands on a graphics calculator. The sequence is given by $t_n = 6 - 2n$.

Thus, $\sum_{k=1}^{12}(6 - 2k) = -84$.

TRY THIS Evaluate $\sum_{k=1}^{15}(22 - 7k)$.

CRITICAL THINKING If an arithmetic sequence has a nonzero constant difference, can any sum of terms in the corresponding arithmetic series be 0? Justify your response with examples.

Exercises

Communicate

1. What information about an arithmetic series is needed to find its sum?
2. Explain how to use summation notation to express the following series:
$$2 + 4 + 6 + 8 + 10 + 12$$
3. In how many different ways can you represent the series 2 + 4 + 6 + 8? Explain.

Guided Skills Practice

APPLICATION

4. **MERCHANDISING** Refer to the pattern for stacking cans described at the beginning of the lesson. How many cans are in an 18-row triangular display of cans stacked in this pattern? ***(EXAMPLE 1)***
5. Given 5 + 12 + 19 + 26 + · · · , find S_{26}. ***(EXAMPLE 2)***
6. Evaluate $\sum_{k=1}^{10}(20 - 3k)$. ***(EXAMPLE 3)***

Practice and Apply

Use the formula for an arithmetic series to find each sum.

7. $2 + 4 + 6 + 8 + 10$
8. $5 + 10 + 15 + 20$
9. $5 + 13 + 21 + 29$
10. $13 + 17 + 21 + 25$
11. $-100 + (-96) + (-92) + (-88)$
12. $-50 + (-47) + (-44) + (-41)$
13. $1 + 2 + 3 + 4 + \cdots + 11$
14. $15 + 21 + 27 + 33 + \cdots + 63$
15. $-4 + (-13) + (-22) + \cdots + (-76)$
16. $10 + 8 + 6 + 4 + 2 + \cdots + (-4)$
17. Find the sum of the first 300 natural numbers.
18. Find the sum of all even numbers from 2 to 200 inclusive.
19. Find the sum of the multiples of 3 from 3 to 99 inclusive.
20. Find the sum of the multiples of 9 from 9 to 657 inclusive.

For each arithmetic series, find S_{25}.

21. $3 + 7 + 11 + 15 + \cdots$

22. $25 + 24 + 23 + 22 + \cdots$

23. $4 + 14 + 24 + 34 + \cdots$

24. $6 + 2 + (-2) + (-6) + \cdots$

25. $5 + 10 + 15 + 20 + \cdots$

26. $3 + 6 + 9 + 12 + \cdots$

27. $-12 + (-6) + 0 + 6 + \cdots$

28. $-17 + (-12) + (-7) + (-2) + 3 + \cdots$

29. $10 + 20 + 30 + 40 + 50 + \cdots$

30. $100 + 200 + 300 + 400 + 500 + \cdots$

31. $-10 + (-15) + (-20) + (-25) + (-30) + \cdots$

32. $-20 + (-22) + (-24) + (-26) + (-28) + \cdots$

33. $\sqrt{2} + 2\sqrt{2} + 3\sqrt{2} + 4\sqrt{2} + 5\sqrt{2} + \cdots$

34. $5\sqrt{3} + 10\sqrt{3} + 15\sqrt{3} + 20\sqrt{3} + \cdots$

35. $2\pi + 3\pi + 4\pi + 5\pi + 6\pi + \cdots$

Evaluate.

36. $\sum_{m=1}^{5} (15 - 2m)$

37. $\sum_{j=1}^{8} (30 - 2j)$

38. $\sum_{k=1}^{6} (10 + k)$

39. $\sum_{m=1}^{4} (5 + m)$

40. $\sum_{n=1}^{5} (100 - 5n)$

41. $\sum_{n=1}^{5} (60 - 4n)$

42. $\sum_{j=1}^{6} (1000 + 25j)$

43. $\sum_{j=1}^{5} (500 + 2j)$

44. $\sum_{k=1}^{10} (40 - 2k)$

45. $\sum_{m=1}^{10} (600 - 10m)$

46. $\sum_{n=1}^{50} (500 + 20n)$

47. $\sum_{k=1}^{10} \left(\frac{2}{5} + \frac{1}{5}k\right)$

48. $\sum_{j=1}^{12} \left(\frac{1}{3} + \frac{1}{6}j\right)$

49. $\sum_{k=1}^{20} (2.2 + 3.1k)$

50. $\sum_{k=1}^{10} (1.2 - 4.1k)$

CHALLENGES

51. For a certain arithmetic series, $S_4 = 50$ and $S_5 = 75$. Find the first five terms.

52. Find the number of and values of the arithmetic means that should be inserted between 1 and 50 in order to make the sum of the resulting series equal to 459.

APPLICATION

53. INVENTORY Pipes are stacked as shown at right.

a. Find the number of pipes in a stack of 6 rows if the bottom row contains 9 pipes.

b. Find the number of pipes in a stack of 7 rows if the bottom row contains 10 pipes.

APPLICATIONS

54. **MERCHANDISING** A pattern for stacking cans is shown at right.
  a. How many cans are in a 7-row display?
  b. If 66 cans are to be stacked in this pattern, how many rows will the display have?

55. **ENTERTAINMENT** A marching band formation consists of 8 rows. The first row has 5 musicians, the second has 7, the third has 9, and so on. How many musicians are in the last row? How many musicians are there in all?

Look Back

Write each pair of parametric equations as a single equation in *x* and *y*. *(LESSON 3.6)*

56. $\begin{cases} x(t) = -3t \\ y(t) = t - 6 \end{cases}$ **57.** $\begin{cases} x(t) = t + 2 \\ y(t) = |t - 2| \end{cases}$ **58.** $\begin{cases} x(t) = 2t - 1 \\ y(t) = 3t + 1 \end{cases}$

Write each product as a polynomial expression in standard form. *(LESSON 7.3)*

59. $2x(3x^2 - 5x^3 + 2x - 6)$ **60.** $(x - 3)^2(x^2 - 2x + 5)$

Write an equation to represent each relationship. Use *k* as the constant of variation. *(LESSON 8.1)*

61. y varies jointly as x and z and inversely as the square of m.
62. y varies directly as x^2 and inversely as z^3.

Find the domain for each radical function. *(LESSON 8.6)*

63. $f(x) = 2\sqrt{x^2 + 36}$ **64.** $f(x) = \sqrt{2(x - 3)} + 1$

65. In how many ways can you choose 6 objects from a collection of 30 distinct objects, if order does not matter? ***(LESSON 10.3)***

66. Two number cubes are rolled. The sum of the numbers appearing on the top faces is recorded. What is the probability that the number rolled on one cube is 4 given that the sum of the numbers is 6? ***(LESSON 10.6)***

Look Beyond

67. The first term of a certain sequence is 2. Each successive term is formed by doubling the previous term. Write the first eight terms of the sequence.

Graph each sequence, and describe the graph.

68.

x	1	2	3	4	5
t_n	3	6	12	24	48

69.

x	1	2	3	4	5
t_n	-4	-2	-1	$-\frac{1}{2}$	$-\frac{1}{4}$

11.4

Geometric Sequences

Why *Geometric sequences can be used to model real-world events such as the depreciation of an automobile.*

Objectives

- Recognize geometric sequences, and find the indicated term of a geometric sequence.
- Find the geometric means between two numbers.

APPLICATION
DEPRECIATION

An automobile that cost $12,500 depreciates, and its value at the end of a given year is 80% of its value at the end of the preceding year. What is it worth after 10 years? You can answer this question by using a *geometric sequence*. *You will answer this question in Example 2.*

Two examples of geometric sequences and their graphs are shown below.

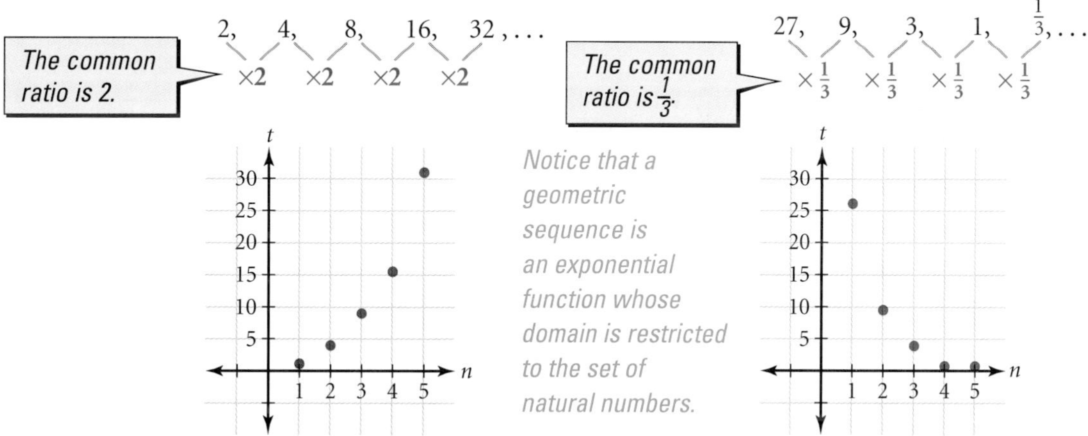

2, 4, 8, 16, 32, . . .
×2 ×2 ×2 ×2
The common ratio is 2.
27, 9, 3, 1, 1/3, . . .
×1/3 ×1/3 ×1/3 ×1/3
The common ratio is 1/3.
t
n
30
25
20
15
10
5
1 2 3 4 5
Notice that a geometric sequence is an exponential function whose domain is restricted to the set of natural numbers.

A **geometric sequence** is a sequence in which the ratio of successive terms is the same number, r, called the **common ratio**. That is, if t_n is any term in a geometric sequence, then the following is true:

$$\frac{t_n}{t_{n-1}} = r, \text{ or } t_n = rt_{n-1}, \text{ where } n \geq 2$$

The formula for the general term, $t_n = rt_{n-1}$, where $n \geq 2$, is a recursive formula because it gives the nth term of a sequence in relation to the previous term and r. You can also write an explicit formula for the nth term of a sequence by using the first term and r.

PROBLEM SOLVING **Look for a pattern** in the recursive formula for the geometric sequence defined by $t_1 = 3$ and $t_n = 4t_{n-1}$, where $n \geq 2$.

Recursive formula	Pattern
$t_1 = 3$	$t_1 = 4^0 \cdot 3$
$t_2 = 4 \cdot 3$	$t_2 = 4^1 \cdot 3$
$t_3 = 4(4 \cdot 3)$	$t_3 = 4^2 \cdot 3$
$t_4 = 4(4 \cdot 4 \cdot 3)$	$t_4 = 4^3 \cdot 3$

From the pattern, the explicit formula is $t_n = 4^{n-1} \cdot 3$, where $n \geq 1$.

*n*th Term of a Geometric Sequence

The *n*th term, t_n, of a geometric sequence whose first term is t_1 and whose common ratio is r is given by the explicit formula $t_n = t_1 r^{n-1}$, where $n \geq 1$.

EXAMPLE 1 **Find the fifth term of the sequence defined by the recursive formula $t_1 = 8$ and $t_n = 3t_{n-1}$.**

Keystroke Guide, page 759

SOLUTION

This is a geometric sequence in which $t_1 = 8$ and $r = 3$. Use the explicit formula for the *n*th term of a geometric sequence to find the fifth term.

$$t_n = t_1 r^{n-1}$$
$$t_5 = 8(3)^{5-1}$$
$$t_5 = 648$$

The fifth term of the sequence is 648.

CHECK

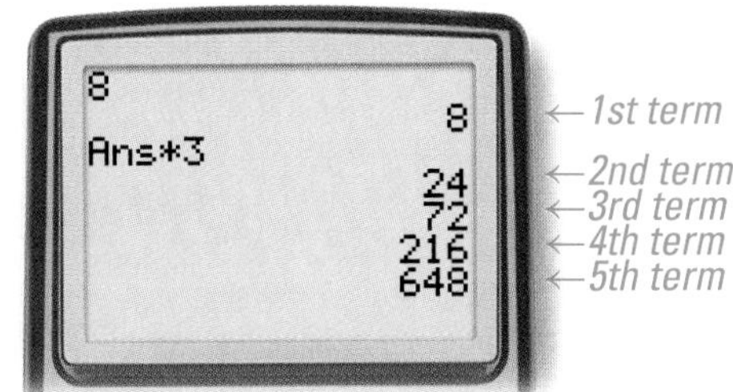

TRY THIS Find the eighth term of the sequence defined by $t_1 = 2.5$ and $t_n = -4t_{n-1}$.

EXAMPLE 2 **Refer to the automobile described at the beginning of the lesson.**

a. Use a recursive formula to find the value of the automobile after 4 years.

b. Use the explicit formula for the *n*th term of a geometric sequence to find the value of the automobile after 10 years.

APPLICATION
DEPRECIATION

TECHNOLOGY
GRAPHICS CALCULATOR
Keystroke Guide, page 759

SOLUTION

a. Initial value (year 0): 12,500

year 1: 12,500(0.80) = 10,000
year 2: 10,000(0.80) = 8000
year 3: 8000(0.80) = 6400
year 4: 6400(0.80) = 5120

The automobile's value after 4 years is $5120.

CHECK

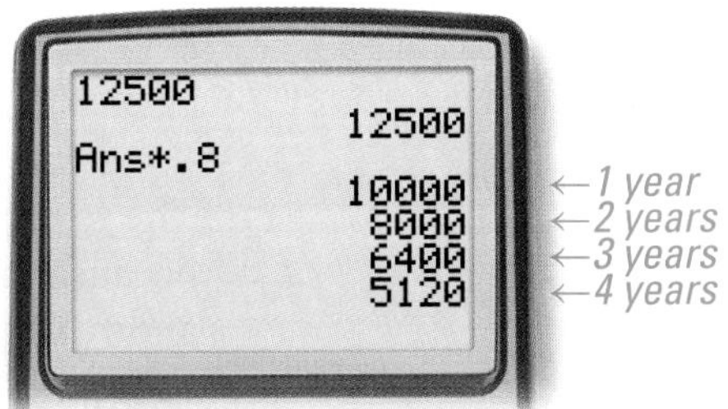

b. At year 10, $n = 11$. Find t_{11}.

$$t_n = t_1 r^{n-1}$$
$$t_{11} = 12{,}500(0.8^{11-1})$$
$$t_{11} \approx 1342.18$$

The automobile's value after 10 years is $1342.18.

TRY THIS An automobile that costs $12,500 depreciates such that its value at the end of a given year is 76% of its value at the end of the preceding year. Use the explicit formula for the *n*th term of a geometric sequence to find the automobile's value after 10 years.

If you know any two terms of a geometric sequence, you can often write all of the terms. However, Example 3 shows that it is possible for two geometric sequences to share terms.

EXAMPLE 3 **Find the eighth term of the geometric sequence in which $t_3 = 36$ and $t_5 = 324$.**

SOLUTION

1. Find the common ratio, r.

n	3	4	5
t_n	36	?	324

(each step multiplies by r, r)

$$\rightarrow 36r^2 = 324$$
$$r = \pm\sqrt{\frac{324}{36}}$$
$$r = \pm 3$$

2. Find t_1 for both r-values. Because $t_5 = 324$, $n = 5$ and $t_n = 324$.

For $r = 3$:

$$t_n = t_1 r^{n-1}$$
$$324 = t_1(3)^{5-1}$$
$$\frac{324}{3^4} = t_1$$
$$4 = t_1$$

For $r = -3$:

$$t_n = t_1 r^{n-1}$$
$$324 = t_1(-3)^{5-1}$$
$$\frac{324}{(-3)^4} = t_1$$
$$4 = t_1$$

3. Find the eighth term.

For $r = 3$:

$$t_n = t_1 r^{n-1}$$
$$t_8 = 4(3)^{8-1}$$
$$t_8 = 8748$$

For $r = -3$:

$$t_n = t_1 r^{n-1}$$
$$t_8 = 4(-3)^{8-1}$$
$$t_8 = -8748$$

CHECK

324
324 ←5th term
Ans*3
972 ←6th term
2916 ←7th term
8748 ←8th term

CHECK

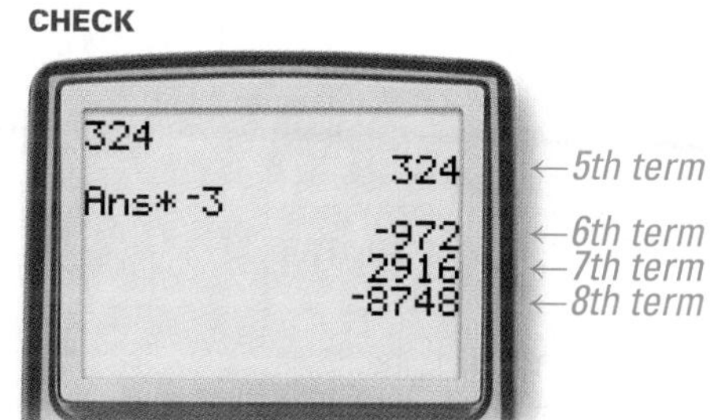

Thus, the eighth term of this geometric sequence is 8748 or −8748.

TRY THIS Find the 12th term of the geometric sequence in which $t_2 = 240$ and $t_5 = 30$.

The terms between any two nonconsecutive terms of a geometric sequence are called the **geometric means** between the two nonconsecutive terms. For example, in the sequence 5, **−10**, **20**, **−40**, 80, −160, . . . , the three geometric means between 5 and 80 are **−10**, **20**, and **−40**.

EXAMPLE 4 **Find three geometric means between 6 and 96.**

SOLUTION

PROBLEM SOLVING

Draw a diagram. Let $t_1 = 6$ and $t_5 = 96$.

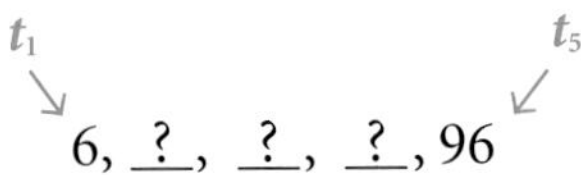

Find the common ratio, r.

$$t_n = t_1 r^{n-1}$$
$$96 = 6r^{5-1} \quad \text{Because } t_5 = 96,\ n = 5 \text{ and } t_n = 96.$$
$$16 = r^4$$
$$\pm 2 = r$$

Use $r = 2$ and $r = -2$ to find the two possible sets of geometric means.

$r = 2$:

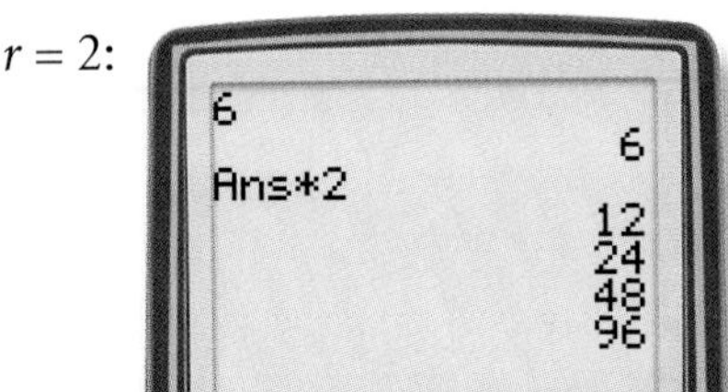

$r = -2$:

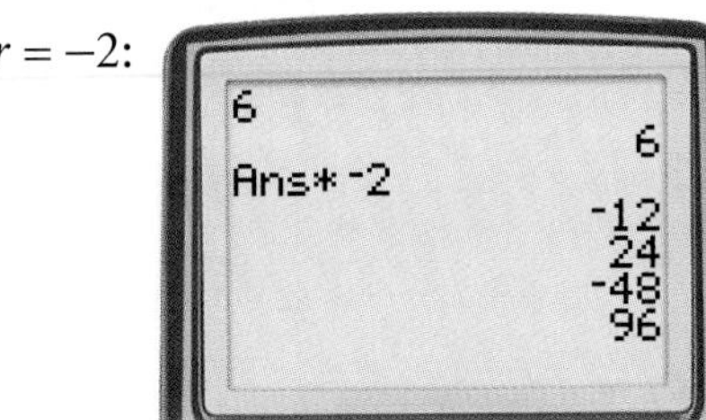

The three geometric means are 12, 24, and 48 or −12, 24, and −48.

TRY THIS Find three geometric means between 64 and 4.

CHECKPOINT ✔ How many sets of two geometric means are possible between $t_3 = -40$ and $t_6 = 5$? Explain.

CRITICAL THINKING In Example 4, there are two possible common ratios. If a geometric sequence were defined to include complex numbers, what two other common ratios would be possible?

Activity
Exploring Geometric Sequences

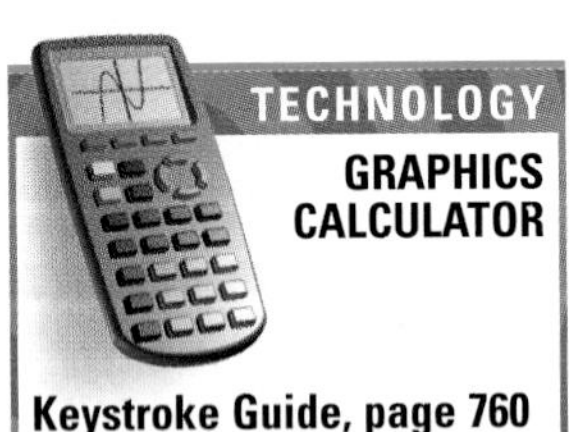
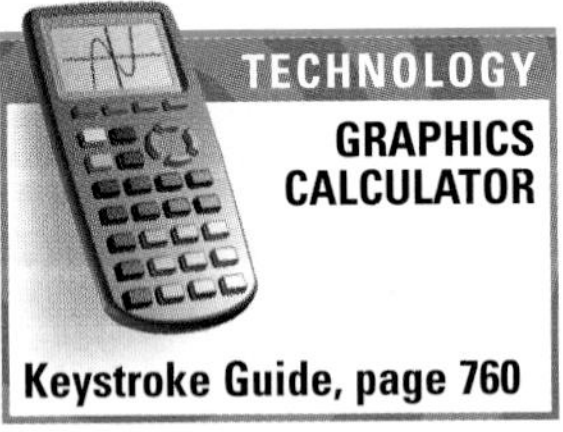

You will need: a graphics calculator

1. Write the first 5 terms of each geometric sequence below.
   a. $t_1 = 1, r = 10$ **b.** $t_1 = 1, r = 2$ **c.** $t_1 = 0.1, r = 1.1$
   d. $t_1 = 1, r = 1.01$ **e.** $t_1 = 1, r = 0.1$ **f.** $t_1 = 1, r = 0.9$
2. Which sequence from Step 1 has the largest 5th term? the smallest 5th term?

CHECKPOINT ✔

3. Describe how the value of r affects the terms of the sequence when $0 < r < 1$. Describe how the value of r affects the terms of the series when $r > 1$.

Exercises

Communicate

1. Describe how to find the nth term of 1, 3, 9, 27, . . .
2. Explain what happens to the terms of a geometric sequence when the common ratio, r, is doubled. Justify your answer.
3. Explain what happens to the terms of a geometric sequence when the first term, t_1, is doubled.

Guided Skills Practice

4. Find the fifth term of the sequence defined by $t_1 = 2$ and $t_n = 2t_{n-1}$. ***(EXAMPLE 1)***

APPLICATION

5. **DEPRECIATION** A new automobile costs $14,000 and retains 85% of its value each year. Find the value of the automobile after 10 years. ***(EXAMPLE 2)***
6. Find the fifth term of the geometric sequence in which $t_4 = 768$ and $t_6 = 192$. ***(EXAMPLE 3)***
7. Find three geometric means between 160 and 10. ***(EXAMPLE 4)***

Practice and Apply

Determine whether each sequence is a geometric sequence. If so, identify the common ratio, *r*, and give the next three terms.

8. 3, 6, 12, 24, . . .
9. 20, 40, 80, 160, . . .
10. 2, 4, 6, 8, . . .
11. 1, 3, 5, 7, . . .
12. $10, 2, \frac{2}{5}, \frac{2}{25}, \ldots$
13. 2, 10, 50, 250, . . .
14. 2, 4, 8, 16, . . .
15. 2, 6, 18, 54, . . .
16. 1, −4, 16, −64, . . .
17. 2, −5, 25, . . .
18. 6, 42, 294, . . .
19. 2, 18, 162, . . .
20. $5, \frac{5}{2}, \frac{5}{4}, \frac{5}{8}, \ldots$
21. $9, 3, 1, \frac{1}{3}, \ldots$
22. 9, 0.9, 0.09, 0.009, . . .
23. $12, 3, \frac{3}{4}, \frac{3}{16}, \ldots$
24. 2, 3, 4.5, 6.75, . . .
25. 16, 20, 25, 31.25, . . .

List the first four terms of each geometric sequence.

26. $t_1 = 3$, $t_n = 2t_{n-1}$
27. $t_1 = -2$, $t_n = 4t_{n-1}$
28. $t_1 = 5$, $t_n = -2t_{n-1}$
29. $t_1 = 4$, $t_n = -3t_{n-1}$
30. $t_1 = 1$, $t_n = 4t_{n-1}$
31. $t_1 = -1$, $t_n = -0.2t_{n-1}$
32. $t_1 = -3$, $t_n = -2.2t_{n-1}$
33. $t_1 = 3$, $t_n = 3.37t_{n-1}$
34. $t_1 = 3$, $t_n = -4.88t_{n-1}$
35. In a geometric sequence, $t_1 = 6$ and $r = 4$. Find t_7.
36. In a geometric sequence, $t_1 = 5$ and $r = -2$. Find t_7.
37. In a geometric sequence, $t_1 = 3$ and $r = \frac{1}{10}$. Find t_{20}.
38. In a geometric sequence, $t_1 = 3$ and $r = -\frac{1}{10}$. Find t_{20}.

Find the sixth term in the geometric sequence that includes each pair of terms.

39. $t_3 = 150$; $t_5 = 3750$

40. $t_4 = 189$; $t_9 = 45{,}927$

41. $t_4 = 36$; $t_8 = 2916$

42. $t_3 = 444$; $t_7 = 7104$

43. $t_5 = 24$; $t_8 = 3$

44. $t_7 = 10{,}935$; $t_{11} = 135$

45. $t_3 = -24$; $t_5 = -54$

46. $t_7 = 4$; $t_{12} = 972$

47. $t_3 = 12\frac{1}{2}$; $t_9 = \frac{25}{128}$

48. $t_2 = 25$; $t_4 = 2\frac{7}{9}$

Write an explicit formula for the *n*th term of each geometric sequence.

49. $2, 4, 8, 16, \ldots$

50. $1, 3, 9, 27, \ldots$

51. $1, \frac{1}{2}, \frac{1}{4}, \frac{1}{8}, \ldots$

52. $1, \frac{1}{3}, \frac{1}{9}, \frac{1}{27}, \ldots$

53. $30, 10, 3\frac{1}{3}, 1\frac{1}{9}, \ldots$

54. $40, 10, 2\frac{1}{2}, \frac{5}{8}, \ldots$

55. $\sqrt{2}, 2, 2\sqrt{2}, 4, \ldots$

56. $\sqrt{3}, 3, 3\sqrt{3}, 9, \ldots$

Find the indicated geometric means.

57. Find two geometric means between 5 and 135.

58. Find two geometric means between 4 and 13.5.

59. Find two geometric means between 5 and 16.875.

60. Find three geometric means between 1 and 81.

61. Find three geometric means between -2 and $-\frac{1}{8}$.

62. Find three geometric means between -6 and $-\frac{3}{8}$.

63. Find three geometric means between 486 and 6.

64. Find three geometric means between -40.5 and -8.

65. Find two geometric means between $41\frac{2}{3}$ and 1125.

List the first four terms of each sequence. Tell whether it is arithmetic, geometric, or neither.

66. $t_n = 4(2)^n$

67. $t_n = 4(3)^n$

68. $t_n = 20\left(\frac{1}{2}\right)^n$

69. $t_n = 9\left(\frac{2}{5}\right)^n$

70. $t_n = 3 + 10^n$

71. $t_n = 2 + 5^n$

72. $t_n = -10(3)^n$

73. $t_n = -100(4)^n$

74. $t_n = 30(-5)^n$

APPLICATION

REAL ESTATE An office building purchased for $1,200,000 is appreciating because of rising property values in the city. At the end of each year its value is 105% of its value at the end of the previous year.

75. Use a recursive formula to determine what the value of the building will be 7 years after it is purchased.

76. Use an explicit formula to find the value of the building 4 years after it is purchased.

CHALLENGE

77. During the eighth year, the building begins to decrease in value at a rate of 8% per year. What would its value be after the 15th year?

APPLICATION

78. MUSIC A piano keyboard has 88 equally spaced musical notes. The first, and lowest, note is assigned the letter A, and it has a frequency of 27.5 hertz (Hz). The 13th note is also assigned the letter A, and it has a frequency twice that of the preceding A note, as does each of the subsequent A notes.

a. Write an explicit formula for the frequencies of all of the A notes.

b. Find the frequency of the seventh A note in the sequence defined in part **a.**

c. Find the frequencies of the 11 equally spaced notes between the first A note and the second A note. Round your answers to the nearest hundredth.

Look Back

Write an equation in slope-intercept form for the line containing the indicated points. ***(LESSON 1.3)***

79. $(-2, 5)$ and $(0, -1)$ **80.** $(9, -4)$ and $(-5, 3)$

Let $A = \begin{bmatrix} 1 & 0.5 \\ 2.4 & 3.8 \end{bmatrix}$, $B = \begin{bmatrix} 1.7 \\ 3.2 \end{bmatrix}$, **and** $C = [3.2 \quad 4.8]$. **Find each product, if it exists.** ***(LESSON 4.2)***

81. AB **82.** CA **83.** BC **84.** CB

APPLICATION

85. SPORTS Liam plans to spend a certain amount of time every day training for the school track team. He wants to run 3 miles and ride his bicycle for 6 miles. If he rides his bicycle an average of 12 miles per hour faster than he runs, at what rate must he run and bike in order to complete his training workout in one hour? ***(LESSON 8.5)***

Simplify. Write each expression with a rational denominator. ***(LESSON 8.7)***

86. $\sqrt{8} + \sqrt{98}$ **87.** $\dfrac{\sqrt{30} + \sqrt{14}}{\sqrt{2}}$ **88.** $\sqrt{6x} + \dfrac{\sqrt{2x}}{\sqrt{3}} - \sqrt{\dfrac{3x}{2}}$

Find the number of permutations of the letters in each word below. ***(LESSON 10.2)***

89. *roommate* **90.** *apple* **91.** *apogee*

Look Beyond

92. Consider the geometric sequence 0.3, 0.03, 0.003, 0.0003, . . .

a. Find the sum of the first 4 terms and the sum of the first 10 terms.

b. What value are the sums approaching?

Geometric Series and Mathematical Induction

Why *Geometric series can be used to solve real-world problems such as finding the right investment to save money for college.*

Objectives

- Find the sum of the first n terms of a geometric series.
- Use mathematical induction to prove statements about natural numbers.

Mr. and Mrs. Sanchez want to invest money for their child's college education. They have decided to invest \$2000 at the beginning of every year for the next 10 years. If the investment is in an account that earns 8% annual interest, compounded once per year, how much will their investment be worth at the end of the 10th year? *You will solve this in Example 2.*

Geometric Series

A **geometric series** is the indicated sum of the terms of a geometric sequence. Consider the sequence 2, 4, 8, 16, 32, . . . The sum of the first five terms, denoted by S_5, is $S_5 = 2 + 4 + 8 + 16 + 32 = 62$.

You can derive a formula for the sum of a geometric series by using the Subtraction Property of Equality, as shown below.

Each side is multiplied by the common ratio, r.

$$\begin{aligned} S_n &= t_1 + t_1r + t_1r^2 + \cdots + t_nr^{n-2} + t_nr^{n-1} \\ \underline{rS_n} &= \underline{t_1r + t_1r^2 + \cdots + t_nr^{n-2} + t_nr^{n-1} + t_nr^n} \\ S_n - rS_n &= t_1 + 0 + 0 + \cdots + 0 + 0 - t_nr^n \\ S_n(1-r) &= t_1 - t_1r^n \\ S_n &= \frac{t_1(1-r^n)}{1-r}, \text{ or } t_1\left(\frac{1-r^n}{1-r}\right) \end{aligned}$$

To divide both sides of the equation by 1 – r, r cannot equal 1.

Notice that S_n is undefined when $r = 1$.

CHECKPOINT ✔ Using the sequence 2, 4, 8, . . . , find S_5 by following the procedure used in the derivation of S_n.

Sum of the First *n* Terms of a Geometric Series

The sum, S_n, of the first n terms of a geometric series is given by

$S_n = t_1\left(\frac{1-r^n}{1-r}\right)$, where t_1 is the first term, r is the common ratio, and $r \neq 1$.

Activity
Exploring Geometric Series

You will need: no special materials

Consider the geometric series $S_n = 1 + 2 + 4 + 8 + \cdots + 2^{n-1}$.

1. Copy and complete the table.

n	1	2	3	4	5	6	7	8
S_n	1	3	7	15	?	?	?	?

2. Compare each sum with 2^n.
3. Predict the sum of the first 10 terms. Check your prediction.

CHECKPOINT ✔ 4. Compare your answer from Step 3 with the formula for S_n when $t_1 = 1$ and $r = 2$.

EXAMPLE 1 **Given the series $3 + 4.5 + 6.75 + 10.125 + \cdots$, find S_{10} to the nearest tenth.**

SOLUTION

1. Find the common ratio, r. $\quad r = \frac{4.5}{3} = \frac{6.75}{4.5} = 1.5$
2. Substitute 3 for t_1, 1.5 for r, and 10 for n in $S_n = t_1\left(\frac{1 - r^n}{1 - r}\right)$.

$$S_{10} = 3\left[\frac{1 - (1.5)^{10}}{1 - 1.5}\right] \approx 340.0$$

CHECK

Define the geometric sequence involved.

$$t_n = t_1 r^{n-1}$$
$$t_n = 3 \times 1.5^{n-1}$$

Then use the summation and sequence commands. Thus, $S_{10} \approx 340.0$.

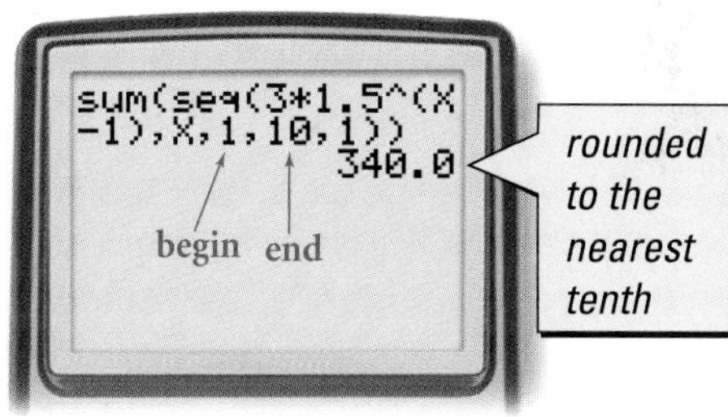

TRY THIS Given the series $400 + 300 + 225 + 168.75 + \ldots$, find S_{16} to the nearest tenth.

EXAMPLE 2 Refer to the investment situation described at the beginning of the lesson. **How much money will be in the account at the end of the 10th year?**

APPLICATION
INVESTMENTS

SOLUTION

After year 1 → $S_1 = 2000(1.08)$

After year 2 → $S_2 = 2000(1.08) + 2000(1.08)^2$

After year 3 → $S_3 = 2000(1.08) + 2000(1.08)^2 + 2000(1.08)^3$

⋮

After year 10 → $S_{10} = 2000(1.08) + 2000(1.08)^2 + \cdots + 2000(1.08)^{10}$

This is a geometric series in which $t_1 = 2000(1.08) = 2160$, $r = 1.08$, and $n = 10$.

$$S_{10} = 2160\left[\frac{1 - (1.08)^{10}}{1 - 1.08}\right] \approx 31{,}290.97$$

At the end of the 10th year, the account will contain $31,290.97.

EXAMPLE 3 Evaluate $\sum_{k=1}^{6} 2(3^{k-1})$.

TECHNOLOGY
GRAPHICS CALCULATOR
Keystroke Guide, page 760

SOLUTION

This summation notation indicates the sum of the first six terms of the geometric series in which $t_1 = 2$ and $r = 3$.

$$S_n = t_1\left(\frac{1 - r^n}{1 - r}\right)$$

$$S_6 = 2\left(\frac{1 - 3^6}{1 - 3}\right)$$

$$S_6 = 728$$

CHECK

TRY THIS Evaluate $\sum_{k=1}^{5} 1.5[(-2)^{k-1}]$.

CRITICAL THINKING Evaluate $\sum_{k=1}^{6} (3^{k-1})$. Compare the result with the result in Example 3. Make a hypothesis about how a series is affected if each term of the corresponding sequence is multiplied by a constant number, c.

Mathematical Induction

How can you determine whether a general statement, such as $1 + 2 + 3 + \cdots + n = \frac{n(n+1)}{2}$, is true for every natural number? Because it is impossible to test every natural number, n, you can use a type of proof called *mathematical induction.*

The principle of mathematical induction is like a line of dominoes that fall over one by one after the first domino is pushed. If you can show that the statement is true for one natural number, then induction will prove it to be true for the next natural number and the next natural number and so on.

To prove that a statement is true for all natural numbers n:

Basis Step: Show that the statement is true for $n = 1$.

Induction Step: Assume the statement is true for a natural number, k. Then prove that it is true for the natural number $k + 1$.

EXAMPLE 4 **Prove the following statement:**

For every natural number n, $1 + 2 + 3 + \cdots + n = \frac{n(n+1)}{2}$.

SOLUTION

1. Basis Step

Show that $1 + 2 + 3 + \cdots + n = \frac{n(n+1)}{2}$ is true for $n = 1$.

$$S_n = \frac{n(n+1)}{2}$$

$$1 \stackrel{?}{=} \frac{1(1+1)}{2}$$

$$1 = 1 \quad \textbf{True}$$

2. Induction Step

Assume the statement is true for a natural number, k.

$$S_k\text{: } 1 + 2 + 3 + \cdots + k = \frac{k(k+1)}{2}$$

Then prove that it is true for the next natural number, $k + 1$.

- Determine the statement to be proved, S_{k+1}:

  Add $k + 1$ to the left side, and substitute $k + 1$ for k on the right.

$$S_k\text{: } 1 + 2 + 3 + \cdots + k = \frac{k(k+1)}{2}$$

$$S_{k+1}\text{: } 1 + 2 + 3 + \cdots + k + (k+1) = \frac{(k+1)[(k+1)+1]}{2}$$

$$1 + 2 + 3 + \cdots + k + (k+1) = \frac{(k+1)(k+2)}{2} \quad \textit{Simplify.}$$

This is the statement to be proved.

- Begin with the statement assumed to be true, S_k, and use properties of equality to prove the statement that you want to prove, S_{k+1}:

$$S_k\text{: } 1 + 2 + 3 + \cdots + k = \frac{k(k+1)}{2}$$

$$1 + 2 + 3 + \cdots + k + (k+1) = \frac{k(k+1)}{2} + (k+1) \quad \textit{Addition Property of Equality}$$

$$= \frac{k(k+1)}{2} + \frac{2(k+1)}{2} \quad \textit{Common denominators}$$

$$= \frac{k^2 + k + 2k + 2}{2} \quad \textit{Add fractions.}$$

$$= \frac{k^2 + 3k + 2}{2} \quad \textit{Combine like terms.}$$

$$= \frac{(k+1)(k+2)}{2} \quad \textit{Factor.}$$

CHECK

Substitute any two consecutive natural numbers for k and $k + 1$.

$$\frac{k(k+1)}{2} + (k+1) = \frac{k(k+1)}{2} + \frac{2(k+1)}{2}$$

$$\frac{3(4)}{2} + 4 \stackrel{?}{=} \frac{3(4)}{2} + \frac{2(4)}{2}$$

$$10 = 10 \quad \textbf{True}$$

TRY THIS Prove the following statement:

For every natural number n, $4 + 8 + 12 + \cdots + 4n = 2n(n+1)$.

Exercises

Communicate

1. How is a geometric series different from an arithmetic series?

2. How would you use summation notation to express the series $2 + 4 + 8 + 16 + 32$? Show three different ways to do this.

3. Explain how to check the results of an induction proof.

4. If you use $n = 3$ for the basis step in an induction proof, is your general proof necessarily true for $n = 1$ and $n = 2$? Explain.

Guided Skills Practice

5. Given the series $2 + 5 + 12.5 + 31.25 + \cdots$, find S_{10} to the nearest tenth. ***(EXAMPLE 1)***

APPLICATION

6. **INVESTMENTS** If a family deposits \$2500 at the beginning of each year for 10 years into an account earning 12% interest, compounded annually, how much would be in the account at the end of the 8th year? ***(EXAMPLE 2)***

7. Evaluate $\sum_{k=1}^{6} 3(2^{k-1})$. ***(EXAMPLE 3)***

8. Prove the following statement: ***(EXAMPLE 4)***

For every natural number n, $\frac{1}{1(2)} + \frac{1}{2(3)} + \cdots + \frac{1}{n(n+1)} = \frac{n}{n+1}$.

Practice and Apply

Find each indicated sum of the geometric series $1 + 2 + 4 + 8 + \cdots$

9. S_3 **10.** S_5 **11.** S_8 **12.** S_{11}

Find each indicated sum of the geometric series $2 + (-6) + 18 + (-54) + \cdots$

13. S_4 **14.** S_6 **15.** S_{15} **16.** S_{20}

Find each indicated sum of the geometric series $4 + 6 + 9 + 13.5 + \cdots$ Give answers to the nearest tenth, if necessary.

17. S_2 **18.** S_3 **19.** S_6 **20.** S_7

21. S_{10} **22.** S_{11} **23.** S_{20} **24.** S_{21}

Use the formula for the sum of the first *n* terms of a geometric series to find each sum. Give answers to the nearest tenth, if necessary.

25. $2 + 4 + 8 + 16 + 32$

26. $3 + 9 + 27 + 81 + 243$

27. $-1 + 2 + (-4) + 8$

28. $-5 + 15 + (-45) + 135$

29. $1 + 1.2 + 1.44 + 1.728$

30. $2 + 4.6 + 10.58 + 24.334$

31. $1 + \frac{2}{5} + \frac{4}{25} + \frac{8}{125}$

32. $\frac{2}{3} + \frac{1}{3} + \frac{1}{6} + \frac{1}{12} + \frac{1}{24}$

For Exercises 33–36, refer to the series $12 + 3 + \frac{3}{4} + \frac{3}{16} + \cdots$

33. Find t_{10}. **34.** Find t_{20}. **35.** Find S_{10}. **36.** Find S_{20}.

Identify t_1, r, and t_n, and evaluate the sum of each series.

37. $\sum_{k=1}^{10} 5^k$ **38.** $\sum_{k=1}^{12} (3 \cdot 2^k)$ **39.** $\sum_{j=1}^{12} \left(\frac{1}{11}\right)^{j-1}$

40. $\sum_{m=1}^{6} \left(\frac{1}{4}\right)^{m-1}$ **41.** $\sum_{n=1}^{8} 2.76^n$ **42.** $\sum_{t=1}^{10} 7.65^{t-1}$

Evaluate. Round answers to the nearest tenth, if necessary.

43. $\sum_{k=1}^{5} 4(2^{k-1})$ **44.** $\sum_{k=1}^{10} 4(5^{k-1})$ **45.** $\sum_{k=1}^{6} \left(\frac{1}{2}\right)^{k-1}$

46. $\sum_{d=1}^{6} \left(\frac{1}{3}\right)^{d-1}$ **47.** $\sum_{m=1}^{7} 3(0.2^{m-1})$ **48.** $\sum_{k=1}^{6} 2(0.3)^{k-1}$

49. $\sum_{k=1}^{7} 5(4^{k-1})$ **50.** $\sum_{k=1}^{8} 10(3^{k-1})$ **51.** $\sum_{k=1}^{12} 6.92^{k-1}$

52. $\sum_{p=1}^{8} 2.87^{p-1}$ **53.** $\sum_{n=1}^{10} \left(\frac{1}{\pi}\right)^{n}$ **54.** $\sum_{k=1}^{10} \left(\frac{1}{\pi}\right)^{k-1}$

Refer to the geometric series in which $t_1 = 5$ and $r = -5$.

55. Find S_4. **56.** Find S_6.

57. Given $t_n = 3125$, find n. **58.** Given $t_n = 125$, find n.

Use mathematical induction to prove that each statement is true for all natural numbers, n.

59. $n < n + 1$ **60.** $2 \le n + 1$

61. $1 + 3 + 5 + \cdots + (2n - 1) = n^2$ **62.** $2 + 4 + 6 + \cdots + 2n = n(n + 1)$

CHALLENGE

Find S_{10} for each series. Round answers to the nearest tenth.

63. $2 + \sqrt{2} + 1 + \frac{\sqrt{2}}{2} + \cdots$ **64.** $2 + 4\pi + 8\pi^2 + 16\pi^3 + \cdots$

CONNECTION

65. GEOMETRY A side of a square is 8 centimeters long. A second square is inscribed in it by joining the midpoints of the sides of the first square. This process is continued as shown in the diagram at right.

a. Write the sequence of side-lengths for the first seven squares.

b. Write an explicit formula for the sequence from part **a.**

c. Find the sum of the side lengths of the first seven squares.

d. Develop a formula in terms of t_1 and n for S_n, the sum of the side lengths of the first n squares.

CONNECTIONS

66. GEOMETRY Smaller and smaller squares are formed consecutively, as shown at right. Find the sum of the perimeters of the first nine squares if the first square is 40 inches wide.

10 in.

20 in.

40 in.

67. GEOMETRY Find the sum of the areas of the first six squares at right if the first square is 40 inches wide.

68. GEOMETRY A piece of wrapping paper is 0.0025 centimeter thick. Assuming that the result after folding is twice as thick, how thick will the paper be if it is folded on top of itself 5 times?

APPLICATIONS

INVESTMENTS Find the value of each investment at the end of the year of the last deposit.

69. \$3000 deposited at the beginning of every year for 10 years at 9% interest, compounded annually

70. \$2000 deposited at the beginning of every year for 20 years at 8% interest, compounded annually

71. \$1500 deposited at the beginning of every year for 50 years at 5% interest, compounded annually

72. DEMOGRAPHICS The population of a city of 100,000 people increases 10% each year for 10 years. What will the population be after 10 years?

73. PHYSICS A ball is dropped from a height of 8 feet. It rebounds to one-half of its original height and falls again. If the ball keeps rebounding in this manner, what is the total distance, to the nearest tenth, that the ball travels after 10 rebounds? (Hint: Draw a diagram, and notice the pattern.)

Look Back

Graph the solution to each system of linear inequalities. ***(LESSON 3.4)***

74. $\begin{cases} x + y \geq 4 \\ 2x \leq y \end{cases}$

75. $\begin{cases} y < 4x + 2 \\ x \leq 2 \\ y > -1 \end{cases}$

76. $\begin{cases} y < 8 - 2x \\ x \geq 1 \\ y \geq 0 \end{cases}$

APPLICATIONS

77. DEPRECIATION Personal computers often rapidly depreciate in value due to advances in technology. Suppose that a computer which originally cost \$3800 loses 10% of its value every 6 months. ***(LESSON 6.2)***

a. What is the multiplier for this exponential decay function?

b. Write a formula for the value of the computer, $V(t)$, after t 6-month periods.

c. What is the value of the computer after 1 year?

d. What is the value of the computer after 18 months?

Identify all asymptotes and holes in the graph of each rational function. ***(LESSON 8.2)***

78. $f(x) = \dfrac{2x + 1}{x - 3}$

79. $g(x) = \dfrac{x - 5}{3x^2}$

80. $h(x) = \dfrac{x + 4}{x^2 + 3x - 4}$

Simplify each rational function. ***(LESSON 8.3)***

81. $f(x) = \dfrac{x - 3}{2x^2 - 5x - 3}$

82. $f(x) = \dfrac{x^2 - 5x + 4}{x^2 + 2x - 3}$

83. MUSIC Maria, a violinist, wants to form a string octet with friends from the school orchestra. She will need 3 more violinists, 2 violists, and 2 cellists. In the orchestra, there are 24 violinists (not including Maria), 7 violists, and 12 cellists. In how many different ways can she pick members of the octet? ***(LESSON 10.3)***

Look Beyond

84. Consider the geometric sequence $\frac{1}{2}, \frac{1}{4}, \frac{1}{8}, \frac{1}{16}, \ldots$ Calculate S_1, S_2, S_3, S_4, and S_5. Plot these points on a number line. Describe the behavior of S_n as n increases.

PORTFOLIO ACTIVITY

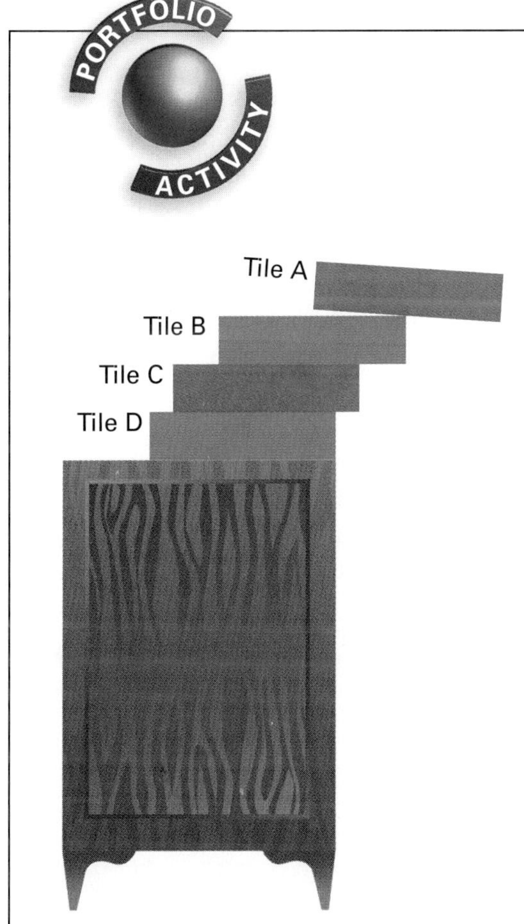

As tiles are moved over the edge of a desk, as shown at left, the center of gravity for the entire stack of tiles moves closer and closer to the edge of the desk. If the tiles are moved in such a way that the center of gravity for the entire stack is shifted beyond the edge of the desk, then the stack of tiles will fall over the edge.

Place four congruent tiles in a neat stack on your desk so that the front edge of each tile is aligned with the edge of the desk. The original center of gravity for these tiles is located half of the length of a tile from the edge of the desk.

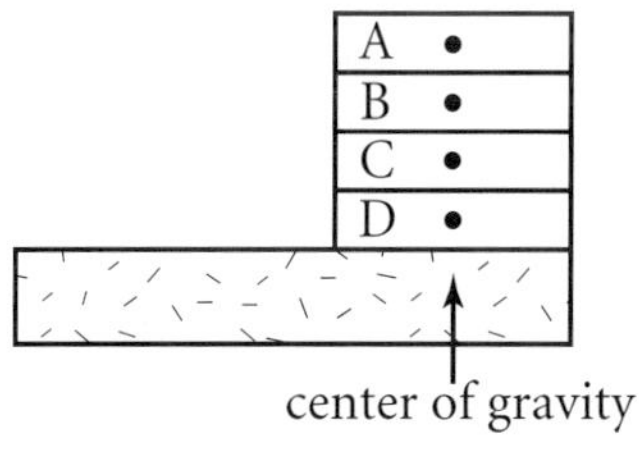

Extend tile A beyond tile B as far as possible while keeping the stack balanced. Keeping the position of tile A on tile B, extend tile B beyond tile C as far as possible while keeping the stack balanced. Continue this process with tiles C and D. Explain what happens to the distance that each successive tile can be extended.

WORKING ON THE CHAPTER PROJECT

You should now be able to complete Activity 2 of the Chapter Project.

11.6

Infinite Geometric Series

Why *Infinite geometric series can be used to describe patterns such as those found in some fractal art and geometric designs.*

Objective

- Find the sum of an infinite geometric series, if one exists.
- Write repeating decimals as fractions.

APPLICATION
ART

Denise is making a design using only equilateral triangles. The outer triangle is 20 inches long on each side. A second equilateral triangle is formed by joining the midpoints of the sides of the outer triangle. The process is continued. The length of the path shown in black in the figure at right can be modeled by the geometric series below.

$$20 + 10 + 5 + 2.5 + 1.25 + 0.625$$

20 in.

If the path were to continue indefinitely, it could be modeled by the *infinite geometric series* below.

$$20 + 10 + 5 + 2.5 + \cdots + t_1 r^{n-1} + \cdots$$

An **infinite geometric series** is a geometric series with infinitely many terms. A **partial sum** of an infinite series is the sum of a given number of terms and not the sum of the entire series. Examine the table and the graph of partial sums for this infinite geometric series.

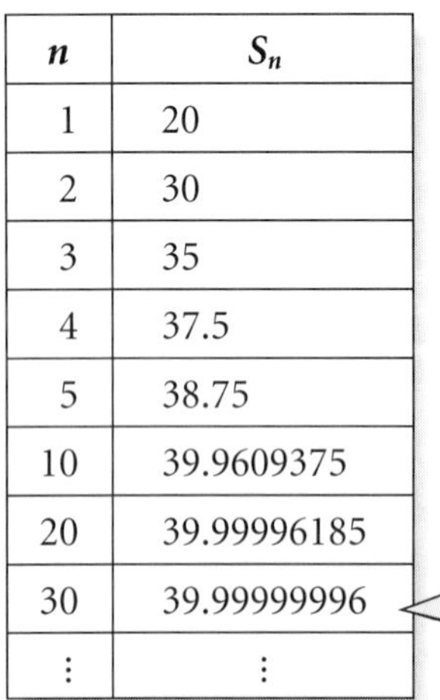

n	S_n
1	20
2	30
3	35
4	37.5
5	38.75
10	39.9609375
20	39.99996185
30	39.99999996
⋮	⋮

Notice that as n gets larger and larger, the sums get closer and closer to the number 40.

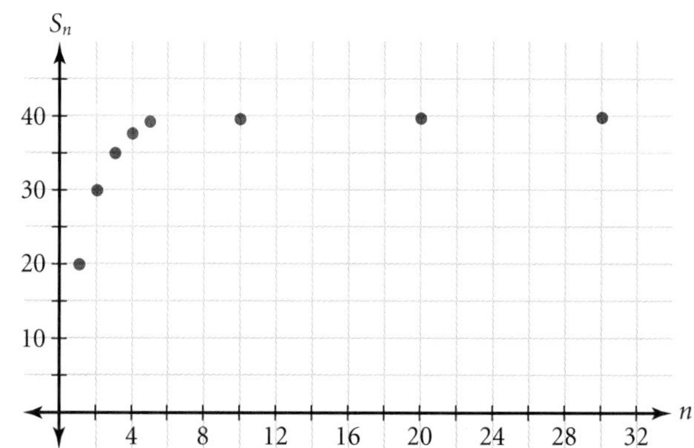

Examine the formula for the sum of a geometric series to see why this sum approaches 40.

$$S_n = t_1\left(\frac{1-r^n}{1-r}\right)$$

$$S_n = 20\left(\frac{1-0.5^n}{1-0.5}\right)$$

$$S_n = 20\left(\frac{1}{1-0.5} - \frac{0.5^n}{1-0.5}\right) \quad \textit{Rewrite } \frac{1-0.5^n}{1-0.5}.$$

$$S_n = \frac{20}{1-0.5} - \frac{20(0.5^n)}{1-0.5}$$

What happens to 0.5^n as n gets larger?

As n gets larger, the rational expression $\frac{20(0.5^n)}{1-0.5}$ gets closer and closer to 0.

Therefore, the partial sums of this geometric series get closer and closer to $\frac{20}{1-0.5}$, or 40.

When the partial sums of an infinite series approach a fixed number as n increases, the infinite geometric series is said to **converge**.

When the partial sums of an infinite series do not approach a fixed number as n increases, the infinite geometric series is said to **diverge.**

Exploring Convergence

TECHNOLOGY
GRAPHICS CALCULATOR
Keystroke Guide, page 760

You will need: a graphics calculator or paper and pencil

1. For each infinite geometric series indicated below, complete a table of values for n and S_n, using n-values of 1, 2, 3, 5, 10, and 100.

a. $t_1 = -5$; $r = -0.25$ **b.** $t_1 = 5$; $r = -0.25$

c. $t_1 = 2$; $r = \frac{1}{3}$ **d.** $t_1 = 2$; $r = -\frac{1}{3}$

2. For each infinite geometric series indicated below, complete a table of values for n and S_n, using n-values of 1, 2, 3, 5, 10, and 100.

a. $t_1 = -5$; $r = -8$ **b.** $t_1 = 5$; $r = -8$

c. $t_1 = 2$; $r = 3$ **d.** $t_1 = 2$; $r = -3$

3. Which of the infinite geometric series from Steps 1 and 2 converge? How are the common ratios of these series alike?

4. Which of the infinite geometric series from Steps 1 and 2 diverge? How are the common ratios of these series alike?

5. Make a conjecture about how the common ratio of an infinite geometric series determines whether or not the series converges. Test your conjecture.

Sum of an Infinite Geometric Series

If a geometric sequence has common ratio r and $|r| < 1$, then the sum, S, of the related infinite geometric series is as follows:

$$S = \frac{t_1}{1-r}$$

If a geometric sequence has common ratio r and $|r| > 1$, then the related infinite geometric series diverges and therefore does not have a sum. Examine the table of values and the graph of the infinite geometric series below in which $t_1 = 5$ and $r = 2$:

$$5 + 10 + 20 + 40 + \cdots + t_1 r^{n-1} + \cdots$$

n	S_n
1	5
2	15
3	35
4	75
5	155
6	315
7	635
8	1275
⋮	⋮

Notice that as n gets larger and larger, the sums also get larger and larger.

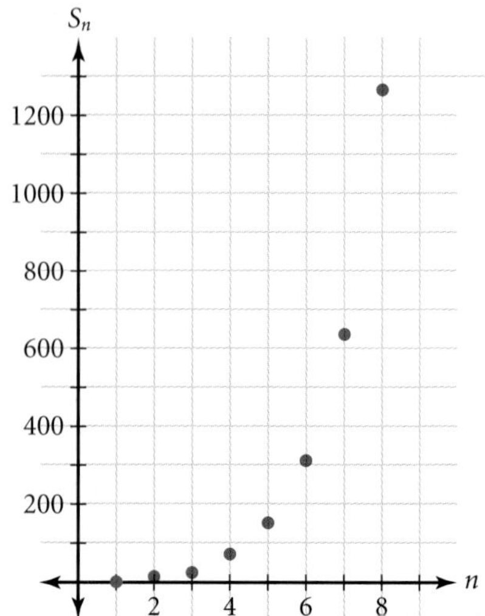

CHECKPOINT ✔ What happens to the partial sums of an infinite geometric series in which $t_1 = 5$ and $r = -2$ as n increases?

CRITICAL THINKING Examine the table and graph for S_n above. Does S_n increase exponentially? Explain.

EXAMPLE 1 **Find the sum of the infinite series $3 + 1.2 + 0.48 + 0.192 + \cdots$, if it exists.**

SOLUTION

1. Determine whether the infinite series is geometric.

$$\frac{t_2}{t_1} = \frac{1.2}{3} = 0.4 \qquad \frac{t_3}{t_2} = \frac{0.48}{1.2} = 0.4 \qquad \frac{t_4}{t_3} = \frac{0.192}{0.48} = 0.4$$

This is an infinite geometric series in which $t_1 = 3$ and $r = 0.4$.

2. Determine whether the series diverges or converges.

Since $|0.4| < 1$, the series converges. The sum is $S = \frac{t_1}{1-r}$.

$$S = \frac{t_1}{1-r} = \frac{3}{1-0.4} = 5$$

The sum of the series is 5. This seems reasonable because $S_4 = 4.872$.

CHECK

Graph the formula for the sum of the nth term of the geometric series in which $t_1 = 3$ and $r = 0.4$.

$$S_n = t_1\left(\frac{1-r^n}{1-r}\right), \text{ or } y = 3\left(\frac{1-0.4^x}{1-0.4}\right)$$

From the graph, you can see that the series converges to a sum of 5.

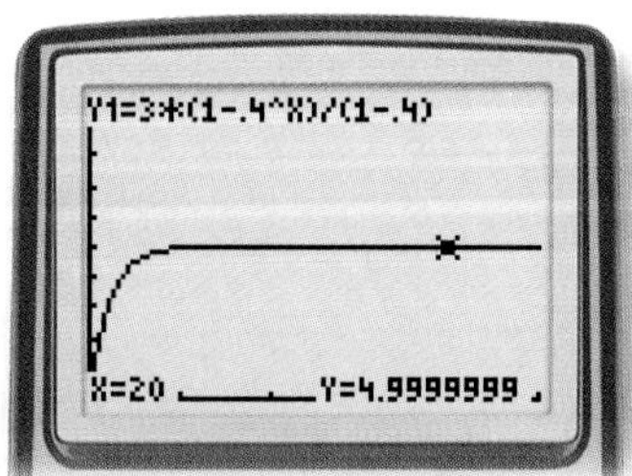

TRY THIS Find the sum of the infinite series $-4 + 2 + (-1) + 0.5 + \cdots$, if it exists.

The mathematical symbol for infinity is ∞. The notation $\sum_{k=1}^{\infty}$ indicates an infinite series.

EXAMPLE 2 **Find the sum of the infinite series $\sum_{k=1}^{\infty} \frac{1}{3^{k+1}}$, if it exists.**

SOLUTION

1. Determine whether the infinite series is geometric.

$$\frac{t_2}{t_1} = \frac{\frac{1}{27}}{\frac{1}{9}} = \frac{1}{3} \qquad \frac{t_3}{t_2} = \frac{\frac{1}{81}}{\frac{1}{27}} = \frac{1}{3}$$

This is a geometric series in which $t_1 = \frac{1}{9}$ and $r = \frac{1}{3}$.

2. Determine whether the series diverges or converges. Because $\left|\frac{1}{3}\right| < 1$, the series converges. The sum is $S = \frac{t_1}{1 - r}$.

$$S = \frac{t_1}{1 - r} = \frac{\frac{1}{9}}{1 - \frac{1}{3}} = \frac{1}{6}$$

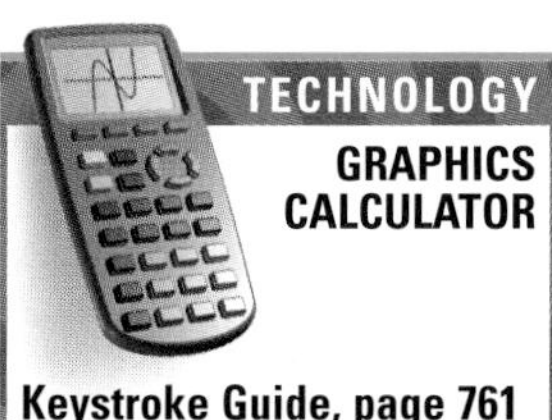

Keystroke Guide, page 761

CHECK

Graph the formula for the sum of the nth term of the geometric series in which $t_1 = \frac{1}{9}$ and $r = \frac{1}{3}$.

From the graph, you can see that the series converges to a sum of $\frac{1}{6}$.

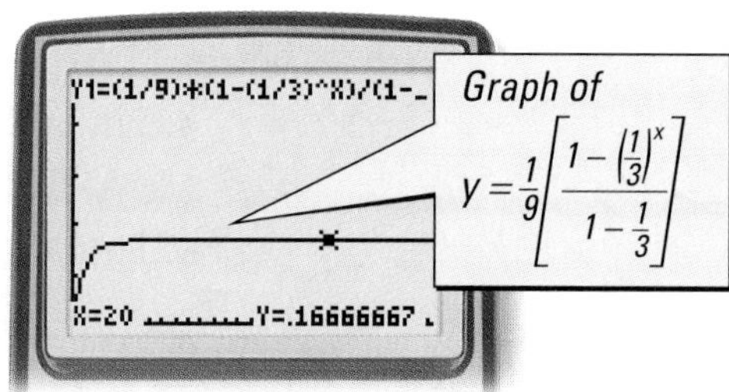

TRY THIS Find the sum of the infinite series $\sum_{k=1}^{\infty} \frac{1}{2^{k+1}}$, if it exists.

Every repeating decimal is a rational number and can therefore be written in the form $\frac{p}{q}$, where p and q are integers with no common factors. Infinite series can be used to convert a repeating decimal into a fraction.

EXAMPLE 3 **Write $0.\overline{2}$ as a fraction in simplest form.**

SOLUTION

1. Write the repeating decimal as an infinite geometric series.

$$\begin{aligned} 0.\overline{2} &= 0.222\ldots \\ &= 0.2 + 0.02 + 0.002 + \cdots \\ &= \frac{2}{10} + \frac{2}{100} + \frac{2}{1000} + \cdots \end{aligned}$$

Notice that $0.\overline{2}$ can be written as an infinite geometric series of decimals or fractions. Thus, $t_1 = 0.2$, or $\frac{2}{10}$, and $r = 0.1$, or $\frac{1}{10}$.

2. Because $|0.1| < 1$, the series converges. The sum is $S = \frac{t_1}{1 - r}$.

$$S = \frac{0.2}{1 - 0.1} = \frac{0.2}{0.9} = \frac{2}{9}$$

CHECK

Use a calculator: $2 \div 9 = 0.222\ldots$ Thus, $0.\overline{2}$ can be written as $\frac{2}{9}$.

TRY THIS Write $0.\overline{5}$ as a fraction in simplest form.

Exercises

Communicate

1. Explain how to determine whether an infinite geometric series has a sum.
2. How can you tell if the series $\sum_{k=1}^{\infty}\left(\frac{1}{2}\right)^k$ and the series $\sum_{k=1}^{\infty}2^k$ converge?
3. Explain how to write a repeating decimal as a fraction.

Guided Skills Practice

4. Find the sum of the infinite series $3 + 2 + \frac{4}{3} + \frac{8}{9} + \cdots$, if it exists. ***(EXAMPLE 1)***
5. Find the sum of the infinite series $\sum_{k=1}^{\infty}\frac{1}{4^{k+1}}$, if it exists. ***(EXAMPLE 2)***
6. Write $0.\overline{3}$ as a fraction in simplest form. ***(EXAMPLE 3)***

Practice and Apply

Find the sum of each infinite geometric series, if it exists.

7. $\frac{1}{3} + \frac{1}{9} + \frac{1}{27} + \frac{1}{81} + \cdots$
8. $1 + \frac{1}{5} + \frac{1}{25} + \frac{1}{125} + \cdots$
9. $2 + 1.5 + 1.125 + 0.84375 + \cdots$
10. $3 + 1.2 + 0.48 + 0.192 + \cdots$
11. $1 + 2 + 4 + 8 + \cdots$
12. $2 + 6 + 18 + 54 + \cdots$
13. $\frac{11}{15} + \frac{1}{15} + \frac{1}{165} + \frac{1}{1815} + \cdots$
14. $\frac{9}{17} + \frac{3}{17} + \frac{1}{17} + \frac{1}{51} + \cdots$
15. $3 + 2.1 + 1.47 + 1.029 + \cdots$
16. $4 + 3.2 + 2.56 + 2.048 + \cdots$
17. $\frac{1}{3} + \frac{4}{9} + \frac{16}{27} + \frac{64}{81} + \cdots$
18. $\frac{2}{5} + \frac{12}{25} + \frac{72}{125} + \frac{432}{625} + \cdots$

Find the sum of each infinite geometric series, if it exists.

19. $\sum_{k=0}^{\infty}\left(\frac{1}{10}\right)^k$
20. $\sum_{k=0}^{\infty}\left(\frac{5}{3}\right)^k$
21. $\sum_{k=1}^{\infty}\left(\frac{1}{8}\right)^k$
22. $\sum_{k=1}^{\infty}(-0.45)^k$
23. $\sum_{k=0}^{\infty}\frac{7}{10^k}$
24. $\sum_{k=1}^{\infty}\frac{3}{5^{k+1}}$
25. $\sum_{k=0}^{\infty}\left(-\frac{3}{7}\right)^k$
26. $\sum_{j=0}^{\infty}\left(-\frac{4}{11}\right)^j$
27. $\sum_{k=1}^{\infty}2.9^k$
28. $\sum_{k=1}^{\infty}4.6^k$
29. $\sum_{k=1}^{\infty}0.7^k$
30. $\sum_{k=1}^{\infty}(-0.73)^k$
31. $\sum_{n=0}^{\infty}3^n$
32. $\sum_{m=0}^{\infty}5^m$
33. $\sum_{k=1}^{\infty}\frac{3^{k-1}}{4^k}$
34. $\sum_{k=1}^{\infty}\frac{4^{k+1}}{3^k}$
35. $\sum_{k=0}^{\infty}\left(\frac{1}{\sqrt{2}}\right)^k$
36. $\sum_{j=0}^{\infty}\left(\frac{2}{\sqrt{3}}\right)^j$
37. $\sum_{j=0}^{\infty}\left(\frac{1}{\pi}\right)^j$
38. $\sum_{k=0}^{\infty}\left(\frac{\sqrt{2}}{\sqrt{3}}\right)^k$

Write an infinite geometric series that converges to the given number.

39. 0.191919... **40.** 57.57575757... **41.** 0.001001001001...

42. 0.219219219... **43.** 0.353535... **44.** 0.898989...

45. 0.819819819... **46.** 0.733733733... **47.** 0.121121121...

Write each decimal as a fraction in simplest form.

48. $0.\overline{5}$ **49.** $0.\overline{4}$ **50.** $0.\overline{72}$ **51.** $0.\overline{36}$

52. $0.\overline{43}$ **53.** $0.\overline{54}$ **54.** $0.\overline{372}$ **55.** $0.\overline{586}$

56. $0.\overline{831}$ **57.** $0.\overline{474}$ **58.** $0.\overline{626}$ **59.** $0.\overline{031}$

60. Derive the formula for the sum of an infinite geometric series by using the examination of the formula shown on the top of page 729, in which n becomes larger and larger.

CONNECTIONS

61. GEOMETRY The midpoints of the sides of a square are joined to create a new square. This process is repeated for each new square. Find the sum of an infinite series of the areas of such squares if the side length of the original square is 10 centimeters.

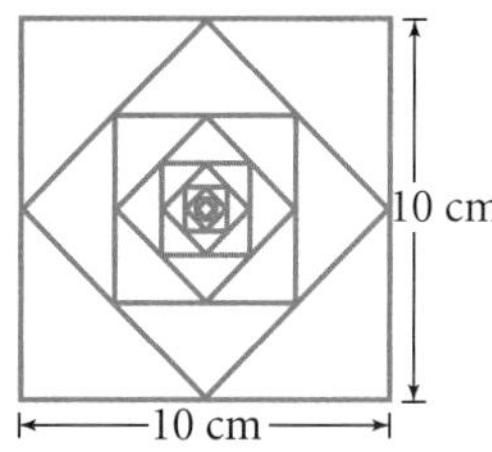

CHALLENGE

Step 1

Step 2

Step 3

Step 4

62. GEOMETRY A Koch curve can be constructed by taking an equilateral triangle and adding a smaller equilateral triangle along the middle third of each side (see Step 2 at left). This process is continued, or *iterated*, infinitely to form a *fractal.*

a. Assume that the original triangle has side lengths of 9. Copy and complete the table below. Step n may contain either recursive or explicit formulas.

	Step 1	Step 2	Step 3	Step 4	...	Step n
Number of sides	3	12	48		...	
Length of each side	9	3	1		...	
Perimeter	27	36	48		...	
Number of new triangles	1	3	12		...	
New area added	$\frac{81\sqrt{3}}{4}$	$\frac{9\sqrt{3}}{4}$	$\frac{\sqrt{3}}{4}$		...	

b. Which of the formulas in Step n describe sequences?

c. If the formulas in Step n describe series, which are convergent and which are divergent?

d. What is the unusual relationship between the perimeter and area of this figure?

APPLICATION

63. INVESTMENTS A *perpetuity* is an investment that pays a fixed amount of money at the end of every period forever. Perpetuities have a finite present value. For example, the present value of a perpetuity that earns 7% interest and that pays \$500 at the end of every year is as follows:

$$P = 500\left(\frac{1}{1.07}\right) + 500\left(\frac{1}{1.07}\right)^2 + 500\left(\frac{1}{1.07}\right)^3 + 500\left(\frac{1}{1.07}\right)^4 + \cdots$$

a. Find P by finding the sum of the infinite geometric series.

b. Find the present value of a perpetuity that earns 8% interest and that pays \$1000 at the end of every year forever.

APPLICATION

64. PHYSICS A golf ball is dropped from a height of 81 inches. It rebounds to $\frac{2}{3}$ of its original height and continues rebounding in this manner. How far does it travel before coming to rest?

Look Back

65 Use a matrix equation to solve the system at right. ***(LESSON 4.4)***

$$\begin{cases} -2x + y + 6z = 18 \\ 5x + 8z = -16 \\ 3x + 2y - 10z = -3 \end{cases}$$

Solve each equation for *x*. Write the exact solution and the approximate solution to the nearest hundredth, when appropriate. ***(LESSONS 6.6 AND 6.7)***

66. $2^{x-2} = 23$ **67.** $3^{-x} = 19$ **68.** $8^x = 0.5$ **69.** $2^x = 7.23$

APPLICATION

70. CONSTRUCTION A manager of a construction company is managing three projects. The probabilities that the three projects will be completed on schedule are 0.85, 0.72, and 0.94. If the events are independent, what is the probability, to the nearest hundredth, that all three projects will be completed on schedule? ***(LESSON 10.5)***

Look Beyond

71. **a.** Write out the first four terms of the infinite geometric series in which $t_1 = 0.14$ and $r_1 = 0.02$.

b. Find the sum of the infinite series from part **a.** Simplify your answer.

c. Write the answer as a repeating decimal with bar notation.

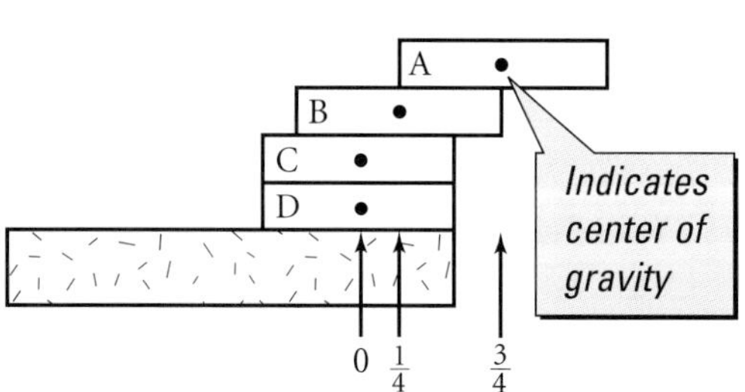

Refer to the diagram of tiles above. The center of gravity for tile A is $\frac{3}{4}$ of the length of a tile to the right of 0. The center of gravity for tile B is $\frac{1}{4}$ of the length of a tile to the right of 0. The centers of gravity for tiles C and D are both 0.

1. Position four tiles as shown in the diagram.
2. Keeping the position of tile A on tile B and tile B on tile C, find the maximum distance, in tile lengths, to the right of 0 that tile C can be moved without the stack of tiles falling. Record your results.
3. While keeping the position of tile A on tile B, tile B on tile C, and tile C on tile D (from Step 2), find the maximum distance to the right of 0 that tile D can be moved without the stack of tiles falling. Record your results.

WORKING ON THE CHAPTER PROJECT

You should now be able to complete Activity 3 of the Chapter Project.

11.7

Pascal's Triangle

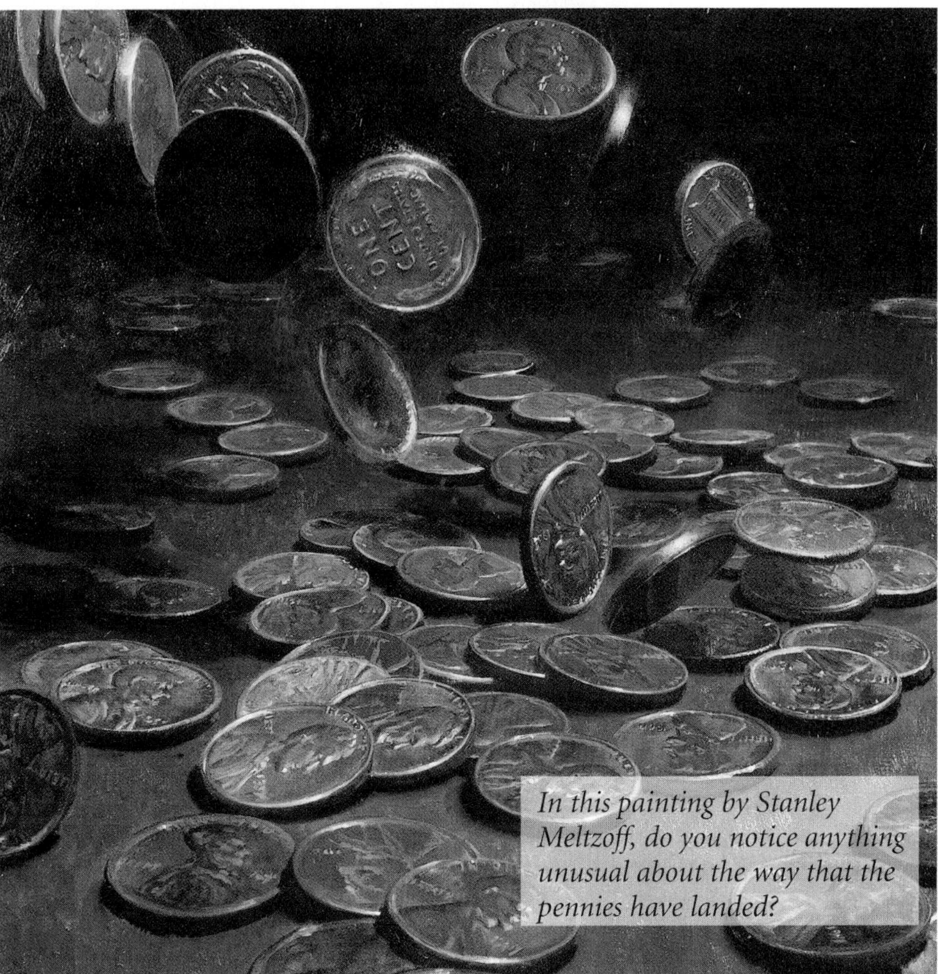
In this painting by Stanley Meltzoff, do you notice anything unusual about the way that the pennies have landed?

Objectives

- Find entries in Pascal's triangle.
- Use Pascal's triangle to find combinations and probabilities.

Why ***The patterns in Pascal's triangle can be used to solve real-world problems involving probability.***

Find the probability that exactly 3 heads or exactly 4 heads appear when a coin is tossed 7 times. *You will answer this question in Example 3.*

In this chapter you have studied the patterns in some sequences and series. A famous pattern in the form of an arithmetic triangle, called **Pascal's triangle,** is shown below.

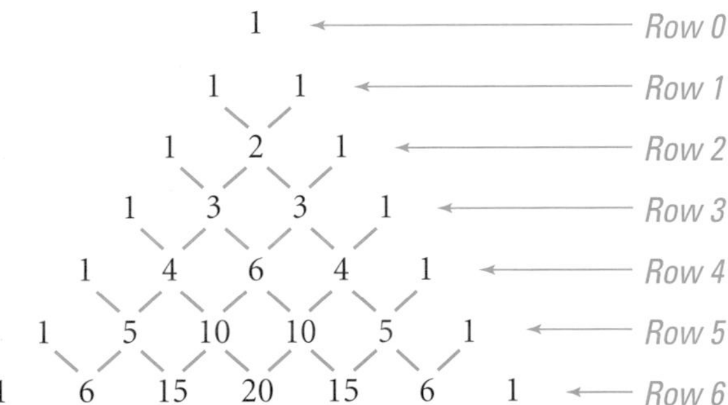

Notice that each row begins with 1 and ends with 1. Each number between the 1s is the sum of the pair of numbers above it in the previous row.

Blaise Pascal (1623–1662)

The arithmetic triangle above is called Pascal's triangle because the French mathematician and theologian Blaise Pascal analyzed the pattern extensively in the seventeenth century.

In the Activity below, you can investigate some of the many interesting patterns in Pascal's triangle.

Exploring Patterns in Pascal's Triangle

You will need: no special tools

1. Make several copies of Pascal's triangle through row 15.
2. Find the sum of the entries in each row of Pascal's triangle.

CHECKPOINT ✓ 3. What patterns do you see in the sums from Step 2?

CHECKPOINT ✓ 4. Notice that 5 divides all of the entries in row 5, except the first and last. Find three more rows in which the row number divides all the entries in that row (except the first and last). Find a rule to predict which rows have this property.

5. Shade all of the even numbers in the triangle.

CHECKPOINT ✓ 6. What shape(s) do you see in the shaded numbers?

The table below shows all of the possible outcomes when a coin is tossed 4 times. It also indicates how many ways each event can occur.

0 heads	1 heads	2 heads	3 heads	4 heads
TTTT	HTTT THTT TTHT TTTH	HHTT HTHT HTTH TTHH THTH THHT	HHHT HHTH HTHH THHH	HHHH
↓	↓	↓	↓	↓
1 way	4 ways	6 ways	4 ways	1 way

Notice that these numbers are the numbers in row 4 of Pascal's Triangle.

The number of ways that each event above can occur can be found by using combinations. For example, the number of ways that 2 heads can occur when a coin is tossed 4 times is a combination of 4 objects taken 2 at a time, or ${}_4C_2$.

Pascal's triangle can also be expressed in combination notation, as shown below.

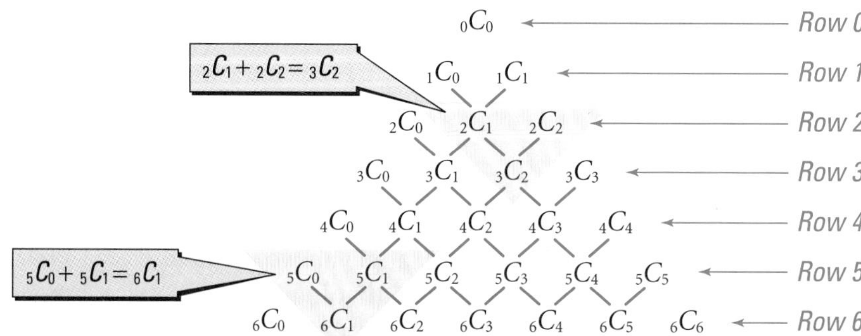

The patterns listed below can be found in Pascal's triangle.

Patterns in Pascal's Triangle

- Row n of Pascal's triangle contains $n + 1$ entries.
- The kth entry in row n of Pascal's triangle is ${}_nC_{k-1}$.
- The sum of all the entries in row n of Pascal's triangle equals 2^n.
- ${}_nC_{k-1} + {}_nC_k = {}_{n+1}C_k$, where $0 < k \leq n$

CHECKPOINT ✔ Verify each equation below by evaluating combinations.

a. ${}_7C_4 + {}_7C_5 = {}_8C_5$ **b.** ${}_8C_1 + {}_8C_2 = {}_9C_2$ **c.** ${}_4C_2 + {}_4C_3 = {}_5C_3$

EXAMPLE 1 **Find the 4th and 10th entries in row 12 of Pascal's triangle.**

SOLUTION

The kth entry in row n of Pascal's triangle is ${}_nC_{k-1}$.

TECHNOLOGY GRAPHICS CALCULATOR
Keystroke Guide, page 761

4th entry in row 12:

$${}_nC_{k-1} = {}_{12}C_3 = \frac{12!}{9!3!} = 220$$

10th entry in row 12:

$${}_nC_{k-1} = {}_{12}C_9 = \frac{12!}{3!9!} = 220$$

The 4th and 10th entries in row 12 of Pascal's triangle are both 220.

CHECK

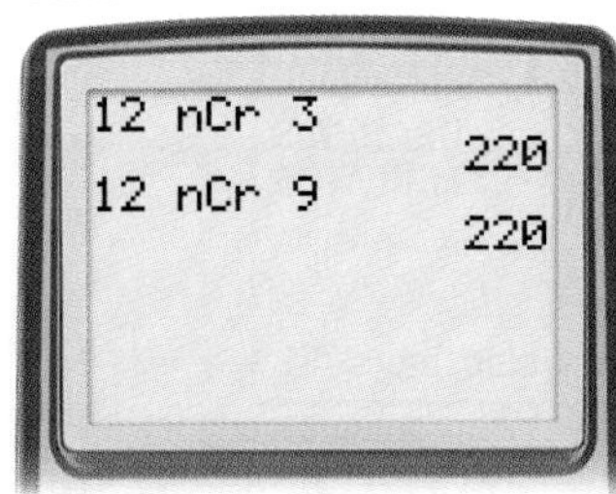

TRY THIS Find the 2nd and 12th entries in row 11 of Pascal's triangle.

You can solve probability problems by using Pascal's triangle.

EXAMPLE 2 **Suppose that a fair coin is tossed 7 times. In how many ways can exactly 0, 1, 2, 3, 4, 5, 6, and 7 heads appear?**

SOLUTION

Because the coin is tossed 7 times, use row 7 of Pascal's triangle.

Heads	0	1	2	3	4	5	6	7
Number of ways	${}_7C_0$ 1	${}_7C_1$ 7	${}_7C_2$ 21	${}_7C_3$ 35	${}_7C_4$ 35	${}_7C_5$ 21	${}_7C_6$ 7	${}_7C_7$ 1

TRY THIS Suppose that a fair coin is tossed 8 times. In how many ways can exactly 0, 1, 2, 3, 4, 5, 6, 7, and 8 heads appear?

Row n of Pascal's triangle indicates the number of ways that each possible outcome can occur when a coin is tossed n times. The sum of all the entries in row n of Pascal's triangle, 2^n, gives the total number of possible outcomes that can occur when a coin is tossed n times.

Pascal's Triangle and Two-Outcome Experiments

If a probability experiment with 2 equally likely outcomes is repeated in n independent trials, the probability $P(A)$ of event A occurring exactly k times is given by $P(A) = \frac{{}_nC_k}{2^n}$.

EXAMPLE 3 **Find the probability that exactly 3 heads or exactly 4 heads appear when a coin is tossed 7 times. Give your answer to the nearest hundredth.**

SOLUTION

The events "3 heads" and "4 heads" are mutually exclusive.

$$P(3 \text{ heads } or \text{ 4 heads}) = P(3 \text{ heads}) + P(4 \text{ heads})$$
$$= \frac{{}_7C_3}{2^7} + \frac{{}_7C_4}{2^7}$$
$$= \frac{35 + 35}{128}$$
$$\approx 0.55$$

TECHNOLOGY
GRAPHICS CALCULATOR

Keystroke Guide, page 761

CHECK

The probability that exactly 3 heads or exactly 4 heads appear when a coin is tossed 7 times is about 0.55.

TRY THIS Find the probability that exactly 4 heads or exactly 6 heads appear when a coin is tossed 8 times. Give your answer to the nearest hundredth.

Exercises

Communicate

1. Describe the patterns that you see in Pascal's triangle when it is written in ${}_nC_r$ notation.
2. Describe two patterns that you see in Pascal's triangle when it is written with integer entries.

3. **PROBABILITY** Explain how Pascal's triangle can be used to find the probability that exactly 4 tails will appear when a coin is tossed 6 times.

Guided Skills Practice

4. Find the third and fifth entries in row 10 of Pascal's triangle. ***(EXAMPLE 1)***

CONNECTIONS

5. **PROBABILITY** Suppose that a fair coin is tossed 6 times. In how many ways can exactly 0, 1, 2, 3, 4, 5, and 6 heads appear? ***(EXAMPLE 2)***

6. **PROBABILITY** Find the probability that exactly 2 heads or exactly 3 heads appear when a coin is tossed 6 times. Give your answer to the nearest hundredth. ***(EXAMPLE 3)***

Practice and Apply

State the location of each entry in Pascal's triangle. Then give the value of each expression.

7. ${}_5C_2$	**8.** ${}_7C_3$	**9.** ${}_8C_5$	**10.** ${}_7C_4$
11. ${}_{11}C_2$	**12.** ${}_{12}C_4$	**13.** ${}_{10}C_3$	**14.** ${}_9C_2$
15. ${}_8C_4$	**16.** ${}_6C_4$	**17.** ${}_7C_2$	**18.** ${}_9C_2$
19. ${}_9C_6$	**20.** ${}_{11}C_4$	**21.** ${}_{13}C_7$	**22.** ${}_{12}C_8$

Find the 4th and 7th entries in the indicated row of Pascal's triangle.

23. row 7	**24.** row 9	**25.** row 11	**26.** row 13

CHALLENGES

27. In the figure below, the sum of each diagonal is at the end of the diagonal.
    a. Find the missing sums.
    b. What is the name of the sequence formed by the sums?

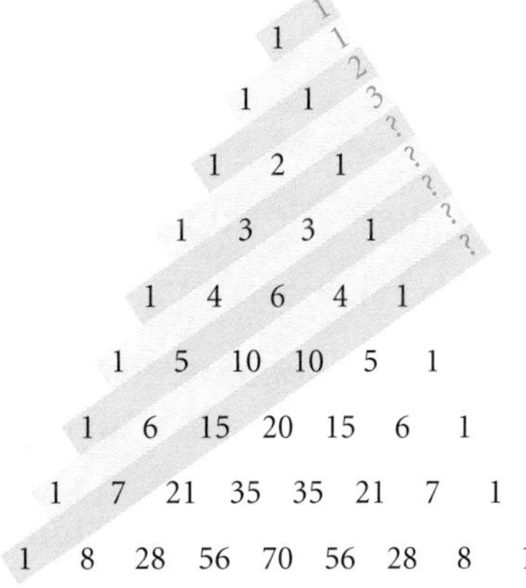

28. Evaluate 11^2, 11^3, and 11^4.
    a. How are these numbers related to Pascal's triangle?
    b. Formulate a rule for multiplying by 11 based on your answer to part **a.** Test your response by multiplying other numbers by 11.

CONNECTION

PROBABILITY **Find the probability of each event.**

29. At least 4 heads appear in 6 tosses of a fair coin.
30. At least 3 heads appear in 5 tosses of a fair coin.
31. No more than 2 heads appear in 5 tosses of a fair coin.
32. No more than 3 heads appear in 6 tosses of a fair coin.
33. Either 4 *or* 5 heads appear in 8 tosses of a fair coin.
34. Either 5 *or* 6 heads appear in 7 tosses of a fair coin.

APPLICATIONS

GENETICS Assume that the genders of children are equally likely. A family has 5 children. Find the probability that the children are the following:

35. exactly 3 girls **36.** exactly 5 girls **37.** at least 4 boys

38. at least 3 boys **39.** at most 3 girls **40.** at most 2 boys

ACADEMICS A student guesses the answers for 5 items on a true-false quiz. Find the probability that the indicated number of answers are correct.

41. exactly 3 **42.** exactly 4 **43.** at least 4

44. at least 3 **45.** at most 3 **46.** at most 4

47. CULTURAL CONNECTION: ASIA In 1303 the Chinese mathematician Chu Shih-Chieh published the book whose cover is shown at right. The caption reads "The Old Method Chart of the Seven Multiplying Squares."

a. Do the numerical symbols appear to correspond to Pascal's triangle? If so, write the symbols that are equivalent to one another.

b. How can the name of the triangle be explained? (Hint: Row 2 is labeled as the first "multiplying square.")

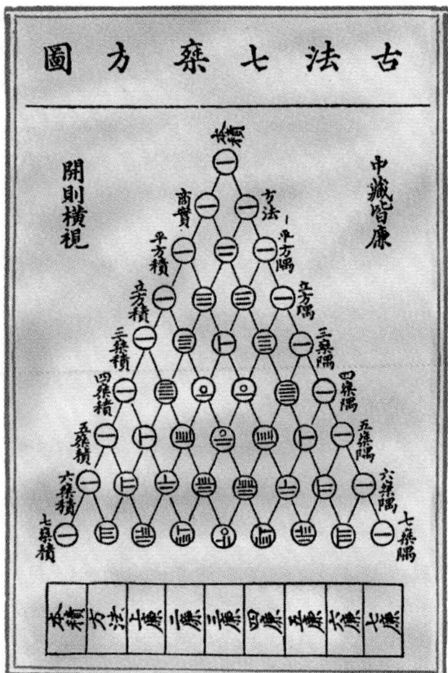

Look Back

Find a quadratic function that fits each list of data points. ***(LESSON 5.7)***

48. (0, 5), (1, 6), (3, 20) **49.** (4, 4), (7, −2), (−3, −7)

Solve each inequality. Graph the solution on a number line. ***(LESSON 5.8)***

50. $x^2 + x - 6 > 0$ **51.** $x^2 + 7x - 18 < 0$ **52.** $6 \leq 5x + x^2$

State whether each situation involves a permutation or a combination. Then solve. ***(LESSONS 10.2 AND 10.3)***

53. the number of ways to award 1st, 2nd, and 3rd prizes to a group of 10 floats entered in a homecoming parade

54. the number of ways to select a committee of 5 senators from a group of 100 senators

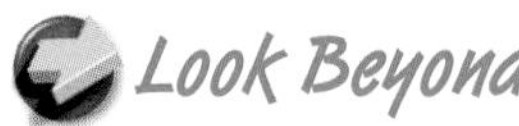

Look Beyond

55. Use multiplication and the Distributive Property to expand $(x + y)^4$ as a polynomial in x and y with decreasing powers of x. Compare the coefficients with Pascal's triangle. Do the entries in one of the rows agree with the coefficients in the expansion? If so, which row?

The Binomial Theorem

Jose Guillen at Shea Stadium, 1998

Objectives

- Use the Binomial Theorem to expand $(x + y)^n$.
- Use the Binomial Theorem to calculate a probability.

Why *The Binomial Theorem can be used to solve real-world problems involving probability such as predicting the future performance of an athlete.*

APPLICATION
SPORTS

At one time during the 1998 season, baseball player Jose Guillen had a season batting average of 0.337. If Guillen were to maintain his 0.337 average, what is the probability that he would get exactly 4 hits in the next 5 at bats? To answer this question, you can use the *Binomial Theorem.* *You will solve this problem in Example 2.*

In Chapters 5 and 7, you worked with linear binomials in x, such as $x + 3$ and $2x - 5$. In this lesson, you will work with linear binomials in x and y, such as $x + y$ and $3x - 2y$. You can use multiplication and the Distributive Property to *expand* linear binomials in x and y that are raised to a power.

$$\begin{aligned}(x + y)^4 &= (x + y)^2(x + y)^2 \\ &= (\mathbf{x^2 + 2xy + y^2})(x^2 + 2xy + y^2) \\ &= \mathbf{x^2}(x^2 + 2xy + y^2) + \mathbf{2xy}(x^2 + 2xy + y^2) + \mathbf{y^2}(x^2 + 2xy + y^2) \\ &= x^4 + 2x^3y + x^2y^2 + 2x^3y + 4x^2y^2 + 2xy^3 + x^2y^2 + 2xy^3 + y^4 \\ &= x^4 + 4x^3y + 6x^2y^2 + 4xy^3 + y^4\end{aligned}$$

Activity

Exploring the Binomial Theorem

You will need: no special tools

The table below shows the expansions of the first three nonnegative integral powers of $x + y$.

1. Copy the table at right.
2. Expand $(x + y)^3$ by multiplying $(x + y)^2$ by $(x + y)$. Add a row to the bottom of the table, and write the full expansion.

Product	Expansion
$(x + y)^0 =$	1
$(x + y)^1 =$	$1x + 1y$
$(x + y)^2 =$	$1x^2 + 2xy + 1y^2$

3. Expand $(x + y)^4$ by multiplying $(x + y)^3$ by $(x + y)$. Write the full expansion below the row from Step 2.
4. Expand $(x + y)^5$ by multiplying $(x + y)^4$ by $(x + y)$. Write the full expansion below the row from Step 3.

CHECKPOINT ✔

5. Write conjectures about the number of terms and about symmetry in the terms of the expansion in any row of the table. Verify your conjecture by filling in the row that would follow Step 4.

Notice that each row of Pascal's triangle also gives you the coefficients for the expansion of $(x + y)^n$ for positive integers n.

The Binomial Theorem stated below enables you to expand a power of a binomial. Notice that the Binomial Theorem makes use of the number of combinations of n objects taken r at a time. Recall from Lesson 10.3 that the notation $\binom{n}{k}$ indicates the combination ${}_nC_k$.

Binomial Theorem

Let n be a positive integer.

$$(x+y)^n = \sum_{k=0}^{n} \binom{n}{k} x^{n-k}y^k$$

$$= \binom{n}{0}x^n y^0 + \binom{n}{1}x^{n-1}y^1 + \cdots + \binom{n}{n-1}x^1 y^{n-1} + \binom{n}{n}x^0 y^n$$

EXAMPLE 1 **Expand $(x + y)^7$.**

SOLUTION

Write the expansion. Then evaluate ${}_nC_k$ for each value of k.

$(x + y)^7$

$$= \binom{7}{0}x^7y^0 + \binom{7}{1}x^6y^1 + \binom{7}{2}x^5y^2 + \binom{7}{3}x^4y^3 + \binom{7}{4}x^3y^4 + \binom{7}{5}x^2y^5 + \binom{7}{6}x^1y^6 + \binom{7}{7}x^0y^7$$

$$= 1x^7y^0 + 7x^6y^1 + 21x^5y^2 + 35x^4y^3 + 35x^3y^4 + 21x^2y^5 + 7x^1y^6 + 1x^0y^7$$

Thus, $(x + y)^7 = x^7 + 7x^6y + 21x^5y^2 + 35x^4y^3 + 35x^3y^4 + 21x^2y^5 + 7xy^6 + y^7$.

Keystroke Guide, page 761

CHECK

Use the sequence command of a graphics calculator to check the coefficients of your answer. Use the right arrow button to view all of the coefficients. Note that ${}_nC_r$ notation is used.

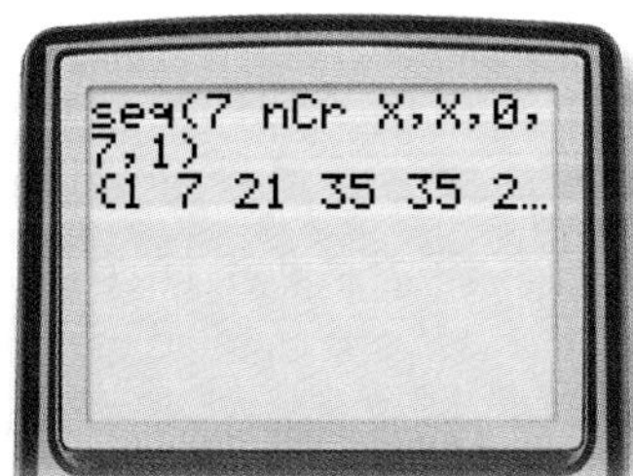

TRY THIS Expand $(m + n)^6$.

CHECKPOINT ✔ Write the power of the binomial $m + n$ given by the expansion $m^8 + 8m^7n + 28m^6n^2 + 56m^5n^3 + 70m^4n^4 + 56m^3n^5 + 28m^2n^6 + 8mn^7 + n^8$.

EXAMPLE 2

APPLICATION
SPORTS

Refer to the batting situation described at the beginning of the lesson.

If Jose Guillen were to maintain his 0.337 average, what is the probability that Jose Guillen would get exactly 4 hits in the next 5 at bats?

SOLUTION

$P(\text{getting a hit}) = 0.337 \qquad P(\text{not getting a hit}) = 0.663$

Use the Binomial Theorem because there are only two possible outcomes.

Substitute 0.337 for x and 0.663 for y in $(x + y)^n$. The number of times at bat, 5, is the exponent.

$$(0.337 + 0.663)^5 = \binom{5}{0}(0.337)^5 + \binom{5}{1}(\mathbf{0.337})^4(0.663) + \binom{5}{2}(0.337)^3(0.663)^2 + \binom{5}{3}(0.337)^2(0.663)^3 + \binom{5}{4}(0.337)(0.663)^4 + \binom{5}{5}(0.663)^5$$

Because you are looking for the probability of 4 *hits*, evaluate the term in which $(\mathbf{0.337})^4$ appears.

$$\binom{5}{1}(0.337)^4(0.663) \approx 0.04$$

Thus, if Jose Guillen maintains his 0.337 batting average in the current season, he has approximately a 4% chance of getting exactly 4 hits in the next 5 at bats.

TRY THIS What is the probability that Jose Guillen will get exactly 2 hits in the next 4 at bats?

EXAMPLE 3

Find the fifth term in the expansion of $(x + y)^{10}$.

SOLUTION

1. Use $(x + y)^n = \sum_{k=0}^{n} \binom{n}{k} x^{n-k}y^k$ to identify n and k.

   For the expansion of $(x + y)^{10}$, $n = 10$.

   For the fifth term, $k = 4$ because k begins at 0.

2. Evaluate $\binom{n}{k}x^{n-k}y^k$ for $n = 10$ and $k = 4$.

$$\binom{n}{k}x^{n-k}y^k = \binom{10}{4}x^{10-4}y^4$$
$$= 210x^6y^4$$

Thus, the fifth term in the expansion of $(x + y)^{10}$ is $210x^6y^4$.

TRY THIS Find the sixth term in the expansion of $(r + s)^8$.

CHECKPOINT ✔ Explain why the expansion of $(x + y)^{12}$ cannot have a term containing x^6y^7. Explain why $24a^4b^5$ cannot be a term in the expansion of $(a + b)^9$.

You can apply the Binomial Theorem to the expansion of a sum or difference of two monomials, as shown in Example 4.

EXAMPLE 4 **Expand $(2x - 3y)^4$.**

SOLUTION

Write $(2x - 3y)^4$ as $[2x + (-3y)]^4$.

$$[2x + (-3y)]^4$$
$$= \binom{4}{0}(2x)^4(-3y)^0 + \binom{4}{1}(2x)^3(-3y)^1 + \binom{4}{2}(2x)^2(-3y)^2 + \binom{4}{3}(2x)^1(-3y)^3 + \binom{4}{4}(2x)^0(-3y)^4$$
$$= 1(2x)^4(-3y)^0 + 4(2x)^3(-3y)^1 + 6(2x)^2(-3y)^2 + 4(2x)^1(-3y)^3 + 1(2x)^0(-3y)^4$$
$$= 1(16x^4)(1) + 4(8x^3)(-3y) + 6(4x^2)(9y^2) + 4(2x)(-27y^3) + 1(1)(81y^4)$$
$$= 16x^4 - 96x^3y + 216x^2y^2 - 216xy^3 + 81y^4$$

TRY THIS Expand $(x - 2y)^5$.

CRITICAL THINKING Can you apply the Binomial Theorem to $\left(\frac{1}{a} + \frac{1}{b}\right)^4$? What is the result?

EXAMPLE 5 A cube has dimensions of $s \cdot s \cdot s$.

Describe all of the pieces that need to be added in order to increase the cube's length, width, and height by 0.1 unit each.

SOLUTION

The expansion of $(s + 0.1)^3$ is shown below.

$$(s + 0.1)^3 = 1s^3(0.1)^0 + 3s^2(0.1)^1 + 3s^1(0.1)^2 + 1s^0(0.1)^3$$

The pieces indicated by this expansion are listed below:

$1s^3(0.1)^0$: 1 piece with dimensions of $s \cdot s \cdot s$ (the original cube)

$3s^2(0.1)^1$: 3 pieces with dimensions of $s \cdot s \cdot (0.1)$

$3s^1(0.1)^2$: 3 pieces with dimensions of $s \cdot (0.1) \cdot (0.1)$

$1s^0(0.1)^3$: 1 piece with dimensions of $(0.1) \cdot (0.1) \cdot (0.1)$

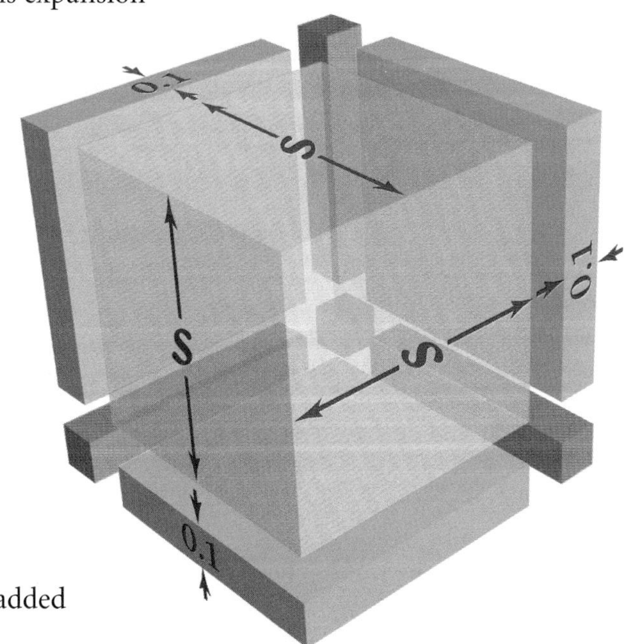

Thus, 7 pieces need to be added to the original cube.

Exercises

Communicate

1. Describe the connection between Pascal's triangle and the Binomial Theorem.

2. Explain how to use the Binomial Theorem to find the fourth term in the expansion of $(x + y)^6$.

3. Explain how to use a binomial expansion to find the probability of exactly 7 heads appearing in a total of 10 coin tosses.

Guided Skills Practice

4. Expand $(a + b)^5$. ***(EXAMPLE 1)***

APPLICATION

5. **METEOROLOGY** If there is a 0.30 probability of rain for each of the next 5 days, what is the probability of it raining exactly 3 out of the 5 days? ***(EXAMPLE 2)***

6. Find the fourth term in the expansion of $(a + b)^{10}$. ***(EXAMPLE 3)***

7. Expand $(3x - 2y)^5$. ***(EXAMPLE 4)***

CONNECTION

8. **GEOMETRY** Refer to Example 5. Describe all of the pieces that need to be added to the cube in order to increase the length, width, and height by 0.2 unit each. ***(EXAMPLE 5)***

Practice and Apply

Expand each binomial raised to a power.

9. $(a + b)^5$ **10.** $(p + q)^6$ **11.** $(a + b)^8$

12. $(p + q)^7$ **13.** $(x + y)^4$ **14.** $(x + y)^5$

15. $(2 + x)^5$ **16.** $(y + 3)^4$ **17.** $(y + 4)^9$

18. $(6 + x)^6$ **19.** $(x - y)^4$ **20.** $(x - y)^5$

Write each summation as a binomial raised to a power. Then write it in expanded form.

21. $\sum_{k=0}^{4} \binom{4}{k} a^{4-k} b^k$ **22.** $\sum_{k=0}^{6} \binom{6}{k} a^{6-k} b^k$

23. $\sum_{k=0}^{5} \binom{5}{k} a^{5-k} b^k$ **24.** $\sum_{k=0}^{8} \binom{8}{k} a^{8-k} b^k$

25. $\sum_{k=0}^{9} \binom{9}{k} x^{9-k} y^k$ **26.** $\sum_{k=0}^{7} \binom{7}{k} x^{7-k} y^k$

For the expansion of $(r + s)^9$, find the indicated term.

27. third term
28. fifth term
29. sixth term
30. second term

For the expansion of $(x + 4)^8$, find the indicated term.

31. fourth term
32. sixth term
33. seventh term
34. fifth term

For the expansion of $(x - y)^7$, find the indicated term.

35. fifth term
36. fourth term
37. sixth term
38. third term

Expand each binomial.

39. $(4a + 3b)^5$
40. $(a + 2b)^4$
41. $(x - 2y)^4$
42. $(2x - y)^5$
43. $(2x + 3)^4$
44. $(x + 3y)^4$
45. $(3x + 2y)^5$
46. $(-x + 2y)^4$
47. $\left(\frac{1}{2}x + \frac{1}{3}y\right)^3$
48. $\left(\frac{2}{3}x + \frac{1}{2}y\right)^4$
49. $(0.7 + x)^4$
50. $(y + 1.2)^5$

51. Find the eighth term in the expansion of $(p + q)^{14}$.

52. How many terms are in the expansion of $(x + y)^{18}$?

53. In the expansion of $(a + b)^{10}$, a certain term contains b^3. What is the exponent of a in this term? What is the term?

54. In the expansion of $(x + y)^{15}$, a certain term contains x^{10}. What is the exponent of y in this term? What is the term?

55. The term $36a^7b^2$ appears in the expansion of $(a + b)^n$. What is the value of n?

56. The value $\binom{10}{7}$ appears as a coefficient of two different terms in the expansion of $(a + b)^{10}$. What are the two terms?

CHALLENGE

57. Let $a + bi = (1 + i)^{11}$, where $i = \sqrt{-1}$. Find a and b by using the Binomial Theorem.

CONNECTION

58. **GEOMETRY** The side length of a cube is a. Describe the pieces that need to be added in order to increase its length, width, and height by 0.3 unit each.

APPLICATION

59. **SPORTS** Refer to the batting problem in Example 2.

a. The probability that Guillen will get at most 3 hits in the next 5 at bats is given by the sum of the last four terms of the expansion of (0.337 + 0.663)5. Find this probability to the nearest hundredth.

b. Find the probability that Guillen will get at least 3 hits in the next 5 at bats.

APPLICATIONS

SPORTS If Guillen goes into a slump and his batting average drops to 0.285, what would be the probability of each event below?

60. exactly 3 hits in the next 6 at bats

CHALLENGE

61. at least 3 hits in the next 6 at bats

METEOROLOGY If there is a 20% probability of rain for each of the next 7 days, what is the probability of each event below?

62. It will rain exactly 1 of the next 7 days.

63. It will rain at least 1 of the next 7 days.

64. It will rain each of the next 7 days.

65. It will not rain each of the next 7 days.

Look Back

APPLICATION

66. ENTERTAINMENT Ricardo won a \$100 gift certificate to a movie theater. The gift certificate can be used for movie tickets, at the snack bar, and in the arcade. Tickets for evening shows cost \$7.50 and tickets for matinees cost \$4. ***(LESSON 3.3)***

a. Write an inequality that describes the total value of x tickets at \$7.50 and y tickets at \$4 that Ricardo could purchase with his gift certificate.
b. Graph the inequality.
c. Describe the values of the variables that are meaningful for this situation.
d. What is the maximum number of \$7.50 tickets he can buy?
e. What is the maximum number of \$4 tickets he can buy?
f. Identify three reasonable solutions of the inequality.

CONNECTION

MAXIMUM/MINIMUM Maximize and minimize each objective function within the given constraints. ***(LESSON 3.5)***

67. $S = 10x + 3y$

$$\begin{cases} 0 \le x \le 10 \\ y \ge 5 \\ y \le -0.3x + 10 \end{cases}$$

68. $I = 100m + 160a$

$$\begin{cases} m + a \le 100 \\ 4m + 6m \le 500 \\ 20m + 10a \le 1600 \\ m \ge 0 \\ a \ge 0 \end{cases}$$

Classify the conic section defined by each equation, and sketch its graph. ***(LESSONS 9.2, 9.3, 9.4, AND 9.5)***

69. $4x^2 + 9y^2 = 36$

70. $\frac{x^2}{100} + \frac{y^2}{36} = 1$

71. $x = y^2 - 6y + 5$

72. $y = -x^2 + 5x + 6$

73. $(x + 2)^2 + (y - 5)^2 = 10$

74. $3x^2 - 2y^2 = 30$

Look Beyond

75. Expand the expression $(x + y + z)^3$.

OVER THE EDGE

Notice the stack of 4 congruent tiles on the desk shown at right. What do you think is the maximum distance that each tile can be extended beyond the tile beneath it without falling over?

Activity 1

All of the weight of an object can be considered to be concentrated at a single point called the *center of gravity*. The Portfolio Activity on page 706 involved slowly sliding a 12-inch ruler over the edge of a desk to find its center of gravity, or balance point, which is located at the 6-inch mark. Use a 12-inch wooden ruler and a quarter for this activity.

1. Tape a quarter to the ruler at the locations described in the table below. Determine the center of gravity for the ruler with the quarter taped at each location. Record your results.

Location of the quarter	none	1 in.	2 in.	3 in.	4 in.	5 in.	6 in.
Location of the center of gravity	6 in.						

2. Let n represent the location of the quarter, and let c represent the location of the center of gravity for the ruler with the quarter. Write a recursive formula and an explicit formula for the sequence that models the relationship between the location of the quarter and the location of the center of gravity for the ruler with the quarter.

Activity 2

1. Place all of the tiles in a stack that is aligned with the edge of the desk so that the center of gravity is above 0. Extend tile A beyond the edge of tile B so that $\frac{1}{2}$ of its length is hanging over the edge of tile B. Now the center of gravity for tile A is located $\frac{1}{2}$ of a tile length to the right of 0.

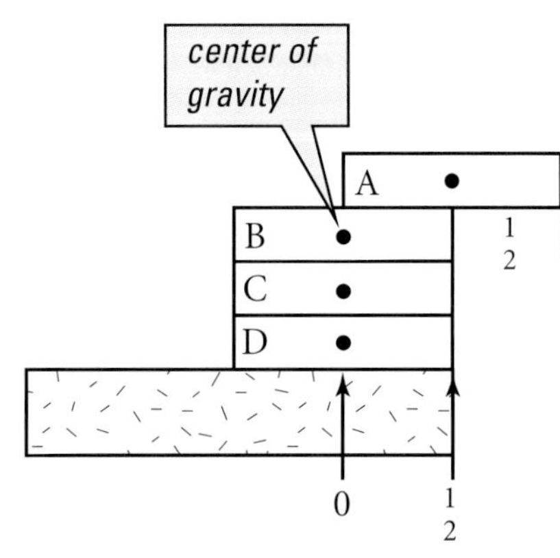

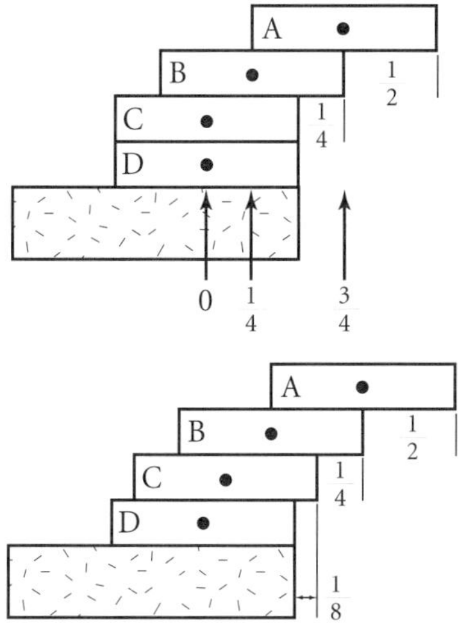

2. While keeping the same position of tile A on tile B, extend tile B so that $\frac{1}{4}$ of its length is hanging over the edge of tile C. The center of gravity for tile A is now $\frac{1}{4} + \frac{1}{2}$, or $\frac{3}{4}$, of a tile length to the right of 0, and the center of gravity for tile B is $\frac{1}{4}$ of a tile length to the right of 0.
3. While keeping the same position of tile A on tile B and tile B on tile C, extend tile C so that $\frac{1}{8}$ of its length is hanging over the edge of tile D. What is the center of gravity for tile A in this position? for tile B? for tile C?
4. Using summation notation, write a geometric series that models the shift in the center of gravity for tile A as each of these extensions is made.

Activity 3

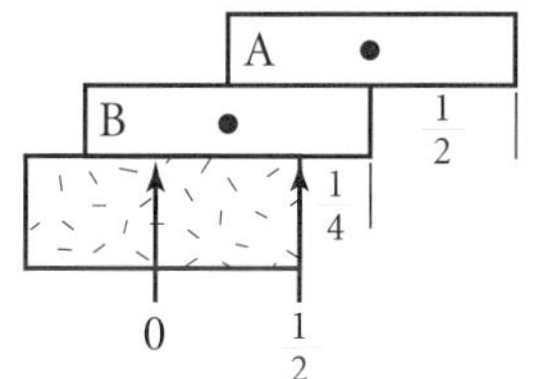

The center of gravity for an entire stack of tiles is the average of the centers of gravity for each tile in the stack. For example, the center of gravity for the 2-tile stack shown at left is to the right of 0 by the following fraction of a tile length:

$$\frac{\left(\frac{1}{2}+\frac{1}{4}\right)+\frac{1}{4}}{2} = \frac{1}{2}$$

The edge of the desk is $\frac{1}{2}$ of a tile length to the right of 0. If the center of gravity for a stack of tiles is less than or equal to $\frac{1}{2}$ of a tile length to the right of 0, then the stack will remain balanced. Since $\frac{1}{2} \leq \frac{1}{2}$, the 2-tile stack remains balanced.
Let n represent the tile number, where $n = 1$ represents the top tile (A), $n = 2$ represents the next tile (B), and so on. Let x represent the fraction of a tile length that the tile extends beyond the tile directly below it. Then the equation $x = \frac{1}{2n}$ models the pattern of tile extensions.

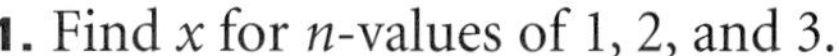

1. Find x for n-values of 1, 2, and 3.
2. Show that the 3-tile stack described by your results in Step 1 remains balanced. Is each stack extended the maximum distance while maintaining the stack's balance?
3. Find x for n-values of 4, 5, and 6.
4. Show that the 6-tile stack described by your results from Steps 1 and 3 remains balanced. Is each tile extended the maximum distance while maintaining the stack's balance?
5. Using summation notation, write a series that models the shift in the center of gravity for the top tile as each of the extensions described in Steps 1 and 3 are made.
6. Place 6 tiles in the position described by your results above. Does the 6-tile stack remain balanced? Describe the relationship between the mathematical results and your experimental results.

11

Chapter Review and Assessment

VOCABULARY

Key Skills & Exercises

LESSON 11.1

Key Skills

Find the terms of a sequence.

You can represent a sequence as follows:

- ordered pairs in a table

n	1	2	3	...
t_n	2	5	8	...

- a list $\{2, 5, 8, \dots\}$
- an explicit formula $t_n = 3n - 1$
- a recursive formula $t_1 = 2$, $t_n = t_{n-1} + 3$, where $n > 2$

Write the first three terms of the sequence defined by the explicit formula $t_n = 2n + 1$.

$$t_1 = 2(1) + 1 = 3$$
$$t_2 = 2(2) + 1 = 5$$
$$t_3 = 2(3) + 1 = 7$$

Write the first three terms of the sequence defined by the recursive formula $t_1 = 4$ and $t_n = 3t_{n-1} - 1$.

$$t_1 = 4$$
$$t_2 = 3(4) - 1 = 11$$
$$t_3 = 3(11) - 1 = 32$$

Evaluate the sum of a series expressed in sigma notation.

Evaluate $\sum_{k=1}^{8}(k^2 + 3k + 1)$.

$$\sum_{k=1}^{8}(k^2 + 3k + 1) = \sum_{k=1}^{8} k^2 + 3\sum_{k=1}^{8} k + \sum_{k=1}^{8} 1$$
$$= \frac{8 \cdot 9 \cdot 17}{6} + 3\left(\frac{8 \cdot 9}{2}\right) + 8$$
$$= 204 + 108 + 8 = 320$$

Exercises

Write the first five terms of each sequence.

1. $t_n = 2n + 3$
2. $t_n = 3n - 4$
3. $t_n = -0.2n + 0.1$
4. $t_n = -2.22n + 1.3$
5. $t_1 = 1$, $t_n = 2t_{n-1} + 2$
6. $t_1 = 1$, $t_n = 5t_{n-1} - 2$
7. $t_1 = 3$, $t_n = -3t_{n-1} + 1$
8. $t_1 = 2$, $t_n = -4t_{n-1} - 3$

Evaluate.

9. $\sum_{k=1}^{5} 6$
10. $\sum_{m=1}^{10} -5$
11. $\sum_{k=1}^{8} -3k$
12. $\sum_{k=1}^{6} 2k$
13. $\sum_{k=1}^{6}(2k^2 + k + 2)$
14. $\sum_{k=1}^{7}(3k^2 + 4k + 2)$

LESSON 11.2

Key Skills

Find the indicated term of an arithmetic sequence.

Find the fifth term of the arithmetic sequence in which $t_1 = 2$ and $t_n = t_{n-1} + 3$.

$$t_n = t_1 + (n - 1)d$$
$$t_5 = 2 + (5 - 1)3 \quad n = 5,\ t_1 = 2, \text{ and } d = 3$$
$$t_5 = 14$$

Find arithmetic means between two nonconsecutive terms.

Find three arithmetic means between 10 and 18.

10, _?_, _?_, _?_, 18

Substitute 10 for t_1, 18 for t_n, and 5 for n.

$$t_n = t_1 + (n - 1)d$$
$$18 = 10 + (5 - 1)d$$
$$d = 2$$

The three arithmetic means are 12, 14, and 16.

Exercises

Find the indicated term.

15. the sixth term of the arithmetic sequence in which $t_1 = 2$ and $t_n = t_{n-1} + 4$

16. the seventh term of the arithmetic sequence in which $t_1 = 1$ and $t_n = t_{n-1} - 2$

17. the fifth term of the arithmetic sequence in which $t_1 = -3$ and $t_n = t_{n-1} - 4$

18. the 10th term of the arithmetic sequence in which $t_1 = 3$ and $t_4 = -9$

Find the indicated arithmetic means.

19. two arithmetic means between 20 and 50

20. three arithmetic means between 100 and 180

21. four arithmetic means between −10 and −35

22. three arithmetic means between −8 and 12

LESSON 11.3

Key Skills

Find the sum of the first *n* terms of an arithmetic series.

For the series $6 + 11 + 16 + 21 + \cdots$, find S_8.

Method 1:

First find t_8.

$$t_n = t_1 + (n - 1)d$$
$$t_8 = 6 + (8 - 1)5$$
$$t_8 = 41$$

Then find S_8.

$$S_n = n\left(\frac{t_1 + t_n}{2}\right)$$
$$S_8 = 8\left(\frac{6 + 41}{2}\right)$$
$$S_8 = 188$$

Method 2:

$$S_n = n\left[\frac{2t_1 + (n - 1)d}{2}\right]$$
$$S_8 = 8\left[\frac{12 + (8 - 1)5}{2}\right]$$
$$S_8 = 188$$

Exercises

For the series $2 + 5 + 8 + 11 + \cdots$, find the indicated sum.

23. S_5

24. S_{10}

25. S_{12}

26. S_{15}

For each arithmetic series, find S_{20}.

27. $8 + 16 + 24 + 32 + \cdots$

28. $14 + 16 + 18 + 20 + 22 + \cdots$

29. $-6 + (-12) + (-18) + (-24) + (-30) + \cdots$

30. $-7 + (-5) + (-3) + (-1) + \cdots$

Evaluate.

31. $\sum_{k=1}^{5} 6k$

32. $\sum_{j=3}^{7} (2j - 5)$

33. $\sum_{k=0}^{4} (5 - 2k)$

34. $\sum_{n=1}^{30} (7 - n)$

LESSON 11.4

Key Skills

Find the indicated term of a geometric sequence.

Find the sixth term of the geometric sequence in which $t_1 = 4$ and $t_n = 2t_{n-1}$.

$$t_n = t_1 r^{n-1}$$
$$t_6 = 4 \cdot 2^{6-1}$$
$$t_6 = 128$$

Find geometric means between two nonconsecutive terms.

Find three geometric means between 10 and 2560.

10, ?, ?, ?, 2560

Substitute 10 for t_1 and 2560 for t_5.

$$t_n = t_1 r^{n-1}$$
$$2560 = 10 \cdot r^{5-1}$$
$$r = \pm 4$$

The three geometric means are 40, 160, and 640 or −40, 160, and −640.

Exercises

Find the indicated term.

35. the sixth term of the sequence in which $t_1 = -4$ and $t_n = 5t_{n-1}$

36. the fifth term of the sequence in which $t_1 = 8$ and $t_n = -3t_{n-1}$

37. the 10th term of the sequence in which $t_1 = \frac{1}{3}$ and $t_n = \frac{1}{2}t_{n-1}$

Find the indicated geometric means.

38. two geometric means between 10 and 1250

39. three geometric means between 5 and 100

40. three geometric means between 20 and 30

LESSON 11.5

Key Skills

Find the sum of the first *n* terms of a geometric series.

Find the sum of the first eight terms in the series $1 + 2 + 4 + 8 + \cdots$

Substitute 2 for r, 1 for t_1, and 8 for n.

$$S_n = t_1\left(\frac{1 - r^n}{1 - r}\right)$$
$$S_8 = 1\left(\frac{1 - 2^8}{1 - 2}\right) = 255$$

Use mathematical induction to prove statements about the natural numbers.

To prove that a statement about natural numbers is true for all natural numbers, use the principle of mathematical induction stated below.

1. Show that the statement is true for $n = 1$.
2. Assume that the statement is true for a natural number k. Then prove that it is true for the natural number $k + 1$.

Exercises

For the series $1 + 1.5 + 2.25 + 3.375 + \cdots$, find each indicated sum to the nearest tenth.

41. S_4 **42.** S_5 **43.** S_{12} **44.** S_{15}

Use the formula for the first *n* terms of a geometric series to find the sum of each geometric series. Give answers to the nearest tenth, if necessary.

45. $-1 + 10 + (-100) + 1000 + (-10{,}000)$

46. $0.4 + 4 + 40 + 400 + 4000$

47. $3 + (-6) + 12 + (-24) + 48 + (-96)$

Evaluate. Give answers to the nearest hundredth, if necessary.

48. $\sum_{p=1}^{4} \frac{1}{6}(3)^p$ **49.** $\sum_{k=5}^{8} (0.2)^{k-4}$

Use mathematical induction to prove each statement for all natural numbers, *n*.

50. $n - 1 < n$

51. $7 + 9 + 11 + \cdots + (2n + 5) = n(n + 6)$

LESSON 11.6

Key Skills

Find the sum of an infinite geometric series, if one exists.

Find the sum of the series $\sum_{k=0}^{\infty} \frac{2}{5^{k+2}}$, if it exists.

$$r = \frac{\frac{2}{125}}{\frac{2}{25}} = \frac{1}{5}$$

If a geometric sequence has common ratio r and $|r| < 1$, then the related infinite geometric series converges and has a sum.

The series converges because $|r| = \left|\frac{1}{5}\right| < 1$.

$$\sum_{k=0}^{\infty} \frac{2}{5^{k+2}} = \frac{t_1}{1-r} = \frac{\frac{2}{25}}{1-\frac{1}{5}} = \frac{1}{10}$$

Exercises

Find the sum of each infinite geometric series, if it exists.

52. $5 + \frac{5}{3} + \frac{5}{9} + \frac{5}{27} + \cdots$

53. $8 + 4 + 2 + 1 + \cdots$

54. $\frac{1}{2} + \left(-\frac{1}{4}\right) + \frac{1}{8} + \left(-\frac{1}{16}\right) + \cdots$

55. $0.5 + 0.05 + 0.005 + 0.0005 + \cdots$

56. $\sum_{k=1}^{\infty} \left(\frac{1}{3}\right)^k$ **57.** $\sum_{k=1}^{\infty} \left(\frac{1}{6}\right)^k$ **58.** $\sum_{k=1}^{\infty} 4^k$

59. $\sum_{k=0}^{\infty} \left(\frac{3}{7}\right)^k$ **60.** $\sum_{k=0}^{\infty} \left(\frac{5}{6}\right)^k$ **61.** $\sum_{k=0}^{\infty} \left(\frac{5}{4}\right)^k$

Write each decimal as a fraction in simplest form.

62. $0.\overline{620}$ **63.** $0.\overline{032}$

LESSON 11.7

Key Skills

Find entries in Pascal's triangle.

Find the seventh entry in row 11 of Pascal's triangle.

The kth entry in the nth row is ${}_nC_{k-1}$.

$$ {}_{11}C_{7-1} = {}_{11}C_6 = \frac{11!}{5!6!} = 462$$

Exercises

Find each entry of Pascal's triangle.

64. sixth entry of row 9

65. eighth entry of row 10

66. fifth entry of row 8

67. fourth entry of row 6

Use Pascal's triangle to find probabilities.

Find the probability that exactly 1 heads *or* exactly 2 heads appears when a coin is tossed 5 times.

Number of possible outcomes $= 2^5$

Probability of exactly 1 heads $= \frac{{}_5C_1}{2^5}$

Probability of exactly 2 heads $= \frac{{}_5C_2}{2^5}$

$$P(1 \text{ heads } or \text{ 2 heads}) = \frac{{}_5C_1}{2^5} + \frac{{}_5C_2}{2^5} \approx 0.47$$

Find the probability of each event.

68. exactly 4 heads when a coin is tossed 4 times

69. exactly 3 tails when a coin is tossed 8 times

70. more than 6 tails when a coin is tossed 8 times

71. exactly 2 *or* exactly 4 heads when a coin is tossed 6 times

LESSON 11.8

Key Skills

Use the Binomial Theorem to expand a binomial raised to a power.

Expand $(a + b)^4$.

$$(a+b)^n = \sum_{k=0}^{n} \binom{n}{k} a^{n-k} b^k$$

$$(a+b)^4 = \binom{4}{0} a^4 b^0 + \binom{4}{1} a^3 b^1 + \binom{4}{2} a^2 b^2 + \binom{4}{3} a^1 b^3 + \binom{4}{4} a^0 b^4$$

$$= a^4 b^0 + 4a^3 b^1 + 6a^2 b^2 + 4a^1 b^3 + a^0 b^4$$

Find a term in a binomial expansion.

Find the seventh term in the expansion of $(a + b)^9$.

For the expansion of $(a + b)^9$, $n = 9$.

For the seventh term, $k = 6$.

$$\binom{n}{k} x^{n-k} y^k = \binom{9}{6} a^3 b^6 = 84a^3 b^6$$

Exercises

Expand each binomial raised to a power.

72. $(5 + y)^4$

73. $(a + 3)^5$

74. $(2x - 2y)^5$

75. $(3x - y)^6$

76. Find the sixth term in the expansion of $(x + y)^7$.

77. Find the eighth term in the expansion of $(a + b)^{10}$.

Write each summation as a binomial raised to a power. Then write it in expanded form.

78. $\sum_{k=0}^{5} \binom{5}{k} a^{5-k} b^k$

79. $\sum_{k=0}^{6} \binom{6}{k} a^{6-k} b^k$

Applications

80. INVESTMENTS Yolanda deposits $1000 in a bank at the beginning of every year for 8 years. Her account earns 8% interest compounded annually. How much is in the account after the last deposit?

81. PHYSICS A ball is dropped from a height of 12 meters. Each time it bounces, it rebounds $\frac{2}{3}$ of the distance it has fallen.

a. How far will it rebound after the third bounce?

b. Theoretically, what is the vertical distance that the ball will travel before coming to rest?

82. MERCHANDISING Boxes are stacked in a display of 21 rows with 2 boxes in the top row, 5 boxes in the second row, 8 boxes in the third row, and so on. How many boxes are there?

83. ENTERTAINMENT A theater has 18 seats in the front row. Each succeeding row has 4 more seats than the row ahead of it. How many seats are there in the first 12 rows? 20 rows?

84. REAL ESTATE A 5-year lease for an apartment calls for a rent of $500 per month the first year with an increase of 6% for each remaining year of the lease. What will be the monthly rent during the last year of the lease?

11 Alternative Assessment

Performance Assessment

1. **ARITHMETIC SEQUENCES**
   a. Create an arithmetic sequence, and give the first seven terms.
   b. Define your sequence with an explicit formula and find the 10th term.
   c. Define your sequence with a recursive formula and find the 20th term.
   d. Explain the difference between an explicit formula and a recursive formula.
2. **SPLITTING STOCK** Jeanine owns 20 shares of stock. If her stock splits, she receives 2 shares for every share she owns.
   a. Write an infinite sequence that represents the number of shares she owns after repeated stock splits.
   b. What type of sequence did you write?
   c. Write a formula for the nth term of this sequence and graph your formula.
   d. How many shares does Jeanine own after 5 stock splits? 10 stock splits?
3. **GEOMETRIC SEQUENCES AND SERIES** A person wearing contact lenses is told to wear them for 3 hours on the first day and for $\frac{1}{2}$ hour longer on each succeeding day.
   a. Write this finite sequence with an explicit formula and a recursive formula.
   b. After how many days can the contacts be worn for 12 hours?

Portfolio Projects

1. **HARMONIC SEQUENCES AND SERIES** When the reciprocals of a sequence, such as $1, \frac{1}{2}, \frac{1}{3}, \frac{1}{4}, \ldots,$ form an arithmetic sequence, the sequence is called a harmonic sequence.
   a. Write the related arithmetic sequence.
   b. Write the related harmonic series in sigma notation.
   c. Create your own harmonic sequence and repeat Steps **a** and **b**.
2. **RESEARCHING MEANS** In mathematics, there are three means defined for a pair of numbers, a and b. They are the arithmetic, geometric, and harmonic means. Research these means and answer each question below.
   a. How is each mean defined?
   b. How is each mean used?
   c. How are the means ordered according to size?
3. **PASCAL'S TRIANGLE** The numbers in a row of Pascal's triangle can be used to generate the next row of numbers, as shown below.

$$\begin{array}{r} 1\ 2\ 1 \\ +\ \ 1\ 2\ 1 \\ \hline 1\ 3\ 3\ 1 \end{array}$$

   Starting with the number 1 in row 0, generate rows 1 through 7 by using this procedure.

internetconnect

The HRW Web site contains many resources to reinforce and expand your knowledge of series and sequences. This Web site also provides Internet links to other sites where you can find information and real-world data for use in research projects, reports, and activities that involve series and sequences. Visit the HRW Web site at **go.hrw.com,** and enter the keyword **MB1 CH11** to access the resources for this chapter.

College Entrance Exam Practice

QUANTITATIVE COMPARISON For Items 1–5, write
A if the quantity in Column A is greater than the quantity in Column B;
B if the quantity in Column B is greater than the quantity in Column A;
C if the quantities are equal; or
D if the relationship cannot be determined from the given information.

	Column A	Column B	Answers
1.	$f(x) = x - 5$, $g(x) = 3x$ $(f \circ g)(3)$	$(g \circ f)(3)$	(A) (B) (C) (D) [Lesson 2.4]
2.	${}_{10}C_2$	${}_{10}C_8$	(A) (B) (C) (D) [Lesson 10.3]
3.	$(5 - 2i)(5 + 2i)$	$6i^2 \cdot 7i^2$	(A) (B) (C) (D) [Lesson 5.6]
4.	The probability of the event rolling an odd number on one roll of a six-sided number cube	rolling a 1, 2, or 3 on one roll of a six-sided number cube	(A) (B) (C) (D) [Lesson 10.1]
5.	The value of x $\begin{cases} 2x + 3y = 21 \\ x - 2y = -7 \end{cases}$	$\begin{cases} -2x + y = 8 \\ 5x - 3y = -21 \end{cases}$	(A) (B) (C) (D) [Lesson 3.1]

6. Which function represents the graph of $f(x) = |x|$ translated 3 units to the right? ***(LESSON 2.7)***

a. $g(x) = |x - 3|$ **b.** $g(x) = |x + 3|$
c. $g(x) = |x| - 3$ **d.** $g(x) = |x| + 3$

7. Solve $|4t - 7| = 5t + 2$. ***(LESSON 1.8)***

a. 9 **b.** −9 **c.** $\frac{5}{9}$ **d.** $9, -\frac{5}{9}$

8. Evaluate $-5^3 - 2 \cdot 3^2 \div 6$. ***(LESSON 2.1)***

a. 122 **b.** −128 **c.** −122 **d.** −23

9. What are the coordinates of the vertex of the graph of $y = -x^2 + 2$? ***(LESSON 5.1)***

a. $(-1, 2)$ **b.** $(0, -2)$
c. $(-1, -2)$ **d.** $(0, 2)$

10. Find the slope of the line that contains $(-2, 5)$ and $(-5, -4)$. ***(LESSON 1.2)***

a. $\frac{1}{3}$ **b.** −3 **c.** 3 **d.** $-\frac{1}{3}$

11. Which single equation represents the pair of parametric equations $\begin{cases} x(t) = 2 + t \\ y(t) = 3 + t \end{cases}$? ***(LESSON 3.6)***

a. $y = x - 1$ **b.** $y = -x - 1$
c. $y = x + 1$ **d.** $y = -x + 1$

12. What is the domain of $g(x) = -\frac{1}{2}x^2 - 4$? ***(LESSON 2.3)***

a. $x > 0$ **b.** all real numbers
c. $x > -4$ **d.** $x < -4$

13. Which is the greatest monomial factor of $2(6x^2 - 14x)$? ***(LESSON 5.3)***

a. 2 **b.** 4 **c.** $2x$ **d.** $4x$

14. The graph of which ellipse has x-intercepts of 2 and -2 and y-intercepts of 5 and -5? ***(LESSON 9.4)***

a. $\frac{x^2}{4} + \frac{y^2}{4} = 1$ **b.** $\frac{x^2}{4} - \frac{y^2}{25} = 1$

c. $\frac{x^2}{4} + \frac{y^2}{25} = 1$ **d.** $\frac{y^2}{25} - \frac{x^2}{4} = 1$

15. Which binomial is a factor of $x^3 - 3x^2 - 2x + 6$? ***(LESSON 7.3)***

a. $x^2 - 2$ **b.** $x^2 + 2$

c. $x + 3$ **d.** $x + 1$

16. Which equation represents $\log_2 \frac{1}{32} = -5$ in exponential form? ***(LESSON 6.3)***

a. $2^{-5} = \frac{1}{32}$ **b.** $2^{-5} = -32$

c. $2^{-5} = 32$ **d.** $2^{-5} = -\frac{1}{32}$

17. If y varies jointly as the cube of m and the square of n and inversely as p, which equation represents this relationship? ***(LESSON 8.1)***

a. $y = \frac{p}{m^3n^2}$ **b.** $y = \frac{km^3n^2}{p}$

c. $y = m^3n^2p$ **d.** $y = km^3n^2p$

18. Which polynomial equation has -2 and $5i$ as roots? ***(LESSON 7.4)***

a. $x^3 - 2x^2 + 25x - 50 = 0$

b. $x^3 + 2x^2 - 5x - 10 = 0$

c. $x^3 + 2x^2 + 25x + 50 = 0$

d. $x^3 - 2x^2 + 5x - 10 = 0$

19. Find the slope, m, of $x = -5$. ***(LESSON 1.2)***

20. Write the equation in slope-intercept form for the line that has a slope of $-\frac{3}{5}$ and contains the point $(-2, -5)$. ***(LESSON 1.3)***

21. Find the inverse of $\{(-1, -1), (-2, 2), (-3, 1), (0, 0)\}$. ***(LESSON 2.5)***

22. Find the zeros of $f(x) = 12x^2 - 8x - 15$. ***(LESSON 5.3)***

23. Graph $2y + x \le 6$. ***(LESSON 3.3)***

24. Find the product $\begin{bmatrix} -1 & 2 & 3 \\ 4 & -2 & 3 \end{bmatrix} \begin{bmatrix} 2 & 1 & 3 \\ -1 & -2 & -3 \\ 4 & 1 & -2 \end{bmatrix}$, if it exists. ***(LESSON 4.2)***

25. Solve $10^{-3x} = 125$ to the nearest hundredth. ***(LESSON 6.7)***

26. Factor $6x^2 - 28x - 10$, if possible. ***(LESSON 5.3)***

27. Find the 100th term of the sequence $-11, -5, 1, \ldots$ ***(LESSON 11.2)***

28. Simplify $\frac{1 - 2i}{2 + i} + 3i$. ***(LESSON 5.6)***

29. Graph $y \ge x^2 - 3x + 5$. ***(LESSON 5.8)***

30. Solve $\begin{cases} 2x - 5y = 15 \\ 3x - 7y = 22 \end{cases}$ by using a matrix equation. ***(LESSON 4.4)***

31. Write $(x - 1)^2(x^2 + 2x + 5)$ as a polynomial expression in standard form. ***(LESSON 7.3)***

32. Simplify $\frac{x^2 + 3x - 18}{2x^2 - 5x - 3} \cdot \frac{1 - 4x^2}{x^2 - 36}$. ***(LESSON 8.3)***

33. Use substitution to solve $\begin{cases} x + y = 18 \\ 4x - 4y = 5 \end{cases}$. ***(LESSON 3.1)***

FREE-RESPONSE GRID The following questions may be answered by using a free-response grid such as that commonly used by standardized-test services.

	/	/	
.	.	.	.
	0	0	0
1	1	1	1
2	2	2	2
3	3	3	3
4	4	4	4
5	5	5	5
6	6	6	6
7	7	7	7
8	8	8	8
9	9	9	9

34. Solve $\sqrt{2x - 3} = \sqrt{5x - 21}$. ***(LESSON 8.8)***

35. Evaluate $\log_{\frac{1}{3}} 27 + 3^{\log_3 5}$ ***(LESSON 6.4)***

36. Find the value of v in $-1 = \log_{10} v$. ***(LESSON 6.3)***

37. Find the perimeter to the nearest hundredth of a triangle whose vertices have the coordinates $(2, 0)$, $(0, 0)$, and $(0, -4)$. ***(LESSON 9.1)***

38. How many 4 letter arrangements can be made with the letters in *meet*? ***(LESSON 10.2)***

PHYSICS A ball is dropped from a height of 12 meters. Each time it bounces on the ground, it rebounds to $\frac{2}{3}$ the distance it has fallen.

39. How many meters will it rebound after the third bounce? ***(LESSON 11.4)***

40. Theoretically, how many meters will the ball travel before coming to rest? ***(LESSON 11.6)***

Keystroke Guide for Chapter 11

Essential keystroke sequences (using the model TI-82 or TI-83 graphics calculator) are presented below for all Activities and Examples found in this chapter that require or recommend the use of a graphics calculator.

internetconnect

Keystrokes for other models of graphics calculators are found on the HRW Web site.

LESSON 11.2

EXAMPLE 1 Page 700

Find the fifth term of the sequence defined by $t_1 = -4$ and $t_n = t_{n-1} + 3$.

(–) 4 ENTER + 3 ENTER ENTER ENTER ENTER

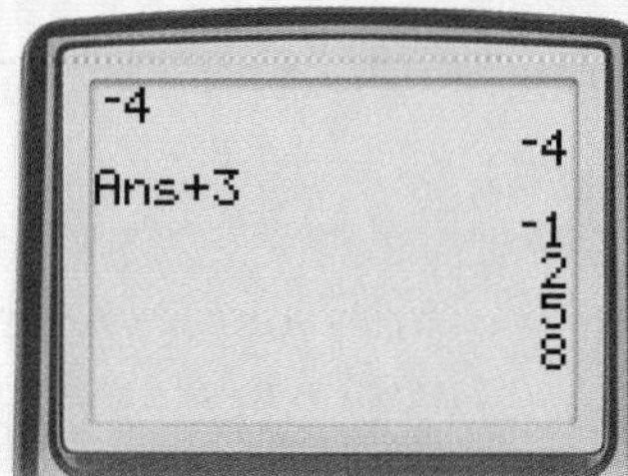

EXAMPLES 2 and 3 Page 701

For Example 2, find the fifth term of the sequence defined by $t_1 = 389.95$ and $t_n = t_{n-1} - 42.50$.

389.95 ENTER – 42.5 ENTER ENTER ENTER ENTER

Use a similar keystroke sequence for Example 3.

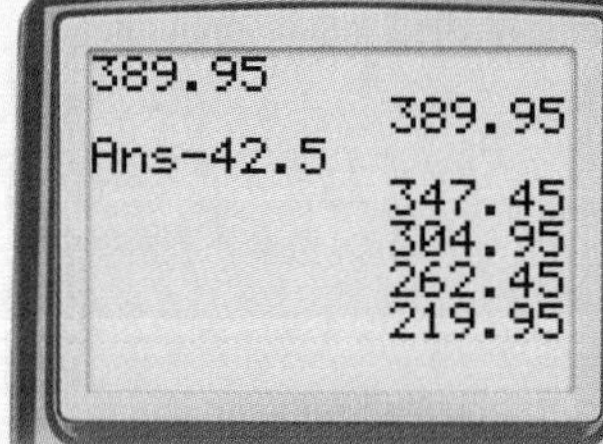

Activity Page 702

For Step 1, part a, use sequence mode to graph the sequence $t_n = 5 + 2n$ for n-values from 1 to 6.

Put the calculator in sequence and dot modes:

MODE Seq ENTER Dot ENTER 2nd MODE (QUIT)

Set the viewing window:

WINDOW (*n*Min=) 1 ENTER (*n*Max=) 6 ENTER (PlotStart=) 1 ENTER (PlotStep=) 1 ENTER (Xmin=) 0 ENTER (Xmax=) 7 ENTER (Xscl=) 1 ENTER (Ymin=) 0 ENTER (Ymax=) 20 ENTER (Yscl=) 4

TI-82:

WINDOW ENTER (U*n*Start=) 7 ENTER ENTER (*n*Start=) 1 ENTER (*n*Min=) 1 ENTER (*n*Max=) 6 ENTER (Xmin=) 0 ENTER (Xmax=) 7 ENTER (Xsc1=) 1 ENTER (Ymin=) 0 ENTER (Ymax=) 20 ENTER (Ysc1=) 4

Graph the sequence:

[Y=] (u(n)=) 5 [+] 2 [X,T,Θ,n] [ENTER] (u(nMin)=) 7 [GRAPH]

⇑TI-82: [2nd] [9] [GRAPH]

For part **b**, use the same viewing window. Use nMin = 1 and u(nMin) = 7.5.

For part **c**, change to Ymax = 40 in the viewing window. Graph the sequence by using nMin = 1 and u(nMin) = 2.

For part **d**, use Ymax = 2, Yscl = 0.5, nMin = 1, and u(nMin) = 1.

For part **e**, use Ymax = 0.4, Yscl = 0.05, nMin = 1, and u(nMin) = 0.3.

For part **f**, use Ymax = 40, Yscl = 4, nMin = 1, and u(nMin) = 1.

LESSON 11.3

EXAMPLES 1 and 2 **Find S_{15} for the series in which $t_1 = 1$ and $d = 3$.**

Pages 708 and 709

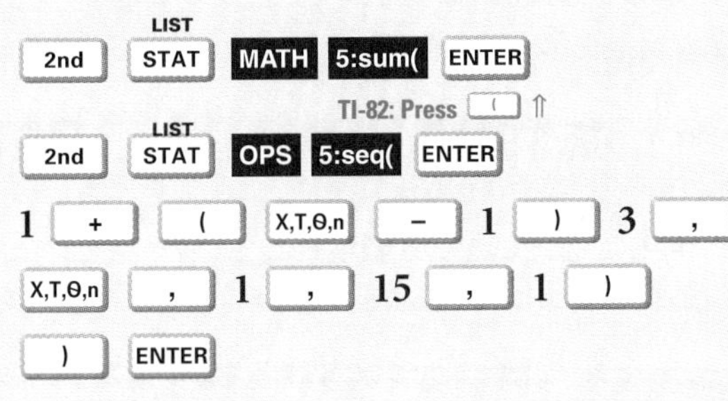

sum(seq(1+(X-1)3
,X,1,15,1))
330

Use a similar keystroke sequence for Example 2.

EXAMPLE 3 **Evaluate $\sum_{k=1}^{12} (6 - 2k)$.**

Page 709

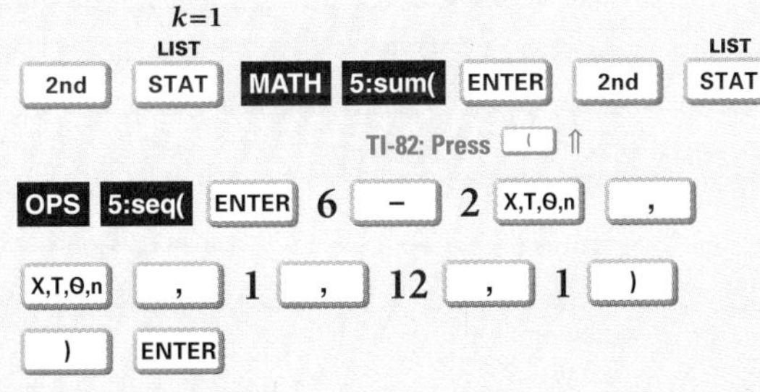

LESSON 11.4

EXAMPLES 1, 2, 3, and 4 **For Example 1, find the fifth term of the sequence defined by $t_1 = 8$ and $r = 3$.**

Pages 714–716

8 [ENTER] [×] 3 [ENTER] [ENTER] [ENTER] [ENTER]

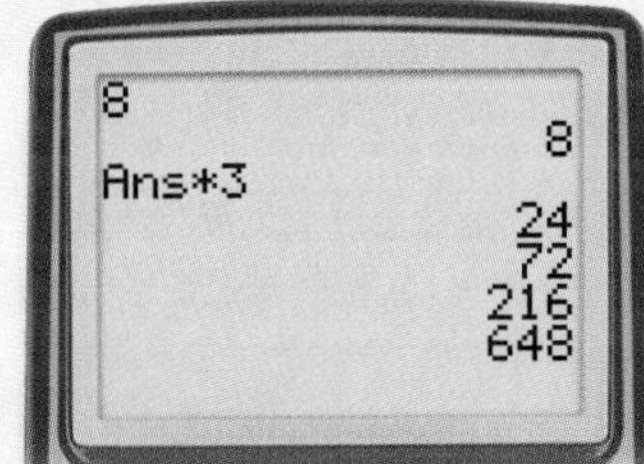

Use a similar keystroke sequence for Examples 2, 3, and 4.

Activity

Page 716

For Step 1, part a, find the first 5 terms of the geometric sequence defined by $t_1 = 1$ and $r = 10$.

1 [ENTER] [×] 10 [ENTER]

Press [ENTER] 18 more times to generate the rest of the terms.

Use a similar keystroke sequence for parts **b–f**.

LESSON 11.5

EXAMPLE 1 Page 721

Find S_{10} to the nearest tenth for the series defined by $t_1 = 3$ and $r = 1.5$.

Set the calculator to round answers to the nearest tenth:

[MODE] [FLOAT] [►] [►] [1] [ENTER] [ENTER]

Find the sum:

[2nd] [STAT] (LIST) [MATH] [5:sum(] [ENTER] [2nd] [STAT] (LIST) [OPS] [5:seq(] [ENTER]

TI-82: Press [(] ⇑

3 [×] 1.5 [^] [(] [X,T,θ,n] [–] 1 [)] [,] [X,T,θ,n] [,] 1 [,] 10 [,] 1 [)] [)] [ENTER]

EXAMPLE 3 Page 722

Evaluate $\sum_{k=1}^{6} 2(3^{k-1})$.

Be sure that your calculator is returned to the floating decimal mode setting.

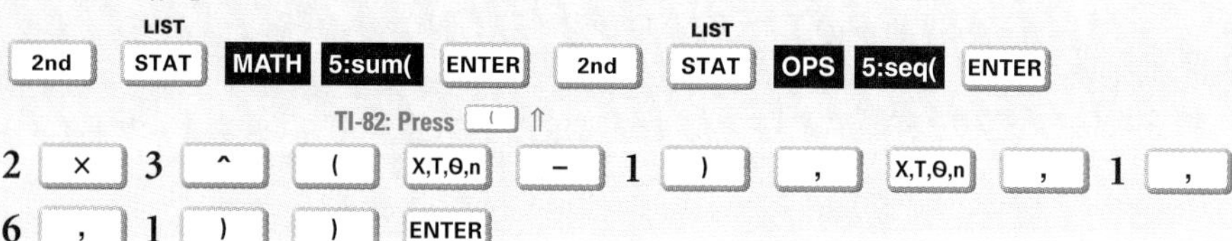

6 [,] 1 [)] [)] [ENTER]

LESSON 11.6

Page 729

For Step 1, part a, create a table of values for n and S_n for the infinite geometric series defined by $t_1 = -5$ and $r = -0.25$. Use n-values of 1, 2, 3, 5, 10, and 100.

First clear old data from Lists 1 and 2.

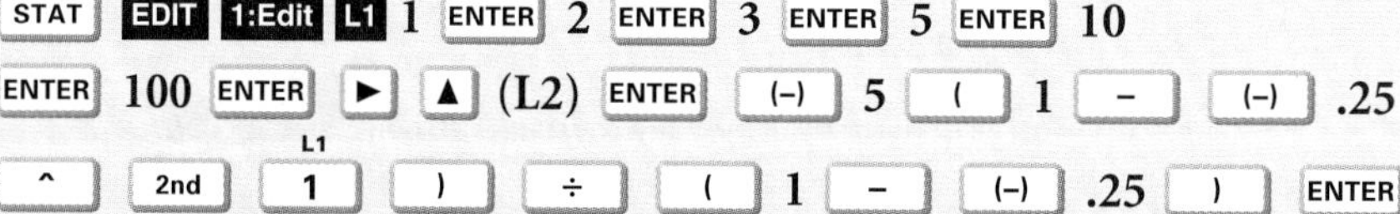

[STAT] [EDIT] [1:Edit] [L1] 1 [ENTER] 2 [ENTER] 3 [ENTER] 5 [ENTER] 10
[ENTER] 100 [ENTER] [►] [▲] (L2) [ENTER] [(–)] 5 [(] 1 [–] [(–)] .25
[^] [2nd] [1] (L1) [)] [÷] [(] 1 [–] [(–)] .25 [)] [ENTER]

Use a similar keystroke sequence for Step 1, parts **b–d**, and for Step 2.

EXAMPLES 1 and 2 For Example 1, graph the formula for the sum of n terms of the geometric series in which $t_1 = 3$ and $r = 0.4$.

Pages 730 and 731

Be sure that your calculator is returned to function mode.

Use friendly viewing window [0, 28.2] by [0, 10].

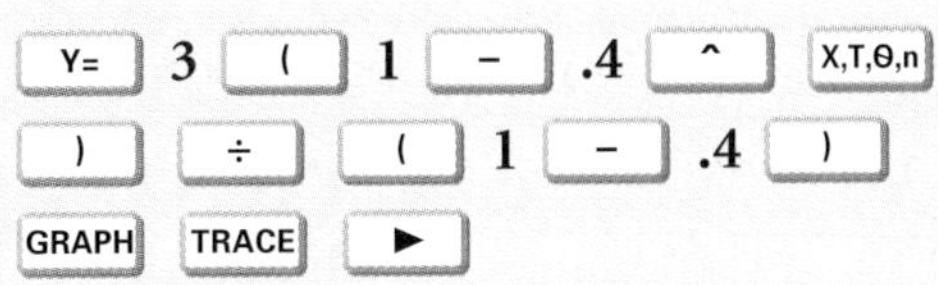

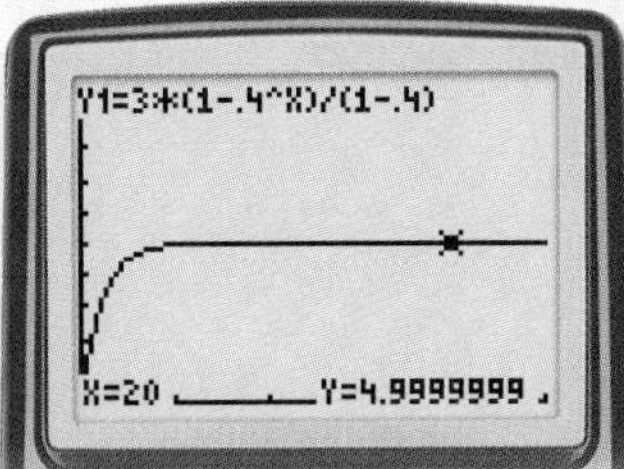

Use a similar keystroke sequence for Example 2. Use friendly viewing window [0, 28.2] by [0, 0.5].

LESSON 11.7

EXAMPLE 1 To find the 4th and 10th entries in row 12 of Pascal's triangle, evaluate $_{12}C_3$ and $_{12}C_9$.

Page 737

12 MATH PRB 3:nCr ENTER 3 ENTER

12 MATH PRB 3:nCr ENTER 9 ENTER

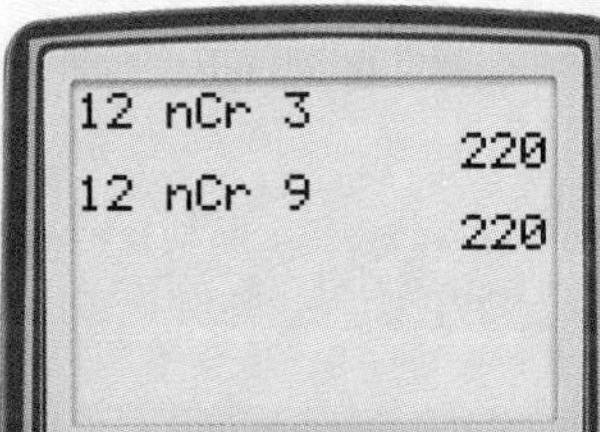

EXAMPLE 3 Evaluate $\frac{_7C_3}{2^7} + \frac{_7C_4}{2^7}$.

Page 738

(7 MATH PRB 3:nCr ENTER 3)

÷ (2 ^ 7) + (

7 MATH PRB 3:nCr ENTER 4) ÷

(2 ^ 7) ENTER

LESSON 11.8

EXAMPLE 1 Find the coefficients in the expansion of $(x + y)^7$.

Page 742

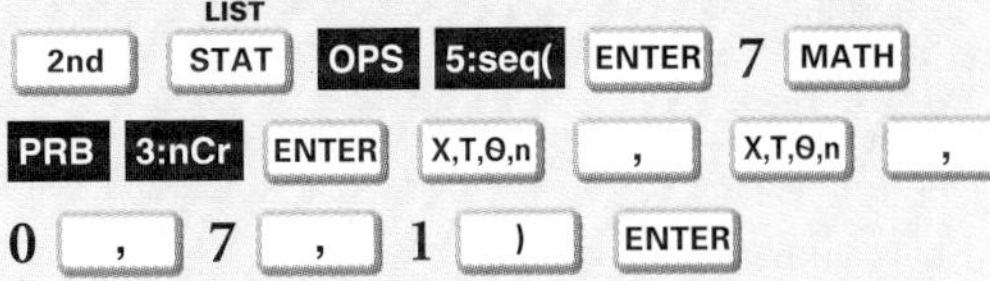

0 , 7 , 1) ENTER

DISCRETE MATHEMATICS Statistics

STATISTICS IS A BRANCH OF APPLIED MATHEMATICS that involves collecting, organizing, interpreting, and making predictions from data. Statistics is categorized as descriptive or inferential. Descriptive statistics uses tables, graphs, and summary measures to describe data. Inferential statistics consists of analyzing and interpreting data to make predictions.

Lessons

Teenagers work various jobs to earn spending money.

USA STATISTICS

Spending Habits of Teenagers

Teenagers obtain money in a variety of ways: jobs, allowances, or relatives. Teens categorized their spending habits as shown at right.

Spend most of it 12%

Save most of it 28%

Spend half and save half 60%

Source: ICR'S Teen EXCEL Survey for Merrill Lynch

About the Chapter Project

To obtain information about a large group, or population, smaller parts, or samples are studied. A sample is any part of a population. A sampling method is a procedure for selecting a sample to represent the population. A sampling method is *biased* if it deliberately or unintentionally favors particular outcomes. In the Chapter Project, *That's Not Fair!*, you will design a sampling method to provide a reasonable representation of a population and use the method to conduct a survey.

After completing the Chapter Project, you will be able to do the following:

- Determine whether a sampling procedure provides a poor or a reasonable representation of the total population.
- Design a sampling method that provides a reasonable representation of the population.
- Use statistics to support conclusions made from results of a survey.

About the Portfolio Activities

Throughout the chapter, you will be given opportunities to complete Portfolio Activities that are designed to support your work on the Chapter Project.

- Comparing measures of central tendency is included in the Portfolio Activity on page 771.
- Collecting data and choosing a method of visual representation for your data is included in the Portfolio Activity on page 780.
- Collecting data and explaining what some features of a box-and-whisker plot tell you about the data is included in the Portfolio Activity on page 789.
- Explaining what the measures of dispersion tell you about data that you have collected is included in the Portfolio Activity on page 798.

Measures of Central Tendency

Why *You can use measures of central tendency to analyze many real-world situations, such as the number of minutes that a commercial radio station devotes to music.*

Objectives

- Find the mean, median, and mode of a data set.
- Find or estimate the mean from a frequency table of data.

APPLICATION
BROADCASTING

Guillermo wondered how many minutes his favorite commercial radio station actually devotes to music. He recorded the broadcast between 3:00 P.M. and 4:00 P.M. for 10 successive weekdays. Guillermo's results, in minutes, were 40, 45, 39, 40, 41, 42, 37, 41, 41, and 40.

Find *measures of central tendency* that summarize this data and compare the measures. *You will solve this problem in Example 1.*

Comparing Central Tendencies

Measures of central tendency are values that are representative of an entire data set. Three commonly used measures of central tendency are the *mean*, *median*, and *mode*.

Measures of Central Tendency

The **mean**, or arithmetic average, denoted $\overline{x}$, of a data set is the sum of all of the values in the data set divided by the number of values.

The **median** of a data set is the numerical middle value when the data values are arranged in ascending or descending order. If there are an even number of values, the median is the mean of the two middle values.

The **mode** of a data set is the value that is repeated most often in the data set. There can be one, more than one, or no mode.

EXAMPLE 1 Refer to the radio station data given at the beginning of the lesson.

APPLICATION
BROADCASTING

Find the measures of central tendency, and compare them.

a. mean **b.** median **c.** mode

SOLUTION

a. $\bar{x} = \frac{40 + 45 + 39 + 40 + 41 + 42 + 37 + 41 + 41 + 40}{10} = \frac{406}{10} = 40.6$

The mean number of minutes devoted to music is 40.6.

PROBLEM SOLVING

b. Make an organized list. Arrange values in the data set in ascending order.

37, 39, 40, 40, **40**, **41**, 41, 41, 42, 45

The median is the mean of the fifth and sixth values, 40 and 41, which is $\frac{40 + 41}{2} = 40.5$. Thus, the median number of minutes is 40.5.

c. The most often repeated values, 40 and 41, both appear the same number of times. Because there are two modes, the data set is called *bimodal.*

The mean (40.6), median (40.5), and modes (40 and 41) are all very similar. Thus, the measures of central tendency for the number of minutes devoted to music during this hour are all between 40 and 41, inclusive.

TRY THIS

Using the data 88, 74, 98, 76, 68, 74, 89, and 92, find the mean, median, and mode, and compare them.

CRITICAL THINKING

What percent of the time does Guillermo's radio station play music? How broadly can this generalization be applied? Explain.

Any of the measures of central tendency can be misleading (not truly representative or typical) for certain data sets, as shown in Example 2.

EXAMPLE 2 **The salaries at a small business with 7 employees are as follows: \$255,000, \$32,000, \$30,000, \$28,000, \$24,000, \$22,000, and \$22,000.**

APPLICATION
BUSINESS

a. Find the mean, median, and mode of the salaries.

b. Explain which measures best represent a typical employee's salary.

SOLUTION

a. mean: $\bar{x} = \frac{255{,}000 + 32{,}000 + 30{,}000 + 28{,}000 + 24{,}000 + 22{,}000 + 22{,}000}{7}$

$= \frac{413{,}000}{7} = 59{,}000$

median: The middle value is \$28,000.

mode: \$22,000

b. The mean, \$59,000, does not represent a typical salary because all except the top salary are much lower. The mode, \$22,000, is a better representation of a typical salary than the mean, but it is still not the best representation because it is the lowest salary. The median, \$28,000, is the best representation of the typical salary.

TRY THIS The yearly bonuses for five managers are \$90,000, \$85,000, \$100,000, \$0, and \$80,000. Find the mean, median, and mode, and explain which measures are most representative.

CHECKPOINT ✔ Suppose that the number of employees in Example 2 increases by 6, and these employees all receive the same salary, \$30,000. Does the one large salary of \$255,000 have as much influence on the new mean as it did on the original mean? Why?

In the Activity below you can explore how the mean, median, and mode are influenced by various changes to the data set.

Exploring Measures of Central Tendency

You will need: two 6-sided number cubes

1. Roll both number cubes and record their sum for 20 trials. Find the mean, median, and mode(s) of the sums.
2. Add 3 to each sum. Find the new mean, median, and mode(s), and describe how the measures have changed.
3. Double each sum from Step 1. Find the new mean, median, and mode, and describe how the measures have changed.
4. Take half of each sum from Step 1, and then subtract 1 from each value. Find the new mean, median, and mode(s), and describe how the measures have changed.

CHECKPOINT ✔ 5. Make a conjecture about what happens to the mean, median, and mode when you add, subtract, multiply, or divide each data value.

CHECKPOINT ✔ 6. Each value in Example 2 ends with three zeros. How can you use your conjecture to find the mean for the values in Example 2 by performing calculations without the final three zeros? Explain.

Frequency Tables

APPLICATION
ECOLOGY

The number of chirps that a cricket makes is related to the temperature according to the following relationship:

$$\text{number of chirps in 15 seconds} + 40 = \text{temperature in degrees Fahrenheit}$$

To verify this relationship, a class of 24 students counted cricket chirps for 15 seconds with the following results:

30	32	30	30	30	30	32	31
30	32	32	30	32	30	32	32
30	30	31	32	31	30	32	31

This *raw data* of cricket chirps can be organized into a **frequency table** that lists the number of times, or frequency, that each data value appears.

To make a frequency table, first list each distinct value. Then make a mark for each value in the data set. Finally, count the number of marks to get the respective frequency for each value, as shown below.

Number of chirps	Tally	Frequency
30	~~||||~~ ~~||||~~ |	11
31	||||	4
32	~~||||~~ ||||	9
	Total	24

Example 3 demonstrates how to find the mean of a data set that is organized in a frequency table.

EXAMPLE 3 **Find the mean number of cricket chirps from the frequency table above. Then estimate the temperature at the time the chirps were counted.**

APPLICATION
ECOLOGY

SOLUTION

Multiply each number of chirps by its corresponding frequency.

Frequency Table for Cricket Chirps

Number of chirps	Frequency	Product
30	11	330
31	4	124
32	9	288
Total	24	742

Add the products, and divide by the total number of values.

$$\overline{x} = \frac{742}{24} \approx 30.9$$

The mean number of cricket chirps during the 15 seconds was 30.9. Thus, according to the given relationship, the temperature should have been $30.9 + 40 = 70.9$, or about 71°F.

CHECKPOINT ✔ Would you obtain the same mean in Example 3 if you added each of the 24 values and then divided this sum by 24? Explain. Would you obtain the same mean if you calculated $\frac{30 + 31 + 32}{3}$? Explain.

TRY THIS Suppose that 9 students counted 30 chirps, 5 students counted 31 chirps, and 10 students counted 32 chirps. Find the mean number of chirps by using a frequency table. Then find the corresponding temperature.

When there are many different values, a *grouped* frequency table is used. In a **grouped frequency table**, the values are grouped into *classes* that contain a range of values. Example 4 shows the procedure for estimating the mean from a grouped frequency table.

EXAMPLE 4

APPLICATION
MUSIC

The grouped frequency table at right lists the results of a survey of 80 musicians who were asked how many hours per week they spend practicing.

Hours	Frequency
1–5	13
6–10	9
11–15	9
16–20	14
21–25	16
26–30	8
31–35	8
36–40	3
Total	80

Estimate the mean number of hours that these musicians practice each week.

SOLUTION

First find the *class mean*, or midpoint value, for each class. Then multiply each class mean by its corresponding frequency. Add the products, and divide by the total number of musicians surveyed.

$$\overline{x} = \frac{1450}{80} = 18.125$$

Hours	Class mean	Frequency	Product
1–5	3	13	39
6–10	8	9	72
11–15	13	9	117
16–20	18	14	252
21–25	23	16	368
26–30	28	8	224
31–35	33	8	264
36–40	38	3	114
	Total	80	1450

Thus, a reasonable estimate of the mean number of hours that these musicians practice each week is 18 hours.

CRITICAL THINKING Explain why the mean of the values in a grouped frequency table is an estimate.

Exercises

Communicate

1. Which measure is the easiest to determine: mean, median, or mode? Which measure is the most difficult? Why?
2. Suppose that the largest and smallest value in a data set are omitted. Will the median change? Will the mean change? Explain.
3. Describe a data set for which the mean is not as representative as the mode or median.

Guided Skills Practice

4. Find the mean, median, and mode for the hourly wages below and then compare the measures. ***(EXAMPLE 1)***

$5.25, $5.00, $6.50, $6.00, $5.00, $6.75, $6.50, $5.00

5. The hours worked in one week by 10 cashiers at a grocery store were 36, 40, 34, 38, 33, 0, 40, 32, 35, and 37. ***(EXAMPLE 2)***

a. Find the mean, median, and mode of the hours worked that week.

b. Explain which measures best represent the number of the hours worked by a typical cashier in that week.

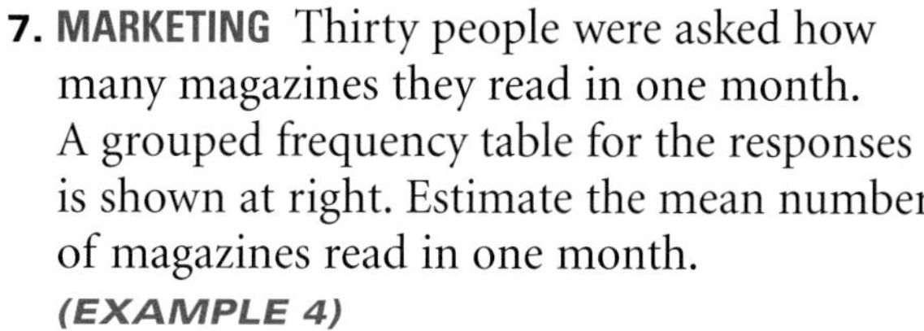

6. Find the mean of the data set given in the horizontal frequency table at right. ***(EXAMPLE 3)***

Value	3	4	5	Total
Frequency	6	11	13	30

7. MARKETING Thirty people were asked how many magazines they read in one month. A grouped frequency table for the responses is shown at right. Estimate the mean number of magazines read in one month. ***(EXAMPLE 4)***

Number	Frequency
0–2	10
3–5	12
6–8	4
9–11	4
Total	30

Practice and Apply

Find the mean, median, and mode of each data set. Give answers to the nearest thousandth, when necessary.

8. 1, 3, 4, 8, 1, 7, 1, 5

9. 2, 5, 3, 6, 3, 1, 3, 4

10. 18, 13, 16, 20, 21, 13, 19

11. 14, 16, 19, 14, 12, 15, 13

12. −5, −1, 2, −6, −2,

13. −12, −10, −13, −9, −11

14. 2.1, 3.4, 3.7, 2.2, 2.1, 2.2

15. 1.7, 1.6, 3.8, 5.1, 1.6, 3.8

16. 0.33, 1.24, 2.71, 7.42, 6.21

17. 4.82, 5.22, 8.32, 3.22, 1.56

18. $\frac{1}{2}, \frac{3}{4}, \frac{5}{8}, \frac{7}{8}$

19. $\frac{1}{3}, \frac{1}{9}, \frac{5}{6}, \frac{5}{9}$

Find the mean, median, and mode of each data set, and compare them.

20. the price of haircuts (rounded to nearest half-dollar):
$6.50, $7.50, $8, $8, $10, $10, $12.50, $14, $16, $16, $20, $24

21. the cost for a gallon of unleaded gasoline (rounded to the nearest cent):
$1.20, $1.23, $1.25, $1.16, $1.32, $1.24, $1.33, $1.23, $1.21, $1.30, $1.20, $1.20, $1.21, $1.28

Make a frequency table for each data set, and find the mean.

22. the number of days students in 4th period were absent:
1, 0, 3, 4, 1, 0, 2, 0, 3, 4, 1, 3, 4, 1, 2, 0, 1, 2, 0, 4, 3, 1, 2, 2, 2, 1, 3, 1, 1, 2

23. the number of pets that students in a class have:
3, 4, 0, 1, 2, 3, 2, 0, 4, 0, 1, 0, 1, 2, 0, 1, 0, 4, 2, 0, 1, 1, 4, 2, 3, 3, 4, 2, 1, 0

Make a grouped frequency table for each data set, and estimate the mean.

24. test scores of a class: 66, 75, 74, 78, 88, 99, 75, 88, 76, 74, 66, 89, 82, 92, 67, 89, 88, 84, 92, 65, 75, 85, 78, 79, 84, 94, 91, 81, 61, 79

25. the miles per gallon for cars driven to school: 30, 21, 18, 19, 23, 24, 26, 32, 30, 22, 12, 15, 21, 28, 27, 18, 16, 19, 23, 29, 24, 25, 16

For each situation described below, decide whether you would represent the data in a frequency table or a grouped frequency table. Explain your choice.

26. the number of pencils carried by each student to class

27. the dollar value of sales recorded by the school store for one month

28. the number of points scored by a basketball team in each game for a season, which vary from 38 to 75

29. the number of brothers and sisters of each student in a class

Survey about 15 students in your class about the topics below, and find the mean, median, and mode of the responses. Then describe which measures are most representative.

30. the distance that students live from school (to the nearest tenth of a mile)

31. the estimated number of movies that students saw last year

32. the time spent sleeping the previous night

33. the time spent studying the previous day

APPLICATIONS

34. BUSINESS A vending company claims that one of its beverage machines dispenses about 8 fluid ounces into each cup. To verify this claim, they measured the amount dispensed into 40 cups. The results are listed below.

7.8	7.9	7.6	8.0	7.8	8.0	7.9	7.6	8.0	8.0	7.5	7.9	7.8	7.9
7.8	8.0	8.2	7.9	7.6	8.0	7.6	8.1	8.1	7.9	7.5	8.0	7.8	7.8
8.0	8.2	7.9	8.1	8.1	7.9	7.5	8.0	7.8	7.8	8.0	8.2		

a. Find the mean, median, and mode, and compare them.

b. Do the results from part **a** support the company's claim?

35. INVENTORY The manager of the women's shoe department recorded the following sizes of shoes sold in one day:

$$5, 6, 5\tfrac{1}{2}, 7, 9, 6, 5, 7\tfrac{1}{2}, 7, 5, 8, 6\tfrac{1}{2}, 7, 8, 6, 4, 6\tfrac{1}{2}, 10, 7$$

a. Find the mean, median, and mode of the shoe sizes sold.

b. Explain which measure of central tendency is the most helpful for the manager.

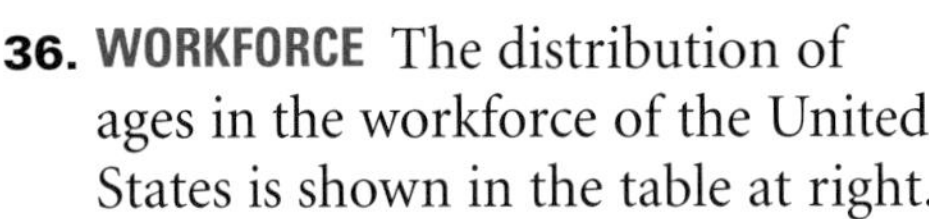

36. WORKFORCE The distribution of ages in the workforce of the United States is shown in the table at right.

a. Make three grouped frequency tables, one for each year.

b. Find the estimated mean age of a worker for each year. Use 60 for the class mean of the 55+ class.

c. Compare the estimated means from part **b**. What do they indicate about the workforce?

Percent of the Labor Force by Age

Age	1979	1992	2005
16–24	24%	16%	16%
25–34	27%	28%	21%
35–44	19%	27%	25%
45–54	16%	18%	24%
55+	14%	12%	14%

[*Source: Bureau of Labor Statistics*]

APPLICATIONS

37. **ACADEMICS** A student's test scores are 86, 72, 85, and 90. What is the lowest score that the student can get on the next test and still have a test average (mean) of at least 80?

CHALLENGE

38. **ACCOUNTING** The record of Jacob's gasoline purchases on a recent vacation is given in the table below. What is the average cost per gallon of gasoline for the entire trip?

Price per gallon	\$1.18	\$1.04	\$1.29	\$1.12	\$1.21
Number of gallons purchased	21	17	16	19	11

39. Given $f(x) = x^3$ and $g(x) = x^3 + 2x - 3$, find $f + g$ and $f - g$. ***(LESSON 2.4)***

Write each equation in logarithmic form. ***(LESSON 6.3)***

40. $16^{\frac{1}{2}} = 4$ 41. $5^4 = 625$ 42. $\left(\frac{1}{3}\right)^2 = \frac{1}{9}$ 43. $2^{-3} = \frac{1}{8}$

Write each equation in exponential form. ***(LESSON 6.3)***

44. $\log_5 125 = 3$ 45. $4 = \log_5 625$ 46. $-4 = \log_3 \frac{1}{81}$

Factor each polynomial expression. ***(LESSON 7.3)***

47. $x^3 + 125$ 48. $x^3 - 27$

Create a data set with at least 5 values for each description below.

49. The mean, median, and mode are all equal.

50. The mean is 4, the median is 5, and the mode is 4.

51. When one data value is deleted, the mean increases by 10.

47	71	75	70	59	78
88	82	89	72	70	74
95	91	74	85	92	62
93	85	98	73	75	97

The scores in Allison's world history class are given above. Allison's score was 78.

1. Find the mean and the median score for this class.
2. Should Allison use the mean or the median to compare her score with the rest of the class when she reports her grade to her parents? Explain.
3. Choose a score that is greater than the median and raise it by 10 points. Find the new mean and median. Explain what happens to each measure.
4. Choose a score that is less than the median and lower it by 10 points. Find the new mean and median. Explain what happens to each measure.

Stem-and-Leaf Plots, Histograms, and Circle Graphs

Why *You can use a variety of visual displays to view the general distribution of real-world data, such as the number of times that an Internet site is visited.*

Objectives

- Make a stem-and-leaf plot, a histogram, or a circle graph for a data set.
- Find and use relative frequencies to solve probability problems.

APPLICATION
MARKETING

73	24	5	72
64	38	66	70
20	41	55	67
8	25	12	37
21	58	54	42
61	45	19	6
19	36	42	14

An Internet site recorded the number of "hits" between 4 P.M. and 6 P.M. on 28 randomly selected weekdays. The results are listed above.

Stem-and-Leaf Plots

Stem	Leaf $4\|1 = 41$
0	5, 6, 8
1	2, 4, 9, 9
2	0, 1, 4, 5
3	2, 6, 8
4	1, 2, 2, 5
5	4, 5, 8
6	1, 4, 6, 7
7	0, 2, 3

This is an ordered stem-and-leaf plot because the leaves of each stem are listed in order.

A *stem-and-leaf plot* of the Internet data is shown at left. A **stem-and-leaf plot** is a quick way to arrange a set of data and view its shape, or general distribution.

In a stem-and-leaf plot, each data value is split into two parts: a *stem* and a *leaf*. The stems and leaves are chosen so that the data is represented in the most informative way.

A key, shown in the upper right corner of a stem-and-leaf plot, explains what the stems and leaves represent. For example, the key at left tells you that the stem 4 and the leaf 1 represent the data value 41.

From the stem-and-leaf plot above, you can easily see that the maximum number of "hits" is 73 and the minimum is 5. You can also see that the data values are fairly evenly distributed, with 3 or 4 leaves in each stem.

CHECKPOINT ✔ Suppose that you want to make a stem-and-leaf plot for values ranging from 105 to 162. What stems would you use? Why? What stems would you use if the values range from 12.4 to 19.3? Why?

CRITICAL THINKING Describe what the fairly even distribution of data values indicates about the Internet site.

You can also find the median and the mode(s) of a data set from a stem-and-leaf plot, as shown in Example 1.

EXAMPLE 1

APPLICATION
RECREATION

Rosa is planning the annual Degollado family reunion. She has collected the ages of family members who plan to attend.

32	32	34	91	38
12	17	62	22	51
27	34	43	44	44
8	30	30	31	40
34	37	38	38	78
50	26	54	28	29
19	6	45		

a. Make a stem-and-leaf plot of the ages.
b. Find the median and mode of the ages.
c. How can the stem-and-leaf plot be used to plan the reunion?

SOLUTION

a. Choose digits in the tens place for the stems, as shown at right.
b. Because there are 33 values, the median is the 17th value, 34. The modes are 34 and 38.
c. The stem-and-leaf plot organizes the ages so that events can be planned for different age groups. For example, you can see that 3 members are 12 or younger, 2 members are teenagers, and 3 members are 60 or older. You can also see that the ages *cluster* around the 30s, forming a *mound-shaped* distribution.

Stem	Leaf $5\|2 = 52$
0	6, 8
1	2, 7, 9
2	2, 6, 7, 8, 9
3	0, 0, 1, 2, 2, 4, 4, 4, 7, 8, 8, 8
4	0, 3, 4, 4, 5
5	0, 1, 4
6	2
7	8
8	
9	1

TRY THIS Make a stem-and-leaf plot for the data at right. Find the median and mode of the data. How many values are between 5.0 and 6.0? Describe the shape of the distribution.

3.3	5.5	5.3	7.7	4.2	2.5	6.5	9.2	5.6
4.2	6.9	2.3	9.1	5.6	4.5	7.0	7.2	4.5
5.1	7.2	5.4	2.3	3.2	6.2	3.2	6.2	2.3

CHECKPOINT ✔ Use the stem-and-leaf plot at right to answer the questions below.

a. How can you find the number of values in the data set?
b. How can you find the maximum, minimum, median, and mode(s)?
c. In what order are the values in the stem-and-leaf plot arranged?

Stem	Leaf $1\|0 = 10$
0	1, 1, 3, 7, 8
1	0, 0, 5, 6, 9
2	1, 2, 3, 5
3	2
4	2, 5, 6

Histograms

A **histogram** is a bar graph that gives the frequency of each value.

In a histogram, the horizontal axis is like a number line divided into equal widths. Each width represents a data value or range of data values. The height of each bar indicates the frequency of that data value or range of data values.

EXAMPLE 2

APPLICATION
BUSINESS

Isaac manages a canoe rental business. He recorded the number of hours that each of 30 customers rented canoes.

Make a frequency table and a histogram for the canoe rental data below.

1	4	5	2	2	2	3	2	3	3
2	3	7	2	3	3	2	6	4	2
1	1	3	5	5	4	4	2	8	2

SOLUTION

PROBLEM SOLVING

Make a table. Organize the data in a frequency table. Make the histogram by measuring 8 equal widths for the number of hours the canoes were rented. Draw vertical bars to the height of the corresponding frequencies.

Hours	Frequency
1	3
2	10
3	7
4	4
5	3
6	1
7	1
8	1

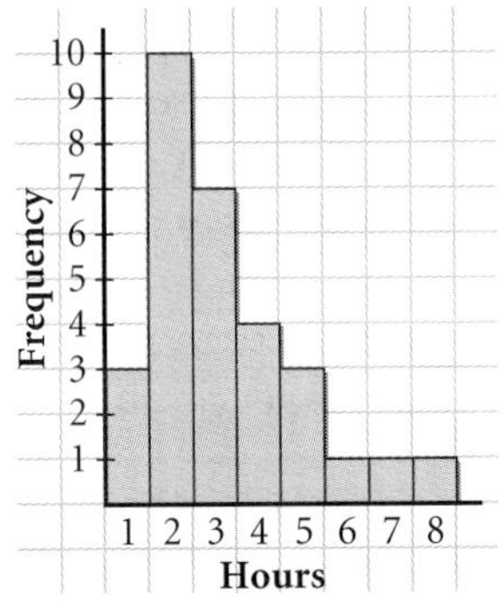

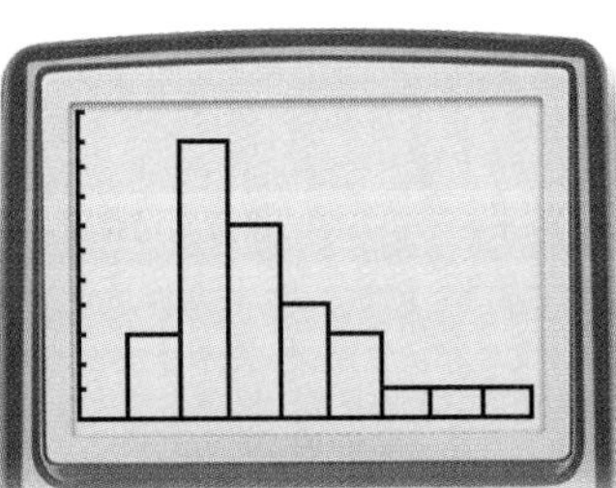

You can also make histograms on your graphics calculator by entering the frequency data into lists.

TRY THIS Make a frequency table and histogram for the data below.

11	12	16	16	12	16	15	11	15	14	13	12
17	15	17	13	14	13	11	13	12	15	13	15

CHECKPOINT ✔ Given a histogram, how can you make a frequency table for the data?

CRITICAL THINKING Describe the histogram for a set of data that has no mode.

Relative frequency tables are frequency tables that include a column that displays how frequently a value appears *relative* to the entire data set. The *relative frequency* column is the percent frequency, or probability. A relative frequency table and histogram are shown below for the canoe rental data.

Relative Frequency Table

Hours	Frequency	Relative frequency
1	3	$\frac{3}{30} = 0.10$, or 10%
2	10	$\frac{10}{30} = 0.\overline{3}$, or 33.3%
3	7	$\frac{7}{30} = 0.2\overline{3}$, or $23.\overline{3}$%
4	4	$\frac{4}{30} = 0.1\overline{3}$, or $13.\overline{3}$%
5	3	$\frac{3}{30} = 0.10$, or 10%
6	1	$\frac{1}{30} = 0.0\overline{3}$, or $3.\overline{3}$%
7	1	$\frac{1}{30} = 0.0\overline{3}$, or $3.\overline{3}$%
8	1	$\frac{1}{30} = 0.0\overline{3}$, or $3.\overline{3}$%
Total	30	$\frac{30}{30} = 1.00$, or 100%

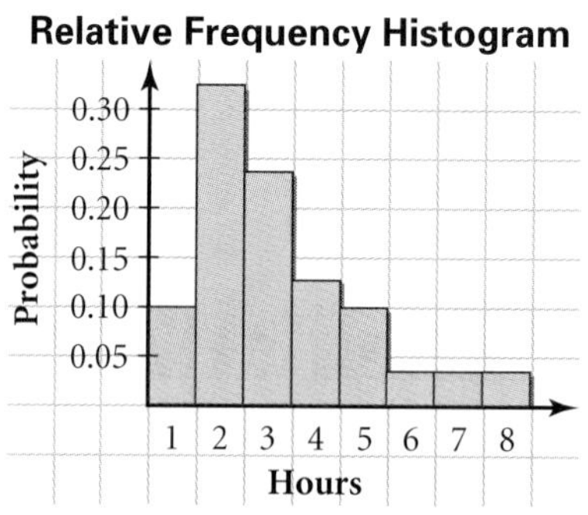

There is a $0.0\overline{3}$ probability that a randomly selected customer will rent a canoe for 8 hours.

EXAMPLE 3 **Use the relative frequencies given above to estimate the probability that a randomly selected customer will rent a canoe for 5 or more hours.**

SOLUTION

Let event $A = 5$ hours, event $B = 6$ hours, event $C = 7$ hours, and event $D = 8$ hours. Assume that events A, B, C and D are mutually exclusive.

$$\begin{aligned} P(A \text{ or } B \text{ or } C \text{ or } D) &= P(A) + P(B) + P(C) + P(D) \\ &= 0.10 + 0.0\overline{3} + 0.0\overline{3} + 0.0\overline{3} \\ &\approx 0.20 \end{aligned}$$

Thus, the probability that a randomly selected customer will rent a canoe for 5 or more hours is approximately 0.20, or about 20%.

TRY THIS Estimate the probability that a randomly selected customer will rent a canoe for less than 4 hours?

Exploring the Shapes of Histograms

You will need: coins and a pair of number cubes

1. Roll a 6-sided number cube and record the result. Repeat this procedure for a total of 20 trials. Make a histogram with the number rolled (1–6) on the horizontal axis.
2. Toss a coin 6 times and record the number of heads that appear. Repeat this procedure for a total of 20 trials. Make a histogram with the number of heads out of 6 tosses on the horizontal axis.

CHECKPOINT ✔

3. Compare the shape of the histogram for Step 1 with the one for Step 2. Which is flatter? Which is more mound-shaped?

4. Suppose that a pair of number cubes are rolled and the sum is recorded for 20 trials. What shape would you expect for the histogram of this data? Explain.

CHECKPOINT ✓ 5. Roll a pair of number cubes as described in Step 4 and record the results. Make a histogram and describe its shape. Is the histogram different from the shape you expected? Explain.

Circle Graphs

You can use a **circle graph** to display the distribution of non-overlapping *parts* of a *whole*, as shown in Example 4.

EXAMPLE 4 **The causes of 1200 fires are listed at right.**

APPLICATION
PUBLIC SAFETY

a. Make a circle graph to represent this data.

b. Find the probability that a given fire was caused by smoking, children, or cooking.

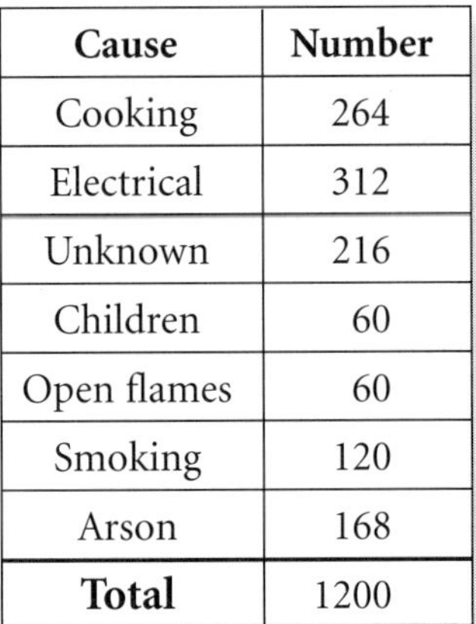

Cause	Number
Cooking	264
Electrical	312
Unknown	216
Children	60
Open flames	60
Smoking	120
Arson	168
Total	1200

SOLUTION

a. Find the relative frequency, or percent, for each cause. Multiply this percent by 360° to obtain the corresponding central angle.

Cause	Relative Frequency	Central Angle
Cooking	$\frac{264}{1200} = 0.22$	$0.22 \times 360° \approx 79°$
Electrical	$\frac{312}{1200} = 0.26$	$0.26 \times 360° \approx 94°$
Unknown	$\frac{216}{1200} = 0.18$	$0.18 \times 360° \approx 65°$
Children	$\frac{60}{1200} = 0.05$	$0.05 \times 360° = 18°$
Open flames	$\frac{60}{1200} = 0.05$	$0.05 \times 360° = 18°$
Smoking	$\frac{120}{1200} = 0.10$	$0.10 \times 360° = 36°$
Arson	$\frac{168}{1200} = 0.14$	$0.14 \times 360° \approx 50°$
Total	$\frac{1200}{1200} = 1.00$	$1.00 \times 360° = 360°$

Use a protractor to measure the central angle for each category.

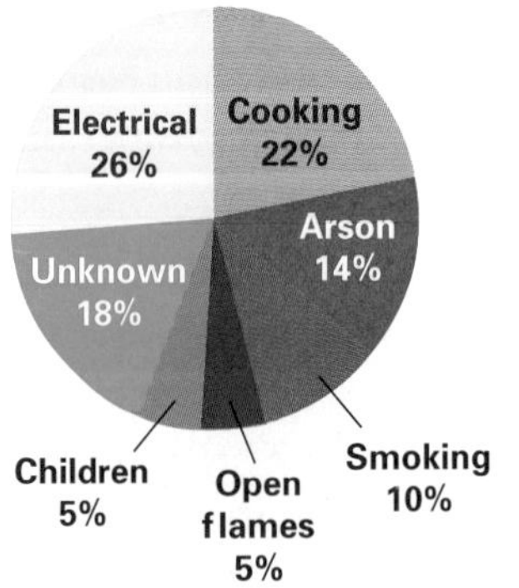

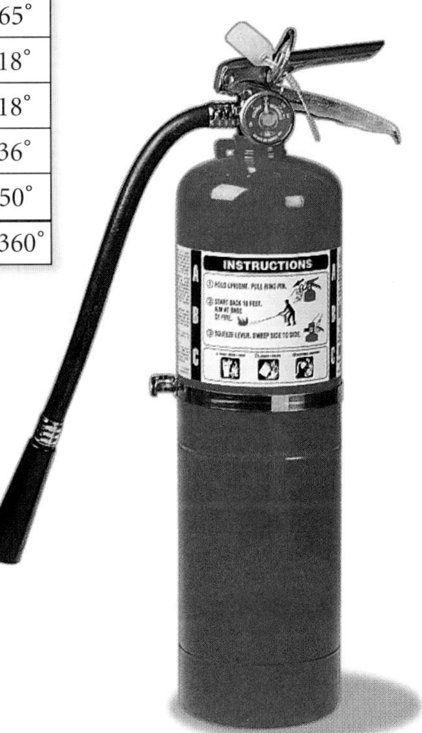

b. Let each event be the cause of a given fire: event A = smoking, event B = children, and event C = cooking. Assume that events A, B, and C are mutually exclusive.

$$\begin{aligned} P(A \text{ or } B \text{ or } C) &= P(A) + P(B) + P(C) \\ &= 0.10 + 0.05 + 0.22 \\ &= 0.37 \end{aligned}$$

Thus, the probability that a fire was caused by smoking, children, or cooking is 0.37, or 37%.

SUMMARY OF DISPLAYS FOR DATA	
Name	**When useful**
stem-and-leaf plot	• to quickly arrange raw data • to show distribution and retain actual values for analysis
histogram	• to show frequency or probability distributions
circle graph	• to show how parts relate to a whole

Exercises

Communicate

1. Describe the different shapes of distributions discussed in the lesson.

2. Which contains more information, a stem-and-leaf plot or a histogram? When is each representation preferred?

3. Explain why the relative frequencies for a data set may also be probabilities.

4. Circle graphs are also called pie charts. Describe the characteristics of a circle graph that are implied by the name *pie chart*.

Guided Skills Practice

APPLICATION

5. BUSINESS The number of calls for customer service during 24 randomly selected days are listed below. ***(EXAMPLE 1)***

22	32	25	42	48	42	36	51	42	53	53	29
31	38	52	51	48	24	39	37	71	51	39	21

a. Make a stem-and-leaf plot of the calls received.
b. Find the median and mode of the number of calls.
c. How could a stem-and-leaf plot of the number of calls be used?

APPLICATIONS

College campus in New York

6. LAW ENFORCEMENT The number of calls that a police department responded to during 24 randomly selected days are listed below. ***(EXAMPLE 2)***

5	7	8	4	9	4	5	6	7	4	6	3
6	7	6	8	5	4	6	8	3	7	5	5

Make a frequency table and a histogram for the number of responses.

7. BUSINESS Refer to the relative frequency table on page 775. Find the probability that a randomly selected customer rents a canoe for 5 hours or less. ***(EXAMPLE 3)***

8. EDUCATION The table at right lists the majors of students at a small college. ***(EXAMPLE 4)***

a. Make a circle graph to represent this data.

b. Find the probability that a randomly selected student is a liberal arts major or undecided.

Major	Number
Liberal arts	891
Natural sciences	627
Undecided	235
Other	122

Practice and Apply

Make a stem-and-leaf plot for each data set. Then find the median and the mode, and describe the distribution of the data.

9. 8.9, 8.8, 7.2, 7.5, 9.2, 7.9, 8.2, 9.1, 8.7, 8.2, 8.5, 8.6, 9.5, 7.5

10. 27.2, 26.3, 30.1, 26.8, 27.3, 28.7, 28.3, 29.8, 29.4, 28.4, 29.1, 28.1, 27.6

11. 359, 357, 348, 347, 337, 347, 340, 335, 338, 348, 339, 356, 336, 358

12. 6.15, 8.55, 7.85, 9.65, 7.85, 8.45, 7.35, 6.35, 8.45, 9.65, 7.85, 9.75, 6.35

Make a frequency table and histogram for each data set.

13. 5, 4, 6, 7, 9, 2, 3, 9, 6, 9, 3, 2, 8, 10, 10

14. 3, 5, 7, 9, 2, 4, 6, 10, 7, 8, 2, 3, 9, 7, 6

15. 1.0, 0.5, 1.5, 2.0, 2.5, 1.0, 1.5, 2.0, 0.5, 1.5, 2.5, 3.0, 2.0, 1.5, 1.0

16. 0.8, 0.4, 0.6, 0.4, 0.2, 0.2, 0.6, 0.6, 0.4, 0.2, 0.4, 0.4, 0.4, 0.8, 0.6

Make a relative frequency table and relative frequency histogram for each data set.

17. 1, 3, 1, 4, 3, 2, 7, 5, 8, 3, 7, 1, 4, 8, 5, 7, 4, 2, 3, 4, 7, 3, 8, 1

18. 40, 60, 80, 30, 70, 80, 80, 60, 60, 40, 30, 40, 70, 100, 60, 70, 30, 40

19. 0.1, 0.3, 0.1, 0.2, 0.4, 0.2, 0.1, 0.5, 0.3, 0.1, 0.1, 0.2, 0.1, 0.3, 0.2

20. 8.1, 8.5, 7.6, 7.9, 8.0, 7.8, 7.9, 8.1, 8.0, 8.1, 8.3, 8.1, 7.9, 7.5, 8.0

Make a histogram with the following intervals for each data set: $0 \le x < 1$, $1 \le x < 2$, $2 \le x < 3$, $3 \le x < 4$, $4 \le x < 5$, and $5 \le x < 6$.

21. 0.2, 1.3, 5.4, 4.3, 2.2, 4.3, 4.6, 3.5, 5.1, 4.8, 1.5, 3.7, 5.4, 4.0, 4.2, 5.2

22. 2.2, 4.6, 3.2, 1.2, 2.8, 3.8, 4.2, 1.2, 2.2, 1.5, 0.5, 2.9, 3.6, 0.9, 1.0

23. 3.4, 4.8, 1.2, 2.5, 3.6, 5.2, 5.0, 4.1, 3.8, 3.5, 4.2, 5.1, 4.8, 4.4, 4.9

24. 0.2, 1.9, 1.2, 0.7, 2.3, 3.1, 2.5, 1.8, 1.6, 1.4, 0.8, 1.3, 0.9, 2.2, 1.7

CONNECTION

25. PATTERNS IN DATA Survey at least 20 students in your class about how they travel to school (walk, bus, car, bike, subway, . . .). Organize your data into a table and make a circle graph. Explain what your graph illustrates.

APPLICATIONS

26. BUSINESS The dollar amount of the total purchases from a vending machine in an office over a 3-month period is shown below for 21 randomly selected individuals.

$10	$43	$5	$18	$8	$63	$10	$6	$30	$22	
$27	$25	$14	$18	$30	$41	$27	$22	$31	$32	$42

a. Make a stem-and-leaf plot of the dollar amounts. Describe the distribution.
b. Find the median and mode of the dollar amounts.
c. Find the probability that a randomly selected individual spent $20 or less on vending machine purchases.

27. INCOME The percent distribution by income of all households in the United States is listed in the table below for 1994.

Under $14,999	$15,000–$24,999	$25,000–$34,999	$35,000–$49,999	$50,000–$74,999	Over $75,000
22.7%	16.7%	14.2%	16.3%	16.5%	13.6%

[*Source: U.S. Bureau of the Census*]

a. Explain whether a histogram or circle graph would best display the data in the table and draw the display.
b. Interpret your display by describing what it illustrates.
c. Find the probability that a randomly selected household in the United States has an income of $50,000 or more.

28. ARMED FORCES The table below lists the location and number of the active-duty military personnel from the United States worldwide.

Location	Number
U.S., U.S. Territories, and special locations	1,397,083
Western and Southern Europe	166,249
East Asia and Pacific	99,022
North Africa, Middle East, and South Asia	11,490
Sub-Saharan Africa	6864
Other Western Hemisphere	17,758

[*Source: The World Almanac and Book of Facts, 1995*]

a. Display this information in your choice of a stem-and-leaf plot, histogram, or circle graph. Justify your choice.
b. Find the probability that a randomly selected active-duty military person from the United States is not located in the United States.

CHALLENGE

29. MARKETING A taste test of three sodas, labeled A, B, and C, included 175 participants. In the test, soda B was selected by twice as many people as soda A, and soda C was selected by twice as many people as soda B. Represent these results in a circle graph.

Look Back

Solve each proportion for *x*. *(LESSON 1.4)*

30. $\frac{3x-2}{4}=\frac{x}{9}$

31. $\frac{-4x}{7}=x+2$

32. $\frac{20x}{-6}=\frac{x-4}{3}$

Factor each expression. *(LESSON 5.3)*

33. $x^2+16x+64$

34. $x^2-10x+25$

35. $3(2x-5)-x(2x-5)$

36. $25a^2-49b^2$

Divide by using synthetic division. *(LESSON 7.3)*

37. $(x^3+x^2-20)\div(x+2)$

38. $(2x^3+10x^2-2x+8)\div(x-3)$

Use a graph, synthetic division, and factoring to find all of the roots of each equation. *(LESSON 7.4)*

39 $x^3-2x^2-4x+8=0$

40 $x^3+x^2-x-1=0$

41 $c^3+5c^2+8c+4=0$

42 $y^3-4y^2+4y=0$

CONNECTION

43. TRANSFORMATIONS Translate the ellipse defined by the equation $25x^2+16y^2=100$ down 2 units and to the right 4 units. Write the standard equation of the resulting ellipse. ***(LESSON 9.4)***

A coin is tossed 3 times. Use a tree diagram to find the probability that 2 of the 3 tosses land tails up, given that each event below occurs. *(LESSON 10.6)*

44. The first coin lands tails up.

45. The first coin lands heads up.

Look Beyond

46. A trick coin with a 0.75 probability of heads is tossed 3 times. What is the probability of getting 2 heads in 3 tosses?

Collect data from the National Weather Service about the average number of days per year that different cities have snowfall. Choose one city in each of the 50 states, including the city in which you reside. Represent the data in a stem-and-leaf plot, a histogram, and a circle graph. Then answer the questions below.

1. How does your city compare with the other cities? Which display—a stem-and-leaf plot, a histogram, or a circle graph—best compares this information? Why?
2. How many cities have the same average number of days of snowfall per year as your city? Which display—a stem-and-leaf plot, a histogram, or a circle graph—best illustrates this information? Why?
3. Which display—a stem-and-leaf plot, a histogram, or a circle graph—do you prefer for this data? Why?

WORKING ON THE CHAPTER PROJECT

You should now be able to complete Activity 1 of the Chapter Project.

Box-and-Whisker Plots

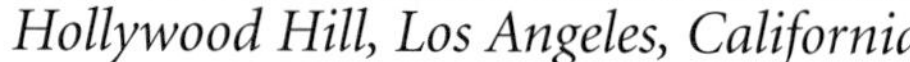

Hollywood Hill, Los Angeles, California

Wrigley Field, home of the Chicago Cubs

Objectives

- Find the range, quartiles, and interquartile range for a data set.
- Make a box-and-whisker plot for a data set.

Why *You can use box-and-whisker plots to compare the distributions of two sets of similar data, such as the monthly mean temperatures for two cities.*

APPLICATION
CLIMATE

The mean monthly temperatures for Los Angeles, California, and Chicago, Illinois, are listed at right. Construct a box-and-whisker plot for the temperatures in each city and compare them. *You will solve the problem in Example 2.*

Los Angeles (1961–1990) Monthly Mean Temperatures (°F)

Month	Temp.
Jan.	55.9
Feb.	57.0
Mar.	58.3
Apr.	60.8
May	63.3
June	66.7
July	70.9
Aug.	71.8
Sep.	70.5
Oct.	66.6
Nov.	62.1
Dec.	57.6

[*Source: U.S. NOAA*]

Chicago (1961–1990) Monthly Mean Temperatures (°F)

Month	Temp.
Jan.	21.0
Feb.	25.5
Mar.	37.0
Apr.	48.6
May	58.8
June	68.5
July	73.0
Aug.	71.6
Sep.	64.4
Oct.	52.7
Nov.	39.9
Dec.	26.6

[*Source: U.S. NOAA*]

Quartiles

Activity

Exploring Quartiles

TECHNOLOGY
SCIENTIFIC CALCULATOR

You will need: a calculator and graph paper

The table below gives the mean monthly precipitation (1961–1990) in inches for Dallas–Fort Worth, Texas. [*Source: U.S. NOAA*]

Jan.	Feb.	Mar.	Apr.	May	Jun.	Jul.	Aug.	Sep.	Oct.	Nov.	Dec.
1.9	2.2	2.8	3.5	4.9	3.0	2.3	2.2	3.4	3.5	2.3	1.8

1. Find the median of the monthly precipitation data. What percent of the data values are *below* the median? *above* the median?

2. Find the median of the lower half of the values. What percent of data values are below this "lower" median?

3. Find the median of the upper half of the values. What percent of data values are above this "upper" median?

CHECKPOINT ✓ 4. Draw a number line and plot each of the medians you calculated in Steps 1–3 along with the highest and lowest values. Write the percent of data values that are between each plotted value.

Related to the median, which divides a data set into halves, are **quartiles** which divide a data set into quarters. The second quartile, Q_2, is the median that divides the lower half of the data values from the upper half. The lower quartile, Q_1, is the median of the lower half of the data values, and the upper quartile, Q_3, is the median of the upper half of the data values.

These five measures are often called the five-point summary of a data set.

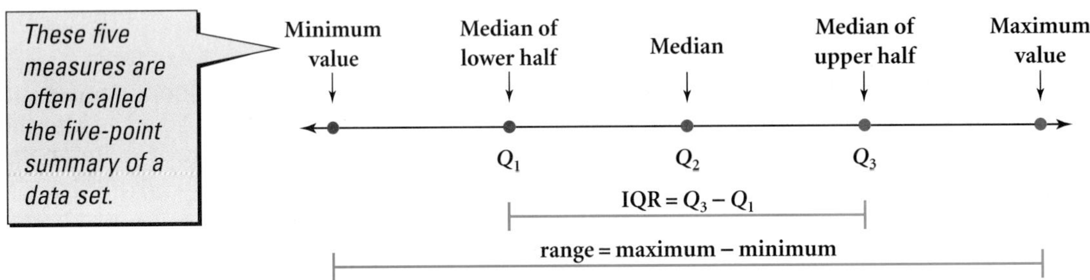

The difference between the maximum value and the minimum value is called the **range**. The difference between the upper and lower quartiles, $Q_3 - Q_1$, is called the **interquartile range**, denoted IQR. When a data value is less than $Q_1 - 1.5(\text{IQR})$ or greater than $Q_3 + 1.5(\text{IQR})$, the data value may be called an **outlier**.

EXAMPLE 1

APPLICATION
SOCIAL SERVICES

The number of calls received by a crisis hotline during 17 randomly selected days is listed at right.

a. Find the minimum and maximum values, quartiles, range, and interquartile range for the data.

b. Identify any outliers.

50	57	77	66
53	72	51	88
82	70	112	107
69	88	98	65
155			

SOLUTION

a. Arrange the values in order. The median is the ninth value, 72. Then find the median of the lower half, $Q_1 = \frac{57 + 65}{2} = 61$, and the median of the upper half, $Q_3 = \frac{88 + 98}{2} = 93$.

50 51 53 57 65 66 69 70 72 77 82 88 88 98 107 112 155

Minimum value: 50; $Q_1 = 61$; $Q_2 = 72$ Median; $Q_3 = 93$; Maximum value: 155

range = maximum − minimum
= 155 − 50 = 105

All data values lie within the range.

$IQR = Q_3 - Q_1$
= 93 − 61 = 32

The middle half of the values lie within the interquartile range.

b. Find any possible outliers below Q_1.

$Q_1 - 1.5(\text{IQR}) = 61 - 1.5(32) = 13$

Find any possible outliers above Q_3.

$Q_3 + 1.5(\text{IQR}) = 93 + 1.5(32) = 141$

There are no values less than or equal to 13. Because the data value 155 is greater than 141, 155 is a possible outlier.

TRY THIS Find the minimum and maximum values, quartiles, range, and interquartile range for the set of data below. Identify any possible outliers.

4	7	9	31	34	2	35	37	24	34	31	50
11	33	36	2	8	13	52	57	60	69	78	83

CRITICAL THINKING What could the possible outlier in Example 1 indicate for the crisis hotline?

Box-and-Whisker Plots

A **box-and-whisker plot** displays how data values are distributed. A box-and-whisker plot is shown below for the crisis-hotline data from Example 1.

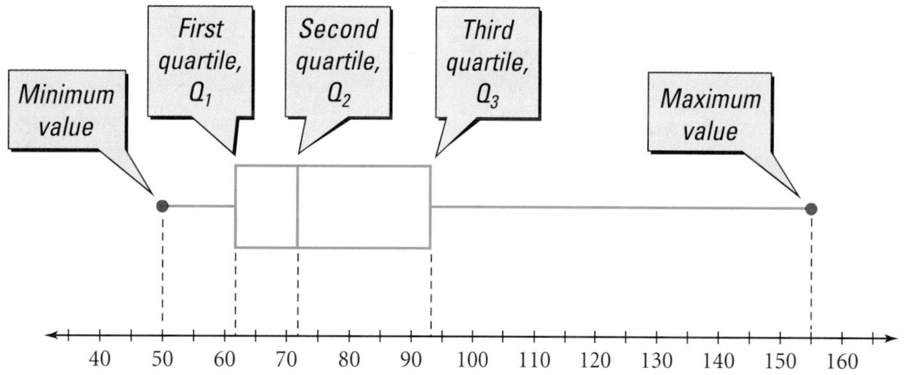

Notice that five measures define a box-and-whisker plot: the minimum value, the maximum value, Q_1, Q_2, and Q_3.

CHECKPOINT ✔ What part of the box-and-whisker plot represents the middle half of the values?

MAKING A BOX-AND-WHISKER PLOT

Step 1. Arrange the values in increasing order and compute Q_1, Q_2, and Q_3.

Step 2. Draw a number line that includes the minimum and maximum values.

Step 3. Make a box whose left end is at Q_1 and whose right end is at Q_3..

Step 4. Draw a vertical line segment to divide the box at, Q_2, the median.

Step 5. Draw a line segment from Q_1 to the minimum value and another line segment from Q_3 to the maximum value for the left and right whiskers.

EXAMPLE 2 **Refer to the temperature data at the beginning of the lesson.**

a. Make a box-and-whisker plot for the temperatures in each city.

b. Compare the box-and-whisker plots.

APPLICATION
CLIMATE

SOLUTION

a. Method 1

Calculate the five measures that define the box-and-whisker plot for each city's temperatures.

	Chicago	LA
minimum	21.0	55.9
Q_1	31.8	57.95
median, Q_2	50.65	62.7
Q_3	66.45	68.6
maximum	73.0	71.8

Then draw both plots as shown below.

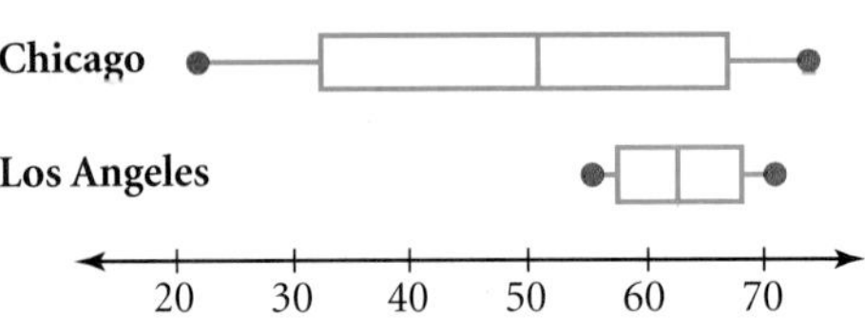

Method 2

Use a graphics calculator. First enter the temperatures for each city into separate lists. Then select box-and-whisker plots for each list of data.

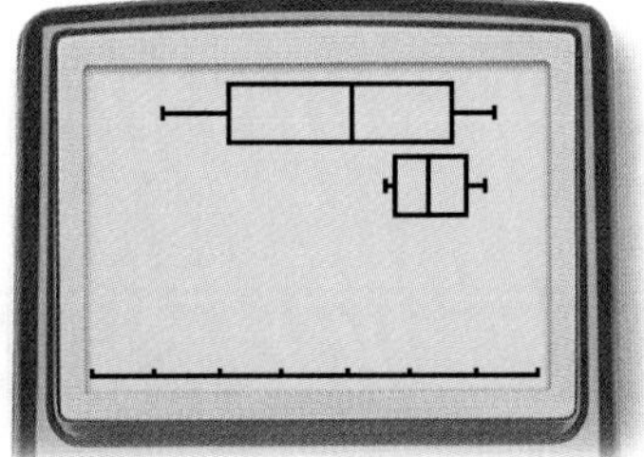

Use the trace feature to identify the maximum, minimum, and quartiles that define each box-and-whisker plot.

TECHNOLOGY
GRAPHICS CALCULATOR
Keystroke Guide, page 822

b. The longer box and longer whiskers for Chicago indicate that the temperature in Chicago varies much more than the temperature in Los Angeles. Over one-half of Chicago's months had an average temperature less than that of any month in Los Angeles. The maximum average monthly temperature in Chicago was also slightly greater than any average monthly temperature in Los Angeles.

CHECKPOINT ✔ Calculate the IQR for Chicago and for Los Angeles in Example 2. What do your results tell you? What can you conjecture about the temperature variation in New York City, which has an IQR of 35.5?

CRITICAL THINKING Can a box-and-whisker plot have only one whisker? no whiskers? Explain.

APPLICATION
SPORTS

The regular-season batting averages for the top 10 players with at least 175 at bats are displayed at right for the teams in the 1997 World Series.

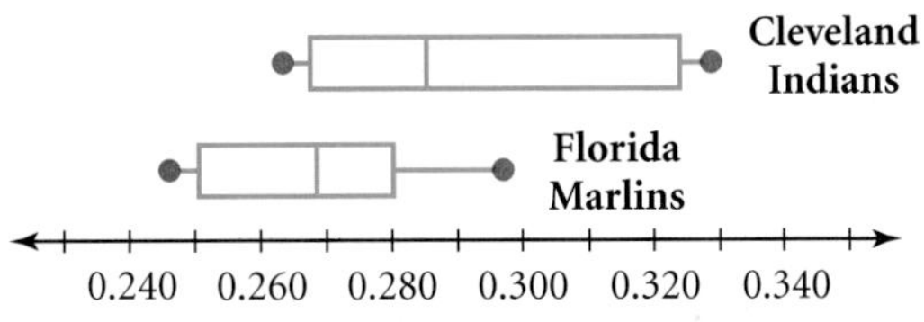

CHECKPOINT ✔ Compare the two box-and-whisker plots above.

Although the graphs show that Cleveland's players had higher batting averages, they lost the 1997 World Series to Florida. Regular-season batting averages are clearly not the only factor to consider when predicting who will win.

Exercises

Communicate

1. Explain how finding the quartiles for a data set with 20 values is different from finding the quartiles for a data set with 15 values.

2. The box-and-whisker plots at right show the test scores for a history class. Explain what the plots indicate about the class performance on the tests.

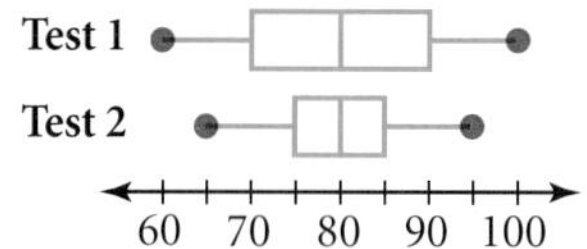

3. What does a box-and-whisker plot tell you about the data set that it represents?

4. Construct two data sets that have the following quartiles: $Q_1 = 5$, $Q_2 = 7$, and $Q_3 = 11$. Explain why you cannot determine from the quartiles what the actual data values are.

Guided Skills Practice

APPLICATIONS

5. **ECOLOGY** The lengths (in centimeters) of 24 American burying beetles are given in the table below. ***(EXAMPLE 1)***

Lengths of American Burying Beetles (cm)

2.5	2.8	3.1	3.6	3.4	3.8	3.0	2.8	3.5	3.3	2.6	3.0
2.9	2.7	3.4	3.2	3.7	2.5	3.1	2.9	2.5	3.1	3.8	2.9

   a. Find the minimum and maximum values, quartiles, range, and interquartile range for the data.
   b. Identify any possible outliers.

6. **CLIMATE** Refer to the temperature data below. ***(EXAMPLE 2)***
   a. Make a box-and-whisker plot for the temperatures in each city.
   b. Compare the box-and-whisker plots.

Honolulu (1961–1990)
Monthly Mean Temperatures (°F)

Jan.	71.8
Feb.	71.8
Mar.	72.5
Apr.	73.9
May	75.7
June	77.5
July	78.6
Aug.	79.3
Sep.	79.2
Oct.	77.9
Nov.	75.6
Dec.	73.2

[*Source: U.S. NOAA*]

Phoenix (1961–1990)
Monthly Mean Temperatures (°F)

Jan.	51.6
Feb.	55.8
Mar.	61.0
Apr.	68.4
May	76.5
June	85.8
July	91.0
Aug.	89.2
Sep.	83.5
Oct.	72.0
Nov.	59.9
Dec.	52.7

[*Source: U.S. NOAA*]

Practice and Apply

Find the minimum and maximum values, quartiles, range, and interquartile range for each data set. Then make a box-and-whisker plot for each data set.

7. 42, 45, 56, 48, 59, 60, 51, 54, 44, 51, 50, 44, 42, 49, 56

8. 2, 16, 4, 11, 14, 8, 17, 19, 13, 19, 9, 15, 8, 13, 17

9. 102, 120, 154, 130, 130, 180, 190, 175, 125, 130

10. 525, 575, 580, 585, 590, 530, 545, 569, 595, 580

11. 22, 50, 78, 22, 77, 93, 27, 86, 14

12. 12, 73, 11, 96, 45, 21, 16, 98, 13

13. 3.2, 4.8, 7.8, 2.2, 7.7, 2.3, 2.7, 8.8, 4.8, 6.5

14. 6.2, 5.1, 4.5, 3.2, 3.5, 5.2, 3.2, 4.8, 8.7, 5.3

Three classes took the same test. Use the box-and-whisker plots below for the scores of each class to answer each question.

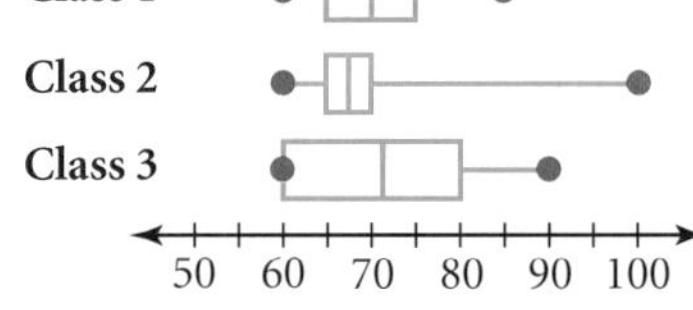

15. Which class had the highest score?

16. Which class had the greatest range?

17. Which class had the highest median?

18. Which class had the highest Q_1?

19. Which class had the greatest IQR?

20. In which class do the middle half of the scores have the smallest range?

21. What percent of scores are greater than Q_1 for each class?

CHALLENGE

22. Colleges report the SAT I scores of the entering freshman class. Instead of a median score, many schools give a range of scores to represent the middle 50% of the class, such as a range from 520 to 610 for math scores. Explain what this range describes as well as the advantages of using it rather than a median score.

CONNECTION

23. PATTERNS IN DATA Research the mean monthly temperatures for your city. Find the quartiles and make a box-and-whisker plot. How does the plot for your city compare with those for Chicago and Los Angeles given at the beginning of the lesson?

APPLICATION

A woman in Japan seeds oysters for pearls.

24. DEMOGRAPHICS The table at right gives the percent of women in the labor force of eight major countries for the years 1980 and 1992. [*Source: Information Please: Almanac, Atlas, and Yearbook, 1996*]

a. Find Q_1, Q_2, and Q_3 for both years.

b. Make box-and-whisker plots for the data from 1980 and from 1992.

c. Compare the two box-and-whisker plots.

Females as a Percent of the Total Labor Force

Country	1980	1992
Australia	36.4	42.1
Canada	39.7	45.5
France	39.5	43.8
Germany	38.0	42.0
Japan	38.4	40.5
Sweden	45.2	48.3
United Kingdom	40.4	44.9
United States	42.4	45.7

APPLICATIONS

DEMOGRAPHICS The table below gives the life expectancy at birth for selected countries in North, Central, and South America for 1994.

Life Expectancy at Birth (years)

Country	Both genders	Male	Female
Brazil	62	57	67
Canada	78	75	82
Chile	75	72	78
Costa Rica	78	76	80
Ecuador	70	67	73
Guatemala	64	62	67
Mexico	73	69	77
Panama	75	72	78
Peru	66	63	68
Trinidad and Tobago	71	68	73
United States	76	73	79
Uruguay	74	71	77
Venezuela	73	70	76

[*Source: Information Please: Almanac, Atlas, and Yearbook, 1996*]

25. a. Find the minimum and maximum values, Q_1, Q_2, and Q_3 for both genders.
b. Make a box-and-whisker plot of the life expectancy for both genders.

26. a. Find the minimum and maximum values, Q_1, Q_2, and Q_3 for males and for females.
b. Using the same number line as in Exercise 25, make a box-and-whisker plot of the life expectancy for males and for females. Then compare them.

27 **GEOGRAPHY** The table below gives the area for each of the 50 states.

Area of States in Square Miles

AL	52,423	HI	10,932	ME	35,387	NJ	8722	SD	77,121
AK	656,424	IA	56,276	MI	96,705	NM	121,598	TN	42,146
AR	53,182	ID	83,574	MN	86,943	NV	110,567	TX	268,601
AZ	114,006	IL	57,918	MO	69,709	NY	54,471	UT	84,904
CA	163,707	IN	36,420	MS	48,434	OH	44,828	VA	42,777
CO	104,100	KS	82,282	MT	147,046	OK	69,903	VT	9615
CT	5544	KY	40,411	NC	53,821	OR	98,386	WA	71,302
DE	2489	LA	51,843	ND	70,704	PA	46,058	WI	65,499
FL	65,756	MA	10,555	NE	77,358	RI	1545	WV	24,231
GA	59,441	MD	12,407	NH	9351	SC	32,008	WY	97,818

[*Source: The World Almanac and Book of Facts, 1996*]

a. Find the minimum and maximum values, Q_1, Q_2, and Q_3 for this data.
b. Make a box-and-whisker plot with the values from part **a**.
c. Identify any possible outliers by naming the corresponding states.

APPLICATION

GOVERNMENT The table below lists the presidents and their ages at inauguration.

John F. Kennedy was 43 years old at inauguration.

Age of the Presidents of the United States at Inauguration

Name	Age	Name	Age
1. Washington	57	**22.** Cleveland	47
2. J. Adams	61	**23.** B. Harrison	55
3. Jefferson	57	**24.** Cleveland	55
4. Madison	57	**25.** McKinley	54
5. Monroe	58	**26.** T. Roosevelt	42
6. J. Q. Adams	57	**27.** Taft	51
7. Jackson	61	**28.** Wilson	56
8. Van Buren	54	**29.** Harding	55
9. W. H. Harrison	68	**30.** Coolidge	51
10. Tyler	51	**31.** Hoover	54
11. Polk	49	**32.** F. D. Roosevelt	51
12. Taylor	64	**33.** Truman	60
13. Filmore	50	**34.** Eisenhower	62
14. Pierce	48	**35.** Kennedy	43
15. Buchanan	65	**36.** L. B. Johnson	55
16. Lincoln	52	**37.** Nixon	56
17. A. Johnson	56	**38.** Ford	61
18. Grant	46	**39.** Carter	52
19. Hayes	54	**40.** Reagan	69
20. Garfield	49	**41.** Bush	64
21. Arthur	50	**42.** Clinton	46

[*Source: Information Please: Almanac, Atlas, and Yearbook, 1996*]

28. **a.** Find the minimum and maximum values, Q_1, Q_2, and Q_3 for the ages of the presidents at inauguration. Are there any possible outliers?
b. Make a box-and-whisker plot for ages of the presidents at inauguration.

29. **a.** Using the same number line, make a box-and-whisker plot for the first 21 presidents and another box-and-whisker plot for the last 21 presidents.
b. Compare the box-and-whisker plots. What do they indicate?

Tell whether each function represents exponential growth or decay. ***(LESSON 6.2)***

30. $f(x) = 0.7^x$ **31.** $f(x) = 0.7^{-x}$ **32.** $f(x) = 7^x$ **33.** $f(x) = 7^{-x}$

34. Write an exponential function that models 8% annual growth with a y-value of 1000 at $x = 0$. ***(LESSON 6.2)***

Describe the end behavior of each function. ***(LESSON 7.2)***

35. $P(x) = x^3 + 2x^2 - x + 1$ **36.** $P(x) = -2x^3 - 5x + 4$

Find the constant of variation, and write the equation for the relationship. ***(LESSON 8.1)***

37. y varies directly as x, and $y = 12$ when $x = 3$.

38. y varies inversely as x, and $y = 20$ when $x = 3$.

39. y varies as the square of x, and $y = 2$ when $x = 3$.

Write the standard equation for each parabola with the given characteristics. ***(LESSON 9.2)***

40. vertex: (0, 0); focus: (3, 0)

41. directrix: $x = 4$; focus: $(-1, 2)$

Write the center, vertices, and co-vertices of each ellipse. ***(LESSON 9.4)***

42. $\frac{(x-1)^2}{4} + \frac{(y+5)^2}{144} = 1$

43. $x^2 + 4x + 9y^2 - 21 = 0$

APPLICATION

44. SECURITY A certain type of blank key has 6 possible notches, each of which can be cut to 4 different heights (including no cut at all). How many different keys can be made from this type of blank key? ***(LESSON 10.1)***

45. In a group of 7 balloons, 2 are red, 3 are blue, and the rest are white. In how many distinct ways can the balloons be arranged in a row? ***(LESSON 10.2)***

46. Find the next three terms of the arithmetic sequence 2, 3.5, 5, 6.5, . . . ***(LESSON 11.2)***

47. Find the next three terms of the geometric sequence 5, 6, 7.2, 8.64, . . . ***(LESSON 11.4)***

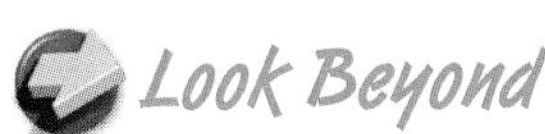

Lewis	Adams
15	20
25	20
30	18
10	22
20	20

48. The table at left shows the points scored by two basketball players in the first five games of the season.

a. Calculate each player's mean points per game.

b. Which player is more consistent, based on this data? Justify your response. Did the player's mean score from part **a** help you to decide which player is more consistent? Why or why not?

Obtain the weekly television ratings from the A. C. Nielsen Company. Explain what the ratings represent. Then make a box-and-whisker plot of the data and answer the questions below.

1. What percent of the ratings are below the median, below the lower quartile, above the upper quartile, in the box, and in the whiskers?
2. Is one whisker longer than the other? If so, what does this indicate? If not, what does this indicate?
3. Is the median centered in the box? If so, what does this indicate? If not, what does this indicate?

WORKING ON THE CHAPTER PROJECT

You should now be able to complete Activity 2 of the Chapter Project.

EYEWITNESS MATH

Is it RANDOM?

The Quest for True Randomness Finally Appears Successful

by James Gleick

One of the strangest quests of modern computer science seems to be reaching its goal; mathematicians believe they have found a process for making perfectly random strings of numbers.

Sequences of truly patternless, truly unpredictable digits have become a perversely valuable commodity, in demand for a wide variety applications in science and industry. Randomness is a tool for insuring fairness in statistical studies or jury selection, for designing safe cryptographic schemes and for helping scientists simulate complex behavior.

Yet random numbers—as unbiased and disorganized as the result of millions of imaginary coin tosses—have long proved extremely hard to make, either with electronic computers or mechanical devices. Consumers of randomness have had to settle for numbers that fall short, always hiding some subtle pattern.

Random number generators are sold for every kind of computer. Every generator now in use has some kind of flaw, though often the flaw can be hard to detect. Furthermore, in a way, the idea of using a predictable electronic machine to create true randomness is nonsense. No string of numbers is really random if it can be produced by a simple computer process. But in a more practical sense, a string is random if there is no way to distinguish it from a string of coin flips.

Several theorists presented details of the apparent breakthrough in random-number generation. The technique will now be subjected to batteries of statistical tests, meant to see whether it performs as well as the theorists believe it will. The way people perceive randomness in the world around them differs sharply from the way mathematicians understand it and test for it.

The need for randomness in human institutions seems to begin at whatever age "eeny-meeny-miny-moe" becomes a practical decision-making procedure: randomness is meant to insure fairness. Like "eeny-meeny-miny-moe," most such procedures prove far from random. Even the most carefully designed mechanical randomness-makers break down under scrutiny.

One such failure, on a dramatic scale, struck the national draft lottery in 1969, its first year. Military officials wrote all the possible birthdays on 366 pieces of paper and put them into 366 capsules. Then they poured the January capsules into a box and mixed them. Then they added the February capsules and mixed again—and so on.

At a public ceremony, the capsules were drawn from the box by hand. Only later did statisticians establish that the procedure had been far from random; people born toward the end of the year had a far greater chance of being drafted than people born in the early months. In general, the problem of mixing or stirring or shuffling things to insure randomness is more complicated than most experts assume.

An expert in exposing the flaws in pseudorandom-number generators, George Marsaglia of Florida State University, has begun to test the new technique. Dr. Marsaglia judges sequences (of numbers) not just by uniformity—a good distribution of numbers in a sequence —but also by "independence." No number or string of numbers should change the probability of the number or numbers that follow, any more than flipping a coin and getting 10 straight tails changes the likelihood of getting heads on the 11th flip.

[*Source:* New York Times, *April 19, 1988*]

How hard can it be to write a bunch of random numbers? Do you think you can write a sequence of 0s and 1s that looks like it came from coin flips? Do you think you could fool a psychologist or mathematician?

To find out, start by writing down a sequence of 120 zeros and ones in an order that you think looks random.

Before you put your made-up sequence to the test, you need to find out how to check for randomness. One way is by breaking the sequence into smaller sequences, such as sets of 3 digits. Then you can see whether some sets occur too often or not enough.

You can visualize these sets of digits by plotting them as points. Think of the first 3 digits in your sequence as an *ordered triple*, the *x*, *y*, and *z* coordinates of a point in space. Using the digits 0 and 1 to model heads and tails, respectively, there are 8 possible ordered triples, as shown.

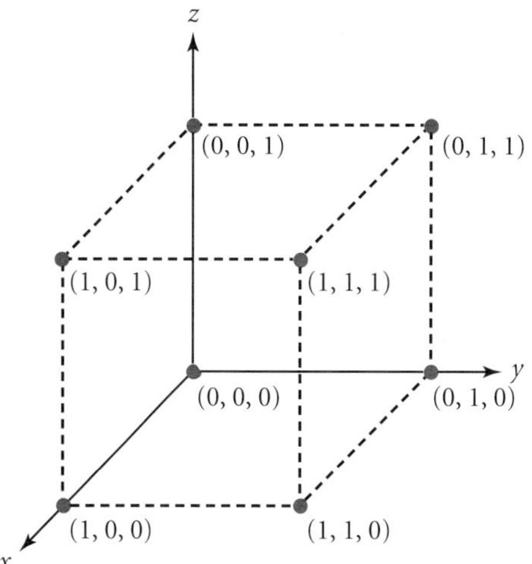

Cooperative Learning

Now you can see whether your classmates are able to distinguish your made-up sequence from an actual sequence.

1. Generate a random sequence of 120 zeros and ones by tossing a coin (heads = 0, tails = 1) or by using a random-number table (even numbers = 0, odd numbers = 1.)

   Exchange this actual sequence and your made-up sequences with another group. (Be sure to mark the sequences so that only you know which one is made up.)

2. Test each sequence you are given by following these steps:
   a. Separate the sequence into 40 ordered triples, as shown here:
   b. Count the number of times the triples **000** and **111** appear. Record your results in a chart.

	Sequence A	Sequence B	Sequence C
0 0 0			
1 1 1			

3. If you flip a coin 3 times, what is the probability of getting 3 heads? 3 tails? Explain.
4. In each new sequence you test, about how many of the 40 triples would you expect to be 000? 111?
5. How might you use your answer to Step 4 to distinguish real random sequences from fake ones?
6. Use your answer to Step 5 to tell which sequence is the fake one. Then find out whether you are correct.
7. Do you think the test would work better if you used sequences of 1200 zeros and ones instead of 120? Why?
8. Write a definition for *random numbers*.

Measures of Dispersion

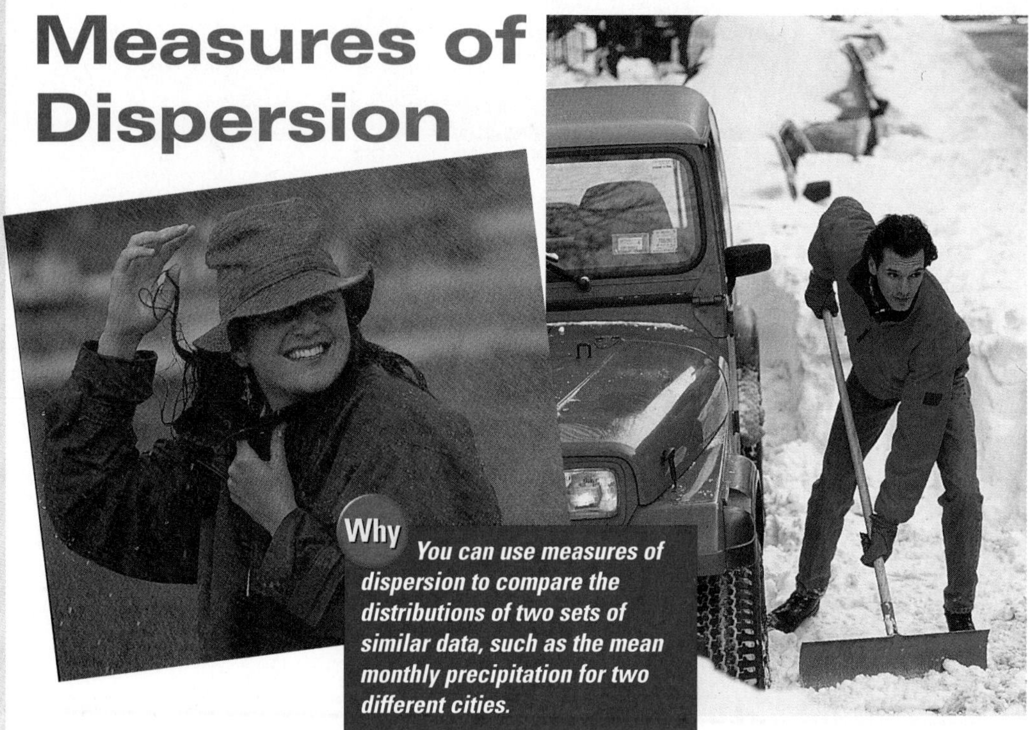

Why
You can use measures of dispersion to compare the distributions of two sets of similar data, such as the mean monthly precipitation for two different cities.

Objective

- Calculate and use measures of dispersion, such as range, mean deviation, variance, and standard deviation.

APPLICATION
CLIMATE

Pittsburgh, Pennsylvania, and Kansas City, Missouri, receive similar amounts of annual precipitation (36.5 and 37.6 inches on average, respectively). However, how the precipitation is spread out, or dispersed, over the year is dramatically different. This is illustrated by the box-and-whisker plots below.

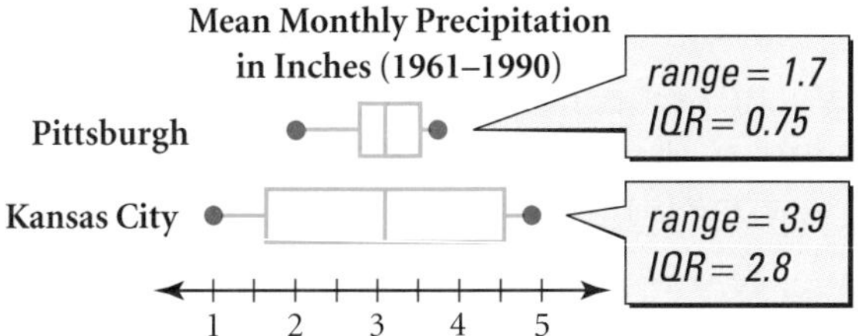

The range and the interquartile range are *measures of dispersion* because they indicate how the monthly precipitation values are *spread* out. **Measures of dispersion** indicate the extent to which values are spread around a central value such as the mean.

As a measure of dispersion, the range is not very reliable because it depends on only two data values, the maximum and the minimum. Likewise, the interquartile range depends on only two values, the first and third quartiles.

Another measure of dispersion, which depends on each data value, is the *mean deviation*. The mean deviation gives the average (mean) amount that the values in a data set differ from the mean.

Mean Deviation

The **mean deviation** of $x_1, x_2, \ldots, x_n$ is the mean of the absolute values of the differences between the data values and the mean, $\overline{x}$.

$$\text{mean deviation} = \frac{1}{n}\sum_{i=1}^{n}|x_i - \overline{x}|$$

EXAMPLE 1 **The number of miles, in thousands, obtained in five tests of two different tires is listed in the table below.**

APPLICATION
MANUFACTURING

Tire A	66	43	37	50	54
Tire B	54	49	47	48	52

a. Find the range and the mean deviation of the number of miles for each tire.

b. Describe what these measures indicate about each tire.

SOLUTION

a. Tire A

range: 66 − 37 = 29
The range is 29,000 miles.

To find the mean deviation, first find the mean.

$$\bar{x} = \frac{66 + 43 + 37 + 50 + 54}{5} = \frac{250}{5} = 50$$

PROBLEM SOLVING

Make a table to find the absolute values of the differences from the mean. Then find and the sum of the absolute values.

x_i	$\|x_i - \bar{x}\|$
66	16
43	7
37	13
50	0
54	4
Total	40

Divide the total by n.

$$n = \frac{40}{5} = 8$$

The mean deviation is 8000 miles.

Tire B

range: 54 − 47 = 7
The range is 7000 miles.

To find the mean deviation, first find the mean.

$$\bar{x} = \frac{54 + 49 + 47 + 48 + 52}{5} = \frac{250}{5} = 50$$

Make a table to find the absolute values of the differences from the mean. Then find and the sum of the absolute values.

x_i	$\|x_i - \bar{x}\|$
54	4
49	1
47	3
48	2
52	2
Total	12

Divide the total by n.

$$n = \frac{12}{5} = 2.4$$

The mean deviation is 2400 miles.

b. Because tire B has a smaller mean deviation than tire A (2400 < 8000), the individual values for tire B deviate less from the mean. This indicates that the mean for tire B is a more reliable measure of its central tendency. Thus, the expected mileage for tire B is more predictable.

TRY THIS Find the range and the mean deviation for the data on tire C below. Then compare these measures with those for tires A and B.

Tire C	64	52	50	49	35

CHECKPOINT ✔ Can two data sets have the same range and different mean deviations? Justify your answer with a sample set of data.

The variance and standard deviation are two more measures of dispersion that are commonly used in comparing and analyzing data.

Variance and Standard Deviation

If a data set has n data values $x_1, x_2, \ldots, x_n$ and mean $\bar{x}$, then the **variance** and **standard deviation** of the data are defined as follows:

$$\text{Variance: } \sigma^2 = \frac{1}{n}\sum_{i=1}^{n}(x_i - \bar{x})^2$$

$$\text{Standard deviation: } \sigma = \sqrt{\sigma^2}$$

EXAMPLE 2 **Find the standard deviation for the tire data in Example 1.**

APPLICATION
MANUFACTURING

SOLUTION

PROBLEM SOLVING

Tire A

$$\bar{x} = \frac{66 + 43 + 37 + 50 + 54}{5} = 50$$

Make a table to organize your calculations.

x_i	$x_i - \bar{x}$	$(x_i - \bar{x})^2$
66	16	256
43	−7	49
37	−13	169
50	0	0
54	4	16
Total	0	490

variance: $\sigma^2 = \frac{490}{5} = 98$
standard deviation: $\sigma = \sqrt{98} \approx 9.9$

The standard deviation is 9900 miles.

Tire B

$$\bar{x} = \frac{54 + 49 + 47 + 48 + 52}{5} = 50$$

Make a table to organize your calculations.

x_i	$x_i - \bar{x}$	$(x_i - \bar{x})^2$
54	4	16
49	−1	1
47	−3	9
48	−2	4
52	2	4
Total	0	34

variance: $\sigma^2 = \frac{34}{5} = 6.8$
standard deviation: $\sigma = \sqrt{6.8} \approx 2.6$

The standard deviation is 2600 miles.

As expected from the results in Example 1, tire B has a lower standard deviation than tire A, which indicates a greater consistency in its individual test scores.

TRY THIS Find the standard deviation for the data on tire C given in the Try This after Example 1.

CHECKPOINT ✔ Suppose that you are given a standard deviation of 1500 miles for tire D. What does this tell you about tire D relative to tires A and B in Example 2?

CRITICAL THINKING Which measure do you think is used most, the variance or the standard deviation? Why?

Investigating Standard Deviation

You will need: a calculator

1. Find the standard deviation for the following data: 0, 5, 10, 15, 20.
2. Add a constant to each data value in Step 1. Find the new standard deviation, and describe how it changed.
3. Multiply each data value in Step 1 by a positive constant. Find the new standard deviation, and describe how it changed.
4. Divide each data value in Step 1 by 2, and then subtract 5. Find the new standard deviation, and describe how it changed.

CHECKPOINT ✔

5. Make a conjecture about what happens to the standard deviation when you add, subtract, multiply, or divide each data value by a constant.

CHECKPOINT ✔

6. Suppose that a basketball player has a mean of 12 points per game with a standard deviation of 2 points. What is a comparable standard deviation for a basketball player who has a mean of 24 points per game? 30 points per game? Explain.

The precipitation data for the box-and-whisker plots from the beginning of the lesson are shown below.

Mean Monthly Precipitation in Inches (1961–1990)

	Jan.	Feb.	Mar.	Apr.	May	Jun.
Pittsburgh	2.0	2.2	2.9	3.1	3.5	3.7
Kansas City	1.1	1.1	2.5	3.1	5.0	4.7

	Jul.	Aug.	Sep.	Oct.	Nov.	Dec.
Pittsburgh	3.5	3.4	3.4	2.5	3.2	3.1
Kansas City	4.4	4.0	4.9	3.3	1.9	1.6

[*Source: U.S. NOAA*]

You can use a graphics calculator to find the standard deviation for the precipitation of each city by entering the data into lists. Then select the appropriate statistical feature.

Pittsburgh, Pennsylvania **Kansas City, Missouri**

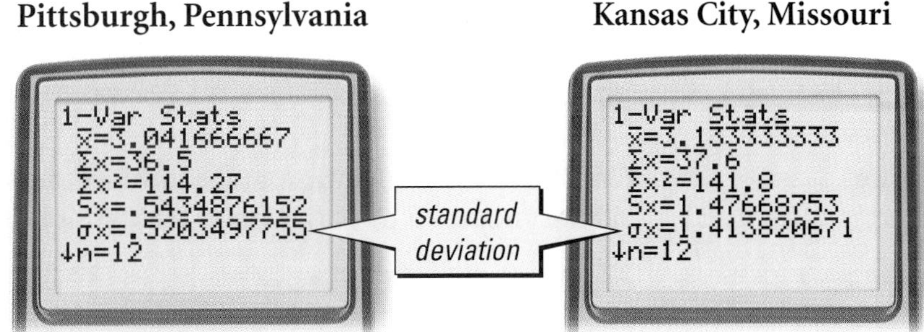

The means are within 0.1 of an inch of each other, but the standard deviations are about 0.5 inches for Pittsburgh and 1.4 inches for Kansas City. Thus, Kansas City's monthly precipitation varies much more than Pittsburgh's monthly precipitation.

Exercises

Communicate

1. Explain why the mean deviation and the standard deviation of a set of data are always nonnegative.
2. Describe the relationship between variance and standard deviation. Is the standard deviation always less than the variance? Explain.
3. Explain why the mean deviation and standard deviation are more reliable measures of dispersion than the range or interquartile range.

Guided Skills Practice

APPLICATION

4. **EDUCATION** The table at right lists five test scores for two students. ***(EXAMPLE 1)***
   a. Find the range and the mean deviation of the scores for each student.
   b. Describe what these measures indicate about each student's test scores.

Tricia	Morgan
81	98
84	68
88	99
82	59
85	96

5. Find the standard deviation of the scores for each student in Exercise 4. ***(EXAMPLE 2)***

Practice and Apply

Find the range and mean deviation for each data set.

6. 8, 10, 3, 9, 10
7. 1, 2, 4, 2, 6
8. 31, 103, 34, 98, 107, 23
9. 32, 23, 68, 74, 26, 93
10. 13.2, 9.4, 7.3, 12.3, 8.6, 7.6
11. 11.1, 14.2, 8.4, 12.2, 15.2, 10.9
12. −1.22, 4.35, −2.42, 2.33, 4.66
13. 8.72, 7.43, −2.92, −3.56, 5.78

Find the variance and standard deviation for each data set.

14. 9, 10, 10, 8, 7, 11, 12, 9
15. 12, 8, 13, 9, 13, 11, 12, 11, 9
16. 8.1, 10.3, 3.4, 9.8, 10.7
17. 19.2, 12.3, 4.8, 22.4, 26
18. 2.42, 7.46, 4.97, 4.22, 6.44
19. 1.34, 2.56, 4.78, 11.89, 8.92
20. −3, 2, −5, 4, −2, 8, 9, −1
21. 2, 4, −8, 8, 7, −2, −4, 3, 7

Find the mean deviation and standard deviation for each data set. Which measure of variation is less affected by an extreme value?

22. 20, 30, 40, 500
23. 0, 500, 510, 520

CHALLENGES

24. Create two data sets with the same range and the same interquartile range, but different standard deviations.
25. Can the standard deviation of a data set be 0? If so, under what conditions? Use sample data sets in your explanation.

CONNECTION

26. **TRANSFORMATIONS** What happens to the standard deviation of a set of data if a constant, c, is added to each value in the data set? What happens to the standard deviation for a data set if each value is multiplied by the same constant, c?

APPLICATIONS

SURVEYS In a survey, 30 people were asked to rank a new soda on a scale from 1 to 10. The results are shown in the table at right.

5	7	9	6	8	10
7	8	8	9	7	8
10	8	7	9	6	8
8	10	9	8	10	10
7	9	8	7	7	9

27. Find the range and the mean deviation of the rankings.

28. Find the standard deviation of the rankings.

MANUFACTURING The table below lists the diameters in millimeters of the ball bearings produced by a certain machine.

5.001	4.9998	4.999	5.002	4.999	5.001	5.002	4.998
4.999	5.000	5.001	4.999	5.000	4.998	4.999	5.003
4.998	4.999	5.001	5.002	5.001	4.999	4.997	5.001
5.001	5.002	5.001	4.998	4.999	5.001	5.002	4.997

29. Find the range and mean deviation.

30. Find the standard deviation.

BUSINESS The tables below list the number of customers for two fast-food locations.

Location 1

12,375	13,890	13,202
12,825	11,982	12,098
11,829	13,234	12,025
12,502	12,654	11,723

Location 2

13,245	13,543	12,983
12,825	12,925	11,924
12,645	11,982	11,728
12,987	13,125	12,887

31. Find the range and the mean deviation of the data for each location. Describe what these measures indicate about each location.

32. Find the standard deviation of the data for each location. Describe what these measures indicate about each location.

SPORTS The winning times (in minutes:seconds.hundredths of a second) for the men's and women's 1500-meter speed-skating competition in several Olympics are shown below.

	1976	1980	1984	1988	1992	1994	1998
Men	1:59.38	1:55.44	1:58.36	1:52.06	1:54.81	1:51.29	1:47.87
Women	2:16.58	2:10.95	2:03.42	2:00.68	2:05.87	2:02.19	1:57.58

33. Find the mean and median winning times for men and for women.

34. Find the range and the mean deviation for men and for women. Describe what these measures indicate about the men's and women's times.

35. Find the standard deviation for men and for women. Describe what these measures indicate about men's and women's times.

Look Back

Solve each system by using a matrix equation. ***(LESSON 4.4)***

36 $\begin{cases} 2.3x + 3.2y = 16.1 \\ 4.2x - 4.6y = 12.3 \end{cases}$

37 $\begin{cases} 7.2x + 10.2y = 20.1 \\ 3.8x + 9.5y = 25.6 \end{cases}$

Use the quadratic formula to solve each equation. Give answers to the nearest tenth if their solutions are irrational. ***(LESSON 5.5)***

38. $3x^2 + 10x + 1 = 0$

39. $2x^2 + 12x - 4 = 0$

Find each value. ***(LESSONS 10.2 AND 10.3)***

40. ${}_8C_3$

41. ${}_{10}C_3$

42. ${}_{17}P_3$

43. ${}_{21}P_3$

Find the sum of each infinite geometric series, if it exists. ***(LESSON 11.6)***

44. $\sum_{k=1}^{\infty} 0.765^k$

45. $\sum_{k=1}^{\infty} 0.45^k$

46. $\sum_{k=1}^{\infty} \left(\frac{3}{2}\right)^k$

47. $\sum_{k=1}^{\infty} 2.7^k$

Look Beyond

48. A sample is often used to make predictions about a larger population. To estimate the mean of a larger population, the mean of the sample is used. However, to estimate the variance or standard deviation of a population, the *sample variance*, denoted S^2, is calculated. The formula for the sample variance is $S^2 = \frac{1}{n-1} \sum_{i=1}^{n} (x_i - \overline{x})^2$. This formula differs from the formula for variance, σ^2, in that the sum is divided by $n - 1$ instead of n.

a. Find the sample variance, S^2, and sample standard deviation, S, for the following sample of a larger population: 15, 18, 7, 16, 5, 12.

b. A random survey of 10 households in a certain city revealed the following numbers of automobiles: 2, 3, 2, 1, 1, 4, 2, 1, 3, 4. Use this sample to estimate the mean number of automobiles per household and the sample standard deviation of the data for the entire city.

Find the mean and the standard deviation for each of the data sets that you collected for the Portfolio Activities on pages 780 and 789. Explain what these measures tell you about the dispersion of each of the data sets.

Binomial Distributions

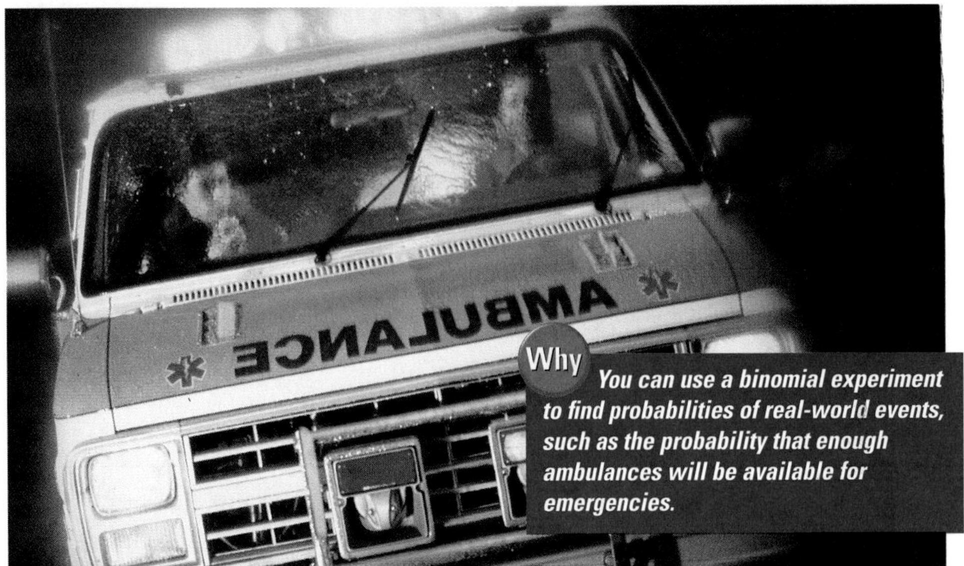

Why *You can use a binomial experiment to find probabilities of real-world events, such as the probability that enough ambulances will be available for emergencies.*

Objective

- Find the probability of r successes in n trials of a binomial experiment.

APPLICATION
EMERGENCY SERVICES

A medical center has 8 ambulances. Given the ambulance's current condition, regular maintenance, and restocking of medical supplies, the probability of an ambulance being operational is 0.96. Find the probability that at least 6 of the 8 ambulances are operational. *You will solve this problem in Example 2.*

The ambulance problem above is an example of a *binomial experiment*.

Binomial Experiment

A probability experiment is a **binomial experiment** if both of the following conditions are met:

- The experiment consists of n trials whose outcomes are either successes (the outcome *is* the event in question) or failures (the outcome is *not* the event in question).
- The trials are identical and independent with a constant probability of success, p, and a constant probability of failure, $1 - p$.

Activity

Exploring Binomial Probability

You will need: a 6-sided number cube

Let a roll of 1 on the number cube be considered a success, S, and the roll of any other number be considered a failure, F.

1. Write a fraction for the probability of a success, $P(\text{S})$, and for the probability of a failure, $P(\text{F})$, in 1 roll of a number cube.
2. For each arrangement of outcomes in 5 rolls of a number cube, write the probability as a product of fractions. Use exponents in your products.
   a. S F F F F **b.** F F S F F **c.** S S F F F **d.** S F F S F

CHECKPOINT ✔ 3. Using combination notation, how many ways can you obtain exactly 1 success in 5 rolls of a number cube? exactly 2 successes?

4. Using your answers from Steps 2 and 3, write each probability below as a product, using combination notation and fractions with exponents.
   a. P(exactly 1 success) **b.** P(exactly 2 successes)

CHECKPOINT ✔ 5. Find the probability of exactly 3 successes in 5 rolls of a number cube.

In the preceding Activity, *a roll of 1* on a 6-sided number cube is considered a success and *a roll of not 1* is considered a failure. In 5 rolls of the number cube, the probability of 2 successes followed by 3 failures is as follows:

$$\frac{1}{6} \times \frac{1}{6} \times \frac{5}{6} \times \frac{5}{6} \times \frac{5}{6} = \left(\frac{1}{6}\right)^2\left(\frac{5}{6}\right)^3$$

Roll number 1 2 3 4 5

However, this probability accounts for only one way in which 2 successes in 5 rolls can occur. All of the ways in which 2 successes can occur is the combination ${}_5C_2$. Thus, the probability of exactly 2 successes in 5 rolls of a number cube is ${}_5C_2\left(\frac{1}{6}\right)^2\left(\frac{5}{6}\right)^3$, or approximately 0.16.

To find the theoretical probability that exactly r successes will occur in n trials of a binomial experiment, you can use the formula below.

Binomial Probability

In a binomial experiment consisting of n trials, the probability, P, of r successes (where $0 \leq r \leq n$, p is the probability of success, and $1 - p$ is the probability of failure) is given by the following formula:

$$P = {}_nC_r p^r (1 - p)^{n-r}$$

EXAMPLE 1 Suppose that the probability a seed will germinate is 80%.

What is the probability that 7 of these seeds will germinate when 10 are planted?

APPLICATION
GARDENING

SOLUTION

$n = 10$, $r = 7$, $p = 0.8$, and $1 - p = 1 - 0.8$

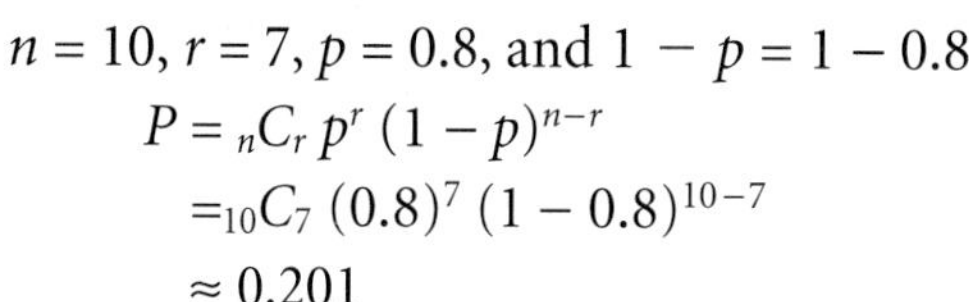

$$P = {}_nC_r\, p^r (1 - p)^{n-r}$$
$$= {}_{10}C_7\, (0.8)^7 (1 - 0.8)^{10-7}$$
$$\approx 0.201$$

TECHNOLOGY
GRAPHICS CALCULATOR
Keystroke Guide, page 823

Thus, the probability that 7 of these seeds will germinate when 10 are planted is about 0.201, or 20.1%.

TRY THIS Suppose that the probability a seed will germinate is 85%. What is the probability that 7 of these seeds will germinate when 10 are planted?

CHECKPOINT ✔ Refer to Example 1. Find the probability that all 10 of these seeds will germinate when 10 are planted. Then find the probability that none of these seeds will germinate when 10 are planted. What happens to the binomial probability formula when $r = n$? when $r = 0$?

In a binomial experiment, the events *r successes* and *s successes* are mutually exclusive. Thus, you can find the probability of exactly r successes or exactly s successes by adding the probabilities.

$$P(r \text{ successes } \textbf{or } s \text{ successes}) = P(r \text{ successes}) + P(s \text{ successes})$$

EXAMPLE 2

APPLICATION
EMERGENCY SERVICES

Refer to the ambulance problem posed at the beginning of the lesson.

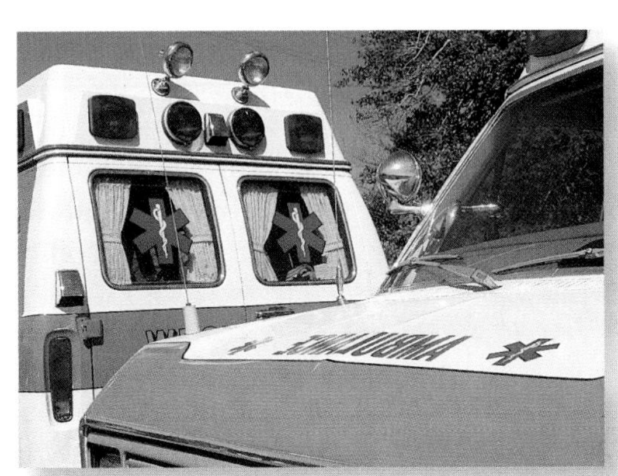

Find the probability that at least 6 of the 8 ambulances are operational. Round to the nearest tenth of a percent.

SOLUTION

At least 6 ambulances are operational when exactly 6, 7, or 8 ambulances are operational.

Find $P(\text{exactly } 6) + P(\text{exactly } 7) + P(\text{exactly } 8)$.

Use $n = 8$, $p = 0.96$, and $1 - p = 1 - 0.96$.

$$P(\text{exactly } 6) = {}_8C_6(0.96)^6(1 - 0.96)^{8-6} \approx 0.0351$$

$$P(\text{exactly } 7) = {}_8C_7(0.96)^7(1 - 0.96)^{8-7} \approx 0.2405$$

$$P(\text{exactly } 8) = {}_8C_8(0.96)^8(1 - 0.96)^{8-8} \approx 0.7214$$

$$P(\text{exactly } 6) + P(\text{exactly } 7) + P(\text{exactly } 8) \approx 0.0351 + 0.2405 + 0.7214 \approx 0.997$$

Thus, the probability is about 99.7%.

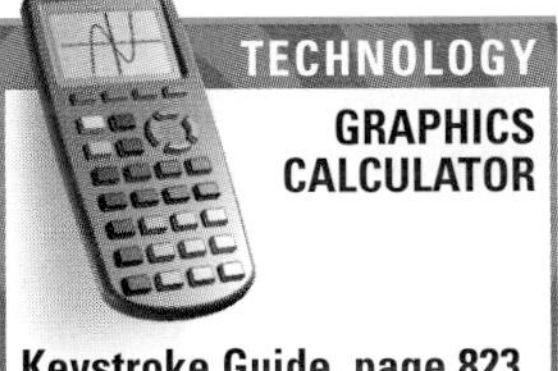

TECHNOLOGY
GRAPHICS CALCULATOR

Keystroke Guide, page 823

CHECK

You can check your answer by using a calculator with a built-in binomial probability feature. In the display at right, the command **binompdf** is used for 6, 7, and 8 successes. The sum gives the desired probability.

binompdf(8,.96,6
)+binompdf(8,.96
,7)+binompdf(8,.
96,8)
.996920321

TRY THIS Find the probability that at least 7 of 8 ambulances are operational, given that the probability of an ambulance being operational is 0.95. Round to the nearest tenth of a percent.

In the binomial experiment of tossing a coin 6 times, success is heads, $n = 6$, $p = 0.5$, and r ranges from 0 heads to 6 heads. The probabilities of tossing each possible number of successes are organized in the table and the relative frequency histogram below.

Heads, r	P(heads), $P = {}_6C_r(0.5)^r(0.5)^{6-r}$
0	≈ 0.016
1	≈ 0.094
2	≈ 0.234
3	≈ 0.312
4	≈ 0.234
5	≈ 0.094
6	≈ 0.016

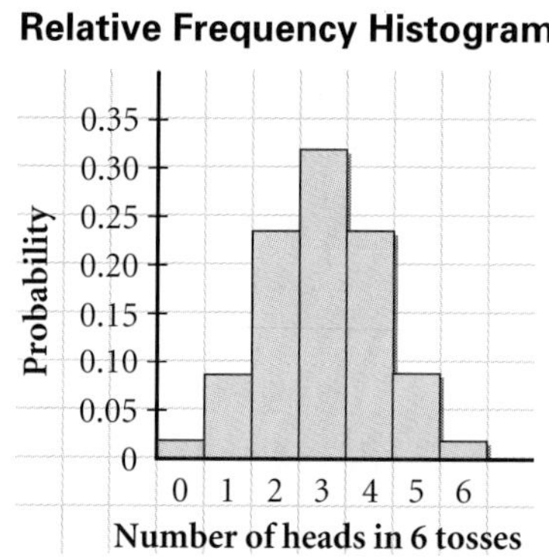

Notice that the distribution of successes is symmetric about the mode because the probabilities of success and failure are equal.

You can use a graphics calculator to generate simulations of tossing a coin 6 times. By graphing the experimental results in a histogram, you can compare the distributions obtained experimentally with the distribution obtained theoretically. Each calculator display below shows the distribution of the results of 100 simulations.

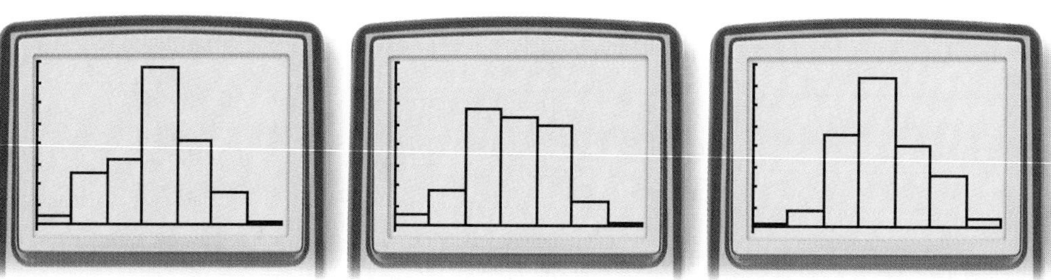

CHECKPOINT ✔ How are the distributions alike and how are they different?

When the probabilities of success and of failure are *not* equal, the binomial distribution obtained by theoretical probability will not be symmetric.

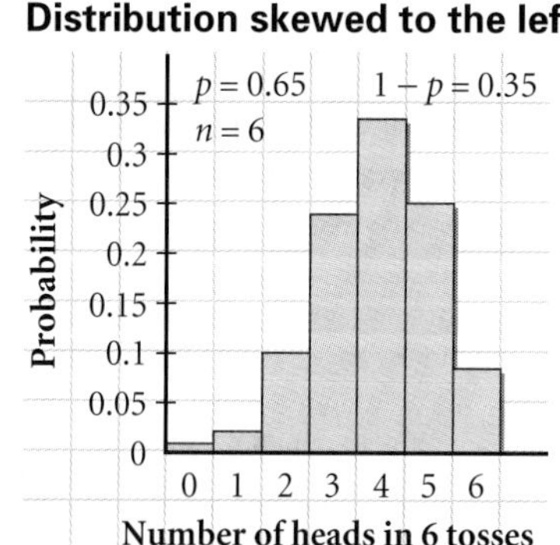

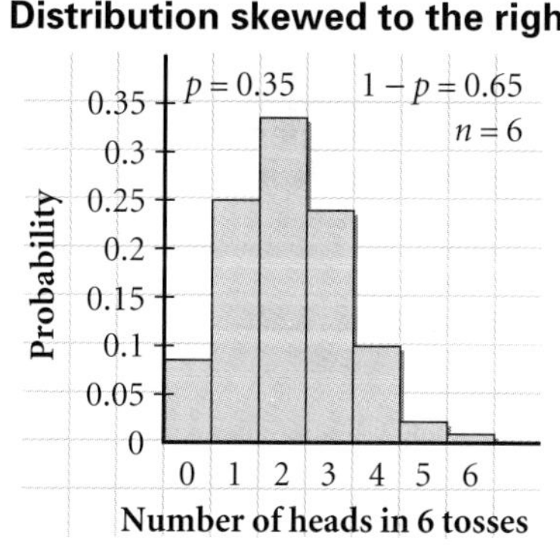

CRITICAL THINKING Explain why the distribution is skewed to the left when $p > 0.5$ and to the right when $p < 0.5$.

Exercises

Communicate

1. Describe the conditions that an experiment must satisfy in order to be a binomial experiment.

2. Explain why ${}_nC_r$ appears in the formula for the probability of a binomial experiment, $P = {}_nC_r p^r(1-p)^{n-r}$.

3. A person randomly selects answers to all 12 questions of a multiple-choice test. Each question has 1 correct and 4 incorrect responses. Describe what n, r, and p represent when finding the binomial probability of 9 answers being correct.

4. Explain the conditions under which a binomial distribution is symmetric and the conditions under which it is skewed.

Guided Skills Practice

APPLICATIONS

5. VETERINARY MEDICINE Suppose that the probability of a sick animal recovering within a week is 70%. What is the probability that 4 out of 6 sick animals will recover within a week? ***(EXAMPLE 1)***

6. PUBLIC SAFETY The probability that a driver is not wearing a seat belt is 0.18. Find the probability that at least 2 of 10 drivers are not wearing seat belts. ***(EXAMPLE 2)***

Practice and Apply

A coin is flipped 8 times. Find the probability of each event.

7. exactly 5 heads
8. exactly 3 heads
9. exactly 2 heads
10. exactly 6 heads
11. exactly 0 heads
12. exactly 8 heads

A family has 4 children. Find the probability of each event, assuming that the probability of a male equals the probability of a female.

13. exactly 2 males
14. exactly 1 male
15. 1 female and 3 males
16. all females

Suppose that 70% of the adults in a certain city are registered voters. In a group of 10 randomly selected adults in the city, find the probability that the indicated number are registered voters.

17. exactly 5
18. exactly 8
19. at least 6
20. at least 8
21. at most 5
22. at most 6
23. 2 are not registered voters
24. 4 are not registered voters

A person randomly selects answers to all 10 questions on a multiple-choice quiz. Each question has 1 correct answer and 3 incorrect answers. Find the probability that the indicated number of answers are correct.

25. exactly 6 **26.** exactly 7 **27.** at least 8

28. at least 5 **29.** at most 3 **30.** at most 4

Find the probability that a batter with each batting average given below will get at least 3 hits in the next 5 at bats.

31. 0.200 **32.** 0.250 **33.** 0.300 **34.** 0.350

Find the probability that a batter with each batting average given below will get at most 3 hits in the next 5 at bats.

35. 0.200 **36.** 0.250 **37.** 0.300 **38.** 0.350

APPLICATIONS

HOSPITAL STATISTICS Suppose that a hospital found an 8.5% probability that the birth of a baby will require the presence of more than one doctor.

39. Find the probability that 2 of the next 20 babies born at the hospital will require the presence of more than one doctor.

40. Find the probability that 3 of the next 20 babies born at the hospital will require the presence of more than one doctor.

SURVEYS In a 1998 survey, 54% of U.S. men and 36% of U.S. women consider themselves basketball fans. [*Source: Bruskin-Goldring Research*]

41. Find the probability that 5 men randomly selected from a group of 10 U.S. men consider themselves basketball fans.

42. Find the probability that 3 women randomly selected from a group of 10 U.S. women consider themselves basketball fans.

SURVEYS In 1997, 40% of U.S. households owned at least one cellular or wireless phone. [*Source: The Wirthin Report*]

43. What is the probability that 2 in 10 U.S. households owned a cellular or wireless phone?

44. What is the probability that at least 2 in 10 U.S. households owned a cellular or wireless phone?

45. What is the probability that at least 2 in 8 U.S. households owned a cellular or wireless phone?

AWARDS Three different prizes are placed in cereal boxes, with no more than 1 prize per box. Prize A is in 10% of the cereal boxes, prize B is in 20%, and prize C is in 30%. Find the probability of each event.

46. 1 prize in 1 box

47. exactly 1 prize in 2 boxes

48. 3 different prizes in 3 boxes

49. at least 2 prizes in 3 boxes

APPLICATION

50. AVIATION A certain twin-engine airplane can fly with only one engine. The probability of engine failure for each of this airplane's engines is 0.002. Determine whether each airplane described below is more likely than this twin-engine airplane to crash due to engine failure.

a. a single-engine airplane with an engine whose probability of failure is 0.001

b. an experimental 3-engine airplane that can fly with only 2 engines, equipped with engines whose probability of failure is 0.001

c. an airplane with 4 engines that can fly with only 2 engines, equipped with engines whose probability of failure is 0.0008.

CHALLENGE

d. Find p such that a single-engine airplane with p probability of engine failure is as safe as the 4-engine airplane described in part **c**.

Look Back

A 6-sided number cube is rolled once. Find each probability. ***(LESSON 10.4)***

51. $P(2 \text{ or } 3)$

52. $P(1 \text{ or } 2 \text{ or } 6)$

53. $P(\text{even or } 6)$

54. $P(\text{not } 6 \text{ or} < 2)$

55. $P(< 5)$

56. $P(> 2 \text{ or } 4)$

57. Construct an arithmetic sequence with a common difference of 6. ***(LESSON 11.2)***

58. Construct a geometric sequence with a common ratio of 6. ***(LESSON 11.4)***

APPLICATION

59. EDUCATION Refer to the data below. ***(LESSON 12.4)***

Percent of Recent High School Graduates Enrolled in College

	1988	1989	1990	1991	1992	1993	1994
Male	57.0	57.6	57.8	57.6	59.6	59.7	60.6
Female	60.8	61.6	62.0	67.1	63.8	65.4	63.2

[*Source: U.S. Department of Education Statistics*]

a. Find the range and mean deviation for the percent enrollments of males and females.

b. Find the standard deviation for the percent enrollments of males and of females.

c. Describe what the measures indicate about the percent enrollments of males and females.

Look Beyond

60. The standard deviation for a binomial distribution is given by $\sigma = \sqrt{np(1-p)}$, where n is the number of trials and p is the probability of a particular event occurring. A number cube is rolled 1000 times. Find the mean ($\overline{x} = np$) and the standard deviation for the event of rolling a 5.

12.6

Normal Distributions

Why You can use the characteristics of a normal distribution to find probabilities of many real-world events, such as the number of deaths caused by lightning each month.

Objectives

- Find the probability of an event given that the data is normally distributed and its mean and standard deviation are known.
- Use z-scores to find probabilities.

APPLICATION
METEOROLOGY

The histogram at right shows that deaths caused by lightning occur much more frequently in the summer months. In fact, about 70% of the deaths occurred in June, July, or August. [*Source: NOAA*]

Because this distribution is nearly symmetric about July, you can say that this data represents a *normal distribution.*

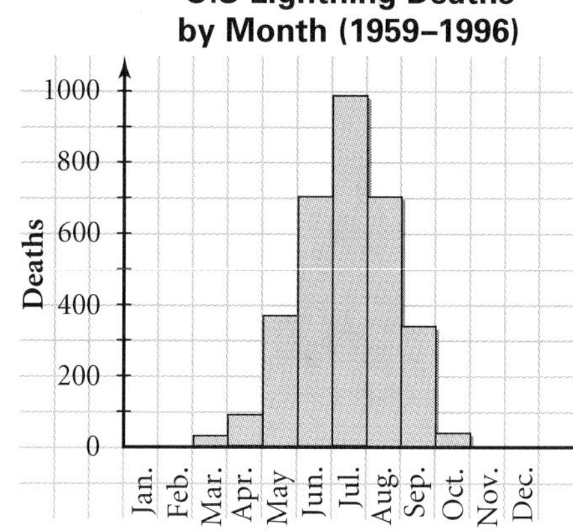

A **normal distribution** of data varies randomly from the mean, creating a mound-shaped pattern that is symmetric about the mean when graphed. Some examples of normally distributed data are human heights and weights.

The model obtained by drawing a curve through the midpoints of the tops of the bars in a histogram of normally distributed data is called a **normal curve.** A normal curve is defined by the mean and the standard deviation. A **standard normal curve** is a normal curve with mean of 0 and standard deviation of 1.

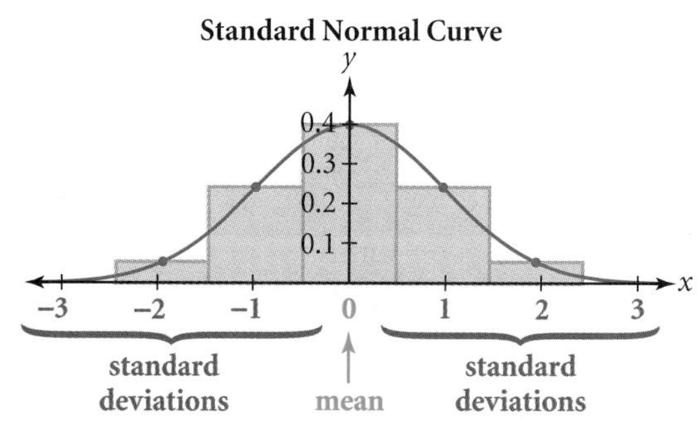

Recall from 12.2 that relative frequency histograms give probabilities. You can use the area under a normal curve (and above the x-axis) to approximate probabilities.

The total area under a normal curve is 1, with an area of 0.5 of the total to the right of the mean and an area of 0.5 of the total to the left of the mean.

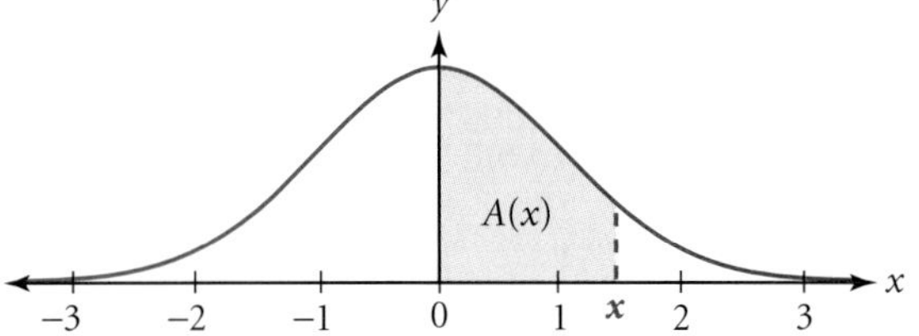

A table of approximate areas, $A(x)$, under the standard normal curve between the mean, 0, and the number of standard deviations, x, is given below.

Standard Normal Curve Areas

x	0	0.2	0.4	0.6	0.8	1.0	1.2	1.4	1.6	1.8	2.0
$A(x)$	0.0000	0.0793	0.1554	0.2257	0.2881	0.3413	0.3849	0.4192	0.4452	0.4641	0.4772

EXAMPLE  **Approximate each probability by using the area table for a standard normal curve.**

a. $P(x \geq 1.6)$ **b.** $P(-2.0 \leq x \leq 0.4)$

SOLUTION

a.

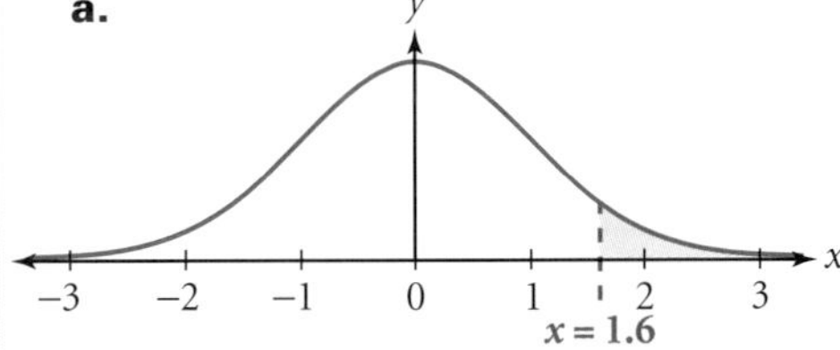

b.

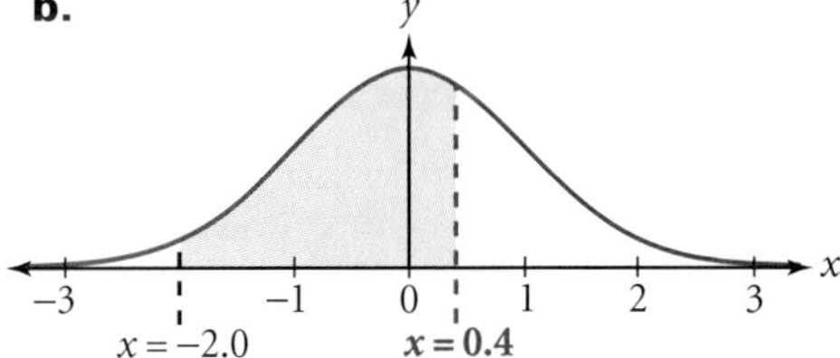

$$P(x \geq 1.6) = 0.5 - P(0 \leq x \leq 1.6)$$
$$\approx 0.5 - 0.4452$$
$$\approx 0.0548$$

$$P(-2.0 \leq x \leq 0.4)$$
$$= P(-2.0 \leq x \leq 0) + P(0 \leq x \leq 0.4)$$
$$= P(0 \leq x \leq 2.0) + P(0 \leq x \leq 0.4)$$
$$\approx 0.4772 + 0.1554$$
$$\approx 0.6326$$

TECHNOLOGY
GRAPHICS CALCULATOR
Keystroke Guide, page 824

CHECK

You can use a graphics calculator to check the probabilities.

TRY THIS Find each probability by using the area table for a standard normal curve.

a. $P(x \leq -0.8)$ **b.** $P(-1.2 \leq x \leq 1.6)$

CHECKPOINT  Using the area table for a standard normal curve, describe the trend for $A(x)$ as x increases.

CRITICAL THINKING Why is 10^99 entered in the graphics calculator for the upper bound in part **a** of Example 1? What would you enter to find $P(x \leq 1.6)$?

Exploring the Standard Normal Curve

You will need: a graphics calculator

1. Graph $f(x) = \frac{1}{\sqrt{2\pi}} e^{\frac{-x^2}{2}}$.

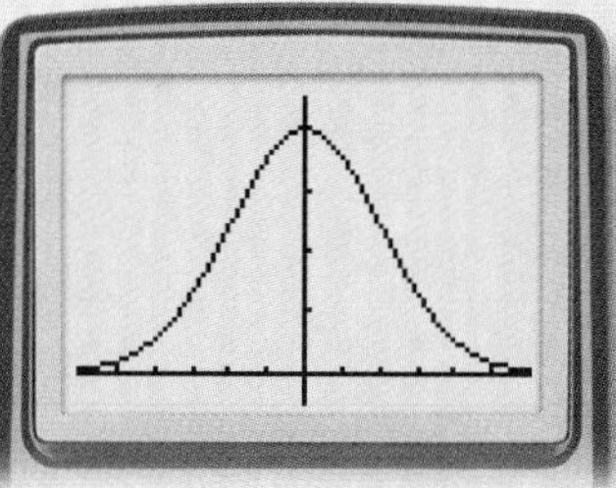

2. Use the trace feature to verify that the graph is symmetric about the y-axis and that the x-axis is a horizontal asymptote.
3. Use the $\int f(x)dx$ feature to find the area under the curve (and above the x-axis) from $x = 0$ to $x = 1$ and from $x = -1$ to $x = 0$.

CHECKPOINT ✔ 4. What area represents 1 standard deviation on either side of the mean ($x = 0$)?

5. Repeat Step 3 for values from $x = 0$ to $x = 2$ and from $x = -2$ to $x = 0$.

CHECKPOINT ✔ 6. What area represents 2 standard deviations on either side of $x = 0$?

7. Repeat Step 3 for values from $x = 0$ to $x = 3$ and from $x = -3$ to $x = 0$.

CHECKPOINT ✔ 8. What area represents 3 standard deviations on either side of $x = 0$?

9. Find the areas corresponding to values less than $x = -3$ and to values greater than $x = 3$.

CHECKPOINT ✔ 10. What probability is represented by the total area under the curve?

All normal distributions have the properties listed below.

Properties of Normal Distributions

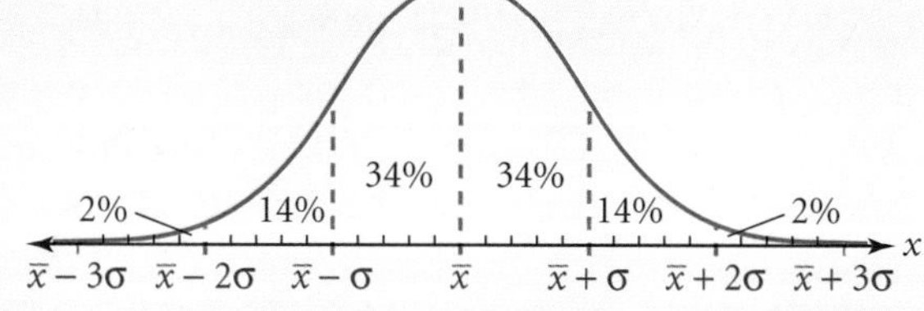

- The curve is symmetric about the mean, $\bar{x}$.
- The total area under the curve is 1.
- The mean, median, and mode are about equal.
- About 68% of the area is within 1 standard deviation (σ) of the mean.
- About 95% of the area is within 2 standard deviations (2σ) of the mean.
- About 99% of the area is within 3 standard deviations (3σ) of the mean.

CHECKPOINT ✔ Examine the two normal curves graphed below. How are the standard deviations different? How does the size of the standard deviation of a normal distribution affect the graph?

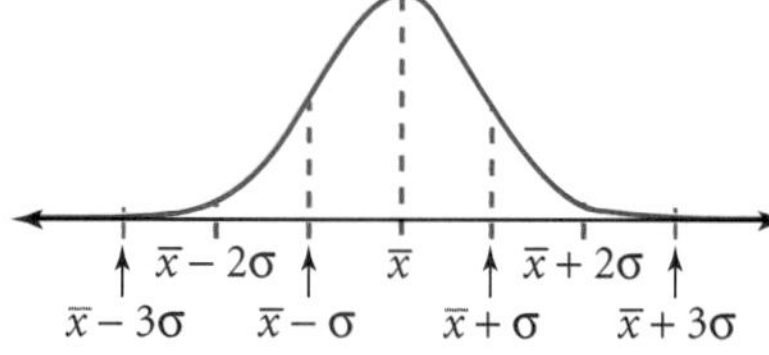

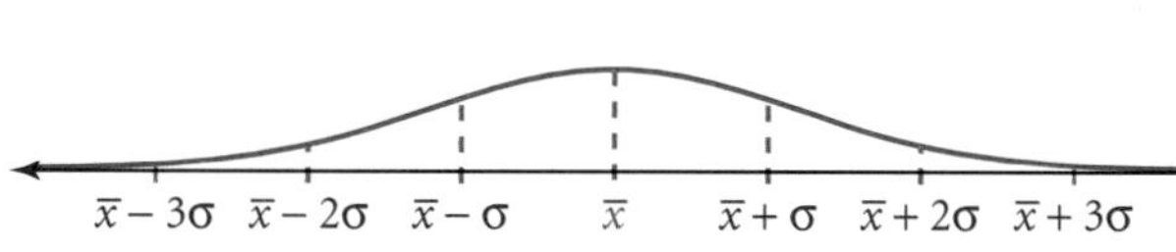

Normal distributions occur in many large data sets. For example, standardized test scores are usually normally distributed, as shown in Example 2.

EXAMPLE 2

APPLICATION
ACADEMICS

Scores for a certain professional exam are approximately normally distributed with a mean of 650 and a standard deviation of 100.

a. What is the probability that a randomly selected test score is between 450 and 850?

b. Out of 1000 randomly selected test scores, how many would you expect to be between 450 and 850?

SOLUTION

a. Because $\bar{x} = 650$ and $\sigma = 100$, the interval from 450 to 850 is $650 - 2\sigma \le \bar{x} \le 650 + 2\sigma$.

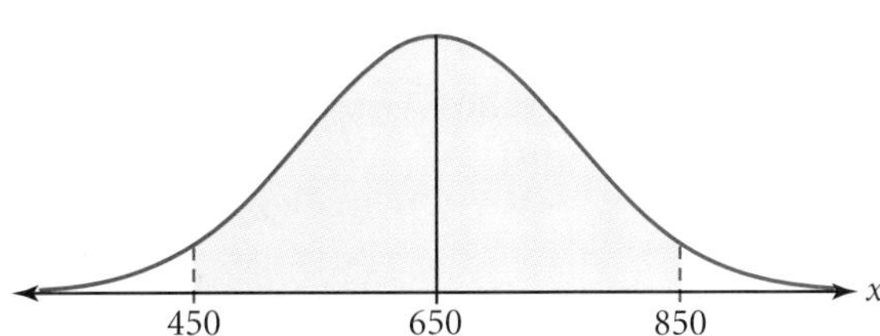

Thus, the probability that a randomly selected test score is between 450 and 850 is about 95%.

b. 95% of 1000 = $0.95 \times 1000 = 950$

Thus, you could expect about 950 out of 1000 randomly selected test scores to be between 450 and 850.

TRY THIS Refer to Example 2 above. Out of 2300 randomly selected scores, how many would you expect to be between 650 and 950?

Using z-Scores

A measure called a *z-score* tells how far a data value is from the mean in terms of standard deviations. For example, if a data set has a mean of 50 and a standard deviation of 10, then a data value of 70 has a *z*-score of 2 because it is 2 standard deviations above the mean. Similarly, a score of 20 has a *z*-score of –3 because it is 3 standard deviations below the mean.

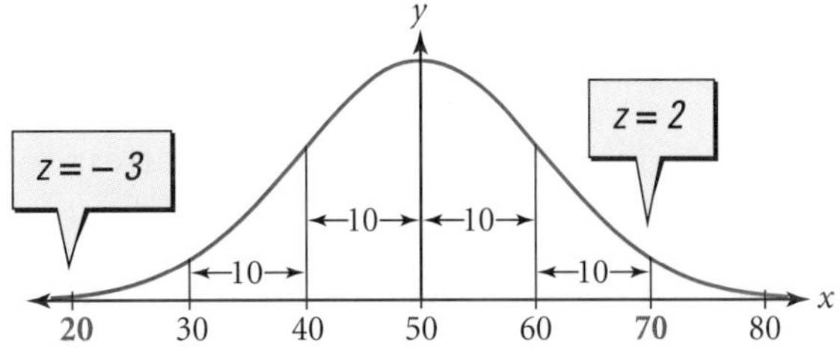

z-Score

If a data set is normally distributed with a mean of $\bar{x}$ and a standard deviation of σ, then the z-score for any data value, x, in that data set is given by $z = \frac{x - \bar{x}}{\sigma}$.

EXAMPLE 3

APPLICATION
TRAVEL

An airline finds that the travel times between two cities have a mean of 85 minutes and a standard deviation of 7 minutes. Assume that the travel times are normally distributed.

Find the probability that a flight from the first city to the second city will take between 75 minutes and 90 minutes.

Keystroke Guide, page 825

SOLUTION

Method 1

Find the area between 75 and 90 under a normal curve with a mean of 85 and a standard deviation of 7.

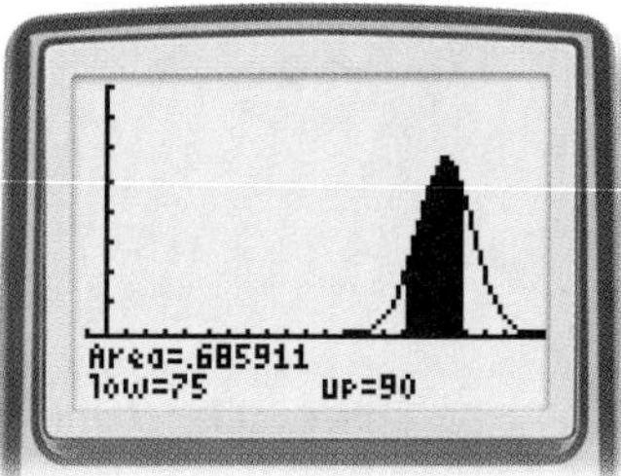

The area is about 0.686.

Method 2

Find the z-scores for $x_1 = 75$ and $x_2 = 90$.

$$z_1 = \frac{x_1 - \bar{x}}{\sigma} = \frac{75 - 85}{7} \approx -1.43 \qquad z_2 = \frac{x_2 - \bar{x}}{\sigma} = \frac{90 - 85}{7} \approx 0.71$$

Find the area between $z_1 \approx -1.43$ and $z_2 \approx 0.71$ under the standard normal curve.

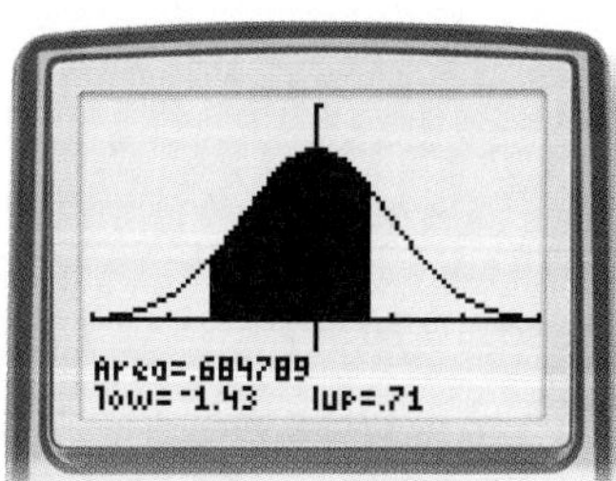

The area is about 0.685.

Thus, there is about a 69% probability that the flight will take between 75 minutes and 90 minutes.

CHECKPOINT ✔ Find the flight times that correspond to $\bar{x} - \sigma$ and $\bar{x} + \sigma$. How do your answers confirm that the solution in Example 3 is reasonable?

TRY THIS Find the probability that a flight from the first city to the second city will take between 82 minutes and 95 minutes.

Exercises

Communicate

1. Describe the characteristics of the normal curve, including the measures that define it.
2. Explain how to find the area between 25 and 50 under a normal curve with a mean of 30 and a standard deviation of 10.
3. Sketch three normal curves that have the same mean but different standard deviations. Explain how the standard deviation affects the shape of the normal curve.

Guided Skills Practice

Find each probability by using the area table for a standard normal curve given on page 807. ***(EXAMPLE 1)***

4. $P(-0.6 \leq x \leq 1.4)$
5. $P(0.2 \leq x \leq 1.8)$

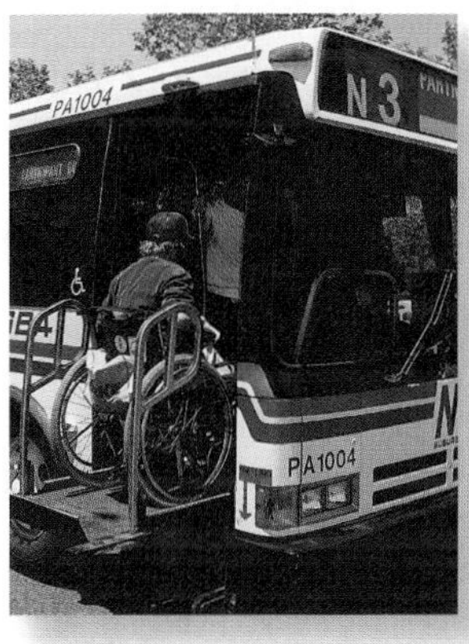

6. **MANUFACTURING** The lengths of a certain bolt are normally distributed with a mean of 8 centimeters and a standard deviation of 0.01 centimeter. ***(EXAMPLE 2)***
   a. What is the probability that a randomly selected bolt is within 0.03 centimeter of 8 centimeters?
   b. Out of 1000 randomly selected bolts, how many can the manufacturer expect to be within 0.03 centimeter of 8 centimeters?
7. **TRANSPORTATION** A bus route takes a mean of 40 minutes to complete, with a standard deviation of 5 minutes. Assume that completion times for the route are normally distributed. Find the probability that it takes between 30 minutes and 45 minutes to complete the route. ***(EXAMPLE 3)***

Practice and Apply

Let *x* be a random variable with a standard normal distribution. Use the area table for a standard normal curve, given on page 807, to find each probability.

8. $P(x \geq 0.8)$
9. $P(x \geq 0.4)$
10. $P(1.0 \leq x \leq 1.6)$
11. $P(0.2 \leq x \leq 1.8)$
12. $P(x \geq 1)$
13. $P(x \geq 2)$
14. $P(x \leq -0.2)$
15. $P(x \leq -1.4)$
16. $P(-0.4 \leq x \leq 0.4)$
17. $P(-0.2 \leq x \leq 0.2)$
18. $P(x \geq -1.6)$
19. $P(x \geq -0.8)$

Let *x* be a random variable with a standard normal distribution. Use a graphics calculator to find each probability. Round answers to the nearest ten-thousandth.

20. $P(0.653 \leq x)$
21. $P(1.456 \leq x)$
22. $P(1.254 \leq x)$
23. $P(1.457 \leq x)$
24. $P(0.842 \leq x \leq 1.233)$
25. $P(0.423 \leq x \leq 1.438)$

A city's annual rainfall is approximately normally distributed with a mean of 40 inches and a standard deviation of 6 inches. Find the probability, to the nearest ten-thousandth, for each amount of annual rainfall in the city.

26. less than 34 inches

27. greater than 46 inches

28. greater than 52 inches

29. less than 28 inches

30. between 34 and 40 inches

31. between 34 and 46 inches

Scores on a professional exam are normally distributed with a mean of 500 and a standard deviation of 50. Out of 28,000 randomly selected exams, find the number of exams that could be expected to have each score.

32. greater than 500

33. greater than 550

34. less than 600

35. less than 400

36. between 450 and 550

37. between 400 and 600

A survey of male shoe sizes is approximately normally distributed with a mean size of 9 and a standard deviation of 1.5. Use *z*-scores to find each probability to the nearest ten-thousandth.

38 $P(9 \leq x \leq 10)$

39 $P(10 \leq x \leq 11)$

40 $P(7 \leq x \leq 11)$

41 $P(7 \leq x \leq 13)$

42 $P(7 \leq x \leq 12)$

43 $P(5 \leq x)$

APPLICATIONS

TRANSPORTATION Tests show that a certain model of a new car averages 36 miles per gallon on the highway with a standard deviation of 3 miles per gallon. Assuming that the distribution is normal, find the probability, to the nearest ten-thousandth, that a car of this model gets the indicated mileage.

44. more than 40 miles per gallon

45. less than 32 miles per gallon

46. between 34 and 38 miles per gallon

MORTGAGE Mortgage statistics indicate that the number of years that a new homeowner will occupy a house before moving or selling is normally distributed with a mean of 6.3 years and a standard deviation of 2.3 years. Find the probability, to the nearest ten-thousandth, of each event.

47. A homeowner will sell or move within 3 years of buying the house.

48. A homeowner will sell or move after 10 years of buying the house.

49. A homeowner will sell or move after 6 to 8 years of buying the house.

50. QUALITY CONTROL A machine fills containers with perfume. When the machine is adjusted properly, it fills the containers with 4 fluid ounces, with a standard deviation of 0.1 fluid ounce. If 400 randomly selected containers are tested, how many containers with less than 3.8 fluid ounces of perfume will indicate that the machine needs to be adjusted?

CHALLENGE

51. **QUALITY CONTROL** The lengths of a mechanical component are normally distributed with a mean of 30.0 inches and standard deviation of 0.2 inch. All components not within 0.4 inch of 30.0 inches are rejected.

a. What percent of the components are acceptable?

b. If one of the *acceptable* components is randomly selected, what is the probability, to the nearest percent, that its length is within 0.1 inch of 30.0 inches?

Look Back

Write an equation in slope-intercept form for the line that contains the given point and is parallel to the given line. ***(LESSON 1.3)***

52. $(9, -4), y = -12x + 3$ **53.** $(1, -4), y = 100x + 12$

Write an equation in slope-intercept form for the line that contains the given point and is perpendicular to the given line. ***(LESSON 1.3)***

54. $(6, -3), y = -2x + 18$ **55.** $(-2, 7), 6x - 7y = 8$

Simplify each expression. ***(LESSON 8.4)***

56. $\frac{1}{x} + \frac{1}{x+2}$ **57.** $\frac{1}{x+1} + \frac{1}{x+2}$ **58.** $\frac{x}{1+x} + \frac{x^2+x}{x}$ **59.** $\frac{1}{x} + \frac{x+1}{x+2}$

Write each expression with a rational denominator and in simplest form. ***(LESSON 8.7)***

60. $\frac{1}{\sqrt{3}}$ **61.** $\frac{1}{\sqrt{5}}$ **62.** $\frac{1}{\sqrt{2}-1}$ **63.** $\frac{1}{1-\sqrt{3}}$

APPLICATION

64. **EDUCATION** The table at right shows the final exam scores for each student in an economics class. ***(LESSON 10.4)***

72	88	96	75	85
98	80	87	78	90
80	87	82	88	93
92	84	97	98	83

a. Find the range and the mean deviation of the scores.

b. Find the variance and the standard deviation of the scores.

Find the indicated sum of the arithmetic series 5 + 7 + 9 + 11 + · · · ***(LESSON 11.3)***

65. S_3 **66.** S_4 **67.** S_{10} **68.** S_{15}

Find the indicated sum of the geometric series $1 + \frac{3}{2} + \frac{9}{4} + \frac{27}{8} + \cdots$ ***(LESSON 11.5)***

69. S_3 **70.** S_4 **71.** S_{10} **72.** S_{15}

Look Beyond

73 *Exponential distributions* are widely used to model lifetimes of electronic components which are generally not affected by how long they have already been operated. Suppose that the lifetime (in months) of a certain fuse can be modeled by the exponential density function $f(x) = \frac{1}{100}e^{\frac{-x}{100}}$ for $x \geq 0$. Graph f and describe its general shape.

Chapter Twelve Project

That's NOT Fair!

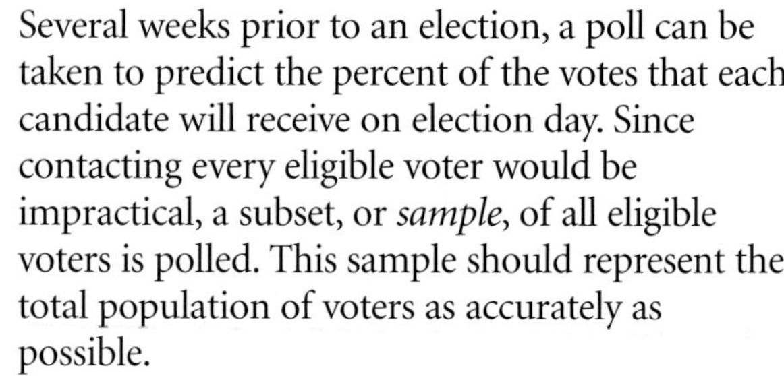

Several weeks prior to an election, a poll can be taken to predict the percent of the votes that each candidate will receive on election day. Since contacting every eligible voter would be impractical, a subset, or *sample*, of all eligible voters is polled. This sample should represent the total population of voters as accurately as possible.

A certain city with 80,000 eligible voters can be divided into four areas that roughly correspond to the annual family incomes shown in the table below.

Area	Number of voters	Family income
Rolling Hills	400	over $100,000
South Park	40,600	$75,000–$100,000
West Side	27,000	$35,000–$74,999
North End	12,000	under $35,000

The sampling methods below will not give a good representation of the total population of voters in this city for the reasons given.

1. **Every home in Rolling Hills** The Rolling Hills area has families with the highest income level. Voters from this area might tend to vote for a candidate who will represent their interests by promising to lower taxes, to provide services based on property and home values, and so on.
2. **100 homes in each of the four areas** The 80,000 eligible voters in the city are not divided equally among the four areas. South Park and West Side would be *under* represented in the sample while Rolling Hills and North End would be *over* represented.
3. **Every 10th person entering the terminal building at the local commercial airport that serves this city** The frequency of airline trips is not a characteristic that is equally distributed among the total population of the city. Business people tend to fly more often than many other people.

In contrast to the faulty sampling methods discussed above, there are efficient methods that provide a more representative sample of a given population. Two examples are:

- Telephone every nth person listed in the telephone book.
- Mail a questionnaire with a stamped return envelope to every nth person in the telephone book. Notice that even these methods are not truly representative. For example, some people don't have telephones, some have unlisted numbers, some might not return their questionnaires, and so on. Still, for a specific city or area, these methods often give a fairly representative sample.

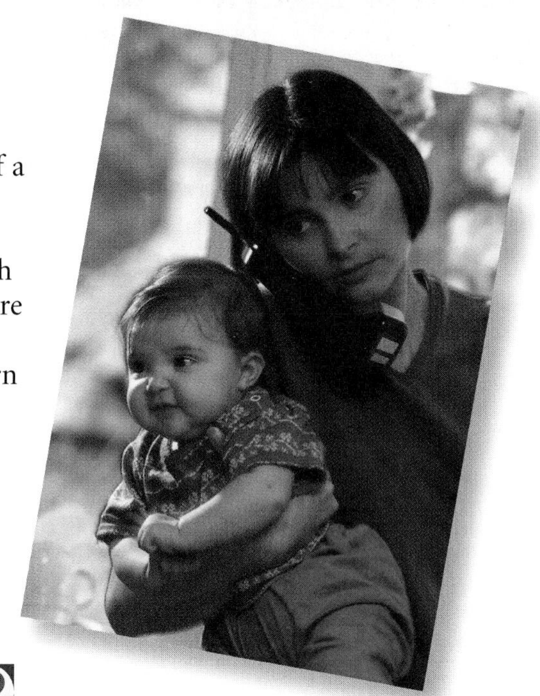

Activity 1

Tell whether each sampling procedure below provides a poor or a reasonable representation of the total population. Justify your answers.

1. To determine the mean (average) weight of all 20-year-old males, find the weight of all 20-year-old males in the U.S. Naval Academy.
2. To determine the majority opinion on whether a city should treat its water supply with fluoride, publish a ballot in the city's newspaper and ask the public to vote and mail the ballot to the newspaper's office.
3. To determine the majority opinion on a very controversial topic, have television viewers telephone in a "yes" or "no" response.
4. To determine the average number of chocolate chips per cookie in a bag of cookies, find the average number in every fifth cookie.
5. To determine the quality of a given model of automobile, test the last one assembled on every Friday of the model year.
6. To estimate the average brightness of the stars in the summer sky, an astronomer measures the brightness of all the stars that she can see and computes the average brightness.
7. To determine whether the effectiveness of a herbicide was less than advertised, a researcher samples a group of 50 randomly selected users of the herbicide for their opinion about its effectiveness.

Activity 2

1. Design a survey to conduct among a sample of your classmates that represents the student population at your school. Describe what you think the results of your survey will reveal. Explain why you think your sample is a reasonable and fair representation of the entire student population.
2. Conduct your survey. Then represent the data in two of the following formats: a stem-and-leaf plot, histogram, circle graph, or box-and-whisker plot. Explain why you chose these two formats to represent your data.
3. What conclusions can you make about the results of your survey? How do statistical measures and graphs support your conclusions? Are the results what you expected?

Chapter Review and Assessment

VOCABULARY

Key Skills & Exercises

LESSON 12.1

Key Skills

Find the mean, median, and mode.

For the data set 8, 7, 4, 5, 9, 4, 5, 4, 2, 3:

mean

$$\bar{x} = \frac{2+3+4+4+4+5+5+7+8+9}{10} = 5.1$$

median

2, 3, 4, 4, **4, 5,** 5, 7, 8, 9

The middle numbers are 4 and 5, so the median is 4.5.

mode

The mode is 4.

Exercises

Find the mean, median, and mode of each data set.

1. 7, 9, 2, 9, 0, 2, 8, 9, 1

2. −3, 8, 2, 3, 2, 4, 3, 2

Make a frequency table for each data set, and find the mean.

3. 5, 4, 6, 5, 4, 6, 6, 5, 4, 7, 4, 5, 6

4. 9, 10, 11, 8, 10, 10, 11, 9, 8, 10

LESSON 12.2

Key Skills

Make a stem-and-leaf plot.

Data: 4, 4, 28, 3, 29, 15, 12, 16, 17, 24, 16, 28, 5, 28, 29

Stems	Leaves 1|2 = 12
0	3, 4, 4, 5
1	2, 5, 6, 6, 7
2	4, 8, 8, 8, 9, 9

Make a histogram.

Data: 5, 2, 3, 3, 6, 1, 3, 4, 2, 3, 1, 5, 5, 2, 4

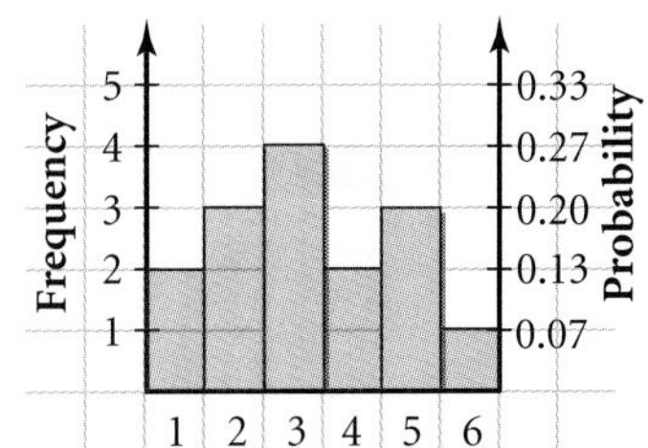

Exercises

Make a stem-and-leaf plot for each data set.

5. 35, 38, 45, 49, 45, 53, 57, 58

6. 67, 87, 82, 73, 81, 78, 79, 69

Make a histogram for each data set.

7. 4, 3, 2, 5, 4, 5, 6, 1, 2, 4, 3, 1

8. 24, 28, 30, 30, 22, 21, 29, 29, 30, 27, 26, 28, 22, 23, 25, 27, 28, 28, 24

Make a relative frequency histogram for each data set.

9. 1, 1, 3, 3, 5, 2, 5, 3

10. 10, 14, 14, 11, 15, 13, 12

Make a circle graph.

For	98
Against	67
Undecided	20

For 53%
Undecided 11%
Against 36%

Divide each category in the table by the total, 185, to find its percent. Then multiply its percent by 360° to find the measure of the central angle.

11. The table below lists the number of people who selected each brand. Make a circle graph of the results.

Brand X	53
Brand Y	32
Brand Z	89

LESSON 12.3

Key Skills

Find the minimum and maximum values, range, quartiles, and interquartile range for a data set.

Data: 5, 6, 9, 2, 3, 7, 2, 9, 8
Arrange the data set in ascending order.

2 2 3 5 6 7 8 9 9

$$Q_1 = \frac{2+3}{2} = 2.5 \quad Q_2 = 6 \quad Q_3 = \frac{8+9}{2} = 8.5$$

$$\text{range} = 9 - 2 = 7 \qquad \text{IQR} = 8.5 - 2.5 = 6$$

Make a box-and-whisker plot.

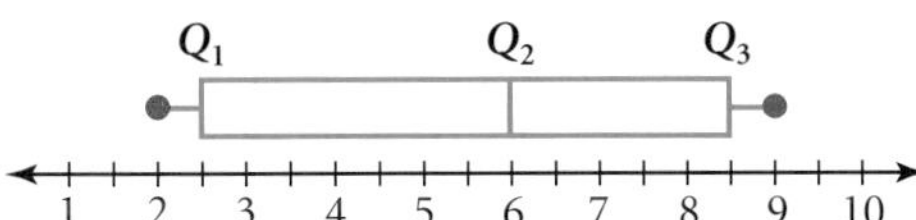

Exercises

Find the quartiles of each data set.

12. 12, 18, 13, 15, 16, 19, 17, 13, 14, 19, 17, 16

13. 23, 28, 34, 36, 34, 29, 35, 31, 45, 22, 23, 25

Make a box-and-whisker plot for each data set.

14. 5, 4, 9, 3, 1, 9, 0, 6, 3, 2

15. 22, 28, 29, 24, 25, 28, 29, 23, 23, 29

LESSON 12.4

Key Skills

Find the range, variance, mean deviation, and standard deviation of a data set.

Data: 3, 2, 3, 5, 7, 5
In ascending order:

2, 3, 3, 5, 5, 7

Range: 7 − 2 = 5

Mean:

$$\frac{2+3+3+5+5+7}{6} \approx 4.167$$

x_i	$\lvert x_i - \overline{x}\rvert$
3	1.167
2	2.167
3	1.167
5	0.833
7	2.833
5	0.833
Total	9

Mean deviation: $\frac{9}{6} = 1.5$

Variance: $\frac{1}{6}\sum_{i=1}^{6}(x_i - \overline{x})^2 \approx 2.8$

Standard deviation: $\sqrt{2.8} \approx 1.7$

Exercises

Find the range and mean deviation of each data set.

16. 6, 10, 12, 4, 14, 8, 11, 14

17. 20, 22, 15, 14, 13, 17

18. 3, 6, −7, 9, −3, 2

19. 4, −8, 12, 13, −22, 24, 21

Find the variance and standard deviation of each data set.

20. 10, 12, 15, 18, 11, 13, 14, 16, 19, 20

21. 100, 140, 130, 180, 80, 160

22. 8, 9, 12, 14, 7, 9, 11, 13, 14

23. 3, 4, 12, 2, 3, 4, 6, 12, 18, 20, 2

LESSON 12.5

Key Skills

Find probabilities of events in a binomial experiment.

A certain trick coin has a probability of 0.75 for heads and 0.25 for tails.

The probability of 3 heads appearing in 5 tosses of the coin is found by using the formula for binomial probability, as shown below.

$$P(\text{exactly 3 heads}) = {}_5C_3(0.75)^3(0.25^{5-3}) \approx 0.26$$

Exercises

Given 10 trials of a binomial experiment with 0.6 probability of success, find each probability below.

24. P(exactly 2 successes)

25. P(exactly 3 successes)

26. P(at least 3 successes)

27. Find the probability of at least 3 heads in 5 tosses of a fair coin.

LESSON 12.6

Key Skills

Find probabilities by using a normal distribution.

Let x be a random variable with a standard normal distribution. To find $P(-1.6 \le x \le 0.4)$, use the area table for a standard normal curve on page 807.

$$P(-1.6 \le x \le 0.4) \approx 0.4452 + 0.1554 \approx 0.6006$$

Use z-scores to find probabilities.

If x is a random data value with a normally distributed data set with a mean of 6 and a standard deviation of 3, find $P(8 \le x \le 11)$.

$$z_1 = \frac{8-6}{3} = \frac{2}{3} \approx 0.667$$

$$z_2 = \frac{11-6}{3} = \frac{5}{3} \approx 1.667$$

$$P(8 \le x \le 11) \approx 0.205$$

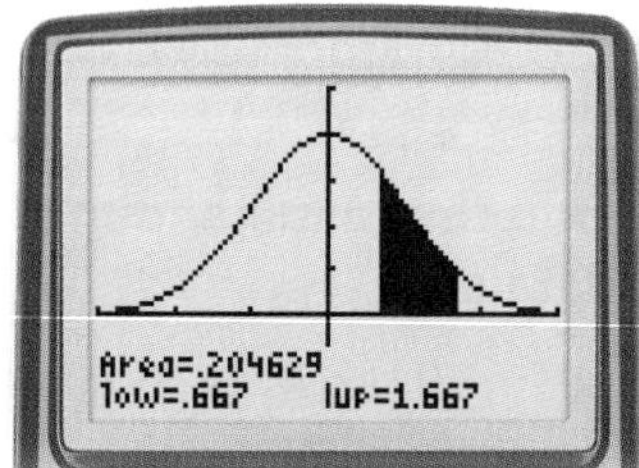

Exercises

Let x be a random variable with a standard normal distribution. Use the area table for a standard normal curve on page 807 to find each probability.

28. $P(x \le 0.4)$

29. $P(x \ge -1.8)$

30. $P(-1.6 \le x \le 1.6)$

31. $P(-0.8 \le x \le 0.8)$

Let x be a random data value with a normally distributed data set with a mean of 20 and a standard deviation of 2. Use z-scores to find each probability to the nearest percent.

32. $P(x \le -21)$

33. $P(x \le 18.6)$

34. $P(16.5 \le x \le 23.5)$

35. $P(17.2 \le x \le 22)$

Applications

36. **AUTOMOBILE DISTRIBUTION** The table at right gives the number of each type of vehicle on a car dealer's lot. Make a circle graph to represent this data.

Type	Number
cars (other than sports cars)	50
sports cars	20
trucks	30
sports utility vehicles	28

Alternative Assessment

Performance Assessment

1. **DEMOGRAPHICS** The number of live births per 1000 women of ages 15–44 in the United States in 1996 is given in the table.

Age	Number
15–17	34.0
18–19	86.5
20–24	111.1
25–29	113.9
30–34	84.5
35–39	35.4
40–44	6.8

[*Source: CDCP*]

   a. Make a frequency table with equal class sizes.

   b. Estimate the mean age for this data.

   c. Make a histogram from the frequency table. Tell what the shape of the histogram indicates.

   d. Make a circle graph from the frequency table. What does it most clearly indicate?

2. **AIR QUALITY** The table below shows ozone readings in parts per million (ppm) for 23 weekdays in July of 1998 in St. Louis, Missouri.

40	61	78	54
90	61	47	50
42	87	50	80
51	44	105	40
102	43	42	48
50	71	29	

[*Source: EPA*]

   a. Make a stem-and-leaf plot for this data.

   b. On how many days were the readings less than 50?

   c. Find the mean, median, and mode for the data set. Which measure is most useful? Why?

   d. Find the range and standard deviation.

   e. Make a box-and-whisker plot of the data.

Portfolio Projects

1. **EVERYDAY USE OF STATISTICS** Examine recent magazines and newspapers for examples of statistical information.

   a. Find examples of numerical statistics. Describe each situation, and explain why statistics were used.

   b. Find examples of circle graphs and histograms (or bar graphs). Why was each particular display used? Is it successful? Justify your responses.

   c. Create a misleading graph for one of the situations that you found. Explain why your graph is misleading.

2. **HEIGHT DISTRIBUTIONS** The heights for males and females are normally distributed according to the data below.

	97.5% are more than	Mean	97.5% are less than
Male	158 cm	172 cm	186 cm
Female	147 cm	161 cm	175 cm

[*Source: Environmental Systems*]

   a. Sketch normal distribution curves for the heights of males and of females. Use the same set of axes for both graphs.

   b. What is the standard deviation for the heights of males? of females? What unit is used to measure the standard deviation?

   c. What is the probability, to the nearest percent, that a randomly selected adult (of the appropriate gender) has the same height as you?

internetconnect

The HRW Web site contains many resources to reinforce and expand your knowledge of statistics. This Web site also provides Internet links to other sites where you can find information and real-world data for use in research projects, reports, and activities that involve statistics. Visit the HRW Web site at **go.hrw.com**, and enter the keyword **MB1 CH12** to access the resources for this chapter.

1–12 College Entrance Exam Practice

QUANTITATIVE COMPARISON For Items 1–5, write
A if the quantity in Column A is greater than the quantity in Column B;
B if the quantity in Column B is greater than the quantity in Column A;
C if the quantities are equal; or
D if the relationship cannot be determined from the given information.

	Column A	Column B	Answers
1.	The value of x: $\frac{2x}{7}=\frac{3x-1}{4}$	The value of x: $\frac{x}{6}=\frac{2x}{5}$	(A) (B) (C) (D) [Lesson 12.1]
2.	$\lceil 3.95 \rceil$	$\lceil 4.95 \rceil$	(A) (B) (C) (D) [Lesson 2.6]
3.	The maximum value of $f(x)=-(x+4)^2+3$	The minimum value of $g(x)=2(x-5)^2-1$	(A) (B) (C) (D) [Lesson 10.3]
4.	${}_5C_3$	${}_5P_3$	(A) (B) (C) (D) [Lesson 5.1]
5.	The mean of 76, 78, 71, 78, 72, 75	The median of 76, 78, 71, 78, 72, 75	(A) (B) (C) (D) [Lesson 1.4]

6. Solve $4(5+2x)=42-3x$. ***(LESSON 1.6)***
a. $x=-2$ **b.** $x=4$
c. $x=2$ **d.** $x=12$

7. Which is the axis of symmetry of the graph of $y=2x^2-8x-1$? ***(LESSON 5.1)***
a. $x=1$ **b.** $x=-1$
c. $x=2$ **d.** $x=-2$

8. Which expression gives the function rule for $f \circ g$, where $f(x)=3-x$ and $g(x)=2x$? ***(LESSON 2.4)***
a. $3-2x$ **b.** $3+2x$
c. $2(3-x)$ **d.** $6-2x$

9. Simplify $\left(-\frac{2a^{-2}}{b^{-1}}\right)^3$. ***(LESSON 2.2)***
a. $\frac{8a^6}{b^3}$ **b.** $\frac{-8b^6}{a^3}$
c. $\frac{-8b^3}{a^6}$ **d.** $-\frac{8a^6}{b^3}$

10. Which property is illustrated by $a+0=a$, where a represents a real number? ***(LESSON 2.1)***
a. Identity **b.** Inverse
c. Reciprocal **d.** Closure

11. How many solutions does a consistent system of linear equations have? ***(LESSON 3.1)***
a. 0 **b.** 1
c. at least 1 **d.** infinite

12. Which expression is equivalent to $|x-2|=6$? ***(LESSON 1.8)***
a. $x=4$ **b.** $x=8$
c. $x=-4$ *or* $x=8$ **d.** $x=8$ *and* $x=-8$

13. Which best describes the roots of $3x^2+2x-5=0$? ***(LESSON 5.6)***
a. 1 real root **b.** 2 rational roots
c. 2 irrational roots **d.** 2 imaginary roots

14. Which function represents exponential decay? **(LESSON 6.2)**

a. $f(x) = 2.5^x$ b. $f(x) = 2(5)^x$
c. $f(x) = 2(0.5)^x$ d. $f(x) = 2x^2$

15. Evaluate $-\frac{1}{3}\sqrt[3]{27}$. **(LESSON 8.6)**

a. 3 b. −3 c. 1 d. −1

16. Which is the remainder when $2x^2 - 5x + 8$ is divided by $x + 4$? **(LESSON 7.3)**

a. 60 b. −44 c. 0 d. 20

17. Which expression is equivalent to $\log_a \frac{xy}{2}$? **(LESSON 6.4)**

a. $\log_a 2xy$ b. $\log_a y + 2 \log_a a$
c. $\log_a xy - \log_a 2$ d. $\log_a xy + \log_a 2$

18. Solve $\begin{cases} 2x^2 + y^2 = 36 \\ x^2 - y^2 = 12 \end{cases}$. **(LESSON 9.6)**

a. $(2\sqrt{13}, 8), (-2\sqrt{13}, 8)$
b. $(8, 2\sqrt{13}), (-8, 2\sqrt{13})$
c. $(2, 4), (2, -4), (-2, 4), (-2, -4)$
d. $(4, 2)(-4, 2), (4, -2), (-4, -2)$

19. Write the equation in slope-intercept form for the line that has a slope of $-\frac{5}{3}$ and contains the point $(8, -3)$. **(LESSON 1.3)**

20. Write the function that represents the graph of $f(x) = |x|$ translated 2 units to the left. **(LESSON 2.7)**

21. Factor $25x^2 - 9$, if possible. **(LESSON 5.3)**

22. Graph $-2 < y \le 3$ in a coordinate plane. **(LESSON 3.4)**

Let $A = \begin{bmatrix} 1 & 4 \\ -3 & -1 \end{bmatrix}$ **and** $B = \begin{bmatrix} 1 & -11 \\ 6 & 15 \end{bmatrix}$**. Perform the indicated operations. (LESSON 4.1)**

23. AB

24. $3BA$

25. $A + B$

26. $B - 2A$

27. Use elimination to solve the system. **(LESSON 3.2)** $\begin{cases} 5x + 11y = -7 \\ -3x + 2y = 30 \end{cases}$

28. Multiply $(5 - 2i)(5 - 2i)$. **(LESSON 5.6)**

29. Find the domain of $g(x) = \frac{x^2 - 1}{x - 5}$. **(LESSON 8.2)**

30. Evaluate $e^{\ln 2} + \ln e^{-7}$. **(LESSON 6.5)**

31. Describe the end behavior of $P(x) = -2x^3 + x^2 - 11x + 4$. **(LESSON 7.2)**

32. If a coin is tossed 10 times, what is the probability that it will land heads up exactly 4 times? **(LESSON 12.5)**

33. Divide by using synthetic division. $(3x^3 - 18x + 12) \div (x - 3)$ **(LESSON 7.3)**

34. Solve $x^2 + 2x - 1 \le 0$, and graph its solution. **(LESSON 5.7)**

35. Solve $\frac{3}{x^2 - 4} = \frac{-2}{5x + 10}$. **(LESSON 8.5)**

36. Find the domain of $g(x) = \sqrt{1 - 2(x + 1)}$. **(LESSON 8.6)**

37. In how many ways can a committee of 5 be chosen from a group of 8? **(LESSON 10.3)**

38. Factor $x^3 + 125$. **(LESSON 7.3)**

FREE-RESPONSE GRID The following questions may be answered by using a free-response grid such as that commonly used by standardized-test services.

39. Simplify $\sqrt{27^{\frac{2}{3}}}$. **(LESSON 8.7)**

40. Evaluate $10^{\log_{10} 1000} - \log_2 2$. **(LESSON 6.4)**

41. Find the value of v in $2 = \log_v 64$. **(LESSON 6.3)**

42. Find the sixth term of the sequence −100, 500, −250, . . . **(LESSON 11.4)**

43. Find the distance between the points $P(-3, 2)$ and $Q(1, 5)$. **(LESSON 9.1)**

ENTERTAINMENT The top 10 movies grossed the dollar amounts (in millions) shown at right in one weekend.

4.0	14.8
3.7	10.6
3.0	6.1
2.9	5.6
2.5	4.2

44. Find the mean for this data set. **(LESSON 12.1)**

45. Find the range for this data set. **(LESSON 12.4)**

Keystroke Guide for Chapter 12

Essential keystroke sequences (using the model TI-82 or TI-83 graphics calculator) are presented below for all Activities and Examples found in this chapter that require or recommend the use of a graphics calculator.

 internet**connect**

Keystrokes for other models of graphics calculators are found on the HRW Web site.

LESSON 12.2

EXAMPLE 2 Make a histogram for the canoe rental data given.

Page 774

First clear old data and old equations.

Use viewing window [0, 9] by [0, 11].

Enter the data:

STAT EDIT 1:Edit ENTER L1 1 ENTER 4 ENTER 5 ENTER 2 ENTER 2 ENTER 2 ENTER 3 ENTER 2 ENTER 3 ENTER . . .

Continue until all of the data values are entered into List 1.

Make a histogram:

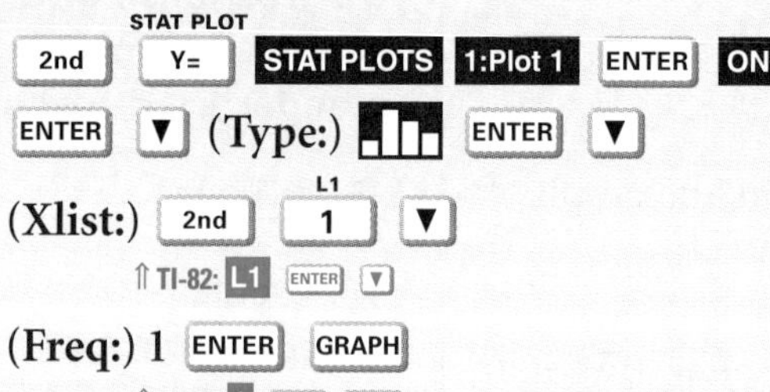

(Freq:) 1 ENTER GRAPH

⇑ TI-82: 1 ENTER GRAPH

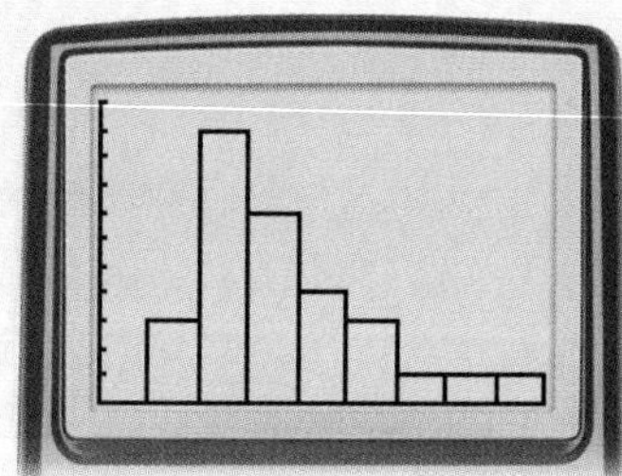

LESSON 12.3

EXAMPLE 2 Make box-and-whisker plots for the temperature data given.

Page 784

Use viewing window [10, 80] by [0, 1].

Enter the data:

STAT EDIT 1:Edit ENTER L1 21 ENTER 25.5 ENTER 37 ENTER 48.6 ENTER . . .

Continue until all of the data values for Chicago are entered into List 1.

► L2 55.9 ENTER 57 ENTER 58.3 ENTER 60.8 ENTER 63.3 ENTER . . .

Continue until all of the data values for Los Angeles are entered into List 2.

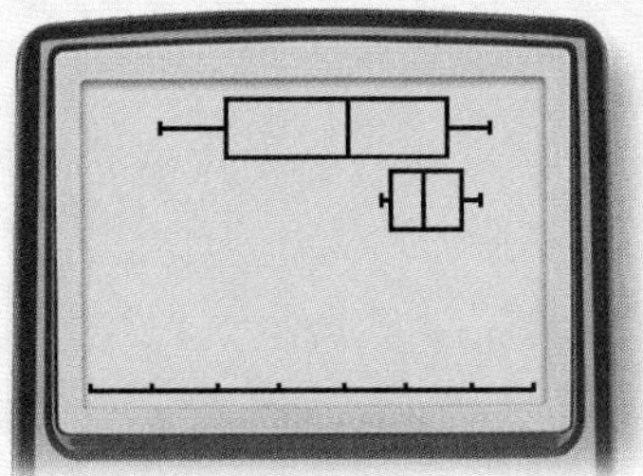

Make the box-and-whisker plots:

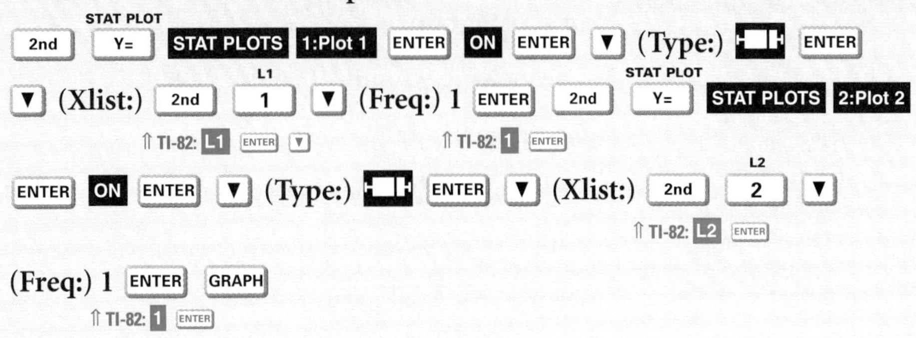

LESSON 12.4

TECHNOLOGY
Page 795

Find the standard deviations for the monthly precipitation data.

Enter the data:

Use a keystroke sequence similar to that in Example 2 of Lesson 12.3 to enter the data into Lists 1 and 2.

Find the standard deviations:

STAT CALC 1:1-Var Stats ENTER 2nd L1 1 ENTER

STAT CALC 1:1-Var Stats ENTER 2nd L2 2 ENTER

LESSON 12.5

EXAMPLE 1
Page 800

Evaluate $P = {}_nC_r\, p^r\,(1-p)^{n-r}$ for $n = 10$, $r = 7$, and $p = 0.8$.

10 MATH PRB 3:nCr ENTER 7 × .8 ^
7 × .2 ^ 3 ENTER

EXAMPLE 2
Page 801

Find the probability of "6 successes" *or* "7 successes" *or* "8 successes" in a binomial experiment in which there are 8 possible outcomes and the probability of success is 0.96.

The TI-82 model does not have a program for finding binomial probabilities.

2nd DISTR VARS DISTR O:binompdf(ENTER 8 ,
.96 , 6) + 2nd DISTR VARS DISTR
O:binompdf(ENTER 8 , .96 , 7)
+ 2nd DISTR VARS DISTR O:binompdf(ENTER
8 , .96 , 8) ENTER

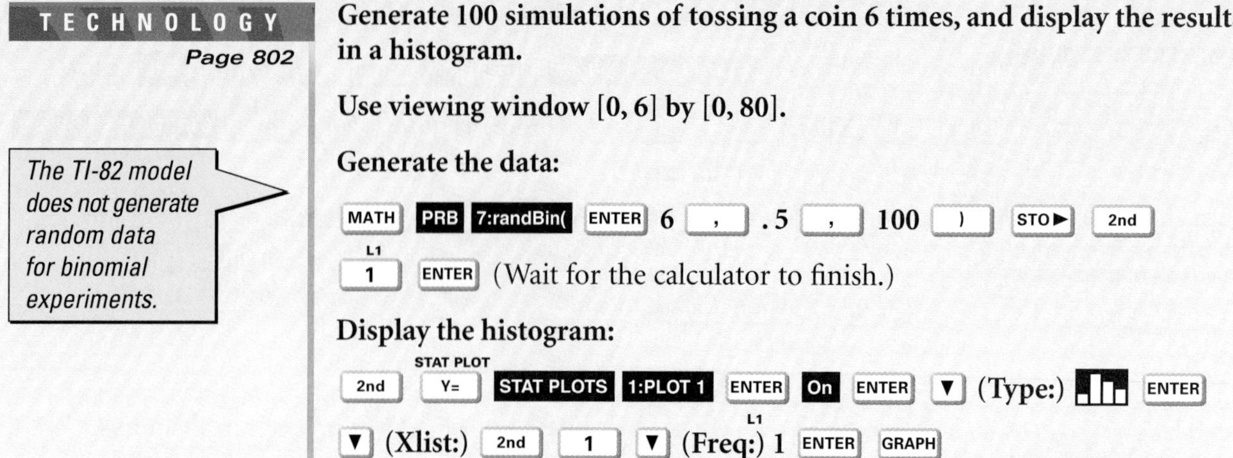

TECHNOLOGY
Page 802

The TI-82 model does not generate random data for binomial experiments.

Generate 100 simulations of tossing a coin 6 times, and display the results in a histogram.

Use viewing window [0, 6] by [0, 80].

Generate the data:

MATH PRB 7:randBin(ENTER 6 , .5 , 100) STO▶ 2nd L1 1 ENTER (Wait for the calculator to finish.)

Display the histogram:

2nd STAT PLOT Y= STAT PLOTS 1:PLOT 1 ENTER On ENTER ▼ (Type:) [histogram] ENTER ▼ (Xlist:) 2nd L1 1 ▼ (Freq:) 1 ENTER GRAPH

LESSON 12.6

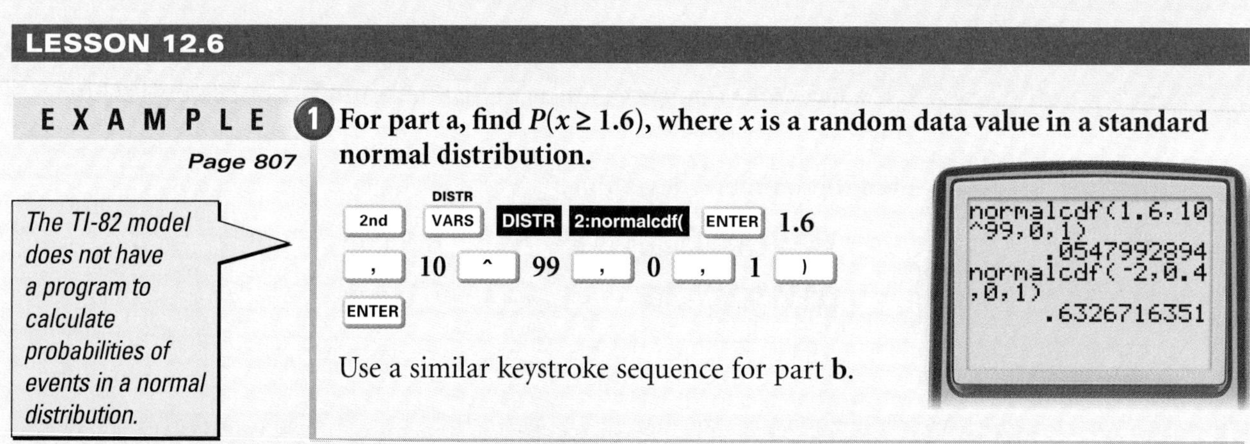

EXAMPLE 1
Page 807

The TI-82 model does not have a program to calculate probabilities of events in a normal distribution.

For part a, find $P(x \geq 1.6)$, where x is a random data value in a standard normal distribution.

2nd DISTR VARS DISTR 2:normalcdf(ENTER 1.6 , 10 ^ 99 , 0 , 1) ENTER

normalcdf(1.6,10
^99,0,1)
.0547992894
normalcdf(-2,0.4
,0,1)
.6326716351

Use a similar keystroke sequence for part **b**.

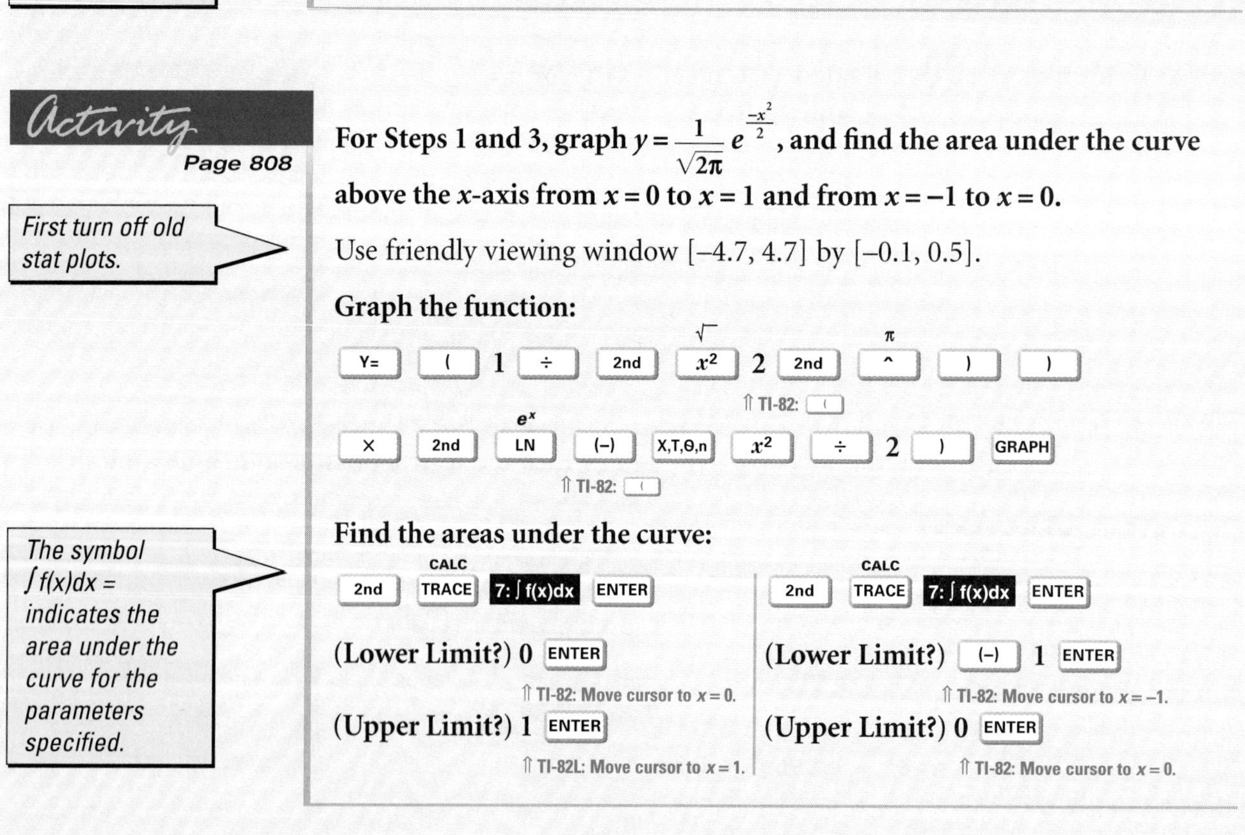

Activity
Page 808

First turn off old stat plots.

For Steps 1 and 3, graph $y = \frac{1}{\sqrt{2\pi}} e^{\frac{-x^2}{2}}$, and find the area under the curve above the x-axis from $x = 0$ to $x = 1$ and from $x = -1$ to $x = 0$.

Use friendly viewing window [–4.7, 4.7] by [–0.1, 0.5].

Graph the function:

Y= (1 ÷ 2nd √ x^2 2 2nd π ^)) (⇑ TI-82: ( )

× 2nd e^x LN (–) X,T,θ,n x^2 ÷ 2) GRAPH (⇑ TI-82: ( )

The symbol ∫ f(x)dx = indicates the area under the curve for the parameters specified.

Find the areas under the curve:

2nd CALC TRACE 7: ∫ f(x)dx ENTER

(Lower Limit?) 0 ENTER
⇑ TI-82: Move cursor to $x = 0$.

(Upper Limit?) 1 ENTER
⇑ TI-82L: Move cursor to $x = 1$.

2nd CALC TRACE 7: ∫ f(x)dx ENTER

(Lower Limit?) (–) 1 ENTER
⇑ TI-82: Move cursor to $x = -1$.

(Upper Limit?) 0 ENTER
⇑ TI-82: Move cursor to $x = 0$.

EXAMPLE 3 For Method 1, find the area between 75 and 90 under a normal curve with a mean of 85 and a standard deviation of 7.

Page 810

To clear anything created through a draw command, press 2nd PRGM (DRAW) 1:ClrDraw ENTER ENTER.

Use viewing window [–5, 110] by [–0.02, 0.08].

To find these areas with a model TI-82, use a keystroke sequence similar to that used in the Activity for Lesson 12.6.

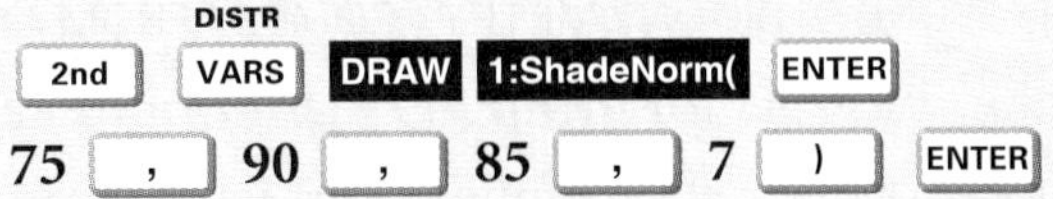

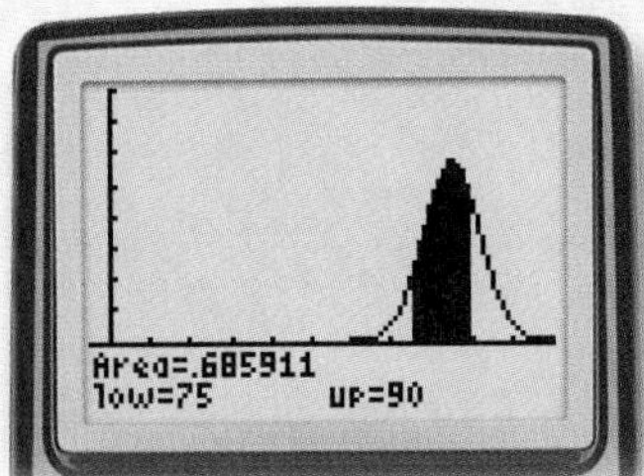

For Method 2, find the area between $x \approx -1.43$ and $x \approx 0.71$ under the standard normal curve.

Use viewing window [–3, 3] by [–0.2, 0.5].

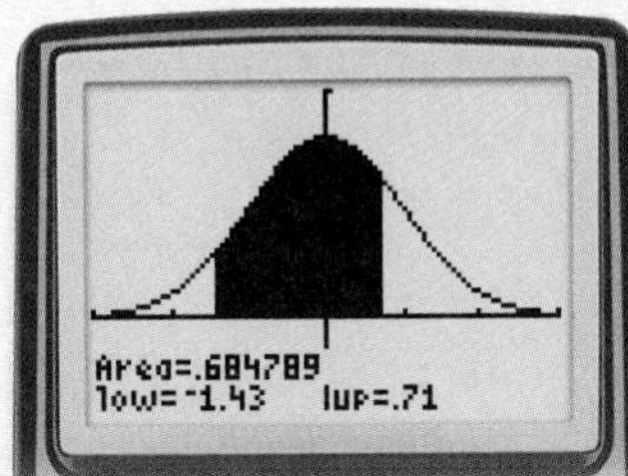

13

Trigonometric Functions

THE WORD TRIGONOMETRY COMES FROM THE Greek words for triangle (*trigonon*) and measure (*metria*). Trigonometry is commonly described as the study of the relationship between the angles and sides of a triangle.

Trigonometry has a wide variety of applications in physics, astronomy, architecture, engineering, and other disciplines. People's understanding and interest in triangles can be observed in the structures shown here.

The Pyramids at Giza, Egypt

Lessons

The Louvre Museum, Paris, France

About the Chapter Project

George W. G. Ferris constructed the first Ferris wheel for the World's Exposition in Chicago in 1893. In the Chapter Project, you will create a model for the altitude of a rider on the Ferris wheel at Chicago's Navy Pier, which is modeled after Ferris's original wheel.

After completing the Chapter Project, you will be able to do the following:

- Model the height of a point on a Ferris wheel as a function of time.
- Interpret the real-world meaning of each parameter in your model.
- Find the speed of a point on a given Ferris wheel.

About the Portfolio Activities

Throughout the chapter, you will be given opportunities to complete Portfolio Activities that are designed to support your work on the Chapter Project.

- Sketching a rough graph for the height of a point on the Ferris wheel (relative to the center of the wheel) as a function of the angle of rotation is included in the Portfolio Activity on page 835.
- Sketching a graph for the altitude of a rider on the Ferris wheel as a function of the angle of rotation is included in the Portfolio Activity on page 850.
- Sketching a graph for the altitude of a rider on the Ferris wheel as a function of time and finding the speed of a rider on the Ferris wheel is included in the Portfolio Activity on page 857.
- Creating and interpreting a model for the altitude of a rider on the Ferris wheel is included in the Portfolio Activity on page 866.

Rock and Roll Hall of Fame, Cleveland, Ohio

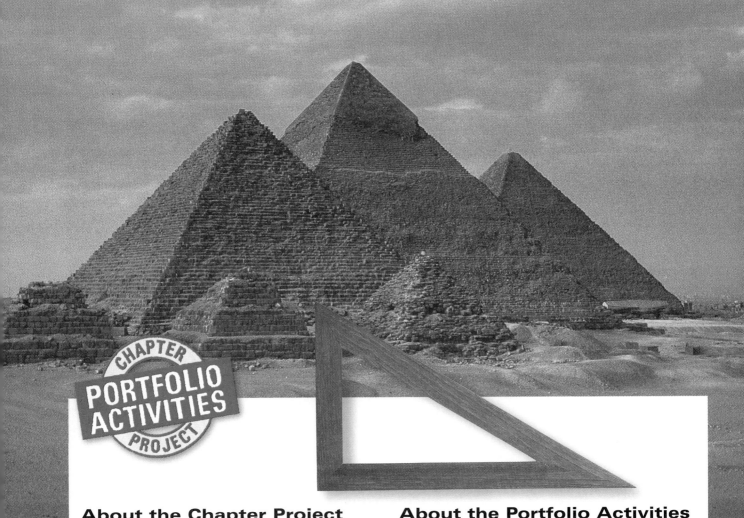

13.1

Right-Triangle Trigonometry

Objectives

- Find the trigonometric functions of acute angles.
- Solve a right triangle by using trigonometric functions.

Why *You can use right-triangle trigonometry to solve real-world problems such as finding the height of the puffins above the water.*

APPLICATION
WILDLIFE

An ornithologist is taking pictures of puffins on the edge of a cliff. To find the height of the puffins above the water, she measures a 28° *angle of elevation* of her line of sight to the puffins. If her position is about 15 feet above the water, and about 40 feet from the cliff, how high above the water are the puffins? *You will solve this problem in Example 3.*

To find the height of the puffins, you can use *trigonometry*. **Trigonometry** can be used to find the measure of an unknown angle or an unknown side length of a right triangle.

Recall from Lesson 5.2 that the *hypotenuse* of a right triangle is the side opposite the right angle. The *legs* of a right triangle are the other two sides. Each leg is opposite one of the two *acute* angles and adjacent to the other. For example, in $\triangle ABC$, $\overline{BC}$ is the leg *opposite* angle A and $\overline{AC}$ is the leg *adjacent* to angle A.

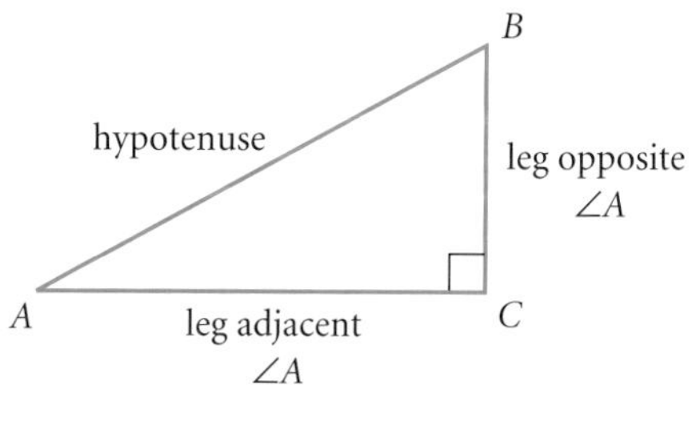

CHECKPOINT ✔ Identify the legs of $\triangle ABC$ above by their relationship to $\angle B$.

Triangle ABC at right shows the abbreviations for the lengths of the sides of a right triangle in terms of $\angle A$. The six trigonometric functions are defined below with these abbreviations.

Trigonometric Functions of $\angle A$

sine of $\angle A = \frac{\text{opp.}}{\text{hyp.}}$	cosecant of $\angle A = \frac{\text{hyp.}}{\text{opp.}}$
cosine of $\angle A = \frac{\text{adj.}}{\text{hyp.}}$	secant of $\angle A = \frac{\text{hyp.}}{\text{adj.}}$
tangent of $\angle A = \frac{\text{opp.}}{\text{adj.}}$	cotangent of $\angle A = \frac{\text{adj.}}{\text{opp.}}$

The six trigonometric functions are abbreviated as sin A, cos A, tan A, csc A, sec A, and cot A.

EXAMPLE 1 **Find the values of the six trigonometric functions of $\angle X$ for $\triangle XYZ$ at right. Give exact answers and answers rounded to the nearest ten-thousandth.**

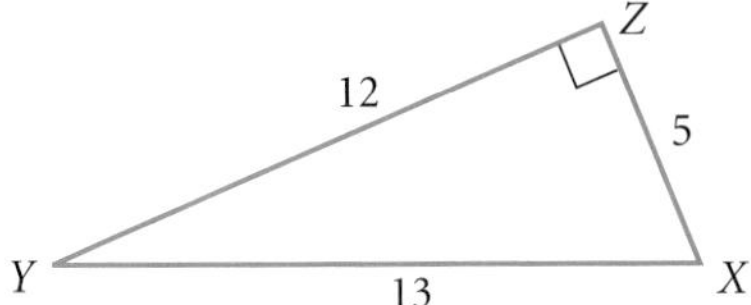

SOLUTION

$\sin X = \frac{\text{opp.}}{\text{hyp.}} = \frac{12}{13} \approx 0.9231$

$\cos X = \frac{\text{adj.}}{\text{hyp.}} = \frac{5}{13} \approx 0.3846$

$\tan X = \frac{\text{opp.}}{\text{adj.}} = \frac{12}{5} = 2.4$

$\csc X = \frac{\text{hyp.}}{\text{opp.}} = \frac{13}{12} \approx 1.0833$

$\sec X = \frac{\text{hyp.}}{\text{adj.}} = \frac{13}{5} = 2.6$

$\cot X = \frac{\text{adj.}}{\text{opp.}} = \frac{5}{12} \approx 0.4167$

TRY THIS Find the values of the six trigonometric functions of $\angle Y$ for $\triangle XYZ$. Give exact answers and answers rounded to the nearest ten-thousandth.

Notice that in the solution to Example 1, the ratios for sin X and csc X are reciprocals. Likewise, the ratios for cos X and sec X are reciprocals, and the ratios for tan X and cot X are reciprocals.

The cosecant, secant, and cotangent ratios can be expressed in terms of the sine, cosine, and tangent ratios, respectively.

$$\csc A = \frac{1}{\sin A} \qquad \sec A = \frac{1}{\cos A} \qquad \cot A = \frac{1}{\tan A}$$

CHECKPOINT ✔ Show that the following statements are also true:

$$\sin A = \frac{1}{\csc A} \qquad \cos A = \frac{1}{\sec A} \qquad \tan A = \frac{1}{\cot A}$$

CRITICAL THINKING Find the number of different possible ratios of the lengths of two sides of a triangle by using permutations. Explain what your result means. Are all possible ratios given by the functions above?

Activity

Exploring Trigonometric Functions

You will need: a protractor, a centimeter ruler, and a calculator

On a sheet of paper, make a large diagram like the one shown below. Place segments $\overline{X_1Y_1}$, $\overline{X_2Y_2}$, and $\overline{X_3Y_3}$ wherever you wish, as long as they are perpendicular to $\overrightarrow{AP}$.

1. Copy and complete the table below by measuring the indicated sides and calculating sin *A*, cos *A*, and tan *A*.
2. Are all of the entries approximately equal in the sin *A* column? in the cos *A* column? in the tan *A* column?

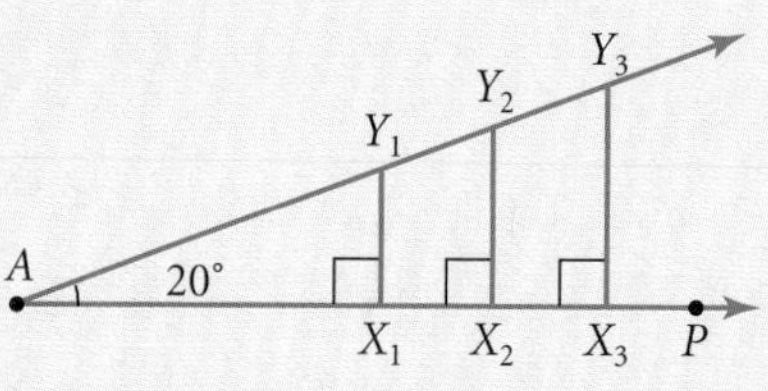

	opp. ∠A	adj. ∠A	hyp.	$\sin A = \frac{\text{opp.}}{\text{hyp.}}$	$\cos A = \frac{\text{adj.}}{\text{hyp.}}$	$\tan A = \frac{\text{opp.}}{\text{adj.}}$
$\triangle AY_1X_1$						
$\triangle AY_2X_2$						
$\triangle AY_3X_3$						

3. Compare your results from Step 2 with your classmates' results.

CHECKPOINT ✓ 4. What can you conjecture about the sine, cosine, and tangent functions for the measure of ∠*A*?

As the results of the Activity suggest, the ratios for the sine, cosine, and tangent of an acute angle in similar triangles does not depend on the lengths of sides. The trigonometric functions depend only on the measure of the acute angle.

For any given angle measure, you can obtain values for the sine, cosine, and tangent of the angle by using a scientific calculator in degree mode. These trigonometric function values can be used to find the unknown lengths of sides, as shown in Example 2.

EXAMPLE 2

For △*ABC* shown at right, find each side length to the nearest tenth.

a. *AB* **b.** *BC*

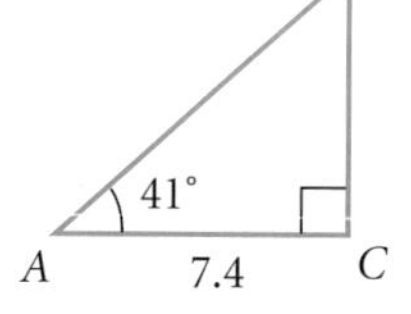

SOLUTION

From the diagram, m∠*A* = 41° and the length of the leg adjacent to ∠*A* is 7.4.

a. To find *AB*, the length of the hypotenuse, use the cosine ratio.

$$\cos A = \frac{\text{adj.}}{\text{hyp.}}$$

$$\cos 41^\circ = \frac{7.4}{AB}$$

$$AB = \frac{7.4}{\cos 41^\circ}$$

$$AB \approx \frac{7.4}{0.7547} \approx 9.8$$

b. To find *BC*, the length of the leg opposite ∠*A*, use the tangent ratio.

$$\tan A = \frac{\text{opp.}}{\text{adj.}}$$

$$\tan 41^\circ = \frac{BC}{7.4}$$

$$7.4 \times \tan 41^\circ = BC$$

$$7.4 \times 0.8693 \approx BC$$

$$BC \approx 6.4$$

TRY THIS For $\triangle KLM$ shown at right, find KL and LM to the nearest tenth.

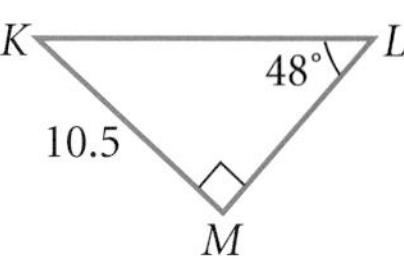

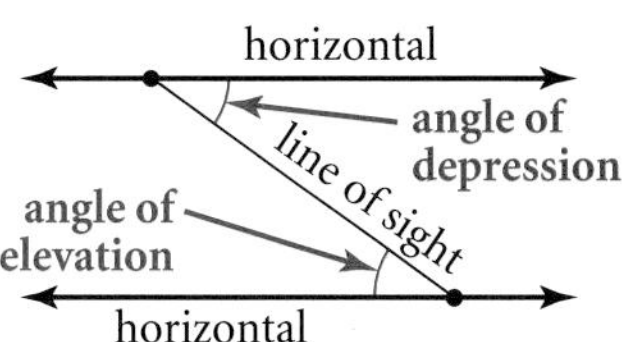

An **angle of elevation** is an angle between a horizontal line and a line of sight to a point above. An **angle of depression** is an angle between a horizontal line and a line of sight to a point below.

EXAMPLE 3 Refer to the ornithologist's problem described at the beginning of the lesson.

APPLICATION
WILDLIFE

How high above the water are the puffins? Give your answer to the nearest foot.

SOLUTION

In the diagram, BE represents the height of the puffins above the water. Because $BE = BA + AE$ and you know that EA is 15, you need to find AB. The angle of elevation is 28°.

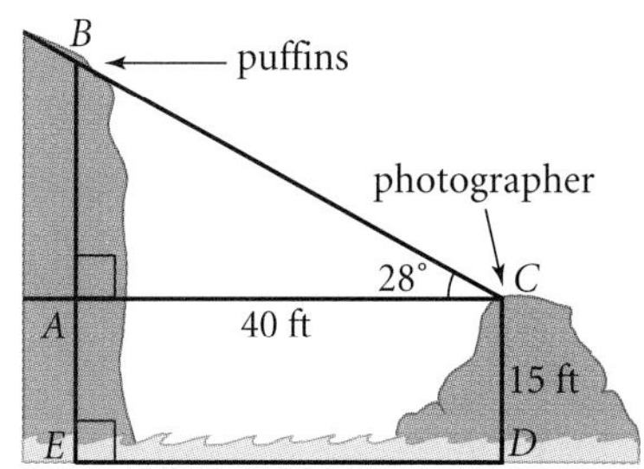

$$\tan 28° = \frac{AB}{40}$$
$$40 \tan 28° = AB$$
$$AB \approx 21.3$$

Then find BE.

$$BE = EA + AB$$
$$\approx 15 + 21.3$$
$$\approx 36.3$$

The puffins are about 36 feet above the water.

When you know the trigonometric ratio of an angle, you can find the measure of that angle by using the *inverse relation* of the trigonometric ratio. For example, if $\tan A$ is $\frac{4}{3}$, then the angle whose tangent is $\frac{4}{3}$ is written $\tan^{-1}\frac{4}{3}$.

$$\tan A = \frac{4}{3}$$
$$m\angle A = \tan^{-1}\frac{4}{3}$$
$$m\angle A \approx 53°$$

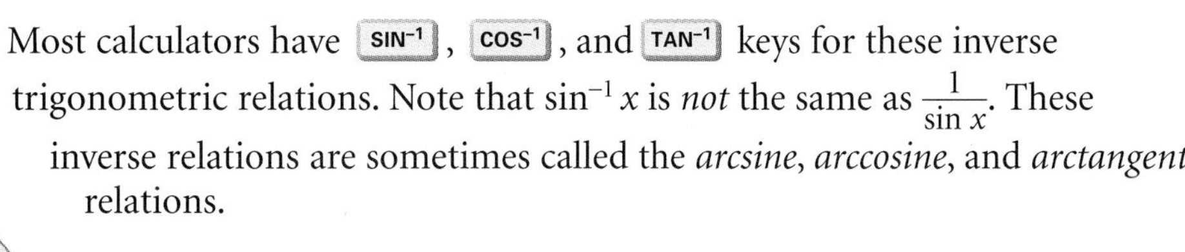

Most calculators have SIN⁻¹, COS⁻¹, and TAN⁻¹ keys for these inverse trigonometric relations. Note that $\sin^{-1} x$ is *not* the same as $\frac{1}{\sin x}$. These inverse relations are sometimes called the *arcsine*, *arccosine*, and *arctangent* relations.

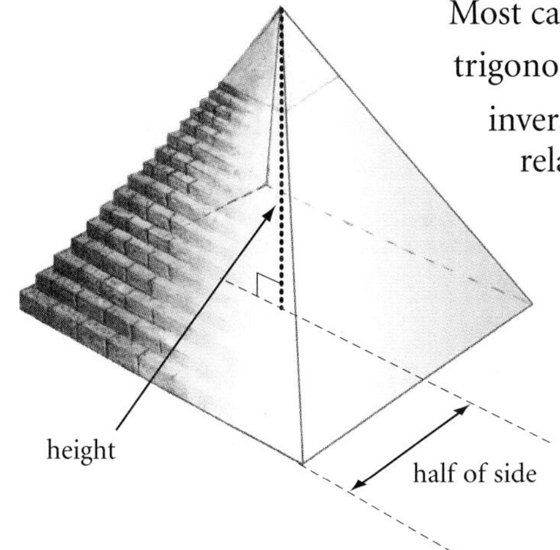

CULTURAL CONNECTION: AFRICA The Egyptians used a triangle relation called the *seked* to denote the slope of the inclined face of a pyramid.

$$\textit{seked} = \frac{\text{half of the pyramid's side length in palms}}{\text{height of the pyramid in cubits, where 1 cubit equals 7 palms}}$$

Today, we use the tangent ratio, which is similar to the reciprocal of the *seked*.

Inverse trigonometric relations are often used to solve a triangle. **Solving a triangle** involves finding the measures of all of the unknown sides and angles of the triangle. A geometry fact used in solving triangles is that the sum of the measures of all the angles in a triangle is 180°. For right triangles, the sum of the measures of the two acute angles is 90°.

EXAMPLE 4 **Solve △*RST*. Give m∠*R* and m∠*S* to the nearest degree, and give *RS* to the nearest tenth of a unit.**

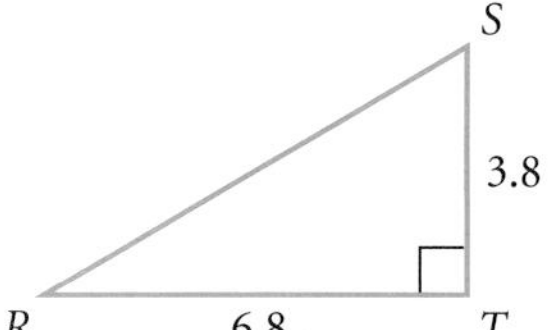

SOLUTION

1. First find m∠*R*.

$$\tan R = \frac{3.8}{6.8}$$
$$R = \tan^{-1}\frac{3.8}{6.8} \approx 29^\circ$$

2. Then find m∠*S*.

$$R + S + T = 180^\circ \qquad \text{or} \qquad R + S = 90^\circ$$
$$29^\circ + S + 90^\circ \approx 180^\circ \qquad\qquad 29^\circ + S \approx 90^\circ$$
$$S \approx 61^\circ \qquad\qquad S \approx 61^\circ$$

3. Use the Pythagorean Theorem to find *RS*.

$$(RS)^2 = (6.8)^2 + (3.8)^2$$
$$RS = \sqrt{(6.8)^2 + (3.8)^2}$$
$$RS \approx 7.8$$

Thus, m∠$R \approx 29^\circ$, m∠$S \approx 61^\circ$, and $RS \approx 7.8$.

TRY THIS Solve △*KLM*. Give m∠*K* and m∠*L* to the nearest degree and *LM* to the nearest tenth of a unit.

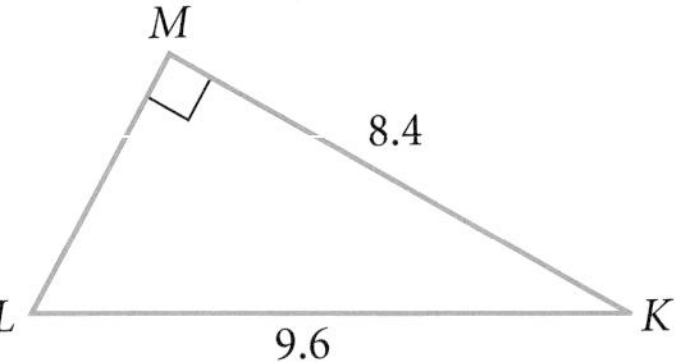

CHECKPOINT ✔ Explain how to solve △*RST* in Example 4 by finding *RS* first and then using the sine or cosine to find m∠*R*.

Exercises

Communicate

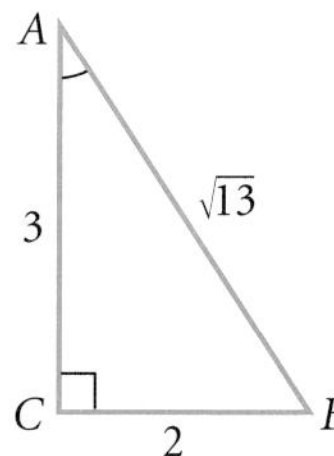

1. Explain how to find the values of the six trigonometric functions of ∠*A* at right.
2. Explain how to find the measures of ∠*A* and ∠*B* in △*ABC* at right.
3. Explain how the expressions $\frac{1}{\sin A}$ and $\sin^{-1} A$ are different.

Guided Skills Practice

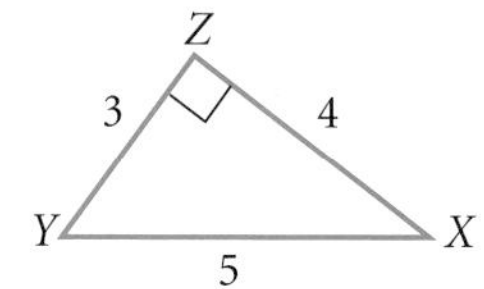

4. Find the values of the six trigonometric functions of $\angle X$ in $\triangle XYZ$ at right. Give exact answers and answers rounded to the nearest ten-thousandth. ***(EXAMPLE 1)***

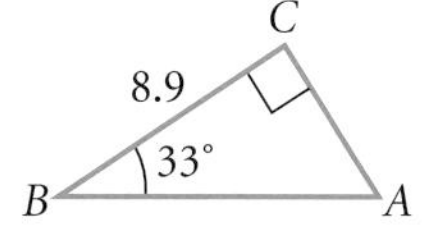

5. For $\triangle ABC$ at left, find AC and BA to the nearest tenth. ***(EXAMPLE 2)***

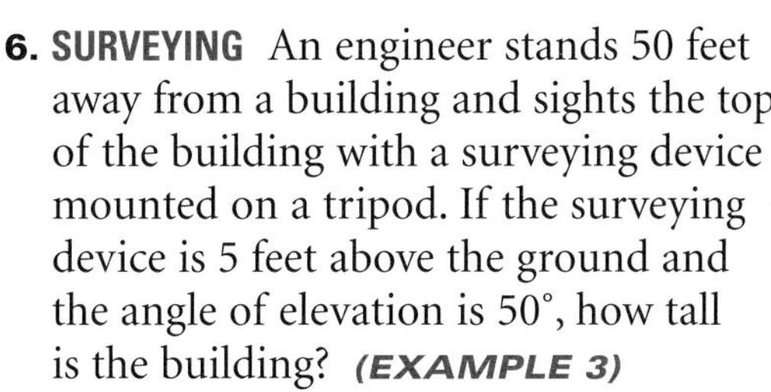

6. SURVEYING An engineer stands 50 feet away from a building and sights the top of the building with a surveying device mounted on a tripod. If the surveying device is 5 feet above the ground and the angle of elevation is 50°, how tall is the building? ***(EXAMPLE 3)***

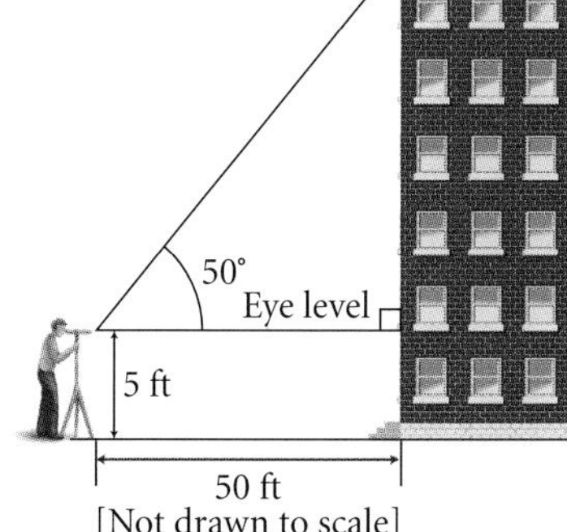

7. Solve $\triangle ABC$ shown below. Give $m\angle A$ and $m\angle B$ to the nearest degree, and give AB to the nearest tenth of a unit. ***(EXAMPLE 4)***

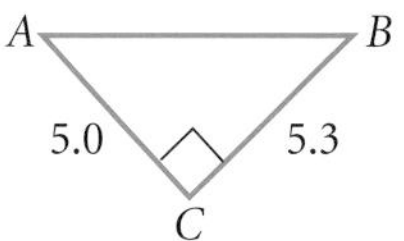

Practice and Apply

Refer to $\triangle JKL$ below to find each value listed. Give exact answers and answers rounded to the nearest ten-thousandth.

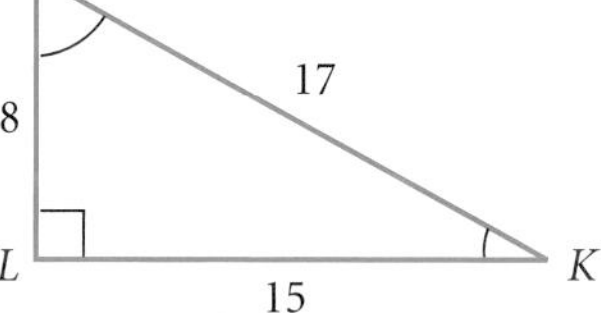

8. $\sin K$ **9.** $\sin J$ **10.** $\cos J$
11. $\cos K$ **12.** $\tan K$ **13.** $\tan J$
14. $\csc J$ **15.** $\csc K$ **16.** $\sec K$
17. $\sec J$ **18.** $\cot J$ **19.** $\cot K$

Refer to $\triangle FGH$ below to find each value listed. Give exact answers and answers rounded to the nearest ten-thousandth.

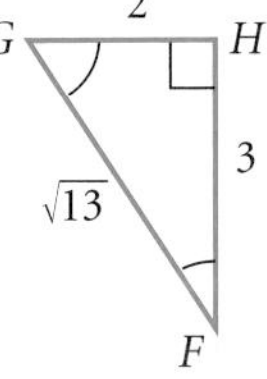

20. $\sin G$ **21.** $\sin F$ **22.** $\cos G$
23. $\cos F$ **24.** $\tan G$ **25.** $\tan F$
26. $\csc G$ **27.** $\csc F$ **28.** $\sec G$
29. $\sec F$ **30.** $\cot G$ **31.** $\cot F$

Find $m\angle A$ by using inverse trigonometric functions.

32.

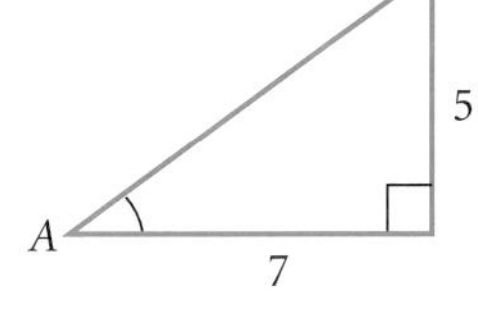

33.

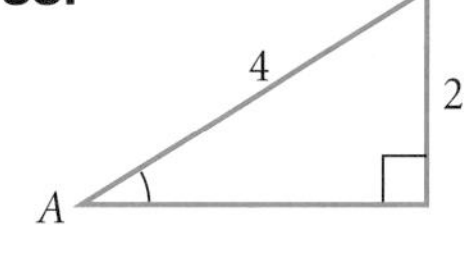

34.

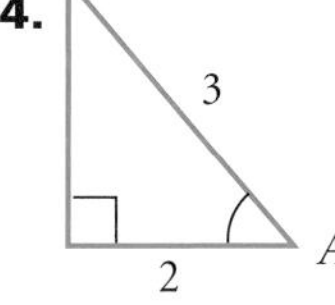

35.

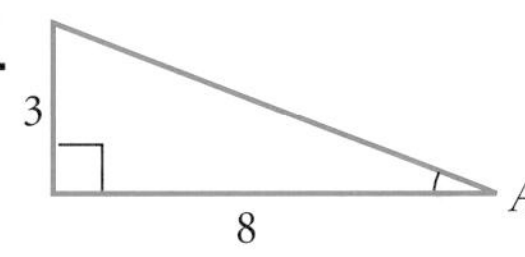

36.

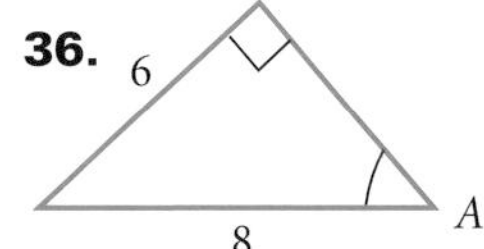

37.

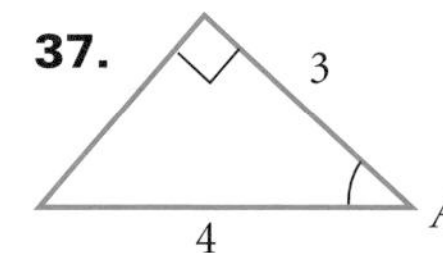

Solve each triangle. Give angle measures to the nearest degree and side lengths to the nearest tenth.

38.

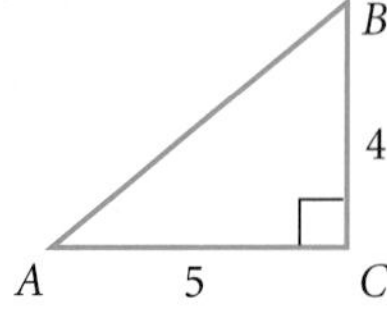

39.

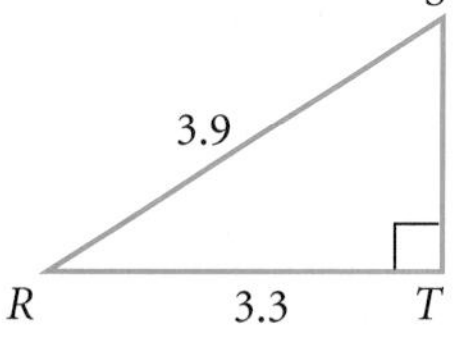

40.

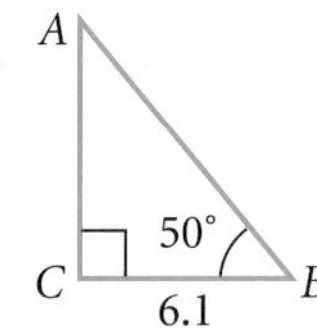

41.

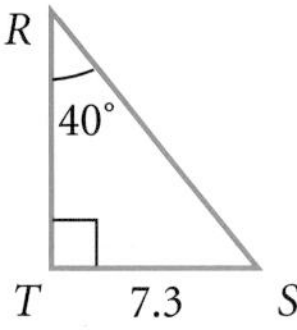

42.

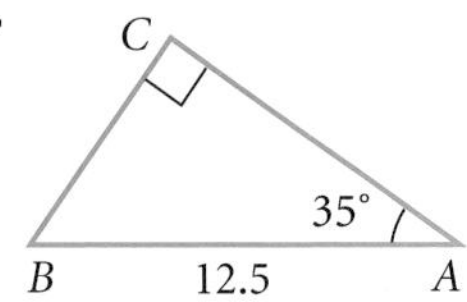

43.

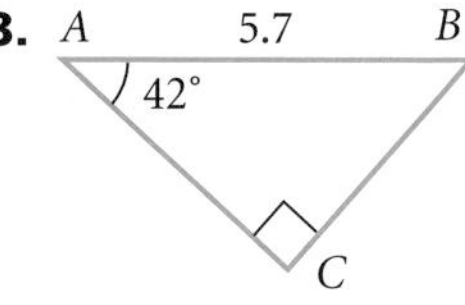

44. Show that $\tan A = \frac{\sin A}{\cos A}$ is true.

CONNECTION

45. GEOMETRY Quadrilateral $ABCD$ at right is a rectangle. Find AD and AC to the nearest tenth of a foot.

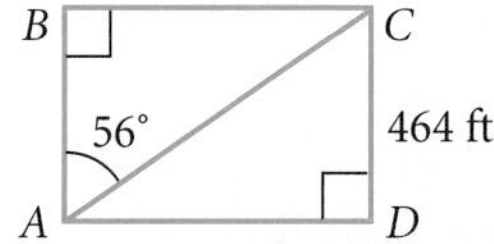

APPLICATIONS

46. HOME IMPROVEMENT Mary and Chris want to build a right-triangular deck behind their house. They would like the hypotenuse of the deck to be 20 feet long, and they would like the other two sides of the deck to be equal in length.

a. Find the length of the sides of the deck.

b. Find the area of the deck.

AVIATION A commercial airline pilot is flying at an altitude of 6.5 miles. To make a gentle descent for landing, the pilot begins descending toward the airport when still fairly far away.

47. If the pilot begins descending 186 miles from the airport (measured on the ground), what angle will the plane's path make with the runway (without further adjustment)?

48. If the plane's path is to make an angle of 5° with the runway (without further adjustment), how far from the airport (measured on the ground) must the pilot begin descending?

CHALLENGE

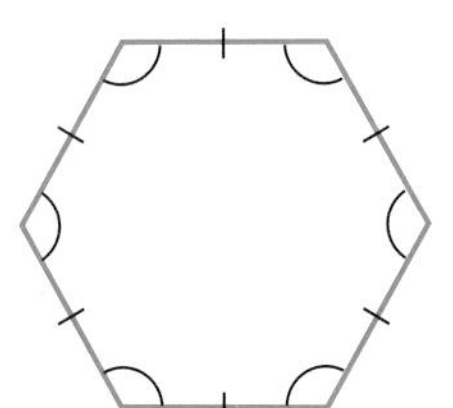

49. CONSTRUCTION The city park manager would like to build a gazebo in the shape of a regular hexagon with sides 10 feet long. (A regular hexagon is a 6-sided polygon with all sides equal in length and all angles equal in measure.) Paving costs $15 per square foot. Use trigonometric ratios to find the cost of paving the hexagonal area.

Determine the degree of each polynomial function. ***(LESSON 7.1)***

50. $f(x) = 3x^5 - 5x^8 + 4x^3 + 2$

51. $f(x) = (x^2 - 9)(x^3 + 4)$

Write each polynomial in factored form. ***(LESSON 7.3)***

52. $2x^3 - 18x$

53. $3x^3 - 7x^2 + 2x$

Write each expression with a rational denominator in simplest form. ***(LESSON 8.7)***

54. $\frac{3}{\sqrt{2}}$

55. $\frac{1}{\sqrt{3}}$

56. $\frac{5}{1 - \sqrt{2}}$

57. $\frac{-2}{\sqrt{2} + \sqrt{3}}$

Find the minimum and maximum values, Q_1, Q_2, and Q_3, and make a box-and-whisker plot for each set of data. ***(LESSON 12.3)***

58. 102, 107, 122, 99, 103, 121, 113, 100, 78, 130, 125, 119, 110

59. 12, 34, 18, 25, 53, 46, 17, 14, 25, 36, 24, 19, 17, 28, 26, 22

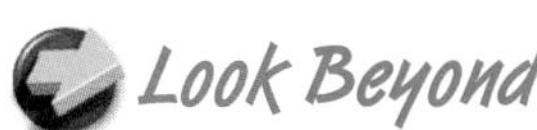

CONNECTION

60. GEOMETRY A 360° angle of rotation creates a circle. What angle of rotation creates a semicircle? a quarter circle?

The world's largest Ferris wheel, as of 1998, is the Cosmoclock 21 in Yokohama City, Japan. Its center is 344.5 feet above the ground and it has a diameter of 328 feet.
[*Source: Guiness Book of World Records, 1998*]

The center of the Cosmoclock 21 is located at the origin of the coordinate plane at right. Assume that a point, *P*, begins its rotation at (164, 0) and that it rotates in a counterclockwise direction.

1. Identify the coordinates of *Q*, *R*, and *S*.

2. Copy and complete the table below.

Rotation (degrees)	0°	90°	180°	270°	...	810°
Height of *P* relative to the *x*-axis (feet)	0	164		−164	...	

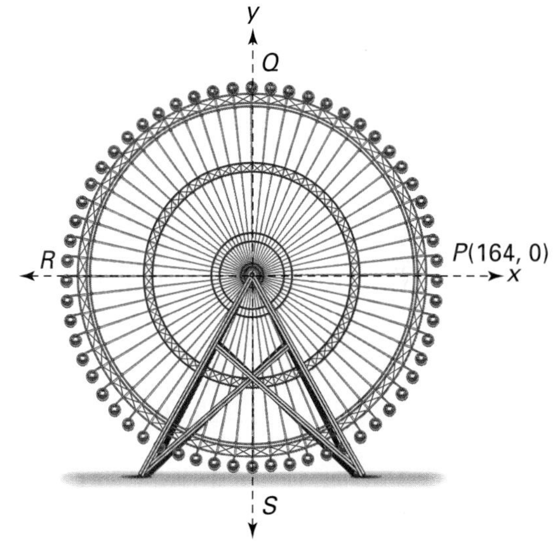

3. Plot the points from your table in a new coordinate plane. Sketch a *smooth curve* through the points.

4. Does your graph appear to be linear, quadratic, exponential, logarithmic, or none of these?

WORKING ON THE CHAPTER PROJECT

You should now be able to complete Activity 1 of the Chapter Project.

Angles of Rotation

Why *You can use angles of rotation to describe the rate at which an airplane propeller rotates.*

Objectives

- Find coterminal and reference angles.
- Find the trigonometric function values of angles in standard position.

APPLICATION
AVIATION

The propeller of an airplane rotates 1100 times per minute. Through how many degrees will a point on the propeller rotate in 1 second? *You will solve this problem in Example 1.*

In geometry, an angle is defined by two rays that have a common endpoint. In trigonometry, an angle is defined by a ray that is rotated around its endpoint. Each position of the rotated ray, relative to its starting position, creates an **angle of rotation.** The Greek letter *theta*, θ, is commonly used to name an angle of rotation.

The initial position of the ray is called the **initial side** of the angle, and the final position is called the **terminal side** of the angle. When the initial side lies along the positive x-axis and its endpoint is at the origin, the angle is said to be in **standard position**.

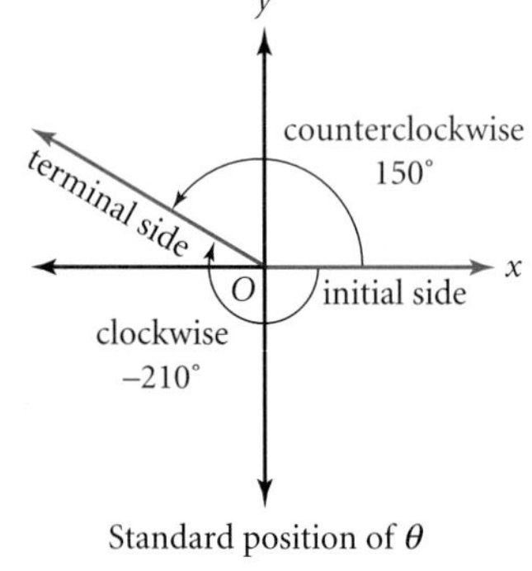

Standard position of θ

If the direction of rotation is counterclockwise, the angle has a **positive measure**. If the direction of rotation is clockwise, the angle has a **negative measure**.

The most common unit for angle measure is the **degree.** A complete rotation of a ray is assigned a measure of 360°. Thus, a measure of 1° is $\frac{1}{360}$ of a complete rotation.

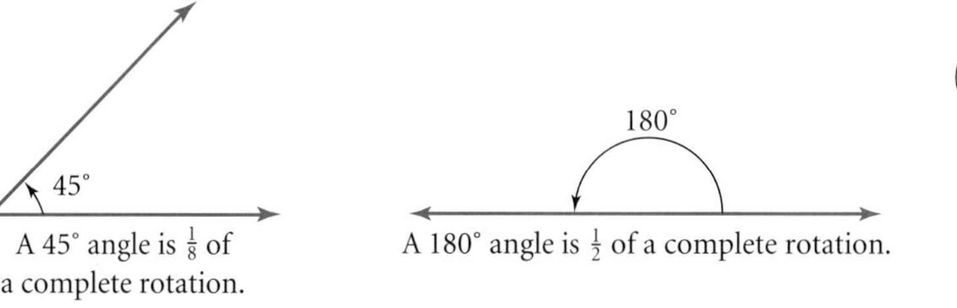

A 45° angle is $\frac{1}{8}$ of a complete rotation.

A 180° angle is $\frac{1}{2}$ of a complete rotation.

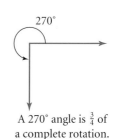

A 270° angle is $\frac{3}{4}$ of a complete rotation.

CHECKPOINT ✔ What direction of rotation generates an angle with a measure of –90°? of 120°? What portion of a complete rotation is –90°? 120°?

EXAMPLE 1

APPLICATION
AVIATION

Refer to the propeller problem at the beginning of the lesson.

Find the number of degrees through which a point on the propeller rotates in 1 second.

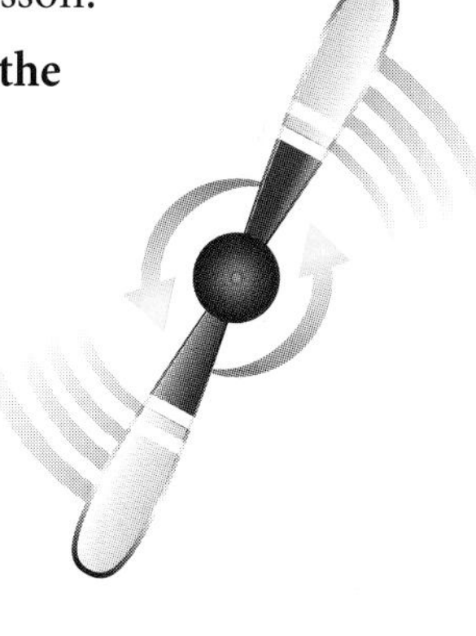

SOLUTION

The propeller rotates 1100 times per minute. The number of degrees through which a point rotates in 1 minute is $1100 \times 360^\circ = 396{,}000^\circ$. The number of degrees through which a point rotates in 1 second is $\frac{396{,}000^\circ}{60} = 6600^\circ$.

TRY THIS A record player makes 33.3 revolutions in 1 minute. Find the number of degrees through which a point on the record rotates in 1 second.

Angles in standard position are **coterminal** if they have the same terminal side.

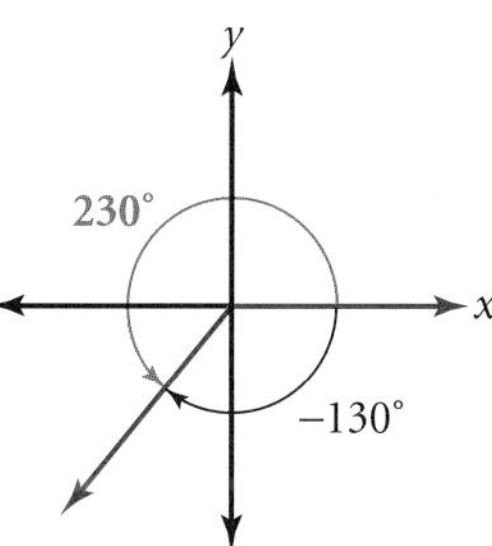

A 230° angle and a −130° angle are coterminal.

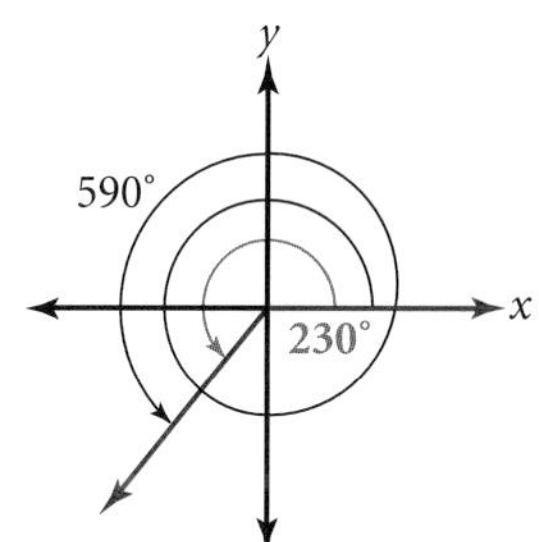

A 230° angle and a 590° angle are coterminal.

You can find coterminal angles by adding or subtracting integer multiples of 360°. This is shown in Example 2.

EXAMPLE 2 **Find the coterminal angle, θ, for each angle below such that $-360^\circ < \theta < 360^\circ$.**

a. 180° **b.** −27°

SOLUTION

Add and subtract 360° from each given angle. Discard answers that are not in the given range, $-360^\circ < \theta < 360^\circ$.

a. $\theta = \sout{180^\circ + 360^\circ = 540^\circ}$
$\theta = 180^\circ - 360^\circ = -180^\circ$
The coterminal angle is −180°.

b. $\theta = -27 + 360^\circ = 333^\circ$
$\theta = \sout{-27 - 360^\circ = 387^\circ}$
The coterminal angle is 333°.

TRY THIS Find the coterminal angle, θ, for 123° and for −185° such that $-360^\circ < \theta < 360^\circ$.

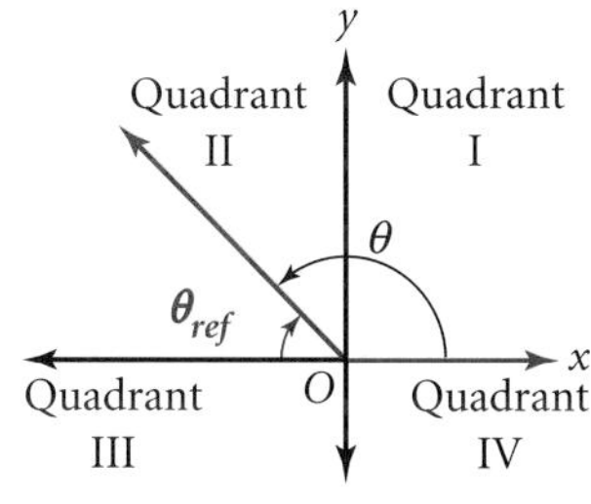

In Lesson 13.3 you will learn how to find trigonometric values for angles in standard position that are larger than 90° (or smaller than 0°). In order to do this, you will need to know how to find the measures of *reference angles.*

For an angle θ in standard position, the **reference angle,** θ_{ref}, is the positive acute angle formed by the terminal side of θ and the nearest part (positive or negative) of the x-axis. Use the positive x-axis for angles in Quadrants I and IV, and use the negative x-axis for angles in Quadrants II and III.

EXAMPLE 3 **Find the reference angle, θ_{ref}, for each angle.**

a. $\theta = 94°$ **b.** $\theta = 245°$ **c.** $\theta = 290°$ **d.** $\theta = -110°$

SOLUTION

a. $\theta = 94°$ is in Quadrant II. Use the negative x-axis.

$\theta_{ref} = |180° - \theta|$

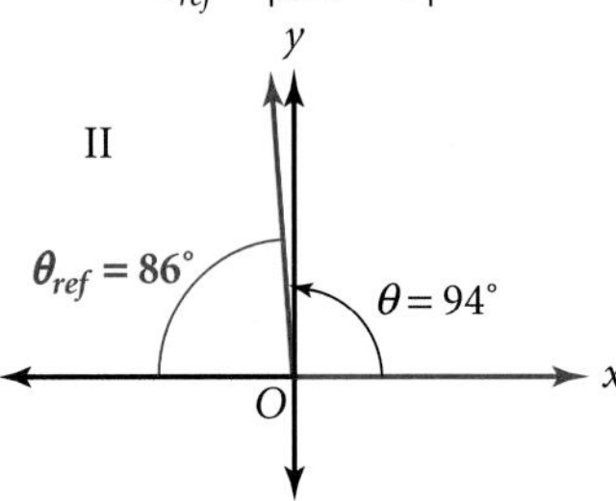

$\theta_{ref} = |180° - 94°| = 86°$

b. $\theta = 245°$ is in Quadrant III. Use the negative x-axis.

$\theta_{ref} = |180° - \theta|$

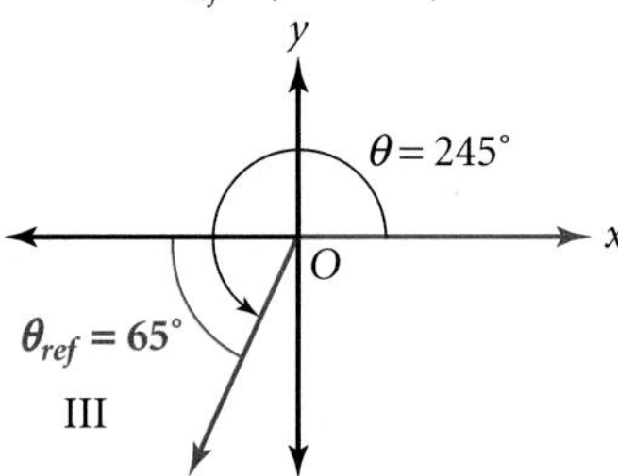

$\theta_{ref} = |180° - 245°| = 65°$

c. $\theta = 290°$ is in Quadrant IV. Use the positive x-axis.

$\theta_{ref} = |360° - \theta|$

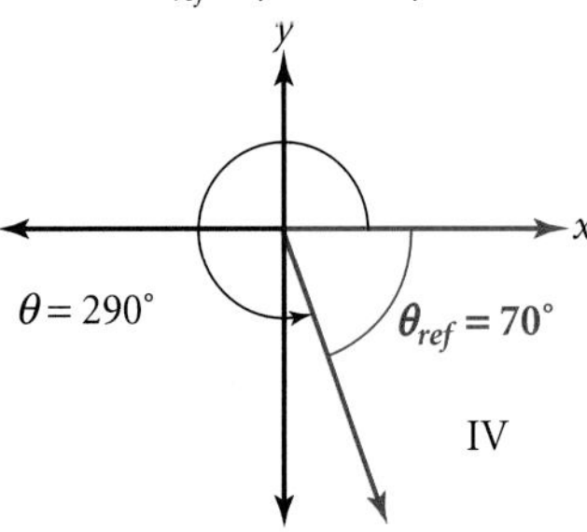

$\theta_{ref} = |360° - 290°| = 70°$

d. $\theta = -110°$ is in Quadrant III. Use the negative x-axis.

$\theta_{ref} = |180° - \theta|$

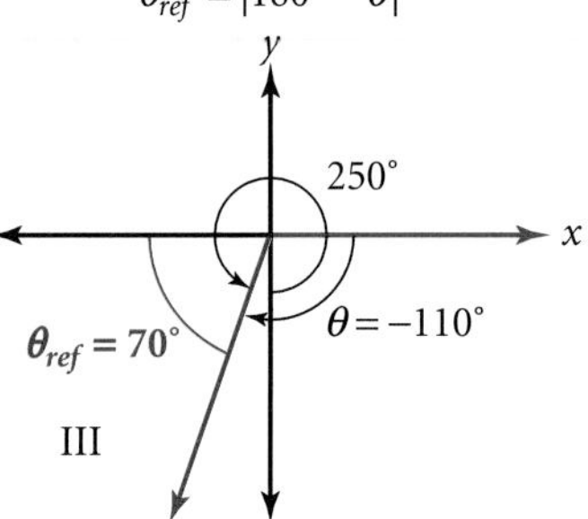

The positive coterminal angle for $-110°$ is $250°$.

$\theta_{ref} = |180° - 250°| = 70°$

TRY THIS Find the reference angle, θ_{ref}, for $\theta = 315°$ and $\theta = -235°$.

CRITICAL THINKING How many angles in standard position between 0° and 360° have the same reference angle?

If you think of x and y as the coordinates of a point on the terminal side of an angle in standard position, you will be able to determine the correct sign of the values for the trigonometric functions.

Trigonometric Functions of θ

Let $P(x, y)$ be a point on the terminal side of θ in standard position. The distance from the origin to P is given by $r = \sqrt{x^2 + y^2}$.

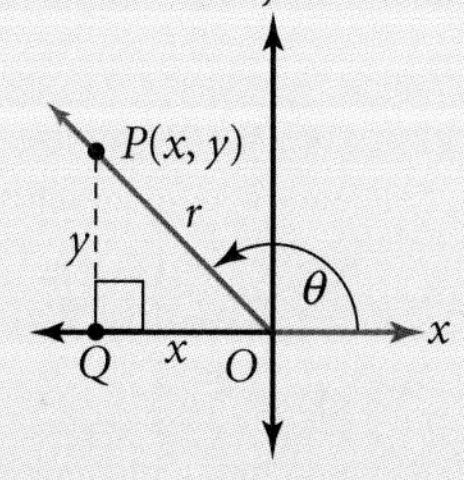

$\sin\theta = \frac{y}{r}$ $\cos\theta = \frac{x}{r}$ $\tan\theta = \frac{y}{x}, x \neq 0$

$\csc\theta = \frac{r}{y}, y \neq 0$ $\sec\theta = \frac{r}{x}, x \neq 0$ $\cot\theta = \frac{x}{y}, y \neq 0$

EXAMPLE 4 **Let $P(-2, -3)$ be a point on the terminal side of θ in standard position. Find the exact values of the six trigonometric functions of θ.**

SOLUTION

PROBLEM SOLVING

Draw a diagram. You know that $x = -2$ and $y = -3$. Find r.

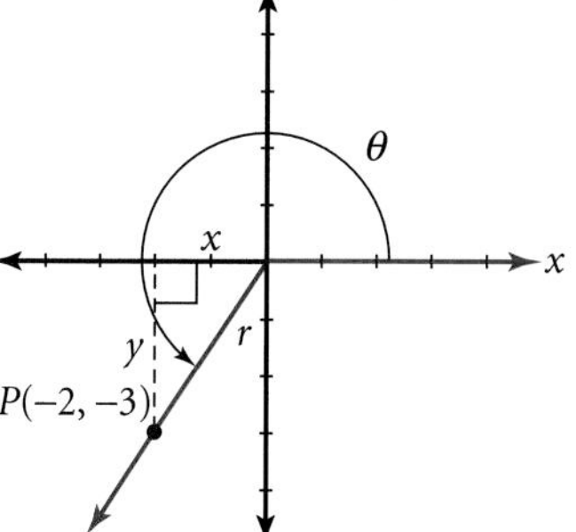

$$r = \sqrt{x^2 + y^2}$$

$$r = \sqrt{(-2)^2 + (-3)^2} = \sqrt{13}$$

$\sin\theta = \frac{y}{r} = \frac{-3}{\sqrt{13}} = -\frac{3\sqrt{13}}{13}$ $\quad$ $\cos\theta = \frac{x}{r} = \frac{-2}{\sqrt{13}} = -\frac{2\sqrt{13}}{13}$ $\quad$ $\tan\theta = \frac{y}{x} = \frac{-3}{-2} = \frac{3}{2}$

To find $\csc\theta$, $\sec\theta$, and $\cot\theta$, use reciprocals.

$\csc\theta = -\frac{\sqrt{13}}{3}$ $\quad$ $\sec\theta = -\frac{\sqrt{13}}{2}$ $\quad$ $\cot\theta = \frac{2}{3}$

TRY THIS Let $P(3, -5)$ be a point on the terminal side of θ in standard position. Find the exact values of the six trigonometric functions of θ.

Investigating the Signs in Each Quadrant

You will need: no special materials

1. Copy and complete the table below with the signs of the trigonometric functions of θ in standard position for each quadrant.

	Quadrant			
Trig value	**I**	**II**	**III**	**IV**
$\sin\theta$ and $\csc\theta$	+			
$\cos\theta$ and $\sec\theta$				
$\tan\theta$ and $\cot\theta$				

y
Quadrant II (−, +) | Quadrant I (+, +)
Quadrant III (−, −) | Quadrant IV (+, −)
x

2. In what quadrant is the terminal side of θ if $\sin\theta = -\frac{2}{7}$? if $\cos\theta = -\frac{2}{7}$? if $\tan\theta = -\frac{1}{5}$? Give all possible answers.

CHECKPOINT ✔
3. Does the value of r affect the sign of any of the trigonometric values? Explain.

CHECKPOINT ✔
4. Which coordinate, x or y, determines the sign of $\sin\theta$ and $\csc\theta$? of $\cos\theta$ and $\sec\theta$? of $\tan\theta$ and $\cot\theta$?

In each quadrant at right are listed the trigonometric function values that are positive for any angle θ in that quadrant. For example, for any angle θ in Quadrant II, $\sin\theta$ and $\csc\theta$ are positive while all other trigonometric function values are negative. This occurs because the sign of $\sin\theta$ and $\csc\theta$ both depend on y, which is positive in Quadrant II.

y
Quadrant II **sin θ csc θ** | Quadrant I **all**
Quadrant III **tan θ cot θ** | Quadrant IV **cos θ sec θ**
x

If you know which quadrant contains the terminal side of θ in standard position and the exact value of one trigonometric function of θ, you can find the values of the other trigonometric functions of θ. This is shown in Example 5.

EXAMPLE 5 **The terminal side of θ in standard position is in Quadrant II, and $\cos\theta = -\frac{3}{5}$. Find the exact values of the six trigonometric functions of θ.**

SOLUTION

PROBLEM SOLVING

Draw a diagram and find the x- and y-coordinates of P.

$$\cos\theta = \frac{x}{r} = -\frac{3}{5}$$

In Quadrant II, x is negative. Thus, $x = -3$ and $r = 5$.

Use the Pythagorean Theorem to find y.

$$5^2 = (-3)^2 + y^2$$
$$y^2 = 25 - 9$$
$$y = \pm\sqrt{16}$$
$$y = 4 \quad \textit{Because P is in Quadrant II, y is positive.}$$

$\sin\theta = \frac{y}{r} = \frac{4}{5}$ $\qquad \cos\theta = \frac{x}{r} = \frac{-3}{5}$ $\qquad \tan\theta = \frac{y}{x} = \frac{4}{-3}$

$\csc\theta = \frac{r}{y} = \frac{5}{4}$ $\qquad \sec\theta = \frac{r}{x} = \frac{5}{-3}$ $\qquad \cot\theta = \frac{x}{y} = \frac{-3}{4}$

TRY THIS The terminal side of θ in standard position is in Quadrant III, and $\sin\theta = -\frac{4}{5}$. Find the exact values of the six trigonometric functions of θ.

If the terminal side of an angle, θ, in standard position coincides with a coordinate axis (such that x or y is 0), some trigonometric functions of θ will be undefined. For example csc 0°, sec 90°, tan 180°, and cot 270° are all undefined because they involve division by zero. These angle measures are excluded values in the domain of the respective functions.

CHECKPOINT ✔ Find the exact values of the six trigonometric functions for $\theta = 90°$.

Exercises

Communicate

1. Describe the differences between angles in right triangles and angles of rotation.
2. Describe the difference that may exist between the trigonometric functions of an angle and those of its reference angle. Explain the reason for this difference.
3. Do you need to know the measure of an angle in order to find the exact values of its trigonometric functions? Explain.

Guided Skills Practice

APPLICATION

4. **AVIATION** The main rotor of a helicopter rotates 430 times per minute. Find the number of degrees through which a point on the main rotor rotates in 1 second. ***(EXAMPLE 1)***

5. Find the coterminal angle, θ, for 271° such that $-360° < \theta < 360°$. ***(EXAMPLE 2)***

6. Find the reference angle for 93°, 280°, and −36°. ***(EXAMPLE 3)***

7. Let $P(3, -2)$ be a point on the terminal side of θ in standard position. Find the exact values of the six trigonometric functions of θ. ***(EXAMPLE 4)***

8. The terminal side of θ in standard position is in Quadrant III, and $\sin\theta = -\frac{12}{13}$. Find the exact values of the six trigonometric functions of θ. ***(EXAMPLE 5)***

Practice and Apply

Sketch each angle in standard position.

9. 115°
10. 280°
11. −300°
12. −130°

For each angle below, find all coterminal angles such that $-360° < \theta < 360°$. Then find the corresponding reference angle, if it exists.

13. 35°
14. 23°
15. 112°
16. 160°
17. 612°
18. 478°
19. −135°
20. −315°
21. 90°
22. −180°
23. −450°
24. −485°
25. 540°
26. 270°
27. 225°
28. 195°
29. 410°
30. 560°
31. −120°
32. −280°
33. −175°
34. −295°
35. −395°
36. −540°

Find the exact values of the six trigonometric functions of θ.

37.

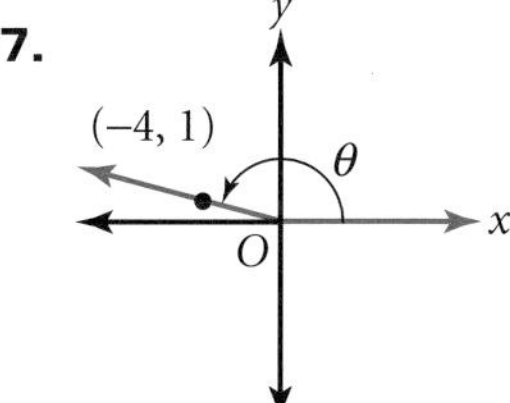

38.

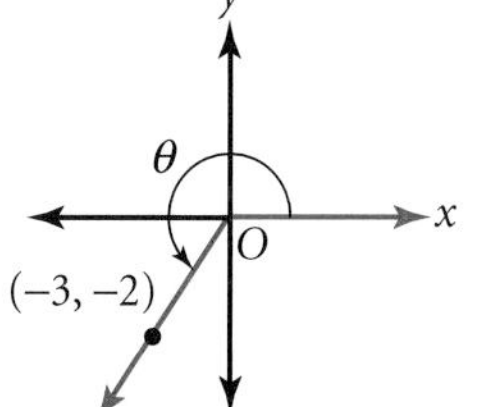

39.

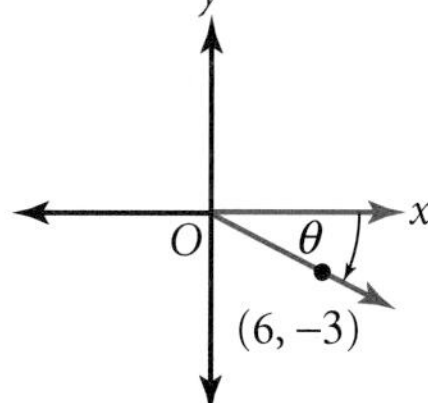

Find the exact values of the six trigonometric functions of θ given each point on the terminal side of θ in standard position.

40. (3, 4)
41. (5, 2)
42. (−4, 2)
43. (−4, 6)
44. $(\sqrt{3}, -3)$
45. $(2\sqrt{5}, -1)$
46. (−4, −3)
47. (−1, −8)

Given the quadrant of θ in standard position and a trigonometric function value of θ, find exact values for the indicated functions.

48. I, $\cos\theta = 0.25$; $\tan\theta$
49. III, $\cos\theta = -\frac{1}{2}$; $\tan\theta$
50. IV, $\tan\theta = -1$; $\csc\theta$
51. I, $\tan\theta = 2$; $\csc\theta$
52. III, $\sin\theta = -\frac{1}{2}$; $\sec\theta$
53. II, $\sin\theta = 0.4$; $\sec\theta$
54. IV, $\cot\theta = -1.2$; $\cos\theta$
55. II, $\cot\theta = -1.75$; $\cos\theta$

Find the number of rotations or the fraction of a rotation represented by each angle below. Indicate whether the rotation is clockwise or counterclockwise.

56. 45° **57.** 90° **58.** −180° **59.** −270°

60. 450° **61.** 720° **62.** −420° **63.** −640°

CHALLENGES

64. Find cos θ if sin $\theta = 0.375$ and tan θ is less than 0.

65. Find tan θ if cos $\theta = 0.809$ and sin θ is less than 0.

CONNECTION

66. PROBABILITY An angle of rotation of 120° is colored red on a circular spinner at a school fair. If the spinner lands anywhere in the red space, the contestant wins. What is the probability of a contestant winning?

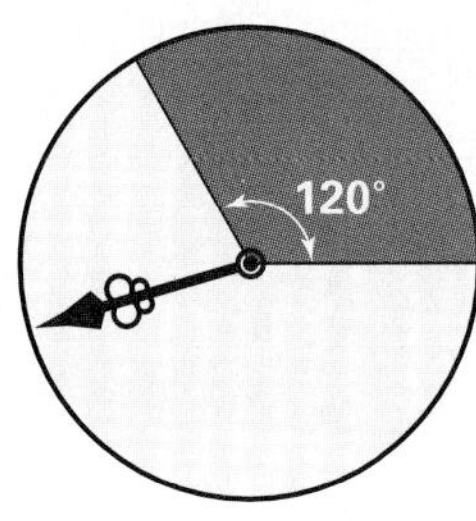

APPLICATIONS

67. ENGINEERING The flywheel of an engine rotates 900 times per minute. Through how many degrees does a point on the flywheel rotate in 1 second?

68. NAVIGATION Airline pilots and sea captains both use *nautical miles* to measure distance. A nautical mile is approximately equal to the arc length intercepted on the surface of the Earth by a central angle measure of 1 *minute* (there are 60 minutes in 1 degree). The diameter of the Earth at the equator is approximately 7926.41 miles.

a. How many minutes are there in the circumference of the Earth?
b. Find the approximate circumference of the Earth in miles.
c. Approximately how many miles are equal to one nautical mile?

Look Back

69. Solve $x^2 - 8 = 188$ for x. ***(LESSONS 5.5 AND 5.6)***

Graph each number and its conjugate in the complex plane. ***(LESSON 5.6)***

70. $-6 + 4i$ **71.** $5i$ **72.** -1 **73.** $-3 - 4i$

Evaluate. ***(LESSON 5.6)***

74. $|1 + i|$ **75.** $|2 + 3i|$ **76.** $\left|\frac{\sqrt{2}}{2} + \frac{\sqrt{2}}{2}i\right|$ **77.** $\left|\frac{\sqrt{3}}{3} + \frac{\sqrt{6}}{3}i\right|$

78. Find the standard equation for the hyperbola centered at (1, 4) with vertices at (−4, 4) and (6, 4) and co-vertices at (1, −5) and (1, 13). Graph the equation. ***(LESSON 9.5)***

79. How many ways are there to choose a committee of 4 from a group of 10 people? ***(LESSON 10.3)***

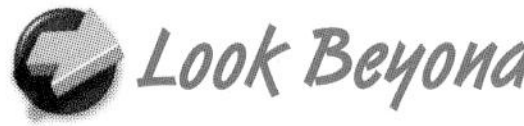

Look Beyond

Find the exact values of the six trigonometric functions of θ given each point on the terminal side of θ in standard position.

80. $\left(\frac{\sqrt{3}}{2}, \frac{1}{2}\right)$ **81.** $\left(\frac{\sqrt{2}}{2}, \frac{\sqrt{2}}{2}\right)$ **82.** $\left(\frac{1}{2}, \frac{\sqrt{3}}{2}\right)$

Trigonometric Functions of Any Angle

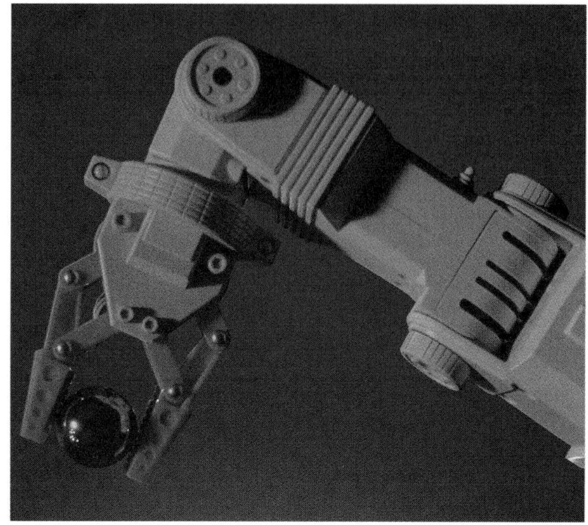

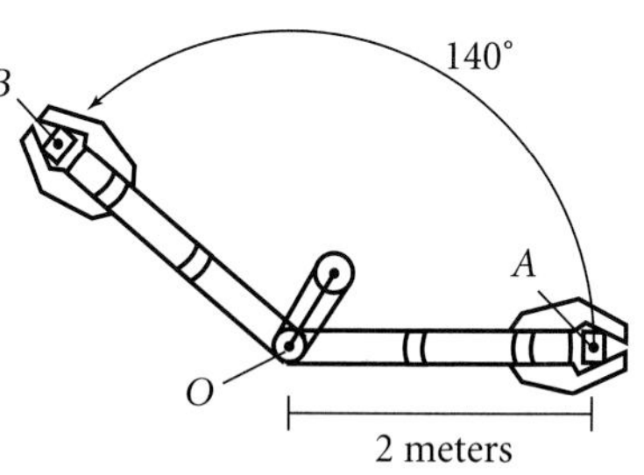

Why *You can use trigonometric functions of any angle to solve real-world problems such as designing the motion of a robotic arm.*

Objective

- Find exact values for trigonometric functions of special angles and their multiples.
- Find approximate values for trigonometric functions of any angle.

APPLICATION
ROBOTICS

Steve is programming a 2-meter long robotic arm. The arm grasps an object at point A, located directly to the right of the pivot point, O. The arm swings through an angle of 140° and releases the object at point B. What is the new position of the object relative to the pivot point? *You will solve this problem in Example 3.*

There are certain angles whose exact trigonometric function values can be found without a calculator. You will explore these angles in the Activity below.

Activity Exploring Special Triangles

CONNECTION
GEOMETRY

You will need: no special materials

1. When a square is bisected along a diagonal, two 45-45-90 triangles are formed, as shown below.

   Find the length of c in terms of a by using the Pythagorean Theorem.

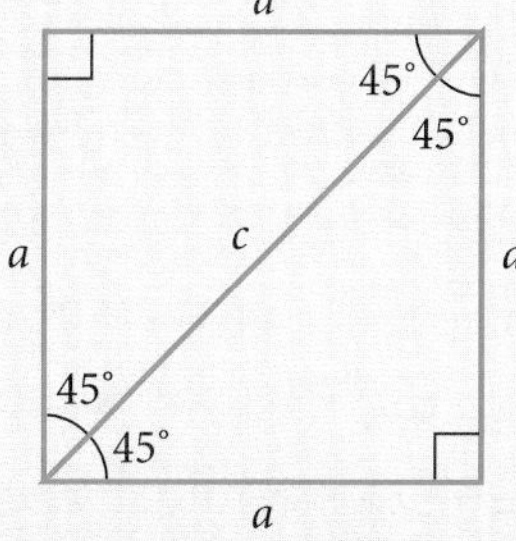

2. An equilateral triangle has three 60° angles. When one angle is bisected, two 30-60-90 triangles are formed, as shown below.

   Find the length of c in terms of a by using the Pythagorean Theorem.

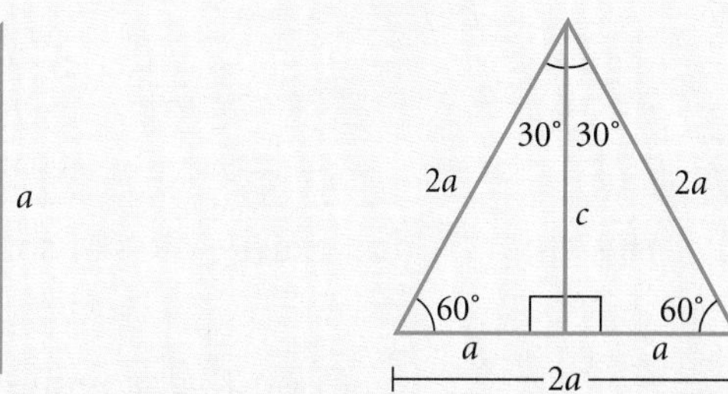

CHECKPOINT  3. State the relationship between the sides of a 45-45-90 triangle and the relationship between the sides of a 30-60-90 triangle.

In the Activity, you found that the lengths of the sides of a 45-45-90 triangle have a ratio of 1 to 1 to $\sqrt{2}$, and the lengths of the sides of a 30-60-90 triangle have a ratio of 1 to $\sqrt{3}$ to 2. You can use these relationships to find the exact values of the sine, cosine, and tangent of 30°, 45°, and 60° angles.

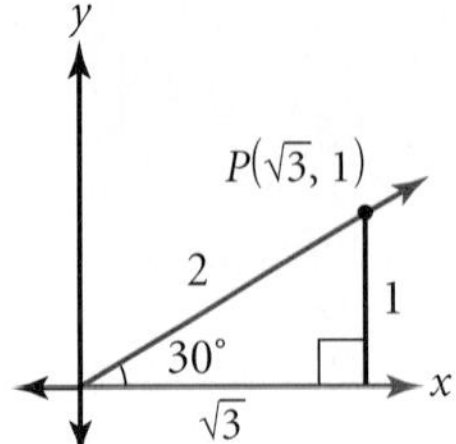

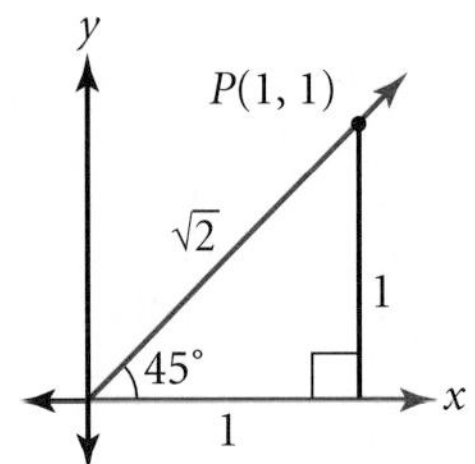

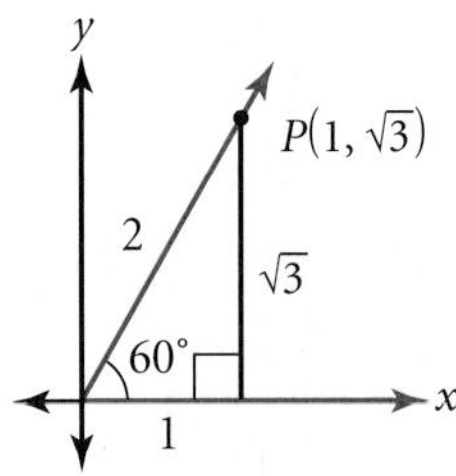

$\sin 30° = \frac{1}{2}$

$\cos 30° = \frac{\sqrt{3}}{2}$

$\tan 30° = \frac{1}{\sqrt{3}}$, or $\frac{\sqrt{3}}{3}$

$\sin 45° = \frac{1}{\sqrt{2}}$, or $\frac{\sqrt{2}}{2}$

$\cos 45° = \frac{1}{\sqrt{2}}$, or $\frac{\sqrt{2}}{2}$

$\tan 45° = 1$

$\sin 60° = \frac{\sqrt{3}}{2}$

$\cos 60° = \frac{1}{2}$

$\tan 60° = \sqrt{3}$

Throughout this chapter it will be helpful to be familiar with the exact values of the sine, cosine, and tangent of 30°, 45°, and 60° angles, given above.

CHECKPOINT ✔ Make a table of the exact values and the decimal approximations of the sine, cosine, and tangent of 30°, 45°, and 60°.

You can use the exact values of the sine, cosine, and tangent given above to evaluate any angle whose reference angle is 30°, 45°, or 60°. This is shown in Example 1.

EXAMPLE 1 **Find exact values of sin 315°, cos 315°, and tan 315°.**

SOLUTION

PROBLEM SOLVING **Draw a diagram** and find the reference angle.

$$\theta_{ref} = |360° - 315°| = 45°$$

Because 315° is in Quadrant IV, where y is negative, the sine and tangent are negative.

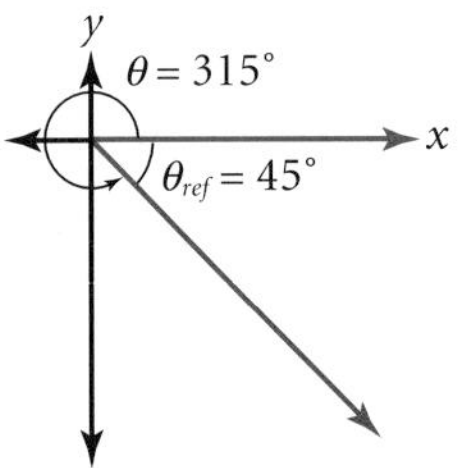

$\sin 315° = -\sin 45°$
$= -\frac{1}{\sqrt{2}}$, or $-\frac{\sqrt{2}}{2}$

$\cos 315° = \cos 45°$
$= \frac{1}{\sqrt{2}}$, or $\frac{\sqrt{2}}{2}$

$\tan 315° = -\tan 45°$
$= -1$

TRY THIS Find exact values of $\sin(-150°)$, $\cos(-150°)$, and $\tan(-150°)$.

In Lesson 13.2, a point on the terminal side of an angle was used to find trigonometric function values. In Example 2 on the next page, trigonometric function values are used to find the exact coordinates of a point on the terminal side of an angle.

EXAMPLE 2

Find the exact coordinates of point P, located at the intersection of a circle with a radius of 5 and the terminal side of a 150° angle in standard position.

SOLUTION

PROBLEM SOLVING

Draw a diagram, and find the reference angle.

$$\theta_{ref} = |180° - 150°| = 30°$$

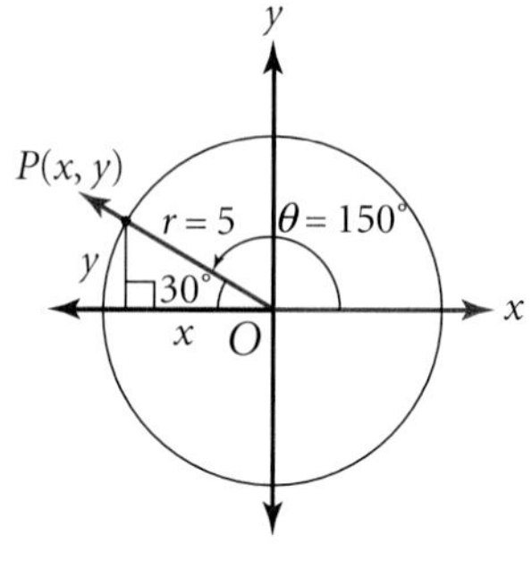

Because P is in Quadrant II, where x is negative, the cosine is negative.

$$\cos 150° = \frac{x}{r} \qquad \sin 150° = \frac{y}{r}$$

$$-\cos 30° = \frac{x}{5} \qquad \sin 30° = \frac{y}{5}$$

$$-\frac{\sqrt{3}}{2} = \frac{x}{5} \qquad \frac{1}{2} = \frac{y}{5}$$

$$-\frac{5\sqrt{3}}{2} = x \qquad \frac{5}{2} = y$$

The exact coordinates of P are $\left(-\frac{5\sqrt{3}}{2}, \frac{5}{2}\right)$.

TRY THIS

Find the exact coordinates of point P, located at the intersection of a circle with a radius of 12 and the terminal side of a 300° angle in standard position.

For any point on the terminal side of an angle in Quadrant I, $\cos \theta = \frac{x}{r}$, so $r \cos \theta = x$, and $\sin \theta = \frac{y}{r}$, so $r \sin \theta = y$. This allows you to find the coordinates of any point on a circle centered at the origin with radius r.

Coordinates of a Point on a Circle

If P lies at the intersection of the terminal side of θ in standard position and a circle with a radius of r centered at the origin, then the coordinates of P are $(r \cos \theta, r \sin \theta)$.

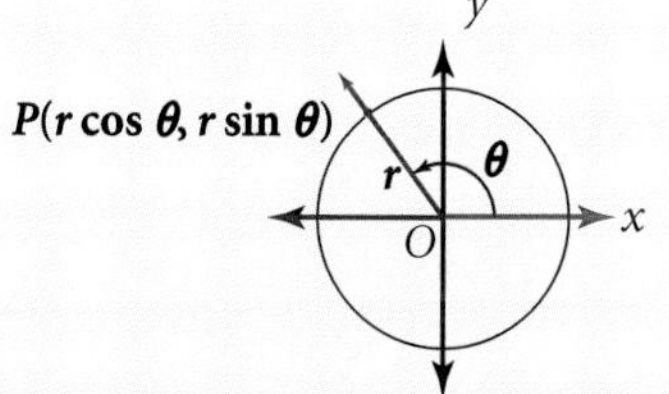

EXAMPLE 3

APPLICATION
ROBOTICS

Refer to the robotic arm described at the beginning of the lesson.

What is the new position of the object relative to the pivot point?

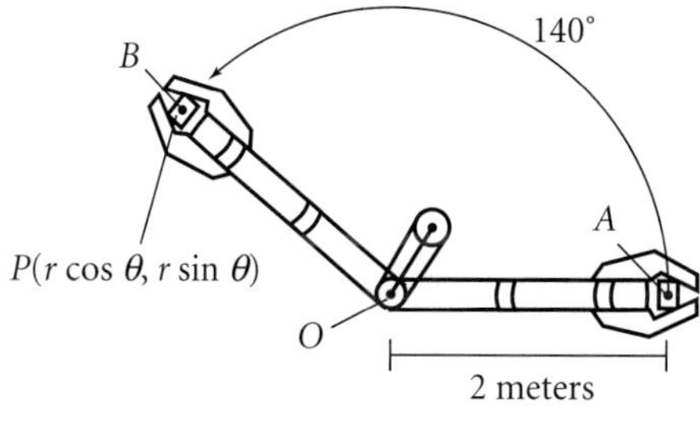

SOLUTION

Place the pivot point at the origin. The new position at point B has the coordinates $(r \cos \theta, r \sin \theta)$. Substitute 2 for r and 140° for θ.

$$B(r \cos \theta, r \sin \theta) = B(2 \cos 140°, 2 \sin 140°)$$
$$\approx B(-1.53, 1.29)$$

Use a scientific calculator in degree mode.

The object is about 1.53 meters to the left of the pivot point and about 1.29 meters above the pivot point.

Unit Circle

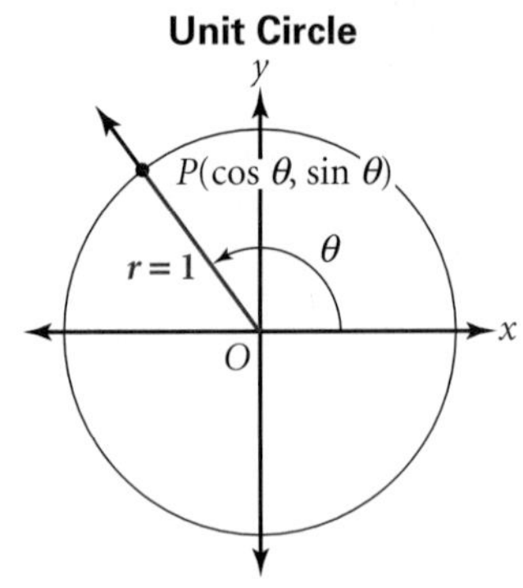

When a circle centered at the origin has a radius of 1, it is called a **unit circle.** Because r is 1, the coordinates of P are $(\cos\theta, \sin\theta)$.

Unit circles are helpful in demonstrating the behavior of trigonometric functions. The unit circle below shows the x- and y-coordinates of P for special angles between 0° and 360°.

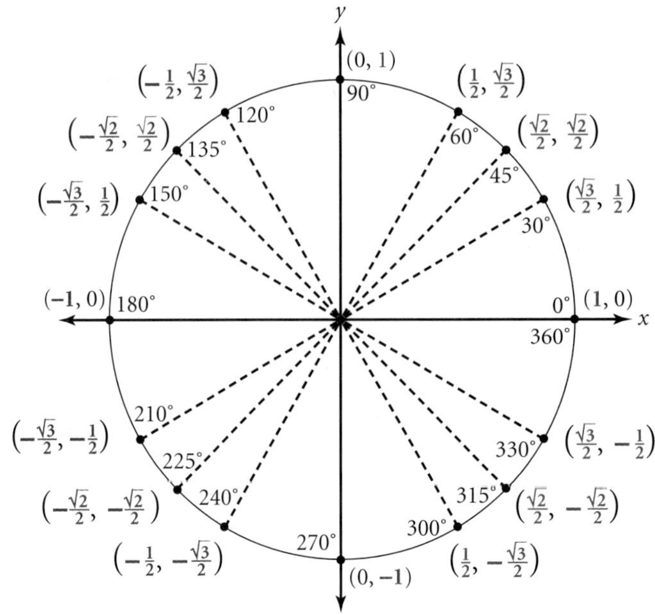

CHECKPOINT ✔ Using the coordinates on the unit circle above, find the following trigonometric function values: sin 90°, cos 60°, sin –45°, cos –30°, sin 360°, and cos 180°.

Recall from Lesson 13.2 that an angle of 90° is coterminal with angles of 450° and 810°. In fact, an angle of 90° is coterminal with any angle whose measure can be represented by $90° + n360°$, where n is an integer. All coterminal angles share the same reference angle and have the same trigonometric function values. Because the values of sine and cosine repeat every 360°, they are called *periodic functions* and their *period* is 360°.

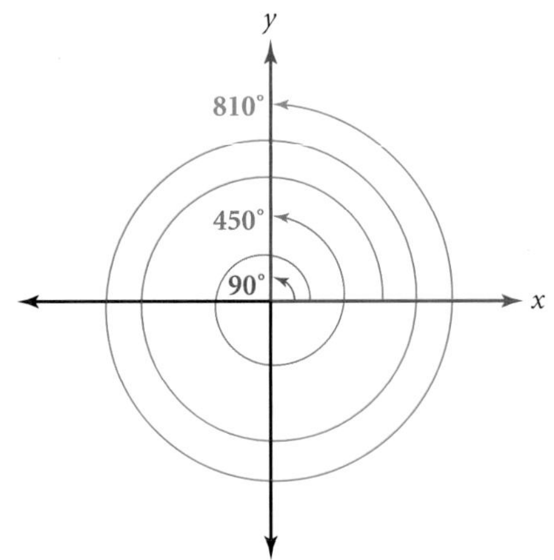

Periodic Functions

A function, f, is **periodic** if there is a number p such that $f(x + p) = f(x)$ for every x in the domain of f.

The smallest positive number p that satisfies the equation above is called the **period** of the function.

CRITICAL THINKING What is the period of the tangent function?

EXAMPLE 4 **Find the exact values of the sine, cosine, and tangent of each angle.**

a. 900° **b.** –930°

SOLUTION

Find a coterminal angle with a positive measure between 0° and 360°.

a.

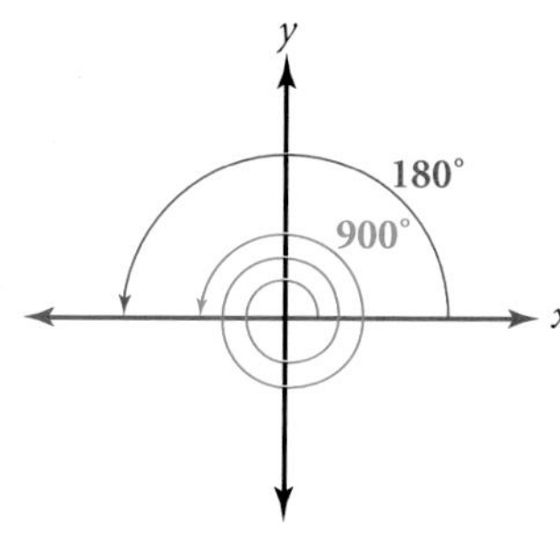

b.

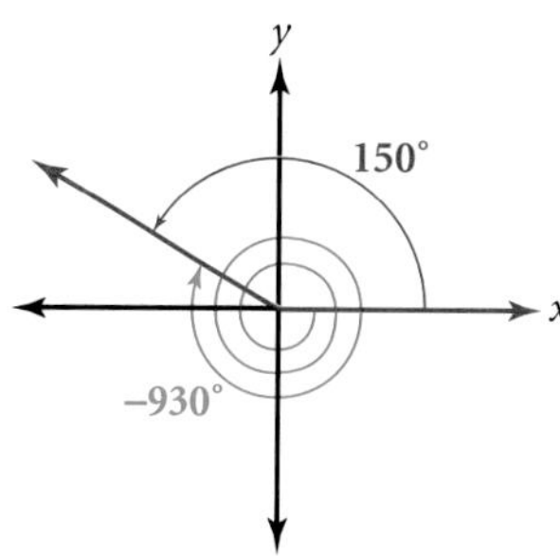

a.	**b.**
$900° - 2 \cdot 360° = 180°$	$-930° + 3 \cdot 360° = 150°$
$\sin 900° = \sin 180° = 0$	$\sin 930° = \sin 150° = \frac{1}{2}$
$\cos 900° = \cos 180° = -1$	$\cos 930° = \cos 150° = -\frac{\sqrt{3}}{2}$
$\tan 900° = \tan 180° = 0$	$\tan 930° = \tan 150° = -\frac{\sqrt{3}}{3}$

TRY THIS Find the exact values of the sine, cosine, and tangent of each angle.

a. 1110° **b.** –1110°

Exercises

Communicate

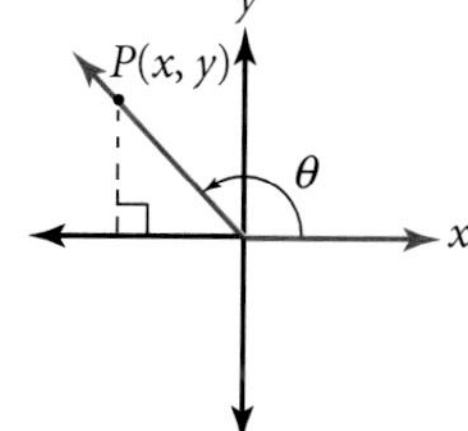

1. Explain when it is possible to use a reference angle rather than a scientific calculator to solve a trigonometric problem.

2. Explain the relationship of the sine and cosine of θ to the coordinates of point P in the diagram at right.

3. Describe how to find the exact value of sin 420°.

Guided Skills Practice

4. Find the exact values of sin 150°, cos 150°, and tan 150°. ***(EXAMPLE 1)***

5. Find the exact coordinates of a point, P, that is located at the intersection of a circle with a radius of 9 and the terminal side of a 315° angle in standard position. ***(EXAMPLE 2)***

APPLICATION

6. ROBOTICS Refer to the robotic arm described at the beginning of the lesson. Find the new position of the object relative to the pivot point after the 2-meter robotic arm swings through an angle of 110° degrees. ***(EXAMPLE 3)***

7. Find the exact values of the sine, cosine, and tangent of –1200°. ***(EXAMPLE 4)***

Practice and Apply

Find the exact values of the sine, cosine, and tangent of each angle.

8. 300° **9.** 210° **10.** 225° **11.** 120°

12. 135° **13.** 240° **14.** –225° **15.** –135°

16. –150° **17.** –330° **18.** –120° **19.** –210°

Point *P* is located at the intersection of a circle with a radius of *r* and the terminal side of angle *θ*. Find the exact coordinates of *P*.

20. $\theta = 60°, r = 3$ **21.** $\theta = 30°, r = 5$ **22.** $\theta = 120°, r = 8$

23. $\theta = 135°, r = 9$ **24.** $\theta = 240°, r = 50$ **25.** $\theta = 180°, r = 45$

26. $\theta = -30°, r = 6.2$ **27.** $\theta = -135°, r = 7.6$ **28.** $\theta = -330°, r = 0.9$

Point *P* is located at the intersection of the unit circle and the terminal side of angle *θ* in standard position. Find the coordinates of *P* to the nearest hundredth.

29. $\theta = 75°$ **30.** $\theta = 205°$ **31.** $\theta = -130°$ **32.** $\theta = -205°$

33. $\theta = 4°$ **34.** $\theta = 87°$ **35.** $\theta = -88°$ **36.** $\theta = -183°$

Find the exact values of the sine, cosine, and tangent of each angle.

37. 405° **38.** 690° **39.** 870° **40.** 855°

41. 1380° **42.** 1305° **43.** –600° **44.** –510°

45. –495° **46.** –480° **47.** –840° **48.** –1020°

Find each trigonometric function value. Give exact answers.

49. sin 135° **50.** cos 120° **51.** tan 150° **52.** sin 240°

53. cos 210° **54.** tan 225° **55.** sin 300° **56.** cos 315°

57. tan 330° **58.** sin 0° **59.** cos 0° **60.** tan 180°

61. sin 90° **62.** cos 90° **63.** tan 270° **64.** sin 180°

65. cos 180° **66.** tan 90° **67.** sin(–90°) **68.** cos(–90°)

69. tan(–180°) **70.** sin 720° **71.** cos 1080° **72.** cos 450°

73. sin 495° **74.** sin(–45°) **75.** cos(–135°) **76.** cos(–270°)

77. sin(–405°) **78.** tan(–150°) **79.** tan(–30°) **80.** sin 1125°

81. cos 810° **82.** tan 390° **83.** tan 780° **84.** csc 135°

85. sec 120° **86.** cot 150° **87.** csc(–660°) **88.** sec(–990°)

89. cot(–765°) **90.** sec 405° **91.** csc 1140° **92.** cot 1500°

CHALLENGE

93. Use the definition of a periodic function to show that the function $f(x) = x$ is not periodic.

CONNECTION

GEOMETRY **Solve each triangle.**

94.

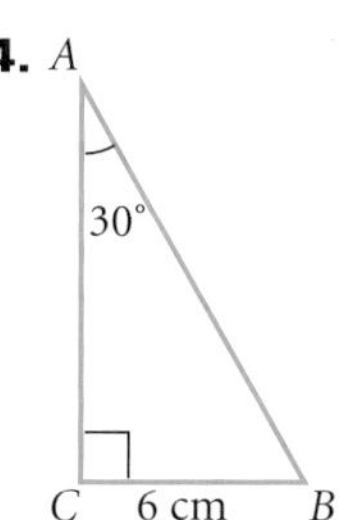

95.

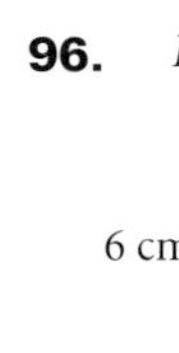

96.

97.

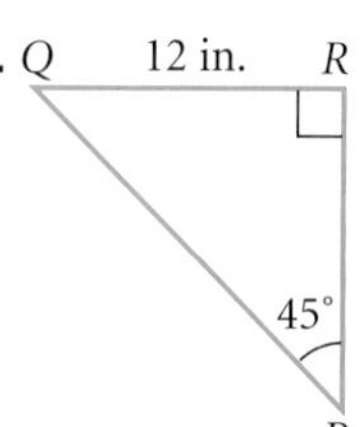

APPLICATIONS

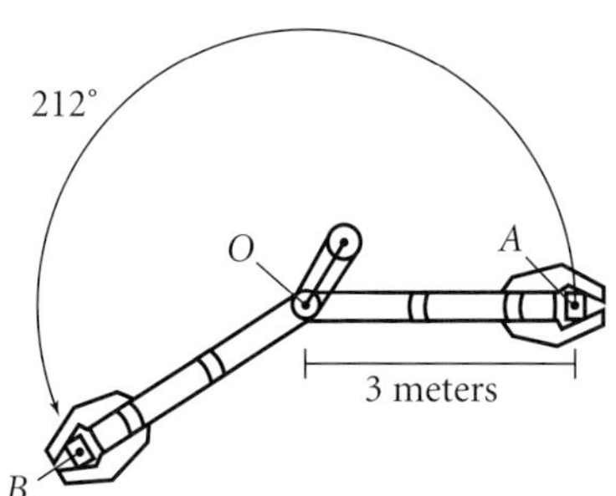

98. **ROBOTICS** A robotic arm attached at point O picks up an object at point A, which is 3 meters to the right of O.

a. The arm rotates through an angle of 212° and releases the object at point B. What is the location of the object at point B relative to O?

b. If the arm lifts an object at A, rotates through an angle of 250°, extends to a length of 4 meters, and then places the object at point C, what is the location of the object at point C relative to O?

c. How far must the arm be extended and through what angle must it swing in order for it to move an object from point A to a point that is located 1 meter to the right of and 2 meters below point O?

99. **BICYCLE DESIGN** The tires of a bicycle have a diameter of 26 inches. In the lowest gear, one complete revolution of the pedals causes the back wheel to rotate through an angle of 106°. How far, in inches, does this cause the bike to move?

100. **CONSTRUCTION** The Williams are building a new fence for their horse pen. The fence will have square sections with diagonal supports, as shown at right. If the height of a square fence section is 3.5 feet, find the length of a diagonal support.

Look Back

Let $f(x) = 3x + 2$ and $g(x) = 4x - 1$. Find each composite function. ***(LESSON 2.4)***

101. $f \circ g$ **102.** $g \circ f$ **103.** $g \circ g$

Matrix J represents the amounts of money that Sheree and her brother Donnell had in their savings and checking accounts at the end of January. ***(LESSON 4.1)***

$$\begin{array}{r} \\ \text{Sheree} \\ \text{Donnell} \end{array} \begin{array}{c} \text{Savings} \quad \text{Checking} \\ \begin{bmatrix} 325 & 512 \\ 408 & 275 \end{bmatrix} \end{array} = J$$

104. What are the dimensions of matrix J?

105. Describe the data in location j_{21}.

106. Find the total amount Sheree had in the bank at the end of January.

CONNECTION

107. COORDINATE GEOMETRY Show that the triangle with vertices at $A(-2, 5)$, $B(4, 13)$, and $C(10, 5)$ is an isosceles triangle. ***(LESSON 9.1)***

Find the mean, median, and mode of each data set. Give answers to the nearest hundredth. ***(LESSON 12.1)***

108. 2, 8, 4, 11, 13, 4, 7, 8, 0

109. 5, 8, 3, 8, 12, 3, 16, 9, 11

Find the mean and standard deviation of each data set. Give answers to the nearest hundredth. ***(LESSON 12.4)***

110. 5, 7, 38, 4, 9, 10, 11, 9, 3

111. 44, 43, 0, 47, 53, 54, 45, 48

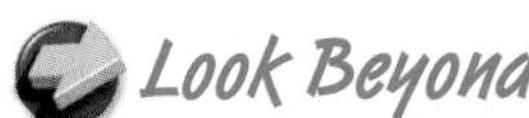

Look Beyond

112. Because the whole unit circle (360°) has a circumference of 2π, an arc intercepted by angle θ will have a length ℓ given by $\ell = \frac{\theta}{360} \cdot 2\pi$. Find ℓ for each angle below.

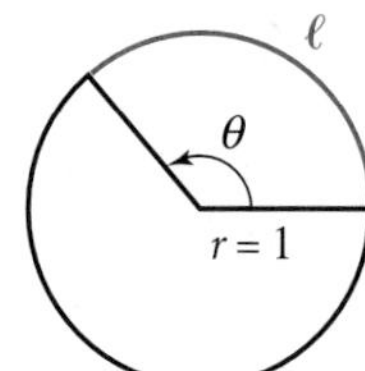

a. $\theta = 180°$ **b.** $\theta = 90°$ **c.** $\theta = 360°$ **d.** $\theta = 45°$

Refer to the Cosmoclock 21 described in the Portfolio Activity on page 835. The center of the Ferris wheel is located at the origin of the coordinate plane at right. Assume that point P begins its rotation at (164, 0) and that it rotates counterclockwise.

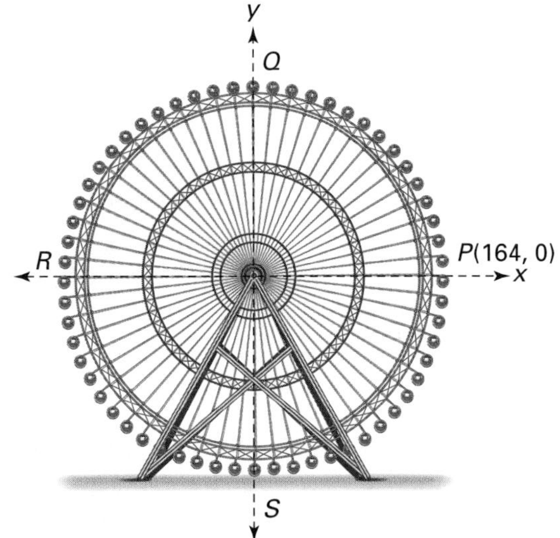

1. Find the height of P relative to the x-axis for each angle of rotation.
   a. 30° **b.** 45° **c.** 60°

2. Find the altitude of P, or height of P relative to the ground, for each angle of rotation given in Step 1.

3. Describe a general rule for converting from the height of P relative to the x-axis to the altitude of P.

4. Create a table of values for the altitude of P. Include all special angle measures for θ such that $0° \le \theta \le 360°$.

5. Plot the points from your table on graph paper. Sketch a *smooth curve* through the points.

6. Describe how the graph that you sketched in Step 5 compares with the graph that you sketched in Step 3 of the Portfolio Activity on page 835.

WORKING ON THE CHAPTER PROJECT

You should now be able to complete Activity 2 of the Chapter Project.

Radian Measure and Arc Length

Objectives

- Convert from degree measure to radian measure and vice versa.
- Find arc length.

Why *Radian measure is used to describe periodic phenomena such as seismic waves, climatic and population cycles, and the motion of circular orbiting objects such as satellites.*

APPLICATION
METEOROLOGY

A weather satellite orbits the Earth at an altitude of approximately 22,200 miles above Earth's surface. If the satellite observes a fixed region on Earth and has a period of revolution of 24 hours, what is the linear speed of the satellite? What is its angular speed? *You will answer these questions in Example 4.*

A useful angle measure other than degrees is *radian* measure. In the Activity below, you can investigate the relationship between measures in a circle, which is fundamental to the definition of radian measure.

Activity
Investigating Circle Ratios

You will need: centimeter measuring tape and various cylindrical cans

1. Measure the circumference and diameter of several cylindrical objects of different sizes. Record your results in a table.
2. Plot your values as ordered pairs, with diameter on the x-axis.
3. Find the least-squares line for this data, and determine its slope.

4. The slope should be approximately equal to a famous number that relates circumference and diameter. What is it? How close were you?

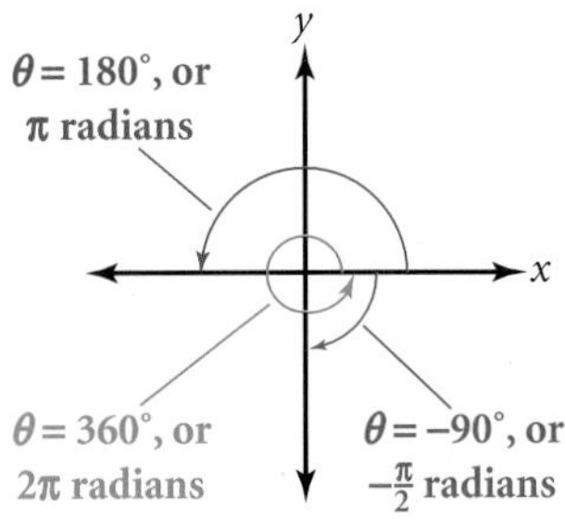

The circumference of a circle with a radius of r is $2\pi r$. Because the radius of a unit circle is 1, its circumference is 2π. The **radian** measure of an angle is equal to the length of the arc on the unit circle that is intercepted by the angle in standard position. Thus, an angle of rotation of 360° has a measure of 2π radians, an angle of 180° has a measure of π radians, and an angle of –90° has a measure of $-\frac{\pi}{2}$ radians.

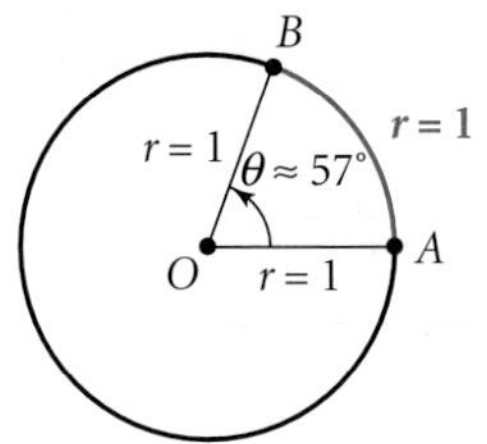

When the length of the arc determined by an angle of rotation equals the radius, the measure of the angle is 1 radian. Because an arc length of 1 radian represents $\frac{1}{2\pi}$ of the entire circumference, 1 radian $= \frac{1}{2\pi} \cdot 360°$, or about 57°.

You can convert from degrees to radians, and vice versa, by using the relationship below to *multiply by 1*.

$$1 = \frac{1 \text{ rotation}}{1 \text{ rotation}} = \frac{2\pi \text{ radians}}{360° \text{ degrees}} = \frac{\pi \text{ radians}}{180° \text{ degrees}}$$

CONVERTING ANGLE MEASURES	
Degrees to radians	**Radians to degrees**
Multiply by $\frac{\pi \text{ radians}}{180°}$.	Multiply by $\frac{180°}{\pi \text{ radians}}$.

EXAMPLE 1 **Convert from degrees to radians and from radians to degrees.**

a. 40° **b.** 3π radians

SOLUTION

a. $40° \cdot \frac{\pi \text{ radians}}{180°} = \frac{2\pi}{9}$ radians

b. $3\pi \cdot \frac{180°}{\pi \text{ radians}} = 540°$

TRY THIS Convert –120° to radians and $-\frac{2}{3}\pi$ radians to degrees.

CHECKPOINT ✓ How many radians correspond to 1°?

EXAMPLE 2 **Evaluate. Give exact values.**

a. $\sin \frac{\pi}{3}$ **b.** $\cos \frac{3\pi}{4}$ **c.** $\tan \frac{4\pi}{3}$

SOLUTION

Convert from radians to degrees. Then evaluate.

a. $\frac{\pi}{3} \times \frac{180°}{\pi} = 60°$

$\sin \frac{\pi}{3} = \sin 60°$
$= \frac{\sqrt{3}}{2}$

b. $\frac{3\pi}{4} \times \frac{180°}{\pi} = 135°$

$\cos \frac{3\pi}{4} = \cos 135°$
$= -\frac{\sqrt{2}}{2}$

c. $\frac{4\pi}{3} \times \frac{180°}{\pi} = 240°$

$\tan \frac{4\pi}{3} = \tan 240°$
$= \sqrt{3}$

TRY THIS Evaluate $\sin \frac{3\pi}{2}$, $\cos \frac{2\pi}{3}$, and $\tan \frac{5\pi}{4}$. Give exact values.

CHECKPOINT ✓ Draw a unit circle and label all of the special angles in radians from 0 to 2π.

Arc Length

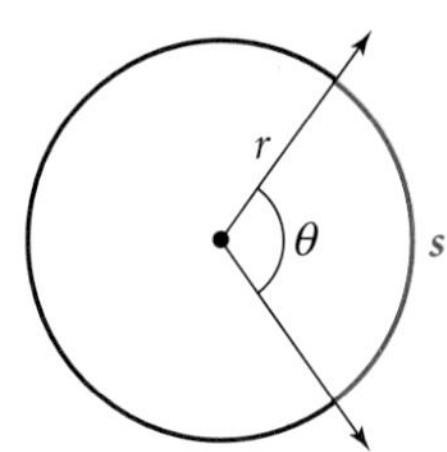

A circle with a radius of r and a central angle of θ, whose vertex at the center of the circle, is shown at right. You can use proportions to find a formula for the length of the intercepted arc, s, as follows:

$$\frac{\theta}{2\pi} = \frac{s}{2\pi r}$$

radian measure of θ → θ; radian measure of circle → 2π; s ← arc length of θ; 2πr ← arc length of circle

$$\theta = \frac{s}{r} \quad \textit{Multiply each side by } 2\pi.$$

$$s = r\theta$$

Arc Length

If θ is the radian measure of a central angle in a circle with a radius of r, then the length, s, of the arc intercepted by θ is $s = r\theta$.

CRITICAL THINKING Define radian measure by using the definition of arc length. What does your definition tell you about the units for radians?

EXAMPLE 3 **A central angle in a circle with a diameter of 30 meters measures $\frac{\pi}{3}$ radians. Find the length of the arc intercepted by this angle.**

SOLUTION

Because the diameter is 30 meters, the radius is 15 meters.

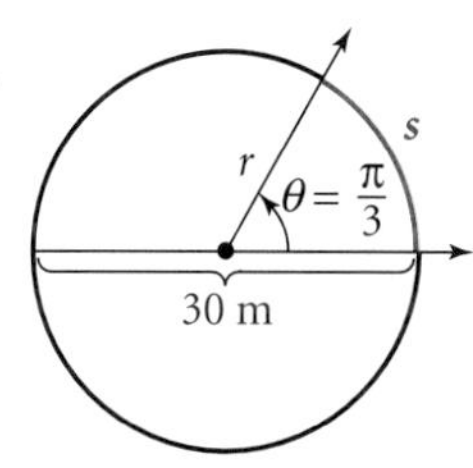

$$s = r\theta$$
$$s = 15\left(\frac{\pi}{3}\right)$$
$$s = 5\pi$$

The arc length is 5π meters, or about 15.7 meters.

TRY THIS A central angle in a circle with a radius of 1.25 feet measures 0.6 radian. Find the length of the arc intercepted by this angle.

Merry-go-round

When an object is moving at a constant speed in a circular path with a radius of r, the **linear speed** of the object is a measure of how fast the position of the object changes and is given by $\frac{s}{t}$, or $\frac{r\theta}{t}$, where t is time and θ is an angle measure in radians. This is a form of the ratio $\frac{\text{distance}}{\text{time}}$.

linear speed
object moves in a circular path
s
r
θ
angular speed

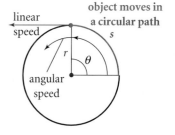

The **angular speed** of the object is a measure of how fast the angle of rotation for the object changes and is given by $\frac{\theta}{t}$, where θ is an angle measure in radians and t is time.

EXAMPLE 4

APPLICATION
METEOROLOGY

Refer to the weather satellite described at the beginning of the lesson. Assume that the radius of the Earth is 3960 miles.

a. What is the linear speed of the satellite?
b. What is the angular speed of the satellite?

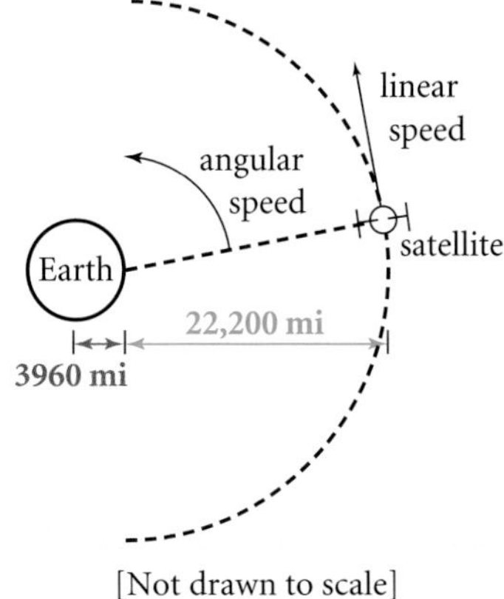

[Not drawn to scale]

SOLUTION

a. Find the radius of the satellite's orbit.

$$\begin{aligned} \text{radius of orbit} &= \text{Earth's radius} + \text{satellite's altitude} \\ &= 3960 + 22{,}200 \\ &= 26{,}160 \end{aligned}$$

Find the linear speed of the satellite if it makes one complete revolution (2π radians) in 24 hours.

$$\begin{aligned} \text{linear speed} &= \frac{r\theta}{t} \\ &= \frac{26{,}160 \cdot 2\pi}{24} \\ &\approx 6848 \end{aligned}$$

The linear speed of the satellite is about 6848 miles per hour.

Computer enhanced image from a weather satellite

b. Use the formula for angular speed.

$$\begin{aligned} \text{angular speed} &= \frac{\theta}{t} \\ &= \frac{2\pi}{24} \\ &= \frac{\pi}{12} \end{aligned}$$

The angular speed of the satellite is $\frac{\pi}{12}$ radians per hour.

TRY THIS Find the linear and angular speeds of a person standing on Earth, 3960 miles from its center.

Exercises

Communicate

1. Explain what the radian measure of an angle is and how it differs from degree measure.
2. Describe how to convert from radians to degrees and vice versa.
3. What happens to the length of an arc intercepted by a given central angle of a circle if the radius of the circle is doubled? Why?
4. Describe the linear and angular speeds associated with circular motion. How do they differ?

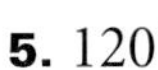

Guided Skills Practice

Convert from degrees to radians and from radians to degrees. ***(EXAMPLE 1)***

5. $120°$ **6.** $\frac{\pi}{4}$ radians

Seattle's Space Needle

Evaluate. Give exact values. ***(EXAMPLE 2)***

7. $\sin \frac{2\pi}{3}$ **8.** $\cos \frac{5\pi}{4}$ **9.** $\tan \frac{5\pi}{3}$

10. A central angle in a circle with a diameter of 90 centimeters measures $\frac{4\pi}{3}$ radians. Find the length of the arc intercepted by this angle. ***(EXAMPLE 3)***

11. ENTERTAINMENT The outer 14 feet of the Space Needle Restaurant in Seattle rotates once every 58 minutes. Find the linear speed in feet per minute of a person sitting by the window of this restaurant if the diameter of the restaurant is 194.5 feet. How fast is this in miles per hour? ***(EXAMPLE 4)***

Practice and Apply

Convert each degree measure to radian measure. Give exact answers.

12. $180°$ **13.** $90°$ **14.** $360°$ **15.** $270°$

16. $-30°$ **17.** $-120°$ **18.** $-210°$ **19.** $-240°$

20. $720°$ **21.** $930°$ **22.** $80°$ **23.** $160°$

Convert each radian measure to degree measure. Round answers to the nearest tenth of a degree.

24. 2π **25.** π **26.** $\frac{\pi}{2}$ **27.** $\frac{\pi}{4}$

28. $\frac{\pi}{3}$ **29.** $\frac{\pi}{6}$ **30.** $-\frac{\pi}{2}$ **31.** $-\frac{\pi}{4}$

32. -3.91 **33.** -9.799 **34.** 9.27 **35.** 4.96

Evaluate each expression. Give exact values.

36. $\sin \pi$ **37.** $\cos \pi$ **38.** $\cos \frac{\pi}{3}$ **39.** $\sin \frac{7\pi}{6}$

40. $\sin\left(-\frac{\pi}{6}\right)$ **41.** $\cos\left(-\frac{5\pi}{3}\right)$ **42.** $\tan \pi$ **43.** $\tan \frac{\pi}{4}$

44. $\cos \frac{2\pi}{3}$ **45.** $\cos\left(-\frac{7\pi}{4}\right)$ **46.** $\sin \frac{11\pi}{2}$ **47.** $\cos 5\pi$

48. $\tan \frac{9\pi}{4}$ **49.** $\sec \frac{\pi}{4}$ **50.** $\cot \frac{\pi}{6}$ **51.** $\csc\left(-\frac{\pi}{3}\right)$

A circle has a diameter of 10 meters. For each central angle measure below, find the length in meters of the arc intercepted by the angle.

52. 3.8 radians **53.** 2.4 radians **54.** 45 radians

55. 72 radians **56.** 4.28 radians **57.** 0.67 radians

58. $\frac{\pi}{3}$ radians **59.** $\frac{2\pi}{3}$ radians **60.** $\frac{\pi}{4}$ radians

61. $\frac{\pi}{2}$ radians **62.** $\frac{7\pi}{4}$ radians **63.** $\frac{7\pi}{6}$ radians

CONNECTION

GEOMETRY The **area of a sector**, *A*, which resembles the slice of a pie, is a fraction $\left(\frac{\theta}{2\pi}\right)$ of the area of a complete circle (πr^2), so $A = \frac{\theta}{2\pi} \cdot \pi r^2 = \frac{1}{2}r^2\theta$, where θ is the measure of the central angle in radians.

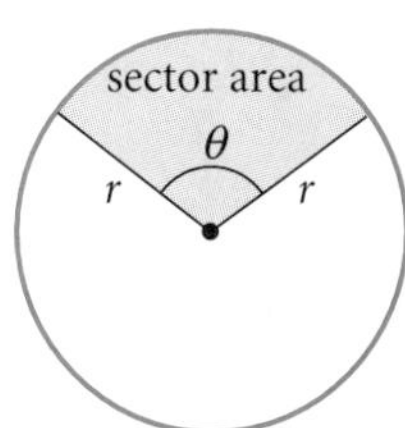

64. Find the area of a sector with a central angle of $\frac{7\pi}{6}$ radians in a circle with a radius of 20 meters.

65. Find the central angle for a sector with an area of 55.5 square inches in a circle with a radius of 12 inches.

APPLICATIONS

ENGINEERING The rear windshield wiper shown below moves through an angle of $\frac{3\pi}{4}$ radians in 0.9 second at normal speed.

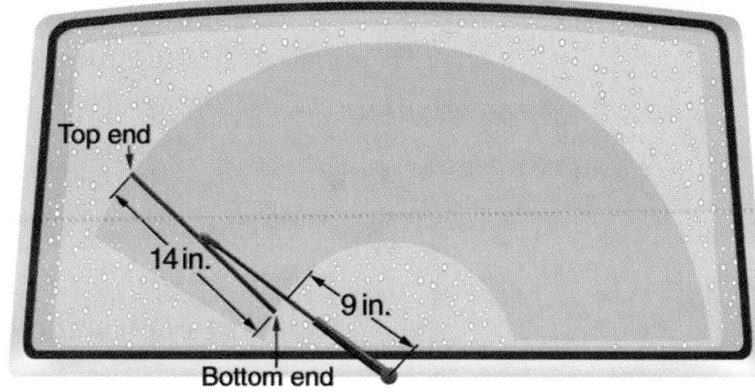

66. Find the approximate distances traveled by a point on the top end of the wiper and by a point on the bottom end of the wiper in one sweep of the wiper.

67. Find the approximate linear speeds in inches per second of a point at the top end of the wiper and of a point at the bottom end of the wiper. What are these speeds in miles per hour?

TECHNOLOGY A CD player rotates a CD at different speeds depending on where the laser is reading the disc. Assume that information is stored within a 6-centimeter diameter on the disc.

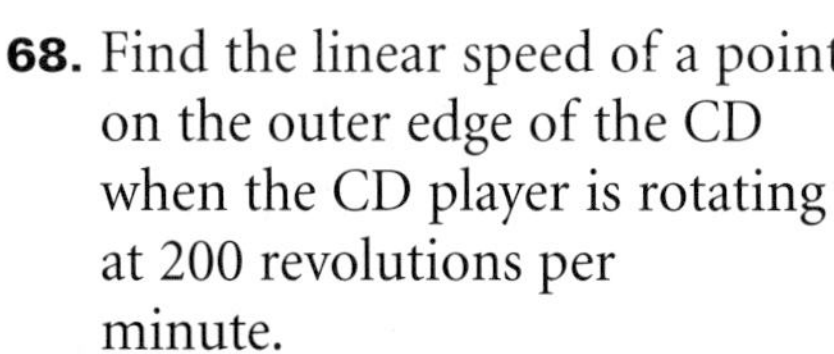

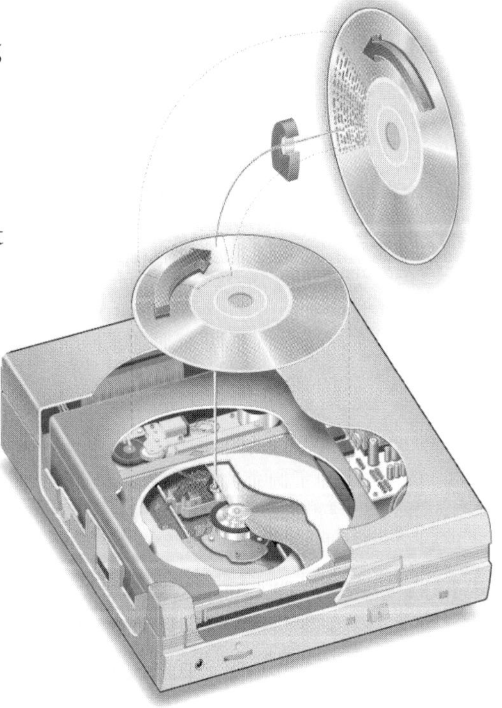

68. Find the linear speed of a point on the outer edge of the CD when the CD player is rotating at 200 revolutions per minute.

69. Find the linear speed of a point 2 centimeters from the outer edge of the CD when the CD player is rotating at 240 revolutions per minute.

AUTO RACING In 17.5 seconds, a car covers an arc intercepted by a central angle of 120° on a circular track with a radius of 300 meters.

70. What is the car's linear speed in meters per second?

71. What is the car's angular speed in radians per second?

CHALLENGE

72. **MACHINERY** The large gear shown at right rotates through angle θ_1 (measured in radians), causing the small gear to rotate through angle θ_2. Find an expression for θ_2 in terms of θ_1, r_1, and r_2.

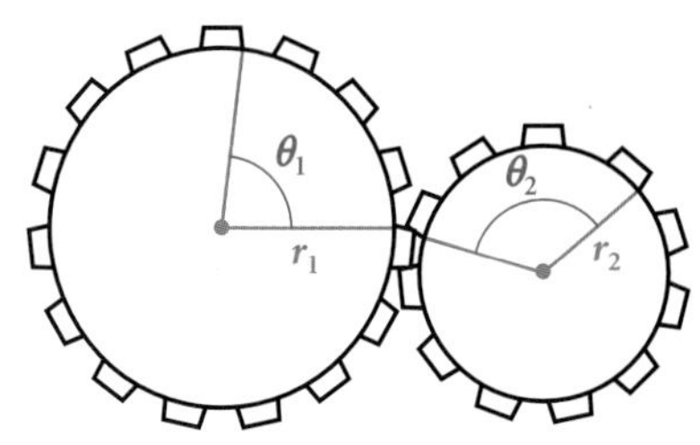

Look Back

Solve each inequality. Graph the solution on a number line. ***(LESSON 1.8)***

73. $|x - 4| \leq -2$ **74.** $|2 - x| > 1$ **75.** $|3x + 5| < 4$

Multiply. ***(LESSON 5.6)***

76. $(1 + i)(2 + 3i)$ **77.** $(1 - 2i)(-2 + i)$ **78.** $(3 + 4i)(2 - 3i)$

Solve each equation. Round your answers to the nearest hundredth. ***(LESSON 6.3)***

79. $4^x = 35$ **80.** $\log x^2 = 4$ **81.** $3 \log(x + 1) = 5$

Solve each rational equation algebraically. Check your solutions by any method. ***(LESSON 8.5)***

82. $\frac{x-3}{x+5} = \frac{x}{x+1}$ **83.** $\frac{x-8}{2x} = \frac{x}{6}$ **84.** $\frac{y}{y-4} - \frac{y}{y+2} = \frac{5}{y^2 - 2y - 8}$

Make relative frequency table and histogram of probabilities for each set of data. ***(LESSON 12.2)***

85. 3, 4, 5, 4, 5, 6, 5, 7, 4, 5, 2, 1, 3, 4, 7, 5, 3, 4, 6, 5, 4, 8, 6, 3, 3

86. 69, 74, 66, 68, 72, 74, 67, 71, 73, 67, 67, 65, 66, 67, 66, 70, 72

Look Beyond

87 Graph $y = \sin x$ and $y = \cos x$ over the interval $-4\pi \leq x \leq 4\pi$, and compare the graphs.

Refer to the Cosmoclock 21 described in the Portfolio Activity on page 835.

1. If the Cosmoclock 21 completes 1.5 revolutions per minute, how many seconds does it take to make 1 complete revolution? $\frac{1}{4}$ of a revolution?
2. Refer to the table of values that you created in Step 4 of the Portfolio Activity on page 850. Find the corresponding time in seconds for each angle of rotation in the table.
3. Plot the altitude of P versus time on graph paper. Sketch a *smooth curve* through the points.
4. What is the period of the graph? What does the period represent?
5. Find the linear speed of a rider on the Cosmoclock 21.

WORKING ON THE CHAPTER PROJECT

You should now be able to complete Activity 3 of the Chapter Project.

Graphing Trigonometric Functions

Why *The graphs of trigonometric functions can be used to model real-world events such as the changes in air pressure that create sounds.*

Objectives

- Graph the sine, cosine, and tangent functions and their transformations.
- Use the sine function to solve problems.

APPLICATION
ACOUSTICS

Sound occurs when an object, such as a speaker, vibrates. This vibration causes small changes in air pressure, which travel away from the object in waves. The sound from an electric keyboard can be modeled by a transformed graph of a trigonometric function. *You will do this in Example 3.*

Activity
Exploring Trigonometric Graphs

Keystroke Guide, page 882

You will need: a graphics calculator

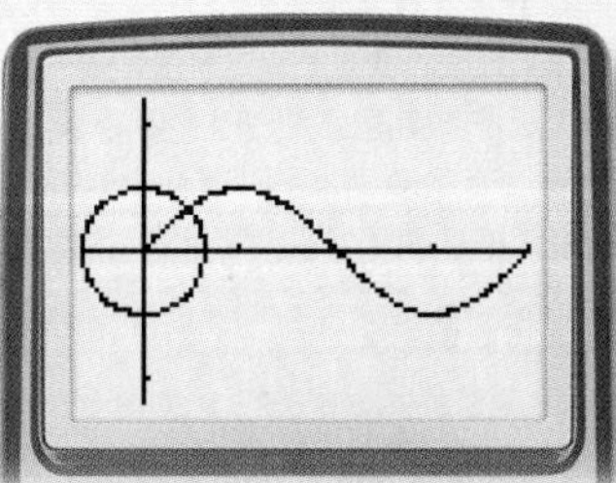

Using radian, parametric, and simultaneous modes, enter $x_{1t} = \cos t$ and $y_{1t} = \sin t$ to generate the unit circle, and enter $x_{2t} = t$ and $y_{2t} = \sin t$ for the function. Set a square viewing window such that t takes on values from 0 to 2π inclusive.

1. Graph the equations and watch as both curves emerge simultaneously. What is the function that you have just graphed?

CHECKPOINT ✔

2. Describe any relationships that you see between the two curves during the graphing process. You can also use the trace feature to compare x- and y-values with t-values.

CHECKPOINT ✔

3. **a.** What is the period of the function?
   b. Predict how the curves will change for $x_{1t} = 2 \cos t$, $y_{1t} = 2 \sin t$, $x_{2t} = t$, and $y_{2t} = 2 \sin t$. Check your prediction by graphing.
   c. Predict how the curves will differ from the original curves for $x_{1t} = \cos 3t$, $y_{1t} = \sin 3t$, $x_{2t} = t$, and $y_{2t} = \sin 3t$. Check your prediction by graphing. (Watch the graphing of the circle carefully.)
4. Repeat Steps 1–3 for $y_{2t} = \cos t$ and $y_{2t} = \tan t$.

The Sine and Cosine Functions

Recall from Lesson 13.3 that one period of the parent function $y = \sin\theta$ or $y = \cos\theta$ is 360°

The table of values at right and the graphs below show one period of the sine and cosine function over the interval $0° \leq \theta \leq 360°$.

The vertical line segments in the unit circle next to the graph below of $y = \sin\theta$ represent selected values of $\sin\theta$ that can be used to construct the graph.

The horizontal line segments in the unit circle next to the graph below of $y = \cos\theta$ represent selected values of $\cos\theta$ that can be used to construct the graph.

	$y = \sin\theta$		$y = \cos\theta$	
θ	Exact	Approx.	Exact	Approx.
0°	0	0.00	1	1.00
30°	$\frac{1}{2}$	0.50	$\frac{\sqrt{3}}{2}$	0.87
45°	$\frac{\sqrt{2}}{2}$	0.71	$\frac{\sqrt{2}}{2}$	0.71
60°	$\frac{\sqrt{3}}{2}$	0.87	$\frac{1}{2}$	0.50
90°	1	1.00	0	0.00
120°	$\frac{\sqrt{3}}{2}$	0.87	$-\frac{1}{2}$	−0.50
135°	$\frac{\sqrt{2}}{2}$	0.71	$-\frac{\sqrt{2}}{2}$	−0.71
150°	$\frac{1}{2}$	0.50	$-\frac{\sqrt{3}}{2}$	−0.87
180°	0	0.00	−1	−1.00
210°	$-\frac{1}{2}$	−0.50	$-\frac{\sqrt{3}}{2}$	−0.87
225°	$-\frac{\sqrt{2}}{2}$	−0.71	$-\frac{\sqrt{2}}{2}$	−0.71
240°	$-\frac{\sqrt{3}}{2}$	−0.87	$-\frac{1}{2}$	−0.50
270°	−1	−1.00	0	0.00
300°	$-\frac{\sqrt{3}}{2}$	−0.87	$\frac{1}{2}$	0.50
315°	$-\frac{\sqrt{2}}{2}$	−0.71	$\frac{\sqrt{2}}{2}$	0.71
330°	$-\frac{1}{2}$	−0.50	$\frac{\sqrt{3}}{2}$	0.87
360°	0	0.00	1	1.00

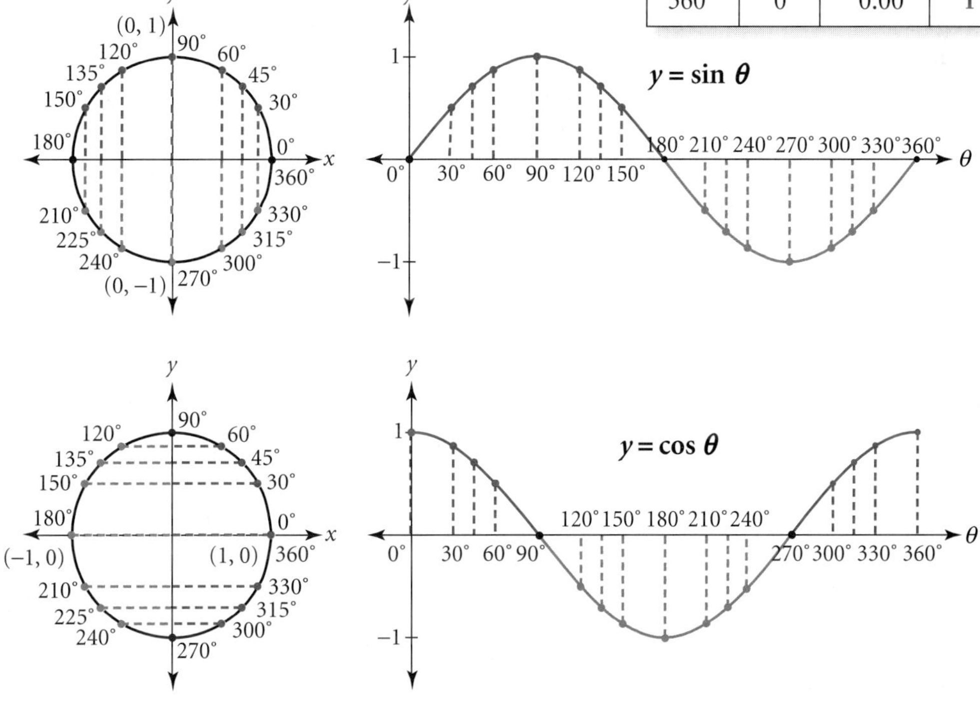

Stretches and Compressions

Transformations of the sine and cosine functions are quite common in real-world applications. Recall from Lesson 2.7 that the graph of the function $y = af(x)$ is a vertical stretch or compression of the graph of the parent function $y = f(x)$ by a factor of a. Similarly, the graph of $y = f(bx)$ is a horizontal stretch or compression of the graph of $y = f(x)$ by a factor of $\frac{1}{|b|}$.

EXAMPLE 1 **Graph at least one period of each trigonometric function along with its parent function.**

CONNECTION
TRANSFORMATIONS

a. $y = 2 \sin \theta$ **b.** $y = \cos \frac{1}{2}\theta$

SOLUTION

a. The 2 causes the function values to be twice as big, so the graph of $y = 2 \sin \theta$ is a vertical stretch of the graph of $y = \sin \theta$ by a factor of 2. Because the zeros are the same as in the parent function, this kind of transformation is relatively easy to graph without creating a table of values.

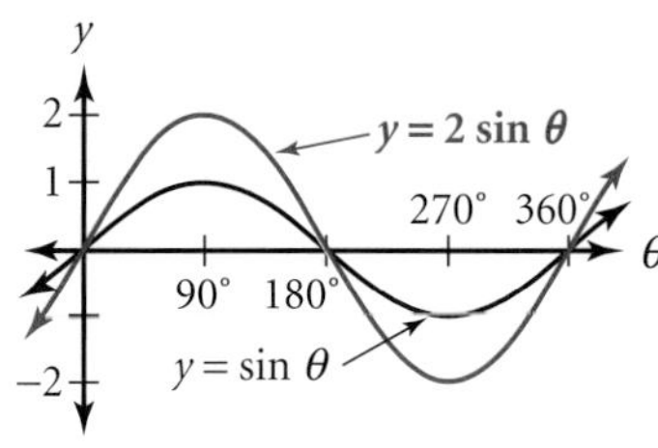

b. The values of θ are multiplied by $\frac{1}{2}$, so the curve "unfolds" half as fast, or takes twice as long to "unfold." The graph of $y = \cos \frac{1}{2}\theta$ is a horizontal stretch of the graph of $y = \cos \theta$ by a factor of 2. Note that the graph of $y = \cos \theta$ completes one period over the interval $0° \leq \theta \leq 360°$, while the graph of $y = \cos \frac{1}{2}\theta$ completes one period over the interval $0° \leq \theta \leq 720°$.

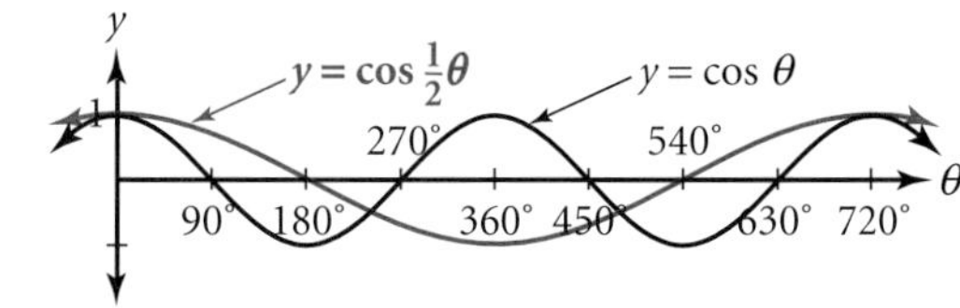

TRY THIS Graph at least one period of each trigonometric function along with its parent function.

a. $y = \frac{1}{3} \cos \theta$ **b.** $y = \sin 3\theta$

The **amplitude** of a periodic function is defined as follows:

$$\text{amplitude} = \frac{1}{2}(\text{maximum value} - \text{minimum value})$$

Because $y = \sin \theta$ and $y = \cos \theta$ each have a minimum of -1 and a maximum of 1, the amplitude of each function is $\frac{1}{2}[1 - (-1)] = 1$.

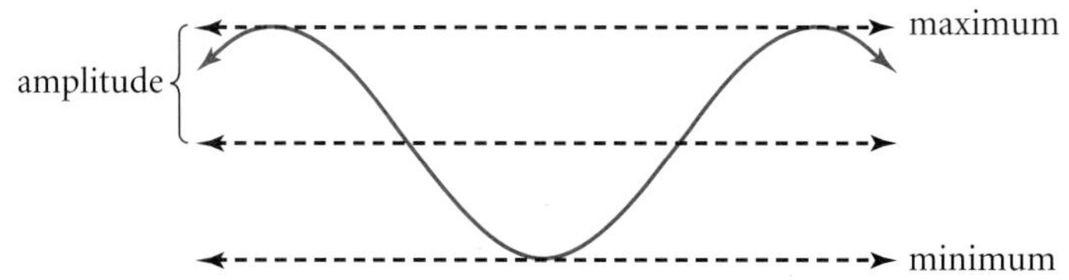

CHECKPOINT ✔ What is the amplitude of $y = 2 \sin \theta$ in Example 1? of $y = \frac{1}{4} \cos 3\theta$?

Translations

Recall from Lesson 2.7 that the graph of $y = f(x - h)$ is a horizontal translation of the graph of $y = f(x)$. The translation is h units to the right for $h > 0$ and $|h|$ units to the left for $h < 0$. A horizontal translation of a sine or cosine function is also called a **phase shift.** The graph of $y = f(x) + k$ is a vertical translation of the graph of $y = f(x)$. The translation is k units up for $k > 0$ and $|k|$ units down for $k < 0$.

EXAMPLE 2 **Graph at least one period of each trigonometric function along with its parent function.**

a. $y = \sin(\theta + 45°)$ **b.** $y = \cos\theta + 1$

CONNECTION
TRANSFORMATIONS

SOLUTION

a. Rewrite $y = \sin(\theta + 45°)$ in the form $y = \sin(\theta - h)$.

$$y = \sin[\theta - (-45°)]$$

The graph of $y = \sin(\theta + 45°)$ is a horizontal translation 45° to the left of the graph of $y = \sin\theta$. This is reasonable because when 45° is added to the values of θ, the graph unfolds 45° *sooner.*

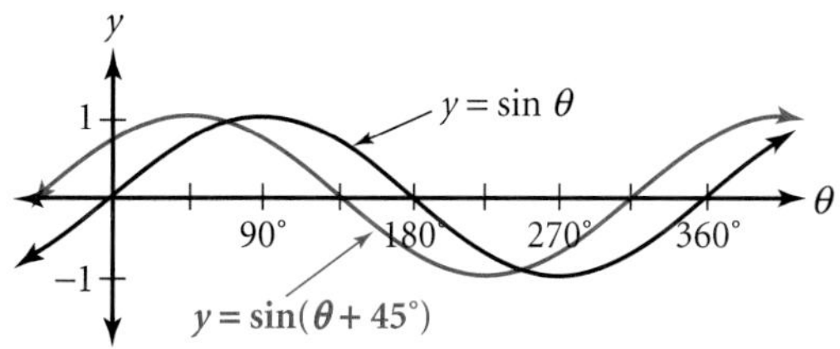

b. The graph of $y = \cos\theta + 1$ is a vertical translation of the graph of $y = \cos\theta$ 1 unit up. This is reasonable because 1 is added to each function value.

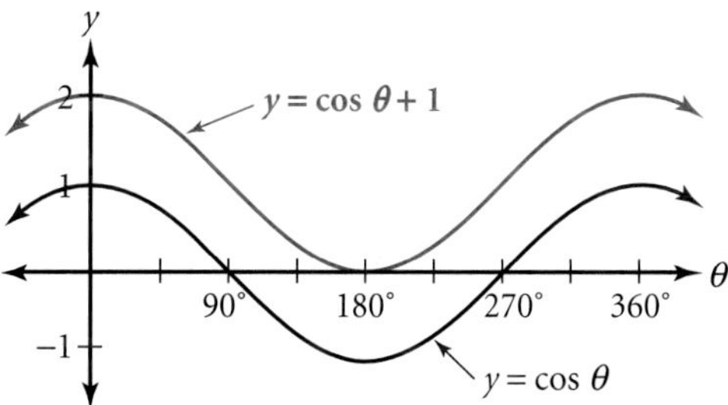

TRY THIS

Graph at least one period of each trigonometric function along with its parent function.

a. $y = \cos(\theta - 45°)$ **b.** $y = \sin\theta - 1$

CRITICAL THINKING

Write the translated sine function and the translated cosine function represented by the graph below.

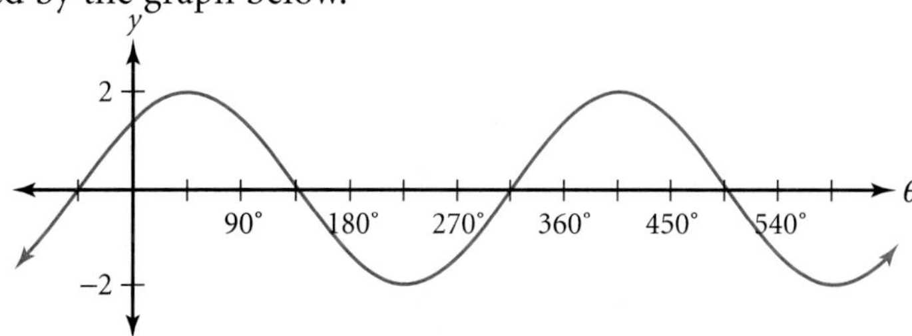

The function $y = a \sin b(t - c)$, where t is in radians and y represents relative air pressure, can represent a particular sound as follows:

- The amplitude of the graph, a, represents the relative *intensity* of the changes in air pressure. A higher intensity results in a louder sound.
- The frequency of the sound wave, measured in units called hertz (Hz), or cycles per second, determines the pitch of the sound. The value of b in the function is equal to the frequency multiplied by 2π.
- The phase shift, c, represents the change in the position of the sound wave over time.
- The period of the sound wave is the reciprocal of the frequency.

EXAMPLE 3

APPLICATION
ACOUSTICS

A particular sound has a frequency of 55 hertz and an amplitude of 3.

a. Write a transformed sine function to represent this sound.

b. Write a new function that represents a phase shift of $\frac{1}{2}$ of a period to the right of the function from part **a**. Then use a graphics calculator to graph at least one period of both functions on the same coordinate plane.

Denyce Graves singing in the opera Carmen

SOLUTION

a. The parent function is $y = \sin t$. Write the transformed function in the form $y = a \sin b(t - c)$.

The amplitude is 3.	$a = 3$
The frequency is related to b.	$b = 2\pi \times 55 = 110\pi$
There is no phase shift.	$c = 0$

Thus, the transformed function is $y = 3 \sin 110\pi t$.

b. The period is the reciprocal of the frequency: $\frac{1}{55}$. One-half of the period is $\frac{1}{2} \times \frac{1}{55} = \frac{1}{110}$. Thus, a phase shift of $\frac{1}{110}$ radian to the right of the function $y = 3 \sin 110\pi t$ is given by $y = 3 \sin 110\pi\left(t - \frac{1}{110}\right)$. Graph both functions in radian mode.

Keystroke Guide, page 883

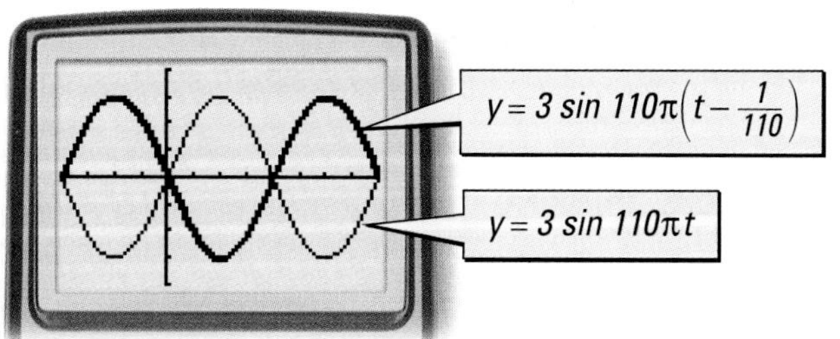

TRY THIS

Write the function for a sound with a frequency of 120 hertz, an amplitude of 1.5, and a phase shift of $\frac{1}{3}$ of a period to the left. Graph at least one period of the function along with its parent function.

The Tangent Function

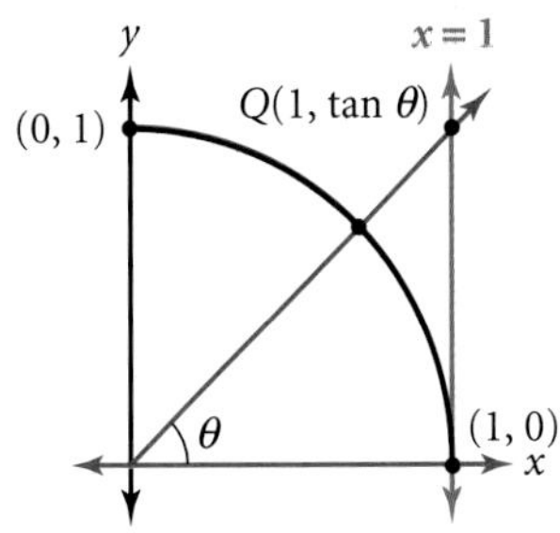

The terminal side of θ intersects the tangent line $x = 1$ at Q.

The sine and cosine functions are related to the coordinates of the points on a unit circle. The tangent function, however, relates to the points on a line *tangent* to the unit circle. Recall from geometry that a **tangent line** is perpendicular to a radius of the circle and touches the circle at only one point.

The table of values and graph for $y = \tan\theta$ below show that its period is 180°. The graph of $y = \tan\theta$ has vertical asymptotes where the function is undefined and has no amplitude because its range is all real numbers.

	θ	−90° 90°	−60° 120°	−45° 135°	−30° 150°	0° 180°	30° 210°	45° 225°	60° 240°
$\tan\theta$	exact	not defined	$-\sqrt{3}$	−1	$-\frac{\sqrt{3}}{3}$	0	$\frac{\sqrt{3}}{3}$	1	$\sqrt{3}$
	approx.	not defined	−1.73	−1	−0.58	0	0.58	1	1.73

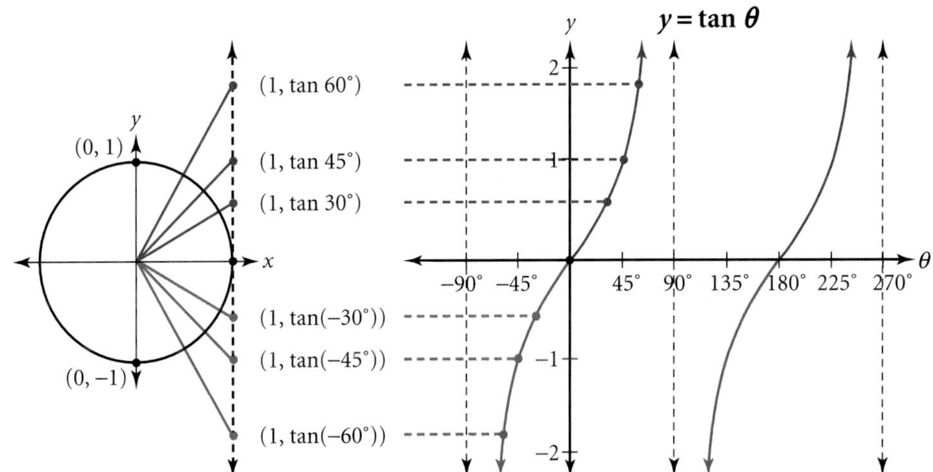

EXAMPLE 4 **Graph at least one period of $y = 3\tan\frac{\theta}{2}$ along with its parent function.**

SOLUTION

Make a table of approximate values. Then graph.

θ	$\frac{\theta}{2}$	$\tan\frac{\theta}{2}$	$3\tan\frac{\theta}{2}$
−180°	−90°	not defined	not defined
−120°	−60°	−1.73	−5.20
−90°	−45°	−1	−3
0°	0°	0	0
90°	45°	1	3
120°	60°	1.73	5.20
180°	90°	not defined	not defined

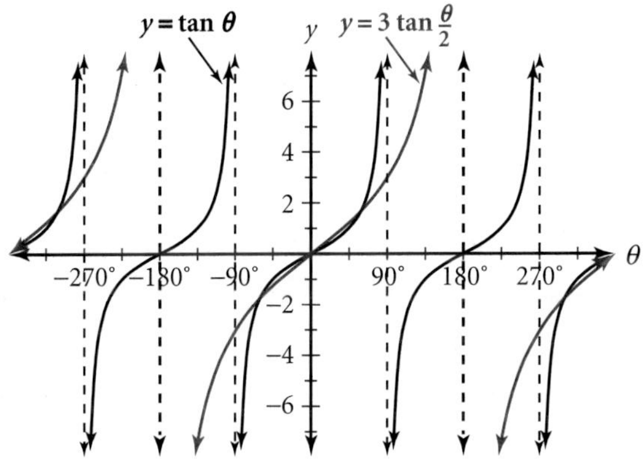

Notice that the graph of $y = 3\tan\frac{\theta}{2}$ is a horizontal stretch of the graph of $y = \tan\theta$ by a factor of 2 and a vertical stretch by a factor of 3.

TRY THIS Graph at least one period of $y = \frac{1}{2}\tan\theta - 3$ along with its parent function.

Exercises

Communicate

1. Compare and contrast the graph of $y = \sin\theta$ with the graph of $y = \cos\theta$.
2. Describe the shape of the graph of the tangent function.
3. Explain why the amplitude of $y = -4\sin\theta$ is larger than that of $y = 3\sin\theta + 2$.
4. Describe at least four ways in which the graph of $y = \tan\theta$ differs from the graph of $y = \sin\theta$.

Guided Skills Practice

Graph at least one period of each trigonometric function along with its parent function. ***(EXAMPLE 1)***

5. $y = \frac{1}{3}\cos\theta$
6. $y = \sin\frac{3}{2}\theta$

Graph at least one period of each trigonometric function along with its parent function. ***(EXAMPLE 2)***

7. $y = \cos(\theta - 90^\circ)$
8. $y = \sin\theta - 1.5$
9. Write the function for a sound with a frequency of 30 hertz, an amplitude of 2, and a phase shift of $\frac{1}{4}$ of a period to the left. Graph at least one period of the function. ***(EXAMPLE 3)***
10. Graph at least one period of the function $y = \frac{3}{2}\tan 3\theta$ along with its parent function. ***(EXAMPLE 4)***

Practice and Apply

Identify the amplitude, if it exists, and the period of each function.

11. $y = 2.5\sin 2\theta$
12. $y = 1.5\sin 4\theta$
13. $y = 4.5\tan 3\theta$
14. $y = -4\tan 3\theta$
15. $y = -5\cos\frac{1}{2}\theta$
16. $y = -6\sin\frac{1}{4}\theta$
17. $y = 3\cos(\theta + 90^\circ)$
18. $y = -2\sin(\theta - 30^\circ)$
19. $y = -\sin(\theta + 45^\circ)$

Identify the phase shift and the vertical translation of each function from its parent function.

20. $y = \sin(\theta - 90^\circ) + 3$
21. $y = \cos(\theta - 45^\circ) - 2$
22. $y = \cos(\theta + 30^\circ) - 2$
23. $y = \sin(\theta + 60^\circ) + 1$
24. $y = 3 - \sin(\theta - 45^\circ)$
25. $y = 2 + \cos(\theta + 30^\circ)$
26. $y = 4\cos[3(\theta + 180^\circ)] + 1$
27. $y = 3\sin[2(\theta - 135^\circ)] - 3$

Describe the transformation of each function from its parent function. Then graph at least one period of the function along with its parent function.

28. $y = 2\cos\theta$

29. $y = 4\sin\theta$

30. $y = -2\sin\theta$

31. $y = -3\cos\theta$

32. $y = \sin(\theta - 90^\circ)$

33. $y = \cos(\theta + 90^\circ)$

34. $y = 3\cos(\theta + 90^\circ)$

35. $y = 2\sin(\theta - 90^\circ)$

36. $y = -4\cos\frac{1}{2}\theta$

37. $y = -2\cos\frac{1}{3}\theta$

38. $y = \frac{1}{2}\sin 3\theta$

39. $y = \frac{1}{3}\sin 2\theta$

40. $y = 3\tan\theta$

41. $y = 2\tan\theta$

42. $y = \tan\theta + 3$

43. $y = \tan\theta - 2$

44. $y = \tan 2\theta$

45. $y = \tan 3\theta$

46. $y = 2\tan\frac{1}{3}\theta$

47. $y = 3\tan\frac{1}{2}\theta$

CHALLENGE

48. Write a function of the form $f(\theta) = a\cos[b(\theta - c)] + d$ for the graph below.

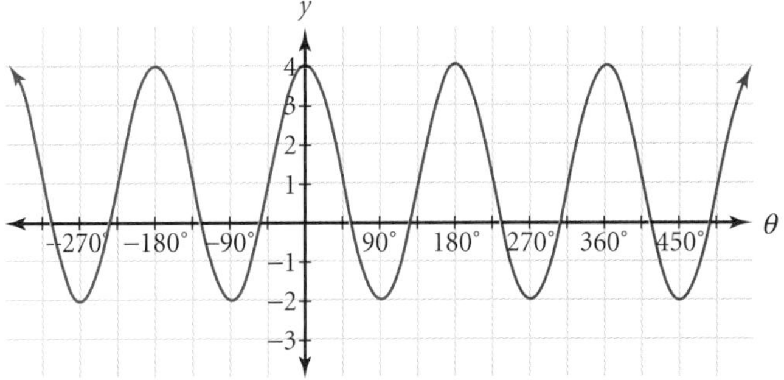

APPLICATIONS

EMPLOYMENT The number of people employed in a resort town can be modeled by the function $g(x) = 1.5\sin\left(\frac{\pi x}{6} + 1\right) + 5.2$, where x is the month of the year (beginning with 1 for January) and $g(x)$ is the number of people (in thousands) employed in the town that month.

49. What type of resort might this be? Explain.

50. About how many people are permanently employed in the town?

51. About how many people are employed in February?

52. Find two months when there are about 4500 people employed in the town.

53. If a major year-round business in the town were to close, which one of the constants in the function model would decrease?

TEMPERATURE The temperature in an air-conditioned office on a hot day can be modeled by the function $t(x) = 1.5\cos\left(\frac{\pi x}{12}\right) + 67$, where x is the time in minutes after the air conditioner is turned on and $t(x)$ is the temperature in degrees Fahrenheit after x minutes.

54. How long does the air conditioner run after being turned on?

55. Find the maximum and minimum temperatures in the office building.

56. Find the temperature 10 minutes after the air conditioner is turned on.

57. Adjust the function to model the temperature in the office when the thermostat is set to a higher temperature.

Look Back

APPLICATION

58. INCOME When Julie baby-sat for 4 hours and did yard work for 4 hours, she made a total of \$47. When she baby-sat for 7 hours and did yard work for 2 hours, she made a total of \$51. How much does Julie get paid for each type of work? ***(LESSON 3.2)***

Write each pair of parametric equations as a single equation in *x* and *y*. ***(LESSON 3.6)***

59. $\begin{cases} x(t) = 2t + 1 \\ y(t) = 2t - 3 \end{cases}$ **60.** $\begin{cases} x(t) = t - 2 \\ y(t) = 4t + 1 \end{cases}$ **61.** $\begin{cases} x(t) = 2t + 1 \\ y(t) = 8t + 13 \end{cases}$

Solve each system of equations by using a matrix equation. Give answers to the nearest hundredth. ***(LESSON 4.4)***

62 $\begin{cases} 2.25x + 3.78y = 11.78 \\ 3.56x + 4.89y = 9.67 \end{cases}$ **63** $\begin{cases} 3.87x + 8.45y = 7.48 \\ 6.67x + 8.36y = 9.85 \end{cases}$

Find *x* to the nearest ten-thousandth. ***(LESSONS 6.3 AND 6.5)***

64. $e^{2x+1} = 13$ **65.** $e^{3x-2} = 25$ **66.** $2^{2x+4} = 20$ **67.** $2^{3x-21} = 31$

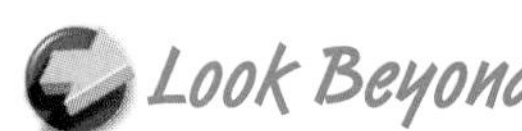

Look Beyond

68 Graph the functions $f(x) = \sin x$ and $f(x) = \dfrac{1}{\sin x}$ on the same axes. Compare their graphs. How are they alike? How are they different?

69 Graph the functions $f(x) = \cos x$ and $f(x) = \dfrac{1}{\cos x}$ on the same axes. Compare their graphs. How are they alike? How are they different?

Using the definitions from Lesson 13.1, make a table of values and graph each function.

70. $y = \sec \theta$ **71.** $y = \csc \theta$ **72.** $y = \cot \theta$

Refer to the data and the graph you created in the Portfolio Activity on page 857.

1. Find the amplitude of your graph. What does the amplitude represent in terms of the Cosmoclock 21?
2. Write an equation of the form $y = a \sin bt$ to model the data that was graphed.
3. Create a scatter plot of the data. Then graph your equation on the same coordinate axes as your scatter plot. Is the equation a good model for the data? Explain.

WORKING ON THE CHAPTER PROJECT

You should now be able to complete Activity 4 of the Chapter Project.

Inverses of Trigonometric Functions

Why *You can use inverses of trigonometric functions to solve real-world problems, such as finding the angle of depression between a supersonic aircraft and the ground.*

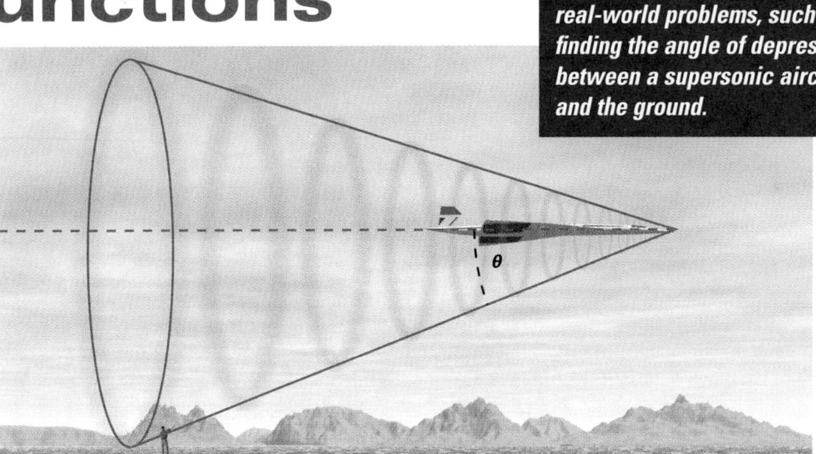

Objective

- Evaluate trigonometric expressions involving inverses.

APPLICATION
AVIATION

When an aircraft flies faster than the speed of sound, which is about 730 miles per hour, shock waves in the shape of a cone are created. When the cone passes a person on the ground, a sonic boom is heard.

The speed of an aircraft can be expressed as a *Mach number*, which gives the aircraft's speed relative to the speed of sound. For example, an aircraft flying at 1000 miles per hour has a speed of $\frac{1000}{730}$, or about Mach 1.4. If θ is the angle of depression between the aircraft and the ground, then θ depends on the speed of the aircraft in Mach numbers as follows:

$$\sin \theta = \frac{1}{\text{speed of aircraft}}$$

What is θ if the speed of the aircraft is Mach 1.3? Mach 1.8? *You will solve this problem in Example 4.*

In Lesson 2.5 you found inverse relations by interchanging the domain and range of the given relation or function. This procedure is used in the following Activity involving trigonometric functions.

Activity

Exploring the Inverse Relation of $y = \sin x$

You will need: graph paper

1. Create a table of values and sketch the graph of $y = \sin x$ over the interval $-2\pi \le x \le 2\pi$. Use x-values of $0, \pm\frac{\pi}{2}, \pm\pi, \pm\frac{3\pi}{2}$, and $\pm 2\pi$.
2. Create a new table of ordered pairs by interchanging the x and y values in your table from Step 1. Plot the new ordered pairs on the same axes, and sketch the resulting curve, which represents $y = \sin^{-1} x$.
3. Add the line $y = x$ to your graph.
4. **CHECKPOINT ✔** Fold the graph paper along the line $y = x$. Describe what happens to the graphs of $y = \sin x$ and $y = \sin^{-1} x$ and what this result means.
5. **CHECKPOINT ✔** Describe what $y = \sin^{-1} x$ represents. Is $y = \sin^{-1} x$ a function? Explain.

Because the trigonometric functions are periodic, many values in their domains have the same function values. For example, examine the sine, cosine, and tangent of 30°, 390°, and −330° shown below.

$\sin 30^\circ = \frac{1}{2}$	$\sin 390^\circ = \frac{1}{2}$	$\sin(-330^\circ) = \frac{1}{2}$
$\cos 30^\circ = \frac{\sqrt{3}}{2}$	$\cos 390^\circ = \frac{\sqrt{3}}{2}$	$\cos(-330^\circ) = \frac{\sqrt{3}}{2}$
$\tan 30^\circ = \frac{1}{\sqrt{3}}$, or $\frac{\sqrt{3}}{3}$	$\tan 390^\circ = \frac{1}{\sqrt{3}}$, or $\frac{\sqrt{3}}{3}$	$\tan(-330^\circ) = \frac{1}{\sqrt{3}}$, or $\frac{\sqrt{3}}{3}$

These repeated function values are readily apparent in the graph of a trigonometric function. For example, examine the graph of $y = \sin \theta$ shown below.

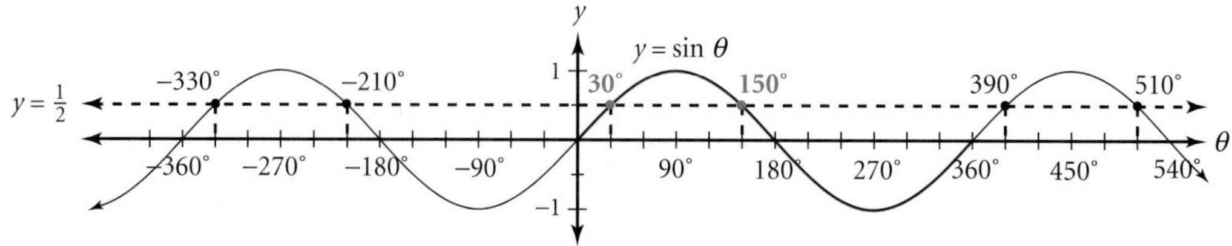

Recall from Lesson 13.1 that the inverse relations of the sine, cosine, and tangent functions are denoted as $y = \sin^{-1} x$, $y = \cos^{-1} x$, and $y = \tan^{-1} x$. To find all possible values of inverse trigonometric function, such as $y = \sin^{-1} \frac{1}{2}$, first find all values that occur within one period. In the period between 0° and 360°, as shown above in blue, $\sin 30^\circ = \frac{1}{2}$ and $\sin 150^\circ = \frac{1}{2}$. Therefore, $\sin^{-1} \frac{1}{2} = 30^\circ$ and $\sin^{-1} \frac{1}{2} = 150^\circ$. The other values of $\sin^{-1} \frac{1}{2}$ occur at values every period before or after 30° and 150°. Thus, if n is an integer, then all possible values of $\sin^{-1} \frac{1}{2}$ occur at $30^\circ + n360^\circ$ and $150^\circ + 360^\circ$.

EXAMPLE 1 Find all possible values of $\cos^{-1} \frac{1}{2}$.

SOLUTION

Find all possible values of $\cos^{-1} \frac{1}{2}$ within one period. The cosine function is positive in Quadrants I and IV.

$\cos 60^\circ = \frac{1}{2}$ *Quadrant I* $\qquad$ $\cos 300^\circ = \frac{1}{2}$ *Quadrant IV*

Thus, all possible values of $\cos^{-1} \frac{1}{2}$ are $60^\circ + n360^\circ$ and $300^\circ + n360^\circ$.

TRY THIS Find all possible values of $\sin^{-1} \frac{\sqrt{2}}{2}$.

The graph of $y = \sin \theta$, shown above, clearly fails the horizontal-line test. Therefore, $y = \sin \theta$ is not a one-to-one function and its inverse cannot be a function. This is true for all trigonometric functions unless their domains are restricted in such a way that their inverses can be functions. The functions *Sine, Cosine,* and *Tangent* (denoted by capital letters) are defined as the sine, cosine, and tangent functions with the restricted domains defined on the next page. The restricted domains are called **principle values.**

Principle Values of Sin θ, Cos θ, and Tan θ

$\text{Sin } \theta = \sin \theta$ for $-90^\circ \le \theta \le 90^\circ$

$\text{Cos } \theta = \cos \theta$ for $0^\circ \le \theta \le 180^\circ$

$\text{Tan } \theta = \tan \theta$ for $-90^\circ < \theta < 90^\circ$

The graph of $y = \sin \theta$ and the portion of the curve that represents $y = \text{Sin } \theta$ are shown below.

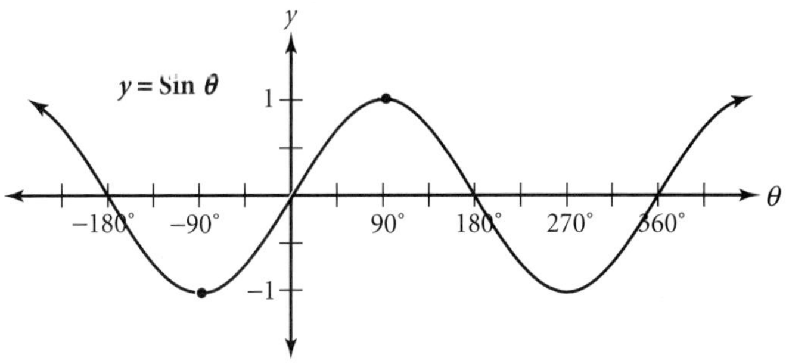

CHECKPOINT ✔ Graph $y = \cos \theta$ and $y = \tan \theta$ and indicate the portion of these curves that represent $y = \text{Cos } \theta$ and $y = \text{Tan } \theta$.

The functions $y = \text{Sin } \theta$, $y = \text{Cos } \theta$, and $y = \text{Tan } \theta$ are one-to-one functions and have inverses that are also functions. The inverse functions are denoted by $y = \text{Sin}^{-1} x$, $y = \text{Cos}^{-1} x$, and $y = \text{Tan}^{-1} x$, respectively.

Inverse Trigonometric Functions

If $y = \text{Sin } x$, then its inverse function is $y = \text{Sin}^{-1} x$.

If $y = \text{Cos } x$, then its inverse function is $y = \text{Cos}^{-1} x$.

If $y = \text{Tan } x$, then its inverse function is $y = \text{Tan}^{-1} x$.

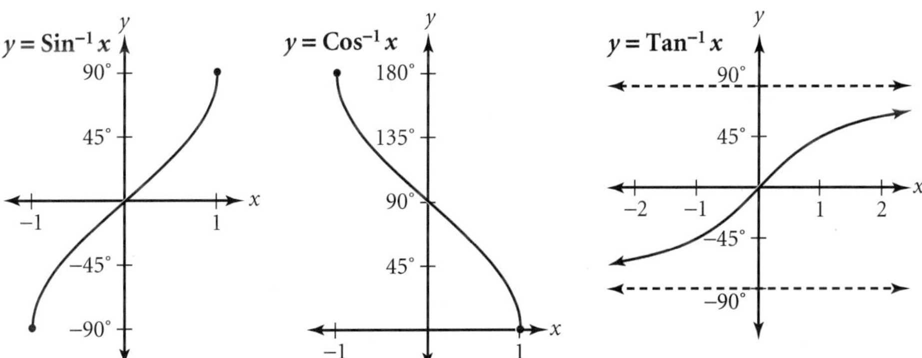

CHECKPOINT ✔ What is the range of $y = \text{Sin}^{-1} x$, of $y = \text{Cos}^{-1} x$, and of $y = \text{Tan}^{-1} x$?

EXAMPLE 2 **Evaluate each inverse trigonometric expression.**

a. $\text{Sin}^{-1}\frac{1}{2}$ **b.** $\text{Cos}^{-1}\left(-\frac{\sqrt{3}}{2}\right)$ **c.** $\text{Tan}^{-1}\left(-\frac{\sqrt{3}}{3}\right)$

SOLUTION

a. Find the angle between the principle values –90° and 90°, inclusive, whose sine is $\frac{1}{2}$. Because $\sin 30° = \frac{1}{2}$, $\text{Sin}^{-1}\frac{1}{2} = 30°$.

b. Find the angle between the principle values 0° and 180°, inclusive, whose cosine is $-\frac{\sqrt{3}}{2}$. Because $\cos 150° = -\frac{\sqrt{3}}{2}$, $\text{Cos}^{-1}\left(-\frac{\sqrt{3}}{2}\right) = 150°$.

c. Find the angle between the principle values –90° and 90°, inclusive, whose tangent is $-\frac{\sqrt{3}}{3}$. Because $\tan(-30°) = -\frac{\sqrt{3}}{3}$, $\text{Tan}^{-1}\left(-\frac{\sqrt{3}}{3}\right) = -30°$.

CHECK

A scientific or graphics calculator returns principle values for inverse trigonometric functions.

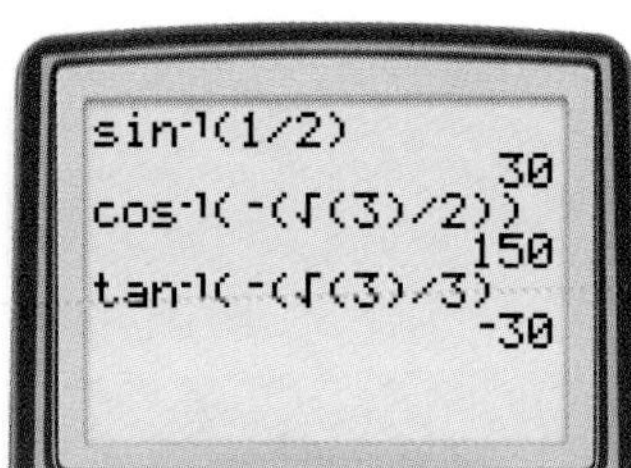

TRY THIS Evaluate each inverse trigonometric expression.

a. $\text{Sin}^{-1}\frac{\sqrt{3}}{2}$ **b.** $\text{Cos}^{-1}\left(-\frac{\sqrt{2}}{2}\right)$ **c.** $\text{Tan}^{-1}\sqrt{3}$

To evaluate an expression such as $\sin\left(\text{Cos}^{-1}\frac{\sqrt{3}}{2}\right)$, first evaluate the expression inside the parentheses. Then evaluate the resulting expression.

EXAMPLE 3 **Evaluate each trigonometric expression.**

a. $\sin\left(\text{Cos}^{-1}\frac{\sqrt{3}}{2}\right)$ **b.** $\text{Tan}^{-1}(\cos 180°)$

SOLUTION

a. Because $\cos 30° = \frac{\sqrt{3}}{2}$, substitute 30° for $\text{Cos}^{-1}\frac{\sqrt{3}}{2}$.

$$\sin\left(\text{Cos}^{-1}\frac{\sqrt{3}}{2}\right) = \sin 30° = \frac{1}{2}$$

b. First evaluate cos 180°. Then use the fact that $\tan(-45°) = -1$.

$$\text{Tan}^{-1}(\cos 180°) = \text{Tan}^{-1}(-1) = -45°$$

TRY THIS Evaluate each trigonometric expression.

a. $\text{Cos}^{-1}(\sin 315°)$ **b.** $\tan\left[\text{Sin}^{-1}\left(-\frac{\sqrt{3}}{2}\right)\right]$

CRITICAL THINKING Explain why $\text{Cos}^{-1}(\cos x) \neq x$, $\text{Sin}^{-1}(\sin x) \neq x$, and $\text{Tan}^{-1}(\tan x) \neq x$ for all values of x.

EXAMPLE 4 Refer to the aviation problem at the beginning of the lesson.

APPLICATION AVIATION

Find the angle of depression, θ, for an airplane flying at each speed.

a. Mach 1.3

b. Mach 1.8

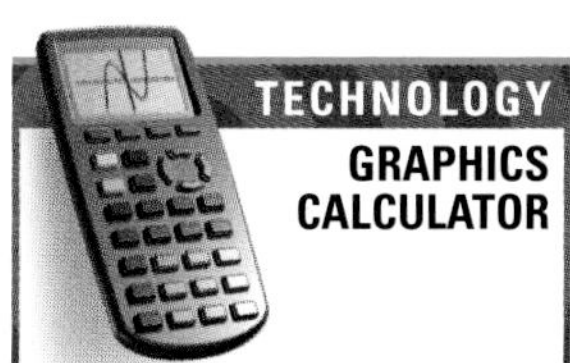

Keystroke Guide, page 883

SOLUTION

a. $\sin\theta = \frac{1}{1.3}$

$\theta = \text{Sin}^{-1}\frac{1}{1.3} \approx 50.28°$

The angle of depression is about 50.28°.

b. $\sin\theta = \frac{1}{1.8}$

$\theta = \text{Sin}^{-1}\frac{1}{1.8} \approx 33.75°$

The angle of depression is about 33.75°.

Exercises

Communicate

1. Describe how Sin θ, Cos θ, and Tan θ are related to sin θ, cos θ, and tan θ, respectively.
2. Describe how $\text{Sin}^{-1} x$, $\text{Cos}^{-1} x$, and $\text{Tan}^{-1} x$ are related to Sin x, Cos x, and Tan x, respectively.
3. Explain why $\text{Sin}^{-1} 5$ is not defined. Is $\text{Tan}^{-1} 5$ defined? Explain.

Guided Skills Practice

4. Find all possible values of $\cos^{-1}\frac{\sqrt{3}}{2}$. ***(EXAMPLE 1)***

Evaluate each inverse trigonometric expression. ***(EXAMPLE 2)***

5. $\text{Sin}^{-1}\left(-\frac{\sqrt{3}}{2}\right)$
6. $\text{Cos}^{-1}\frac{1}{2}$
7. $\text{Tan}^{-1}\left(-\sqrt{3}\right)$

Evaluate each trigonometric expression. ***(EXAMPLE 3)***

8. $\sin\left(\text{Cos}^{-1}\frac{1}{2}\right)$
9. $\text{Cos}^{-1}(\sin 30°)$
10. $\text{Tan}^{-1}(\tan 150°)$

11. Find the angle of depression, θ, for an airplane flying at Mach 1.5. ***(EXAMPLE 4)***

Practice and Apply

Find all possible values for each expression.

12. $\cos^{-1}\left(-\frac{1}{2}\right)$
13. $\sin^{-1}\left(-\frac{\sqrt{2}}{2}\right)$
14. $\tan^{-1}\left(-\frac{\sqrt{3}}{3}\right)$
15. $\tan^{-1}\sqrt{3}$
16. $\sin^{-1} 1$
17. $\cos^{-1} 0$
18. $\sin^{-1}\frac{\sqrt{3}}{2}$
19. $\cos^{-1}\frac{\sqrt{2}}{2}$
20. $\tan^{-1} 0$

Evaluate each trigonometric expression.

21. $\text{Sin}^{-1}\left(-\frac{1}{2}\right)$

22. $\text{Sin}^{-1}\frac{\sqrt{2}}{2}$

23. $\text{Cos}^{-1}\frac{\sqrt{2}}{2}$

24. $\text{Cos}^{-1}\left(-\frac{\sqrt{3}}{2}\right)$

25. $\text{Tan}^{-1}\sqrt{3}$

26. $\text{Tan}^{-1}\frac{\sqrt{3}}{3}$

27. $\text{Sin}^{-1}\frac{\sqrt{3}}{2}$

28. $\text{Sin}^{-1} 1$

29. $\text{Cos}^{-1}(-1)$

30. $\text{Cos}^{-1}\frac{1}{2}$

31. $\text{Tan}^{-1} 1$

32. $\text{Tan}^{-1}(-1)$

Evaluate each trigonometric expression.

33. $\tan\left(\text{Sin}^{-1}\frac{\sqrt{2}}{2}\right)$

34. $\cos\left(\text{Sin}^{-1}\frac{1}{2}\right)$

35. $\sin(\text{Tan}^{-1} 1)$

36. $\cos\left(\text{Tan}^{-1}\frac{\sqrt{3}}{2}\right)$

37. $\tan\left(\text{Cos}^{-1}\frac{1}{2}\right)$

38. $\tan\left(\text{Cos}^{-1}\frac{\sqrt{2}}{2}\right)$

39. $\text{Tan}^{-1}(\sin 30^\circ)$

40. $\text{Tan}^{-1}(\cos 135^\circ)$

41. $\text{Cos}^{-1}(\tan 225^\circ)$

42. $\text{Cos}^{-1}(\sin 60^\circ)$

43. $\text{Sin}^{-1}(\cos 120^\circ)$

44. $\text{Sin}^{-1}(\cos 300^\circ)$

CHALLENGE

Prove each statement.

45. $\text{Sin}^{-1}(\text{Sin}\,\theta) = \theta$

46. $\cos(\text{Cos}^{-1} x) = x$

APPLICATIONS

47. FORESTRY A tree casts a 35-foot shadow on the ground when the angle of elevation from the edge of the shadow to the sun is about 40°. How tall is the tree? Draw a diagram to illustrate this situation.

48. ASTRONOMY Katie is setting up a new telescope in her backyard. Her neighbor's house, which is 50 feet away from the telescope, is 30 feet tall, and the eyepiece of the telescope is 5 feet above the ground. What is the minimum angle that the telescope must make with the horizon in the direction of her neighbor's house in order to see over the house?

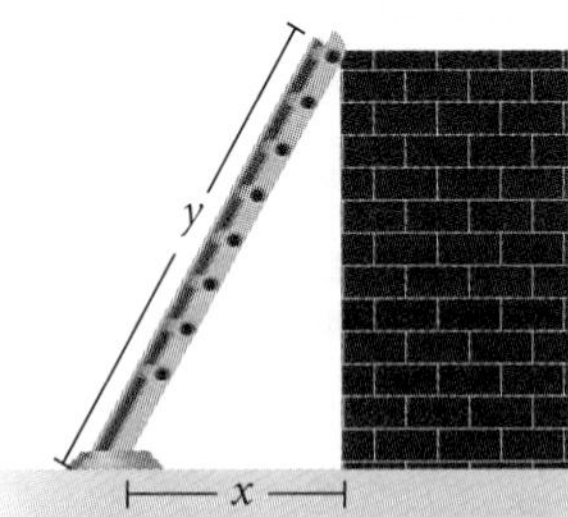

49. CARPENTRY When using a ladder, it is recommended that the distance from the base of the ladder to the structure, x, be $\frac{1}{4}$ of the distance from the base of the ladder to the support for the top of the ladder, y. Find the measure of the angle formed by the ladder and the ground.

50. ARCHITECTURE A person's eyes are 6 feet above the ground and 15 feet from a building. The angle of elevation from the person's line of sight to the top of the building is 75°.

a. How tall is the building?

b. What would be the angle of elevation if the person were standing 50 feet from the building? 100 feet?

APPLICATIONS

51. HIKING Sandra wants to find the height of a mountain. From her first location on the ground, she finds the angle of elevation to the top of the mountain to be about 35°. After moving 1000 meters closer to the mountain on level ground, she finds the angle of elevation to be 50°. Find the height of the mountain to the nearest meter. (Hint: Find two equations with two unknowns, and solve them for each unknown.)

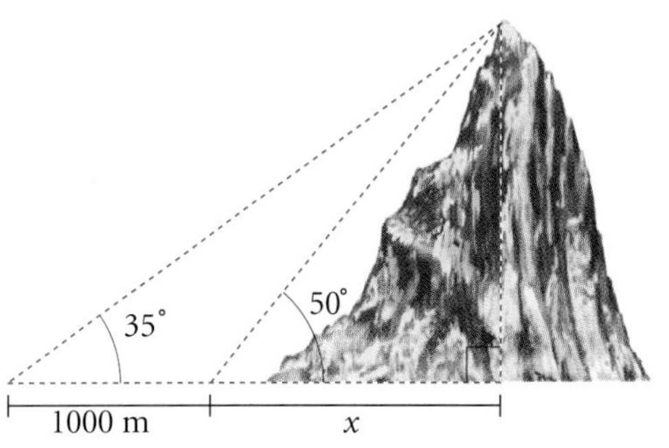

52. PUBLIC SAFETY A driver approaching an intersection sees the word *STOP* written on the road. The driver's eyes are 3.5 feet above the road and 50 feet from the nearest edge of the 8-foot long letters. What angle, θ, does the word make with the driver's eyes?

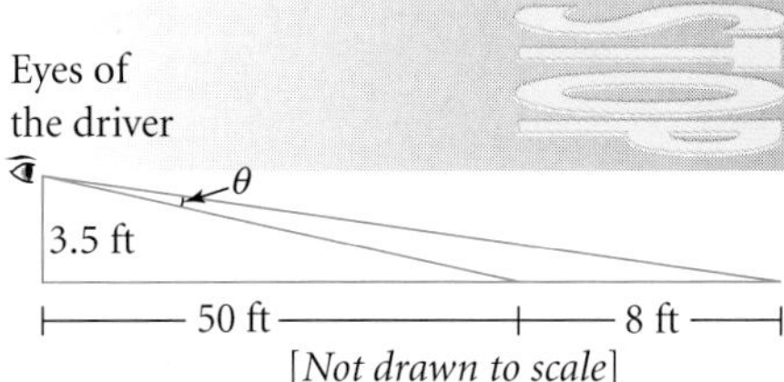

[*Not drawn to scale*]

To simulate the driver's perspective, look at the page from its left edge.

Look Back

53 Solve the system of equations by using a matrix equation. ***(LESSON 4.4)***

$$\begin{cases} 2x + 3y + 5z = 16 \\ -4x + 2y + 3z = -5 \\ 3x - y - z = 5 \end{cases}$$

Solve each equation for *x*. *(LESSON 6.7)*

54. $5e^{2x-1} = 60$

55. $2 \log_3 x + \log_3 9 = 4$

56. Find the zeros of the function $f(x) = x^3 + 5x^2 - 8x - 12$. ***(LESSON 7.5)***

Find the reference angle for each angle below. *(LESSON 13.2)*

57. 337°

58. −118°

59. −23°

60. 520°

Convert from radians to degrees. *(LESSON 13.4)*

61. $\frac{5\pi}{12}$ radians

62. $\frac{7\pi}{8}$ radians

63. 2.38 radians

64. 4.72 radians

Look Beyond

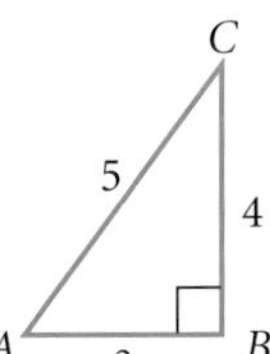

65. Evaluate $\sin^2 x + \cos^2 x$ for $x = \frac{\pi}{2}$, $x = \frac{\pi}{3}$, and $x = 0$. Then evaluate this expression for three other values of x. Make a conjecture about the value of $\sin^2 x + \cos^2 x$ for any value of x.

66. Verify that $\frac{\sin A}{4} = \frac{\sin B}{5} = \frac{\sin C}{3}$ is true for the triangle at left.

Reinventing the Wheel

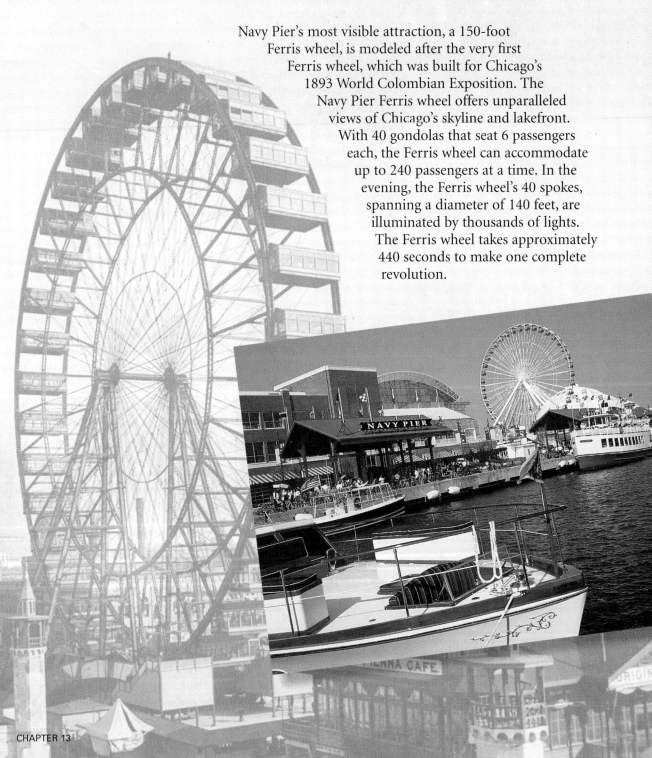

Navy Pier's most visible attraction, a 150-foot Ferris wheel, is modeled after the very first Ferris wheel, which was built for Chicago's 1893 World Colombian Exposition. The Navy Pier Ferris wheel offers unparalleled views of Chicago's skyline and lakefront. With 40 gondolas that seat 6 passengers each, the Ferris wheel can accommodate up to 240 passengers at a time. In the evening, the Ferris wheel's 40 spokes, spanning a diameter of 140 feet, are illuminated by thousands of lights. The Ferris wheel takes approximately 440 seconds to make one complete revolution.

Activity 1

Graph a representation of the Navy Pier Ferris wheel on a coordinate plane with its center at the origin. Create a table of values for the distance from a point on the Ferris wheel to the x-axis. Use the following angles of counterclockwise rotation: 0°, 90°, 180°, 270°, . . . , 810°. Graph the resulting ordered pairs, and sketch a *smooth curve* through the points.

George W. G. Ferris (1859–1896)

Activity 2

Create a table of values for the altitude (height above the ground) of a rider on the Ferris wheel. Let the independent variable include all common angle measures for θ such that $0° \le \theta \le 810°$. Graph the points, and sketch a *smooth curve* through the points.

Activity 3

1. Using the table of values that you created in Activity 2 and the fact that one complete revolution takes 440 seconds, convert the units of the independent variable from degrees to time in seconds. Graph the points, and sketch a *smooth curve* through the points.
2. Find the linear speed, in miles per hour, of a rider on the Ferris wheel.

Activity 4

Write an equation of the form $y = a \sin bt$ to model the altitude of a rider on the Ferris wheel as a function of time. Describe what each variable in your model represents.

13 Chapter Review and Assessment

VOCABULARY

Key Skills & Exercises

LESSON 13.1

Key Skills

Solve a right triangle by using trigonometric functions.

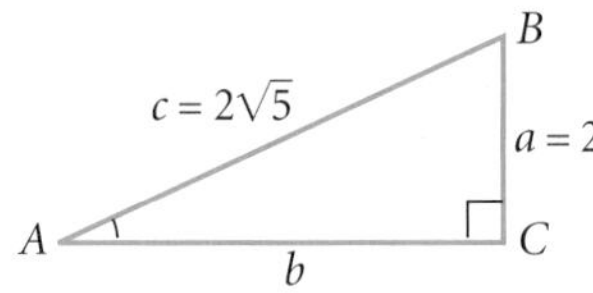

$$\sin A = \frac{2}{2\sqrt{5}}$$

$$A = \sin^{-1} \frac{2}{2\sqrt{5}}$$

$$A \approx 26.6^\circ$$

$$2^2 + b^2 = (2\sqrt{5})^2$$

$$b = \sqrt{(2\sqrt{5})^2 - 2^2}$$

$$b = 4$$

$$A + B = 90^\circ$$

$$B \approx 90^\circ - 26.6^\circ \approx 63.4^\circ$$

Exercises

Solve each triangle.

1.

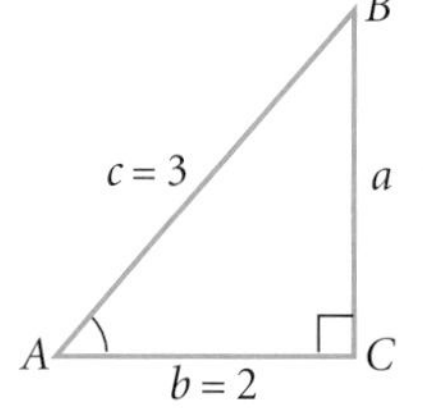

2.

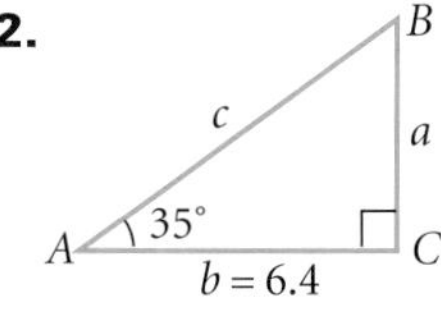

3.

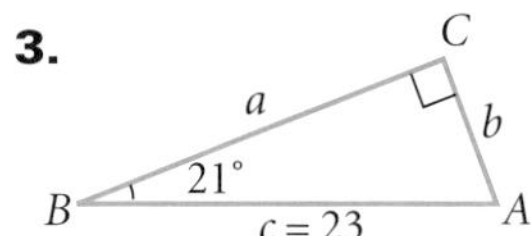

4.

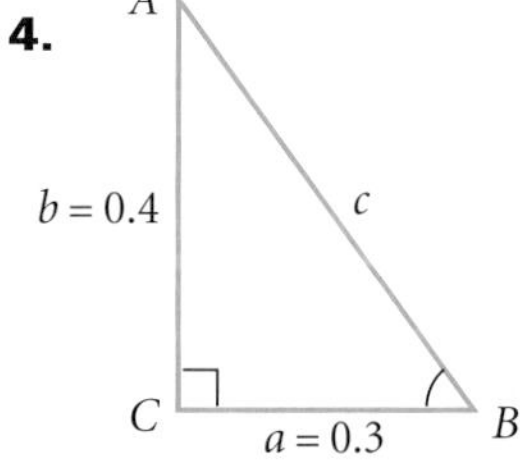

LESSON 13.2

Key Skills

Find coterminal angles and reference angles.

Coterminal angles of 480°, such that $-360^\circ < \theta < 360^\circ$, are found as follows:

$$480^\circ - 360^\circ = 120^\circ$$

$$480^\circ - (2)(360^\circ) = -240^\circ$$

$$\theta_{ref} = |180^\circ - 120^\circ|$$

$$= 60^\circ$$

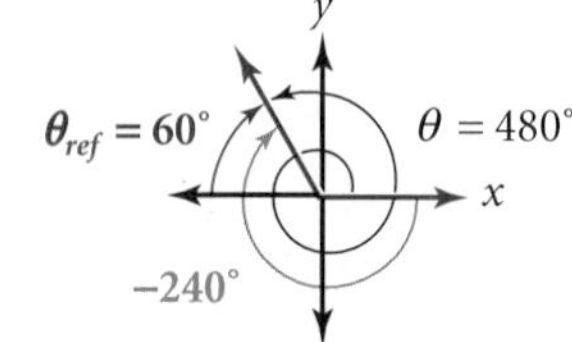

Exercises

For each angle below, find all coterminal angles such that $-360^\circ < \theta < 360^\circ$. Then find their corresponding reference angles.

5. 270°

6. 150°

7. −135°

8. −225°

9. 380°

10. 440°

11. 1028°

12. 973°

13. −515°

14. −612°

Find the trigonometric function values of angles in standard position.

The terminal side of θ in standard position is in Quadrant IV, and $\cos \theta = \frac{5}{13}$. To find $\sin \theta$, find the length of the longer leg. Use the Pythagorean Theorem.

$$y = \pm\sqrt{13^2 - 5^2} = -12$$

Because P is in Quadrant IV, y is negative.

Thus, $\sin \theta = \frac{y}{r} = -\frac{12}{13}$.

Find the exact values of the six trigonometric functions of θ, given each point on the terminal side of θ in standard position.

15. $P(3, -4)$ **16.** $P(-2, 5)$

17. $P(-1, -8)$ **18.** $P(6, 2)$

Given the quadrant of θ in standard position and a trigonometric function value of θ, find exact values for the indicated functions.

19. III, $\sin \theta = -\frac{2}{7}$; $\tan \theta$

20. IV, $\cos \theta = \frac{1}{3}$; $\sin \theta$

21. I, $\tan \theta = 1$; $\cos \theta$

22. II, $\tan \theta = -\sqrt{3}$; $\sin \theta$

LESSON 13.3

Key Skills

Find exact values for trigonometric functions of special angles and their multiples.

$$\begin{aligned}\cos 390^\circ &= \cos(390^\circ - 360^\circ)\\ &= \cos 30^\circ\\ &= \frac{\sqrt{3}}{2}\end{aligned}$$

Find the coordinates of a point on a circle given an angle of rotation and the radius of the circle.

The coordinates of $P(x, y)$ shown at right are $P(r \cos \theta, r \sin \theta)$.

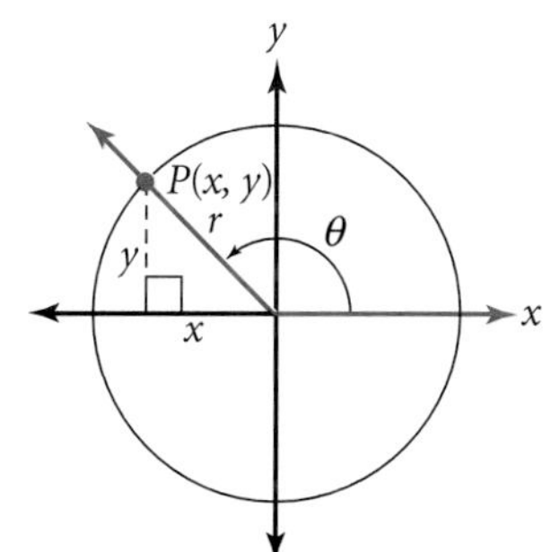

Exercises

Find each trigonometric function value. Give exact answers.

23. $\cos 135^\circ$ **24.** $\sin 315^\circ$

25. $\tan 225^\circ$ **26.** $\cos 0^\circ$

27. $\sin(-270^\circ)$ **28.** $\cos(-180^\circ)$

29. $\tan(-90^\circ)$ **30.** $\cos 675^\circ$

31. $\sin 600^\circ$ **32.** $\tan 765^\circ$

Point P is located at the intersection of a circle with a radius of r and the terminal side of angle θ in standard position. Find the exact coordinates of P.

33. $\theta = 60^\circ, r = 1$ **34.** $\theta = -30^\circ, r = 2$

35. $\theta = 240^\circ, r = 5$ **36.** $\theta = -240^\circ, r = 3$

LESSON 13.4

Key Skills

Convert from degrees to radians and vice versa.

Multiply degrees by $\frac{\pi \text{ radians}}{180^\circ}$.

Multiply radians by $\frac{180^\circ}{\pi \text{ radians}}$.

Find arc length.

Use $s = r\theta$, where s is the arc length, r is the radius, and θ is the angle measure in radians.

Exercises

Convert each degree measure to radian measure, giving exact answers. Convert each radian measure to degree measure, rounding answers to the nearest tenth of a degree.

37. 78° **38.** 334.61° **39.** -23°

40. $\frac{\pi}{7}$ radians **41.** $-\frac{15\pi}{16}$ radians **42.** 8.87 radians

43. Find the length of the arc intercepted by a central angle of 30° in a circle with a radius of 4.5 meters.

LESSON 13.5

Key Skills

Graph transformations of trigonometric functions.

For $y = a\sin(b\theta - c) + d$ and $y = a\cos(b\theta - c) + d$, $|a|$ is the amplitude; $\frac{2\pi}{|b|}$, where $b \neq 0$, is the period; $|c|$ is the phase shift (to the right for $c > 0$ and to the left for $c < 0$); and $|d|$ is the vertical shift (upward for $d > 0$ and downward for $d < 0$).

For $y = a\tan(b\theta - c) + d$, there is no amplitude, but a represents a vertical stretch or compression, and $\frac{\pi}{|b|}$, where $b \neq 0$, is the period. The phase shift and vertical shift are the same as those of sine and cosine.

Exercises

Identify the amplitude, if it exists, and the period of each trigonometric function.

44. $y = -3\sin\theta$

45. $y = -4\sin\theta$

46. $y = \frac{1}{2}\sin 3\theta$

47. $y = 2\tan\frac{1}{3}\theta$

Identify the phase shift and the vertical shift of each function from its parent function.

48. $y = 2\sin(\theta - 90°)$

49. $y = -4\cos(\theta + 45°)$

50. $y = \sin(\theta - 215°) + 3$

51. $y = \cos(\theta + 120°) - 2$

Describe the transformation of each function from its parent function. Then graph at least one period of the function along with its parent function.

52. $y = \cos 4\theta$

53. $y = \tan\frac{1}{2}\theta$

54. $2\sin(\theta - 45°)$

55. $y = 3\cos(\theta + 45°)$

LESSON 13.6

Key Skills

Evaluate trigonometric expressions involving inverses.

Find all possible values of $\sin^{-1}\frac{\sqrt{2}}{2}$.

For $0° \leq \theta < 360°$, $\sin^{-1}\frac{\sqrt{2}}{2} = 45°$ and $\sin^{-1}\frac{\sqrt{2}}{2} = 135°$.

Thus, all possible values are $45° + n360°$ and $135° + n360°$, where n is an integer.

Evaluate composite trigonometric functions.

$$\cos\left(\text{Sin}^{-1}\frac{\sqrt{3}}{2}\right) = \cos 60° = \frac{1}{2}$$

Exercises

Find all possible values for each expression.

56. $\sin^{-1} 0$

57. $\cos^{-1} 1$

58. $\tan^{-1}\left(-\frac{\sqrt{3}}{3}\right)$

59. $\cos^{-1}\left(-\frac{\sqrt{2}}{2}\right)$

60. $\sin^{-1}\left(-\frac{\sqrt{3}}{2}\right)$

61. $\tan^{-1} 1$

Evaluate each trigonometric expression.

62. $\text{Sin}^{-1}\frac{1}{2}$

63. $\text{Cos}^{-1}\left(-\frac{\sqrt{3}}{2}\right)$

64. $\text{Tan}^{-1}\sqrt{3}$

65. $\text{Sin}^{-1}\left(-\frac{\sqrt{2}}{2}\right)$

66. $\tan\left(\text{Sin}^{-1}\frac{1}{2}\right)$

67. $\cos[\text{Tan}^{-1}(-\sqrt{3})]$

68. $\text{Tan}^{-1}(\cos 135°)$

69. $\text{Sin}^{-1}[\sin(-120°)]$

Applications

70. MAPMAKING A map maker is making a map of a park. She would like to find the distance across a river. She marks a point on the bank of the river at C and then walks 200 meters up the river to point A, where she measures an angle of 50° between points B and C. What is the distance from point B to point C across the river?

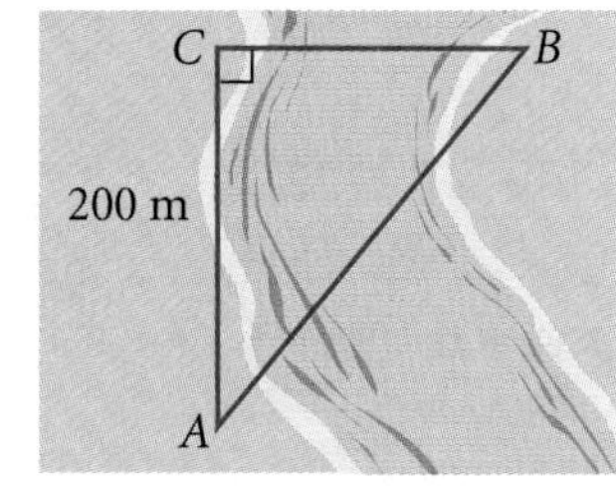

Alternative Assessment

Performance Assessment

1. **NAVIGATION** In ocean and air navigation, it is customary to measure *bearings* with clockwise angles of rotation in degrees from the north axis. Suppose that an airplane is flying at a bearing of 140°. Sketch this situation. If the positive y-axis corresponds with north, what angle of rotation, in standard position, corresponds to this bearing? What bearing corresponds to an angle of rotation of 135°?
2. **DESCRIBING ANGLES** Sketch and give the degree measure of each angle described below.
   - $1\frac{1}{3}$ rotations clockwise
   - the reference angle for a –240° angle
   - the angle coterminal with 40° that makes 5 complete clockwise rotations
3. **SOLVING RIGHT TRIANGLES** A flagpole is on top of a building. A line of sight from a point 450 feet from the base of the building forms a 60° angle of elevation to the top of the flagpole and a 55° angle of elevation to the top of the building.
   a. Draw a sketch of the situation.
   b. Find the height of the building to the nearest foot.
   c. Find the height of the flagpole to the nearest foot.
4. **COMPARING SINE AND COSINE FUNCTIONS**
   a. Describe how the sine function values compare with the cosine function values in each of the four quadrants.
   b. Compare the inverse cosine function with the inverse sine function as the values in their domains increase.

Portfolio Projects

1. **HIGHWAY GRADES** The grade of a highway indicates its slope. For example, a highway with a 6% grade has a slope of $\frac{6}{100}$.
   a. Find the angle of elevation for a highway with a 6% grade.
   b. Find the grade that corresponds to an angle of elevation of 5°.
   c. Make a generalization about the slope of a highway and its angle of elevation.
2. **TRIANGLE TRIGONOMETRY** Find a real-world situation that can be represented with a right triangle. Sketch a right triangle to represent your situation, and label one side and one acute angle of your triangle. Solve your triangle and describe the results. Explain when to apply the sine, cosine, and tangent ratios to solve a triangle.
3. **ANGLE RELATIONSHIPS** Draw and label figures with the types of angles listed below.
   - right angle
   - acute angle
   - straight angle
   - obtuse angle
   - coterminal angles
   - reference angle
   - complementary angles
   - supplementary angles
4. **MEASURING KITES** When a kite is flying, its string forms a curve instead of a straight line. Devise a method for measuring the height of a kite that does not involve measuring the length of its string. Include sketches and procedures for implementing your measurement method.

internetconnect

HRW The HRW Web site contains many resources to reinforce and expand your knowledge of trigonometric functions. This Web site also provides Internet links to other sites where you can find information and real-world data for use in research projects, reports, and activities that involve trigonometric functions. Visit the HRW Web site at **go.hrw.com,** and enter the keyword **MB1 CH13** to access the resources for this chapter.

CHAPTERS 1–13 CUMULATIVE ASSESSMENT

College Entrance Exam Practice

QUANTITATIVE COMPARISON For Items 1–6, write
A if the quantity in Column A is greater than the quantity in Column B;
B if the quantity in Column B is greater than the quantity in Column A;
C if the quantities are equal; or
D if the relationship cannot be determined from the given information.

	Column A	Column B	Answers
1.	6^{-2}	2^{-6}	Ⓐ Ⓑ Ⓒ Ⓓ [Lesson 2.2]
2.	The x-coordinate of the center of the circle $(x+2)^2+y^2=1$	The x-coordinate of the center of the circle $x^2+y^2-4x+4=1$	Ⓐ Ⓑ Ⓒ Ⓓ [Lesson 9.3]
3.	The degree of the polynomial $3x^3-2x^4+1$	The degree of the polynomial $(3x-2)(2x+1)^2$	Ⓐ Ⓑ Ⓒ Ⓓ [Lesson 7.1]
4.	$\frac{5\pi}{3}$ radians	$305°$	Ⓐ Ⓑ Ⓒ Ⓓ [Lesson 13.4]
5.	${}_{10}C_2$	${}_{10}C_8$	Ⓐ Ⓑ Ⓒ Ⓓ [Lesson 10.3]
6.	$\lvert -1\rvert - \lvert -3\rvert$	$[-2.01]-[-1.33]$	Ⓐ Ⓑ Ⓒ Ⓓ [Lesson 2.6]

7. The domain of $f(x)=\frac{2x-3}{x+1}$ includes all real numbers except which value? ***(LESSON 8.2)***

a. 1 **b.** -1 **c.** $-\frac{3}{2}$ **d.** $\frac{3}{2}$

8. Which expression is not equivalent to the others? ***(LESSON 6.4)***

a. $\log_3 (2x)^{\frac{1}{4}}$ **b.** $\frac{1}{4}\log_3 2x$

c. $\log_3 \sqrt[4]{2x}$ **d.** $3^{\frac{1}{4}\log_3 2x}$

9. Which represents $(2x^3-x^4)+(3x^2-5)-(x^2-x^4+1)$ as a polynomial in standard form? ***(LESSON 7.1)***

a. $-2x^4+2x^3+3x^2-6$
b. $2x^3+2x^2-6$
c. $2x^3+2x^2-4$
d. $2x^3+3x^2+4$

10. Which is the value of x at the vertex of the graph of $f(x)=2x^2-4x+1$? ***(LESSON 5.1)***

a. -1 **b.** 1 **c.** 2 **d.** $-\frac{1}{2}$

11. Which describes a number that cannot be written as the ratio of two integers? ***(LESSON 2.1)***

a. prime **b.** integer
c. rational **d.** irrational

12. Which of the following is the complex conjugate of $3-2i$? ***(LESSON 5.6)***

a. $-3+2i$ **b.** $3+2i$
c. $2i-3$ **d.** $-3-2i$

13. Solve $\lvert 2x+5\rvert=11$. ***(LESSON 1.8)***

a. $3, -3$ **b.** $8, -8$ **c.** $3, -8$ **d.** $8, -3$

14. If y varies directly as x and y is 8 when x is 4, which of the following is the constant of variation? ***(LESSON 1.4)***

a. $\frac{1}{2}$ **b.** 2 **c.** 32 **d.** -2

15. If an entire population of 100 bacteria doubles every hour, how many bacteria are in the population after 3 hours? ***(LESSON 6.1)***

a. 200 **b.** 300 **c.** 400 **d.** 800

16. Which of the following is true of the ellipse given by $\frac{x^2}{36} + \frac{y^2}{4} = 1$? ***(LESSON 9.4)***

a. The major axis is horizontal.
b. The major axis is vertical.
c. The foci are $(0, \pm 4\sqrt{2})$.
d. The length of the major axis is 6.

17. Which equation defines the inverse of $f(x) = \frac{1}{3}x + 1$? ***(LESSON 2.5)***

a. $y = -\frac{1}{3}x + 1$ **b.** $y + 1 = \frac{1}{3}x$
c. $y + 3 = 3x$ **d.** $y + 3x = 3$

18. Graph $y \leq \frac{1}{4}x - 6$. ***(LESSON 3.3)***

19. Evaluate $3(\sqrt{45})^2$. ***(LESSON 8.6)***

20. Write the function represented by the graph of $f(x) = x^2$ translated 3 units to the left. ***(LESSON 2.7)***

Use the diagram below to find each value. Give exact answers. ***(LESSON 13.1)***

21. $\sin A$

22. $\cos A$

23. $\tan B$

24. $\cot A$

25. $\sec B$

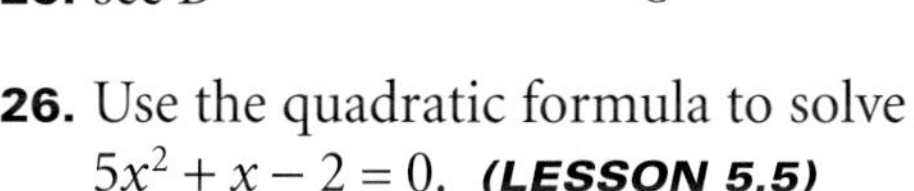

26. Use the quadratic formula to solve $5x^2 + x - 2 = 0$. ***(LESSON 5.5)***

27. Write the pair of parametric equations as a single equation in only x and y. ***(LESSON 3.6)***

$$\begin{cases} x(t) = 3t \\ y(t) = 5 - 2t \end{cases}$$

28. Solve $\frac{6}{x-2} > \frac{5}{x-3}$. ***(LESSON 8.5)***

29. Write an equation in standard form for the line that contains $(-3, 4)$ and is perpendicular to $y = 3x - 5$. ***(LESSON 1.3)***

30. Simplify $\frac{x}{x+4} \div \frac{6x^2}{3x+12}$. ***(LESSON 8.3)***

31. State the domain of $f(x) = \sqrt{2 - 3x}$. ***(LESSON 8.6)***

32. Factor $3y(5x + 2) - 4(5x + 2)$, if possible. ***(LESSON 5.3)***

33. Find the product $\begin{bmatrix} 2 & -2 & 4 \\ -1 & 3 & 5 \end{bmatrix} \begin{bmatrix} 3 & 5 \\ 2 & -2 \\ -1 & 4 \end{bmatrix}$, if it exists. ***(LESSON 4.2)***

FREE-RESPONSE GRID The following questions may be answered by using a free-response grid such as that commonly used by standardized-test services.

	/	/	
.	.	.	.
	0	0	0
1	1	1	1
2	2	2	2
3	3	3	3
4	4	4	4
5	5	5	5
6	6	6	6
7	7	7	7
8	8	8	8
9	9	9	9

34. Solve $\ln(2x - 7) = \ln 13$. ***(LESSON 6.7)***

35. Evaluate $\sum_{n=1}^{3} 8$. ***(LESSON 11.1)***

36. Evaluate $\sin\left(\mathrm{Cos}^{-1}\frac{1}{2}\right)$. ***(LESSON 13.6)***

37. Give the exact value of $\sin\left(\frac{\pi}{2}\right)$. ***(LESSON 13.4)***

38. Evaluate $\log_{10} 10^5 + 7^{\log_7 6}$. ***(LESSON 6.4)***

39. Find the reference angle, θ_{ref}, for 640°. ***(LESSON 13.2)***

40. Find the value of v in $\frac{1}{2} = \log_v 4$. ***(LESSON 6.3)***

41. **PROBABILITY** In how many different ways can a committee chairman and vice-chairman be selected from 15 members? ***(LESSON 10.2)***

42. What is the minimum value of $f(x) = 3 + 2\cos\left(x + \frac{\pi}{2}\right)$? ***(LESSON 13.5)***

43. What is the 13th term of the arithmetic sequence 50, 46, 42, . . . ? ***(LESSON 11.2)***

Keystroke Guide for Chapter 13

Essential keystroke sequences (using the model TI-82 or TI-83 graphics calculator) are presented below for all Activities and Examples found in this chapter that require or recommend the use of a graphics calculator.

internet**connect**

Keystrokes for other models of graphics calculators are found on the HRW Web site.

LESSON 13.5

Page 858

For Step 1, use radian, parametric, and simultaneous modes to graph the parametric equations $x_1(t) = \cos t$ and $y_1(t) = \sin t$ in order to generate the unit circle and $x_2(t) = t$ and $y_2(t) = \sin t$ in order to generate the basic sine function.

Set the modes:

Set the viewing window:

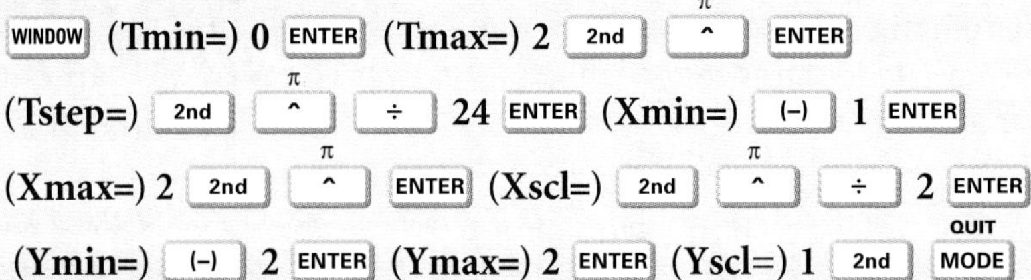

WINDOW (Tmin=) 0 ENTER (Tmax=) 2 2nd π ^ ENTER
(Tstep=) 2nd π ^ ÷ 24 ENTER (Xmin=) (-) 1 ENTER
(Xmax=) 2 2nd π ^ ENTER (Xscl=) 2nd π ^ ÷ 2 ENTER
(Ymin=) (-) 2 ENTER (Ymax=) 2 ENTER (Yscl=) 1 2nd QUIT MODE

Graph the parametric equations:

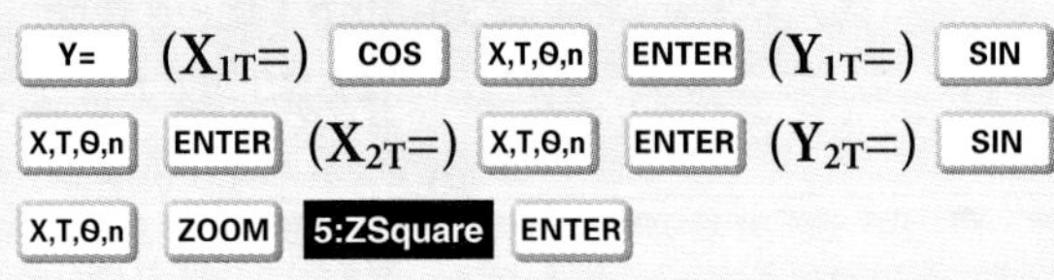

Y= (X_{1T}=) COS X,T,θ,n ENTER (Y_{1T}=) SIN
X,T,θ,n ENTER (X_{2T}=) X,T,θ,n ENTER (Y_{2T}=) SIN
X,T,θ,n ZOOM 5:ZSquare ENTER

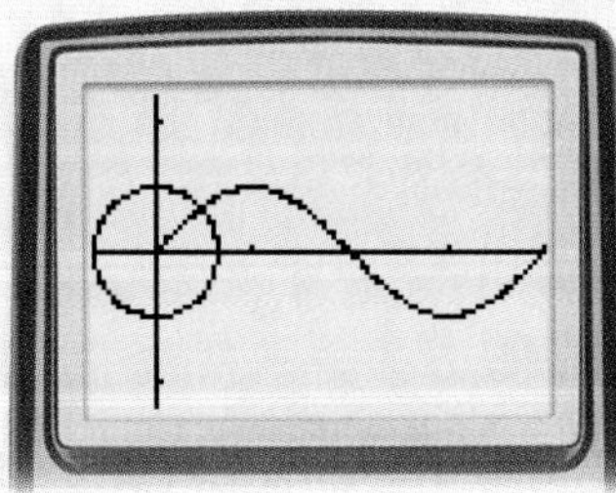

For Step 2, use the trace feature to compare the x-values and y-values for various t-values.

Use TRACE and the cursor keys. The ◄ and ► keys move the cursor along the graph. The ▲ and ▼ keys move the cursor to and from corresponding points on the two curves.

For part b of Step 3, graph the parametric equations $x_1(t) = 2 \cos t$, $y_1(t) = 2 \sin t$, $x_2(t) = t$, and $y_2(t) = 2 \sin t$.
Change Xmin to –2 in the viewing window, and use a keystroke sequence similar to that for Step 1.

For part c of Step 3, graph the parametric equations $x_1(t) = 3 \cos t$, $y_1(t) = 3 \sin t$, $x_2(t) = t$, and $y_2(t) = 3 \sin t$.
Change Xmin to –3 in the viewing window, and use a keystroke sequence similar to that for Step 1.

EXAMPLE 3 Page 862

In radian, function, and sequential modes, graph $y = 3 \sin 110\pi x$ and $y = 3 \sin 110\pi\left(x - \frac{1}{110}\right)$ on the same screen.

Use a viewing window $\left[-\frac{1}{110}, \frac{2}{110}\right]$ by [–4, 4] and an x-scale of $\frac{1}{440}$.

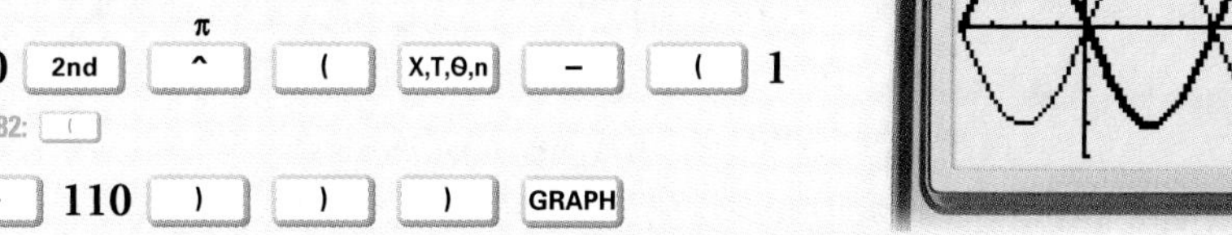
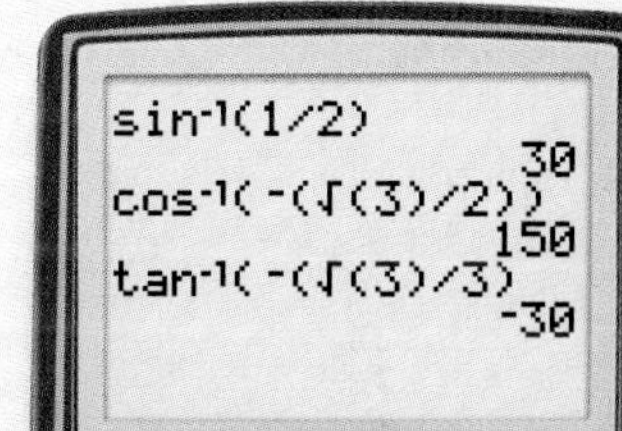

LESSON 13.6

EXAMPLE 2 Page 870

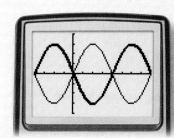

Evaluate $\text{Sin}^{-1} \frac{1}{2}$, $\text{Cos}^{-1}\left(-\frac{\sqrt{3}}{2}\right)$, and $\text{Tan}^{-1}\left(-\frac{\sqrt{3}}{3}\right)$.

Set the mode:

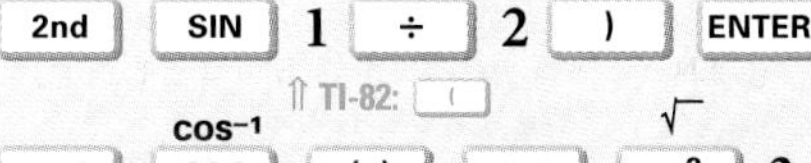
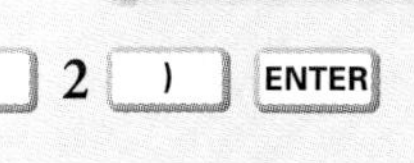

Evaluate:

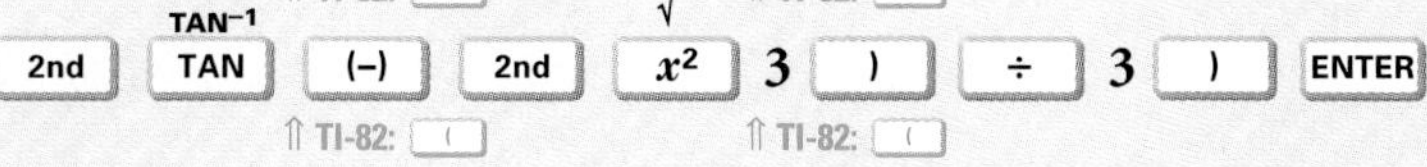

EXAMPLE 4 Page 871

For part a, find $\text{Sin}^{-1} \frac{1}{1.3}$ in degrees.

Set the mode:

Evaluate:

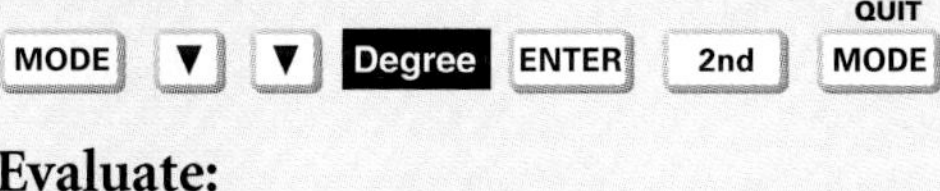
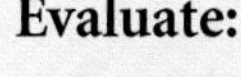

14 Further Topics in Trigonometry

IN THIS SECOND CHAPTER ON TRIGONOMETRY, YOU will study additional uses of trigonometry and several relationships among the trigonometric functions. For example, the law of sines and the law of cosines will enable you to solve more general triangles. A classic application of trigonometry is ship navigation, which involves the instruments shown here.

Lessons

14.1 • The Law of Sines

14.2 • The Law of Cosines

14.3 • Fundamental Trigonometric Identities

14.4 • Sum and Difference Identities

14.5 • Double-Angle and Half-Angle Identities

14.6 • Solving Trigonometric Equations

Chapter Project
Gearing Up

The astrolabe, an astronomical instrument useful for ship navigation, consisted of circles marked with angular measurements. This brass Islamic astrolabe is from the period 1350–1450.

A present-day sextant, which is used to find the position of a ship

About the Chapter Project

Gear design has evolved over hundreds of years and can involve some complex mechanical engineering. The Chapter Project, *Gearing Up*, will give you some insight into the mathematics that allow gears to mesh smoothly.

After completing the Chapter Project, you will be able to:

- Determine a gear tooth profile and the spacing of gear teeth around a base circle.
- Design a gear template for a set of gears.
- Make a working model of a set of gears that mesh together smoothly.

About the Portfolio Activities

Throughout the chapter, you will be given opportunities to complete the Portfolio Activities that are designed to support your work on the Chapter Project.

- Sketching an involute gear profile and determining the radius of the curved edge of a gear tooth is included in the Portfolio Activity on page 901.
- Using rotation matrices to find the positions of gear teeth on a gear's base circle is included in the Portfolio Activity on page 916.

14.1

The Law of Sines

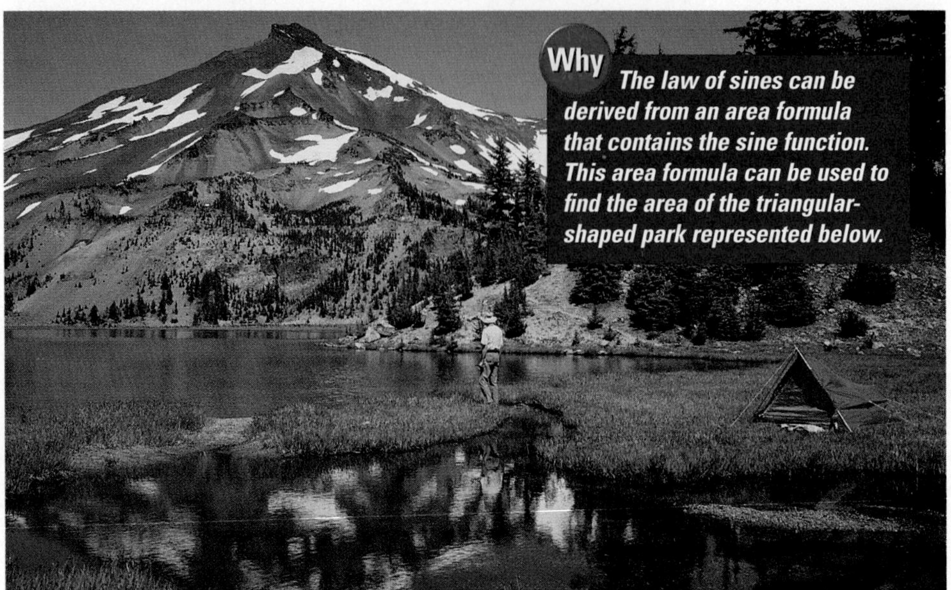

Why *The law of sines can be derived from an area formula that contains the sine function. This area formula can be used to find the area of the triangular-shaped park represented below.*

Objective

- Solve mathematical and real-world problems by using the law of sines.

The triangular piece of land represented at right will be used for a new park. What is the approximate area of the land?

Let K represent the area of $\triangle ABC$.

$$K = \frac{1}{2} \times \text{base} \times \text{height}$$

$$K = \frac{1}{2} \times AC \times BD$$

$$K = \frac{1}{2} \times 2.5 \times (2 \sin 32^\circ)$$ *Because* $\sin 32^\circ = \frac{BD}{2}$, *substitute* $2 \sin 32^\circ$ *for* BD.

$$K \approx 1.3$$

The area of the triangular piece of land is about 1.3 square miles.

The information given in the park problem above includes AC, BC, and the measure of the included angle, C. This information is known as side-angle-side, or SAS, information. Given SAS information for a triangle, you can always find its area with one of the formulas below.

Area of a Triangle

The area, K, of $\triangle ABC$ is given by the equations below.

$$K = \frac{1}{2}bc \sin A \qquad K = \frac{1}{2}ac \sin B$$

$$K = \frac{1}{2}ab \sin C$$

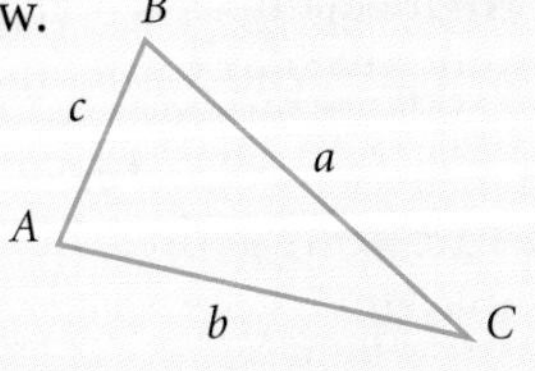

When labeling triangles, it is customary to use capital letters for the angles or angle measures, and lowercase letters for the sides or side lengths. Furthermore, an angle and the side opposite that angle are labeled with the same letter.

EXAMPLE 1 **Find the area of $\triangle RST$ to the nearest tenth of a square unit.**

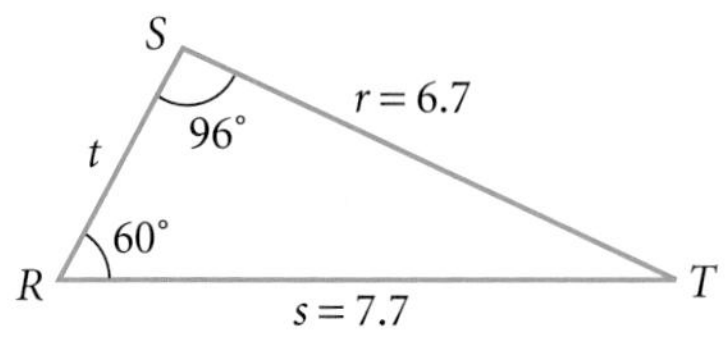

SOLUTION

In order to have SAS information, you need to know T. Recall that the sum of the angle measures of any triangle is 180°.

$$R + S + T = 180°$$
$$60° + 96° + T = 180°$$
$$T = 24°$$

With SAS information, you can use one of the area formulas from the previous page to find the area of $\triangle RST$.

$$K = \frac{1}{2}sr \sin T$$
$$K = \frac{1}{2}(7.7)(6.7) \sin 24°$$
$$K \approx 10.5$$

Thus, the area of $\triangle RST$ is about 10.5 square units.

TRY THIS Find the area of $\triangle XYZ$ to the nearest tenth of a square unit.

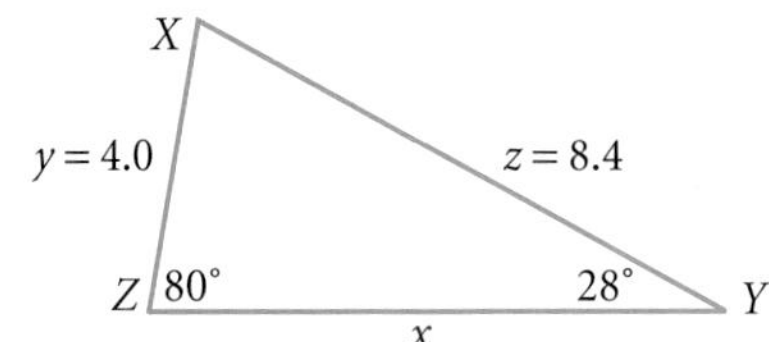

Law of Sines

Using the area formulas, you can derive the *law of sines*. Because the formulas $K = \frac{1}{2}bc \sin A$, $K = \frac{1}{2}ac \sin B$, and $K = \frac{1}{2}ab \sin C$ all represent the area of $\triangle ABC$, they are equal.

$$\frac{1}{2}bc \sin A = \frac{1}{2}ac \sin B = \frac{1}{2}ab \sin C$$
$$bc \sin A = ac \sin B = ab \sin C$$
$$\frac{bc \sin A}{abc} = \frac{ac \sin B}{abc} = \frac{ab \sin C}{abc}$$
$$\frac{\sin A}{a} = \frac{\sin B}{b} = \frac{\sin C}{c}$$

Law of Sines

For $\triangle ABC$, the **law of sines** states the following:

$$\frac{\sin A}{a} = \frac{\sin B}{b} = \frac{\sin C}{c}$$

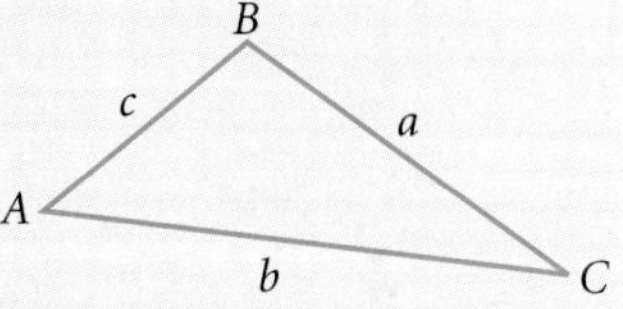

CRITICAL THINKING Show that $\frac{\sin A + \sin B}{\sin B} = \frac{a + b}{b}$ is true for any $\triangle ABC$.

When you are given the measures of two angles and the length of the included side in a triangle, this is called angle-side-angle (ASA) information. Given ASA information, you can use the law of sines to solve triangles, as shown in Example 2.

EXAMPLE 2 **Solve $\triangle ABC$. Give answers to the nearest tenth, if necessary.**

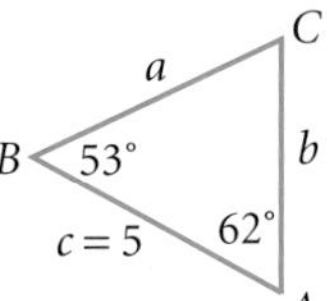

SOLUTION

First find C.

$$A + B + C = 180^\circ$$
$$62^\circ + 53^\circ + C = 180^\circ$$
$$C = 65^\circ$$

Now apply the law of sines to find sides a and b.

$$\frac{\sin A}{a} = \frac{\sin C}{c} \qquad \frac{\sin B}{b} = \frac{\sin C}{c}$$
$$\frac{\sin 62^\circ}{a} = \frac{\sin 65^\circ}{5} \qquad \frac{\sin 53^\circ}{b} = \frac{\sin 65^\circ}{5}$$
$$a = \frac{5 \sin 62^\circ}{\sin 65^\circ} \qquad b = \frac{5 \sin 53^\circ}{\sin 65^\circ}$$
$$a \approx 4.9 \qquad b \approx 4.4$$

TRY THIS Solve $\triangle DEF$. Give answers to the nearest tenth, if necessary.

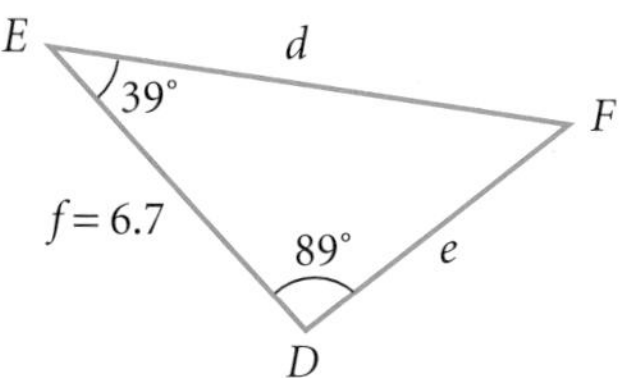

Example 3 shows how you can use the law of sines to solve a triangle for which you are given side-angle-angle (SAA) information.

EXAMPLE 3 A surveying crew needs to find the distance between two points, A and B. They cannot measure the distance directly because there is a hill between the two points. The surveyors obtain the information shown in the diagram at right.

APPLICATION
SURVEYING

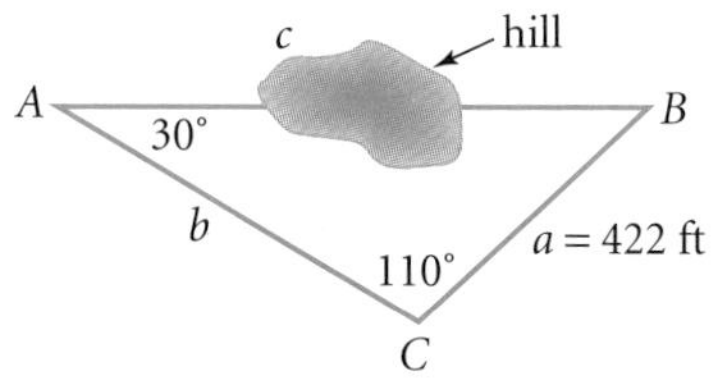

Find c to the nearest foot.

SOLUTION

$$\frac{\sin C}{c} = \frac{\sin A}{a}$$
$$\frac{\sin 110^\circ}{c} = \frac{\sin 30^\circ}{422} \qquad \textit{Substitute } A = 30^\circ, a = 422, \textit{ and } C = 110^\circ.$$
$$c = \frac{422 \sin 110^\circ}{\sin 30^\circ}$$
$$c \approx 793$$

Thus, the distance between points A and B is approximately 793 feet.

TRY THIS In $\triangle KLM$ at right, find m to the nearest whole number.

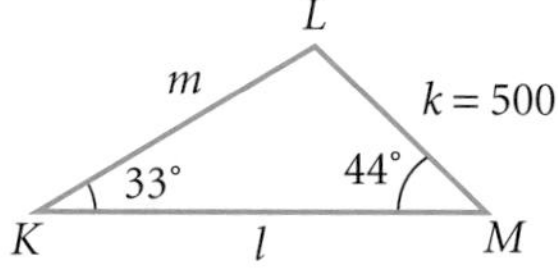

The Ambiguous Case

When you are given two side lengths and the measure of an angle that is not between the sides, the given information is called side-side-angle (SSA) information.

Activity
Exploring SSA Information

You will need: no special materials

1. The figure below illustrates SSA triangle information. Side a is free to pivot about C. How many triangles can be formed when $a < h$, where h is the altitude of the triangle? Use the illustration to explain your answer.

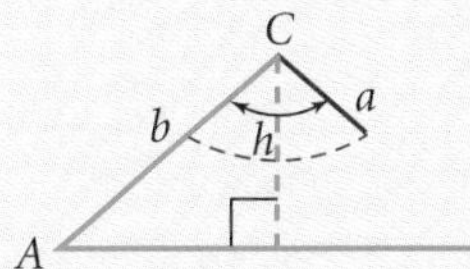

2. How many triangles can be formed when $a = h$? Use the illustration to explain your answer.

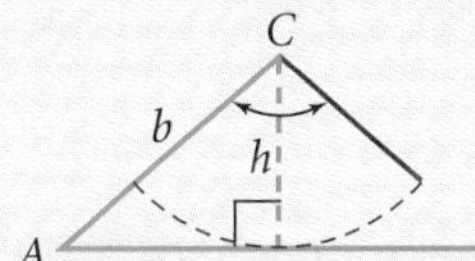

3. How many triangles can be formed when $a > h$ and $a < b$? Use the illustration to explain your answer.

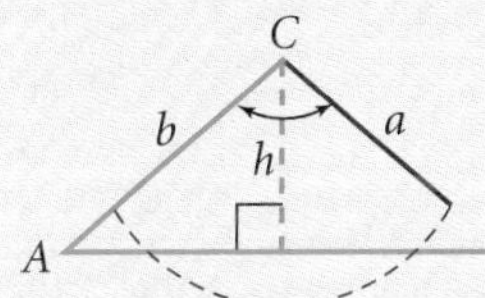

4. How many triangles may be formed when $a > h$ and $a > b$? Use the illustration to explain your answer.

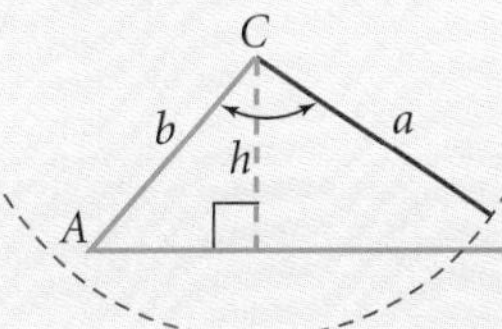

CHECKPOINT ✔ 5. Explain how you may find 0, 1, or 2 triangles, given SSA information.

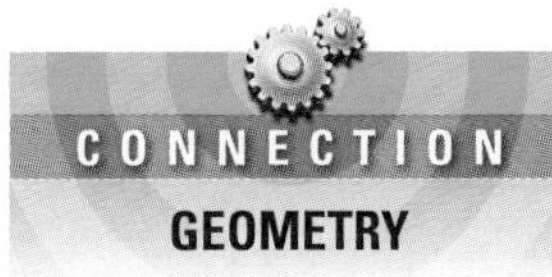

Recall from geometry that SSA information is not sufficient to prove triangle congruence. With SSA information, 0, 1, or 2 triangles may be possible.

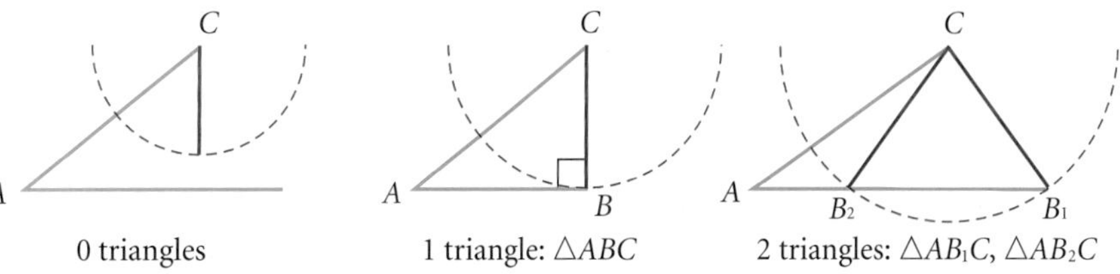

0 triangles | 1 triangle: $\triangle ABC$ | 2 triangles: $\triangle AB_1C$, $\triangle AB_2C$

EXAMPLE 4 **Determine whether the given SSA information defines 0, 1, or 2 triangles.**

a. $b = 2$, $c = 8$, and $B = 120°$ **b.** $c = 10$, $a = 6$, and $A = 28°$

SOLUTION

a.
$$\frac{\sin C}{c} = \frac{\sin B}{b}$$
$$\frac{\sin C}{8} = \frac{\sin 120°}{2}$$
$$\sin C = \frac{8 \sin 120°}{2}$$
$$\sin C \approx 3.4641$$

The range of $y = \sin \theta$ is $-1 \leq y \leq 1$. Because there is no angle whose sine is 3.4641, no triangle can be formed.

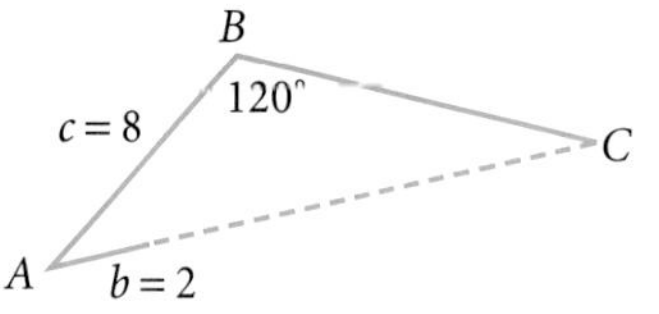

b.
$$\frac{\sin C}{c} = \frac{\sin A}{a}$$
$$\frac{\sin C}{10} = \frac{\sin 28°}{6}$$
$$\sin C = \frac{10 \sin 28°}{6}$$
$$\sin C \approx 0.7825$$

Recall from Lesson 13.3 that there are two possible values of θ between 0° and 180° for which $\sin \theta \approx 0.7825$. Thus, there are two possible triangles.

$C \approx 51.5°$ *or* $C \approx 180° - 51.5°$
$C \approx 128.5°$

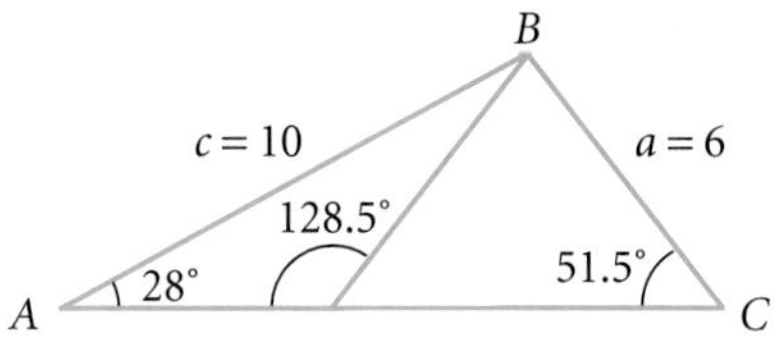

TRY THIS Determine whether the given SSA information defines 0, 1, or 2 triangles.

a. $a = 10$, $c = 4$, and $C = 148°$ **b.** $a = 2.4$, $b = 3.1$, and $A = 24°$

LAW OF SINES			
Given	**You can**	**Given**	**You can**
SAS	find the area of a triangle	SAA	solve a triangle
ASA	solve a triangle	SSA	define 0, 1, or 2 triangles

Exercises

Communicate

1. Explain how to solve a triangle when ASA information is known.

2. Explain how to solve a triangle when SAA information is known.

3. Explain under what circumstances SSA information does *not* determine a triangle.

4. Explain how information about sides and angles may determine two different triangles.

Guided Skills Practice

5. Find the area of $\triangle RST$ to the nearest tenth of a square unit. ***(EXAMPLE 1)***

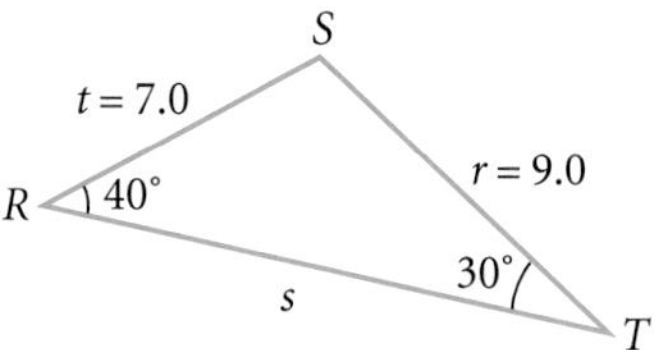

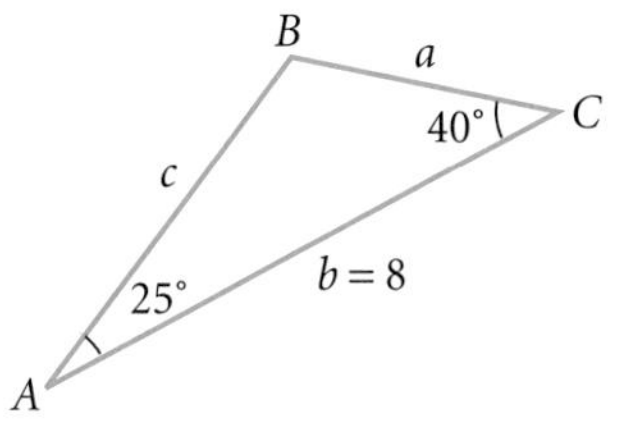

6. Solve $\triangle ABC$ at left. Give answers to the nearest tenth, if necessary. ***(EXAMPLE 2)***

7. In $\triangle XYZ$ at right, find x to the nearest tenth. ***(EXAMPLE 3)***

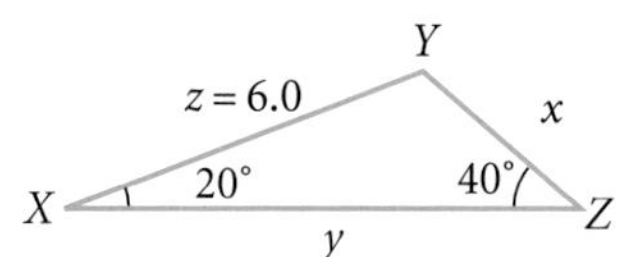

Determine whether the given SSA information defines 0, 1, or 2 triangles. ***(EXAMPLE 4)***

8. $a = 12$, $b = 15$, and $A = 30°$

9. $c = 2$, $b = 20$, and $C = 150°$

Practice and Apply

Find the area of $\triangle ABC$ to the nearest tenth of a square unit.

10. $b = 5$ in., $c = 8$ in., $A = 45°$
11. $a = 10$ ft, $c = 12$ ft, $B = 30°$
12. $a = 9$ in., $b = 11$ in., $C = 60°$
13. $b = 7$ cm, $c = 10$ cm, $A = 45°$
14. $a = 6$ km, $c = 10$ km, $B = 57°$
15. $a = 25$ ft, $b = 32$ ft, $C = 67°$
16. $b = 13$ in., $c = 16$ in., $A = 110°$
17. $a = 17$ m, $c = 22$ m, $B = 121°$
18. $a = 19$ ft, $b = 8$ ft, $C = 102.32°$
19. $b = 5$ cm, $c = 8$ cm, $A = 94.75°$
20. $a = 5$ km, $c = 9$ km, $B = 67.23°$
21. $a = 87$ ft, $b = 42$ ft, $C = 73.97°$
22. $a = 7$ m, $c = 10$ m, $C = 23°$
23. $a = 33$ ft, $c = 49$ ft, $B = 63.34°$

Use the given information to find the indicated side length in $\triangle ABC$. Give answers to the nearest tenth.

24. Given $A = 42°$, $B = 35°$, and $a = 10$, find b.
25. Given $A = 50°$, $C = 25°$, and $a = 15$, find c.
26. Given $B = 60°$, $C = 70°$, and $c = 15$, find b.
27. Given $C = 55°$, $A = 100°$, and $c = 8$, find a.
28. Given $A = 115°$, $B = 30°$, and $c = 10$, find a.
29. Given $A = 40°$, $C = 80°$, and $b = 15$, find c.

Solve each triangle. Give answers to the nearest tenth, if necessary.

30. $A = 43°, B = 52°, b = 20$
31. $B = 27°, C = 52°, c = 6$
32. $A = 20°, C = 60°, a = 10$
33. $A = 35°, B = 62°, a = 8$
34. $A = 23°, B = 62°, c = 15$
35. $B = 80°, C = 20°, a = 10$
36. $A = 60°, B = 40°, a = 10$
37. $B = 35°, C = 48°, b = 12$
38. $B = 40°, C = 60°, b = 8$
39. $A = 37°, C = 42°, b = 20$
40. $A = 40°, B = 45°, c = 16$
41. $C = 42°, B = 58°, c = 9$
42. $B = 30°, C = 45°, a = 9$
43. $A = 45°, C = 23°, b = 11$

State the number of triangles determined by the given information. If 1 or 2 triangles are formed, solve the triangle(s). Give answers to the nearest tenth, if necessary.

44. $A = 45°, c = 10, a = 2$

45. $A = 30°, c = 2, a = 1.5$

46. $A = 45°, c = 4, a = 5$

47. $A = 60°, c = 8, a = 2$

48. $A = 30°, c = 2, a = 1$

49. $A = 45°, c = 5, a = \frac{5\sqrt{2}}{2}$

CHALLENGE

50. Find the length of side x in the figure at right to the nearest tenth.

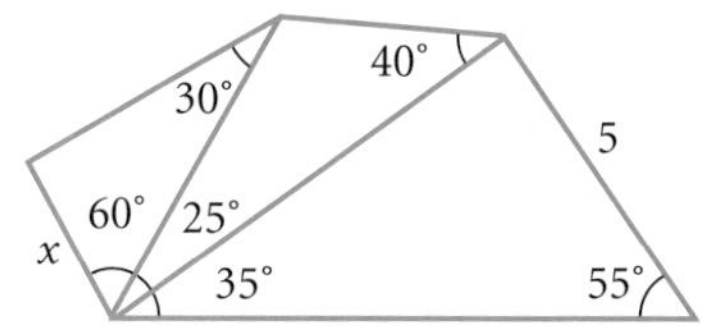

CONNECTION

51. **GEOMETRY** In the figure at right, $CD = 100$ centimeters, $m\angle 1 = 33°$, $m\angle 2 = 42°$, $m\angle 3 = m\angle 1 + m\angle 2$, $m\angle 4 = 37°$, $m\angle 5 = 78°$, and $m \angle 6 = 50°$. Find AB to the nearest centimeter.

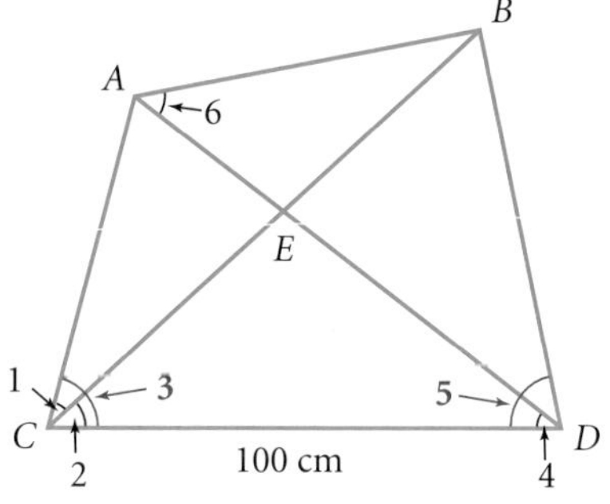

APPLICATIONS

52. **FIRE FIGHTING** Two rangers, one at station A and one at station B, observe a fire in the forest. The angle at station A formed by the lines of sight to station B and to the fire is 65.23°. The angle at station B formed by the lines of sight to station A and to the fire is 56.47°. The stations are 10 kilometers apart.

a. How far from station A is the fire?

b. How far from station B is the fire?

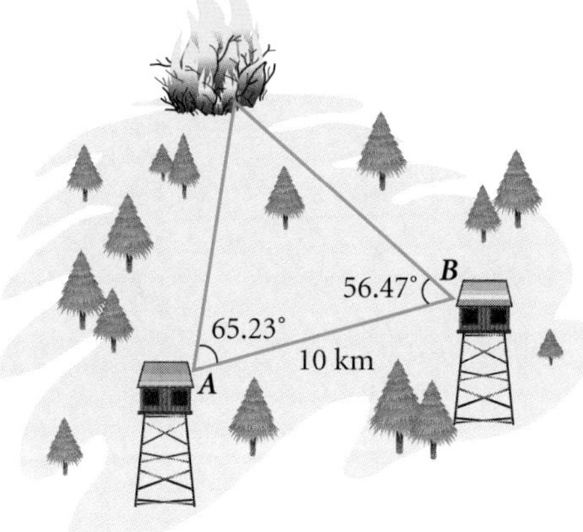

53. **SURVEYING** Refer to the diagram below. Find the distance from point A to point B across the river. Give your answer to the nearest meter.

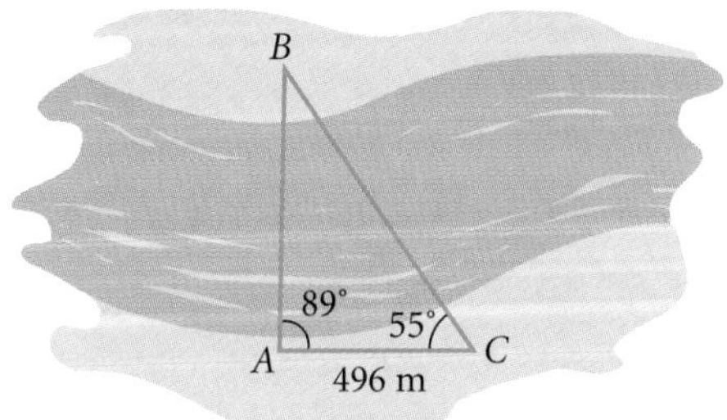

54. **FORESTRY** The angle of elevation between a straight path and a horizontal is 6°. A tree at the higher end of the path casts a 6.5-meter shadow down the path. The angle of elevation from the end of the shadow to the top of the tree is 32°. How tall is the tree?

APPLICATIONS

The U.S. Coast Guard aids vessels in distress.

55. RESCUE A boat in distress at sea is sighted from two coast guard observation posts, A and B, on the shore. The angle at post A formed by the lines of sight to post B and to the boat is 41.67°. The angle at post B formed by the lines of sight to post A and to the boat is 36.17°. Find the distance, to the nearest tenth of a kilometer, from observation post A to the boat.

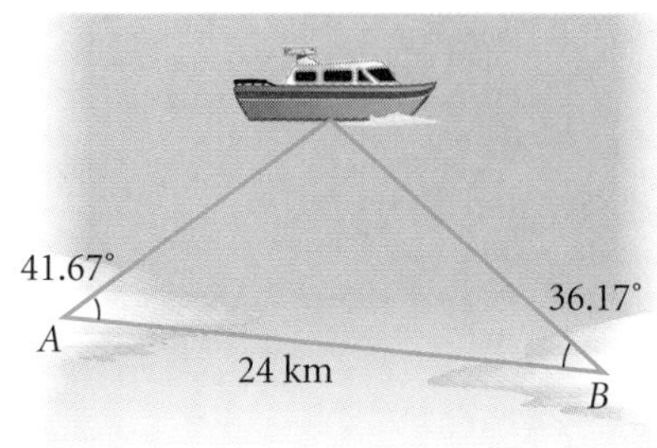

56. SURVEYING Surveyors made the angle and distance measurements shown at right.

a. Find distance c to the nearest meter.

b. Find distance a to the nearest meter.

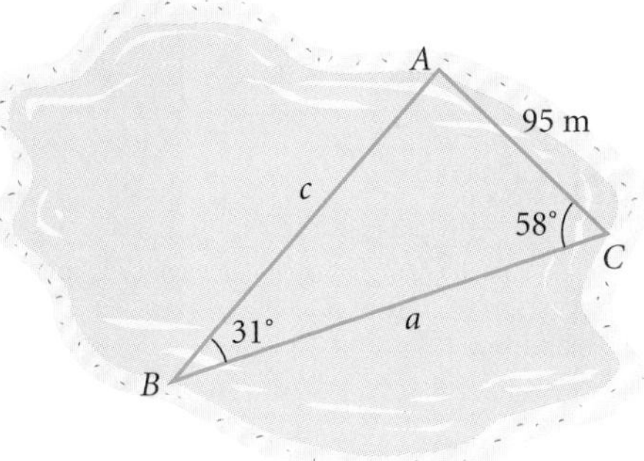

Look Back

APPLICATION

57. INVESTMENTS How long does it take for an investment to double at an annual interest rate of 5% compounded continuously? ***(LESSON 6.6)***

Factor each polynomial. ***(LESSON 7.3)***

58. $3x^3 - 12x$ **59.** $2x^4 - 12x^3 + 18x^2$

60. Identify all asymptotes and holes in the graph of $f(x) = \frac{2x^2 + 10x}{x^2 + 2x - 15}$. ***(LESSON 8.2)***

Convert each degree measure to radian measure. Give exact answers. ***(LESSON 13.4)***

61. 90° **62.** −180° **63.** 135° **64.** 120°

Convert each radian measure to degree measure. Round answers to the nearest tenth of a degree. ***(LESSON 13.4)***

65. $-\frac{\pi}{5}$ **66.** $\frac{3\pi}{7}$ **67.** 4.1802 **68.** −2.3221

Look Beyond

69. For each triangle, verify that $c^2 = a^2 + b^2 - 2ab \cos C$.

a.

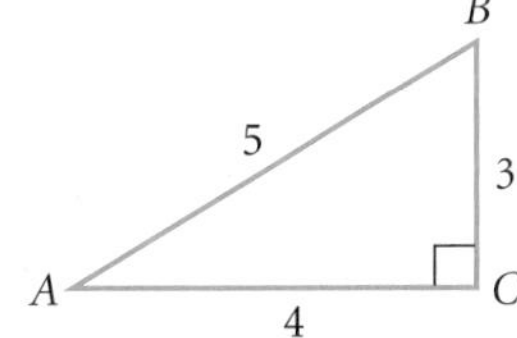

b.

B
5.4006
3
100°
C
A
4

14.2 The Law of Cosines

Objective

- Use the law of cosines to solve triangles.

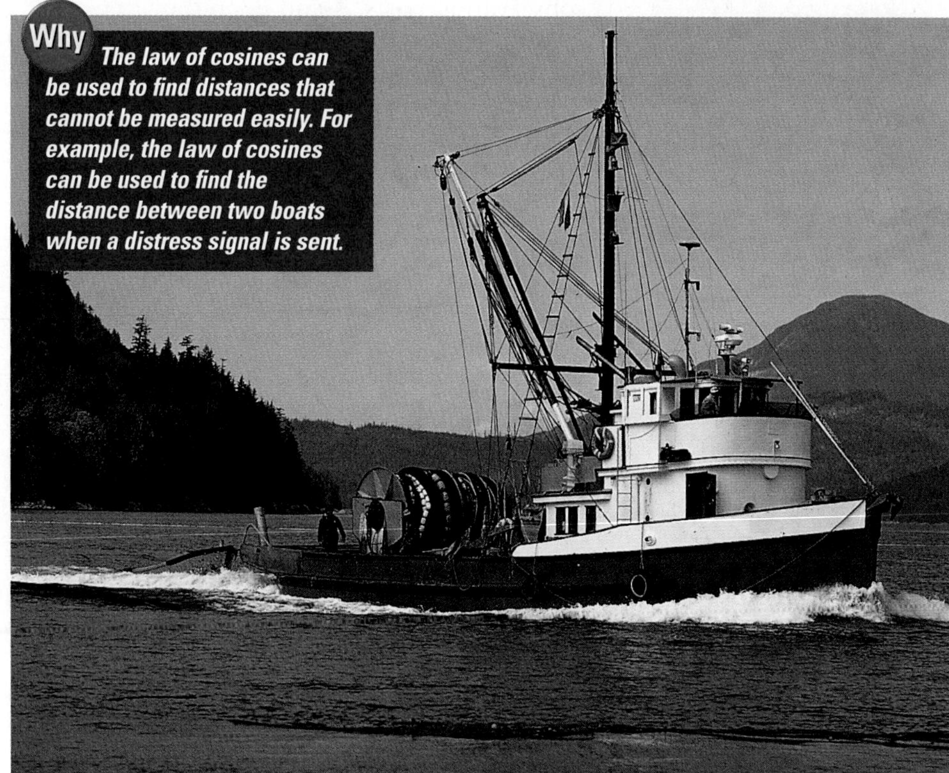

Why
The law of cosines can be used to find distances that cannot be measured easily. For example, the law of cosines can be used to find the distance between two boats when a distress signal is sent.

APPLICATION
NAVIGATION

Two fishing boats, the *Tina Anna* and the *Melissa Jane*, leave the same dock at the same time. The *Tina Anna* sails at 15 nautical miles per hour and the *Melissa Jane* sails at 17 nautical miles per hour in directions that create a 115° angle between their paths.

After 3 hours, the *Tina Anna* sends a distress signal to the *Melissa Jane*. How far apart are the two boats when the distress signal is sent? As soon as the signal is sent, the *Tina Anna* stops and the *Melissa Jane* sails at 17 nautical miles per hour directly toward the *Tina Anna*. How long will it take for the *Melissa Jane* to reach the *Tina Anna*? To answer these questions, you can use the *law of cosines*. *You will solve this problem in Example 2.*

The law of cosines is used in solving triangles for which side-side-side (SSS) or side-angle-side (SAS) information is given. In these cases, the law of sines can be used only after more information is found by using the law of cosines.

To derive the law of cosines, consider $\triangle ABC$ with altitude $\overline{BD}$ whose length is h.

B, c, a, h, A, x, D, b − x, C, b

In $\triangle ABD$:

$c^2 = x^2 + h^2$ and $\cos A = \frac{x}{c}$, or $x = c \cos A$

In $\triangle CBD$:

$$a^2 = (b - x)^2 + h^2$$
$$a^2 = b^2 - 2bx + x^2 + h^2$$
$$a^2 = b^2 - 2bx + c^2 \qquad \textit{Substitute } c^2 \textit{ for } x^2 + h^2.$$
$$a^2 = b^2 - 2b(\mathbf{c \cos A}) + c^2 \qquad \textit{Substitute } c \cos A \textit{ for } x.$$
$$a^2 = b^2 + c^2 - 2bc \cos A \qquad \textit{Simplify.}$$

The two other formulas for the law of cosines can be derived in a similar fashion.

Law of Cosines

In any triangle $\triangle ABC$, the law of cosines states the following:

$$a^2 = b^2 + c^2 - 2bc \cos A$$
$$b^2 = a^2 + c^2 - 2ac \cos B$$
$$c^2 = a^2 + b^2 - 2ab \cos C$$

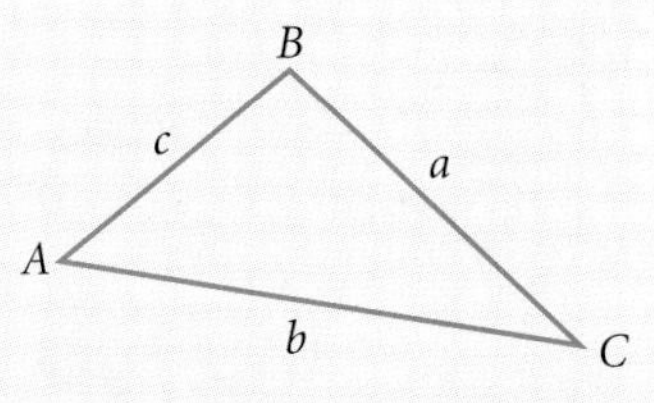

CRITICAL THINKING Show that the Pythagorean Theorem is a special case of the law of cosines. Then show that if $c^2 = a^2 + b^2$, then $\triangle ABC$ is a right triangle in which C is the right angle.

Example 1 below shows you how to use the law of cosines in two situations to find the unknown length of a side of a triangle when given SAS information and the unknown measure of an angle when given SSS information.

EXAMPLE 1 **Find the indicated measure to the nearest tenth for $\triangle ABC$.**

a. Given $a = 123$, $c = 97$, and $B = 22°$, find b.

b. Given $a = 11.3$, $b = 7.2$, and $c = 14.8$, find A.

SOLUTION

PROBLEM SOLVING

a. Draw a diagram.

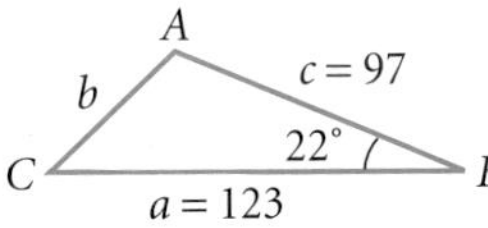

You are given SAS information. Use the law of cosines to find b.

$$b^2 = a^2 + c^2 - 2ac \cos B$$

$$b^2 = 123^2 + 97^2 - 2(123)(97) \cos 22°$$

$$b = \sqrt{123^2 + 97^2 - 2(123)(97) \cos 22°}$$

$$b \approx 49.1$$

CHECK

Note that the side opposite the smallest angle has the shortest length.

b. Draw a diagram.

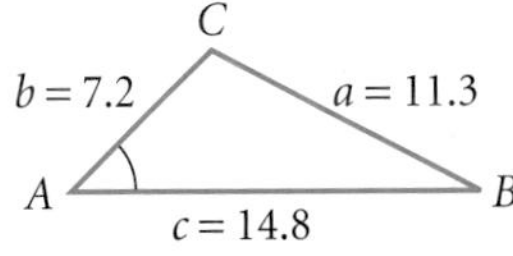

You are given SSS information. Use the law of cosines to find A.

$$a^2 = b^2 + c^2 - 2bc \cos A$$

$$11.3^2 = 7.2^2 + 14.8^2 - 2(7.2)(14.8) \cos A$$

$$\cos A = \frac{11.3^2 - 7.2^2 - 14.8^2}{-2(7.2)(14.8)}$$

$$\cos A \approx 0.6719$$

$$A \approx \cos^{-1}(0.6719)$$

$$A \approx 47.8°$$

TRY THIS Find the indicated measure, to the nearest tenth, for $\triangle XYZ$.

a. Given $x = 82$, $z = 63.2$, and $Y = 114°$, find y.

b. Given $x = 2.47$, $y = 3.80$, and $z = 4.24$, find X.

EXAMPLE 2 Refer to the two fishing boats described at the beginning of the lesson. The boats leave the dock at the same time, and after 3 hours the *Tina Anna* sends a distress signal to the *Melissa Jane.*

APPLICATION
NAVIGATION

a. How far apart are the two boats when the distress signal is sent? Give your answer to the nearest tenth of a nautical mile.

b. If the *Tina Anna* stops and the *Melissa Jane* sails at 17 nautical miles per hour toward the *Tina Anna*, about how long will it take for the *Melissa Jane* to reach the *Tina Anna*?

Tina Anna
T
15 nautical miles per hour
115°
D
17 nautical miles per hour
M
Melissa Jane

SOLUTION

PROBLEM SOLVING

a. Draw a diagram. Use the formula *distance* = *rate* × *time* to find *TD* and *MD*.

T
45
115°
D
51
M

$TD = 15(3) = 45$

$MD = 17(3) = 51$

Use the law of cosines to find *MT*.

$$(MT)^2 = (TD)^2 + (MD)^2 - 2(TD)(MD)\cos D$$
$$(MT)^2 = (45)^2 + (51)^2 - 2(45)(51)\cos 115^\circ$$
$$MT = \sqrt{(45)^2 + (51)^2 - 2(45)(51)\cos 115^\circ}$$
$$MT \approx 81.0$$

The boats are about 81.0 nautical miles apart.

b. To find the time, use the formula *distance* = *rate* × *time*.

$$d = rt$$
$$81.0 = 17t$$
$$t = \frac{81.0}{17}$$
$$t \approx 4.8$$

It will take the *Melissa Jane* about 4.8 hours, or 4 hours and 48 minutes, to reach the *Tina Anna*.

Activity

Using Graphs to Explore Solutions

You will need: a graphics calculator or graph paper

1. Graph $y = \sin\theta$ for $0^\circ \le \theta \le 180^\circ$.
2. How many times does $\sin\theta = \frac{1}{2}$ on this interval?

CHECKPOINT ✔ 3. What is the maximum number of solutions that are possible when finding an angle of a triangle by using the law of sines? Explain.

4. Graph $y = \cos\theta$ for $0^\circ \le \theta \le 180^\circ$.
5. How many times does $\cos\theta = \frac{1}{2}$ on this interval?

CHECKPOINT ✔ 6. What is the maximum number of solutions that are possible when finding an angle of a triangle by using the law of cosines? Explain.

Example 3 below shows you how to use the law of cosines and the law of sines with SAS information to solve a triangle.

EXAMPLE 3 **Solve $\triangle DFG$ at right. Give answers to the nearest tenth.**

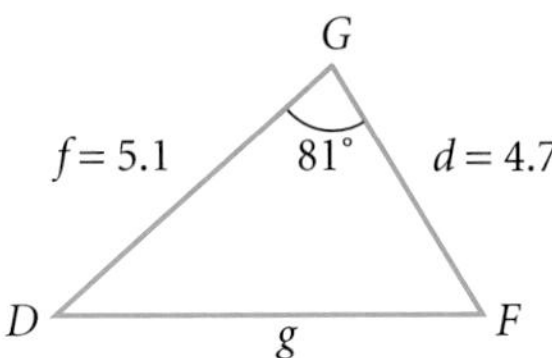

SOLUTION

1. Use the law of cosines to find g.

$$g^2 = d^2 + f^2 - 2df \cos G$$
$$g^2 = (4.7)^2 + (5.1)^2 - 2(4.7)(5.1) \cos 81^\circ$$
$$g = \sqrt{(4.7)^2 + (5.1)^2 - 2(4.7)(5.1) \cos 81^\circ}$$
$$g \approx 6.4$$

2. Then use the law of sines to find a second angle. Find D.

$$\frac{\sin D}{d} = \frac{\sin G}{g}$$
$$\frac{\sin D}{4.7} = \frac{\sin 81^\circ}{6.4}$$
$$\sin D = \frac{4.7 \sin 81^\circ}{6.4}$$
$$\sin D = 0.7253$$
$$D \approx 46.5^\circ \quad or \quad D \approx 133.5^\circ$$

If $d < g$, then $D < G$. Therefore, $D \approx 46.5^\circ$.

Remember to consider both possible angle measures when using the law of sines.

3. Find G.

$$D + G + F = 180^\circ$$
$$F \approx 180^\circ - 81^\circ - 46.5^\circ$$
$$F \approx 52.5^\circ$$

Thus, $g \approx 6.4$, $D \approx 46^\circ$, and $F \approx 53^\circ$.

TRY THIS Solve $\triangle XYZ$ at right. Give answers to the nearest tenth.

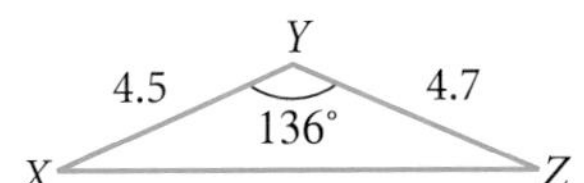

Example 4 below shows you how to use the law of cosines and the law of sines with SSS information to solve a triangle.

EXAMPLE 4 **Solve $\triangle ABC$ at right. Give answers to the nearest tenth.**

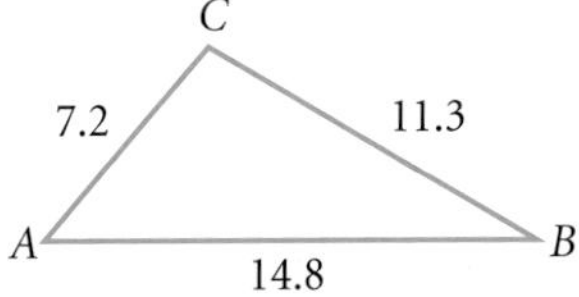

SOLUTION

The angle opposite the largest side can be either obtuse or acute. If you begin by using the law of cosines to find this angle, then you can use the law of sines to find the next angle without having to consider the ambiguous case.

1.

$$c^2 = a^2 + b^2 - 2ab \cos C$$
$$(14.8)^2 = (11.3)^2 + (7.2)^2 - 2(11.3)(7.2) \cos C$$
$$(14.8)^2 - (11.3)^2 - (7.2)^2 = -2(11.3)(7.2) \cos C$$
$$\cos C = \frac{(14.8)^2 - (11.3)^2 - (7.2)^2}{-2(11.3)(7.2)}$$
$$\cos C \approx -0.2428$$
$$C \approx 104.1^\circ$$

PROBLEM SOLVING

Identify the wanted, given, and needed information. You could continue to use the law of cosines to find the measure of the second angle, but the law of sines is the easier method to use. Because C is obtuse, you know that the other angles are acute, so there will be no guessing involved when using the law of sines.

2. Find the measure of one of the other angles.

$$\frac{\sin B}{b} = \frac{\sin C}{c}$$
$$\frac{\sin B}{7.2} = \frac{\sin 104.1°}{14.8}$$
$$\sin B = \frac{7.2 \sin 104.1°}{14.8}$$
$$\sin B = 0.4718$$
$$B \approx 28.2°$$

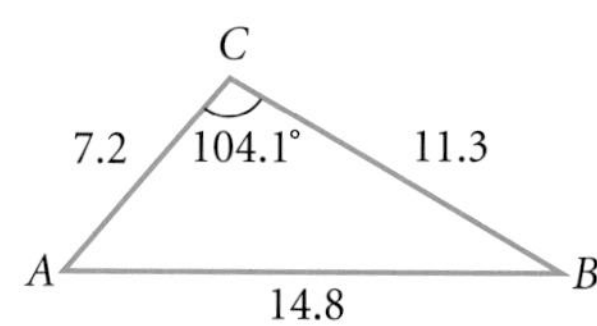

3. Find the measure of the remaining angle.

$$A + B + C = 180°$$
$$A + 28.2 + 104.1 \approx 180°$$
$$A \approx 180° - 28.2° - 104.1°$$
$$A \approx 47.7°$$

SOLVING A TRIANGLE	
Given:	**Use:**
SSS	law of cosines, then law of sines
SSA	law of sines (ambiguous)
SAA	law of sines
ASA	law of sines
SAS	law of cosines, then law of sines
AAA	not possible

Exercises

1. What variables appear in each of the three versions of the law of cosines, and what do these variables represent?

2. Explain how to solve a triangle by using the law of cosines if the lengths of the three sides of the triangle are known.

3. Explain how to solve a triangle by using the law of cosines if the lengths of two sides and the measure of the angle between them are known.

CONNECTION

4. GEOMETRY Explain why it is not possible to solve a triangle by using AAA information.

Guided Skills Practice

5. Find the indicated measure to the nearest tenth for $\triangle ABC$. ***(EXAMPLE 1)***

a. Given $a = 65$, $c = 52$, and $B = 31°$, find b.

b. Given $a = 8$, $b = 12.1$, and $c = 9.4$, find A.

APPLICATION

6. **NAVIGATION** Refer to the two boats described at the beginning of the lesson and continued in Example 2. Assume that $D = 128°$, the *Tina Anna* sails at 21 nautical miles per hour and the *Melissa Jane* sails at 18.5 nautical miles per hour. How far apart are the boats when the distress signal is sent? How long will it take the *Melissa Jane* to reach the *Tina Anna*? ***(EXAMPLE 2)***

7. Solve $\triangle DEF$. Give answers to the nearest tenth. ***(EXAMPLE 3)***

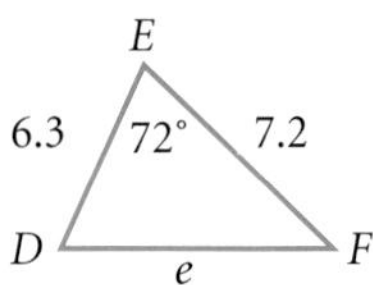

8. Solve $\triangle ABC$ at right. Give answers to the nearest tenth. ***(EXAMPLE 4)***

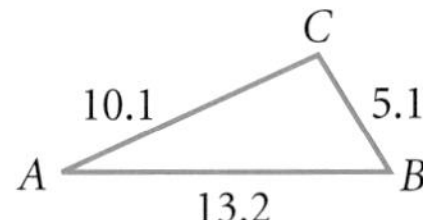

Practice and Apply

Classify the type of information given, and then find the measure of *A* in each triangle. Give answers to the nearest tenth.

9.

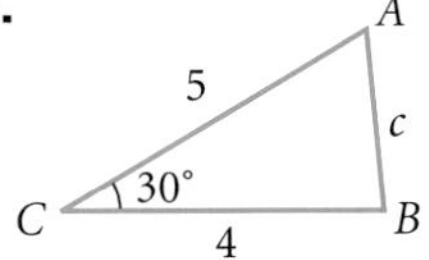

10.

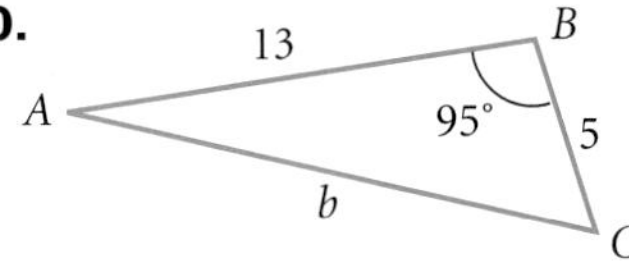

11.

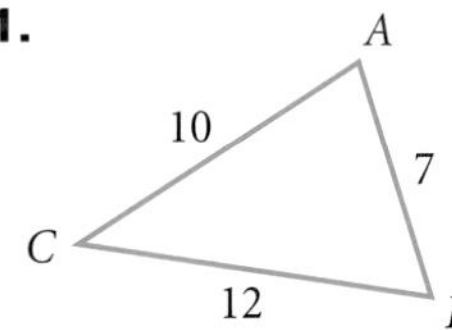

12.

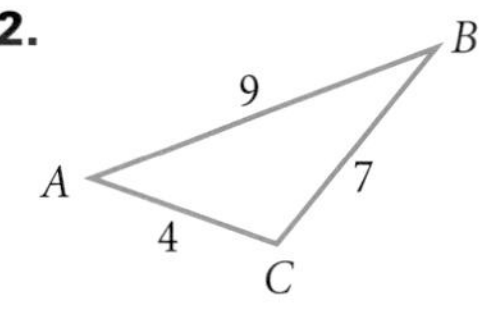

Classify the type of information given, and then use the law of cosines to find the missing side length of $\triangle ABC$ to the nearest tenth.

13. $a = 10$, $b = 15$, $C = 24°$

14. $b = 20$, $c = 14$, $A = 21°$

15. $a = 24.4$, $c = 16.2$, $B = 112°$

16. $a = 47.5$, $b = 58.0$, $C = 74°$

17. $A = 78°$, $b = 2$, $c = 4$

18. $B = 108°$, $a = 7$, $b = 10$

Solve each triangle. Give answers to the nearest tenth.

19. $a = 35$, $b = 49$, $c = 45$

20. $a = 8$, $b = 9$, $c = 33$

21. $a = 12.3$, $b = 14.0$, $c = 15.7$

22. $a = 18.1$, $b = 21.0$, $c = 23.7$

23. $a = 0.7$, $b = 0.9$, $c = 1.2$

24. $a = 8.4$, $b = 9.6$, $c = 11.4$

Classify the type of information given, and then solve $\triangle ABC$. Give answers to the nearest tenth. If no such triangle exists, write *not possible*.

25. $a = 30, b = 25, c = 22$

26. $a = 10, b = 20, c = 15$

27. $a = 123, c = 97, B = 22°$

28. $b = 123, c = 63.2, A = 114°$

29. $B = 30°, a = 4, c = 6$

30. $B = 45°, a = 3, c = 5$

31. $a = 7, b = 9, c = 18$

32. $a = 8, b = 12, c = 21$

33. $C = 60°, a = 7, b = 5$

34. $C = 30°, a = 4, b = 10$

35. $a = 6, b = 3, c = 5$

36. $a = 8, b = 7, c = 6$

37. $A = 58°, a = 10, b = 8$

38. $A = 42°, a = 9, b = 12$

39. $a = 9, b = 15, c = 5$

40. $a = 4, b = 8, c = 13$

41. $a = 11, b = 13, c = 12$

42. $a = 29, b = 25, c = 23$

CHALLENGE

43. Find x in the figure at right.

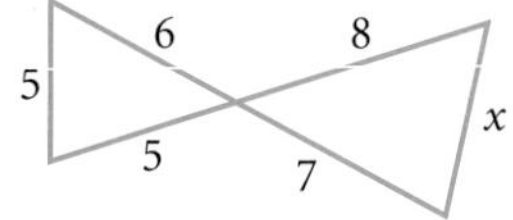

CONNECTIONS

44. GEOMETRY In parallelogram $ABCD$, $AC = 8.4$, $BD = 5.6$, and $m\angle CED = 80°$. Find the length of the sides of parallelogram $ABCD$ to the nearest tenth.

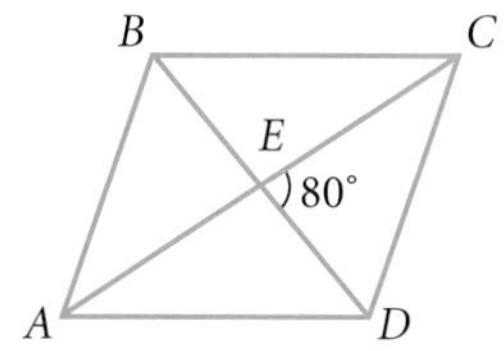

45. GEOMETRY Find all of the angle measures in an isosceles triangle whose base is $\frac{1}{3}$ as long as its legs.

MAXIMUM/MINIMUM A TV antenna is to be installed on a roof that has a pitch of 5 in 12, or a rise of 5 feet for every 12 feet of run, as shown below. The manufacturer's instructions state that the angle that each of the two guy wires make with the pole should be no less than 30°.

46. What is the minimum length of each guy wire that could be used? Round your answer to the nearest foot.

47. What is the height to the nearest tenth of a foot of the longest antenna pole that could fit on the roof shown at right if the roof attachment point can vary? What is the length to the nearest foot of the guy wire that will be required for an antenna pole of this length?

48. Is it possible for the guy wire to make a 40° angle with a 13-foot antenna pole?

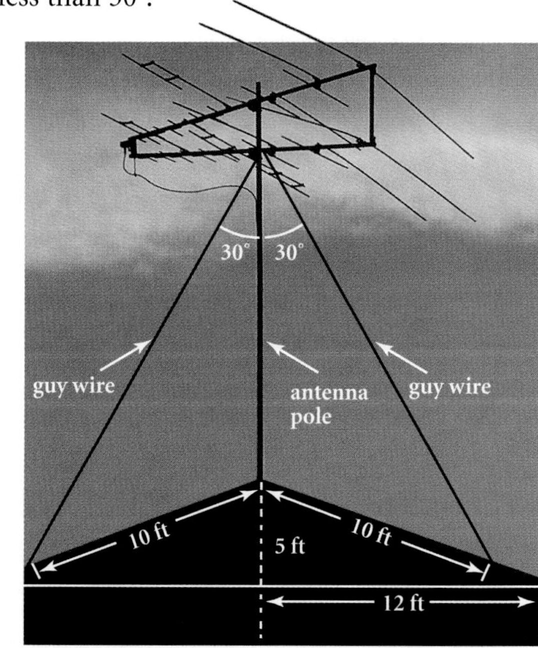

APPLICATIONS

49. SURVEYING A surveying crew needs to find the distance between two points, A and B, but a boulder blocks the path. The surveyors obtain the information shown in the diagram at right. Find AB. Give your answer to the nearest foot.

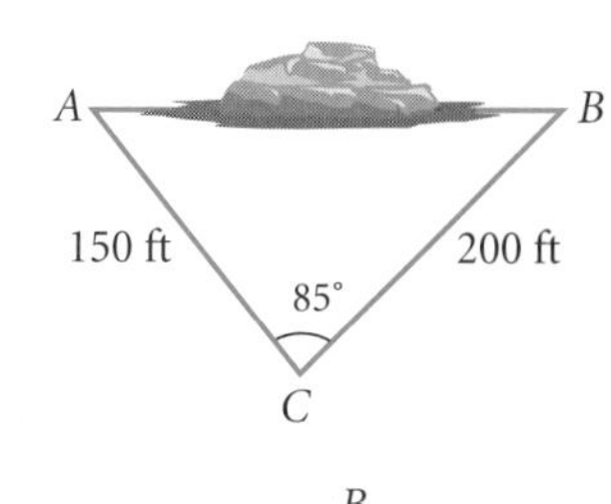

50. MANUFACTURING A piece of sheet metal is to be cut using a blowtorch so that it forms a triangle with the side lengths shown at right. Find the measures of angles A, B, and C.

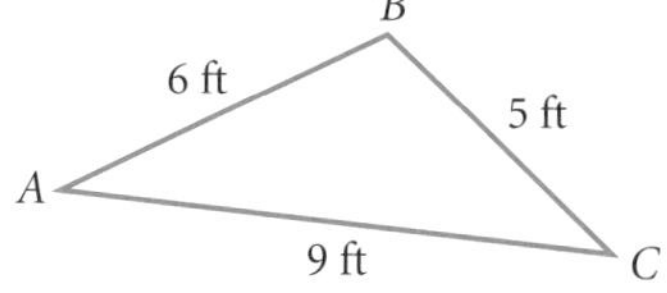

Look Back

Graph each pair of parametric equations for the given interval of *t*. *(LESSON 3.6)*

51. $\begin{cases} x(t) = 4t \\ y(t) = 2 - t \end{cases}$ for $2 \le t \le 6$

52. $\begin{cases} x(t) = 2t - 1 \\ y(t) = \frac{1}{2}t \end{cases}$ for $-4 \le t \le 4$

Use the quadratic formula to solve each equation. Give exact answers. *(LESSON 5.5)*

53. $y = 6x^2 - x - 12$

54. $y = 2x^2 + 5x + 2$

55. $y = x^2 + 3x - 2$

56. $y = 2x^2 + 3x$

Look Beyond

57. Graph the function $y = \sin^2 x + \cos^2 x$ for x-values from 0 to 2π. Describe the graph.

Gear-Tooth Design Gear makers often shape the sides of gear teeth so that they curve toward each other. This gear design allows gears to mesh smoothly without seizing up or jamming.

On gear tooth $ABCD$, $\overset{\frown}{BC}$ is the arc of a circle with its center at A and radius AC. In the diagram, $\theta = 13.5°$. The radius of the gear's base circle is 6 centimeters and the radius of the outer circle is 7 centimeters.

1. Make a sketch like the gear tooth above by using the given lengths and angle measures.

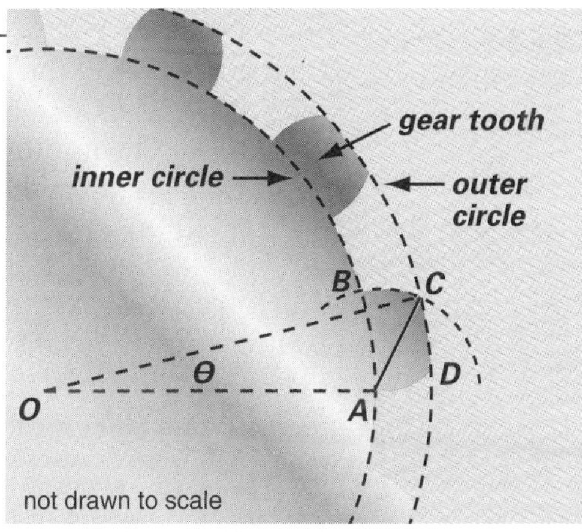

2. Use the law of cosines to find AC, the radius of the circle that generates $\overset{\frown}{BC}$.

WORKING ON THE CHAPTER PROJECT

You should now be able to complete Activity 1 of the Chapter Project.

Fundamental Trigonometric Identities

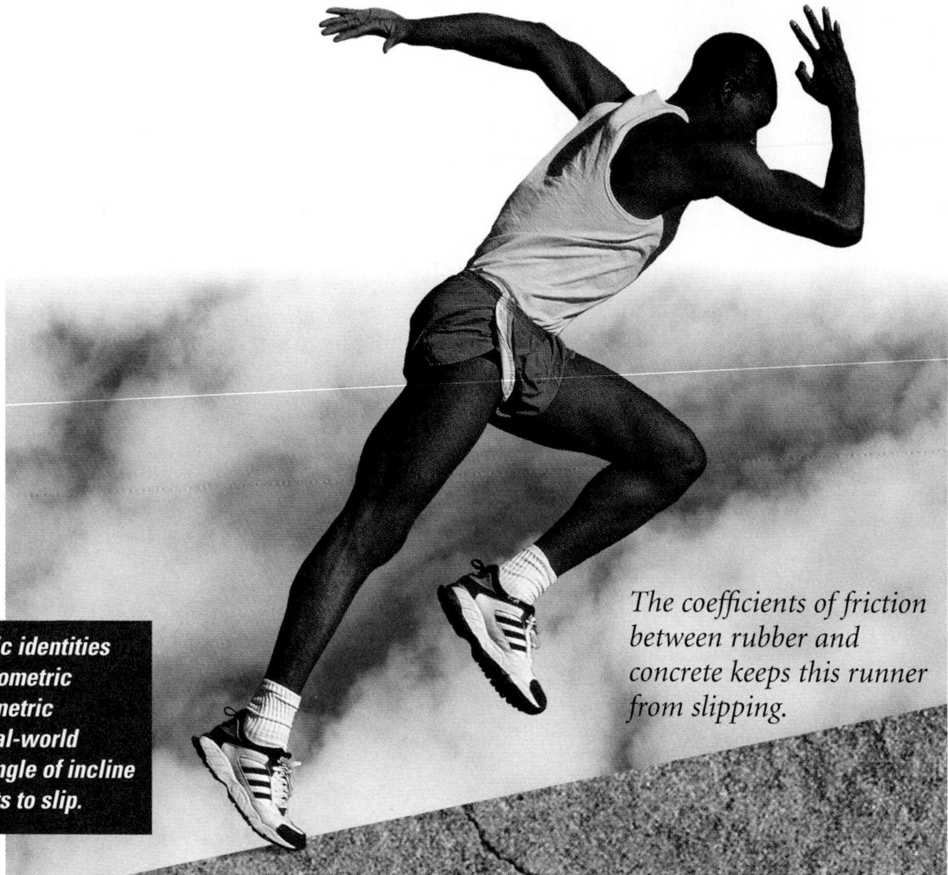

The coefficients of friction between rubber and concrete keeps this runner from slipping.

Objectives

- Prove fundamental trigonometric identities.
- Use fundamental trigonometric identities to rewrite expressions.

Why *Fundamental trigonometric identities can be used to rewrite a trigonometric expression as a single trigonometric function. This lets you solve real-world problems such as finding the angle of incline where rubber on concrete starts to slip.*

APPLICATION
PHYSICS

A block of rubber rests on a concrete platform. One end of the platform is slowly elevated. At what angle, θ, will the block of rubber begin to slide down the concrete platform? This angle is used to find the *coefficient of static friction,* μ_s (read "*mu* sub *s*"), between the rubber block and the cement. For a rubber block on concrete, this number is $\mu_s = 1.4$.

The force of friction that prevents the block from sliding is equal to $\mu_s mg \cos \theta$, where m is the mass of the block and g is the acceleration due to gravity. The force that causes the block to slide is $mg \sin \theta$. At the instant that the block begins to slide, both forces are equal, as shown below.

$$mg \sin \theta = 1.4mg \cos \theta$$

Use this equation to find the angle, θ, at which the block begins to slide. *You will solve this problem in Example 5.*

Trigonometric identities are equations that are true for all values of the variables for which the expressions on each side of the equation are defined. Recall from Chapter 13 that if $P(x, y)$ is a point on the terminal side of θ in standard position, then $\tan \theta = \frac{x}{y}$ and $P(x, y) = P(r \cos \theta, r \sin \theta)$. You can use these definitions to prove the identity $\tan \theta = \frac{\sin \theta}{\cos \theta}$.

EXAMPLE 1 **Prove the identity $\tan\theta = \frac{\sin\theta}{\cos\theta}$.**

SOLUTION

$\tan\theta = \frac{y}{x}$ *Use the definition of tan θ.*

$\tan\theta = \frac{r\sin\theta}{r\cos\theta}$ *Use substitution.*

$\tan\theta = \frac{\sin\theta}{\cos\theta}$

CHECK

In degree mode, graph $y = \tan x$ and $y = \frac{\sin x}{\cos x}$ on the same screen. The graphs appear to be the same. Note that this does not prove the identity, it only verifies it.

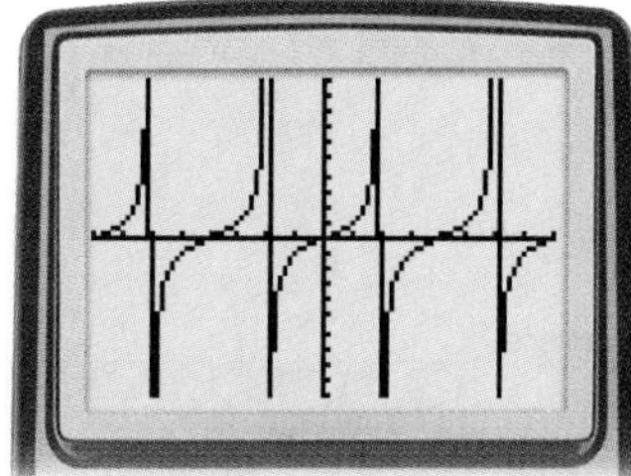

TRY THIS Prove the identity $\cot\theta = \frac{\cos\theta}{\sin\theta}$.

You can use a procedure similar to that shown in Example 1 to prove *ratio identities* and *reciprocal identities*. You can use the Pythagorean Theorem and the definitions of the trigonometric functions to prove the *Pythagorean identities*.

Fundamental Identities

Ratio identities	Reciprocal identities	Pythagorean identities
$\tan\theta = \frac{\sin\theta}{\cos\theta}$	$\csc\theta = \frac{1}{\sin\theta}$	$\cos^2\theta + \sin^2\theta = 1$
		$\sin^2\theta = 1 - \cos^2\theta$
$\cot\theta = \frac{\cos\theta}{\sin\theta}$	$\sec\theta = \frac{1}{\cos\theta}$	$\cos^2\theta = 1 - \sin^2\theta$
		$\tan^2\theta + 1 = \sec^2\theta$
	$\cot\theta = \frac{1}{\tan\theta}$	$1 + \cot^2\theta = \csc^2\theta$

Note that the square of $\sin\theta$ is written as $\sin^2\theta$. This form is used for all trigonometric functions.

EXAMPLE 2 **Prove the identity $\cos^2\theta + \sin^2\theta = 1$.**

SOLUTION

$\cos^2\theta + \sin^2\theta = \left(\frac{x}{r}\right)^2 + \left(\frac{y}{r}\right)^2$ *Use definitions of cos θ and sin θ.*

$\cos^2\theta + \sin^2\theta = \frac{x^2+y^2}{r^2}$

$\cos^2\theta + \sin^2\theta = \frac{r^2}{r^2}$ *By the Pythagorean Theorem, $x^2 + y^2 = r^2$.*

$\cos^2\theta + \sin^2\theta = 1$

TRY THIS Prove the identity $\tan^2\theta + 1 = \sec^2\theta$.

You can use the fundamental identities to rewrite trigonometric expressions in terms of a single trigonometric function.

EXAMPLE 3 **Write $\frac{\sin^2\theta}{1-\cos\theta}$ in terms of a single trigonometric function.**

SOLUTION

$$\frac{\sin^2\theta}{1-\cos\theta} = \frac{1-\cos^2\theta}{1-\cos\theta}$$ *Use $\sin^2\theta = 1-\cos^2\theta$.*

$$= \frac{(1+\cos\theta)(1-\cos\theta)}{1-\cos\theta}$$ *Factor the difference of two squares.*

$$= \frac{(1+\cos\theta)\cancel{(1-\cos\theta)}}{\cancel{1-\cos\theta}}$$

$$= 1+\cos\theta$$

TECHNOLOGY GRAPHICS CALCULATOR

Keystroke Guide, page 936

CHECK

Graph $y = \frac{\sin^2\theta}{1-\cos\theta}$ and $y = 1+\cos\theta$ on the same screen. The graphs appear to coincide.

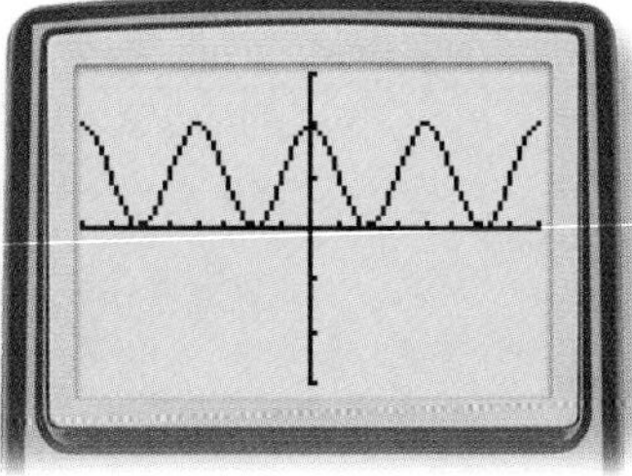

TRY THIS

Write $\frac{\cos^2\theta}{1-\sin\theta}$ in terms of a single trigonometric function.

Exploring Graphing Methods

You will need: a graphics calculator

1. Graph $y = (\csc\theta)(1-\cos\theta)(1+\cos\theta)$.
2. Write a simple function involving only $\sin\theta$ or $\cos\theta$ for the graph in Step 1.
3. Show algebraically that setting your function rule from Step 2 equal to $(\csc\theta)(1-\cos\theta)(1+\cos\theta)$ results in an identity.
4. Repeat Steps 1–3, using $y = \tan\theta(\csc\theta - \tan\theta\cos\theta)$.

CHECKPOINT ✔

5. Describe one advantage to graphing the related function for a trigonometric expression to help simplify the expression.
6. Use your own example to illustrate how a graph can help you simplify a trigonometric expression.

TECHNOLOGY GRAPHICS CALCULATOR

Keystroke Guide, page 937

CONNECTION TRANSFORMATIONS

You can use a graphics calculator to get hints on the outcome of rewriting a trigonometric expression. For example, you can graph $y = \frac{\sin^2\theta}{1-\cos\theta}$ from Example 3 before rewriting the expression to see that it appears to be the graph of $y = \cos\theta$ translated 1 unit up.

CHECKPOINT ✔ Graph $y = \tan^2\theta - \sec^2\theta$. What does it suggest to you about the result of rewriting the expression $\tan^2\theta - \sec^2\theta$?

EXAMPLE 4 **Write $\sec\theta - \tan\theta\sin\theta$ in terms of $\cos\theta$.**

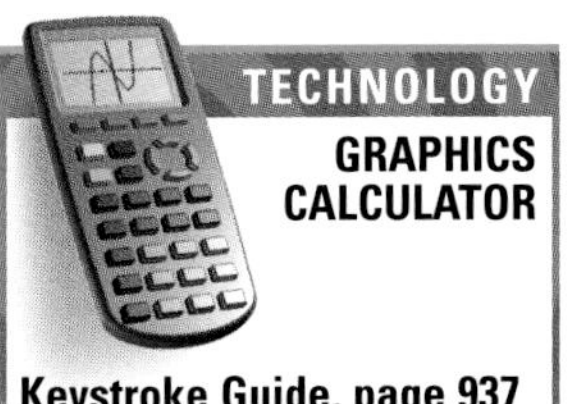

SOLUTION

Graph $y = \sec\theta - \tan\theta\sin\theta$.

Notice that the graph appears to be the same as $y = \cos\theta$.

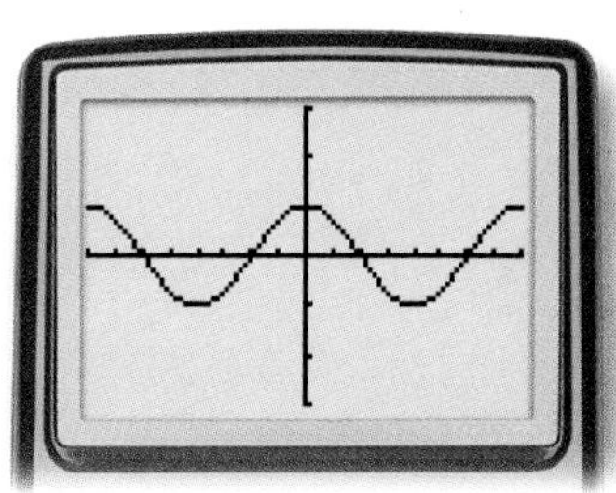

Use algebra to verify this.

$$\begin{aligned}\sec\theta - \tan\theta\sin\theta &= \frac{1}{\cos\theta} - \left(\frac{\sin\theta}{\cos\theta}\right)(\sin\theta) && \text{Use reciprocal and ratio identities.}\\ &= \frac{1}{\cos\theta} - \frac{\sin^2\theta}{\cos\theta}\\ &= \frac{1-\sin^2\theta}{\cos\theta}\\ &= \frac{\cos^2\theta}{\cos\theta} && \text{Use a Pythagorean identity.}\\ &= \cos\theta\end{aligned}$$

TRY THIS Write $\frac{1}{\sec^2\theta}$ in terms of $\sin\theta$.

CRITICAL THINKING Write $\tan\theta$ in terms of $\sin\theta$.

Example 5 uses substitution of equivalent trigonometric expressions to solve problems.

EXAMPLE 5 Refer to the friction problem at the beginning of the lesson.

APPLICATION
PHYSICS

Use the equation $mg\sin\theta = \mu_s mg\cos\theta$ to determine the angle at which each material begins to slide.

a. rubber block on cement: $\mu_s = 1.4$

b. glass block on lubricated metal: $\mu_s = 0.25$

SOLUTION

a.
$$\begin{aligned}mg\sin\theta &= \mu_s mg\cos\theta\\ mg\sin\theta &= 1.4mg\cos\theta\\ \sin\theta &= 1.4\cos\theta\\ \frac{\sin\theta}{\cos\theta} &= 1.4\\ \tan\theta &= 1.4\\ \theta &\approx 54.5^\circ\end{aligned}$$

Thus, rubber will begin to slide on cement at an angle of about 54.5°.

b.
$$\begin{aligned}mg\sin\theta &= \mu_s mg\cos\theta\\ mg\sin\theta &= 0.25mg\cos\theta\\ \sin\theta &= 0.25\cos\theta\\ \frac{\sin\theta}{\cos\theta} &= 0.25\\ \tan\theta &= 0.25\\ \theta &\approx 14.4^\circ\end{aligned}$$

Thus, glass will begin to slide on lubricated metal at an angle of about 14.4°.

TRY THIS The coefficient of static friction for a certain type of leather on metal is $\mu_s = 0.8$. At what angle will a block of this type of leather begin to slide on a metal platform?

Exercises

Communicate

1. How is the tangent function related to the sine and cosine functions?
2. Describe two strategies that can be used to rewrite trigonometric expressions.

CONNECTION

3. **GEOMETRY** Explain how the trigonometric Pythagorean identity $\sin^2 \theta + \cos^2 \theta = 1$ is related to the Pythagorean Theorem.

Guided Skills Practice

4. Prove the identity $\sec \theta = \frac{1}{\cos \theta}$, for $\cos \theta \neq 0$. ***(EXAMPLE 1)***
5. Prove the identity $\sin^2 \theta = 1 - \cos^2 \theta$. ***(EXAMPLE 2)***
6. Write $\frac{\cos^2 \theta}{1 + \sin \theta}$ in terms of a single trigonometric function. ***(EXAMPLE 3)***
7. Write $\cot^2 \theta$ in terms of $\sin \theta$. ***(EXAMPLE 4)***

APPLICATION

8. **PHYSICS** The coefficient of static friction for a certain type of rubber on concrete is $\mu_s = 1.2$. At what angle will a block of this type of rubber begin to slide on a concrete platform? ***(EXAMPLE 5)***

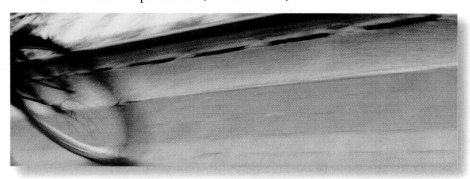

Practice and Apply

Use definitions to prove each identity.

9. $\cot \theta = \frac{1}{\tan \theta}$, $\tan \theta \neq 0$
10. $\csc \theta = \frac{1}{\sin \theta}$, $\sin \theta \neq 0$
11. $\cos^2 \theta = 1 - \sin^2 \theta$
12. $1 + \cot^2 \theta = \csc^2 \theta$

Write each expression in terms of a single trigonometric function.

13. $\cot \theta \sin \theta$
14. $\tan \theta \cos \theta$
15. $\tan \theta \csc \theta$
16. $\tan \theta \sec \theta \sin \theta$
17. $\csc \theta \sin^2 \theta$
18. $\sec \theta \cos^2 \theta$
19. $\left(\frac{\sin^2 \theta}{\cos \theta}\right)(\csc \theta)$
20. $\left(\frac{\cos^3 \theta}{\sin \theta}\right)(\sec^2 \theta)$
21. $\frac{\sin \theta}{\tan \theta}$
22. $\frac{\cos \theta}{\cot \theta}$
23. $\frac{\csc^2 \theta}{\cot^2 \theta}$
24. $\frac{\sec^2 \theta}{\tan^2 \theta}$
25. $\left(\frac{\sin \theta}{\cot \theta}\right)(\cos \theta)$
26. $\left(\frac{\cos \theta}{\tan \theta}\right)(\sin \theta)$

Write each expression in terms of cos θ.

27. $2 \sin^2 \theta - 1$

28. $(1 - \sin^2 \theta)(1 + \sec^2 \theta)$

29. $(1 - \cot^2 \theta)(\cot^2 \theta + 1)$

30. $\frac{\tan \theta}{\sin \theta}$

Write each expression in terms of sin θ.

31. $\cot \theta \cos \theta$

32. $\cot^2 \theta$

33. $\tan^2 \theta \cos^2 \theta + \csc \theta$

34. $\frac{1}{\sec^2 \theta}$

Use identities to verify that each statement is true.

35. $\frac{\sec \theta}{\csc \theta} = \tan \theta$

36. $\frac{\csc \theta}{\sec \theta} = \cot \theta$

37. $\frac{\tan^2 \theta}{\sec^2 \theta} = \sin^2 \theta$

38. $\frac{\cot^2 \theta}{\csc^2 \theta} = \cos^2 \theta$

39. $\cot^2 \theta = \cos^2 \theta \csc^2 \theta$

40. $\tan^2 \theta = \sin^2 \theta \sec^2 \theta$

41. $\frac{\sec \theta}{\cos \theta} = \sec^2 \theta$

42. $\frac{\csc \theta}{\sin \theta} = \csc^2 \theta$

43. $\frac{\cos \theta}{1 - \sin^2 \theta} = \sec \theta$

44. $\frac{\sin \theta}{1 - \cos^2 \theta} = \csc \theta$

45. $(\sec \theta)(1 - \sin^2 \theta) = \cos \theta$

46. $(\csc \theta)(1 - \cos^2 \theta) = \sin \theta$

47. $(\tan \theta)(\csc \theta)(\sec \theta) = \sec^2 \theta$

48. $(\cot \theta)(\csc \theta)(\sec \theta) = \csc^2 \theta$

49. Write $\tan^2 \theta - 2 \sec \theta \sin \theta$ in terms of $\sin \theta$ and $\cos \theta$.

50. Write $\tan^2 \theta - 2 \sec \theta \sin \theta$ in terms of $\tan \theta$.

Write each expression in terms of cos θ.

51. $\sin \theta$

52. $\csc \theta$

53. $\tan \theta$

54. $\cot \theta$

CHALLENGE

Write all of the trigonometric functions in terms of each given function.

55. $\sin \theta$

56. $\tan \theta$

57. $\cot \theta$

58. $\sec \theta$

APPLICATION

PHYSICS Refer to the friction problem described at the beginning of the lesson and continued in Example 5. Use the equation $mg \sin \theta = \mu_s mg \cos \theta$ to determine the angle at which each material begins to slide.

59. waxed wood on wet snow: $\mu_s = 0.14$

60. wood on wood: $\mu_s = 0.4$

61. wood on brick: $\mu_s = 0.6$

62. silk on silk: $\mu_s = 0.25$

Friction slows the motion of a skier, allowing them to turn and stop.

Look Back

63 Write the matrix equation that represents the system at right and solve the system, if possible. ***(LESSON 4.4)***

$$\begin{cases} 2x + y - 6z = -12 \\ -x + y + z = -7 \\ 5x - 3y + 7z = 11 \end{cases}$$

APPLICATION

GEOLOGY Recall from Lesson 6.7 that on the Richter scale, the magnitude, M, of an earthquake depends on the amount of energy, E, in ergs released by the earthquake as given by the equation $M = \frac{2}{3} \log \frac{E}{10^{11.8}}$. The list below gives information about some earthquakes that have occurred in the recent past.

Central square of Leninakan, Armenia, in 1988

Year	Location	Richter magnitude
1976	Tangshan, China	8.2
1978	Northeast Iran	7.7
1985	Mexico City, Mexico	8.1
1988	Northwest Armenia	6.8
1989	San Francisco, CA	7.1
1990	Northwest Iran	7.7
1993	South India	6.4
1994	Northridge, CA	6.8
1995	Kobe, Japan	7.2

Compare the amounts of energy released by the earthquakes listed for the indicated years. How much more energy was released by the greater earthquake? *(LESSON 6.7)*

64. 1976 and 1989

65. 1976 and 1985

66. 1978 and 1993

67. 1990 and 1993

68. 1976 and 1995

69. 1985 and 1994

70. Graph $y = 2(x - 3)^2 + 5$. Label the vertex, focus, and directrix. ***(LESSON 9.2)***

71. Graph $\frac{x^2}{4} + \frac{y^2}{9} = 1$. Label the center, vertices, co-vertices, and foci. ***(LESSON 9.4)***

72. In the diagram at right, $\angle BAC$ is the angle of depression. Point A represents the eyes of a person who is standing on top of a building and sees a traffic accident at C. How far from the base of the building, D, is the accident? Give your answer to the nearest foot. ***(LESSON 13.1)***

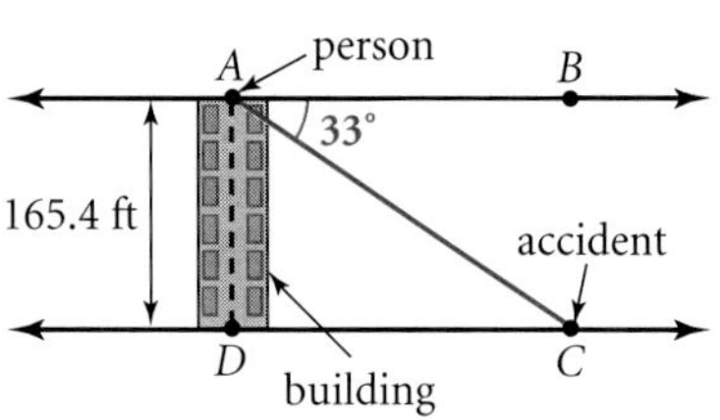

Look Beyond

73. Carry out the procedure below by using radian measure.

a. On the same axes, graph $y = \sin x$ and $y = x$ for $-0.3 \leq x \leq 0.3$. Does this suggest that $\sin x = x$?

b. Repeat part **a** for $-2 \leq x \leq 2$.

c. Draw a conclusion about using a graph to verify identities.

Sum and Difference Identities

Objectives

- Evaluate expressions by using the sum and difference identities.
- Use matrix multiplication with sum and difference identities to perform rotations.

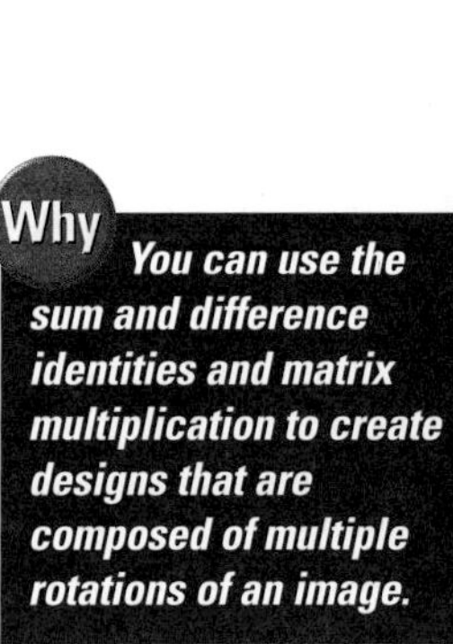

Why *You can use the sum and difference identities and matrix multiplication to create designs that are composed of multiple rotations of an image.*

APPLICATION
DESIGN

A design is made by rotating a rectangular figure as shown at left below. The figure on the positive x-axis has the vertices A, B, C, and D, shown at right below.

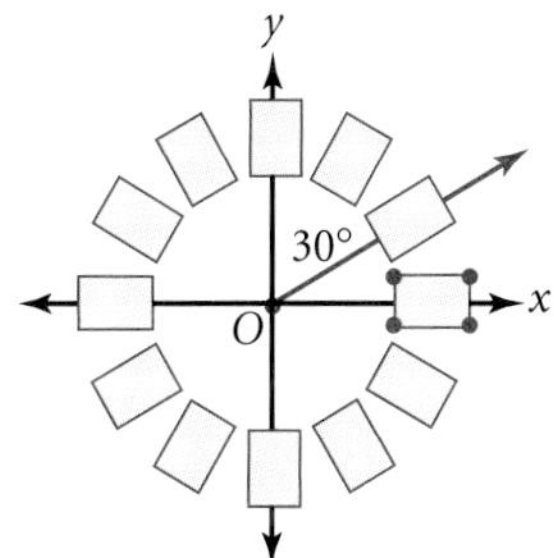

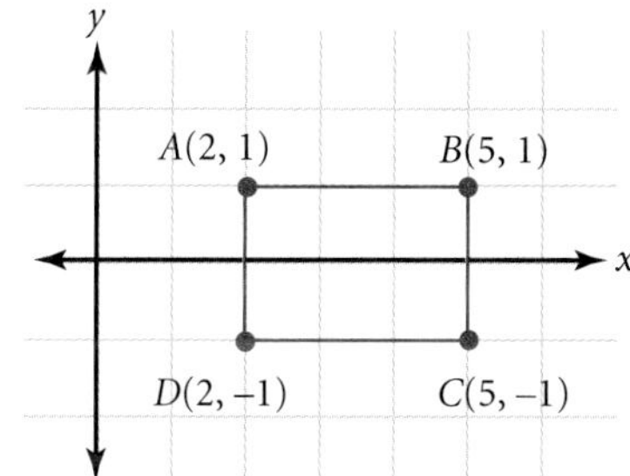

Find the coordinates of the vertices after a 30° rotation about the origin.
You will solve this problem in Example 5.

To solve the problem above, you can use a rotation matrix. The entries in the matrix are found by using the trigonometric *sum and difference identities.*

Activity

Proving the Difference Identity for Cosine

You will need: no special materials

In the diagram at left, $m\angle POQ = \alpha - \beta$.

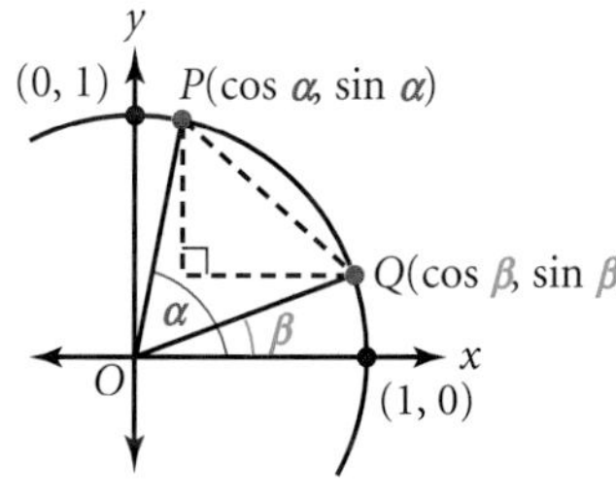

1. Using the distance formula, $d = \sqrt{(x_2 - x_1)^2 + (y_2 - y_1)^2}$, you can write the equation below.

$$(PQ)^2 = (\cos \alpha - \cos \beta)^2 + (\sin \alpha - \sin \beta)^2$$

a. Show that the right side of the equation can be rewritten as $2 - 2 \cos \alpha \cos \beta - 2 \sin \alpha \sin \beta$.

b. What identity did you use in part **a**?

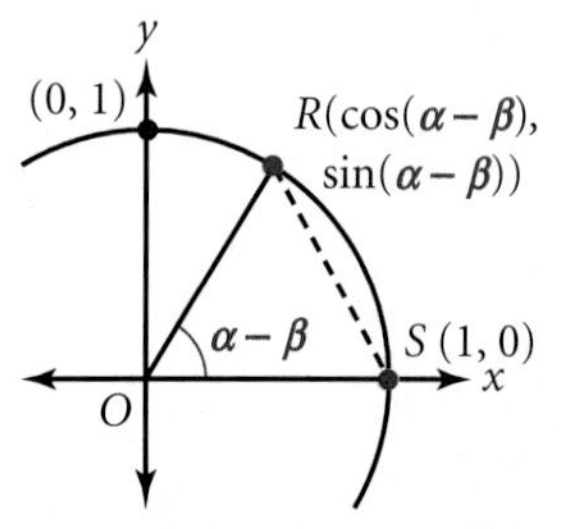

In the diagram at left, $m\angle ROS = \alpha - \beta$.

2. Using the distance formula, you can write the equation below.

$$(RS)^2 = [\cos(\alpha - \beta) - 1]^2 + [\sin(\alpha - \beta) - 0]^2$$

a. Show that the right side of the equation can be rewritten as $2 - 2\cos(\alpha - \beta)$.

b. What identity did you use in part **a**?

CHECKPOINT ✔ **3.** Does $PQ = RS$? Explain. Does $(PQ)^2 = (RS)^2$? Explain.

CHECKPOINT ✔ **4.** Using $(PQ)^2 = (RS)^2$ and the expressions for $(PQ)^2$ and $(RS)^2$ given in Step 1**a** and 2**a**, derive an expression for $\cos(\alpha - \beta)$ that includes $\sin\alpha$, $\sin\beta$, $\cos\alpha$, and $\cos\beta$.

All of the sum and difference identities can be proved in a manner similar to that explored in the Activity.

Sum and Difference Identities

$$\sin(A + B) = \sin A\cos B + \cos A\sin B$$
$$\sin(A - B) = \sin A\cos B - \cos A\sin B$$

$$\cos(A + B) = \cos A\cos B - \sin A\sin B$$
$$\cos(A - B) = \cos A\cos B + \sin A\sin B$$

EXAMPLE 1 **Find the exact value of each expression.**

a. $\sin(120° + 45°)$ **b.** $\cos(120° + 45°)$

SOLUTION

a.
$$\begin{aligned}\sin(120° + 45°) &= (\sin 120°)(\cos 45°) + (\cos 120°)(\sin 45°)\\ &= \left(\frac{\sqrt{3}}{2}\right)\left(\frac{\sqrt{2}}{2}\right) + \left(-\frac{1}{2}\right)\left(\frac{\sqrt{2}}{2}\right)\\ &= \frac{\sqrt{6}}{4} - \frac{\sqrt{2}}{4}\\ &= \frac{\sqrt{6} - \sqrt{2}}{4}\end{aligned}$$

b.
$$\begin{aligned}\cos(120° + 45°) &= (\cos 120°)(\cos 45°) - (\sin 120°)(\sin 45°)\\ &= \left(-\frac{1}{2}\right)\left(\frac{\sqrt{2}}{2}\right) - \left(\frac{\sqrt{3}}{2}\right)\left(\frac{\sqrt{2}}{2}\right)\\ &= \frac{-\sqrt{2}}{4} - \frac{\sqrt{6}}{4}\\ &= \frac{-\sqrt{2} - \sqrt{6}}{4}\end{aligned}$$

TRY THIS Find the exact value of each expression.

a. $\cos(210° - 30°)$ **b.** $\sin(330° - 135°)$

You can use the difference identities to derive other identities.

EXAMPLE 2 **Prove the identity $\sin(180° - \theta) = \sin\theta$.**

SOLUTION

$$\begin{aligned}\sin(180° - \theta) &= (\sin 180°)(\cos\theta) - (\cos 180°)(\sin\theta)\\ &= (0)(\cos\theta) - (-1)(\sin\theta)\\ &= \sin\theta\end{aligned}$$

TRY THIS Prove the identity $\sin(90° - \theta) = \cos\theta$.

A function, f, is **even** if $f(-x) = f(x)$ for all values of x in its domain. A function f is **odd** if $f(-x) = -f(x)$ for all x in its domain. You can use the difference identities to show that cosine is an even function and sine is an odd function.

$$\begin{aligned}\cos(-\theta) &= \cos(0° - \theta)\\ &= \cos 0° \cos\theta + \sin 0° \sin\theta\\ &= (1)(\cos\theta) + (0)\sin\theta\\ &= \cos\theta\end{aligned}$$

$$\begin{aligned}\sin(-\theta) &= \sin(0° - \theta)\\ &= \sin 0° \cos\theta - \cos 0° \sin\theta\\ &= (0)(\cos\theta) - (1)(\sin\theta)\\ &= -\sin\theta\end{aligned}$$

Thus, the cosine function is an even function and the sine function is an odd function.

CHECKPOINT ✔ Use the reciprocal identities to determine whether the secant and cosecant functions are odd or even.

EXAMPLE 3 **Find the exact value of each expression.**

a. $\sin(-165°)$ **b.** $\sin 195°$

SOLUTION

a.
$$\begin{aligned}\sin(-165°) &= -\sin 165°\\ &= -\sin(120° + 45°)\\ &= -[(\sin 120°)(\cos 45°) + (\cos 120°)(\sin 45°)]\\ &= -\left[\left(\frac{\sqrt{3}}{2}\right)\left(\frac{\sqrt{2}}{2}\right) + \left(-\frac{1}{2}\right)\left(\frac{\sqrt{2}}{2}\right)\right]\\ &= -\left(\frac{\sqrt{6} - \sqrt{2}}{4}\right)\\ &= \frac{\sqrt{2} - \sqrt{6}}{4}\end{aligned}$$

b.
$$\begin{aligned}\cos 195° &= \cos(150° + 45°)\\ &= (\cos 150°)(\cos 45°) - (\sin 150°)(\sin 45°)\\ &= \left(-\frac{\sqrt{3}}{2}\right)\left(\frac{\sqrt{2}}{2}\right) - \left(\frac{1}{2}\right)\left(\frac{\sqrt{2}}{2}\right)\\ &= \frac{-\sqrt{6} - \sqrt{2}}{4}\end{aligned}$$

TRY THIS Find the exact value of each expression.

a. $\cos(-105°)$ **b.** $\sin 285°$

EXAMPLE 4 **Graph $y = \sin(30^\circ - \theta)$.**

SOLUTION

$$
\begin{aligned}
y &= \sin(30^\circ - \theta) \\
&= \sin[-(\theta - 30^\circ)] \\
&= -\sin(\theta - 30^\circ) \quad \textit{The sine function is odd.}
\end{aligned}
$$

Graph $y = \sin \theta$.

Then translate the graph 30° to the right, and reflect the graph across the x-axis.

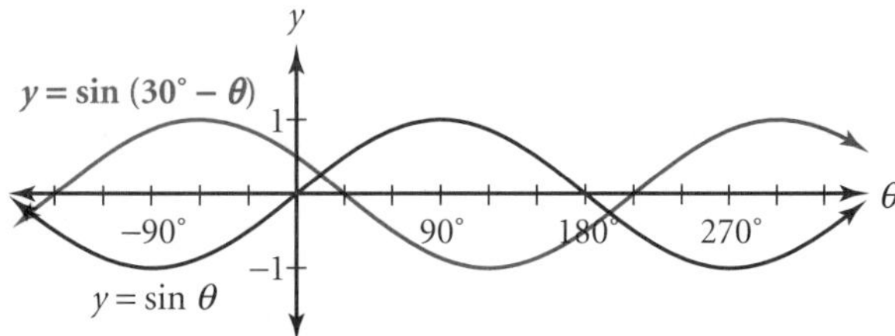

TRY THIS Graph $y = \cos(45^\circ - \theta)$.

Rotation Matrices

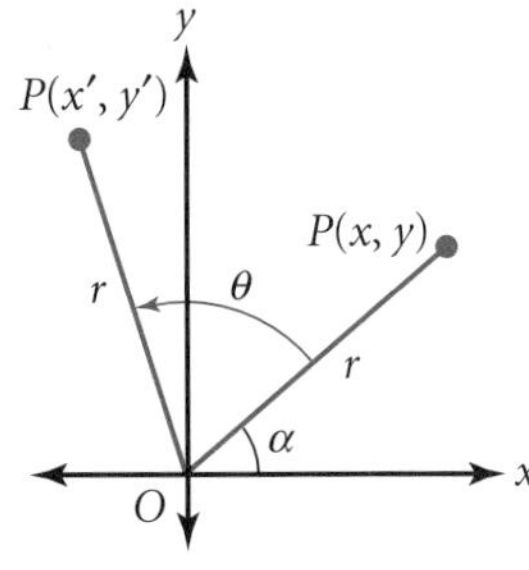

Matrix multiplication can be used in combination with sum and difference identities to determine the coordinates of points rotated on a plane about the origin. In the diagram at left, $P'(x', y')$ is the image of $P(x, y)$ after a rotation of θ degrees.

Recall from Lesson 13.3 that the coordinates of P are $(r \cos \alpha, r \sin \alpha)$. The coordinates of P' are found below.

$$
\begin{aligned}
x' &= r\cos(\alpha + \theta) \\
&= r[(\cos \alpha)(\cos \theta) - (\sin \alpha)(\sin \theta)] \\
&= (\mathbf{r \cos \alpha})(\cos \theta) - (\mathbf{r \sin \alpha})(\sin \theta) \\
&= \mathbf{x}(\cos \theta) - \mathbf{y}(\sin \theta) \\
&= x \cos \theta - y \sin \theta
\end{aligned}
$$

$$
\begin{aligned}
y' &= r\sin(\alpha + \theta) \\
&= r[(\sin \alpha)(\cos \theta) + (\cos \alpha)(\sin \theta)] \\
&= (\mathbf{r \sin \alpha})(\cos \theta) + (\mathbf{r \cos \alpha})(\sin \theta) \\
&= \mathbf{y}(\cos \theta) + \mathbf{x}(\sin \theta) \\
&= x \sin \theta + y \cos \theta
\end{aligned}
$$

Thus, you can find the coordinates of the image point, $P'(x', y')$, by using a *rotation matrix.*

$$
\begin{aligned}
\begin{bmatrix} x' \\ y' \end{bmatrix} &= \begin{bmatrix} x \cos \theta - y \sin \theta \\ x \sin \theta + y \cos \theta \end{bmatrix} \\
&= \begin{bmatrix} \cos \theta & -\sin \theta \\ \sin \theta & \cos \theta \end{bmatrix} \begin{bmatrix} x \\ y \end{bmatrix}
\end{aligned}
$$

Rotation Matrix

If $P(x, y)$ is any point in a plane, then the coordinates of the image of point $P'(x', y')$ after a rotation of θ degrees about the origin can be found by using a *rotation matrix* as follows:

$$
\begin{bmatrix} \cos \theta & -\sin \theta \\ \sin \theta & \cos \theta \end{bmatrix} \begin{bmatrix} x \\ y \end{bmatrix} = \begin{bmatrix} x' \\ y' \end{bmatrix}
$$

CHECKPOINT ✔ Write the rotation matrix for each angle of rotation.

a. 90° **b.** 180° **c.** 270°

EXAMPLE 5 Refer to the rectangular figure described at the beginning of the lesson.

APPLICATION
DESIGN

Find the coordinates to the nearest hundredth of the vertices after a 30° rotation about the origin.

SOLUTION

The rectangular figure has vertices at $A(2, 1)$, $B(5, 1)$, $C(5, -1)$, and $D(2, -1)$.

Write matrices for a 30° rotation and for the vertices of figure $ABCD$.

$$R_{30^\circ} = \begin{bmatrix} \cos 30^\circ & -\sin 30^\circ \\ \sin 30^\circ & \cos 30^\circ \end{bmatrix} \qquad S = \begin{bmatrix} 2 & 5 & 5 & 2 \\ 1 & 1 & -1 & -1 \end{bmatrix}$$

Keystroke Guide, page 937

Find the matrix product.

$$R_{30^\circ} \times S = \begin{bmatrix} \cos 30^\circ & -\sin 30^\circ \\ \sin 30^\circ & \cos 30^\circ \end{bmatrix} \begin{bmatrix} 2 & 5 & 5 & 2 \\ 1 & 1 & -1 & -1 \end{bmatrix}$$

$$\approx \begin{bmatrix} 1.23 & 3.83 & 4.83 & 2.23 \\ 1.87 & 3.37 & 1.63 & 0.13 \end{bmatrix}$$

The approximate coordinates of the vertices for the image of figure $ABCD$ are $A'(1.23, 1.87)$, $B'(3.83, 3.37)$, $C'(4.83, 1.63)$, and $D'(2.23, 0.13)$.

TRY THIS Given the figure described in Example 5, find the coordinates of the vertices for the image of this figure after a 60° rotation about the origin.

CRITICAL THINKING Show that a 90° rotation about the origin is the same as a 60° rotation about the origin followed by a 30° rotation.

Exercises

Communicate

1. Explain how to use sum or difference identities to find the exact value of cos 75°.

2. Explain how to use sum or difference identities to find the exact value of sin(−15°).

3. Explain how a matrix can be used to rotate the point $P(2, 3)$ at right 45° about the origin.

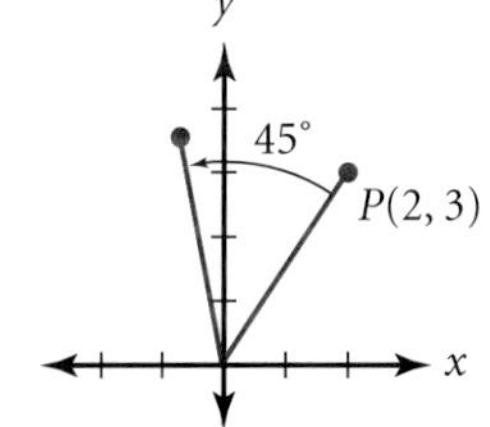

Guided Skills Practice

Find the exact value of each expression. ***(EXAMPLE 1)***

4. $\sin(145° + 60°)$

5. $\cos(60° - 45°)$

6. Prove the identity $-\cos(\theta + 180°) = \cos\theta$. ***(EXAMPLE 2)***

Find the exact value of each expression. ***(EXAMPLE 3)***

7. $\cos(-270°)$

8. $\sin(-240°)$

CONNECTION

9. TRANSFORMATIONS Graph $y = \sin(45° - \theta)$. ***(EXAMPLE 4)***

APPLICATION

10. DESIGN Refer to the design problem described at the beginning of the lesson. Find the coordinates to the nearest hundredth of the vertices after a 120° rotation about the origin. ***(EXAMPLE 5)***

Practice and Apply

Find the exact value of each expression.

11. $\sin(30° + 45°)$

12. $\sin(30° + 135°)$

13. $\cos(30° + 135°)$

14. $\cos(30° + 45°)$

15. $\sin(135° + 180°)$

16. $\sin(135° + 180°)$

17. $\cos(120° - 45°)$

18. $\cos(150° - 45°)$

19. $\sin(210° - 315°)$

20. $\sin(240° - 315°)$

21. $\cos(225° - 330°)$

22. $\cos(135° - 330°)$

Prove each identity.

23. $\sin(90° - \theta) = \cos\theta$

24. $\cos(90° - \theta) = \sin\theta$

25. $\cos(90° + \theta) = -\sin\theta$

26. $\sin(270° + \theta) = -\cos\theta$

27. $\sin(180° - \theta) = \sin\theta$

28. $\cos(180° - \theta) = -\cos\theta$

Use substitution to verify each statement.

29. $\sin(A + B) \neq \sin A + \sin B$

30. $\cos(A + B) \neq \cos A + \cos B$

31. $\sin(A - B) \neq \sin A - \sin B$

32. $\sin(A - B) \neq \cos A - \cos B$

Find the exact value of each expression.

33. $\sin 105°$

34. $\sin 165°$

35. $\cos 195°$

36. $\cos 225°$

37. $\sin 15°$

38. $\sin 75°$

39. $\cos 165°$

40. $\cos 285°$

41. $\sin(-135°)$

42. $\sin(-210°)$

43. $\cos(-235°)$

44. $\cos(-15°)$

Find the rotation matrix for each angle of rotation. Round entries to the nearest hundredth, if necessary.

45. 45°

46. 60°

47. 320°

48. 224°

49. −120°

50. −200°

51. −135°

52. −320°

Graph each function.

53. $y = \sin(\theta - 60°)$

54. $y = \sin(\theta - 45°)$

55. $y = \cos(30° - \theta)$

56. $y = \cos(180° - \theta)$

57. $y = \sin(120° - \theta)$

58. $y = \cos(135° - \theta)$

Find the coordinates of the image of each point after a 135° rotation.

59. $P(2, 3)$ **60.** $P(1, 5)$ **61.** $P(-3, 2)$ **62.** $P(4, -5)$

Find the coordinates of the image of each point after a –30° rotation.

63. $P(-1, 2)$ **64.** $P(2, -3)$ **65.** $P(10, 23)$ **66.** $P(7, 35)$

CHALLENGES

67. Use the sum and difference identities for the sine function to show that $\sin(A + B) + \sin(A - B) = 2 \sin A \cos B$ is true.

68. Use the definition of an inverse matrix to verify that the rotation matrix for θ degrees and the rotation matrix for $-\theta$ degrees are inverse matrices.

CONNECTION

TRANSFORMATIONS A rectangular figure has vertices at $W(3, 0)$, $X(3, 2)$, $Y(6, 2)$, and $Z(6, 0)$. Find the coordinates, to the nearest hundredth, of the vertices after the indicated rotation.

69. 60° counterclockwise **70.** 120° counterclockwise

71. 30° clockwise **72.** 150° clockwise

73. 225° clockwise **74.** 330° clockwise

75. 270° counterclockwise **76.** 240° counterclockwise

APPLICATIONS

The up-and-down motion of a pogo stick spring can illustrate simple harmonic motion.

77. PHYSICS The function $f(t) = a \cos(At + B)$ represents simple harmonic motion, where t is time, a is the amplitude of the motion, A is the angular frequency in radians, and B is the phase shift in radians. Show that f can be expressed in terms of a difference of the cosine and sine functions when $a = 3$, $A = 1$, and $B = \frac{\pi}{4}$.

78 PHYSICS The *superposition principle* states that if two or more waves are traveling in the same medium (air, water, and so on) the resulting wave is found by adding together the displacements of the individual waves. For instance, for waves f and g, the resulting wave is $y = f(x) + g(x)$.

a. Graph $f(x) = \cos 2x$ and $g(x) = \cos(2x - 1)$ over the interval $0 \le x \le 2\pi$. How do the graphs of f and g differ?

b. Graph $h(x) = f(x) + g(x)$ in the same screen as f and g. Describe the behavior of the graph of h.

c. Compare the periods of f, g, and h.

d. The identity $\cos x + \cos y = 2 \cos \frac{1}{2}(x + y) \cos \frac{1}{2}(x - y)$ can be derived from the identities of this lesson. Use this identity to simplify h.

Ocean waves generally pass through one another without being altered. However, a momentary combination of waves can result in an unusually tall wave.

Look Back

79. Find an equation for the inverse of $f(x) = -3x + 7$. Then use composition to verify that the equation you wrote is the inverse. ***(LESSON 2.5)***

APPLICATION

80. LAW ENFORCEMENT An explosion is heard by two law enforcement officers who are 2000 meters apart. Electronic equipment allows them to determine that one officer heard the explosion 1.8 seconds after the other officer. The speed of sound in air (at 20°C) is approximately 340 meters per second. Write an equation for the possible locations of the explosions relative to the two law enforcement officers. ***(LESSON 9.5)***

81. Solve $\triangle ABC$ given that $a = 2.96$, $b = 3.78$, and $c = 4.54$. ***(LESSON 14.2)***

Look Beyond

82. Is $\sin \frac{A}{2} = \frac{\sin A}{2}$ true for all angle measures A? Justify your response.

83. Is $\sin 2A = 2 \sin A$ true for all angle measures A? Justify your response.

PROGRAMMING A machine-tool operator needs to program a gear-cutting machine to cut a gear with 12 teeth. The teeth are to be positioned at 30° intervals. The coordinates for the vertices of the gear-tooth profile are $A(8.00, 0.00)$, $B(7.52, 2.74)$, $C(9.72, 2.33)$, and $D(9.94, 1.13)$.

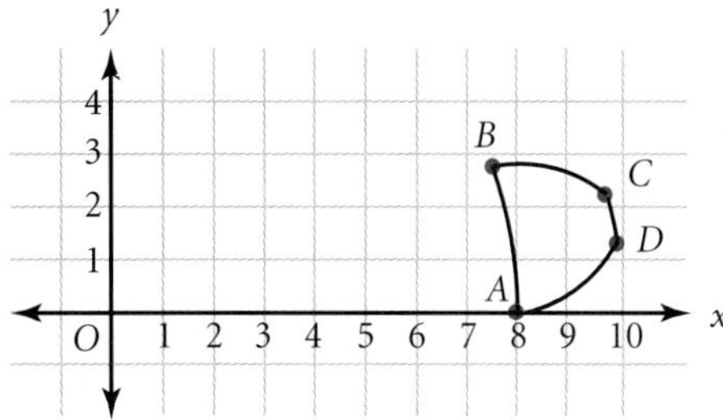

1. Find the coordinates for the image of the gear-tooth profile after a 30° rotation about the origin.

  a. Write matrices for a 30° rotation and for the vertices of the gear-tooth profile.

  b. Find the matrix product.

2. Find the coordinates to the nearest hundredth for the image of the gear-tooth profile after a 60° rotation about the origin.

WORKING ON THE CHAPTER PROJECT

You should now be able to complete Activity 2 of the Chapter project.

Double-Angle and Half-Angle Identities

Objective

- Evaluate and simplify expressions by using double-angle and half-angle identities.

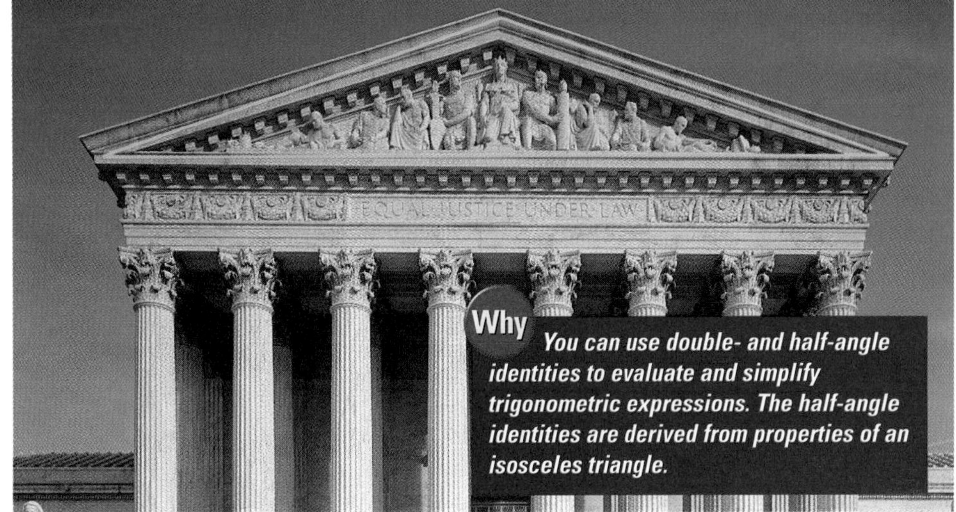

EQUAL JUSTICE UNDER LAW
Why
You can use double- and half-angle identities to evaluate and simplify trigonometric expressions. The half-angle identities are derived from properties of an isosceles triangle.

U.S. Supreme Court, Washington, D.C.

APPLICATION
ARCHITECTURE

An isosceles roof system, such as the one shown above, is represented at right. The width, s, can be written in terms of a and θ as follows:

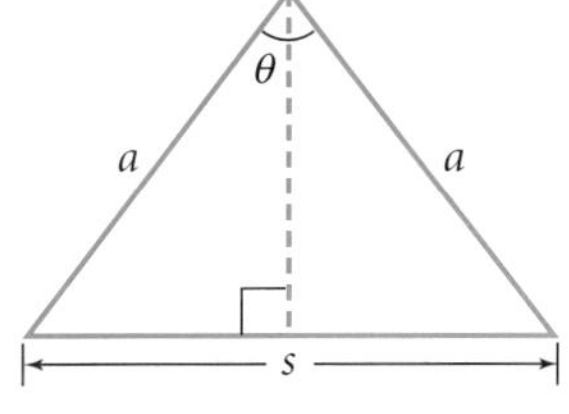

$$\sin\frac{\theta}{2} = \frac{\left(\frac{s}{2}\right)}{a}$$

$$s = 2a\sin\frac{\theta}{2}$$

Another expression for s can be derived from the law of cosines.

$$s^2 = a^2 + a^2 - 2aa\cos\theta$$
$$s^2 = 2a^2 - 2a^2\cos\theta$$
$$s^2 = a^2(2 - 2\cos\theta)$$
$$s = a\sqrt{2 - 2\cos\theta}$$

By equating these two expressions for s, you can write what is called a *half-angle identity* for the sine function. This is shown on page 919.

Double-Angle Identities

You can use sum identities to prove the *double-angle identities* for the sine and cosine functions.

$$\begin{aligned}\sin 2\theta &= \sin(\theta + \theta)\\ &= \sin\theta\cos\theta + \cos\theta\sin\theta\\ &= 2\sin\theta\cos\theta\end{aligned}$$

$$\begin{aligned}\cos 2\theta &= \cos(\theta + \theta)\\ &= \cos\theta\cos\theta - \sin\theta\sin\theta\\ &= \cos^2\theta - \sin^2\theta\end{aligned}$$

Double-Angle Identities

$$\sin 2\theta = 2\sin\theta\cos\theta \qquad \cos 2\theta = \cos^2\theta - \sin^2\theta$$

You can use double-angle identities to simplify a trigonometric expression, as shown in Example 1.

EXAMPLE 1 **Simplify $(\cos\theta + \sin\theta)^2$.**

SOLUTION

$$
\begin{aligned}
(\cos\theta + \sin\theta)^2 &= \cos^2\theta + 2\cos\theta\sin\theta + \sin^2\theta && \textit{Expand.}\\
&= \cos^2\theta + \sin^2\theta + 2\sin\theta\cos\theta && \textit{Rearrange terms.}\\
&= 1 + \sin 2\theta && \textit{Use substitution.}
\end{aligned}
$$

CRITICAL THINKING Use a double-angle identity to write $\sin 3\theta$ in terms of $\sin\theta$ and $\cos\theta$.

You can use double-angle identities to find the exact value of a double-angle given certain information.

EXAMPLE 2 **Given $90^\circ \le \theta \le 180^\circ$ and $\cos\theta = -\frac{3}{4}$, find the exact value of $\cos 2\theta$.**

SOLUTION

PROBLEM SOLVING **Draw a diagram** and find the exact value of $\sin\theta$.

$$
\begin{aligned}
x^2 + y^2 &= r^2\\
(-3)^2 + y^2 &= 4^2\\
y &= \pm\sqrt{4^2 - (-3)^2}\\
y &= \sqrt{7} && \textit{y is positive in Quadrant II.}
\end{aligned}
$$

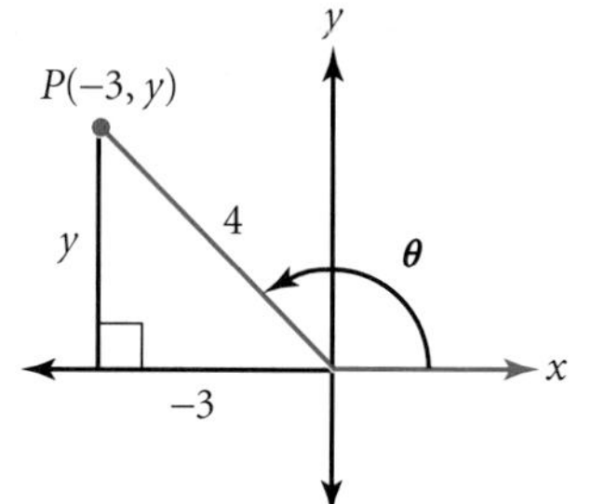

Thus, $\sin\theta = \frac{y}{r} = \frac{\sqrt{7}}{4}$.

Use the double-angle identity.

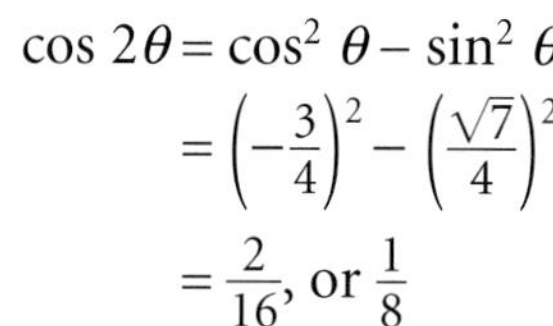

$$
\begin{aligned}
\cos 2\theta &= \cos^2\theta - \sin^2\theta\\
&= \left(-\frac{3}{4}\right)^2 - \left(\frac{\sqrt{7}}{4}\right)^2\\
&= \frac{2}{16}, \text{ or } \frac{1}{8}
\end{aligned}
$$

TRY THIS Given $270^\circ \le \theta \le 360^\circ$ and $\cos\theta = \frac{1}{4}$, find the exact value of $\sin 2\theta$.

You can use the identity $\cos^2\theta = 1 - \sin^2\theta$ or $\sin^2\theta = 1 - \cos^2\theta$ to write alternative identities for $\cos 2\theta$.

$$
\begin{aligned}
\cos 2\theta &= \cos^2\theta - \sin^2\theta\\
&= (1 - \sin^2\theta) - \sin^2\theta\\
&= 1 - 2\sin^2\theta
\end{aligned}
\qquad\qquad
\begin{aligned}
\cos 2\theta &= \cos^2\theta - \sin^2\theta\\
&= \cos^2\theta - (1 - \cos^2\theta)\\
&= 2\cos^2\theta - 1
\end{aligned}
$$

Alternative Double-Angle Identities for Cosine

$\cos 2\theta = 1 - 2\sin^2\theta$ $\qquad\qquad$ $\cos 2\theta = 2\cos^2\theta - 1$

CHECKPOINT ✔ Solve the problem in Example 2 by using each of the alternative double-angle identities for cosine.

Half-Angle Identities

APPLICATION
ARCHITECTURE

Refer to the isosceles triangle described at the beginning of the lesson. A half-angle identity for the sine function can be found by solving the two expressions for s that relate $\sin\frac{\theta}{2}$ and $\cos\theta$.

$$2a\sin\frac{\theta}{2} = a\sqrt{2-2\cos\theta} \quad (0^\circ < \theta < 180^\circ \text{ and } a > 0)$$

$$\sin\frac{\theta}{2} = \frac{\sqrt{2-2\cos\theta}}{2}$$

$$\sin\frac{\theta}{2} = \sqrt{\frac{2-2\cos\theta}{4}}$$

$$\sin\frac{\theta}{2} = \sqrt{\frac{1-\cos\theta}{2}}$$

The *half-angle identities* for the sine and cosine of any angle are given below.

Half-Angle Identities

$$\sin\frac{\theta}{2} = \pm\sqrt{\frac{1-\cos\theta}{2}} \qquad \cos\frac{\theta}{2} = \pm\sqrt{\frac{1+\cos\theta}{2}}$$

Choose + or – depending on the sign of the value for $\sin\frac{\theta}{2}$ or $\cos\frac{\theta}{2}$.

EXAMPLE 3 **Given $180^\circ \le \theta \le 270^\circ$ and $\sin\theta = -\frac{2}{3}$, find the exact value of $\cos\frac{\theta}{2}$.**

SOLUTION

PROBLEM SOLVING

Draw a diagram and find the exact value of $\cos\theta$.

$$x^2 + y^2 = r^2$$

$$x^2 + (-2)^2 = 3^2$$

$$x = \pm\sqrt{3^2 - (-2)^2}$$

$$x = -\sqrt{5} \qquad \textit{x is negative in Quadrant III.}$$

Thus, $\cos\theta = \frac{x}{r} = \frac{-\sqrt{5}}{3}$.

Use the half-angle identity for cosine. If $180^\circ \le \theta \le 270^\circ$, then $\frac{180^\circ}{2} \le \frac{\theta}{2} \le \frac{270^\circ}{2}$, or $90^\circ \le \theta \le 135^\circ$. Therefore, the sign of the value for $\cos\frac{\theta}{2}$ will be negative.

$$\cos\frac{\theta}{2} = -\sqrt{\frac{1+\cos\theta}{2}}$$

$$= -\sqrt{\frac{1+\left(\frac{-\sqrt{5}}{3}\right)}{2}}$$

$$= -\sqrt{\frac{1}{2}\left(1-\frac{\sqrt{5}}{3}\right)}$$

$$= -\sqrt{\frac{1}{2}-\frac{\sqrt{5}}{6}}$$

TRY THIS Given $90^\circ \le \theta \le 180^\circ$ and $\cos\theta = -\frac{1}{3}$, find the exact value of $\sin\frac{\theta}{2}$.

CULTURAL CONNECTION: AFRICA Ptolemy was an astronomer who lived and worked in the North African city of Alexandria during the second century C.E. Ptolemy wrote the most authoritative work on trigonometry of that time, called the *Almagest*, which included the double-angle identities for the sine of an angle.

Ptolemy, a second century astronomer

CRITICAL THINKING Use identities to show that $\cos 2\left(\frac{\theta}{2}\right) = 2\cos^2\frac{\theta}{2} - 1$ can be rewritten as the identity $\cos\frac{\theta}{2} = \pm\sqrt{\frac{1+\cos\theta}{2}}$.

Exercises

Communicate

1. Use the range of $y = \sin\theta$ to explain why $\sin 2\theta$ is not, in general, equivalent to $2\sin\theta$.
2. Describe how to determine the sign of the value of $\sin\frac{\theta}{2}$ or $\cos\frac{\theta}{2}$ if you are given $0^\circ < \theta < 360^\circ$ and the quadrant in which θ terminates.

Guided Skills Practice

3. Simplify $\cos^4\theta - \sin^4\theta$. ***(EXAMPLE 1)***

Given $0^\circ \le \theta \le 90^\circ$ and $\sin\theta = \frac{2}{5}$, find the exact value of each expression. ***(EXAMPLES 2 AND 3)***

4. $\cos 2\theta$
5. $\sin 2\theta$
6. $\cos\frac{\theta}{2}$
7. $\sin\frac{\theta}{2}$

Practice and Apply

Simplify.

8. $\frac{\sin 2\theta}{\cos\theta}$
9. $\cos 2\theta + 1$
10. $\cos 2\theta + 2\sin^2\theta$
11. $\frac{\cos\theta\sin 2\theta}{1+\cos 2\theta}$
12. $\frac{\cos 2\theta}{\cos\theta + \sin\theta}$
13. $\frac{\cos 2\theta}{\cos\theta - \sin\theta} - \sin\theta$

Write each expression in terms of trigonometric functions of θ rather than multiples of θ.

14. $\sin^2 2\theta$
15. $\sin 4\theta$
16. $\cos^2 2\theta$
17. $\cos 4\theta$
18. $\sin 2\theta - 1 + \cos^2\theta$
19. $\frac{\sin^2\theta}{\sin 2\theta}$

Write each expression in terms of a single trigonometric function.

20. $\sin\theta\cos\theta$
21. $2\cos^2\theta - 2\sin^2\theta$
22. $2\cos^2\theta - \sin^2\theta$

CHALLENGE

23. Find the exact value of $\sin 7.5^\circ$.

Use the information given to find the exact value of sin 2θ and cos 2θ.

24. $90° \leq \theta \leq 180°$; $\cos \theta = -\frac{3}{5}$

25. $90° \leq \theta \leq 180°$; $\sin \theta = \frac{3}{5}$

26. $270° \leq \theta \leq 360°$; $\cos \theta = \frac{2}{5}$

27. $270° \leq \theta \leq 360°$; $\sin \theta = -\frac{2}{5}$

28. $0° \leq \theta \leq 90°$; $\sin \theta = \frac{1}{4}$

29. $0° \leq \theta \leq 90°$; $\cos \theta = \frac{1}{4}$

30. $180° \leq \theta \leq 270°$; $\sin \theta = -\frac{\sqrt{5}}{4}$

31. $180° \leq \theta \leq 270°$; $\cos \theta = -\frac{\sqrt{5}}{4}$

Use the information given to find the exact value of sin $\frac{\theta}{2}$ and cos $\frac{\theta}{2}$.

32. $0° \leq \theta \leq 90°$; $\sin \theta = \frac{1}{5}$

33. $0° \leq \theta \leq 90°$; $\cos \theta = \frac{1}{5}$

34. $90° \leq \theta \leq 180°$; $\cos \theta = -\frac{5}{6}$

35. $90° \leq \theta \leq 180°$; $\sin \theta = \frac{5}{6}$

36. $180° \leq \theta \leq 270°$; $\sin \theta = -\frac{\sqrt{5}}{3}$

37. $180° \leq \theta \leq 270°$; $\cos \theta = -\frac{\sqrt{5}}{3}$

38. $270° \leq \theta \leq 360°$; $\cos \theta = \frac{3}{8}$

39. $270° \leq \theta \leq 360°$; $\sin \theta = -\frac{3}{8}$

APPLICATION

SPORTS A golf ball is struck with an initial velocity of v_0, in feet per second, and leaves the ground at angle x. The distance that the ball travels is given by the function $d(x) = \frac{(v_0)^2 \sin x \cos x}{16}$.

40. Write the function, d, in terms of the double angle, $2x$.

41. At what angle must a golf ball be hit in order to achieve the maximum possible distance for a given initial velocity? Explain.

Tiger Woods, 1997

Look Back

State whether each relation represents a function. ***(LESSON 2.3)***

42. $\{(-1, 6), (0, 3), (1, 3), (2, 6)\}$

43. $\{(1, 2), (2, 3), (2, 4), (3, 5)\}$

Evaluate. ***(LESSONS 10.2 AND 10.3)***

44. $\frac{5!}{2!}$

45. $0!$

46. ${}_{12}C_4$

47. ${}_{13}C_3$

48. ${}_{10}P_4$

49. ${}_{15}P_3$

50. $\binom{7}{3}$

51. $\binom{10}{2}$

CONNECTION

52. TRANSFORMATIONS For the function $f(\theta) = 3\sin(2\theta - 60°)$, describe the transformation from its parent function. Then graph at least one period of the function along with the parent function. ***(LESSON 13.5)***

Look Beyond

53. Consider the equation $\sin^2 \theta + 2\sin \theta - 3 = 0$. Substitute x for $\sin \theta$, and solve the resulting equation for x. Then solve for θ given that $0° \leq \theta \leq 360°$.

Solving Trigonometric Equations

Objectives

- Solve trigonometric equations algebraically and graphically.
- Solve real-world problems by using trigonometric equations.

Why *Trigonometric equations can be used to solve real-world problems such as finding the angle at which a batter hits a ball.*

APPLICATION
SPORTS

When a batter hits a baseball, the ball travels in a parabolic path. For a certain hit, the path of the ball in terms of time, t, in seconds is represented by the parametric equations below.

$$\begin{cases} x(t) = 122t \cos \theta & x(t) \text{ is the distance in feet.} \\ y(t) = 122t \sin \theta - 16t^2 & y(t) \text{ is the height in feet.} \end{cases}$$

At what angle is the ball hit if it has a height of 15 feet after 3 seconds? *You will answer this question in Example 4.*

Notice that each of the parametric equations is a trigonometric equation. A **trigonometric equation** is an equation that contains at least one trigonometric function. Each of the equations below are trigonometric equations.

$$\cos \theta = 0.5 \qquad \sin^2\left(2x - \frac{\pi}{3}\right) = \frac{\sqrt{3}}{2} \qquad \cos^2 x - 2 \cos x + 3 = 0$$

A solution to a trigonometric equation is any value of the variable for which the equation is true.

Exploring Trigonometric Equations

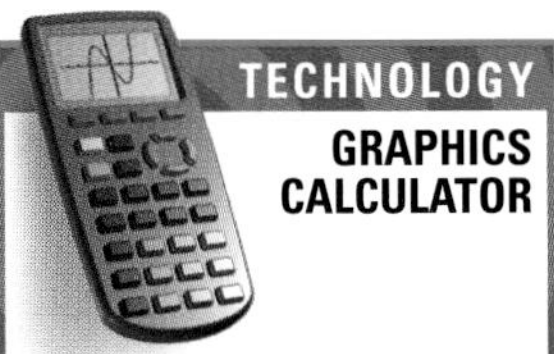

You will need: a graphics calculator in degree mode

1. Graph $y = \sin \theta$ for the interval $0^\circ \le \theta < 360^\circ$. Over this range, how many values of θ satisfy $\sin \theta = 1$? What are these values?
2. Graph $y = \sin \theta$ for the interval $0^\circ \le \theta < 720^\circ$. Over this range, how many values of θ satisfy $\sin \theta = 0.5$? What are these values?
3. Copy and complete the table below. Based on the table, write a complete solution to $\sin \theta = 1$ in general terms.

Interval	$0^\circ \le \theta < 360^\circ$	$0^\circ \le \theta < 720^\circ$	$0^\circ \le \theta < 1080^\circ$	$0^\circ \le \theta < 1440^\circ$
Number of solutions				
Solutions				

CHECKPOINT ✔

4. Let $\sin \theta = a$, where θ is any real number and a is a fixed real number. Find one value of a for which $\sin \theta = a$ has no solution.
5. Is there a value of a for which there is exactly one solution to $\sin \theta = a$? Justify your response.
6. If $\sin \theta = a$ has at least one solution, must it have infinitely many solutions? Explain your response.

Trigonometric equations are true only for certain values of the variables, unlike trigonometric identities, which are true for all values of the variables. Example 1 shows you how to find all possible solutions of a trigonometric equation.

EXAMPLE 1 **Find all solutions of $\cos \theta = \sqrt{3} - \cos \theta$.**

SOLUTION

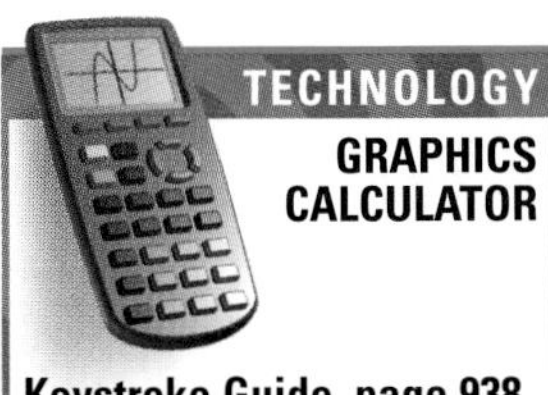

Method 1 Use algebra.

First solve for $0^\circ \le \theta < 360^\circ$.

$$\cos \theta = \sqrt{3} - \cos \theta$$
$$2 \cos \theta = \sqrt{3}$$
$$\cos \theta = \frac{\sqrt{3}}{2}$$
$$\theta = 30^\circ \text{ or } \theta = 330^\circ$$

Method 2 Use a graph.

Graph $y = \cos \theta$ and $y = \sqrt{3} - \cos \theta$ on the same screen over the interval $0^\circ \le \theta < 360^\circ$, and find any points of intersection.

The graphs intersect at $\theta = 30^\circ$ and at $\theta = 330^\circ$.

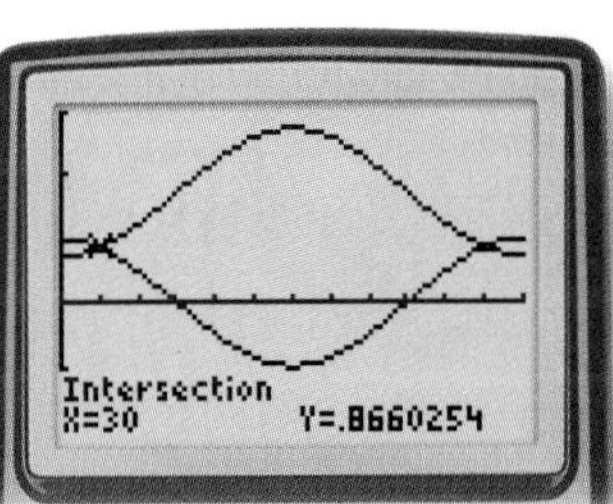

Thus, $\theta = 30^\circ + n360^\circ$ *or* $\theta = 330^\circ + n360^\circ$.

TRY THIS Find all solutions of $1 - 2 \sin \theta = 0$.

A trigonometric equation may also be solved by using methods for solving quadratic equations.

EXAMPLE 2 **Find the exact solutions of $\sin^2 \theta - 2 \sin \theta - 3 = 0$ for $0° \leq \theta < 360°$.**

SOLUTION

$$\begin{aligned} \sin^2 \theta - 2 \sin \theta - 3 &= 0 \\ (\sin \theta)^2 - 2(\sin \theta) - 3 &= 0 \\ u^2 - 2u - 3 &= 0 && \textit{Substitute u for sin } \theta. \\ (u+1)(u-3) &= 0 && \textit{Factor the quadratic expression.} \\ (\sin \theta + 1)(\sin \theta - 3) &= 0 && \textit{Substitute sin } \theta \textit{ for u.} \\ \sin \theta = -1 \text{ or } \sin \theta &= 3 && \textit{Apply the Zero-Product Property.} \end{aligned}$$

For $\sin \theta = -1$, $\theta = 270°$. The equation $\sin \theta = 3$ has no solution.

Thus, the solution for $0° \leq \theta < 360°$ is $\theta = 270°$.

TRY THIS Find the exact solutions of $\cos^2 \theta - \sqrt{2} \cos \theta + \frac{1}{2} = 0$ for $0° \leq \theta < 360°$.

CRITICAL THINKING Use substitution to find the exact solutions of $\sin 3\theta = \frac{1}{2}$ for $0° \leq \theta < 360°$.

A trigonometric equation may contain two trigonometric functions. You can often use trigonometric identities to write the equation in terms of only one of the functions. This is shown in Example 3.

EXAMPLE 3 **Solve $2 \cos^2 \theta = \sin \theta + 1$ for $0° \leq \theta < 360°$.**

SOLUTION

$$\begin{aligned} 2 \cos^2 \theta &= \sin \theta + 1 \\ 2(1 - \sin^2 \theta) &= \sin \theta + 1 && \textit{Substitute } 1 - \sin^2 \theta \textit{ for } \cos^2 \theta = 1. \\ 2 - 2\sin^2 \theta &= \sin \theta + 1 \\ 2 \sin^2 \theta + \sin \theta - 1 &= 0 \\ 2u^2 + u - 1 &= 0 && \textit{Substitute u for sin } \theta. \\ (u+1)(2u-1) &= 0 && \textit{Factor.} \\ (\sin \theta + 1)(2 \sin \theta - 1) &= 0 \end{aligned}$$

$$\sin \theta = -1 \quad \text{or} \quad \sin \theta = \frac{1}{2}$$

$$\theta = 270° \quad \text{or} \quad \theta = 30° \quad \text{or} \quad \theta = 150°$$

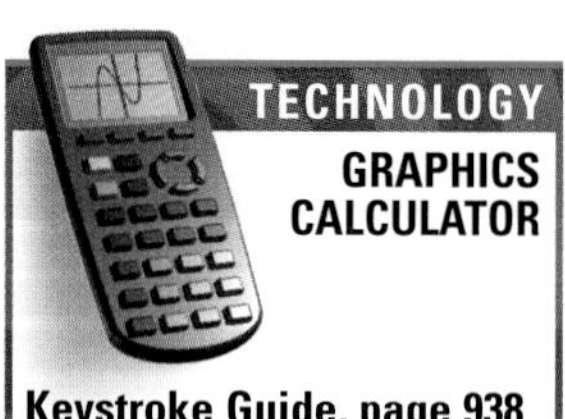

CHECK

Graph $y = 2 \cos^2 x$ and $y = \sin x + 1$ on the same screen for $0° \leq x < 360°$, and find any points of intersection.

The graph shows intersections at $x = 30°$, $x = 150°$, and $x = 270°$.

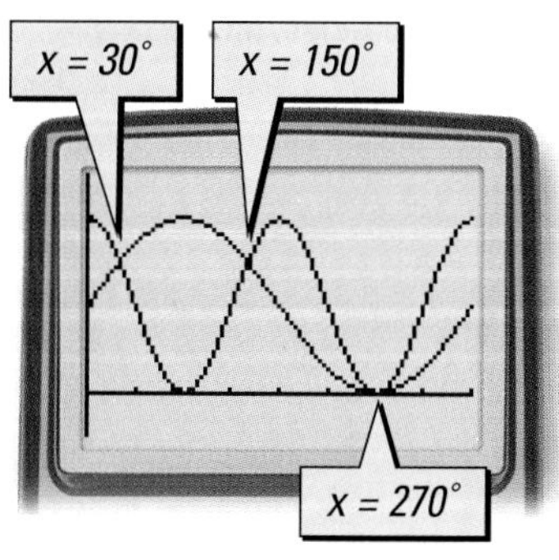

TRY THIS Solve $1 + \tan^2 \theta + \sec \theta = 0$ for $0° \leq \theta < 360°$.

EXAMPLE 4 Refer to the baseball problem at the beginning of the lesson.

APPLICATION SPORTS

At what angle is the ball hit if it has a height of 15 feet after 3 seconds?

SOLUTION

Substitute 15 for $y(t)$ and 3 for t in the equation for the height.

$$y(t) = 122t \sin \theta - 16t^2$$
$$15 = 122(3) \sin \theta - 16(3)^2$$
$$15 = 366 \sin \theta - 144$$
$$\sin \theta = \frac{15 + 144}{366}$$
$$\theta \approx \sin^{-1}(0.4344)$$
$$\approx 25.7^\circ$$

Keystroke Guide, page 939

CHECK

Graph $y = 366 \sin x - 144$ and $y = 15$ on the same screen, and look for any points of intersection.

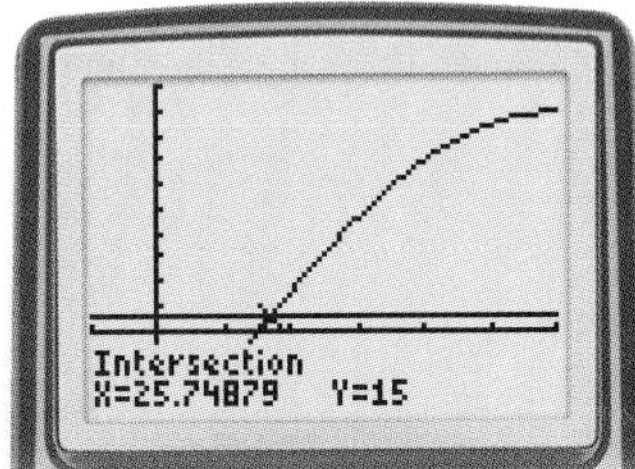

The graph shows an intersection at $\theta \approx 25.7^\circ$.

CHECKPOINT ✔ What distance has the ball traveled if it has a height of 15 feet after 3 seconds? Is the hit a home run if the fence is 325 feet from home plate and 15 feet tall?

Exercises

Communicate

1. Describe how trigonometric equations differ from trigonometric identities.
2. Give the number of solutions to $\sin x = -1$ and $\cos x = 2$, and explain why they differ.
3. Summarize the different methods used to solve trigonometric equations in Examples 1, 2, and 3.

Guided Skills Practice

4. Find all solutions of $4 \cos \theta + 1 = 3$. ***(EXAMPLE 1)***
5. Find the exact solutions of $\cos^2 \theta - \cos \theta - 2 = 0$ for $0 \le \theta < 360^\circ$. ***(EXAMPLE 2)***
6. Solve $1 - 2 \cos \theta + \cos^2 \theta = \sin^2 \theta$ for $0 \le \theta < 360^\circ$. ***(EXAMPLE 3)***
7. **SPORTS** Refer to the baseball problem at the beginning of the lesson. At what angle is the ball hit if it has a height of 20 feet after 3 seconds? ***(EXAMPLE 4)***

Practice and Apply

Find all solutions of each equation.

8. $2 \sin \theta - 1 = 0$

9. $2 \cos \theta + 1 = 0$

10. $4 \sin \theta + 2\sqrt{3} = 0$

11. $4 \cos \theta - 2 = 0$

12. $\sin \theta = \sqrt{2} - \sin \theta$

13. $1 - \sin \theta = \sin \theta$

14. $2 - 3 \cos \theta = \cos \theta + 2$

15. $1 + 5 \cos \theta = 2 \cos \theta - 2$

16. $\tan \theta - \sqrt{3} = 0$

17. $\cot \theta + 1 = 0$

18. $6 \cos \theta - 1 = 3 + 4 \cos \theta$

19. $1 - 2 \sin \theta = \sin \theta - \sqrt{3}$

Find the exact solutions of each equation for $0° \le \theta < 360°$.

20. $2 \cos^2 \theta - \cos \theta = 1$

21. $2 \sin^2 \theta = 1 - \sin \theta$

22. $2 \sin^2 \theta - 5 \sin \theta = -2$

23. $2 \cos^2 \theta - 3 \cos \theta = 2$

24. $3 \cos \theta + 2 = -\cos^2 \theta$

25. $3 - \sin \theta = -\sin^2 \theta$

26. $\sin \theta + \sin \theta \cos \theta = 0$

27. $\cos^2 \theta + \cos \theta = 0$

28. $6 \sin^2 \theta - 3 \sin \theta = 0$

29. $2 \cos^2 \theta + \sqrt{3} \cos \theta = 0$

30. $\cos^2 \theta + 2 \cos \theta = -2$

31. $25 \sin^2 \theta + 8 \sin \theta = -8$

32. $2 \cos^2 \theta = \sin^2 \theta + 2$

33. $\cos^2 \theta = \sin^2 \theta + 1$

34. $\cos \theta \tan \theta = -1$

35. $\sec \theta \cos^2 \theta - 1 = 0$

36. $2 \tan^2 \theta = \sec^2 \theta$

37. $\sec^2 \theta + 2 \cot^2 \theta = 3$

38. $\cos \theta - \sin^2 \theta = 1$

39. $3 + 3 \sin \theta = \cos^2 \theta$

40. $2 \cos^2 \theta = \sin \theta + 1$

41. $-\cos \theta - \sin^2 \theta = 1$

42. $2 \cos^2 \theta - 2 \cos \theta = -\sin^2 \theta$

43. $1 - \cos^2 \theta = \cos^2 \theta + 2 \cos \theta + 1$

Solve each equation to the nearest tenth of a degree for $0° \le \theta < 360°$.

44 $2 \cos^2 \theta - \sin \theta - 1 = 0$

45 $\tan^2 \theta + \cot^2 \theta + 2 = 0$

46 $\cos 2\theta - \sin \theta = 0$

47 $\sin 2\theta + \sin \theta = 0$

48 $\cos^2 \theta + 5 \cos \theta + 2 = 0$

49 $4 \sin^2 \theta - 3 \sin \theta - 2 = 0$

CHALLENGE

50. Solve $|\sin \theta| = \sin \theta$ and $|\cos \theta| = \cos \theta$ over the interval $-360° \le \theta < 360°$.

CONNECTION

51. GEOMETRY A circular cap is formed by subtracting the area of the triangle (with legs of length r and angle θ in radians) from the area of the sector, as shown in the figure at right. The area of a circular cap is given by the formula $A = \frac{1}{2}r^2(\theta - \sin \theta)$. A circular sector with a radius of 5 and angle θ has a circular cap whose area is 20. What is the measure of angle θ in radians?

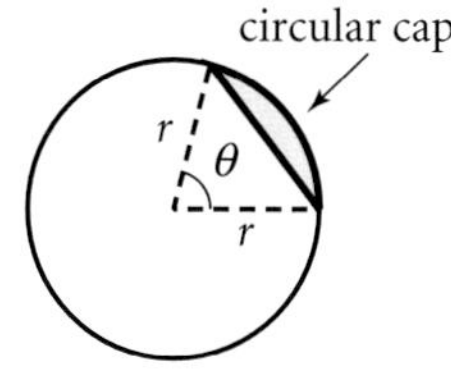

APPLICATION

PHYSICS The position of a weight attached to an oscillating spring is given by $y = 5 \cos \pi t$, where t is time in seconds and y is vertical distance in centimeters. Rest position is at the point where $y = 0$.

52. Find the times at which the weight is 5 centimeters above its rest position.

53. Find the times at which the weight is 4 centimeters above its rest position.

APPLICATION

PHYSICS When light travels from one medium to another, the path of the light ray changes direction. Snell's law states that a light ray traveling from air to water changes direction according to the equation $\frac{\sin \theta_{air}}{\sin \theta_{water}} = n_{water}$, where θ_{air} and θ_{water} are the angles shown in the diagram below, and n_{water} is a constant called the *index of refraction*.

For example, when looking at a fish underwater, a bird hovering in the air perceives the fish to be nearer to the water's surface than it actually is. Conversely, the fish perceives the bird in the air to be farther away from the water's surface than it actually is.

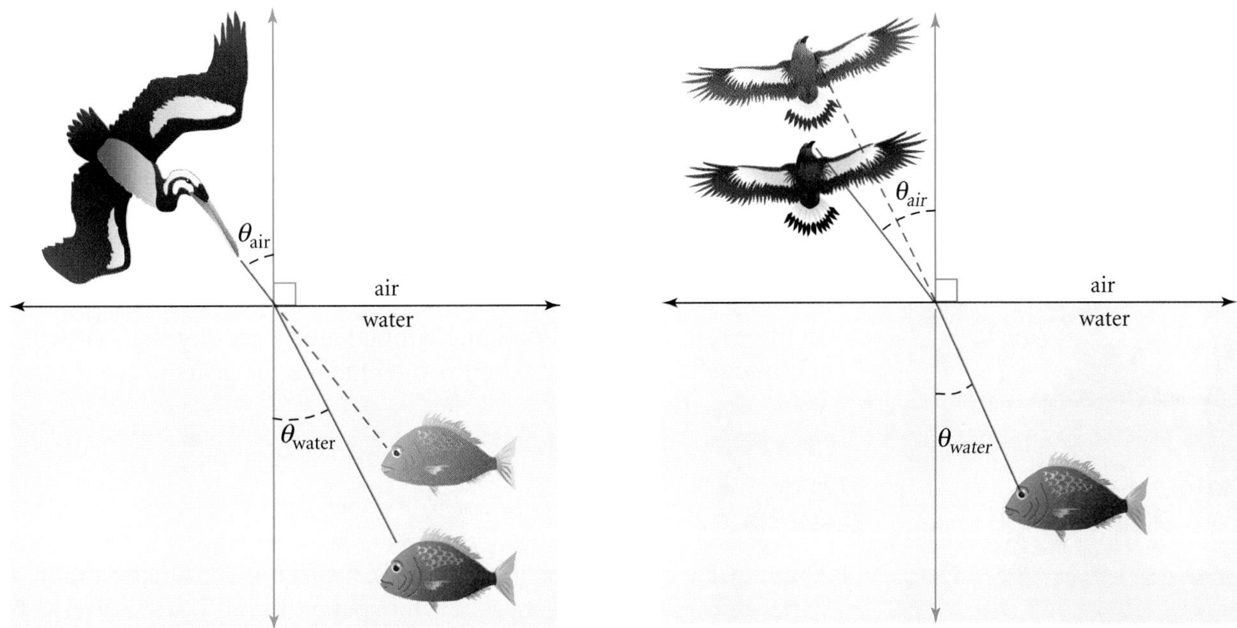

Given the index of refraction for water, n_{water}, is approximately 1.33, find each indicated angle.

54. θ_{air} if θ_{water} is 30°.

55. θ_{water} if θ_{air} is 60°.

56. θ_{water} if θ_{air} is 42°.

57. θ_{air} if θ_{water} is 25°.

Look Back

Let $A = \begin{bmatrix} 5 & -4 \\ 7 & 3 \end{bmatrix}$, $B = \begin{bmatrix} 3 \\ -5 \end{bmatrix}$, and $C = \begin{bmatrix} 7 \\ -3 \end{bmatrix}$. Find each product. If the product does not exist, write *none*. ***(LESSON 4.2)***

58. AC

59. BA

60. BC

61. Solve $\triangle ABC$ given that $a = 12.7$, $c = 10.4$, and $B = 26.5°$. Give answers to the nearest tenth. ***(LESSON 14.2)***

A pencil in a glass of water appears bent or broken because of the bending of light, or refraction.

Look Beyond

62. In calculus, it can be proved that $\sin x = x - \frac{x^3}{3!} + \frac{x^5}{5!} - \frac{x^7}{7!} + \cdots$ and $\cos x = 1 - \frac{x^2}{2!} + \frac{x^4}{4!} - \frac{x^6}{6!} + \cdots$ (where x is expressed in radians) are true. Use the first five terms of these series, called the *Taylor series*, to approximate the value of $\sin \frac{\pi}{6}$ and $\cos \pi$. Compare your answers with the exact values.

GEARING UP

Much of the activity in today's world depends on electricity. This modern technology is in turn equally dependent on a much older technology that you will study in this Chapter Project. Electricity flows into our homes because turbines turn, and the smooth and efficient transfer of this mechanical energy to electricity often depends on systems of gears.

A gear is usually classified as a "simple machine"—a wheel with teeth. But what size and shape should the teeth be so that a system of gears will mesh together properly? It turns out that this is not a simple question to answer.

In this project, you will design a template for a set of gears that will mesh together smoothly. Then you will make the gears to see if they work properly.

Activity 1

You may lay out your gear template on a sheet of centimeter graph paper or on an unlined sheet of white paper. In both cases, orient the paper horizontally rather than vertically.

1. Mark and label point O in the center of the graph paper, and draw the x-axis and y-axis.
2. Use a compass to draw a *base circle* centered at point O with a radius of 8 centimeters and an *outer circle* centered at point O with a radius of 10 centimeters. Mark and label point $A(8, 0)$. If you are using unlined paper, place point A anywhere on the base circle.
3. Set a compass to draw a radius of 2.8 centimeters. Put the compass point on A and draw an arc that passes through the base circle and the outer circle. Mark and label point B, the arc's intersection with the base circle, and point C, the arc's intersection with the outer circle.
4. With the compass point on B and the pencil point on A, draw an arc that passes through the outer circle, and label the point of intersection D. Quadrilateral $ABCD$ constitutes the *gear tooth profile.*
5. Use the Law of Cosines to determine the measure of arc AB on the base circle to the nearest degree.

Activity 2

In this activity you will complete the gear template you began in Activity 1.

1. Use the coordinates from the Portfolio Activity on page 916 for the images of the original gear tooth profile under a 30° and a 60° rotation about the origin. Carefully plot these coordinates on the base circle and on the outer circle.
2. Use matrix multiplication to determine the coordinates for the images of the original gear tooth profile under rotations of 90°, 120°, 150°, 180°, 210°, 240°, 270°, 300°, and 330° about the origin. Carefully plot these coordinates on the base circle and on the outer circle. Note: Plot the points as carefully as you can. Rounding error and the precision of the centimeter grid will often make your vertices fall just above or below the base circle and the outer circle. Use these circles as guides for positioning the vertices of the gear teeth.
3. Use a compass to draw arcs for the curved sides of each gear tooth. (See Steps 3 and 4 in Activity 1.)

Activity 3

Make working models of the gears.

1. Cut out the gear template that you completed in Activity 3.
2. Pin the gear template to cardboard or fiberboard, and carefully trace around it. Then outline a second gear.
3. Cut out the gears. Position them on a piece of cardboard so that their teeth mesh, and pin them at their centers to keep them in place. The gears should turn smoothly in opposite directions. Observe how the curved surfaces touch each other when the gear teeth engage.

14 Chapter Review and Assessment

VOCABULARY

Key Skills & Exercises

LESSON 14.1

Key Skills

Use the law of sines to solve triangles.

Solve triangle $\triangle ABC$ given that $A = 42^\circ$, $B = 52^\circ$, and $a = 10$.

$$\frac{\sin A}{a} = \frac{\sin B}{b}$$
$$\frac{\sin 42^\circ}{10} = \frac{\sin 52^\circ}{b}$$
$$b = \frac{10 \sin 52^\circ}{\sin 42^\circ} \approx 11.8$$

Determine whether the given SSA information defines 0, 1, or 2 triangles.

SSA information: $c = 12$, $a = 8$, and $A = 30^\circ$

$$\frac{\sin A}{a} = \frac{\sin C}{c}$$
$$\frac{\sin 30^\circ}{8} = \frac{\sin C}{12}$$
$$\sin C \approx 0.75$$
$$C \approx 48.6^\circ \text{ or } C \approx 131.4^\circ$$

There are 2 possible triangles.

Exercises

Solve each triangle. Give answers to the nearest tenth, if necessary.

1. $A = 35^\circ, B = 45^\circ, a = 12$
2. $B = 27^\circ, C = 40^\circ, b = 20$
3. $A = 30^\circ, c = 10, B = 50^\circ$
4. $B = 42^\circ, a = 14, C = 57^\circ$

State the number of triangles determined by the given information. If 1 or 2 triangles are formed, solve the triangle(s). Give answers to the nearest tenth, if necessary.

5. $A = 40^\circ, c = 20, a = 5$
6. $A = 60^\circ, c = 10, a = 5\sqrt{3}$
7. $B = 30^\circ, b = 3, c = 5$
8. $B = 75^\circ, c = 9, b = 3$

LESSON 14.2

Key Skills

Use the law of cosines to solve triangles.

$$a^2 = b^2 + c^2 - 2bc \cos A$$
$$b^2 = a^2 + c^2 - 2ac \cos B$$
$$c^2 = a^2 + b^2 - 2ab \cos C$$

Given:	Use:
SSS	law of cosines, then law of sines
SSA	law of sines (ambiguous)
SAA	law of sines
ASA	law of sines
SAS	law of cosines, then law of sines
AAA	not possible

Exercises

Classify the type of information given, and then solve $\triangle ABC$ to the nearest tenth.

9. $A = 37^\circ, b = 10, c = 14$
10. $B = 63^\circ, a = 12, c = 15$
11. $a = 6, b = 3, c = 5$
12. $a = 9, b = 4, c = 12$
13. $A = 35^\circ, c = 30, a = 20$

LESSON 14.3

Key Skills

Use fundamental trigonometric identities to rewrite expressions.

Verify the identity $(\tan\theta)\dfrac{\cos\theta}{\sin^2\theta} = \csc\theta$.

$$(\tan\theta)\frac{\cos\theta}{\sin^2\theta} = \frac{\sin\theta}{\cos\theta} \bullet \frac{\cos\theta}{\sin^2\theta} = \frac{1}{\sin\theta} = \csc\theta$$

Exercises

Write each expression in terms of a single trigonometric function.

14. $(\sec\theta)(\cos^2\theta)$

15. $(\csc\theta)(\tan\theta)$

16. $\dfrac{2\cos^2\theta}{1-\sin^2\theta}$

17. $\dfrac{-3\tan^2\theta}{1+\sec^2\theta}$

LESSON 14.4

Key Skills

Use the sum and difference identities.

Find the exact value of $\sin(30^\circ - 45^\circ)$.

$$\begin{aligned}&\sin(30^\circ - 45^\circ)\\ &= (\sin 30^\circ)(\cos 45^\circ) - (\cos 30^\circ)(\sin 45^\circ)\\ &= \left(\frac{1}{2}\right)\left(\frac{\sqrt{2}}{2}\right) - \left(\frac{\sqrt{3}}{2}\right)\left(\frac{\sqrt{2}}{2}\right) = \frac{\sqrt{2}-\sqrt{6}}{4}\end{aligned}$$

Use rotation matrices.

Find the coordinates of the image of $P(-3, 4)$ after a 20° rotation about the origin.

$$\begin{bmatrix}\cos 20^\circ & -\sin 20^\circ\\ \sin 20^\circ & \cos 20^\circ\end{bmatrix}\begin{bmatrix}-3\\ 4\end{bmatrix} \approx \begin{bmatrix}-4.2\\ 2.7\end{bmatrix}$$

Exercises

Find the exact value of each expression.

18. $\sin(45^\circ - 210^\circ)$

19. $\sin(60^\circ + 270^\circ)$

20. $\cos(90^\circ + 60^\circ)$

21. $\cos(120^\circ - 135^\circ)$

22. $\sin 195^\circ$

23. $\cos 75^\circ$

24. $\cos(-210^\circ)$

25. $\sin(-15^\circ)$

Find the coordinates of the image of each point after a 120° rotation.

26. $(3, -5)$

27. $(-2, 7)$

LESSON 14.5

Key Skills

Use the double- and half-angle identities.

$$\sin 2\theta = 2\sin\theta\cos\theta \qquad \sin\frac{\theta}{2} = \pm\sqrt{\frac{1-\cos\theta}{2}}$$

$$\cos 2\theta = \cos^2\theta - \sin^2\theta \qquad \cos\frac{\theta}{2} = \pm\sqrt{\frac{1+\cos\theta}{2}}$$

Given $180^\circ \le \theta \le 270^\circ$ and $\sin\theta = -\frac{4}{7}$, find the exact value of $\cos\frac{\theta}{2}$.

Find $\cos\theta$:

$$\begin{aligned}x^2 + y^2 &= r^2\\ x^2 + (-4)^2 &= 7^2\\ x &= -\sqrt{33} \leftarrow \textit{Quadrant III}\end{aligned}$$

$$\cos\theta = \frac{-\sqrt{33}}{7}$$

$$\begin{aligned}\cos\frac{\theta}{2} &= \pm\sqrt{\frac{1+\cos\theta}{2}}\\ &= -\sqrt{\frac{1+\left(-\frac{\sqrt{33}}{7}\right)}{2}} \leftarrow 90^\circ \le \tfrac{\theta}{2} \le 135^\circ\\ &= -\sqrt{\frac{1}{2} - \frac{\sqrt{33}}{14}}\end{aligned}$$

Exercises

Given $0^\circ \le \theta \le 90^\circ$ and $\cos\theta = \frac{1}{8}$, find the exact value of each expression.

28. $\cos 2\theta$

29. $\sin 2\theta$

30. $\cos\frac{\theta}{2}$

31. $\sin\frac{\theta}{2}$

Given $270^\circ \le \theta \le 360^\circ$ and $\sin\theta = -\frac{5}{8}$, find the exact value of each expression.

32. $\sin 2\theta$

33. $\cos 2\theta$

34. $\sin\frac{\theta}{2}$

35. $\cos\frac{\theta}{2}$

Write each expression in terms of trigonometric functions of θ rather than multiples of θ.

36. $\sin 2\theta + \cos 2\theta$

37. $\cos 4\theta$

LESSON 14.6

Key Skills

Solve trigonometric equations.

Find the exact solutions of $-\cos^2\theta = 1 + 5\sin\theta$ for $0° \leq \theta < 360°$.

$$-2\cos^2\theta = 1 + 5\sin\theta$$
$$-2(1 - \sin^2\theta) = 1 + 5\sin\theta$$
$$2\sin^2\theta - 5\sin\theta - 3 = 0$$
$$(2\sin\theta + 1)(\sin\theta - 3) = 0$$
$$\sin\theta = -\frac{1}{2} \quad or \quad \sin\theta = 3$$

For $\sin\theta = -\frac{1}{2}$, $\theta = 225°$ *or* $\theta = 315°$. For $\sin\theta = 3$, there is no solution.

Exercises

Find the exact solutions of each equation for $0° \leq \theta < 360°$.

38. $2\cos\theta - \sqrt{2} = 0$

39. $\sin^2\theta + \sin\theta = 2$

40. $2\cos^2\theta - \cos\theta - 1 = 0$

41. $\cos^2\theta - \sin^2\theta + 1 = 0$

42. $4\sin^2\theta + 4\cos\theta - 1 = 0$

43. $4\sin^2\theta - 2(\sqrt{2} + 1)\sin\theta + \sqrt{2} = 0$

Applications

44. SURVEYING A map maker makes the measurements shown in the diagram at right. Find the distance across the river from B to C.

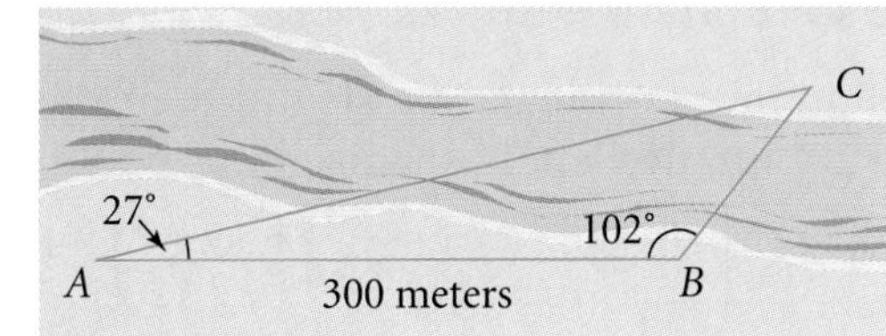

RECREATION At a distance of 3000 yards from the base of a mountain, the angle of elevation to the top is 20°. At a distance of 1000 yards from the base of the mountain, a tram ride goes to the top of the mountain at an inclination of 35°.

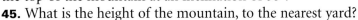

45. What is the height of the mountain, to the nearest yard?

46. What is the length of the tram ride to the nearest yard?

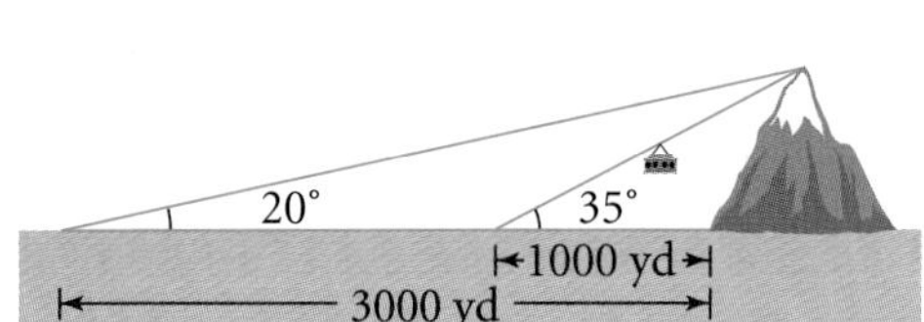

47. REAL ESTATE A triangular lot has sides of 215 feet, 185 feet, and 125 feet. Find the measures of the angles at its corners.

48. SURVEYING A tunnel from point A to point B runs through a mountain. From point C, both ends of the tunnel can be observed. If $AC = 165$ meters, $BC = 115$ meters, and $C = 74°$, find AB, the length of the tunnel.

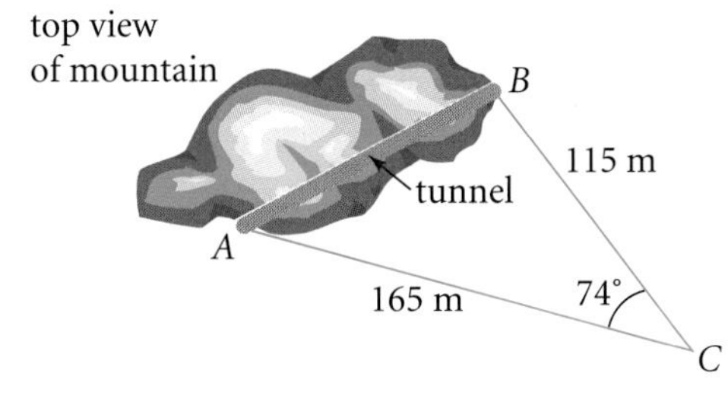

49. SPACE SCIENCE Two space-monitoring stations are located at two different points, A and B, on Earth's surface. The inscribed angle at the Earth's center is $C = 110°$. The radius of the Earth is about 3960 miles. Find the straight-line distance, AB, between the two stations.

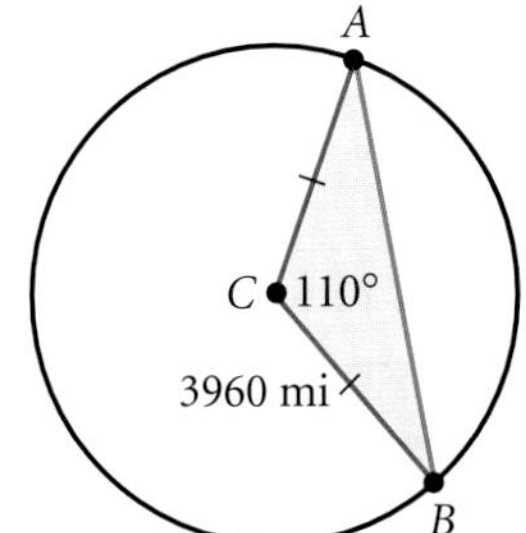

Alternative Assessment

Performance Assessment

1. **TRIANGLE AREA** For $\triangle ABC$, $a = 10$, $A = 85°$, $B = 60°$, and $C = 35°$.

   a. Sketch $\triangle ABC$ and label its angles and side.
   b. Use the law of sines to find the length of a second side of $\triangle ABC$.
   c. Given SAS information, find the area of $\triangle ABC$ by using the area formula.
   d. Using your results from parts **b** and **c**, write a formula for the area of any triangle given one side and all three angles.
   e. Given the lengths of three sides of a triangle ABC, you can use *Heron's formula* below to find the triangle's area. Verify this formula by finding the area of $\triangle ABC$.

   $$K = \sqrt{s(s-a)(s-b)(s-c)},$$

   where s is the semiperimeter, $\left(s = \frac{a+b+c}{2}\right)$

2. **FINDING HEIGHTS** The angle of elevation from point P on the ground to point S at the top of a mountain is 24°. The angle of depression from point S to point Q on the ground, which is 1350 feet closer to the mountain than P, is 61°.

   a. Draw and label a sketch of the situation.
   b. What is needed to find QS by using the law of sines? Find QS to the nearest foot.
   c. Find the height of the mountain to the nearest foot.
   d. Write a single formula for finding the height of a mountain given the same three pieces of information.

Portfolio Projects

1. **GEOMETRY** Helen wants to construct a tabletop in the shape of either a regular pentagon or a regular hexagon. She wants each side of the tabletop to have a length of at least 2 feet.

   a. Find the length of a diagonal for the pentagonal table.
   b. Find the area of the pentagonal table.
   c. Find the length of a diagonal for the hexagonal table.
   d. Find the area of the hexagonal table.
   e. Which table should Helen construct? Explain your reasoning.

2. **TRIGONOMETRIC REFLECTIONS**

   a. Sketch $y = \sin\theta$, $y = \sin(-\theta)$, and $y = -\sin\theta$ on the same coordinate plane.
      1. How is $y = \sin(-\theta)$ a reflection of the graph of $y = \sin\theta$?
      2. How is $y = -\sin\theta$ a reflection of the graph of $y = \sin\theta$?
   b. Sketch $y = \cos\theta$, $y = \cos(-\theta)$, and $y = -\cos\theta$ on the same coordinate plane. Then answer the questions in Steps 1 and 2 of part **a**.
   c. Discuss how the results from the reflections of $y = \sin\theta$ and $y = \cos\theta$ differ.

3. **PROVING IDENTITIES** Prove that each identity is true for any angle θ or any triangle ABC.

   a. $\tan 2\theta = \frac{2\tan\theta}{1-\tan^2\theta}$
   b. $\tan\frac{\theta}{2} = \frac{1-\cos\theta}{\sin\theta}$
   c. $\frac{a}{b} = \frac{\sin A}{\sin B}$
   d. $\frac{a-b}{b} = \frac{\sin A - \sin B}{\sin B}$

internetconnect

HRW The HRW Web site contains many resources to reinforce and expand your knowledge of additional trigonometric topics. This Web site also provides Internet links to other sites where you can find information and real-world data for use in research projects, reports, and activities that involve additional trigonometric topics. Visit the HRW Web site at **go.hrw.com,** and enter the keyword **MB1 CH14** to access the resources for this chapter.

College Entrance Exam Practice

QUANTITATIVE COMPARISON For Items 1–6, write
A if the quantity in Column A is greater than the quantity in Column B;
B if the quantity in Column B is greater than the quantity in Column A;
C if the quantities are equal; or
D if the relationship cannot be determined from the given information.

	Column A	Column B	Answers
1.	The period of f $f(\theta) = 2 + 2\cos 5\theta$	$f(\theta) = -3\sin\frac{\theta}{2}$	(A) (B) (C) (D) [Lesson 13.5]
2.	$\sum_{n=1}^{5} 4n$	$\sum_{n=1}^{4} 5n$	(A) (B) (C) (D) [Lesson 11.1]
3.	The number of real-number solutions $2x^2 - 3x - 3 = 0$	$4x^2 - 4x + 1 = 0$	(A) (B) (C) (D) [Lesson 5.6]
4.	$\ln x$	$\log x$	(A) (B) (C) (D) [Lesson 6.6]
5.	The given measure for 76, 78, 71, 78, 72, and 75 mean	median	(A) (B) (C) (D) [Lesson 12.1]
6.	$3x - 5y = 6$ slope	y-intercept	(A) (B) (C) (D) [Lesson 1.2]

7. Which word describes the number $\frac{1}{12}$? ***(LESSON 2.1)***
a. prime **b.** integer
c. rational **d.** irrational

8. Simplify $(x^3 - 8x^2 + 17x - 6) \div (x^2 - 5x + 2)$. ***(LESSON 7.3)***
a. $x + 3$ **b.** $x - 3$ **c.** $x + 1$ **d.** $x - 1$

9. Which equation below has a graph that opens downward? ***(LESSON 5.1)***
a. $y = 5x^2$ **b.** $y = 5 - x^2$
c. $y - x^2 = 5$ **d.** $y = x^2 - 5$

10. Which equation represents the line that has a slope of $\frac{1}{2}$ and contains the point $P(2, -2)$? ***(LESSON 1.3)***
a. $y + 2 = \frac{1}{2}(x - 2)$ **b.** $y - 2 = \frac{1}{2}(x - 2)$
c. $y - 2 = \frac{1}{2}(x + 2)$ **d.** $y + 2 = \frac{1}{2}(x + 2)$

11. Which expression represents $(a^3 - 1) - (a^3 - a^2 + 5)$ in standard form? ***(LESSON 7.1)***
a. $2a^3 + a^2 - 6$ **b.** $-a^2 + 6$
c. $a^2 - 6$ **d.** $-2a^3 + 4$

12. What is the amplitude of $y = 3 \sin(2\theta - 5)$? ***(LESSON 13.5)***

a. 1 **b.** 3 **c.** 2 **d.** 5

13. Simplify $(4 - 5i) + (-7 - 5i)$. ***(LESSON 5.6)***

a. $-(7 + i)$ **b.** $-3 - 10i$

c. $-3 + i$ **d.** -3

14. Which ellipse has a horizontal major axis that is 18 units long? ***(LESSON 9.4)***

a. $\frac{x^2}{4} + \frac{y^2}{81} = 1$ **b.** $\frac{x^2}{9} + \frac{y^2}{4} = 1$

c. $4x^2 + 81y^2 = 324$ **d.** $81x^2 + 4y^2 = 324$

15. A committee of 3 is selected from 8 eligible members. How many different committees are possible? ***(LESSON 10.3)***

a. $8!$ **b.** $3!$ **c.** $\frac{8!}{5!}$ **d.** $\frac{8!}{3!5!}$

16. Find A in $\triangle ABC$ if $a = 6$, $b = 9$, and $C = 30°$. ***(LESSON 14.2)***

a. $\approx 68.3°$ **b.** $\approx 38.3°$

c. $\approx 111.7°$ **d.** $60°$

17. Which expression is not equivalent to the others? ***(LESSON 6.4)***

a. $3 \log_5 2x$ **b.** $\log_5 2x^3$

c. $\log_5 (2x)^3$ **d.** $\log_5 8x^3$

For Items 18–19, state the property that is illustrated in each statement. All variables represent real numbers. *(LESSON 2.1)*

18. $3(x^2 - 1) = 3x^2 - 3$

19. $-4 + 4 = 0$

20. Simplify $\frac{-9x - 3}{x^2 - 11x + 18} + \frac{x + 3}{x - 9}$. ***(LESSON 8.4)***

21. Find the area of $\triangle ABC$ to the nearest tenth of a square unit if $a = 4.5$, $c = 8.3$, and $B = 55°$. ***(LESSON 14.1)***

22. Find the inverse of $f(x) = -\frac{1}{4}x + 2$. ***(LESSON 2.5)***

23. Solve the literal equation $R = \frac{S + F + P}{S + P}$ for S. ***(LESSON 1.6)***

24. Solve $\begin{cases} 3x - 4y = -14 \\ 3x + 2y = 16 \end{cases}$. ***(LESSON 3.2)***

25. Use the quadratic formula to solve $x^2 - 2x + 4 = 0$. ***(LESSON 5.6)***

26. Graph the solution of $\begin{cases} x < 2 \\ y \le 3x - 4 \end{cases}$. ***(LESSON 3.4)***

27. Simplify the complex fraction $\frac{\frac{3x}{5}}{\frac{x}{2}}$. ***(LESSON 8.3)***

28. Factor $4x^4 - 17x^2 + 4$ completely. ***(LESSON 7.3)***

29. Find the domain of $f(x) = \frac{x^2 - 4}{x - 2}$. ***(LESSON 8.2)***

FREE-RESPONSE GRID The following questions may be answered by using a free-response grid such as that commonly used by standardized-test services.

30. Solve $\frac{3x}{4} - 12 = \frac{3(x - 12)}{5}$. ***(LESSON 8.5)***

31. A coin is flipped 10 times. Find the probability of exactly 4 heads appearing. ***(LESSON 11.7)***

32. Find the coterminal angle, θ, for 255° such that $-360° < \theta < 360°$. ***(LESSON 13.2)***

33. Find the value of v if $v = \log_3 1$. ***(LESSON 6.3)***

34. Convert $\frac{3\pi}{5}$ radians to degrees. ***(LESSON 13.4)***

35. Find the final amount of a $1000 investment earning 5% interest compounded annually for 10 years. Round answer to the nearest dollar. ***(LESSON 6.2)***

36. Evaluate $\text{Cos}^{-1}(\sin 30°)$. ***(LESSON 13.6)***

37. Evaluate $\log_5 73.25$ to the nearest hundredth. ***(LESSON 6.4)***

38. Evaluate $\sum_{n=1}^{4}(8 - 5n)$. ***(LESSON 11.3)***

39. **PROBABILITY** A 6-sided number cube is rolled once. Find the probability of getting an even number *or* 1. ***(LESSON 10.4)***

40. **PROBABILITY** A coin is flipped 5 times. Find the probability of exactly 3 heads appearing. ***(LESSON 12.5)***

Keystroke Guide for Chapter 14

Essential keystroke sequences (using the model TI-82 or TI-83 graphics calculator) are presented below for all Activities and Examples found in this chapter that require or recommend the use of a graphics calculator.

 internet**connect**

Keystrokes for other models of graphics calculators are found on the HRW Web site.

LESSON 14.2

Activity
Page 896

For Steps 1 and 2, graph $y = \sin x$ and $y = \frac{1}{2}$ on the same screen for $0° \le x \le 180°$.

Use viewing window [0, 180] by [−2, 2] in degree mode.

[Y=] [SIN] [X,T,θ,n] [ENTER] (Y2=) 1 [÷] 2 [GRAPH]

Use a similar keystroke sequence for Steps 4 and 5.

LESSON 14.3

EXAMPLE 1
Page 903

Graph $y = \tan x$ and $y = \frac{\sin x}{\cos x}$ on the same screen.

Use viewing window [−360, 360] by [−10, 10] in degree mode.

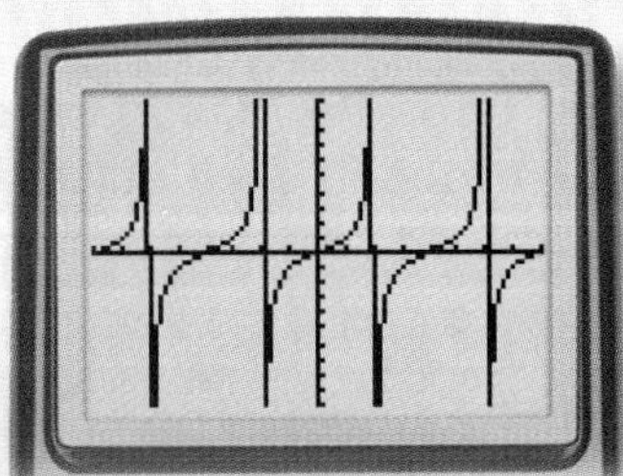

[Y=] [TAN] [X,T,θ,n] [ENTER] (Y2=) [SIN]

[X,T,θ,n] [)] [÷] [COS] [X,T,θ,n] [)] [GRAPH]

⇑ TI-82: [(]   ⇑ TI-82: [(]

EXAMPLE 3
Page 904

Graph $y = \frac{\sin^2 x}{1 - \cos x}$ and $y = 1 + \cos x$ on the same screen.

Use viewing window [−720, 720] by [−3, 3] in degree mode.

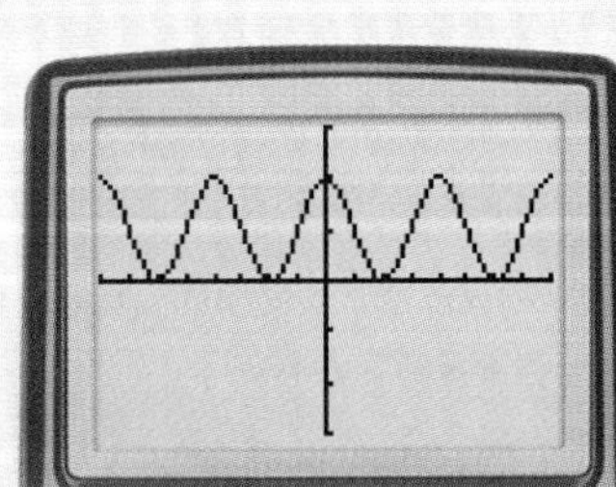

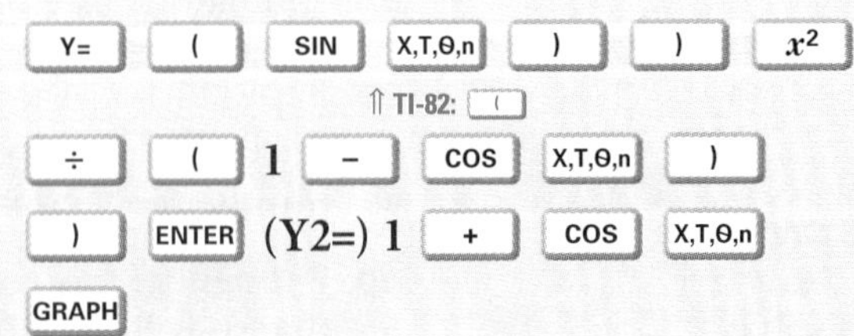

[Y=] [(] [SIN] [X,T,θ,n] [)] [)] [x^2]

⇑ TI-82: [(]

[÷] [(] 1 [−] [COS] [X,T,θ,n] [)]

[)] [ENTER] (Y2=) 1 [+] [COS] [X,T,θ,n]

[GRAPH]

Activity

Page 904

For Step 1, graph $y = (\csc x)(1 - \cos x)(1 + \cos x)$.

Use viewing window [–360, 360] by [–3, 3] in degree mode.

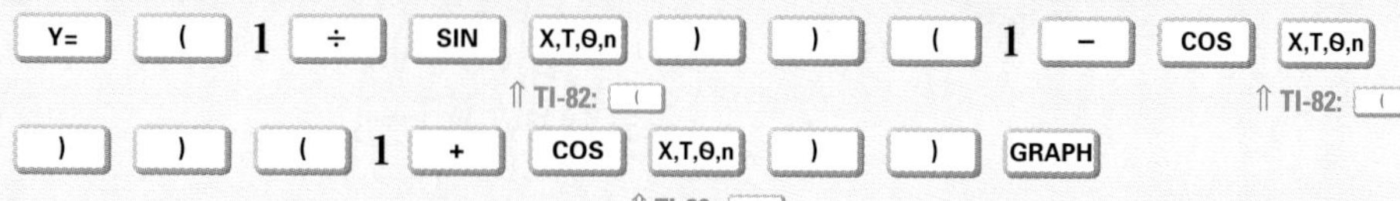

For Step 3, use the same viewing window and a similar keystroke sequence.

EXAMPLE 4

Page 905

Graph $y = \sec x - \tan x \sin x$.

Use viewing window [–360, 360] by [–3, 3] in degree mode.

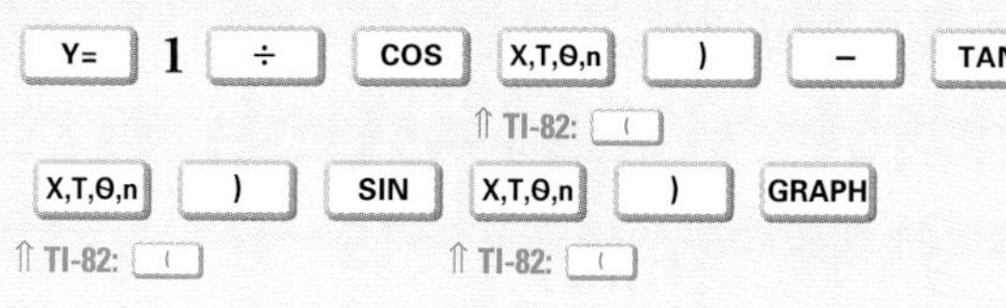

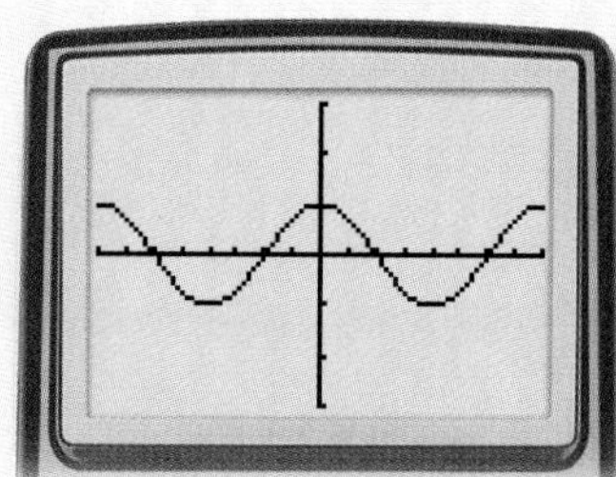

LESSON 14.4

EXAMPLE 5

Page 913

Find the product $\begin{bmatrix} \cos 30° & -\sin 30° \\ \sin 30° & \cos 30° \end{bmatrix} \begin{bmatrix} 2 & 5 & 5 & 2 \\ 1 & 1 & -1 & -1 \end{bmatrix}$.

Set the mode:

Enter the matrices:

For TI-83 Plus, press 2nd x^{-1} (MATRX) to access the matrix menu.

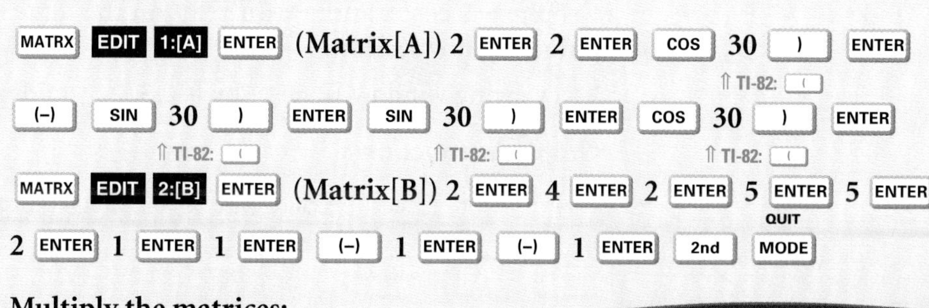

Multiply the matrices:

Page 923

Graph $y = \sin x$ and $y = 1$ on the same screen.

Use viewing window [0, 360] by [−3, 3] in degree mode.

Y= SIN X,T,θ,n ENTER (Y2=) 1 GRAPH

For Step 2 use viewing window [0, 720] by [−3, 3].

EXAMPLE 1

Page 923

Graph $y = \cos x$ and $y = \sqrt{3} - \cos x$ on the same screen, and find any points of intersection.

Use viewing window [0, 360] by [−2, 3] in degree mode.

Graph the functions:

Y= COS X,T,θ,n ENTER (Y2=) 2nd x^2 ($\sqrt{\ }$) 3) − COS X,T,θ,n GRAPH

Find any points of intersection:

2nd TRACE (CALC) 5:intersect (First curve?) ENTER (Second curve?) ENTER (Guess?) ENTER

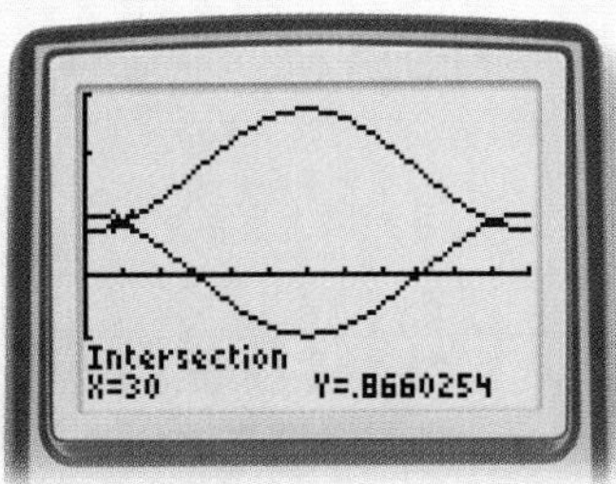

EXAMPLE 3

Page 924

Graph $y = 2\cos^2 x$ and $y = \sin x + 1$ on the same screen, and find any points of intersection.

Use viewing window [0, 360] by [−0.5, 2.5] in degree mode.

Graph the functions:

Y= 2 (COS X,T,θ,n)) x^2 ENTER (Y2=) SIN X,T,θ,n) + 1 GRAPH

⇑ TI-82: (⇑ TI-82: (

Find any points of intersection:

2nd TRACE (CALC) 5:intersect (First curve?) ENTER (Second curve?) ENTER (Guess?) ENTER

The calculator may return an error message when looking for the intersection point (270°, 0).

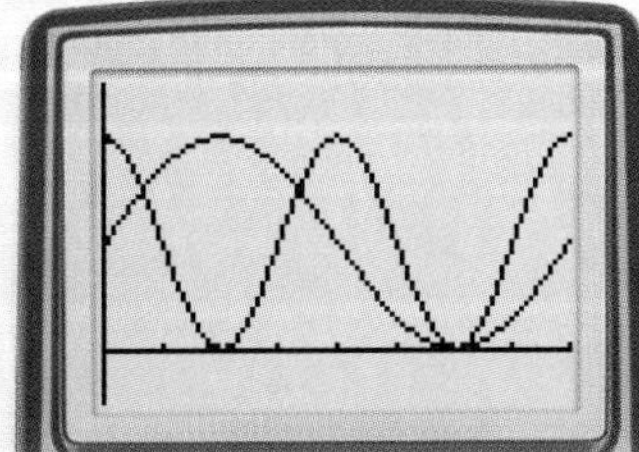

EXAMPLE 4 Graph $y = 366 \sin x - 144$ and $y = 15$ on the same screen, and find any points of intersection.

Page 925

Use viewing window [−15, 90] by [−75, 250] in degree mode.

Graph the functions:

Y= 366 SIN X,T,θ,n − 144 ENTER (Y2=) 15 GRAPH

Find any points of intersection:

2nd CALC TRACE 5:intersect (First curve?) ENTER (Second curve?) ENTER (Guess?) ENTER

Intersection
X=25.74879 Y=15

Extra Practice
Tables
Parent Functions
Selected Answers
Index

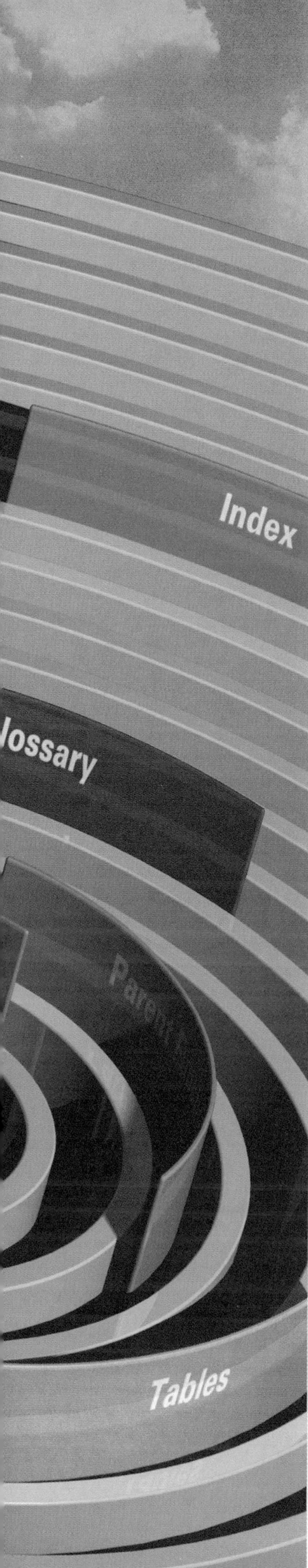

Info Bank

Extra Practice

Extra Practice

Chapter 1

LESSON 1.1

State whether each equation is a linear equation.

1. $y = 2x$ **2.** $y = -3x - 1$ **3.** $y = x + 3$ **4.** $y = \frac{3}{4}x + 1$

5. $y = 10 - x$ **6.** $y = \frac{4x}{5}$ **7.** $y = 7 + x^2$ **8.** $y = 2 - x^3$

Determine whether each table represents a linear relationship between *x* and *y*. If the relationship is linear, write the next ordered pair that would appear in the table.

9.

x	0	1	2	3
y	1	6	11	16

10.

x	−2	−1	0	1
y	4	1	0	1

11.

x	2	4	6	8
y	7	13	19	25

For each graph, make a table of values to represent the points. Does the table represent a linear relationship? Explain.

12.

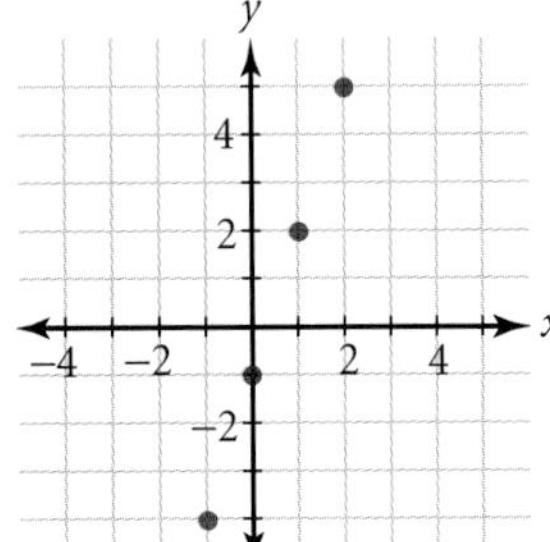

13.

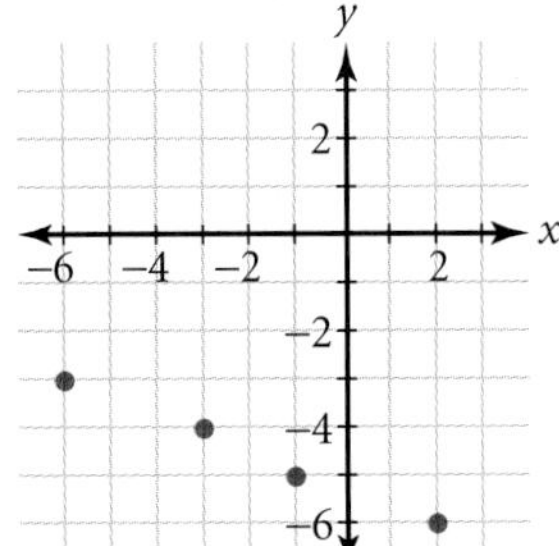

14.

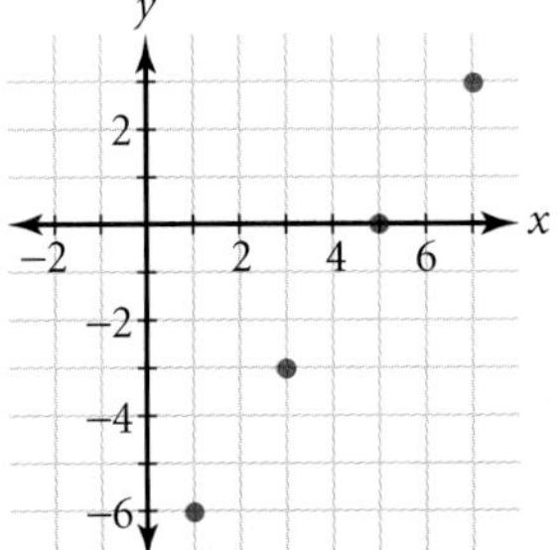

LESSON 1.2

Write an equation in slope-intercept form for the line that has the indicated slope, *m*, and *y*-intercept, *b*.

1. $m = -3, b = 6$ **2.** $m = -2, b = 0$ **3.** $m = 0, b = \frac{1}{2}$ **4.** $m = \frac{4}{5}, b = 1$

Find the slope of the line containing the indicated points.

5. (0, 0) and (−2, −8) **6.** (1, 2) and (2, 6) **7.** (−4, 5) and (1, 5)

Identify the slope, *m*, and the *y*-intercept, *b*, for each line. Then graph.

8. $x = 1.5$ **9.** $-2x + y = 1$ **10.** $3x - y = 2$ **11.** $y = -3$

Write an equation in slope-intercept form for each line.

12.

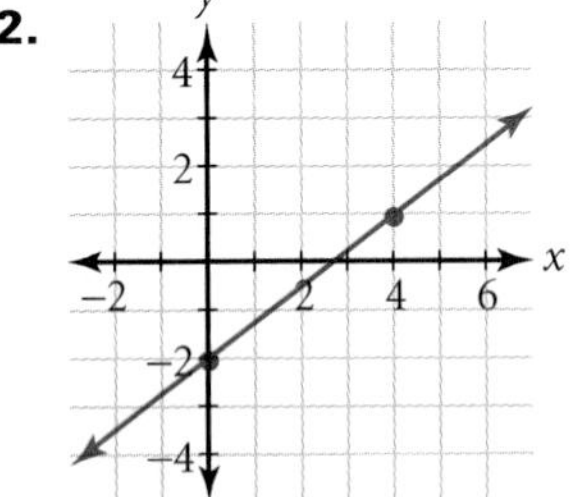

13.

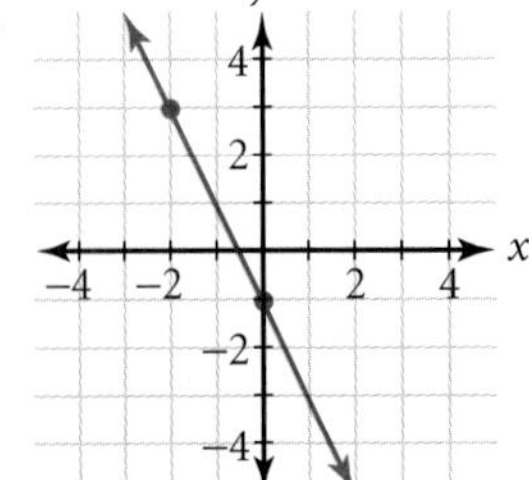

14.

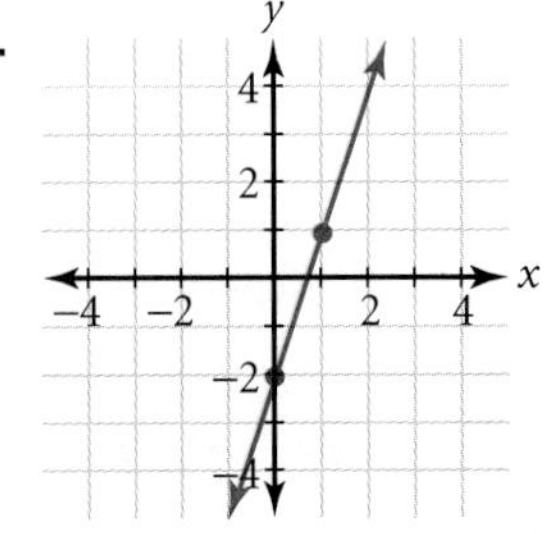

LESSON 1.3

Write an equation in slope-intercept form for the line containing the indicated points.

1. $(4, -7)$ and $(9, 3)$

2. $(3, 10)$ and $(-8, -12)$

3. $(8, -11)$ and $(13, -11)$

4. $(3, -17)$ and $(-4, 18)$

5. $(-7, -1)$ and $(5, 7)$

6. $(0, 13)$ and $(4, -11)$

Write an equation in slope-intercept form for the line that has the indicated slope, *m*, and that contains the given point.

7. $m = -8$; $(-1, -2)$

8. $m = -\frac{1}{2}$; $(4, 6)$

9. $m = -13$; $(5, 1)$

10. $m = \frac{5}{6}$; $(-12, 8)$

Write an equation in slope-intercept form for the line that contains the given point and is parallel to the given line.

11. $(0, 7)$; $y = 5x - 3$

12. $(-11, 8)$; $y = -x + 5$

13. $\left(4\frac{1}{2}, 9\right)$; $y = -2x + 15$

14. $(9, 7)$; $y = \frac{2}{3}x - 1$

15. $(-2, -3)$; $3x + 4y = 9$

16. $(-7, 2)$; $-x + 3y = 1$

Write an equation in slope-intercept form for the line that contains the given point and is perpendicular to the given line.

17. $(3, -6)$; $y = \frac{1}{2}x + 7$

18. $(4, 5)$; $y = -\frac{1}{8}x + 17$

19. $(-3, 9)$; $y = 5x + \frac{1}{4}$

20. $(0, 7)$; $x - 4y = 3$

21. $(3, -3)$; $5x + 2y = 1$

22. $(6, -4)$; $3x - y = 0.5$

LESSON 1.4

In Exercises 1–6, *y* varies directly as *x*. Find the constant of variation, and write an equation of direct variation that relates the two variables.

1. $y = 32$ when $x = 8$

2. $y = -12$ when $x = -4$

3. $y = 4.2$ when $x = 0.7$

4. $y = 65$ when $x = 13$

5. $y = -3$ when $x = 11$

6. $y = \frac{1}{4}$ when $x = \frac{1}{2}$

Solve each proportion for the indicated variable. Check your answers.

7. $\frac{5}{32} = \frac{10}{x}$

8. $\frac{w}{14} = \frac{14}{49}$

9. $\frac{0.7}{10} = \frac{21}{k}$

10. $\frac{4}{5} = \frac{t}{8}$

11. $\frac{n+1}{7} = \frac{3}{5}$

12. $\frac{3y+4}{10} = \frac{y}{5}$

13. $\frac{z+2}{7} = \frac{z}{6}$

14. $\frac{m-2}{15} = \frac{m+2}{6}$

15. $\frac{5x-3}{7} = \frac{2x}{3}$

Determine whether the values in each table are related by a direct variation. If so, write an equation for the variation. If not, explain.

16.

x	1	2	3	4	5
y	1.5	3	4.5	6	7.5

17.

x	1	2	3	4	6
y	24	12	8	6	4

18.

x	5	6	7	8	9
y	6	7.2	8.4	9.6	10.8

19.

x	−2	−1	0	1	2
y	14	7	0	−7	−14

Extra Practice

LESSON 1.5

Create a scatter plot of the data in each table. Describe the correlation. Then find an equation for the least-squares line.

1.

x	5	8	4	9	7	6	3	2	6	6	4	3	3	9
y	17	20	12	28	17	15	6	8	11	18	14	10	8	24

2.

x	1	2	2	3	4	5	6	7	8	8	4	8	9	9
y	70	55	75	72	66	58	38	45	17	19	52	15	15	10

The table lists the total weight lifted by the winners in eight weight classes of the 1996 Women's National Weightlifting Championship.

Weight class (kg)	46	50	54	59	64	70	76	83
Total lifted (kg)	140.0	127.5	167.5	167.5	192.5	185.0	197.5	200.0

3 Let x represent weight class, and let y represent the total weight lifted. Enter the data into a graphics calculator, and find an equation of the least-squares line.

4 Find the correlation coefficient, r, to the nearest tenth.

5 Suppose that there were a 68-kilogram weight class. Predict the total weight lifted by the winner.

LESSON 1.6

Solve each equation.

1. $x - 9 = -23$

2. $\frac{1}{2}x - 3 = 11$

3. $3x - 2 = 13$

4. $-3x + 5 = 19$

5. $12 - 5x = -8$

6. $\frac{3}{4}x + \frac{1}{4} = 9$

7. $\frac{9}{10}x - 17 = 19$

8. $\frac{16}{15}x + 78 = 14$

9. $\frac{5}{12}x - 12 = 48$

10. $7x + 8 = 11x$

11. $4x + 12 = 7x$

12. $9x - 42 = 3x$

13. $4x + 5 = x - 3$

14. $7x - 22 = 3x + 18$

15. $\frac{x + 3}{2} = x - 4$

16. $8\left(\frac{3}{4}x + \frac{1}{2}\right) = 5x$

17. $8x = 6x - 11$

18. $\frac{2}{3}x - 7 = 3$

19. $-3x + 5 = 5x - 3$

20. $18 = 6x + 8$

21. $x + \frac{15}{8} = \frac{3x}{2}$

22. $0.7x + 0.3x = 2x - 4$

23. $\frac{1}{2}x + 6 = x - 4$

24. $x - 7 = 3\frac{1}{2} + 2x$

Solve each literal equation for the indicated variable.

25. $S = 180(n - 2)$ for n

26. $A = \frac{1}{2}pr$ for p

27. $V = \frac{1}{3}Bh$ for h

28. $m = \frac{1}{2}(a - b)$ for a

29. $m = \frac{1}{2}(a - b)$ for b

30. $\frac{x}{a} + \frac{y}{b} = 1$ for a

31. $m = \frac{y_2 - y_1}{x_2 - x_1}$ for x_1

32. $F = \frac{W}{d}$ for d

33. $E = IR$ for R

34. $t = -0.55\left(\frac{a}{1000}\right)$ for a

35. $R = \frac{s^2}{A}$ for A

36. $S = \frac{1}{2}(a + b + c)$ for b

37. Given the equation $x = 4 + y$, use substitution to solve $3y - x = -14$ for y.

38. Given the equation $x - 2y = 8$, use substitution to solve $6y = -3x$ for x.

LESSON 1.7

Write an inequality that describes each graph.

1. −6 −4 −2 0 2 4 6

2. −2 0 2 4 6 8

3. −10 −8 −6 −4 −2 0 2

4. 0 1 2 3 4 5 6

5. −20 −18 −16 −14 −12 −10 −8

6. 30 32 34 36 38 40 42

Solve each inequality, and graph the solution on a number line.

7. $8x < 64$ **8.** $14x \leq -42$ **9.** $x + 15 > 7$

10. $-3x > -21$ **11.** $x - 9 \geq 1$ **12.** $3x - 2 \leq 13$

13. $11 - x < 7$ **14.** $6 - 7x \geq -8$ **15.** $-\frac{x}{4} \geq 3$

16. $7x - 2 < 3x + 4$ **17.** $4 - 2(x + 1) \leq -3$ **18.** $3(x - 2) + 5 \geq 7 + x$

Graph the solution of each compound inequality on a number line.

19. $x \geq -5$ *and* $x < 3$ **20.** $2x + 1 \leq 7$ *and* $-3x + 1 < -5$

21. $x + 5 \geq 2$ *and* $x - 3 < 2$ **22.** $7 - x < 4$ *or* $2x + 1 < -2$

23. $4x < -20$ *or* $5x - 2 \geq 3$ **24.** $3x - 6 < 12$ *and* $1 - 2x \leq 17$

25. $\frac{1}{3}(x + 9) \geq 4$ *or* $3 < -2x - 5$ **26.** $\frac{3}{4}(12 - 2x) \leq 0$ *or* $8 - x > 3$

LESSON 1.8

Match each statement on the left with a statement on the right.

1. $|x - 3| = -4$ **a.** $x = -1$ *or* $x = 7$

2. $|x - 3| \leq 4$ **b.** $x \geq -1$ *and* $x \leq 7$

3. $|x - 3| \geq -4$ **c.** $x \leq -1$ *or* $x \geq 7$

4. $|x - 3| = 4$ **d.** There is no solution.

5. $|x - 3| \geq 4$ **e.** All real numbers are solutions.

6. $|x - 3| \leq -4$

Solve each absolute-value equation. If the equation has no solution, write *no solution.*

7. $|x - 1| = 3$ **8.** $|x + 9| = 13$ **9.** $|x - 6| = 9$

10. $|7 + x| = 13$ **11.** $|2x - 2| = 5$ **12.** $|4x + 1| = 10$

13. $|3x| = -14$ **14.** $|3x - 5| + 7 = 4$ **15.** $|10x + 5| - 7 = 8$

16. $3 = \left|\frac{1}{5}(2 - x)\right|$ **17.** $\left|\frac{2}{3}x\right| = \frac{1}{12}$ **18.** $|1 - x| = 8$

Solve each absolute-value inequality. Graph the solution on a number line.

19. $|2x| < 8$ **20.** $|x - 1| \geq 4$ **21.** $|2 - x| \leq 6$

22. $|3x + 5| > 2$ **23.** $|5x - 10| > 0$ **24.** $|6x + 3| \leq -7$

25. $|6 - 12x| \leq -7$ **26.** $|4x + 3| > 5$ **27.** $|6 - 3x| \leq 2$

28. $|2x - 6| < 4$ **29.** $|3x - 7| \geq 2$ **30.** $|4x + 3| - 2 > 4$

Extra Practice

Chapter 2

LESSON 2.1

Classify each number in as many ways as possible.

1. 47
2. 12.86
3. $\sqrt{7}$
4. $-\sqrt{100}$
5. $\frac{7}{9}$
6. $0.\overline{456}$
7. 123.45678 . . .
8. 12.888888 . . .

State the property that is illustrated in each statement. All variables represent real numbers.

9. $z + 1.09 = 1.09 + z$
10. $152 + 0 = 152$
11. $23(x + 34) = 23x + 23(34)$
12. $-7 + (19 + 2) = (-7 + 19) + 2$
13. $-42y = y(-42)$
14. $\frac{12}{y} \cdot \frac{y}{12} = 1$, where $y \neq 0$
15. $1 \cdot 77 = 77$
16. $422 + (-422) = 0$

Evaluate each expression by using the order of operations.

17. $24 \div 8 + 4$
18. $2 + 7^2$
19. $3(11 + 2^2) + 1$
20. $(29 + 7) + 12 \div 6$
21. $8 + 2 \times 5 + 7$
22. $1 + 2 \times 7 - 5$
23. $\frac{15 + 10}{5} - 16 \div 4$
24. $\frac{7^2 - 1}{3 + 5}$
25. $16 \times 2 \div (1 - 5)$
26. $1 - \frac{4}{2 \cdot 7 + 4}$
27. $\frac{13 - 2 \cdot 6}{5 + 2 \cdot 3}$
28. $3 + \frac{4(3 - 1)}{8}$
29. $\frac{5}{8} + \frac{6}{2(7 + 1)}$
30. $\frac{2(7 - 3)}{3(4 + 5)}$
31. $20 \cdot 9 + \frac{8 - 3}{5}$

LESSON 2.2

Evaluate each expression.

1. 12^1
2. $(-27)^0$
3. 5^{-1}
4. $\left(\frac{4}{5}\right)^{-2}$
5. $\left(\frac{1}{3}\right)^{-2}$
6. $\left(\frac{2}{3}\right)^{-4}$
7. $8^{\frac{1}{3}}$
8. $\left(\frac{1}{8}\right)^{-3}$
9. $81^{\frac{3}{4}}$
10. $27^{\frac{2}{3}}$
11. $\left(100^{\frac{2}{3}}\right)^{\frac{3}{4}}$
12. $125^{\frac{1}{3}}$

Simplify each expression, assuming that no variable equals zero. Write your answer with positive exponents only.

13. z^5z^{-3}
14. $\left(\frac{a^{\frac{-2}{3}}}{b^8}\right)^{-2}$
15. $3b^3 \cdot b^4 \cdot b^{-2}$
16. $\left(\frac{9z^4}{16w^8}\right)^{-2}$
17. $2xy(-3x^2y^3)$
18. $(-6ab^2c^5)^2$
19. $\frac{k^7}{k^5}$
20. $\frac{n^{-3}}{n^4}$
21. $\left(\frac{3x^{-4}}{y^3}\right)^2$
22. $(x^{-1}y^{-2}z^3)^{-2}(x^2y^{-4}z^6)$
23. $(a^{-3}b^{-4})^{-2}(a^9b^{-7})^0$
24. $\left(\frac{24x^4y^{-5}}{-4x^{-2}y^{-1}}\right)^{-3}$
25. $\frac{(x^3y^2)^{-2}}{x^2y^4}$
26. $\left(\frac{a^{-3}}{b^{-5}}\right)^{-2}\left(\frac{b^3}{a^2}\right)^{-1}$
27. $\left(\frac{5c^{-2}}{z^3}\right)^2\left(\frac{c^3z^3}{x}\right)^{-2}$

LESSON 2.3

State whether each relation represents a function. Explain.

1.

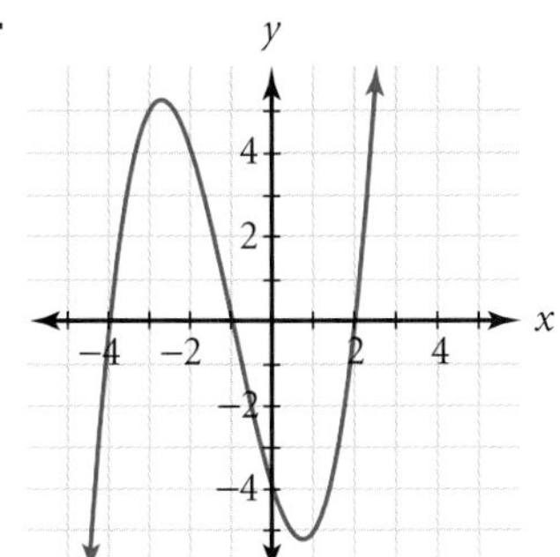

2.

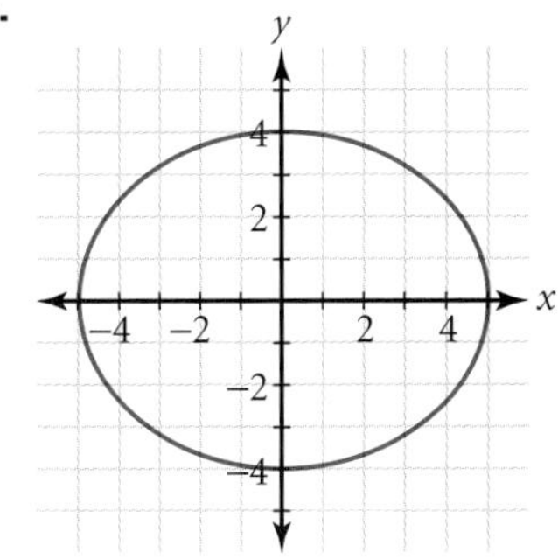

3.

x	y
−2	8
−2	7
−1	6
0	5

4. $\{(32, 1), (48, 15), (56, 19)\}$ **5.** $\{(-8, 25), (-8, 24), (-8, 23)\}$ **6.** $\{(7, 8), (9, 10), (11, 12)\}$

State the domain and range of each function.

7. $\{(-2, 8), (3, 13)\}$

8. $\{(0, 1), (1, 4), (2, 7), (3, 10)\}$

9. $\{(-4, 16), (0, 0), (2, 4)(4, 16)\}$

10. $\{(1.1, 5), (2.2, 10), (3.3, 15), (4.4, 20)\}$

Evaluate each function for the given values of *x*.

11. $f(x) = 1 - 2x$ for $x = -3$ and $x = 1$

12. $f(x) = \frac{x-1}{4}$ for $x = 7$ and $x = -3$

13. $f(x) = 10x - 7$ for $x = -1$ and $x = 0$

14. $f(x) = x^2 + 2x + 1$ for $x = 3$ and $x = 4$

15. $f(x) = -\frac{3x}{5}$ for $x = 10$ and $x = -2$

16. $f(x) = -2x^2 - x$ for $x = -3$ and $x = \frac{1}{4}$

LESSON 2.4

Let $f(x) = x^2$ and $g(x) = 2x - 1$. Find each new function, and state any domain restrictions.

1. $f + g$ **2.** $f - g$ **3.** $g - f$

4. $f \cdot g$ **5.** $\frac{f}{g}$ **6.** $\frac{g}{f}$

Let $f(x) = -2x^2$ and $g(x) = x + 1$. Find each new function, and state any domain restrictions.

7. $f + g$ **8.** $f - g$ **9.** $g - f$

10. $f \cdot g$ **11.** $\frac{f}{g}$ **12.** $\frac{g}{f}$

Find $f \circ g$ and $g \circ f$.

13. $f(x) = 4x$ and $g(x) = x^2 - 2$

14. $f(x) = x^2 - 3x$ and $g(x) = 2x$

15. $f(x) = -3x$ and $g(x) = 2x^2 - 3x$

16. $f(x) = \frac{1}{3}x$ and $g(x) = -9x^2$

Let $f(x) = 3x$, $g(x) = -2x^2$, and $h(x) = x^2 - 1$. Evaluate each composite function.

17. $(f \circ g)(3)$ **18.** $(f \circ h)(2)$ **19.** $(g \circ f)(1)$

20. $(h \circ f)(0)$ **21.** $(f \circ f)(1)$ **22.** $(h \circ g)(-2)$

LESSON 2.5

Find the inverse of each relation. State whether the relation is a function. State whether the inverse is a function.

1. $\{(1, 2), (2, 2), (3, 2), (4, 2)\}$ **2.** $\{(1, 0), (1, 2), (4, 3), (4, -2)\}$

3. $\{(1, 6), (2, 9), (3, 12), (4, 19)\}$ **4.** $\{(-2, 9), (-1, 8), (0, 7), (1, 6)\}$

For each function, find an equation for the inverse. Then use composition to verify that the equation you wrote is the inverse.

5. $f(x) = 10x - 6$ **6.** $g(x) = -6x + 5$ **7.** $h(x) = 0.5x + 2.5$

8. $g(x) = 9.5 - x$ **9.** $h(x) = \frac{x-2}{6}$ **10.** $f(x) = 14.4x$

Graph each function, and use the horizontal-line test to determine whether the inverse is a function.

11 $f(x) = 10x - 6$ **12** $h(x) = 1 - 2x^2$ **13** $g(x) = \frac{1}{2}x + 4$

14 $g(x) = x^3 + 1$ **15** $f(x) = \frac{1}{x}$ **16** $f(x) = \frac{1}{x^2}$

LESSON 2.6

Graph each function.

1. $g(x) = \begin{cases} x & \text{if } x \leq 0 \\ -x & \text{if } x > 0 \end{cases}$ **2.** $f(x) = \begin{cases} -2x + 1 & \text{if } x \leq 2 \\ 4x + 1 & \text{if } x > 2 \end{cases}$ **3.** $h(x) = \begin{cases} 9 & \text{if } x < -3 \\ x^2 & \text{if } -3 \leq x \leq 3 \\ 9 & \text{if } x > 3 \end{cases}$

4. $g(x) = |x| - 2$ **5.** $f(x) = \lceil x \rceil + 1$ **6.** $g(x) = -[x]$

Write the piecewise function represented by each graph.

7.

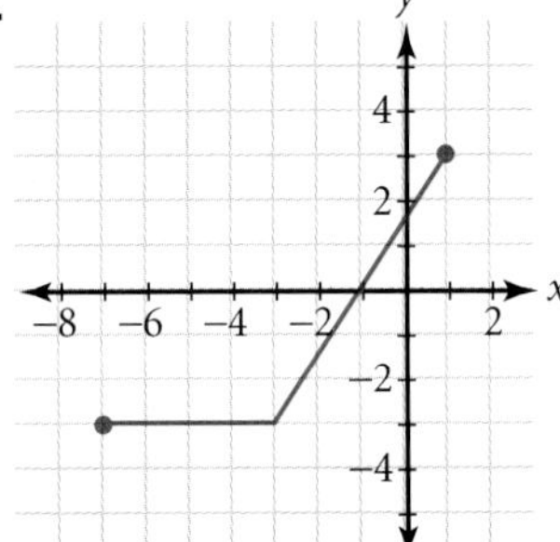

8.

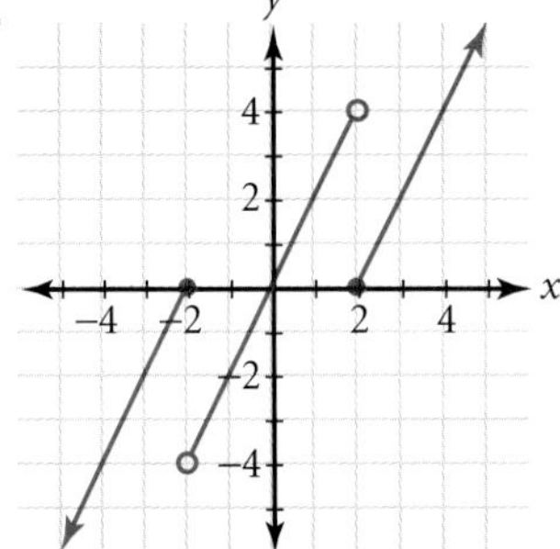

9.

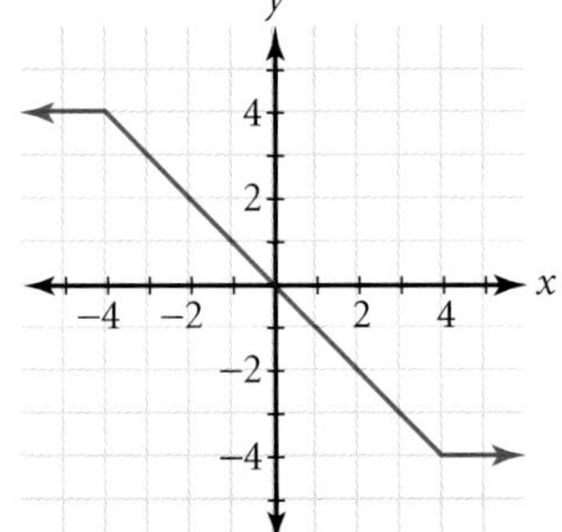

10.

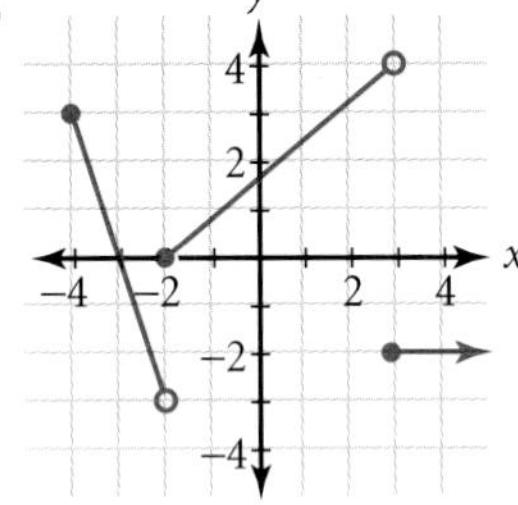

11.

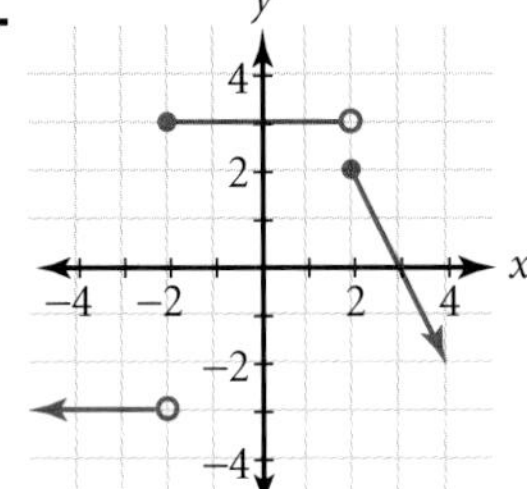

12.

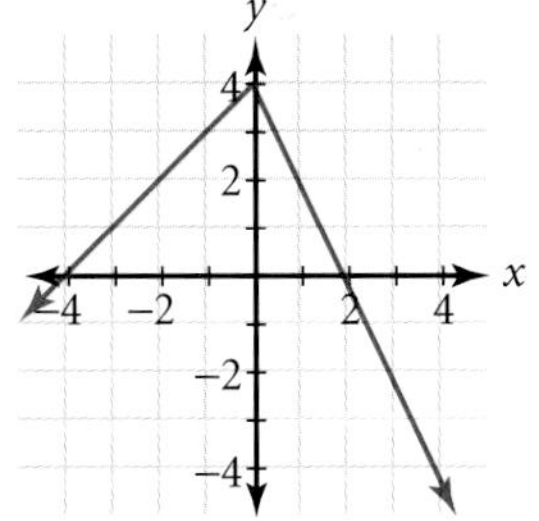

Evaluate.

13. $\lceil 14.07 \rceil$ **14.** $[14.07]$ **15.** $\lceil -8.65 \rceil$ **16.** $[72.4] + |-6|$

17. $\lceil 23.4 \rceil + [23.4]$ **18.** $[12.6] - [9.2]$ **19.** $|-12| + |12|$ **20.** $\lceil -7 \rceil - |-7|$

LESSON 2.7

Identify each transformation from the parent function $f(x) = x^4$ to g.

1. $g(x) = 8x^4$ **2.** $g(x) = (x + 11)^4$ **3.** $g(x) = -x^4$

4. $g(x) = (-6x)^4$ **5.** $g(x) = x^4 - 16$ **6.** $g(x) = x^4 + 5$

7. $g(x) = (-x)^4 + 13$ **8.** $g(x) = 7(x - 4)^4$ **9.** $g(x) = 2(x + 3)^4$

Identify each transformation from the parent function $f(x) = |x|$ to g.

10. $g(x) = |34x|$ **11.** $g(x) = |x - 19|$ **12.** $g(x) = |x| - 19$

13. $g(x) = 2|3x|$ **14.** $g(x) = \left|\frac{1}{3}x\right|$ **15.** $g(x) = 24|x| + 9$

Write a function g for the graph described.

16. the graph of $f(x) = x^2$ translated 18 units down

17. the graph of $f(x) = |x|$ vertically stretched by a factor of 10

18. the graph of $f(x) = \sqrt{x}$ reflected across the x-axis

19. the graph of $f(x) = 21x + 17$ reflected across the y-axis

20. the graph of $f(x) = x^2$ horizontally stretched by a factor of 6

21. the graph of $f(x) = x^2$ translated 3.5 units to the left

22. the graph of $f(x) = x^3$ translated 11 units up

23. the graph of $f(x) = |x|$ horizontally compressed by a factor of $\frac{1}{3}$

Chapter 3

LESSON 3.1

Graph and classify each system. Then find the solution from the graph.

1 $\begin{cases} y = 7x + 8 \\ y = 3x \end{cases}$ **2** $\begin{cases} 3x - 2y = 9 \\ 2y - 3x = 6 \end{cases}$ **3** $\begin{cases} 2x + y = -1 \\ 2y = -4x - 2 \end{cases}$

4 $\begin{cases} 4x + 5y = 2 \\ x + y = 1 \end{cases}$ **5** $\begin{cases} x - 2y = 1 \\ 2x - 5y = -1 \end{cases}$ **6** $\begin{cases} 4x - y = 5 \\ y = 4x + 3 \end{cases}$

7 $\begin{cases} 5x + 2y = 6 \\ x - y = -3 \end{cases}$ **8** $\begin{cases} 3x - 2y = -2 \\ x + 2y = -6 \end{cases}$ **9** $\begin{cases} 2x - y = 5 \\ 3x + 2y = 4 \end{cases}$

10 $\begin{cases} y - x = 1 \\ 2x + y = -5 \end{cases}$ **11** $\begin{cases} y - 2x = -1 \\ x + 3y = 4 \end{cases}$ **12** $\begin{cases} 2x + 3y = -4 \\ y = \frac{1}{2}x + 1 \end{cases}$

Use substitution to solve each system.

13. $\begin{cases} y = x - 13 \\ 2x + 3y = 1 \end{cases}$ **14.** $\begin{cases} x + y = 12 \\ x - y = 8 \end{cases}$ **15.** $\begin{cases} y = 2x - 7 \\ x + y = 5 \end{cases}$

16. $\begin{cases} y = \frac{1}{2}x - 3 \\ x = y + 1 \end{cases}$ **17.** $\begin{cases} 6x - 2y = 0 \\ x - y = 12 \end{cases}$ **18.** $\begin{cases} \frac{2}{3}x + \frac{1}{2}y = 2 \\ x - y = 10 \end{cases}$

19. $\begin{cases} y = 4x - 9 \\ y = 3x + 5 \end{cases}$ **20.** $\begin{cases} 2x - y = -1 \\ x + y = -17 \end{cases}$ **21.** $\begin{cases} x + 3y = 12 \\ x - 2y = -8 \end{cases}$

22. $\begin{cases} 2x + 5y + z = -4 \\ 4y + z = 0 \\ z = 8 \end{cases}$ **23.** $\begin{cases} x - 2y + 3z = 9 \\ x + y = -3 \\ x = -2 \end{cases}$ **24.** $\begin{cases} x + y + z = 10 \\ x + z = 8 \\ z = 5 \end{cases}$

LESSON 3.2

Use elimination to solve each system. Check your solution.

1. $\begin{cases} 13x - 2y = 10 \\ 8x + y = 24 \end{cases}$

2. $\begin{cases} 7x - y = 5 \\ 3x + y = 15 \end{cases}$

3. $\begin{cases} -2x - y = 7 \\ x - 3y = 14 \end{cases}$

4. $\begin{cases} 3x - 4y = 12 \\ 8y - 6x = -24 \end{cases}$

5. $\begin{cases} \frac{1}{2}x - y = 5 \\ x + 2y = -2 \end{cases}$

6. $\begin{cases} 7x - 4y = -9 \\ 3x + 2y = -15 \end{cases}$

7. $\begin{cases} 7x - 3y = 5 \\ 3y - 7x = 8 \end{cases}$

8. $\begin{cases} \frac{3}{4}x + \frac{1}{2}y = 11 \\ 3x - y = 14 \end{cases}$

9. $\begin{cases} 2x + 11y = 18 \\ 5x + 3y = -4 \end{cases}$

Use any method to solve each system. Check your solution.

10. $\begin{cases} y = 12x - 3 \\ 4x - y = -1 \end{cases}$

11. $\begin{cases} 2x + 5y = 43 \\ 7x - y = -16 \end{cases}$

12. $\begin{cases} 2x + y = -3 \\ 2x - y = -17 \end{cases}$

13. $\begin{cases} -3x + 2y = 1 \\ 4y - 6x = 2 \end{cases}$

14. $\begin{cases} y = 4x - 2 \\ y = 2x + 8 \end{cases}$

15. $\begin{cases} \frac{3}{4}x - y = 2 \\ 3x - 4y = 3 \end{cases}$

16. $\begin{cases} 9x + 3y = -3 \\ y - x = 11 \end{cases}$

17. $\begin{cases} 5y - 7x = -13 \\ 2x + 3y = 17 \end{cases}$

18. $\begin{cases} 17 - 5y = 3x \\ x + y = 5 \end{cases}$

LESSON 3.3

Graph each linear inequality.

1. $y < 2x - 4$

2. $y \geq -x + 3$

3. $y \leq 4x - 1$

4. $y > 4x + 4$

5. $-y \geq -3x$

6. $-y < 3x$

7. $x + 2y \leq 5$

8. $2x + y > -1$

9. $x + 4y < 8$

10. $3x + 2y \leq 6$

11. $5x - y > 6$

12. $\frac{2}{3}x + y \geq -2$

13. $x \geq -3$

14. $y < 0$

15. $x > 2$

16. $x + 5 < 0$

17. $-\frac{1}{2}y \leq 3$

18. $-\frac{2}{3}y \leq -4$

Write an inequality for each graph.

19.

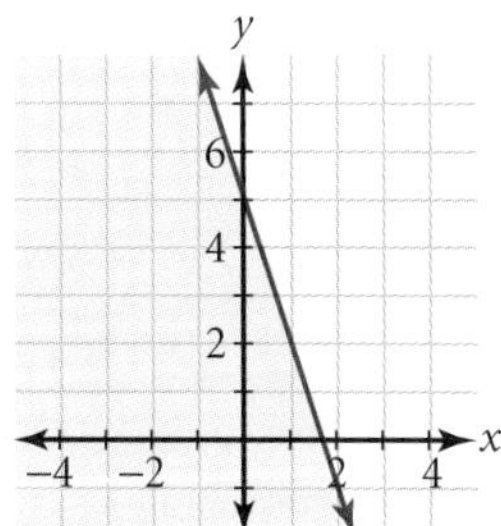

20.

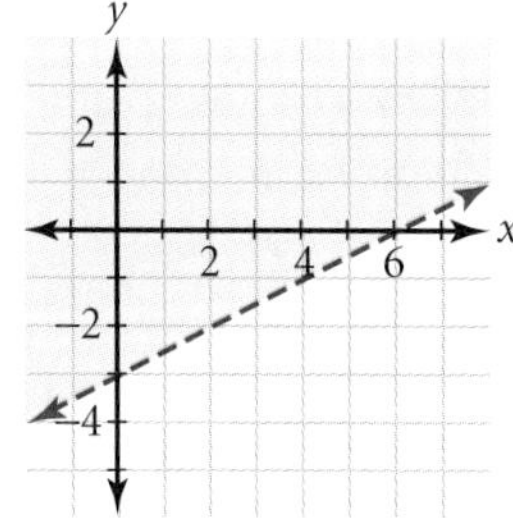

21.

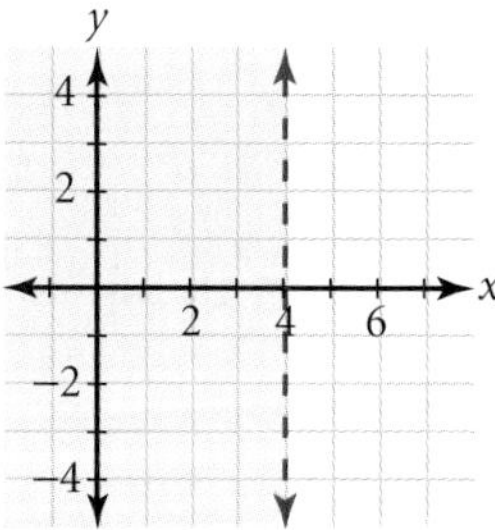

22.

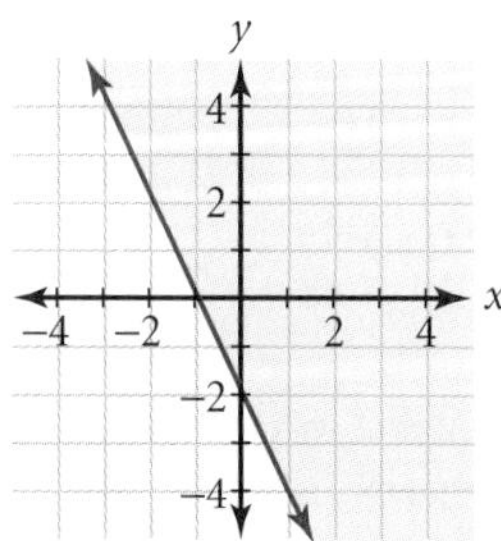

23.

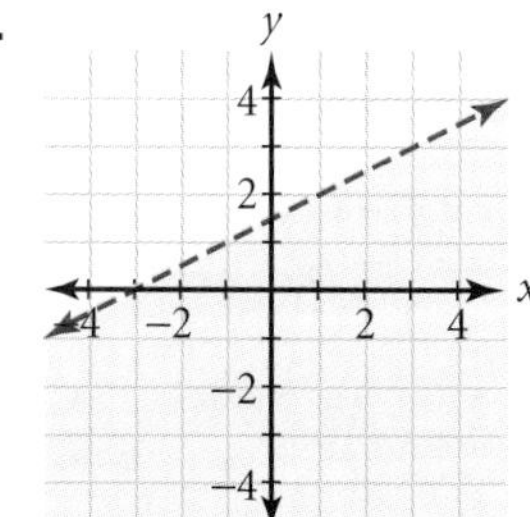

24.

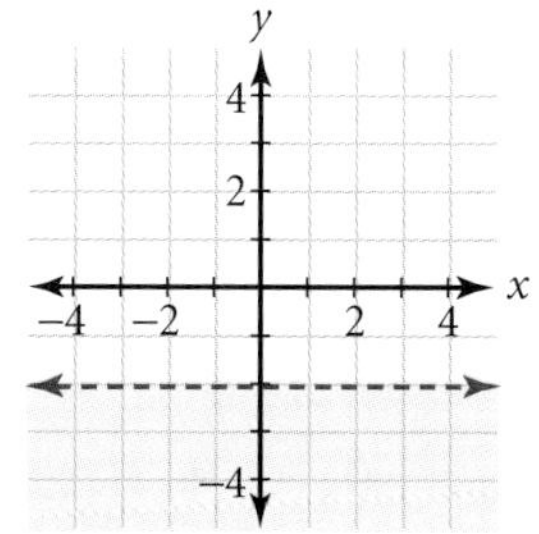

LESSON 3.4

Graph each compound inequality in a coordinate plane.

1. $-3 \le x \le 0$ **2.** $-4 < x < -1$ **3.** $-6 < y < -1$

4. $-2 \le y \le 4$ **5.** $2 \le x < 5$ **6.** $1 < y \le 4$

Graph each system of linear inequalities.

7. $\begin{cases} y < 3 \\ y \ge 2x - 1 \end{cases}$ **8.** $\begin{cases} x \le 2 \\ y > x \end{cases}$ **9.** $\begin{cases} y < 5 - x \\ y > 2x + 1 \end{cases}$

10. $\begin{cases} x > 1 \\ y \le 4 \\ y < 2x + 1 \end{cases}$ **11.** $\begin{cases} x > 0 \\ y < -x + 5 \\ y > x - 5 \end{cases}$ **12.** $\begin{cases} x \ge 2 \\ y \ge 0 \\ y \ge -x + 3 \\ y \le x + 1 \end{cases}$

Write the system of inequalities whose solution is graphed. Assume that each vertex has integer coordinates.

13.

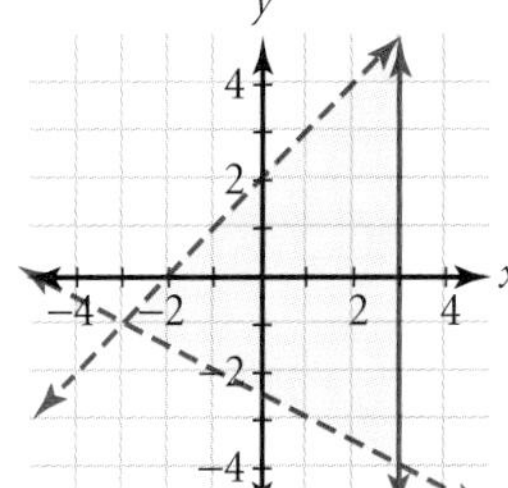

14.

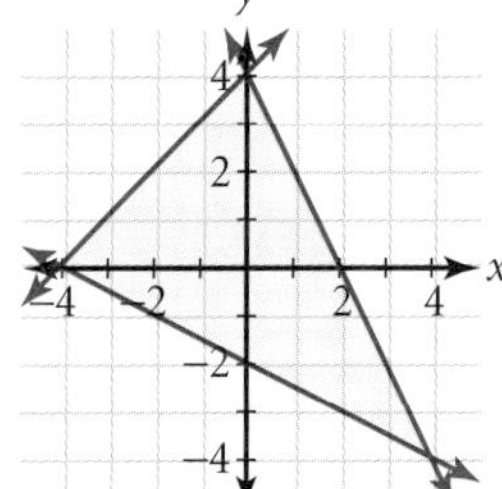

15.

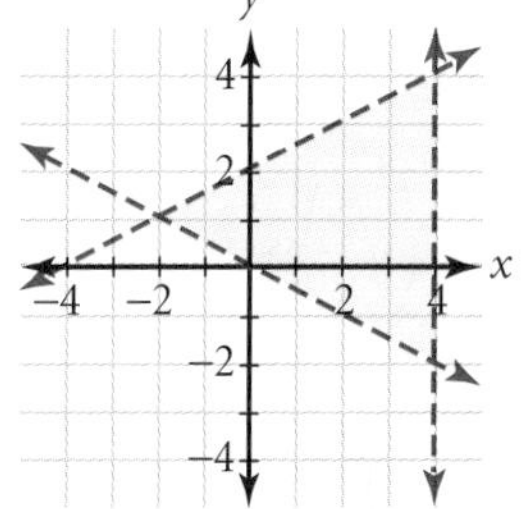

LESSON 3.5

Graph the feasible region for each set of constraints.

1. $\begin{cases} x + y \le 5 \\ 2x + y \le 9 \\ x \ge 0 \\ y \ge 0 \end{cases}$ **2.** $\begin{cases} 2x + 3y \le 15 \\ x - y \le 4 \\ x \ge 0 \\ y \ge 0 \end{cases}$ **3.** $\begin{cases} y \le \frac{1}{2}x + 4 \\ y \ge \frac{1}{2}x - 2 \\ 0 \le x < 6 \end{cases}$

The feasible region for a set of constraints has vertices at (0, 0), (60, 0), (60, 30), and (10, 50). Given this feasible region, find the maximum and minimum values of each objective function.

4. $C = 100x + 25y$ **5.** $P = 40x + 65y$

Find the maximum and minimum values, if they exist, of each objective function for the given constraints.

6. $P = 5x + 2y$
Constraints:
$\begin{cases} x + y \le 7 \\ x - y \le 5 \\ x \ge 0 \\ y \ge 0 \end{cases}$

7. $P = 10x + y$
Constraints:
$\begin{cases} 5x + 2y \le 20 \\ x - y \le 4 \\ x \ge 0 \\ y \ge 0 \end{cases}$

8. $E = 4x + 5y$
Constraints:
$\begin{cases} x + 2y \ge 6 \\ x + 2y \le 12 \\ x \ge 0 \\ y \ge 0 \end{cases}$

LESSON 3.6

Graph each pair of parametric equations for the given interval of *t*.

1. $\begin{cases} x(t) = t + 4 \\ y(t) = t - 3 \end{cases}$ for $-4 \le t \le 4$

2. $\begin{cases} x(t) = -4t \\ y(t) = t + 2 \end{cases}$ for $-3 \le t \le 3$

3. $\begin{cases} x(t) = 2t + 1 \\ y(t) = t - 4 \end{cases}$ for $-3 \le t \le 3$

4. $\begin{cases} x(t) = 2 - t \\ y(t) = \frac{1}{2}t + 1 \end{cases}$ for $-4 \le t \le 4$

Write each pair of parametric equations as a single equation in *x* and *y*.

5. $\begin{cases} x(t) = 2 - t \\ y(t) = 3 + t \end{cases}$

6. $\begin{cases} x(t) = t + 4 \\ y(t) = 1 - 2t \end{cases}$

7. $\begin{cases} x(t) = 4 - t \\ y(t) = t + 1 \end{cases}$

8. $\begin{cases} x(t) = 4t \\ y(t) = 3t - 1 \end{cases}$

9. $\begin{cases} x(t) = 2t \\ y(t) = \frac{t}{3} \end{cases}$

10. $\begin{cases} x(t) = 3t \\ y(t) = t^2 \end{cases}$

Graph the function represented by each pair of parametric equations. Then graph its inverse in the same coordinate plane.

11. $\begin{cases} x(t) = t^2 - 4 \\ y(t) = t \end{cases}$

12. $\begin{cases} x(t) = t^2 \\ y(t) = t - 4 \end{cases}$

13. $\begin{cases} x(t) = t^2 + 2 \\ y(t) = 1 - t \end{cases}$

14. $\begin{cases} x(t) = 2 - t^2 \\ y(t) = t + 1 \end{cases}$

15. $\begin{cases} x(t) = t^2 + 3t - 1 \\ y(t) = t + 2 \end{cases}$

16. $\begin{cases} x(t) = t^2 - 4t + 2 \\ y(t) = 1 - t \end{cases}$

Chapter 4

LESSON 4.1

For Exercises 1–14, let $A = \begin{bmatrix} 2 & 3 & -2 \\ 1 & 4 & 5 \\ 0 & 1 & 7 \end{bmatrix}$, $B = \begin{bmatrix} -3 & -2 & 1 \\ 0 & 5 & 5 \\ 1 & 2 & -1 \end{bmatrix}$, **and** $C = \begin{bmatrix} 8 & 0 & 1 \\ -6 & 4 & 3 \end{bmatrix}$.

Give the dimensions of each matrix.

1. A **2.** B **3.** C

Give the entry at the indicated address in matrix *A*, *B*, or *C*.

4. a_{13} **5.** c_{21} **6.** b_{31}

Perform the indicated matrix operations. If it is not possible, explain why.

7. $-A$ **8.** $A + B$ **9.** $-2C$ **10.** $B - A$

11. $A + C$ **12.** $2A - B$ **13.** $2B + A$ **14.** $4C$

Solve for *x* and *y*.

15. $\begin{bmatrix} x+3 & -3 \\ 2 & 3y+1 \end{bmatrix} = \begin{bmatrix} 10 & -3 \\ 2 & 10 \end{bmatrix}$

16. $\begin{bmatrix} -4 & 21 \\ -4y-3 & 1 \end{bmatrix} = \begin{bmatrix} -4 & -2x+5 \\ -19 & 1 \end{bmatrix}$

17. Quadrilateral $ABCD$ has vertices at $A(0, 0)$, $B(1, 4)$, $C(4, 2)$, and $D(2, 0)$.
- **a.** Represent quadrilateral $ABCD$ in a matrix called Q.
- **b.** Find $-2Q$.
- **c.** Sketch quadrilateral $ABCD$ and its image, $A'B'C'D'$, represented by $-2Q$. Describe the transformation.

LESSON 4.2

Find each product, if it exists.

1. $\begin{bmatrix} 2 & 4 & 3 \end{bmatrix}\begin{bmatrix} -4 \\ 0 \\ 6 \end{bmatrix}$

2. $\begin{bmatrix} -2 & -1 \\ 0 & 4 \\ 0 & -4 \end{bmatrix}\begin{bmatrix} 8 \\ 0 \\ 12 \end{bmatrix}$

3. $\begin{bmatrix} -6 & 2 \\ 4 & 0 \end{bmatrix}\begin{bmatrix} 3 & 2 \\ 1 & -1 \end{bmatrix}$

4. $\begin{bmatrix} -7 & 2 \\ 2 & 3 \end{bmatrix}\begin{bmatrix} 8 & -1 & 2 \\ 3 & 2 & 4 \\ -3 & 5 & 1 \end{bmatrix}$

5. $\begin{bmatrix} -3 & -3 & 7 \end{bmatrix}\begin{bmatrix} 9 & 1 \\ 0 & 3 \\ 3 & 5 \end{bmatrix}$

6. $\begin{bmatrix} 2 & 1 & 0 & 3 \end{bmatrix}\begin{bmatrix} -5 & 4 \\ 4 & 9 \\ 2 & 7 \\ -3 & -6 \end{bmatrix}$

7. $\begin{bmatrix} 1 & 4 \\ 2 & 3 \\ -3 & -3 \end{bmatrix}\begin{bmatrix} -5 & 3 & 4 \\ 1 & 1 & 0 \end{bmatrix}$

8. $\begin{bmatrix} 1 & 0 & 4 \\ -2 & 2 & 3 \end{bmatrix}\begin{bmatrix} 6 \\ 2 \\ 5 \end{bmatrix}$

9. $\begin{bmatrix} 9 & 4 & 1 \end{bmatrix}\begin{bmatrix} -5 & 1 \\ 0.5 & 4 \\ 2 & 1 \end{bmatrix}$

10. Triangle DEF has vertices at $D(-2, 4)$, $E(4, 0)$, and $F(0, -4)$.

a. Represent $\triangle DEF$ in a matrix called T.

b. Multiply T by the transformation matrix $S = \begin{bmatrix} \frac{3}{4} & 0 \\ 0 & \frac{3}{4} \end{bmatrix}$.

c. Sketch $\triangle DEF$ and its image, $\triangle D'E'F'$, represented by ST. Describe the transformation.

LESSON 4.3

Determine whether each pair of matrices are inverses of each other.

1. $\begin{bmatrix} 5 & -4 \\ 1 & 6 \end{bmatrix}$ and $\begin{bmatrix} -5 & 4 \\ -1 & 6 \end{bmatrix}$

2. $\begin{bmatrix} 2 & 4 \\ 0 & -3 \end{bmatrix}$ and $\begin{bmatrix} \frac{1}{2} & \frac{2}{3} \\ 0 & -\frac{1}{3} \end{bmatrix}$

3. $\begin{bmatrix} 2 & -3 \\ -1 & 2 \end{bmatrix}$ and $\begin{bmatrix} 2 & 3 \\ 1 & 2 \end{bmatrix}$

4. $\begin{bmatrix} 3 & 2 \\ 5 & 4 \end{bmatrix}$ and $\begin{bmatrix} 2 & -1 \\ -2.5 & 1.5 \end{bmatrix}$

Find the determinant, and state whether each matrix has an inverse.

5. $\begin{bmatrix} 5 & 3 \\ 2 & 1 \end{bmatrix}$

6. $\begin{bmatrix} 4 & 2 \\ 3 & 2 \end{bmatrix}$

7. $\begin{bmatrix} 4 & 2 \\ 6 & 3 \end{bmatrix}$

8. $\begin{bmatrix} -3 & 1 \\ 7 & 4 \end{bmatrix}$

9. $\begin{bmatrix} \frac{1}{2} & -\frac{1}{4} \\ \frac{3}{4} & \frac{5}{2} \end{bmatrix}$

10. $\begin{bmatrix} \frac{2}{3} & -\frac{3}{4} \\ \frac{1}{3} & -5 \end{bmatrix}$

Find the inverse matrix, if it exists. Round entries to the nearest hundredth, if necessary. If the inverse matrix does not exist, write *no inverse*.

11 $\begin{bmatrix} 5 & 8 \\ 2 & 3 \end{bmatrix}$

12 $\begin{bmatrix} 2.5 & 5 \\ 2 & 4 \end{bmatrix}$

13 $\begin{bmatrix} 8 & 3 \\ 4 & 2 \end{bmatrix}$

14 $\begin{bmatrix} 12 & 9 \\ 4 & 3 \end{bmatrix}$

15 $\begin{bmatrix} 3 & 2 \\ 13 & 8 \end{bmatrix}$

16 $\begin{bmatrix} 3 & 8 \\ 4 & 12 \end{bmatrix}$

17 $\begin{bmatrix} 4 & -2 & 1 \\ 1 & 1 & 3 \\ 1 & -1 & 1 \end{bmatrix}$

18 $\begin{bmatrix} 6 & 1 & -7 \\ -2 & 0 & 4 \\ 4 & 5 & -3 \end{bmatrix}$

19 $\begin{bmatrix} \frac{1}{3} & \frac{2}{3} & 0 \\ -\frac{1}{2} & 3 & -1 \\ 4 & -\frac{1}{4} & 3 \end{bmatrix}$

Extra Practice

LESSON 4.4

Write the matrix equation that represents each system.

1. $\begin{cases} 2x + y = 2 \\ 5x - 3y = -17 \end{cases}$

2. $\begin{cases} 8x + 2y = 10 \\ 5x + y = 7 \end{cases}$

3. $\begin{cases} 3x - 2y = 4 \\ x - 4y = 15 \end{cases}$

4. $\begin{cases} 2x + y + z = 1 \\ x + 3y - 4z = 19 \\ 4x - 2y + 3z = -9 \end{cases}$

5. $\begin{cases} 2x - 3y + z = 3 \\ x - 5y + 2z = 4 \\ 4x - y - z = -1 \end{cases}$

6. $\begin{cases} 3x - y + 2z = 3 \\ 2x + 5y - 3z = -12 \\ x - 3y + 4z = 8 \end{cases}$

Write the system of equations represented by each matrix equation.

7. $\begin{bmatrix} -2 & 1 & -1 \\ 5 & -1 & 2 \\ 3 & 4 & 1 \end{bmatrix}\begin{bmatrix} x \\ y \\ z \end{bmatrix} = \begin{bmatrix} 4 \\ -6 \\ 10 \end{bmatrix}$

8. $\begin{bmatrix} 0.5 & -2 & -1 \\ 3 & -6 & 2 \\ 1 & 1 & -5 \end{bmatrix}\begin{bmatrix} x \\ y \\ z \end{bmatrix} = \begin{bmatrix} -1 \\ 8 \\ 0 \end{bmatrix}$

Write the matrix equation that represents each system, and solve the system, if possible, by using a matrix equation.

9. $\begin{cases} 15x - 7y = 9 \\ 11x + 5y = 37 \end{cases}$

10. $\begin{cases} x + y - z = 2 \\ 2x - y + z = 7 \\ x + y = 10 \end{cases}$

11. $\begin{cases} 2x + y + z = 5 \\ x - y + 3z = -11 \\ y + z = 1 \end{cases}$

12. $\begin{cases} x - 2y + 3z = -6 \\ 2x + y - 4z = -7 \\ 5x + 3y - 2z = 10 \end{cases}$

13. $\begin{cases} 4x - 3y + z = 9 \\ 2x + y - 3z = -7 \\ 3x + 2y + z = 12 \end{cases}$

14. $\begin{cases} x + y - z = 15 \\ 2x - y + z = 0 \\ 3x + 2y - 3z = 38 \end{cases}$

LESSON 4.5

Write the augmented matrix for each system of equations.

1. $\begin{cases} 4x - 3y = 7 \\ 2x - y = 5 \end{cases}$

2. $\begin{cases} 11x - 5y + z = 9 \\ 3x + 7y - z = 3 \\ x - y + 4z = 8 \end{cases}$

3. $\begin{cases} 6x - y + z = 6 \\ 3x + 4y - z = 3 \\ 9x - 3y + 2z = 9 \end{cases}$

Find the reduced row-echelon form of each matrix.

4. $\left[\begin{array}{ccc|c} 2 & 1 & -1 & -1 \\ 1 & -1 & 3 & 8 \\ 1 & 1 & 1 & 2 \end{array}\right]$

5. $\left[\begin{array}{ccc|c} 1 & 1 & 2 & 2 \\ 1 & 0 & 2 & -3 \\ -1 & 0 & 3 & 5 \end{array}\right]$

6. $\left[\begin{array}{ccc|c} -1 & -2 & 0 & -4 \\ 1 & 2 & 1 & 7 \\ 3 & 6 & 3 & 21 \end{array}\right]$

Solve each system of equations by using the row-reduction method. Show each step.

7. $\begin{cases} 8x - 5y = -6 \\ 4x + 3y = 8 \end{cases}$

8. $\begin{cases} 2x - 5y = 4 \\ 5x - 7y = -1 \end{cases}$

9. $\begin{cases} 7x - 3y = 29 \\ 10x + 3y = 5 \end{cases}$

10. $\begin{cases} 2x - y + 3z = -7 \\ x + 4y - 2z = 17 \\ 3x + y + 2z = 2 \end{cases}$

11. $\begin{cases} x + 5y - 3z = 14 \\ 2x + y - z = 10 \\ x - 2y + z = 0 \end{cases}$

12. $\begin{cases} -x - 3y + 2z = -10 \\ 2x + y + z = 5 \\ 3x - 2y + 3z = -5 \end{cases}$

Classify each system as inconsistent, dependent, or independent.

13 $\begin{cases} -y - z = -1 \\ x + y + z = -2 \\ 2x - y - z = -7 \end{cases}$

14 $\begin{cases} x - 2y + 3z = 13 \\ 2x + 5y - 3z = -19 \\ x + 4y - 5z = -21 \end{cases}$

15 $\begin{cases} x - y + z = 4 \\ -2x + y - 2z = -7 \\ x + z = 6 \end{cases}$

Chapter 5

LESSON 5.1

Show that each function is a quadratic function by writing it in the form $f(x) = ax^2 + bx + c$ and identifying *a*, *b*, and *c*.

1. $f(x) = (x + 1)(x - 7)$

2. $f(x) = (x - 11)(x + 2)$

3. $f(x) = (2x + 1)(x - 4)$

4. $f(x) = (12 - x)(1 + x)$

5. $f(x) = (2x + 7)(x - 5)$

6. $f(x) = (x - 2)^2 + 9$

Identify whether each function is a quadratic function. Use a graph to check your answers.

7. $g(x) = 5 - 2x + x^2$

8. $h(x) = (x - 1)(x^2 + 1)$

9. $f(x) = x^2 - (x + 1)^2$

10. $g(x) = 3x(-x + 4)$

State whether each parabola opens up or down and whether the *y*-coordinate of the vertex is the minimum value or the maximum value of the function.

11. $f(x) = 16 - x^2$

12. $h(x) = x^2 - x - 12$

13. $g(x) = (4 - x)(6 - x)$

14. $f(x) = (x - 4)^2 - 2x^2$

Graph each function and give the approximate coordinates of the vertex.

15 $f(x) = 4 + 2x + x^2$

16 $h(x) = 3x^2 + x - 3$

17 $k(x) = \frac{1}{2}x^2 + 5$

18 $g(x) = (x - 3)^2$

19 $f(x) = 0.5x + x^2$

20 $h(x) = -(x - 2)(x - 3)$

LESSON 5.2

Solve each equation. Give exact solutions. Then approximate each solution to the nearest hundredth, if necessary.

1. $x^2 = 51$

2. $16x^2 = 49$

3. $3x^2 = 39$

4. $x^2 - 44 = 0$

5. $7x^2 + 3 = 29$

6. $(x - 4)^2 = 19$

Find the unknown length in each triangle. Give answers to the nearest tenth.

7.

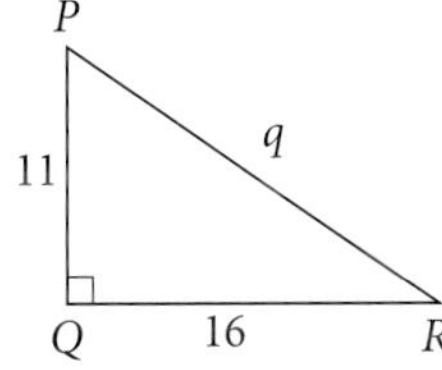

8.

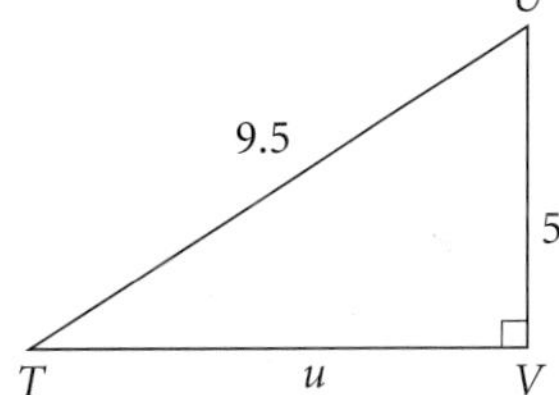

9.

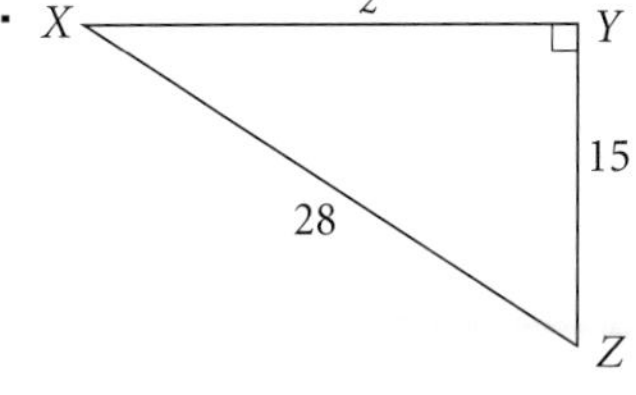

Find the missing side length in right triangle *ABC*. Round answers to the nearest tenth, if necessary.

10. $a = 17$ and $b = 8$

11. $a = 20$ and $c = 32$

12. $b = 7.2$ and $c = 13$

13. $b = 4.5$ and $c = 16$

14. $c = \sqrt{102}$ and $a = 6$

15. $a = 9$ and $b = 11$

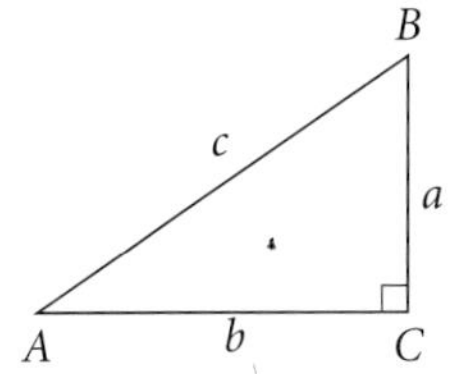

LESSON 5.3

Factor each expression.

1. $7x + 49$
2. $36x + 108x^2$
3. $4x^2 - 28x$
4. $-9x^2 + 3x$
5. $14(3 - x^2) + x(3 - x^2)$
6. $3x(x - 8) + 7(x - 8)$
7. $-3x^3 - 12x^2$
8. $(9 - 2x)3x - 8(9 - 2x)$

Factor each quadratic expression.

9. $x^2 + 14x + 49$
10. $x^2 - 13x + 30$
11. $x^2 + 17x + 42$
12. $x^2 - 7x - 60$
13. $3x^2 + 8x + 4$
14. $2x^2 - 7x + 6$
15. $5x - 2x^2 - 3$
16. $x + 2 - 6x^2$

Solve each equation by factoring and applying the Zero-Product Property.

17. $x^2 - 144 = 0$
18. $x^2 - 18x + 81 = 0$
19. $16x^2 - 25 = 0$
20. $x^2 + 3x - 4 = 0$
21. $9x^2 - 6x + 1 = 0$
22. $x^2 + 10x + 25 = 0$

Use factoring and the Zero-Product Property to find the zeros of each quadratic function.

23. $h(x) = x^2 - 12x$
24. $k(x) = x^2 - 4x - 21$
25. $g(x) = 2x^2 + 17x - 9$
26. $f(x) = x^2 + 16x + 55$
27. $h(x) = x^2 - 12x + 35$
28. $a(x) = 2x^2 + 9x - 5$

LESSON 5.4

Complete the square for each quadratic expression in order to form a perfect-square trinomial. Then write the new expression as a binomial squared.

1. $x^2 + x$
2. $x^2 + 18x$
3. $x^2 - 10x$
4. $x^2 + 26x$
5. $x^2 - 9x$
6. $x^2 + 3x$
7. $x^2 - 22x$
8. $x^2 + 17x$
9. $x^2 - 0.5x$

Solve each equation by completing the square. Give exact solutions.

10. $x^2 - 10x + 4 = 0$
11. $x^2 + 2x - 7 = 0$
12. $x^2 - 12x = 20$
13. $x^2 = 8x + 12$
14. $0 = x^2 - 14x + 2$
15. $21 = x^2 - 16x$
16. $x^2 + 5x = 7$
17. $x^2 + 3x + 6 = 17$
18. $x^2 - 7x = 15 - x$
19. $2x^2 - 15 = 8x$
20. $4x^2 + 12x = 14$
21. $x^2 + x - 3 = 0$

Write each quadratic function in vertex form. Give the coordinates of the vertex and the equation of the axis of symmetry.

22. $f(x) = 9x^2$
23. $f(x) = x^2 - 3$
24. $f(x) = -x^2 + 12$
25. $f(x) = x^2 + 4x$
26. $f(x) = -x^2 + 3x + 1$
27. $f(x) = x^2 + 6x + 5$
28. $f(x) = x^2 + 12x + 42$
29. $f(x) = 2x^2 + 4x - 3$
30. $f(x) = -x^2 - 3x + 7$

LESSON 5.5

Use the quadratic formula to solve each equation. Give exact solutions.

1. $x^2 - 8x + 15 = 0$
2. $x^2 + 14x = 0$
3. $x^2 - 5x + 1 = 0$
4. $x^2 - x = 12$
5. $x^2 - 10x + 14 = 5$
6. $x^2 + 5x + 3 = 0$
7. $x^2 - 7 = 2x$
8. $2x^2 + 3x - 1 = 0$
9. $(x - 3)(x + 4) = 5$
10. $3x^2 - 2x - 5 = 0$
11. $7x^2 - 2x - 8 = 0$
12. $-2x^2 + 3x + 1 = 0$
13. $4x + x^2 - 9 = 0$
14. $4x^2 = x + 6$
15. $x^2 - 14 = x$

For each quadratic function, write the equation for the axis of symmetry and find the coordinates of the vertex.

16. $y = 3x^2 + 6x - 2$
17. $y = x^2 + 4x - 11$
18. $y = -x^2 + 8x + 12$
19. $y = 2x^2 + 3x - 5$
20. $y = 6 + 2x - x^2$
21. $y = x^2 + x - 9$
22. $y = -3x^2 + 2x + 8$
23. $y = -3x^2 - 4x + 2$
24. $y = 5x^2 + 10x + 3$
25. $y = 4x^2 + 2x - 1$
26. $y = -7 + 6x + x^2$
27. $y = 3x^2 - 9x + 5$
28. $y = -x^2 + 8x - 16$
29. $y = 4x^2 - 3x - 5$
30. $y = -5x^2 - 4x + 7$

LESSON 5.6

Find the discriminant and determine the number of real solutions. Then solve.

1. $x^2 - 3x - 5 = 0$
2. $2x^2 - 4x + 3 = 0$
3. $x^2 - 7x + 17 = 0$
4. $3x^2 - 5x + 8 = 0$
5. $4x - 8x^2 = 3$
6. $x^2 - 5x + 10 = 0$
7. $4x^2 + 9 = 2x$
8. $x - x^2 = 11$
9. $-3x^2 = 6x - 2$

Write the conjugate of each complex number.

10. -2
11. $13 - 5i$
12. $7 + 2i$
13. $-3i + 4$
14. $i - 1$
15. $3i$

Simplify.

16. $(6 + 5i) + (13 - 4i)$
17. $(-2 + 14i) - (-7 + 12i)$
18. $(17 + 8i) + (-4 + i)$
19. $(6i + 2) + (3i - 1)$
20. $(3i - 1) - (-2i + 1)$
21. $(-5 - 3i) + (2i - 6)$
22. $(20 - 16i) - (9 + 2i)$
23. $(15 - 6i) + (15 + 6i)$
24. $(14 + 3i) - (3 + i)$
25. $3(-9 + 12i)$
26. $2i(-4 - 8i)$
27. $(7 + 3i)(2 - 5i)$
28. $(2 - 4i)(7 + i)$
29. $(-3i + 2)(4 - i)$
30. $(3 + 5i)(-2i - 4)$
31. $\frac{5 - i}{3 + i}$
32. $\frac{4 - 7i}{-1 + i}$
33. $\frac{6 - 2i}{-4 + i}$
34. $\frac{5 + i}{i}$
35. $\frac{4 + 3i}{2i}$
36. $\frac{2i + 5}{-3i}$
37. $(2i - 9)^2$
38. $(-3 + 10i)^2$
39. $(4 - 5i)^2$

Graph each number and its conjugate in the complex plane.

40. $4 + i$
41. $4i$
42. 4
43. $i + 2$
44. $-i - 3$
45. -6

Extra Practice

LESSON 5.7

Solve a system of equations in order to find a quadratic function that fits each set of data points exactly.

1. $(-7, 51), (5, 27), (-4, 18)$
2. $(-2, 9), (6, -47), (-1, 9)$
3. $(-4, -13), (-2, -11), (2, 17)$
4. $(-3, 14), (2, 19), (4, 49)$
5. $(0, 6), (1, 8), (3, 18)$
6. $(-5, 19), (-3, 7), (6, 52)$
7. $(-3, 4), (-2, -19), (9, -140)$
8. $(-6, -114), (-5, -81), (4, -54)$
9. $(2, 7), (4, 19), (-6, -1)$
10. $(3, 47), (-1, 13), (0, 1)$
11. $(4, 0), (6, -12), (-2, -12)$
12. $(1, 4), (2, -20), (-1, -8)$
13. $(4, 3), (-4, 7), (2, 1)$
14. $(-3, 51), (3, 27), (0, 3)$
15. $(-8, -28), (6, 0), (3, 10.5)$
16. $(-5, 17), (5, 47), (3, 25)$

Randall plays baseball for his high school team. The table shows the height, *y*, of the ball *x* seconds after Randall hit it.

17. Find a quadratic function that fits the data by solving a system.
18. Find the height of the ball 2.5 seconds after it was hit.
19. After how many seconds did the ball hit the ground?

Time (seconds)	Height (feet)
1	48
2	60
3	40

LESSON 5.8

Solve each inequality. Graph the solution on a number line.

1. $x^2 - 9 < 0$
2. $x^2 - 25 \geq 0$
3. $x^2 + 11x + 18 \leq 0$
4. $x^2 - 11x + 30 < 0$
5. $x^2 + x - 12 > 0$
6. $x^2 - 5x + 4 \geq 0$
7. $x^2 - 8x + 16 \leq 0$
8. $x^2 - 6x + 9 \leq 0$
9. $x^2 - 6x - 7 > 0$
10. $x^2 + 4x - 1 > 0$
11. $x^2 - 3x - 5 \leq 0$
12. $x^2 + 2x + \frac{1}{2} < 0$

Sketch the graph of each inequality. Then decide which of the given points are in the solution region.

13. $y < (x + 2)^2 - 3$ $\quad A(-3, -1) \quad B(-3, -2) \quad C(-3, -4)$
14. $y \leq -(x + 1)^2 + 4$ $\quad A(1, 2) \quad B(1, -2) \quad C(1, -5)$
15. $y > -(x - 4)^2 + 3$ $\quad A(3, 2) \quad B(4, -3) \quad C(7, -5)$

Graph each inequality and shade the solution region.

16. $y \geq (x - 3)^2$
17. $y \leq (x - 1)^2$
18. $y > -x^2 + 2x - 1$
19. $y \leq x^2 + 4x + 3$
20. $y \geq x^2 + 5x + 4$
21. $y \leq (x + 2)^2 + 2$
22. $y > x^2 + 2x - 4$
23. $y < 2x^2 + 2x - 2$
24. $y > -(x + 4)^2$
25. $y < (x - 4)^2 - 1$
26. $y \geq 2x^2 + 6x + 9$
27. $y < x^2 + 4x + 1$

Chapter 6

LESSON 6.1

Find the multiplier for each rate of exponential growth or decay.

1. 3% growth
2. 2.4% growth
3. 10% decay
4. 4% decay
5. 0.7% growth
6. 1.4% growth
7. 18% growth
8. 9% decay
9. 0.04% growth
10. 7.2% decay
11. 1.15% growth
12. 0.7% decay

Evaluate each expression to the nearest thousandth for the given value of *x*.

13. 2^x for $x = 1.5$
14. $40(2)^{2x}$ for $x = 2.5$
15. $30(0.5)^x$ for $x = 3$
16. $20(2)^{x+1}$ for $x = 0.5$
17. 2^{3x} for $x = 0.8$
18. $50(0.5)^{2x}$ for $x = 0.75$
19. $3(0.5)^x$ for $x = 5$
20. $10(2)^x$ for $x = 2.4$

21. A physician gives a patient 250 milligrams of an antibiotic that is eliminated from the bloodstream at a rate of 15% per hour. Predict the number of milligrams remaining after 3 hours.

22. A lab sample contains 400 bacteria that double every 15 minutes. Predict the number of bacteria after 3 hours.

23. The population of a city was approximately 450,000 in the year 2000 and was projected to grow at an annual rate of 2.3%. Predict the population, to the nearest ten thousand, for the year 2006.

LESSON 6.2

Identify each function as linear, quadratic, or exponential.

1. $f(x) = x^2 - 12$
2. $g(x) = 2x - 12$
3. $h(x) = (x + 3)^2$
4. $k(x) = \left(\frac{5}{4}\right)^{2x}$
5. $p(x) = 3x + 2^2$
6. $q(x) = 3^{x+2}$

Tell whether each function represents exponential growth or decay.

7. $b(x) = 40(3.8)^x$
8. $f(x) = 100(0.18)^x$
9. $g(x) = \left(\frac{1}{5}\right)^x$
10. $w(x) = 3.5(1.01)^x$
11. $z(x) = 0.4^x$
12. $m(x) = 450(2.04)^x$
13. $k(x) = 500(0.99)^x$
14. $h(x) = 20(1.75)^x$
15. $f(x) = 17(4)^{-x}$

Find the final amount for each investment.

16. $1200 earning 5% interest compounded annually for 10 years

17. $900 earning 6% interest compounded annually for 15 years

18. $5000 earning 6.5% interest compounded semiannually for 12 years

19. $500 earning 5.5% interest compounded semiannually for 3 years

20. $8000 earning 8% interest compounded quarterly for 5 years

21. $600 earning 7.5% interest compounded quarterly for 2 years

22. $10,000 earning 8% interest compounded daily for 1 year

23. $4000 earning 5.25% interest compounded daily for 2 years

LESSON 6.3

Write each equation in logarithmic form.

1. $3^4 = 81$ **2.** $4^3 = 64$ **3.** $\left(\frac{1}{2}\right)^7 = \frac{1}{128}$

4. $\left(\frac{1}{4}\right)^3 = \frac{1}{64}$ **5.** $\left(\frac{1}{3}\right)^{-4} = 81$ **6.** $\left(\frac{1}{15}\right)^{-2} = 225$

7. $5^{-3} = \frac{1}{125}$ **8.** $10^{-2} = 0.01$ **9.** $9^{-2} = \frac{1}{81}$

Write each equation in exponential form.

10. $\log_{14} 196 = 2$ **11.** $\log_7 2401 = 4$ **12.** $\log_8 \frac{1}{512} = -3$

13. $\log_6 \frac{1}{1296} = -4$ **14.** $\log_3 81 = 4$ **15.** $\log_2 256 = 8$

16. $\log_{17} 289 = 2$ **17.** $\log_{10} 0.0001 = -4$ **18.** $\log_{10} 10{,}000 = 4$

Solve each equation for *x*. Round your answers to the nearest hundredth.

19. $10^x = 15$ **20.** $10^x = 72$ **21.** $10^x = 4.5$

22. $10^x = 7.8$ **23.** $10^x = 1042$ **24.** $10^x = 2509$

25. $10^x - 0.835$ **26.** $10^x = 0.007$ **27.** $10^x = 14.2$

Find the value of *v* in each equation.

28. $v = \log_4 1024$ **29.** $v = \log_{13} 1$ **30.** $\log_6 \frac{1}{36} = v$

31. $4 = \log_5 v$ **32.** $\log_4 v = -3$ **33.** $-6 = \log_2 v$

34. $-3 = \log_v \frac{1}{27}$ **35.** $\log_v \frac{1}{625} = -4$ **36.** $7 = \log_v 128$

LESSON 6.4

Write each expression as a sum or difference of logarithms. Then simplify, if possible.

1. $\log_3 9x$ **2.** $\log_3 27x$ **3.** $\log_4(2 \cdot 3 \cdot 4)$

4. $\log_2 \frac{16}{y}$ **5.** $\log_5 \frac{4}{5}$ **6.** $\log_{10} \frac{xy}{10}$

Write each expression as a single logarithm. Then simplify, if possible.

7. $\log_2 3 + \log_2 7$ **8.** $\log_6 12 + \log_6 15 - \log_6 5$

9. $2 \log_4 5 - \log_4 6$ **10.** $\log_9 x - 3 \log_9 y$

11. $3 \log_5 3 - \log_5 5.4$ **12.** $\frac{1}{2} \log_b 25 + 3 \log_b z$

Evaluate each expression.

13. $\log_3 3^4 - \log_8 8^4$ **14.** $\log_7 7^5 + \log_6 6^3$ **15.** $4^{\log_4 87} + \log_5 25$

16. $8^{\log_8 9} - \log_4 16$ **17.** $\log_3 \frac{1}{81} + \log_4 64$ **18.** $\log_2 64 - 7^{\log_7 1}$

Solve for *x*, and check your answers. If the equation has no solution, write *no solution*.

19. $\log_8(x+1) = \log_8(2x-2)$ **20.** $\log_3(3x-4) = \log_3(8-5x)$

21. $\log_7(6x+4) = \log_7(-3x-5)$ **22.** $\log_{10}(6x+3) = \log_{10} 3x$

23. $\log_2 x + \log_2(x-4) = 5$ **24.** $\log_8(3x+1) + \log_8(x-1) = 2$

25. $2 \log_b x = \log_b 2 + \log_b(2x-2)$ **26.** $2 \log_b x = \log_b(x-1) + \log_b 4$

LESSON 6.5

Evaluate each logarithmic expression to the nearest hundredth.

1. $\log_2 51$ **2.** $\log_5 64$ **3.** $\log_6 0.5$

4. $\log_4 9$ **5.** $\log_9 14$ **6.** $\log_7 32$

7. $\log_8 0.23$ **8.** $\log_{\frac{1}{2}} 15$ **9.** $\log_2 0.72$

10. $\log_{\frac{1}{4}} 16$ **11.** $2 - \log_5 7$ **12.** $\log_9 10$

13. $\log_6 \frac{2}{3}$ **14.** $\log_8 50$ **15.** $3 + \log_3 22$

16. $\log_7 \frac{3}{4}$ **17.** $\log_8 \frac{1}{3}$ **18.** $\log_7 8$

19. $10 + \log_4 25$ **20.** $\log_{15} 40$ **21.** $\log_9 \frac{3}{4}$

Solve each equation. Round your answers to the nearest hundredth.

22. $5^x = 24$ **23.** $6^x = 44$ **24.** $8^x = 0.9$

25. $2^x = 3.5$ **26.** $9^x = 17$ **27.** $3^x = 41$

28. $8^{-x} = 0.25$ **29.** $4^x = 22$ **30.** $9^x = 2$

31. $2.5^x = 17$ **32.** $7^x = 3$ **33.** $12^x = 140$

34. $1 + 3^x = 14$ **35.** $3^{-x} = 0.9$ **36.** $4^{x+1} = 64$

37. $5^{2x} = 114$ **38.** $7 - 2^x = 1$ **39.** $4 + 4^x = 14$

40. $5^{x-2} = 70$ **41.** $5^x = 20.5$ **42.** $7^x = 22$

LESSON 6.6

Evaluate each expression, if possible, to the nearest thousandth.

1. e^3 **2.** e^{-2} **3.** $e^{4.5}$ **4.** $e^{0.6}$

5. $e^{\sqrt{3}}$ **6.** $\ln 17$ **7.** $\ln \sqrt{7}$ **8.** $\ln 45$

9. $\ln(-12)$ **10.** $\ln(-5)$ **11.** $\ln 0.8$ **12.** $\ln \sqrt{3}$

Write an equivalent logarithmic or exponential equation.

13. $e^{3.22} \approx 25.03$ **14.** $e^5 \approx 148.41$ **15.** $\ln 50 \approx 3.91$

16. $\ln 3.6 \approx 1.28$ **17.** $e^{3.4} \approx 29.96$ **18.** $\ln 5 \approx 1.61$

19. $\ln 25 \approx 3.22$ **20.** $e^{\frac{1}{2}} \approx 1.65$ **21.** $e^{\frac{2}{3}} \approx 1.95$

22. $e^{-7} \approx 0.000912$ **23.** $\ln\left(\frac{1}{4}\right) \approx -1.39$ **24.** $\ln\left(\frac{3}{4}\right) \approx -0.29$

Solve each equation for *x* by using the natural logarithm function. Round your answers to the nearest hundredth.

25. $15^x = 27$ **26.** $4.2^x = 15$ **27.** $7^{-x} = 120$

28. $0.5^x = 11$ **29.** $8^{\frac{-x}{2}} = 21$ **30.** $9^{-x} = 0.2$

31. $\left(\frac{1}{3}\right)^{-2x} = 125$ **32.** $\left(\frac{2}{3}\right)^x = 12$ **33.** $1.5^{3x} = 1500$

34. $2.3^x = 15$ **35.** $7^x = 14{,}000$ **36.** $11^{-2x} = 15{,}000$

37. An investor puts $5000 in an account that earns 6.5% annual interest which is compounded continuously. Find the amount that will be in the account at the end of 5 years if no deposits or withdrawals are made.

LESSON 6.7

Solve each equation for *x*. Write the exact solution and the approximate solution to the nearest hundredth, when appropriate.

1. $2^x = 2^5$
2. $\log_6 216 = x$
3. $3^{x-1} = 3^4$
4. $\log x = 2.1$
5. $x = \log_3 27$
6. $\log_9 x = 2$
7. $5 = \log_x 32$
8. $\log_x \frac{1}{4} = -1$
9. $3^x = 4$
10. $\log_4(x - 2) = 2$
11. $10^{x-1} = 121$
12. $e^{x+1} = 14$
13. $e^{2x-1} = 9$
14. $\ln(x + 1) = \ln 7$
15. $\ln(x - 5) = \ln(3x + 1)$
16. $2 \ln\left(x + \frac{1}{2}\right) = \ln \frac{1}{4}$
17. $e^{-3x+4} = 22$
18. $2 \ln x = \ln(2x - 1)$

In Exercises 19 and 20, use the equation $M = \frac{2}{3} \log \frac{E}{10^{11.8}}$.

19. On October 15, 1997, an earthquake with a magnitude of 6.8 struck parts of Chile and Argentina. Find the amount of energy released by the earthquake.

20. From December 1811 to early 1812, a series of earthquakes shook the Mississippi Valley near New Madrid, Missouri. One of the earthquakes released about 2.5×10^{24} ergs of energy. Find the earthquake's magnitude on the Richter scale. Round your answer to the nearest tenth.

Chapter 7

LESSON 7.1

Determine whether each expression is a polynomial. If so, classify the polynomial by degree and by number of terms.

1. $12x^3 - 2x^2 + \frac{1}{2}$
2. $\frac{x^3}{11} + \frac{x^2}{8}$
3. $\frac{11}{x^3} + \frac{8}{x^2}$
4. $4x - 2^{2x} + 3^{5x}$
5. $0.66x^4 - 1$
6. $10x^3 + 6x^7 - 15x$

Evaluate each polynomial expression for the indicated value of *x*.

7. $x^3 - 3x^2 + 4x$ for $x = -2$
8. $4 - 2x + 3x^2 - x^4$ for $x = -1$
9. $\frac{3}{4}x^4 + \frac{1}{2}x^2 - \frac{1}{4}x + \frac{1}{2}$ for $x = 2$
10. $-x^4 - x^3 - x^2 + 12$ for $x = 5$
11. $0.5x^4 + 2.5x^3 - x^2$ for $x = 4$
12. $x^4 - 3x^3 + 3x^2 - 9$ for $x = 3$

Write each sum or difference as a polynomial expression in standard form. Then classify the polynomial by degree and by number of terms.

13. $(-2x^3 + 5x^2 - 3x + 7) + (5x^3 + x^2 + 9)$
14. $(7x^4 - 3x^3 + 5x) - (2x^4 + x^3 + x^2 + 3x - 2)$
15. $(4.1x^3 + 3.5x - 6x^2 - 11) - (3x^2 - 4x^3 + 9)$
16. $(5x^3 - 2x^4 + 3x - 6) + (x^4 - 7x^2 + 3x - 9)$
17. $(3x^5 - 4x^2 + 2x^3) - (4x^4 + 3x^3 - 9x^2 - 7)$
18. $(7.5x^3 + 3.2x^4 + 5.1x^2 + x) + (x^4 - 7x^2 - 3x)$

Graph each function. Describe the general shape of the graph.

19 $f(x) = x^3 - x^2 - x + 1$
20 $g(x) = -2x^3 + 3x - 1$
21 $k(x) = x^4 - x^3 - 3x^2 + 1$
22 $h(x) = 0.5x^4 - 3x^2$

LESSON 7.2

Graph each function. Approximate any local maxima or minima to the nearest tenth.

1 $P(x) = 10x - 8x^2$

2 $P(x) = x^2 - 3x - 2$

3 $P(x) = x^4 - x^3 - x^2$

4 $P(x) = 5x - x^3 + 1$

Graph each function. Approximate any local maxima or minima to the nearest tenth. Find the intervals over which the function is increasing and decreasing.

5 $P(x) = x^3 + x^2; -6 \le x \le 6$

6 $P(x) = 0.5x^4 + x^2 - 3; -5 \le x \le 5$

7 $P(x) = -2x^4 + 3x^3 + 2x^2; -4 \le x \le 4$

8 $P(x) = x^3 - 4x^2 + 1; -5 \le x \le 5$

9 $P(x) = 0.2x^3 - 6x + 4; -6 \le x \le 6$

10 $P(x) = 3x^4 - 8x^2 - 2; -2 \le x \le 2$

Describe the end behavior of each function.

11. $P(x) = 17x^2 - 8x^3 - 6$

12. $P(x) = 9 - 2x - x^2 + 5x^3$

13. $P(x) = 4x^4 - 6x^3 + 2x^2 - x$

14. $P(x) = -8 + x^3 - 5x^4$

15 The number (in thousands) of federal employees in the United States is given in the table below. Find a quartic regression model for the data by using $x = 0$ for 1982. [*Source: U.S. Bureau of the Census*]

1982	1983	1984	1985	1986	1987	1988	1989
15,841	16,034	16,436	16,690	16,933	17,212	17,588	18,369

LESSON 7.3

Write each product as a polynomial in standard form.

1. $2x^3(-5x^4 + 3x^3 - 2x - 6)$

2. $(4x - 7)(3x + 4)$

3. $(x - 6)(x^2 + 3x - 5)$

4. $(2x - 3)(x + 4)^2$

5. $(2x - 1)^3$

6. $(x + 7)(2x^2 - 3x - 4)$

Use substitution to determine whether the given linear expression is a factor of the polynomial.

7. $2x^3 + 7x^2 - 15x; x + 5$

8. $x^3 - 4x^2 - 20x - 7; x - 7$

9. $2x^3 + 15x^2 - 9x - 10; x + 8$

Divide by using long division.

10. $(2x^3 + 3x^2 - 6x - 3) \div (2x - 3)$

11. $(x^3 + 3x + 4) \div (x + 1)$

12. $(x^2 - 27x + x^3 + 28) \div (x - 4)$

13. $\left(\frac{1}{2}x^2 - 5x + 3x^3 + 2\right) \div \left(x - \frac{1}{2}\right)$

Divide by using synthetic division.

14. $(x^2 + 9x - 36) \div (x - 3)$

15. $(x^3 - 5x^2 - 2x + 24) \div (x - 3)$

16. $(x^3 + 8) \div (x - 4)$

17. $(9x - 17x^2 - 9 + 5x^3) \div (x - 3)$

For each function, use both synthetic division and substitution to find the indicated value.

18. $P(x) = x^4 + 3x^3 - 2x + 1; P(2)$

19. $P(x) = x^3 - 8; P(-2)$

20. $P(x) = 5x^2 - 4x + 3; P(-1)$

21. $P(x) = -3x^3 + 4 - x^2; P(3)$

LESSON 7.4

Use factoring to solve each equation.

1. $x^3 + 3x^2 - 10x = 0$ **2.** $x^3 - 64x = 0$ **3.** $x^3 + 49x = 14x^2$

4. $2x^3 - 22x^2 + 56x = 0$ **5.** $3x^3 + 3x^2 = 6x$ **6.** $x^3 - 77x + 4x^2 = 0$

Use a graph, synthetic division, and factoring to find all of the roots of each equation.

7 $x^3 - 2x^2 - 4x + 8 = 0$ **8** $x^3 - 3x^2 - x + 3 = 0$ **9** $x^3 - 2x^2 - 13x - 10 = 0$

10 $x^3 + 5x^2 = x + 5$ **11** $x^3 + x + 6 = 4x^2$ **12** $x^3 - 9x^2 + 15x - 7 = 0$

Use variable substitution and factoring to find all of the roots of each equation.

13. $x^4 - 14x^2 + 45 = 0$ **14.** $x^4 - 16x^2 + 15 = 0$ **15.** $x^4 + 12 = 13x^2$

16. $x^4 - 25x^2 + 144 = 0$ **17.** $x^4 + 33 = 14x^2$ **18.** $x^4 - 8x^2 + 7 = 0$

Use a graph and the Location Principle to find the real zeros of each function. Give approximate values to the nearest hundredth, if necessary.

19 $g(x) = x^3 - 5x^2 + 7x$ **20** $b(x) = 0.8x^4 - 2x^2 + 1$ **21** $f(x) = x^3 - 4x + 2$

LESSON 7.5

Find all of the rational roots of each polynomial equation.

1. $3x^2 - 14x + 8 = 0$ **2.** $2x^2 - 5x - 3 = 0$ **3.** $10x^3 - 31x^2 + 25x - 6 = 0$

4. $2x^3 - 9x^2 + 7x + 6 = 0$ **5.** $4x^3 - 9x^2 - x + 6 = 0$ **6.** $15x^3 - 47x^2 + 38x - 8 = 0$

Find all zeros of each polynomial function.

7 $M(x) = x^3 - x^2 - 7x + 3$ **8** $H(x) = x^3 - 3x^2 - 5x + 15$

9 $J(x) = x^3 - 2x^2 + 7x - 14$ **10** $R(x) = x^4 - 3x^3 - x^2 - 9x - 12$

11 $F(x) = x^4 - 5x^2 - 24$ **12** $H(x) = x^4 + 5x^3 + x^2 - 20x - 20$

Find all real values of *x* for which the functions are equal. Give your answers to the nearest hundredth.

13 $P(x) = x^4 + 3x^2 + 2x$ and $Q(x) = x + 2$

14 $P(x) = -x^2 + 6x - 2$ and $Q(x) = 0.2x^4 + x^3 - 3$

15 $P(x) = x^4 - 3x^2$ and $Q(x) = x^2 + 3x - 5$

16 $P(x) = x^4 - x^3 + 1$ and $Q(x) = x^2 - 2x + 3$

Write a polynomial function, *P*, in factored form and in standard form by using the given information.

17. P is of degree 3; $P(0) = 2$; zeros: $-1, 1, 2$

18. P is of degree 4; $P(0) = 6$; zeros: $2, -3, \frac{1}{2}, -\frac{1}{2}$

19. P is of degree 4; $P(0) = -9$; zeros: $\frac{1}{2}$ (multiplicity 2), $\frac{3}{2}, -\frac{3}{2}$

20. P is of degree 3; $P(0) = -1$; zeros: $\frac{1}{2}, \frac{1}{3}$ (multiplicity 2)

21. P is of degree 3; $P(0) = -36$; zeros: $2, 3i$

22. P is of degree 4; $P(0) = 24$; zeros: $2, 3, i$

Chapter 8

LESSON 8.1

For Exercises 1–4, y varies inversely as x. Write the appropriate inverse-variation equation, and find y for the given values of x.

1. $y = 18$ when $x = 8$; $x = 4, 9, 15$, and 20

2. $y = 7.5$ when $x = 8$; $x = 4, 5, 6$, and 18

3. $y = 0.32$ when $x = 5$; $x = 0.1, 0.2, 4$, and 8

4. $y = 9.5$ when $x = 4$; $x = 1.9, 5, 6$, and 20

For Exercises 5–8, y varies jointly as x and z. Write the appropriate joint-variation equation, and find y for the given values of x and z.

5. $y = 18$ when $x = 4$ and $z = 3$; $x = 4.5$ and $z = 6$

6. $y = 375$ when $x = 6$ and $z = 5$; $x = 0.4$ and $z = 30$

7. $y = 24$ when $x = 2$ and $z = -4$; $x = -3$ and $z = 0.8$

8. $y = 1.5$ when $x = 1.5$ and $z = 6$; $x = 8$ and $z = 0.4$

For Exercises 9–12, z varies jointly as x and y and inversely as w. Write the appropriate inverse-variation equation, and find z for the given values of x, y, and w.

9. $z = 82.5$ when $x = 12, y = 5$, and $w = 4$; $x = 8, y = 4.5$, and $w = 10$

10. $z = 19.2$ when $x = 20, y = 4.2$, and $w = 3.5$; $x = 16, y = 9$, and $w = 5$

11. $z = 6$ when $x = 12, y = -2$, and $w = 5$; $x = 7, y = 0.2$, and $w = 14$

12. $z = 2.5$ when $x = -6, y = 5$, and $w = 4$; $x = 3, y = -0.6$, and $w = 2$

13. The time, t, that it takes to travel a given distance, d, varies inversely as r, the rate of speed. A certain trip can be made in 7.5 hours at a rate of 60 miles per hour. Find the constant of variation, and write an inverse-variation equation. Find t to the nearest tenth when r is 40, 45, 50, and 55.

LESSON 8.2

Determine whether each function is a rational function. If so, find the domain. If not, explain.

1. $f(x) = \frac{x - 0.5}{(x+2)(x+5)}$

2. $g(x) = \frac{2^{x+1}}{x^2+1}$

3. $h(x) = \frac{x^2+3x+1}{x^2-9}$

Identify all asymptotes and holes in the graph of each rational function.

4. $b(x) = \frac{x+6}{2x-1}$

5. $m(x) = \frac{x-5}{x^2-3}$

6. $k(x) = \frac{2x}{x^2-x-2}$

7. $f(x) = \frac{2x^3+6x^2}{x^2-x-12}$

8. $f(x) = \frac{-x^3+x^2}{x^2+x-2}$

9. $f(x) = \frac{x^2+2x-15}{x-3}$

10. $f(x) = \frac{x^2-2x-3}{x+1}$

11. $f(x) = \frac{x^2-4}{2x^2-5x+2}$

12. $f(x) = \frac{3x^2+x-4}{x^2+2x-3}$

Find the domain of each rational function. Identify all asymptotes and holes in the graph of each function. Then graph.

13. $h(x) = \frac{x+4}{x-4}$

14. $f(x) = \frac{x}{3x(x-1)}$

15. $g(x) = \frac{x+3}{x^2+8x+15}$

16. $f(x) = \frac{1}{x+2}$

17. $b(x) = \frac{x-1}{x+2}$

18. $d(x) = \frac{x-1}{x^2-5x+4}$

Extra Practice

LESSON 8.3

Simplify each rational expression.

1. $\frac{7x(12x^5)}{3x^2(28x^2)}$
2. $\frac{x^2+8x-9}{x^2-81}$
3. $\frac{x^2+10x+24}{x^2+x-12}$
4. $\frac{x^2+4x-12}{3x^2-12x+12}$
5. $\frac{x^2-8x-20}{12x-x^2-20}$
6. $\frac{x^2-25}{2x^2-7x-15}$

Simplify each product or quotient.

7. $\frac{2x^2-x-1}{3x^2-2x-1} \cdot \frac{15x^3+5x^2}{4x^2-1}$
8. $\frac{x^2-2x-3}{x^2+x-20} \div \frac{x^2+2x+1}{x^2+6x+5}$
9. $\frac{4x+8}{5x-20} \div \frac{10+3x-x^2}{x^2-4x}$
10. $\frac{2x^2-12x-14}{x^3-16x} \cdot \frac{-16-4x}{6x-42}$
11. $\frac{3x^2+10x-8}{3x^2-17x+10} \cdot \frac{5+9x-2x^2}{x^2+3x-4}$
12. $\frac{3x^2+14x-5}{x^2+2x-15} \div \frac{3x^2-25x+8}{8+15x-2x^2}$

Simplify each complex fraction.

13. $\dfrac{\frac{x^2-49}{x^2-100}}{\frac{x-7}{x+10}}$
14. $\dfrac{\frac{(x+7)^2}{(2x-3)^2}}{\frac{x^2-49}{2x^2-17x+21}}$
15. $\dfrac{\frac{x^2+8x-33}{x^2-x-6}}{\frac{x^2+10x-11}{x^2+9x+14}}$

Simplify each product or quotient involving complex fractions.

16. $\dfrac{\frac{1}{x+1}}{\frac{x}{x^2-1}} \cdot \frac{x}{x-1}$
17. $\frac{x-3}{x-4} \cdot \dfrac{\frac{2x-8}{x^2-9}}{\frac{x+5}{x+3}}$
18. $\frac{x+4}{x^2-9} \div \dfrac{\frac{x^2+4x}{x+3}}{\frac{x-3}{x}}$
19. $\dfrac{\frac{-2x-5}{x^2-1}}{\frac{x+1}{x-3}} \cdot \frac{x^2-1}{2x^2-x-15}$
20. $\frac{x}{x+4} \cdot \dfrac{\frac{x^2+6x+8}{x+10}}{\frac{x^2}{2x+20}}$
21. $\dfrac{\frac{x^2+4x-32}{x^2-12x+35}}{\frac{16x-4x^2}{x^2-4x-21}} \cdot \frac{x^2-10x}{x^2+11x+24}$

LESSON 8.4

Simplify each sum or difference.

1. $\frac{3x}{2x+5} - \frac{2x}{2x+5}$
2. $\frac{2x+1}{3x-4} + \frac{x-1}{3x-4}$
3. $\frac{3x^2+x}{12} - \frac{x^2+1}{4}$
4. $\frac{5x-15}{x^2-9} - \frac{2}{x+3}$
5. $\frac{2x-1}{x+8} + \frac{34x}{x^2-64}$
6. $\frac{2}{x-8} + \frac{1}{x+2}$
7. $\frac{3x-10}{x^2+4x-12} - \frac{2}{x+6}$
8. $\frac{-2x-3}{x^2-3x} - \frac{-x}{x-3}$
9. $\frac{2x+1}{5-x} + \frac{1}{3x+2}$

Simplify each sum or difference involving complex fractions.

10. $\dfrac{5}{\frac{x}{3x+1}} - \frac{7x^2+3x}{x}$
11. $\dfrac{\frac{3}{2x-1}}{\frac{6x}{2x-1}} + \frac{3}{x}$
12. $\dfrac{\frac{x+1}{x-2}}{\frac{x+2}{2}} - \frac{x}{x^2-4}$
13. $\dfrac{\frac{7x}{x^2-4}}{\frac{6}{x-2}} - \dfrac{\frac{2x-6}{x+2}}{\frac{x-3}{2x}}$
14. $\dfrac{\frac{2}{x+5}}{\frac{x-5}{x}} + \dfrac{\frac{5x-10}{x-5}}{\frac{x^2+3x-10}{2}}$
15. $\dfrac{\frac{2}{x^2+2x-3}}{\frac{x-4}{x^3-x^2}} + \dfrac{\frac{6}{x^2+5x+6}}{\frac{x-4}{x+2}}$

Write each expression as a single rational expression in simplest form.

16. $\frac{3}{x+7} - \frac{2x+8}{x+7} + \frac{4x+19}{x+7}$
17. $\frac{8x-5}{2x+3} + \frac{x+4}{2x+3} - \frac{3x-10}{2x+3}$
18. $\frac{3x}{x+2} - \frac{3x}{x+5} + \frac{18}{x^2+7x+10}$
19. $\frac{2x-1}{x+5} + \frac{x}{x-2} - \frac{5x+4}{x^2+3x-10}$

LESSON 8.5

Solve each equation. Check your solution.

1. $\frac{x-3}{x-1} = \frac{x}{x+4}$

2. $\frac{x+1}{x-2} = \frac{x+3}{x-1}$

3. $\frac{x-7}{x+3} = \frac{x-9}{x-3}$

4. $\frac{1}{x} - \frac{5}{6x} = \frac{2}{3}$

5. $\frac{3}{2} - \frac{3}{x} = \frac{9}{2x}$

6. $\frac{x-7}{x+1} - \frac{x-4}{3x-2} = 0$

7. $\frac{3}{x-2} + \frac{5}{x+2} = \frac{4x^2}{x^2-4}$

8. $\frac{3}{x-1} - \frac{1}{x+1} = \frac{3}{x^2-1}$

9. $5 - \frac{26}{x+2} = \frac{27}{x^2-4}$

10. $\frac{2x-3}{4} + 2 = \frac{2x+1}{3}$

11. $\frac{3x}{4} - \frac{2x-1}{2} = \frac{x-7}{6}$

12. $\frac{x+1}{x-3} = \frac{3}{x} + \frac{12}{x^2-3x}$

13. $\frac{4}{x^2-8x+12} = \frac{x}{x-2} + \frac{1}{x-6}$

14. $\frac{2x-3}{x-5} = \frac{x}{x+4} + \frac{20x-37}{x^2-x-20}$

15. $\frac{x-2}{x+1} = \frac{x-3}{x^2-5x-6} - \frac{2x-7}{x-6}$

Solve each inequality. Check your solution.

16. $\frac{x-2}{x+6} > 4$

17. $\frac{3x+2}{2x} < 1$

18. $\frac{3x+3}{2x} > 1$

19. $\frac{4x}{3x-2} > \frac{1}{2}$

20. $\frac{x-2}{x+2} < 3$

21. $\frac{3x+5}{2x-3} < 6$

Use a graphics calculator to solve each rational inequality. Round answers to the nearest tenth.

22 $\frac{3x+5}{2x-3} < 0$

23 $\frac{2}{x} > x^2 + 1$

24 $\frac{3}{2x} < x^2 + 2$

25 $\frac{x+4}{x-2} < x$

26 $\frac{x+3}{x+1} > 2x$

27 $x^2 - 3 \ge \frac{1}{x^2}$

28 $\frac{x+5}{x-2} < \frac{36}{x^2-4}$

29 $\frac{x+1}{6-x} \le \frac{2-x}{x+1}$

30 $\frac{x}{x+1} + \frac{2x}{x-1} > \frac{2}{x^2-1}$

LESSON 8.6

Evaluate each expression.

1. $\frac{3}{5}\sqrt[3]{-27}$

2. $0.25\sqrt[4]{16}$

3. $3\left(\sqrt[3]{-512}\right)^2$

4. $\frac{3}{2}\left(\sqrt[3]{-1000}\right)^2$

5. $\frac{1}{3}\left(\sqrt[3]{64}\right)^2$

6. $5\left(\sqrt{81}\right)^{-2}$

7. $\frac{1}{2}\left(\sqrt[3]{-512}\right)^{-1}$

8. $\left(\sqrt[4]{1296} - 2\right)^{\frac{1}{2}}$

9. $3\left(\sqrt[4]{625} + 3\right)^{\frac{1}{3}}$

10. $\frac{1}{3}\left(\sqrt[5]{-243}\right)^2 - 3$

11. $\frac{2}{3}\left(\sqrt[4]{\frac{21}{8}}\right)^4 + \frac{1}{4}$

12. $\frac{3}{5}\left(\sqrt[4]{\frac{35}{9}}\right)^4 + \frac{2}{3}$

Find the domain of each radical function.

13. $f(x) = \sqrt{x^2 - 16}$

14. $f(x) = \sqrt{3x + 6}$

15. $f(x) = \sqrt{4(x-1)}$

16. $f(x) = \sqrt{4x^2 - 9}$

17. $f(x) = \sqrt{x^2 + 2x + 1}$

18. $f(x) = \sqrt{x^2 + 7x + 12}$

Find the inverse of each quadratic function. Then graph the function and its inverse in the same coordinate plane.

19. $y = x^2 + 4$

20. $y = x^2 - 3$

21. $y = x^2 + 4x$

22. $y = x^2 - 8x + 16$

23. $y = x^2 - 6x + 9$

24. $y = x^2 - 4x + 1$

25. The speed of an ocean wave depends on the depth of the water in which it travels. A wave's speed, in miles per hour, in water that is x feet deep is given by the function $f(x) = \sqrt{21.92x}$. Find the speed of a wave in water that is 25, 50, and 100 feet deep. Round your answers to the nearest tenth.

Extra Practice

LESSON 8.7

Simplify each radical expression by using the Properties of *n*th Roots.

1. $\sqrt{125}$ **2.** $\sqrt[3]{162x^6y^3}$ **3.** $\sqrt[4]{80x^8z^{10}}$

4. $\sqrt[3]{-56x^4y^4z^3}$ **5.** $(75x^2y^3z)^{\frac{1}{2}}$ **6.** $(54x^5)^{\frac{1}{3}}$

Simplify each product or quotient. Assume that the value of each variable is positive.

7. $\sqrt[3]{9x^2} \cdot \sqrt[3]{3x}$ **8.** $\sqrt[3]{4x^5} \cdot \sqrt[3]{54xy^2}$ **9.** $\sqrt{8x^3} \cdot (2xz^5)^{\frac{1}{2}} \cdot \sqrt{4x^3z^4}$

10. $\dfrac{(81y^5)^{\frac{1}{4}}}{\sqrt[4]{x^4y}}$ **11.** $\dfrac{\sqrt[3]{48x^2y^4z^4}}{\sqrt[3]{6x}}$ **12.** $\dfrac{\sqrt{15x^9y^3}}{\sqrt{5x^5y}}$

13. $\sqrt[4]{8x^5} \cdot \sqrt[4]{4x^7}$ **14.** $\dfrac{\sqrt{9b^7}}{(12b^5)^{\frac{1}{2}}}$ **15.** $\dfrac{\sqrt[4]{8x^5}}{(20x^2)^{-\frac{1}{4}}}$

Find each sum, difference, or product. Give your answer in simplest radical form.

16. $(12 - \sqrt{2}) + (15 + \sqrt{2})$ **17.** $(9 + 2\sqrt{5}) - (1 + \sqrt{45})$

18. $(7 - 2\sqrt{6})(7 + 2\sqrt{6})$ **19.** $(3 - \sqrt{8})(5 + \sqrt{2})$

20. $(4 + \sqrt{3})(-2 + \sqrt{2})$ **21.** $6\sqrt{3}(2\sqrt{5} + 4\sqrt{6})$

22. $7\sqrt{20} + 8\sqrt{5} - 2\sqrt{45}$ **23.** $6\sqrt{8} - (\sqrt{24} - 3\sqrt{72} + \sqrt{54})$

24. $4\sqrt{2}(\sqrt{12} - 3\sqrt{2} + 4\sqrt{8})$ **25.** $(4\sqrt{2} - 2\sqrt{3})(5\sqrt{2} - \sqrt{3})$

Write each expression with a rational denominator and in simplest form.

26. $\dfrac{3}{\sqrt{15}}$ **27.** $\dfrac{\sqrt{135}}{\sqrt{15}}$ **28.** $\dfrac{5}{1-\sqrt{6}}$ **29.** $\dfrac{-3}{\sqrt{6}-\sqrt{2}}$

30. $\dfrac{14}{\sqrt{5}+\sqrt{3}}$ **31.** $\dfrac{\sqrt{3}-\sqrt{2}}{\sqrt{3}+\sqrt{2}}$ **32.** $\dfrac{2\sqrt{5}-\sqrt{3}}{\sqrt{5}+\sqrt{3}}$ **33.** $\dfrac{2\sqrt{x}}{3\sqrt{x}-4\sqrt{y}}$

LESSON 8.8

Solve each radical equation by using algebra. If the equation has no real solution, write *no solution*. Check your solutions.

1. $\sqrt{x-5} = 3$ **2.** $\sqrt{x^2 - 15} = 7$ **3.** $\sqrt{x-4} = \sqrt{x+4}$

4. $\sqrt{2x-5} + 4 = 3$ **5.** $\sqrt{3x-5} = 5$ **6.** $\sqrt{5x-11} = x - 1$

7. $\sqrt{2x-1} = x$ **8.** $\sqrt[3]{x+5} = \sqrt[3]{3x-2}$ **9.** $\sqrt{x^2 - 4x - 5} = \sqrt{5x - x^2}$

Solve each radical inequality by using algebra. If the inequality has no real solution, write *no solution*. Check your solution.

10. $\sqrt{x-3} \ge 2$ **11.** $3 > \sqrt{2x}$ **12.** $\sqrt{4x-1} > 2$

13. $3 \ge \sqrt{x^2 - 4x + 4}$ **14.** $\sqrt{1-x} > 3$ **15.** $\sqrt{3x-2} \le 2$

16. $4 \le \sqrt{7-x}$ **17.** $\sqrt{5x-6} > 12$ **18.** $\sqrt{4x+1} \ge 5$

Solve each radical equation or inequality by graphing. Round solutions to the nearest tenth. Check your solutions by any method.

19 $2\sqrt{x} \le 3x - 4$ **20** $3\sqrt{x+2} \ge \sqrt{x^2+4}$ **21** $0.25\sqrt{3x-1} < x + 2$

22 $\sqrt[3]{x^2+1} = x$ **23** $\sqrt[3]{x+2} = \sqrt{x}$ **24** $\sqrt[3]{2x-1} > 2\sqrt{x-4}$

Chapter 9

LESSON 9.1

Graph each equation and identify the conic section.

1 $x^2 + y^2 = 4$
2 $y^2 - 9x = 0$
3 $9x^2 - 4y^2 = 25$
4 $x^2 + 4y^2 = 16$
5 $x^2 - y^2 = 16$
6 $4x^2 - y = 0$
7 $16x^2 + y^2 = 81$
8 $x^2 + y^2 = 144$
9 $9x^2 - 16y^2 = 144$

Find the distance between P and Q and the coordinates of M, the midpoint of $\overline{PQ}$. Give exact answers and approximate answers to the nearest hundredth when appropriate.

10. $P(-6, 4)$ and $Q(2, -2)$
11. $P(6, -2)$ and $Q(2, 4)$
12. $P(8, -4)$ and $Q(6, 0)$
13. $P(0, 1)$ and $Q(4, 7)$
14. $P(-2, 3)$ and $Q(5, 4)$
15. $P(\sqrt{2}, 4)$ and $Q(3\sqrt{2}, 0)$

Find the center, circumference, and area of a circle whose diameter has the given endpoints.

16. $P(12, -8)$ and $Q(6, 0)$
17. $P(3, 4)$ and $Q(10, -20)$
18. $P(0, 10)$ and $Q(2, -6)$
19. $P(14, 8)$ and $Q(-2, -8)$
20. $P(4, -5)$ and $Q(8, 3)$
21. $P(24, 16)$ and $Q(-2, 18)$

LESSON 9.2

Write the standard equation for each parabola below.

1.

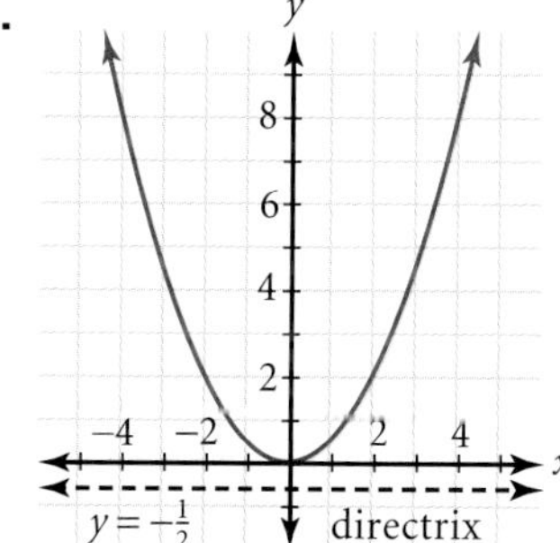

2.

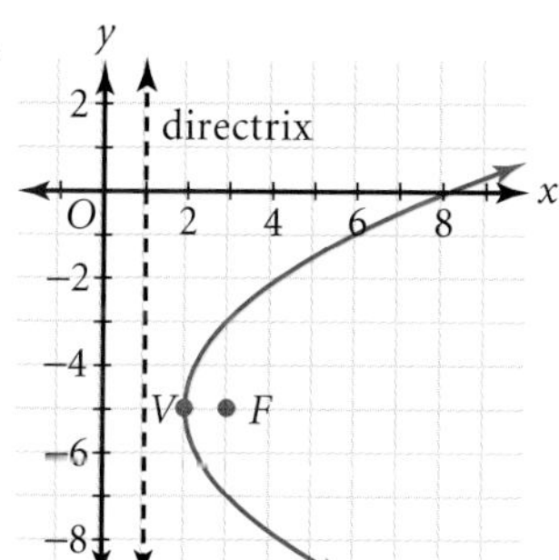

3.

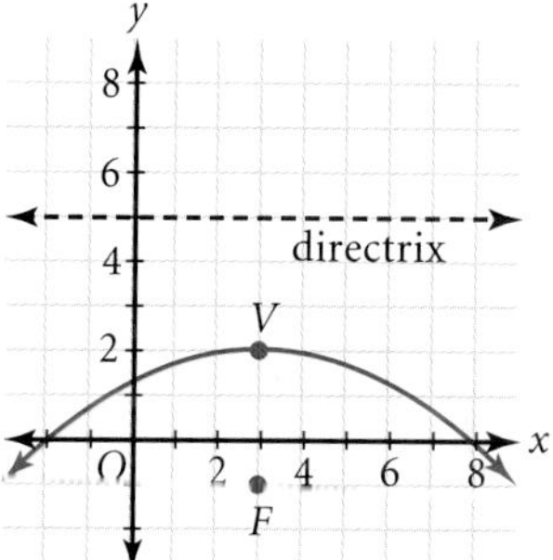

Graph each equation. Label the vertex, focus, and directrix.

4. $y = \frac{1}{2}x^2$
5. $x = -\frac{1}{4}y^2$
6. $y = -\frac{1}{12}x^2$
7. $y - 2 = (x - 2)^2$
8. $x + 3 = \frac{1}{8}(y - 1)^2$
9. $y - x^2 + 6x = 0$
10. $y - x^2 + 2x = 0$
11. $y - x^2 - 10x = 27$
12. $x^2 + 2x - 3y = 5$

Write the standard equation for a parabola with the given characteristics.

13. vertex: $(0, 0)$
directrix: $x = -15$

14. focus: $(-2, 3)$
directrix: $x = 2$

15. vertex: $(0, 2)$
directrix: $y = -4$

16. vertex: $(2, 0)$
focus: $(6, 0)$

17. focus: $(1, 1)$
directrix: $y = 0$

18. vertex: $(3, 2)$
focus: $(6, 2)$

19. The parabola defined by the equation $y = -2x^2 + 12x - 13$ is translated 3 units up and 2 units to the left. Write the standard equation of the resulting parabola.

Extra Practice

LESSON 9.3

Write the standard equation for each circle below.

1.

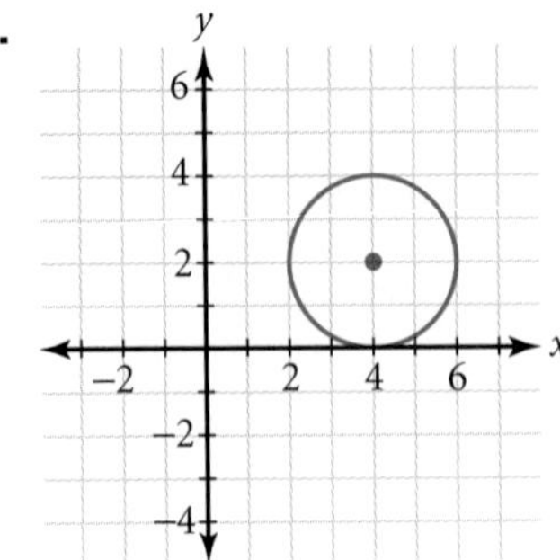

2.

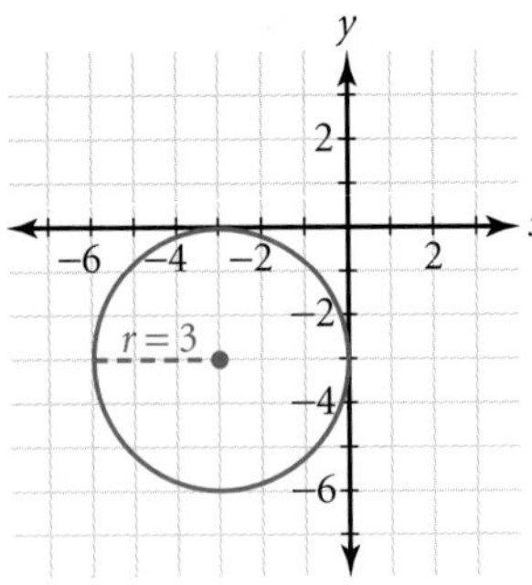

3.

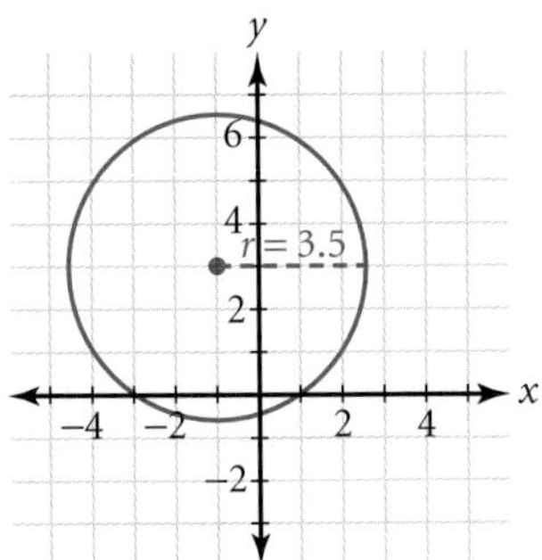

Write the standard equation of a circle with each given radius and center.

4. $r = 5$; $C\,(0, 4)$ **5.** $r = 4.5$; $C(0, 0)$ **6.** $r = 1.5$; $C(-3, -5)$

Write the standard equation for each circle. Then state the coordinates of its center and give its radius.

7. $x^2 + y^2 - 16x + 4y = -43$ **8.** $x^2 - 8x + y^2 = 33$ **9.** $x^2 + y^2 - 20x - 10y + 61 = 0$

Graph each equation. Label the center and the radius.

10. $\left(x - \frac{5}{2}\right)2 + y^2 = \frac{25}{4}$ **11.** $(x - 5)^2 + (y - 9)^2 = 100$ **12.** $x^2 + (y - 7)^2 = \frac{49}{4}$

13. State whether $C(-1, 3)$ is inside, outside, or on the circle whose equation is $x^2 + y^2 - 12x - 2y = 8$.

LESSON 9.4

Write the standard equation for each ellipse below.

1.

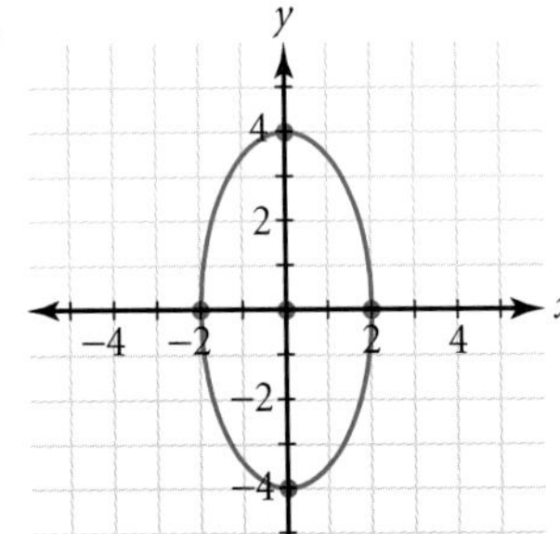

2.

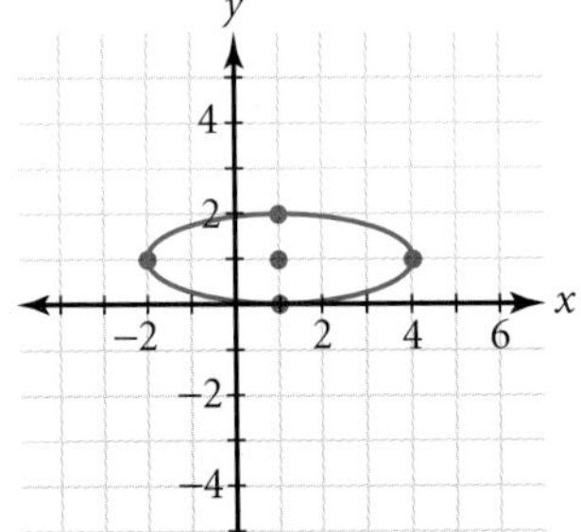

3.

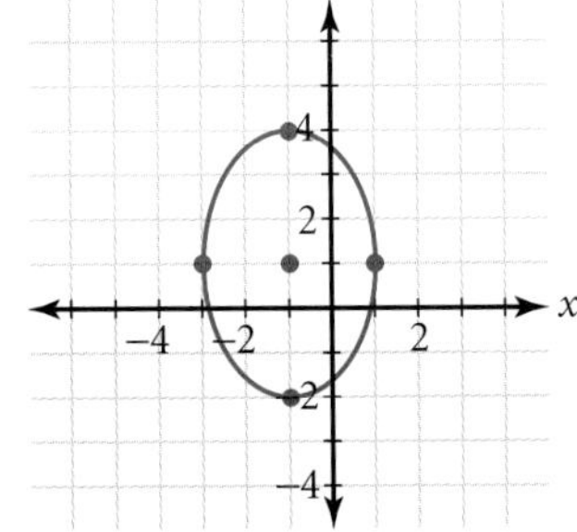

Write the standard equation of each ellipse. Find the coordinates of its center, vertices, co-vertices, and foci.

4. $25x^2 + 9y^2 = 225$ **5.** $49x^2 + y^2 = 49$ **6.** $x^2 + 4y^2 = 64$

7. $x^2 - 2x + 9y^2 - 8 = 0$ **8.** $x^2 + 4y^2 - 18x - 8y + 81 = 0$ **9.** $9x^2 + 4y^2 - 144x - 8y = -544$

Write the standard equation for an ellipse with the given characteristics.

10. foci: $(-2, 0)$, $(2, 0)$; vertices: $(-6, 0)$, $(6, 0)$ **11.** foci: $(0, -3)$, $(0, 3)$; vertices: $(0, -4)$, $(0, 4)$

Graph each ellipse. Label the center, foci, vertices, and co-vertices.

12. $\frac{x^2}{100} + \frac{y^2}{25} = 1$ **13.** $\frac{x^2}{4} + \frac{y^2}{25} = 1$ **14.** $\frac{(x-2)^2}{16} + \frac{(y-1)^2}{25} = 1$

LESSON 9.5

Write the standard equation for each hyperbola below.

1.

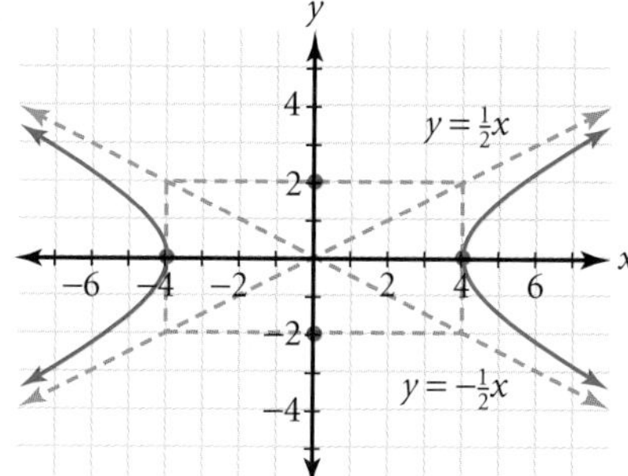

2.

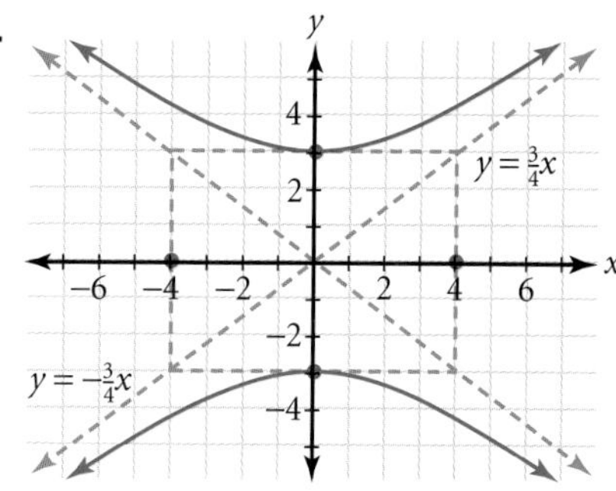

Write the standard equation for each hyperbola. Give the coordinates of the center, vertices, co-vertices, and foci.

3. $x^2 - 100y^2 = 100$

4. $25y^2 - 100y + 100 - x^2 = 25$

5. $9x^2 - 4y^2 - 18x + 8y = 31$

Write the standard equation for a hyperbola with the given characteristics.

6. vertices: $(-6, 0)$ and $(6, 0)$; foci: $(-8, 0)$ and $(8, 0)$

7. vertices: $(0, -12)$ and $(0, 12)$; co-vertices: $(-11, 0)$ and $(11, 0)$

Graph each hyperbola. Label the center, vertices, co-vertices, foci, and asymptotes.

8. $\frac{x^2}{9} - \frac{y^2}{4} = 1$

9. $\frac{y^2}{36} - \frac{x^2}{9} = 1$

10. $\frac{(x-2)^2}{4} - (y-1)^2 = 1$

11. The hyperbola defined by the equation $25x^2 - 36y^2 = 900$ is translated 4 units up and 3 units to the right. Write the standard equation of the resulting ellipse.

LESSON 9.6

Use the substitution method to solve each system. If there are no real solutions, write *none*.

1. $\begin{cases} y = 7 - x \\ y = x^2 + 1 \end{cases}$

2. $\begin{cases} y = 12 - 6x \\ x^2 + y = 4 \end{cases}$

3. $\begin{cases} x = 12y - 4 \\ x^2 - 16y^2 = 16 \end{cases}$

Use the elimination method to solve each system. If there are no real solutions, write *none*.

4. $\begin{cases} 4x^2 + y^2 = 20 \\ x^2 + 4y^2 = 20 \end{cases}$

5. $\begin{cases} x^2 + y^2 = 36 \\ 9x^2 + 4y^2 = 16 \end{cases}$

6. $\begin{cases} 16x^2 + 9y^2 = 144 \\ -48x^2 + y^2 = 144 \end{cases}$

Solve each system by graphing. Round answers to the nearest hundredth, if necessary. If there are no real solutions, write *none*.

7. $\begin{cases} x^2 + y^2 = 16 \\ 2x^2 - y^2 = -4 \end{cases}$

8. $\begin{cases} 3y^2 - 4x^2 = 1 \\ x^2 + y^2 = 9 \end{cases}$

9. $\begin{cases} 9x^2 + 16y^2 = 144 \\ 3x^2 - 2y^2 = 6 \end{cases}$

Classify the conic section defined by each equation. Write the standard equation of the conic section, and sketch the graph.

10. $x^2 - 8x + y = -2$

11. $x^2 + y^2 - 6x - 10y = 2$

12. $x^2 + 10x - 8y = -73$

13. $9x^2 + 4y^2 - 72x - 32y = -172$

14. $9x^2 - 4y^2 + 54x + 8y + 41 = 0$

15. $4x^2 + 25y^2 + 16x + 50y - 59 = 0$

Extra Practice

Chapter 10

LESSON 10.1

Find the probability of each event.

1. A yellow marble is drawn at random from a bag containing 3 white, 2 yellow, 1 green, and 4 blue marbles.
2. Arden arrives at home at 10:07 P.M. and is there to receive a package that was expected at any time between 10:00 P.M. and 10:15 P.M.
3. When a 6-sided number cube is rolled, a number less than 5 appears.
4. A card chosen at random from a standard deck is red.
5. When an 8-sided number cube is rolled, a multiple of 3 appears.
6. A card chosen at random from a standard deck is a jack, queen, king, or ace.

A spinner is divided into three colored regions. The results of 125 spins are recorded in the table at right. Find the probability of each event.

red	53
blue	32
yellow	40

7. red
8. blue
9. yellow

Find the number of possible passwords (with no letters or digits excluded) for each of the following conditions:

10. 2 letters followed by 3 digits, with no letters or digits excluded
11. 3 letters followed by 3 digits, with only vowels and even digits allowed (Consider *y* a consonant.)
12. 2 letters followed by 2 digits followed by 3 letters, with no letters or digits excluded
13. In a 5-digit U.S. zip code, the last 2 digits identify the local delivery area. How many local delivery areas can be designated if any digit can be used?
14. For a given telephone area code, how many 7-digit telephone numbers are possible if the first digit cannot be 0?

LESSON 10.2

A city recreation program has one summer job available at each of its 6 parks. In how many ways can the 6 jobs be assigned if the given number of employees are available?

1. 6
2. 10
3. 12
4. 15

Find the number of permutations of the digits 1–5 for each situation.

5. using all 5 digits
6. taking 3 digits at a time
7. taking 4 digits at a time
8. taking 2 digits at a time

Find the number of permutations of the letters in each word.

9. *heptagon*
10. *pentagon*
11. *circle*
12. *textbook*

13. The United Nations Security Council has 15 member nations. In how many ways can the representatives be seated around a circular table if each nation has one representative?
14. The 8 winning entries in a school art contest are to be displayed in a row. In how many different orders can the entries be displayed?
15. A shoe store has 6 different models of running shoes on sale. In how many ways can a rotating display of the models be arranged?

LESSON 10.3

Find the number of ways in which each committee can be selected.

1. 2 people from a group of 5 people
2. 4 people from a group of 7 people
3. 3 people from a group of 8 people
4. 1 person from a group of 9 people

A take-out restaurant offers a selection of 5 main dishes, 4 vegetables, and 3 desserts. In how many ways can a family choose a meal consisting of the following?

5. 2 different main dishes, 3 different vegetables, and 1 dessert
6. 3 different main dishes, 2 different vegetables, and 3 different desserts
7. 5 different main dishes, 4 different vegetables, and 3 different desserts

Four marbles are chosen at random (without replacement) from a bag containing 4 white marbles and 6 green marbles. Find the probability of selecting each combination.

8. 4 green
9. 2 white *and* 2 green
10. 1 white *and* 3 green

Fifteen students are entered in a public-speaking contest. Determine whether each situation involves a permutation or a combination.

11. The order in which the contestants speak must be chosen.
12. First, second, and third prizes are awarded.
13. Two of the 15 represent the school in a regional contest.
14. In a survey of 50 voters, 33 favor a policy change, and 17 oppose it or have no opinion. Find the probability that in a random sample of 10 respondents from this survey, exactly 8 favor the proposed regulation and 2 oppose it or have no opinion.

LESSON 10.4

A card is drawn at random from a standard deck of playing cards. State whether the events *A* and *B* are inclusive or mutually exclusive. Then find *P*(*A or B*). (Note: A standard deck of 52 cards has 12 face cards, 4 of which are kings. Also, exactly half of the cards are red, including 6 of the face cards and 2 of the kings.)

1. *A*: The card is a queen.
   B: The card is a king.
2. *A*: The card is red.
   B: The card is a king.
3. *A*: The card is red.
   B: The card is not a king.
4. *A*: The card is a face card.
   B: The card is not a king.
5. *A*: The card is red.
   B: The card is not red.
6. *A*: The card is a face card.
   B: The card is a king.

A number cube is rolled once, and the number on the top face is recorded. Find the probability of each pair of events.

7. The number is even *or* greater than 5.
8. The number is 5 *or* a multiple of 3.
9. The number is odd *or* greater than 4.
10. The number is greater than 2 *or* less than 5.

Each of the digits from 0 to 9 is written on a card. The cards are placed in a sack, and one is drawn at random. Find the probability of each pair of events.

11. digit is odd *or* a multiple of 3
12. digit is less than 2 *or* greater than 8
13. digit is odd *or* less than 5
14. digit is greater than 7 *or* even

LESSON 10.5

A coin is tossed 3 times. Find the probability of each event.

1. All 3 tosses are heads.
2. The first toss is heads, but the second and the third are tails.

Events Q, R, and S are independent, and $P(Q) = 0.2$, $P(R) = 0.4$, and $P(S) = 0.1$. Find each probability.

3. $P(Q \text{ and } R)$
4. $P(Q \text{ and } S)$
5. $P(R \text{ and } S)$

A red number cube and a green number cube are rolled. Find the probability of each event.

6. The red cube is a 3, *and* the green cube is greater than 3.
7. The red cube is greater than 1, *and* the green cube is less than 6.
8. The red cube is less than or equal to 4, *and* the green cube is greater than or equal to 5.
9. The green cube is less than or equal to 6, *and* the red cube is greater than or equal to 1.

A bag contains 3 red, 2 green, and 5 blue marbles. A marble is picked at random and is replaced. A second marble is picked at random. Find the probability of each event.

10. Both marbles are red.
11. The first marble is green, *and* the second is blue.
12. Neither marble is green.
13. The first marble is blue, *and* the second is not blue.

A number cube is rolled twice. On each roll, the number on the top face of the cube is recorded. Find the probability of each event.

14. The first number is even, *and* the second number is greater than 3.
15. The first number is greater than 4, *and* the second number is less than 3.

LESSON 10.6

A bag contains 5 red, 7 blue, and 4 white marbles. Two consecutive draws are made from the bag without replacement of the first draw. Find each probability.

1. red first *and* blue second
2. red first *and* white second
3. blue first *and* red second
4. white first *and* white second

Two number cubes are rolled, and the first cube shows a 3. Find the probability of each event below.

5. a sum of 8
6. one even number *and* one odd number
7. a sum of less than 6
8. a sum of greater than 5 *and* less than 9

For one roll of a number cube, let A be the event "even" and let B be the event "4". Find each probability.

9. $P(A)$
10. $P(B)$
11. $P(A \text{ and } B)$
12. $P(A \text{ or } B)$
13. $P(A \mid B)$
14. $P(B \mid A)$

For one roll of a number cube, let A be the event "less than 4" and let B be the event "1 *or* 2". Find each probability.

15. $P(A)$
16. $P(B)$
17. $P(A \text{ and } B)$
18. $P(A \text{ or } B)$
19. $P(A \mid B)$
20. $P(B \mid A)$

21. Given that $P(A \text{ and } B) = 0.2$ and $P(A) = 0.5$, find $P(B \mid A)$.
22. Given that $P(B \mid A) = 0.8$ and $P(A \text{ and } B) = 0.6$, find $P(A)$.

LESSON 10.7

Use a simulation with 20 trials to estimate each probability. Simulation results may vary.

1. In 3 tosses of a coin, 2 consecutive heads will appear.
2. In 4 tosses of a coin, tails will appear exactly once.
3. In 3 rolls of a number cube, the number 3 will appear exactly twice.
4. In 5 rolls of a number cube, the number 4 will appear exactly 3 times.
5. In 6 rolls of a number cube, the number 1 will not appear.

Of 150 motorists observed at an intersection, 47 turned left, 72 went straight, and 31 turned right. Use a simulation with 10 trials to estimate the probability of each event.

6. At least 2 out of every 5 consecutive motorists go straight.
7. More than 1 out of every 5 consecutive motorists turn left.
8. Less than 3 out of every 5 consecutive motorists turn right.
9. At least 3 out of every 5 consecutive motorists do not go straight.
10. No more than 1 out of every 5 consecutive motorists goes left.

11. Assume that a person who is learning to play darts has acquired enough skill to hit the target but is just as likely to hit any one spot on the target as any other. Use a simulation with 10 trials to estimate the probability that exactly 3 out of 5 darts that land on the square target shown at right land inside the circle.

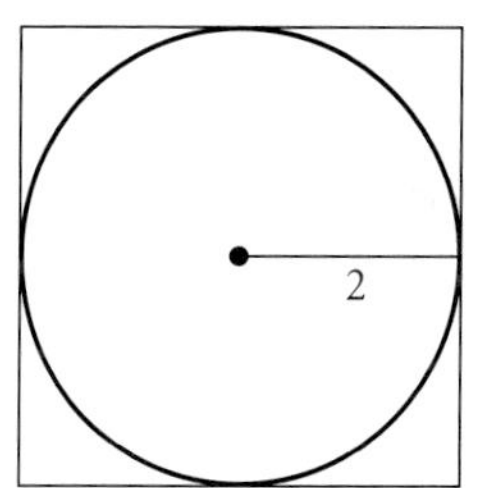

Chapter 11

LESSON 11.1

Write the first five terms of each sequence.

1. $t_n = -3n + 8$
2. $t_n = 4n - 12$
3. $t_n = 2n^2$
4. $t_1 = 1$
   $t_n = t_{n-1} + 5$
5. $t_1 = 16$
   $t_n = t_{n-1} - 6$
6. $t_1 = 3$
   $t_n = 2t_{n-1}$

Write a recursive formula for each sequence and find the next three terms.

7. 1, 10, 19, 28, . . .
8. 2, 7, 12, 17, . . .
9. 4, 9, 19, 34, . . .

Write the terms of each series and then evaluate the sum.

10. $\sum_{n=1}^{6}(12n + 1)$
11. $\sum_{j=1}^{5}(j - 1)^2$
12. $\sum_{k=1}^{4}(3k^2 + 4k)$

Evaluate.

13. $\sum_{m=1}^{6} 5m$
14. $\sum_{n=1}^{5}(10n - 3)$
15. $\sum_{j=1}^{4}(2j^2 - 3j + 1)$

LESSON 11.2

Based on the terms given, state whether each sequence is arithmetic. If it is, identify the common difference, *d*.

1. 5, 7, 10, 14, 19, . . .
2. −8, −5, −2, 1, 4, . . .
3. 1, 8, 27, 64, 125, . . .
4. 0.1, 0.2, 0.3, 0.4, 0.5, . . .
5. 4.4, 5.5, 6.6, 7.7, . . .
6. 1.2, 3.4, 5.6, 7.8, . . .

Write an explicit formula for the *n*th term of each arithmetic sequence.

7. 5, 8, 11, 14, 17, . . .
8. 7, 3, −1, −5, −9, . . .
9. 10, 16, 22, 28, 34, . . .
10. 30, 37, 44, 51, 58, . . .
11. −12, −8, −4, 0, 4, . . .
12. 40, 33, 26, 19, 12, . . .

List the first four terms of each arithmetic sequence.

13. $t_1 = 5, t_n = t_{n-1} + 11$
14. $t_1 = -13, t_n = t_{n-1} + 10$
15. $t_1 = 0, t_n = t_{n-1} + 20$
16. $t_n = 5n - 8$
17. $t_n = -8n - 4$
18. $t_n = 6n - 10$

Find the indicated number of arithmetic means between the two given numbers.

19. three arithmetic means between 5 and 29
20. four arithmetic means between −12 and 28
21. two arithmetic means between 6.5 and 15.8
22. three arithmetic means between −6 and 4

LESSON 11.3

Use the formula for an arithmetic series to find each sum.

1. $3 + 6 + 9 + 12 + 15$
2. $-8 + (-15) + (-22) + (-29) + (-36)$
3. $40 + 42 + 44 + \cdots + 68$
4. $-45 + (-40) + (-35) + (-30) + \cdots + 25$
5. Find the sum of the first 175 natural numbers.
6. Find the sum of the multiples of 6 from 18 to 120 inclusive.
7. Find the sum of the multiples of 8 from 40 to 480 inclusive.

For each arithmetic series, find S_{20}.

8. 4, 8, 12, 16, 20, 24, . . .
9. 3, 8, 13, 18, 23, . . .
10. −15, −12, −9, −6, −3, . . .
11. −20, −40, −60, −80, −100, . . .
12. $\pi, 3\pi, 5\pi, 7\pi, 9\pi, \ldots$
13. $\sqrt{7}, 4\sqrt{7}, 7\sqrt{7}, 10\sqrt{7}, \ldots$

Evaluate.

14. $\sum_{j=1}^{5} (24 - 3j)$
15. $\sum_{n=1}^{8} (15n - 1)$
16. $\sum_{k=1}^{10} (3k + 50)$
17. $\sum_{m=1}^{20} (120 - 10m)$
18. $\sum_{n=1}^{12} (25n + 4)$
19. $\sum_{k=1}^{15} (10 + 20k)$

LESSON 11.4

Determine whether each sequence is a geometric sequence. If so, identify the common ratio, *r*, and give the next three terms.

1. $12, 6, 3, \frac{3}{2}, \ldots$

2. $11, 22, 44, 88, \ldots$

3. $-2, -6, -18, -54, \ldots$

4. $27, 9, 3, 1, \ldots$

5. $25, 36, 49, 64, \ldots$

6. $25, 2.5, 0.25, 0.025, \ldots$

List the first four terms of each geometric sequence.

7. $t_1 = 5$, $t_n = 0.2t_{n-1}$

8. $t_1 = 4$, $t_n = 10t_{n-1}$

9. $t_1 = -2$, $t_n = -4.5t_{n-1}$

Find the fifth term in the geometric sequence that includes the given terms.

10. $t_2 = 48$; $t_3 = 144$

11. $t_2 = 224$; $t_4 = 14$

12. $t_3 = 75$; $t_8 = 234{,}375$

Write an explicit formula for the *n*th term of each geometric sequence.

13. $0.04, 0.2, 1, 5, \ldots$

14. $16, 8, 4, 2, \ldots$

15. $\sqrt{6}, 6, 6\sqrt{6}, 36, \ldots$

Find the indicated number of geometric means between the two given numbers.

16. two geometric means between 12 and 324

17. two geometric means between 6.4 and 21.6

18. three geometric means between 16 and 81

19. three geometric means between 8 and 312.5

LESSON 11.5

Find each sum. Round answers to the nearest tenth, if necessary.

1. S_{10} for the geometric series $3 + 6 + 12 + 24 + \cdots$

2. S_8 for the geometric series $-32 + 16 + (-8) + 4 + (-2) + \cdots$

3. $\frac{3}{4} + \frac{3}{8} + \frac{3}{16} + \frac{3}{32} + \frac{3}{64} + \frac{3}{128}$

4. $-0.48 + 2.4 - 12 + 60 - 300$

For Exercises 5–8, refer to the series $0.2 + 0.6 + 1.8 + 5.4 + \cdots$

5. Find t_8.

6. Find t_{16}.

7. Find S_8.

8. Find S_{16}.

Evaluate. Round answers to the nearest tenth, if necessary.

9. $\sum_{k=1}^{8} 2(3^k - 1)$

10. $\sum_{n=1}^{6} 4(0.5^n)$

11. $\sum_{k=1}^{10} 3.5^{k-1}$

12. $\sum_{k=1}^{20} 0.5(2^{k-1})$

Use mathematical induction to prove that each statement is true for every natural number, *n*.

13. $\frac{1}{2} + \frac{1}{2^2} + \frac{1}{2^3} + \cdots + \frac{1}{2^n} = 1 - \frac{1}{2^n}$

14. $1^3 + 3^3 + 5^3 + \cdots + (2n - 1)^3 = n^2(2n^2 - 1)$

LESSON 11.6

Find the sum of each infinite geometric series, if it exists.

1. $\frac{1}{5} + \frac{1}{25} + \frac{1}{125} + \frac{1}{625} + \cdots$

2. $20 + 12 + 7.2 + 4.32 + \cdots$

3. $0.2 + 0.4 + 0.8 + 1 + \cdots$

4. $5 + \frac{5}{7} + \frac{5}{49} + \frac{5}{343} + \cdots$

Find the sum of each infinite geometric series, if it exists.

5. $\sum_{n=0}^{\infty} 4^n$

6. $\sum_{k=1}^{\infty} \frac{3}{5^k}$

7. $\sum_{n=1}^{\infty} 0.4^n - 1$

8. $\sum_{k=0}^{\infty} (-0.25)^k$

Write each decimal as a fraction in simplest form.

9. $0.\overline{7}$

10. $0.\overline{23}$

11. $0.\overline{321}$

12. $0.\overline{726}$

Write an infinite geometric series that converges to the given number.

13. 0.3131313131 . . .

14. 0.4747474747 . . .

15. 0.357357357 . . .

LESSON 11.7

State the location of each entry in Pascal's triangle. Then give the value of each expression.

1. ${}_4C_2$

2. ${}_9C_5$

3. ${}_8C_3$

4. ${}_6C_5$

5. ${}_{10}C_7$

6. ${}_{15}C_7$

7. ${}_{11}C_8$

8. ${}_{20}C_{10}$

Find the fifth and eighth entries in the indicated row of Pascal's triangle.

9. row 8

10. row 10

11. row 13

12. row 16

Find the probability of each event.

13. exactly 3 heads in 4 tosses of a fair coin

14. 3 *or* 4 heads in 8 tosses of a fair coin

15. no more than 3 heads in 7 tosses of a fair coin

16. no fewer than 4 heads in 9 tosses of a fair coin

17. 3 *or* 4 *or* 5 heads in 10 tosses of a fair coin

A student guesses the answers for 8 items on a true-false quiz. Find the probability that the indicated number of answers is correct.

18. exactly 6

19. at least 5

20. at most 4

LESSON 11.8

Expand each binomial.

1. $(a + b)^4$
2. $(w + z)^5$
3. $(c + d)^6$
4. $(1 + x)^3$
5. $(y + 2)^5$
6. $(z + 1)^4$

For Exercises 7–8, refer to the expansion of $(x + y)^{12}$.

7. How many terms are in the expansion?
8. What is the exponent of x in the term containing y^7? What is the term?

Expand each binomial.

9. $(2x + y)^5$
10. $(3z - 2)^4$
11. $(x - 2y)^4$
12. $(3y - 2z)^5$
13. $\left(\frac{1}{2}x + 2y\right)^3$
14. $\left(\frac{2}{3}x - y\right)^3$

Use the Binomial Theorem to find each theoretical probability for a baseball player with a batting average of 0.250.

15. exactly 4 hits in 5 at bats
16. no more than 3 hits in 5 at bats
17. exactly 2 hits in 6 at bats
18. no more than 3 hits in 6 at bats

Chapter 12

LESSON 12.1

Find the mean, median, and mode of each data set. Round answers to the nearest thousandth, if necessary.

1. 12, 16, 22, 45, 30, 58, 11, 21, 29, 37
2. 92, 90, 88, 88, 99, 70, 55, 85, 92, 93, 90
3. 12.6, 8.5, 7.7, 9.9, 12.8, 12.6, 12.5, 13.2
4. 5, 5, 6, 16, 24, 32, 5, 66, 7, 10, 22, 6

Find the mean, median, and mode of each data set and compare the three measures.

5. minimum starting salaries (in dollars per year) in selected professional specialties: 35,700; 24,700; 34,100; 35,700; 22,900; 29,300; 28,300
6. number of people (in millions) viewing prime-time television in a given week: 94.5, 93.2, 85.2, 88.8, 79.2, 77.6, 92.8

Make a frequency table for each data set and find the mean.

7. workers' sick days in one year: 0, 5, 2, 1, 3, 5, 5, 10, 22, 0, 0, 4, 3, 2, 0, 0, 1, 1, 1, 8
8. the number of bicycles in students' families: 1, 4, 3, 3, 6, 2, 4, 4, 3, 1, 1, 1, 2, 2, 2, 3, 5, 4, 4, 3

Make a grouped frequency table for each data set and estimate the mean.

9. class test scores: 88, 72, 65, 58, 90, 71, 66, 82, 76, 75, 77, 91, 56, 70, 92, 80, 66, 86, 84, 75
10. the number of hours worked per week: 40, 32, 30, 44, 40, 52, 30, 25, 20, 42, 46, 38, 35, 27, 55, 51

LESSON 12.2

Make a stem-and-leaf plot for each data set. Then find the median and the mode, and describe the distribution of the data.

1. 16, 22, 26, 43, 30, 12, 15, 40, 47, 25, 46, 33, 32, 12

2. 55, 87, 92, 50, 54, 58, 57, 72, 88, 96, 90, 78, 74, 55, 60, 61, 76

Make a frequency table and a histogram for each data set.

3. 3, 5, 7, 2, 2, 3, 5, 5, 6, 6, 6, 2, 3, 4, 1, 5, 7, 5, 4, 6, 7, 7, 2, 1, 2, 7, 5, 3

4. 13, 16, 15, 12, 12, 15, 18, 20, 17, 16, 15, 16, 12, 13, 17, 19, 20, 15, 15, 14

Make a relative frequency table and a histogram of probabilities for each data set.

5. 20, 22, 25, 21, 24, 22, 25, 23, 23, 20, 21, 25, 22, 21, 24, 21, 22, 23, 25, 22

6. 5, 4, 8, 5, 8, 4, 6, 8, 4, 5, 8, 8, 4, 8, 4, 8, 6, 5, 5, 5, 7, 6, 5, 7, 5

The table below lists the number of United States military personnel by branch.

United States Military Personnel, 1996

Army	Air Force	Navy	Marine Corps
493,330	389,400	436,608	172,287

7a. Make a circle graph to represent this data.

b. Find the probability that a randomly selected person in the U.S. military is in the marines or the navy.

LESSON 12.3

Find the minimum and maximum values, quartiles, range, and interquartile range for each data set. Then make a box-and-whisker plot for each data set.

1. 12, 35, 22, 18, 16, 21, 19, 33, 7, 10, 14, 28, 27, 16, 13

2. 5.4, 7.8, 1.1, 9.2, 12.6, 15.5, 18.0, 16.2, 18.8, 12.1, 13.2, 13.2, 15.0, 16.3, 20.2

3. 210, 185, 340, 715, 224, 290, 168, 312, 272, 300

4. 47, 40, 31, 22, 62, 50, 43, 28, 47, 35, 32, 44, 29, 28, 56, 50, 52, 54, 36, 20, 22

5. 5.0, 6.5, 8.0, 3.2, 8.1, 7.4, 6.7, 6.2, 5.0, 12.3, 5.7, 6.3, 6.8, 5.7, 7.2, 8.4

The box-and-whisker plots below compare the state per capita personal incomes in dollars for 1990 and 1995. Refer to the box-and-whisker plots for Exercises 6–8.

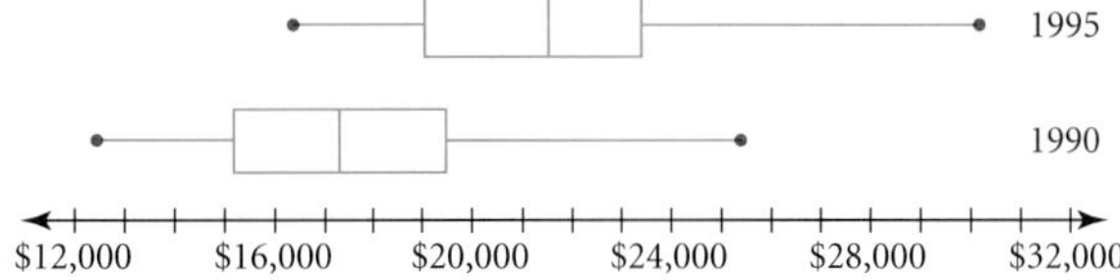

6. Which data set has the greater range?

7. Compare the interquartile ranges for the two data sets.

8. Q_1 for the 1995 data and Q_3 for the 1990 data are about the same. Describe what this means in terms of the distribution of the data.

LESSON 12.4

Find the range and the mean deviation for each data set.

1. 6, 5, 3, 2, 4, 6, 8, 6

2. 20, 22, 20, 21, 23, 26

3. 5, 8, 10, 16, 9, 12

4. 28, 40, 20, 32, 30, 54

5. −12, 25, 17, −8, 15

6. 3.5, 4.0, 2.8, 3.8, 7.2, 7.5

Find the variance and the standard deviation for each data set.

7. 52, 61, 54, 48, 72

8. 115, 120, 132, 140, 113

9. 61, 20, 93, 72, 30, 24

10. 0.4, 1.1, 6.9, 9.8, 6.3

11. 9, 7, 3, 1, 2, 8

12. 59, 60, 7, 37, 69

The table below shows the number of free throws made by the 15 best free-throw shooters in the National Basketball Association for the 1995–1996 season. Refer to the table for Exercises 13–14.

146	259	338	130	167	425	430	132
125	342	137	146	135	247	172	

13. Find the range and the mean deviation of the data.

14. Find the standard deviation of the data.

LESSON 12.5

A coin is flipped 5 times. Find the probability of each event.

1. exactly 3 heads

2. exactly 2 heads

3. at least 4 heads

4. at most 4 heads

5. at most 1 heads

6. at least 2 heads

A spinner is divided into 6 congruent segments, each labeled with one of the letters *A–F*. Find each of the following probabilities:

7. exactly 3 *A*s in 5 spins

8. exactly 2 *D*s in 4 spins

9. more than 2 *B*s in 5 spins

10. no more than 2 *C*s in 4 spins

Find the probability that a batter will get *exactly* 3 hits in her next 6 at bats given each batting average below.

11. 0.300

12. 0.280

13. 0.312

Find the probability that a batter will get *at least* 3 hits in his next 6 at bats given each batting average below.

14. 0.290

15. 0.285

16. 0.315

LESSON 12.6

Let x be a random variable with a standard normal distribution. Use the area table for a standard normal curve, given on page 807, to find each probability.

1. $P(x \leq 0.4)$

2. $P(x \geq 0.6)$

3. $P(1.4 \leq x \leq 1.8)$

4. $P(x \leq -0.8)$

5. $P(-0.2 \leq x \leq 1.4)$

6. $P(x \geq -0.6)$

At one university, the ages of first-year students are approximately normally distributed with a mean of 19 and a standard deviation of 1. A first-year student is chosen at random. Find the probability that the student is

7. not less than 21 years old.

8. 19 or younger.

9. between 18 and 20 inclusive.

10. between 19 and 21 inclusive.

On an assembly line, the time required to perform a certain task is approximately normally distributed with a mean of 140 seconds and a standard deviation of 10 seconds. Of 1000 separate tasks, how many can be expected to take the given number of seconds?

11. more than 150 seconds

12. less than 150 seconds

13. between 120 and 150 seconds

14. more than 160 seconds

Chapter 13

LESSON 13.1

Refer to $\triangle XYZ$ at right in order to find each value below. Give exact answers and answers rounded to the nearest ten-thousandth.

1. sin Y

2. sin X

3. cos Y

4. cos X

5. tan Y

6. tan X

7. csc Y

8. csc X

9. sec Y

10. sec X

11. cot Y

12. cot X

Solve each triangle. Round angle measures to the nearest degree and side lengths to the nearest tenth.

13.

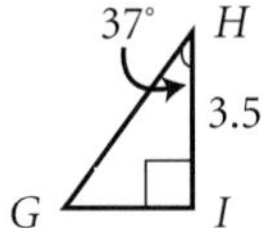

14.

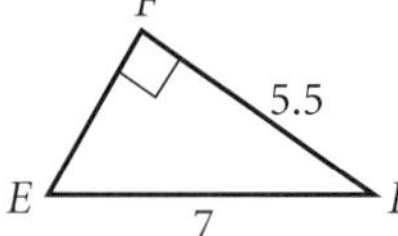

15.

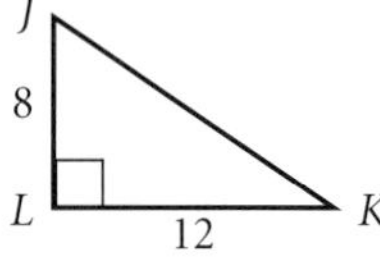

16.

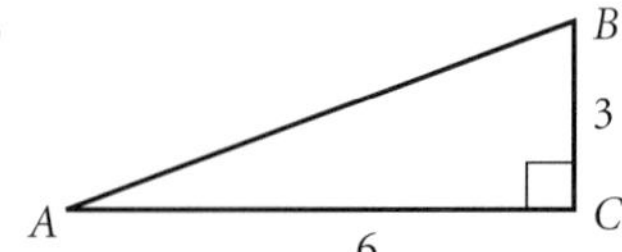

17.

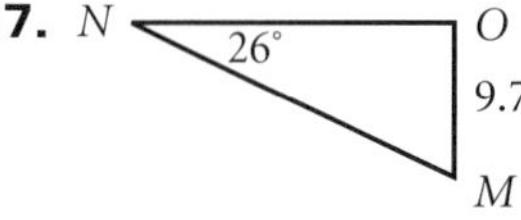

18.

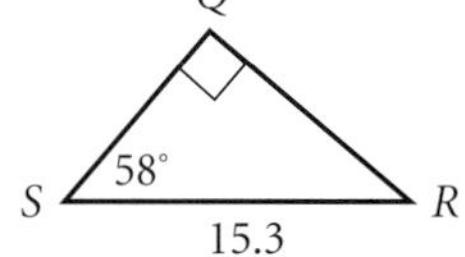

LESSON 13.2

For each angle below, find all coterminal angles such that $-360^\circ < \theta < 360^\circ$.

1. 114° **2.** 22° **3.** -53°

4. -272° **5.** 512° **6.** -495°

Find the reference angle for each angle below.

7. 117° **8.** -78° **9.** 1024°

10. -512° **11.** 245° **12.** 311°

Given each point on the terminal side of θ in standard position, find the exact values of the six trigonometric functions of θ.

13. $(3, 6)$ **14.** $(-4, 5)$ **15.** $(3, -8)$

16. $(2, -\sqrt{2})$ **17.** $(-4, -3)$ **18.** $(6, 5)$

Given the quadrant of θ in standard position and a trigonometric function value of θ, find the exact values for the indicated function.

19. I, $\tan\theta = \sqrt{3}$; $\cos\theta$ **20.** III, $\sin\theta = -\frac{5}{13}$; $\cos\theta$ **21.** IV, $\csc\theta = -\frac{4}{3}$; $\tan\theta$

LESSON 13.3

Point *P* is located at the intersection of a circle with a radius of *r* and the terminal side of angle θ in standard position. Find the exact coordinates of *P*.

1. $\theta = -60^\circ, r = 10$ **2.** $\theta = 120^\circ, r = 6$ **3.** $\theta = 45^\circ, r = 100$

4. $\theta = 300^\circ, r = 2$ **5.** $\theta = 135^\circ, r = 20$ **6.** $\theta = 330^\circ, r = 50$

Point *P* is located at the intersection of a unit circle and the terminal side of angle θ in standard position. Find the coordinates of *P* to the nearest hundredth.

7. $\theta = 50^\circ$ **8.** $\theta = -95^\circ$ **9.** $\theta = 345^\circ$

Find the exact values of the sine, cosine, and tangent of each angle.

10. -300° **11.** 405° **12.** -420° **13.** 1380°

14. 495° **15.** 330° **16.** -1800° **17.** 930°

Find each trigonometric value. Give exact answers.

18. $\cos 495^\circ$ **19.** $\tan 870^\circ$ **20.** $\sin 780^\circ$

21. $\sin 330^\circ$ **22.** $\cos 405^\circ$ **23.** $\sin 570^\circ$

24. $\tan 405^\circ$ **25.** $\cos 660^\circ$ **26.** $\tan 420^\circ$

27. $\tan 1395^\circ$ **28.** $\sin(-1485^\circ)$ **29.** $\cos 660^\circ$

30. $\sin 1110^\circ$ **31.** $\sec 780^\circ$ **32.** $\cot 300^\circ$

33. $\sin 390^\circ$ **34.** $\csc(-765^\circ)$ **35.** $\cot(-210^\circ)$

Extra Practice

LESSON 13.4

Convert each degree measure to radian measure. Give exact answers.

1. 30° **2.** −90° **3.** 20°

4. 400° **5.** 1080° **6.** 50°

Convert each radian measure to degree measure. Round answers to the nearest tenth of a degree, if necessary.

7. $\frac{2\pi}{3}$ radians **8.** $-\frac{\pi}{9}$ radian **9.** 3π radians

10. $-\frac{3\pi}{4}$ radians **11.** 3.245 radians **12.** −6.122 radians

Evaluate each expression. Give the values.

13. $\sin \frac{3\pi}{4}$ **14.** $\csc \frac{\pi}{6}$ **15.** $\tan(-2\pi)$ **16.** $\cos \frac{5\pi}{6}$

17. $\cos \frac{\pi}{3}$ **18.** $\tan\left(-\frac{3\pi}{4}\right)$ **19.** $\cot \frac{\pi}{4}$ **20.** $\cos\left(-\frac{11\pi}{6}\right)$

A circle has a diameter of 8 meters. For each central angle measure below, find the length in meters of the arc intercepted by the angle.

21. $\frac{5\pi}{6}$ radians **22.** $\frac{\pi}{12}$ radians **23.** 2.5 radians **24.** 1.2 radians

LESSON 13.5

Identify the amplitude, if it exists, and the period of each function.

1. $y = 3.5 \sin 4\theta$ **2.** $y = 8 \tan x$ **3.** $y = -6\cos(-x)$

4. $y = 7 \cos \frac{1}{2}\theta$ **5.** $y = \frac{2}{3} \sin 3\theta$ **6.** $y = -\frac{1}{2} \tan 6\theta$

Identify the phase shift and vertical translation of each function from its parent function.

7. $y = \cos(\theta + 45°) + 1$ **8.** $y = \sin(\theta + 180°) - 3$ **9.** $y = \tan(\theta - 90°)$

10. $y = 3 \cos(\theta - 30°) - 1$ **11.** $y = 3 + \sin(\theta - 45°)$ **12.** $y = 2 - \tan(\theta + 30°)$

Describe the transformation of each function from its parent function. Then graph at least one period of the given function and its parent function.

13. $y = 5 \sin \theta$ **14.** $y = \cos(\theta + 90°)$ **15.** $y = \tan 2\theta$

16. The sales of a seasonal product are modeled by the function $s(x) = 40 \sin \frac{\pi}{6}x + 74$, where s is thousands of units and x is time in months (beginning with 1 for January). Identify the amplitude, period, and phase shift of the function. Sketch a graph of the function for at least one period. In what month is greatest number of units sold?

LESSON 13.6

Find all possible values for each expression.

1. $\sin^{-1} \frac{\sqrt{3}}{2}$
2. $\cos^{-1} \frac{1}{2}$
3. $\cos^{-1}\left(-\frac{\sqrt{2}}{2}\right)$
4. $\tan^{-1} 1$
5. $\tan^{-1} -1$
6. $\sin^{-1} 0$

Evaluate each trigonometric expression.

7. $\mathrm{Cos}^{-1} 0$
8. $\mathrm{Sin}^{-1}\left(-\frac{1}{2}\right)$
9. $\mathrm{Cos}^{-1} \frac{\sqrt{3}}{2}$
10. $\mathrm{Tan}^{-1}(-\sqrt{3})$
11. $\mathrm{Sin}^{-1}\left(-\frac{\sqrt{2}}{2}\right)$
12. $\mathrm{Tan}^{-1} 0$

Evaluate each trigonometric expression.

13. $\tan\left(\mathrm{Sin}^{-1} \frac{\sqrt{3}}{2}\right)$
14. $\cos(\mathrm{Tan}^{-1} 1)$
15. $\sin\left[\mathrm{Cos}^{-1}\left(-\frac{\sqrt{2}}{2}\right)\right]$
16. $\mathrm{Sin}^{-1}(\cos 45^\circ)$
17. $\mathrm{Tan}^{-1}(\cos 90^\circ)$
18. $\mathrm{Sin}^{-1}(\cos 30^\circ)$
19. At one point in the day, a 15-foot flagpole casts a 19.5-foot shadow. Find the angle of elevation between the sun and the far end of the shadow.

Chapter 14

LESSON 14.1

Find the area of $\triangle ABC$ to the nearest tenth of a square unit.

1. $b = 18$ in., $c = 24$ in., $A = 42^\circ$
2. $a = 4$ m, $c = 9$ m, $B = 67^\circ$
3. $c = 20$ cm, $a = 10$ cm, $B = 110^\circ$
4. $b = 5$ in., $c = 4$ in., $A = 120^\circ$

Use the given information to find the indicated side length of $\triangle ABC$. Round answers to the nearest tenth, if necessary.

5. Given $A = 38^\circ$, $B = 50^\circ$, and $a = 7$, find b.
6. Given $B = 120^\circ$, $C = 42^\circ$, and $b = 70$, find c.
7. Given $A = 52^\circ$, $C = 88^\circ$, and $a = 6$, find c.
8. Given $C = 59^\circ$, $B = 63^\circ$, and $c = 15$, find b.

Solve each triangle. Round answers to the nearest tenth, if necessary.

9. $A = 65^\circ$, $C = 20^\circ$, $b = 9$
10. $C = 37^\circ$, $B = 20^\circ$, $a = 40$
11. $A = 21^\circ$, $C = 104^\circ$, $b = 10$
12. $B = 50^\circ$, $C = 32^\circ$, $a = 35$
13. $A = 50^\circ$, $C = 44^\circ$, $a = 12$
14. $A = 65^\circ$, $C = 70^\circ$, $b = 15$

State the number of triangles determined by the given information. If 1 or 2 triangles are fomed, solve the triangle(s). Round the angle measures and sides lengths to the nearest tenth.

15. $A = 117^\circ$, $b = 40$, $a = 28$
16. $B = 39^\circ$, $a = 4$, $b = 3$

17. A surveyor marks the corners of a triangular lot and labels them as A, B, and C. If $\overline{AC} = 110$ feet, $\overline{BC} = 158$ feet, and the measure of the angle between $\overline{AC}$ and $\overline{BC}$ is 65°, find the area of the park to the nearest hundredth of a square foot.

LESSON 14.2

Classify the type of information given, and then use the law of cosines to find the missing side length of $\triangle ABC$ to the nearest tenth.

1. $b = 64, c = 80, A = 80°$

2. $a = 5, b = 12, C = 46°$

3. $a = 7, c = 9, B = 100°$

4. $b = 42, c = 30, A = 56°$

5. $b = 90, c = 120, A = 55°$

6. $a = 4, b = 6, C = 130°$

Solve each triangle. Round answers to the nearest tenth.

7. $a = 13, b = 15, c = 9$

8. $a = 8, b = 12, c = 7$

9. $a = 20, b = 24, c = 32$

10. $a = 24, b = 22, c = 30$

11. $a = 40, b = 50, c = 80$

12. $a = 10, b = 12, c = 20$

Classify the type of information given, and then solve $\triangle ABC$, if possible. Round answers to the nearest tenth. If no such triangle exists, write *not possible*.

13. $a = 5.8, b = 6.4, c = 7.5$

14. $A = 39°, b = 42, a = 16$

15. $B = 72°, a = 8.2, b = 10$

16. $C = 50°, a = 102, b = 95$

17. $A = 40°, a = 5, b = 20$

18. $A = 70°, a = 6, b = 2$

19. A piece of gold cord 42 inches long will be used to trim the edges of a banner in the shape of an isosceles triangle. If the base of the triangle is 20 inches, find the measure of each angle of the triangle to the nearest tenth of a degree.

LESSON 14.3

Use definitions to prove each identity.

1. $(\sec\theta)(\sin\theta) = \tan\theta$

2. $\sin^2\theta + \cos^2\theta = \sec^2\theta - \tan^2\theta$

3. $\tan\theta = \dfrac{1}{\cot\theta}$

4. $1 + \cot^2\theta = \csc^2\theta$

Write each expression in terms of a single trigonometric function, if possible.

5. $(\cos\theta)(\sec\theta) - \cos^2\theta$

6. $\dfrac{\tan\theta}{\sin\theta}$

7. $\dfrac{(\sin\theta)(\sec\theta)}{\tan\theta}$

8. $(\csc\theta)(\cos\theta)(\sin\theta)$

9. $\sec^2\theta - \tan^2\theta + \cot^2\theta$

10. $\dfrac{\tan\theta + 1}{\tan\theta}$

Write each expression in terms of only the sine and cosine functions. Then simplify, if possible.

11. $\dfrac{\sec\theta - \cos\theta}{\tan\theta}$

12. $\sec^2\theta - \tan^2\theta$

13. $(\cot\theta)(1 - \sin\theta) + \cos\theta$

14. $(\sec\theta)(\sec\theta - \cos\theta)$

15. $\dfrac{\sin\theta + \tan\theta}{1 + \sec\theta}$

16. $\dfrac{1 + \cot^2\theta}{1 + \tan^2\theta}$

LESSON 14.4

Find the exact value of each expression.

1. $\sin(45° - 30°)$

2. $\sin(225° + 60°)$

3. $\cos(120° + 45°)$

4. $\cos(150° - 135°)$

5. $\sin(90° - 120°)$

6. $\cos(30° + 120°)$

7. $\sin 210°$

8. $\cos 105°$

9. $\sin 285°$

10. $\cos 75°$

11. $\cos 15°$

12. $\sin 195°$

Find the rotation matrix for each angle of rotation.

13. $30°$

14. $-45°$

15. $80°$

16. A rectangle has vertices at (4, 2), (4, 8), (10, 8), and (10, 2). Find the coordinates, to the nearest hundredth, of the vertices for the image of the rectangle after a 45° rotation about the origin.

LESSON 14.5

Write each expression in terms of trigonometric functions of θ rather than multiples of θ.

1. $\cos 4\theta$

2. $\frac{1 - \cos 2\theta}{2}$

3. $\cos 2\theta + \sin^2 \theta$

Write each expression in terms of a single trigonometric function.

4. $\frac{\sin^2 \theta}{\sin 2\theta}$

5. $\frac{\cos 2\theta}{\cos \theta + \sin \theta} + \sin \theta$

6. $\frac{\sin 2\theta}{1 - \cos 2\theta}$

Use the information given to find the exact value of $\sin 2\theta$ and $\cos 2\theta$.

7. $0° \le \theta \le 360°$; $\cos\theta = \frac{4}{5}$

8. $90° \le \theta \le 180°$; $\sin \theta = \frac{1}{4}$

Use the information given to find the exact value of $\sin \frac{1}{2}\theta$ and $\cos \frac{1}{2}\theta$.

9. $0° \le \theta \le 180°$; $\tan\theta = \frac{4}{3}$

10. $180° \le \theta \le 270°$; $\cos\theta = -\frac{3}{8}$

LESSON 14.6

Find all solutions of each equation.

1. $2 \sin \theta + \sqrt{2} = 0$

2. $6 \sin \theta + 3 = 0$

3. $\sqrt{3} - \sin \theta = \sin \theta$

Find the exact solutions of each equation for $0° \le \theta < 360°$.

4. $\sec^2 \theta - 4 = 0$

5. $\sin 2\theta = \sin \theta$

6. $\sec^2 \theta + 2 \sec \theta = 0$

7. $\cos 2\theta = 3 \cos \theta + 1$

8. $2 \cos^2 \theta - \cos \theta - 1 = 0$

9. $2 \sin \theta \cos \theta = \tan \theta$

Solve each equation to the nearest tenth of a degree for $0° \le \theta < 360°$.

10 $4 \cos \theta - 5 \sin \theta = 0$

11 $3 \sin^2 \theta - 2 \sin \theta - 1 = 0$

Parent Functions and Their Graphs

The simplest form of any function is called the parent function. Each parent function has a distinctive graph. These two pages summarize the basic graphs of some parent functions.

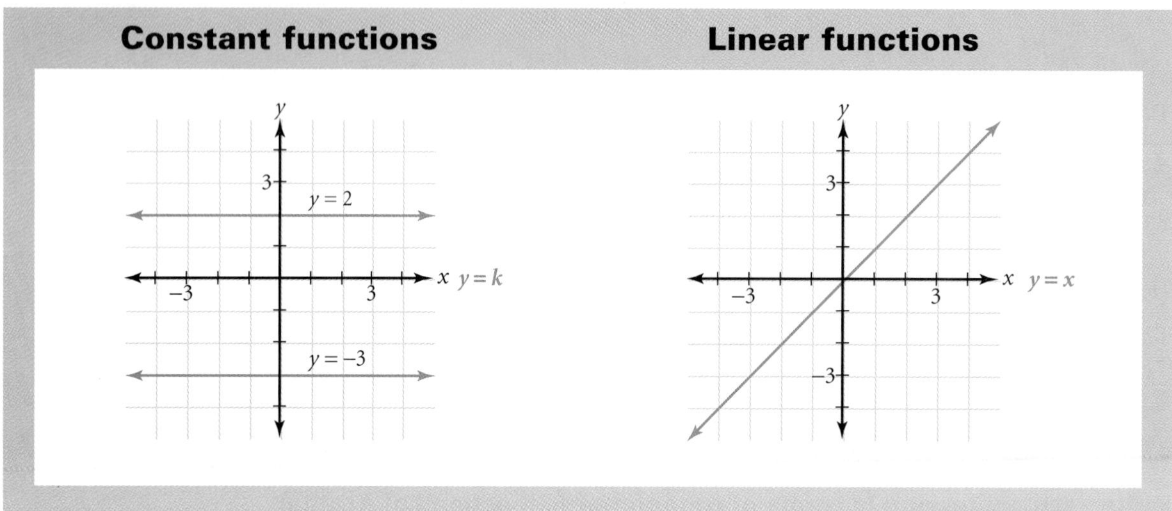

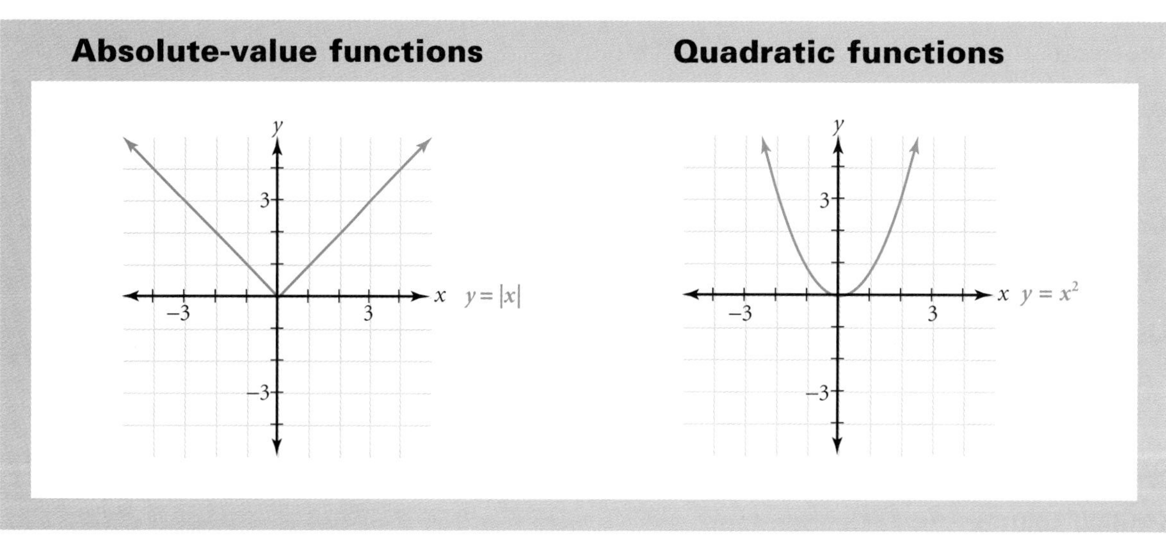

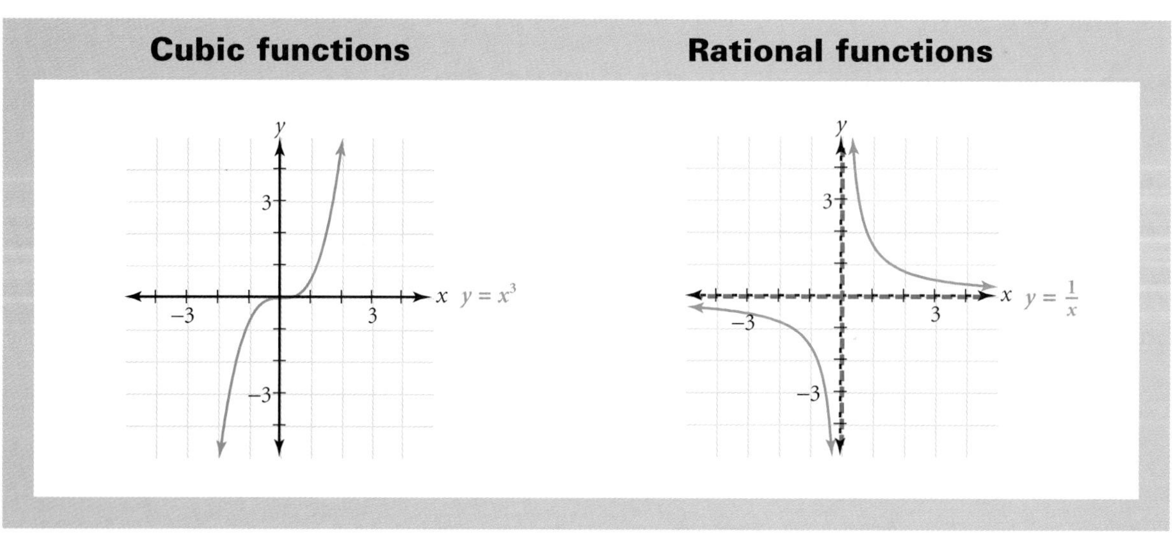

Radical functions

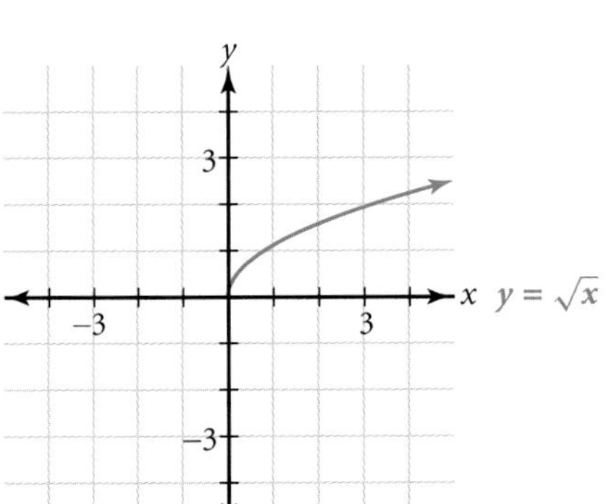

Exponential functions

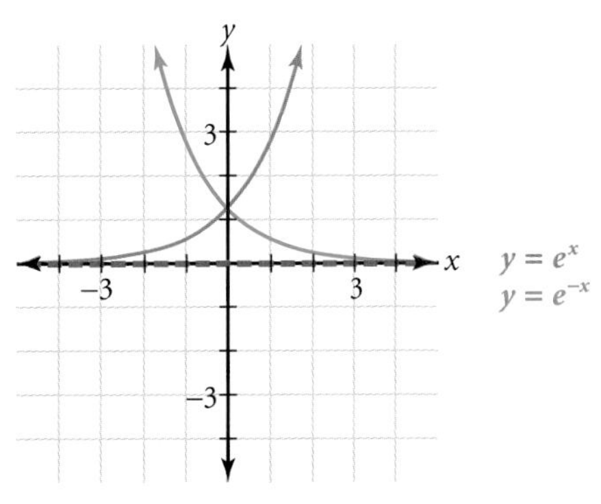

Logarithmic functions

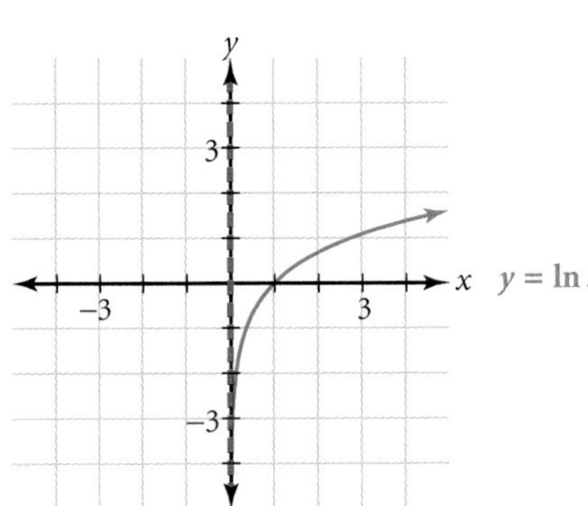

Sine functions

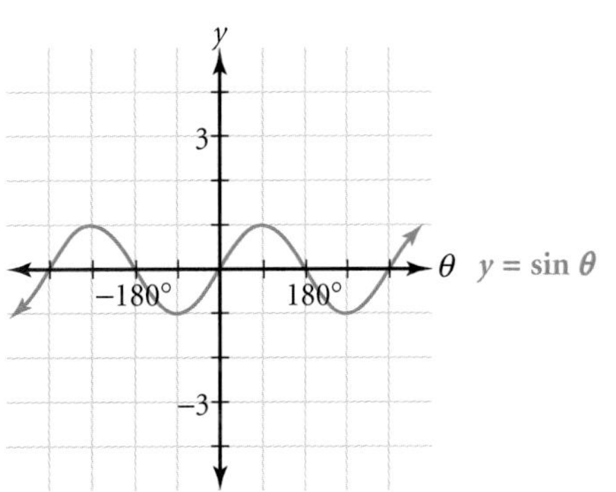

Cosine functions

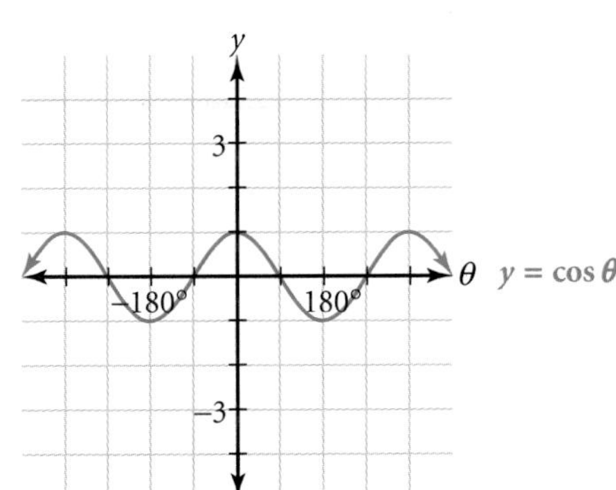

Tangent functions

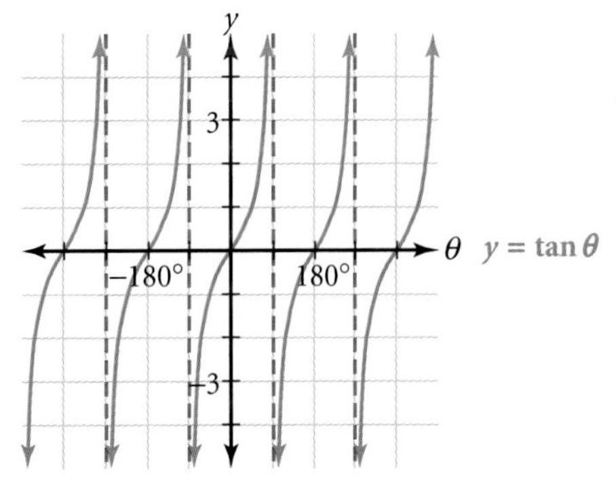

Transformations of Parent Functions

A transformation of a parent function is an alteration of its function rule that results in an alteration of its graph. The new graph retains the distinctive features of the graph of the parent function. These two pages summarize transformations.

Translations

Vertical

If $y = f(x)$, then $y = f(x) + k$ gives a vertical translation of the graph of f. The translation is k units up for $k > 0$ and $|k|$ units down for $k < 0$.

Horizontal

If $y = f(x)$, then $y = f(x - h)$ gives a horizontal translation of the graph of f. The translation is h units to the right for $h > 0$ and $|h|$ units to the left for $h < 0$.

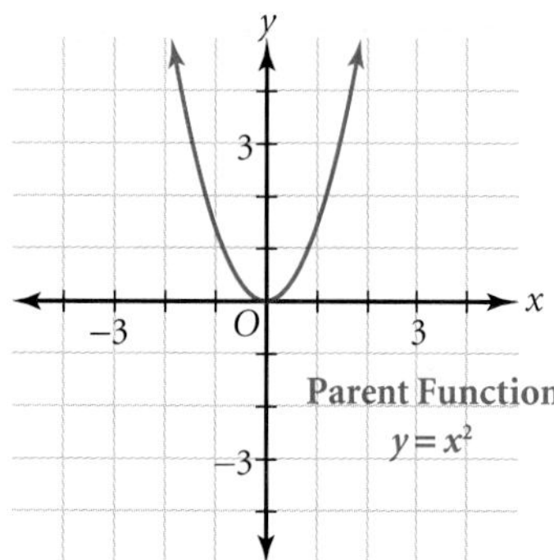

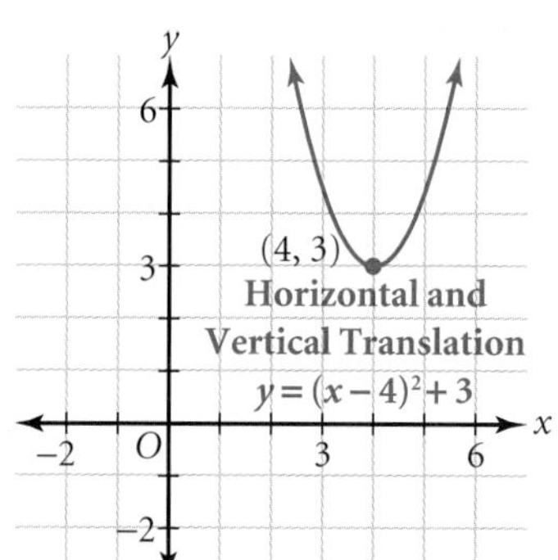

Vertical Stretches and Compressions

If $y = f(x)$, then $y = af(x)$ gives a vertical stretch or vertical compression of the graph of f.

If $a > 1$, the graph is stretched vertically by a factor of a.
If $a < 1$, the graph is compressed vertically by a factor of a.

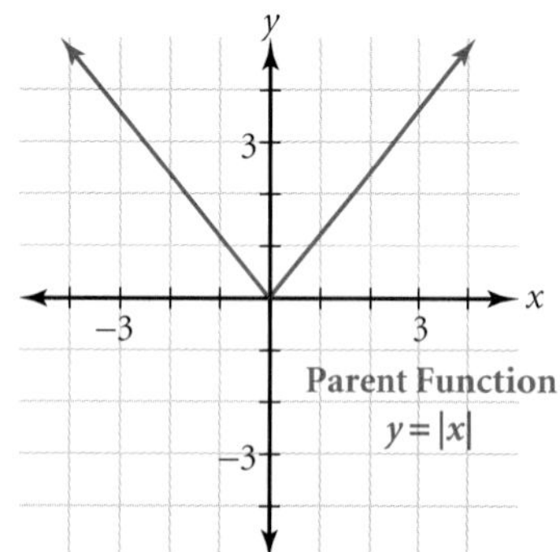

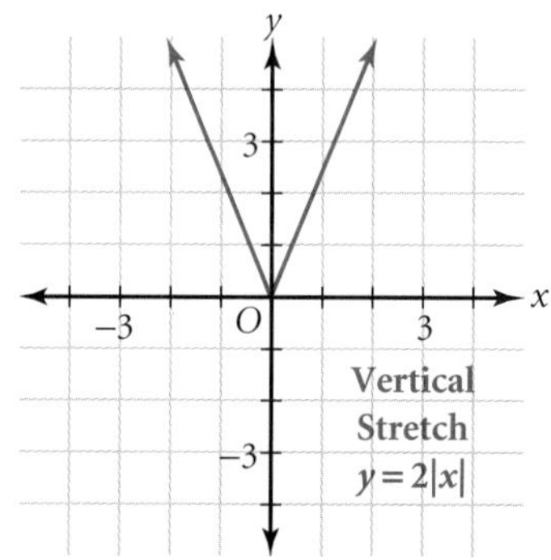

Horizontal Stretches and Compressions

If $y = f(x)$, then $y = f(bx)$ gives a horizontal stretch or horizontal compression of the graph of f.

If $b > 1$, the graph is compressed horizontally by a factor of $\frac{1}{b}$.
If $0 < b < 1$, the graph is stretched horizontally by a factor of $\frac{1}{b}$.

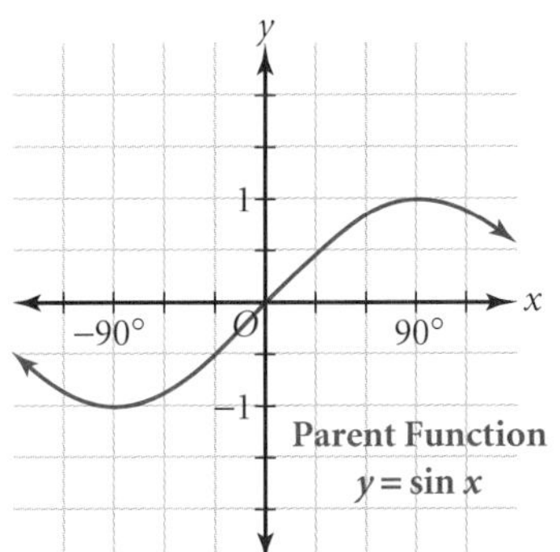

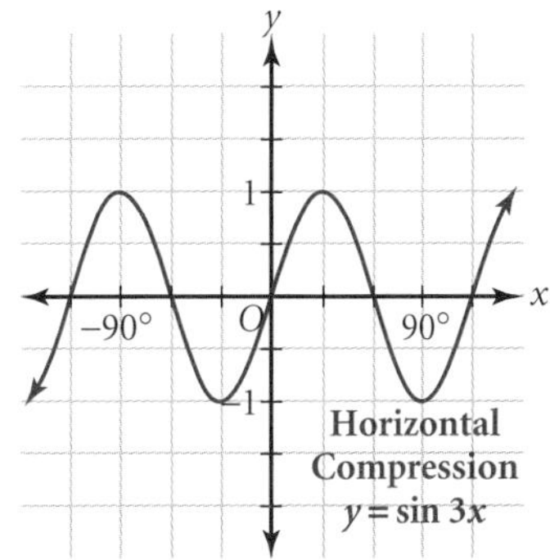

Reflections

If $y = f(x)$, then $y = -f(x)$ gives a reflection of the graph of f across the x-axis.
If $y = f(x)$, then $y = f(-x)$ gives a reflection of the graph of f across the y-axis.

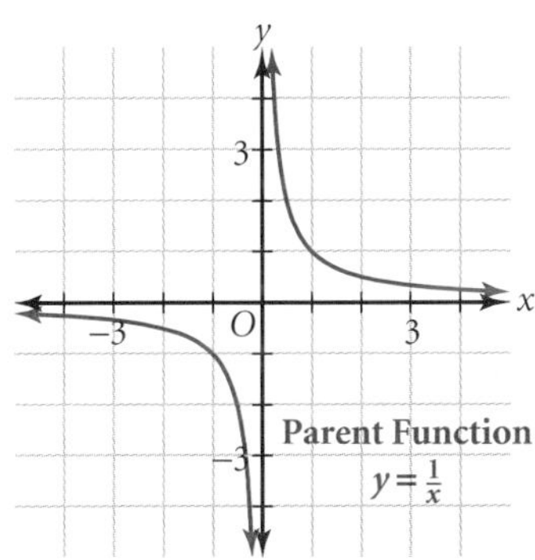

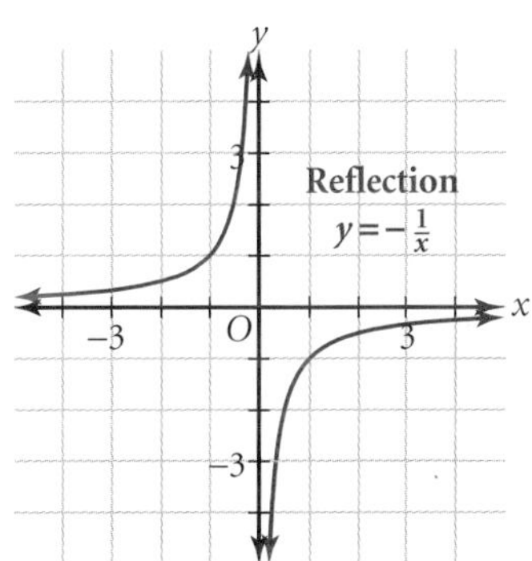

Combining Transformations

Any number of the above transformations can be combined. For example, the graph at right represents $y = -2(x - 4)^2 + 3$. It is a vertical stretch, a horizontal and vertical translation, and a reflection of the graph of the parent function, $y = x^2$.

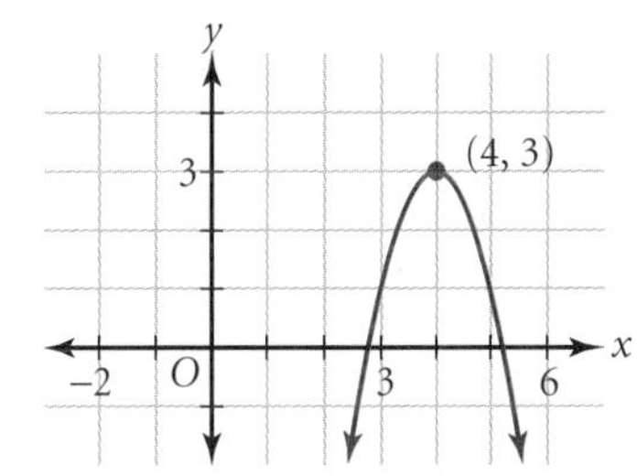

Table of Random Digits

Column / Line	(1)	(2)	(3)	(4)	(5)	(6)	(7)	(8)	(9)	(10)	(11)	(12)	(13)	(14)
1	10480	15011	01536	02011	81647	91646	69179	14194	62590	36207	20969	99570	91291	90700
2	22368	46573	25595	85393	30995	89198	27982	53402	93965	34095	52666	19174	39615	99505
3	24130	48360	22527	97265	76393	64809	15179	24830	49340	32081	30680	19655	63348	58629
4	42167	93093	06243	61680	07856	16376	39440	53537	71341	57004	00849	74917	97758	16379
5	37570	39975	81837	16656	06121	91782	60468	81305	49684	60672	14110	06927	01263	54613
6	77921	06907	11008	42751	27756	53498	18602	70659	90655	15053	21916	81825	44394	42880
7	99562	72905	56420	69994	98872	31016	71194	18738	44013	48840	63213	21069	10634	12952
8	96301	91977	05463	07972	18876	20922	94595	56869	69014	60045	18425	84903	42508	32307
9	89579	14342	63661	10281	17453	18103	57740	84378	25331	12566	58678	44947	05585	56941
10	85475	36857	53342	53988	53060	59533	38867	62300	08158	17983	16439	11458	18593	64952
11	28918	69578	88231	33276	70997	79936	56865	05859	90106	31595	01547	85590	91610	78188
12	63553	40961	48235	03427	49626	69445	18663	72695	52180	20847	12234	90511	33703	90322
13	09429	93969	52636	92737	88974	33488	36320	17617	30015	08272	84115	27156	30613	74952
14	10365	61129	87529	85689	48237	52267	67689	93394	01511	26358	85104	20285	29975	89868
15	07119	97336	71048	08178	77233	13916	47564	81056	97735	85977	29372	74461	28551	90707
16	51085	12765	51821	51259	77452	16308	60756	92144	49442	53900	70960	63990	75601	40719
17	02368	21382	52404	60268	89368	19885	55322	44819	01188	65225	64835	44919	05944	55157
18	01011	54092	33362	94904	31273	04146	18594	29852	71585	85030	51132	01915	92747	64951
19	52162	53916	46369	58586	23216	14513	83149	98736	23495	64350	94738	17752	35156	35749
20	07056	97628	33787	09998	42698	06691	76988	13602	51851	46104	88916	19509	25625	58104
21	48663	91245	85828	14346	09172	30168	90229	04734	59193	22178	30421	61666	99904	32812
22	54164	58492	22421	74103	47070	25306	76468	26384	58151	06646	21524	15227	96909	44592
23	32639	32363	05597	24200	13363	38005	94342	28728	35806	06912	17012	64161	18296	22851
24	29334	27001	87637	87308	58731	00256	45834	15398	46557	41135	10367	07684	36188	18510
25	02488	33062	28834	07351	19731	92420	60952	61280	50001	67658	32586	86679	50720	94953
26	81525	72295	04839	96423	24878	82651	66566	14778	76797	14780	13300	87074	79666	95725
27	29676	20591	68086	26432	46901	20849	89768	81536	86645	12659	92259	57102	80428	25280
28	00742	57392	39064	66432	84673	40027	32832	61362	98947	96067	64760	64584	96096	98253
29	05366	04213	25669	26422	44407	44048	37937	63904	45766	66134	75470	66520	34693	90449
30	91921	26418	64117	94305	26766	25940	39972	22209	71500	64568	91402	42416	07844	69618
31	00582	04711	87917	77341	42206	35126	74087	99547	81817	42607	43808	76655	62028	76630
32	00725	69884	62797	56170	86324	88072	76222	36086	84637	93161	76038	65855	77919	88006
33	69011	65795	95876	55293	18988	27354	26575	08625	40801	59920	29841	80150	12777	48501
34	25976	57948	29888	88604	67917	48708	18912	82271	65424	69774	33611	54262	85963	03547
35	09763	83473	73577	12908	30883	18317	28290	35797	05998	41688	34952	37888	38917	88050
36	91567	42595	27958	30134	04024	86385	29880	99730	55536	84855	29080	09250	79656	73211
37	17955	56349	90999	49127	20044	59931	06115	20542	18059	02008	73708	83517	36103	42791
38	46503	18584	18845	49618	02304	51038	20655	58727	28168	15475	56942	53389	20562	87338
39	92157	89634	94824	78171	84610	82834	09922	25417	44137	48413	25555	21246	35509	20468
40	14577	62765	35605	81263	39667	47358	56873	56307	61607	49518	89656	20103	77490	18062
41	98427	07523	33362	64270	01638	92477	66969	98420	04880	45585	46565	04102	46880	45709
42	34914	63976	88720	82765	34476	17032	87589	40836	32427	70002	70663	88863	77775	69348
43	70060	28277	39475	46473	23219	53416	94970	25832	69975	94884	19661	72828	00102	66794
44	53976	54914	06990	67245	68350	82948	11398	42878	80287	88267	47363	46634	06541	97809
45	76072	29515	40980	07391	58745	25774	22987	80059	39911	96189	41151	14222	60697	59583
46	90725	52210	83974	29992	65831	38857	50490	83765	55657	14361	31720	57375	56228	41546
47	64364	67412	33339	31926	14883	24413	59744	92351	97473	89286	35931	04110	23726	51900
48	08962	00358	31662	25388	61642	34072	81249	35648	56891	69352	48373	45578	78547	81788
49	95012	68379	93526	70765	10592	04542	76463	54328	02349	17247	28865	14777	62730	92277
50	15664	10493	20492	38391	91132	21999	59516	81652	27195	48223	46751	22923	32261	85653

Standard Normal Curve Areas

The table below gives the area under the standard normal curve between the mean, 0, and the desired number of standard deviations, *a*.

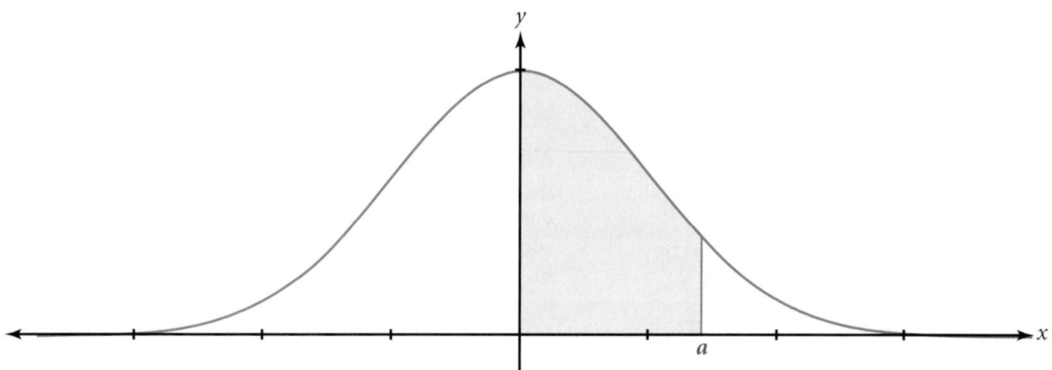

$P(x < a)$ for $a \geq 0$

a	0	1	2	3	4	5	6	7	8	9
0.0	.0000	.0040	.0080	.0120	.0160	.0199	.0239	.0279	.0319	.0359
0.1	.0398	.0438	.0478	.0517	.0557	.0596	.0636	.0675	.0714	.0753
0.2	.0793	.0832	.0871	.0910	.0948	.0987	.1026	.1064	.1103	.1141
0.3	.1179	.1217	.1255	.1293	.1331	.1368	.1406	.1443	.1480	.1517
0.4	.1554	.1591	.1628	.1664	.1700	.1736	.1772	.1808	.1844	.1879
0.5	.1915	.1950	.1985	.2019	.2054	.2088	.2123	.2157	.2190	.2224
0.6	.2257	.2291	.2324	.2357	.2389	.2422	.2454	.2486	.2518	.2549
0.7	.2580	.2612	.2642	.2673	.2704	.2734	.2764	.2794	.2823	.2852
0.8	.2881	.2910	.2939	.2967	.2995	.3023	.3051	.3078	.3106	.3133
0.9	.3159	.3186	.3212	.3238	.3264	.3289	.3315	.3340	.3365	.3389
1.0	.3413	.3438	.3461	.3485	.3508	.3531	.3554	.3577	.3599	.3621
1.1	.3643	.3665	.3686	.3708	.3729	.3749	.3770	.3790	.3810	.3830
1.2	.3849	.3869	.3888	.3907	.3925	.3944	.3962	.3980	.3997	.4015
1.3	.4032	.4049	.4066	.4082	.4099	.4115	.4131	.4147	.4162	.4177
1.4	.4192	.4207	.4222	.4236	.4251	.4265	.4279	.4292	.4306	.4319
1.5	.4332	.4345	.4357	.4370	.4382	.4394	.4406	.4418	.4429	.4441
1.6	.4452	.4463	.4474	.4484	.4495	.4505	.4515	.4525	.4535	.4545
1.7	.4554	.4564	.4573	.4582	.4591	.4599	.4608	.4616	.4625	.4633
1.8	.4641	.4649	.4656	.4664	.4671	.4678	.4686	.4693	.4699	.4706
1.9	.4713	.4719	.4726	.4732	.4738	.4744	.4750	.4756	.4761	.4767
2.0	.4772	.4778	.4783	.4788	.4793	.4798	.4803	.4808	.4812	.4817
2.1	.4821	.4826	.4830	.4834	.4838	.4842	.4846	.4850	.4854	.4857
2.2	.4861	.4864	.4868	.4871	.4875	.4878	.4881	.4884	.4887	.4890
2.3	.4893	.4896	.4898	.4901	.4904	.4906	.4909	.4911	.4913	.4916
2.4	.4918	.4920	.4922	.4925	.4927	.4929	.4931	.4932	.4934	.4936
2.5	.4938	.4940	.4941	.4943	.4945	.4946	.4948	.4949	.4951	.4952
2.6	.4953	.4955	.4956	.4957	.4959	.4960	.4961	.4962	.4963	.4964
2.7	.4965	.4966	.4967	.4968	.4969	.4970	.4971	.4972	.4973	.4974
2.8	.4974	.4975	.4976	.4977	.4977	.4978	.4979	.4979	.4980	.4981
2.9	.4981	.4982	.4982	.4983	.4984	.4984	.4985	.4985	.4986	.4986
3.0	.4986	.4987	.4987	.4988	.4988	.4989	.4989	.4989	.4990	.4990

Glossary

absolute value For any real number x, $|x| = x$ if $x \geq 0$ and $|x| = -x$ if $x < 0$. On a number line, $|x|$ is the distance from x to 0. (62)

absolute value of a complex number The distance of the complex number $a + bi$ from the origin in the complex plane, denoted $|a + bi| = \sqrt{a^2 + b^2}$. (318)

absolute-value function A function described by $f(x) = |x|$. (127)

additive inverse matrix The scalar product of a matrix and -1. (219)

adjacency matrix A representation of a network that indicates how many one-stage (direct) paths are possible from one vertex to another. (228)

amplitude The amplitude of a periodic function is one-half of the difference between the maximum and minimum function values and is always positive. (860)

angle of depression The angle formed by a horizontal line and a line of sight to a point below. (831)

angle of elevation The angle formed by a horizontal line and a line of sight to a point above. (831)

angle of rotation The angle formed by a ray that is rotated around its endpoint. (836)

arc length The length of the arc intercepted by a central angle with a radian measure of θ in a circle with a radius of r is given by the equation $s = r\theta$. (853)

arithmetic means The terms between any two nonconsecutive terms of an arithmetic sequence. (702)

arithmetic sequence A sequence whose successive terms differ by the same number, d, called the common difference. (700)

arithmetic series The indicated sum of the terms of an arithmetic sequence. (707)

asymptote A line that a curve approaches (but does not reach) as its x- or y-values become very large or very small. (362)

asymptotes of a hyperbola The diagonals of the rectangle that is determined by the vertices and co-vertices. (597)

augmented matrix A matrix that consists of the coefficients and the constant terms in a system of linear equations. (251)

axis of symmetry of a parabola A line that divides the parabola into two parts that are mirror images of each other. (276, 310)

B

base In an exponential expression of the form b^x, b is the base. (94, 362)

binomial A polynomial with exactly two terms. (425)

binomial experiment A probability experiment that meets the following conditions: The experiment consists of n trials whose outcomes are either successes or failures, and the trials are identical and independent with a constant probability of success, p, and a constant probability of failure, $1 - p$. (799)

binomial probability In a binomial experiment consisting of n trials, the probability, P, of r successes (where $0 \leq r \leq n$, p is the probability is of success, and $1 - p$ is the probability of failure) is given by the equation $P = {}_nC_r\, p^5(1 - p)^{n-r}$. (800)

Binomial Theorem A theorem that tells how to expand a positive integer power of a binomial. (742)

box-and-whisker plot A summary display of how values are distributed within a data set. (783)

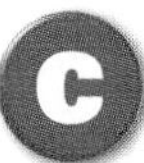

center A fixed point that is used to define a circle, ellipse, or hyperbola. (579, 587, 596)

change-of-base formula For any positive real numbers $a \neq 1$, $b \neq 1$, and $x > 0$, $\log_b x = \frac{\log_a x}{\log_a b}$. (388)

circle graph A display of the distribution of non-overlapping parts of a whole by using sectors of a circle. (776)

circle The set of all points in a plane that are at a constant distance, called the radius, from a fixed point, called the center. (579)

circular permutation An arrangement of distinct objects in a specified order around a circle. (639)

coefficient The numerical factor of a monomial. (425)

combination An arrangement of a group of objects in which order is *not* important. (643)

combined variation A relationship containing both direct and inverse variation. (484)

common difference The number by which successive terms of an arithmetic sequence differ. (700)

common logarithm A logarithm whose base is 10. (385)

common ratio The ratio by which successive terms of a geometric sequence differ. (713)

complement The complement of event A consists of all outcomes in the sample space that are not in A, denoted A^c. (654)

completing the square A process used to form a perfect-square trinomial. (300)

Complex Conjugate Root Theorem If P is a polynomial function with real-number coefficients and $a + bi$ (where $b \neq 0$) is a root of $P(x) = 0$, then $a - bi$ is also a root of $P(x) = 0$. (461)

complex fraction A quotient that contains one or more fractions in the numerator, the denominator, or both. (500)

complex number Any number that can be written as $a + bi$, where a and b are real numbers and $i = \sqrt{-1}$. (316)

complex plane A set of coordinates axes in which the horizontal axis is the real axis and the vertical axis is the imaginary axis; used to graph complex numbers. (318)

composition of functions The composition of functions f and g, $(f \circ g)(x)$, is defined as $(f(g(x)))$. The domain of f must include the range of g. (113)

compound inequalities A pair of inequalities combined by the words *and* or *or*. (56)

conditional probability The probability of event B, given that event A has happened (or will occur), denoted $P(B|A)$. (665)

conic section A plane figure formed by the intersection of a double cone and a plane. (562)

conjugate axis The axis of symmetry of a hyperbola that is perpendicular to the transverse axis. (596)

conjugate of a complex number The conjugate of a complex number $a + bi$ is $a - bi$, denoted $\overline{a + bi}$. (318)

consistent system A system of equations or inequalities that has at least one solution. (157)

constant A monomial with no variables. (425)

constant function A constant function is a function of the form $f(x) = k$. (125)

constant of variation The constant k in an inverse-, joint-, or combined-variation equation. (480)

constraints The inequalities that form the feasible region in a linear-programming problem. (187)

continuous compounding formula If P dollars are invested at an interest rate, r, that is compounded continuously, then the amount, A, of the investment at time t is given by $A = Pe^{rt}$. (393)

continuous function A function whose graph is an unbroken line or smooth curve. (105, 434)

converge Describes a infinite series whose partial sums approach a fixed number as n increases. (729)

Corner-Point Principle A principle in linear programming that identifies the maximum and minimum values of the objective function as occurring at one of the vertices of the feasible region. (189)

correlation coefficient A number represented by the variable r, where $-1 \leq r \leq 1$, that describes how closely points in a scatter plot cluster around the least-squares line. (39)

coterminal angle Describes angles that have the same terminal side when in standard position. (837)

co-vertices The endpoints of the minor axis of an ellipse; the endpoints of the conjugate axis of a hyperbola. (587, 596)

cube root A number, $\sqrt[3]{x}$, that when multiplied by itself three times produces the given number, x. (523)

decreasing function For a function f and any numbers x_1 and x_2 in the domain of f, the function f is decreasing over an open interval if for every $x_1 < x_2$ in the interval, $f(x_1) > f(x_2)$. (433)

degree of a monomial The sum of the exponents of the variables in the monomial. (425)

degree of a polynomial The degree of the monomial with the highest degree after simplification. (425)

degree The most common unit for angle measure; one degree, 1°, is defined as $\frac{1}{360}$ of a complete rotation of a ray. (836)

dependent events Two events are dependent if the occurrence of one event affects the occurrence of the other, or if the events are not independent. (660)

dependent system A system of equations that has infinitely many solutions. (157)

dependent variable The output of a function. For $y = f(x)$, $f(x)$ is the dependent variable. (106)

determinant A real number associated with a square matrix. (238)

diameter A chord of a circle that contains the center of the circle. (566)

dimensions of a matrix A matrix of m horizontal rows and n vertical columns has the dimension $m \times n$. (216)

direct variation The equation $y = kx$ describes a direct variation, where y varies directly as x, k is the constant of variation, and $k \neq 0$. (29)

directrix A fixed line used to define a parabola. (570)

discontinuous function A function whose graph has breaks or holes in it. (434)

discrete function A function whose graph consists of points that are not connected. (105)

discriminant The discriminant of a quadratic equation $ax^2 + bx + c = 0$ is $b^2 - 4ac$. (314)

distance formula The distance, d, between $P(x_1, y_1)$ and $Q(x_2, y_2)$ is $d = \sqrt{(x_2 - x_1)^2 + (y_2 - y_1)^2}$. (563)

diverge Describes a infinite series whose partial sums do not approach a fixed number as n increases. (729)

domain The set of possible values for the first coordinate of a function. (102, 104)

double root For a quadratic equation, if $b^2 - 4ac = 0$, the equation has only one solution, called a double root. (314)

effective yield The annually compounded interest rate that yields the final amount of an investment. (365)

elementary row operations Operations performed on a matrix that result in an equivalent matrix. (252)

elimination method A method of solving a system of equations by multiplying and combining the equations in the system in order to eliminate a variable. (164)

ellipse The set of all points P in a plane such that the sum of the distances from P to two fixed points, F_1 and F_2, called the foci, is a constant. (587)

end behavior What happens to a polynomial function as its domain values get very small and very large. (435)

entry Each value in a matrix; also called an element. (216)

equation A statement of equality between two expressions that may be true or false. (45)

equivalent equations Equations that have the same solution set. (48)

even function A function f for which $f(-x) = f(x)$ for all values of x in its domain. (911)

event An individual outcome or any specified combination of outcomes. (628)

excluded values Real numbers for which a rational function is not defined. (491)

experimental probability A probability approximated by performing trials and recording the ratio of the number of occurrences of the event to the number of trials. (629)

explicit formula A formula that defines the nth term, or general term, of a sequence. (691)

exponential expression An algebraic expression in which the exponent is a variable and the base is a fixed number. (355)

exponential function A function of the form $f(x) = b^x$, where b is a positive real number other than 1 and x is any real number. (362)

exponential growth and decay Represented by a function of the form $f(x) = b^x$, where $b > 1$ or $0 < b < 1$, respectively. (363)

Exponential-Logarithmic Inverse Property For $b > 0$ and $b \neq 0$, $\log_b b^x = x$ and $b^{\log_b x} = x$ for $x > 0$. (380)

extraneous solution A solution to a derived equation that is not a solution to the original equation. (514)

Factor Theorem For a polynomial $P(x)$, if and only if $P(r) = 0$, then $x - r$ is a factor $P(x)$. (442)

factorial If n is a positive integer, then n factorial, written $n!$, is given by $n \times (n-1) \times (n-2) \times \cdots \times 2 \times 1$. (636)

factoring The process that allows a sum to be written as a product. (290)

feasible region The solution set of a linear-programming problem. (187)

finite sequence A sequence that ends and therefore has a last term. (691)

foci Fixed points that are used to define an ellipse or hyperbola. (587, 595)

focus A fixed point used to define a parabola. (570)

frequency table A table that lists the number of times, or frequency, that each data value appears. (767)

function A relation in which, for each first coordinate, there is exactly *one* corresponding second coordinate. (102)

function notation A function is usually defined in terms of x and y, where $y = f(x)$, x is the independent variable, and $f(x)$ is the dependent variable. (106)

Fundamental Counting Principle If there are m ways that one event can occur and n ways that another event can occur, then there are $m \times n$ ways that both events can occur. (631)

Fundamental Theorem of Algebra Every polynomial function with degree $n \geq 1$ has at least one complex zero. Corollary: Every polynomial function with degree $n \geq 1$ has exactly n complex zeros, counting multiplicities. (462)

geometric means The terms between any two nonconsecutive terms of a geometric sequence. (716)

geometric sequence A sequence in which the ratio of successive terms is the same number, r, called the common ratio. (713)

geometric series The indicated sum of the terms of a geometric sequence. (720)

greatest-integer function A function denoted by $f(x) = [x]$ that converts a real number, x, into the largest integer that is less than or equal to x. (125)

grouped frequency table A frequency table in which the values are grouped into classes that contain a range of data values. (767)

histogram A bar graph that gives the frequency of each value in a data set. (774)

hole in the graph If the factor $x - b$ is a factor of both the numerator and denominator of a rational function, then a hole occurs in the graph of the rational function when $x = b$. (494)

horizontal line A line with slope of 0. (16)

horizontal-line test If a horizontal line crosses the graph of a function in more than one point, the inverse of the function is not a function. (120)

hyperbola The set of all points P in a plane such that the absolute value of the difference between the distances from P to two fixed points in the plane, F_1 and F_2, called the foci, is a constant. (595)

identity function A linear function defined by $I(x) = x$. (120)

identity matrix for multiplication An $n \times n$ matrix with 1s along the main diagonal (upper left entry to lower right entry) and 0s elsewhere. (235)

imaginary axis The vertical axis in the complex plane. (318)

imaginary part of a complex number For a complex number $a + bi$, b is the imaginary part. (316)

imaginary unit The imaginary unit i is defined as $i = \sqrt{-1}$ and $i^2 = -1$. (315)

inclusive events Events which can occur at the same time. (652)

inconsistent system A system of equations or inequalities that has no solution. (157)

increasing function For a function f and any numbers x_1 and x_2 in the domain of f, the function f is increasing over an open interval if for every $x_1 < x_2$ in the interval, $f(x_1) < f(x_2)$. (433)

independent events Two events are independent if the occurrence (or non-occurrence) of one event has no effect on the likelihood of the occurrence of the other event. (660)

independent system A system of equations that has exactly one solution. (157)

independent variable The input of a function. For $y = f(x)$, x is the independent variable. (106)

inequality A mathematical sentence that contains $>, <, \geq, \leq$, or $\neq$. (54)

infinite geometric series A geometric series with infinitely many terms. (729)

infinite sequence A sequence that continues without end. (691)

initial side The initial position of a rotated ray. (836)

interquartile range (IQR) The difference between the upper and lower quartiles of a data set. (782)

inverse of a matrix If A is an $n \times n$ matrix with an inverse, then A^{-1} is its inverse matrix, and $AA^{-1} = A^{-1}A = I$. (235)

inverse of a relation The inverse of a relation consisting of the ordered pairs (x, y) is the set of all ordered pairs (y, x). (118)

inverse variation Two variables, x and y, have an inverse-variation relationship if there is a nonzero number k such that $xy = k$, or $y = \frac{k}{x}$. (480)

irrational number A number whose decimal part does not terminate or repeat. (86)

joint variation If $y = kxz$ where k is a nonzero constant, then y varies jointly as x and z ($x \neq 0$ and $z \neq 0$). (482)

law of cosines For $\triangle ABC$, $a^2 = b^2 + c^2 - 2bc \cos A$, $b^2 = a^2 + c^2 - 2ac \cos B$, $c^2 = a^2 + b^2 - 2ab \cos C$. (895)

law of sines For $\triangle ABC$, $\frac{\sin A}{a} = \frac{\sin B}{b} = \frac{\sin C}{c}$. (887)

leading coefficient The coefficient of the term with the highest degree. (435)

least-squares line A linear model that fits a data set. (38)

like terms Two or more monomials that can only differ in their coefficients. (46)

linear equation An equation whose graph is a line. (5)

linear permutation A arrangement of objects in a specified order in a straight line. (636)

linear programming A method of finding a maximum or a minimum value that satisfies all of the given conditions of a particular situation. (187)

linearly related A relationship in which a constant difference in consecutive x-values results in a constant difference in consecutive y-values. (5)

literal equation An equation that contains two or more variables. (47)

local maximum For a function f, $f(a)$ is a local maximum if there is an interval around a such that $f(a) > f(x)$ for all values of x in the interval, where $x \neq a$. (433)

local minimum For a function f, $f(a)$ is a local minimum if there is an interval around a such that $f(a) < f(x)$ for all values of x in the interval, where $x \neq a$. (433)

Location Principle If P is a polynomial function and $P(x_1)$ and $P(x_2)$ have opposite signs, then there is a real number r between x_1 and x_2 that is a zero of P, that is $P(r) = 0$. (450)

logarithmic function A function of the form $y = \log_b x$ with base b, or $x = b^y$, which is the inverse of the exponential function $y = b^x$, where $b \neq 1$ and $b > 0$. (372)

major axis The longer axis of an ellipse. (587)

mathematical induction A type of mathematical proof that uses the following two steps to prove a statement for all natural numbers n: the basis step, which shows that the statement is true for $n = 1$, and the induction step, which assumes that the statement is true for a natural number, k, and proves that the statement is true for the natural number $k + 1$. (722)

matrix Any rectangular array of numbers enclosed in a single set of brackets. (216)

matrix equation An equation of the form $AX = B$, where A is the coefficient matrix, X is the variable matrix, and B is the constant matrix. (244)

matrix multiplication If matrix A has dimension $m \times n$ and matrix B has dimensions $n \times r$, then the product AB has dimensions $m \times r$. (226)

mean The sum of all of the values in a data set divided by the number of values; also called arithmetic average. (764)

mean deviation The average amount that the values in a data set differ from the mean. (792)

median The middle value, denoted Q_2, in a data set that is arranged in ascending or descending order. If there are an even number of data values, the median is the mean of the two middle values. (764)

midpoint formula The coordinates of the midpoint, M, between two points $P(x_1, y_1)$ and $Q(x_2, y_2)$ are $M\left(\frac{x_1 + x_2}{2}, \frac{y_1 + y_2}{2}\right)$. (565)

minor axis The shorter axis of an ellipse. (587)

mode The value in a data set that occurs most often. There can be one, more than one, or no mode. (764)

monomial A numeral, variable, or product of a numeral and one or more variables. (425)

multiplicity The number of times that a factor is repeated in the factorization of a polynomial expression. (449)

multiplier The base of an exponential expression. (355)

mutually exclusive events Events that cannot occur at the same time. (652)

natural base The irrational number e, which is approximately equal to 2.71828… (393)

natural exponential function An exponential function with base e; $f(x) = e^x$. (393)

natural logarithmic function The function $y = \log_e x$, the inverse of the natural exponential function. (394)

normal distribution Data that varies randomly from the mean, creating a bell-shaped pattern that is symmetric about the mean when graphed. (806)

objective function The function to be maximized or minimized in a linear-programming problem. (187)

odd function A function f for which $f(-x) = -f(x)$ for all values of x in its domain. (911)

one-to-one A one-to-one function can be intersected by a horizontal line at no more than one point. The inverse of a one-to-one function is also a function. (120)

One-to-One Property of Exponents If $b^x = b^y$, then $x = y$. (372)

One-to-One Property of Logarithms If $\log_b x = \log_b y$, then $x = y$. (380)

outlier A data value that is less than $Q_1 - 1.5(\text{IQR})$ or greater than $Q_3 + 1.5(\text{IQR})$. (782)

parabola The graph of a quadratic function. (276) The set of all points $P(x, y)$ in the plane whose distance to a point, called the focus, equals the distance to a fixed line, called the directrix. (570)

parallel lines Two lines (in the same plane) that have the same slope. All vertical lines are parallel and all horizontal lines are parallel. (23)

parametric equations A pair of continuous functions that define the x- and y-coordinates of a point in a coordinate plane in terms of a third variable. (196)

partial sum The sum of a specified number of terms of an infinite geometric series. (728)

Pascal's triangle A triangular pattern formed by the coefficients of binomial expansion. (735)

period The smallest positive number p that satisfies the equation in the definition of a periodic function. (846)

periodic function Describes functions for which there is a number p such that $f(x + p) = f(x)$ for every x in the domain of f. (846)

permutation An arrangement of objects in a specified order. (636)

perpendicular lines Two lines whose slopes are negative reciprocals of one another. All vertical and horizontal lines are perpendicular. (24)

phase shift A horizontal translation of a sine or cosine function. (861)

piecewise function A function that consists of different function rules for different parts of the domain. (124)

point-slope form The point-slope form of a line is $y - y_1 = m(x - x_1)$, where m is the slope and (x_1, y_1) is the coordinates of a point on the line. (22)

polynomial A monomial or a sum of terms that are monomials. (425)

polynomial function A function that is defined by a polynomial. (427)

power An expression of the form a^n. (94)

Power Property of Logarithms For $m > 0, b > 0, b \neq 1$, and any real number p, $\log_b m^p = p \log_b m$. (379)

Principle of Powers If $a = b$ and n is a positive integer, then $a^n = b^n$. (536)

principal square root The positive square root of a number a, denoted $\sqrt{a}$. (281)

principle values The restricted domains of the Sine, Cosine, and Tangent functions. (868)

probability The overall likelihood of the occurrence of an event. (628)

Product Property of Logarithms For $m > 0, n > 0$, and $b \neq 1$, $\log_b(mn) = \log_b m + \log_b n$. (378)

Product Property of Radicals For $a \geq 0$. $b \geq 0$, and a positive integer n, $\sqrt[n]{ab} = \sqrt[n]{a} \cdot \sqrt[n]{b}$ (529)

Product Property of Square Roots If $a \geq 0$ and $b \geq 0$, then $\sqrt{ab} = \sqrt{a} \cdot \sqrt{b}$. (281)

Properties of nth Roots For any real number a, $\sqrt[n]{a^n} = |a|$ if n is a positive even integer, and $\sqrt[n]{a^n} = a$ if n is a positive odd integer. (529)

proportion An equation that states that two ratios are equal. (31)

Pythagorean Theorem If $\triangle ABC$ is a right triangle with the right angle at C, the $a^2 + b^2 = c^2$. (284)

quadratic expression An expression of the form $ax^2 + bx + c$, where $a \neq 0$. (275)

quadratic formula The quadratic formula, $\frac{-b \pm \sqrt{b^2 - 4ac}}{2a}$, gives the solutions of the quadratic equation $ax^2 + bx + c = 0$ and $a \neq 0$. (308)

quadratic function Any function that can be written in the form $f(x) = ax^2 + bx + c$, where $a \neq 0$. (275)

quadratic inequality in two variables An inequality that can be written in one of the following forms, where a, b, and c are real numbers and $a \neq 0$: $y \geq ax^2 + bx + c$, $y > ax^2 + bx + c$, $y \leq ax^2 + bx + c$, and $y < ax^2 + bx + c$. (333)

quartiles Two values that, along with the median (Q_2), divide a data set into quarters; there is a lower quartile, Q_1, and an upper quartile, Q_3. (782)

Quotient Property of Logarithms For $m > 0, n > 0$, and $b \neq 1$, $\log_b \frac{m}{n} = \log_b m - \log_b n$. (378)

Quotient Property of Radicals For $a \geq 0$. $b \geq 0$, and a positive integer n, $\sqrt[n]{\frac{a}{b}} = \frac{\sqrt[n]{a}}{\sqrt[n]{b}}$, where $b \neq 0$. (529)

Quotient Property of Square Roots If $a \geq 0$ and $b \geq 0$, then $\sqrt{\frac{a}{b}} = \frac{\sqrt{a}}{\sqrt{b}}$. (281)

radian A unit of angle measure that is equal to $\frac{1}{2\pi}$ of the circumference of the unit circle; 1 radian is equal to approximately 57°. (852)

radical equation An equation that contains at least one radical expression with a variable in the radicand. (536)

radical expression An expression that contains at least one radical symbol. (524)

radical function A function that contains at least one radical expression. (524)

radical inequality An inequality that contains at least one radical expression. (540)

radical symbol The symbol $\sqrt{\ }$ in a radical expression. (524)

radicand The number or expression under a radical symbol. (524)

radius A segment with one endpoint at the center of the circle and the other endpoint on the circle. (566)

random Describes outcomes whose occurrences are all equally likely. (628)

range The set of possible values for the second coordinate of a function. (102, 104) The absolute value of the difference between the largest value and the smallest value of a data set. (782)

rational equation An equation that contains at least one rational expression. (512)

rational expression The quotient of two polynomials. (489)

rational function A function defined by a rational expression. (489)

rational inequality An inequality that contains at least one rational expression. (515)

rational number A number that can be expressed as the quotient of two integers, where the denominator is not equal to zero. (86)

Rational Root Theorem Let P be a polynomial function with integers coefficients in standard form. If $\frac{p}{q}$ (in lowest terms) is a root of $P(x) = 0$, then p is a factor of the constant term of P and q is a factor of the leading coefficient of P. (458)

rationalizing the denominator The process of removing an imaginary number from the denominator of a quotient. (318) A procedure that involves transforming a quotient with a radical in the denominator into an expression with no radical in the denominator. (532)

real axis The horizontal axis in the complex plane. (318)

real number Any rational or irrational number. (86)

real part of a complex number For a complex number $a + bi$, a is the real part. (316)

recursive formula A formula for a sequence in which one or more previous terms are used to generate the next term. (691)

reduced row-echelon form An augmented matrix is in this form if the coefficient columns form an identity matrix. (252)

reference angle For an angle in standard position, the reference angle, θ_{ref}, is the positive acute angle formed by the terminal side of θ and the nearest part (positive or negative) of the x-axis. (837)

relation Any set of ordered pairs. (104)

relative frequency table A frequency table that includes a column showing how frequently each value appears relative to the entire data set. (775)

Remainder Theorem If the polynomial expression that defines the function P is divided by $x - a$, then the remainder is the number $P(a)$. (444)

roots Solutions to an equation. (449)

rounding-up function The function, denoted $f(x) = \lceil x \rceil$, that converts a real number, x, into the smallest integer greater than or equal to x. (125)

row-reduction method The process of performing elementary row operations on an augmented matrix to solve a system of equations and determine whether the system is independent, dependent, or inconsistent. (251)

sample space The set of all possible outcomes of an event. (628)

scalar multiplication Multiplication of each entry in a matrix by the same real number. (218)

scatter plot The graph of the ordered pairs that describe a relationship between two sets of data. (37)

sequence An ordered list of numbers. (691)

series The indicated sum of the terms of a sequence. (693)

sigma The Greek letter Σ, used to denote a series. (693)

simplest radical form The expression $\sqrt{a}$ is in simplest radical form if no factor of a is a perfect square. (530)

simulation A representation of events that are likely to occur in the real world that can be used to find experimental probabilities. (672)

slope-intercept form A linear equation in the form $y = mx + b$, where m represents the slope and b represents the y-intercept. (14)

slope of a line The ratio of the change in vertical direction to the corresponding change in the horizontal direction. (13)

solution A value that can replace a variable that makes an equation or inequality true. (45, 55)

solving a triangle Finding the measures of all of the unknown sides and angles of the triangle. (832)

square matrix A matrix that has the same number of columns and rows. (234)

square root A number, $\sqrt{x}$, that when multiplied by itself produces the given number, x. (520)

standard deviation A measure of dispersion for a data set, given by the formula $\sigma = \sqrt{\sigma^2}$. (794)

standard form The standard form of a linear equation is $Ax + By = C$, where A, B, and C are not both 0. (15)

standard form of a quadratic equation A quadratic equation of the form $ax^2 + bx + c = 0$. (294)

standard normal curve A normal curve with a mean of 0 and a standard deviation of 1. (806)

standard position An angle is in standard position when its initial side lies along the x-axis and its endpoint is at the origin. (836)

stem-and-leaf plot A way of displaying a data set in which each data value is split into two parts, a stem and a leaf. (772)

step function A function whose graph looks like a series of steps. (125)

Substitution Property If $a = b$, then a may replace b in any statement containing a and the resulting statement will be true. (46)

summation notation A way to express a series in an abbreviated form by using the Greek letter sigma, Σ. (693)

synthetic division A method of division of a polynomial by a binomial in which only coefficients are used. (442)

system of equations A set of equations in the same variables. (156)

system of linear inequalities A set of linear inequalities in the same variables. (179)

system of nonlinear equations A set of equations in which at least one equation is nonlinear. (606)

tangent line A line that is perpendicular to a radius of a circle and that touches the circle at only one point. (863)

terminal side The final position of a rotated ray. (836)

terms Parts of an algebraic expression separated by addition or subtraction signs. (46) The numbers in a sequence. (691)

theoretical probability The theoretical probability of event A is defined by $P(A) = \frac{\text{number of outcomes in event } A}{\text{number of outcomes in the sample space}}$. (629)

transformation An alteration in the function rule and its graph. (133)

transverse axis The axis of symmetry of a hyperbola that contains vertices and foci. (596)

trial A systematic opportunity for an event to occur. (628)

trigonometric equation An equation that includes at least one trigonometric function. (922)

trigonometric functions A function that uses one of the six trigonometric ratios to assign values to the measures of the acute angles of a right triangle, or angles of rotation. (829, 838)

trigonometric identity An equation that includes trigonometric functions and that is true for all values of the variables for which the expressions on each side of the equation are defined. (902)

trinomial A polynomial with three terms. (425)

turning points The points on the graph of a polynomial function that correspond to local maxima and minima. (433)

unit circle A circle centered at the origin with a radius of 1. (846)

variable A symbol used to represent one or many different numbers. (45)

variance A measure of dispersion for a data set, given by the formula $\sigma^2 = \frac{1}{n}\sum_{i=1}^{n}(x_i - \bar{x})^2$ where n is the number of values in the data set and $\bar{x}$ is the mean. (794)

vertex A point in a finite set of connected points called a network. (228)

vertex form of a parabola If the coordinates of the vertex of the graph of $y = ax^2 + bx + c$, where $a \neq 0$, are (h, k), then the parabola can be represented in vertex form as $y = a(x - h)^2 + k$. (302)

vertex of a parabola Either the lowest point on the graph or the highest point on the graph. (276) The midpoint between the focus and directrix. (571)

vertical-line test If a vertical line crosses the graph of a relation in more than one point, the relation is not a function. (103)

vertical line A line that has an undefined slope. (16)

vertices The endpoints of the major axis of an ellipse; the endpoints of the transverse axis of a hyperbola. (587, 596)

***x*-intercept** The x-coordinate of the point where the graph crosses the x-axis. (15)

***y*-intercept** The y-coordinate of the point where the graph of a line crosses the y-axis. (14)

zero of a function Any number r such that $f(r) = 0$. (294, 434)

Zero-Product Property If $pq = 0$, then $p = 0$ or $q = 0$. (294)

***z*-score** A measure of how far a value is from the mean in terms of the standard deviation. (809)

Selected Answers

Chapter 1

LESSON 1.1

TRY THIS (p. 5)

a.

Time (min)	1	2	3	4
Volume (gal)	64	73	82	91

b.

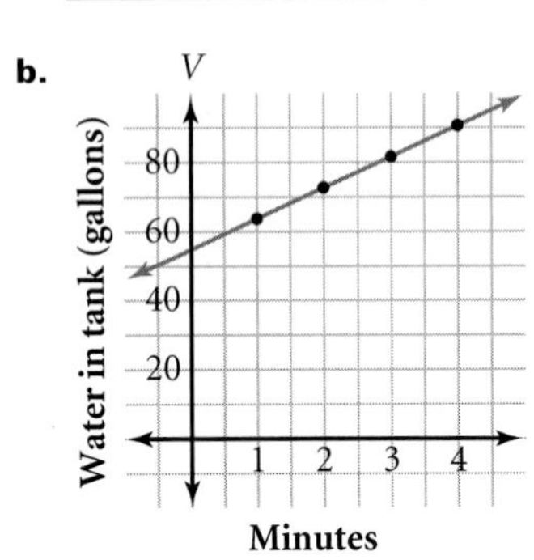

c. $V = 9t + 55$, where V is volume in gallons and t is time in minutes.

d. 235 gallons

TRY THIS (p. 6)

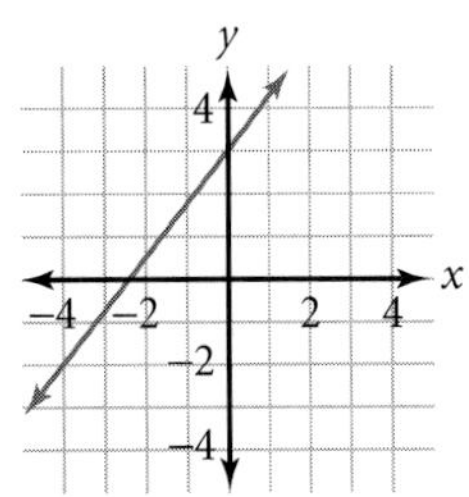

TRY THIS (p. 7)

The relationship is not linear because there is not a constant difference in the y-values.

Exercises

4a.

Weekly sales, x	Weekly income, y
100	$50 + (0.15)(100) = 65$
200	$50 + (0.15)(200) = 80$
300	$50 + (0.15)(300) = 95$
400	$50 + (0.15)(400) = 110$
x	$50 + (0.15)x = 0.15x + 50$

b.

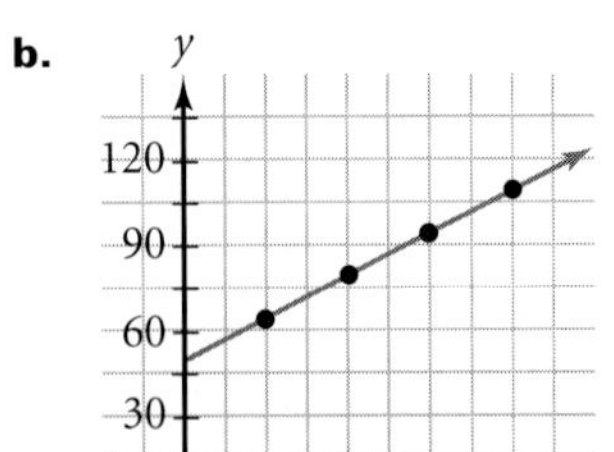

c. $y = 0.15x + 50$

d. $230

5.

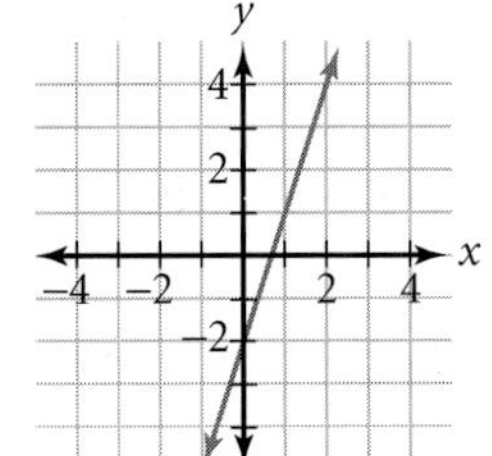

6. yes; (26, 49) **7.** linear **9.** linear **11.** linear **13.** not linear **15.** not linear **17.** linear

19.

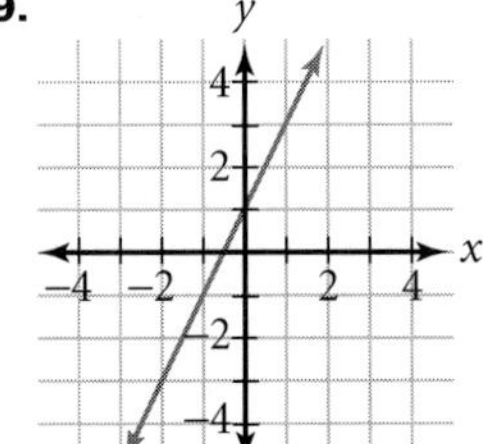

21.

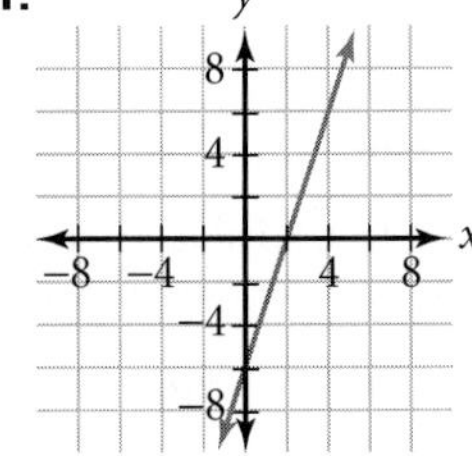

23.

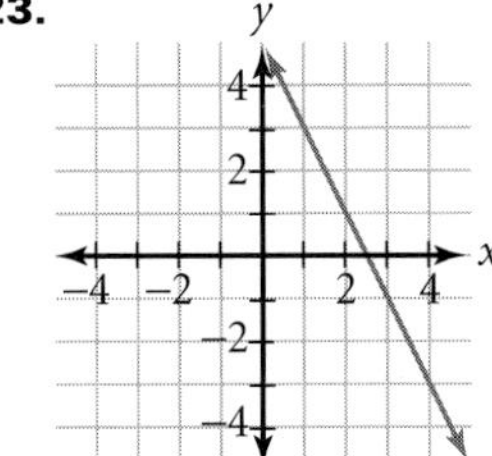

25.

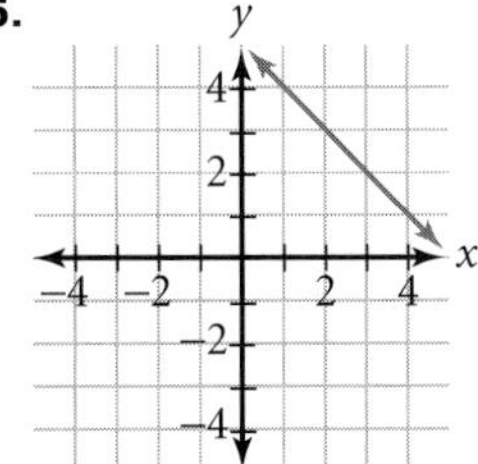

27.

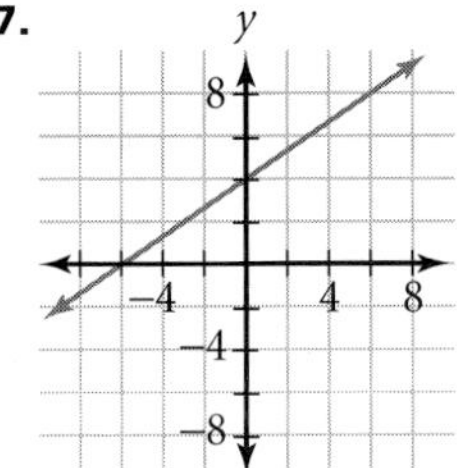

29.

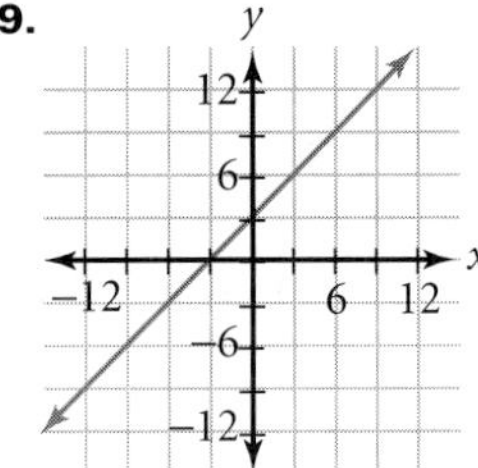

31. linear; (4, 58) **33.** not linear **35.** linear; (0, 4) **37.** not linear

39.

x	y
0	0
2	3
4	6
6	9

This is a linear relationship, because there is a constant difference of 2 in consecutive x-values and a constant difference of 3 in consecutive y-values.

41.

x	y
0	1
1	3
2	7

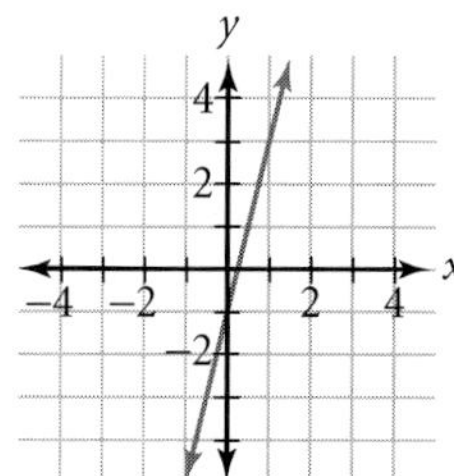

The point (2, 6) is not on the line because $x = 2$ is paired with $y = 7$ in the table. The point (2, 6) also does not make the equation true. Finally, the point (2, 6) is not a point on the graph of $y = 4x - 1$.

43.

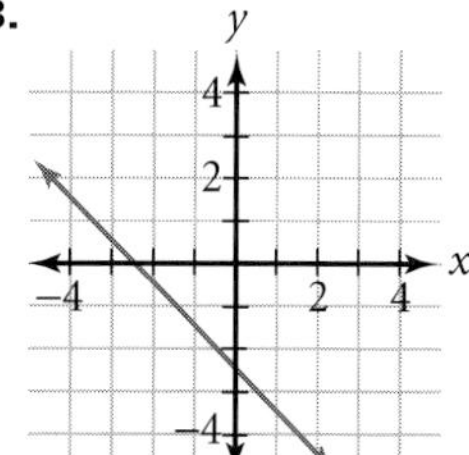

45.

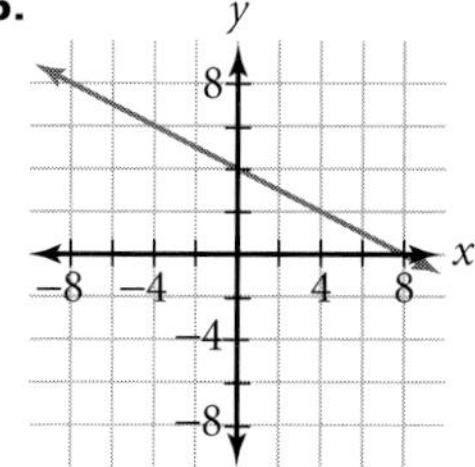

47.

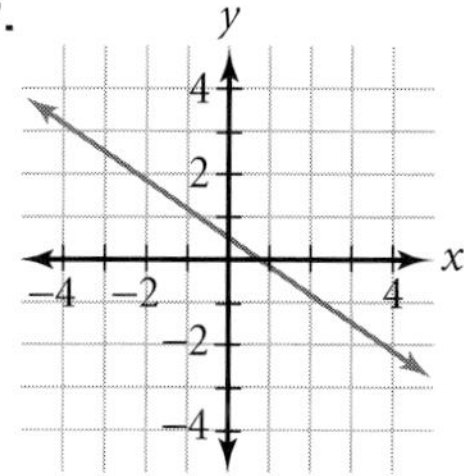

49a.

x	y
0	6
1	9
2	12
3	15

b. \$51 **c.** 7 videos **d.** The answers to parts **b** and **c** could also be found by continuing the table and the graph until the desired ordered pairs are found.

51a.

Half-hours	Total charge (\$)
0	$2 + (1)(0) = 2$
1	$2 + (1)(1) = 3$
2	$2 + (1)(2) = 4$
3	$2 + (1)(3) = 5$
10	$2 + (1)(10) = 12$

b.

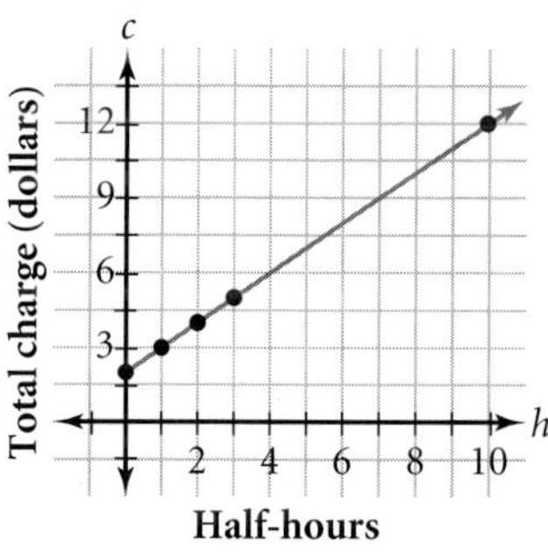

c. $c = 2 + h$ **d.** 144; \$146

53a.

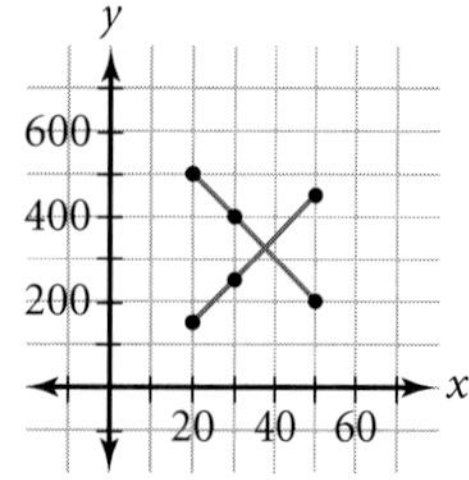

b. about \$37; about \$350 **c.** When the price is higher, supply is greater than demand. When the price is lower, supply is less than demand.

55. $a = 9, b = 4$ **57.** $a = 41, b = 2$ **59.** $a = 8, b = 16$ **61.** $a = 16, b = 3$ **63.** $\frac{2}{7}$ **65.** 2 **67.** 8 **69.** 24

LESSON 1.2

TRY THIS (p. 13)

$-\frac{7}{8}$

TRY THIS (p. 15, Ex. 2)

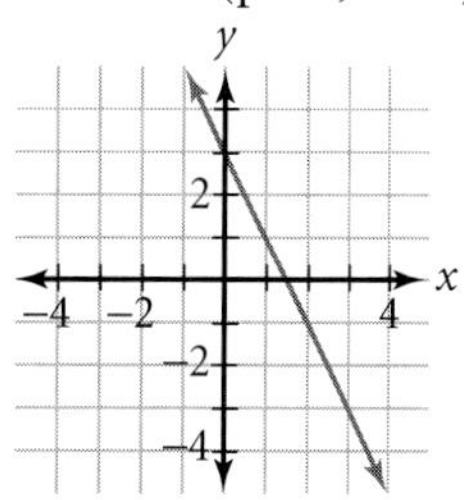

TRY THIS (p. 15, Ex. 3)

$y = x + 3$

TRY THIS (p. 16)

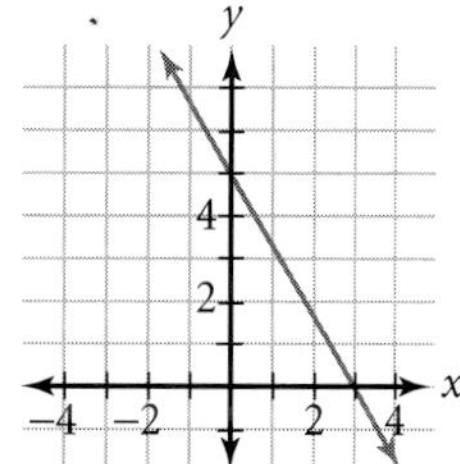

Exercises

5. $-\frac{7}{10}$

6.

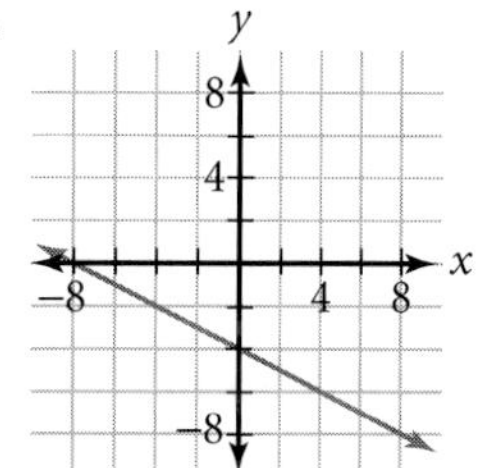

7. $y = \frac{1}{2}x - 3$

Selected Answers

8.

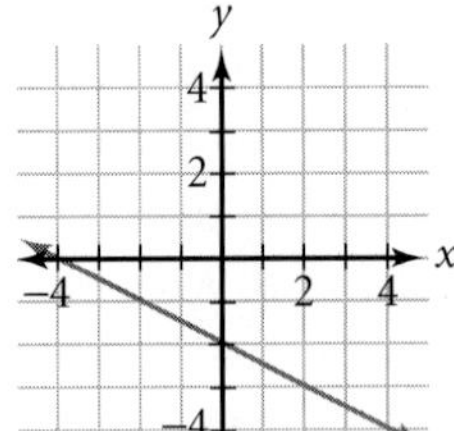

9.

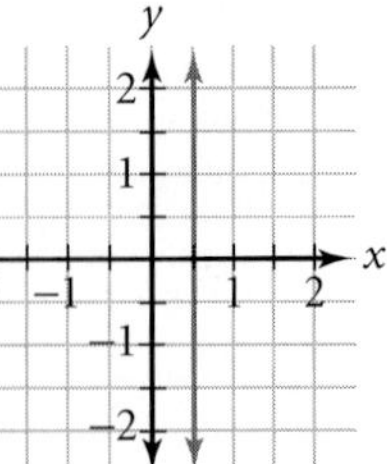

10.

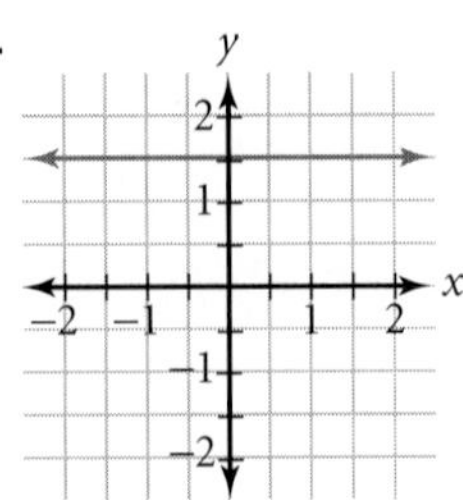

11. $y = 2x + 0.75$ **13.** $y = -3$ **15.** $y = -3x + 7$

17. $y = \frac{1}{4}x - \frac{3}{4}$ **19.** 10 **21.** 7 **23.** $\frac{7}{3}$ **25.** 1

27. $m = -2; b = 0$

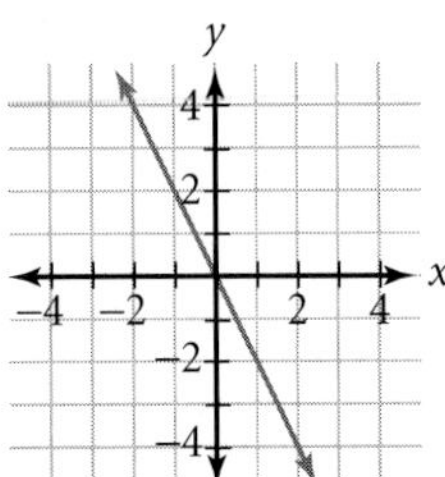

29. $m = \frac{1}{3}; b = -7$

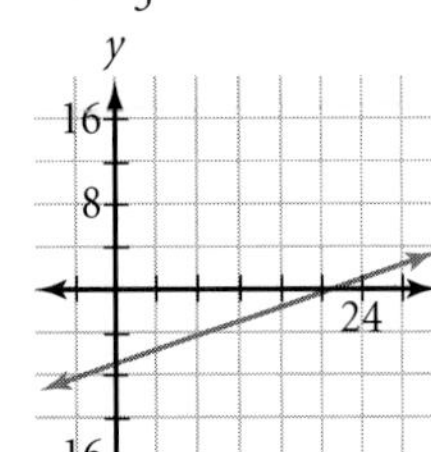

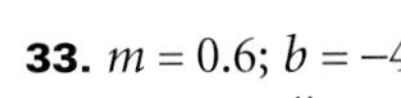

31. $m = 1; b = 0$

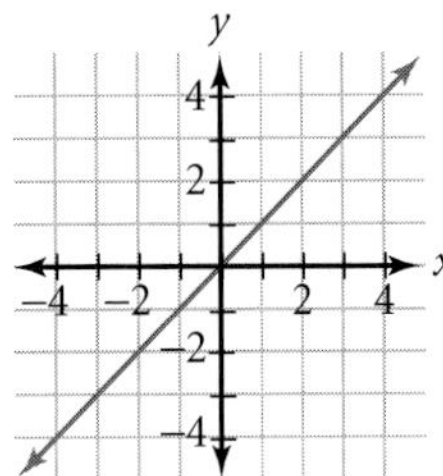

33. $m = 0.6; b = -4$

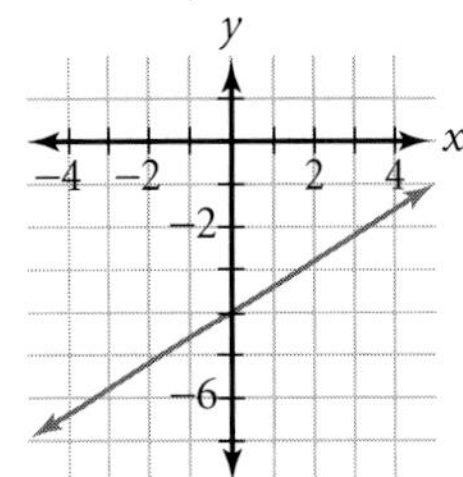

35. m is undefined; there is no y-intercept.

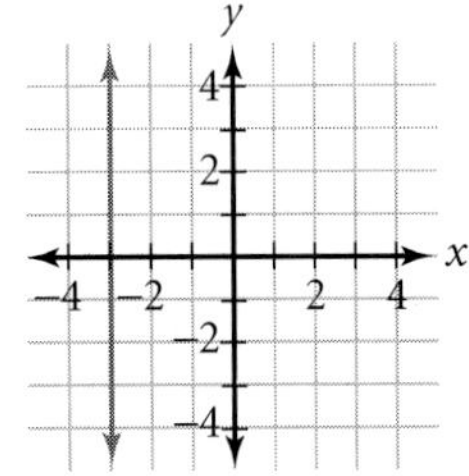

37. $y = \frac{3}{2}x - 1$ **39.** $y = -3x + 2$

41.

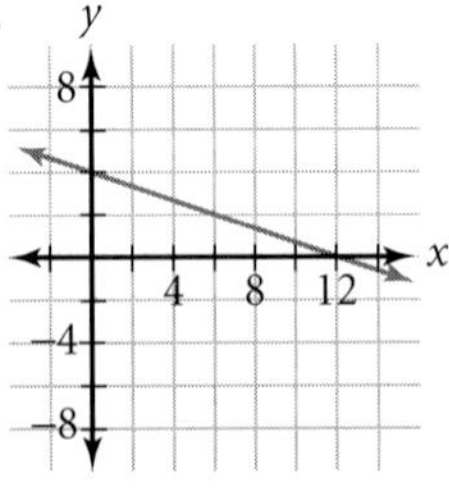

43.

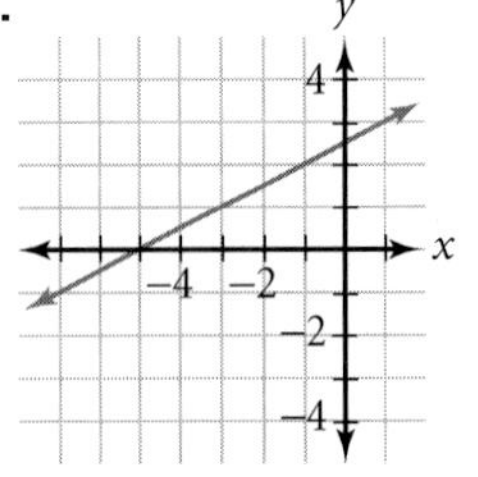

45.

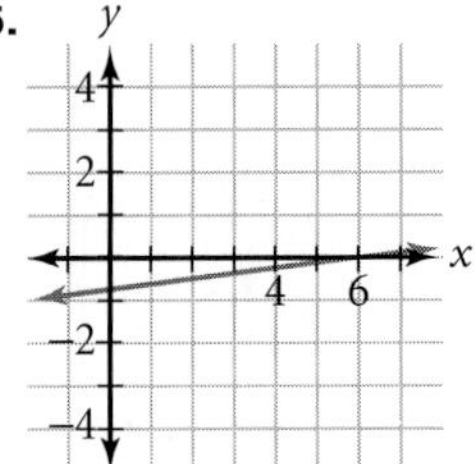

47.

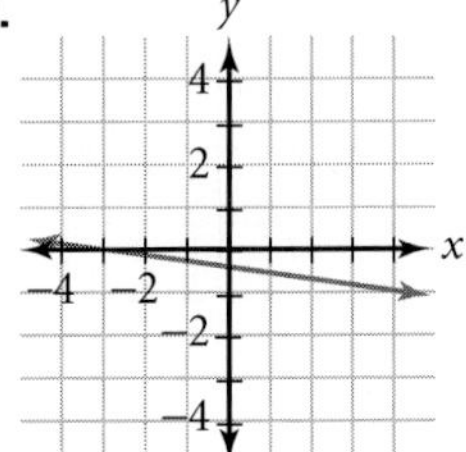

49.

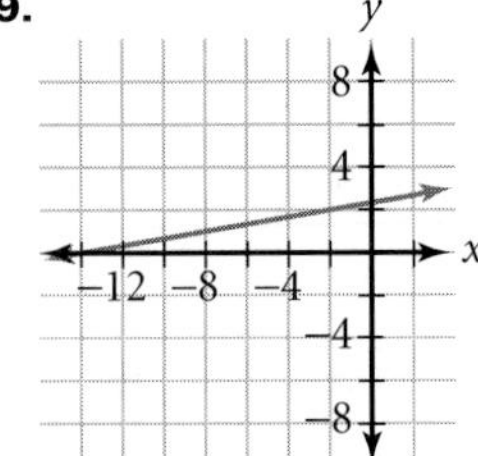

51.

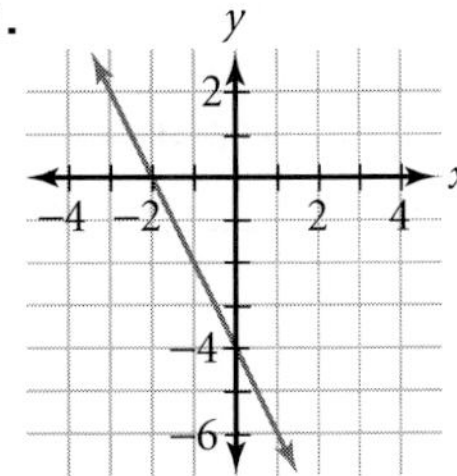

53. Slope is undefined.

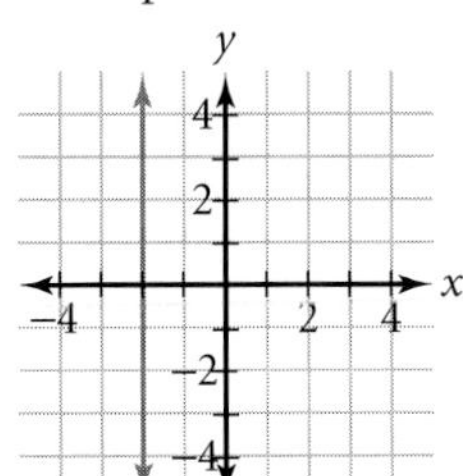

55. slope = 0

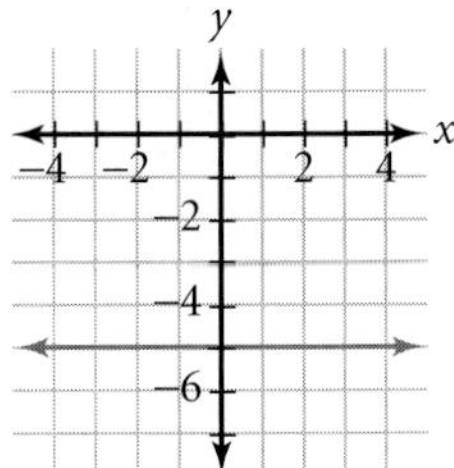

57. Slope is undefined.

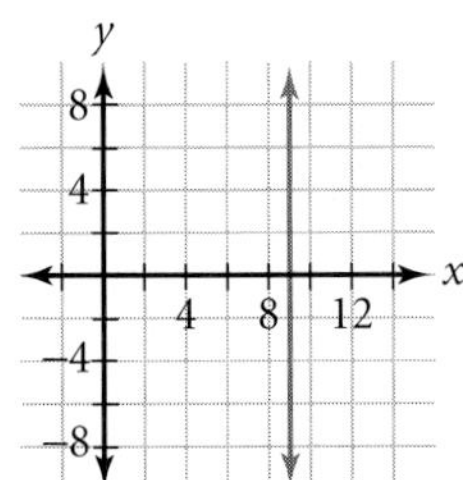

59. slope = 0

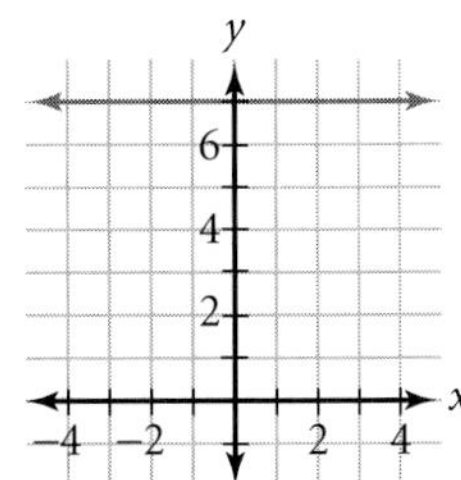

61. Slope is undefined.

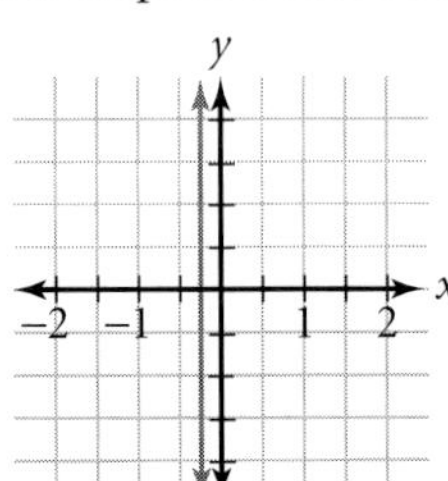

63. slope = 0

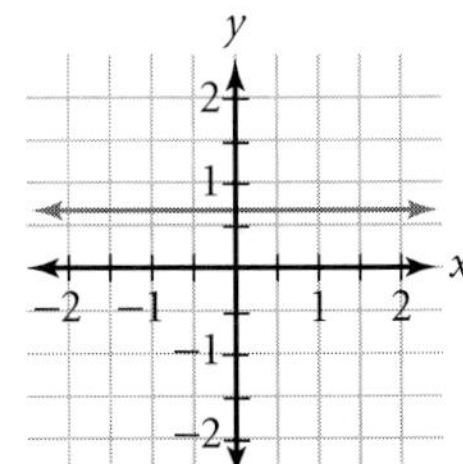

65a. $m = -600$ **b.** $b = 3600$ **c.** $y = -600x + 3600$, where $0 \leq x \leq 6$ **d.** $y = 900$

67a. Answers may vary. sample answer: 50°F = 10°C, 32°F = 0°C

b.

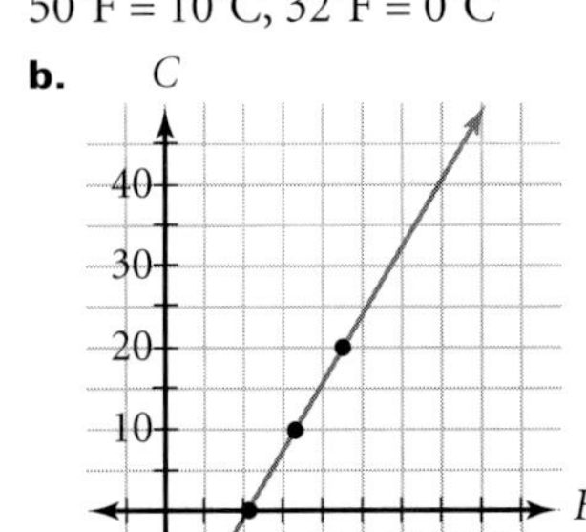

c. $m = \frac{5}{9}; b = -\frac{160}{9}$

d. $C = \frac{5}{9}F - \frac{160}{9}$

69a.

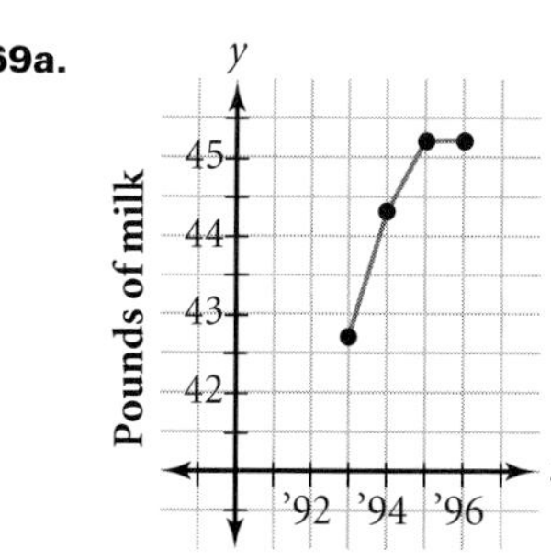

b. 1993–1994; 1.6 pounds per day **c.** 1995–1996; 0 pounds per day

71. \$160 **73.** Yes; there is a constant difference of 3 in the x-values and a constant difference of –2 in the y-values; (10, –3).

LESSON 1.3

TRY THIS (p. 24)
$y = -4x - 16$

TRY THIS (p. 25)
$y = \frac{1}{4}x + \frac{21}{4}$

Exercises

5. $y = \frac{1}{2}x + \frac{3}{2}$ **6.** $y = 3x - 5$ **7.** 20 miles **8.** $y = \frac{2}{5}x - \frac{37}{5}$ **9.** $y = \frac{5}{2}x + \frac{41}{2}$ **11.** $y = -x - 2$ **13.** $y = \frac{1}{7}x - \frac{18}{7}$ **15.** $x = -2$ **17.** $y = -\frac{3}{8}x$ **19.** $y = x - \frac{7}{2}$ **21.** $x = -5$ **23.** $y = -\frac{2}{3}x - 1$ **25.** $y = 5x + 2$ **27.** $y = 8$ **29.** $y = 3x + 21$ **31.** $y = -\frac{2}{3}x - \frac{2}{3}$ **33.** $y = 2.5x + 4$; slope represents average cost in dollars per item. **35.** $y = -3x - 3$ **37.** $y = \frac{1}{2}x - 4$ **39.** $y = -\frac{2}{5}x - \frac{17}{5}$ **41.** $y = \frac{1}{2}x - \frac{3}{2}$ **43.** $y = \frac{1}{2}x + 6$ **45.** $y = x - 3$ **47.** $y = \frac{1}{3}x + \frac{13}{3}$ **49.** $y = -6x - 8$ **51.** $y = \frac{5}{2}x + 3$, or $5x - 2y = -6$ **53.** ℓ_1 is parallel to ℓ_2. **55.** ℓ_1 is perpendicular to ℓ_3. **57.** ℓ_2 is not perpendicular to ℓ_4.

59. $m_1 = \frac{4-1}{2-4} = \frac{3}{-2}$ $\quad m_2 = \frac{0-(-3)}{-4-(-2)} = \frac{3}{-2}$

$m_3 = \frac{4-0}{2-(-4)} = \frac{2}{3}$ $\quad m_4 = \frac{1-(-3)}{4-(-2)} = \frac{2}{3}$

There are two pairs of parallel sides, so the quadrilateral is a parallelogram.

61. slope of $D_1 = \frac{a-0}{0-a} = -1$; slope of $D_2 = \frac{a-0}{a-0} = 1$; the slopes are negative reciprocals of each other, so the diagonals are perpendicular.

63a. $y = \frac{3}{4}x + 30$ **b.** 64 **c.** 72

	Fraction	Decimal	Percent
65.	$\frac{1}{3}$	$0.0\overline{3}$	$33\frac{1}{3}\%$
67.	$\frac{1}{50}$	0.02	2%
69.	$\frac{1}{8}$	0.125	$12\frac{1}{2}\%$
71.	$\frac{1}{6}$	$0.1\overline{6}$	$16\frac{2}{3}\%$
73.	$\frac{4}{5}$	0.80	80%
75.	$\frac{9}{20}$	0.45	45%

77. 200 meters

LESSON 1.4

TRY THIS (p. 29)
$k = 5$; $y = 5x$

TRY THIS (p. 30)
72 minutes

TRY THIS (p. 32)
$x = 4$

Exercises

8. $k = 5$; $y = 5x$ **9.** 8375 feet **10a.** 20 **b.** $y = 6.35x$; the constant of variation is the hourly wage. **11.** $x = 2$ **12.** $x = -3$ **13.** $x = 4$ **15.** $k = 2$; $y = 2x$ **17.** $k = 3$; $y = 3x$ **19.** $k = \frac{5}{3}$; $y = \frac{5}{3}x$ **21.** $k = -50$; $y = -50x$ **23.** $k = -0.4$; $y = -0.4x$ **25.** $k = 48$; $y = 48x$ **27.** $k = 20$; $y = 20x$ **29.** $k = -0.3$; $y = -0.3x$ **31.** $a = kb$ **33.** $b = 60$ **35.** $a = -\frac{1}{2}$ **37.** $w = 3\frac{1}{3}$ **39.** $x = 12\frac{1}{2}$ **41.** $x = -2\frac{1}{10}$ **43.** $x = 9\frac{1}{3}$ **45.** $x = 5$ **47.** $x = -2$ **49.** $x = 8$ **51.** $x = 3$ **53.** yes; $y = 0.02x$ **55.** yes; $y = -\frac{1}{2}x$ **57.** No; there is no value of k such that $y = kx$ for every x in the table. **59.** If a varies directly as c, then $a = k_1c$ for some nonzero constant, k_1. If b varies directly as c, then $b = k_2c$ for some nonzero constant, k_2. Add each side of these equations together in order to get $a + b = (k_1 + k_2)c$. Because $k_1 + k_2$ is a nonzero constant, $a + b$ varies directly as c. **61.** $k = 0.11$; $m = 0.11g$ **63.** 35.2 grams **65.** 35 kilometers, 30 kilometers **67.** 10 amperes **69.** 0.29 ampere **71a.** 0.1875; $s = 0.1875w$; the constant represents the "stretchiness" of the spring as compared with that of other springs. **b.** 16 pounds **c.** 7.5 inches **73.** $2^2 \cdot 5 \cdot 43$ **75.** $2^2 \cdot 3^2 \cdot 5$ **77.** $2 \cdot 5 \cdot 7^2$ **79.** $\frac{2}{3}$ **81.** $-\frac{5}{14}$

LESSON 1.5

TRY THIS (p. 40)
about 13.66 minutes, or about 13:39.93

Exercises

9. strong negative correlation; $y \approx -0.8x + 9.2$ **10.** fairly strong positive correlation; $y \approx 0.83x + 1.1$ **11.** No reliable correlation; the calculator gives a least-squares line with equation $y \approx 0.8x + 1.4$, but the correlation coefficient is about –0.1. **12.** 112.58 **13.** fairly strong positive correlation; $y \approx 0.8x + 1.36$ **15.** $r = -1$ **17.** $r = 1$ **19.** $r \approx 0.63$ **21.** *Interpolate*—to estimate values (of a function) between two known values. *Extrapolate*—to predict by projecting past known data. **23a.** $y \approx 0.17x - 2.97$ **b.** $y \approx 0.52x - 26.91$

c. $r \approx 0.3$ for women; $r \approx 0.9$ for men; the data set for men is almost linear and has most of its data points clustered around the least-squares line. The data set for women is not very linear and has many of its data points away from the least-squares line. **d.** about a size 7.5 shoe **e.** about a size 11.5 shoe **f.** about 6 feet and 3 inches **g.** about 5 feet and 5 inches **25a.** $y \approx -0.57x + 77.12$ **b.** $y \approx -0.94x + 111.97$ **c.** $r \approx -0.89$ for women; $r \approx -0.95$ for men; the data for men is more linear than the data for women. **d.** about 32% **e.** about 46% **f.** about 1966 **g.** about 1996 **27.** $0.\overline{3}$ **29.** 4.25 **31.** 0.35 **33.** 25 **35.** $m = -1.6$

LESSON 1.6

TRY THIS (p. 47, Ex. 2)
$x = \frac{3}{2}$

TRY THIS (p. 47, Ex. 3)
$x \approx 1.25$

Exercises

6. $x = 2$ **7.** $x = 5$ **8.** $x = -1$ **9.** $x = 2$ **10.** $x \approx -1.28$ **11.** $y = -\frac{A}{B}x + \frac{C}{B}$ **13.** $x = -8$ **15.** $x = \frac{8}{3}$ **17.** $x = 3$ **19.** $x = -3$ **21.** $x = -8$ **23.** $x = \frac{5}{9}$ **25.** $x = -2$ **27.** $x = -5$ **29.** $x = 3$ **31.** $x = \frac{40}{3}$ **33.** $x = 3$ **35.** $x = \frac{12}{11}$ **37.** $x = \frac{78}{7}$ **39.** $x = \frac{2}{3}$ **41.** $x \approx 1.12$ **43.** $x \approx 10.75$ **45.** $x \approx 11.08$ **47.** $b = \frac{2A}{h}$ **49.** $r_2 = -\frac{r_1R}{R - r_1}$, or $\frac{Rr_1}{r_1 - R}$ **51.** $h = \frac{2A}{b_1 + b_2}$ **53.** $x = -\frac{b-d}{a-c}$, or $\frac{d-b}{a-c}$ **55.** $r = \frac{I-P}{Pt}$ **57.** $v = \frac{x}{t}$ **59.** $v = \frac{2y}{x}$ **61.** $x = 13$ **63.** $s = \frac{A - \pi r^2}{\pi r}$ **65.** 7 years **67.** 30 pairs of shoes **69.** 8 hours

71. about 35 hours

73. slope $= -\frac{3}{4}$; y-intercept $= \frac{9}{4}$

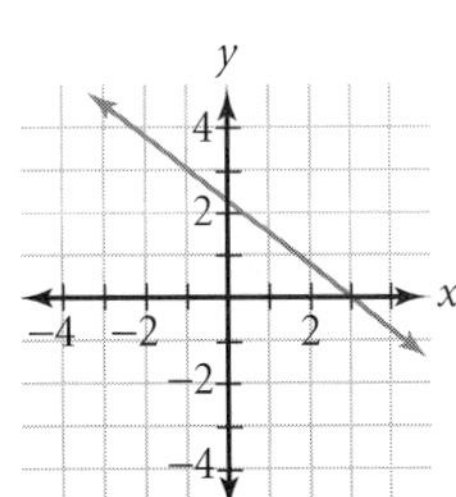

75. 57,360 **77.** 46,720,000 **79.** 2.5×10^4 **81.** 2.6007×10^2 **83.** 5×10^{-2}

LESSON 1.7

TRY THIS (p. 55, Ex. 1)
$x < \frac{11}{3}$

TRY THIS (p. 55, Ex. 2)
$t < -1$

−6 −5 −4 −3 −2 −1 0 1 2 3 4 5 6

TRY THIS (p. 57, Ex. 4)
$x \leq 1$ *and* $x > -7$

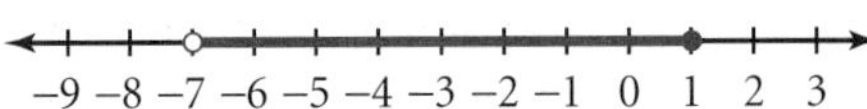

TRY THIS (p. 57, Ex. 5)
$x \leq \frac{5}{2}$ *or* $x > 5$

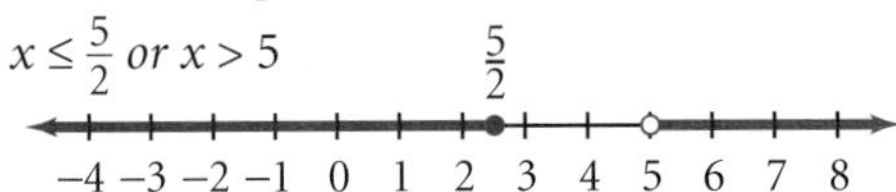

Exercises

5. $x < 4$

6. $q > 5$

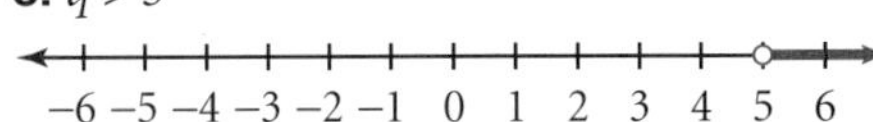

7. $t \geq 76$

8. $x \geq -2$ *and* $x < 6$

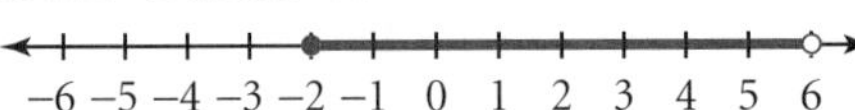

9. $x \geq -7$ *or* $x > 5$

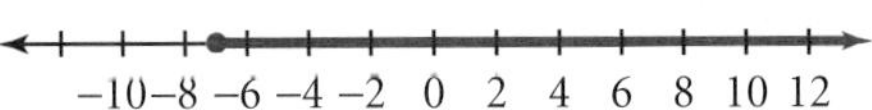

11. $x > -1$ **13.** $x \geq -1$ **15.** $x \leq 5$ **17.** $x \geq 2$ **19.** $x < 3$

21. $x > 2$

−6 −5 −4 −3 −2 −1 0 1 2 3 4 5 6

23. $x < -2$

−6 −5 −4 −3 −2 −1 0 1 2 3 4 5 6

25. $x < 2$

−6 −5 −4 −3 −2 −1 0 1 2 3 4 5 6

27. $y < -8$

−10 −8 −6 −4 −2 0 2 4 6 8 10 12

29. $x \geq 11$

−12 −8 −4 0 4 8 12

31. $x \leq 150$

−300 −200 −100 0 100 200 300

33. $x \geq -6$

−6 −5 −4 −3 −2 −1 0 1 2 3 4 5 6

35. $x < -15$

−30 −15 0 15 30

37. $x \leq 9$

39. $t > -64$

41. $x \le \frac{1}{4}$

43. $a < 5$

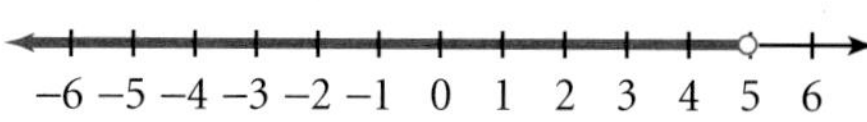

45. $x \ge 15$

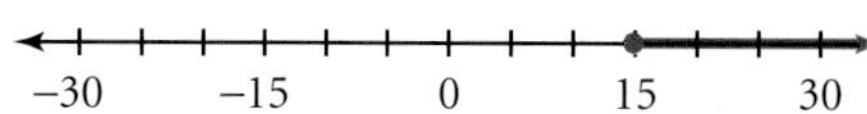

47. $x \ge -4$

49. $x \le -\frac{6}{19}$

51a. $x < -4$

b. no solution

c. $x < 2$

d. $x < -4$ *or* $x > 2$

53. $y < 6$ *and* $y > 3$

55. $x < -3$ *or* $x > 4$

57. $y \ge 3$ *and* $y \ge -6$

59. $x \le -4$ *or* $x \ge 3$

61. $t > 2$ *and* $t < 4$

63. $d > -8$ *and* $d < 1$

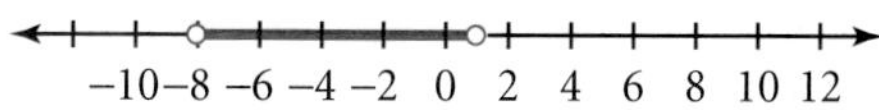

65. $x \ge 4$ *or* $x \le -3$

67. $x > -4$ *or* $x \le -5$

69. $m > -\frac{9}{4}$ *and* $m \le -\frac{5}{2}$; no solution

71. $x > -5$ *or* $x \le 4$; all real numbers

73. \$50 or greater **75.** less than 370 fat calories

77. slope $= -2$ **79.** slope $= \frac{1}{3}$ **81.** $y = -\frac{3}{2}x + \frac{7}{2}$

83. $y = -\frac{8}{3}x - \frac{26}{3}$ **85.** 60,000 voters **87.** $t = \frac{A - p}{pr}$

LESSON 1.8

TRY THIS (p. 63)

$x = -4$ *or* $x = \frac{2}{3}$

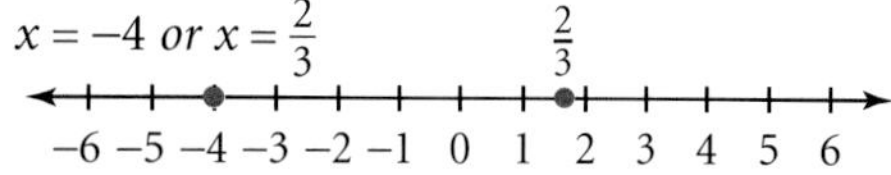

TRY THIS (p. 64)

$x = \frac{3}{2}$

TRY THIS (p. 65, Ex. 3)

$x \le -\frac{4}{3}$ *or* $x \ge \frac{2}{5}$

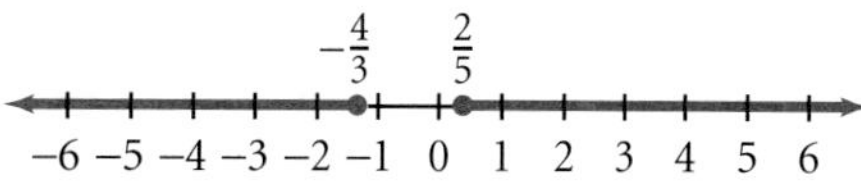

TRY THIS (p. 65, Ex. 4)

$x \ge -\frac{4}{3}$ *and* $x \le \frac{2}{5}$, or $-\frac{4}{3} \le x \le \frac{2}{5}$

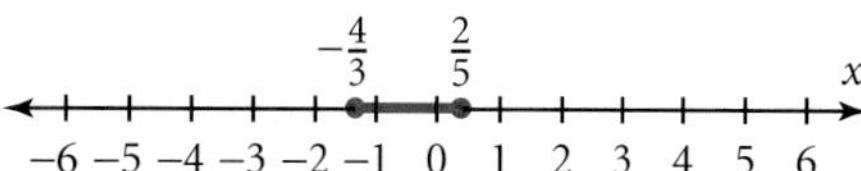

TRY THIS (p. 66)

$|t - 12.00| \le 0.01$

Exercises

6. $x = 14$ *or* $x = 6$ **7.** $x = 4$ *or* $x = 1$ **8.** $x = -1$ *or* $x = \frac{17}{3}$

9. $x = -1$ **10.** $x = 8$ *or* $x = 0$ **11.** no solution

12. $x < 2$ *or* $x > 6$

13. $x \le -3$ *or* $x \ge 2$

14. $-\frac{11}{2} < x < -\frac{9}{2}$

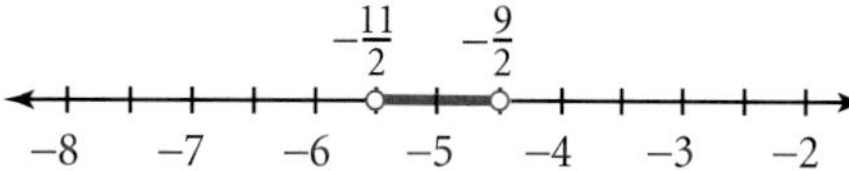

15. $x \le -1$ *or* $x \ge 1$

16. $x \ge -\frac{3}{2}$

17. all real numbers

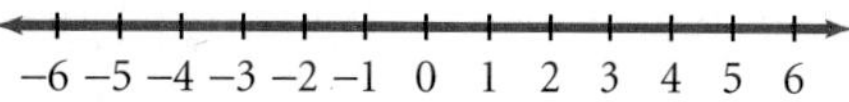

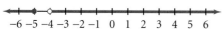

18a. $|x - 25| \leq 2$ *or* $|25 - x| \leq 2$ **b.** $23 \leq x \leq 27$

18 19 20 21 22 23 24 25 26 27 28 29 30

19. b **21.** d **23.** c **25.** $x = 4$ *or* $x = -12$

27. $x = 8$ *or* $x = -12$ **29.** $x = -7$ *or* $x = 11$ **31.** $x = 2$ *or* $x = 13$ **33.** $x = -4\frac{1}{2}$ *or* $x = 9\frac{1}{2}$ **35.** $x = \frac{4}{5}$ *or* $x = \frac{8}{5}$

37. $x = -\frac{4}{5}$ *or* $x = \frac{2}{5}$ **39.** no solution

41. $x \geq -12$ *and* $x \leq 2$

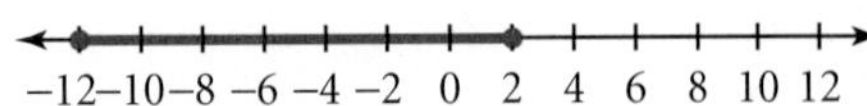

43. $x \geq -6$ *and* $x \leq 6$

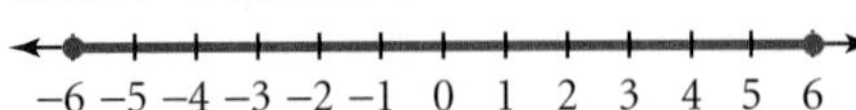

45. all real numbers

–6 –5 –4 –3 –2 –1 0 1 2 3 4 5 6

47. $x > -4$ *and* $x < 7$

7

–12–10–8 –6 –4 –2 0 2 4 6 8 10 12

49. $x < \frac{12}{7}$

$\frac{12}{7}$

–6 –5 –4 –3 –2 –1 0 1 2 3 4 5 6

51. all real numbers

–6 –5 –4 –3 –2 –1 0 1 2 3 4 5 6

53. no solution

55. $x < 2$ *or* $x > \frac{8}{3}$

2 $\frac{8}{3}$

–6 –5 –4 –3 –2 –1 0 1 2 3 4 5 6

57. no solution

59. The distance between x and 4 is less than 1.

–4 –3 –2 –1 0 1 2 3 4 5 6 7 8

61. $x \geq -\frac{3}{2}$ **63.** He is either 7.25 or 12.75 feet away from the end of the rope. **65.** 65%; 71%

67. 6 runs **69.** $x = 6$ **71.** $h = \frac{2A}{b}$

73. $x < \frac{9}{2}$

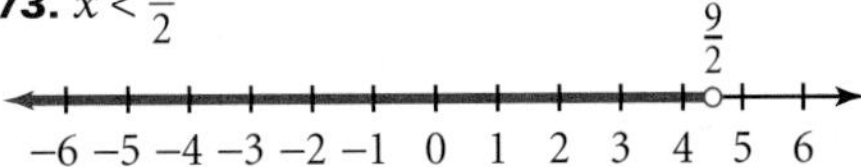

75. $-1 < x < 5$

–4 –3 –2 –1 0 1 2 3 4 5 6 7 8

77. $x \leq -2$ *or* $x > 4$

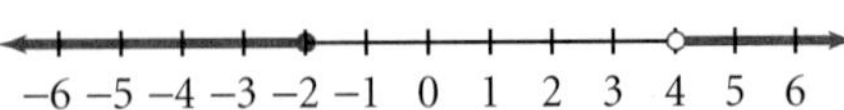

CHAPTER REVIEW AND ASSESSMENT

1. not linear **3.** linear; (35, 25)

5.

Mental age	IQ
10	67
14	94
15	100
19	127
25	167
m	$\frac{100}{15}m$

$y = \frac{100}{15}m$

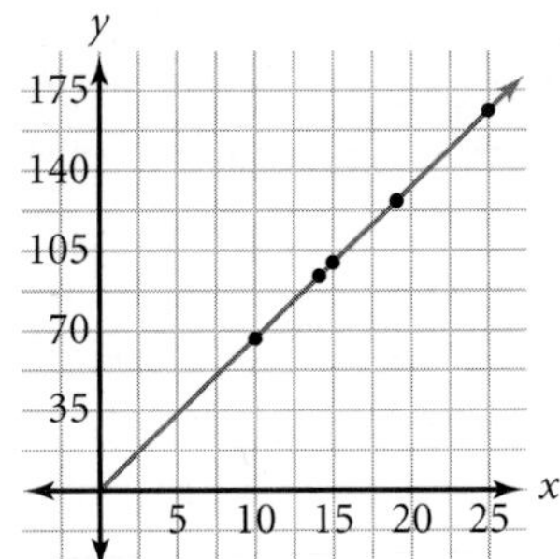

7.

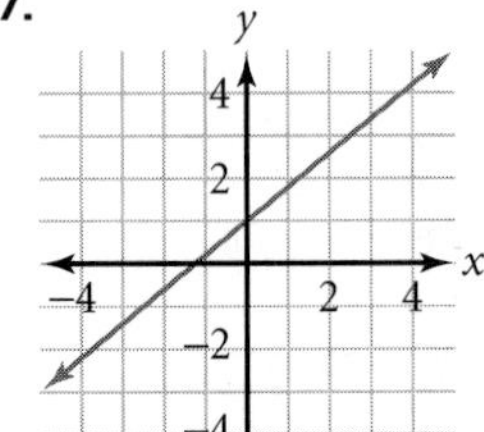

9.

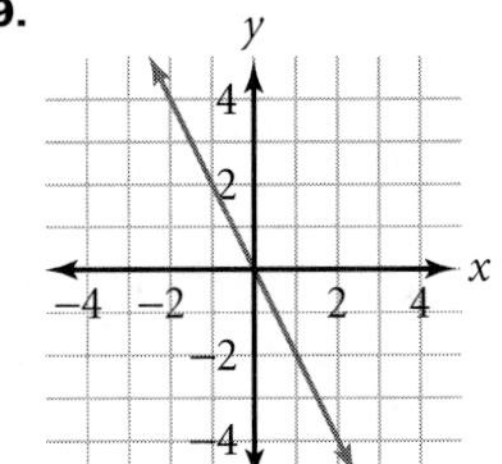

11.

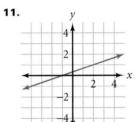

13.

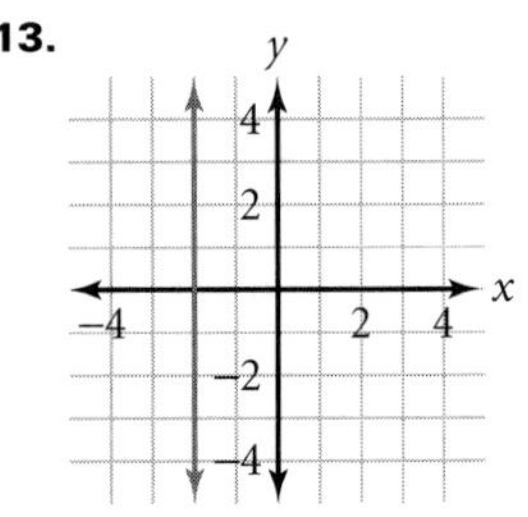

15. $y = 100x + 398$ **17.** $y = 4$ **19.** $x = -2$

21. $y = -1.25x + 10.5$ **23.** $y = \frac{1}{3}x - 1$ **25.** $x = 4$

27. $k = 0.005$; $y = 0.005x$ **29.** 50 millimeters

31. The correlation is negative. **33.** $t = h + 15$

35. $C = \frac{5}{9}F - \frac{160}{9}$ **37.** $f = \frac{f_1 f_2}{f_1 + f_2}$

39. $2(10) + 2l \leq 140$; $l \leq 60$ meters

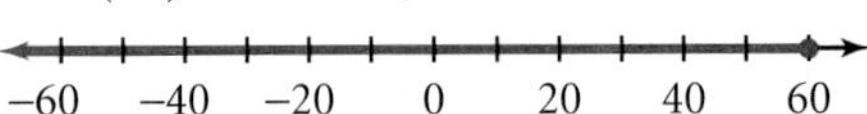

41. $x < 8$ *and* $x > 3$

–12–10–8 –6 –4 –2 0 2 4 6 8 10 12

43. $x < 8$ *or* $x > 3$

–6 –5 –4 –3 –2 –1 0 1 2 3 4 5 6

45. $x = -40$ *or* $x = 40$

–60–50–40–30–20–10 0 10 20 30 40 50 60

47. $x = -4.5$ *or* $x = 4.5$

–6 –5 –4 –3 –2 –1 0 1 2 3 4 5 6

49. $x < -40$ *or* $x > 40$

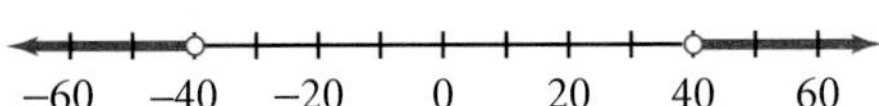

51. all real numbers

53. $k = 2$; $h = 2s$ **55.** $2850 < \frac{1}{10}I$, where $I > 0$

Chapter 2

LESSON 2.1

TRY THIS (p. 88, Ex. 2)

$(a + b)(c - d) = a(c - d) + b(c - d)$ Distributive Property

$= ac - ad + bc - bd$ Distributive Property

or

$(a + b)(c - d) = (a + b)c - (a + b)d$ Distributive Property

$= ac + bc - (ad + bd)$ Distributive Property

$= ac + bc - ad - bd$ Distributive Property

TRY THIS (p. 88, Ex. 3)

$T = c + 0.06c$

$T = 1c + 0.06c$ Use the Identity Property.

$T = (1 + 0.06)c$ Use the Distributive Property.

$T = 1.06c$ Add.

TRY THIS (p. 89)

$\frac{4}{3}$

Exercises

4. $\frac{3}{2}$ is a rational and real number; $-2.101001000\ldots$ is an irrational and real number. **5.** $2b + 2d$ **6.** 0 **7.** 15 **8.** 2 **9.** 5 **10.** $-20t^2$

11. $m = \frac{p}{12} + \frac{0.06p}{12}$

$m = \frac{1p}{12} + \frac{0.06p}{12}$ Use the Identity Property.

$m = \frac{(1 + 0.06)p}{12}$ Use the Distributive Property.

$m = \frac{1.06p}{12}$ Add.

12. 25 **13.** −4 **14.** $\frac{35}{6}$ **15.** −122 **17.** −5.1 is a rational and real number. **19.** $\sqrt{2}$ is an irrational and real number. **21.** $\frac{3}{9}$ is a rational and real number. **23.** $-1.\overline{063}$ is a rational and real number. **25.** $\sqrt{25}$, or 5, is a natural number, a whole number, an integer, a rational number, and a real number. **27.** 1 is a natural number, a whole number, an integer, a rational number, and a real number. **29.** $-\pi$ is an irrational and real number. **31.** $\sqrt{28}$ is an irrational and real number.

33.

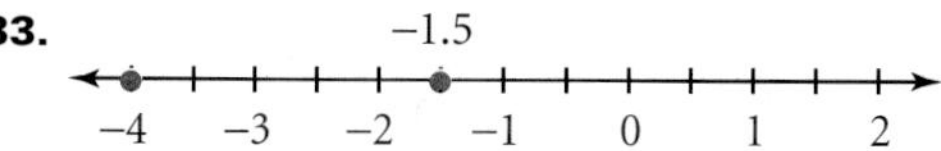

35. $4\frac{3}{8}$

−1 0 1 2 3 4 5

37. $\sqrt{7}$, or ≈2.65

−2 −1 0 1 2 3 4

39. Associative Property of Multiplication **41.** Commutative Property of Addition **43.** Associative Property of Addition **45.** Inverse Property of Multiplication **47.** Inverse Property of Addition **49.** Identity Property of Multiplication **51.** Identity Property of Addition **53.** Distributive Property **55.** Commutative Property of Multiplication **57.** 4 **59.** 15 **61.** 5 **63.** 26 **65.** 7 **67.** 6 **69.** 5 **71a.** Answers may vary. **b.** In general, whole, rational, and real numbers are represented. Sometimes negative integers are also represented. **c.** Answers may vary. sample answers: integers: 0 through 10 on the phone, 0 on a scale; rational: 3.5-ounce bag of microwave popcorn, $\frac{1}{4}$-cup marking on a measuring cup **73a.** No; Ron calculated $8 + 10 + 14 + \frac{16}{4}$, not $\frac{8 + 10 + 14 + 16}{4}$. **b.** Ron should have entered (8 + 10 + 14 + 16) ÷ 4, which would have given an answer of 12. **75.** The annual premium is \$5376. **77.** $\frac{14.6}{1000} = \frac{146}{10{,}000}$, which is rational. **79.** 13%; $\frac{13}{100}$; rational; real **81.** $m = -3$ **83.** $m = \frac{3}{4}$ **85.** $m = \frac{3}{4}$ **87.** $x = \frac{19}{3}$ **89.** $x = -\frac{17}{4}$

91. $x = \frac{12}{5}$ *or* $x = -\frac{12}{5}$

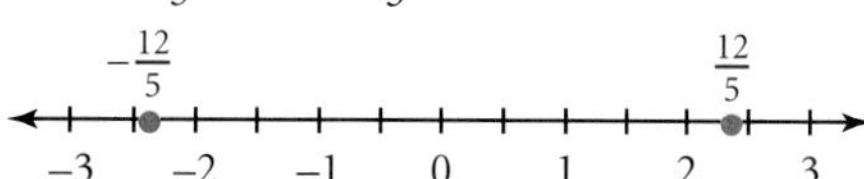

93. $x < -1$ *or* $x > \frac{1}{3}$

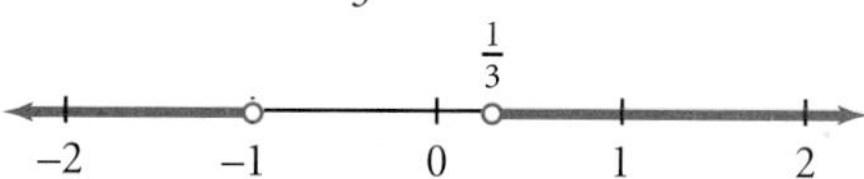

LESSON 2.2

TRY THIS (p. 95)

9.5 feet per second squared

TRY THIS (p. 96, Ex. 2)

$\frac{30x^2}{z^2}$

TRY THIS (p. 96, Ex. 3)

$\frac{-27c^9}{b^{15}}$

TRY THIS (p. 97)

4; 216

TRY THIS (p. 98)

about 1.8 square meters

Exercises

5. 140 feet per second squared **6.** x^6 **7.** z^6 **8.** y^{18} **9.** $a^{12}b^{28}$ **10.** y^{12} **11.** $\frac{4y^2}{25x^8}$ **12.** $\frac{b^6}{a^{10}}$ **13.** $\frac{y^3}{x}$ **14.** 10 **15.** 27 **16.** 3 **17.** 16 **18.** 1.60 square meters **19.** 1 **21.** 1 **23.** $\frac{1}{6}$ **25.** $\frac{81}{625}$ **27.** 4 **29.** −27 **31.** 7 **33.** 256 **35.** 216 **37.** −16 **39.** y^7 **41.** $-10xy^7$ **43.** m^4 **45.** $\frac{1}{x^7}$ **47.** $8x^{12}y^3$ **49.** $25w^8v^{10}$ **51.** $-\frac{128z^{14}}{x^{21}}$ **53.** $-\frac{8p^{15}}{q^{21}}$ **55.** $243x^{20}y^{10}$ **57.** $\frac{1}{5r^2s}$ **59.** $\frac{1}{5xy}$ **61.** $\frac{b^{10}}{16a^8}$ **63.** $\frac{y}{x^3}$ **65.** $\frac{1}{ab^8}$ **67.** $\frac{8x^{47}y^{18}z^{11}}{3}$ **69.** $\frac{b^{30}}{a^9c^6}$ **71.** 3,382,159.1 **73.** 1.1 **75.** 68.1 **77.** For all values of a and b, $-(a-b) = b-a$; therefore, $y^{a-b} = y^{-(b-a)} = \frac{1}{y^{b-a}}$ **79a.** 11.9 centimeters **b.** $\frac{3V}{\pi r^2}$ **81a.** 2,633,744.9 **b.** $\frac{2l}{3r^4}$ **83.** 99.7% **85.** 97.2% **87.** 12.4 pounds per square inch

89. $x > -3$ *and* $x < 1$

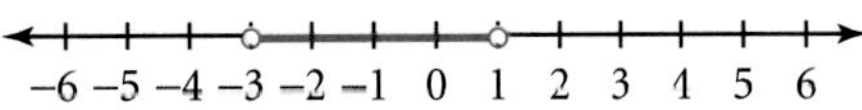

91. all real numbers

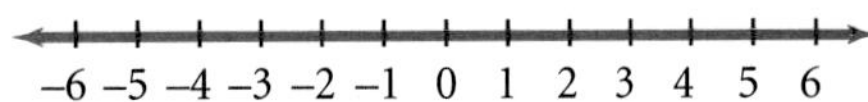

93. 9.373737… is a rational and real number. **95.** 5.38388388838888… is an irrational and real number. **97.** 5 **99.** 63

LESSON 2.3

TRY THIS (p. 104)
A customer with checking and savings accounts has at least one account number, so the correspondence is a relation. Some customers may have both a checking account number and a savings account number, so the relation is not a function.

TRY THIS (p. 105)
a. domain: {−4, −3, −1, 2, 3, 5}; range: {−3, 0, 1, 2}
b. domain: $x \geq -2$; range: $y \geq -1$

Exercises

5. no; (5, 3) and (5, 7) **6.** yes **7.** yes **8.** no; (2, 2) and (2, 1) **9.** yes **10.** No; for example, the y-axis crosses the graph at two points. **11.** A registered automobile has at least one license plate number. Thus, the correspondence is a relation. Each registered automobile may not have more than one license plate number, so the relation is also a function. **12.** domain: $x \geq -3$; range: $y \leq 4$ **13.** domain: {−3, −1, 1, 3}; range: {−2, −1, 0, 1} **14.** $f(3) = 14$; $f(1.5) = 4.25$ **15a.** $w(h) = 24.00h + 20.00$ **b.** For 5.5 hours of work, the plumber earns $152.00. **17.** yes **19.** yes **21.** yes **23.** yes **25.** No; for the first coordinate, −1, there is more than one second coordinate, 8 and 7. **27.** yes **29.** yes **31.** yes **33.** No; for example, the points (−2, −1) and (−2, 2) are on the graph. For the first coordinate, −2, there is more than one second coordinate, −1 and 2. **35.** yes **37.** domain: {0, 3}; range: {2, 4} **39.** domain: {7, 8, 9}; range: {−1, −2, −3} **41.** domain: {4, 5, 6}; range: {−6, −5, −4} **43.** $f(1) = -4$; $f(3) = 0$ **45.** $g(-1) = -1$; $g(1) = \frac{1}{3}$ **47.** $f(3) = 9$; $f(-2.5) = 20$ **49.** $f(-1) = \frac{1}{3}$; $f\left(\frac{3}{4}\right) = \frac{3}{16}$ **51.** domain: all real numbers; range: all real numbers **53.** domain: all real numbers; range: $y \geq 0$ **55.** domain: all real numbers; range: $y = 4$ **57.** domain: all real numbers; range: all real numbers **59.** Answers may vary.
sample answer:

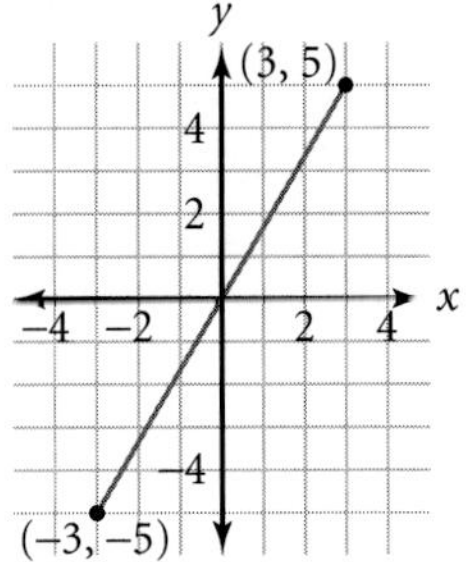

61. $f(\sqrt{2}) = -1$ **63.** $f(a+\sqrt{2}) = a^2 + (2\sqrt{2})a - 1$ **65.** $A(3) = 3^2 = 9$ square meters **67.** $S(P) = 0.7P$ **69.** The sale price of the items was $36.40. **71.** $y = -3x + 13$ **73.** $y = -\frac{2}{3}x - \frac{25}{3}$ **75.** $y = x + 2$ **77.** $y = \frac{4}{7}x - \frac{27}{7}$ **79.** $y = 2x + 13$ **81.** 15,625

LESSON 2.4

TRY THIS (p. 112, Ex. 1)
$(f+g)(x) = 12x - 2.5$; $(f-g)(x) = -14x^2 + 12x + 7.5$

TRY THIS (p. 112, Ex. 2)
$(f \cdot g)(x) = 15x^3 - 6x^2 + 5x - 2$; $\left(\frac{f}{g}\right)(x) = \frac{3x^2+1}{5x-2}$, where $x \neq \frac{2}{5}$

TRY THIS (p. 113)
$(f \circ g)(x) = -8x^2 + 3$; $(g \circ f)(x) = 4x^2 - 6$

Exercises

4. $(f+g)(x) = \frac{7}{2}x + 1$ **5.** $(f-g)(x) = -\frac{5}{2}x - 1$ **6.** $(f \cdot g)(x) = \frac{3}{2}x^2 + \frac{x}{2}$ **7.** $\left(\frac{f}{g}\right)(x) = \frac{x}{2(3x+1)}$, where $x \neq -\frac{1}{3}$ **8.** $(f \circ g)(x) = \frac{3x+1}{2}$ **9.** $(g \circ f)(x) = \frac{3}{2}x + 1$

10. Let x be the total cost of the meal.

$R(x) = x - 5$ and $T(x) = x + 0.15x = 1.15x$

$$\begin{aligned}(R \circ T)(x) &= R(T(x)) = R(1.15x)\\ &= 1.15x - 5\\ (T \circ R)(x) &= (T(R(x)) = T(x - 5)\\ &= 1.15(x - 5)\\ &= 1.15x - 5.75\end{aligned}$$

$(R \circ T)(x)$ represents the total cost of the meal, plus the tip, minus \$5. $(T \circ R)(x)$ represents the total cost of the meal, plus the tip, minus \$5.75. $(R \circ T)(x)$ represents the conditions of the coupon.

11. $(f + g)(x) = 4x + 8$; $(f - g)(x) = 4x - 2$
13. $(f + g)(x) = x^2 + 5x - 6$; $(f - g)(x) = x^2 - x + 4$
15. $(f + g)(x) = -3x^2 + x + 2$; $(f - g)(x) = 3x^2 + x - 6$
17. $(f \cdot g)(x) = 3x^3 - 24x^2$; $\left(\frac{f}{g}\right)(x) = \frac{3x^2}{x - 8}$, $x \neq 8$
19. $(f \cdot g)(x) = -3x^3$; $\left(\frac{f}{g}\right)(x) = -\frac{x}{3}$, $x \neq 0$
21. $(f \cdot g)(x) = 14x^2 - 2x^3$; $\left(\frac{f}{g}\right)(x) = \frac{2x^2}{7 - x}$, $x \neq 7$
23. $(f \cdot g)(x) = 3x^3 - 14x^2 - 5x$; $\left(\frac{f}{g}\right)(x) = \frac{-3x^2 - x}{5 - x}$, $x \neq 5$

25.
$$\begin{aligned}(f + g)(x) &= f(x) + g(x)\\ &= (x^2 - 1) + (2x - 3) \quad \text{Substitution}\\ &= x^2 - 1 + 2x - 3 \quad \text{Commutative Property}\\ &= x^2 + 2x - 4 \quad \text{Combine like terms.}\end{aligned}$$

27.
$$\begin{aligned}(g - f)(x) &= g(x) - f(x)\\ &= (2x - 3) - (x^2 - 1) \quad \text{Substitution}\\ &= 2x - 3 - x^2 + 1 \quad \text{Distributive Property}\\ &= -x^2 + 2x - 2 \quad \text{Combine like terms.}\end{aligned}$$

29. $\left(\frac{f}{g}\right)(x) = \frac{f(x)}{g(x)} = \frac{x^2 - 1}{2x - 3}$, where $x \neq \frac{3}{2}$ (Substitution)

31.
$$\begin{aligned}(f - g)(x) &= f(x) - g(x)\\ &= (x - 3) - (x^2 - 9) \quad \text{Substitution}\\ &= x - 3 - x^2 + 9 \quad \text{Distributive Property}\\ &= -x^2 + x + 6 \quad \text{Combine like terms.}\end{aligned}$$

33.
$$\begin{aligned}(f \cdot g)(x) &= f(x) \cdot g(x)\\ &= (x - 3)(x^2 - 9) \quad \text{Substitution}\\ &= x^3 - 9x - 3x^2 + 27 \quad \text{Distributive Property}\\ &= x^3 - 3x^2 - 9x + 27 \quad \text{Combine like terms.}\end{aligned}$$

35. $(f \circ g)(x) = 2x + 1$; $(g + f)(x) = 2x + 2$
37. $(f \circ g)(x) = 3x + 4$; $(g + f)(x) = 3x$
39. $(f \circ g)(x) = -75x^2 - 1$; $(g \circ f)(x) = 15x^2 + 5$
41. $(f \circ g)(x) = -28$; $(g + f)(x) = 3$ **43.** $(f \circ g)(2) = -16$
45. $(f \circ f)(2) = 2$ **47.** $(g \circ g)(2) = -16$
49. $(g \circ f)(0) = -16$ **51.** $(f \circ g)(x) = 2x^2 + 4$
53. $(f \circ h)(x) = -8x + 6$ **55.** $(f \circ f)(x) = 4x$

57. $(h \circ (h \circ g))(x) = 16x^2 + 23$ **59.** Answers may vary. Sample answer: Let $f(x) = x - 9$ and $g(x) = x^2$. Then $f \circ g = h$. **61a.** $C(t) = 360t + 850$ **b.** \$2650 **c.** 450 **63a.** $C(n) = 0.10n + 125.00$ **b.** $I(n) = 0.25n$ **c.** $P(n) = 0.15n - 125.00$ **d.** 1500 buttons **65.** $y = -\frac{1}{2}x - \frac{1}{2}$ **67.** almost no correlation **69.** weak positive correlation **71.** domain: all real numbers; range: all real numbers

LESSON 2.5

TRY THIS (p. 119)

$y = \frac{1}{4}x + \frac{5}{4}$

TRY THIS (p. 121)

$$\begin{aligned}(f \circ g)(x) &= f(g(x))\\ &= f\left(-\frac{1}{5}x + \frac{7}{5}\right)\\ &= -5\left(-\frac{1}{5}x + \frac{7}{5}\right) + 7\\ &= x - 7 + 7\\ &= x\end{aligned}$$

$$\begin{aligned}(g \circ f)(x) &= g(f(x))\\ &= g(-5x + 7)\\ &= -\frac{1}{5}(-5x + 7) + \frac{7}{5}\\ &= x - \frac{7}{5} + \frac{7}{5}\\ &= x\end{aligned}$$

Exercises

5. $F = \frac{9}{5}(K - 273) + 32$ **6.** Inverse: {(3, 8), (2, 2), (3, 4)}; the relation is a function; the inverse is not a function. **7.** Inverse: {(2, 3), (5, 9), (3, 2), (7, 4)}; the relation is a function; the inverse is a function. **8.** $y = \frac{1}{3}x - 3$ **9.** $y = -\frac{1}{3}x + \frac{5}{3}$

10.
$$\begin{aligned}(f \circ g)(x) &= f\left(\frac{1}{6}x + \frac{5}{6}\right)\\ &= 6\left(\frac{1}{6}x + \frac{5}{6}\right) - 5\\ &= (x + 5) - 5\\ (f \circ g)(x) &= x\end{aligned}$$

$$\begin{aligned}(g \circ f)(x) &= g(6x - 5)\\ &= \frac{1}{6}(6x - 5) + \frac{5}{6}\\ &= \left(x - \frac{5}{6}\right) + \frac{5}{6}\\ (g \circ f)(x) &= x\end{aligned}$$

Thus, f and g are inverses.

11. {(5, 3), (10, 6), (15, 9)}; yes; yes **13.** {(2, 5), (3, 4), (4, 3), (5, 2)}; yes; yes **15.** {(−6, −3), (2, −1), (2, 1), (6, 3)}; yes; no **17.** {(2, 1), (4, 3), (4, −3), (2, −1)}; yes; no **19.** {(0, −1), (1, 2), (3, 4), (4, 3)}; yes **21.** {(2, 1), (3, 2), (2, 3), (1, 4)}; no **23.** {(2, 5), (3, 4), (5, 3), (3, 2)}; no **25.** {(2, 0), (3, 2), (4, 3), (1, 1)}; yes **27.** The inverse is a function. **29.** $f^{-1}(x) = \frac{1}{5}x - \frac{1}{5}$ **31.** $h^{-1}(x) = -2x + 6$ **33.** $h^{-1}(x) = 3x - 8$ **35.** $f^{-1}(x) = \frac{4x + 3}{2}$ **37.** $g^{-1}(x) = \frac{4}{5}x$ **39.** $g^{-1}(x) = 2(x + 3) - 2$, or $g^{-1}(x) = 2x + 4$ **41.** No, the inverse is not a function. **43.** Yes, the inverse is a function. **45.** No, the inverse is not a function. **47.** No, the inverse is not a function. **49.** Yes, the inverse is a function. **51a.** $c = 17.50s + 50$ **b.** $s = \frac{c - 50}{17.50}$ **c.** 82 square yards of carpeting can be installed for \$1485.

53. Let a be your age and g be the guess. Then the guess, g, can be represented by the function $g = \frac{2(a+4)-6}{2}$. Now solve for a:

$$g = \frac{2(a+4)-6}{2}$$
$$2g = 2(a+4) - 6$$
$$2g + 6 = 2(a+4)$$
$$g + 3 = a + 4$$
$$g - 1 = a$$

In other words, your age is found by subtracting 1 from the guess.

55. 256 **57.** 729 **59.** $(f \cdot g)(x) = 15x^2 - 4x - 4$
61. 143

LESSON 2.6

TRY THIS (p. 125)

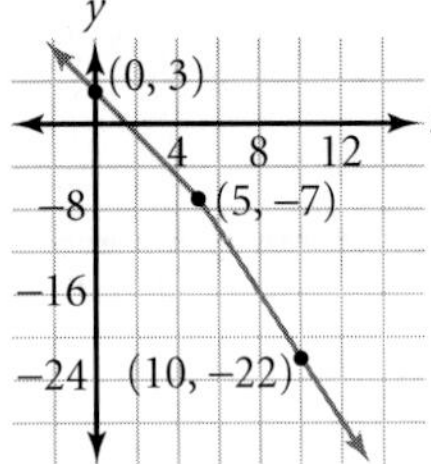

TRY THIS (p. 126, Ex. 2)
\$0.32; \$0.78

TRY THIS (p. 126, Ex. 3)

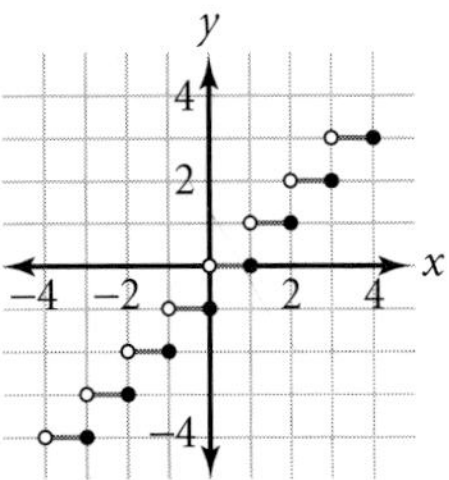

TRY THIS (p. 127)

x	$f(x) = \frac{1}{2}\lvert x\rvert + 1$
−2	2
−1	1.5
0	1
1	1.5
2	2

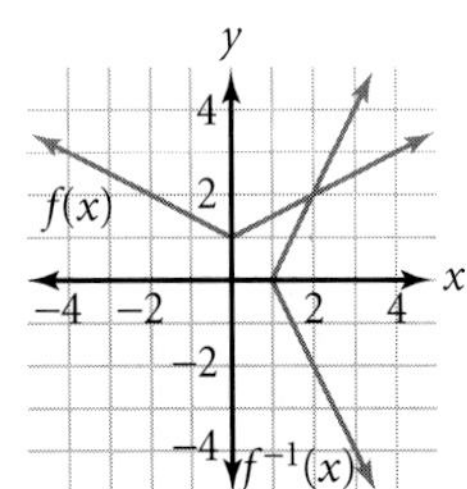

TRY THIS (p. 128)
The relative error is about 0.00125, or 0.125%.

Exercises

5.

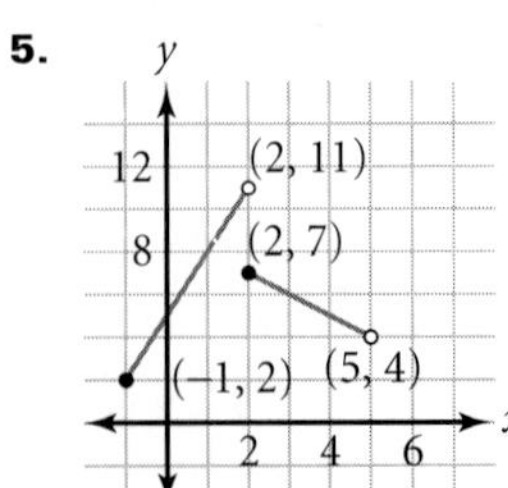

6.

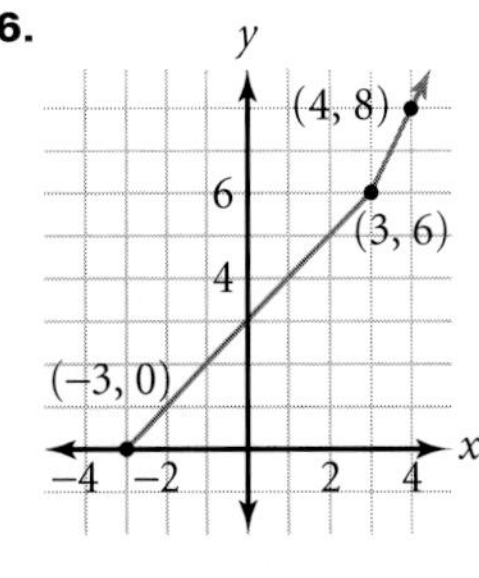

7. \$3.08 **8.** \$1.40 **9.** \$4.76 **10.** \$0.14

11.

Interval of x	$g(x) = -4[x]$
$-3 \le x < -2$	$-4(-3) = 12$
$-2 \le x < -1$	$-4(-2) = 8$
$-1 \le x < 0$	$-4(-1) = 4$
$0 \le x < 1$	$-4(0) = 0$
$1 \le x < 2$	$-4(1) = -4$
$2 \le x < 3$	$-4(2) = -8$
$3 \le x < 4$	$-4(3) = -12$

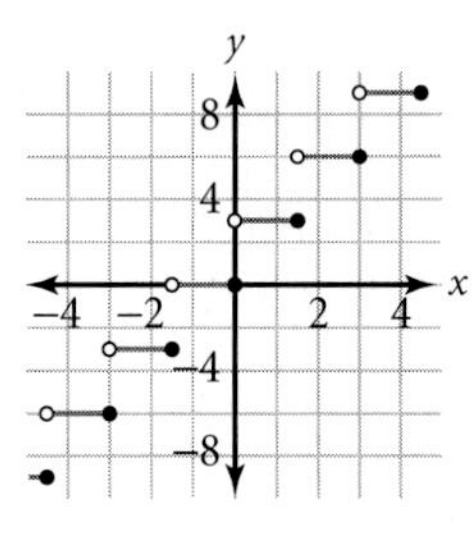

12.

Interval of x	$f(x) = -3\lceil x\rceil$
$-4 < x \le -3$	$3(-3) = -9$
$-3 < x \le -2$	$3(-2) = -6$
$-2 < x \le -1$	$3(-1) = -3$
$-1 < x \le 0$	$3(0) = 0$
$0 < x \le 1$	$3(1) = 3$
$1 < x \le 2$	$3(2) = 6$
$2 < x \le 3$	$3(3) = 0$

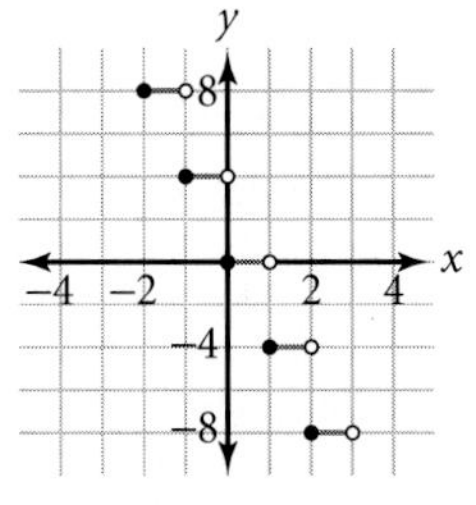

13.

x	$f(x) = \lvert x\rvert + 2$
−3	$\lvert -3\rvert + 2 = 5$
−2	$\lvert -2\rvert + 2 = 4$
−1	$\lvert -1\rvert + 2 = 3$
0	$\lvert 0\rvert + 2 = 2$
1	$\lvert 1\rvert + 2 = 3$
2	$\lvert 2\rvert + 2 = 4$
3	$\lvert 3\rvert + 2 = 5$

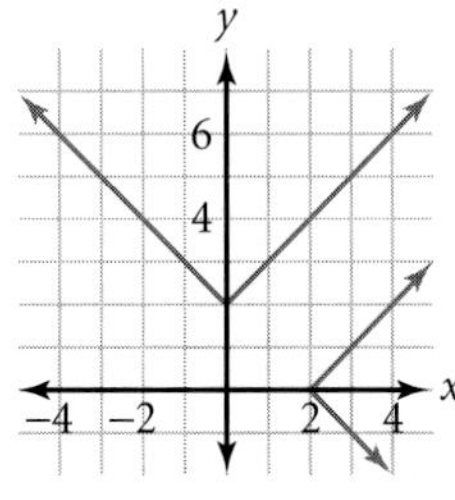

14.

x	$g(x) = 2\lvert x\rvert - 1$
−3	$2\lvert -3\rvert - 1 = 5$
−2	$2\lvert -2\rvert - 1 = 3$
−1	$2\lvert -1\rvert - 1 = 1$
0	$2\lvert 0\rvert - 1 = -1$
1	$2\lvert 1\rvert - 1 = 1$
2	$2\lvert 2\rvert - 1 = 3$
3	$2\lvert 3\rvert - 1 = 5$

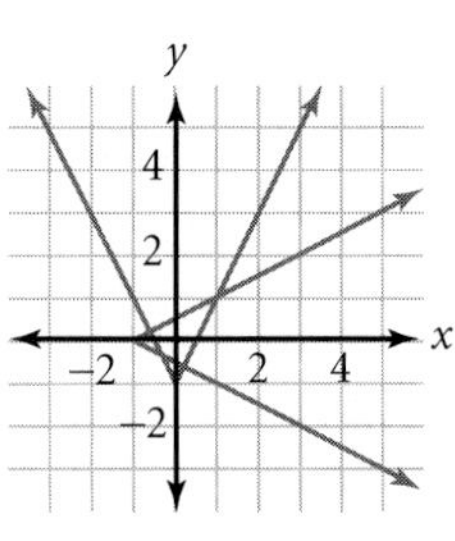

15. 0.002, or 0.2%

17.

(6, 14) (12, 8) (0, −4)

19.

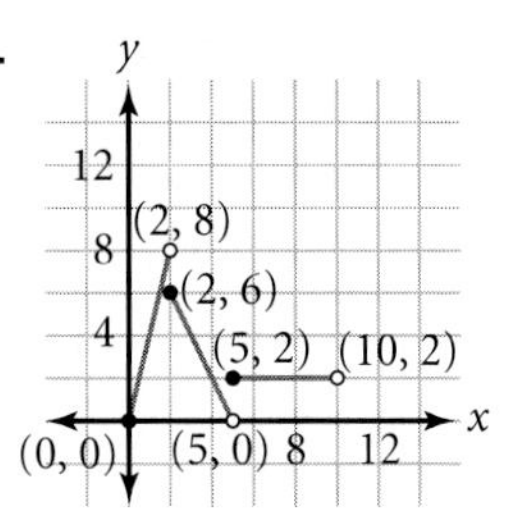

21.

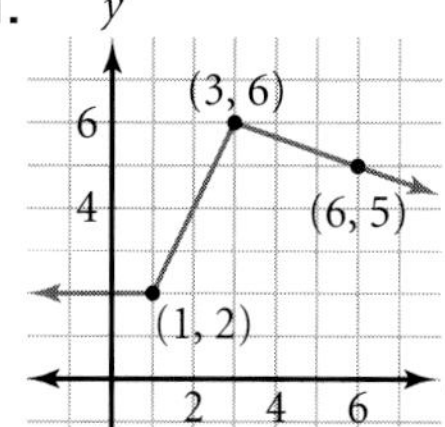

23.
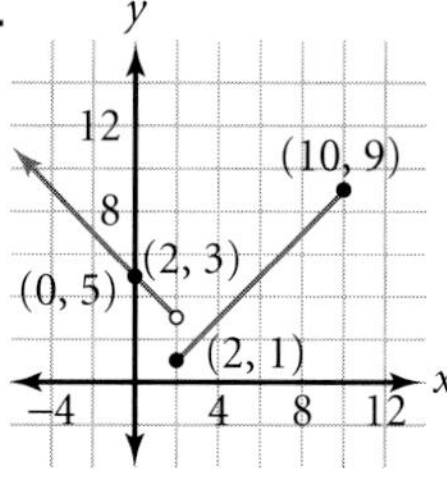

25. $g(x) = \begin{cases} \frac{5}{4}x + 2 & \text{if } -4 < x \le 0 \\ -\frac{1}{2}x & \text{if } 0 < x \le 4 \end{cases}$

27. $g(x) = \begin{cases} -x & \text{if } -3 < x \le 2 \\ -x + 5 & \text{if } x > 2 \end{cases}$

29. −7 **31.** −6 **33.** 2 **35.** 4 **37.** −1 **39.** −4 **41.** −10 **43.** 2 **45.** 1 **47.** 1.8 **49.** −2 **51.** 3.33

53.
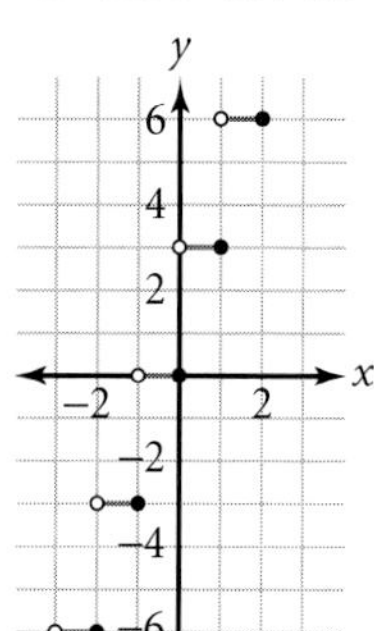

55.
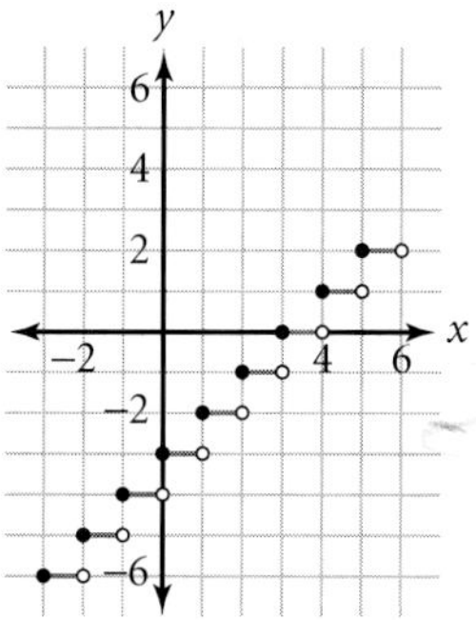

57.
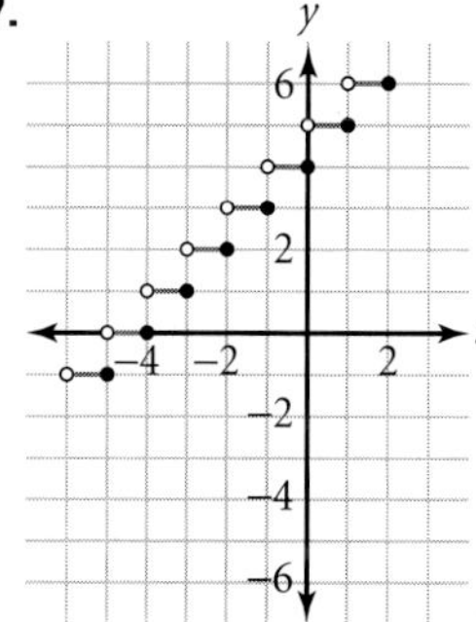

59.
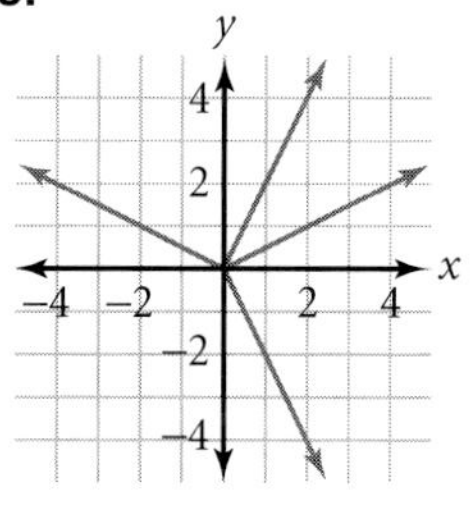

61. false; for example: $|(-1) + 1| = |0| = 0$ and $|-1| + |1| = 1 + 1 = 2$ **63.** true for all values of x and y

65.
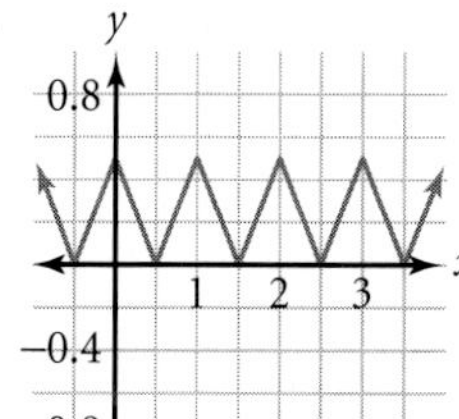

The shape of the graph is a sawtooth.

67. $f(x) = \frac{1}{10}\lceil 10x \rceil$ will round x up to the nearest tenth. $g(x) = \frac{1}{100}[100x]$ will round x down to the nearest hundredth. **69.** 0.6% **71.** 2.5%

73a.

Coffee (lb)	Cost ($)
1	9.89
2	19.78
3	29.67
4	39.56
5	49.45
6	57.43
7	65.41
8	73.39
9	81.37
10	89.35

b.
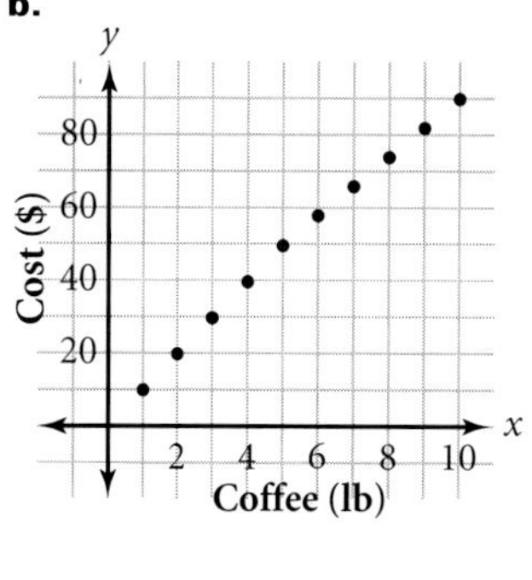

c. $c(x) = \begin{cases} 9.98x & \text{if } x \le 5 \\ 49.45 + 7.98(x - 5) & \text{if } x > 5 \end{cases}$ **d.** $53.44

75a.

Labor hours	Repair charges
0.5	45
1.0	45
1.5	65
2.0	85
2.5	105
3.0	125
3.5	145
4.0	165
4.5	185
5.0	205

b.
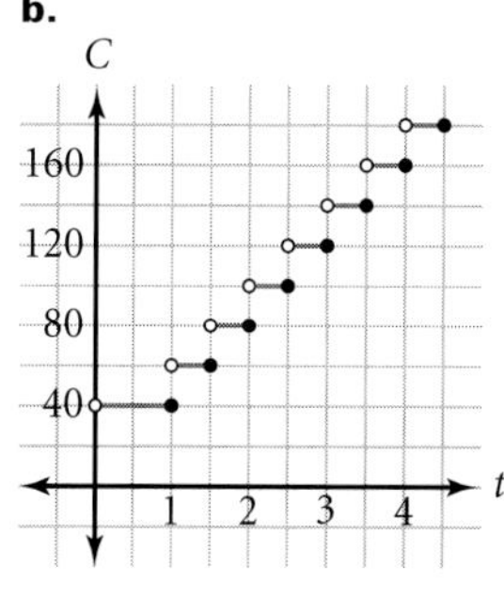

c. $C(t) = \begin{cases} 45 & \text{if } 0 < t \le 1 \\ 45 + 20\lceil 2(t-1) \rceil & \text{if } t > 1 \end{cases}$

d. $165 **77a.** $c(x) = 2.11 + 1.50x$ **b.** $7.25

79. $(g \circ f)(x) = 3x + 6$ **81.** $(g \circ g)(x) = 9x$

83. $(f + g)(x) = 4x + 2$ **85.** $\left(\frac{f}{g}\right) = \frac{x+2}{3x}, x \neq 0$

87. $a^{-1}(x) = \frac{4}{3}x + 2$ **89.** $g^{-1}(x) = 8 - x$

LESSON 2.7

TRY THIS (p. 134)

a. vertical translation 2 units down

b. horizontal translation 3 units to the right

TRY THIS (p. 135)

a. vertical stretch by a factor of 3

b. vertical compression by a factor of $\frac{1}{3}$

TRY THIS (p. 136)

a. horizontal compression by a factor of $\frac{1}{3}$

b. horizontal stretch by a factor of 4

TRY THIS (p. 137)

a. reflection across the x-axis

b. reflection across the y-axis

TRY THIS (p. 138)

a. translation 1 unit to the right; vertical stretch by a factor of 3

b. vertical compression by a factor of $\frac{1}{2}$; vertical translation 2 units down

Exercises

6. vertical translation 3 units down **7.** vertical stretch by a factor of $\frac{4}{3}$ **8.** horizontal compression by a factor of 2 **9.** reflection across the y-axis **10.** horizontal translation 3 units to the right and vertical translation 1 unit up **11.** vertical stretch by a factor of 4 **13.** horizontal compression by a factor of $\frac{1}{4}$ **15.** vertical compression by a factor of $\frac{1}{2}$ and reflection across the x-axis **17.** vertical translation 2 units down **19.** horizontal translation 2 units to the right **21.** horizontal compression by a factor of $\frac{1}{5}$, vertical translation 2 units up, and reflection across the y-axis **23.** vertical compression by a factor of $\frac{1}{3}$ and vertical translation 1 unit down **25.** horizontal translation 4 units to the left, vertical stretch by a factor of 2, reflection across the x-axis, and vertical translation 1 unit up **27.** vertical stretch by a factor of 4 **29.** vertical compression by a factor of $\frac{1}{4}$ and reflection across the x-axis **31.** horizontal compression by a factor of $\frac{1}{4}$ and reflection across the y-axis **33.** vertical translation 4 units up **35.** horizontal translation 4 units to the left **37.** horizontal compression by a factor of $\frac{1}{2}$, reflection across the y-axis, and vertical translation 1 unit up **39.** horizontal translation 4 units to the right, reflection across the x-axis, and vertical translation 3 units up **41.** reflection across the x-axis and reflection across the y-axis **43.** $g(x) = (x - 2)^2$ **45.** $g(x) = x^2 - 6$ **47.** $g(x) = \frac{1}{3}\sqrt{x}$ **49.** $g(x) = \sqrt{\frac{1}{4}x}$ **51.** $g(x) = 2(-x) - 1$ **53.** $g(x) = -|3x| - 3$ **55.** $g(x) = x^2 + 5$ **57.** $g(x) = \left(-\frac{1}{2}x\right)^2$ **59.** Answers may vary. Consider the vertical compression of the graph of $f(x) = x^2$ given by $\frac{1}{4}f(x) = \frac{1}{4}x^2$ and the horizontal stretch given by $f\left(\frac{1}{2}x\right) = \left(\frac{1}{2}x\right)^2$. Because $\left(\frac{1}{2}x\right)^2 = \left(\frac{1}{2}\right)^2 x^2 = \frac{1}{4}x^2$, the effect of the vertical compression by a factor of $\frac{1}{4}$ and the horizontal stretch by a factor of 2 are identical.

61.

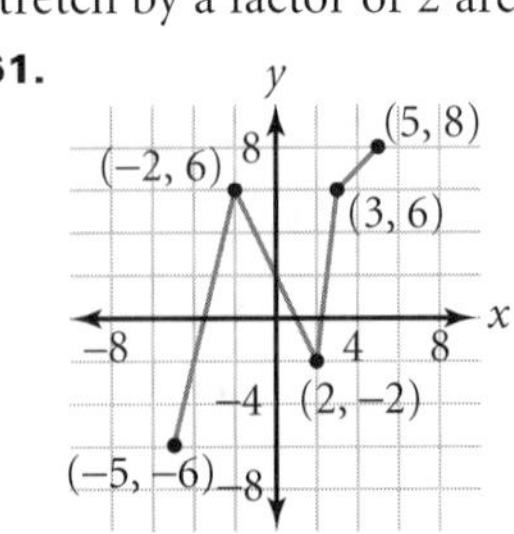

63.

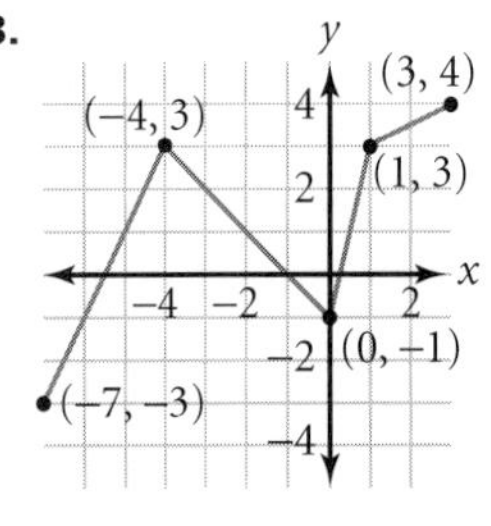

65.

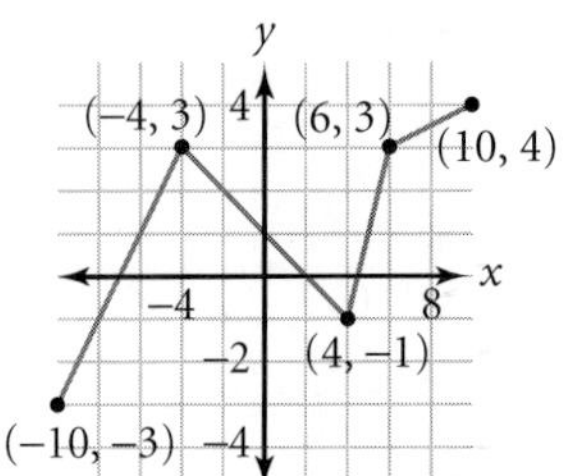

67. $y = 2x + 10$ **69.** $s = \frac{4D}{\pi b^2 n}$ **71.** 14.393939… is a rational and real number.

73. The relation is a function; the inverse, $\{(100, 1), (200, 2), (300, 3), (400, 4)\}$, is a function because each domain value is paired with exactly one range value.

75.

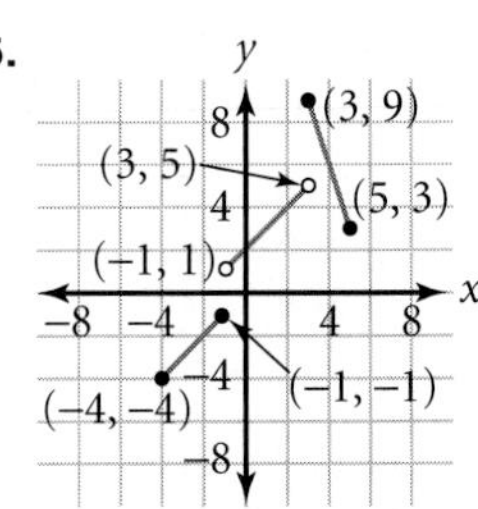

CHAPTER REVIEW AND ASSESSMENT

1. Commutative Property of Multiplication **3.** Inverse Property of Multiplication **5.** Identity Property of Addition **7.** Commutative Property of Addition **9.** −75 **11.** $-\frac{10}{9}$ **13.** $9x^6$ **15.** u^6v **17.** $\frac{8x^9}{27y^2}$ **19.** yes **21.** no **23.** domain: $\{-1, 0, 2, 4\}$; range: $\{2, 6, 7, -7\}$ **25.** $g(1) = 9$; $g(-1) = -13$ **27.** $h(1) = -1$; $h(-1) = 5$ **29.** $(f - g)(x) = \frac{5x}{2} + 1$ **31.** $(f \circ g)(x) = \frac{3x^2}{2} - 17x + 20$ **33.** $\left(\frac{g}{f}\right)(x) = \frac{\frac{x}{2} - 5}{3x - 4}, x \neq \frac{4}{3}$ **35.** $(g \circ f)(x) = -2x + 2$ **37.** $(g \circ g)(x) = x$ **39.** −45 **41.** $\{(0, -2), (1, -1), (0, 0), (1, 1), (0, 2)\}$ **43.** $f^{-1}(x) = -\frac{3}{2}x + 6$ **45.** Yes, the inverse is a function. **47.** Yes, the inverse is a function.

49.

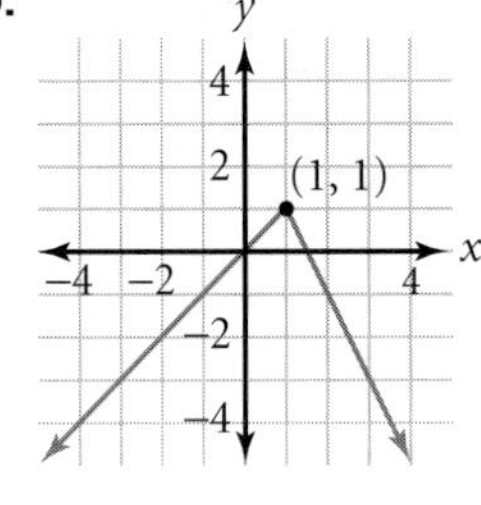

51.

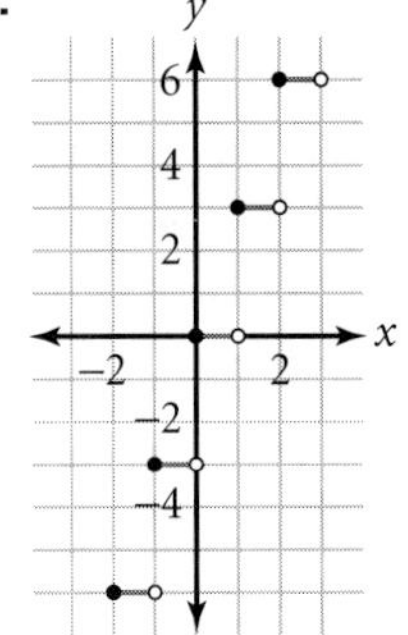

53. −78 **55.** 4 **57.** 8 **59.** horizontal translation 2 units to the right **61.** horizontal translation 3 units to the left and reflection across the x-axis **63.** vertical stretch by a factor of 9.8, reflection across the x-axis, and vertical translation 1.5 units up

Chapter 3

LESSON 3.1

TRY THIS (p. 157)
The system is consistent and independent. The solution is $x = 0$ and $y = 4$.

TRY THIS (p. 158)
$(-1, 11)$

TRY THIS (p. 159)
approximately 167 milliliters of the 7% solution and 333 milliliters of the 4% solution

TRY THIS (p. 160)
$(5, 3, -3)$

Exercises

5. This is a consistent, independent system with the unique solution $(1, 5)$. **6.** This is a dependent system, so there are infinitely many solutions. **7.** $(-12, 32)$ **8.** 480 pounds of \$2.00 candy; 520 pounds of \$0.75 candy **9.** $(1, 1, -3)$ **11.** dependent; infinitely many solutions **13.** dependent; infinitely many solutions **15.** independent; $(3, 5)$ **17.** inconsistent; no solution **19.** independent; $(0, 4)$ **21.** independent; $(2, -3)$ **23.** inconsistent; no solution **25.** $(7, 10)$ **27.** $(4, 2)$ **29.** $(4, 2)$ **31.** $\left(\frac{11}{3}, \frac{2}{3}\right)$ **33.** $(4, 2)$ **35.** $(42, 17)$ **37.** $\left(-\frac{7}{3}, -\frac{13}{15}\right)$ **39.** independent; $\left(-\frac{1}{6}, -\frac{3}{2}\right)$ **41.** $(5, -2, 4)$ **43.** $(-2, 3, -1)$ **45.** $\left(-2, \frac{3}{5}, 2\right)$ **47.** independent; $(0.29, 4.17)$ **49.** independent; $(0.67, 0.17)$ **51.** independent; $(4.15, 5.86)$ **53.** $x = \frac{c - be}{a + bd}, y = d\frac{c - be}{a + bd} + e$; $(3, 5)$ **55.** 750 square yards **57.** The two options will be equal for 2 hours of parking, and the cost will be \$11. If Armando stays less than 2 hours, the second option is less expensive; for more than 2 hours, the first option is less expensive. **59.** 7 2-point baskets and 3 3-point baskets **61.** $-3 \le x \le 7$ **63.** Distributive Property **65.** Additive Inverse **67.** 5 **69.** $\frac{1}{5}$ **71.** $4x^{10}$ **73.** $-\frac{1}{2ab}$ **75.** $\{(4, 1), (4, -3), (0, 2)\}$; not a function **77.** $\{(4, 3), (3, 4), (-1, 3), (-3, 11)\}$; function

LESSON 3.2

TRY THIS (p. 165)
$r = 1$ and $s = -3$, or $(1, -3)$

TRY THIS (p. 166)
90 small frames and 100 large frames

TRY THIS (p. 167)
$0 = 2$; the statement is false, so the system is inconsistent. There is no solution.

TRY THIS (p. 168)
The resulting statement, $0 = 0$, is true, so the system is dependent. There are infinitely many solutions.

Exercises

5. $(2, 1)$ **6.** 85 small picture frames and 60 large ones **7.** no solution **8.** all points on the graph of either equation **9.** $(6, -4)$ **11.** $(4, -2)$ **13.** $(-9, -8)$ **15.** $(3, 1)$ **17.** $(-2, -1)$ **19.** $(3, 2)$ **21.** no solution **23.** all points on the graph of either equation **25.** $\left(\frac{2}{3}, \frac{3}{4}\right)$ **27.** all points on the graph of either equation **29.** $(-4, 3)$ **31.** $(2, 0)$ **33.** $(4, -3)$ **35.** $\left(-\frac{5}{7}, -\frac{73}{84}\right)$ **37.** no solution **39.** $\frac{25}{2}$, or 12.5, acres of good land and $\frac{175}{2}$, or 87.5, acres of bad land **41.** \$3875 at 5% and \$625 at 9% **43.** 7 packages under 3 pounds and 5 packages weighing 3 pounds or more **45.** approximately 5.4 units of whole-wheat flour and 0.5 unit of whole milk **47.** \$124.80 **49.** positive correlation **51.** $x = -\frac{15}{2}$

53. $x > \frac{3}{2}$

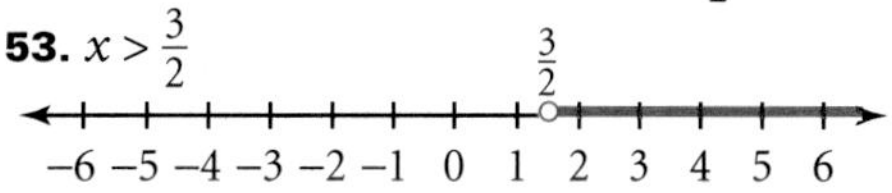

55. $x \ge -10$

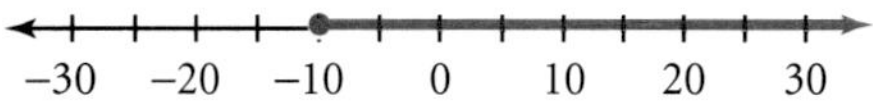

57. $-6 \le y \le 2$

59. all real numbers

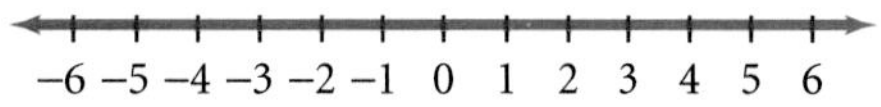

61. -25

LESSON 3.3

TRY THIS (p. 173, Ex. 1)

a.

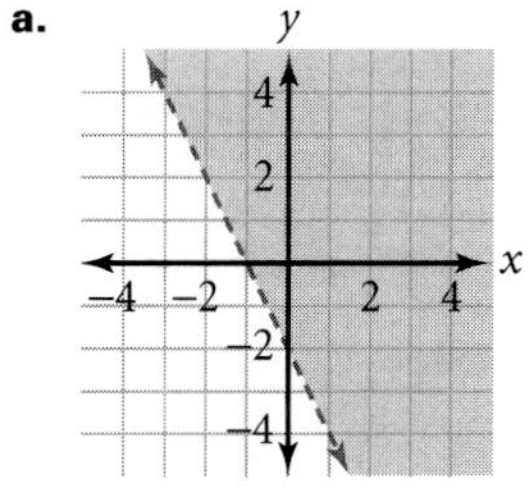

b.

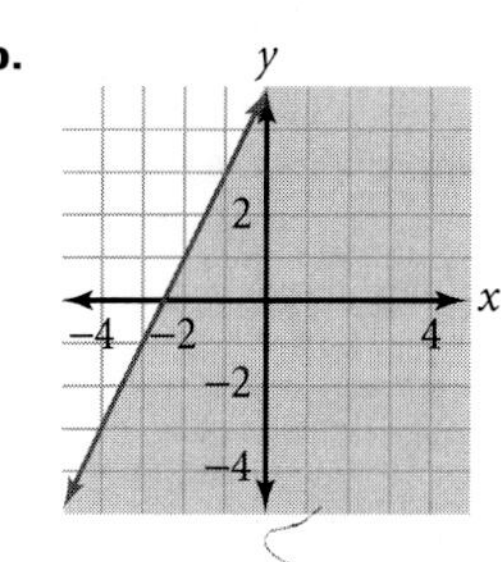

Selected Answers

TRY THIS (p. 173, Ex. 2)

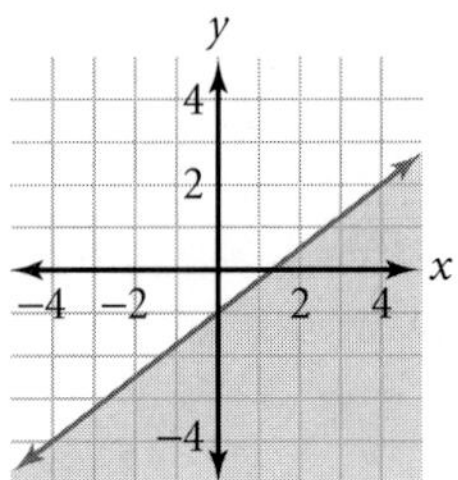

TRY THIS (p. 174)

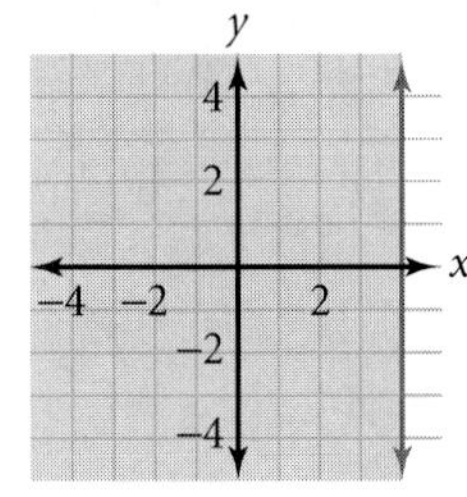

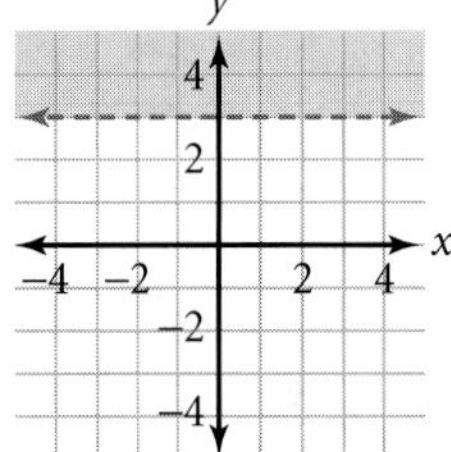

Exercises

4.

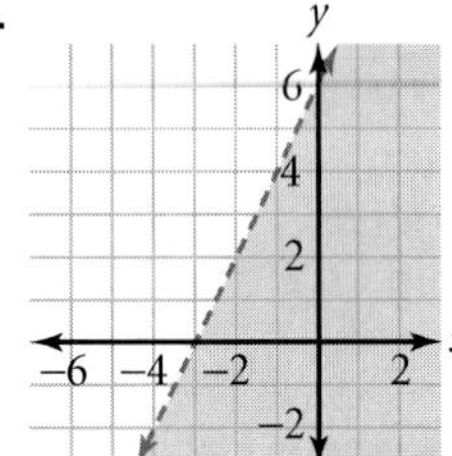

5.

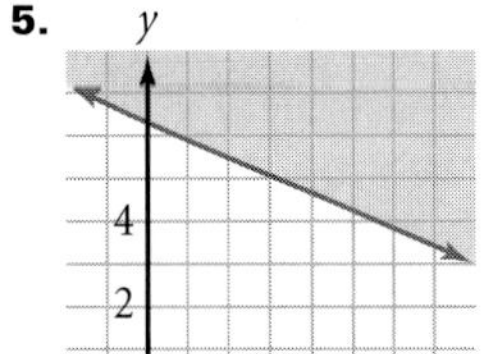

6.

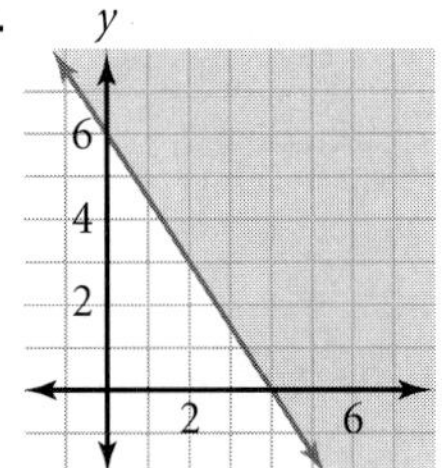

7.

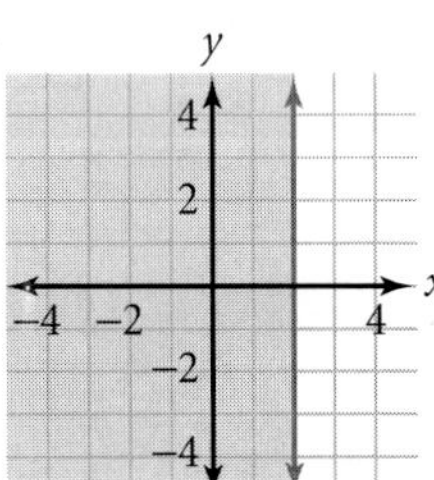

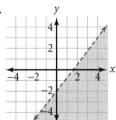

8. Yes, (25, 400) is in the solution region.

9.

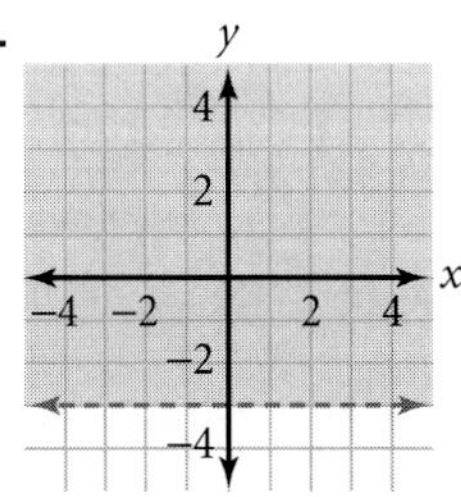

10.

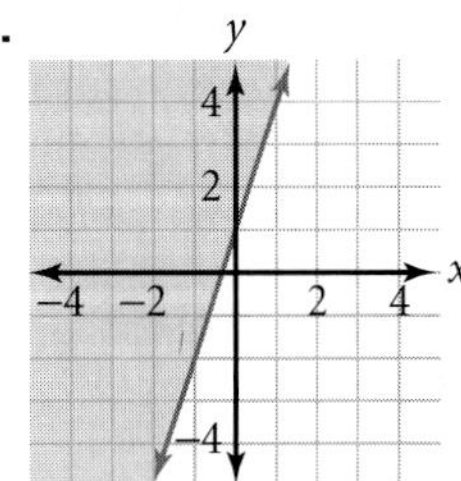

11.

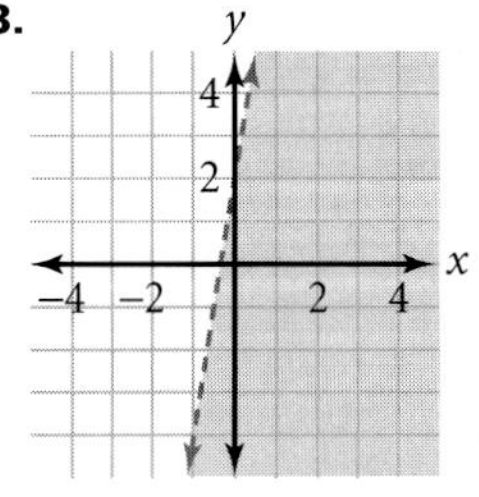

13.

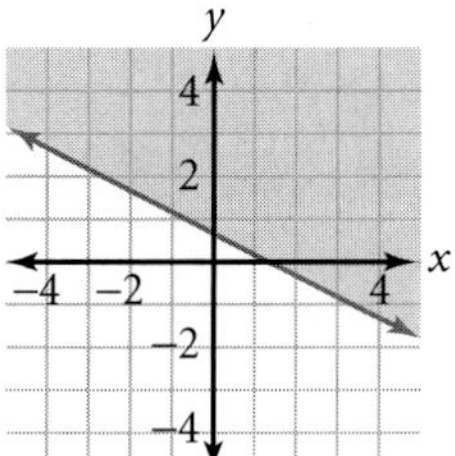

15.

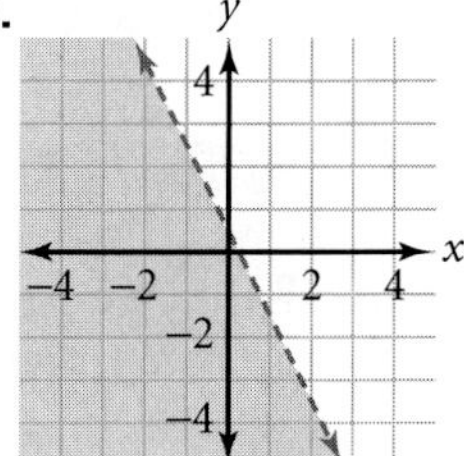

17.

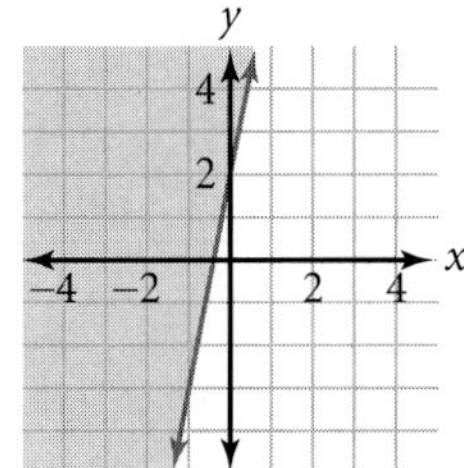

19.

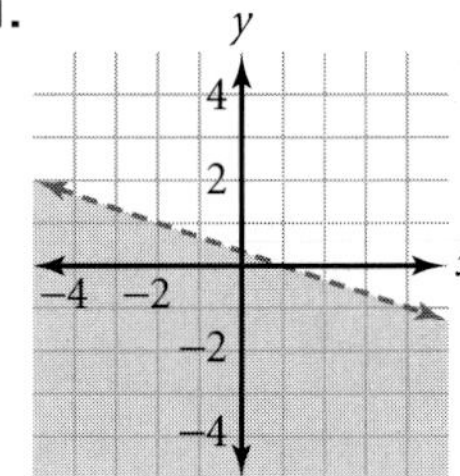

21.

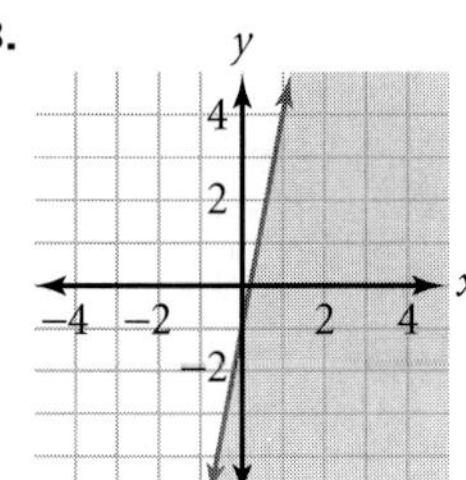

23.

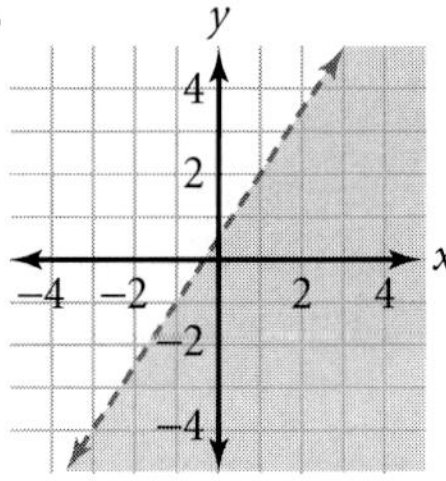

25.

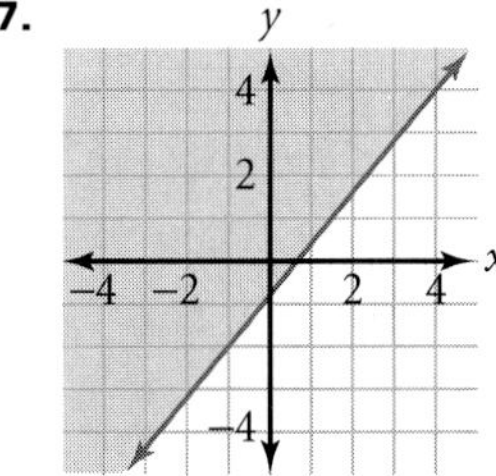

27.

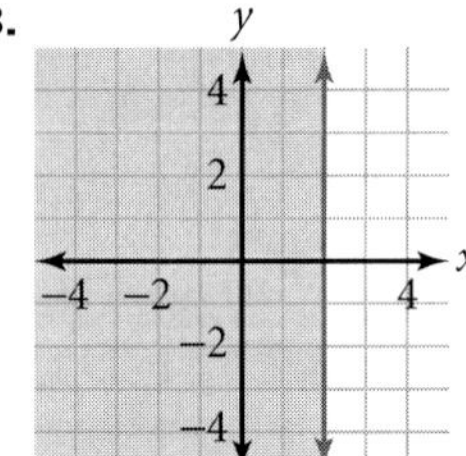

29. $y < 3x + 2$

31. $x \leq -1$

33.

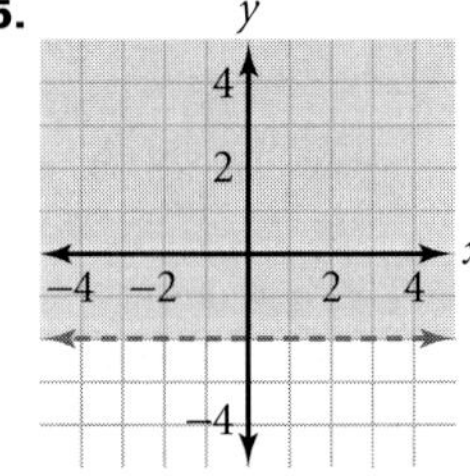

35.

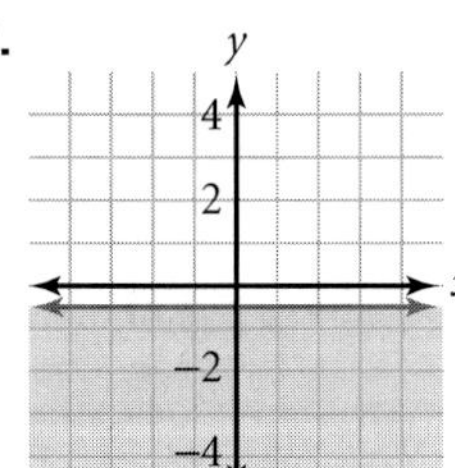

37.

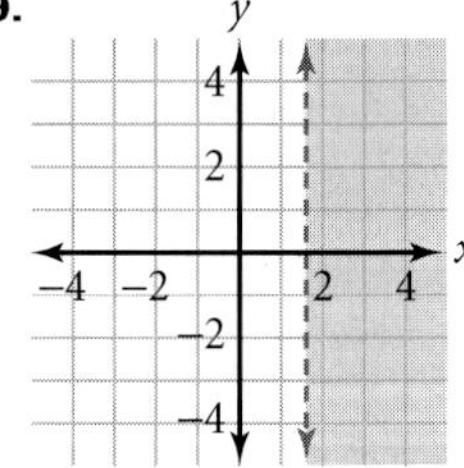

39.

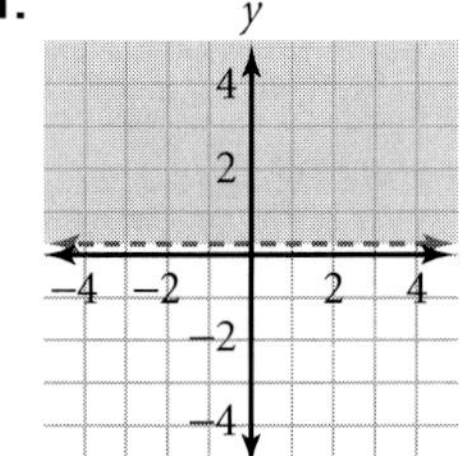

41.

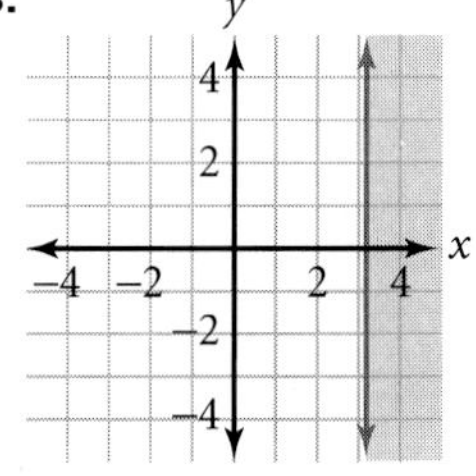

43.

45. $x < n$, where $n = 1, 2, 3$, and 4, is a series of half-planes that lie to the left of the dashed vertical lines $x = 1, x = 2, x = 3$, and $x = 4$. **47.** $ny \leq 2x$, where $n = 1, 2, 3$, and 4, or $y \leq \frac{2}{n}x$, where $n = 1, 2, 3$, and 4, is the series of half-planes below the successive solid lines $y = 2x$, $y = x$, $y = \frac{2}{3}x$, and $y = \frac{1}{2}x$.

49. $2x + 3y < 24$, where x and y are nonnegative integers

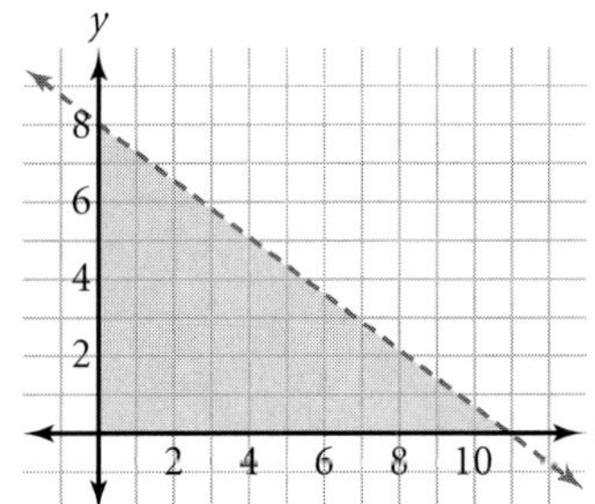

51. $2x + 3y > 24$ or $2x + 3y \geq 25$, where x and y are nonnegative integers

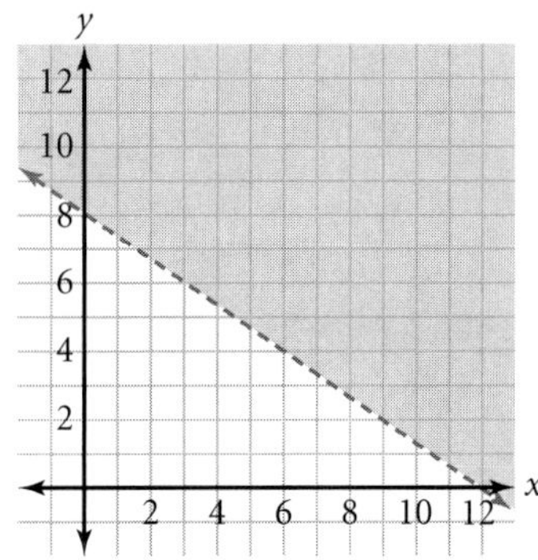

53a. $3x + 2y \leq 60$, where x and y are nonnegative integers

b.

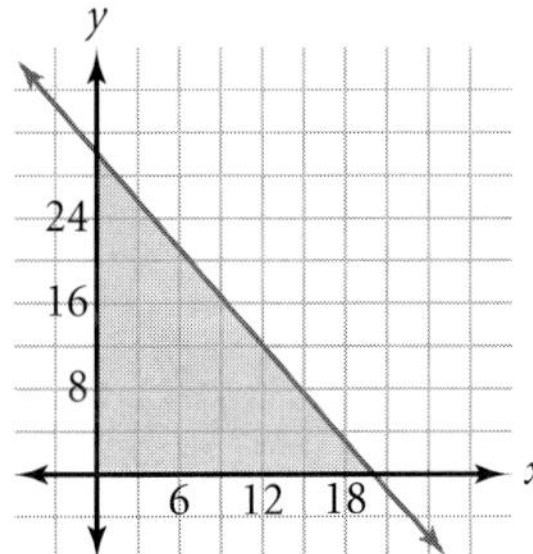

c. 20 pounds
d. 30 pounds

55a. $0.95x + 1.25y \leq 5.75$, where x and y are nonnegative integers **b.** $y \leq -0.76x + 4.6$

c.

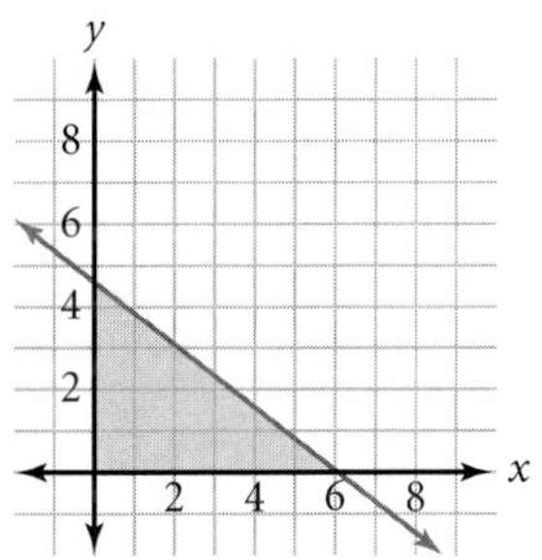

57. $k = 8$; $y = 8x$ **59.** $k = -270$; $y = -270x$ **61.** $x = \frac{4}{9}$
63. independent; $(1, -1)$ **65.** independent; $(4, 5)$
67. $(1, 7)$ **69.** $\left(\frac{3}{2}, 2\right)$ **71.** $(3, 1)$

LESSON 3.4

TRY THIS (p. 180, Ex. 1)

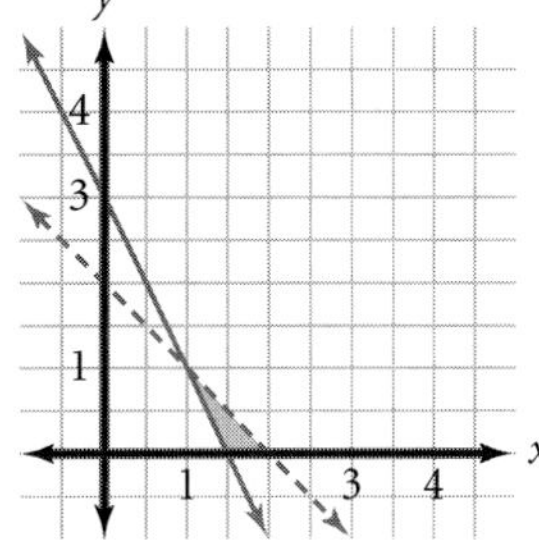

TRY THIS (p. 180, Ex. 2)

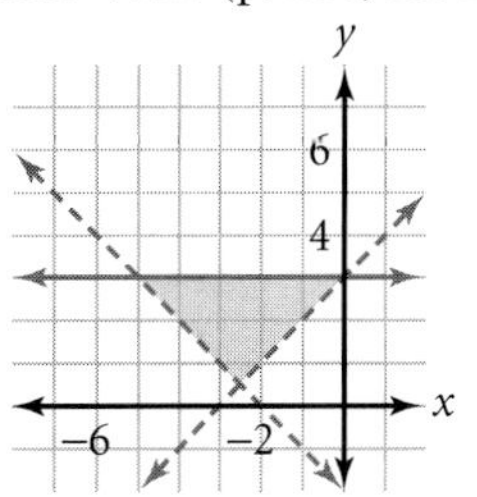

TRY THIS (p. 181)

a.

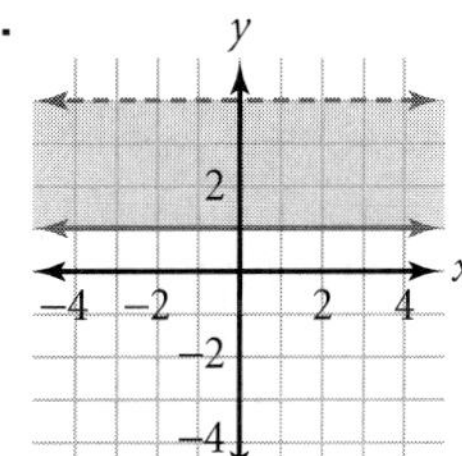

b.

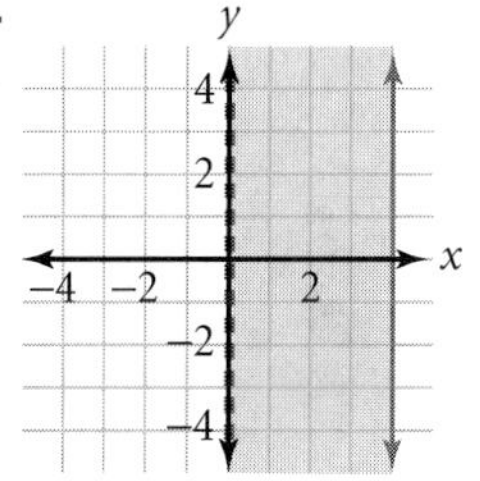

Exercises

4.

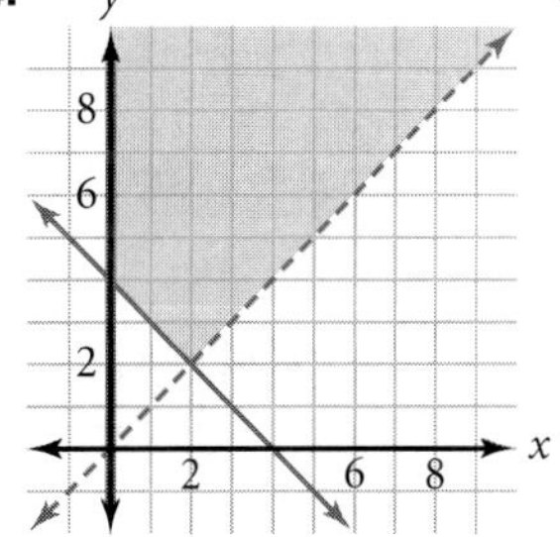

5.

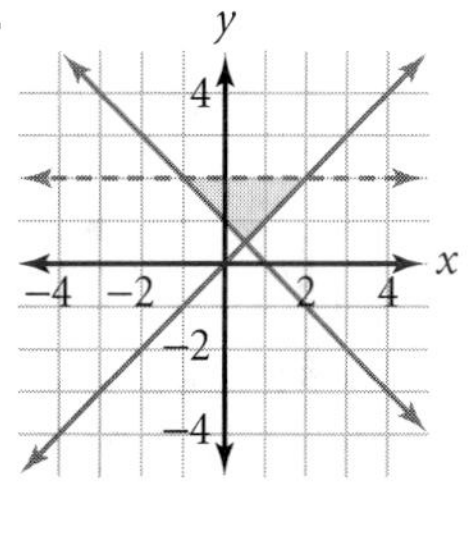

6.

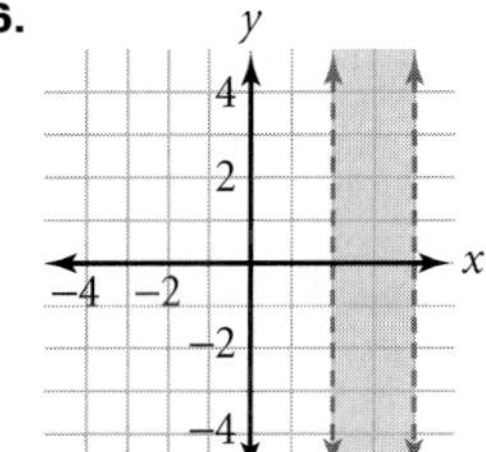

7.

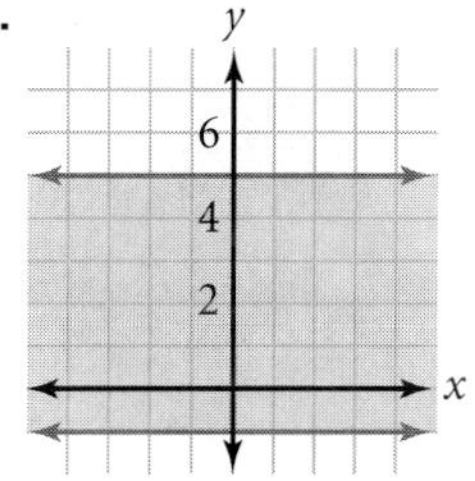

8. $\begin{cases} x \geq 0 \\ y \geq 0 \\ y \leq \frac{2}{5}x + 2 \\ y \leq -4x + 24 \end{cases}$

9.

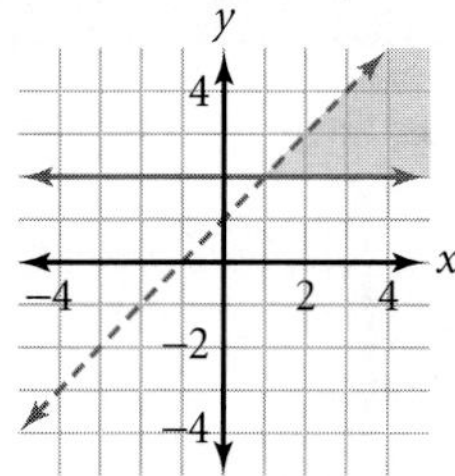

11.

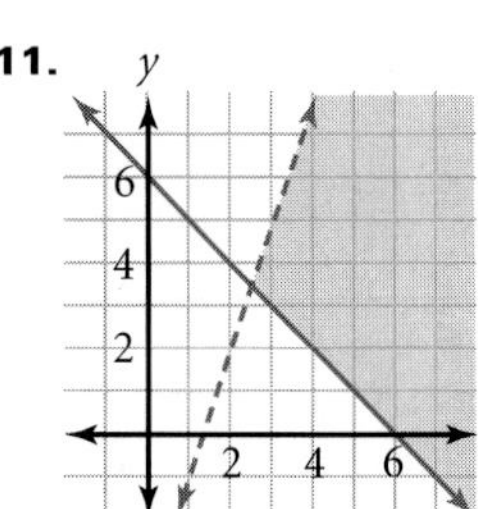

13.

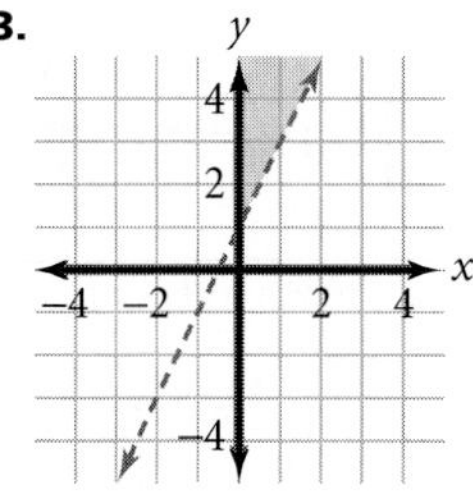

15.

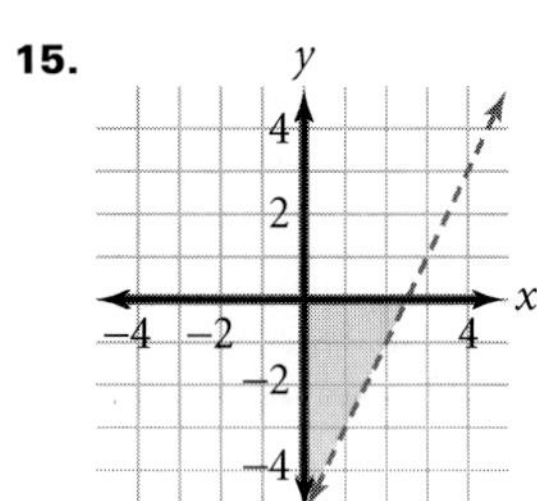

17.

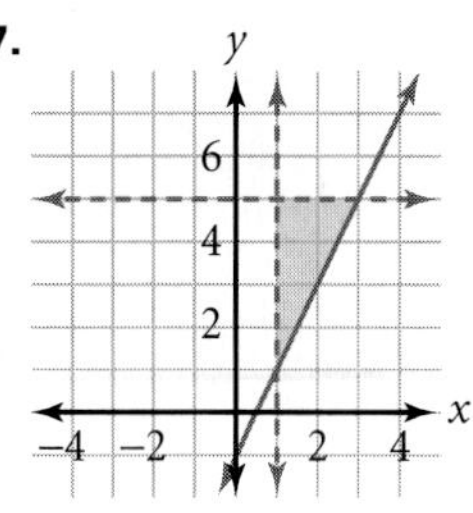

19.

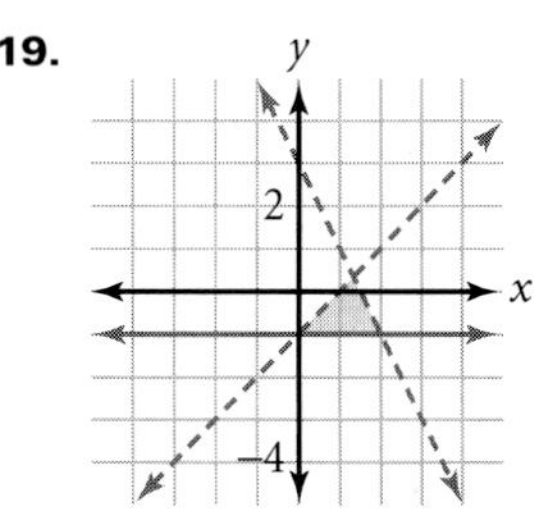

21.

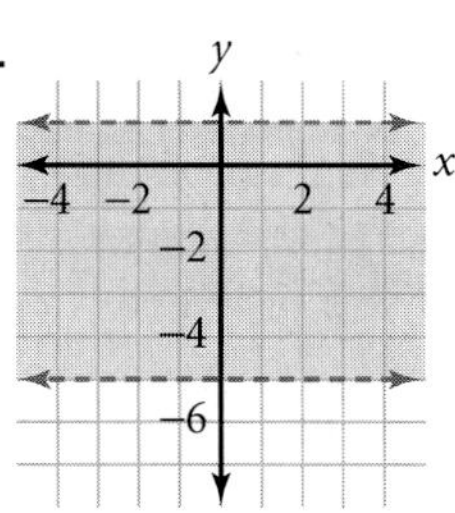

23.

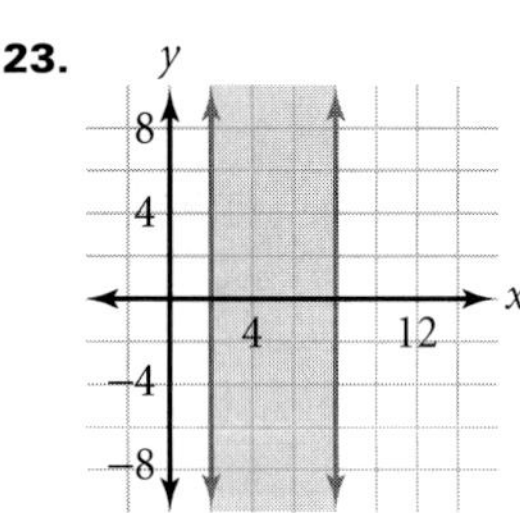

25.

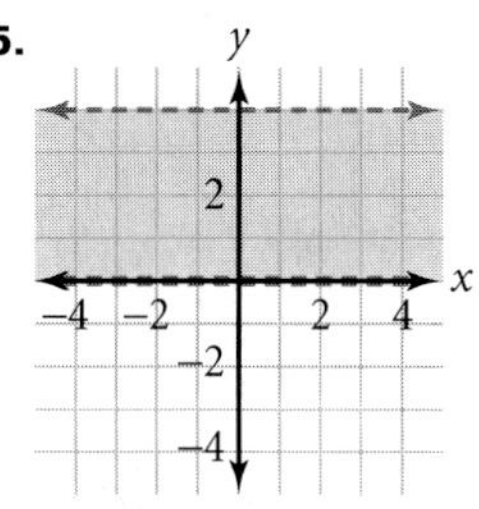

27.

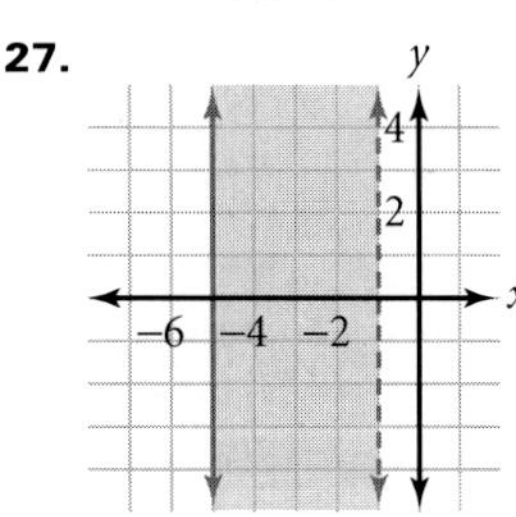

29.

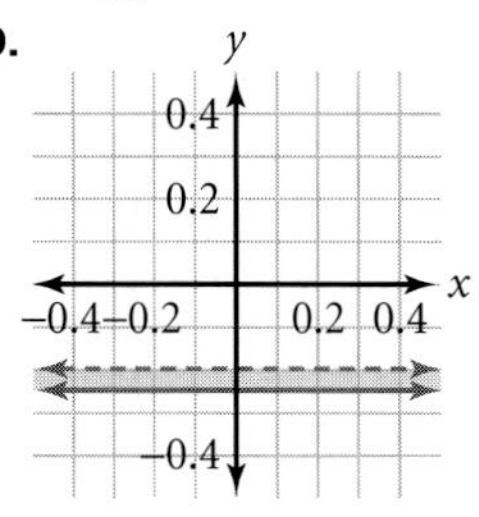

31.

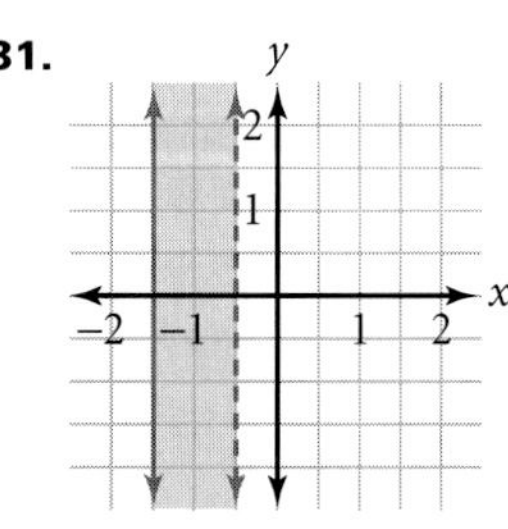

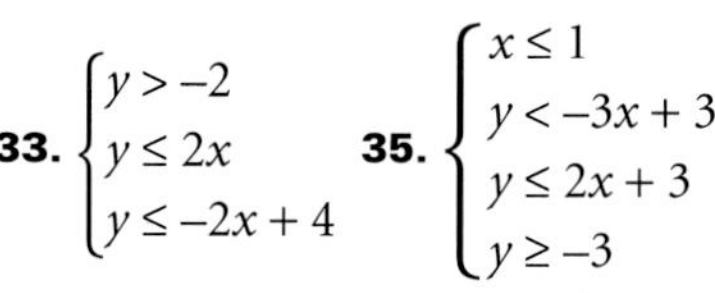

33. $\begin{cases} y > -2 \\ y \leq 2x \\ y \leq -2x + 4 \end{cases}$ **35.** $\begin{cases} x \leq 1 \\ y < -3x + 3 \\ y \leq 2x + 3 \\ y \geq -3 \end{cases}$

37.

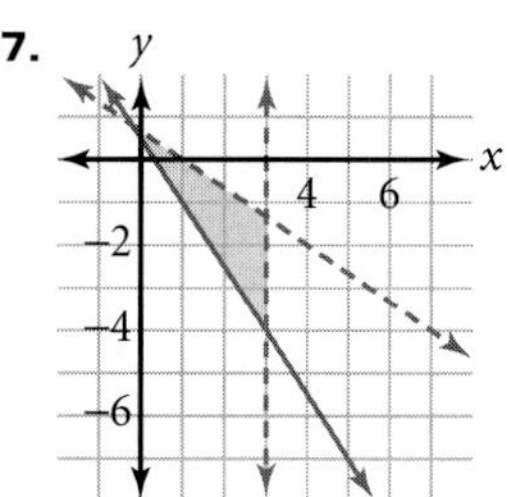

39.

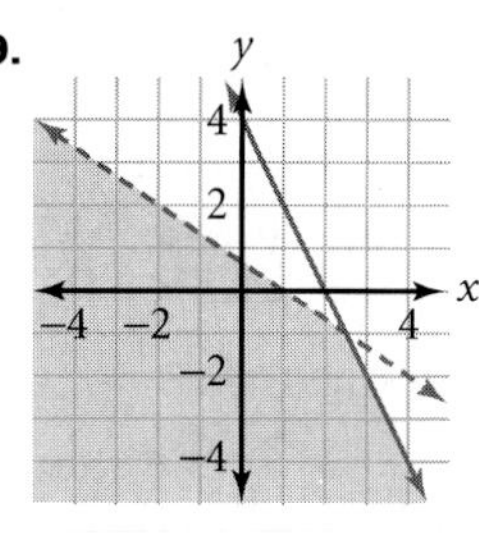

41.

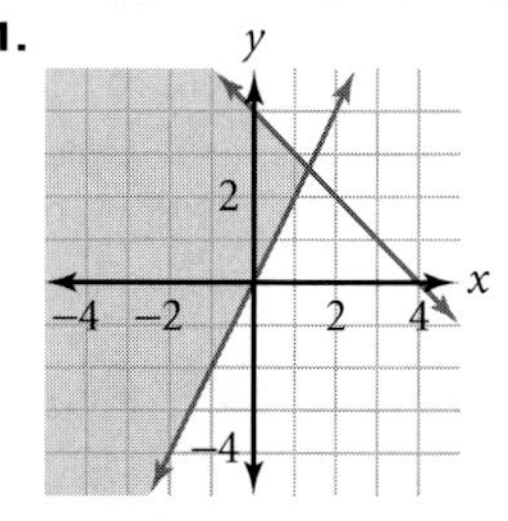

43.

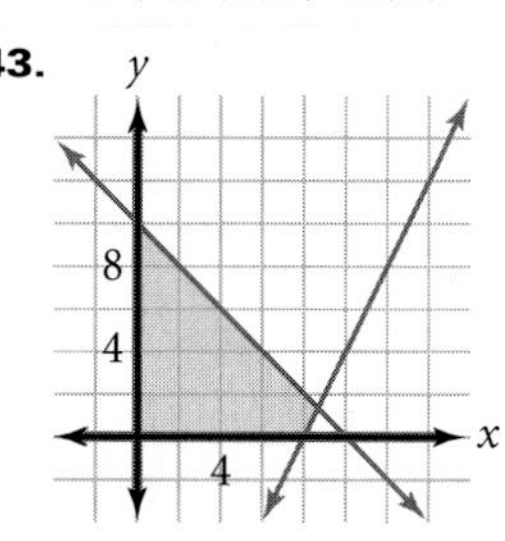

45.

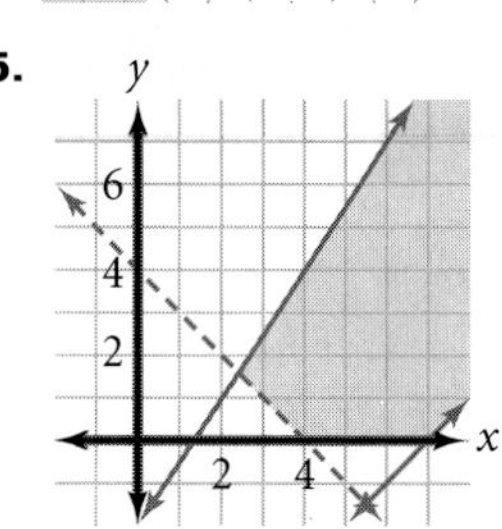

47. The figure is an isosceles right triangle.

49a. $\begin{cases} 9 \leq x \leq 10 \\ 5 \leq y \leq 5\frac{1}{2} \end{cases}$

b.

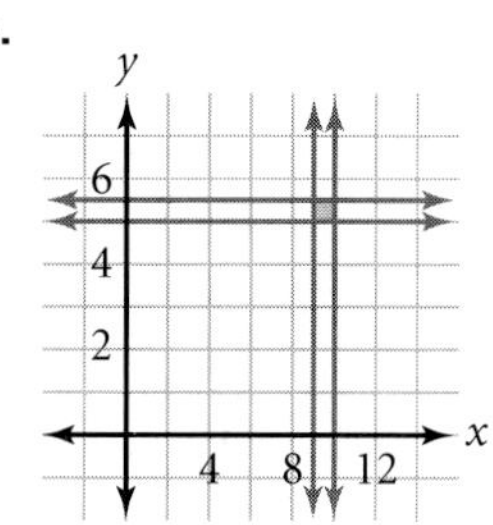

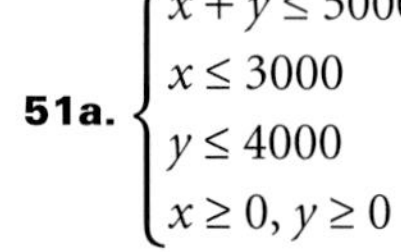

51a. $\begin{cases} x + y \leq 5000 \\ x \leq 3000 \\ y \leq 4000 \\ x \geq 0, y \geq 0 \end{cases}$

b.

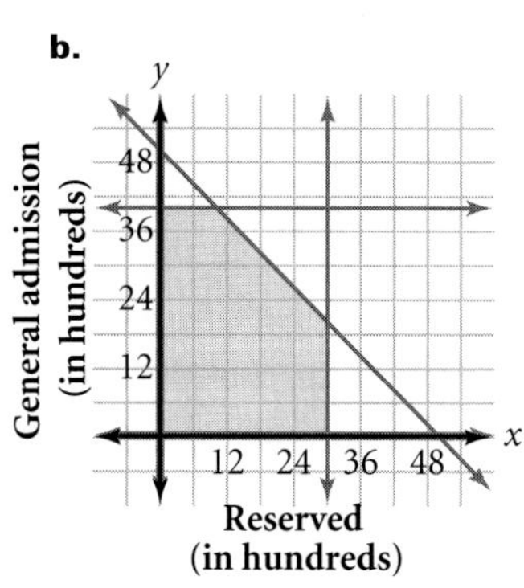

c. The change increases the number of possible combinations.

53.

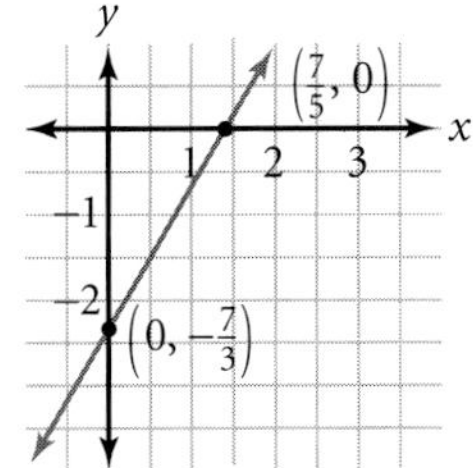

55. $x = \frac{5}{6}$ **57.** $x = -\frac{37}{9}$ **59.** $x = \frac{13}{9}$

61. $(f - g)(x) = 4x - 3$ **63.** $\left(\frac{f}{g}\right)(x) = \frac{3x + 2}{5 - x}, x \neq 5$

65. $\left(\frac{2}{15}, -\frac{5}{13}\right)$; independent **67.** infinitely many solutions; dependent

LESSON 3.5

Exercises

4. Let x be the number of acres of corn and y be the number of acres of soybeans. The constraints are

$$\begin{cases} x + y \leq 150 \\ 40 \leq x \leq 120 \\ 0 \leq y \leq 100 \end{cases}.$$

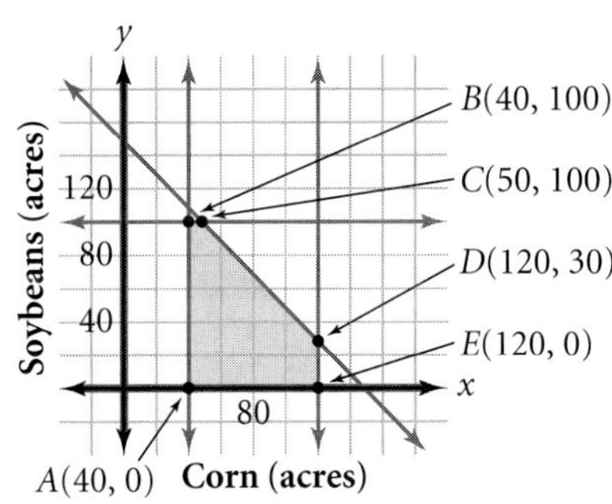

The objective function is $R = 357.525x + 237.32y$.

5. Let x be the number of acres of wheat and y be the number of acres of soybeans. The constraints are

$$\begin{cases} x + y \leq 220 \\ 100 \leq x \leq 200. \\ 0 \leq y \leq 75 \end{cases}$$

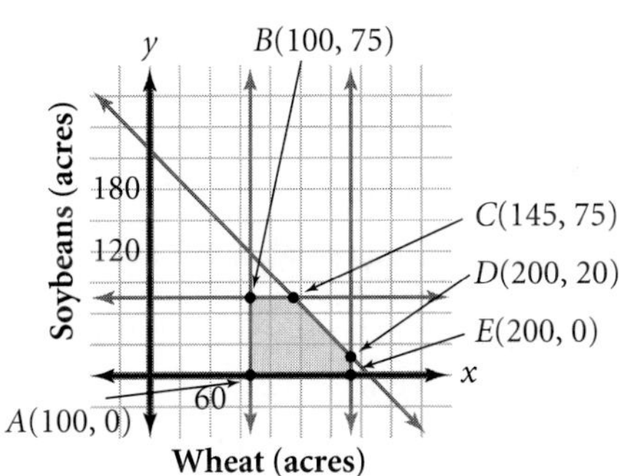

The objective function is $R = 159.31x + 237.32y$.

6. 120 acres of corn and 30 acres of soybeans **7.** 145 acres of wheat and 75 acres of soybeans

8. maximum value = 48, minimum value = 23

9. no maximum value, minimum value = 34

11.

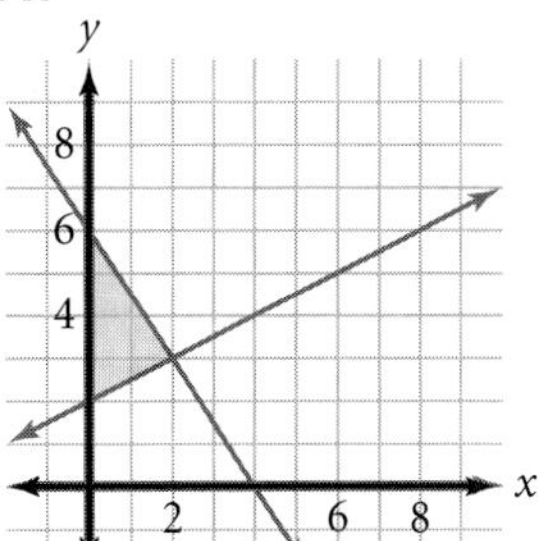

13.

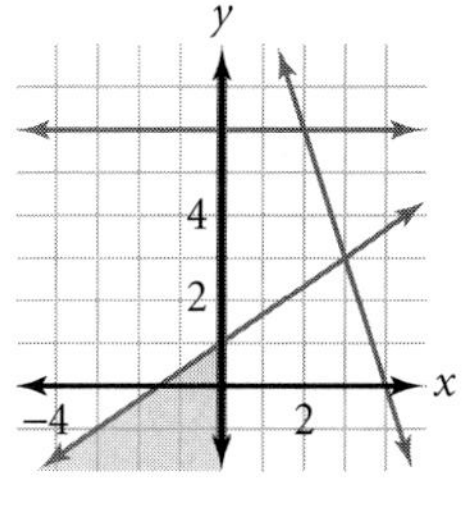

15. (0, 2), (0, 6), and (2, 3) **17.** (0, 1)

19. maximum value = 6, minimum value = −2

21. maximum value = 23, minimum value = −6

23. maximum value = 12, minimum value = 3

25. maximum value = 36, minimum value = 2

27. no maximum value, minimum value = 2

29. maximum value = 10, minimum value = −5

31. Answers may vary. Sample answers are given.

a. The objective function, $P = 2x + 3y$, has its maximum value, 6, at (0, 2) and at $\left(\frac{6}{5}, \frac{6}{5}\right)$.

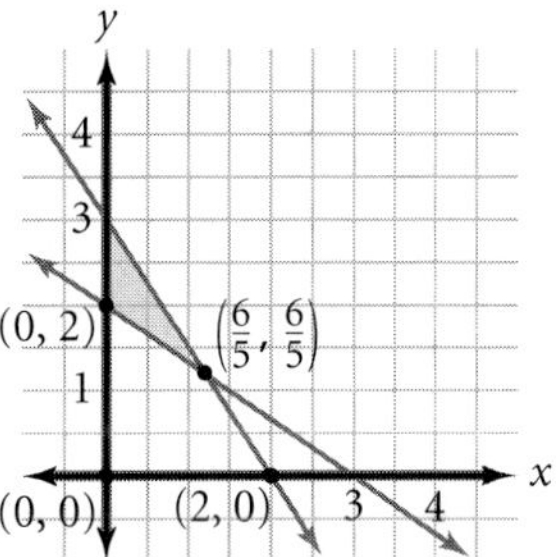

b. The objective function, $P = 2x + 3y$, has its minimum value, 6, at $\left(\frac{6}{5}, \frac{6}{5}\right)$ and at (3, 0).

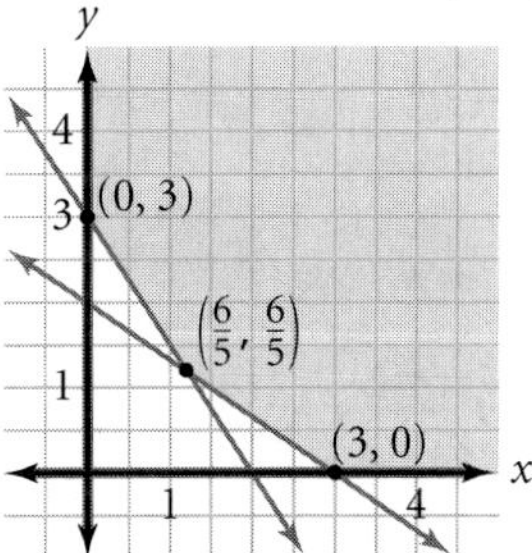

33a. $\begin{cases} 10{,}000x + 20{,}000y \leq 100{,}000 \\ 100x + 75y \leq 500 \\ x \geq 0, y \geq 0 \end{cases}$

b.

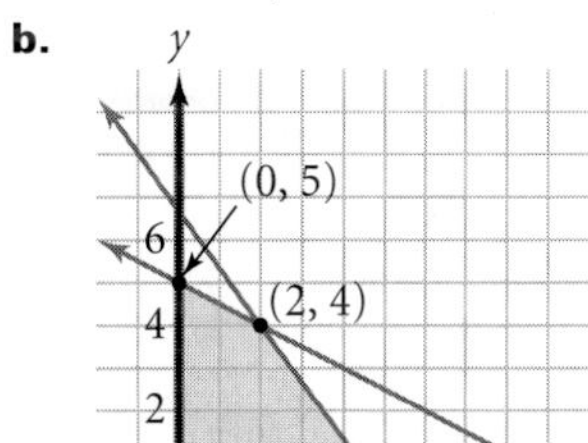

c. The objective function is $P = 7x + 15y$. The maximum number of passengers is 75.

35a. $\begin{cases} 45x + 9y \geq 45 \\ 10x + 6y \geq 20 \\ x \geq 0, y \geq 0 \end{cases}$

b.

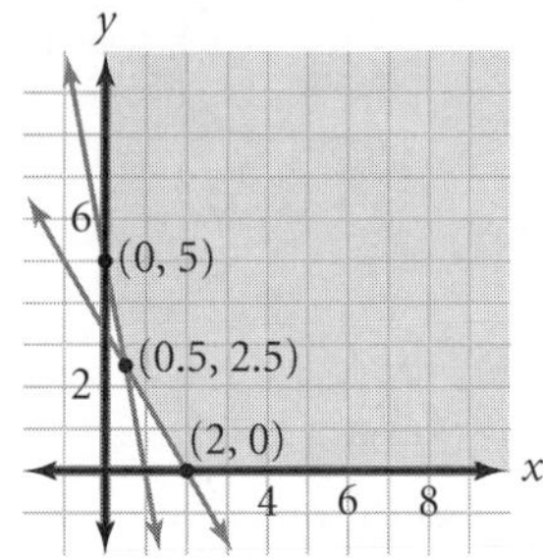

c. The objective function is $M = 4x + 2y$. The minimum number of fat grams is 7.

37a. $\begin{cases} 6x + 2y \leq 24 \\ x \geq 2 \\ y \geq 2 \end{cases}$

b.

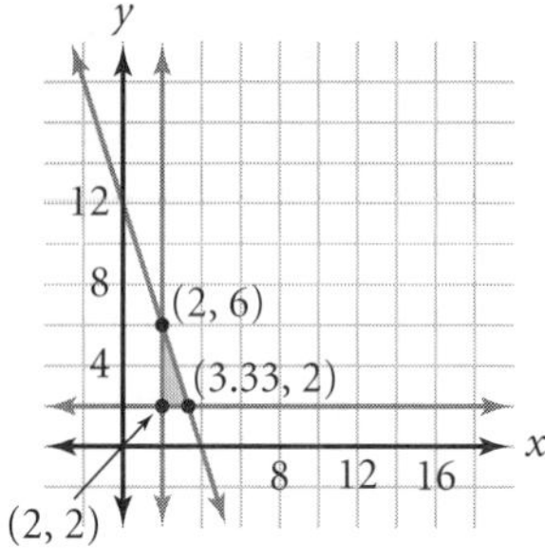

c. The objective function is $P = 50x + 20y$. The maximum profit is $220. **39.** linear; $(-5, 10)$

41.

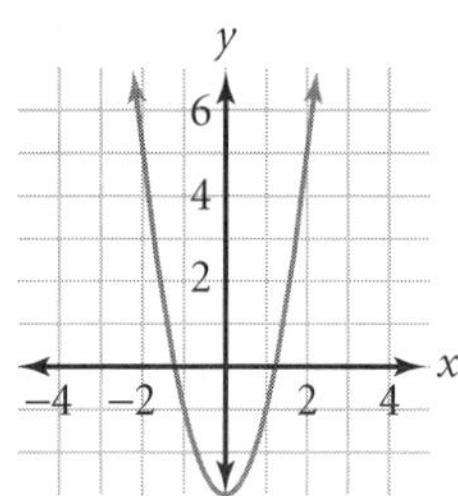

domain: all real numbers; range: $g(x) \geq -3$

43. $g^{-1}(x) = -\frac{1}{2}x + \frac{1}{8}$ **45.** $g^{-1}(x) = 4x + 24$

LESSON 3.6

TRY THIS (p. 196)

$\begin{cases} x(t) = -2t + 2 \\ y(t) = -t - 2 \end{cases}$ for $-4 \leq t \leq 4$

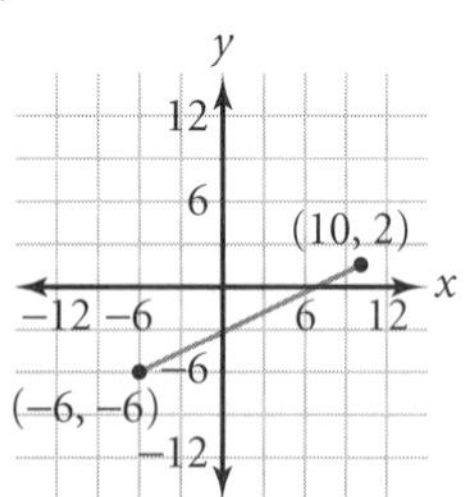

TRY THIS (p. 197)

$y = -\frac{3}{2}x - 10$

TRY THIS (p. 198)

a. after about 0.95 seconds **b.** no

Exercises

4.

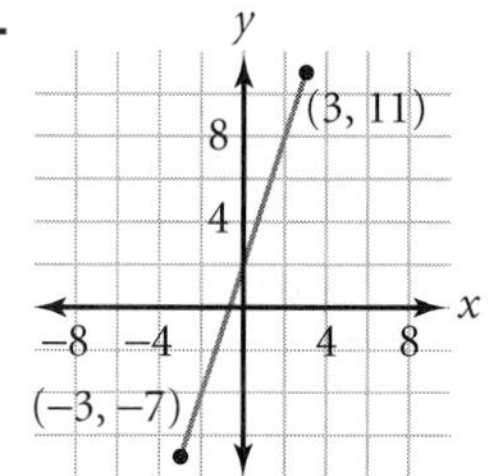

5.

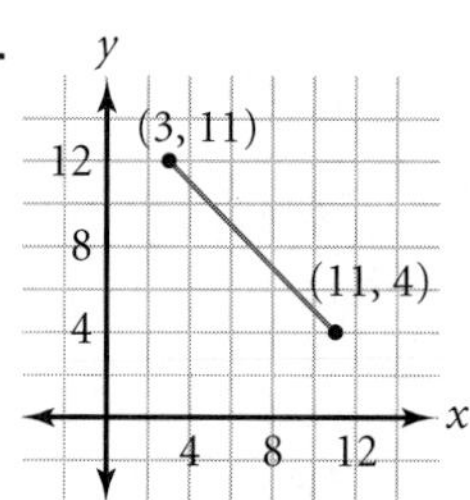

6. $y = \frac{3}{5}x + \frac{23}{5}$ **7.** $y = -x + 8$ **8a.** approximately 2.6 seconds **b.** yes

9.

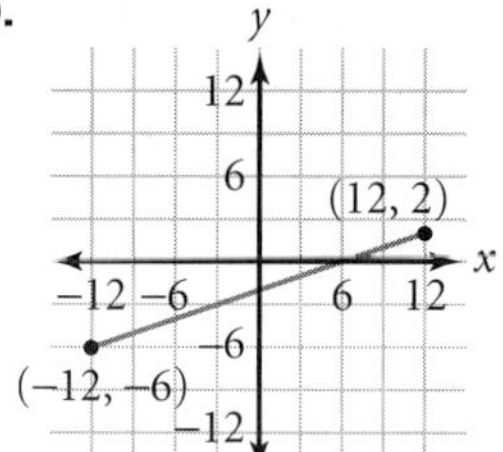

11.

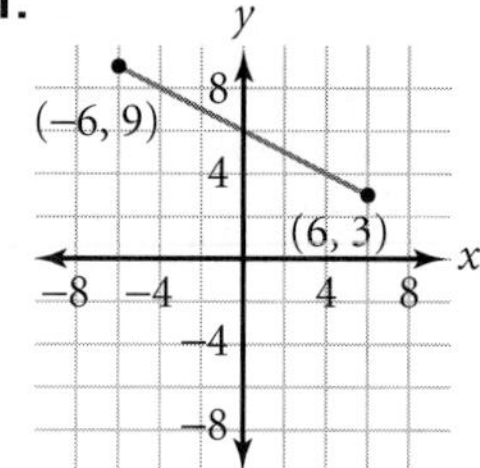

13.

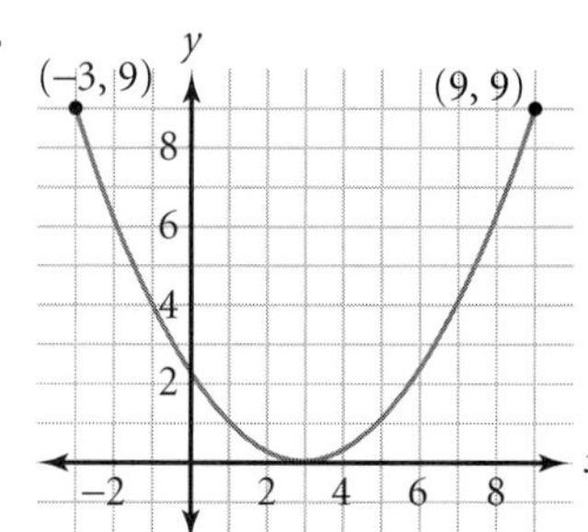

15. $y = \frac{1}{2}x - 1$ **17.** $y = \frac{1}{2}x + \frac{9}{2}$ **19.** $y = 1 - \frac{1}{3}x$

21. $y = \frac{1}{4}x^2 - 1$ **23.** $y = 9x^2$ **25.** $x = 5 - \frac{4}{9}y^2$

27. inverse parametric equations: $\begin{cases} x(t) = t \\ y(t) = t^2 - 2 \end{cases}$

29. inverse parametric equations: $\begin{cases} x(t) = 6 - t^2 \\ y(t) = t \end{cases}$

31. inverse parametric equations: $\begin{cases} x(t) = t + 1 \\ y(t) = t^2 + 5t - 1 \end{cases}$

33. $x(t) = t$, $y(t) = 3t - 17$ **35a.** 31.5 feet high after 1.25 seconds **b.** The ball hits the ground 159.2 feet away after 2.65 seconds. **37a.** $x(t) = 160t$, $y(t) = 2000 - 15t$ **b.** about 133 seconds **c.** about 21,300 feet **39.** $(f \circ g)(x) = 3 - x$ **41.** $(f \circ f)(x) = x + 4$ **43.** a vertical stretch by a factor of 12 followed by a vertical translation 3 units up **45.** a horizontal stretch by a factor of 2, a reflection across the x-axis, and then a vertical translation 4 units up **47.** $g(x) = |x - 2|$ **49.** $g(x) = \frac{1}{5}x^2$

CHAPTER REVIEW AND ASSESSMENT

1. independent; (4, 2) **3.** dependent; infinitely many solutions **5.** independent; (4, −1) **7.** $x = 2$ and $y = 0$ **9.** $x = \frac{1}{6}$ and $y = \frac{1}{12}$ **11.** $x = 0$ and $y = 3$ **13.** $x = -2$ and $y = -1$ **15.** $x = -4$ and $y = 4$ **17.** infinitely many solutions **19.** no solution

21.

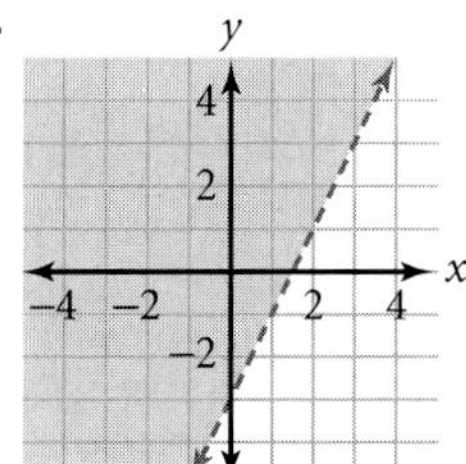

23.

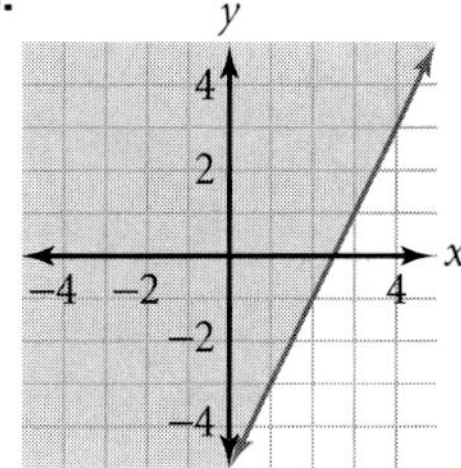

25.

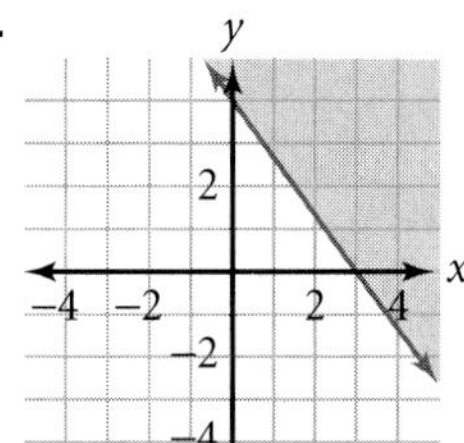

27.

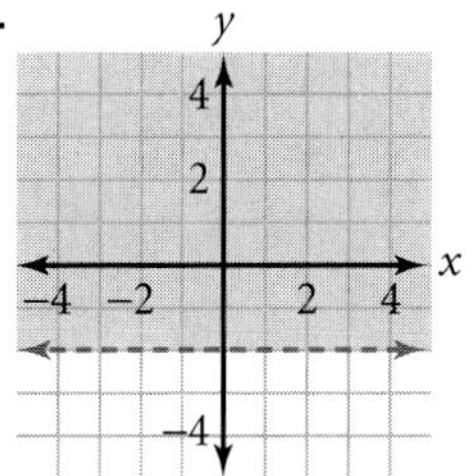

29.

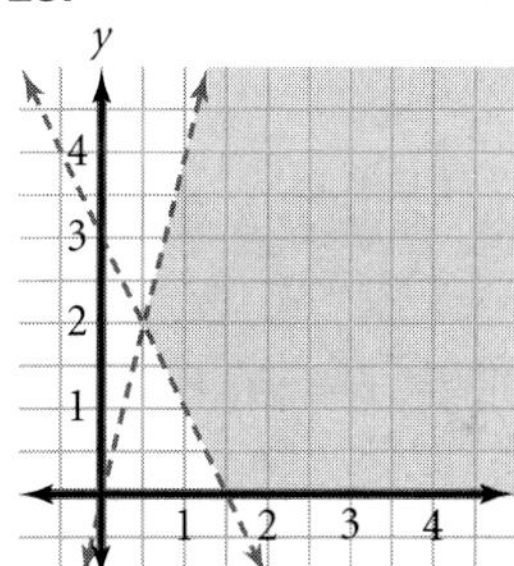

31.

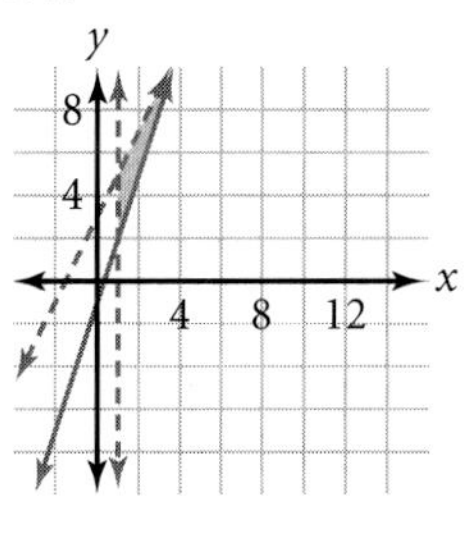

33. 13.5 minutes **35.** $y = 3x - 10$ **37.** $y = 4x - 23$

39. $\begin{cases} 5x + 12y \le 1000 \\ 8x + 12y \le 1500 \end{cases}$

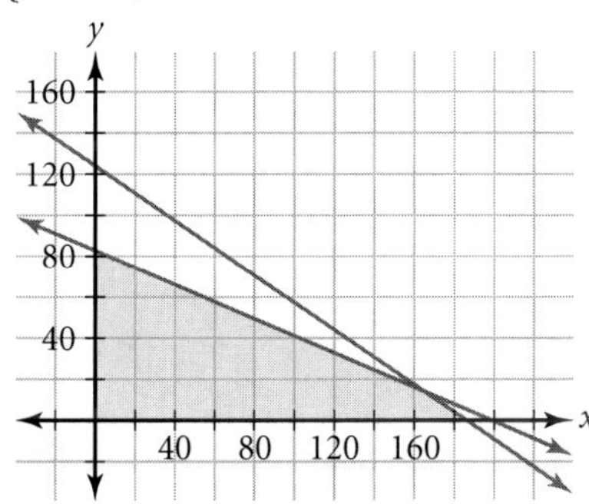

Chapter 4

LESSON 4.1

TRY THIS (p. 216)

	Small	Large
Picnic tables	15	20
Barbecue grills	18	24

$d_{21} = 18$; in June, 18 small barbecue grills were delivered.

TRY THIS (p. 217, Ex. 2)

$x = 6$ and $y = 5$

TRY THIS (p. 217, Ex. 3)

a. $\begin{bmatrix} 10 & -5 \\ 4 & -3 \\ 4 & -8 \end{bmatrix}$ **b.** $\begin{bmatrix} -10 & 5 \\ 4 & 5 \\ -10 & -2 \end{bmatrix}$

TRY THIS (p. 218)

$\begin{bmatrix} -1 & 9 \\ 0 & -9 \end{bmatrix}$

TRY THIS (p. 220)

a.

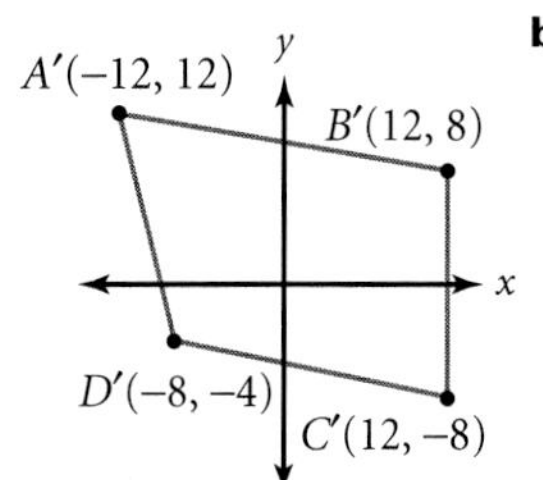

b.

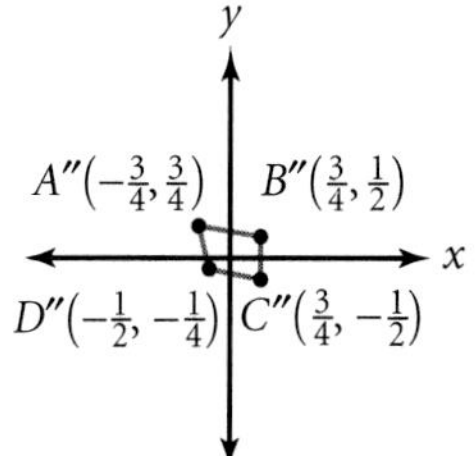

Exercises

5. $M = \begin{bmatrix} 12 & 28 & 17 \\ 15 & 32 & 45 \\ 6 & 20 & 30 \end{bmatrix}$, there are 45 large T-shirts in the inventory. **6.** $x = 3$ and $y = -4$

7a. $\begin{bmatrix} 11 & -7 \\ -7 & 5 \\ 0 & 6 \end{bmatrix}$ **b.** $\begin{bmatrix} -5 & 11 \\ -3 & -7 \\ -14 & 12 \end{bmatrix}$ **8.** $\begin{bmatrix} -3 & -9 & -9 \\ -12 & -1 & 15 \end{bmatrix}$

9. $\begin{bmatrix} \frac{1}{2} & 0 & -4 \\ -3 & 2 & -\frac{5}{2} \end{bmatrix}$ **10.** $Q = \begin{bmatrix} -3 & 2 & 1 & -4 \\ 3 & 3 & -3 & -3 \end{bmatrix}$

11a.

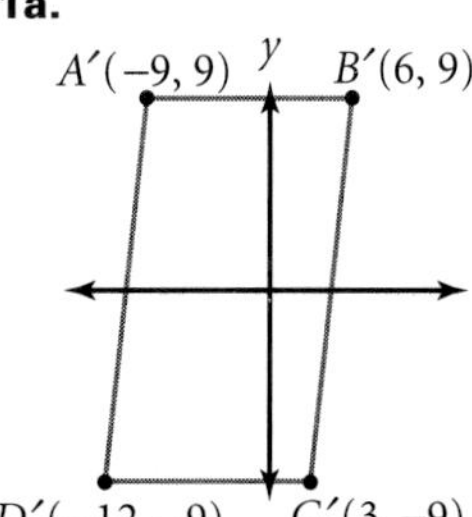

b.

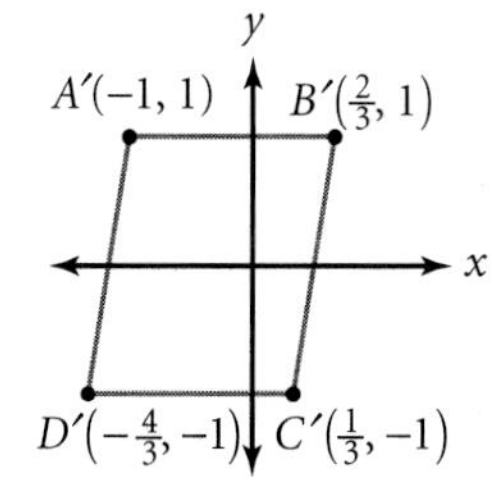

13. 4×3 **15.** 8 **17.** 6 **19.** $\begin{bmatrix} -28 \\ -8 \\ -24 \end{bmatrix}$ **21.** $\begin{bmatrix} -8 & 5 & -2 \\ 1 & -4 & 2 \\ 0 & 5 & -3 \\ -5 & -7 & 6 \end{bmatrix}$

23. $\begin{bmatrix} 4 & -\frac{5}{2} & 1 \\ -\frac{1}{2} & 2 & -1 \\ 0 & -\frac{5}{2} & \frac{3}{2} \\ \frac{5}{2} & \frac{7}{2} & -3 \end{bmatrix}$ **25.** $x = -7$ and $y = -18$

27. $x = 9$ and $y = 8$ **29.** $x = 4$ and $y = 3$

31. $\begin{bmatrix} 1 & 3 & -12 & 8 \\ 3 & 6 & 8 & -13 \end{bmatrix}$ **33.** $\begin{bmatrix} -18 & 0 & -33 & 9 \\ 15 & -6 & 24 & -27 \end{bmatrix}$

35. $\begin{bmatrix} 6 & 0 & 11 & -3 \\ -5 & 2 & -8 & 9 \end{bmatrix}$ **37.** $\begin{bmatrix} 20 & 6 & 9 & 7 \\ -9 & 18 & -8 & 1 \end{bmatrix}$

39. $\begin{bmatrix} 27 & 9 & 8 & 12 \\ -11 & 26 & -8 & -3 \end{bmatrix}$

41. $\begin{bmatrix} -46 & -12 & -29 & -11 \\ 23 & -38 & 24 & -11 \end{bmatrix}$

43. $\begin{bmatrix} 32 & 6 & 31 & 1 \\ -19 & 22 & -24 & 19 \end{bmatrix}$

45. $\begin{bmatrix} \frac{98}{3} & 14 & -\frac{14}{3} & \frac{70}{3} \\ -\frac{28}{3} & \frac{112}{3} & 0 & -\frac{56}{3} \end{bmatrix}$ **47a.** $\begin{bmatrix} -2 & 3 & 0 \\ 3 & 4 & 0 \end{bmatrix}$

b.

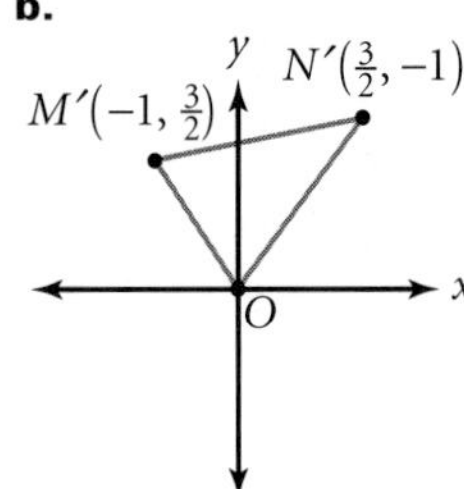

c.

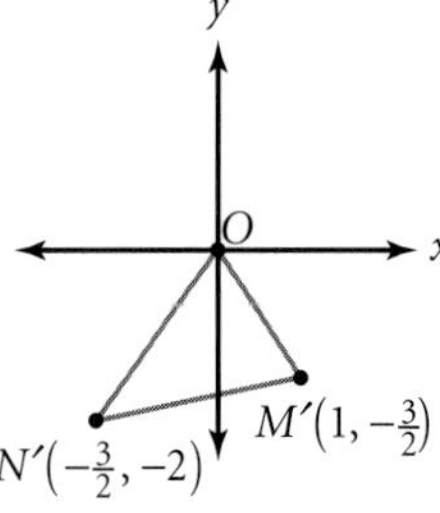

d.

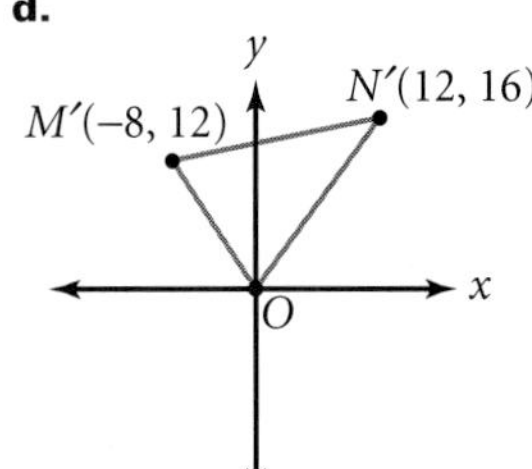

49a. $\begin{bmatrix} 0 & -3 & -3 \\ 0 & -3 & 0 \end{bmatrix}$ **b.**

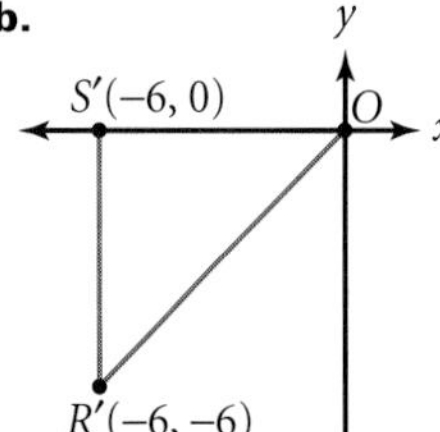

c. **d.**

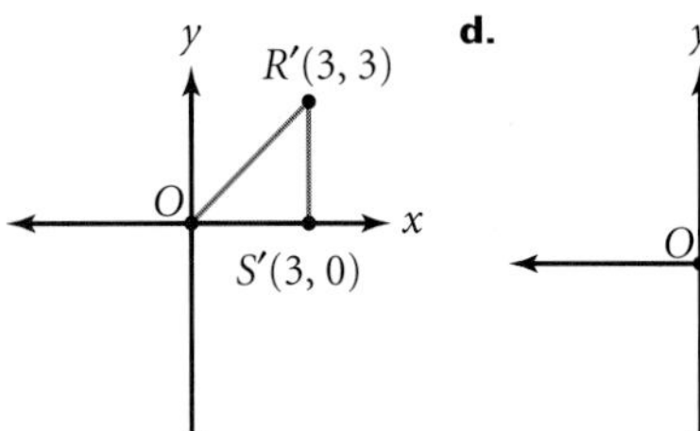

51. $m_{42} = 5$; there are 5 maps of Africa from the 1970s. **53.** 23 **55.** $P = \begin{bmatrix} 27 & 31 & 24 & 18 \\ 48 & 72 & 61 & 25 \end{bmatrix}$ **57.** p_{21}, which represents the number of squash Jane sold **59.** 3×5 **61.** 6 **63.** Answers may vary. sample answer: records: 10 country, 15 jazz, 5 rock, 8 blues, 3 classical; tapes: 5 country, 9 jazz, 1 rock, 13 blues, 6 classical; compact discs: 3 country, 1 jazz, 9 rock, 5 blues, 10 classical **65.** Answers may vary. In matrix M above, $m_{23} = 1$ rock tape. **67.** $y = 4x - 37$ **69.** $y = \frac{x+1}{2}$ **71.** $y = -3x + 15$, or $x = 5 - \frac{1}{3}y$

LESSON 4.2

TRY THIS (p. 226)

a. $\begin{bmatrix} -2 & -21 \\ 20 & 35 \\ -10 & 0 \end{bmatrix}$ **b.** does not exist

Exercises

4a. $[-15]$ **b.** $\begin{bmatrix} 4 & -12 & -20 \\ -2 & 6 & 10 \\ 5 & -15 & -25 \end{bmatrix}$

5a. $\begin{bmatrix} 4 & 3 & 2 \\ 2 & 3 & 4 \end{bmatrix}$ **b.** $\begin{bmatrix} 52 & 69 & 86 \\ 302 & 258 & 214 \\ 108 & 159 & 210 \end{bmatrix}$

c. The trail mix has the most protein. The sport mix has the most carbohydrates.

6. $\begin{matrix} X \\ Y \\ Z \end{matrix} \begin{bmatrix} 1 & 1 & 1 \\ 1 & 0 & 1 \\ 2 & 1 & 0 \end{bmatrix} = M$ (columns X, Y, Z)

a. $\begin{bmatrix} 4 & 2 & 2 \\ 3 & 2 & 1 \\ 3 & 2 & 3 \end{bmatrix}$ **b.** $m_{22} = 2$, which is the number of two-stage paths from Y to Y: $Y \to Z \to Y$ and $Y \to X \to Y$.

7. $\begin{bmatrix} 2 & -6 & 8 \\ 0 & 0 & 0 \\ 6 & -18 & 24 \end{bmatrix}$ **9.** $\begin{bmatrix} 20 & 13 & 4 \\ 0 & 1 & 3 \end{bmatrix}$ **11.** $\begin{bmatrix} 30 & 27 \\ 13 & -3 \end{bmatrix}$

13. $\begin{bmatrix} 19 & 18 & -3 \\ -1 & 30 & 9 \end{bmatrix}$ **15.** $\begin{bmatrix} -12 & 62 \\ 6 & 13 \\ -16 & 0 \\ -10 & 77 \end{bmatrix}$

17. does not exist **19.** $\begin{bmatrix} -188 & 222 \\ 12 & 794 \\ 60 & -142 \end{bmatrix}$

21a. $A'(-1, 0)$, $B'\left(\frac{3}{2}, 0\right)$, $C'(0, -2)$

b.

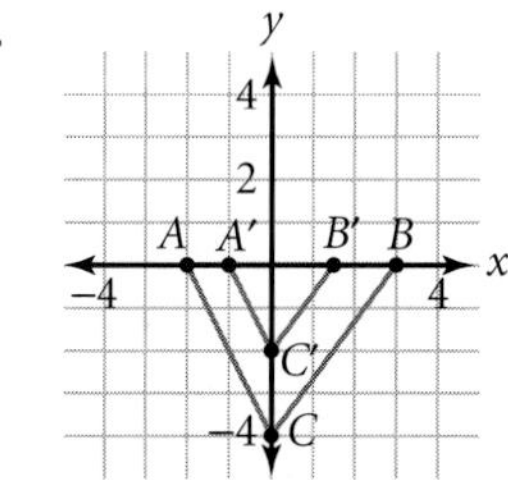

c. This transformation is the same as multiplying the original matrix by a scalar factor of $\frac{1}{2}$.

23a. $\begin{bmatrix} -3 & 3 & 3 & -2 \\ -3 & -2 & 2 & 1 \end{bmatrix}$ **b.**

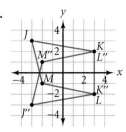

c. Answers may vary. Sample answer: The geometric figure is reflected across the x-axis.

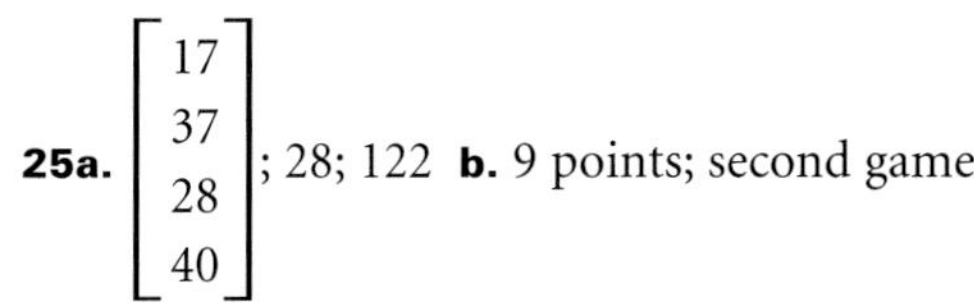

25a. $\begin{bmatrix} 17 \\ 37 \\ 28 \\ 40 \end{bmatrix}$; 28; 122 **b.** 9 points; second game

c. 9 rows and 1 column

27a. $\begin{bmatrix} 833\frac{1}{3} & 1166\frac{2}{3} \end{bmatrix}$; 833 cars in NY and 1167 cars in LA **b.** $\begin{bmatrix} 805\frac{5}{9} & 1194\frac{4}{9} \end{bmatrix}$; 806 cars in NY and 1194 cars in LA **c.** 800 cars in NY and 1200 cars in LA; 4 months have passed.

29a.

	R	S	T
R	3	2	0
S	1	2	1
T	1	3	2

b. 15 two-stage paths **c.** R to S to R, R to T to R, R to T to R, R to S to S, R to T to S, S to S to R, S to S to S, S to R to S, S to R to T, T to S to R, T to S to S, T to R to S, T to R to S, T to R to T, and T to R to T

31. undefined; no y-intercept **33.** −18; 0 **35.** true **37.** true **39.** $10x + 13$ **41.** 59

LESSON 4.3

TRY THIS (p. 238)

a. −19; has an inverse **b.** 0; has no inverse

Exercises

5. $\begin{bmatrix} 2 & 1 \\ 1 & 1 \end{bmatrix}\begin{bmatrix} 1 & -1 \\ -1 & 2 \end{bmatrix} = \begin{bmatrix} 1 & 0 \\ 0 & 1 \end{bmatrix}$

$\begin{bmatrix} 1 & -1 \\ -1 & 2 \end{bmatrix}\begin{bmatrix} 2 & 1 \\ 1 & 1 \end{bmatrix} = \begin{bmatrix} 1 & 0 \\ 0 & 1 \end{bmatrix}$ **6.** $\begin{bmatrix} 4 & -5 \\ -7 & 9 \end{bmatrix}$

7. WAY TO GO **8.** 0; no **9.** 4; yes **11.** yes **13.** 1; yes **15.** 0; no **17.** 0; no **19.** 2; yes

21. $\begin{bmatrix} 4 & -2 & 3 \\ 8 & -3 & 5 \\ 7 & -2 & 4 \end{bmatrix}$ **23.** no inverse **25.** $\begin{bmatrix} \frac{1}{2} & -\frac{1}{6} \\ 0 & \frac{1}{3} \end{bmatrix}$

27. $\begin{bmatrix} \frac{10}{33} & -\frac{1}{11} \\ -\frac{3}{11} & \frac{2}{11} \end{bmatrix}$ **29.** $\begin{bmatrix} 5 & -7 \\ -2 & 3 \end{bmatrix}$ **31.** $\begin{bmatrix} 1 & -1 \\ -1 & 2 \end{bmatrix}$

33. $\begin{bmatrix} 3 & 7 \\ 2 & 5 \end{bmatrix}$ **35.** $\begin{bmatrix} 8 & -2 \\ -10 & 4 \end{bmatrix}$ **37.** $\begin{bmatrix} 2 & 0 \\ -8 & 4 \end{bmatrix}$

39. $\begin{bmatrix} -0.86 & 2.57 \\ 2.57 & -1.71 \end{bmatrix}$ **41.** $\begin{bmatrix} -0.54 & 0.23 & -0.08 \\ 0.77 & -0.62 & 0.54 \\ 0.69 & -0.15 & 0.38 \end{bmatrix}$

43. $\begin{bmatrix} 0.27 & -0.05 & 0.10 \\ 0.02 & 0.13 & -0.10 \\ -0.12 & 0.12 & 0.12 \end{bmatrix}$ **45a.** 10 **b.** 0 **c.** 59

47. $A^{-1} = \begin{bmatrix} \frac{1}{2} & 0 \\ 0 & 1 \end{bmatrix}$; $\begin{bmatrix} \frac{1}{2} & 0 \\ 0 & 1 \end{bmatrix}\begin{bmatrix} 2 & 2 & -2 & -2 \\ 2 & -2 & -2 & 2 \end{bmatrix} = \begin{bmatrix} 1 & 1 & -1 & -1 \\ 2 & -2 & -2 & 2 \end{bmatrix}$

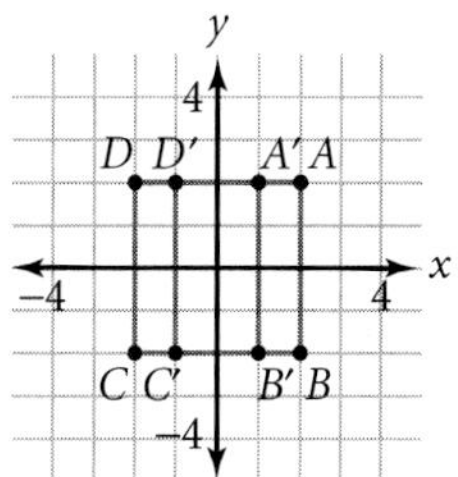

49. $\begin{bmatrix} 82 & 70 & 59 & 80 & 24 \\ 52 & 45 & 39 & 52 & 16 \end{bmatrix}$, or

82 | 70 | 59 | 80 | 24 | 52 | 45 | 39 | 52 | 16

51. $\begin{bmatrix} 15 & 43 & 32 & 149 & 40 \\ 9 & 27 & 21 & 93 & 25 \end{bmatrix}$, or

15 | 43 | 32 | 149 | 40 | 9 | 27 | 21 | 93 | 25

53. MAN DOWN **55.** CHARGE AT NOON

57. $y = \frac{9}{2}x + 3$ **59.** $-\frac{1}{2} = x$ **61.** $x = 1.5$

63. $x = 3$ **65.** $x = \frac{35}{6}$ and $y = \frac{17}{42}$

67.

LESSON 4.4

TRY THIS (p. 245)

$33,333.33 at 5% and $16,666.67 at 14%

TRY THIS (p. 246)

(1, −1, −3)

TRY THIS (p. 247)

no inverse; dependent

Exercises

7. $2500 at 6% and $7500 at 8%

8. $x = -7$ and $y = 15$ **9.** inconsistent **10.** inconsistent

11. $\begin{bmatrix} 3 & -5 \\ 2 & 1 \end{bmatrix}\begin{bmatrix} x \\ y \end{bmatrix} = \begin{bmatrix} 1 \\ -2 \end{bmatrix}$ **13.** $\begin{bmatrix} 2 & 4 \\ 1 & -1 \end{bmatrix}\begin{bmatrix} a \\ b \end{bmatrix} = \begin{bmatrix} -3 \\ 9 \end{bmatrix}$

15. $\begin{bmatrix} 0 & 1 & 5 \\ -2 & 3 & -1 \\ 6 & 0 & -3 \end{bmatrix}\begin{bmatrix} x \\ y \\ z \end{bmatrix} = \begin{bmatrix} -14 \\ 2 \\ 21 \end{bmatrix}$

17. $\begin{cases} 2x - y + 3z = 4 \\ -3x - z = 1 \\ x - 3y + z = 5 \end{cases}$ **19.** $x = 4$, $y = 3$, and $z = -7$

21. $x = 3$, $y = 0$, and $z = 0$ **23.** $x = 1.4$, $y = -2.4$, and $z = 1.6$ **25.** not possible **27.** $x = -2$, $y = 0$, and $z = 1$ **29.** $x = 1$, $y = 2$, $z = 3$, and $w = 4$ **31.** Answers may vary. sample answers:

$\begin{bmatrix} 1 & 0 \\ 0 & -1 \end{bmatrix}, \begin{bmatrix} 0 & -1 \\ -1 & 0 \end{bmatrix}$, or $\begin{bmatrix} 0 & 1 \\ 1 & 0 \end{bmatrix}$ **33.** 70 children, 35 adults, and 15 seniors **35.** 1 liter of 4% acid and 2 liters of 7% acid **37.** domain: all real numbers; range: all real numbers ≥ 2

39. $4x^2 + 6x + 1$ **41.**

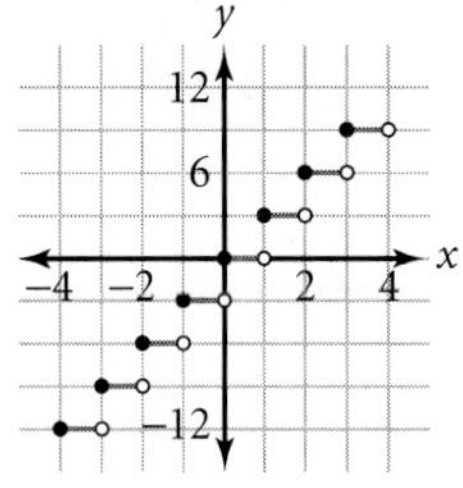

LESSON 4.5

TRY THIS (p. 254)

$(8z - 28, 18 - 5z, z)$; dependent

TRY THIS (p. 255)

no solution; inconsistent

Exercises

5a. $\begin{cases} x + y = 120 \\ 200x + 50y = 12{,}750 \end{cases}$ **b.** 45 leather jackets and 75 imitation leather jackets **6.** no solution; inconsistent **7.** $(6, -3, -2)$; independent

9. $\begin{bmatrix} -1 & 2 & -5 & \vdots & 23 \\ 2 & 0 & 7 & \vdots & 19 \\ 5 & -2 & 1 & \vdots & -10 \end{bmatrix}$

11. $R_2 = [0 \quad 13 \quad -17 \quad \vdots \quad 15]$ **13.** $\begin{bmatrix} 1 & 0 & \vdots & 2 \\ 0 & 1 & \vdots & 3 \end{bmatrix}$

15. $\begin{bmatrix} 1 & 0 & \vdots & 4 \\ 0 & 1 & \vdots & 4 \end{bmatrix}$ **17.** $\begin{bmatrix} 1 & 0 & 0 & \vdots & -2 \\ 0 & 1 & 0 & \vdots & 2 \\ 0 & 0 & 1 & \vdots & 2 \end{bmatrix}$

19. $x = 1$, $y = -1$ **21.** $x = 1$, $y = -1$ **23.** $x = -3$, $y = 5$, $z = -1$ **25.** $x = -\frac{5}{7}$, $y = \frac{27}{7}$, $z = -\frac{1}{7}$ **27.** $x = 0$, $y = 0$, $z = 1$ **29.** $x = \frac{2}{3}$, $y = -\frac{4}{3}$, $z = \frac{10}{3}$ **31.** dependent

33. independent **35.** dependent **37a.** $E = \begin{bmatrix} 2 & 0 \\ 0 & 1 \end{bmatrix}$; $EA = \begin{bmatrix} 2 & 4 \\ 3 & 4 \end{bmatrix}$ **b.** $E = \begin{bmatrix} 0 & 1 \\ 1 & 0 \end{bmatrix}$; $EA = \begin{bmatrix} 3 & 4 \\ 1 & 2 \end{bmatrix}$

c. $E = \begin{bmatrix} 1 & 0 \\ 2 & 1 \end{bmatrix}$; $EA = \begin{bmatrix} 1 & 2 \\ 5 & 8 \end{bmatrix}$ **39.** $p_1 = \frac{2}{3}$, $p_2 = \frac{1}{6}$, and $p_3 = \frac{1}{6}$ **41.** 3 days in Peru, 2 days in Bolivia, and 5 days in Chile **43.** not linear **45.** function

47. function

49.

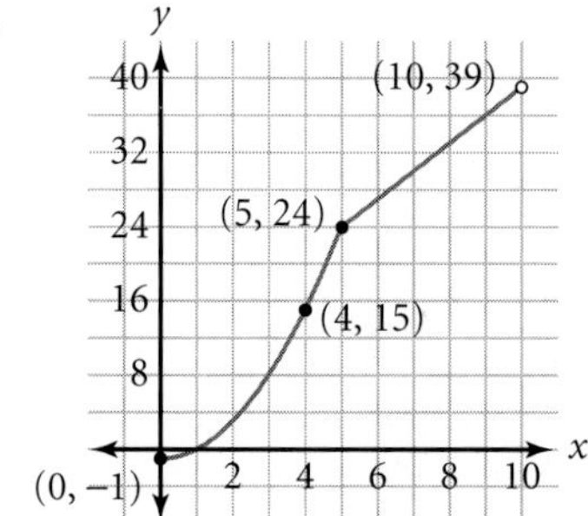

51.

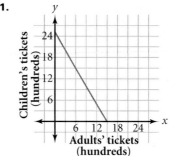

y
24
18
12
6
Children's tickets (hundreds)
6 12 18 24
x
Adults' tickets (hundreds)

53a. $\begin{bmatrix} -4 & 3 & 15 \\ 17 & 5 & -13 \\ 8 & -4 & -9 \end{bmatrix}$ **b.** $\begin{bmatrix} 8 & 9 & 11 \\ -7 & 0 & 0 \\ 17 & 1 & -16 \end{bmatrix}$ **c.** no

CHAPTER REVIEW AND ASSESSMENT

1. $\begin{bmatrix} 5 & -7 & 5 \\ 1 & 5 & 10 \end{bmatrix}$ **3.** $\begin{bmatrix} 0 & 0 & 0 \\ 0 & 0 & 0 \end{bmatrix}$

5. $\begin{bmatrix} 0 & -11 & -22 \\ 22 & 44 & 77 \end{bmatrix}$ **7.** $\begin{bmatrix} 3 & -7 & -5 \\ 2 & -11 & -2 \end{bmatrix}$

9. $\begin{bmatrix} -12 & 19 & -6 \\ -4 & -4 & -21 \end{bmatrix}$ **11.** not possible

13. $\begin{bmatrix} -16 & 13 \\ 22 & -3 \\ -27 & 6 \end{bmatrix}$ **15.** not possible

17. -15; $\begin{bmatrix} 0 & 0.2 \\ 0.\overline{3} & 0.1\overline{3} \end{bmatrix}$ **19.** 0; no inverse

21. 24; $\begin{bmatrix} 0.208\overline{3} & 0.041\overline{6} \\ 0.041\overline{6} & 0.208\overline{3} \end{bmatrix}$ **23.** 5; $\begin{bmatrix} -0.6 & 0.8 \\ 0.2 & -0.6 \end{bmatrix}$

25. 0; no inverse **27.** not possible **29.** $x = 0$, $y = 1$, $z = -5$ **31.** $x = 0$, $y = 1$, $z = -5$ **33.** $(0, 1, -3)$; independent **35.** no solution; inconsistent **37.** $(0, 0, 0)$; independent **39.** 70 regular tickets, 110 student tickets, and 30 child tickets

Chapter 5

LESSON 5.1

TRY THIS (p. 275)
$g(x) = 2x^2 - 9x + 10$ has the form $g(x) = ax^2 + bx + c$, where $a = 2$, $b = -9$, and $c = 10$.

TRY THIS (p. 276)
maximum; $(-1, 3)$

Exercises

4. $f(x) = x^2 - 6x - 7$; $a = 1$, $b = -6$, and $c = -7$
5. $g(x) = x^2 + 7x + 10$; $a = 1$, $b = 7$, and $c = 10$
6. $f(x)\ 6x^2 + 17x + 5$; $a = 6$, $b = 17$, and $c = 5$
7. minimum; $x = 1.5$, $y = 2.75$ **8.** maximum; $x = -1.5$ and $y = 4.25$ **9.** minimum; $x = -2.5$ and $y = -3.25$ **10.** opens up; minimum **11.** opens down; maximum **12.** opens down; maximum
13. $f(x) = x^2 + 5x - 24$; $a = 1$, $b = 5$, $c = -24$
15. $g(x) = -x^2 - 3x + 28$; $a = -1$, $b = -3$, $c = 28$
17. $g(x) = -x^2 -4x + 12$; $a = -1$, $b = -4$, $c = 12$
19. $f(x) = 3x^2 - 3x - 6$; $a = 3$, $b = -3$, $c = -6$
21. $h(x) = x^2 - 3x$; $a = 1$, $b = -3$, $c = 0$
23. $g(x) = -2x^2 + 5x + 12$; $a = -2$, $b = 5$, $c = 12$
25. $h(x) = x^2 - 16$; $a = 1$, $b = 0$, $c = -16$
27. quadratic **29.** quadratic **31.** not quadratic **33.** opens down; maximum **35.** opens down; maximum **37.** opens down; maximum **39.** opens down; maximum **41.** $x = 0.5$, $y = 8.75$ **43.** $x = 0.25$, $y = 1.75$ **45.** $x = 2$, $y = -1$ **47.** The axis of symmetry of the parabola will lie midway between the values of a and $-a$. Therefore, the vertex will occur when $x = 0$ and $y = f(0) = -a^2$.

49a.

Width (yd)	Length (yd)	Area (yd²)
3	14	42
4	12	48
x	$20 - 2x$	$20x - 2x^2$

b. $0 < x < 10$ **c.** $l(x) = 20 - 2x$, where $0 < x < 10$ **d.** $A(x) = -2x^2 + 20x$ **e.** domain: $0 < x < 10$; range: $0 < A(x) < 50$ **f.** Maximum area will be 50 square yards when the width is 5 yards and the length is 10 yards. **51.** slope $= -4$ **53.** $y = 11$

LESSON 5.2

TRY THIS (p. 282, Ex. 1)
$x = \pm 5\sqrt{2} \approx \pm 7.07$

TRY THIS (p. 282, Ex. 2)
$x = -\frac{11}{2}$ *or* $x = \frac{3}{2}$

TRY THIS (p. 283)
about 1.5 seconds

TRY THIS (p. 285, Ex. 4)
a. about 8.1 units
b. about 9.3 units

TRY THIS (p. 285, Ex. 5)
$PQ \approx 1207$ meters

Exercises

4. $\pm\sqrt{29}$; ± 5.39 **5.** $\pm\sqrt{11}$; ± 3.32 **6.** $-4, 2$ **7.** $2 \pm \sqrt{7}$; $-0.65, 4.65$ **8.** $\pm\sqrt{10}$; ± 3.16 **9.** $\pm\sqrt{24}$; ± 4.90 **10.** about 2.6 seconds **11.** $e \approx 3.7$ **12.** $n \approx 17.7$ **13.** 107.6 meters **15.** $\pm\sqrt{32}$; ± 5.66 **17.** $\pm\sqrt{5}$; ± 2.24 **19.** $\pm\sqrt{12}$; ± 3.46 **21.** ± 6 **23.** $\pm\sqrt{\frac{11}{2}}$; ± 2.35 **25.** $\pm\sqrt{2}$; ± 1.41 **27.** 1, 9 **29.** $\pm\sqrt{126}$; ± 11.22 **31.** $-1 \pm \sqrt{5}$; $-3.24, 1.24$ **33.** $t \approx 2.2$ **35.** $d \approx 5.3$ **37.** $v \approx 24.2$ **39.** $c \approx 8.9$ **41.** $a = 2$ **43.** $b = 5$ **45.** $x^2 - 17 = 0$ **47.** about 4.47 inches **49a.** $a \approx 4.24$ feet **b.** $b \approx 5.20$ feet **51.** 1.43 seconds **53.** 127.28 feet **55.** 120.93 feet **57.** 19.49 feet **59.** 14 feet **61.** linear; (9, 15) **63.** $m = \frac{4}{9}$; $y = \frac{4}{9}x + \frac{11}{3}$ **65.** $\frac{1}{25}$ **67.** domain: all real numbers; range: all real numbers ≥ -7 **69.** domain: all real numbers; range: all real numbers ≥ 0

LESSON 5.3

TRY THIS (p. 290)
a. $5x(x + 3)$
b. $(2x - 1)(4 + x)$

TRY THIS (p. 292, Ex. 2)
$(x + 4)(x + 5)$

TRY THIS (p. 292, Ex. 3)
$(x + 1)(x - 11)$

TRY THIS (p. 293, Ex. 4)
$(3x + 4)(x - 5)$

TRY THIS (p. 293, Ex. 5)
$9x^2 - 49 = (3x + 7)(3x - 7)$
$3x^2 + 6x + 3 = 3(x + 1)^2$

TRY THIS (p. 294)
a. $x = 0$ *or* $x = -4$
b. $x = -7$ *or* $x = 3$

Exercises

4. $2x(x - 4)$ **5.** $2y(y - 3)$ **6.** $5ax(x - 3a)$
7. $(4x - 7)(x + 3)$ **8.** $(4r + 7)(3 - 2r)$
9. $(9s - 5)(8s + 3)$ **10.** $(x + 3)(x + 2)$
11. $(x + 7)(x + 1)$ **12.** $(y - 4)(y - 1)$
13. $(x + 2)(x - 6)$ **14.** $(y + 3)(y - 12)$
15. $(x + 12)(x - 2)$ **16.** $(2x + 5)(x + 2)$
17. $(3x + 2)(x + 1)$ **18.** $(x + 3)(5x - 2)$
19. $2(4x - 7)(x + 3)$ **20.** $(3r - 2)(4r + 7)$
21. $4(2s - 1)(9s - 7)$ **22.** $(x^2 + 9)(x + 3)(x - 3)$
23. $2(x + 2)(x - 2)$ **24.** $(4x + 5)(4x - 5)$ **25.** $(x + 4)^2$
26. $x = 0$ *or* $x = -7$ **27.** $x = -3$ **28.** $t = -5$ *or* $t = 2$
29. 9 points **31.** $3(x^2 + 6)$ **33.** $x(1 - 4x)$
35. $-3y(y + 5)$ **37.** $(x + 3)(2x + 7)$ **39.** $2ab(2b - 3a)$
41. $(x + 4)^2$ **43.** $(x + 8)(x - 4)$ **45.** $(x - 12)(x + 2)$
47. $(x + 6)(x - 4)$ **49.** $-(x + 4)(x - 14)$
51. $-(x + 2)(x - 12)$ **53.** $(2x + 1)(x + 2)$
55. $(3x + 1)(x + 2)$ **57.** $(3x + 1)(x - 2)$
59. $x = -\frac{1}{3}$ *or* $x = 2$ **61.** $x = \frac{1}{3}$ *or* $x = 3$
63. $x = \frac{4}{3}$ *or* $x = \frac{3}{2}$ **65.** $t = -3$ *or* $t = 3$

67. $x = -1$ *or* $x = 1$ **69.** $x = -\frac{4}{5}$ *or* $x = \frac{4}{5}$ **71.** $x = -2$ **73.** $x = \frac{1}{2}$ **75.** $x = -\frac{5}{4}$ **77.** $x = 3$ **79.** $t = -3$ *or* $t = 5$ **81.** $x = -\frac{3}{2}$ *or* $x = 1$ **83.** $x = 8$ *or* $x = 7$ **85.** $x = -5$ *or* $x = 8$ **87.** $x = \frac{3}{2}$ *or* $x = \frac{1}{2}$ **89.** $t = -2$ *or* $t = 6$ **91.** $x = -4$ *or* $x = -2$ **93.** $x = -0.5$ *or* $x = 6$

95. $(x^n + 1)(x^n - 1)$ **97.** 7 centimeters **99.** 6 inches **101.** 4 seconds

103. $x < -5\frac{1}{3}$

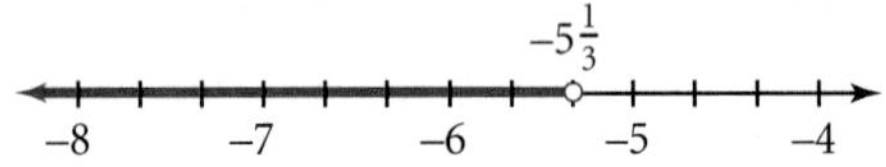

105. $x \le -1\frac{1}{19}$

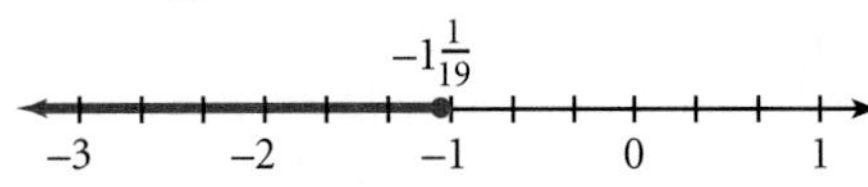

107a. $\begin{cases} 40{,}000x + 25{,}000y \le 1{,}270{,}000 \\ x + y \ge 40 \\ x \ge 0 \\ y \ge 0 \end{cases}$

b.

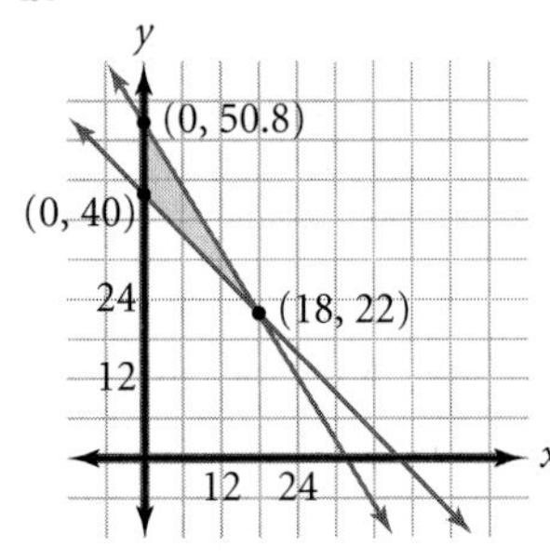

c. Answers may vary. Sample answer: The point (18, 22) is a solution to the system. This point represents buying 18 commercials in the $40,000 time slot and 22 commercials in the $25,000 time slot.

109. $\begin{bmatrix} 0 & -1 & -4 \\ -\frac{1}{2} & -2 & -\frac{3}{2} \\ 1 & 0 & \frac{1}{2} \end{bmatrix}$ **111.** $\begin{bmatrix} -3 & 5 & 16 \\ 4 & 14 & 2 \\ 1 & -2 & -1 \end{bmatrix}$

113. $8x^2 - 50x + 63$

LESSON 5.4

TRY THIS (p. 300)

a. $x^2 - 7x + \left(\frac{7}{2}\right)^2 = \left(x - \frac{7}{2}\right)^2$ **b.** $x^2 + 16x + 8^2 = (x + 8)^2$

TRY THIS (p. 301, Ex. 2)

$x = -12$ *or* $x = 2$

TRY THIS (p. 301, Ex. 3)

$x = -\frac{5}{2} \pm \sqrt{\frac{37}{4}} \approx 0.54$ *or* -5.54

TRY THIS (p. 302)

$g(x) = 3\left(x - \frac{3}{2}\right)^2 + \left(-\frac{35}{4}\right)$; $\left(\frac{3}{2}, -\frac{35}{4}\right)$; $x = \frac{3}{2}$. g is f stretched by a factor of 3, translated $\frac{35}{4}$ units down and $\frac{3}{2}$ units to the right.

Exercises

5. $x^2 - 12x + 36 = (x - 6)^2$ **6.** $x^2 + 5x + \frac{25}{4} = \left(x + \frac{5}{2}\right)^2$ **7.** $x = -3$ *or* $x = 7$ **8.** $x = -3$ *or* $x = \frac{1}{2}$ **9.** $g(x) = [x - (-6)]^2 + (-16)$; vertex: $(-6, -16)$; axis of symmetry: $x = -6$. The graph of g is the graph of f translated 16 units down and 6 units to the left. **10.** $h(t) = -16(t - 1)^2 + 21$; 21 feet **11.** $x^2 + 10x + 25 = (x + 5)^2$ **13.** $x^2 - 8x + 16 = (x - 4)^2$ **15.** $x^2 + 13x + \frac{169}{4} = \left(x + \frac{13}{2}\right)^2$ **17.** $x = 4 \pm \sqrt{19}$ **19.** $x = 1 \pm \sqrt{6}$ **21.** $x = \frac{-7}{2} \pm \sqrt{\frac{153}{4}}$ **23.** $x = -5$ *or* $x = -2$ **25.** $x = -5$ *or* $x = 6$ **27.** $x = -3$ *or* $x = 10$ **29.** $x = 2$ *or* $x = 6$ **31.** $x = -5 \pm \sqrt{29}$ **33.** $x = \frac{-7}{2} \pm \sqrt{\frac{41}{4}}$ **35.** $x = \frac{11}{2} \pm \sqrt{\frac{99}{4}}$ **37.** $x = \frac{3}{4} \pm \sqrt{\frac{105}{16}}$ **39.** $g(x) = -(x - 0)^2 + 2$; $(0, 2)$; $x = 0$; g is f reflected across the y-axis and translated up 2 units. **41.** $g(x) = [x - (-4)]^2 + (-5)$; $(-4, -5)$; $x = -4$; g is f horizontally translated 4 units left and vertically translated down 5 units. **43.** $g(x) = -(x - 2)^2 + 6$; $(2, 6)$; $x = 2$; g is f reflected across the y-axis, translated right 2 units and translated up 6 units. **45.** $g(x) = -3(x - 1)^2 + (-6)$; $(1, -6)$; $x = 1$; g is f reflected across the y-axis, stretched by a factor of 3, translated 1 unit right and 6 units down. **47.** Answers may vary. sample answers:
$f(x) = (x - 2)^2 + 5 = x^2 - 4x + 9$
$g(x) = -2(x - 2)^2 + 5 = -2x^2 + 8x - 3$
$h(x) = 5(x - 2)^2 + 5 = 5x^2 - 20x + 25$
49. $-2 + \sqrt{30} \approx 3.5$ centimeters **51a.** 6:00 A.M. **b.** 174 megawatts **c.** 3rd hour (between 2:00 and 3:00 A.M.) and 10th hour (between 9:00 and 10:00 A.M.) **53.** $x = 5$ **55.** $x = 5$ **57.** function **59.** function **61.** $g(2) = -1$; $g(-3) = 19$ **63.** $g(x) = x^2 - 6$ **65.** $g(x) = -|3x|$

LESSON 5.5

TRY THIS (p. 308, Ex. 1)

$x = 1$ *or* $x = 6$

TRY THIS (p. 308, Ex. 2)

$x = \frac{3 \pm \sqrt{3}}{2}$; $x \approx -0.6$ *or* $x \approx 2.4$

TRY THIS (p. 309)

7.9 feet

TRY THIS (p. 310)

$x = 2$; $(2, -3)$

Exercises

4. $x = 1$ *or* $x = 4$ **5.** $x = -\frac{1}{2}$ *or* $x = 3$ **6.** $x = \frac{3 \pm \sqrt{57}}{6}$; $x \approx -0.8$ *or* $x \approx 1.8$ **7.** 10.7 feet **8.** $x = \frac{1}{2}$; $\left(\frac{1}{2}, -\frac{9}{4}\right)$ **9.** $x = 3$; $(3, -7)$ **11.** $x = -6$ *or* $x = 0$ **13.** $x = \frac{-1 \pm \sqrt{109}}{2}$ **15.** $x = \frac{3 \pm \sqrt{13}}{2}$ **17.** $x = -3$ *or* $x = 8$ **19.** $x = -\frac{3}{2}$ *or* $x = -\frac{1}{2}$ **21.** $x = \frac{-5 \pm \sqrt{33}}{2}$

23. $x = -5 \pm \frac{\sqrt{120}}{2}$ **25.** $x = -\frac{3}{5}$ *or* $x = 1$ **27.** $x = \frac{3 \pm \sqrt{13}}{-2}$
29. $x = -\frac{9}{2}$; $\left(-\frac{9}{2}, -\frac{25}{4}\right)$ **31.** $x = -\frac{3}{2}$; $\left(-\frac{3}{2}, -\frac{85}{4}\right)$
33. $x = 2$; $(2, 22)$ **35.** $x = -3$; $(-3, 11)$ **37.** $x = \frac{3}{4}$; $\left(\frac{3}{4}, \frac{1}{8}\right)$
39. $x = 2$; $(2, 21)$ **41.** $x = \frac{1}{3}$; $\left(\frac{1}{3}, -\frac{7}{3}\right)$ **43.** $x = -1$; $(-1, -3)$ **45.** $x = 0$; $(0, 9)$ **47.** $x = -\frac{1}{5}$; $\left(-\frac{1}{5}, -\frac{16}{5}\right)$
49. 6 seconds **51.** Answers may vary. Sample answer: The pyrotechnician should begin firing after 6 – 2.5, or 3.5, seconds. **53.** 3 inches **55.** \$2687.50
57. $\$30.35 < x < \$219.65$ **59a.** $a = \frac{b \pm b\sqrt{5}}{2}$ **b.** ≈ 1.62
61. $y = -\frac{1}{2}x - 4$ **63.** $y = -5x - 22$
65. $x > -2$ *and* $x < 8$

67. $x \le 1$ *or* $x \ge 7$

69. $\begin{bmatrix} 0.28 & 0.32 \\ 0.16 & 0.04 \end{bmatrix}$ **71.** $x = -\sqrt{8}$ *or* $x = \sqrt{8}$
73. $x = -\sqrt{18}$ *or* $x = \sqrt{18}$

LESSON 5.6

TRY THIS (p. 315)
$216 > 0$, so there are 2 real solutions.

TRY THIS (p. 316, Ex. 2)
$x = \frac{5}{8} + \frac{i\sqrt{23}}{8}$ *or* $x = \frac{5}{8} - \frac{i\sqrt{23}}{8}$

TRY THIS (p. 316, Ex. 3)
$x = -4$ and $y = \frac{10}{3}$

TRY THIS (p. 317)
$14 - 44i$

TRY THIS (p. 318)
$\frac{2}{5} - \frac{11}{5}i$

TRY THIS (p. 319)
$\sqrt{34}$

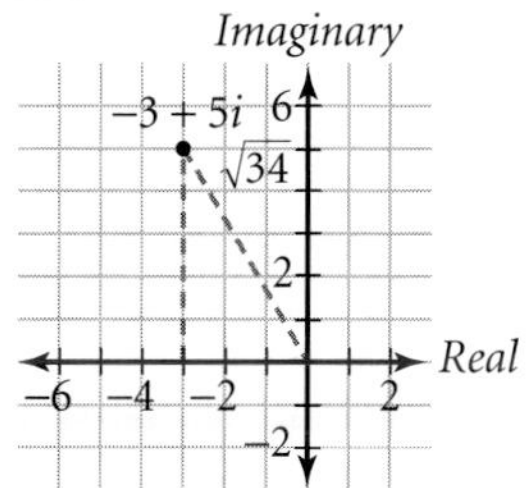

Exercises

4. 1 real solution **5.** no real solutions **6.** 2 real solutions **7.** $x = -\frac{5}{4} \pm \frac{i\sqrt{7}}{4}$ **8.** $x = -1$ and $y = 2$
9. $6 + 10i$ **10.** $5 + 2i$ **11.** $-11 + 2i$ **12.** $\frac{10}{13} + \frac{11}{13}i$
13. 5

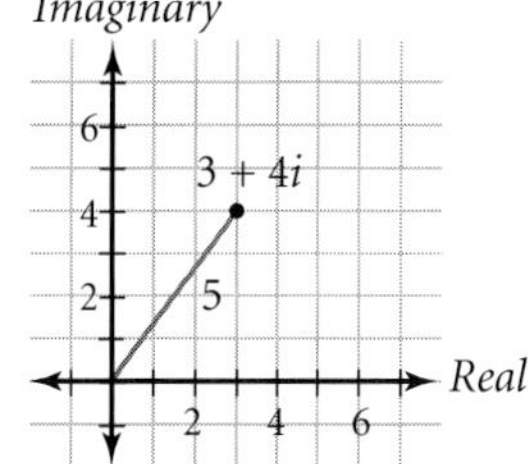

15. 2 is the real part, and 1 is the imaginary part.
17. 0 is the real part, and 4 is the imaginary part.
19. $10i$ **21.** $i\sqrt{17}$ **23.** -49 **25.** -23; no real solutions; $x = \frac{5}{6} \pm \frac{i\sqrt{23}}{6}$ **27.** -15; no real solutions; $x = \frac{1}{2} \pm \frac{i\sqrt{15}}{10}$
29. 37; 2 real solutions; $x = \frac{3}{2} \pm \frac{\sqrt{37}}{2}$ **31.** -4; no real solutions; $x = \frac{3}{2} \pm \frac{i}{2}$ **33.** 9; 2 real solutions; $x = 0$ *or* $x = -\frac{3}{2}$ **35.** -3; no real solutions; $x = -\frac{1}{2} \pm \frac{i\sqrt{3}}{2}$
37. 0; 1 real solution; $x = 7$ **39.** -39; no real solutions; $x = -\frac{5}{16} \pm \frac{i\sqrt{39}}{16}$ **41.** 0; 1 real solution; $x = \frac{1}{3}$
43. $x = \frac{4}{3}$ and $y = -1$ **45.** $-3 - i$ **47.** $1 + \frac{1}{5}i$ **49.** $9 - i$
51. $-1 + 2i$ **53.** $12 - 8i$ **55.** $-13 - 84i$ **57.** $-4 - 2i\sqrt{5}$
59. $-14 - 12i\sqrt{2}$ **61.** 8 **63.** $8 + 3i$ **65.** $\frac{17}{26} + \frac{7}{26}i$
67. $\frac{132}{25} - \frac{24}{25}i$ **69.** 1 **71.** $\frac{30}{17} + \frac{18}{17}i$ **73.** -4 **75.** i

77.

79.

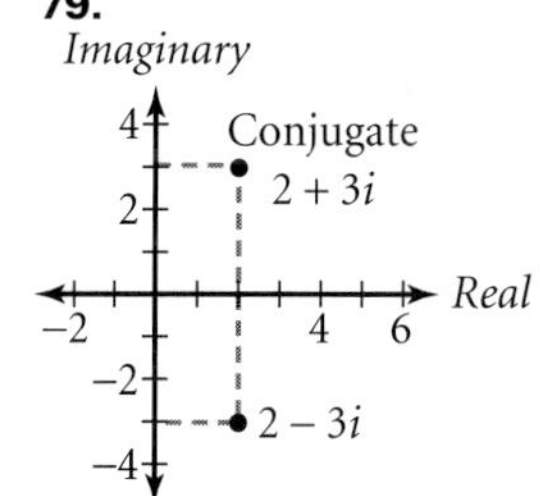

81.

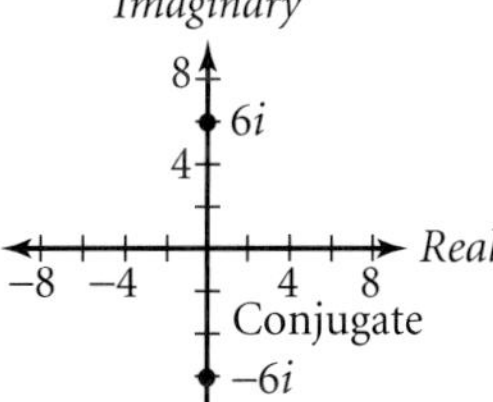

83.

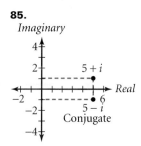

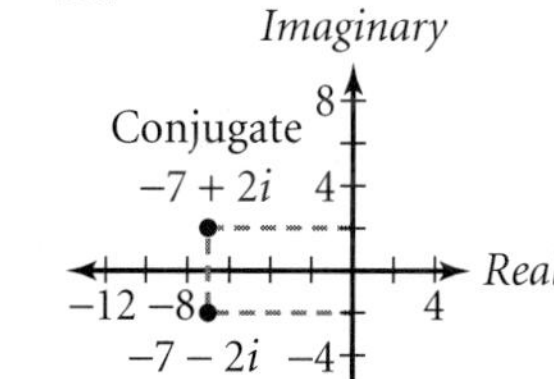

85.

87.

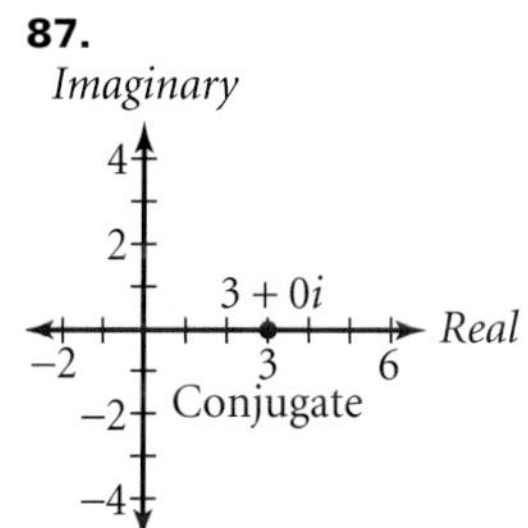

89. 1

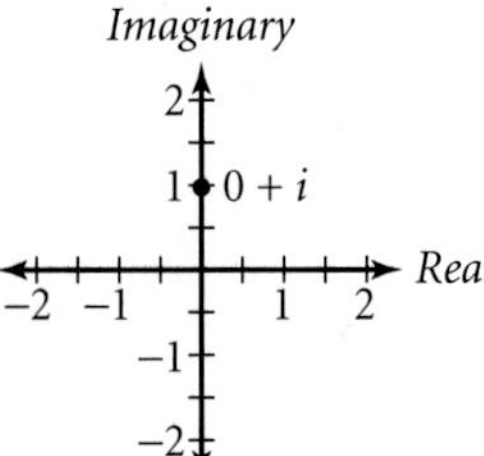

91. $\sqrt{1.0001}$

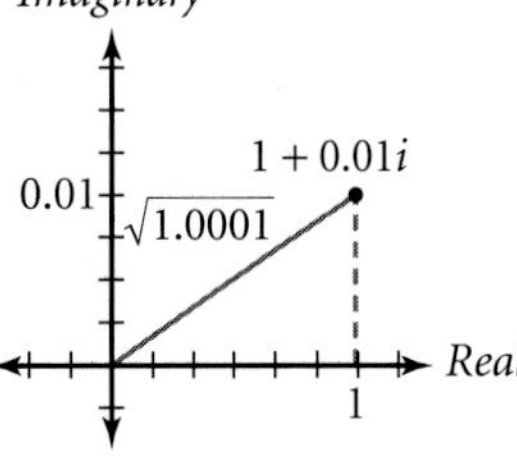

93. $\sqrt{13}$

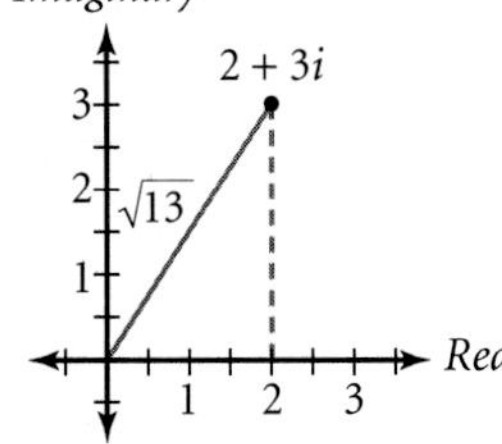

95. 1

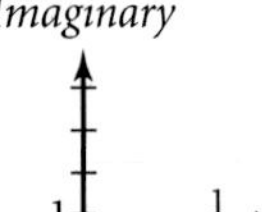

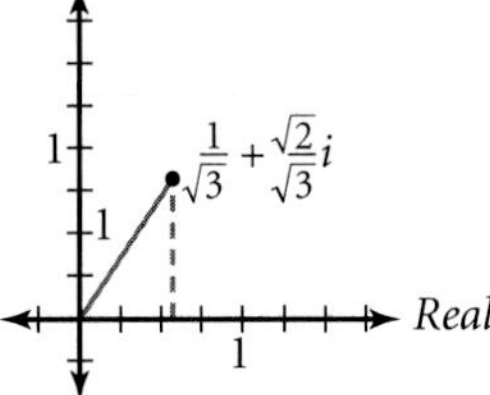

97. (3, 1), (−2, −4), (−3, 3)

99. rectangle

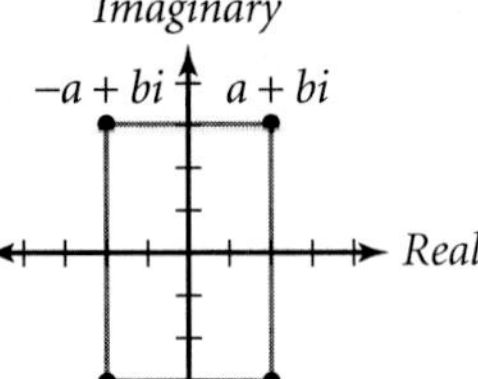

101.

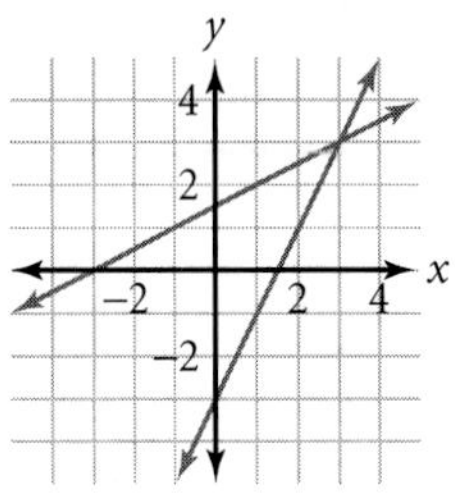

103.

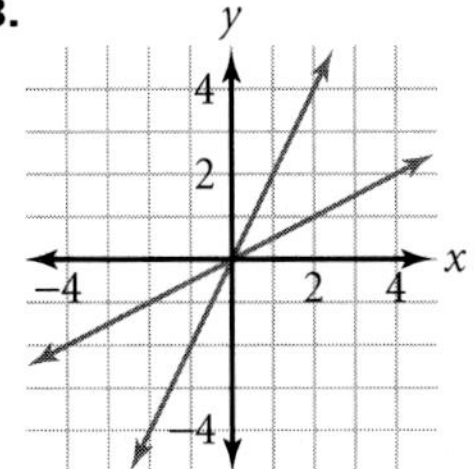

105. $(f \circ f^{-1})(x) = x$ **107.** 5 framed prints

LESSON 5.7

TRY THIS (p. 323)

$f(x) = -x^2 + 9x - 17$

Exercises

3. $f(x) \approx 2x^2 - 11x + 6$

4a.

Number of people, *n*	Number of handshakes, *h*
2	1
3	3
4	6
5	10
6	15

The first differences for the number of handshakes are 2, 3, 4, and 5; the second differences are all equal to 1, indicating a quadratic relationship.

b. $h(n) = 0.5n^2 - 0.5n$ **c.** 45 handshakes

5a.

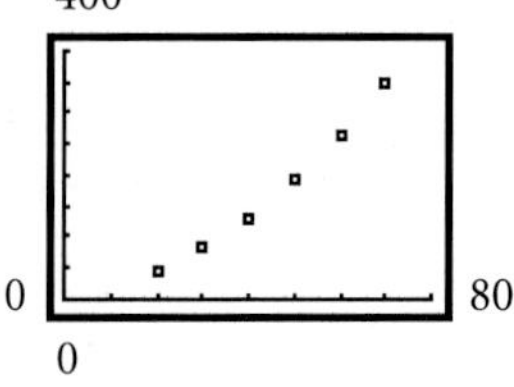

b. yes; $d \approx 0.06x^2 + 1.10x + 0.06$

7. $y = x^2 + 3x - 5$ **9.** $y = -x^2 + 6x + 10$

11. $y = 3x^2 - 2x + 4$ **13.** $y = 2x^2 - 9x + 15$

15. $y = 2x^2 - 18x + 49$ **17.** $y = -0.5x^2 + 4x + 7$

19. $y = -0.5x^2 - 0.5x + 6$ **21.** $y = 2x^2 - 5x + 7$

23. $h(t) = -6t^2 + 20t + 5$ **25.** $1\frac{2}{3}$ seconds **27.** about 3.57 seconds **29.** 0.69 second, 2.64 seconds

31. $h(t) \approx -15.11t^2 + 15.19t + 1.65$

33. yes **35.** yes **37.** yes **39.** −4 **41.** 8; yes

43. $-\frac{1}{12}$; yes

LESSON 5.8

TRY THIS (p. 331)

$2 \le x \le 6$

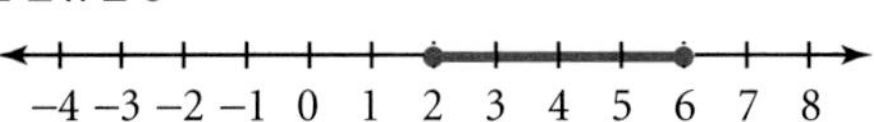

TRY THIS (p. 332)

no solution

TRY THIS (p. 333)

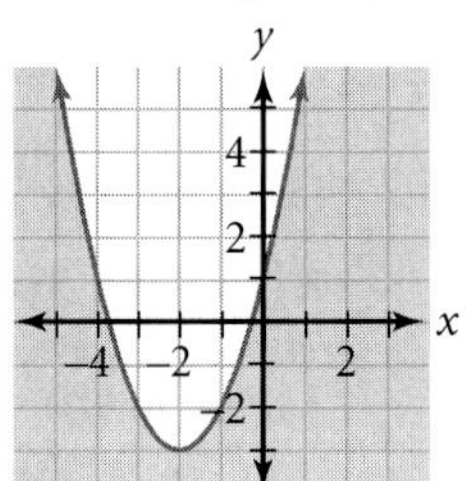

Exercises

6. $x \le 3$ *or* $x \ge 4$

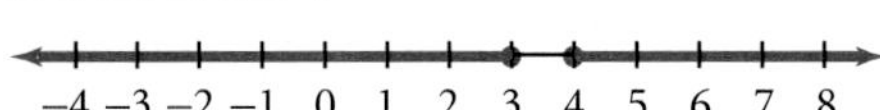

7. 5, 6, and 7 **8.** no solution **9.** all real numbers except 5 **10.** no solution

11.

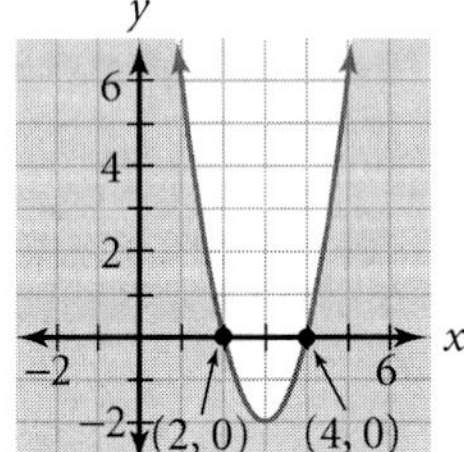

13. $2 < x < 3$

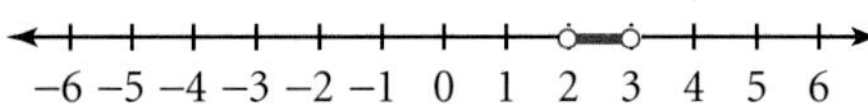

15. $-1 < x < 5$

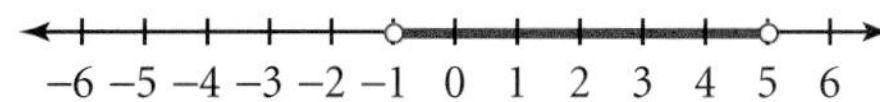

17. $x < 5$ *or* $x > 10$

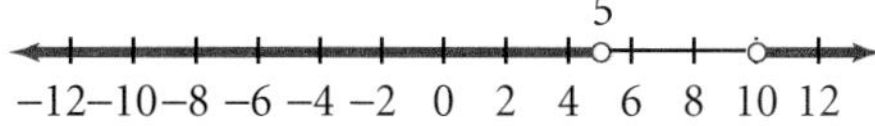

19. $-3 \leq x \leq 4$

−6 −5 −4 −3 −2 −1 0 1 2 3 4 5 6

21. $x < -2$ *or* $x > 6$

−6 −5 −4 −3 −2 −1 0 1 2 3 4 5 6

23. $-3 \leq x \leq 2$

−6 −5 −4 −3 −2 −1 0 1 2 3 4 5 6

25. $1 \leq x \leq 6$

−6 −5 −4 −3 −2 −1 0 1 2 3 4 5 6

27. $-10 \leq x \leq 1$

−10 −9 −8 −7 −6 −5 −4 −3 −2 −1 0 1 2

29. $x < -6$ *or* $x > 3$

−6 −5 −4 −3 −2 −1 0 1 2 3 4 5 6

31. $x \leq -7$ *or* $x \geq 1$

−10 −9 −8 −7 −6 −5 −4 −3 −2 −1 0 1 2

33. $x < \frac{3}{2} - \frac{\sqrt{33}}{2}$ *or* $x > \frac{3}{2} + \frac{\sqrt{33}}{2}$

$\frac{3}{2} - \frac{\sqrt{33}}{2}$ $\frac{3}{2} + \frac{\sqrt{33}}{2}$

−6 −5 −4 −3 −2 −1 0 1 2 3 4 5 6

35. $-\frac{1}{2} - \frac{\sqrt{29}}{2} < x < -\frac{1}{2} + \frac{\sqrt{29}}{2}$

$-\frac{1}{2} - \frac{\sqrt{29}}{2}$ $-\frac{1}{2} + \frac{\sqrt{29}}{2}$

−6 −5 −4 −3 −2 −1 0 1 2 3 4 5 6

37.

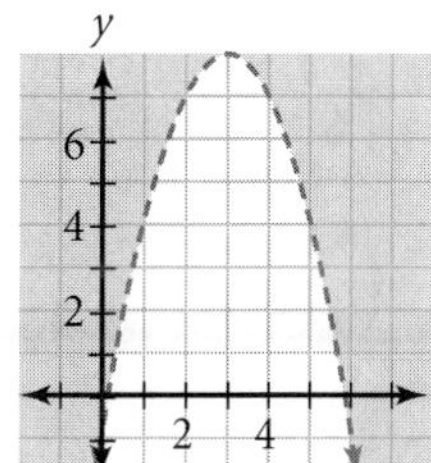

C

39.

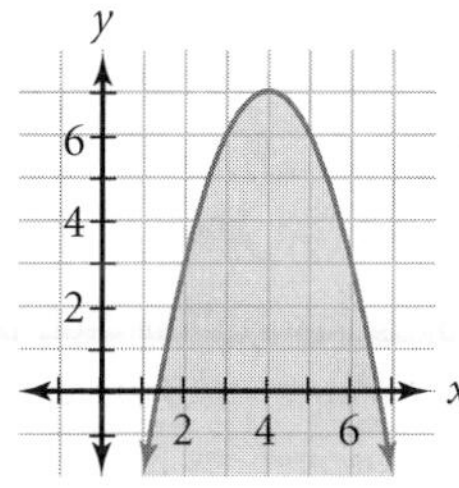

A and *B*

41.

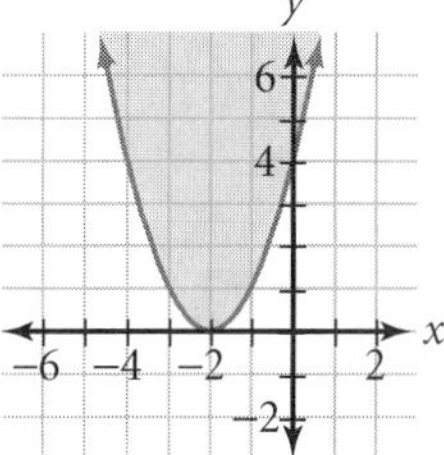

43.

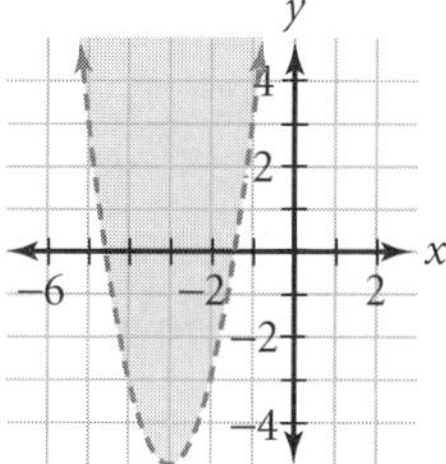

45.

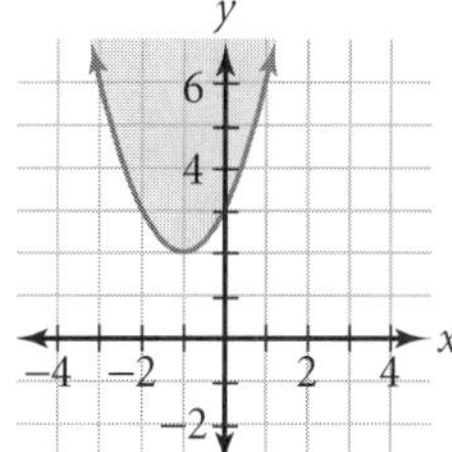

47.

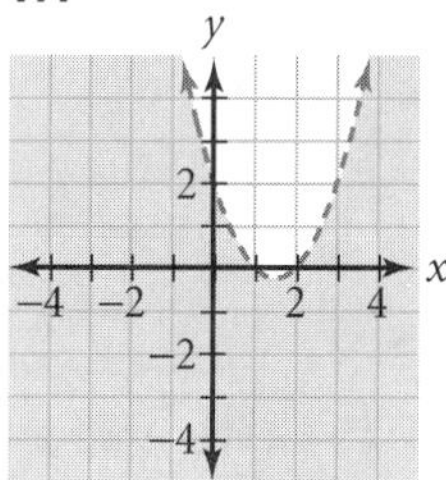

49.

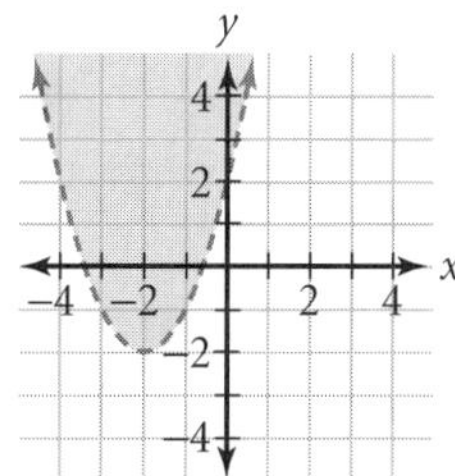

51.

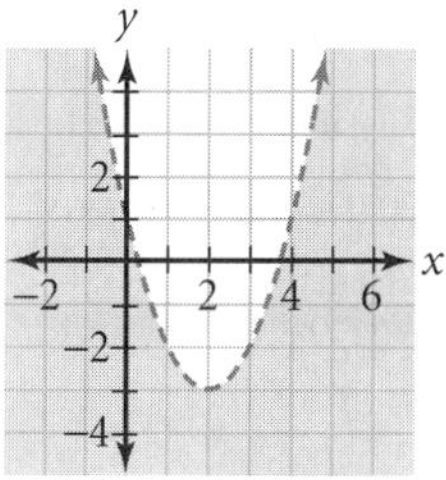

53.

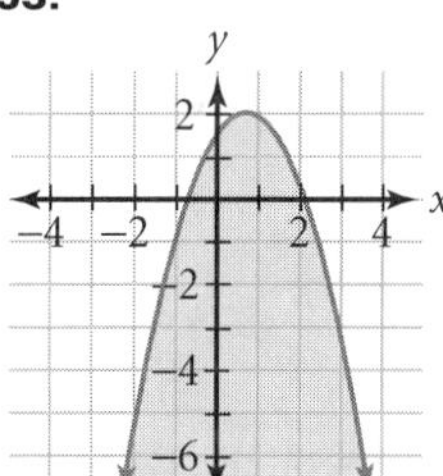

55.

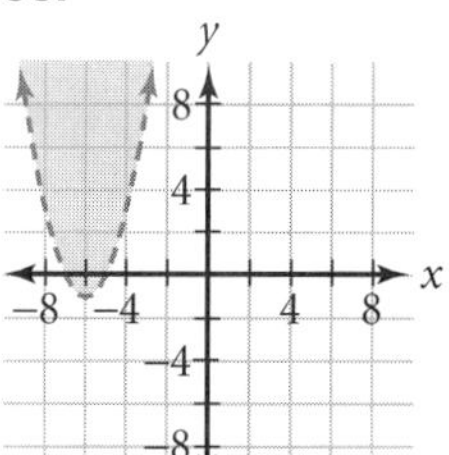

57.

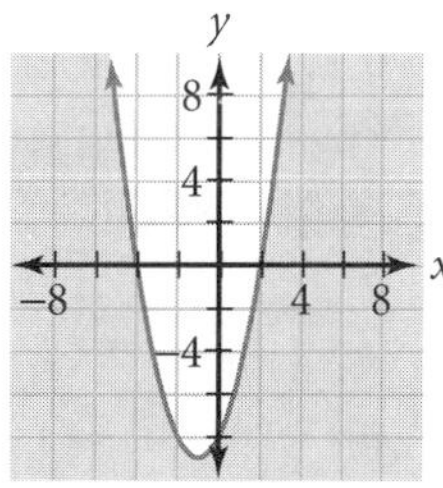

59. $x^2 - 10x + 21 > 0$ **61.** $0.2 \leq t \leq 1.3$ seconds **63a.** from 0 to 33,000 **b.** 20,000 **c.** No; the cost increases as the number of backpacks increases.

d.

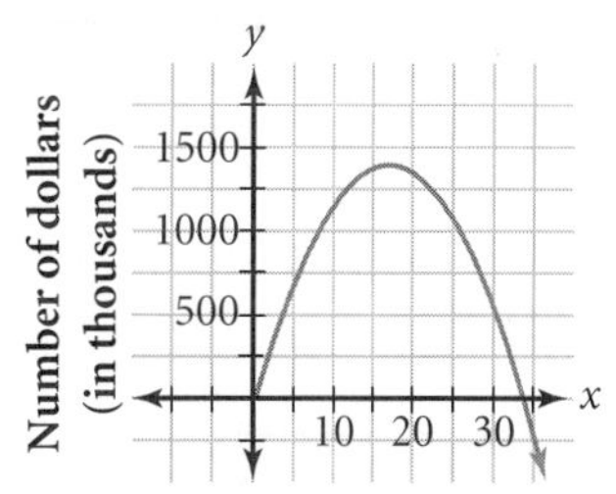

e. from 1000 to 33,000; same as part **a**
f. 17,000; yes
g. after 33,000

65. approximately $0 \le t < 2.48$ **67.** about 2.32 seconds **69.** between 16 and 159 pairs, inclusive **71.** yes **73.** yes **75.** $x = \pm\sqrt{8}$ **77.** $x = \pm\sqrt{18}$ **79.** $-1 + 4i$ **81.** $6 + i$

CHAPTER REVIEW AND ASSESSMENT

1. $f(x) = -x^2 + 3x + 4$; $a = -1$, $b = 3$, and $c = 4$ **3.** $(1.5, 1.25)$ **5.** opens down; maximum **7.** $x = \pm\sqrt{8}$; $x \approx \pm 2.83$ **9.** $x \approx \pm 7$ **11.** $x = -5$ *or* $x = 11$ **13.** $x = -1 \pm \frac{\sqrt{54}}{7}$; $x \approx -3.78$ *or* $x \approx 1.78$ **15.** $c \approx 6.4$ **17.** $a \approx 9.7$ **19.** $a \approx 24.5$ **21.** $b \approx 0.7$ **23.** $7x(x - 3)$ **25.** $(x + 5)(x + 2)$ **27.** $(t + 3)(t - 8)$ **29.** $(x + 2)(x - 10)$ **31.** $(x + 5)(x - 4)$ **33.** $(3y + 2)(y - 1)$ **35.** $(4 + 3x)(4 - 3x)$ **37.** $(x - 8)^2$ **39.** $x = 4$ *or* $x = 6$ **41.** $t = -\frac{5}{2}$ *or* $t = \frac{2}{3}$ **43.** $x = \frac{1}{5} \pm \frac{\sqrt{24}}{10}$ **45.** $x = -12$ *or* $x = 7$ **47.** $x = -4$ *or* $x = \frac{1}{2}$ **49.** $x = -\frac{4}{3}$ *or* $x = 2$ **51.** $y = -3(x + 1)^2 - 4$; $(-1, -4)$ **53.** $y = 4\left(x - \frac{9}{8}\right)^2 - \frac{49}{16}$; $\left(\frac{9}{8}, -\frac{49}{16}\right)$ **55.** $x = -\frac{3}{5} \pm \frac{\sqrt{76}}{10}$ **57.** $x = -4$ *or* $x = -2$ **59.** $x = \frac{1}{12} \pm \frac{\sqrt{73}}{12}$ **61.** $x = -\frac{1}{2} \pm \frac{\sqrt{5}}{2}$ **63.** $\left(\frac{1}{2}, -\frac{49}{4}\right)$ **65.** $(-6, -31)$ **67.** 2 real solutions **69.** no real solutions **71.** $x = -5 - 3i$ *or* $x = -5 + 3i$ **73.** $x = 3 \pm \frac{i\sqrt{8}}{2}$ **75.** $x = \frac{1}{3} \pm \frac{i\sqrt{20}}{6}$ **77.** $1 - 7i$ **79.** -1 **81.** $6 - 9i$ **83.** $2 - 4i$

85. $\sqrt{10}$

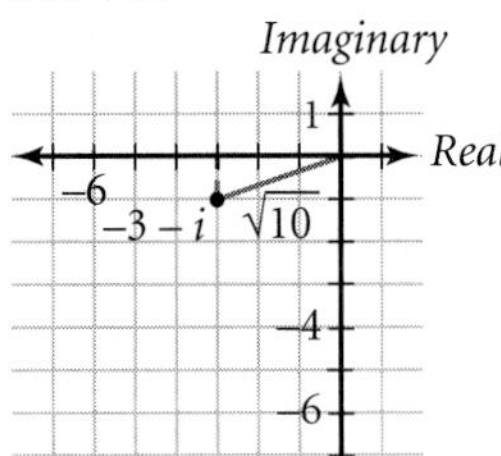

87. $\sqrt{2}$

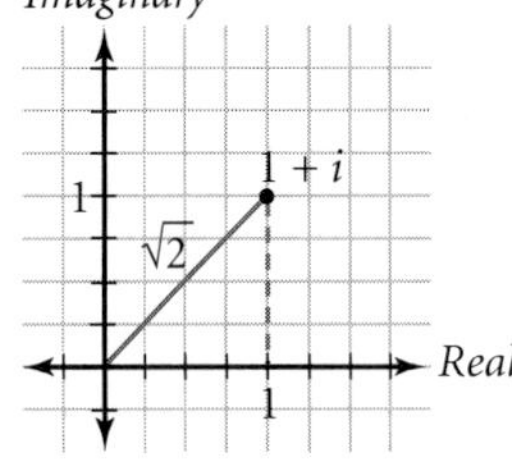

89. $f(x) = 5x^2 + 2x - 9$ **91.** $f(x) = -5x^2 - x + 6$ **93.** $f(x) = 3x^2 - 3x - 3$ **95.** $f(x) = 7x^2 - 1$ **97.** $f(x) \approx -0.7x^2 + 1.5x - 3.1$ **99.** $x < -2$ *or* $x > 6$

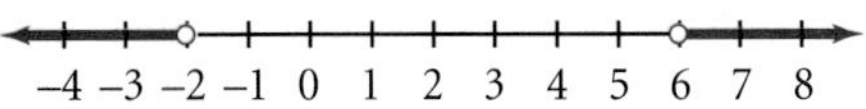

101. $x \le -5$ *or* $x \ge -2$

−6 −5 −4 −3 −2 −1 0 1 2 3 4 5 6

103. $x < -\frac{3}{4}$ *or* $x > 3$

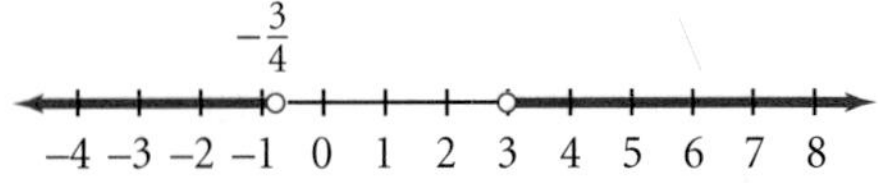

105. $0 \le x \le \frac{5}{2}$

5/2

−6 −5 −4 −3 −2 −1 0 1 2 3 4 5 6

107.

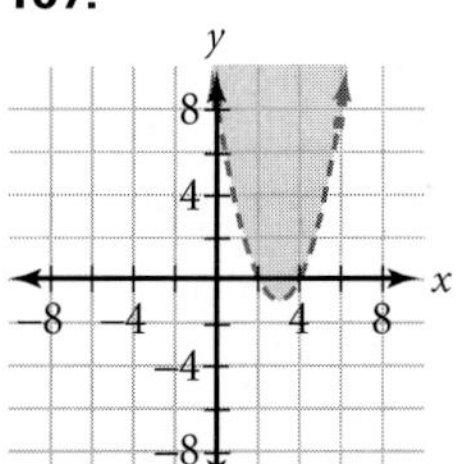

109.

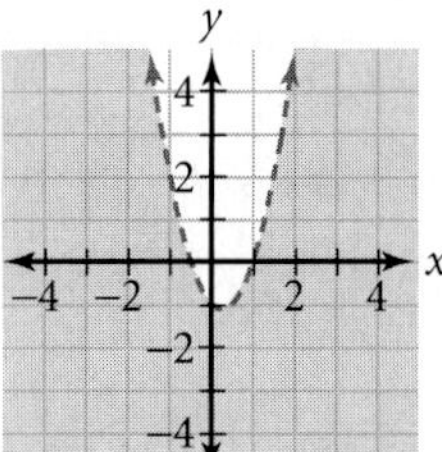

111.

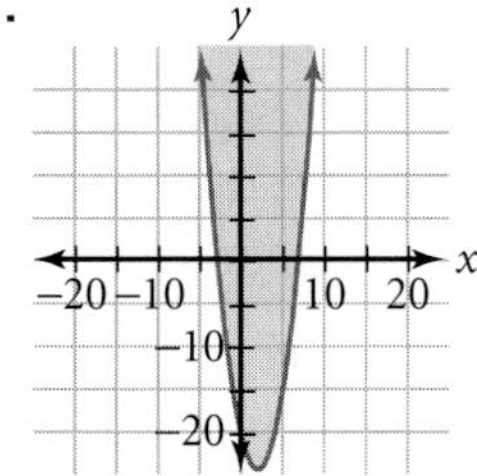

113. about 2.8 seconds

Chapter 6

LESSON 6.1

TRY THIS (p. 356)
188,700,000; 194,400,000

TRY THIS (p. 357)
192 milligrams, 62.9 milligrams

Exercises

5. 1.055 **6.** 1.0025 **7.** 0.97 **8.** 0.995 **9.** 8 **10.** 1350 **11.** 0.512 **12.** 42.1875 **13.** 31,400,000 **14.** 31.0 milligrams and 27.3 milligrams **15.** 1.07 **17.** 0.94 **19.** 1.065 **21.** 0.9995 **23.** 1.00075 **25.** 1.9 **27.** 1,638,400 **29.** 37.9 **31.** 394.0 **33.** 941,013.7 **35.** 32.6 **37a.** 8000 bacteria **b.** 32,000 bacteria **39a.** 1200 bacteria **b.** 4800 bacteria **41a.** 6975 bacteria **b.** 62,775 bacteria **43.** exponential **45.** linear **47.** 278,700,000 **49.** 1,359,600,000 and 1,399,800,000 **51a.** 1,002,600,000 and 1,140,800,000 **b.** 13.79% **c.** 1,107,500,000 **53.** 310,000 gallons **55.** 2 **57.** 7 **59.** $\frac{m^3}{n^{15}}$ **61.** $\frac{1}{12xy^2}$ **63.** reflection across *y*-axis and horizontal compression by a factor of $\frac{1}{2}$ **65.** reflection across *x*-axis, horizontal stretch by a factor of 2, and vertical translation 3 units up **67.** reflection across *x*-axis, vertical stretch by a factor of 5, horizontal translation 2 units to the right, and vertical translation 2 units down **69.** opens down; maximum value

LESSON 6.2

TRY THIS (p. 364)
a. exponential growth; $\frac{1}{3}$
b. exponential decay; $\frac{1}{4}$

TRY THIS (p. 366)
7.2%

Exercises

5. exponential decay; 1 **6.** exponential growth; 3 **7.** exponential decay; 5 **8.** \$334.56, \$336.71, and \$337.46 **9.** 4.7% **11.** quadratic **13.** exponential **15.** quadratic **17.** growth **19.** decay **21.** decay **23.** decay **25.** d **27.** b **29.** \$3207.14 **31.** \$2013.80 **33.** \$2132.45 **35a.** $h(x) = 8^x$; $f(x) = 2^x$ **b.** 1 **c.** Both functions have a domain of all real numbers and a range of all positive real numbers. **37.** when $a = 0$ or when $b = 1$ **39.** g is f compressed vertically by a factor of $\frac{1}{2}$. **41.** g is f stretched vertically by a factor of 2 and translated vertically 3 units down. **43.** g is f translated 1 unit to the right and stretched vertically by a factor of 5. **45.** g is f stretched vertically by a factor of 2. **47.** 3.8% **49.** 1.3% **51.** \$2615.16 **53a.** Final amount is doubled: \$114,674. **b.** Final amount is more than 10 times larger: \$586,954.26. **c.** Final amount is more than 11 times larger: \$657,506.29. **d.** doubling the investment period **55.** $\{(2, 7), (-1, 3), (2, 2), (0, 0)\}$; not a function **57.** $y = \pm\frac{\sqrt{x}}{3}$; not a function **59.** $y = \pm\sqrt{-x}$; not a function

61.

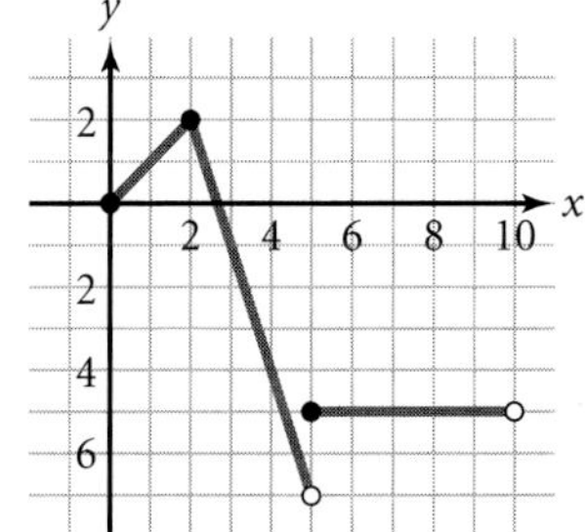

63. does not exist **65.** $\begin{bmatrix} -2 & 40 & -38 \\ 51 & 52 & -9 \end{bmatrix}$

67. $\begin{bmatrix} -32 & 14 \\ -27 & 12 \end{bmatrix}$ **69.** $y = 3x^2 - 2x + 4$

LESSON 6.3

TRY THIS (p. 371, Ex. 1)

Exponential form	Logarithmic form
$2^5 = 32$	$\log_2 32 = 5$
$10^3 = 1000$	$\log_{10} 1000 = 3$
$3^{-2} = \frac{1}{9}$	$\log_3 \frac{1}{9} = -2$
$16^{\frac{1}{2}} = 4$	$\log_{16} 4 = \frac{1}{2}$

TRY THIS (p. 371, Ex. 2)
−2.037

TRY THIS (p. 373, Ex. 3)
a. $v = 3$ **b.** $v = 5$ **c.** $v = 729$

TRY THIS (p. 373, Ex. 4)
$[H^+] \approx 0.00018$ moles per liter

Exercises

4. $\log_4 16 = 2$ **5.** $5^2 = 25$ **6.** 2.754 **7.** −2.699 **8.** 2 **9.** 12 **10.** 16 **11.** 10^{-5}, or 0.00001 **13.** $\log_5 625 = 4$ **15.** $\log_6 216 = 3$ **17.** $\log_7 \frac{1}{49} = -2$ **19.** $\log_{16} 2 = \frac{1}{4}$ **21.** $\log_{\frac{1}{9}} 81 = -2$ **23.** $\log_{\frac{1}{2}} \frac{1}{8} = 3$ **25.** $10^3 = 1000$ **27.** $10^{-1} = 0.1$ **29.** $7^3 = 343$ **31.** $2^{-5} = \frac{1}{32}$ **33.** $3^{-3} = \frac{1}{27}$ **35.** $144^{\frac{1}{2}} = 12$ **37.** 2 **39.** 4 **41.** 0 **43.** −4 **45.** 1.08 **47.** 3.55 **49.** 0.28 **51.** −1.46 **53.** −3.04 **55.** −1.35 **57.** 3 **59.** 2 **61.** 1 **63.** −2 **65.** −2 **67.** 0 **69.** 49 **71.** 3 **73.** 2 **75.** $\frac{1}{64}$ **77.** 1 **79.** 5 **81.** 64 **83.** 2 **85.** 3

87.

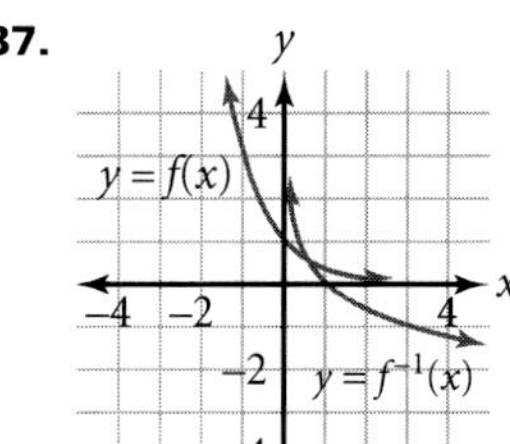

Tables may vary. Sample tables provided.

x	$f(x) = 3^{-x}$
−3	27
−2	9
−1	3
0	1
1	$\frac{1}{3}$
2	$\frac{1}{9}$
3	$\frac{1}{27}$

x	$f^{-1}(x) = \log_{\frac{1}{3}} x$
27	−3
9	−2
3	−1
1	0
$\frac{1}{3}$	1
$\frac{1}{9}$	2
$\frac{1}{27}$	3

89. 4.5 **91.** stretched vertically by a factor of 3 **93.** compressed vertically by a factor of $\frac{1}{2}$ and translated 1 unit up **95.** reflected across the x-axis and translated 2 units to the right **97.** 10^{-10} moles per liter **99.** 3.98×10^{-8} moles per liter **101.** 5261.1 feet **103.** Identity Property of Multiplication **105.** Commutative Property of Addition **107.** Inverse Property of Multiplication **109.** $A^{-1} \approx \begin{bmatrix} 0.364 & 0.273 \\ 0.091 & -0.182 \end{bmatrix}$ **111.** $\pm i$

LESSON 6.4

TRY THIS (p. 379, Ex. 1)
a. 4.17 **b.** −0.4150

TRY THIS (p. 379, Ex. 2)
a. $\log_4 3$ **b.** $\log_b \frac{4x}{3}$

TRY THIS (p. 380, Ex. 3)
300

TRY THIS (p. 380, Ex. 4)
a. 7 **b.** 13

Exercises

5. 3.5424 **6.** −0.7712 **7.** $\log_3 \frac{xz}{y}$ **8.** $\log_2 \frac{9}{5}$ **9.** 16

10. 12 **11.** 3 **12.** $x = 4$ **13.** $\log_8 5 + 1$ **15.** $\log_3 x - 2$ **17.** 1.9535 **19.** 4.8074 **21.** 2.9535 **23.** 2.9191 **25.** −0.3685 **27.** 0.1610 **29.** $\log_2 35$ **31.** $\log_3 5$ **33.** $\log_2 \frac{x}{2}$ **35.** $\log_7 2y$ **37.** $\log_2 \frac{m^5}{n^2}$ **39.** $\log_b \frac{m^4 n^{\frac{1}{2}}}{8p^3}$ **41.** $\log_7 \frac{7}{x^2}$ **43.** 8 **45.** 5 **47.** 12 **49.** 8 **51.** 5 **53.** −5 **55.** $x = 3$ *or* $x = 4$ **57.** $x = 8$ **59.** $x = 3$ **61.** $x = 3$ **63.** always **65.** always **67.** never **69.** always **71.** sometimes **73.** $x = 243$ **75.** 1.83 times greater **77.** 12

79. $\begin{bmatrix} 3 & 2 & -1 \\ 5 & 3 & -2 \\ 2 & 3 & -1 \end{bmatrix}\begin{bmatrix} x \\ y \\ z \end{bmatrix} = \begin{bmatrix} 7 \\ -12 \\ -5 \end{bmatrix}$ **81.** $\begin{bmatrix} -3 & 2 & 11 \\ 4 & 1 & 5 \end{bmatrix}$

83. $\begin{bmatrix} 0.5 & 0.3 & 0 & 2.2 \\ 0 & -8.5 & 1.2 & -24.4 \\ 1.3 & 0 & 3.3 & 29 \end{bmatrix}$

85. \$802.35; \$866.99; \$936.49

LESSON 6.5

TRY THIS (p. 387)
$x \approx 3.21$

TRY THIS (p. 388)
1.72

Exercises

4. 18.75 **5.** 10^{13} times louder **6.** 0.67 **7.** 3.08 **8.** 5.52 **9.** 0.43 **11.** 5.61 **13.** 2.64 **15.** 2.05 **17.** −1.23 **19.** 1.96 **21.** 0.16 **23.** 10 **25.** 4.81 **27.** 3.66 **29.** 2.49 **31.** 2.46 **33.** 0.43 **35.** 0.53 **37.** 0.16 **39.** −3 **41.** −2.01 **43.** −0.89 **45.** 7 **47.** 105 decibels **49.** $10^{11.5}$ times louder **51.** 30 decibels **53.** $10^{12.8}$ times louder **55.** $10^{-14} < [H^+] < 10^{-7}$ **57.** ≈1.3 **59.** ≈10.5 **61.** (5, 2) **63.** (−3, 2) **65.** $g(x) = 2x^2 - 8x - 10$ **67.** $f(x) = -3x^2 - 2x + 1$ **69.** −5 or 3 **71.** exponential growth **73.** exponential growth

LESSON 6.6

TRY THIS (p. 393)
403.429; 0.717

TRY THIS (p. 394)
\$716.66

TRY THIS (p. 395)
about 15.26 years

Exercises

5. 20.086 **6.** 33.115 **7.** \$2250.88; \$2260.23 **8.** 1.609 **9.** 0.916 **10.** about 9.24 years **11.** about 20,066 years old **13.** 8103.084 **15.** 29.964 **17.** 3.154 **19.** 2.320 **21.** 1.284 **23.** 1.946 **25.** 11.513 **27.** −0.006 **29.** 0.805 **31.** undefined **33.** $\ln \frac{1}{2}$, ln 1, e^0, e **35.** log 1.3, ln 1.3, $e^{1.3}$, $10^{1.3}$ **37.** always true **39.** sometimes true **41.** 5 **43.** 25 **45.** 4 **47.** 8 **49.** $\ln 1 = x$ **51.** $\frac{1}{3} \approx \ln 1.40$ **53.** $\ln 1.99 \approx 0.69$ **55.** 7.93 **57.** 0.42 **59.** −9.97 **61.** vertical stretch by a factor of 6 and vertical translation 1 unit up **63.** horizontal translation 1 unit to the left, horizontal compression by a factor of $\frac{1}{4}$, and vertical compression by a factor of 0.25 **65.** vertical stretch by a factor of 3 and vertical translation 1 unit to the left **67.** horizontal compression by a factor of $\frac{1}{5}$, vertical compression by a factor of 0.5, and vertical translation of 2 units down **69.** f to h: reflection across the y-axis and horizontal compression by a factor of $\frac{1}{2}$; g to h: reflection across the y-axis; i to h: horizontal compression by a factor of $\frac{1}{2}$ **71.** The only changes are the following: **a.** no changes **b.** x-intercept: changes **c.** domain: real numbers greater than the value of the translation; asymptotes: x is the value of the translation; x-intercept: value of the translation plus 1 **d.** x-intercept: changes **73a.** \$285,000,000 **b.** during 1999 **75.** No; according to the tests, the chest is only about 700 years old. **77.** almost 11 years and 7 months **79.** 18.7% **81.** $x \geq 5$ *or* $x \leq -5$

−6 −5 −4 −3 −2 −1 0 1 2 3 4 5 6

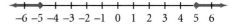

83. $x \geq 6$ *or* $x \leq -\frac{22}{3}$

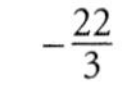

−12 −10 −8 −6 −4 −2 0 2 4 6 8 10 12

85.

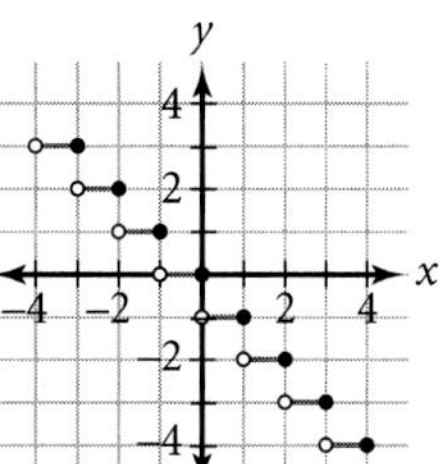

87.

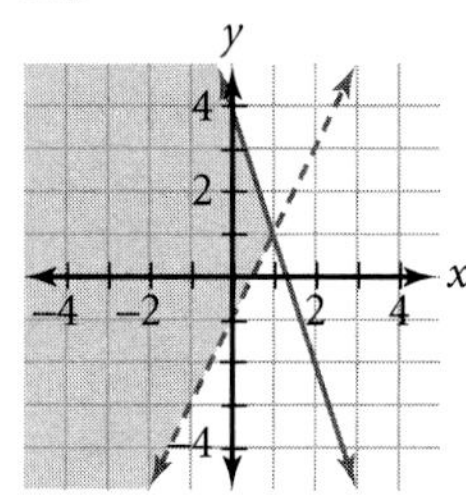

89.

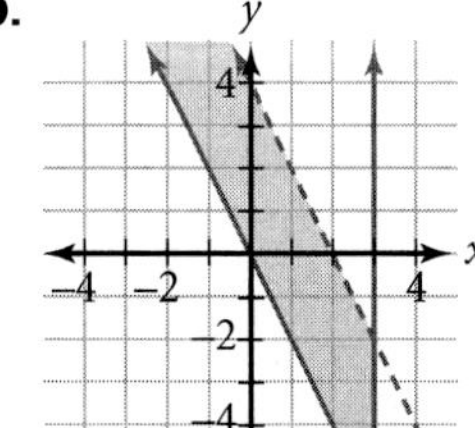

91. $3(x - 1)^2$

LESSON 6.7

TRY THIS (p. 404)

Method 1

$$\log(x + 48) + \log x = 2$$
$$\log[x(x + 48)] = 2$$
$$x(x + 48) = 10^2$$
$$x^2 + 48x - 100 = 0$$
$$(x + 50)(x - 2) = 0$$
$$x = -50 \text{ or } x = 2$$

Check: Let $x = -50$.

$\log(x + 48) + \log x = 2$

$\log(-2) + \log(-50) = 2$ Undefined

Let $x = 2$.

$\log(x + 48) + \log x = 2$

$\log 50 + \log 2 = 2$

$2 = 2$ True

The solution is 2.

Method 2

Graph $y = \log(x + 48) + \log x$ and $y = 2$, and find the point of intersection. The solution is 2.

Exercises

4. 2.82×10^{22} ergs **5.** $x = 100$ **6.** $x \approx 54.78$ **7a.** $T(t) = 70 + 100e^{-0.7133t}$, or $T(t) = 70 + 100(0.7)^{2t}$ **b.** 119°F **c.** about 2.26 hours, or about 2 hours and 16 minutes **9.** 2 **11.** –3 **13.** 4 **15.** $\frac{\ln 20}{2} \approx 1.50$ **17.** 12 **19.** $\frac{\log 75}{2} \approx 0.94$ **21.** 2 **23.** $e^{-\frac{1}{2}} \approx 0.61$ **25.** $10^{-\frac{2}{3}} \approx 0.22$ **27.** 1; $10^{-\sqrt{3}} \approx 0.02$; $10^{\sqrt{3}} \approx 53.96$ **29.** 5.4 **31.** about 31.6 times **33a.** $P(t) = 10{,}000e^{0.46t}$ **b.** 2,500,000 bacteria **c.** 623,000,000 bacteria **35a.** $0.40N_0 = N_0e^{-0.00012t}$ **b.** 7636 years old

37.

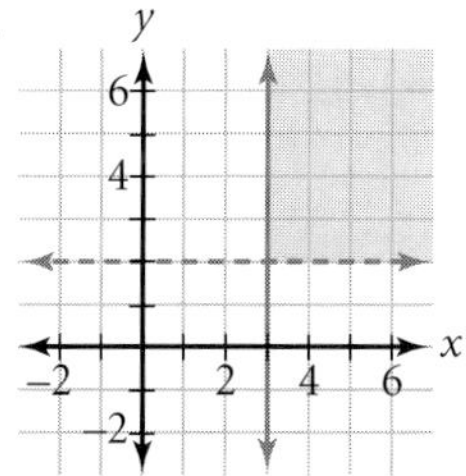

39. $x = 7$ *or* $x = -7$ **41.** $x = 5$ **43.** $x = \frac{1}{2}$ *and* $x = 2$ **45.** ≈13.86 years **47.** 18.7%

CHAPTER REVIEW AND ASSESSMENT

1. $12{,}000(1.08)^t$; about \$38,066 **3.** exponential decay **5.** exponential growth **7.** \$4070.12 **9.** \$4118.28 **11.** $3^3 = 27$ **13.** 2 **15.** 144 **17.** $\frac{1}{8}$ **19.** 7 **21.** 1.9563 **23.** 1.8271 **25.** log 98 **27.** 3 **29.** 100,000,000.00 **31.** no solution **33.** 2.77 **35.** 2.40 **37.** –2.59 **39.** $10^{-2.5}$ **41.** 0.007 **43.** –2.996 **45.** 2 **47.** –1 **49.** about 2 days **51.** 85 decibels

Chapter 7

LESSON 7.1

TRY THIS (p. 425)

a. cubic polynomial

b. quintic trinomial

TRY THIS (p. 425, Ex. 2)

17.6875

TRY THIS (p. 425, Ex. 3)

$4x^3 - 7x^2 + 13x - 12$

TRY THIS (p. 427)

$3x^3 - 11x^2 - 10x - 7$

TRY THIS (p. 428)

a. The graph of this cubic function is S-shaped and has 2 turns.

b. The graph of this quartic function is W-shaped and has 3 turns.

Exercises

4. quartic trinomial **5.** quintic polynomial **6.** 15 **7.** $2x^3 + 3x + 7$ **8.** $3x^3 - 3x^2 + 7x + 5$ **9.** S-shaped with 2 turns **10.** W-shaped with 3 turns **11.** $5x^3 + 2x^2 + 4x + 1$ **13.** $3.3x^8 + 2.7x^3 + 4.1x^2$ **15.** $\frac{x^9}{7} + \frac{x^7}{13} - \frac{2}{3}$ **17.** yes; quintic polynomial **19.** no **21.** yes; quartic trinomial **23.** no **25.** yes; trinomial of degree 6 **27.** no **29.** –17 **31.** –138 **33.** 414 **35.** $8\frac{5}{8}$ **37.** –39.625 **39.** $3x^3 + 4x^2 + 2x + 4$; cubic polynomial **41.** $-2x^4 - 4x^3 + 10x^2 - 5x + 1$; quartic polynomial **43.** $4x^3 + 8x^2 - 7x + 8$; cubic polynomial **45.** $-2x^3 + 5x^2 + 4$; cubic trinomial **47.** $\frac{2}{3}x^3 + \frac{1}{3}x^2 + x + \frac{5}{3}$; cubic polynomial **49.** $2.5x^4 + 7.6x^3 - 3.2x^2 + 7.8x$; quartic polynomial **51.** S-shaped with 2 turns **53.** W-shaped with 3 turns **55.** S-shaped with 2 turns **57.** W-shaped with 3 turns **59.** $a = -2, b = 4, c = 7, d = -7$ **61.** $28x^2 + 54x$ **63.** \$23,996,445 **65.** $\begin{bmatrix} -2 & 5 \\ 5 & 1 \end{bmatrix}$ **67.** $\begin{bmatrix} -2 & 8 \\ 10 & 6 \end{bmatrix}$ **69.** $\begin{bmatrix} -1 & 9 \\ 5 & 1 \end{bmatrix}$ **71.** $\begin{bmatrix} -4 & 7 \\ 5 & -3 \end{bmatrix}$ **73.** $x = -3$ *or* $x = 5$ **75.** $x = -9$ *or* $x = -8$ **77.** $x = -2$ *or* $x = -\frac{1}{3}$ **79.** $x = \frac{-1 - i\sqrt{19}}{5}$ *or* $x = \frac{-1 + i\sqrt{19}}{5}$

LESSON 7.2

TRY THIS (p. 434)

a. maximum of 6.6
minimum of 3.9

b. decreases for all values of x except over the interval of approximately $-0.2 < x < 1.5$, where it increases

TRY THIS (p. 436)

a. falls on the left and rises on the right

b. rises on the left and the right

TRY THIS (p. 437)

$y \approx -0.10x^4 + 2.74x^3 - 26.16x^2 + 100.55x - 112.79$

Exercises

5. maximum of 2.1, minimum of –0.6; increases for all values of x except over the interval of approximately $-1.2 < x < 0.5$, where it decreases **6.** rises on the left and the right **7.** rises on the left and falls on the right

8. $f(x) \approx 0.125x^4 - 0.917x^3 + 1.375x^2 + 1.417x$ **9.** maximum of 5.0, minimum of 1.0 **11.** maximum of 3.2, minimum of −1.2 **13.** no maximum, minimum of 2.0 **15.** maximum of 2.0, minima of −4.3 and −4.3 **17.** maximum of 4.3, minima of 1.9 and 1.0 **19.** maximum of 3.1, minimum of −3.1; increases for all values of x except over the interval of approximately $-1.2 < x < 1.2$, where it decreases **21.** maximum of 2.0, minima of 1.0 and 1.0; decreases for $-\infty < x < -1.0$ and $0.0 < x < 1.0$, increases for $-1.0 < x < 0.0$ and $1.0 < x < \infty$ **23.** maximum of 3.0, no minimum; increases for $-\infty < x < 2.0$, decreases for $2.0 < x < \infty$ **25.** maximum of 4.3, minima of 1.9 and 1.0; decreases for $-\infty < x < -0.5$ and $0.7 < x < 2.1$, increases for $-0.5 < x < 0.7$ and $2.1 < x < \infty$ **27.** maximum of 5.0, minimum of 1.0; increases for all values of x except over the interval of approximately $-1.0 < x < 1.0$, where it decreases **29.** falls on the left and rises on the right **31.** falls on the left and the right **33.** falls on the left and rises on the right **35.** rises on the left and falls on the right **37.** The end behavior of the graph should be rising on the left and the right. The graph shown falls to the left. A more appropriate window may be [−20, 10] by [−3000, 1000].
39. $f(x) \approx 1.17x^4 - 14.33x^3 + 60.83x^2 - 102.67x + 56$
41. $f(x) \approx 0.12x^4 - 2.89x^3 + 23.51x^2 - 76.96x + 84$
43. $f(x) \approx 0.176x^4 - 8.677x^3 + 156.139x^2 - 1199.023x + 3662.963$ **45.** no inverse **47.** $\begin{bmatrix} 5.5 & -2.5 \\ -2 & 1 \end{bmatrix}$
49. $x = -5\sqrt{2}$ *or* $x = 5\sqrt{2}$ **51.** $x = -1$ *or* $x = 3$
53. $x = 2$ **55.** $x > 0$

LESSON 7.3

TRY THIS (p. 441, Ex. 1)
$2x^5 - 6x^4 + 4x^3 - 12x^2$

TRY THIS (p. 441, Ex. 2)
$x^3 - 9x = x(x + 3)(x - 3)$;
$x^3 - x^2 + 2x - 2 = (x - 1)(x^2 + 2)$

TRY THIS (p. 441, Ex. 3)
$x^3 + 1000 = (x + 10)(x^2 - 10x + 100)$;
$x^3 - 125 = (x - 5)(x^2 + 5x + 25)$

TRY THIS (p. 442)
$(-3)^3 - 3(-3)^2 - 6(-3) + 8 = -28$, so $x + 3$ is not a factor.

TRY THIS (p. 443)
$x + 5$

TRY THIS (p. 444, Ex. 6)
$(x + 3)(x - 4)(x + 1)$

TRY THIS (p. 444, Ex. 7)
$P(3) = 94$

Exercises

4. $P(x) = -x^3 + 8x^2 + 20x$ **5.** $x(x - 2)(x - 3)$
6. $(x^2 + 3)(x + 5)$ **7.** $(x - 6)(x^2 + 6x + 36)$
8. $f(-2) = (-2)^3 + 4(-2)^2 + 5(-2) + 2 = 0$; yes
9. $x + 3$ **10.** $(x + 3)(x^2 - 3x - 5)$
11. $(x + 3)(x^2 - 3x - 5)$ **12.** 37 **13.** 37
15. $8x^6 - 4x^5 + 2x^4 + 6x^3$ **17.** $5x^2 + 32x - 21$
19. $2x^4 + 9x^3 + 9x^2 + x + 3$ **21.** $2x^3 - 7x^2 - 10x - 3$
23. $-3x^4 + 15x^3 - 4x^2 + 19x + 5$
25. $-2x^3 + 7x^2 + 3x - 18$ **27.** $2x^3 - 6x - 4$
29. $27x^3 + 54x^2 + 36x + 8$ **31.** $-3x^4 - 7x^3 - 3x^2 + 3x + 2$
33. $\frac{2}{3}x^3 + \frac{1}{6}x^2 + \frac{7}{12}x - \frac{1}{6}$ **35.** $x(x + 2)(x + 4)$
37. $x(x + 3)(x - 1)$ **39.** $x(x - 3)(x + 1)$ **41.** $2x(3x - 5)^2$
43. $(x^2 + 4)(x - 3)$ **45.** $(x^2 - 5)(x - 2)$
47. $(1 + x^2)(1 - x)$ **49.** $(x^2 + 2)(x + 1)$
51. $(x + 10)(x^2 - 10x + 100)$ **53.** $(x^2 + 3)(x^4 - 3x^2 + 9)$
55. $(x - 6)(x^2 + 6x + 36)$ **57.** $(3x - 5)(9x^2 + 15x + 25)$
59. $(4 - x)(16 + 4x + x^2)$ **61.** not a factor **63.** factor
65. factor **67.** factor **69.** factor **71.** $x + 2$
73. $x^2 - x - 6$ **75.** $x - 1$ **77.** $x - 6$ **79.** $x + \frac{1}{3}$
81. $x^2 - \frac{12}{x - 4}$ **83.** $x^2 - 9$ **85.** $x^2 + 2x - 6$
87. $x^2 + x + 1 + \frac{4}{x - 1}$ **89.** $x^3 + 4x^2 + 8x + 13 + \frac{20}{x - 2}$
91. 2 **93.** 6 **95.** 33 **97.** 392 **99.** $k = -18$
101a. $4x^3 - 92x^2 + 448x$ **b.** 560 cubic inches
103. $3 \le x$

−6 −5 −4 −3 −2 −1 0 1 2 3 4 5 6

105. $5(a + b)(a - b)$ **107.** $(n + 4)(n - 3)$
109. $(2x + 1)^2$ **111.** $x \approx 1.51$ **113.** $x \approx 1.61$

LESSON 7.4

TRY THIS (p. 449, Ex. 1)
$x(2x - 3)(x + 2) = 0$
$x = 0$ *or* $x = \frac{3}{2}$ *or* $x = -2$

TRY THIS (p. 449, Ex. 2)

$$\begin{array}{r|rrrr} 2 & 1 & 2 & -4 & -8 \\ & & 2 & 8 & 8 \\ \hline & 1 & 4 & 4 & \boxed{0} \end{array}$$

The quotient is $x^2 + 4x + 4 = (x + 2)^2$.
$x^3 + 2x^2 - 4x - 8 = (x - 2)(x + 2)^2$

TRY THIS (p. 450)
$x = \pm\sqrt{7}$ *and* $x = \pm\sqrt{2}$

Exercises

4. $x = 0$ *or* $x = 4$ *or* $x = -3$ **5.** $y = 0$ *or* $y = -6$ *or* $y = -9$
6. $x = 0, x = \frac{5 + \sqrt{13}}{2}, x = \frac{5 - \sqrt{13}}{2}$
7. $x = 2, x = -1, x = -1$ **8.** $x = \pm 2$ **9.** $x = \pm 1$
10. 4.9 feet **11.** $x = 0, x = 5, x = -7$
13. $y = 0, y = -3, y = 9$ **15.** $x = 0, x = 5, x = 8$

17. $x = 0, x = 5, x = -5$ **19.** $x = 0, x = -5, x = 10$ **21.** $y = 0, y = -9, y = 6$ **23.** $x = 0, x = -11, x = 5$ **25.** $a = 0, a = \frac{7}{3}, a = -4$ **27.** $a = 3, a = -1$ **29.** $x = 1, x = -3$ **31.** $b = 0, b = -4$ **33.** $x = 2, x = -1$ **35.** $x = -3, x = 2, x = 3$ **37.** $n = 2, n = -2$ **39.** $x = \pm\sqrt{2}$ **41.** $y = \pm 3$ **43.** $x = \pm 3$ *or* $x = \pm 2$ **45.** $x = \pm 2\sqrt{2}$ *or* $x = \pm 1$ *or* $x = 0$ **47.** $x = \pm\sqrt{6}$ **49.** $h = \pm\sqrt{3}$ *or* $h = \pm 2$ **51.** There are zeros of f between 8 and 9 (about 8.97) and between 1 and 2 (about 1.45). **53.** There are zeros of f at $a = -3$ and $a = 2$. **55.** There is a zero of m at $n = 2$. **57.** There are zeros of g between -2 and -1 (about -1.49) and between 0 and 1 (about 0.44). **59.** There are zeros of f at $x = 0$, between -1 and 0 (about -0.68), and between 0 and 1 (about 0.88). **61.** $0 < c < 5$ **63.** 2 feet by 6 feet by 3 feet **65.** $x = 9$ *or* $x = -7$ **67.** $x = 4$ *or* $x = 5$ **69.** $9i$ **71.** $6 + 2i$ **73.** 5

75.

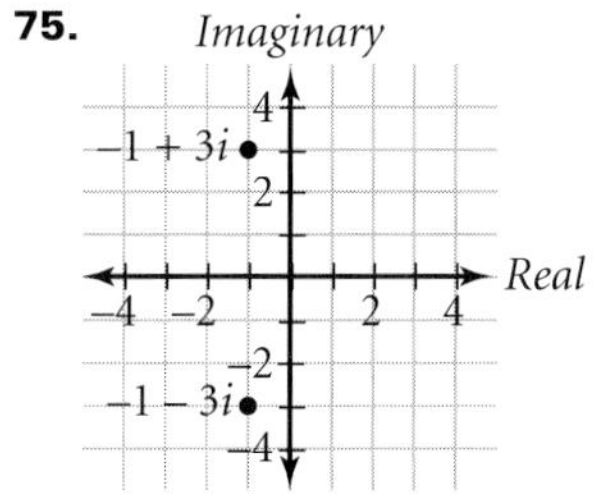

77. $-1 \pm i\sqrt{6}$ **79.** $\frac{3}{2} \pm \frac{3\sqrt{3}}{2}i$

LESSON 7.5

TRY THIS (p. 459)
one rational root, $\frac{5}{3}$

TRY THIS (p. 460, Ex. 2)
The zeros are 2, $2 + \sqrt{5}$, and $2 - \sqrt{5}$.

TRY THIS (p. 460, Ex. 3)
The zeros are 5, $2 + 5i$, and $2 - 5i$.

TRY THIS (p. 463)
$P(x) = -2(x - 1)(x^2 - 6x + 25)$
$= -2x^3 + 14x^2 - 62x + 50$

Exercises

5. $5, -\frac{5}{2}$, and $\frac{1}{6}$ **6.** $2, -\frac{5}{2} + \frac{\sqrt{17}}{2}$, and $-\frac{5}{2} - \frac{\sqrt{17}}{2}$
7. $3, -\frac{1}{2} + \frac{1}{2}i$, and $-\frac{1}{2} - \frac{1}{2}i$ **8.** $x = 2$
9. $P(x) = -\frac{2}{75}(x - 3)^2(x^2 - 6x + 25)$
$= -\frac{2}{75}x^4 + \frac{8}{25}x^3 - \frac{28}{15}x^2 + \frac{136}{25}x - 6$
11. $6, -\frac{3}{2}$, and $\frac{1}{3}$ **13.** $-2, 2$, and $\frac{2}{3}$ **15.** -1
17. $-7, -\frac{2}{5}$, and $\frac{1}{2}$ **19.** $-\frac{3}{5}, -\frac{1}{2}$, and $\frac{2}{5}$
21. $3, 6, -\frac{1}{5}$, and $\frac{3}{2}$ **23.** $\frac{1}{3}, -2\sqrt{2}$, and $2\sqrt{2}$
25. $-8, \frac{\sqrt{5}}{3}$, and $-\frac{\sqrt{5}}{3}$ **27.** 5, $12i$, and $-12i$
29. 5, $3i$, and $-3i$ **31.** 3, $2i\sqrt{3}$, and $-2i\sqrt{3}$
33. $-5, 1, 2i$, and $-2i$ **35.** $x = 2$ **37.** $x = 0, x = -1.65$
39. $x = -2.14, x = -0.66, x = 0.66, x = 2.14$
41. $P(x) = 2(x - 2)(x - 3)$
$= 2x^2 - 10x + 12$
43. $P(x) = 5(x + 2)(x - 1)(x - 2)$
$= 5x^3 - 5x^2 - 20x + 20$
45. $P(x) = \frac{1}{4}(x - 1)^2(x - 2)^2$
$= \frac{1}{4}x^4 - \frac{3}{2}x^3 + \frac{13}{4}x^2 - 3x + 1$
47. $P(x) = (x - 1)(x - i)(x + i)$
$= x^3 - x^2 + x - 1$
49. $P(x) = \frac{3}{50}(x - 1)(x - 2)(x - 5i)(x + 5i)$
$= \frac{3}{50}x^4 - \frac{9}{50}x^3 + \frac{81}{50}x^2 - \frac{9}{2}x + 3$
51. Because $P(\sqrt{3}) = (\sqrt{3})^2 - 3 = 3 - 3 = 0$, $\sqrt{3}$ is a root of P. By the Rational Root Theorem, if $\sqrt{3} = \frac{p}{q}$, where p and q are integers, then p is a factor of -3 and q is a factor of 1. However, the only possible values of $\frac{p}{q}$ are ± 3 and ± 1. Therefore, $\sqrt{3}$ is irrational. **53.** about 143 seconds **55.** $-2 - 5x$ **57.** 24 **59.** 29 **61.** axis of symmetry: $x = -\frac{5}{4}$; vertex: $\left(-\frac{5}{4}, -\frac{9}{8}\right)$ **63.** The graph of f falls on the left and rises on the right. It has a turning point at $(1, -3)$ and a zero at about $(2.2, 0)$. **65.** $3x^3 + 3x^2 - x + 1$

CHAPTER REVIEW AND ASSESSMENT

1. cubic polynomial **3.** quartic polynomial **5.** 6; 3 **7.** -6; -21 **9.** $14x^3 - 6x^2 + 10x - 2$; cubic polynomial **11.** The leading coefficient is negative and the degree is even, so the graph falls on both sides. **13.** The leading coefficient is positive and the degree is even, so the graph rises on both sides.
15. The graph of f has a local minimum of 8 at $x = 1$, is decreasing when $x < 1$, and is increasing when $x > 1$. **17.** The graph of f has a local maximum of about 3.6 at $a = -1\frac{2}{3}$ and a local minimum of -1 at $a = 0$. The graph is increasing when $a < -1\frac{2}{3}$ and when $a > 0$. The graph is decreasing when $-1\frac{2}{3} < a < 0$. **19.** $-10x^7 + 2x^6 - 2x^5 + 6x^4 + 12x^3$
21. $x(x + 5)(x - 1)$ **23.** $(x - 5)(x^2 + 5x + 25)$
25. factor **27.** $x^2 + 8x + 15$ **29.** $x^2 + 6x - 16$
31. $x = \pm 2$ **33.** $x = \pm 1$ *or* $x = \pm 3$ **35.** $x = \pm\sqrt{6}$ *or* $x = 1$
37. $x = 1$ *or* $x = -2$ **39.** -2 **41.** 2 and 5 **43.** $-\frac{2}{5}$ and $\frac{1}{3}$
45. 2
47. $P(x) = (x - 2)(x + 1)^2(x - 3)$
$= x^4 - 3x^3 - 3x^2 + 7x + 6$
49. $P(x) = -(x - 3)^2[x - (2 + i)][x - (2 - i)]$
$= x^4 + 10x^3 - 38x^2 + 66x - 45$ **51.** $\approx 8.3\%$

Chapter 8

LESSON 8.1

TRY THIS (p. 482)
$k = 780$; $y = \frac{780}{x}$; 520; $173.3\overline{3}$; 97.5; 62.4; ≈55.7

TRY THIS (p. 483, Ex. 2)
a. $V = 12wh$; volume varies jointly as the width, w, and the height, h; $k = 12$ **b.** 96 cubic inches

TRY THIS (p. 483, Ex. 3)
a. $A = \pi r^2$; area varies directly as the square of r; $k = \pi$ **b.** ≈7.07, ≈19.63, ≈38.48, and ≈63.62 sq units

TRY THIS (p. 484)
about 8.5 miles per hour

Exercises
7. $k = 1980$; $y = \frac{1980}{x}$; 1320, 990, 792, 660, ≈565.71 **8.** $V = 2.5\ell h$; volume varies jointly as length, ℓ, and height, h; $k = 2.5$ **9.** 40 cubic centimeters **10.** $A = 3x^2$; area varies directly as the square of the side, x; $k = 3$ **11.** 6.75, 18.75, 36.75, 60.75, 90.75, and 126.75 sq units **12.** about 20.8 miles per hour. **13.** $y = \frac{324}{x}$; 108, 81, 64.8, 54, ≈46.3 **15.** $y = \frac{4}{x}$; 0.8, 1, ≈1.3, 2, 4 **17.** $y = \frac{112}{x}$; 11.2, ≈7.47, 5.6 **19.** $y = \frac{200}{x}$; 2, 0.2, 0.02 **21.** $y = 9xz$; −108 **23.** $y = \frac{10}{9}xz$; 60 **25.** $y = \frac{3}{4}xz$; 283.5 **27.** $y = 10xz$; 10^8 **29.** $z = \frac{2xy}{w}$; −21 **31.** $z = \frac{6xy}{w}$; 216 **33.** $z = \frac{2xy}{7w}$; $\frac{8}{9} \approx 0.89$ **35.** $x = 9.6$ **37.** $y = 2.5$ **39.** $y = 6$ *or* $y = -6$ **41.** If $x_1y_1 = k$ and $x_2y_2 = k$, then by substitution, $x_1y_1 = x_2y_2$. Divide both sides by x_2y_1, which results in $\frac{x_1}{x_2} = \frac{y_2}{y_1}$. Multiply both sides by y_1, which results in $y_2 = y_1\left(\frac{x_1}{x_2}\right)$ **43.** The distance remains the same, 6 feet. **45.** 5625 calories **47.** $\frac{1}{x}$ **49.** $\frac{y^2}{x^2}$ **51.** $\frac{1}{x^{18}}$ **53.** vertex: (−1, −4); axis of symmetry: $x = -1$ **55.** vertex: (0, 2); axis of symmetry: $x = 0$ **57.** vertex: $\left(\frac{3}{4}, \frac{7}{8}\right)$; axis of symmetry: $t = \frac{3}{4}$ **59.** 3 **61.** The graph rises on the left and the right.

LESSON 8.2

TRY THIS (p. 490)
all real numbers except −3 and 1

TRY THIS (p. 491)
$x = -2$ and $x = -3$

TRY THIS (p. 493)
$x = -3$ and $x = 4$; $y = 2$

TRY THIS (p. 494)
hole when $x = -3$; vertical asymptote: $x = 1$; no horizontal asymptote

Exercises
5. $C(x) = \frac{13.5}{90 + x}$; 5.6% **6.** all real numbers except $x = 3$ and $x = 4$ **7.** no holes; vertical asymptotes: $x = -\frac{3}{2}$ and $x = \frac{3}{2}$; horizontal asymptote: $y = 0$ **8.** no holes; vertical asymptotes: $x = -3$ and $x = 3$; horizontal asymptote: $y = 2$ **9.** hole when $x = 3$; vertical asymptote: $x = 2$; horizontal asymptote: $y = 1$
10.

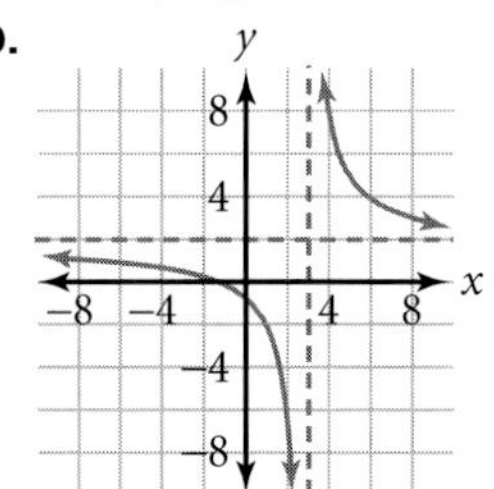

11. a rational function; all real numbers except $x = \frac{7}{2}$ **13.** not a rational function because the numerator is not a polynomial **15.** not a rational function because the numerator is not a polynomial **17.** no holes; vertical asymptote at $x = 2$; horizontal asymptote at $y = 3$ **19.** hole when $x = 2$; vertical asymptote at $x = 2$; horizontal asymptote at $y = 1$ **21.** hole when $x = 4$; vertical asymptote $x = 1$; horizontal asymptote: $y = 1$ **23.** domain of all real numbers except $x = -1$; vertical asymptote: $x = -1$; horizontal asymptote: $y = 1$; no holes

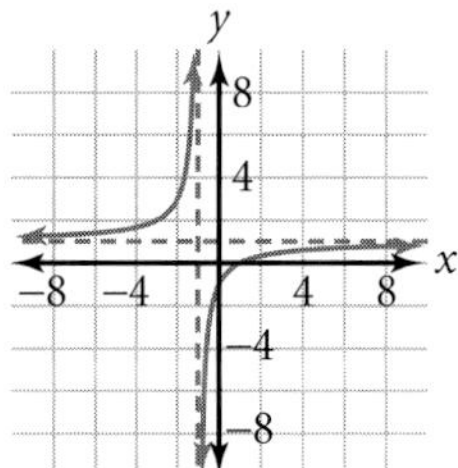

25. domain of all real numbers except $x = -2$; no vertical asymptote; no horizontal asymptote; hole when $x = -2$

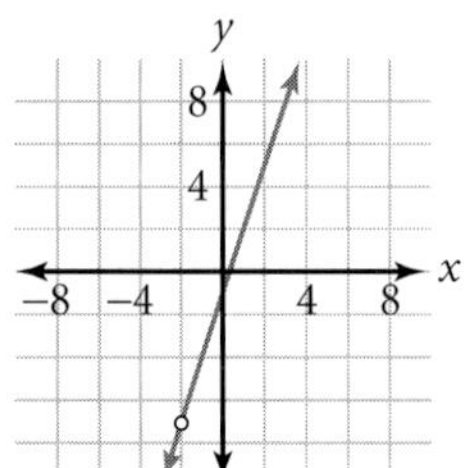

27. domain of all real numbers except $x = -2$ and $x = 2$; vertical asymptotes: $x = -2$ and $x = 2$; horizontal asymptote: $y = 0$; no holes

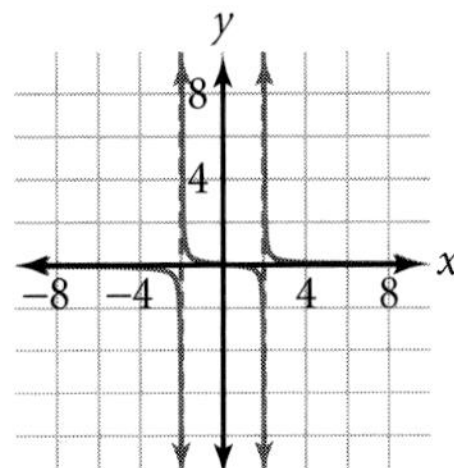

29. domain of all real numbers; no vertical asymptotes; horizontal asymptote: $y = 0$; no holes

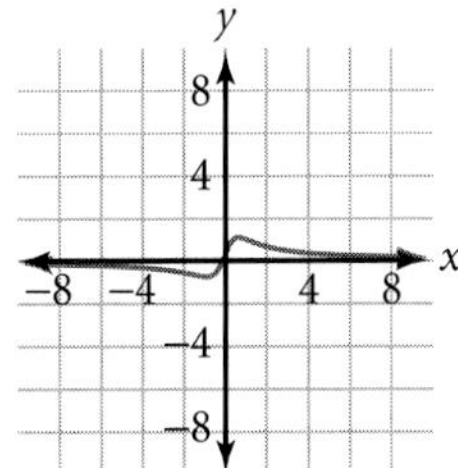

31. domain of all real numbers except $x = 1$ and $x = 6$; vertical asymptotes: $x = 1$ and $x = 6$; no horizontal asymptote; no holes

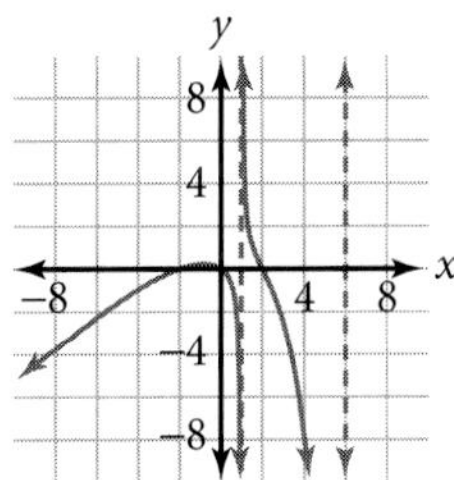

33. domain of all real numbers except $x = 0$ and $x = 4$; vertical asymptote: $x = 4$; horizontal asymptote: $y = 0$; hole when $x = 0$

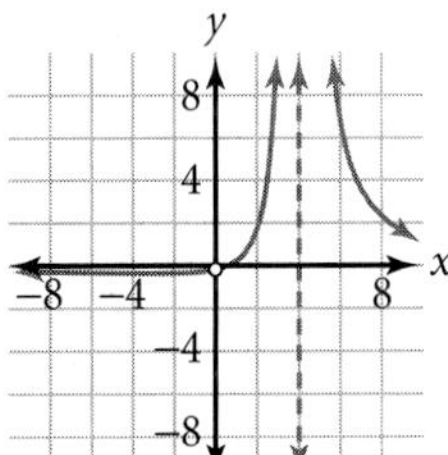

35. $f(x) = \frac{3x}{x-2}$ **37.** $f(x) = \frac{3x^3}{2x^3 - 2x}$ **39.** $f(x) = \frac{x^3 - 2x^2}{x^2 - 2x}$

41a. $c > \frac{9}{4}$; if $b^2 - 4ac = 9 - 4c < 0$, then $x^2 - 3x + c = 0$ has no solutions and there are no vertical asymptotes. **b.** $c = \frac{9}{4}$; if $x^2 - 3x + c = 0 - 4c = 0$, then $x^2 - 3x + c = 0$ has 1 solution and there is 1 vertical asymptote. **c.** $c < \frac{9}{4}$; if $x^2 - 3x + c = 0 - 4c > 0$, then $x^2 - 3x + c = 0$ has 2 solutions and there are 2 vertical asymptotes. **43a.** $R(x) = \frac{2}{x}$ **b.** all real numbers greater than 0; all real numbers greater than 0; all real numbers greater than 0

45a. $T(x) = 11.45x + 250$

b. $C(x) = \frac{T(x)}{x} = \frac{11.45x + 250}{x}$ **47.** $x < \frac{4}{5}$ *or* $x > \frac{8}{5}$

49. $-\frac{4}{5} \leq x \leq 2$ **51.** $-36x^2 + 24x$ **53.** $-5x^2 + 49x - 36$

55. $9x^2 - 16$ **57.** $3x(x - 2)$ **59.** $(3x + 7)(3x - 7)$

61. $(x + 6)^2$

LESSON 8.3

TRY THIS (p. 498)
$\frac{b+7}{b-1}$

TRY THIS (p. 499, Ex. 2)
$\frac{4}{49a^2}$

TRY THIS (p. 499, Ex. 3)
$\frac{x^2 - 3x - 10}{x^2 - 6x + 9}$

TRY THIS (p. 500)
$x + 3$

TRY THIS (p. 501)
$\frac{x^2 - x - 6}{x - 2}$

Exercises

4. $\frac{x+5}{x-5}$ **5.** $8x$ **6.** $\frac{x+2}{x-3}$ **7.** $\frac{x-1}{x+4}$ **8.** $\frac{2x^2+2}{x^2+8x+15}$

9. $4x + 4$ **11.** $5x^2$ **13.** $\frac{x-9}{x+3}$ **15.** $\frac{5}{2x^5}$ **17.** $\frac{x+1}{x-1}$

19. $\frac{2x^2 - 2x}{x^2 - x - 6}$ **21.** $\frac{x^2 + 2x + 1}{x^2 + 2x - 3}$ **23.** $\frac{8x^2 - 18}{3x + 2}$

25. $\frac{a-b}{a+b}$ **27.** $3y$ **29.** $\frac{(x+2)^3}{(x+3)^3}$ **31.** $\frac{x^2 - 4x + 4}{x^2 - 2x + 1}$

33. $\frac{x^2}{x+1}$ **35.** 3 **37.** $\frac{x+3}{x}$ **39.** 1 **41.** $\frac{x-9}{x-2}$ **43.** $\frac{x-y}{x+y}$

45a. $V = \ell \times w \times h$; $V = (20 - 2x)(16 - 2x)x$; $V = x(20 - 2x)(16 - 2x)$
b. Total Area $A = (20 - 2x)(16 - 2x) + 2x(20 - 2x) + 2x(16 - 2x) = 320 - 40x - 32x + 4x^2 + 40x - 4x^2 + 32x - 4x^2 = 320 - 4x^2$ **c.** $R(x) = \frac{x^3 - 18x^2 + 80x}{80 - x^2}$
d. $R(x)$ increases **47a.** $a = \frac{d_2t_1 - d_1t_2}{t_1t_2(t_2 - t_1)}$
b. feet per second per second **49.** $y = -5x + 20$

51.

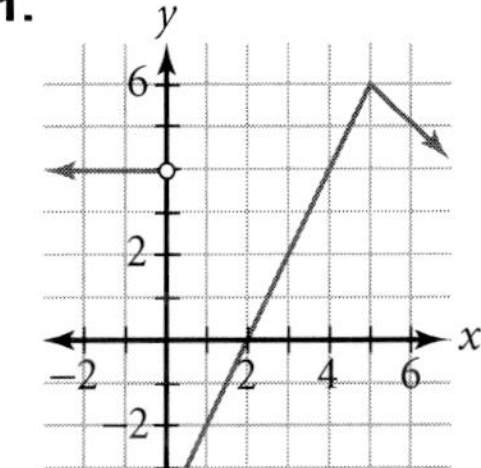

53. $3(4x^2 - x + 2)$ **55.** $\frac{8}{13} - \frac{1}{13}i$ **57.** $\frac{1}{2} - \frac{1}{2}i$

59. $3x^4 - 7x^3 - 4x^2 + 12x$ **61.** $(x - 1)(x^2 + x + 1)$

63. $x(x^2 - 6x - 8)$ **65.** $\frac{4}{x}$ **67.** $\frac{11}{6x}$

LESSON 8.4

TRY THIS (p. 505)
a. $\frac{5x+4}{2x-1}$ **b.** 2

TRY THIS (p. 506)
$\frac{x^2-5x-5}{(x+5)(x-5)}=\frac{x^2-5x-5}{x^2-25}$

TRY THIS (p. 507, Ex. 3)
$\frac{5x+12}{x(x-2)(x+2)}=\frac{5x+12}{x^3-4x}$

TRY THIS (p. 507, Ex. 4)
$\frac{2a^2}{(a+1)(a-1)(a^2+1)}=\frac{2a^2}{a^4-1}$

Exercises

4. $\frac{3x+2}{x-1}$ **5.** 2 **6.** $\frac{4x+8}{(x+1)(x-1)}=\frac{4x+8}{x^2-1}$
7. $\frac{-3x^2}{(2x-1)(x-1)}=\frac{-3x^2}{2x^2-3x+1}$ **8.** $\frac{t}{t-1}$ **9.** 43.9 mph
11. 4 **13.** $\frac{-x+20}{9}$ **15.** $\frac{2x^2+5x+3}{(x+3)^2}=\frac{2x^2+5x+3}{x^2+6x+9}$
17. $\frac{-4x-16}{(x+2)(x-2)}=\frac{-4x-16}{x^2-4}$
19. $\frac{37x-11}{(3x-5)(2x+3)}=\frac{37x-11}{6x^2-x-15}$
21. $\frac{-3x^2+3x-2}{(2x-1)(x-1)}=\frac{-3x^2+3x-2}{2x^2-3x+1}$
23. $\frac{x^2-2x+3}{(x-1)^2}=\frac{x^2-2x+3}{x^2-2x+1}$
25. $\frac{3x}{2x-1}$ **27.** $\frac{2x+1}{x-1}$ **29.** $\frac{x^2+4x+1}{(x-1)(x+1)}=\frac{x^2+4x+1}{x^2-1}$
31. x **33.** $\frac{b-a}{b+a}$ **35.** $\frac{6}{x-1}$
37. $\frac{x^2+x+16}{(x-3)(x+4)}=\frac{x^2+x+16}{x^2+x-12}$
39. $\frac{4ab}{(a-b)^2(a+b)^2}=\frac{4ab}{a^4-2a^2b^2+b^4}$
41. $\frac{2r^2+5rs+2s^2}{(2r-s)(2r+s)}=\frac{2r^2+5rs+2s}{4r^2-s^2}$ **43.** $B=1$ and $D=-2$
45. $A=\frac{1}{6}$, $C=\frac{5}{6}$, and $D=-\frac{7}{3}$ **47a.** ≈2.45 ohms
b. $R_T=\frac{R_AR_BR_C}{R_BR_C+R_AR_C+R_AR_B}$ **49.** ≈48.8 mph
51. Distributive Property **53.** –7; 0; $x=\frac{3}{2}\pm\frac{i\sqrt{7}}{2}$
55. 121; 2; $x=\frac{3}{2}$ *or* $x=-4$ **57.** $\log_2\frac{32}{8}$, or $\log_2 4$; 2
59. $x=-1$ *or* $x=3$ *or* $x=4$
61. $x=2$ *or* $x=-1$ *or* $x=-3$

LESSON 8.5

TRY THIS (p. 513)
$x=-1$ or $x=3$

TRY THIS (p. 514)
$x=-\frac{1}{2}$

TRY THIS (p. 515)
$x>-2$ or $x<-\frac{7}{2}$

TRY THIS (p. 516)
$x<1$

Exercises

4. Rachel must swim at about 3.6 miles per hour, bicycle at about 6(3.6), or 21.6, miles per hour, and run at about 5 + 3.6, or 8.6, miles per hour.
5. $x=-1$ *or* $x=1$ **6.** no solution **7.** $x<0$
8. $-3<x<-2$ **9.** $x=12$ **11.** $n=0$ **13.** $z=8$
15. $y=-7$ **17.** $x=2$ **19.** $x=-\frac{1}{10}\pm\frac{\sqrt{41}}{10}$
21. $x=3\pm\sqrt{17}$ **23.** no solution **25.** $b=-2$ **27.** no solution **29.** $0<x<\frac{2}{3}$ **31.** $0<x<\frac{1}{2}$ **33.** $2<x<\frac{9}{2}$
35. $-2\le x<0$ **37.** $-\frac{2}{3}<x<4$ **39.** $x<0$ *or* $x\ge 1.3$
41. $-2.1\le x<0$ *or* $0<x\le 2.1$
43. $-1\le x<-\frac{1}{2}$ *or* $x\ge 0$
45. $a<-3$ *or* $-2\le a<0$ *or* $a\ge 5$ **47.** always
49. never **51.** sometimes **53.** all real numbers except $x=1$ **55.** $2.5\le w\le 10$ and $\ell=w+5$; thus, $7.5\le\ell\le 15$. **57.** about 4530 km **59.** 1 **61.** 3
63. {(–4, –1), (–3, –2), (–2, –3), (–1, 0)}; function
65. $h^{-1}(x)=5-2x$; function **67.** a horizontal translation of 2 units to the right **69.** a vertical stretch by a factor of 3 and then a vertical translation of 5 units down **71.** a horizontal translation 4 units to the right, a reflection across the y-axis, a vertical stretch by a factor of 2, and a vertical translation 6 units down

LESSON 8.6

TRY THIS (p. 521)
$x\ge-\frac{18}{5}$ or $x\ge-3.6$

TRY THIS (p. 522)
a. a vertical stretch by a factor of 3, a vertical translation 2 units down, and a horizontal translation 1 unit to the right **b.** a horizontal compression by a factor of $\frac{1}{2}$, a vertical translation 3 units up, and a horizontal translation $\frac{1}{2}$ unit to the left

TRY THIS (p. 523)
Interchange the roles of x and y.
$y=x^2+3x-4\rightarrow x=y^2+3y-4$
$y=\frac{-3\pm\sqrt{25+4x}}{2}$

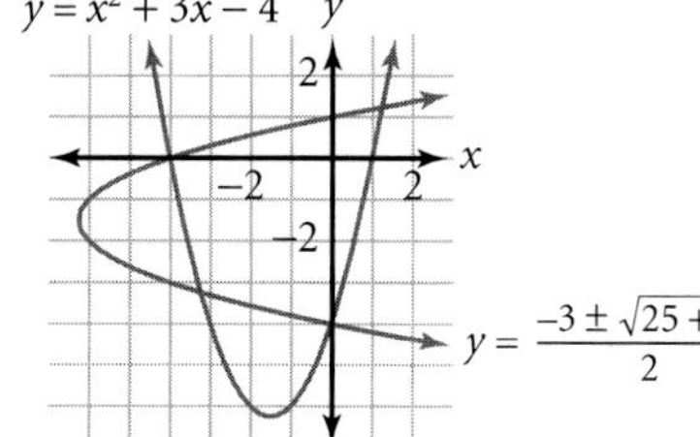

TRY THIS (p. 524)
0, 26

Exercises

4. $x \le \frac{3}{2}$ **5.** a horizontal translation 1 unit to the right, a vertical stretch by a factor of 2, and a vertical translation 2 units down **6.** a horizontal translation $\frac{1}{2}$ unit to the left, a horizontal compression by a factor of $\frac{1}{2}$, and a vertical translation 2 units up

7. $y = \frac{1 \pm \sqrt{1 + 16x}}{8}$

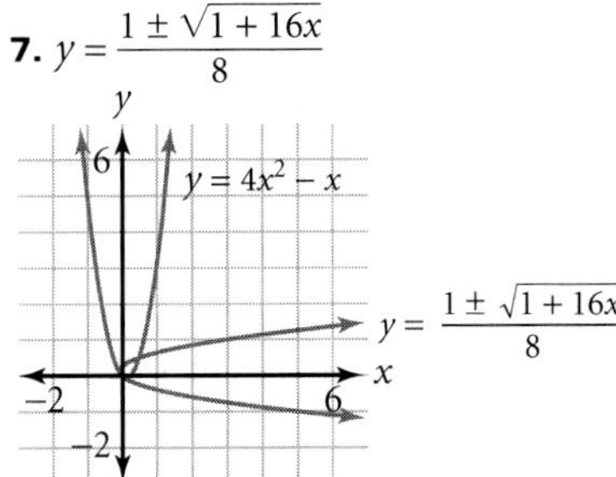

8. 0.4 second; 0.5 second; 0.6 second **9.** −5 **10.** −35 **11.** $x \ge -2$ **13.** $x \ge 2$ **15.** $x \le -\frac{1}{3}$ **17.** $x \le -5$ *or* $x \ge 5$ **19.** $x \le -3$ *or* $x \ge -2$ **21.** $x \le -4$ *or* $x \ge \frac{3}{2}$
23. $x \le \frac{1}{2}$ *or* $x \ge \frac{5}{3}$
25. $y = \pm\sqrt{x + 1}$

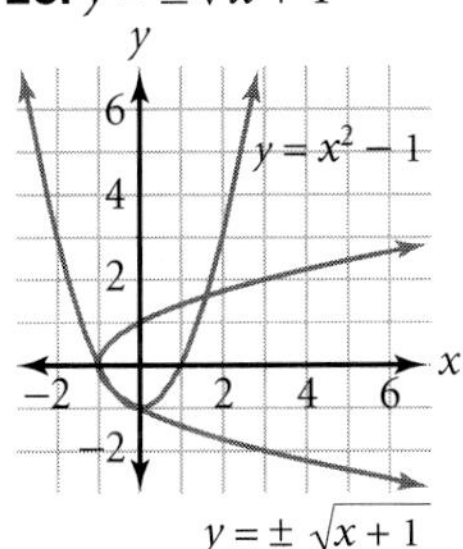

27. $y = \frac{-1 \pm \sqrt{1 + 12x}}{6}$

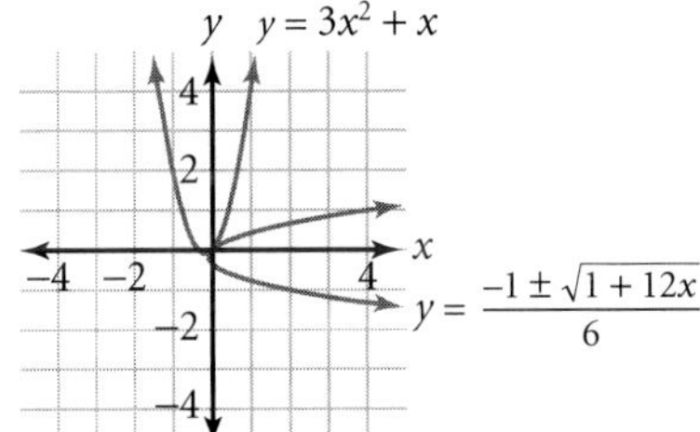

29. $y = -2 \pm \sqrt{x}$

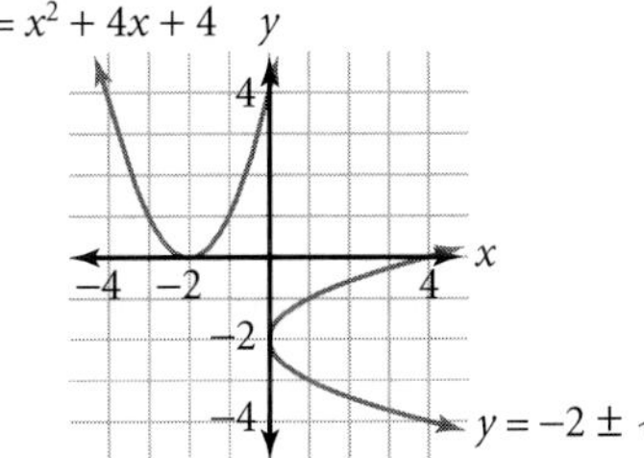

31. $y = 1 \pm \sqrt{x}$

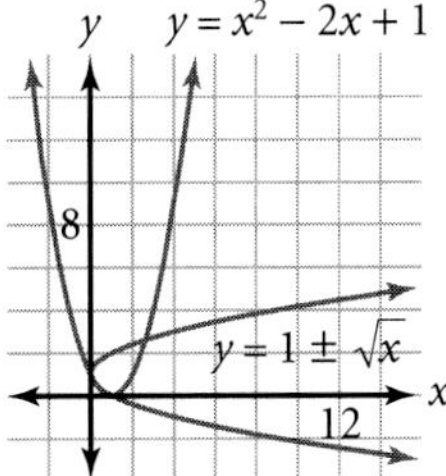

33. $y = \frac{3 \pm \sqrt{25 - 4x}}{2}$

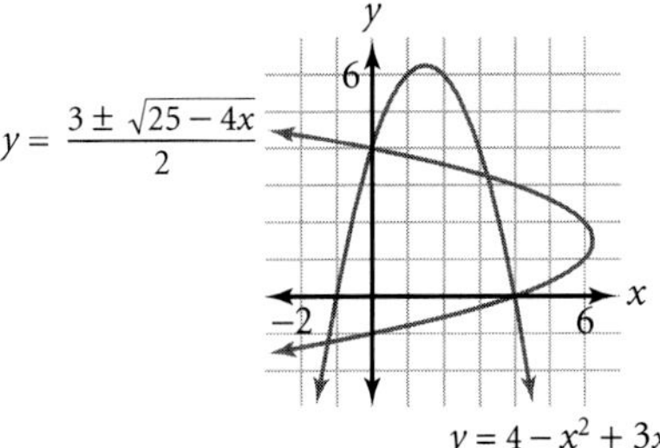

35. $y = \frac{-1 \pm \sqrt{9 + 8x}}{4}$

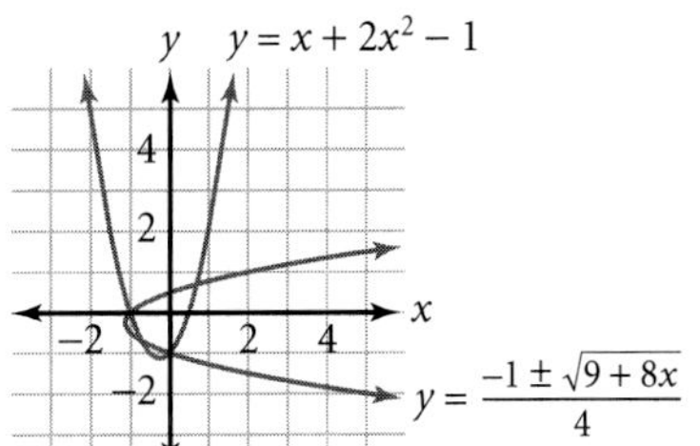

37. 32 **39.** 2 **41.** 8 **43.** −15 **45.** 9999 **47.** 648 **49.** 3 **51.** −12 **53.** $y = -\frac{b}{2a}$
55. a horizontal translation 4 units to the right

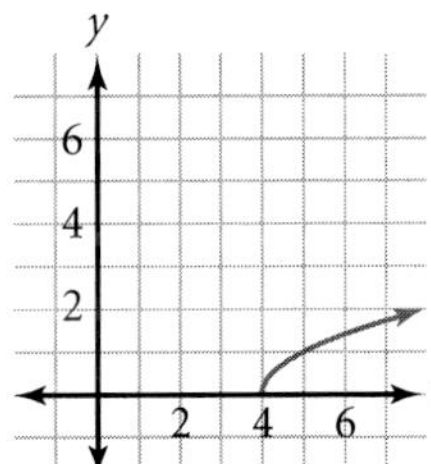

57. a horizontal translation 4 units to the right, a vertical compression by a factor of $\frac{1}{5}$, and a reflection across the x-axis

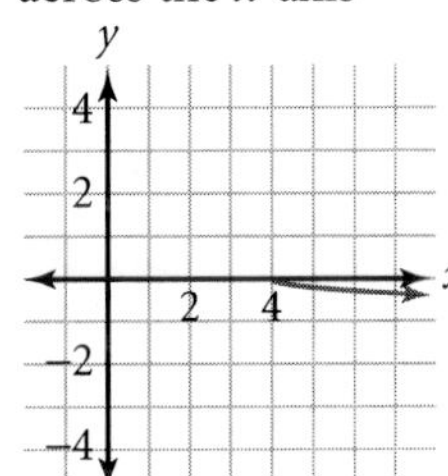

59. a horizontal translation 2 units to the left and a vertical translation 5 units up

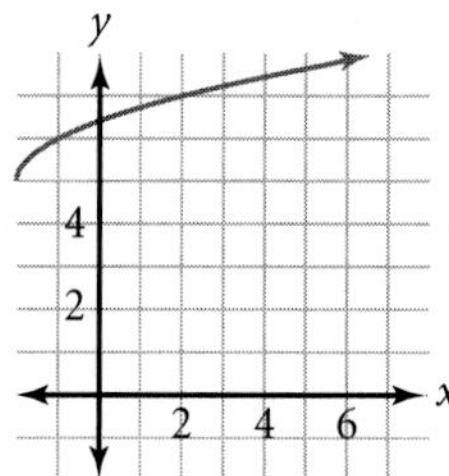

61. a horizontal translation 3 units to the left, a vertical translation 2 units down, and a vertical stretch by a factor of 2

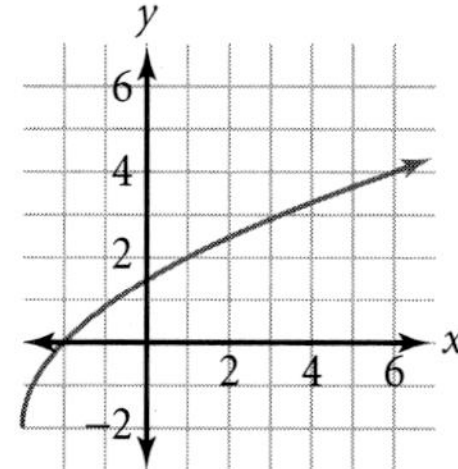

63. a horizontal translation 2 units to the left, a vertical compression by a factor of $\frac{1}{3}$, and a vertical translation 3 units up

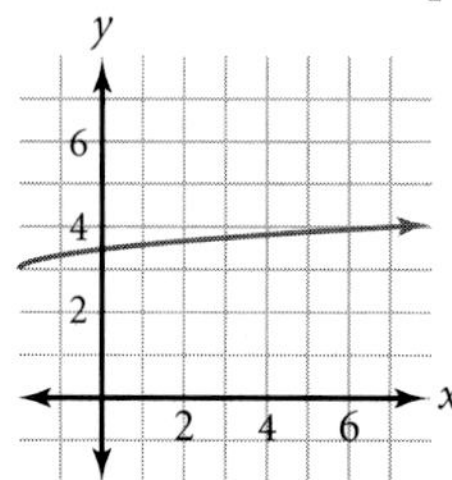

65a. $T \approx \frac{29{,}250 \pm \sqrt{5(12{,}500 + 29E)}}{290}$ **b.** 99°C or 103°C; choose 99°C because the boiling point is lower at higher elevations. **67.** $4y^{16}$ **69.** $5^{-1}x^2y^{-4}$ or $\frac{x^2}{5y^4}$ **71.** $-\frac{1}{4m^2}$ **73.** $-4 + 7i$ **75.** $-7 + 3i$ **77.** $\log 2 + \log x$ **79.** $\log x + \log z - \log y$

LESSON 8.7

TRY THIS (p. 529)
a. $8a^2|c|\sqrt{bc}$ **b.** $-2fg\sqrt[5]{fh^2}$

TRY THIS (p. 530)
a. $3rs^2\sqrt[3]{r^2s}$ **b.** $3x\sqrt{2y}$

TRY THIS (p. 531, Ex. 1)
$(\sqrt[5]{2})^3 = \sqrt[5]{2^3} = \sqrt[5]{8}$
a. $3 + 11\sqrt{2}$ **b.** $10 - 5\sqrt{5}$

TRY THIS (p. 531, Ex. 2)
a. $-162 + 38\sqrt{5}$ **b.** $77 - 23\sqrt{6}$

TRY THIS (p. 532)
a. $\frac{3\sqrt{5}}{5}$ **b.** $-6 - 2\sqrt{2}$

Exercises
4. $8|b|c^2\sqrt{2ac}$ **5.** $-3xy^3\sqrt[3]{2x^2}$ **6.** $9a^2b\sqrt[3]{3b}$ **7.** $2|x|\sqrt{5}$ **8.** $10\sqrt[3]{3}$, or about 14.42 feet **9.** $18\sqrt{2}$ **10.** $20 - 5\sqrt{3}$ **11.** $-96 + 21\sqrt{5}$ **12.** $\frac{2\sqrt{7}}{7}$ **13.** $\frac{-15 - 3\sqrt{3}}{22}$ **15.** $8\sqrt{2}$ **17.** $-2\sqrt[3]{6}$ **19.** $3|x|\sqrt{2x}$ **21.** $-3x^2\sqrt[3]{3x}$ **23.** $5|a|b^2\sqrt{2a}$ **25.** $5r^2t\sqrt[3]{2rs^2}$ **27.** $2|x|\sqrt[4]{x^2}$ **29.** $2x^3\sqrt{2}$ **31.** $5x$ **33.** $12r^2s^3\sqrt{rs}$ **35.** $4y\sqrt[3]{y}$ **37.** $2x$ **39.** $2x\sqrt[4]{4x^2}$, or $2x\sqrt{2x}$ **41.** $3x^3y^5\sqrt{7y}$ **43.** $4yt\sqrt[3]{y^2c}$ **45.** $6 + 2\sqrt{3}$ **47.** $2 - \sqrt{2}$ **49.** $-1 - 10\sqrt{2}$ **51.** $-12 - \sqrt{3}$ **53.** $1 + \sqrt{3}$ **55.** $12 - 10\sqrt{3}$ **57.** $11 + 6\sqrt{2}$ **59.** $-16 + 8\sqrt{3}$ **61.** $-86 + 14\sqrt{3}$ **63.** $16 + 2\sqrt{2}$ **65.** $x + 7 - 6\sqrt{2}$ **67.** $24 - 14\sqrt{6}$ **69.** $30 - 16\sqrt{3}$ **71.** $40 - 8\sqrt{6}$ **73.** $\frac{2\sqrt{5}}{5}$ **75.** $\frac{2\sqrt{6}}{3}$ **77.** $\sqrt{3}$ **79.** $\frac{\sqrt{15}}{15}$ **81.** 2 **83.** $\frac{\sqrt{6}}{2}$ **85.** $\frac{16 - 4\sqrt{2}}{7}$ **87.** $6 - 3\sqrt{3}$ **89.** $2\sqrt{7} - 2\sqrt{2}$ **91.** $-\frac{3x + 5x\sqrt{2} + 82 + 123\sqrt{2}}{41}$ **93.** $6\sqrt{2}$, or about 8.49 miles **95a.** $s = 2\sqrt{3d}$, or $\approx 3.5\sqrt{d}$ mph **b.** about 49 mph **c.** The speed is not double; ≈69 mph. **97.** $x = \pm 4$ **99.** $(x + 5)(x + 1)$ **101.** $(x + 5)(x - 8)$ **103.** $x = 5$ *or* $x = 6$ **105.** $x = -6$ *or* $x = -3$ **107.** $x = -3$ *or* $x = 6$ **109.** $x \le 5$ **113.** $\frac{2 - 2\sqrt[3]{x} + 2\sqrt[3]{x^2}}{1 + x}$

LESSON 8.8

TRY THIS (p. 537, Ex. 1)
$x = \frac{5}{2}$

TRY THIS (p. 537, Ex. 2)
$x = 1$

TRY THIS (p. 538)
$x = \frac{5 - \sqrt{5}}{2}$, or ≈ 1.38

TRY THIS (p. 539)
no real solutions

TRY THIS (p. 540)
Square both sides of the equation, isolate the radical expression, and then square both sides again. Check answers for extraneous solutions.
$\frac{3}{2} \le x < 14$

TRY THIS (p. 541)
$x < -5.4$ *or* $-0.6 < x < 9.0$

Exercises
4. $x = \frac{445}{18}$, or $24\frac{13}{18}$ **5.** $x = 2$ **6.** $x = \frac{1 \pm \sqrt{13}}{2}$, or $x \approx 2.30$ *or* $x \approx -1.30$ **7.** about 58.5 feet **8.** no solution **9.** $\frac{2}{3} \le x \le 22$ **10.** $x \ge 0.7$ **11.** $x = 16$ **13.** $x = \pm 3$ **15.** $x = \frac{2}{15}$ **17.** $x = 6$ **19.** $x = -3$ **21.** no solution **23.** $x = 0$ **25.** $x \ge 1$ **27.** $\frac{1}{2} \le x \le 1$ **29.** $x \ge 0$ **31.** $\frac{1}{3} \le x < \frac{10}{27}$ **33.** no solution **35.** $0 \le x < 2$ **37.** $0 \le x \le 1$ **39.** $x \approx 0.5$ *or* $x = 1$ **41.** $x = -1$ *or* $x \approx 0.5$ **43.** $x = 0$ *or* $x = 1$ **45.** $0 \le x \le 0.3$ **47.** $x \approx -1.9$ *or* $x \approx 1.9$ **49.** $x \ge 1.3$

51. $-1.4 \leq x \leq -1$ *or* $1 \leq x \leq -1.6$ **53.** never **55.** never **57.** sometimes **59.** always **61a.** $a < 0$ **b.** $a \geq 0$ **63a.** 191,916 feet **b.** 36.3 miles **c.** 698 feet **65.** $y = 2x - 7$ **67.** $x = -2$ *or* $x = -3$ **69.** $x = 0.8$ *or* $x = -2.1$ **71.** $x^2 - 6x - 27$ **73.** $24x^6y^6\sqrt{2x}$ **75.** $x\sqrt{5}$ **77.** $2x\sqrt{10}$

CHAPTER 8 REVIEW

1. $y = 2$ **3.** $a = \frac{10}{27}$ **5.** excluded values: $x = 2$ and $x = 6$; no holes; vertical asymptotes: $x = 2$ and $x = 6$; horizontal asymptote: $y = 0$ **7.** excluded values: $x = -7$ and $x = 2$; no holes; vertical asymptotes: $x = -7$ and $x = 2$; horizontal asymptote: $y = 1$ **9.** excluded value: $x = -\frac{5}{3}$; no holes; vertical asymptote: $x = -\frac{5}{3}$; no horizontal asymptote **11.** excluded values: $y = 0$ and $y = 3$; hole when $y = 0$; vertical asymptote: $y = 3$; horizontal asymptote: $h = 0$ **13.** $\frac{2x}{5x - 30}$ **15.** $\frac{4a^2 + 8a}{5a^2 + 15a - 50}$ **17.** $\frac{z^2}{z^2 + 3z + 2}$ **19.** $\frac{x + 2}{x^2 + x}$ **21.** $\frac{23y - 29}{10y - 30}$ **23.** $\frac{-3x^2 + x - 3}{x^2 - 3x}$ **25.** $\frac{23}{x}$ **27.** $x = \pm 1$ **29.** $x = \frac{-5 \pm \sqrt{29}}{2}$ **31.** $x = \pm\sqrt{2}$ **33.** $x > 1$ *or* $x < 0$ **35.** $x < -1$ *or* $x > 1$ **37.** $x < -2$ *or* $x > -\frac{3}{2}$ **39.** $x \leq -1$ *or* $0 < x \leq 1$ **41.** $x < -2$ *or* $-1 < x \leq 0.5$ **43.** $-1.7 < x < -1$ *or* $-1 < x < -0.3$ **45.** $y = \frac{-3 \pm \sqrt{9 + 4x}}{2}$ **47.** $y = \frac{8 \pm \sqrt{49 + 3x}}{3}$ **49.** The parent function is vertically compressed by a factor of $\frac{1}{3}$. **51.** The parent function is horizontally translated $\frac{3}{2}$ units to the right and horizontally compressed by a factor of $\frac{1}{2}$. **53.** The parent function is horizontally compressed by a factor of $\frac{1}{3}$, vertically stretched by a factor 2, reflected across the x-axis, and vertically translated 6 units down. **55.** 45 **57.** $3x^3y^2\sqrt{2xy}$ **59.** $cd^2\sqrt[3]{7}$ **61.** $3x^3y^5\sqrt{y}$ **63.** $\frac{\sqrt{5}}{5}$ **65.** $6 + 3\sqrt{3}$ **67.** $\frac{3 + \sqrt{6} + \sqrt{3} + 3\sqrt{2}}{6}$ **69.** no solution **71.** $x = -10$ **73.** $x = 0$ *or* $x = \frac{1}{4}$ **75.** $x = \frac{3}{2}$ **77.** $x = 1$ **79.** no solution **81.** $0 \leq x \leq 25$ **83.** $x \geq 25$ **85.** $x \geq 3$ **87.** $x > 2$ **89.** no solution **91.** $x \geq 0$ **93.** ≈ 169.9 pounds

Chapter 9

LESSON 9.1

TRY THIS (p. 563)
a. ellipse $\left(y = \pm\frac{1}{3}\sqrt{36 - 4x^2}\right)$
b. parabola $\left(y = \pm\sqrt{6x}\right)$

TRY THIS (p. 564)
$\sqrt{194}$, or about 13.93

TRY THIS (p. 565)
(5.5, 0.5)

TRY THIS (p. 566)
center: (1, 3); $C = 2\sqrt{17}\pi$; $A = 17\pi$

Exercises

4. hyperbola **5.** circle **6.** $\sqrt{218} \approx 14.76$ **7.** $\sqrt{13} \approx 3.61$ miles **8.** $M\left(\frac{3}{2}, -1\right)$ **9.** $(-1, 3)$; $C = 2\pi\sqrt{17}$; $A = 17\pi$ **11.** circle **13.** hyperbola **15.** ellipse **17.** parabola **19.** circle **21.** hyperbola **23.** 7; $M\left(-5, \frac{3}{2}\right)$ **25.** $\sqrt{65} \approx 8.06$; $M\left(1, -\frac{9}{2}\right)$ **27.** $\sqrt{17} \approx 4.12$; $M\left(\frac{1}{2}, \frac{5}{2}\right)$ **29.** $2\sqrt{2} \approx 2.83$; $M(9, 1)$ **31.** $3\sqrt{3} \approx 5.20$; $M\left(\frac{3\sqrt{2}}{2}, \frac{5}{2}\right) \approx M(2.12, 2.5)$ **33.** $\sqrt{\frac{113}{2}} \approx 7.52$; $M\left(-\frac{9}{4}, \frac{1}{2}\right)$ **35.** $\sqrt{114} \approx 10.68$; $M\left(\frac{3\sqrt{2}}{2}, 3\sqrt{7}\right) \approx M(2.12, 7.94)$ **37.** $|a|\sqrt{17} \approx 4.12|a|$; $M\left(\frac{3a}{2}, -a\right)$ **39.** $\left(-\frac{1}{2}, 10\right)$; $C = 13\pi$; $A = \frac{169\pi}{4}$ **41.** $(-6, -4)$; $C = 4\pi\sqrt{13}$; $A = 52\pi$ **43.** $(3, -1)$; $C = 2\pi\sqrt{29}$; $A = 29\pi$ **45.** $(-12, 5)$ **47.** $(-14, 14)$ **49.** $AB = 2\sqrt{5}$; $BC = \sqrt{10}$; $AC = \sqrt{58}$; not collinear **51.** $AB = \sqrt{89}$; $BC = \sqrt{89}$; $AC = 2\sqrt{89}$; collinear **53a.** $AB = 2\sqrt{17}$; $BC = 7$; $CD = 2\sqrt{17}$; $DA = 7$ **b.** yes **55a.** $\overline{AB}$: $m = -\frac{1}{4}$; $\overline{CD}$: $m = -\frac{1}{4}$; the slopes of $\overline{AD}$ and $\overline{BC}$ are undefined. **b.** Yes, because $\overline{AB}$ and $\overline{CD}$ have the same slope, and $\overline{AD}$ and $\overline{BC}$ are both vertical. **57.** scalene **59.** $y = \frac{7}{5}x - \frac{4}{5}$ **61.** 1 **63.** $x = 3$ *or* $x = 5$ **65.** $x = 3 \pm \sqrt{29}$ **67.** $x = \frac{1}{6}$ *or* $x = 1$ **69.** $4x^3 - 3x^2 + 2x + 1$ **71.** 25

LESSON 9.2

TRY THIS (p. 572, Ex. 1)

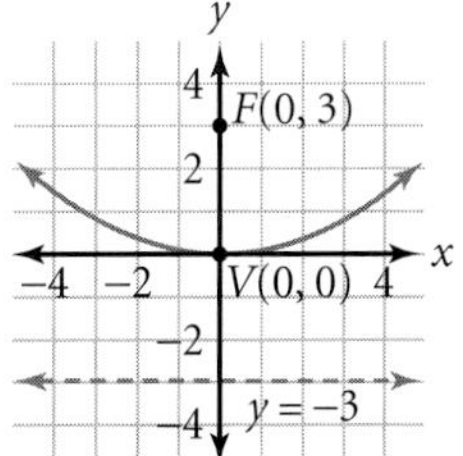

TRY THIS (p. 572, Ex. 2)
$x = -\frac{1}{16}y^2$

TRY THIS (p. 575, Ex. 4)
$x + 2 = -\frac{1}{16}(y - 4)^2$

TRY THIS (p. 575, Ex. 5)

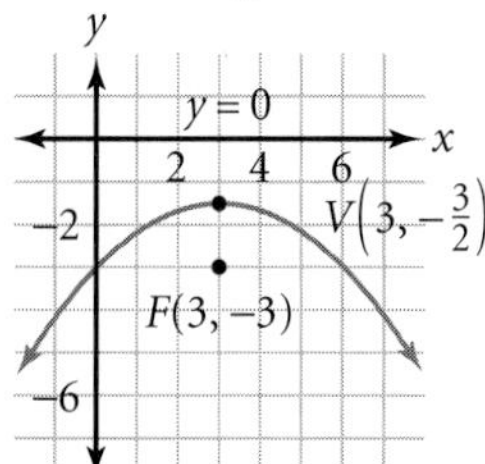

Exercises

4.

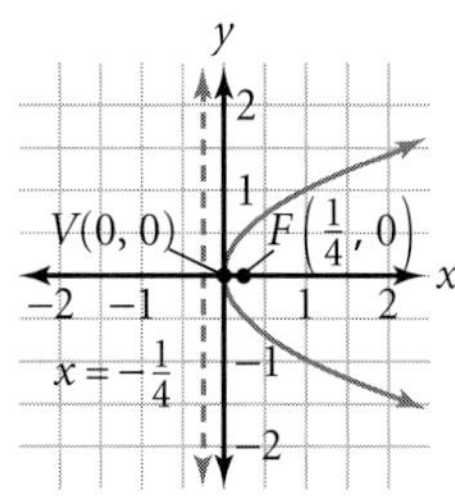

5. $x = -\frac{1}{12}y^2$ **6.** $x = \frac{1}{48}y^2$ **7.** $x - \frac{1}{2} = -\frac{1}{10}(y - 3)^2$

8.

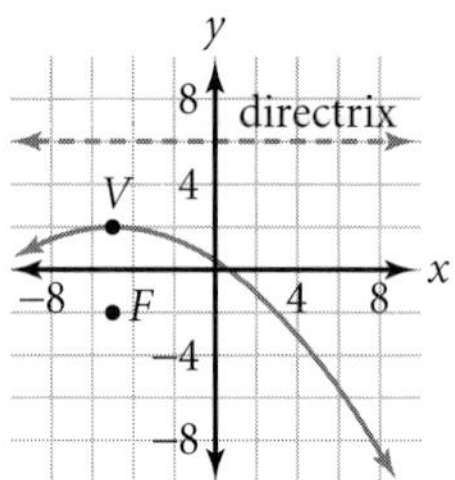

vertex: (−5, 2); focus: (−5, −2); directrix: $y = 6$

9. $y = -\frac{1}{4}x^2$ **11.** $x = -\frac{1}{8}y^2$ **13.** $x - 1 = -\frac{1}{8}(y - 2)^2$

15.

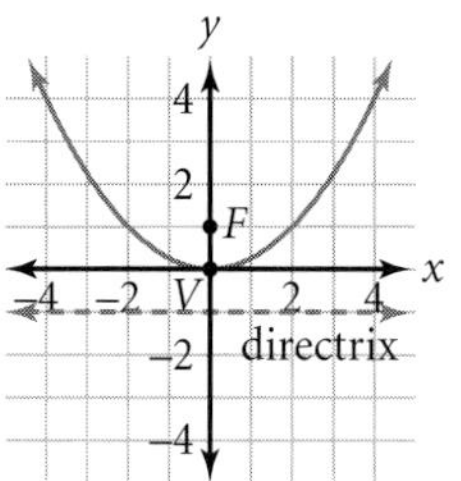

vertex: (0, 1); focus: (0, 0); directrix: $y = -1$

17.

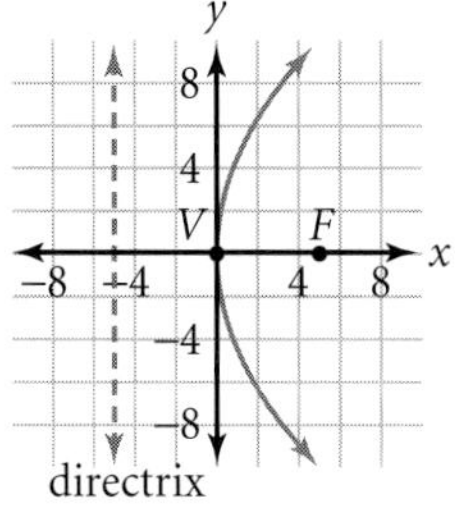

vertex: (0, 0); focus: (5, 0); directrix: $x = -5$

19.

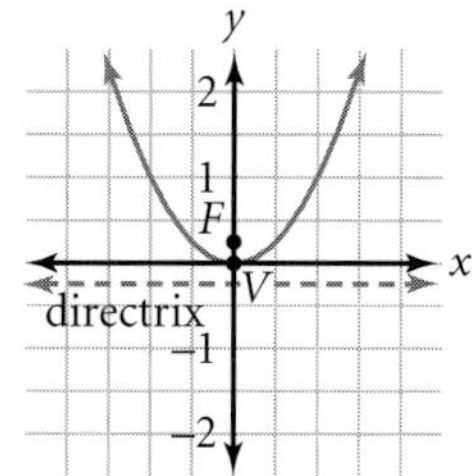

vertex: (0, 0); focus: $\left(0, \frac{1}{4}\right)$; directrix: $y = -\frac{1}{4}$

21.

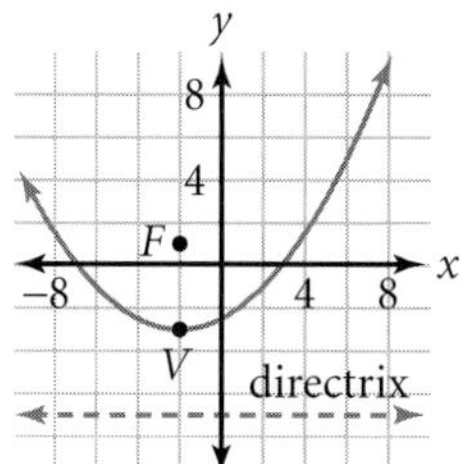

vertex: (−2, −3); focus: (−2, 1); directrix: $y = -7$

23.

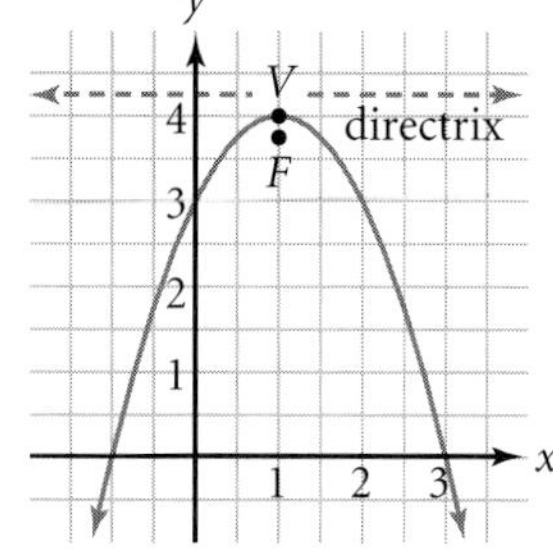

vertex: (1, 4); focus: $\left(1, \frac{15}{4}\right)$; directrix: $y = \frac{17}{4}$

25.

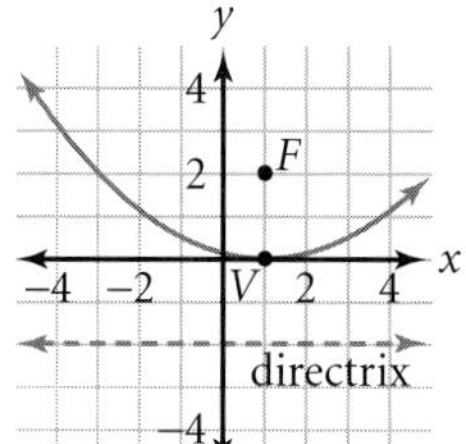

vertex: (1, 0); focus: (1, 2); directrix: $y = -2$

27.

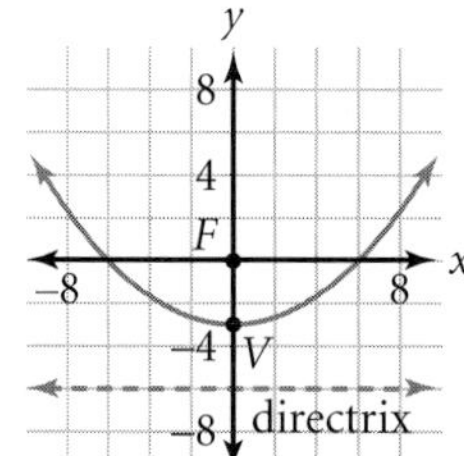

vertex: (0, −3); focus: (0, 0); directrix: $y = -6$

29.

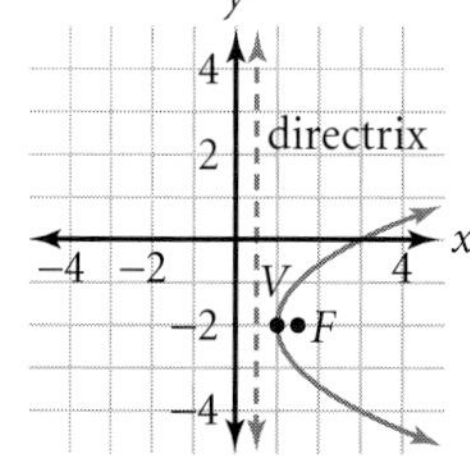

vertex: (1, −2); focus: $\left(\frac{3}{2}, -2\right)$; directrix: $x = \frac{1}{2}$

31.

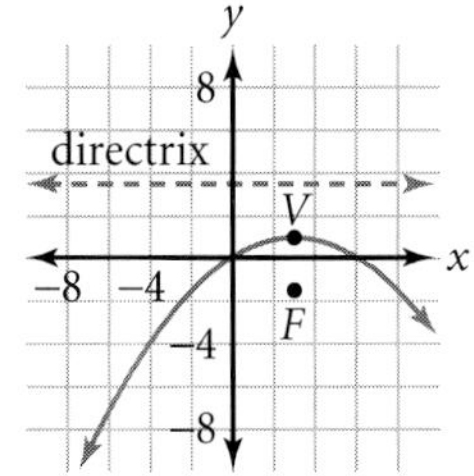

vertex: (3, 1); focus: $\left(3, -\frac{3}{2}\right)$; directrix: $y = \frac{7}{2}$

33.

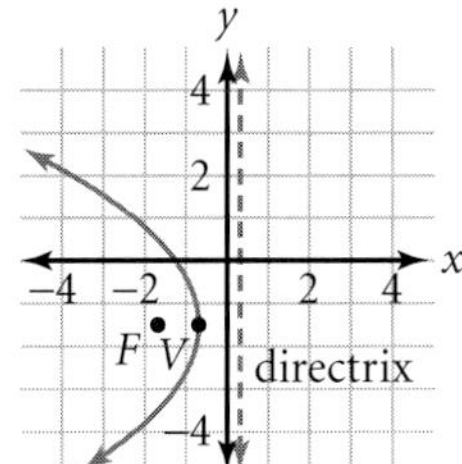

vertex: (1, 1); focus: (1, 2); directrix: $y = 0$

35.

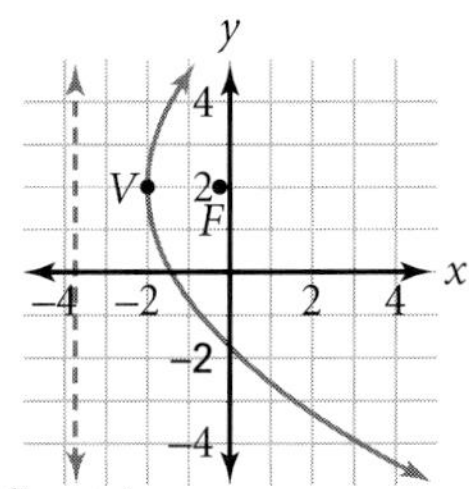

vertex: (−2, 2); focus: $\left(-\frac{1}{4}, 2\right)$; directrix: $x = -\frac{15}{4}$

37. $y = -\frac{1}{20}x^2$ **39.** $x = -\frac{1}{16}y^2$ **41.** $x = \frac{1}{8}y^2$
43. $y = -\frac{1}{48}x^2$ **45.** $x = \frac{1}{12}y^2$ **47.** $x = -\frac{1}{32}y^2$
49. $x - \frac{1}{2} = -\frac{1}{4}(y - 5)^2$ **51.** If the parabola opens to the right and has its vertex at the origin, the equation is $x = \frac{1}{4}y^2$. **53.** $y = \frac{1}{2}x^2$ **55.** $3a(a + 1)$
57. $mn(m + 7mn - 3)$ **59.** $(y - 2)(y - 10)$
61. $5(x - 2)(x - 1)$ **63.** $(3y + 5)(2y - 5)$
65. $\frac{x^3 + 3x^2 + 3x + 2}{x + 1}$ **67.** $\frac{1}{x + 3}$

LESSON 9.3

TRY THIS (p. 580)
$x^2 + y^2 = 4$

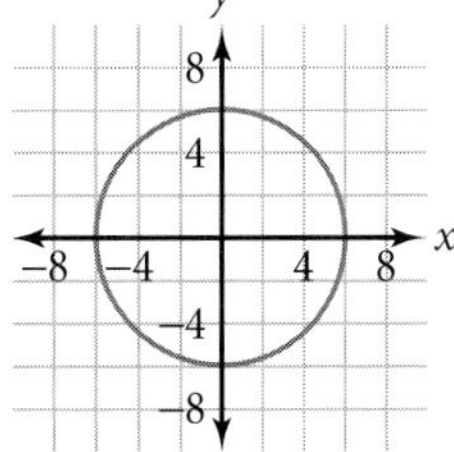

TRY THIS (p. 581)
outside

TRY THIS (p. 582)
$(x - 1)^2 + (y + 1)^2 = 9$; center: (1, −1); $r = 3$

Exercises
4. $x^2 + y^2 = 36$

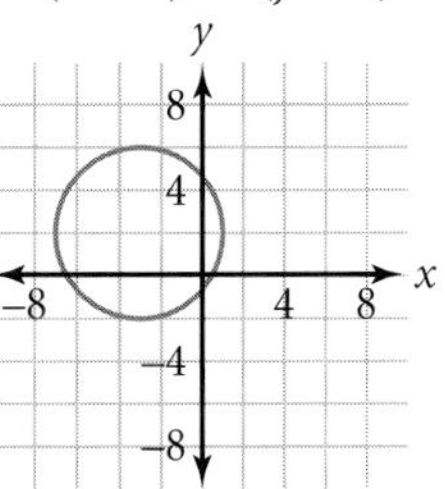

5. $(x - 3)^2 + (y - 2)^2 = 25$ **6.** yes
7. $(x + 3)^2 + (y - 2)^2 = 16$; $C(-3, 2)$; $r = 4$

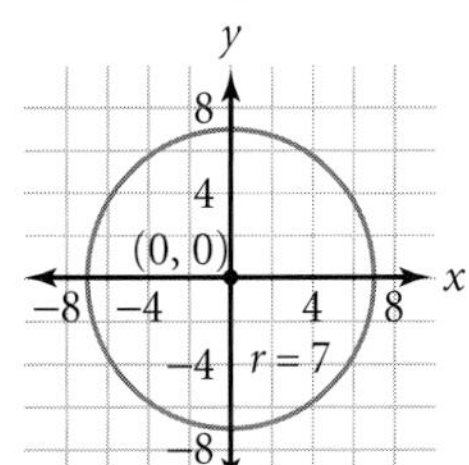

9. $x^2 + y^2 = 1$ **11.** $(x + 2)^2 + (y + 4)^2 = 9$
13. $(x + 1)^2 + (y - 2)^2 = 6.25$ **15.** $x^2 + y^2 = 25$
17. $x^2 + y^2 = 49$ **19.** $(x - 3)^2 + (y - 5)^2 = 144$
21. $(x + 5)^2 + (y + 1)^2 = 25$
23. $(x + 6)^2 + (y - 9)^2 = 225$ **25.** $x^2 + (y - 4)^2 = 9$
27. $(x - 3)^2 + (y - 3)^2 = 4$ **29.** $(x - 1)^2 + y^2 = \frac{1}{16}$
31. $(x - a)^2 + (y + 2a)^2 = 4$

33.

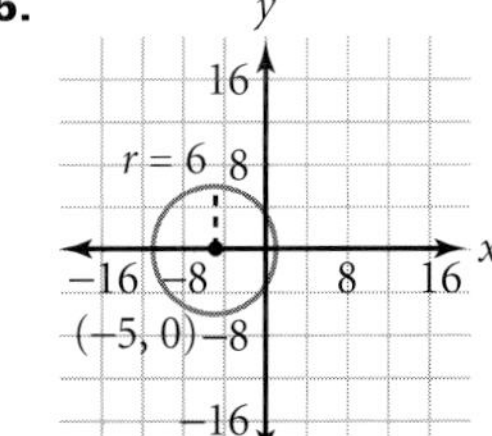

35.

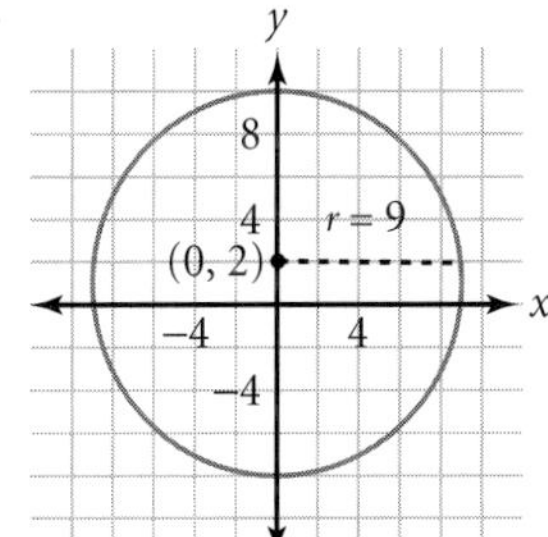

37.

39.

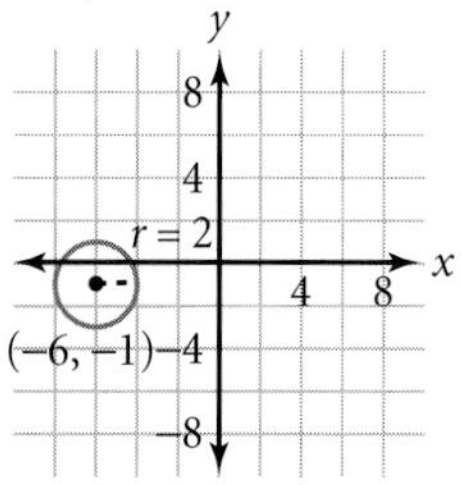

41.

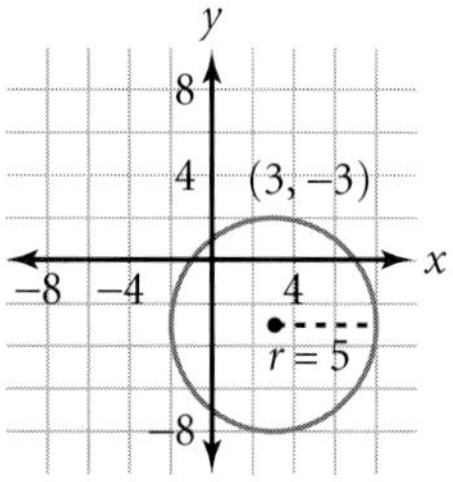

43.

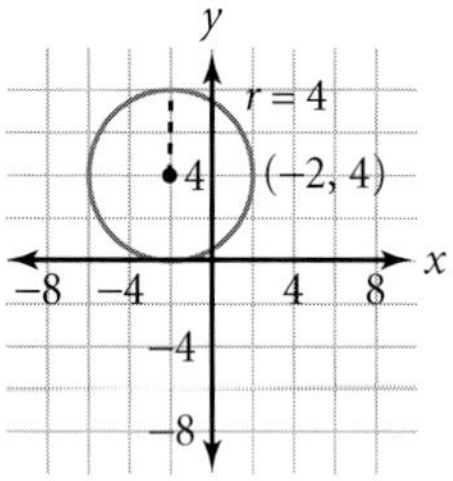

45. $(x-1)^2+y^2=9$; $C(1,0)$; $r=3$
47. $(x+1)^2+(y+3)^2=16$; $C(-1,-3)$; $r=4$
49. $(x-6)^2+(y+3)^2=64$; $C(6,-3)$; $r=8$
51. $x^2+(y-10)^2=81$; $C(0,10)$; $r=9$
53. $\left(x-\frac{1}{2}\right)^2+\left(y+\frac{1}{2}\right)^2=\frac{1}{2}$; $C\left(\frac{1}{2},-\frac{1}{2}\right)$; $r=\frac{\sqrt{2}}{2}\approx 0.71$
55. $(x-0.5)^2+(y+3.5)^2=25$; $C(0.5,-3.5)$; $r=5$
57. $(x-3)^2+(y-5)^2=36$; $C(3,5)$; $r=6$
59. $(x-5)^2+(y+3)^2=34$; $C(5,-3)$; $r=\sqrt{34}\approx 5.83$
61. Circle; the equation can be written as $x^2+y^2=12$, which has the form $x^2+y^2=r^2$, where $r=\sqrt{12}=2\sqrt{3}$. **63.** Parabola; the equation has the form $x=\frac{1}{4p}y^2$, where $p=\frac{1}{4}$. **65.** Parabola; the equation can be written as $x-2=2y^2$, which has the form $(x-h)=\frac{1}{4p}(y-k)^2$, where $h=2$, $k=0$, and $p=\frac{1}{8}$. **67.** Circle; the equation can be written as $(x-2)^2+(y+2)^2=15$, which has the form $(x-h)^2+(y-k)^2=r^2$, where $h=2$, $k=-2$, and $r=\sqrt{15}$. **69.** Inside; because $1^2+6^2=37$, $1^2+6^2<49$. **71.** Inside; the equation can be written as $(x-2)^2+(y+3)^2=25$. $P(2,-3)$ is the center of the circle, so it is inside the circle.
73. Outside; the equation can be written as $(x-6)^2+(y+1)^2=49$. Because $(12-6)^2+(3+1)^2=52$, $(12-6)^2+(3+1)^2>49$.
75. Outside; because $1.5^2+3.5^2=14.5$, $1.5^2+3.5^2>6$. **77a.** Answers may vary. Sample answer: The centers of the circles are at (3, 3) and (3, 1), which are 2 units apart. C_1 will be completely enclosed by C_2 if $r_2-r_1>2$. For example, let $r_1=4$ and $r_2=1$. **b.** Answers may vary. Sample answer: If $r_1=\sqrt{2}$ and $r_2=\sqrt{2}$, the circles intersect at (2, 2) and (4, 2). **c.** If $r_1+r_2=2$, then the circles will intersect at one point. For example, if $r_1=1$ and $r_2=1$, then the circles will intersect at (3, 2).
79. $(x-8)^2+(y-8)^2=11$ **81.** yes **83.** $x=\frac{11}{2}$; $\left(\frac{11}{2},-\frac{9}{4}\right)$ **85.** $x=-\frac{3}{2}$; $\left(-\frac{3}{2},\frac{49}{4}\right)$ **87.** $x=\frac{\ln 12}{-3}\approx 0.83$
89. $a=4$ **91.** $x=24$ **93.** Translate the graph 4 units to the left, stretch it horizontally by a factor of 2, and then translate it 3 units down.

LESSON 9.4

TRY THIS (p. 588)

$\frac{x^2}{169}+\frac{y^2}{25}=1$

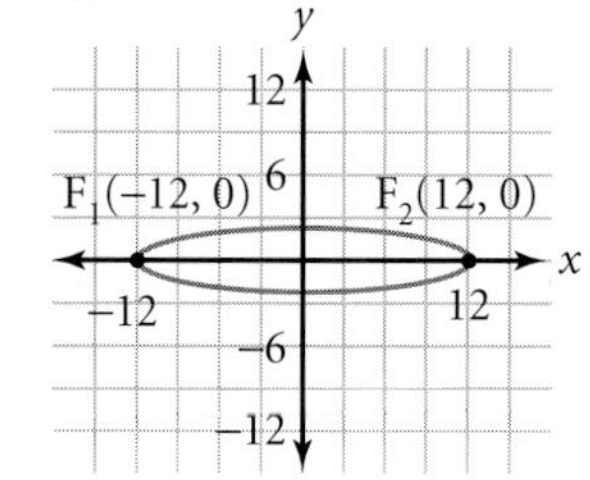

TRY THIS (p. 589)

$\frac{x^2}{4509.1}+\frac{y^2}{4508.9}=1$

TRY THIS (p. 590)

$\frac{(x+1)^2}{4}+\frac{(y+2)^2}{16}=1$

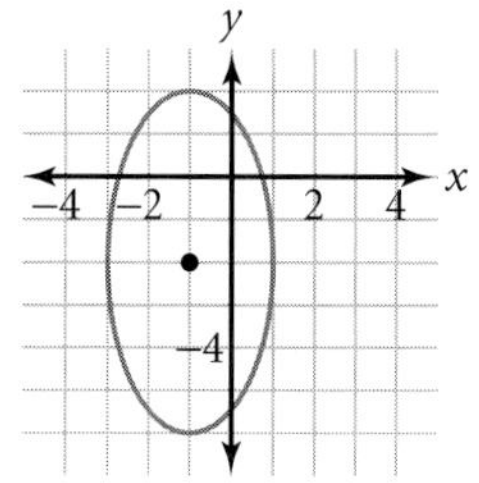

Exercises

5. $\frac{x^2}{41}+\frac{y^2}{16}=1$

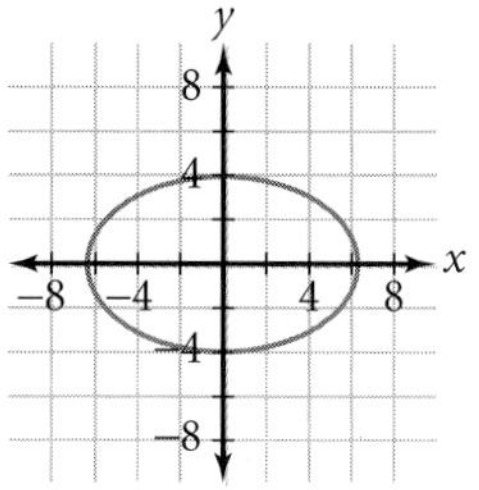

6. $\frac{x^2}{233{,}578.89}+\frac{y^2}{233{,}026.64}=1$

7. $\frac{(x-1)^2}{4} + \frac{(y+2)^2}{9} = 1$

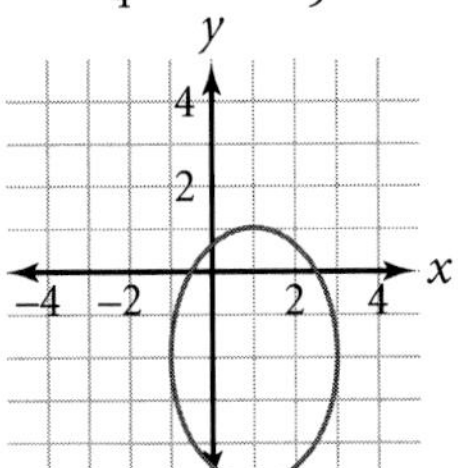

8. $\frac{(x+1)^2}{4} + \frac{(y-1)^2}{25} = 1$; center: $(-1, 1)$; vertices: $(-1, -4)$ and $(-1, 6)$; co-vertices: $(-3, 1)$ and $(1, 1)$; foci: $\left(-1, 1-\sqrt{21}\right)$ and $\left(-1, 1+\sqrt{21}\right)$

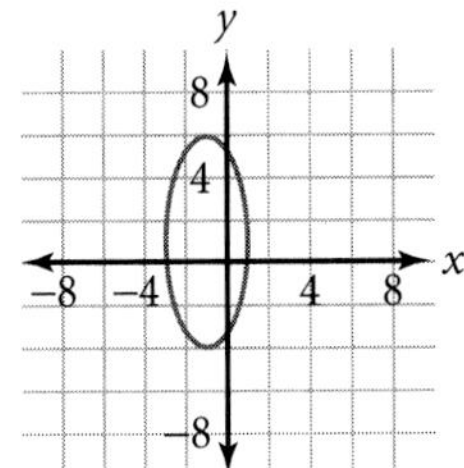

9. vertices: $(-5, 0)$ and $(5, 0)$; co-vertices: $(0, -3)$ and $(0, 3)$ **11.** vertices: $(-9, 0)$ and $(9, 0)$; co-vertices: $(0, -2)$ and $(0, 2)$ **13.** vertices: $(0, -8)$ and $(0, 8)$; co-vertices: $(-1, 0)$ and $(1, 0)$ **15.** $\frac{x^2}{4} + \frac{y^2}{1} = 1$; center: $(0, 0)$; vertices: $(-2, 0)$ and $(2, 0)$; co-vertices: $(0, -1)$ and $(0, 1)$; foci: $\left(-\sqrt{3}, 0\right)$ and $\left(\sqrt{3}, 0\right)$
17. $\frac{x^2}{\frac{28}{3}} + \frac{y^2}{4} = 1$; center: $(0, 0)$; vertices: $\left(-\frac{2\sqrt{21}}{3}, 0\right)$ and $\left(\frac{2\sqrt{21}}{3}, 0\right)$; co-vertices: $(0, -2)$ and $(0, 2)$; foci: $\left(-\frac{4\sqrt{3}}{3}, 0\right)$ and $\left(\frac{4\sqrt{3}}{3}, 0\right)$ **19.** $\frac{x^2}{16} + \frac{y^2}{36} = 1$; center: $(0, 0)$; vertices: $(0, -6)$ and $(0, 6)$; co-vertices: $(-4, 0)$ and $(4, 0)$; foci: $\left(0, -2\sqrt{5}\right)$ and $\left(0, 2\sqrt{5}\right)$
21. $\frac{x^2}{36} + \frac{y^2}{25} = 1$ **23.** $\frac{(x-3)^2}{16} + \frac{(y-3)^2}{9} = 1$
25. $\frac{(x+2)^2}{4} + \frac{(y-2)^2}{9} = 1$
27. center: $(0, 0)$; vertices: $(-5, 0)$ and $(5, 0)$; co-vertices: $(0, -2)$ and $(0, 2)$; foci: $\left(-\sqrt{21}, 0\right)$ and $\left(\sqrt{21}, 0\right)$

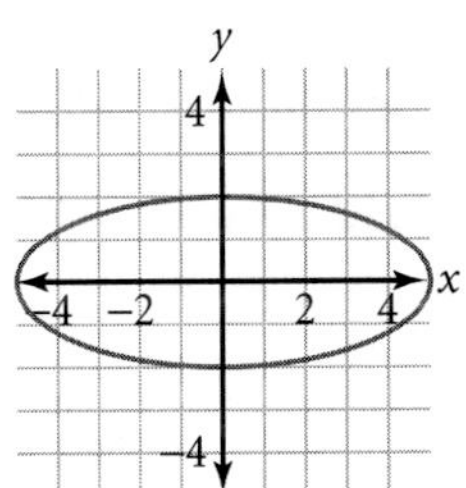

29. center: $(0, 0)$; vertices: $(0, -3)$ and $(0, 3)$; co-vertices: $(-2, 0)$ and $(2, 0)$; foci: $\left(0, -\sqrt{5}\right)$, $\left(0, \sqrt{5}\right)$

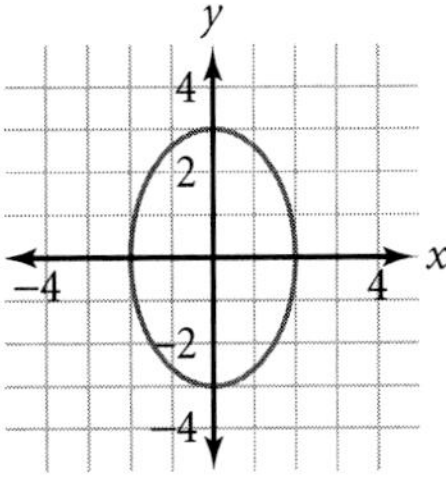

31. center: $(-2, -1)$; vertices: $(-2, -4)$ and $(-2, 2)$; co-vertices: $(-4, -1)$ and $(0, -1)$; foci: $\left(-2, -1-\sqrt{5}\right)$ and $\left(-2, -1+\sqrt{5}\right)$

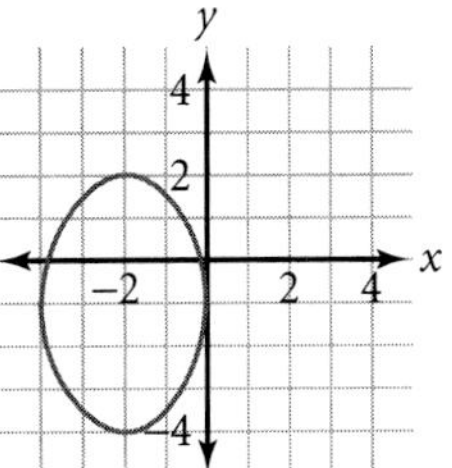

33. center: $(0, -2)$; vertices: $(0, -5)$ and $(0, 1)$; co-vertices: $(-1, -2)$ and $(1, -2)$; foci: $\left(0, -2-2\sqrt{2}\right)$ and $\left(0, -2+2\sqrt{2}\right)$

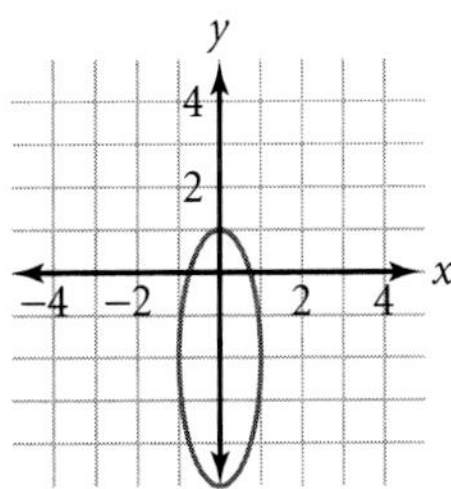

35. The graph is a circle with its center at $(1, 1)$ and a radius of 2.

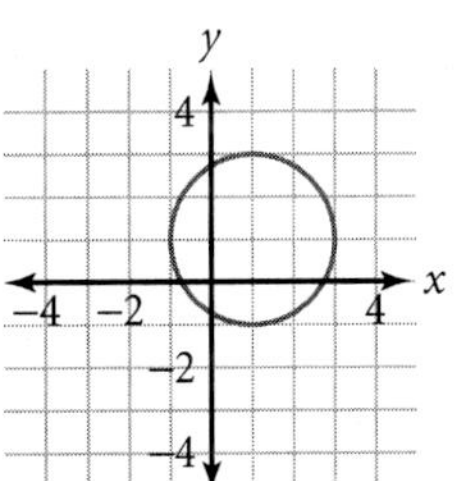

37. center: $(1, -2)$; vertices: $(-4, -2)$ and $(6, -2)$; co-vertices: $(1, -5)$ and $(1, 1)$; foci: $(-3, -2)$ and $(5, -2)$

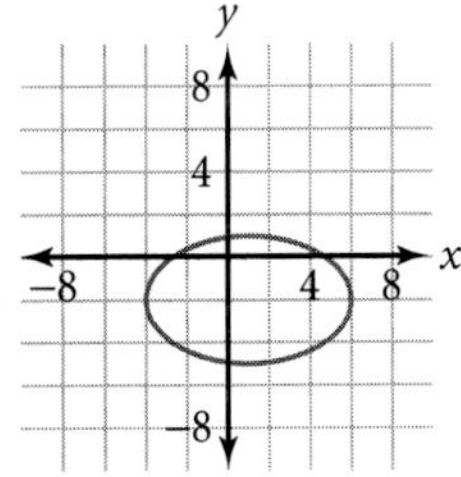

39. center: (0, 0); vertices: (0, –5) and (0, 5); co-vertices: (–3, 0) and (3, 0); foci: (0, –4) and (0, 4)

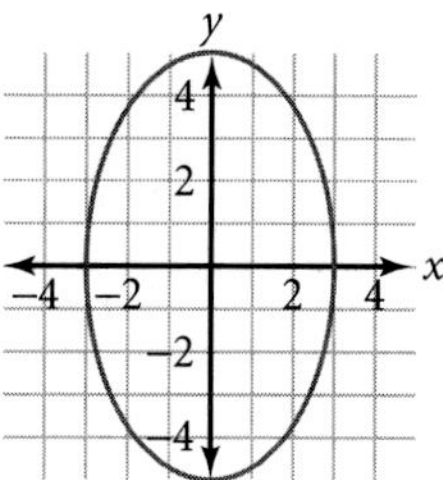

41. $\frac{x^2}{48} + \frac{y^2}{64} = 1$ **43.** $\frac{x^2}{1} + \frac{y^2}{10} = 1$ **45.** $\frac{x^2}{25} + \frac{y^2}{16} = 1$

47. parabola **49.** ellipse **51.** $\frac{(x+1)^2}{4} + \frac{(y-1)^2}{16} = 1$; center: (–1, 1); vertices: (–1, –3) and (–1, 5); co-vertices: (–3, 1) and (1, 1); foci: $(-1, 1 - 2\sqrt{3})$ and $(-1, 1 + 2\sqrt{3})$ **53.** $\frac{(x-1)^2}{1} + \frac{y^2}{25} = 1$; center: (1, 0); vertices: (1, –5) and (1, 5); co-vertices: (0, 0) and (2, 0); foci: $(1, -2\sqrt{6})$ and $(1, 2\sqrt{6})$

55. $\frac{(x+2)^2}{9} + \frac{(y+1)^2}{25} = 1$; center: (–2, –1); vertices: (–2, –6) and (–2, 4); co-vertices: (–5, –1) and (1, –1); foci: (–2, –5) and (–2, 3)

57. $\frac{(x-1)^2}{25} + \frac{(y+2)^2}{36} = 1$; center: (1, –2); vertices: (1, –8) and (1, 4); co-vertices: (–4, –2) and (6, –2); foci: $(1, -2 - \sqrt{11})$ and $(1, -2 + \sqrt{11})$

59. $\frac{(x+10)^2}{4} + \frac{(y+5)^2}{16} = 1$ **61.** the point (–2, 1)

63. $\frac{x^2}{1739.6} + \frac{y^2}{1369} = 1$ **65.** $8x^2y^7$ **67.** $\frac{36y^8}{25x^2z^{12}}$

69. $x \approx 1.50$ **71.** $25a^3 - 5a^2 - 14a + 11$

73. $4x^2y^2 - 15xy + 34y^2$

LESSON 9.5

TRY THIS (p. 597)

$\frac{x^2}{49} - \frac{y^2}{16} = 1$

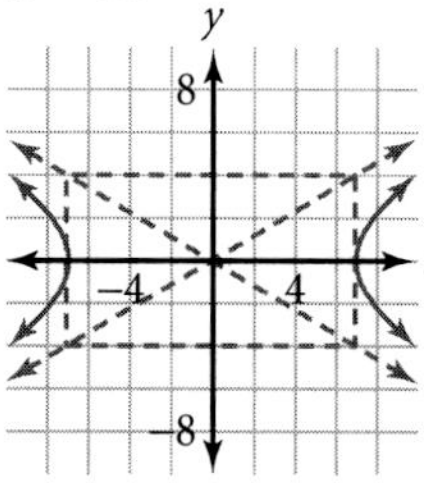

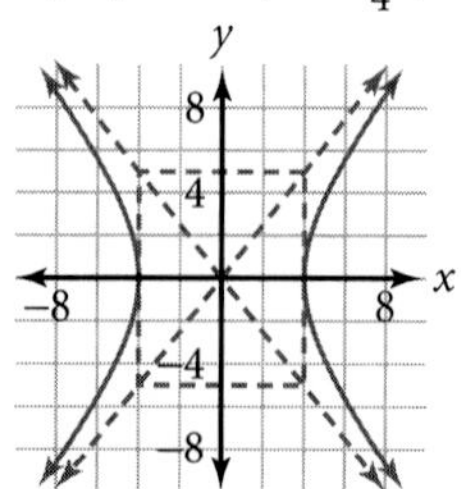

TRY THIS (p. 598)

asymptotes: $y = \pm\frac{5}{4}x$; vertices: (–4, 0) and (4, 0)

TRY THIS (p. 599)

$\frac{(y-2)^2}{9} - \frac{(x-3)^2}{16} = 1$

TRY THIS (p. 600)

$\frac{(x-1)^2}{25} - \frac{(y-2)^2}{4} = 1$; center: (1, 2); vertices: (–4, 2) and (6, 2); co-vertices: (1, 0) and (1, 4); foci: $(1 - \sqrt{29}, 2)$ and $(1 + \sqrt{29}, 2)$

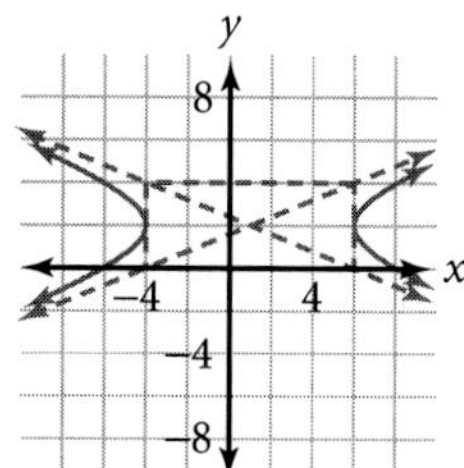

Exercises

3. $\frac{x^2}{16} - \frac{y^2}{4} = 1$

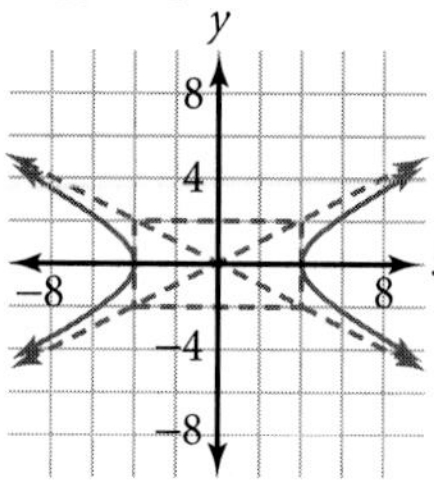

4. asymptotes: $y = \frac{5}{3}x$ and $y = -\frac{5}{3}x$; vertices: (–3, 0) and (3, 0)

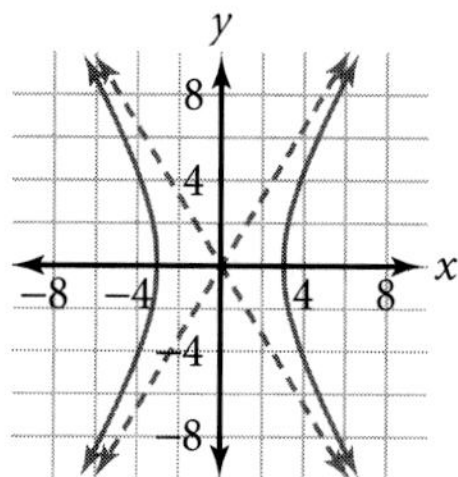

5. $\frac{(x-3)^2}{4} - \frac{(y-4)^2}{5} = 1$ **6.** $\frac{(x+1)^2}{11} - \frac{(y-2)^2}{11} = 1$; center: (–1, 2); vertices: $(-1 - \sqrt{11}, 2)$ and $(-1 + \sqrt{11}, 2)$; co-vertices: $(-1, 2 - \sqrt{11})$ and $(-1, 2 + \sqrt{11})$; foci: $(-1 - 2\sqrt{11}, 2)$ and $(-1 + 2\sqrt{11}, 2)$

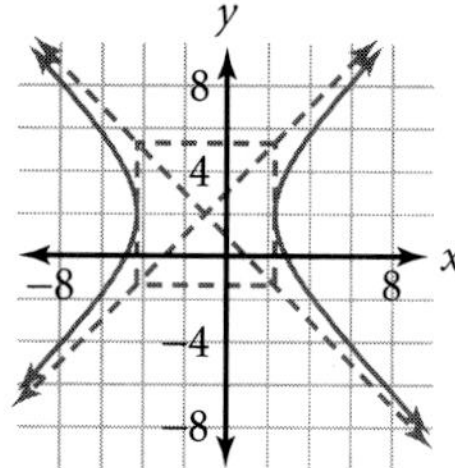

7. $\frac{x^2}{9} - \frac{y^2}{25} = 1$ **9.** $\frac{y^2}{1} - \frac{(x+1)^2}{9} = 1$ **11.** $\frac{y^2}{4} - \frac{x^2}{9} = 1$

13. center: (0, 0); vertices: (−1, 0) and (1, 0); co-vertices: (0, −1) and (0, 1); foci: $\left(-\sqrt{2}, 0\right)$ and $\left(\sqrt{2}, 0\right)$; asymptotes: $y = -x$ and $y = x$

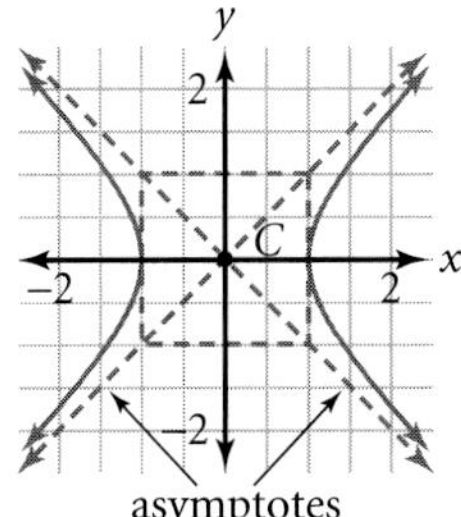

15. center: (0, 0); vertices: (0, −3) and (0, 3); co-vertices: (−5, 0) and (5, 0); foci: $\left(0, -\sqrt{34}\right)$ and $\left(0, \sqrt{34}\right)$; asymptotes: $y = -\frac{3x}{5}$ and $y = \frac{3x}{5}$

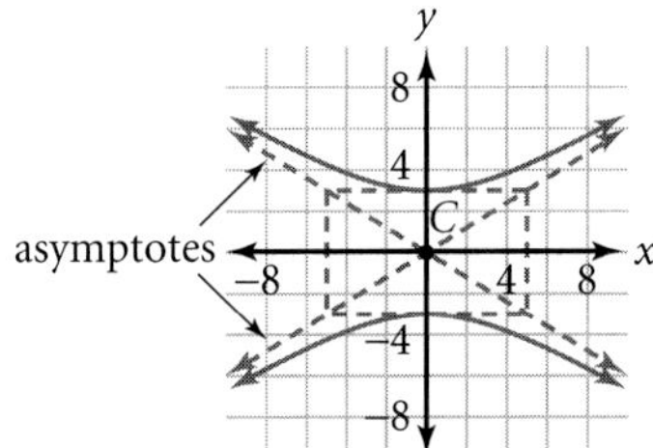

17. center: (0, 0); vertices: (−1, 0) and (1, 0); co-vertices: (0, −2) and (0, 2); foci: $\left(-\sqrt{5}, 0\right)$ and $\left(\sqrt{5}, 0\right)$; asymptotes: $y = -2x$ and $y = 2x$

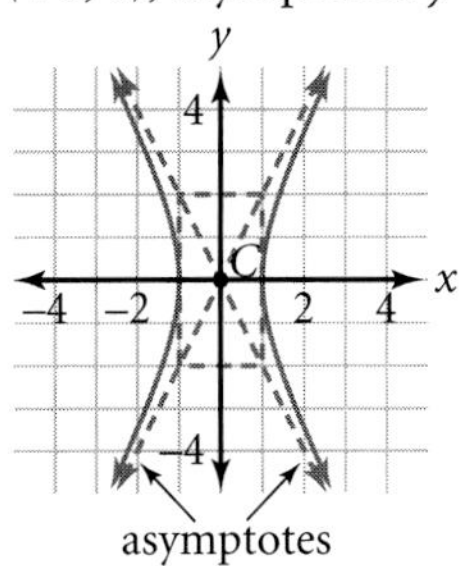

19. center: (0, 0); vertices: (0, −10) and (0, 10); co-vertices: (−8, 0) and (8, 0); foci: $\left(0, -2\sqrt{41}\right)$ and $\left(0, 2\sqrt{41}\right)$; asymptotes: $y = -\frac{5x}{4}$ and $y = \frac{5x}{4}$

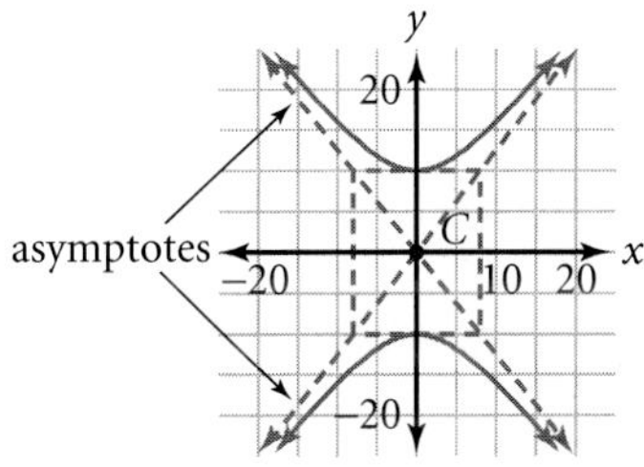

21. center: (0, 0); vertices: (−5, 0) and (5, 0); co-vertices: (0, −2) and (0, 2); foci: $\left(-\sqrt{29}, 0\right)$ and $\left(\sqrt{29}, 0\right)$; asymptotes: $y = -\frac{2x}{5}$ and $y = \frac{2x}{5}$

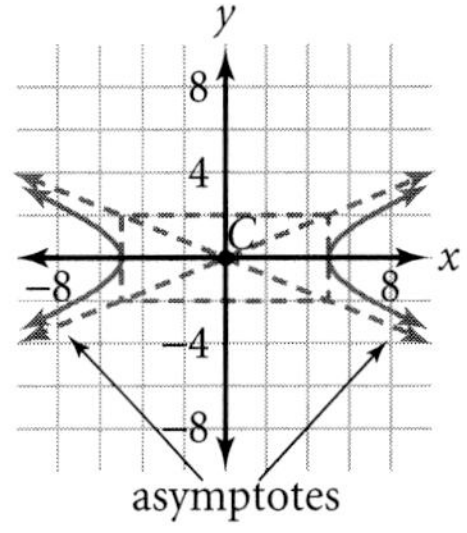

23. center: (1, −2); vertices: (−1, −2) and (3, −2); co-vertices: (1, −5) and (1, 1); foci: $\left(1 - \sqrt{13}, -2\right)$ and $\left(1 + \sqrt{13}, -2\right)$; asymptotes: $y = -\frac{3x}{2} - \frac{1}{2}$ and $y = \frac{3x}{2} - \frac{7}{2}$

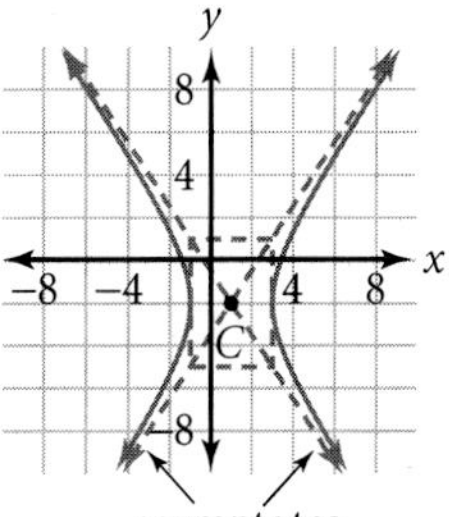

asymptotes

25. $\frac{x^2}{9} - \frac{y^2}{25} = 1$ **27.** $\frac{y^2}{16} - \frac{x^2}{9} = 1$ **29.** $\frac{x^2}{5} - \frac{y^2}{4} = 1$

31. $\frac{(x-2)^2}{9} - \frac{(y-3)^2}{25} = 1$ **33.** $\frac{(x-1)^2}{9} - \frac{(y-3)^2}{4} = 1$; center: (1, 3); vertices: (−2, 3) and (4, 3); co-vertices: (1, 1) and (1, 5); foci: $\left(1 - \sqrt{13}, 3\right)$ and $\left(1 + \sqrt{13}, 3\right)$

35. $\frac{(y+1)^2}{36} - \frac{(x+1)^2}{4} = 1$; center: (−1, −1); vertices: (−1, −7) and (−1, 5); co-vertices: (−3, −1) and (1, −1); foci: $\left(-1, -1 - 2\sqrt{10}\right)$ and $\left(-1, -1 + 2\sqrt{10}\right)$

37. $\frac{(y-3)^2}{9} - \frac{(x+2)^2}{1} = 1$; center: (−2, 3); vertices: (−2, 0) and (−2, 6); co-vertices: (−3, 3) and (−1, 3); foci: $\left(-2, 3 - \sqrt{10}\right)$ and $\left(2, 3 + \sqrt{10}\right)$

39. $\frac{(x+2)^2}{16} - \frac{(y-2)^2}{16} = 1$; center: (−2, 2); vertices: (−6, 2) and (2, 2); co-vertices: (−2, −2) and (−2, 6); foci: $\left(-2 - 4\sqrt{2}, 2\right)$ and $\left(-2 + 4\sqrt{2}, 2\right)$

41. $\frac{(y-2)^2}{5} - \frac{(x-2)^2}{3} = 1$; center: (2, 2); vertices: $\left(2, 2 - \sqrt{5}\right)$ and $\left(2, 2 + \sqrt{5}\right)$; co-vertices: $\left(2 - \sqrt{3}, 2\right)$ and $\left(2 + \sqrt{3}, 2\right)$; foci: $\left(2, 2 - 2\sqrt{2}\right)$ and $\left(2, 2 + 2\sqrt{2}\right)$

43. $\frac{x^2}{25} - \frac{y^2}{16} = 1$ or $\frac{y^2}{16} - \frac{x^2}{25} = 1$

45. $\frac{(x-6)^2}{25} - \frac{\left(y - \frac{13}{2}\right)^2}{\frac{121}{4}} = 1$ or

$$\frac{\left(y - \frac{13}{2}\right)^2}{\frac{121}{4}} - \frac{(x-6)^2}{25} = 1$$

47a. vertices: $V_1(-a, 0)$ and $V_2(a, 0)$; co-vertices: $C_1(0, -a)$ and $C_2(0, a)$
b. square **c.** Answers may vary. Sample answer:

Side	Length	Slope
$\overline{V_1C_1}$	$\sqrt{[0-(-a)]^2+(-a-0)^2}=\sqrt{2a^2}=a\sqrt{2}$	$\frac{-a-0}{0-(-a)}=-1$
$\overline{C_1V_2}$	$\sqrt{(a-0)^2+[0-(-a)]^2}=\sqrt{2a^2}=a\sqrt{2}$	$\frac{0-(-a)}{a-0}=1$
$\overline{V_2C_2}$	$\sqrt{(0-a)^2+(a-0)^2}=\sqrt{2a^2}=a\sqrt{2}$	$\frac{a-0}{0-a}=-1$
$\overline{C_2V_1}$	$\sqrt{(-a-0)^2+(0-a)^2}=\sqrt{2a^2}=a\sqrt{2}$	$\frac{0-a}{-a-0}=1$

The table shows that the sides all have the same length and that the sides meet at right angles because the slopes of adjacent sides are negative reciprocals. Therefore, quadrilateral $V_1C_1V_2C_2$ is a square.

49. $\frac{(x+9)^2}{4}-\frac{(y-3)^2}{9}=1$ **51.** $(3, 2)$ **53.** $\left(\frac{1}{5}, 5\right)$

55. $(3, -2)$ **57.** $\begin{bmatrix}-8 & 0 & 10\\ 4 & 0 & -5\\ 20 & 0 & -25\end{bmatrix}$ **59.** $[-7 \quad 6 \quad -41]$

61. does not exist **63.** does not exist

LESSON 9.6

TRY THIS (p. 608)
$\left(\frac{1}{2}-\frac{\sqrt{61}}{2}, \pm\sqrt{\frac{1}{2}+\frac{\sqrt{61}}{2}}\right)$, $\left(\frac{1}{2}+\frac{\sqrt{61}}{2}, \pm i\sqrt{\frac{\sqrt{61}}{2}-\frac{1}{2}}\right)$, or approximately $(-3.41, \pm 2.10)$, $(4.41, \pm 1.85i)$

TRY THIS (p. 609)
4 solutions: $\left(\pm 3\sqrt{\frac{13}{85}}, \pm 12\sqrt{\frac{2}{85}}\right)$, or approximately $(\pm 1.17, \pm 1.84)$

TRY THIS (p. 610)
a. ellipse
b. $\frac{(x+1)^2}{4}+\frac{(y+1)^2}{9}=1$
c.

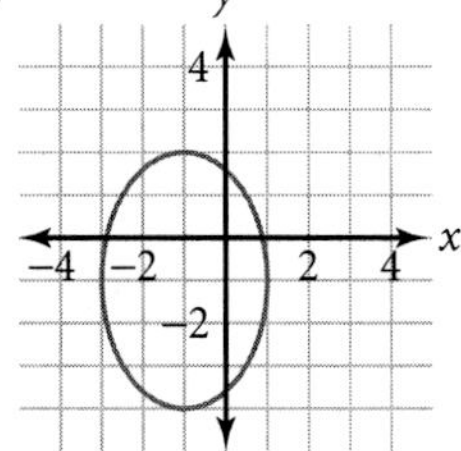

Exercises
5. $(-5, \pm 3i)$ and $(3, \pm\sqrt{7})$ **6.** width: $\frac{12\sqrt{5}}{5}\approx 5.37$ inches; length: $\frac{24\sqrt{5}}{5}\approx 10.73$ inches
7. $\left(\pm\frac{6\sqrt{26}}{13}, \pm\frac{2\sqrt{65}}{13}i\right)$

8. ellipse; $\frac{(x+1)^2}{9}+\frac{(y+1)^2}{4}=1$

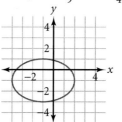

9. $(\pm\sqrt{5}, 5)$ **11.** $(0, 0)$ and $(2, 4)$ **13.** $(-\sqrt{2}, -\sqrt{2})$ and $(\sqrt{2}, \sqrt{2})$ **15.** none **17.** $\left(\pm\sqrt{-\frac{1}{2}+\frac{\sqrt{5}}{2}}, -\frac{1}{2}+\frac{\sqrt{5}}{2}\right)$
19. none **21.** $(0, \pm 1)$ **23.** none **25.** $(\pm 5, 0)$
27. none **29.** 4 solutions: $\left(\pm\frac{6\sqrt{130}}{13}, \pm\frac{6\sqrt{39}}{13}\right)$
31. $(\pm 3, 0)$ **33.** $(0, 0)$, $(1, 1)$ **35.** 4 solutions: $\left(\pm\frac{\sqrt{5}}{2}, \pm\frac{3}{2}\right)$ **37.** 4 solutions: $(\pm 6, \pm 2)$ **39.** none
41. none **43.** 4 approximate solutions: $(\pm 1.85, \pm 1.89)$
45. infinitely many solutions:
47. circle; $(x-1)^2+(y-1)^2=8$

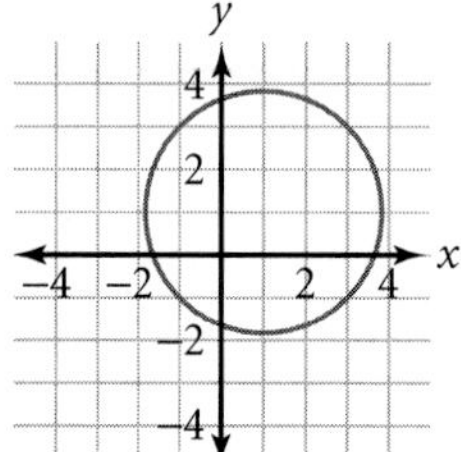

49. ellipse; $\frac{(x+2)^2}{9}+\frac{(y-2)^2}{4}=1$

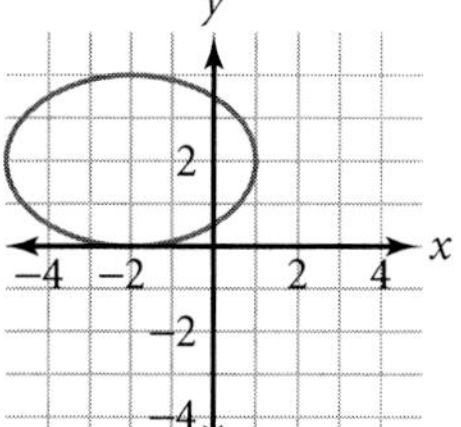

51. hyperbola; $\frac{(x+1)^2}{9}-\frac{(y-2)^2}{4}=1$

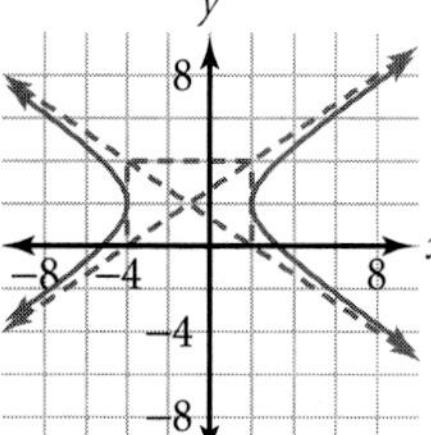

53. ellipse; $\frac{(x-3)^2}{9}+\frac{(y+1)^2}{4}=1$

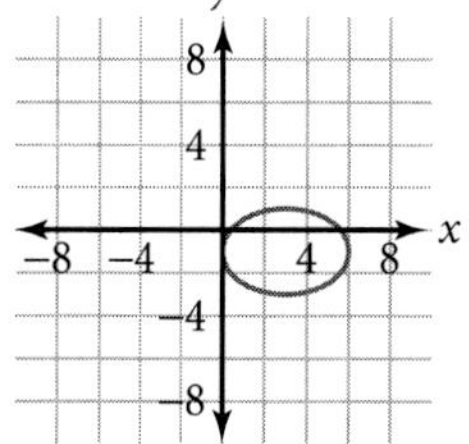

55. parabola; $x + 2 = \frac{1}{2}(y - 3)^2$

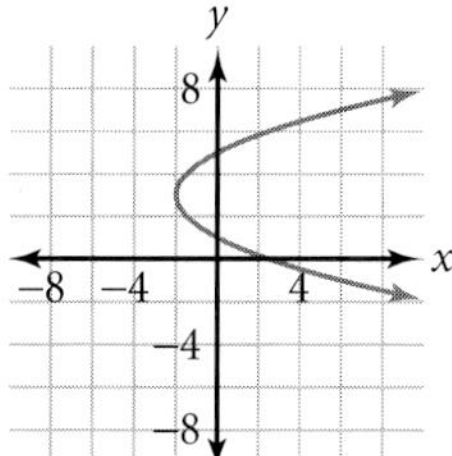

57. hyperbola; $\frac{x^2}{123} - \frac{(y+2)^2}{123} = 1$

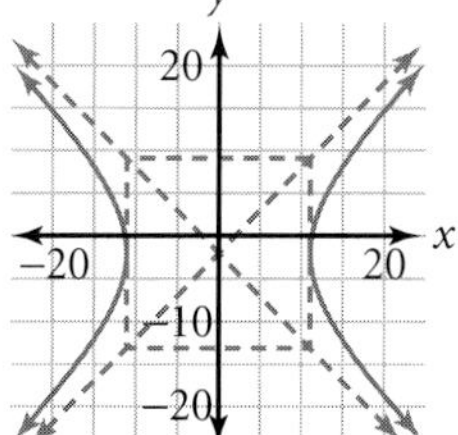

59. $\left(-\frac{5}{3}, 2 \pm \frac{4\sqrt{5}}{3}\right)$ **61.** none **63.** (0, –2) and (0, 4)
65. $\left(\frac{5}{2} + \frac{5\sqrt{247}}{26}, \frac{1}{2} - \frac{\sqrt{247}}{25}\right)$ and $\left(\frac{5}{2} - \frac{5\sqrt{247}}{26}, \frac{1}{2} + \frac{\sqrt{247}}{26}\right)$, or about (5.52, –0.10) and (–0.52, 1.10) **67.** 51 **69.** $x^2 = 9, y^2 = 0; x = \pm 3, y = 0$
71. 3 feet by 4 feet **73.** $6 - 2\sqrt{6}$ inches by $6 + 2\sqrt{6}$ inches, or about 1.10 inches by 10.90 inches
75. $\frac{32\sqrt{5}}{5}$ inches by $\frac{16\sqrt{5}}{5}$ inches, or about 14.31 inches by 7.16 inches **77.** $\frac{27\sqrt{10}}{5}$ inches by $\frac{9\sqrt{10}}{5}$ inches, or about 17.08 inches by 5.69 inches
79. –2, –1, and 1 **81.** no rational zeros
83. $\frac{1}{2}$, $1 - \sqrt{2}$, and $1 + \sqrt{2}$ **85.** $-\frac{1}{3}$, 1, $i\sqrt{3}$, $-i\sqrt{3}$
87. $\frac{x^2 + 3x + 4}{x^3 - 4x}$ **89.** $x = \frac{17}{8}$ **91.** $x > \frac{23}{3}$
93. no solution

CHAPTER REVIEW AND ASSESSMENT

1. 5; $M\left(\frac{3}{2}, 2\right)$ **3.** $PQ = 2\sqrt{13} \approx 7.21$; $M(0, 3)$
5. $PQ = \sqrt{185} \approx 13.60$; $M\left(\frac{9}{2}, -7\right)$
7. $x + 23 = (y - 5)^2$; vertex: (–23, 5); focus: $\left(-\frac{91}{4}, 5\right)$; directrix: $x = -\frac{93}{4}$

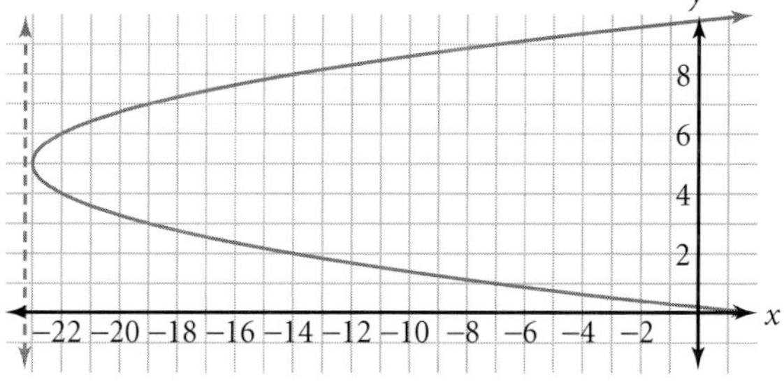

9. $y - 4 = (x + 4)^2$; vertex: (–4, 4); focus: $\left(-4, \frac{17}{4}\right)$; directrix: $y = \frac{15}{4}$

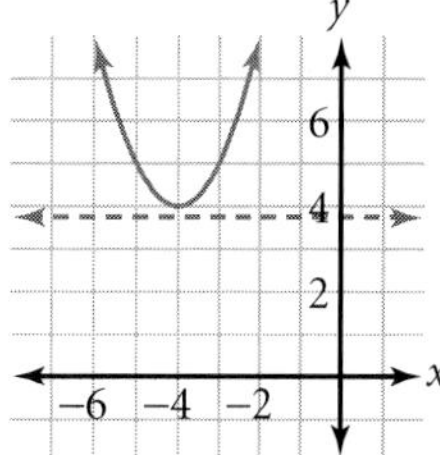

11. $x^2 + y^2 = 100$; $C(0, 0)$; $r = 10$

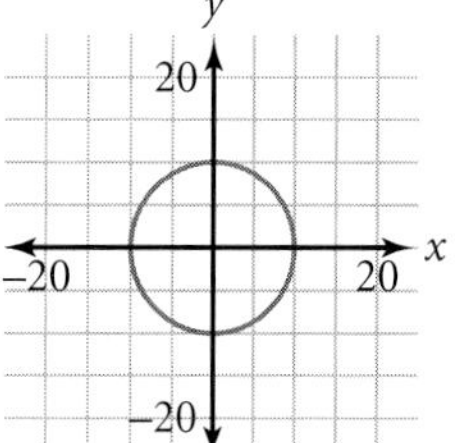

13. $(x - 1)^2 + (y - 49)^2 = 81$; $C(1, 49)$; $r = 9$

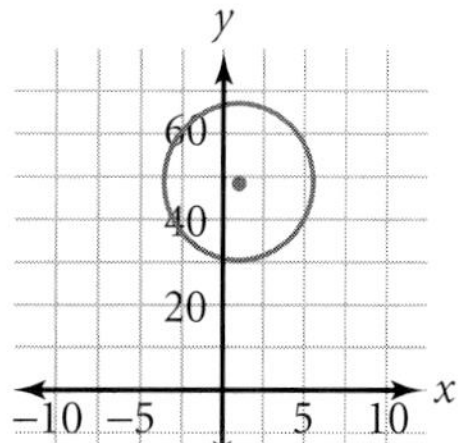

15. $(x + 2)^2 + (y + 4)^2 = 25$; $C(-2, -4)$; $r = 5$

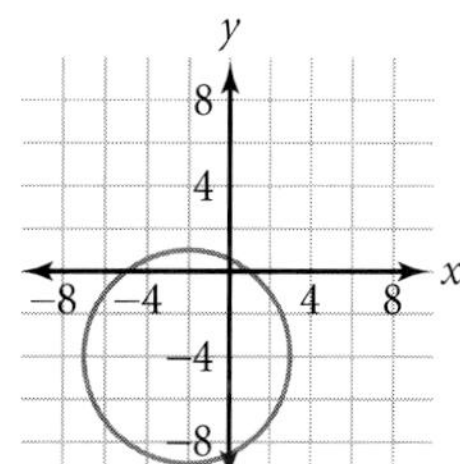

17. $\frac{(x-4)^2}{9} + \frac{(y+1)^2}{25} = 1$; center: (4, –1); vertices: (4, –6) and (4, 4); co-vertices: (1, –1) and (7, –1); foci: (4, –5) and (4, 3)

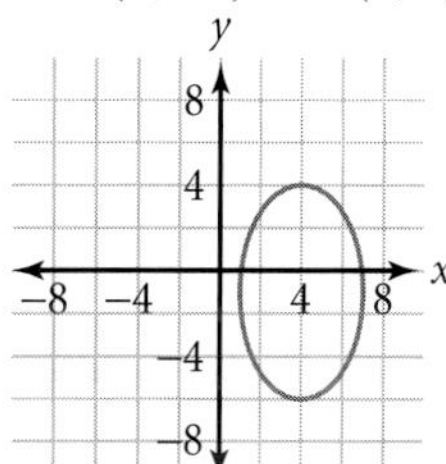

Selected Answers

Selected Answers

19. $\frac{(x+5)^2}{16} + \frac{(y+3)^2}{4} = 1$; center: $(-5, -3)$; vertices: $(-9, -3)$ and $(-1, -3)$; co-vertices: $(-5, -5)$ and $(-5, -1)$; foci: $(-5 - 2\sqrt{3}, -3)$ and $(-5 + 2\sqrt{3}, -3)$

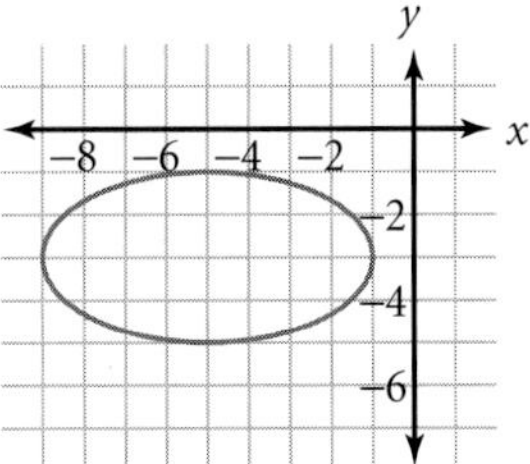

21. $\frac{(x+5)^2}{36} - \frac{(y-1)^2}{64} = 1$; center: $(-5, 1)$; vertices: $(-11, 1)$ and $(1, 1)$; co-vertices: $(-5, -7)$ and $(-5, 9)$; foci: $(-15, 1)$ and $(5, 1)$

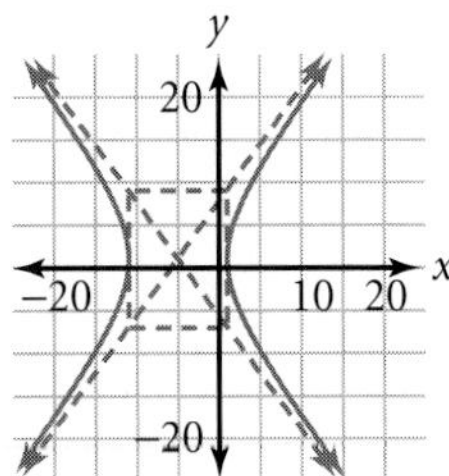

23. $\frac{y^2}{25} - \frac{x^2}{4} = 1$; center: $(0, 0)$; vertices: $(0, -5)$ and $(0, 5)$; co-vertices: $(-2, 0)$ and $(2, 0)$; foci: $(0, -\sqrt{29})$ and $(0, \sqrt{29})$

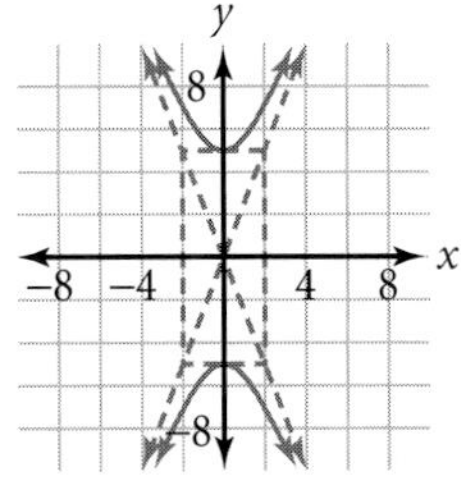

25. $\frac{(y+3)^2}{4} - \frac{(x+5)^2}{36} = 1$; center: $(-5, -3)$; vertices: $(-5, -5)$ and $(-5, -1)$; co-vertices: $(-11, -3)$ and $(1, -3)$; foci: $(-5, -3 - 2\sqrt{10})$ and $(-5, -3 + 2\sqrt{10})$

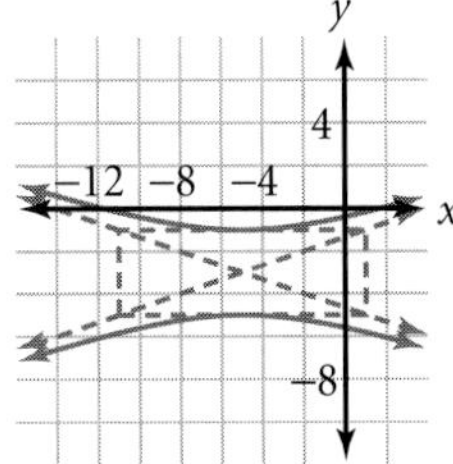

27. 4 solutions: $(\pm 2, \pm\sqrt{2})$, or about $(\pm 2, \pm 1.41)$

29. $\left(-\frac{16}{5}, \frac{9}{5}\right)$ **31.** hyperbola; $\frac{(x-3)^2}{9} - \frac{(y+1)^2}{4} = 1$

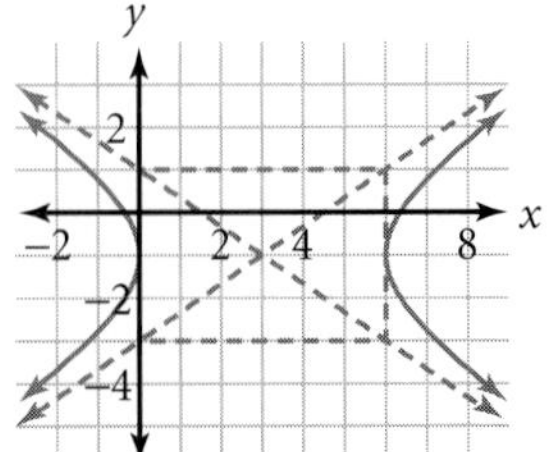

33. $\frac{2420}{3}$ watts, or about 806.7 watts **35a.** Answers may vary. Sample answer: Assuming that distances are measured in feet and that the microphones are located on the x-axis, $\frac{x^2}{1{,}562{,}500} - \frac{y^2}{7{,}437{,}500} = 1$.
b. 1750 feet

Chapter 10

LESSON 10.1

TRY THIS (p. 629)
$\frac{4}{9}$, or ≈44%

TRY THIS (p. 630, Ex. 2)
$\frac{1}{3}$, or ≈33.3%

TRY THIS (p. 630, Ex. 3)
a. $\frac{1}{3}$, or ≈33.3%
b. $\frac{1}{15}$, or ≈6.7%

Exercises

4. $\frac{3}{9}$, or ≈33.3% **5.** $\frac{1}{9}$, or ≈11.1% **6.** $\frac{1}{4}$, or 25% **7.** 455,625 **8.** $\frac{1}{50}$, or 2% **9.** $\frac{3}{10}$, or 30% **11.** $\frac{1}{2}$, or 50% **13.** $\frac{1}{6}$, or ≈16.7% **15.** $\frac{1}{2}$, or 50% **17.** $\frac{1}{2}$, or 50% **19.** $\frac{5}{6}$, or ≈83.3% **21.** $\frac{3}{5}$, or 60% **23.** $\frac{2}{5}$, or 40%

25.

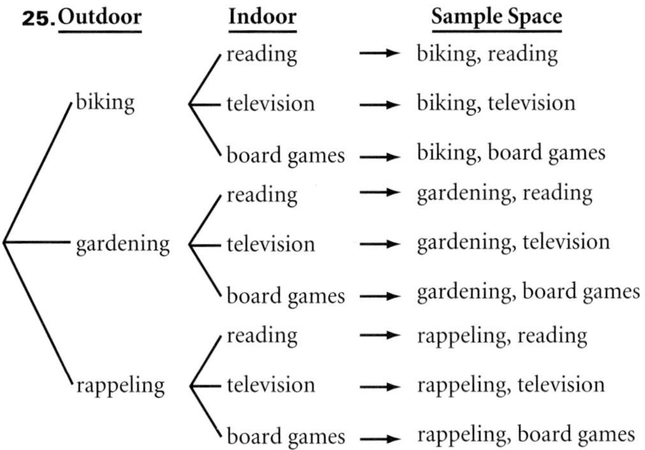

27. 6,760,000 **29.** 6,760,000 **31.** $\frac{4}{9}$, or ≈44.4% **33.** $\frac{1}{21}$, or ≈4.8% **35.** 25% **37.** 35.7% **39.** 268,435,456 **41.** ≈14.0% **43.** ≈29.7% **45.** at least 7 letters long **47.** $g^{-1}(x) = \frac{6x+2}{3}$ **49.** a vertical compression by a factor of $\frac{1}{2}$ and a vertical translation 5 units down **51.** a horizontal compression by a factor of $\frac{1}{2}$ and a vertical translation 1 unit up

LESSON 10.2

TRY THIS (p. 637, Ex. 1)
There are 5040 ways to arrange the letters.

TRY THIS (p. 637, Ex. 2)
There are 1680 ways to listen to 4 out of 8 CDs.

TRY THIS (p. 639, Ex. 3)
There are 462 ways to plant the flowers.

TRY THIS (p. 639, Ex. 4)
There are 39,916,800 ways to choose the seats.

Exercises

5. 720 **6.** 210 **7.** 2520 **8.** 39,916,800 **9.** 4920 **11.** 2 **13.** 56 **15.** 20 **17.** 604,800 **19.** 50 **21.** 132 **23.** 60,480 **25.** 6720 **27.** 1680 **29.** 8 **31.** 40,320 **33.** 1,814,400 **35.** 13,366,080 **37.** 271,252,800 **39.** 720 **41.** 60 **43.** 10,080 **45.** 151,200 **47.** 908,107,200 **49.** 720 **51a.** 10,000 **b.** 5040 **53.** 5040 **55.** 72 **57.** 120 **59.** 720 **61.** 210 **63.** 120 **65.** $3 - 4i$ **67.** $-\frac{42}{29} - \frac{11}{29}i$ **69.** $\log_b 4$ **71.** -1 **73.** ≈194.1 cubic inches

LESSON 10.3

TRY THIS (p. 644)
36

TRY THIS (p. 645, Ex. 2)
21; 42

TRY THIS (p. 645, Ex. 3)
90

TRY THIS (p. 646)
≈0.6%

Exercises

4. 126 **5a.** 220 **b.** 1320 **6.** 2800 **7.** ≈7.6% **9.** 70 **11.** 126 **13.** 11 **15.** 1 **17.** 504 **19.** ≈0.053 **21.** 8 **23.** 210 **25.** 15,504 **27.** 378 **29.** 252 **31.** ≈26.8% **33.** ≈17.9% **35.** combination **37.** permutation **39a.** 2,598,960 **b.** $\frac{1}{649,740} \approx 0.00000154\%$ **41.** ${}_6C_1 = 6$; ${}_6C_2 = 15$; ${}_6C_3 = 20$; ${}_6C_4 = 15$; ${}_6C_5 = 6$; ${}_6C_6 = 1$ **43a.** $\frac{1}{15,890,700} \approx 0.0000000629$
b. Undergoing an audit this year is about 158,907 times more likely, being hit by lightning is about 1746 times more likely, and being hit by a baseball in a major league game is about 53 times more likely than winning the lottery.

45.

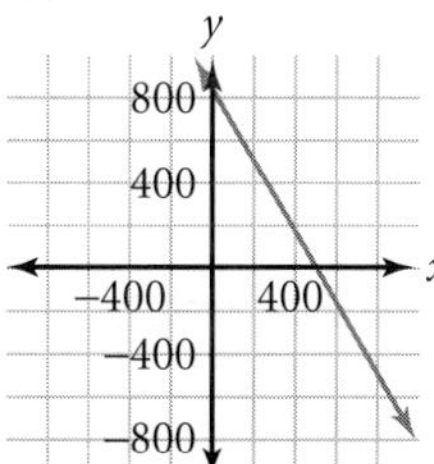

47.

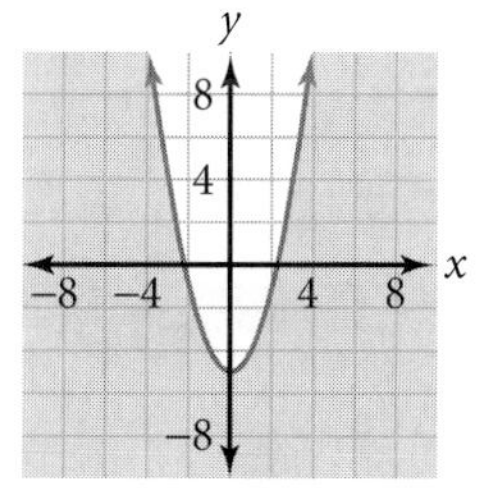

49.

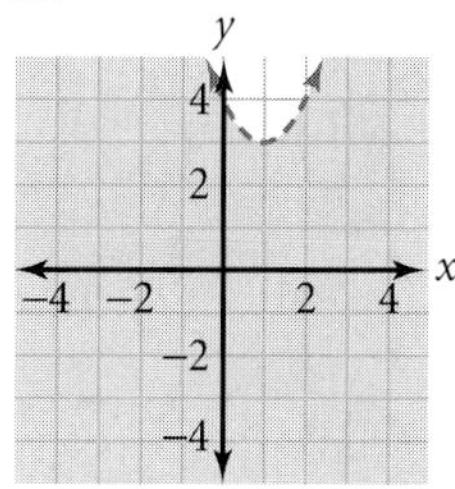

LESSON 10.4

TRY THIS (p. 654, Ex. 1)
63%

TRY THIS (p. 654, Ex. 2)
70%

TRY THIS (p. 655)
≈47%

Exercises

4. 64% **5.** 59% **6.** ≈60.9% **7.** $\frac{1}{3}$ **9.** $\frac{2}{3}$ **11.** $\frac{1}{2}$ **13.** $\frac{5}{6}$ **15.** 1 **17.** mutually exclusive; $\frac{1}{6}$ **19.** mutually exclusive; $\frac{25}{36}$ **21.** inclusive; $\frac{5}{6}$ **23.** inclusive; 1 **25.** mutually exclusive; $\frac{13}{18}$ **27.** inclusive; 1 **29a.** 1100 **b.** $\frac{24}{35}$ **31.** $\frac{7}{11}$ **33.** 0.676 **35.** 0 **37.** $\frac{1}{2}$ **39.** $\frac{5}{16}$ **41.** ≈3.3% **43.** ≈49.9% **45.** ≈60.2% **47.** ≈75.1% **49.** ≈59.4%
51.

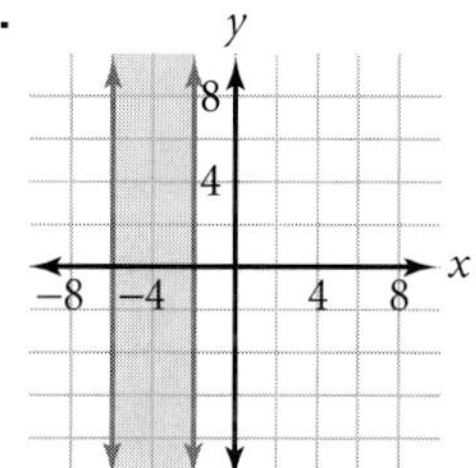

53. $(x + 6)(x - 7)$ **55.** $(9x + 1)^2$ **57.** $x = \frac{5}{2}$ *or* $x = 8$

LESSON 10.5

TRY THIS (p. 661)
≈94.1%

Exercises

4. $\frac{1}{6}$ **5.** $\frac{1}{418}$, or ≈0.24% **6.** ≈89% **7.** 0.125 **9.** 0.1875 **11.** 0.05 **13.** dependent **15.** dependent **17.** $\frac{1}{8}$, or 12.5% **19.** $\frac{9}{64}$, or ≈14.1% **21.** 76% **23.** 89.24% **25.** 0.06 **27.** $\frac{27y^6}{x}$ **29.** $\frac{9}{25y^6}$ **31.** ≈1.10 **33.** ≈1.20 **35.** $y = -\frac{1}{16}(x - 1)^2$

LESSON 10.6

TRY THIS (p. 666)
≈39.4%

TRY THIS (p. 667)
≈53.2%

Exercises

4. $\frac{5}{18}$, or ≈27.8% **5.** $\frac{25}{289}$, or ≈8.7% **6.** $\frac{5}{68}$, or ≈7.4% **7.** ≈41.1% **8.** ≈93.4% **9.** $\frac{4}{33}$, or ≈12.1% **11.** $\frac{20}{231}$, or ≈8.6% **13.** $\frac{12}{77}$, or ≈15.6% **15.** $\frac{15}{154}$, or ≈9.7% **17.** $\frac{1}{6}$, or ≈16.7% **19.** $\frac{1}{3}$, or ≈33.3% **21a.** $\frac{1}{6}$ **b.** $\frac{1}{6}$ **c.** 1 **23a.** $\frac{1}{3}$ **b.** $\frac{1}{3}$ **c.** 1 **25.** $\frac{2}{3}$ **27.** 0.205 **29.** $\frac{5}{6}$ **31a.** $\frac{1}{100}$, or 1% **b.** $\frac{1}{4\pi}$, or ≈8.0% **33.** $\frac{14,320}{37,543}$, or ≈38.1% **35.** $\frac{4850}{44,229}$, or ≈11.0% **37.** $\frac{11,106}{64,323}$, or ≈17.3% **39.** 53.2% **41.** $\frac{2}{3}$ **43.** $x = -\frac{4}{3}$ or $x = \frac{4}{3}$ **45.** $2x(x-6)^2$ **47.** $a = \frac{5 \pm \sqrt{33}}{2}$ **49.** $x \geq 1$ **51.** $x \leq \frac{1}{3}$ **53.** $M(-5, 4.5)$ **55.** $\frac{1}{2}$, or 50%

LESSON 10.7

TRY THIS (p. 674)
Answers may vary. The estimated probability should be close to 0.4.

Exercises

For Exercises 4–6, answers may vary but should be close to those given below.
4. about 60% **5.** about 99% **6.** about 30%

For Exercises 7–27, answers may vary but should be close to those given below.
7. on average about 6 tosses **9.** on average about 4 rolls **11.** about 24% **13.** about 73% **15.** about 25% **17.** on average about 8 **19.** about 8% **21.** about 19 square units **23.** about 32 square units **25.** about 3 times **27.** about 2 times **29.** (−1, −5) **31.** $\left(\frac{\sqrt{10}}{5}, \frac{3\sqrt{10}}{5}\right), \left(-\frac{\sqrt{10}}{5}, -\frac{3\sqrt{10}}{5}\right)$ **33.** $\left(\frac{2\sqrt{15}}{15}, \frac{2\sqrt{210}}{15}\right), \left(-\frac{2\sqrt{15}}{15}, \frac{2\sqrt{210}}{15}\right), \left(\frac{2\sqrt{15}}{15}, -\frac{2\sqrt{210}}{15}\right), \left(-\frac{2\sqrt{15}}{15}, -\frac{2\sqrt{210}}{15}\right)$ **35.** $\frac{11}{25}$ **37.** $\frac{21}{25}$

CHAPTER REVIEW AND ASSESSMENT

1. $\frac{3}{8}$ **3.** $\frac{1}{6}$ **5.** $\frac{1}{10}$ **7.** 625 **9.** 6720 **11.** 95,040 **13.** 24 **15.** 45 **17.** 161,700 **19.** $\frac{1}{3}$ **21.** $\frac{5}{6}$ **23.** $\frac{2}{3}$ **25.** $\frac{1}{4}$ **27.** 0
29. Answers may vary but should be close to 0.5.
31. ≈69%

Chapter 11

LESSON 11.1

TRY THIS (p. 693)

n	1	2	3	4	5	6
t_n	1	7	17	31	49	71

TRY THIS (p. 694)
1, 2, 5, 14, 41, 122

TRY THIS (p. 693)

a. $\sum_{k=1}^{5} 4k = 4 + 8 + 12 + 16 + 20$
$= 60$

b. $\frac{1}{2}\sum_{k=1}^{4} k = \frac{1}{2}(1 + 2 + 3 + 4)$
$= 5$

TRY THIS (p. 695)
$\sum_{j=1}^{5}(-j^2 + 2j + 5) = 0$

Exercises

4. 1, 4, 7, 10, 13, 16 **5.** 1, 4, 13, 40, 121, 364 **6a.** 13, 15, 17, 19, 21 **b.** $t_1 = 3, t_n = t_{n-1} + 2$ **7.** 24 **8.** 50 **9.** 126 **11.** 5, 9, 13, 17 **13.** −5, −9, −13, −17 **15.** 4, 9, 14, 19 **17.** 4, 0, −4, −8 **19.** $\frac{3}{2}$, 2, $\frac{5}{2}$, 3 **21.** 12.42, 21.17, 29.92, 38.67 **23.** 1, 8, 27, 64 **25.** −2, −8, −18, −32 **27.** 2, 4, 6, 8, 10, 12 **29.** −6, 15, −27, 57, −111, 225 **31.** 10, 51, 256, 1281, 6406, 32,031 **33.** 8, 22, 64, 190, 568, 1702 **35.** 3.34, 6.348, 12.9656, 27.52432, 59.553504, 130.0177088 **37.** $\frac{5}{7}, \frac{10}{21}, \frac{3}{7}, \frac{44}{105}, \frac{73}{175}, \frac{1094}{2625}$ **39.** $t_1 = 3, t_n = t_{n-1} + 6$; 27, 33, 39 **41.** $t_1 = 3, t_n = 2t_{n-1} + 1$; 63, 127, 255 **43.** 10 + 10 + 10 + 10 = 40 **45.** 4 + 8 + 12 = 24 **47.** −5 − 10 − 15 − 20 = −50 **49.** $\frac{1}{3} + \frac{4}{3} + \frac{9}{3} + \frac{16}{3} + \frac{25}{3} = \frac{55}{3}$ **51.** $\frac{3}{4} + 1 + \frac{3}{4} = \frac{5}{2}$ **53.** −2 − 5 − 8 = −15 **55.** 3 + 7 + 13 = 23 **57.** 12 **59.** 84 **61.** 42 **63.** 39 **65.** 164 **67.** 6 **69.** $-\frac{88}{21}$ **71.** $50\pi + 8$ **73.** 68 **75.** $t_1 = 0.4$, $t_n = 0.3(2^{n-2}) + 0.4$, or $t_n = \frac{3(2^{n-2}) + 4}{10}$, where $n \geq 2$ **77.** 90° **79.** 120° **81.** 7.00, 7.30, 7.60, 7.90, 8.20, 8.50, 8.80, 9.10; $t_n = 7.00 + 0.30(n-1)$ **83.** $\sum_{n=0}^{6} 12 + 4n = 168$ flowers **85.** $y = \frac{2}{3}x + \frac{14}{3}$ **87.** 0; 1 real solution; $\frac{1}{2}$ **89.** $\left(\frac{2}{5}, \frac{1}{5}\right)$ and $\left(\frac{1}{2}, 0\right)$ **91.** (4, −3) and (−52, 11) **93.** 72 **95.** 70

LESSON 11.2

TRY THIS (p. 700)
−15.5

TRY THIS (p. 701, Ex. 2)
$12.45

TRY THIS (p. 701, Ex. 3)
35

TRY THIS (p. 702)
27, 30, 33, 36

Exercises

4. $t_4 = 2$ **5.** \$575.65 **6.** $\frac{22}{3}$ **7.** 10, 14, 18, and 22 **9.** yes; $d = 2$ **11.** yes; $d = 3$ **13.** no **15.** yes; $d = -6$ **17.** no **19.** no **21.** yes; $d = \frac{1}{3}$ **23.** no **25.** no **27.** no **29.** no **31.** 18; 15; 12; 9 **33.** 1; 3; 5; 7 **35.** −4; −1; 2; 5 **37.** 7, 8, 9, 10 **39.** 4, 7, 10, 13 **41.** −1, 2, 5, 8 **43.** −3, −8, −13, −18 **45.** −3, 2, 7, 12 **47.** $\frac{2}{3}, 1, \frac{4}{3}, \frac{5}{3}$ **49.** $\pi + 4, 2\pi + 4, 3\pi + 4, 4\pi + 4$ **51.** $t_5 = 18$ **53.** $t_{10} = 1.29$ **55.** $t_1 = \frac{5}{6}$ **57.** $t_n = 6 + (n-1)(2)$ **59.** $t_n = 1 + (n-1)(-7)$ **61.** $t_n = 23 + (n-1)(8)$ **63.** $t_n = 20 + (n-1)(-5)$ **65.** $t_n = 100 + (n-1)(5)$ **67.** $t_n = -50 + (n-1)(5)$ **69.** 8, 11, and 14 **71.** 11, 4, and −3 **73.** 5.62 and 5.98 **75.** 9, 6, 3, 0 and −3 **77.** 27 dots **79.** Let *a*, *b*, and *c* represent the sides of a triangle. $a = a$; $b = a + d$; $c = a + 2d$; Let $a = 3$ and $d = 1$. $b = a + d = 3 + 1 = 4$; $c = a + 2d = 3 + 2 = 5$ **81a.** $t_n = 30{,}000 + (n-1)(800)$ **b.** \$37,200 **83.** $(x+3)^2$ **85.** $(x+7)^2$ **87.** $4 < x \le 7$ **89.** $-1 < x < 1$ **91.** $(x+2)^2 + (y-5)^2 = 16$; $C(-2, 5)$; $r = 4$ **93.** $\frac{x^2}{25} + \frac{(y-2)^2}{9} = 1$ **95.** {*MF*, *FM*, *FF*}; $\frac{3}{4}$ **97.** {*MF*, *FM*}; $\frac{1}{2}$

LESSON 11.3

TRY THIS (p. 709)
440

TRY THIS (p. 710)
−510

Exercises

4. 477 cans **5.** 2405 **6.** 35 **7.** 30 **9.** 68 **11.** −376 **13.** 66 **15.** −360 **17.** 45,150 **19.** 1683 **21.** 1275 **23.** 3100 **25.** 1625 **27.** 1500 **29.** 3250 **31.** −1750 **33.** $325\sqrt{2}$ **35.** 350π **37.** 168 **39.** 30 **41.** 240 **43.** 2530 **45.** 5450 **47.** 15 **49.** 695 **51.** 5, 10, 15, 20, 25 **53a.** 39 pipes **b.** 49 pipes **55.** 19 musicians; 96 musicians **57.** $y = |x - 4|$ **59.** $-10x^4 + 6x^3 + 4x^2 - 12x$ **61.** $y = k\frac{xz}{m^2}$ **63.** all real numbers **65.** 593,775

LESSON 11.4

TRY THIS (p. 714)
−40,960

TRY THIS (p. 715, Ex. 2)
\$803.61

TRY THIS (p. 715, Ex. 3)
$\frac{15}{16}$

TRY THIS (p. 716)
32, 16, and 8 or −32, 16, and −8

Exercises

4. 32 **5.** \$2756.24 **6.** ±384 **7.** 80, 40, and 20 or −80, 40, and −20 **9.** yes; $r = 2$; 320, 640, 1280 **11.** no **13.** yes; $r = 5$; 1250, 6250, 31,250 **15.** yes; $r = 3$; 162, 486, 1458 **17.** no **19.** yes; $r = 9$; 1458, 13,122, 118,098 **21.** yes; $r = \frac{1}{3}$; $\frac{1}{9}, \frac{1}{27}, \frac{1}{81}$ **23.** yes; $r = \frac{1}{4}$; $\frac{3}{64}, \frac{3}{256}, \frac{3}{1024}$ **25.** yes; $r = 1.25$; 39.0625, 48.828125, 61.03515625 **27.** −2, −8, −32, −128 **29.** 4, −12, 36, −108 **31.** −1, 0.2, −0.04, 0.008 **33.** 3, 10.11, 34.0707, 114.818259 **35.** 24,576 **37.** $\frac{3}{10{,}000{,}000{,}000{,}000{,}000{,}000} = 3.0 \times 10^{-19}$ **39.** 18,750 or −18,750 **41.** 324 **43.** 12 **45.** −81 **47.** $\frac{25}{16}$ or $-\frac{25}{16}$ **49.** $t_n = 2(2)^{n-1}$ or $t_n = 2^n$ **51.** $t_n = \left(\frac{1}{2}\right)^{n-1}$ **53.** $t_n = 30\left(\frac{1}{3}\right)^{n-1}$ **55.** $t_n = \sqrt{2}(\sqrt{2})^{n-1}$ or $t_n = (\sqrt{2})^n$ **57.** 15 and 45 **59.** 7.5 and 11.25 **61.** $-1, -\frac{1}{2}$, and $-\frac{1}{4}$ or $1, -\frac{1}{2}$, and $\frac{1}{4}$ **63.** 162, 54, and 18 or −162, 54, and −18 **65.** 125 and 375 **67.** 12, 36, 108, 324; geometric **69.** $\frac{18}{5}, \frac{36}{25}, \frac{72}{125}, \frac{144}{625}$; geometric **71.** 7, 27, 127, 627; neither **73.** −400, −1600, −6400, −25,600; geometric **75.** \$1,688,520.51 **77.** \$866,580.59 **79.** $y = -3x - 1$ **81.** $\begin{bmatrix} 3.3 \\ 16.24 \end{bmatrix}$ **83.** $\begin{bmatrix} 5.44 & 8.16 \\ 10.24 & 15.36 \end{bmatrix}$ **85.** run: 4.68 mph; bike: 16.68 mph **87.** $\sqrt{15} + \sqrt{7}$ **89.** 10,080 **91.** 360

LESSON 11.5

TRY THIS (p. 721)
1584.0

TRY THIS (p. 722)
16.5

TRY THIS (p. 723)

Basis Step

Show that $4 + 8 + 12 + \cdots + 4n = 2n(n+1)$ is true for $n = 1$.

$4 = 2(1)(2)$ True

Induction Step

Assume the statement is true for a natural number *k*.

$4 + 8 + 12 + \cdots + 4k = 2k(k+1)$

Determine the statement to be proved: Add $4(k+1)$ to the left side, and substitute $k + 1$ for *k* on the right.

$$4 + 8 + 12 + \cdots + 4k = 2k(k+1)$$
$$4 + 8 + 12 + \cdots + 4k + 4(k+1) = 2(k+1)[(k+1)+1]$$
$$4 + 8 + 12 + \cdots + 4k + 4(k+1) = 2(k+1)(k+2)$$

Rewrite the left-hand side by using the statement assumed to be true.

$$\begin{aligned} 4 + 8 + 12 + \cdots + 4k + 4(k+1) &= 2k(k+1) + 4(k+1) \\ &= (k+1)(2k+4) \\ &= (k+1)2(k+2) \\ &= 2(k+1)(k+2) \end{aligned}$$

True

Exercises

5. 12,714.3 **6.** \$30,749.25 **7.** 189

8. Basis Step

Show that $\frac{1}{1 \cdot 2} + \frac{1}{2 \cdot 3} + \cdots + \frac{1}{n(n+1)} = \frac{n}{n+1}$ is true for $n = 1$.

$\frac{1}{1 \cdot 2} = \frac{1}{1+1}$ True

Induction Step

Assume the statement is true for a natural number k.

$\frac{1}{1 \cdot 2} + \frac{1}{2 \cdot 3} + \cdots + \frac{1}{k(k+1)} = \frac{k}{k+1}$

Determine the statement to be proved: Add $\frac{1}{(k+1)(k+2)}$ to the left side, and substitute $k + 1$ for k on the right.

$\frac{1}{1 \cdot 2} + \frac{1}{2 \cdot 3} + \cdots + \frac{1}{k(k+1)} + \frac{1}{(k+1)(k+2)} = \frac{k+1}{[(k+1)+1]}$

$\frac{1}{1 \cdot 2} + \frac{1}{2 \cdot 3} + \cdots + \frac{1}{k(k+1)} + \frac{1}{(k+1)(k+2)} = \frac{k+1}{k+2}$

Rewrite the left side by using the statement assumed to be true.

$$\begin{aligned}\frac{1}{1 \cdot 2} + \frac{1}{2 \cdot 3} + \cdots + \frac{1}{k(k+1)} + \frac{1}{(k+1)(k+2)} &= \frac{k}{k+1} + \frac{1}{(k+1)(k+2)} \\ &= \frac{k}{k+1}\left(\frac{k+2}{k+2}\right) + \frac{1}{(k+1)(k+2)} \\ &= \frac{k(k+2)+1}{(k+1)(k+2)} \\ &= \frac{k^2+2k+1}{(k+1)(k+2)} \\ &= \frac{(k+1)^2}{(k+1)(k+2)} \\ &= \frac{k+1}{k+2} \quad \text{True}\end{aligned}$$

9. 7 **11.** 255 **13.** –40 **15.** 7,174,454 **17.** 10 **19.** 83.1 **21.** 453.3 **23.** 26,594.1 **25.** 62 **27.** 5 **29.** 5.4 **31.** $\frac{203}{125}$

33. $\frac{3}{65{,}536} \approx 4.58 \times 10^{-5}$ **35.** $\frac{1{,}048{,}575}{65{,}536} \approx 16.0$

37. $t_1 = 5$; $r = 5$; $t_{10} = 9{,}765{,}625$; $S_{10} = 12{,}207{,}030$

39. $t_1 = 1$; $r = \frac{\frac{1}{121}}{\frac{1}{11}} = \frac{1}{11}$; $t_{12} = \frac{1}{285{,}311{,}670{,}611}$; $S_{12} = \frac{11}{10}$

41. $t_1 = 2.76$; $r = 2.76$; $t_8 = 3367.23$; $S_8 = 5278.86$

43. 124 **45.** $\frac{63}{32}$ **47.** 3.8 **49.** 27,305

51. 2,036,814,259 **53.** 0.5 **55.** –520 **57.** $n = 5$

59. $n < n + 1$

Basis Step

Show that $n < n + 1$ is true for $n = 1$.

$1 < 1 + 1$ True

Induction Step

Assume the statement is true for a natural number k.

$k < k + 1$

Determine the statement to be proved.

$k + 1 < k + 2$

Rewrite the inequality by using the statement assumed to be true.

$k + 1 < k + 2$

$(k) + 1 < (k + 1) + 1$ True

61. $1 + 3 + 5 + \cdots + (2n - 1) = n^2$

Basis Step

Show that $1 + 3 + 5 + \cdots + (2n - 1) = n^2$ is true for $n = 1$.

$1 = 1^2$ True

Induction Step

Assume the statement is true for a natural number k.

$1 + 3 + 5 + \cdots + (2k - 1) = k^2$

Determine the statement to be proved: Add $2(k + 1) - 1$ to the left side and substitute $k + 1$ for k on the right side.

$1 + 3 + 5 + \cdots + (2k - 1) + [2(k + 1) - 1] = (k + 1)^2$

$1 + 3 + 5 + \cdots + (2k - 1) + (2k + 1) = (k + 1)^2$

Rewrite the left side by using the statement assumed to be true.

$$\begin{aligned}1 + 3 + 5 + \cdots + (2k - 1) + (2k + 1) &= k^2 + (2k + 1) \\ &= k^2 + 2k + 1 \\ &= (k + 1)^2 \quad \text{True}\end{aligned}$$

63. 6.6 **65a.** $8, 4\sqrt{2}, 4, 2\sqrt{2}, 2, \sqrt{2}, 1$

b. $t_n = 8\left(\frac{\sqrt{2}}{2}\right)^{n-1}$ **c.** $S_7 = 15 + 7\sqrt{2} \approx 24.90$

d. $S_n = \sum_{k=1}^{n} 8\left(\frac{\sqrt{2}}{2}\right)^{n-1}$, or $S_n = 8\left(\frac{1 - \left(\frac{\sqrt{2}}{2}\right)^n}{1 - \frac{\sqrt{2}}{2}}\right)$

67. 2132.8125 in.^{2} **69.** \$49,680.88 **71.** \$329,723.09

73. about 24.0 feet

75.

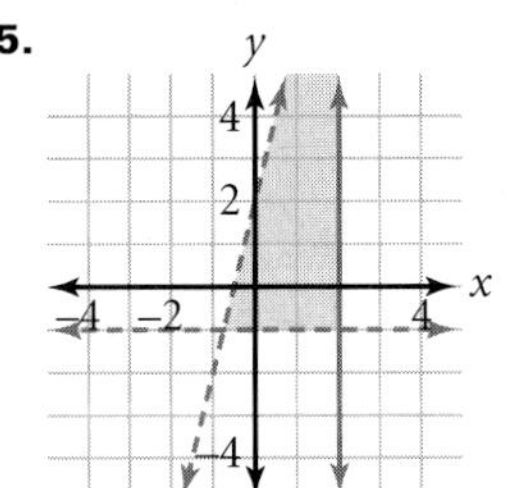

77a. 0.9 **b.** $V(t) = 3800(0.9)^t$ **c.** \$3078 **d.** \$2770.20

79. vertical asymptote: $x = 0$; horizontal asymptote: $y = 0$; no holes **81.** $\frac{1}{2x+1}$ **83.** 2,805,264 ways

LESSON 11.6

TRY THIS (p. 730)

$-\frac{8}{3}$

TRY THIS (p. 731)

$\frac{1}{2}$

TRY THIS (p. 732)

$\frac{5}{9}$

Exercises

4. 9 **5.** $\frac{1}{12}$ **6.** $\frac{1}{3}$ **7.** $\frac{1}{2}$ **9.** 8 **11.** does not converge

13. $\frac{121}{150}$ **15.** 10 **17.** does not converge **19.** $\frac{10}{9}$ **21.** $\frac{1}{7}$

23. $\frac{70}{9}$, or $7.\overline{7}$ **25.** $\frac{7}{10}$ **27.** does not converge **29.** $\frac{7}{3}$

31. does not converge **33.** 1 **35.** $2 + \sqrt{2}$, or about 3.4142 **37.** $\frac{\pi}{\pi - 1}$, or about 1.4669 **39.** $\sum_{k=1}^{\infty} 19\left(\frac{1}{100}\right)^k$ **41.** $\sum_{k=1}^{\infty} \left(\frac{1}{1000}\right)^k$ **43.** $\sum_{k=1}^{\infty} 35\left(\frac{1}{100}\right)^k$ **45.** $\sum_{k=1}^{\infty} 819\left(\frac{1}{1000}\right)^k$ **47.** $\sum_{k=1}^{\infty} 121\left(\frac{1}{1000}\right)^k$ **49.** $\frac{4}{9}$ **51.** $\frac{4}{11}$ **53.** $\frac{6}{11}$ **55.** $\frac{586}{999}$ **57.** $\frac{158}{333}$ **59.** $\frac{31}{999}$ **61.** 200 square centimeters **63a.** \$7142.86 **b.** \$12,500 **65.** $x = -4$, $y = 7$, and $z = 0.5$ **67.** $x = \frac{\ln 19}{\ln 3}$, $x \approx -2.68$ **69.** $x = \frac{\ln 7.23}{\ln 2}$, $x \approx 2.85$

LESSON 11.7

TRY THIS (p. 737, Ex. 1)
11, 1

TRY THIS (p. 737, Ex. 2)
1, 8, 28, 56, 70, 56, 28, 8, 1

TRY THIS (p. 738)
0.38

Exercises

4. ${}_{10}C_2 = 45$ and ${}_{10}C_4 = 210$ **5.** ${}_6C_0 = 1$, ${}_6C_1 = 6$, ${}_6C_2 = 15$, ${}_6C_3 = 20$, ${}_6C_4 = 15$, ${}_6C_5 = 6$, ${}_6C_6 = 1$
6. 0.55 **7.** ${}_5C_2$ is the third entry in the fifth row; ${}_5C_2 = 10$. **9.** ${}_8C_5$ is the sixth entry in the eighth row; ${}_8C_5 = 56$. **11.** ${}_{11}C_2$ is the third entry in the 11th row; ${}_{11}C_2 = 55$. **13.** ${}_{10}C_3$ is the fourth entry in the tenth row; ${}_{10}C_3 = 120$. **15.** ${}_8C_4$ is the fifth entry in the eighth row; ${}_8C_4 = 70$. **17.** ${}_7C_2$ is the third entry in the seventh row; ${}_7C_2 = 21$. **19.** ${}_9C_6$ is the seventh entry in the ninth row; ${}_9C_6 = 84$. **21.** ${}_{13}C_7$ is the eighth entry in the 13th row; ${}_{13}C_7 = 1716$. **23.** 35; 7 **25.** 165; 462
27a. 5, 8, 13, 21, 34 **b.** a Fibonacci sequence
29. ≈0.34 **31.** 0.5 **33.** ≈0.49 **35.** ≈0.31 **37.** ≈0.19
39. ≈0.81 **41.** ≈0.31 **43.** ≈0.19 **45.** ≈0.81
47a. yes; —1, =2, ≡3, ≣4, ≣5, ⊢6, ⊨7, ⊫8, ⫠10, 𝍧15, ≗20, ⊥21, ⩮28, 𝍤35, 𝍥56, ⊣70

b. Answers may vary. Sample answer: The sums of the rows are multiples of 2. **49.** $f(x) = -\frac{5}{14}x^2 + \frac{27}{14}x + 2$
51. $-9 < x < 2$

−9 −8 −7 −6 −5 −4 −3 −2 −1 0 1 2 3

53. permutations; ${}_{10}P_3 = 720$

LESSON 11.8

TRY THIS (p. 741)
$m^6 + 6m^5n + 15m^4n^2 + 20m^3n^3 + 15m^2n^4 + 6mn^5 + n^6$

TRY THIS (p. 742, Ex. 2)
$\binom{4}{2}(0.337)^2(0.663)^2 \approx 0.30$

TRY THIS (p. 742, Ex. 3)
$\binom{8}{5}r^{8-5}s^5 = 56r^3s^5$

TRY THIS (p. 744)
$x^5 - 10x^4y + 40x^3y^2 - 80x^2y^3 + 80xy^4 - 32y^5$

Exercises

4. $a^5 + 5a^4b + 10a^3b^2 + 10a^2b^3 + 5ab^4 + b^5$
5. $\binom{5}{2}(0.30)^3(0.70)^2 \approx 0.13$ **6.** $120a^7b^3$
7. $243x^5 - 810x^4y + 1080x^3y^2 - 720x^2y^3 + 240xy^4 - 32y^5$
8. 7 pieces need to be added: 3 pieces with dimensions $s \cdot s \cdot (0.2)$, 3 pieces with dimensions $s \cdot (0.2) \cdot (0.2)$, and 1 piece with dimensions $(0.2) \cdot (0.2) \cdot (0.2)$.
9. $a^5 + 5a^4b + 10a^3b^2 + 10a^2b^3 + 5ab^4 + b^5$
11. $a^8 + 8a^7b + 28a^6b^2 + 56a^5b^3 + 70a^4b^4 + 56a^3b^5 + 28a^2b^6 + 8ab^7 + b^8$
13. $x^4 + 4x^3y + 6x^2y^2 + 4xy^3 + y^4$
15. $32 + 80x + 80x^2 + 40x^3 + 10x^4 + x^5$
17. $y^9 + 36y^8 + 576y^7 + 5376y^6 + 32{,}256y^5 + 129{,}024y^4 + 344{,}064y^3 + 589{,}824y^2 + 589{,}824y + 262{,}144$
19. $x^4 - 4x^3y + 6x^2y^2 - 4xy^3 + y^4$
21. $(a + b)^4 = a^4 + 4a^3b + 6a^2b^2 + 4ab^3 + b^4$
23. $(a + b)^5 = a^5 + 5a^4b + 10a^3b^2 + 10a^2b^3 + 5ab^4 + b^5$
25. $(x + y)^9 = x^9 + 9x^8y + 36x^7y^2 + 84x^6y^3 + 126x^5y^4 + 126x^4y^5 + 84x^3y^6 + 36x^2y^7 + 9xy^8 + y^9$
27. $36r^7s^2$ **29.** $126r^4s^5$ **31.** $3584x^5$ **33.** $114{,}688x^2$
35. $35x^3y^4$ **37.** $-21x^2y^5$
39. $1024a^5 + 3840a^4b + 5760a^3b^2 + 4320a^2b^3 + 1620ab^4 + 243b^5$
41. $x^4 - 8x^3y + 24x^2y^2 - 32xy^3 + 16y^4$
43. $16x^4 + 96x^3 + 216x^2 + 216x + 81$
45. $243x^5 - 810x^4y + 1080x^3y^2 - 720x^2y^3 + 240xy^4 - 32y^5$
47. $\frac{1}{8}x^3 + \frac{1}{4}x^2y + \frac{1}{6}xy^2 + \frac{1}{27}y^3$
49. $0.2401 + 1.372x + 2.94x^2 + 2.8x^3 + x^4$
51. $3432p^7q^7$ **53.** 7; $120a^7b^3$ **55.** $n = 9$
57. $a = -32$ and $b = 32$ **59a.** 0.95 **b.** 0.22
61. 0.36 **63.** 0.79 **65.** 0.21

67.

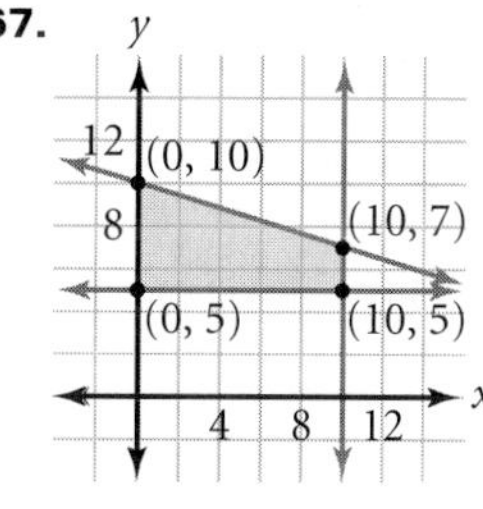
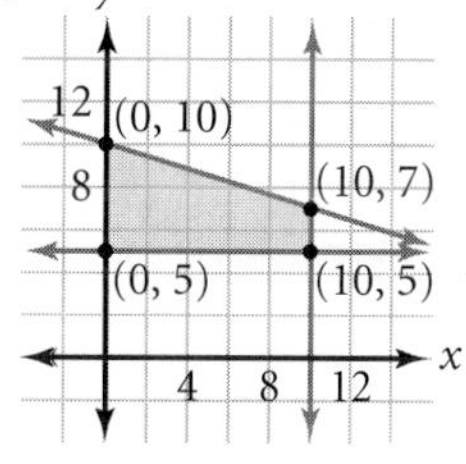

121; 15

69.

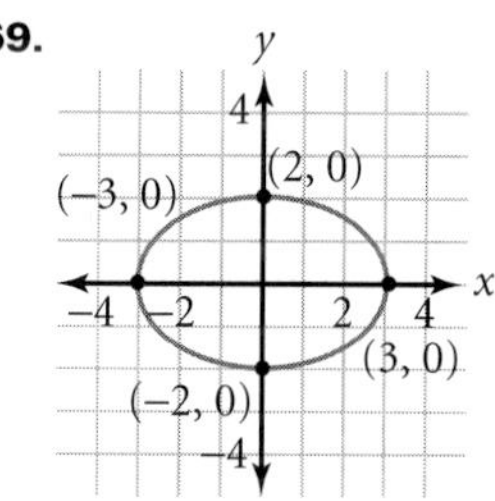

ellipse

71.

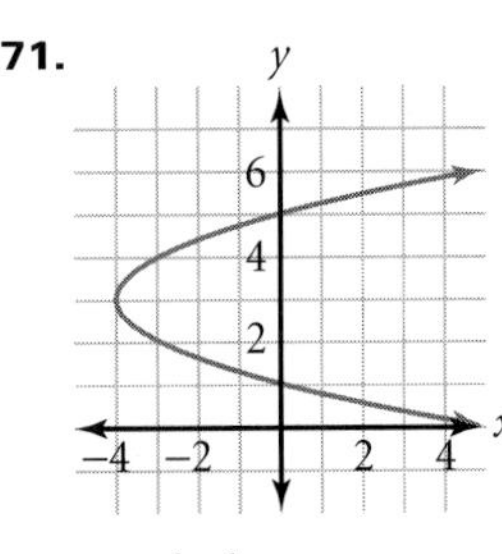

parabola

73.

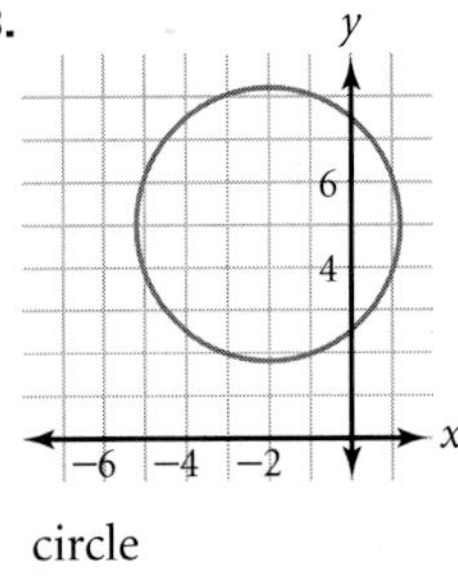

circle

CHAPTER REVIEW AND ASSESSMENT

1. 5, 7, 9, 11, 13 **3.** –0.1, –0.3, –0.5, –0.7, –0.9 **5.** 1, 4, 10, 22, 46 **7.** 3, –8, 25, –74, 223 **9.** 30 **11.** –108 **13.** 215 **15.** 22 **17.** –19 **19.** 30 and 40 **21.** –15, –20, –25, and –30 **23.** 40 **25.** 222 **27.** 1680 **29.** –1260 **31.** 90 **33.** 5 **35.** –12,500 **37.** $\frac{1}{1536}$ **39.** $5(20)^{\frac{1}{4}}$, $5(20)^{\frac{1}{2}}$, and $5(20)^{\frac{3}{4}}$ or $-5(20)^{\frac{1}{4}}$, $5(20)^{\frac{1}{2}}$, and $-5(20)^{\frac{3}{4}}$ **41.** 8.1 **43.** 257.5 **45.** –9091 **47.** –63 **49.** 0.2

51. Basis Step

Show that $7 + 9 + 11 + \cdots + (2n + 5) = n(n + 6)$ is true for $n = 1$.

$7 = 1(1 + 6) = 7$ True

Induction Step

Assume the statement is true for a natural number k.

$7 + 9 + 11 + \cdots + (2k + 5) = k(k + 6)$

Then prove that it is true for the next natural number, $k + 1$.

Determine the statement to be proved.

$$7+9+11+\cdots+[2(k+1)+5]=(k+1)[(k+1)+6]$$
$$7+9+11+\ldots+(2k+7)=(k+1)(k+7)$$

Begin with the statement assumed to be true and use properties of equality.

$$7+9+11+\cdots+(2k+5)+(2k+7)=(k+1)(k+7)$$
$$k(k+6)+(2k+7)=(k+1)(k+7)$$
$$k^2+8k+7=(k+1)(k+7)$$
$$(k+1)(k+7)=(k+1)(k+7) \text{ True}$$

53. 16 **55.** $\frac{5}{9}$ **57.** $\frac{1}{5}$ **59.** $\frac{7}{4}$ **61.** does not converge **63.** $\frac{32}{999}$ **65.** 120 **67.** 20 **69.** 0.22 **71.** 0.47

73. $a^5 + 15a^4 + 90a^3 + 270a^2 + 405a + 243$

75. $729x^6 - 1458x^5y + 1215x^4y^2 - 540x^3y^3 + 135x^2y^4 - 18xy^5 + y^6$

77. $120a^3b^7$

79. $(a + b)^6 = a^6 + 6a^5b + 15a^4b^2 + 20a^3b^3 + 15a^2b^4 + 6ab^5 + b^6$

81a. ≈3.6 meters **b.** 60 meters **83.** 480 seats; 1120 seats

Chapter 12

LESSON 12.1

TRY THIS (p. 765)

$\bar{x} = 82.375$, median = 82, mode = 74; the mean and median are very close, but the mode is lower than the others.

TRY THIS (p. 766)

$\bar{x}$ = \$71,000, median = \$85,000, no mode; the median is the best measure because the mean is below every value except \$0.

TRY THIS (p. 767)

$\bar{x} \approx 31.0$, temperature ≈ 71.0°F

Exercises

4. $\bar{x}$ = \$5.75; median = \$5.625; mode = \$5.00; the mean and median are close, but the mode is the smallest value in the data set. **5a.** $\bar{x}$ = 32.5 hours; median = 35.5 hours; mode = 40 hours **b.** The median best represents the data because mean is more influenced by the extreme value, 0. The mode is the largest value, which happens to occur twice. **6.** $\bar{x} \approx 4.23$ **7.** $x = 4.2$ magazines per month **9.** $\bar{x} = 3.375$; median = 3; mode = 3 **11.** $\bar{x} \approx 14.714$; median = 14; mode = 14 **13.** $\bar{x} = -11$; median = –11; no mode **15.** $\bar{x} \approx 2.933$; median = 2.75; modes = 1.6 and 3.8 **17.** $\bar{x} = 4.628$; median = 4.82; no mode **19.** $\bar{x} = \frac{11}{24} \approx 0.458$; median = $\frac{4}{9} \approx 0.444$; no mode **21.** $\bar{x}$ = \$1.24; median = \$1.23; mode = \$1.20; all three measures are similar and seem to be good measures of central tendency.

23.

Number of pets	Frequency
0	8
1	7
2	6
3	4
4	5
Total	30

$\bar{x} = 1.7$ pets

25. Answers may vary due to arrangement of groups. sample answers:

Miles per gallon	Class mean	Frequency
10–14	12	1
15–19	17	7
20–24	22	7
25–29	27	5
30–35	32	3
	Total	23

Estimate of the mean is 22 miles per gallon.

27. Grouped frequency table; there will be many different values that can be grouped into classes. **29.** Frequency table; number of brothers and sisters should be from about 0 to 6. **31 and 33.** Answers will vary. Find the following measures:

mean = $\frac{\text{sum of data values}}{\text{number of values}}$, median = numerical middle value, or average of the two middle values if there are an even number of values, and mode = the value or values repeated most often. The most representative measures will depend on the data collected. **35a.** $\bar{x} = 6.632$; median = $6\frac{1}{2}$; mode = 7; the mean and median are similar, but the mode is a bit higher. **b.** The mode will be the most helpful because the manager should stock the most of this size. **37.** 67 **39.** $2x^3 + 2x - 3$; $-2x + 3$

41. $\log_5 625 = 4$ **43.** $\log_2 \frac{1}{8} = -3$ **45.** $5^4 = 625$

47. $(x + 5)(x^2 - 5x + 25)$ **49 and 51.** Answers may vary. Sample answers are given. **49.** 2, 2, 2, 2, 2 or 2, 3, 3, 3, 4 **51.** −10, 20, 30, 40, 70; $\bar{x} = 30$; 20, 30, 40, 70; $\bar{x} = 40$

LESSON 12.2

TRY THIS (p. 773)

Stem	Leaf 2|3 = 2.3
2	3, 3, 3, 5
3	2, 2, 3
4	2, 2, 5, 5
5	1, 3, 4, 5, 6, 6
6	2, 2, 5, 9
7	0, 2, 2, 7
8	
9	1, 2

median = 5.4; mode = 2.3; there are 6 data values between 5.0 and 6.0; the graph is slightly mound-shaped with a gap between 7.7 and 9.1.

TRY THIS (p. 774)

Data	Frequency
11	3
12	4
13	5
14	2
15	5
16	3
17	2

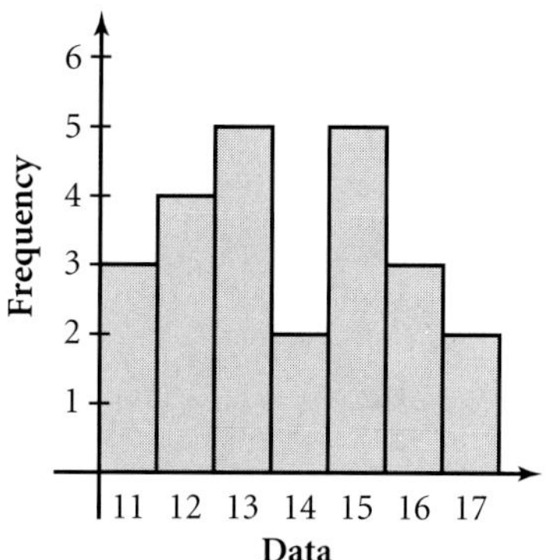

TRY THIS (p. 775)
about 66.7%

Exercises

5a.

Stem	Leaf 2|1 = 21
2	1, 2, 4, 5, 9
3	1, 2, 6, 7, 8, 9, 9
4	2, 2, 2, 8, 8
5	1, 1, 1, 2, 3, 3
6	
7	1

b. median = 40.5; modes = 42 and 51 **c.** possible answer: to determine how many people should be available to answer calls

6a.

Responses	Frequency
3	2
4	4
5	5
6	5
7	4
8	3
9	1

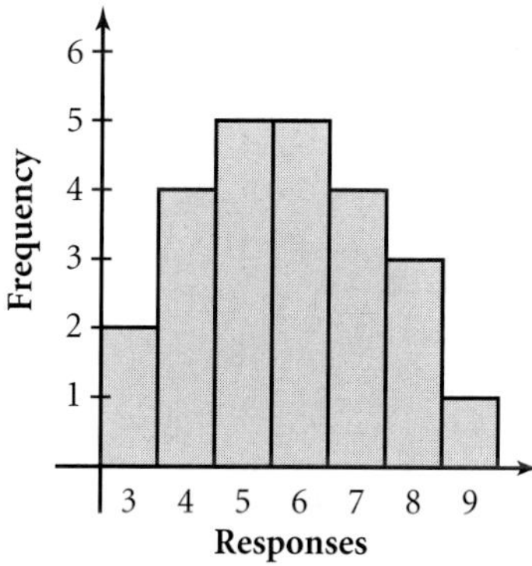

7. 0.9

8a.

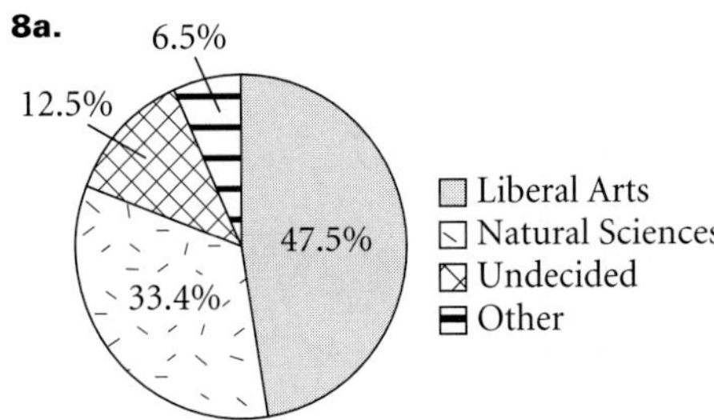

b. 0.6

9.

Stem	Leaf 7|2 = 7.2
7	2, 5, 5, 9
8	2, 2, 5, 6, 7, 8, 9
9	1, 2, 5

median = 8.55; modes = 7.5 and 8.2; mound-shaped

11.

Stem	Leaf 33|5 = 335
33	5, 6, 7, 8, 9
34	0, 7, 7, 8, 8
35	6, 7, 8, 9

median = 347; modes = 347 and 348; flat-shaped

13.

Data	Frequency
2	2
3	2
4	1
5	1
6	2
7	1
8	1
9	3
10	2

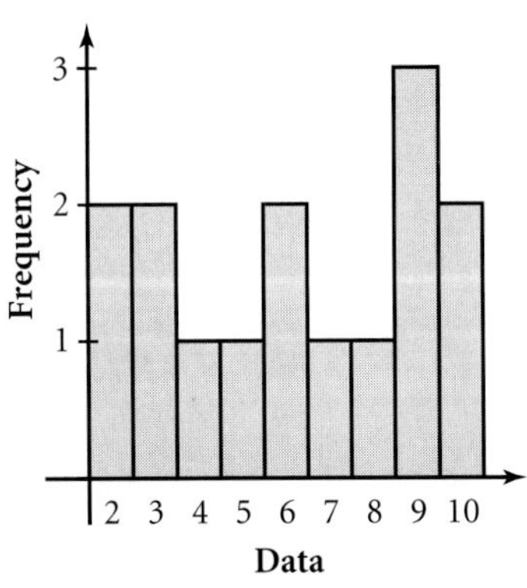

15.

Data	Frequency
0.5	2
1.0	3
1.5	4
2.0	3
2.5	2
3.0	1

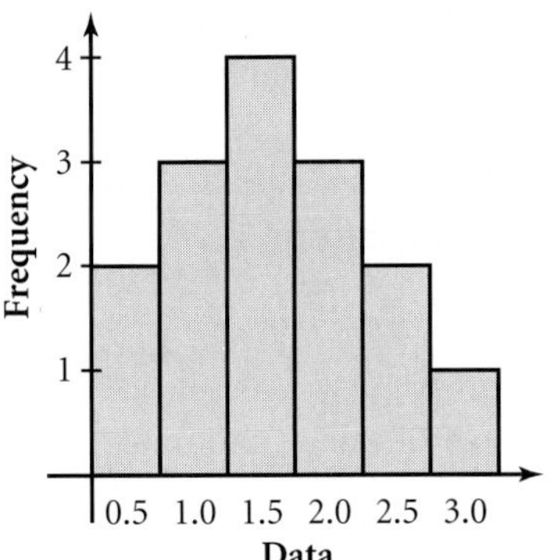

17.

Data	Frequency	Relative Frequency
1	4	$\frac{4}{24} = 0.1\overline{6}$
2	2	$\frac{2}{24} = 0.08\overline{3}$
3	5	$\frac{5}{24} = 0.208\overline{3}$
4	4	$\frac{4}{24} = 0.1\overline{6}$
5	2	$\frac{2}{24} = 0.08\overline{3}$
6	0	$\frac{0}{24} = 0$
7	4	$\frac{4}{24} = 0.1\overline{6}$
8	3	$\frac{3}{24} = 0.125$
Total	24	1

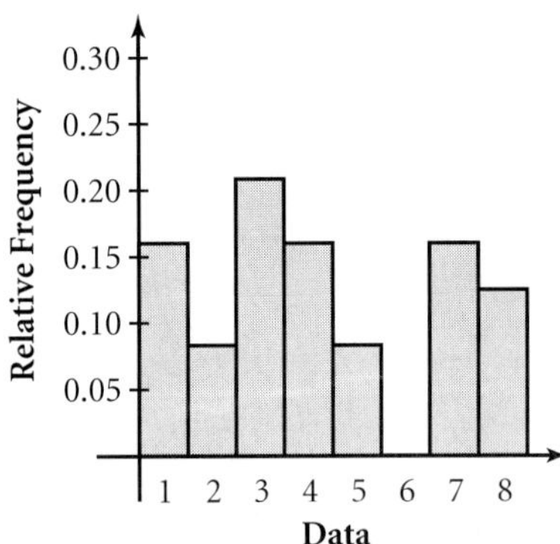

19.

Data	Frequency	Relative Frequency
0.1	6	$\frac{6}{15} = 0.4$
0.2	4	$\frac{4}{15} = 0.2\overline{6}$
0.3	3	$\frac{3}{15} = 0.2$
0.4	1	$\frac{1}{15} = 0.0\overline{6}$
0.5	1	$\frac{1}{15} = 0.0\overline{6}$
Total	15	1

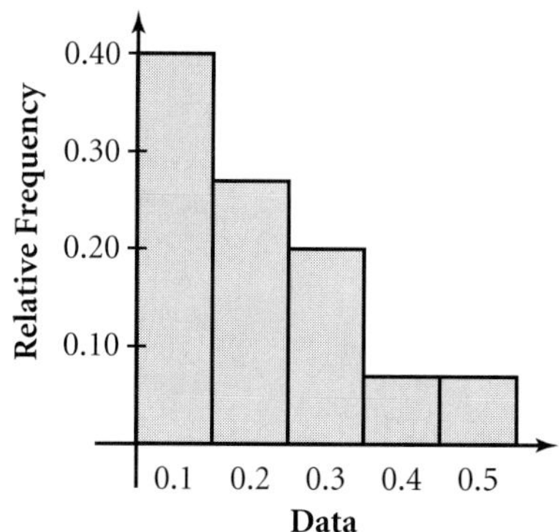

21.

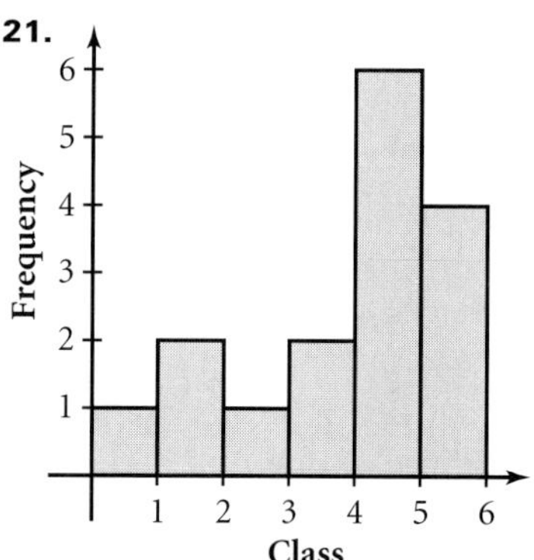

23.

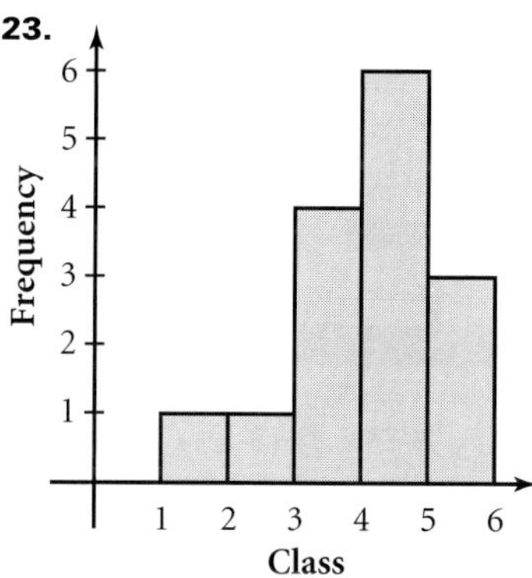

25. Answers may vary. **27a.** Answers may vary. Sample answers: A histogram most effectively shows how the incomes are divided into fairly even percents. Alternatively, a circle graph best illustrates that the incomes represent the entire United States and have fairly even parts that represent the percent in each income.

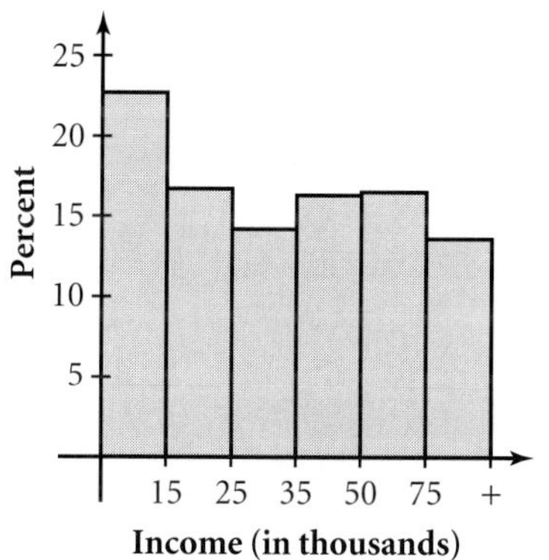

b. Distribution is fairly even. **c.** 30.1%

29.

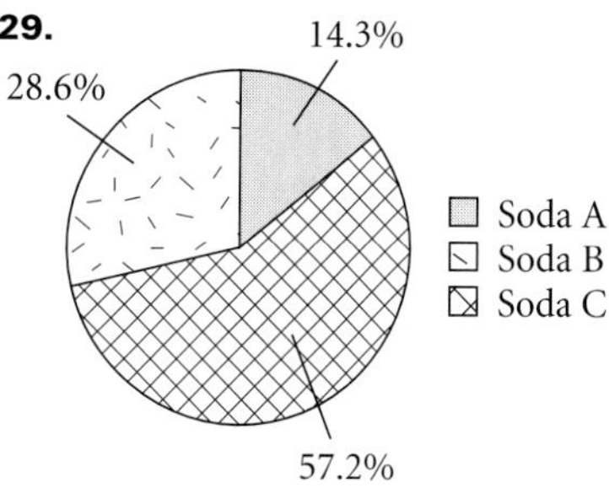

31. $-\frac{14}{11}$ **33.** $(x + 8)^2$ **35.** $(3 - x)(2x - 5)$

37. $x^2 - x + 2 - \frac{24}{x + 2}$ **39.** −2, 2 **41.** −2, −1

43. $\frac{(x - 4)^2}{4} + \frac{(y - 2)^2}{6.25} = 1$ **45.** $\frac{1}{4}$

LESSON 12.3

TRY THIS (p. 783)

minimum = 2; maximum = 83; $Q_1 = 10$; $Q_2 = 33.5$; $Q_3 = 51$; range = 81; IQR = 41; no possible outliers

Exercises

5a. minimum = 2.5; $Q_1 = 2.8$; $Q_2 = 3.05$; $Q_3 = 3.4$; maximum = 3.8; range = 1.3; IQR = 0.6 **b.** no outliers

6a.

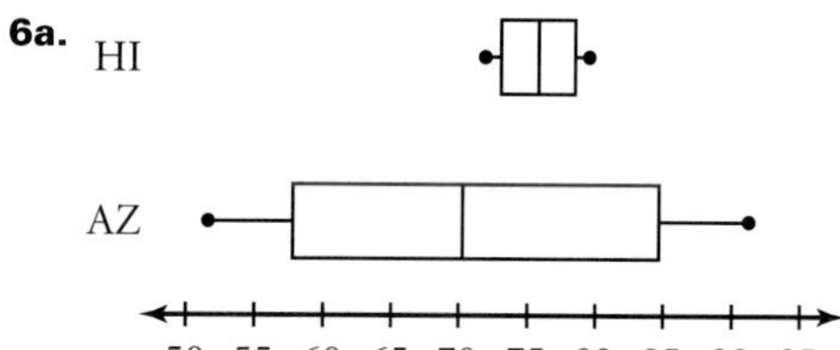

b. Hawaii's median temperature is higher than Arizona's. Arizona's temperature is more variable than Hawaii's.

7. minimum = 42; $Q_1 = 44$; $Q_2 = 50$; $Q_3 = 56$; maximum = 60; range = 18; IQR = 12

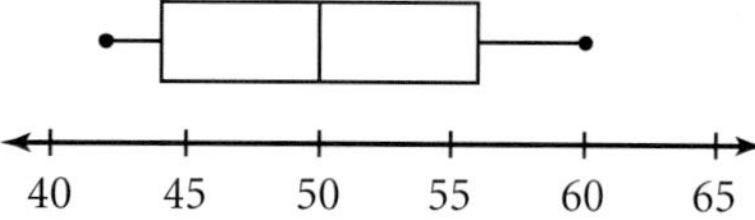

9. minimum = 102; $Q_1 = 125$; $Q_2 = 130$; $Q_3 = 175$; maximum = 190; range = 88; IQR = 50

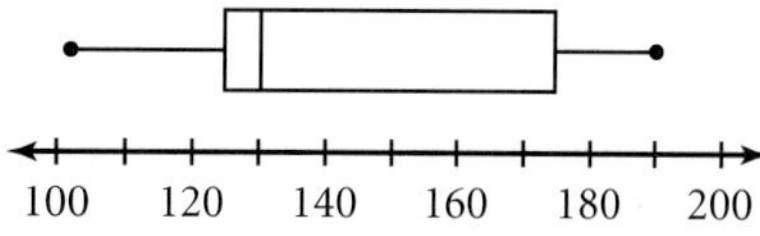

11. minimum = 14; $Q_1 = 22$; $Q_2 = 50$; $Q_3 = 82$; maximum = 93; range = 79; IQR = 60

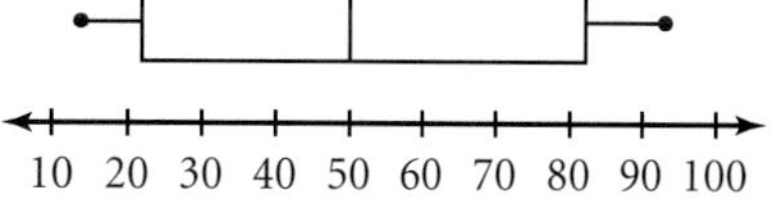

13. minimum = 2.2; $Q_1 = 2.7$; $Q_2 = 4.8$; $Q_3 = 7.7$; maximum = 8.8; range = 6.6; IQR = 5.0

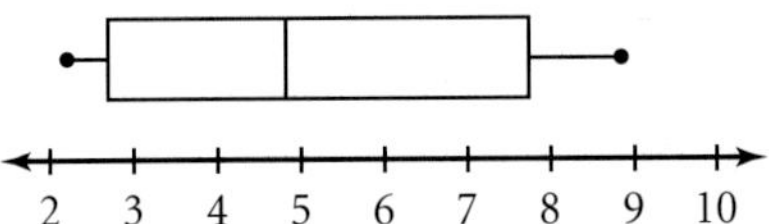

2 3 4 5 6 7 8 9 10

15. class 2 **17.** class 3 **19.** class 3 **21.** 75% **23.** Answers may vary. **25a.** minimum = 62; $Q_1 = 68$; $Q_2 = 73$; $Q_3 = 75.5$; maximum = 78

b.

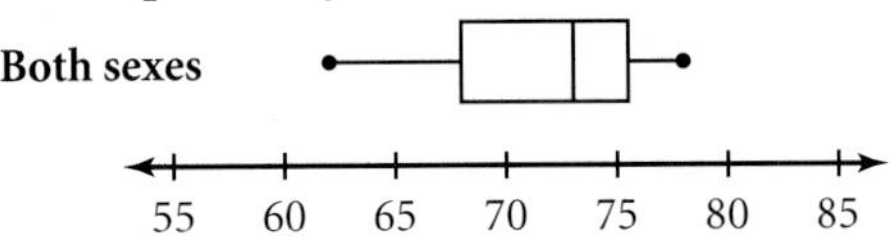

27a. minimum value = 1545; $Q_1 = 36{,}420$; $Q_2 = 57{,}097$; $Q_3 = 84{,}904$; maximum value = 656,424

b.

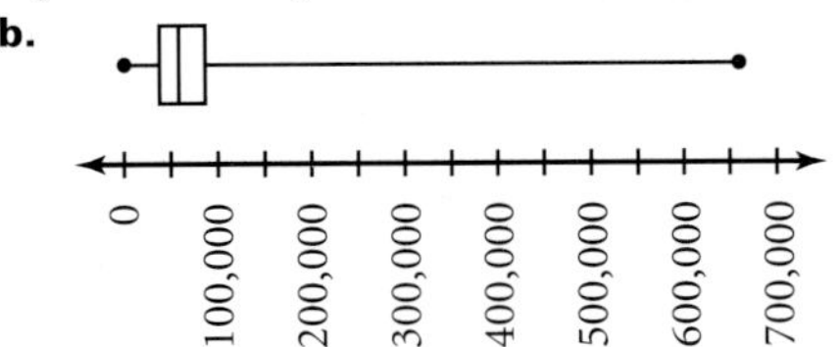

c. yes; Alaska, California, and Texas

29a.

1st 21

2nd 21

40 45 50 55 60 65 70

b. The distributions of the ages of the presidents at inauguration are all fairly similar. The perception of how old a president should be has not changed much over the last 200 years. **31.** growth **33.** decay **35.** falls to the left and rises to the right **37.** $k = 4$; $y = 4x$ **39.** $k = \frac{2}{9}$; $y = \frac{2}{9}x^2$ **41.** $x - \frac{3}{2} = -\frac{1}{10}(y-2)^2$ **43.** $C(-2, 0)$; vertices: $(-7, 0)$ and $(3, 0)$; co-vertices: $\left(-2, -\frac{5}{3}\right)$ and $\left(-2, \frac{5}{3}\right)$ **45.** 210 ways **47.** 10.368, 12.4416, 14.92992

LESSON 12.4

TRY THIS (p. 793)
range = 29,000 miles; mean deviation = 6400 miles; The range for tire C is the same as the range for tire A, which is larger than the range for tire B. The mean deviation for tire C is larger than the mean deviation for tire B and smaller than the mean deviation for tire A.

TRY THIS (p. 794)
$\sigma \approx 9230$ miles

Exercises

4a. Tricia: range = 7; mean deviation = 2
Morgan: range = 40; mean deviation = 16.4
b. Tricia's scores are less variable (more consistent) than those of Morgan. **5.** Tricia: $\sigma \approx 2.45$; Morgan: $\sigma \approx 17.01$ **7.** range = 5; mean deviation = 1.6 **9.** range = 70; mean deviation ≈ 25.7 **11.** range = 6.8; mean deviation ≈ 1.87 **13.** range = 12.28; mean deviation = 5.064 **15.** $\sigma^2 \approx 2.99$; $\sigma \approx 1.73$ **17.** $\sigma^2 \approx 57.18$; $\sigma \approx 7.56$ **19.** $\sigma^2 \approx 15.64$; $\sigma \approx 3.95$ **21.** $\sigma^2 \approx 26.99$; $\sigma \approx 5.19$ **23.** mean deviation = 191.25; standard deviation ≈ 220.95; mean deviation is slightly less affected. **25.** yes; if all the data values are the same **27.** range = 5; mean deviation ≈ 1.02 **29.** range = 0.006 mm; mean deviation ≈ 0.0014 mm **31.** location 1: range = 2167 customers, mean deviation ≈ 527.3 customers; location 2: range = 1815 customers, mean deviation ≈ 442.3 customers; the sales at location 1 are more variable, or less consistent, than those at location 2. **33.** men: $\bar{x} = 1{:}54.17$, median = 1:54.81; women: $\bar{x} = 2{:}05.32$, median = 2:03.42 **35.** men: $\sigma = 3.7637$; women: $\sigma = 6.0194$; the men's times are more consistent, and the women's times are more variable. **37.** (≈–2.37, ≈3.64) **39.** $x \approx -6.3$ *or* $x \approx 0.3$ **41.** 120 **43.** 7980 **45.** $\frac{9}{11} = 0.\overline{81}$ **47.** does not exist

LESSON 12.5

TRY THIS (p. 800)
about 0.130, or 13.0%

TRY THIS (p. 801)
about 0.943, or 94.3%

Exercises

5. about 0.324, or 32.4% **6.** about 0.561, or 56.1% **7.** ≈0.219 **9.** ≈0.109 **11.** ≈0.004 **13.** 0.375 **15.** 0.25 **17.** ≈0.103 **19.** ≈0.849 **21.** ≈0.151 **23.** ≈0.233 **25.** ≈0.016 **27.** ≈0.0004 **29.** ≈0.776 **31.** ≈0.058 **33.** ≈0.163 **35.** ≈0.993 **37.** ≈0.969 **39.** ≈0.277 **41.** ≈0.238 **43.** ≈0.121 **45.** ≈0.894 **47.** 0.48 **49.** 0.648 **51.** $\frac{1}{3}$ **53.** $\frac{1}{2}$ **55.** $\frac{2}{3}$ **57.** Answers may vary. sample answer: –3, 3, 9, 15, . . . **59a.** male: range = 3.6, mean deviation ≈ 1.21; female: range = 6.3, mean deviation ≈ 1.73 **b.** male: $\sigma \approx 1.276$; female: $\sigma \approx 2.065$ **c.** The percent of female enrollment is more variable than that of the male enrollment.

LESSON 12.6

TRY THIS (p. 807)
a. 0.2119
b. 0.5245

TRY THIS (p. 809)
about 1140

TRY THIS (p. 810)
about 59% of the time

Exercises

4. 0.6449 **5.** 0.3848 **6a.** about 0.99 **b.** about 990 **7.** 0.8185 **9.** 0.3446 **11.** 0.3848 **13.** 0.0228 **15.** 0.0808 **17.** 0.1586 **19.** 0.7881 **21.** 0.0727 **23.** 0.0726 **25.** 0.2609 **27.** 0.1587 **29.** 0.0228 **31.** 0.6826 **33.** 4480 **35.** 560 **37.** 26,600 **39.** 0.1596 **41.** 0.9044 **43.** 0.9962 **45.** 0.0918 **47.** 0.0764 **49.** 0.3221 **51a.** 95% **b.** 40% **53.** $y = 100x - 104$ **55.** $y = -\frac{7}{6}x + \frac{14}{3}$ **57.** $\frac{2x+3}{x^2+3x+2}$ **59.** $\frac{x^2+2x+2}{x^2+2x}$ **61.** $\frac{\sqrt{5}}{5}$ **63.** $-\frac{1+\sqrt{3}}{2}$ **65.** 21 **67.** 140 **69.** $\frac{19}{4} \approx 4.75$ **71.** $\frac{58{,}025}{512} \approx 113.33$

CHAPTER REVIEW AND ASSESSMENT

1. mean = $5.\overline{2}$; median = 7; mode = 9

3.

Data	Frequency
4	4
5	4
6	4
7	1
Total	13

mean = 5.15

5.

Stems	Leaves 3|5 = 35
3	5 8
4	5 5 9
5	3 7 8

7.

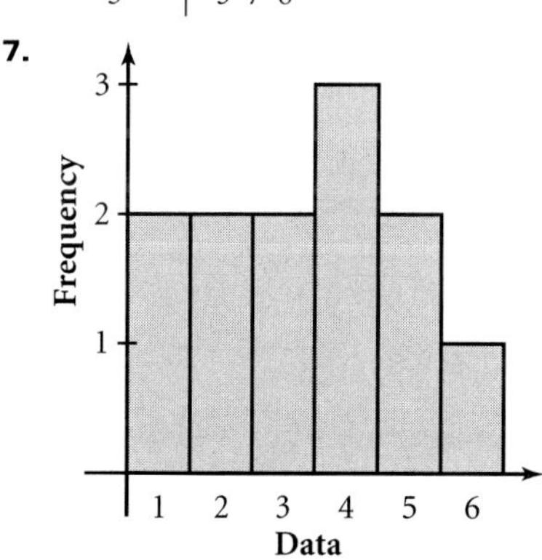

9.

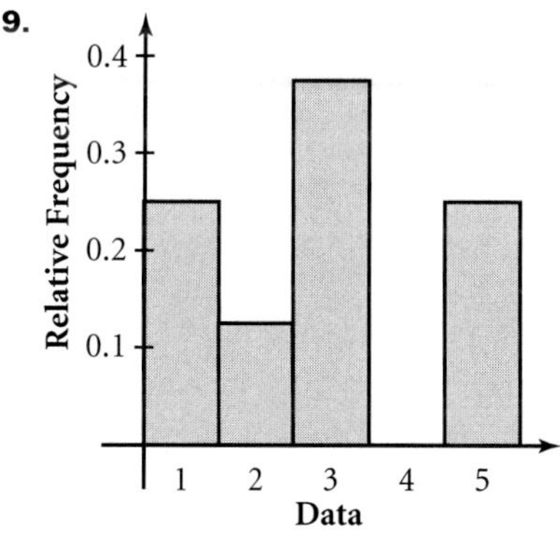

11.

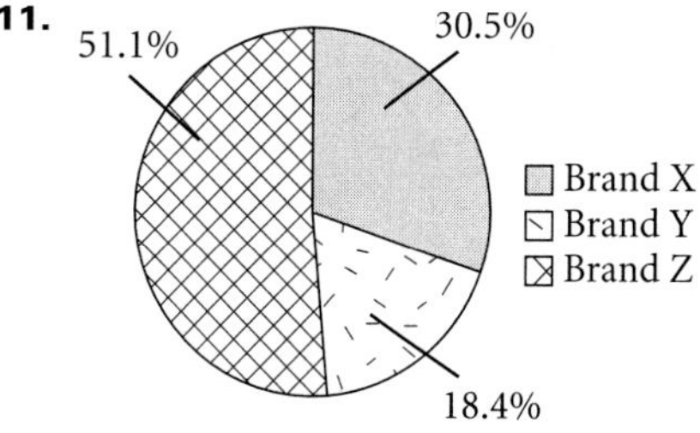

13. $Q_1 = 24$; $Q_2 = 30$; $Q_3 = 34.5$

15.

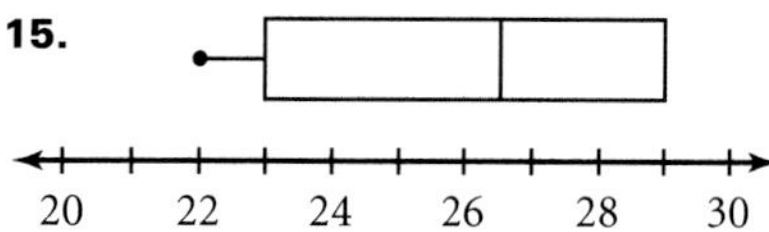

17. range = 9; mean deviation ≈ 2.83 **19.** range = 46; mean deviation ≈ 12.82 **21.** $\sigma^2 \approx 1147.22$; $\sigma \approx 33.87$ **23.** $\sigma^2 \approx 39.42$; $\sigma \approx 6.28$ **25.** ≈0.0425 **27.** 0.5 **29.** 0.9641 **31.** 0.5762 **33.** 0.2420 **35.** 0.7606

Chapter 13

LESSON 13.1

TRY THIS (p. 828)
$\csc Y = \frac{13}{5} \approx 2.6$
$\cos Y = \frac{12}{13} \approx 0.9231$ $\sec Y = \frac{13}{12} = 1.0833$
$\tan Y = \frac{5}{12} \approx 0.4167$ $\cot Y = \frac{12}{5} = 2.4$

TRY THIS (p. 831)
$KL \approx 14.1$
$LM \approx 9.5$

TRY THIS (p. 832)
$m\angle K \approx 29°$
$m\angle L \approx 61°$
$LM = 4.6$

Exercises

4. $\sin x = \frac{3}{5} = 0.6$; $\cos x = \frac{4}{5} = 0.8$; $\tan x = \frac{3}{4} = 0.75$; $\csc x = \frac{5}{3} \approx 1.6667$; $\sec x = \frac{5}{4} = 1.25$; $\cot x = \frac{4}{5} \approx 1.3333$ **5.** $BA \approx 10.6$; $AC \approx 5.8$ **6.** about 64.6 feet **7.** $m\angle A \approx 47°$; $m\angle B \approx 43°$; $AB \approx 7.3$ **9.** $\frac{15}{17} \approx 0.8824$ **11.** $\frac{15}{17} \approx 0.8824$ **13.** $\frac{15}{8} = 1.875$ **15.** $\frac{17}{8} = 2.125$ **17.** $\frac{17}{8} = 2.125$ **19.** $\frac{15}{8} = 1.875$ **21.** $\frac{2}{\sqrt{13}} \approx 0.5547$ **23.** $\frac{3}{\sqrt{13}} \approx 0.8321$ **25.** $\frac{2}{3} \approx 0.6667$ **27.** $\frac{\sqrt{13}}{2} \approx 1.8028$ **29.** $\frac{\sqrt{13}}{3} \approx 1.2019$ **31.** $\frac{3}{2} = 1.5$ **33.** 30° **35.** 20.6° **37.** 41.4° **39.** $m\angle R \approx 32°$; $m\angle S \approx 58°$; $ST \approx 2.1$ **41.** $m\angle S = 50°$; $RS \approx 11.4$; $RT \approx 8.7$ **43.** $m\angle B = 48°$; $BC \approx 3.8$; $AC \approx 4.2$ **45.** $AD \approx 687.9$ ft; $AC \approx 829.8$ ft **47.** 2° **49.** \$3897 **51.** 5 **53.** $x(3x-1)(x-2)$ **55.** $\frac{\sqrt{3}}{3}$ **57.** $2\sqrt{2} - 2\sqrt{3}$

59. $Q_1 = 17.5$; $Q_2 = 24.5$; $Q_3 = 31$; range = 41; IQR = 12.5

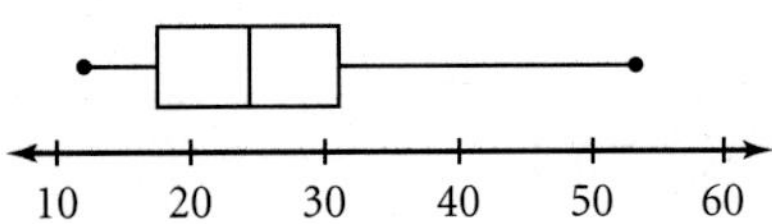

LESSON 13.2

TRY THIS (p. 837, Ex. 1)
199.8° in 1 second

TRY THIS (p. 837, Ex. 2)
–237°; 175°

TRY THIS (p. 837, Ex. 3)
45°; 55°

TRY THIS (p. 837, Ex. 4)

$\sin\theta = -\frac{5\sqrt{34}}{34}$ $\quad\csc\theta = -\frac{\sqrt{34}}{5}$

$\cos\theta = \frac{3\sqrt{34}}{34}$ $\quad\sec\theta = \frac{\sqrt{34}}{3}$

$\tan\theta = -\frac{5}{3}$ $\quad\cot\theta = -\frac{3}{5}$

TRY THIS (p. 840)

$\sin\theta = -\frac{4}{5}$ $\quad\csc\theta = -\frac{5}{4}$

$\cos\theta = -\frac{3}{5}$ $\quad\sec\theta = -\frac{5}{3}$

$\tan\theta = \frac{4}{3}$ $\quad\cot\theta = \frac{3}{4}$

Exercises

4. 2580°/s **5.** –89° **6.** 87°; 80°; 36°

7. $\sin\theta = -\frac{2\sqrt{13}}{13}$; $\cos\theta = \frac{3\sqrt{13}}{13}$; $\tan\theta = -\frac{2}{3}$; $\csc\theta = -\frac{\sqrt{13}}{2}$; $\sec\theta = \frac{\sqrt{13}}{3}$; $\cot\theta = -\frac{3}{2}$ **8.** $\sin\theta = -\frac{12}{13}$; $\cos\theta = -\frac{5}{13}$; $\tan\theta = \frac{12}{5}$; $\csc\theta = -\frac{13}{12}$; $\sec\theta = -\frac{13}{5}$; $\cot\theta = \frac{5}{12}$

9.

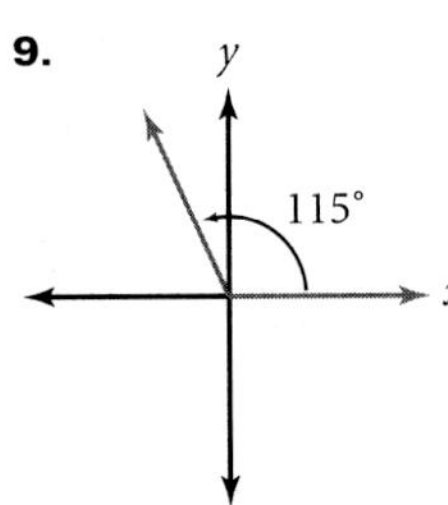

11.

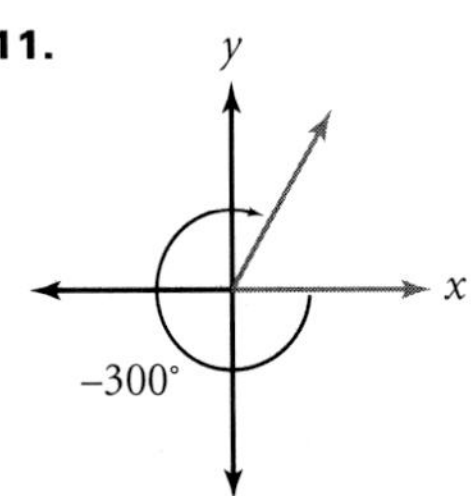

13. –325°; $\theta_{ref} = 35°$ **15.** –248°; $\theta_{ref} = 68°$ **17.** 252°; –108°; $\theta_{ref} = 72°$ **19.** 225°; $\theta_{ref} = 45°$ **21.** –270°; $\theta_{ref} = 90°$ **23.** –90°; 270°; $\theta_{ref} = 90°$ **25.** 180°; –180°; $\theta_{ref} = 0°$ **27.** –135°; $\theta_{ref} = 45°$ **29.** 50°; –310°; $\theta_{ref} = 50°$ **31.** 240°; $\theta_{ref} = 60°$ **33.** 185°; $\theta_{ref} = 5°$ **35.** –35°; 325°; $\theta_{ref} = 35°$ **37.** $\sin\theta = \frac{1}{\sqrt{17}} = \frac{\sqrt{17}}{17}$; $\cos\theta = -\frac{4}{\sqrt{17}} = -\frac{4\sqrt{17}}{17}$; $\tan\theta = -\frac{1}{4}$; $\csc\theta = \sqrt{17}$; $\sec\theta = -\frac{\sqrt{17}}{4}$; $\cot\theta = -4$ **39.** $\sin\theta = -\frac{1}{\sqrt{5}} = -\frac{\sqrt{5}}{5}$; $\cos\theta = \frac{2}{\sqrt{5}} = \frac{2\sqrt{5}}{5}$; $\tan\theta = -\frac{1}{2}$; $\csc\theta = -\sqrt{5}$; $\sec\theta = \frac{\sqrt{5}}{2}$; $\cot\theta = -2$ **41.** $\sin\theta = \frac{2\sqrt{29}}{29}$; $\cos\theta = \frac{5\sqrt{29}}{29}$; $\tan\theta = \frac{2}{5}$; $\csc\theta = \frac{\sqrt{29}}{2}$; $\sec\theta = \frac{\sqrt{29}}{5}$; $\cot\theta = \frac{5}{2}$

43. $\sin\theta = \frac{3\sqrt{13}}{13}$; $\cos\theta = -\frac{2\sqrt{13}}{13}$; $\tan\theta = -\frac{3}{2}$; $\csc\theta = \frac{\sqrt{13}}{3}$; $\sec\theta = -\frac{\sqrt{13}}{2}$; $\cot\theta = -\frac{2}{3}$

45. $\sin\theta = -\frac{\sqrt{21}}{21}$; $\cos\theta = \frac{2\sqrt{105}}{21}$; $\tan\theta = -\frac{\sqrt{5}}{10}$; $\csc\theta = -\sqrt{21}$; $\sec\theta = \frac{\sqrt{105}}{10}$; $\cot\theta = -2\sqrt{5}$

47. $\sin\theta = -\frac{8\sqrt{65}}{65}$; $\cos\theta = -\frac{\sqrt{65}}{65}$; $\tan\theta = 8$; $\csc\theta = -\frac{\sqrt{65}}{8}$; $\sec\theta = -\sqrt{65}$; $\cot\theta = \frac{1}{8}$ **49.** $\sqrt{3}$

51. $\frac{\sqrt{5}}{2}$ **53.** $-\frac{5\sqrt{21}}{21}$ **55.** $-\frac{7\sqrt{65}}{65}$ **57.** $\frac{1}{4}$ rotation counterclockwise **59.** $\frac{3}{4}$ rotation clockwise **61.** 2 rotations counterclockwise **63.** $1\frac{7}{9}$ rotations clockwise **65.** ≈–0.7266 **67.** 5400°/s **69.** ±14

71.

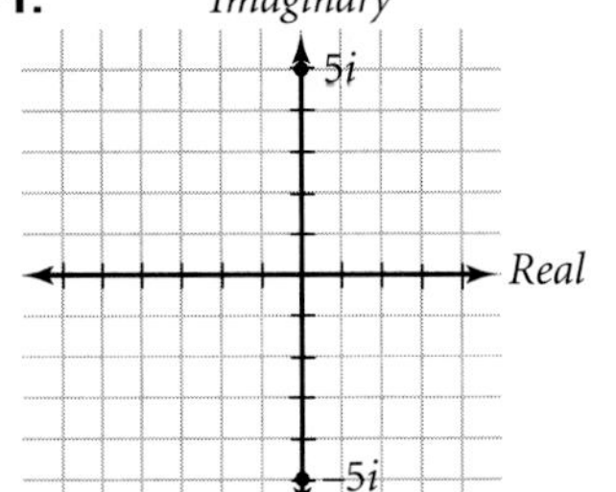

73.

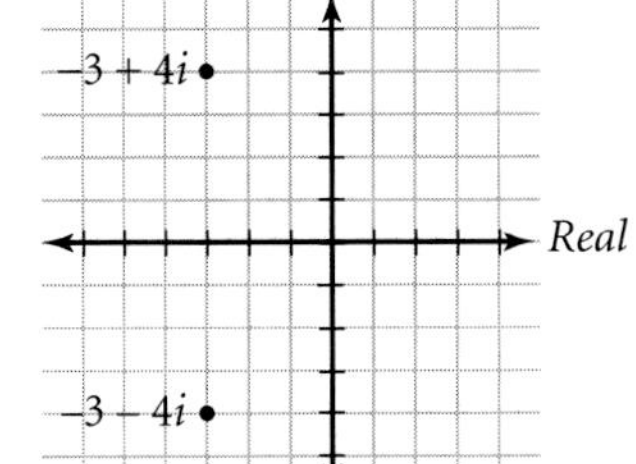

75. $\sqrt{13}$ **77.** 1 **79.** 210

LESSON 13.3

TRY THIS (p. 844)

$\sin(-150°) = -\frac{1}{2}$

$\cos(-150°) = -\frac{\sqrt{3}}{2}$

$\tan(-150°) = \frac{\sqrt{3}}{2}$

TRY THIS (p. 845)

$(6, -6\sqrt{3})$

TRY THIS (p. 847)

a. $\sin 1110° = \frac{1}{2}$

$\cos 1110° = \frac{\sqrt{3}}{2}$

$\tan 1110° = \frac{\sqrt{3}}{3}$

b. $\sin(-1110°) = -\frac{1}{2}$

$\cos(-1110°) = \frac{\sqrt{3}}{2}$

$\tan(-1110°) = -\frac{\sqrt{3}}{3}$

Exercises

4. $\sin 150° = \frac{1}{2}$; $\cos 150° = -\frac{\sqrt{3}}{2}$; $\tan 150° = -\frac{\sqrt{3}}{3}$ **5.** $\left(\frac{9\sqrt{2}}{2}, -\frac{9\sqrt{2}}{2}\right)$ **6.** $(-0.68, 1.88)$ **7.** $\sin(-1200°) = -\frac{\sqrt{3}}{2}$; $\cos(-1200°) = -\frac{1}{2}$; $\tan(-1200°) = \sqrt{3}$ **9.** $\sin 210° = -\frac{1}{2}$; $\cos 210° = -\frac{\sqrt{3}}{2}$; $\tan 210° = \frac{\sqrt{3}}{3}$ **11.** $\sin 120° = \frac{\sqrt{3}}{2}$; $\cos 120° = -\frac{1}{2}$; $\tan 120° = -\sqrt{3}$ **13.** $\sin 240° = -\frac{\sqrt{3}}{2}$; $\cos 240° = -\frac{1}{2}$; $\tan 240° = \sqrt{3}$ **15.** $\sin(-135°) = -\frac{\sqrt{2}}{2}$; $\cos(-135°) = -\frac{\sqrt{2}}{2}$; $\tan(-135°) = 1$ **17.** $\sin(-330°) = \frac{1}{2}$; $\cos(-330°) = \frac{\sqrt{3}}{2}$; $\tan(-330°) = \frac{\sqrt{3}}{3}$ **19.** $\sin(-210°) = \frac{1}{2}$; $\cos(-210°) = -\frac{\sqrt{3}}{2}$; $\tan(-210°) = -\frac{\sqrt{3}}{3}$ **21.** $P\left(\frac{5\sqrt{3}}{2}, \frac{5}{2}\right)$ **23.** $P\left(-\frac{9\sqrt{2}}{2}, \frac{9\sqrt{2}}{2}\right)$ **25.** $P(-45, 0)$ **27.** $P(-3.8\sqrt{2}, -3.8\sqrt{2})$ **29.** $P(0.26, 0.97)$ **31.** $P(-0.64, -0.77)$ **33.** $P(1.00, 0.07)$ **35.** $P(0.03, -1.00)$ **37.** $\sin 405° = \frac{\sqrt{2}}{2}$; $\cos 405° = \frac{\sqrt{2}}{2}$; $\tan 405° = 1$ **39.** $\sin 870° = \frac{1}{2}$; $\cos 870° = -\frac{\sqrt{3}}{2}$; $\tan 870° = -\frac{\sqrt{3}}{3}$ **41.** $\sin 1380° = -\frac{\sqrt{3}}{2}$; $\cos 1380° = \frac{1}{2}$; $\tan 1380° = -\sqrt{3}$ **43.** $\sin(-600°) = \frac{\sqrt{3}}{2}$; $\cos(-600°) = -\frac{1}{2}$; $\tan(-600°) = -\sqrt{3}$ **45.** $\sin(-495°) = -\frac{\sqrt{2}}{2}$; $\cos(-495°) = -\frac{\sqrt{2}}{2}$; $\tan(-495°) = 1$ **47.** $\sin(-840°) = -\frac{\sqrt{3}}{2}$; $\cos(-840°) = -\frac{1}{2}$; $\tan(-840°) = \sqrt{3}$ **49.** $\frac{\sqrt{2}}{2}$ **51.** $-\frac{\sqrt{3}}{3}$ **53.** $-\frac{\sqrt{3}}{2}$ **55.** $-\frac{\sqrt{3}}{2}$ **57.** $-\frac{\sqrt{3}}{3}$ **59.** 1 **61.** 1 **63.** undefined **65.** −1 **67.** −1 **69.** 0 **71.** 1 **73.** $\frac{\sqrt{2}}{2}$ **75.** $-\frac{\sqrt{2}}{2}$ **77.** $-\frac{\sqrt{2}}{2}$ **79.** $-\frac{\sqrt{3}}{3}$ **81.** 0 **83.** $\sqrt{3}$ **85.** −2 **87.** $\frac{2\sqrt{3}}{3}$ **89.** −1 **91.** $\frac{2\sqrt{3}}{3}$ **93.** If f is periodic, then there is a function f such that $f(x + p) = f(x)$. Then for the function $f(x) = x$, $f(x + p) = x + p$ and $x + p = x$ for some p, which is not possible unless $p = 0$. **95.** $JL = 15$ cm; $KL = 15\sqrt{3}$ cm; $m\angle K = 30°$ **97.** $PR = 12$ in.; $PQ = 12\sqrt{2}$ in.; $m\angle Q = 45°$ **99.** ≈24 in. **101.** $12x - 1$ **103.** $16x - 5$ **105.** 2nd row, 1st column; the amount that Donnell has in his savings account, $408 **107.** $AB = BC$, therefore triangle ABC is isosceles. **109.** mean = $8\frac{1}{3}$; median = 8; modes = 3 and 8 **111.** mean = 41.75; standard deviation ≈ 16.22

LESSON 13.4

TRY THIS (p. 852, Ex. 1)
$-120° = -\frac{2\pi}{3}$ radians
$-\frac{2}{3}\pi$ radians $= -120°$

TRY THIS (p. 852, Ex. 2)
$\sin \frac{3\pi}{2} = -1$
$\cos \frac{2\pi}{3} = -0.5$
$\tan \frac{5\pi}{4} = 1$

TRY THIS (p. 853)
0.75 feet

TRY THIS (p. 854)
linear speed ≈ 1037 miles per hour; angular speed ≈ $\frac{\pi}{12}$ radians per hour

Exercises

5. $\frac{2\pi}{3}$ radians **6.** 45° **7.** $\frac{\sqrt{3}}{2}$ **8.** $-\frac{\sqrt{2}}{2}$ **9.** $-\sqrt{3}$ **10.** 60π, or 188.5 cm **11.** $10.54\ \frac{\text{ft}}{\text{min}}$; $0.12\ \frac{\text{mi}}{\text{hr}}$ **13.** $\frac{\pi}{2}$ radians **15.** $\frac{3\pi}{2}$ radians **17.** $-\frac{2\pi}{3}$ radians **19.** $-\frac{4\pi}{3}$ radians **21.** $\frac{31\pi}{6}$ radians **23.** $\frac{8\pi}{9}$ radians **25.** 180° **27.** 45° **29.** 30° **31.** −45° **33.** −561.4° **35.** 284.2° **37.** −1 **39.** $-\frac{1}{2}$ **41.** $\frac{1}{2}$ **43.** 1 **45.** $\frac{\sqrt{2}}{2}$ **47.** −1 **49.** $\sqrt{2}$ **51.** $-\frac{2\sqrt{3}}{3}$ **53.** 12 m **55.** 360 m **57.** 3.35 m **59.** $\frac{10\pi}{3}$ m **61.** $\frac{5\pi}{2}$ m **63.** $\frac{35\pi}{6}$ m **65.** $\frac{37}{48}$ rad **67.** top: 60.2 in./s; bottom: 23.6 in./s; $3.42\ \frac{\text{mi}}{\text{hr}}$; $1.34\ \frac{\text{mi}}{\text{hr}}$ **69.** 480π, or ≈1508 cm/min **71.** 0.12 rad/s **73.** no solution **75.** $-3 < x < -\frac{1}{3}$

$-\frac{1}{3}$
−6 −5 −4 −3 −2 −1 0 1 2 3 4 5 6

77. $5i$ **79.** 2.56 **81.** 45.42 **83.** $x = \frac{3 \pm i\sqrt{87}}{2}$

85.

Data	Frequency	Relative Frequency
1	1	$\frac{1}{25}$ = 0.04, or 4%
2	1	$\frac{1}{25}$ = 0.04, or 4%
3	5	$\frac{5}{25}$ = 0.20, or 20%
4	6	$\frac{6}{25}$ = 0.24, or 24%
5	6	$\frac{6}{25}$ = 0.24, or 24%
6	3	$\frac{3}{25}$ = 0.12, or 12%
7	2	$\frac{2}{25}$ = 0.08, or 8%
8	1	$\frac{1}{25}$ = 0.04, or 4%
Total	25	1, or 100%

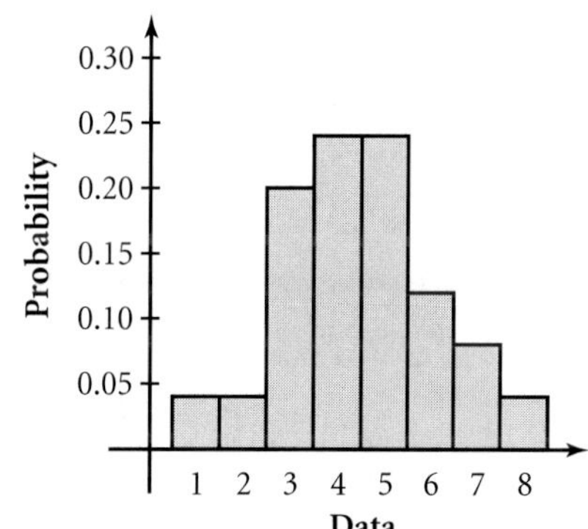

LESSON 13.5

TRY THIS (p. 860)

a.

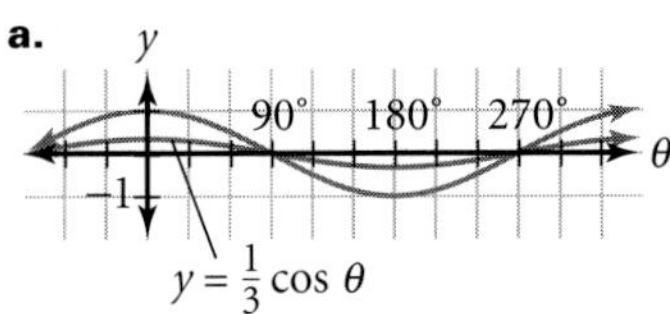

b.

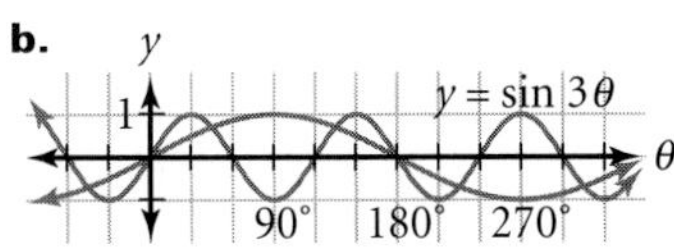

TRY THIS (p. 861)

a.

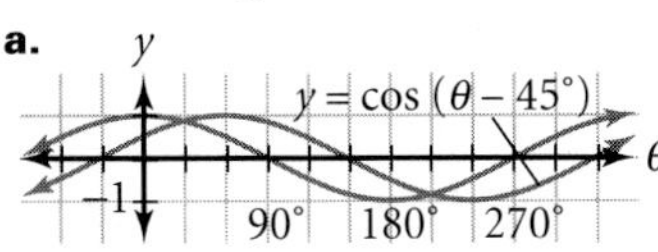

b.

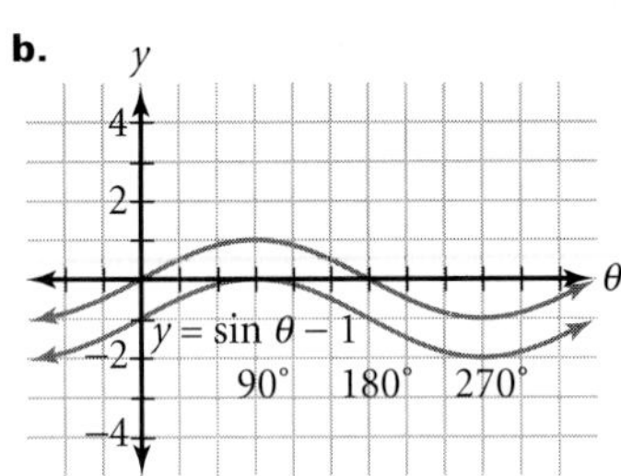

TRY THIS (p. 862)

$y = 1.5 \sin 240\pi\left(t + \frac{1}{360}\right)$

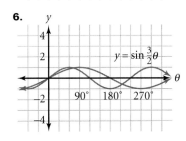

TRY THIS (p. 863)

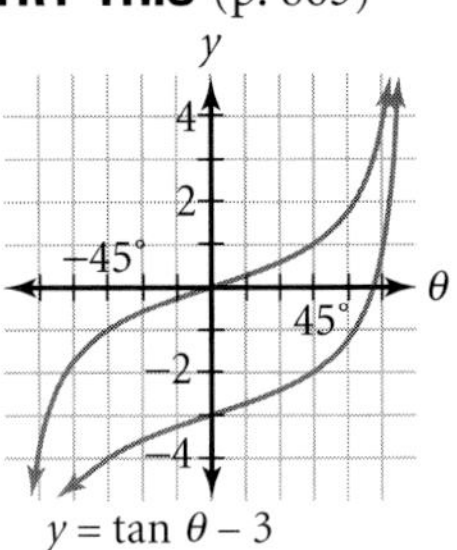

Exercises

5.

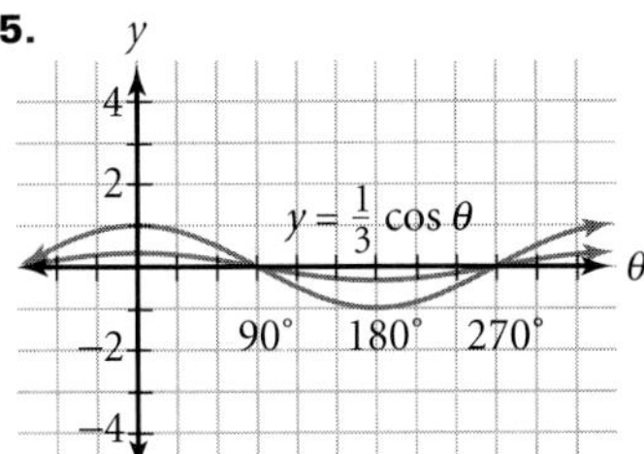

6.

y 4 2 $y = \sin\frac{3}{2}\theta$ θ −2 90° 180° 270° −4

7.

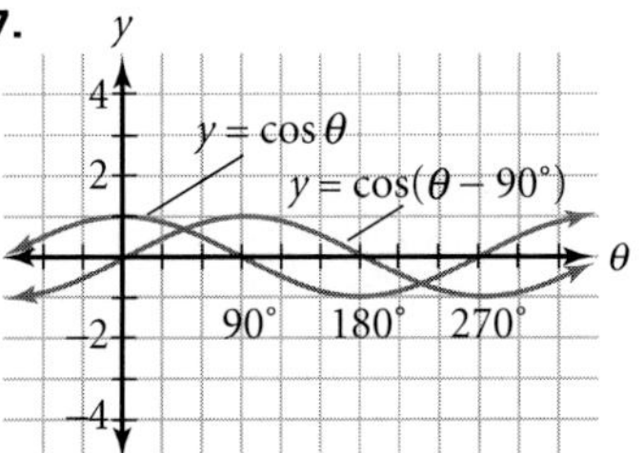

8.

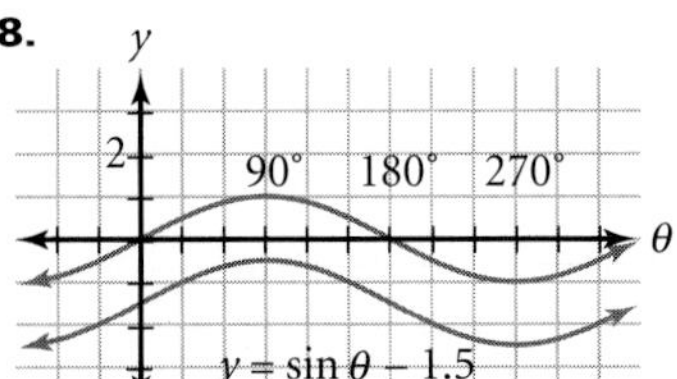

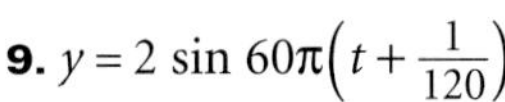

9. $y = 2 \sin 60\pi\left(t + \frac{1}{120}\right)$

10.

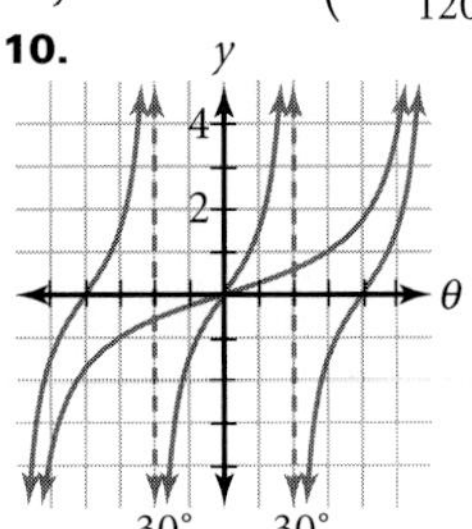

11. amplitude: 2.5; period: π **13.** amplitude: none; period: $\frac{\pi}{3}$ **15.** amplitude: 5; period: 4π

17. amplitude: 3; period: 2π **19.** amplitude: 1; period: 2π **21.** phase shift: 45° to the right; vertical translation: 2 units down **23.** phase shift: 60° to the left; vertical translation: 1 unit up **25.** phase shift: 30° to the left; vertical translation: 2 units up

27. phase shift: 135° to the right; vertical translation: 3 units down

29. stretched vertically by a factor of 4

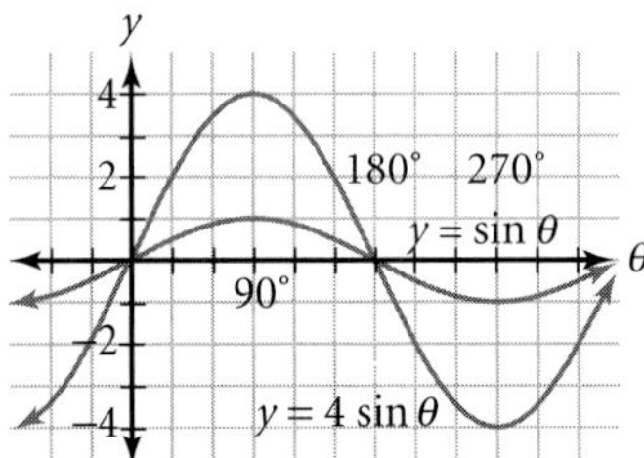

31. reflected across θ-axis and stretched vertically by a factor of 3

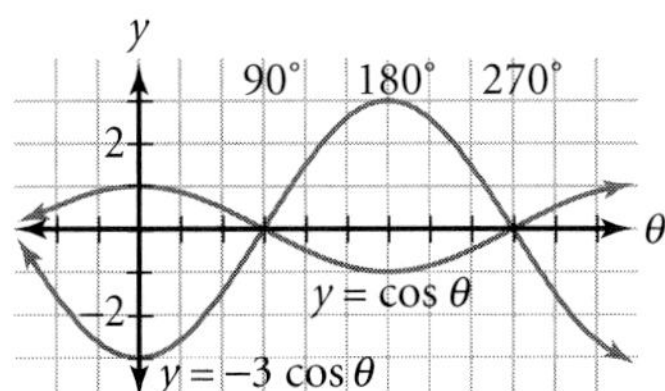

33. translated 90° to the left

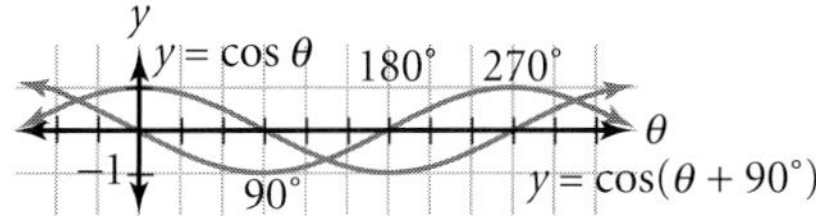

35. stretched vertically by a factor of 2 and translated 90° to the right

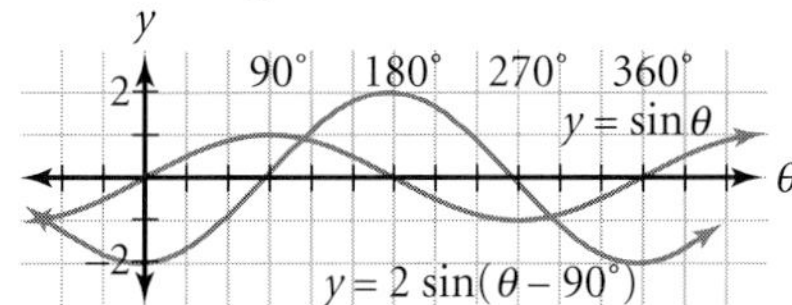

37. reflected across the θ-axis, stretched vertically by a factor of 2, and stretched horizontally by a factor of 3

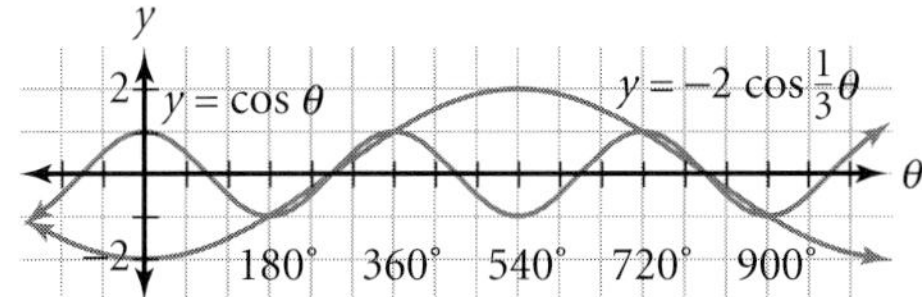

39. compressed vertically by a factor of $\frac{1}{3}$ and compressed horizontally by a factor of $\frac{1}{2}$

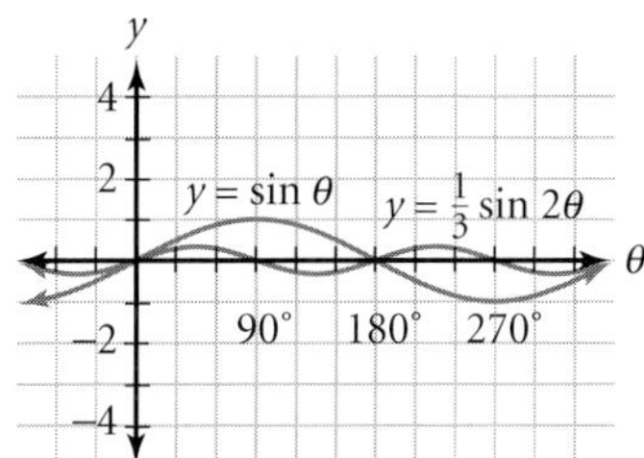

41. stretched vertically by a factor of 2

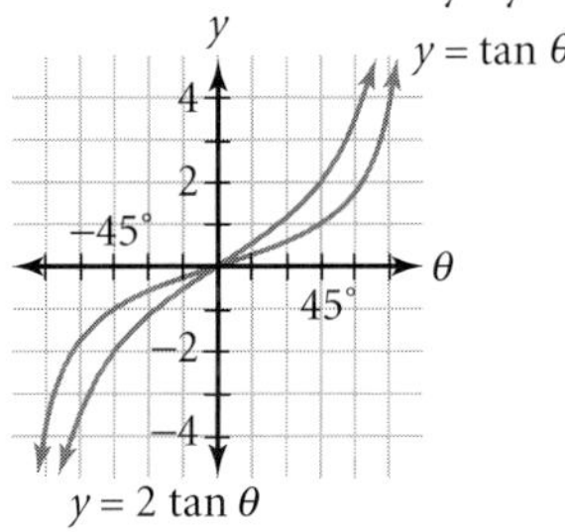

43. translated down 2 units

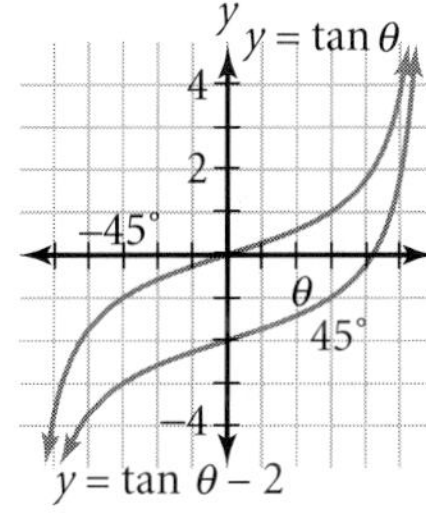

45. compressed horizontally by a factor of $\frac{1}{3}$

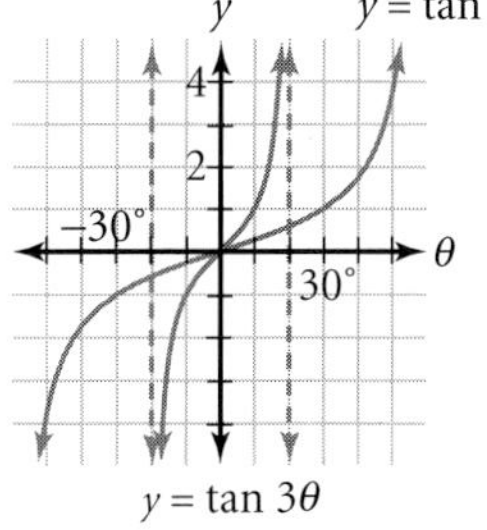

47. stretched vertically by a factor of 3 and stretched horizontally by a factor of 2

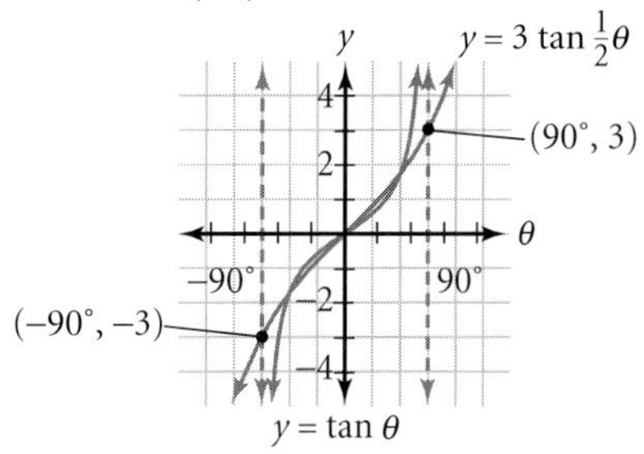

49. a ski resort or a tropical resort because the population of the town is highest in January **51.** ≈6533 **53.** 5.2 **55.** max: 68.5°F; min: 65.5°F **57.** Answers may vary, but the number 67 should be increased. **59.** $x - y = 4$ **61.** $4x - y = -9$ **63.** (0.86, 0.49) **65.** $x \approx 1.7396$ **67.** $x \approx 8.6514$

LESSON 13.6

TRY THIS (p. 868)
45° + n360° and 135° + n360, where n is an integer

TRY THIS (p. 870, Ex. 2)

a. $\text{Sin}^{-1} \frac{\sqrt{3}}{2} = 60°$

b. $\text{Cos}^{-1} -\frac{\sqrt{2}}{2} = 135°$

c. $\text{Tan}^{-1} \sqrt{3} = 60°$

TRY THIS (p. 870, Ex. 3)

a. $\text{Cos}^{-1}(\sin 315°) = 135°$

b. $\tan\left[\text{Sin}^{-1}\left(-\frac{\sqrt{3}}{2}\right)\right] = -\sqrt{3}$

Exercises

4. 30° + n360° and 330° + n360°, where n is an integer **5.** −60° **6.** 60° **7.** −60° **8.** $\frac{\sqrt{3}}{2}$ **9.** 60° **10.** −30° **11.** 41.81° **13.** 225° + n360° and 315° + n360°, where n is an integer **15.** 60° + n360° and 240° + n360°, where n is an integer **17.** 90° + n360° and 270° + n360°, where n is an integer **19.** 45° + n360° and 315° + n360°, where n is an integer **21.** −30° **23.** 45° **25.** 60° **27.** 60° **29.** 180° **31.** 45° **33.** 1 **35.** $\frac{\sqrt{2}}{2}$ **37.** $\sqrt{3}$ **39.** 26.57° **41.** 0° **43.** −30°
45. Let $f(\theta) = \text{Sin}\ \theta$. $(f^{-1} \circ f)(\theta) = (f \circ f^{-1})(\theta) = \theta$ Definition of inverse functions; $(\text{Sin}^{-1} \circ \text{Sin}\ \theta)(\theta) = (\text{Sin} \circ \text{Sin}\ \theta^{-1})(\theta) = \theta$ Substitute Sin for f. $(\text{Sin}^{-1} \circ \text{Sin}\ \theta)(\theta) = \theta$

47. Let x be the height of the tree.

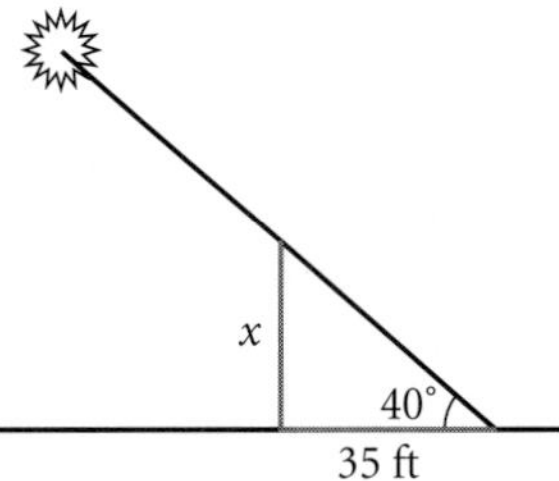

≈ 29.4 feet

49. $\approx 75.5°$ **51.** ≈ 1698 feet **53.** $(3, 5, -1)$ **55.** 3
57. 23° **59.** 23° **61.** 75° **63.** $\approx 136.4°$

CHAPTER REVIEW AND ASSESSMENT

1. $a = \sqrt{5}$; $A \approx 48.2°$; $B \approx 41.8°$ **3.** $b \approx 8.2°$; $a \approx 21.5$; $A = 69°$ **5.** $-90°$; $90°$ **7.** $225°$; $45°$ **9.** $20°$ and $-340°$; $20°$ **11.** $308°$ and $-52°$; $52°$ **13.** $205°$ and $-155°$; $25°$ **15.** $\sin\theta = -\frac{4}{5}$; $\cos\theta = \frac{3}{5}$; $\tan\theta = -\frac{4}{3}$; $\csc\theta = -\frac{5}{4}$; $\sec\theta = \frac{5}{3}$; $\cot\theta = -\frac{3}{4}$ **17.** $\sin\theta = -\frac{8\sqrt{65}}{65}$; $\cos\theta = -\frac{\sqrt{65}}{65}$; $\tan\theta = 8$; $\csc\theta = -\frac{\sqrt{65}}{8}$; $\sec\theta = -\sqrt{65}$; $\cot\theta = \frac{1}{8}$ **19.** $\tan\theta = \frac{2\sqrt{5}}{15}$ **21.** $\cos\theta = \frac{\sqrt{2}}{2}$ **23.** $-\frac{\sqrt{2}}{2}$ **25.** 1 **27.** 1 **29.** undefined **31.** $-\frac{\sqrt{3}}{2}$ **33.** $\left(\frac{1}{2}, \frac{\sqrt{3}}{2}\right)$ **35.** $\left(-\frac{5}{2}, -\frac{5\sqrt{3}}{2}\right)$ **37.** $\frac{13\pi}{30}$ radians **39.** $-\frac{23\pi}{180}$ radians **41.** $-450°$ **43.** ≈ 2.36 meters **45.** 4; 2π **47.** amplitude does not exist; 3π **49.** 45° to the left; no vertical translation

51. 120° to the left; 2 units down

52. $y = \cos 4\theta$ is $y = \cos\theta$ compressed horizontally by a factor of $\frac{1}{4}$.

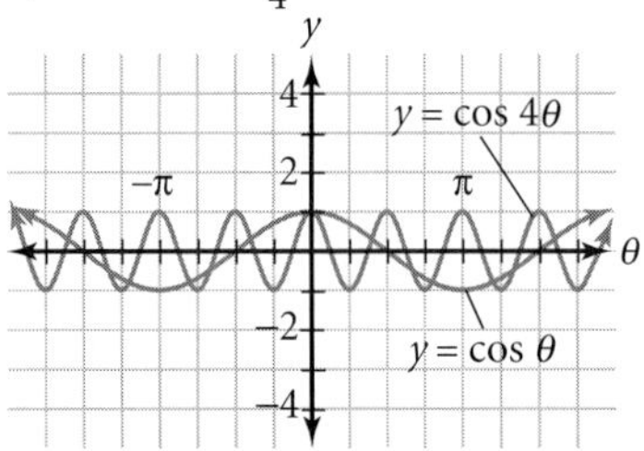

53. $y = \tan\frac{1}{2}\theta$ is $\tan\theta$ stretched horizontally by a factor of 2.

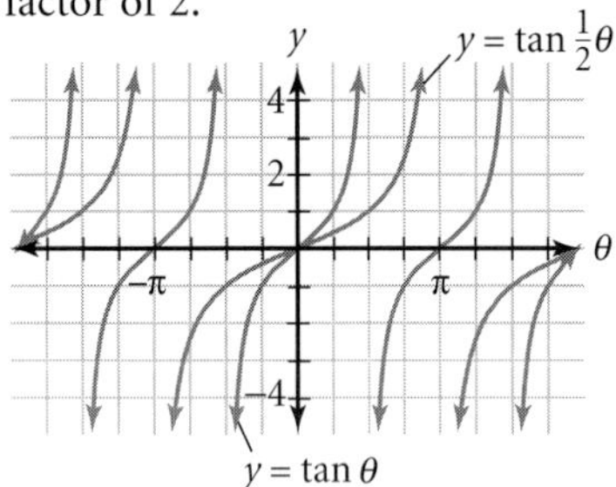

54. $y = 2\sin(\theta - 45°)$ is $y = \sin\theta$ stretched vertically by a factor of 2 and translated 45° to the right.

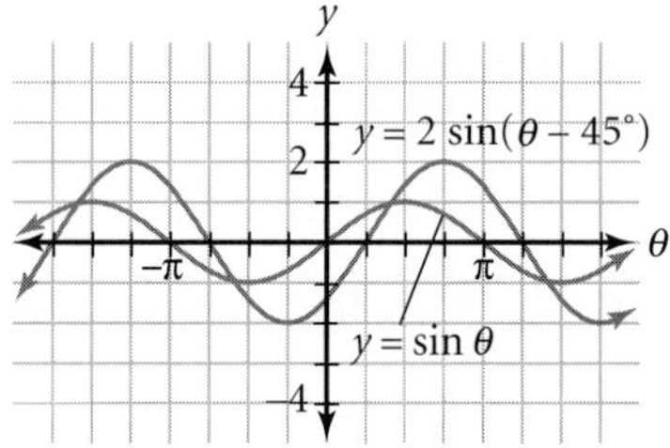

55. $y = 3\cos(\theta + 45°)$ is $y = \cos\theta$ stretched vertically by a factor of 3 and translated 45° to the left.

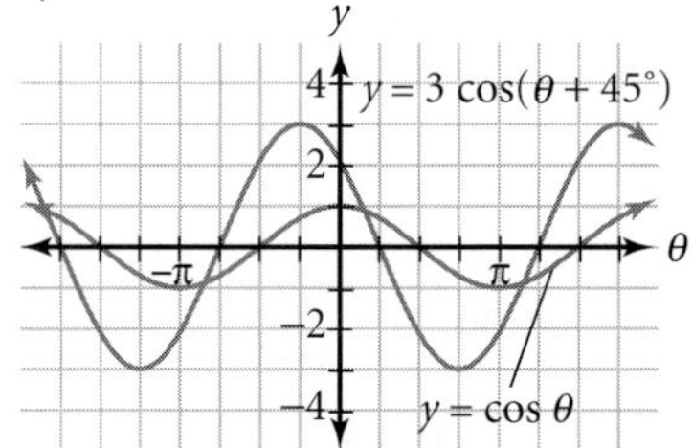

56. $n180°$ (or $0° + n360°$ and $180° + n360°$), where n is an integer **57.** $n360°$, where n is an integer **58.** $150° + n360°$ and $330° + n360°$, where n is an integer **59.** $135° + n360°$ and $225° + n360°$, where n is an integer **60.** $240° + n360°$ and $300° + n360°$, where n is an integer **61.** $45° + n360°$ and $225° + n360°$, where n is an integer **62.** 30° **63.** 150° **64.** 60° **65.** $-45°$ **66.** $\frac{\sqrt{3}}{3}$ **67.** $\frac{1}{2}$ **68.** $\approx -35.26°$ **69.** $-60°$ **70.** ≈ 238.4 meters

Chapter 14

LESSON 14.1

TRY THIS (p. 887)
$K \approx 16.0$ square units

TRY THIS (p. 888, Ex. 2)
$F = 52°$, $d \approx 8.5$, $e \approx 5.4$

TRY THIS (p. 888, Ex. 3)
$m \approx 638$

TRY THIS (p. 890)
a. 0 triangles
b. 2 triangles

Exercises

5. 29.6 square units **6.** $B = 115°$; $a \approx 3.7$; $c \approx 5.7$ **7.** $x \approx 3.2$ **8.** 2 possible triangles **9.** 0 possible triangles **11.** 30 ft^2 **13.** 24.7 cm^2 **15.** 368.2 ft^2 **17.** 160.3 m^2 **19.** 19.9 cm^2 **21.** 1756.0 ft^2 **23.** 722.5 ft^2 **25.** 8.3 **27.** 9.6 **29.** 17.1 **31.** $A = 101°$; $b \approx 3.5$; $a \approx 7.5$ **33.** $C = 83°$; $b \approx 12.3$; $c \approx 13.8$ **35.** $A = 80°$; $b = 10$; $c \approx 3.5$ **37.** $A = 97°$; $a \approx 20.8$; $c \approx 15.5$ **39.** $B = 101°$; $a \approx 12.3$; $c \approx 13.6$ **41.** $A = 80°$; $a \approx 13.2$; $b \approx 11.4$ **43.** $B = 112°$; $a \approx 8.4$; $c \approx 4.6$ **45.** 2 possible triangles: $A = 30°$, $B = 108.2°$, $C = 41.8°$, $a = 1.5$, $b = 2.8$, $c = 2$ and $A = 30°$, $B = 11.8°$, $C = 138.2°$, $a = 1.5$, $b = 0.6$, $c = 2$
47. 0 possible triangles

49. 1 possible triangle: $A = 45°$, $B = 45°$, $C = 90°$, $a = \frac{5\sqrt{2}}{2}$, $b = 3.5$, $c = 5$ **51.** 73 cm **53.** 691 meters **55.** 14.5 km **57.** about 14 years **59.** $2x^2(x-3)^2$ **61.** $\frac{\pi}{2}$ **63.** $\frac{3\pi}{2}$ **65.** $-36°$ **67.** 239.5°

LESSON 14.2

TRY THIS (p. 895)
a. $y \approx 122.2$
b. $X \approx 35.2°$

TRY THIS (p. 897)
$y \approx 8.5$, $X \approx 22.4°$, $Z \approx 21.6°$

Exercises

5a. 33.7 **b.** 41.3° **6.** about 106.6 nautical miles apart; about 5.8 hours, or 5 hours and 48 minutes **7.** $e \approx 8.0$; $D \approx 59°$; $F \approx 49°$ **8.** $A = 20.2°$; $B \approx 43.1°$; $C \approx 116.7°$ **9.** SAS; $A \approx 52.5$ **11.** SSS; $A \approx 88.0°$ **13.** SAS; $c \approx 7.1$ **15.** SAS; $b \approx 34.0$ **17.** SAS; $a \approx 4.1$ **19.** $A \approx 43.5°$; $B \approx 74.4°$; $C \approx 62.1°$ **21.** $A \approx 48.5°$; $B \approx 58.5°$; $C \approx 73.0°$ **23.** $A \approx 35.4°$; $B \approx 48.2°$; $C \approx 96.4°$ **25.** SSS; $A \approx 79.0°$, $B \approx 54.9°$, $C \approx 46.1°$ **27.** SAS; $b \approx 49.1$, $A \approx 110.3°$, $C \approx 47.7°$ **29.** SAS; $b \approx 3.2$, $A \approx 38.7°$, $C \approx 111.3°$ **31.** SSS; not possible **33.** SAS; $c \approx 6.2$, $A \approx 77.9°$, $B \approx 42.1°$ **35.** SSS; $A \approx 93.8°$, $B \approx 29.9°$, $C \approx 56.3°$ **37.** SSA; $B = 42.7°$, $C \approx 79.3°$, $c \approx 11.6°$ **39.** SSS; not possible **41.** SSS; $A \approx 52.0°$, $B \approx 68.6°$, $C \approx 59.4°$ **43.** $x \approx 6.8$ **45.** 19.2°, 80.4°, 80.4° **47.** The longest pole is 15.8 feet. The guy wire should be 24.0 feet. **49.** 239 feet

51.

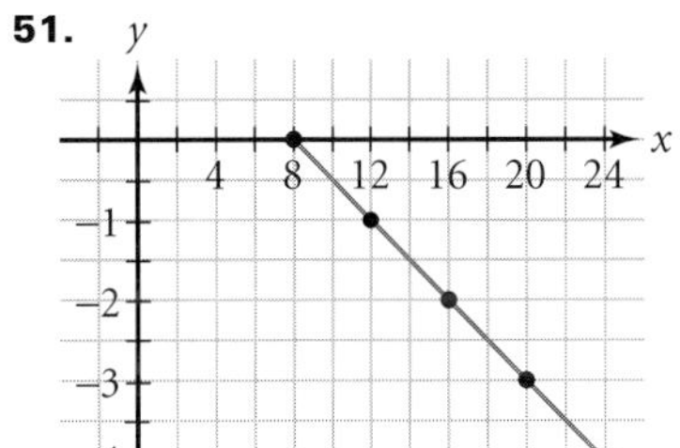

53. $x = -\frac{4}{3}$ *or* $x = \frac{3}{2}$ **55.** $x = \frac{-3-\sqrt{17}}{2}$ *or* $x = \frac{-3+\sqrt{17}}{2}$

LESSON 14.3

TRY THIS (p. 903, Ex. 1)

$\cot\theta = \frac{y}{x}$	Definition of cot θ
$\cot\theta = \frac{r\cos\theta}{r\sin\theta}$	Substitution
$\cot\theta = \frac{\cos\theta}{\sin\theta}$	Simplify.

TRY THIS (p. 903, Ex. 2)

$\tan^2\theta + 1 = \left(\frac{x}{y}\right)^2 + 1$	Definition of tan θ
$\tan^2\theta + 1 = \frac{x^2+y^2}{y^2}$	
$\tan^2\theta + 1 = \frac{r^2}{y^2}$	Substitution
$\tan^2\theta + 1 = \left(\frac{r}{y}\right)^2$	
$\tan^2\theta + 1 = \sec^2\theta$	

TRY THIS (p. 904)
$1 + \sin\theta$

TRY THIS (p. 905, Ex. 4)
$1 - \sin^2\theta$

TRY THIS (p. 905, Ex. 5)
38.7°

Exercises

4. $\sec\theta = \frac{r}{x}$ (by definition of sec θ) $= \frac{1}{\frac{x}{r}} = \frac{1}{\cos\theta}$

5. $\sin^2\theta = \left(\frac{y}{r}\right)^2 = \frac{y^2}{r^2} = \frac{r^2-x^2}{r^2} = \frac{r^2}{r^2} - \frac{x^2}{r^2} = 1 - \left(\frac{x}{r}\right)^2$
$= 1 - \cos^2\theta$

6. $1 - \sin\theta$ **7.** $\frac{1-\sin^2\theta}{\sin^2\theta}$ **8.** 50.2° **9.** $\sec\theta = \frac{r}{x}$ (by definition of sec θ) $= \frac{1}{\frac{x}{r}} = \frac{1}{\cos\theta}$

11. $\cos^2\theta = \left(\frac{x}{r}\right)^2 = \frac{x^2}{r^2} = \frac{r^2-y^2}{r^2} = \frac{r^2}{r^2} - \frac{y^2}{r^2} = 1 - \left(\frac{y}{r}\right)^2$
$= 1 - \sin^2\theta$

13. $\cos\theta$ **15.** $\sec\theta$ **17.** $\sin\theta$ **19.** $\tan\theta$ **21.** $\cos\theta$ **23.** $\sec^2\theta$ **25.** $\sin^2\theta$ **27.** $1 - 2\cos^2\theta$

29. $\frac{1-2\cos^2\theta}{(1-\cos^2\theta)^2}$ **31.** $\frac{1-\sin^2\theta}{\sin\theta}$ **33.** $\sin^2\theta + \frac{1}{\sin\theta}$

35. $\tan\theta = \frac{\sec\theta}{\csc\theta} = \frac{\frac{1}{\cos\theta}}{\frac{1}{\sin\theta}} = \frac{\sin\theta}{\cos\theta} = \tan\theta$

37. $\sin^2\theta = \frac{\tan^2\theta}{\sec^2\theta} = \frac{\frac{\sin^2\theta}{\cos^2\theta}}{\frac{1}{\cos^2\theta}} = \sin^2\theta$

39. $\cot^2\theta = \cos^2\theta\csc^2\theta = \cos^2\theta\left(\frac{1}{\sin^2\theta}\right) = \frac{\cos^2\theta}{\sin^2\theta}$
$= \cot^2\theta$

41. $\frac{\sec\theta}{\cos\theta} = \frac{\frac{1}{\cos\theta}}{\cos\theta} = \frac{1}{\cos^2\theta} = \sec^2\theta$

43. $\frac{\cos\theta}{1-\sin^2\theta} = \frac{\cos\theta}{\cos^2\theta} = \frac{1}{\cos\theta} = \sec\theta$

45. $(\sec\theta)(1-\sin^2\theta) = \left(\frac{1}{\cos\theta}\right)(\cos^2\theta) = \cos\theta$

47. $(\tan\theta)(\csc\theta)(\sec\theta) = \left(\frac{\sin\theta}{\cos\theta}\right)\left(\frac{1}{\sin\theta}\right)\left(\frac{1}{\cos\theta}\right)$
$= \frac{1}{\cos^2\theta} = \sec^2\theta$

49. $\frac{\sin^2\theta - 2\sin\theta\cos\theta}{\cos^2\theta}$, or $\frac{\sin^2\theta}{\cos^2\theta} - \frac{2\sin\theta}{\cos\theta}$

51. $\pm\sqrt{1-\cos^2\theta}$ **53.** $\pm\frac{\sqrt{1-\cos^2\theta}}{\cos\theta}$

55. $\cos\theta = \pm\sqrt{1-\sin^2\theta}$; $\tan\theta = \pm\frac{\sin\theta}{\sqrt{1-\sin^2\theta}}$;

$\csc\theta = \frac{1}{\sin\theta}$; $\sec\theta = \pm\frac{1}{\sqrt{1-\sin^2\theta}}$; $\cot\theta = \pm\frac{\sqrt{1-\sin^2\theta}}{\sin\theta}$

57. $\sin\theta = \pm\frac{1}{\cot\theta\sqrt{1-\frac{1}{\cot^2\theta}}}$; $\cos\theta = \pm\frac{\cot\theta}{\sqrt{1+\cot^2\theta}}$;

$\tan\theta = \frac{1}{\cot\theta}$; $\csc\theta = \pm\cot\theta\sqrt{1-\frac{1}{\cot^2\theta}}$;

$\sec\theta = \pm\frac{\sqrt{1+\cot^2\theta}}{\cot^2\theta}$ **59.** 8.0° **61.** 31.0°

63. $\begin{bmatrix} 2 & 1 & -6 \\ -1 & 1 & 1 \\ 5 & -3 & 7 \end{bmatrix}\begin{bmatrix} x \\ y \\ z \end{bmatrix} = \begin{bmatrix} -12 \\ -7 \\ 11 \end{bmatrix}$; $\left(-\frac{30}{11}, -\frac{102}{11}, -\frac{5}{11}\right)$,
or about (−2.7, −9.3, −0.5)

65. The earthquake in 1976 released about 1.4 times more energy than the one in 1985. **67.** The earthquake in 1990 released about 89.1 times more energy than the one in 1993. **69.** The earthquake in 1985 released about 89.1 times more energy than the one in 1994.

71.

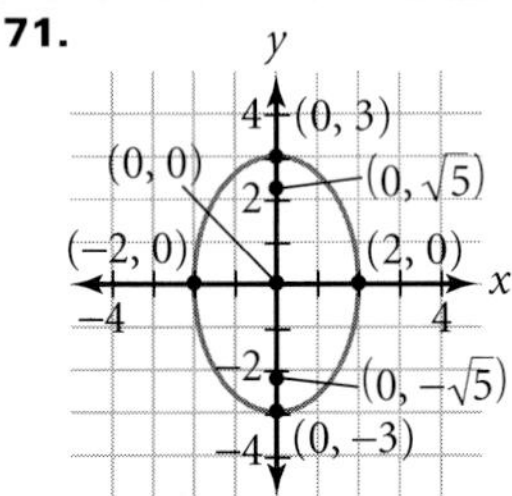

center: (0, 0); foci: $(0, -\sqrt{5})$ and $(0, \sqrt{5})$; vertices: (0, −3) and (0, 3); co-vertices: (−2, 0) and (2, 0)

LESSON 14.4

TRY THIS (p. 910)

a. −1 **b.** $\frac{\sqrt{2}-\sqrt{6}}{4}$

TRY THIS (p. 911, Ex. 2)

$\sin(90° - \theta) = \sin 90° \cos\theta - \cos 90° \sin\theta$
$= 1 \cdot \cos\theta - 0 \cdot \sin\theta$
$= \cos\theta$

TRY THIS (p. 911, Ex. 3)

a. $\frac{\sqrt{2}-\sqrt{6}}{4}$ **b.** $\frac{-\sqrt{2}-\sqrt{6}}{4}$

TRY THIS (p. 912)

$y = \cos(45° - \theta)$

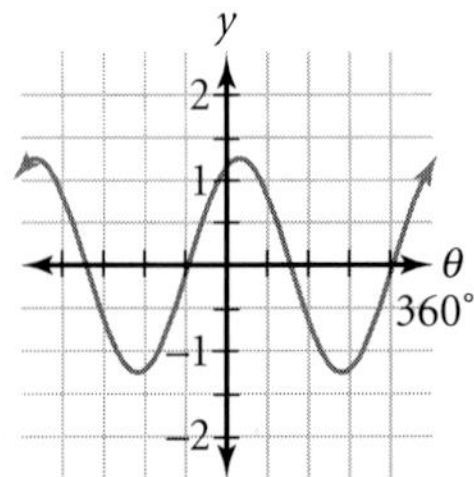

TRY THIS (p. 913)

$A'(0.13, 2.23)$; $B'(1.63, 4.83)$; $C'(3.37, 3.83)$; $D'(1.87, 1.23)$

Exercises

4. $\frac{\sqrt{2}-\sqrt{6}}{4}$ **5.** $\frac{\sqrt{2}+\sqrt{6}}{4}$

6. $-\cos(\theta + 180°) = -[\cos\theta\cos 180° - \sin\theta\sin 180°]$
$= -[\cos\theta(-1) - \sin\theta(0)]$
$= -(-\cos\theta) = \cos\theta$

7. 0 **8.** $\frac{\sqrt{3}}{2}$

9.

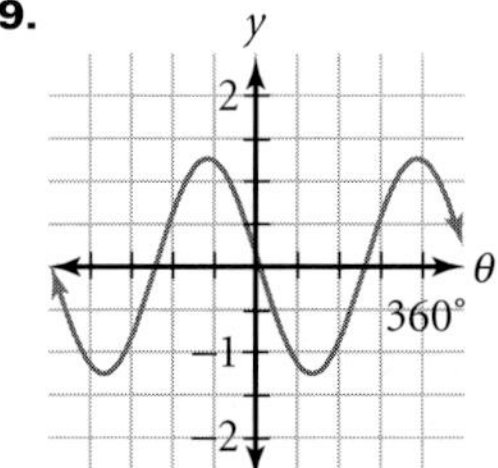

10. $A'(-1.87, 1.23)$, $B'(-3.37, 3.83)$, $C'(-1.63, 4.83)$, $D'(-0.13, 2.23)$ **11.** $\frac{\sqrt{2}+\sqrt{6}}{4}$ **13.** $\frac{-\sqrt{6}-\sqrt{2}}{4}$ **15.** $-\frac{\sqrt{2}}{2}$

17. $\frac{-\sqrt{2}+\sqrt{6}}{4}$ **19.** $\frac{-\sqrt{2}-\sqrt{6}}{4}$ **21.** $\frac{-\sqrt{6}+\sqrt{2}}{4}$

23. $\sin(90° - \theta) = \sin 90° \cos\theta - \cos 90° \sin\theta$
$= 1 \cdot \cos\theta - 0 \cdot \sin\theta = \cos\theta$

25. $\cos(90° + \theta) = \cos 90° \cos\theta - \sin 90° \sin\theta$
$= 0 \cdot \cos\theta - 1 \cdot \sin\theta = -\sin\theta$

27. $\sin(180° - \theta) = \sin 180° \cos\theta - \cos 180° \sin\theta$
$= 0 \cdot \cos\theta - (-1)\sin\theta = \sin\theta$

29. Answers may vary. Sample answer: $\sin(30° + 60°) = 1$; $\sin 30° + \sin 60° = \frac{1+\sqrt{3}}{2}$; So, $\sin(A + B) \neq \sin A + \sin B$. **31.** Answers may vary. Sample answer: $\sin(60° - 30°) = \frac{1}{2}$; $\sin 60° - \sin 30° = \frac{\sqrt{3}-1}{2}$; So, $\sin(A - B) \neq \sin A - \sin B$.

33. $\frac{\sqrt{2}+\sqrt{6}}{4}$ **35.** $\frac{-\sqrt{2}-\sqrt{6}}{4}$ **37.** $\frac{\sqrt{6}-\sqrt{2}}{4}$ **39.** $\frac{-\sqrt{2}-\sqrt{6}}{4}$

41. $-\frac{\sqrt{2}}{2}$ **43.** $-\frac{\sqrt{2}}{2}$ **45.** $\begin{bmatrix} \frac{\sqrt{2}}{2} & -\frac{\sqrt{2}}{2} \\ \frac{\sqrt{2}}{2} & \frac{\sqrt{2}}{2} \end{bmatrix}$

47. $\approx\begin{bmatrix} 0.766 & 0.643 \\ -0.643 & 0.766 \end{bmatrix}$ **49.** $\begin{bmatrix} -\frac{1}{2} & \frac{\sqrt{3}}{2} \\ -\frac{\sqrt{3}}{2} & -\frac{1}{2} \end{bmatrix}$

51. $\begin{bmatrix} -\frac{\sqrt{2}}{2} & \frac{\sqrt{2}}{2} \\ -\frac{\sqrt{2}}{2} & -\frac{\sqrt{2}}{2} \end{bmatrix}$

53.

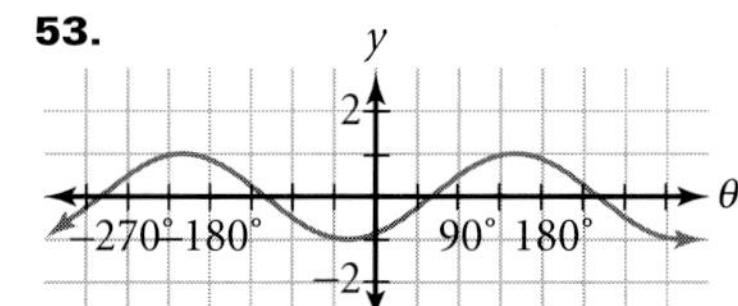

55.

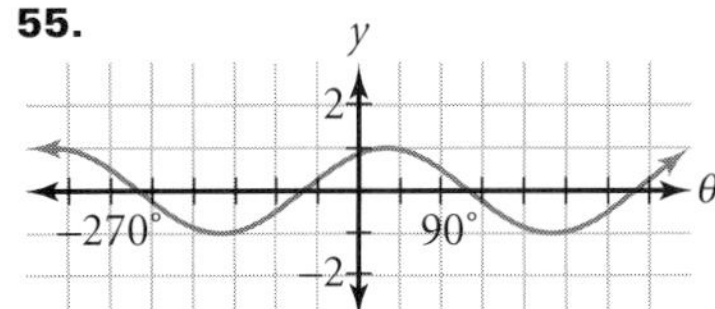

57.

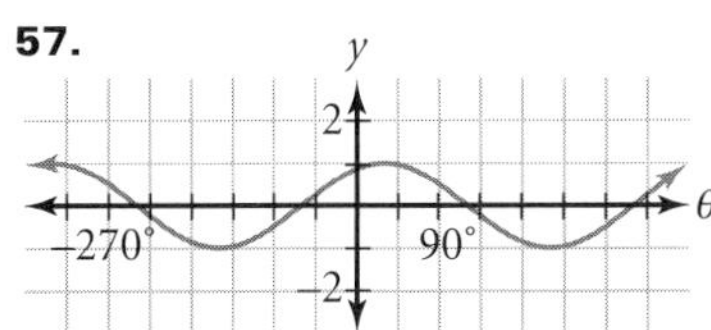

59. $P'\left(-\frac{5\sqrt{2}}{2}, -\frac{\sqrt{2}}{2}\right)$ **61.** $P'\left(\frac{\sqrt{2}}{2}, -\frac{5\sqrt{2}}{2}\right)$

63. $P'\left(\frac{-\sqrt{3}+2}{2}, \frac{1+2\sqrt{3}}{2}\right)$

65. $P'\left(\frac{10\sqrt{3}+23}{2}, \frac{-10+23\sqrt{3}}{2}\right)$

67. $\sin(A+B) + \sin(A-B) = \sin A \cos B + \cos A \sin B + \sin A \cos B - \cos A \sin B = (\sin A \cos B + \sin A \cos B) + (\cos A \sin B - \cos A \sin B) = 2 \sin A \cos B + 0 = 2 \sin A \cos B$ **69.** $W'(1.50, 2.60)$, $X'(-0.23, 3.60)$, $Y'(1.27, 6.20)$, $Z'(3.00, 5.20)$ **71.** $W'(2.60, -1.50)$, $X'(3.60, 0.23)$, $Y'(6.20, -1.27)$, $Z'(5.20, -3.00)$ **73.** $W'(-2.12, 2.12)$, $X'(-3.54, 0.71)$, $Y'(-5.66, 2.83)$, $Z'(-4.24, 4.24)$ **75.** $W'(0, -3)$, $X'(2, -3)$, $Y'(2, -6)$, $Z'(0, -6)$ **77.** $\frac{3\sqrt{2}}{2}(\cos t - \sin t)$ **79.** $f^{-1}(x) = \frac{7-x}{3}$ **81.** $A \approx 40.4°, B \approx 55.9°, C \approx 83.7°$

LESSON 14.5

TRY THIS (p. 918) $-\frac{\sqrt{15}}{8}$

TRY THIS (p. 919) $\sqrt{\frac{2}{3}}$

Exercises

3. $\cos^4\theta - \sin^4\theta = (\cos^2\theta + \sin^2\theta)(\cos^2\theta - \sin^2\theta) = 1(\cos 2\theta) = \cos 2\theta$

4. $\frac{17}{25}$ **5.** $\frac{4\sqrt{21}}{25}$ **6.** $\sqrt{\frac{1}{2} + \frac{\sqrt{21}}{10}}$ **7.** $\sqrt{\frac{1}{2} - \frac{\sqrt{21}}{10}}$ **9.** $2\cos^2\theta$ **11.** $\sin\theta$ **13.** $\cos\theta$ **15.** $4\sin\theta\cos^3\theta - 4\sin^3\theta\cos\theta$ **17.** $\cos^4\theta - 6\sin^2\theta\cos^2\theta + \sin^4\theta$ **19.** $\frac{\sin\theta}{2\cos\theta}$ **21.** $2\cos 2\theta$ **23.** $\sqrt{\frac{4-\sqrt{6}-\sqrt{2}}{8}}$ **25.** $\sin 2\theta = -\frac{24}{25}$; $\cos 2\theta = \frac{7}{25}$ **27.** $\sin 2\theta = -\frac{4\sqrt{21}}{25}$; $\cos 2\theta = \frac{17}{25}$ **29.** $\sin 2\theta = \frac{\sqrt{15}}{8}$; $\cos 2\theta = -\frac{7}{8}$ **31.** $\sin 2\theta = \frac{\sqrt{55}}{8}$; $\cos 2\theta = -\frac{3}{8}$ **33.** $\sin\frac{\theta}{2} = \sqrt{\frac{2}{5}}$; $\cos\frac{\theta}{2} = \sqrt{\frac{3}{5}}$

35. $\sin\frac{\theta}{2} = \sqrt{\frac{1}{2} + \frac{\sqrt{11}}{12}}$; $\cos\frac{\theta}{2} = \sqrt{\frac{1}{2} - \frac{\sqrt{11}}{12}}$

37. $\sin\frac{\theta}{2} = \sqrt{\frac{1}{2} + \frac{\sqrt{5}}{6}}$; $\cos\frac{\theta}{2} = \sqrt{\frac{1}{2} - \frac{\sqrt{5}}{6}}$

39. $\sin\frac{\theta}{2} = \sqrt{\frac{1}{2} - \frac{\sqrt{55}}{16}}$; $\cos\frac{\theta}{2} = -\sqrt{\frac{1}{2} + \frac{\sqrt{55}}{16}}$

41. 45°; Sample answer: The graph of the function reaches its maximum at 45°. **43.** not a function **45.** 1 **47.** 286 **49.** 2730 **51.** 45

LESSON 14.6

TRY THIS (p. 923)
$\theta = 30° + n360°$ *or* $\theta = 150° + n360°$

TRY THIS (p. 924, Ex. 2)
$\theta = 45°$ *or* $\theta = 315°$

TRY THIS (p. 924, Ex. 3)
$\theta = 180°$

Exercises

4. $\theta = 60° + n360°$ *or* $\theta = 300° + n360°$ **5.** $\theta = 180°$ **6.** $\theta = 0°, 90°, 270°$ **7.** $\theta \approx 26.6°$ **9.** $\theta = 120° + n360°$ *or* $\theta = 240° + n360°$ **11.** $\theta = 60° + n360°$ *or* $\theta = 300° + n360°$ **13.** $\theta = 30° + n360°$ *or* $\theta = 150° + n360°$ **15.** $\theta = 180° + n360°$ **17.** $\theta = 135° + n360°$ *or* $\theta = 315° + n360°$ **19.** $\theta \approx 65.6° + n360°$ *or* $\theta \approx 114.4° + n360°$ **21.** $\theta = 30°, 150°, 270°$ **23.** $\theta = 120°, 240°$ **25.** no solution **27.** $\theta = 90°, 180°, 270°$ **29.** $\theta = 90°, 150°, 210°, 270°$ **31.** no solution **33.** $\theta = 0°, 180°$ **35.** $\theta = 0°$ **37.** no solution **39.** $\theta = 270°$ **41.** $\theta = 180°$ **43.** $\theta = 90°, 180°, 270°$ **45.** no solution **47.** $\theta = 0°, 120°, 180°, 240°$ **49.** $\theta \approx 205.2°, 334.8°$ **51.** $\theta \approx 1.6$ radians, or $\approx 91.7°$ **53.** $t \approx 0.2 + 2n$ *or* $t \approx 1.8 + 2n$ seconds **55.** $\theta_{water} \approx 40.6°$ **57.** $\theta_{air} \approx 34.2°$ **59.** none **61.** $b \approx 5.7, A \approx 83.8°, c \approx 69.7°$

CHAPTER REVIEW AND ASSESSMENT

1. $b \approx 14.8, c \approx 20.6, C = 100°$ **3.** $a \approx 5.1, b \approx 7.8, C = 100°$ **5.** 0 possible triangles **7.** 2 possible triangles: $C \approx 56.4°, A \approx 93.6°, a \approx 6.0$ or $C \approx 123.6°, A \approx 26.4°, a \approx 2.7$ **9.** SAS; $a \approx 8.5, B \approx 45.0°, C \approx 98.0°$ **11.** SSS; $A \approx 93.8°, B \approx 29.9°, C \approx 56.3°$ **13.** SSA; $B \approx 85.6°, C \approx 59.4°, b \approx 34.8$ or $B \approx 24.4°, C \approx 120.6°, b \approx 14.4$ **15.** $\sec\theta$ **17.** $\frac{-3\tan^2\theta}{2+\tan^2\theta}$ **19.** $-\frac{1}{2}$

21. $\frac{\sqrt{2}+\sqrt{6}}{4}$ **23.** $\frac{\sqrt{6}-\sqrt{2}}{4}$ **25.** $\frac{\sqrt{2}-\sqrt{6}}{4}$

27. $(-5.06, -5.23)$ **29.** $\frac{\sqrt{63}}{32}$ **31.** $\frac{\sqrt{7}}{4}$ **33.** $\frac{7}{32}$

35. $-\frac{\sqrt{8+\sqrt{39}}}{4}$ **37.** $\cos^4\theta - 6\cos^2\theta\sin^2\theta + \sin^4\theta$

39. $\theta = 90°$ **41.** $\theta = 90°, 270°$ **43.** $\theta = 30°, 45°, 135°, 150°$ **45.** 1516 yards **47.** 85.5°, 59.1°, 35.4° **49.** 6487.7 miles

Extra Practice

CHAPTER 1

Lesson 1.1

1. linear **3.** linear **5.** linear **7.** not linear **9.** linear; (4, 21) **11.** linear; (10, 31)

13.

x	−6	−3	−1	2
y	−3	−4	−5	−6

No; there is no constant difference in the x-values.

Lesson 1.2

1. $y = -3x + 6$ **3.** $y = \frac{1}{2}$ **5.** 4 **7.** 0

9. $m = 2$; $b = 1$ **11.** $m = 0$; $b = -3$

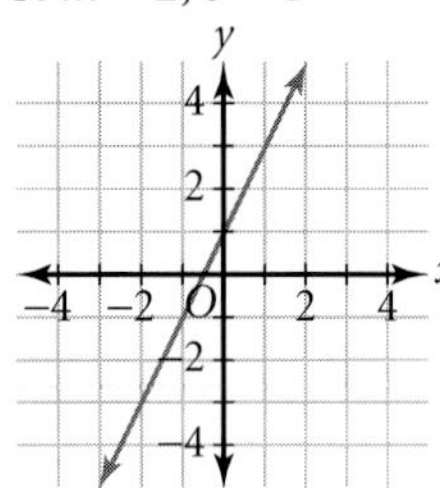

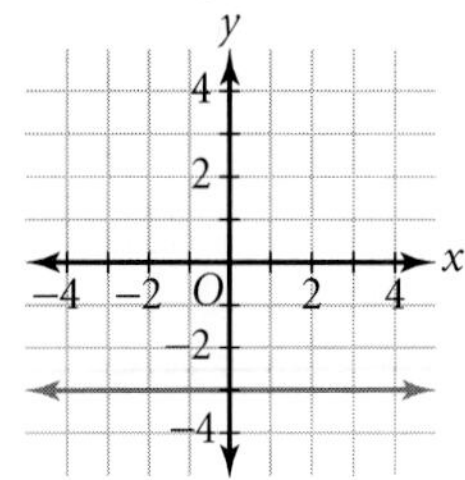

13. $y = -2x - 1$

Lesson 1.3

1. $y = 2x - 15$ **3.** $y = -11$ **5.** $y = \frac{2}{3}x + \frac{11}{3}$

7. $y = -8x - 10$ **9.** $y = -13x + 66$ **11.** $y = 5x + 7$

13. $y = -2x + 18$ **15.** $y = -\frac{3}{4}x - \frac{9}{2}$ **17.** $y = -2x$

19. $y = -\frac{1}{5}x + \frac{42}{5}$ **21.** $y = \frac{2}{5}x - \frac{21}{5}$

Lesson 1.4

1. 4; $y = 4x$ **3.** 6; $y = 6x$ **5.** $-\frac{3}{11}$; $y = -\frac{3}{11}x$ **7.** $x = 64$

9. $k = 300$ **11.** $n = \frac{16}{5}$, or 3.2 **13.** $z = 12$ **15.** $x = 9$

17. The variables are not related by a direct variation. For example, $\frac{24}{1} \neq \frac{12}{2}$. **19.** The variables are related by the direct-variation equation $y = -7x$.

Lesson 1.5

1.

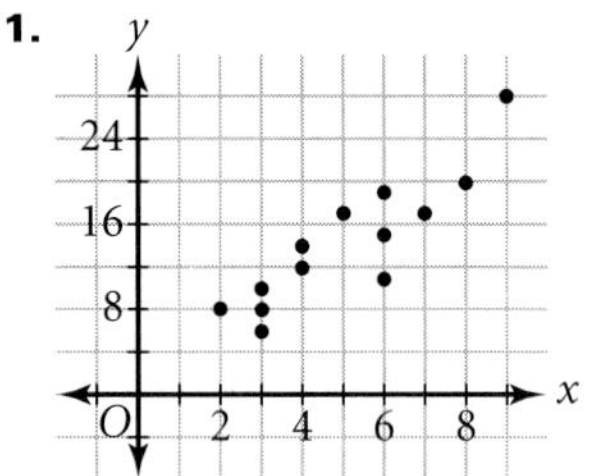

The correlation is positive; $y \approx 2.51x + 1.41$.

3. $y \approx 1.86x + 55.38$ **5.** ≈180 kg

Lesson 1.6

1. $x = -14$ **3.** $x = 5$ **5.** $x = 4$ **7.** $x = 40$ **9.** $x = 144$

11. $x = 4$ **13.** $x = -\frac{8}{3}$, or $-2\frac{2}{3}$ **15.** $x = 11$

17. $x = -\frac{11}{2}$, or $-5\frac{1}{2}$ **19.** $x = 1$ **21.** $x = \frac{15}{4}$, or $3\frac{3}{4}$

23. $x = 20$ **25.** $n = \frac{S}{180} + 2$ **27.** $h = \frac{3V}{B}$

29. $b = a - 2m$ **31.** $x_1 = \frac{y_1 - y_2}{m} + x_2$ **33.** $R = \frac{E}{I}$

35. $A = \frac{s^2}{R}$ **37.** $y = -5$

Lesson 1.7

1. $x < -2$ **3.** $x > -7$ **5.** $x \geq -14$

7. $x < 8$

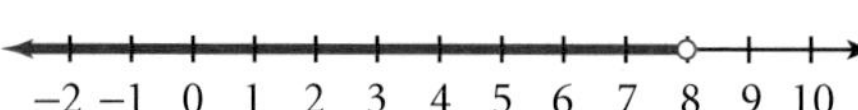

9. $x > -8$

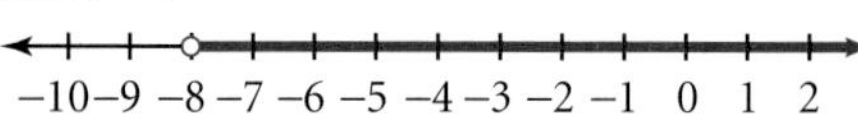

11. $x \geq 10$

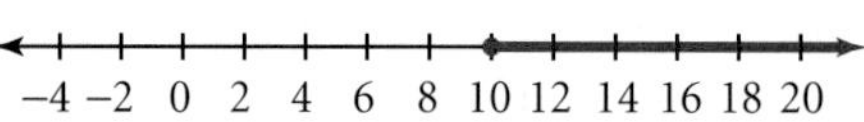

13. $x > 4$

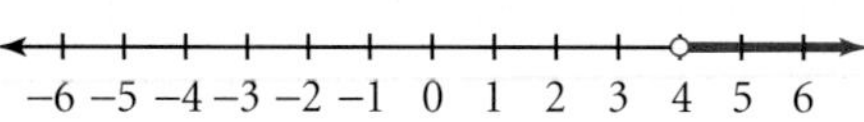

15. $x \leq -12$

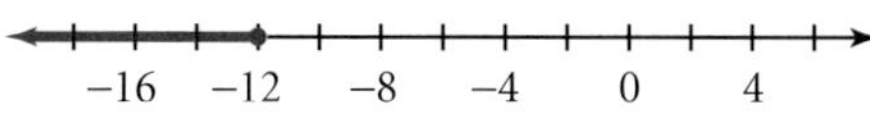

17. $x \geq 2\frac{1}{2}$

19. $-5 \leq x < 3$

21. $-3 \leq x < 5$

23. $x < -5$ *or* $x \geq 1$

25. $x < -4$ *or* $x \geq 3$

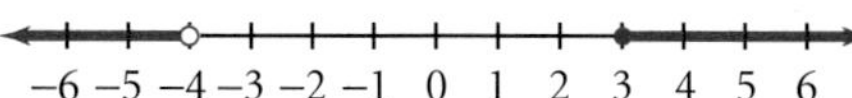

Lesson 1.8

1. d **3.** e **5.** c **7.** $x = -2$ *or* $x = 4$ **9.** $x = -3$ *or* $x = 15$

11. $x = -1\frac{1}{2}$ *or* $x = 3\frac{1}{2}$ **13.** no solution **15.** $x = -2$ *or* $x = 1$ **17.** $x = \frac{1}{8}$ *or* $x = -\frac{1}{8}$

19. $-4 < x < 4$

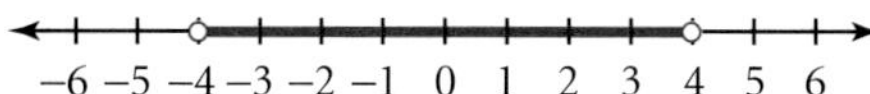

21. $-4 \leq x \leq 8$

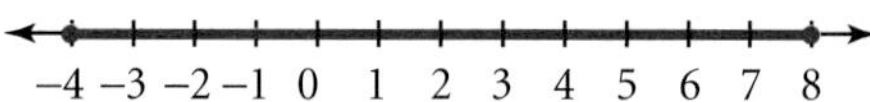

23. $x < 2$ *or* $x > 2$

25. no solution

27. $\frac{4}{3} \le x \le \frac{8}{3}$

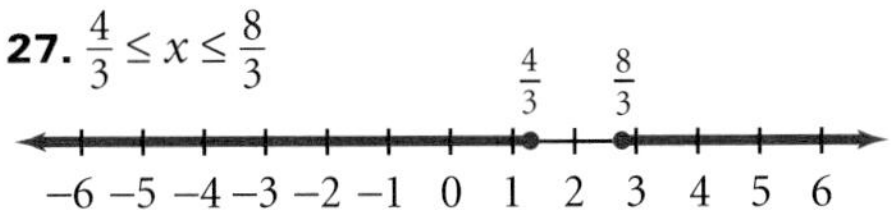

29. $x \le \frac{5}{3}$ *or* $x \ge 3$

−6 −5 −4 −3 −2 −1 0 1 2 3 4 5 6

CHAPTER 2

Lesson 2.1

1. natural, whole, integer, rational, real **3.** irrational, real **5.** rational, real **7.** irrational, real **9.** Commutative Property of Addition **11.** Distributive Property **13.** Commutative Property of Multiplication **15.** Identity Property of Multiplication **17.** 7 **19.** 46 **21.** 25 **23.** 1 **25.** −8 **27.** $\frac{1}{11}$ **29.** 1 **31.** 181

Lesson 2.2

1. 12 **3.** $\frac{1}{5}$ **5.** 9 **7.** 2 **9.** 27 **11.** 10 **13.** z^2 **15.** $3b^5$ **17.** $-6x^3y^4$ **19.** k^2 **21.** $\frac{9}{x^8y^6}$ **23.** a^6b^8 **25.** $\frac{1}{x^8y^8}$ **27.** $\frac{25x^2}{c^{10}z^{12}}$

Lesson 2.3

1. Yes; no vertical line intersects the graph at more than one point. **3.** No; two different y-values are paired with the x-value −2. **5.** No; three different y-values are paired with the x-value −8. **7.** domain: {−2, 3}; range: {8, 13} **9.** domain: {−4, 0, 2, 4}; range: {0, 4, 16} **11.** $f(-3) = 7$ and $f(1) = -1$ **13.** $f(-1) = -17$ and $f(0) = -7$ **15.** $f(10) = -6$ and $f(-2) = \frac{6}{5}$

Lesson 2.4

1. $(f+g)(x) = x^2 + 2x - 1$ **3.** $(g-f)(x) = -x^2 + 2x - 1$ **5.** $\left(\frac{f}{g}\right)(x) = \frac{x^2}{2x-1}, x \ne \frac{1}{2}$ **7.** $(f+g)(x) = -2x^2 + x + 1$ **9.** $(g-f)(x) = 2x^2 + x + 1$ **11.** $\left(\frac{f}{g}\right)(x) = -\frac{2x^2}{x+1}, x \ne -1$ **13.** $(f \circ g)(x) = 4x^2 - 8$; $(g \circ f)(x) = 16x^2 - 2$ **15.** $(f \circ g)(x) = -6x^2 + 9x$; $(g \circ f)(x) = 18x^2 + 9x$ **17.** −54 **19.** −18 **21.** 9

Lesson 2.5

1. {(2, 1), (2, 2), (2, 3), (2, 4)}; yes; no **3.** {(6, 1), (9, 2), (12, 3), (19, 4)}; yes; yes **5.** $y = \frac{x+6}{10}$ **7.** $y = 2x - 5$ **9.** $y = 6x + 2$ **11.** yes **13.** yes **15.** yes

Lesson 2.6

1.

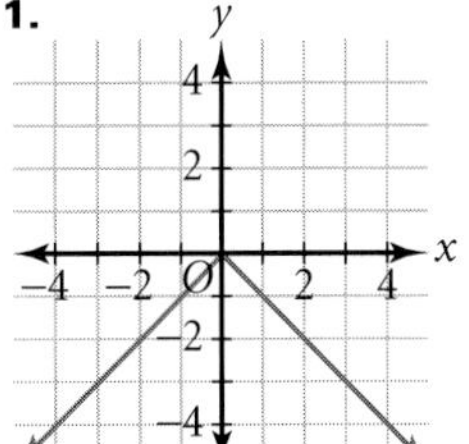

3.

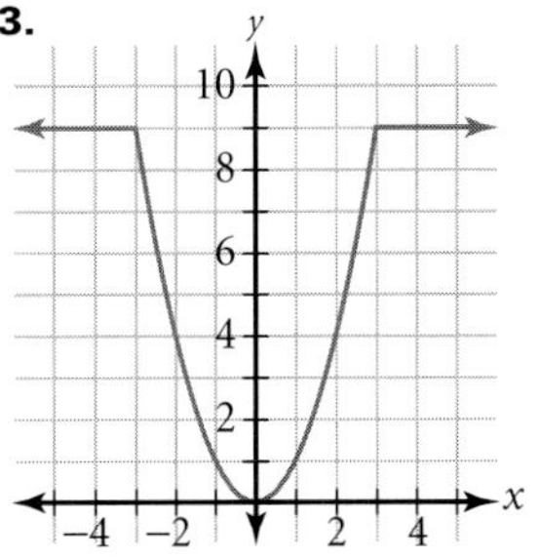

5.

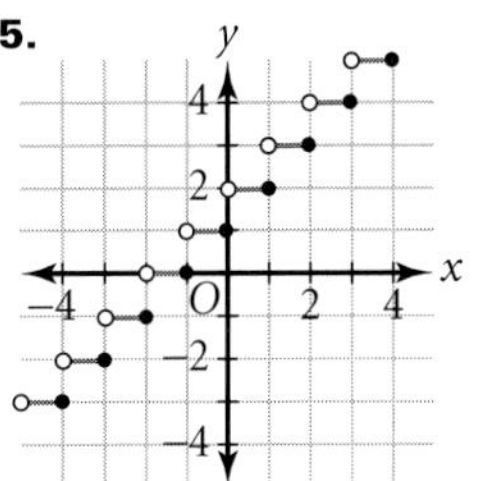

7. $f(x) = \begin{cases} -3 & \text{if } -7 \le x \le -3 \\ \frac{3}{2}x + \frac{3}{2} & \text{if } -3 < x \le 1 \end{cases}$

9. $f(x) = \begin{cases} 4 & \text{if } x < -4 \\ -x & \text{if } -4 \le x \le 4 \\ -4 & \text{if } x > -4 \end{cases}$

11. $f(x) = \begin{cases} -3 & \text{if } x < -2 \\ 3 & \text{if } -2 \le x < 2 \\ -2x + 6 & \text{if } x \ge 2 \end{cases}$

13. 15 **15.** −8 **17.** 47 **19.** 24

Lesson 2.7

1. a vertical stretch by a factor of 8 **3.** a reflection across the x-axis **5.** a vertical translation 16 units down **7.** a reflection across the y-axis and a vertical translation 13 units up **9.** a vertical stretch by a factor of 2 and a horizontal translation 3 units to the left **11.** a horizontal translation 19 units to the right **13.** a horizontal compression by a factor of $\frac{1}{3}$ and a vertical stretch by a factor of 2 **15.** a vertical stretch by a factor of 24 and a vertical translation 9 units up **17.** $g(x) = 10|x|$ **19.** $g(x) = 21(-x) + 17$ **21.** $g(x) = (x + 3.5)^2$ **23.** $g(x) = |3x|$

CHAPTER 3

Lesson 3.1

1. independent; $(-2, -6)$ **3.** dependent; infinitely many solutions **5.** independent; $(7, 3)$ **7.** independent; $(0, 3)$ **9.** independent; $(2, -1)$ **11.** independent; $(1, 1)$ **13.** $(8, -5)$ **15.** $(4, 1)$ **17.** $(-6, -18)$ **19.** $(14, 47)$ **21.** $(0, 4)$ **23.** $(-2, -1, 3)$

Lesson 3.2

1. $(2, 8)$ **3.** $(-1, -5)$ **5.** $(4, -3)$ **7.** no solution **9.** $(-2, 2)$ **11.** $(-1, 9)$ **13.** infinitely many solutions **15.** no solution **17.** $(4, 3)$

Lesson 3.3

1.

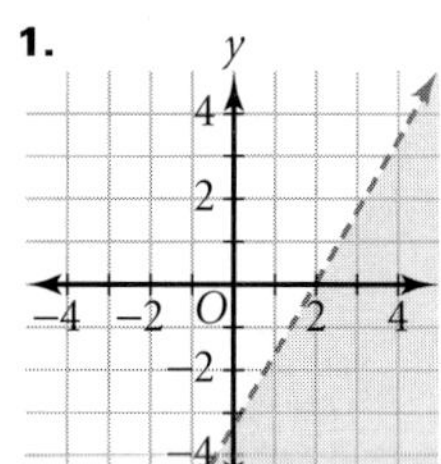

3.

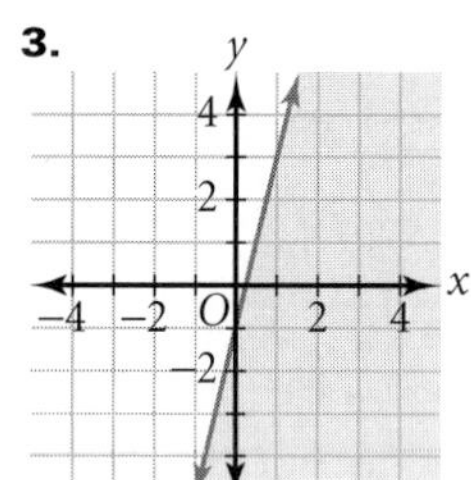

5.

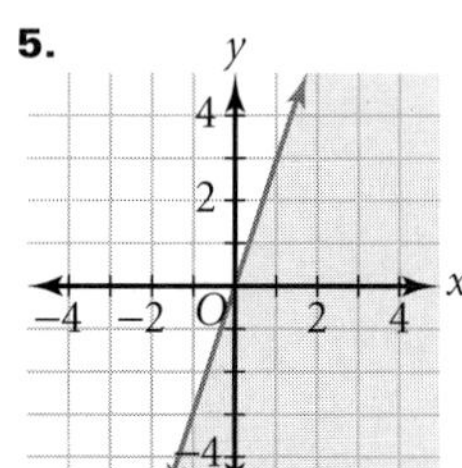

7.

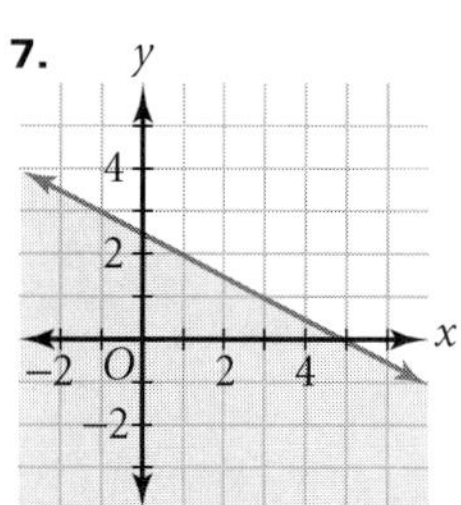

9.

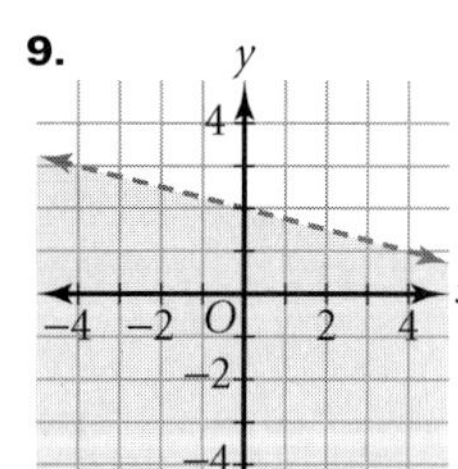

11.

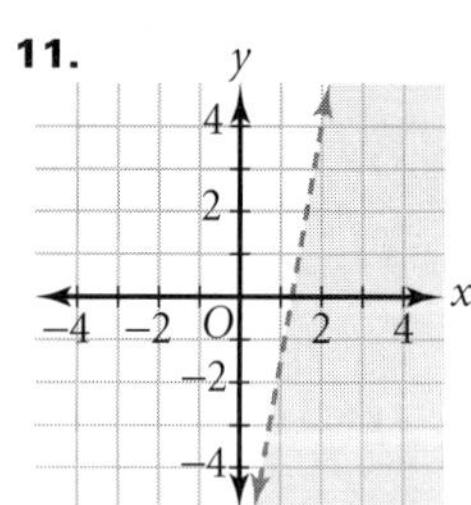

13.

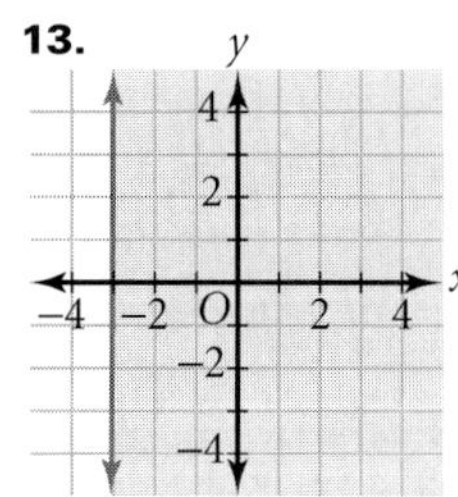

15.

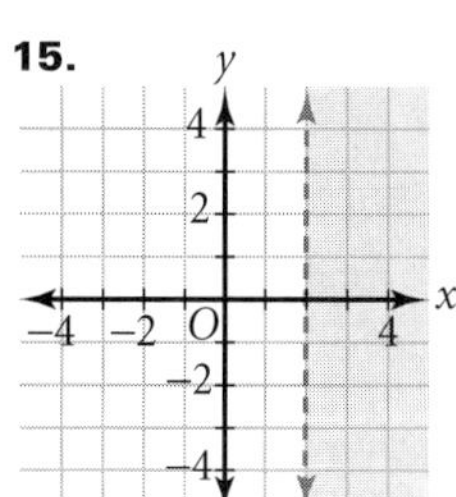

17.

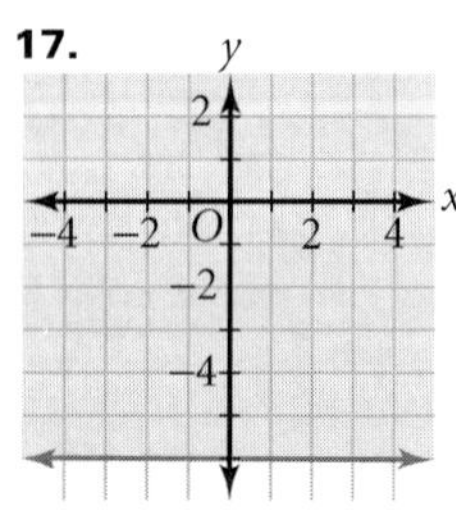

19. $y \le -3x + 5$ **21.** $x < 4$ **23.** $y < \frac{1}{2}x + \frac{3}{2}$

Lesson 3.4

1.

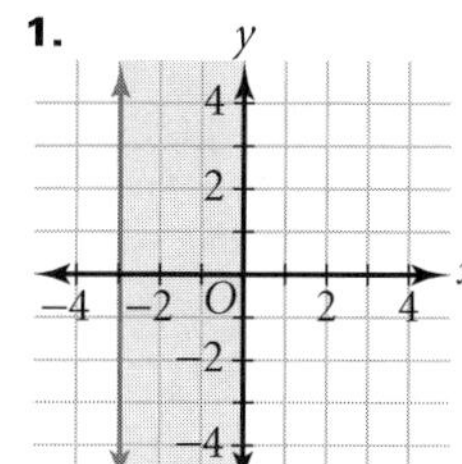

3.

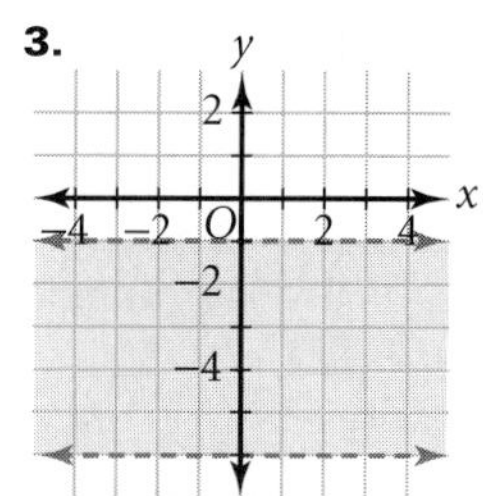

5.

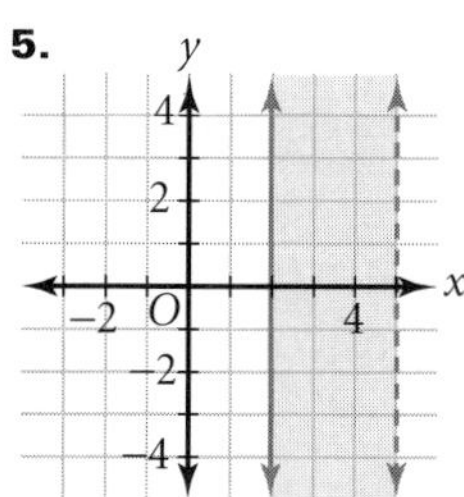

7.

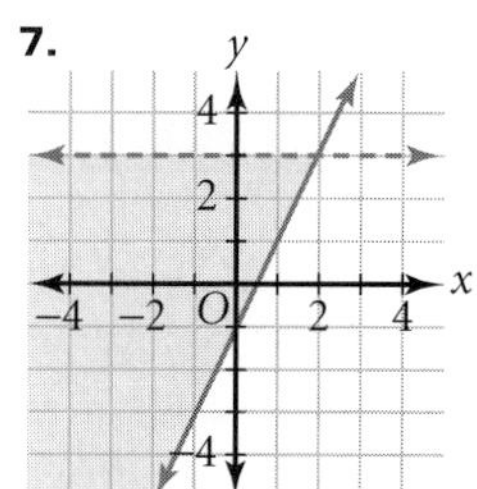

9.

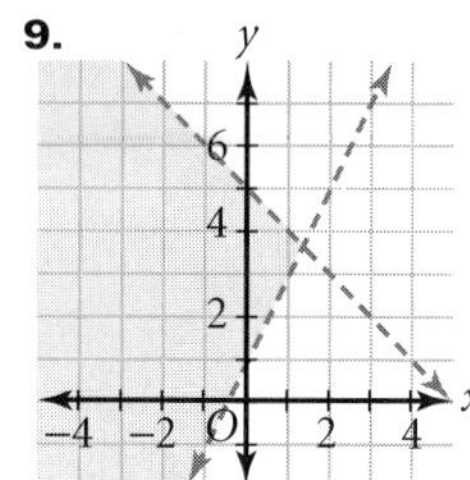

11.

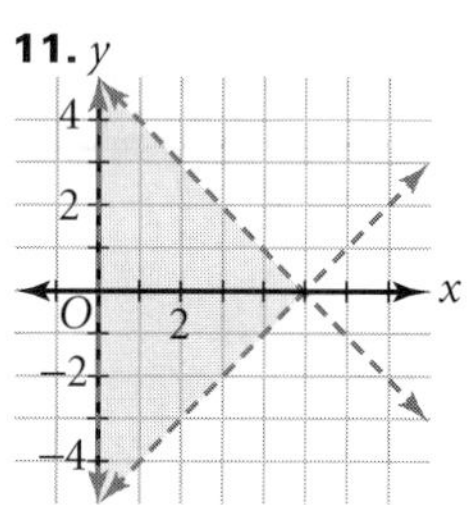

13. $\begin{cases} x \le 3 \\ y < x + 2 \\ y > -\frac{1}{2}x - \frac{5}{2} \end{cases}$ **15.** $\begin{cases} y \le \frac{1}{2}x + 2 \\ y > -\frac{1}{2}x \\ x < 4 \end{cases}$

Lesson 3.5

1.

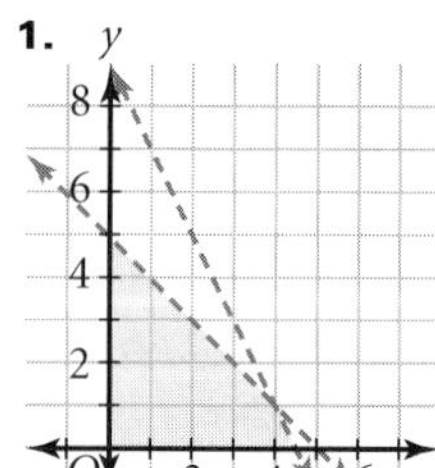

3.

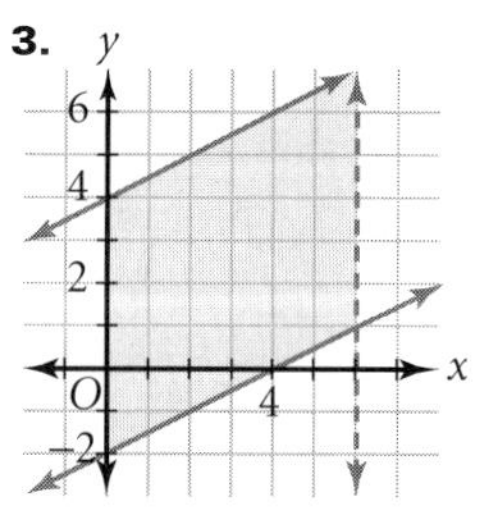

5. max = 4350; min = 0 **7.** max = 40; min = 0

Lesson 3.6

1.

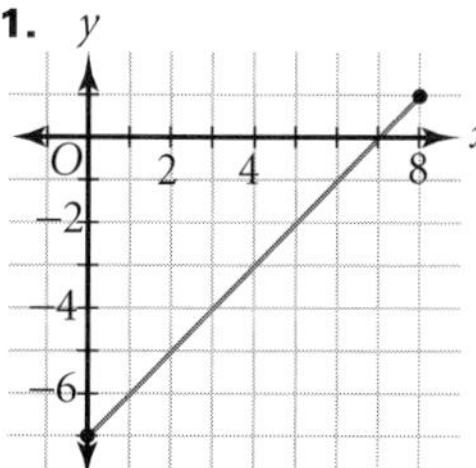

3.

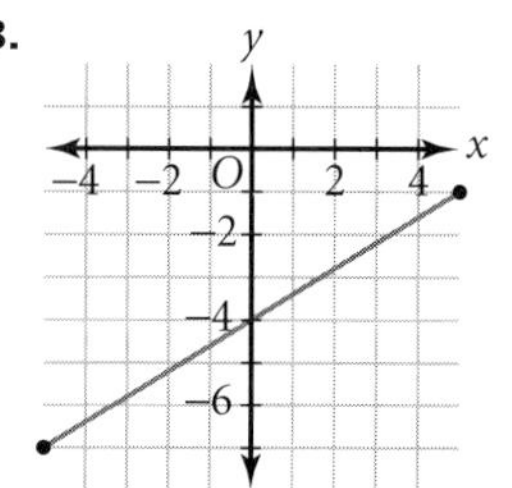

5. $y = 5 - x$ **7.** $y = 5 - x$ **9.** $y = \frac{x}{6}$

11.

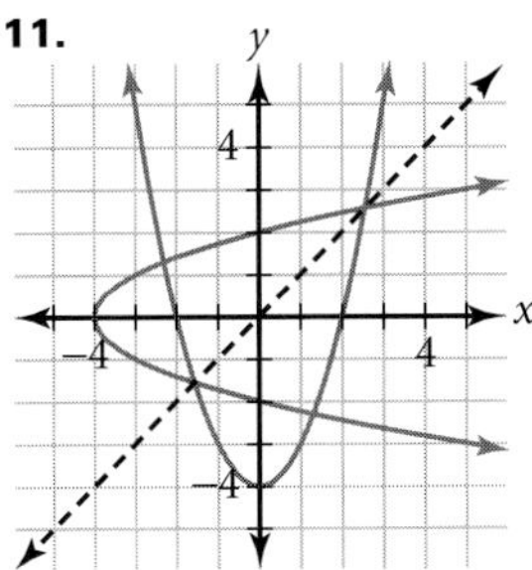

13.

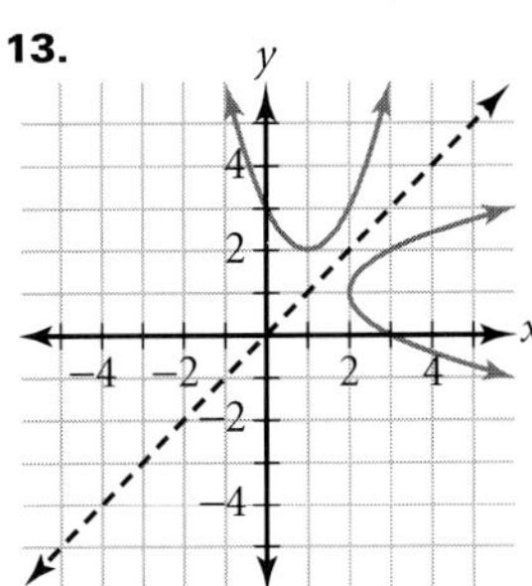

15.

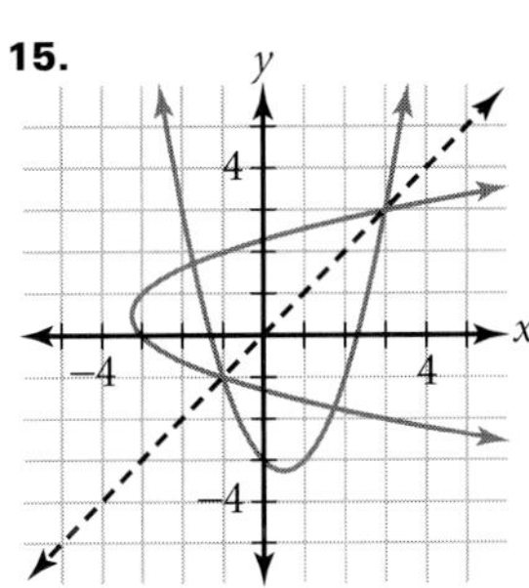

CHAPTER 4

Lesson 4.1

1. 3×3 **3.** 2×3 **5.** -6

7. $\begin{bmatrix} -2 & -3 & 2 \\ -1 & -4 & -5 \\ 0 & -1 & -7 \end{bmatrix}$ **9.** $\begin{bmatrix} -16 & 0 & -2 \\ 12 & -8 & -6 \end{bmatrix}$

11. Not possible; the matrices do not have the same dimensions.

13. $\begin{bmatrix} -4 & -1 & 0 \\ 1 & 14 & 15 \\ 2 & 5 & 5 \end{bmatrix}$ **15.** $x = 7, y = 3$

17a. $Q = \begin{bmatrix} 0 & 1 & 4 & 2 \\ 0 & 4 & 2 & 0 \end{bmatrix}$

b. $-2Q = \begin{bmatrix} 0 & -2 & -8 & -4 \\ 0 & -8 & -4 & 0 \end{bmatrix}$

c.

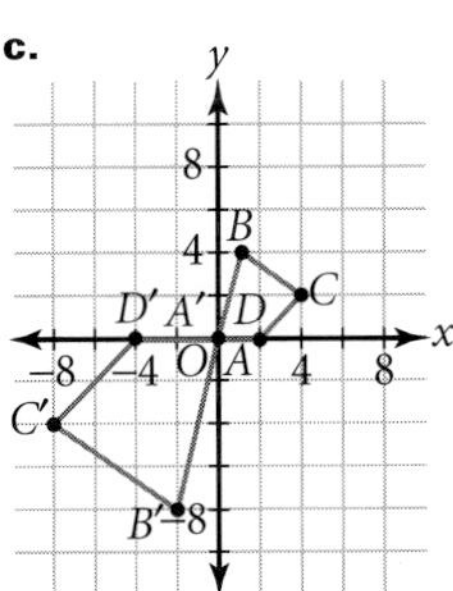

Lesson 4.2

1. $[10]$ **3.** $\begin{bmatrix} -16 & -14 \\ 12 & 8 \end{bmatrix}$ **5.** $[-6 \quad 23]$

7. $\begin{bmatrix} -1 & 7 & 4 \\ -7 & 9 & 8 \\ 12 & -12 & -12 \end{bmatrix}$ **9.** $[-41 \quad 26]$

Lesson 4.3

1. no **3.** yes **5.** –1; yes **7.** 0; no **9.** 1.4375; yes

11. $\begin{bmatrix} -3 & 8 \\ 2 & -5 \end{bmatrix}$ **13.** $\begin{bmatrix} 0.5 & -0.75 \\ -1 & 2 \end{bmatrix}$

15. $\begin{bmatrix} -4 & 1 \\ 6.5 & -1.5 \end{bmatrix}$ **17.** $\begin{bmatrix} 0.4 & 0.1 & -0.7 \\ 0.2 & 0.3 & -1.1 \\ -0.2 & 0.2 & 0.6 \end{bmatrix}$

19. $\begin{bmatrix} 7 & -1.6 & -0.53 \\ -2 & 0.8 & 0.27 \\ -9.5 & 2.2 & 1.07 \end{bmatrix}$

Lesson 4.4

1. $\begin{bmatrix} 2 & 1 \\ 5 & -3 \end{bmatrix}\begin{bmatrix} x \\ y \end{bmatrix} = \begin{bmatrix} 2 \\ -17 \end{bmatrix}$ **3.** $\begin{bmatrix} 3 & -2 \\ 1 & -4 \end{bmatrix}\begin{bmatrix} x \\ y \end{bmatrix} = \begin{bmatrix} 4 \\ 15 \end{bmatrix}$

5. $\begin{bmatrix} 2 & -3 & 1 \\ 1 & -5 & 2 \\ 4 & -1 & -1 \end{bmatrix}\begin{bmatrix} x \\ y \\ z \end{bmatrix} = \begin{bmatrix} 3 \\ 4 \\ -1 \end{bmatrix}$

7. $\begin{cases} -2x + y - z = 4 \\ 5x - y + 2z = -6 \\ 3x + 4y + z = 10 \end{cases}$ **9.** $\begin{bmatrix} 15 & -7 \\ 11 & 5 \end{bmatrix}\begin{bmatrix} x \\ y \end{bmatrix} = \begin{bmatrix} 9 \\ 37 \end{bmatrix}$; (2, 3)

11. $\begin{bmatrix} 2 & 1 & 1 \\ 1 & -1 & 3 \\ 0 & 1 & 1 \end{bmatrix}\begin{bmatrix} x \\ y \\ z \end{bmatrix} = \begin{bmatrix} 5 \\ -11 \\ 1 \end{bmatrix}$; (2, 4, –3)

13. $\begin{bmatrix} 4 & -3 & 1 \\ 2 & 1 & -3 \\ 3 & 2 & 1 \end{bmatrix}\begin{bmatrix} x \\ y \\ z \end{bmatrix} = \begin{bmatrix} 9 \\ -7 \\ 12 \end{bmatrix}$; (2, 1, 4)

Lesson 4.5

1. $\left[\begin{array}{cc|c} 4 & -3 & 7 \\ 2 & -1 & 5 \end{array}\right]$ **3.** $\left[\begin{array}{ccc|c} 6 & -1 & 1 & 6 \\ 3 & 4 & -1 & 3 \\ 9 & -3 & 2 & 9 \end{array}\right]$

5. $\left[\begin{array}{ccc|c} 1 & 0 & 2 & -3.8 \\ 0 & 1 & 0 & 5 \\ 0 & 0 & 1 & 0.4 \end{array}\right]$ **7.** $\left(\frac{1}{2}, 2\right)$ **9.** (2, –5)

11. (4, 2, 0) **13.** dependent **15.** inconsistent

CHAPTER 5

Lesson 5.1

1. $f(x) = x^2 - 6x - 7$; $a = 1, b = -6, c = -7$
3. $f(x) = 2x^2 - 7x - 4$; $a = 2, b = -7, c = -4$
5. $f(x) = 2x^2 - 3x - 35$; $a = 2, b = -3, c = -35$
7. yes **9.** no **11.** down; maximum **13.** up; minimum **15.** (–1, 3) **17.** (0, 5)
19. (–0.25, –0.0625)

Lesson 5.2

1. $\pm\sqrt{51} \approx \pm 7.14$ **3.** $\pm\sqrt{13} \approx \pm 3.61$ **5.** $\pm\frac{\sqrt{182}}{7} \approx \pm 1.93$ **7.** $q \approx 19.4$ **9.** $z \approx 23.6$ **11.** $b \approx 25.0$ **13.** $a \approx 15.4$ **15.** $c \approx 14.2$

Lesson 5.3

1. $7(x+7)$ **3.** $4x(x-7)$ **5.** $(14+x)(3-x^2)$ **7.** $-3x^2(x+4)$ **9.** $(x+7)^2$ **11.** $(x+3)(x+14)$ **13.** $(3x+2)(x+2)$ **15.** $(3-2x)(x-1)$ **17.** ± 12 **19.** $\pm\frac{5}{4}$ **21.** $\frac{1}{3}$ **23.** 0 or 12 **25.** -9 or 0.5 **27.** 5 or 7

Lesson 5.4

1. $x^2 + x + \frac{1}{4}$; $\left(x + \frac{1}{2}\right)^2$ **3.** $x^2 - 10x + 25$; $(x-5)^2$ **5.** $x^2 - 9x + \frac{81}{4}$; $\left(x - \frac{9}{2}\right)^2$ **7.** $x^2 - 22x + 121$; $(x-11)^2$ **9.** $x^2 - 0.5x + 0.0625$; $(x - 0.25)^2$ **11.** $-1 \pm 2\sqrt{2}$ **13.** $4 \pm 2\sqrt{7}$ **15.** $8 \pm \sqrt{85}$ **17.** $-\frac{3}{2} \pm \frac{\sqrt{53}}{2}$ **19.** $2 \pm \frac{\sqrt{46}}{2}$ **21.** $-\frac{1}{2} \pm \frac{\sqrt{13}}{2}$ **23.** $f(x) = x^2 + (-3)$; $(0, -3)$ **25.** $f(x) = [x - (-2)]^2 + (-4)$; $(-2, -4)$ **27.** $f(x) = [x - (-3)]^2 + (-4)$; $(-3, -4)$ **29.** $f(x) = 2[x - (-1)]^2 + (-5)$; $(-1, -5)$

Lesson 5.5

1. 3 or 5 **3.** $\frac{5 \pm \sqrt{21}}{2}$ **5.** 1 or 9 **7.** $1 \pm 2\sqrt{2}$ **9.** $\frac{-1 \pm \sqrt{69}}{2}$ **11.** $\frac{1 \pm \sqrt{57}}{7}$ **13.** $-2 \pm \sqrt{13}$ **15.** $\frac{1 \pm \sqrt{57}}{2}$ **17.** $x = -2$; $(-2, -15)$ **19.** $x = -\frac{3}{4}$; $\left(-\frac{3}{4}, -6\frac{1}{8}\right)$ **21.** $x = -\frac{1}{2}$; $\left(-\frac{1}{2}, -9\frac{1}{4}\right)$ **23.** $x = -\frac{2}{3}$; $\left(-\frac{2}{3}, 3\frac{1}{3}\right)$ **25.** $x = -\frac{1}{4}$; $\left(-\frac{1}{4}, -1\frac{1}{4}\right)$ **27.** $x = \frac{3}{2}$; $\left(\frac{3}{2}, -1\frac{3}{4}\right)$ **29.** $x = \frac{3}{8}$; $\left(\frac{3}{8}, -5\frac{9}{16}\right)$

Lesson 5.6

1. 29; 2 solutions; $\frac{3}{2} \pm \frac{\sqrt{29}}{2}$ **3.** -19; 0 solutions; $\frac{7}{2} \pm \frac{i\sqrt{19}}{2}$ **5.** -80; 0 solutions; $\frac{1}{4} \pm \frac{i\sqrt{5}}{4}$ **7.** -140; 0 solutions; $\frac{1}{4} \pm \frac{i\sqrt{35}}{4}$ **9.** 60; 2; $-1 \pm \frac{\sqrt{15}}{3}$

11. $13 + 5i$ **13.** $3i + 4$ **15.** $-3i$ **17.** $5 + 2i$ **19.** $1 + 9i$ **21.** $-11 - i$ **23.** 30 **25.** $-27 + 36i$ **27.** $29 - 29i$ **29.** $5 - 14i$ **31.** $\frac{7}{5} - \frac{4i}{5}$ **33.** $-\frac{26 - 2i}{17}$ **35.** $\frac{3}{2} - 2i$ **37.** $77 - 36i$ **39.** $-9 - 40i$

41.

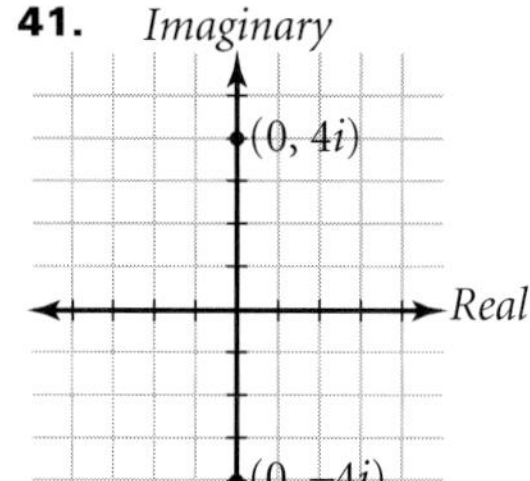

43.

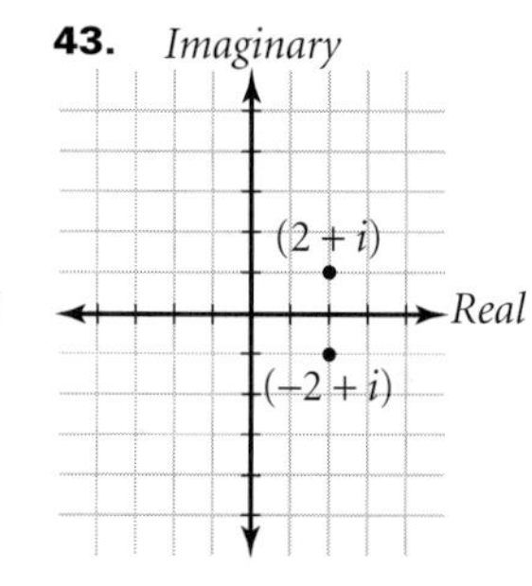

45.

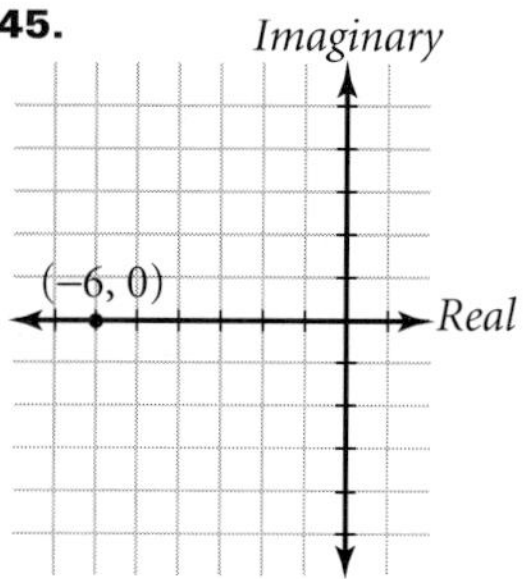

Lesson 5.7

1. $f(x) = x^2 + 2$ **3.** $f(x) = x^2 + 7x - 1$ **5.** $f(x) = x^2 + x + 6$ **7.** $f(x) = x^2 - 18x - 59$ **9.** $f(x) = 0.5x^2 + 3x - 1$ **11.** $f(x) = -x^2 + 4x$ **13.** $f(x) = 0.25x^2 - 0.5x + 1$ **15.** $f(x) = -0.5x^2 + x + 12$ **17.** $f(x) = -16x^2 + 60x + 4$ **19.** about 3.8 seconds

Lesson 5.8

1. $-3 < x < 3$

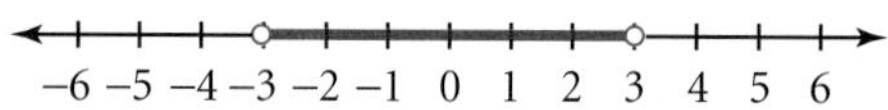

3. $-9 \le x \le -2$

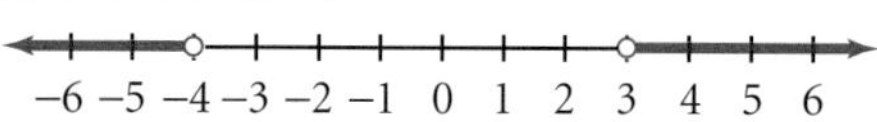

5. $x < -4$ *or* $x > 3$

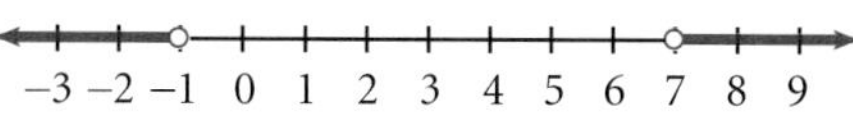

7. $x = 4$

−6 −5 −4 −3 −2 −1 0 1 2 3 4 5 6

9. $x < -1$ *or* $x > 7$

−3 −2 −1 0 1 2 3 4 5 6 7 8 9

11. $\frac{3}{2} - \frac{\sqrt{29}}{2} \le x \le \frac{3}{2} + \frac{\sqrt{29}}{2}$

−6 −5 −4 −3 −2 −1 0 1 2 3 4 5 6

13.

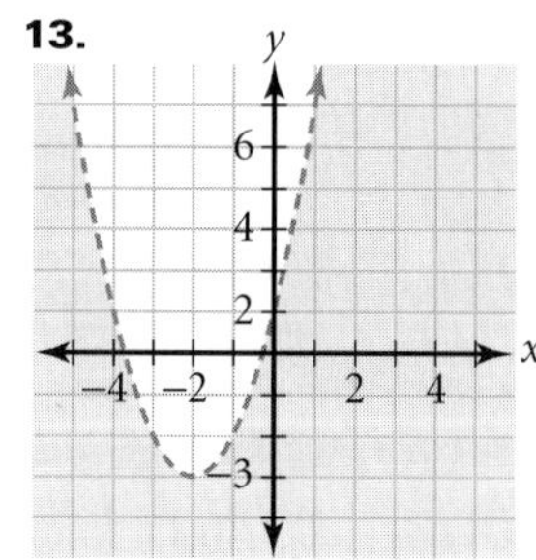

C

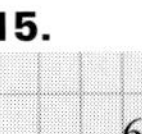

15.

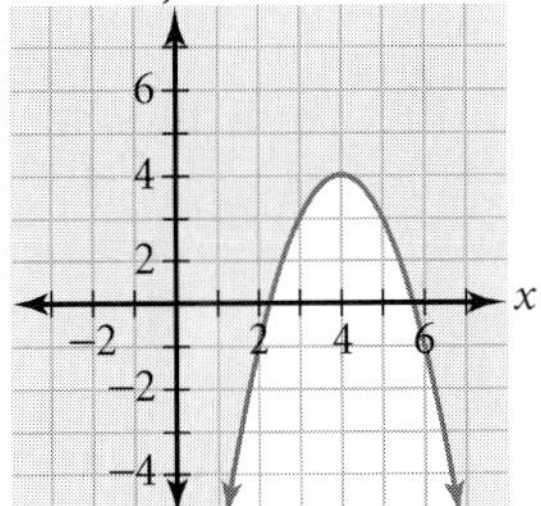

C

17.

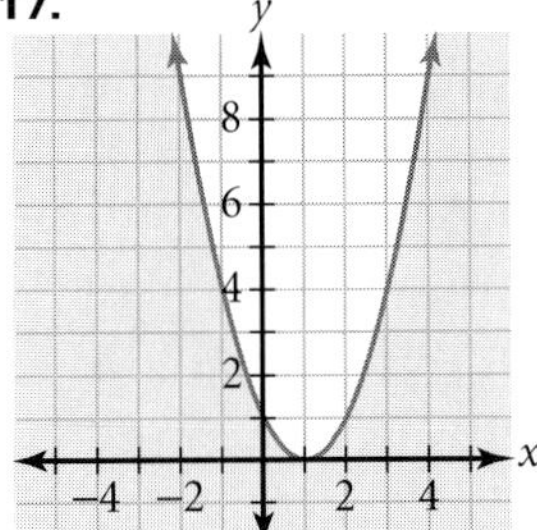

19.

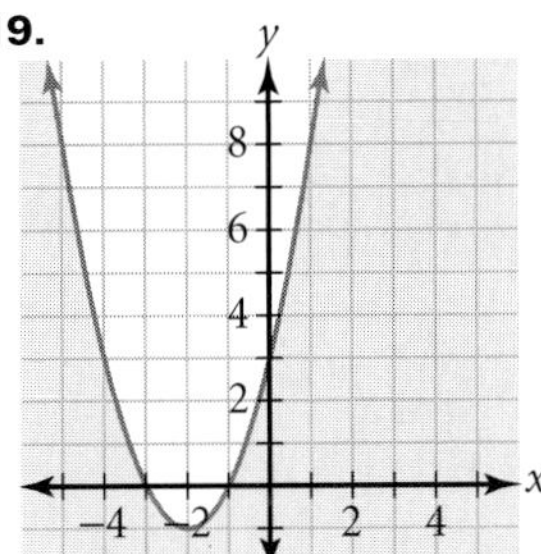

21.

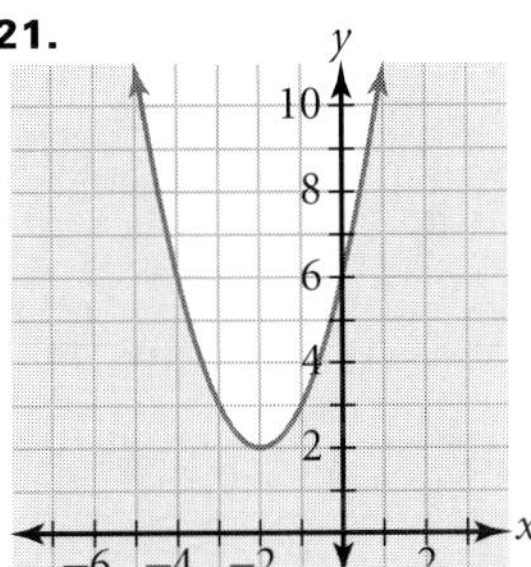

23.

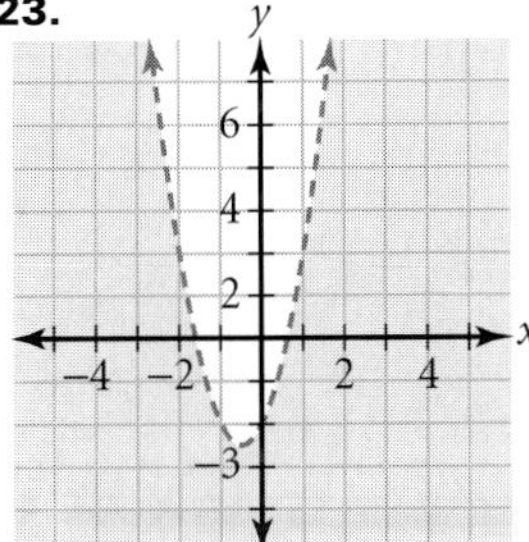

25.

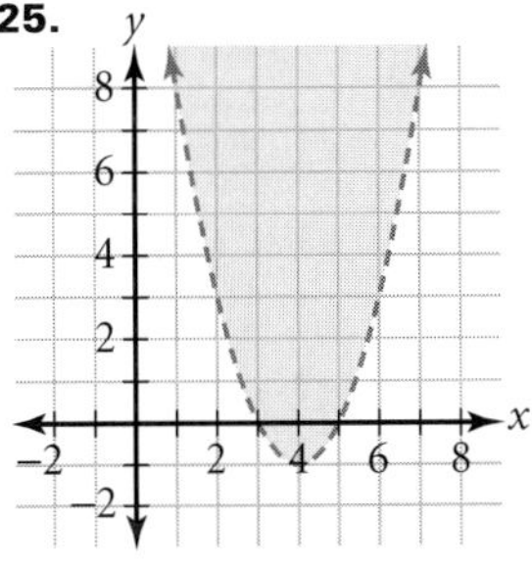

27.

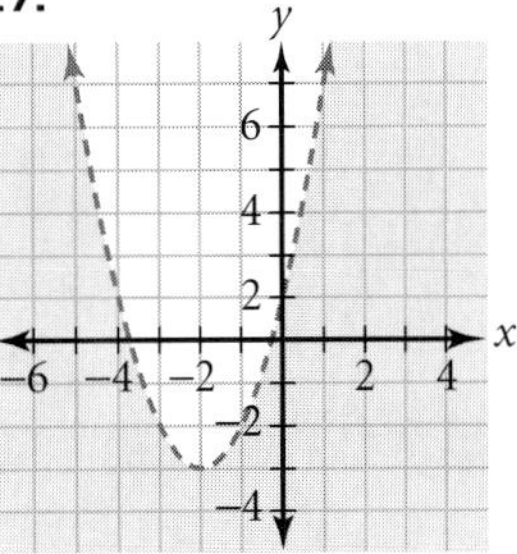

CHAPTER 6

Lesson 6.1

1. 1.03 **3.** 0.9 **5.** 1.007 **7.** 1.18 **9.** 1.0004 **11.** 1.0115 **13.** 2.828 **15.** 3.750 **17.** 5.278 **19.** 0.094 **21.** 153.53 milligrams **23.** 520,000

Lesson 6.2

1. quadratic **3.** quadratic **5.** linear **7.** exponential growth **9.** exponential decay **11.** exponential decay **13.** exponential decay **15.** exponential decay **17.** \$2156.90 **19.** \$588.38 **21.** \$696.13 **23.** \$4442.81

Lesson 6.3

1. $\log_3 81 = 4$ **3.** $\log_{\frac{1}{2}} \frac{1}{128} = 7$ **5.** $\log_{(\frac{1}{3})} 81 = -4$ **7.** $\log_5 \frac{1}{125} = -3$ **9.** $\log_9 \frac{1}{81} = -2$ **11.** $7^4 = 2401$ **13.** $6^{-4} = \frac{1}{1296}$ **15.** $2^8 = 256$ **17.** $10^{-4} = 0.0001$ **19.** $x \approx 1.18$ **21.** $x \approx 0.65$ **23.** $x \approx 3.02$ **25.** $x \approx -0.08$ **27.** $x \approx 1.15$ **29.** $v = 0$ **31.** $v = 625$ **33.** $v = \frac{1}{64}$ **35.** $v = 5$

Lesson 6.4

1. $\log_3 9 + \log_3 x = 2 + \log_3 x$
3. $\log_4 2 + \log_4 3 + \log_4 4 = 1.5 + \log_4 3$
5. $\log_5 4 - \log_5 5 = \log_5 4 - 1$ **7.** $\log_2 21$ **9.** $\log_4 \frac{25}{6}$ **11.** $\log_5 5 = 1$ **13.** 0 **15.** 89 **17.** −1 **19.** $x = 3$ **21.** no solution **23.** $x = 8$ **25.** $x = 2$

Lesson 6.5

1. 5.67 **3.** −0.39 **5.** 1.20 **7.** −0.71 **9.** −0.47 **11.** 0.79 **13.** −0.23 **15.** 5.81 **17.** −0.53 **19.** 12.32 **21.** −0.13 **23.** $x \approx 2.11$ **25.** $x \approx 1.81$ **27.** $x \approx 3.38$ **29.** $x \approx 2.23$ **31.** $x \approx 3.09$ **33.** $x \approx 1.99$ **35.** $x \approx 0.10$ **37.** $x \approx 1.47$ **39.** $x \approx 1.66$ **41.** $x \approx 1.88$

Lesson 6.6

1. 20.086 **3.** 90.017 **5.** 5.652 **7.** 0.973 **9.** not defined **11.** −0.223 **13.** $\ln 25.03 \approx 3.22$ **15.** $e^{3.91} \approx 50$ **17.** $\ln 29.96 \approx 3.4$ **19.** $e^{3.22} \approx 25$ **21.** $\ln 1.95 \approx \frac{2}{3}$ **23.** $e^{-1.39} \approx \frac{1}{4}$ **25.** $x \approx 1.22$ **27.** $x \approx -2.46$ **29.** $x \approx -2.93$ **31.** $x \approx 2.20$ **33.** $x \approx 6.01$ **35.** $x \approx 4.91$ **37.** \$6920.15

Lesson 6.7

1. $x = 5$ **3.** $x = 5$ **5.** $x = 3$ **7.** $x = 2$ **9.** $x = \frac{\ln 4}{\ln 3} \approx 1.26$ **11.** $x = 1 + \log 121 \approx 3.08$ **13.** $x = \frac{1}{2}(1 + \ln 9) \approx 1.60$ **15.** no solution **17.** $x = \frac{1}{3}(4 - \ln 22) \approx 0.30$ **19.** 10^{22} ergs

CHAPTER 7

Lesson 7.1

1. yes; 3 **3.** no **5.** yes; 4 **7.** −28 **9.** 14 **11.** 272 **13.** $3x^3 + 6x^2 - 3x + 16$; cubic polynomial **15.** $8.1x^3 - 9x^2 + 3.5x - 20$; cubic polynomial **17.** $3x^5 - 4x^4 - x^3 + 5x^2 + 7$; quintic polynomial **19.** S-shape **21.** W-shape

Lesson 7.2

1. local maximum of 3.1 **3.** local maximum of 0; local minima of −1.1 and −0.1 **5.** local maximum of 0.1; local minimum of 0; increasing for $-6 < x < -0.7$ and $0 < x < 6$, decreasing for $-0.7 < x < 0$ **7.** local maxima of 0.1 and 4.5; local minimum of 0; increasing for $-4 < x < -0.3$ and $0 < x < 1.5$, decreasing for $-0.3 < x < 0$ and $1.5 < x < 4$ **9.** local maximum of 16.6; local minimum of −8.6; increasing for $x < -3.2$ and $x > 3.2$, decreasing for $-3.2 < x < 3.2$ **11.** rises on the left, falls on the right **13.** rises on the left and the right **15.** $f(x) = 3.83x^4 - 44.15x^3 + 156.86x^2 + 112.93x + 15{,}833.87$

Lesson 7.3

1. $-10x^7 + 6x^6 - 4x^4 - 12x^3$ **3.** $x^3 - 3x^2 - 23x + 30$ **5.** $8x^3 - 12x^2 + 6x - 1$ **7.** yes **9.** no **11.** $x^2 - x + 4$ **13.** $3x^2 + 2x - 4$ **15.** $x^2 - 2x - 8$ **17.** $5x^2 - 2x + 3$ **19.** −16 **21.** −86

Lesson 7.4

1. 0, −5, 2 **3.** 0, 7 (multiplicity 2) **5.** −2, 0, 1 **7.** −2 and 2 (multiplicity 2) **9.** −1, −2, and 5 **11.** −1, 2, and 3 **13.** −3, 3, $-\sqrt{5}$, and $\sqrt{5}$ **15.** −1, 1, $-2\sqrt{3}$, and $2\sqrt{3}$ **17.** $-\sqrt{11}$, $\sqrt{11}$, $-\sqrt{3}$, and $\sqrt{3}$ **19.** 0 **21.** −2.21, 0.54, and 1.68

Lesson 7.5

1. $\frac{2}{3}$ and 4 **3.** $\frac{1}{2}$, $\frac{3}{5}$, and 2 **5.** $-\frac{3}{4}$, 1, and 2 **7.** $-1 - \sqrt{2}$, $-1 + \sqrt{2}$, and 3 **9.** 2, $-i\sqrt{7}$, and $i\sqrt{7}$ **11.** $-2\sqrt{2}$, $2\sqrt{2}$, $-i\sqrt{3}$, and $i\sqrt{3}$ **13.** −0.87 and 0.6 **15.** 0.86 and 2.07

17. $P(x) = (x + 1)(x - 1)(x - 2) = x^3 - 2x^2 - x + 2$

19. $P(x) = 16\left(x - \frac{1}{2}\right)^2\left(x - \frac{3}{2}\right)\left(x + \frac{3}{2}\right)$
$= 16x^4 - 16x^3 - 32x^2 + 36x - 9$

21. $P(x) = 2(x - 2)(x - 3i)(x + 3i)$
$= 2x^3 - 4x^2 + 18x - 36$

CHAPTER 8

Lesson 8.1

1. $y = \frac{144}{x}$; 36, 16, 9.6, 7.2 **3.** $y = \frac{1.6}{x}$; 16, 8, 0.4, 0.2 **5.** $y = 1.5xz$; 40.5 **7.** $y = -3xz$; 7.2 **9.** $z = \frac{5.5xy}{w}$; 19.8 **11.** $z = \frac{-1.25xy}{w}$; −0.125 **13.** 450; $t = \frac{450}{r}$; 11.3, 10, 9, and 8.2 hours

Lesson 8.2

1. yes; all real numbers except −2 and −5 **3.** yes; all real numbers except −3 and 3 **5.** vertical asymptotes: $x = -\sqrt{3}$, $x = \sqrt{3}$; horizontal asymptote: $y = 0$ **7.** vertical asymptote: $x = 4$; no horizontal asymptotes; hole when $x = -3$ **9.** no vertical asymptotes; no horizontal asymptotes; hole when $x = 3$ **11.** vertical asymptote: $x = \frac{1}{2}$; horizontal asymptote: $y = \frac{1}{2}$; hole when $x = 2$

13. all real numbers except 4; vertical asymptote: $x = 4$; horizontal asymptote: $y = 1$; no holes

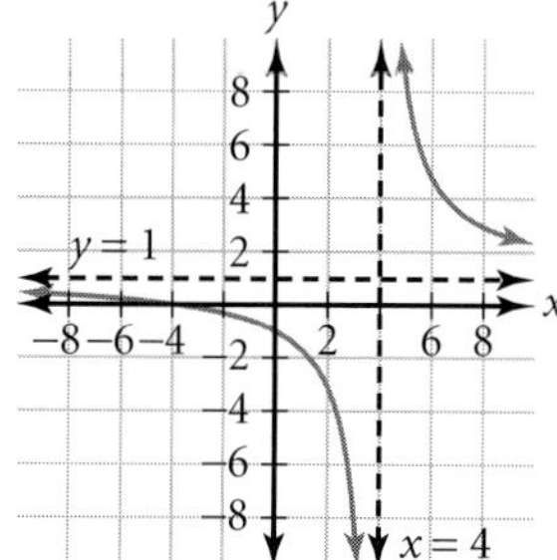

15. all real numbers except −3 and −5; vertical asymptote: $x = 1$; horizontal asymptote: $y = 0$; hole when $x = -3$

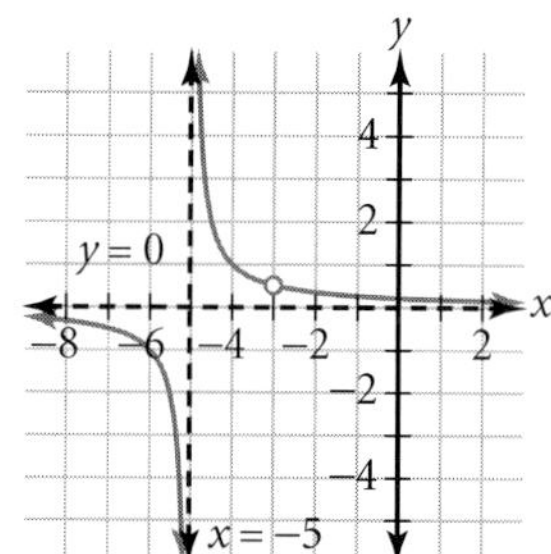

17. all real numbers except −2; vertical asymptote: $x = -2$; horizontal asymptote: $y = 1$; no holes

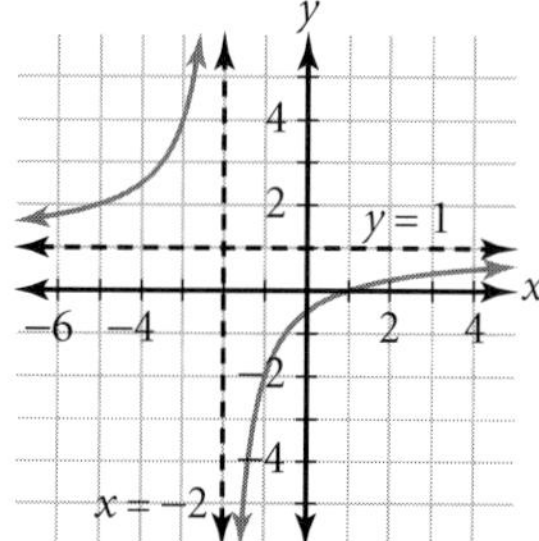

Lesson 8.3

1. x^2 **3.** $\frac{x + 6}{x - 3}$ **5.** $-\frac{x + 2}{x - 2}$ **7.** $\frac{5x^2}{2x - 1}$ **9.** $-\frac{4x}{5x - 25}$

11. $-\frac{2x+1}{x-1}$ **13.** $\frac{x+7}{x-10}$ **15.** $\frac{x+7}{x-1}$ **17.** $\frac{2}{x+5}$ **19.** $-\frac{1}{x+1}$
21. $-\frac{x-10}{4x-20}$

Lesson 8.4

1. $\frac{x}{2x+5}$ **3.** $\frac{x-3}{12}$ **5.** $\frac{2x+1}{x-8}$ **7.** $\frac{x-6}{x^2+4x-12}$
9. $-\frac{6x^2+6x+7}{3x^2-13x-10}$ **11.** $\frac{7}{2x}$ **13.** $-\frac{17}{6x+12}$ **15.** $\frac{2x^2+6}{x^2-x-12}$
17. 3 **19.** $\frac{3x+1}{x+5}$

Lesson 8.5

1. $x=6$ **3.** $x=12$ **5.** $x=5$ **7.** $x=1$ **9.** $\frac{1}{5}$ or 5 **11.** 4
13. -1 **15.** 4 or $\frac{2}{3}$ **17.** $-2<x<0$ **19.** $x<-\frac{2}{5}$ *or* $x>\frac{2}{3}$
21. $x<\frac{3}{2}$ *or* $x>\frac{23}{9}$ **23.** $0<x<1$ **25.** $-1<x<2$ *or* $x>4$
27. $x\le-1.8$ *or* $x\ge1.8$ **29.** $-1<x\le1.1$ *or* $x>6$

Lesson 8.6

1. $-\frac{9}{5}$ **3.** 192 **5.** $\frac{16}{3}$ **7.** $-\frac{1}{16}$ **9.** 6 **11.** 2
13. $x\le-4$ *or* $x\ge4$ **15.** $x\ge1$ **17.** all real numbers
19. $y=-\sqrt{x-4}$, $y=\sqrt{x-4}$

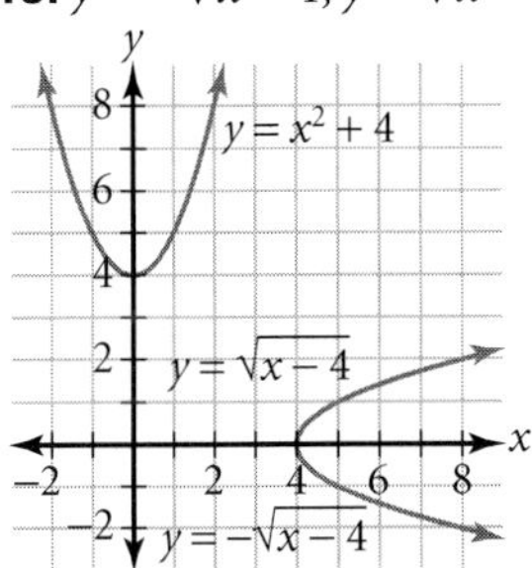

21. $y=-2-\sqrt{x+4}$, $y=-2+\sqrt{x+4}$

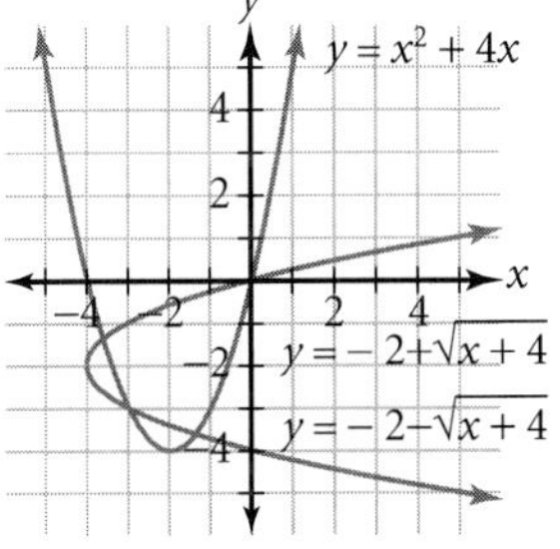

23. $y=3-\sqrt{x}$, $y=3+\sqrt{x}$

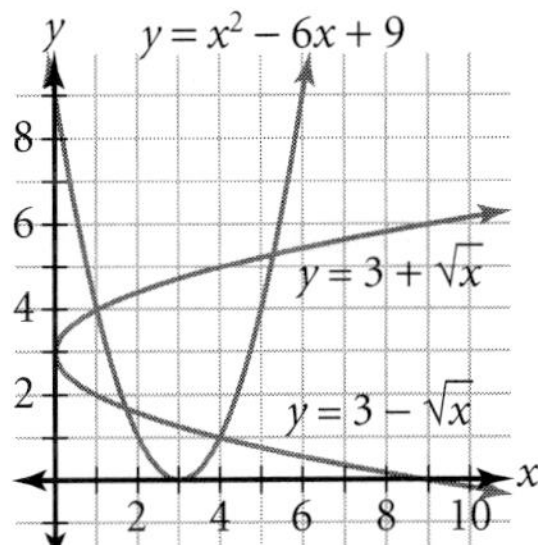

25. 23.4 mph; 33.1 mph; 46.8 mph

Lesson 8.7

1. $5\sqrt{5}$ **3.** $2x^2z^2\sqrt[4]{5z^2}$ **5.** $5|xy|\sqrt{3yz}$ **7.** $3x$ **9.** $8x^3z^4\sqrt{xz}$
11. $2yz\sqrt[3]{xyz}$ **13.** $2x^3\sqrt[4]{2}$ **15.** $2x\sqrt[4]{10x^3}$ **17.** $8-\sqrt{5}$
19. $11-7\sqrt{2}$ **21.** $12\sqrt{15}+72\sqrt{2}$ **23.** $30\sqrt{2}-5\sqrt{6}$
25. $46-14\sqrt{6}$ **27.** 3 **29.** $\frac{-3\sqrt{6}-3\sqrt{2}}{4}$ **31.** $5-2\sqrt{6}$
33. $\frac{6x+8\sqrt{xy}}{9x-16y}$

Lesson 8.8

1. $x=14$ **3.** $x=5$ **5.** $x=10$ **7.** $x=1$ **9.** 5
11. $0<x<4.5$ **13.** $2\le x\le5$ **15.** $\frac{2}{3}\le x\le2$ **17.** $x>30$
19. $x\ge2.4$ **21.** $x\ge\frac{1}{3}$ **23.** $x=2.9$

CHAPTER 9

Lesson 9.1

1. circle **3.** hyperbola **5.** hyperbola **7.** ellipse
9. hyperbola **11.** $2\sqrt{13}\approx7.21$; $M(4,1)$
13. $2\sqrt{13}\approx7.21$; $M(2,4)$ **15.** $2\sqrt{6}\approx4.90$;
$M(2\sqrt{2},2)\approx M(2.83,2)$ **17.** $\left(\frac{13}{2},-8\right)$; 25π; 156.25π
19. $(6,0)$; $16\pi\sqrt{2}$; 128π **21.** $(11,17)$; $2\pi\sqrt{170}$; 170π

Lesson 9.2

1. $y=\frac{1}{2}x^2$ **3.** $y-2=-\frac{1}{12}(x-3)^2$

5.

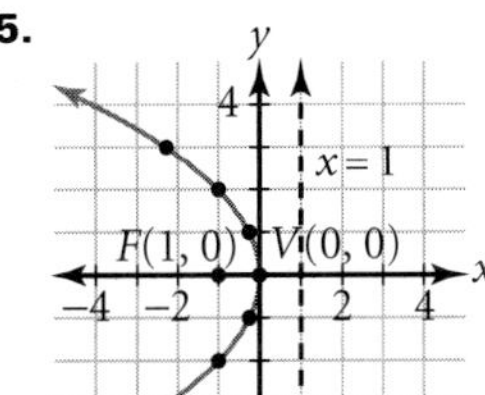

7.

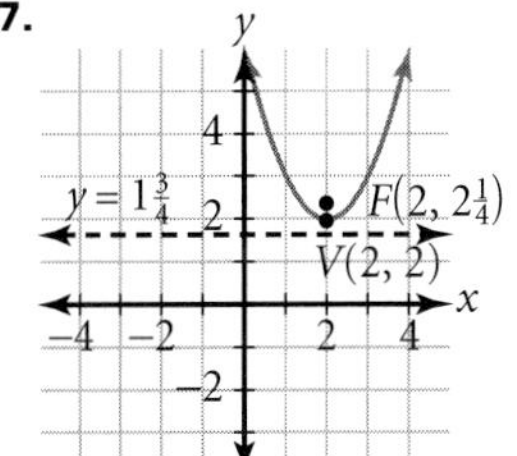

9.

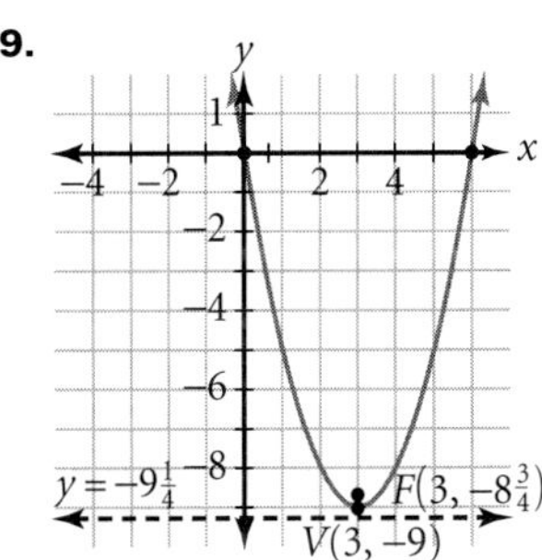

11.

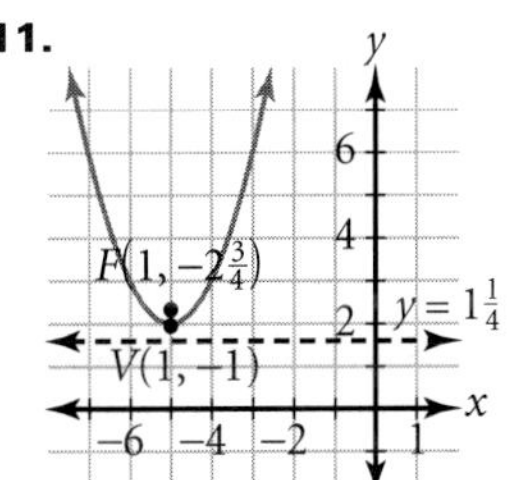

13. $x=\frac{1}{60}y^2$ **15.** $y-2=\frac{1}{24}x^2$ **17.** $y-\frac{1}{2}=\frac{1}{2}(x-1)^2$
19. $y-8=-2(x-1)^2$

Lesson 9.3

1. $(x-4)^2+(y-2)^2=4$ **3.** $(x+1)^2+(y-3)^2=\frac{49}{4}$
5. $x^2+y^2=20.25$ **7.** $(x-8)^2+(y+2)^2=25$; $r=5$;
$C(8,-2)$ **9.** $(x-10)^2+(y-5)^2=64$; $r=8$; $C(10,5)$

11.

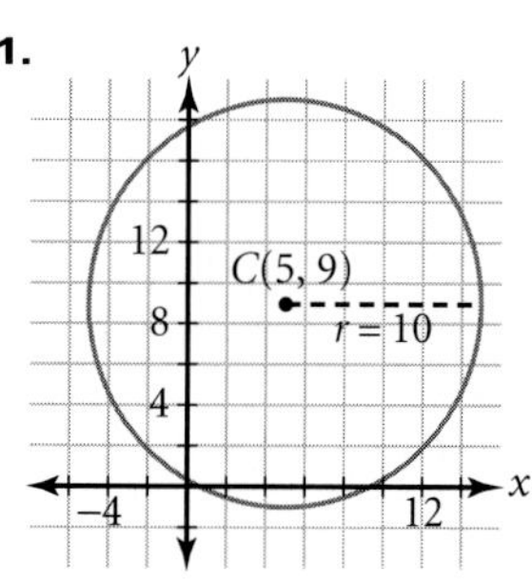

13. outside

Lesson 9.4

1. $\frac{x^2}{4} + \frac{y^2}{16} = 1$ **3.** $\frac{(x+1)^2}{4} + \frac{(y-1)^2}{9} = 1$ **5.** $x^2 + \frac{y^2}{49} = 1$; vertices: (0, −7) and (0, 7); co-vertices: (−1, 0) and (1, 0); foci: $(0, -4\sqrt{3})$ and $(0, 4\sqrt{3})$ **7.** $\frac{(x-1)^2}{9} + y^2 = 1$; center: (1, 0); vertices: (−2, 0) and (4, 0); co-vertices: (1, 1) and (1, −1); foci: $(1 - 2\sqrt{2}, 0)$ and $(1 + 2\sqrt{2}, 0)$ **9.** $\frac{(x-8)^2}{4} + \frac{(y-1)^2}{9} = 1$; center: (8, 1); vertices: (8, −2) and (8, 4); co-vertices: (6, 1) and (10, 1); foci: $(8, 1 - \sqrt{5})$ and $(8, 1 + \sqrt{5})$ **11.** $\frac{x^2}{16} + \frac{y^2}{7} = 1$

13.

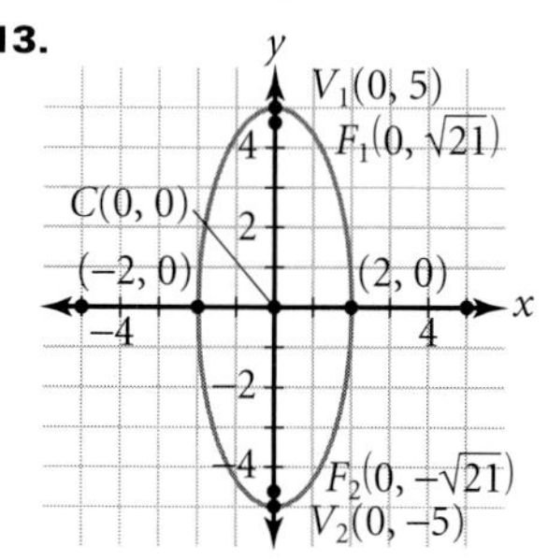

Lesson 9.5

1. $\frac{x^2}{16} - \frac{y^2}{4} = 1$ **3.** $\frac{x^2}{100} - y^2 = 1$; center: (0, 0); vertices: (−10, 0) and (10, 0); co-vertices: (0, −1) and (0, 1); foci: $(\sqrt{101}, 0)$ and $(-\sqrt{101}, 0)$

5. $\frac{(x-1)^2}{4} - \frac{(y-1)^2}{9} = 1$; center: (1, 1); vertices: (−1, 1) and (3, 1) co-vertices: (1, −2) and (1, 4); foci: $(1 + \sqrt{13}, 1)$ and $(1 - \sqrt{13}, 1)$ **7.** $\frac{y^2}{144} - \frac{x^2}{121} = 1$

9.

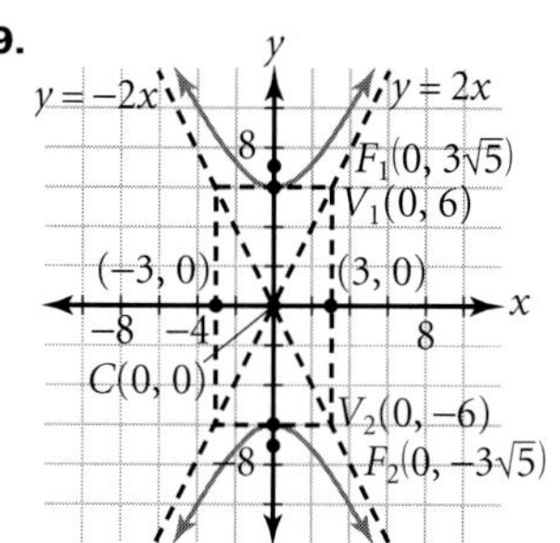

11. $\frac{(x-3)^2}{36} - \frac{(y-4)^2}{25} = 1$

Lesson 9.6

1. (−3, 10) and (2, 5) **3.** (−4, 0) and $\left(5, \frac{3}{4}\right)$ **5.** none

7. (−2, −3.46), (−2, 3.46), (2, −3.46), and (2, 3.46)

9. (−2.41, −2.39), (−2.41, 2.39), (2.41, −2.39), and (2.41, 2.39)

11. circle; $(x-3)^2 + (y-5)^2 = 36$

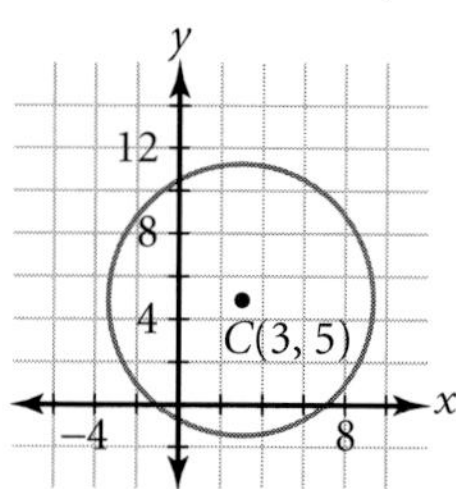

13. ellipse; $\frac{(x-4)^2}{4} + \frac{(y-4)^2}{9} = 1$

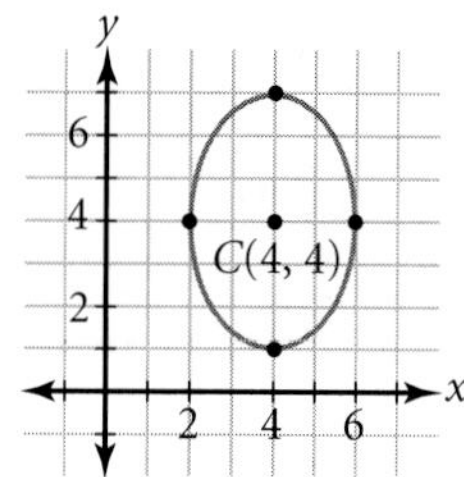

15. ellipse; $\frac{(x+2)^2}{25} + \frac{(y+1)^2}{4} = 1$

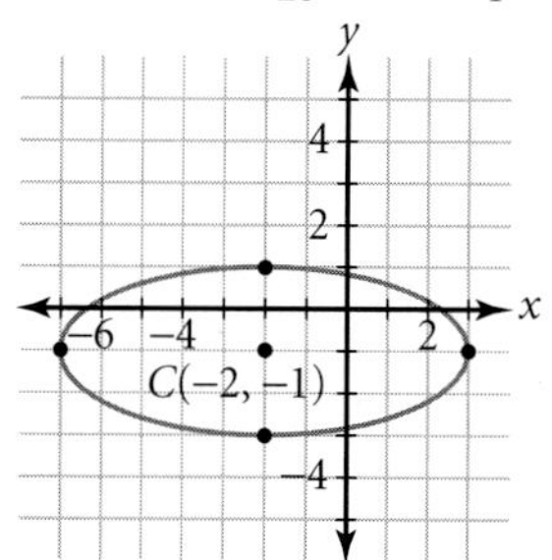

CHAPTER 10

Lesson 10.1

1. $\frac{1}{5} = 20\%$ **3.** $\frac{2}{3} \approx 67\%$ **5.** $\frac{1}{4} = 25\%$ **7.** $\frac{53}{125} = 42.4\%$

9. $\frac{8}{25} = 32\%$ **11.** 15,625 **13.** 100

Lesson 10.2

1. 720 **3.** 665,280 **5.** 120 **7.** 120 **9.** 40,320 **11.** 360

13. about 8.7×10^{10} **15.** 120

Lesson 10.3

1. 10 **3.** 56 **5.** 120 **7.** 1 **9.** about 43%

11. permutation **13.** combination

Lesson 10.4

1. mutually exclusive; $\frac{2}{13} \approx 15\%$ **3.** inclusive; $\frac{25}{26} \approx 96\%$

5. mutually exclusive; 1 = 100% **7.** $\frac{1}{2} = 50\%$

9. $\frac{2}{3} \approx 67\%$ **11.** $\frac{3}{5} = 60\%$ **13.** $\frac{4}{5} = 80\%$

Lesson 10.5

1. $\frac{1}{8} = 12.5\%$ **3.** $0.08 = 8\%$ **5.** $0.04 = 4\%$ **7.** $\frac{25}{36} \approx 69.4\%$ **9.** $1 = 100\%$ **11.** $0.1 = 10\%$ **13.** $0.25 = 25\%$ **15.** $\frac{1}{9} \approx 11.1\%$

Lesson 10.6

1. $\frac{7}{48} \approx 14.6\%$ **3.** $\frac{7}{48} \approx 14.6\%$ **5.** $\frac{1}{6} \approx 17\%$ **7.** $\frac{1}{3} \approx 33\%$ **9.** $\frac{1}{2} = 50\%$ **11.** $\frac{1}{6} \approx 17\%$ **13.** $1 = 100\%$ **15.** $\frac{1}{2} = 50\%$ **17.** $\frac{1}{3} \approx 33\%$ **19.** $1 = 100\%$ **21.** $0.4 = 40\%$

Lesson 10.7

Simulation results may vary.

1. about 38% **3.** about 7% **5.** about 33% **7.** about 50% **9.** about 54% **11.** about 22%

CHAPTER 11

Lesson 11.1

1. 5, 2, −1, −4, −7 **3.** 2, 8, 18, 32, 50 **5.** 16, 10, 4, −2, −8 **7.** $t_1 = 1, t_n = t_{n-1} + 9$; 37, 46, 55 **9.** $t_1 = 4$, $t_n = t_{n-1} + 5(n-1)$; 54, 79, 109 **11.** 0, 1, 4, 9, 16; 30 **13.** 105 **15.** 34

Lesson 11.2

1. no **3.** no **5.** yes; 1.1 **7.** $t_n = 3n + 2$ **9.** $t_n = 6n + 4$ **11.** $t_n = 4n - 16$ **13.** 5, 16, 27, 38 **15.** 0, 20, 40, 60 **17.** −12, −20, −28, −36 **19.** 11, 17, and 23 **21.** 9.6 and 12.7

Lesson 11.3

1. 45 **3.** 810 **5.** 15,400 **7.** 14,560 **9.** 1010 **11.** −4200 **13.** $590\sqrt{7} \approx 1561$ **15.** 532 **17.** 300 **19.** 2550

Lesson 11.4

1. yes; $\frac{1}{2}, \frac{3}{4}, \frac{3}{8}, \frac{3}{16}$ **3.** no **5.** no **7.** 5, 1, 0.2, 0.04 **9.** −2, 9, −40.5, 182.25, −820.125 **11.** 3.5 **13.** $t_n = 0.04 \cdot 5^{n-1}$ **15.** $t_n = 6^{\frac{n}{2}}$, or $(\sqrt{6})^n$ **17.** 9.6 and 14.4 **19.** 20, 50, and 125 or −20, 150, and −125

Lesson 11.5

1. 3069 **3.** $\frac{189}{128} \approx 1.5$ **5.** 437.4 **7.** 656 **9.** 19,664 **11.** 110,341.5 **13.** $\frac{1}{2} = 1 - \frac{1}{2}$, so the statement is true for $n = 1$. Assume that the statement is true for an integer k. Then $\frac{1}{2} + \frac{1}{2^2} + \frac{1}{2^3} + \cdots + \frac{1}{2^k} = 1 - \frac{1}{2^k}$ and $\frac{1}{2} + \frac{1}{2^2} + \frac{1}{2^3} + \cdots + \frac{1}{2^k} + \frac{1}{2^{k+1}} = 1 - \frac{1}{2^k} + \frac{1}{2^{k+1}} = 1 - \left(\frac{1}{2^k} - \frac{1}{2^{k+1}}\right) = 1 - \left(\frac{2}{2^{k+1}} - \frac{1}{2^{k+1}}\right) = 1 - \frac{1}{2^{k+1}}$ and the statement is true for $k + 1$

Lesson 11.6

1. $\frac{1}{4}$ **3.** none **5.** none **7.** $-\frac{1}{3} \approx -0.33$ **9.** $\frac{7}{9}$ **11.** $\frac{107}{333}$ **13.** $\sum_{k=1}^{\infty} 31\left(\frac{1}{100}\right)^k$ **15.** $\sum_{k=1}^{\infty} 357\left(\frac{1}{1000}\right)^k$

Lesson 11.7

1. third entry, row 4; 6 **3.** fourth entry, row 8; 56 **5.** eighth entry, row 10; 120 **7.** ninth entry, row 11; 165 **9.** 70; 8 **11.** 715; 1716 **13.** 0.25 **15.** 0.5 **17.** about 0.57 **19.** about 0.36

Lesson 11.8

1. $a^4 + 4a^3b + 6a^2b^2 + 4ab^3 + b^4$ **3.** $c^6 + 6c^5d + 15c^4d^2 + 20c^3d^3 + 15c^2d^4 + 6cd^5 + d^6$ **5.** $y^5 + 10y^4 + 40y^3 + 80y^2 + 80y + 32$ **7.** 13 terms **9.** $32x^5 + 80x^4y + 80x^3y^2 + 40x^2y^3 + 10xy^4 + y^5$ **11.** $x^4 - 8x^3y + 24x^2y^2 - 32xy^3 + 16y^4$ **13.** $\frac{1}{8}x^3 + \frac{3}{2}x^2y + 6xy^2 + 8y^3$ **15.** about 0.01 **17.** about 0.30

CHAPTER 12

Lesson 12.1

1. 28.1; 25.5; no mode **3.** 11.225; 12.55; 12.6 **5.** 30,100; 29,300; 35,700; sample answer: The mode is too high, but the mean and median are reasonable values to describe the data.

7.

Number of days	Tally	Frequency
0	~~||||~~	5
1	||||	4
2	||	2
3	||	2
4	|	1
5	|||	3
8	|	1
10	|	1
22	|	1

mean: 3.65

9.

Score	Class mean	Freq.	Product
50–59	54.5	2	109
60–69	64.5	3	193.5
70–79	74.5	7	521.5
80–89	84.5	5	422.5
90–99	94.5	3	283.5

estimated mean: 76.5

Lesson 12.2

1.

Stem	Leaf 3|0 = 30
1	2, 2, 5, 6
2	2, 5, 6
3	0, 2, 3
4	0, 3, 6, 7

28; 12; flat-shaped

3.

Number	Frequency
1	2
2	5
3	4
4	2
5	6
6	4
7	5

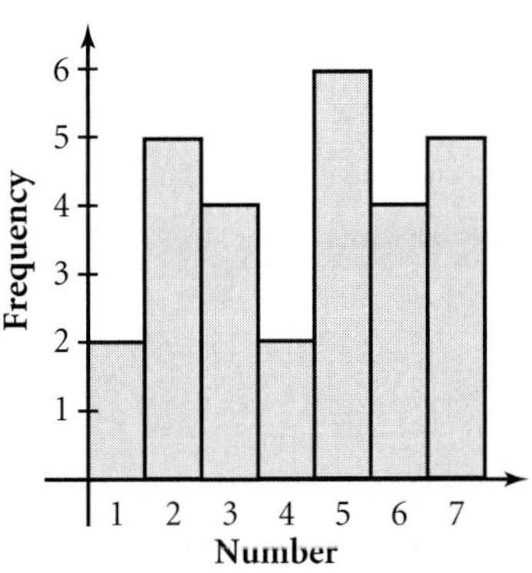

5.

Number	Frequency	Rel. Freq.
20	2	10%
21	4	20%
22	5	25%
23	3	15%
24	2	10%
25	4	20%

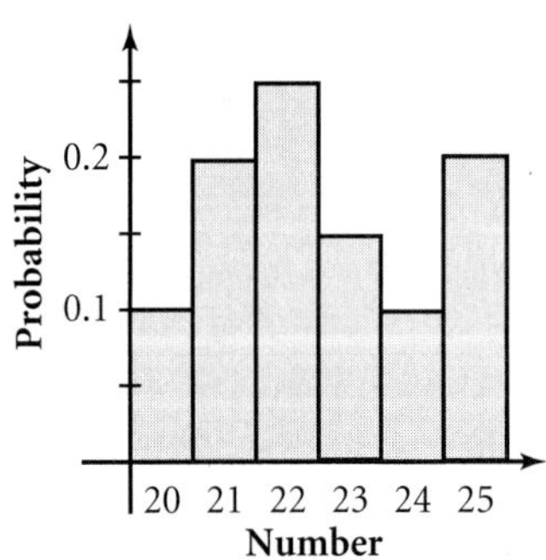

7a.

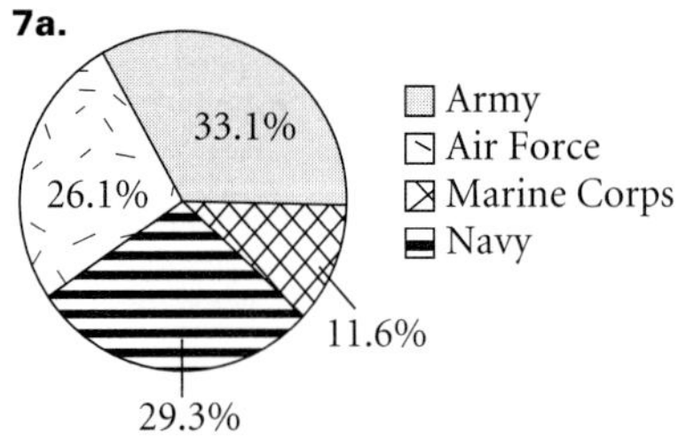

b. 0.41

Lesson 12.3

1. min = 7; $Q_1 = 13$; $Q_2 = 18$; $Q_3 = 27$; max = 35; range = 28; IQR = 14

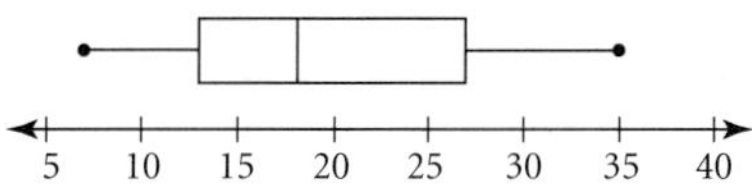

3. min = 168; $Q_1 = 210$; $Q_2 = 281$; $Q_3 = 312$; max = 715; range = 547; IQR = 102

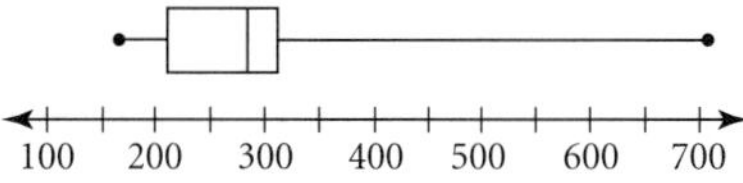

5. min = 3.2; $Q_1 = 5.7$; $Q_2 = 6.6$; $Q_3 = 7.7$; max = 12.3; range = 9.1; IQR = 2

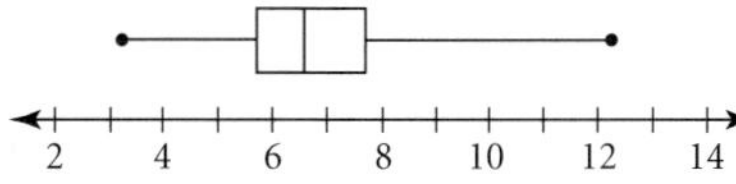

7. They are about the same.

Lesson 12.4

1. 6; 1.5 **3.** 11; 2.7 **5.** 37; 13.9 **7.** 71.04; about 8.4 **9.** 738.3; about 27.2 **11.** 9.7; about 3.1 **13.** 305; about 94.5

Lesson 12.5

1. 31.25% **3.** 18.75% **5.** 18.75% **7.** about 3.2% **9.** about 3.5% **11.** about 18.5% **13.** about 19.8% **15.** about 22.8%

Lesson 12.6

1. 0.6554 **3.** 0.0449 **5.** 0.4986 **7.** ≈0.02 **9.** ≈0.68 **11.** about 160 **13.** about 820

CHAPTER 13

Lesson 13.1

1. $\frac{20}{29}$; 0.6897 **3.** $\frac{21}{29}$; 0.7241 **5.** $\frac{20}{21}$; 0.9524 **7.** $\frac{29}{20}$; 1.45 **9.** $\frac{29}{21}$; 1.3810 **11.** $\frac{21}{20}$; 1.05 **13.** $m\angle G = 53°$; $GI \approx 2.6$; $GH \approx 4.4$ **15.** $JK \approx 14.4$; $m\angle J \approx 56°$; $m\angle K \approx 34°$ **17.** $m\angle M = 64°$; $MN \approx 22.1$; $NO \approx 19.9$

Lesson 13.2

1. −246° **3.** 307° **5.** 152°, −208° **7.** 63° **9.** 56° **11.** 65°

13–17. Answers are given in order as follows: sin, cos, tan, csc, sec, cot.

13. $\frac{2\sqrt{5}}{5}$; $\frac{\sqrt{5}}{5}$; 2; $\frac{\sqrt{5}}{2}$; $\sqrt{5}$; $\frac{1}{2}$

15. $-\frac{8\sqrt{73}}{73}$; $\frac{3\sqrt{73}}{73}$; $-\frac{8}{3}$; $-\frac{\sqrt{73}}{8}$; $\frac{\sqrt{73}}{3}$; $-\frac{3}{8}$

17. $-\frac{3}{5}$; $-\frac{4}{5}$; $\frac{3}{4}$; $-\frac{5}{3}$; $-\frac{5}{4}$; $\frac{4}{3}$ **19.** $\frac{1}{2}$ **21.** $-\frac{3\sqrt{7}}{7}$

Lesson 13.3

1. $(5, -5\sqrt{3})$ **3.** $(50\sqrt{2}, 50\sqrt{2})$ **5.** $(-10\sqrt{2}, 10\sqrt{2})$

7. (0.64, 0.77) **9.** (0.97, –0.26) **11.** $\frac{\sqrt{2}}{2}$; $\frac{\sqrt{2}}{2}$; 1
13. $-\frac{\sqrt{3}}{2}$; $\frac{1}{2}$; $-\sqrt{3}$ **15.** $-\frac{1}{2}$; $\frac{\sqrt{3}}{2}$; $-\frac{\sqrt{3}}{3}$ **17.** $-\frac{1}{2}$; $-\frac{\sqrt{3}}{2}$; $\frac{\sqrt{3}}{3}$
19. $-\frac{\sqrt{3}}{3}$ **21.** $-\frac{1}{2}$ **23.** $-\frac{1}{2}$ **25.** $\frac{1}{2}$ **27.** –1 **29.** $\frac{1}{2}$ **31.** 2
33. $\frac{1}{2}$ **35.** $-\sqrt{3}$

Lesson 13.4

1. $\frac{\pi}{6}$ radians **3.** $\frac{\pi}{9}$ radians **5.** 6π radians **7.** 120°
9. 540° **11.** 185.9° **13.** $\frac{\sqrt{2}}{2}$ **15.** 0 **17.** $\frac{1}{2}$ **19.** 1
21. ≈10.5 m **23.** 10 m

Lesson 13.5

1. 3.5; 90° **3.** 6; 360° **5.** $\frac{2}{3}$; 120° **7.** 45° left; 1 unit up
9. 90° right; no vertical translation **11.** 45° right; 3 units up
13. vertical stretch by factor of 5

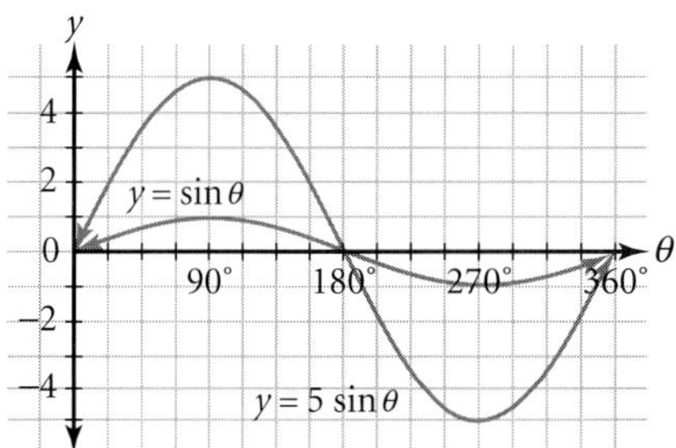

15. horizontal compression by a factor of $\frac{1}{2}$

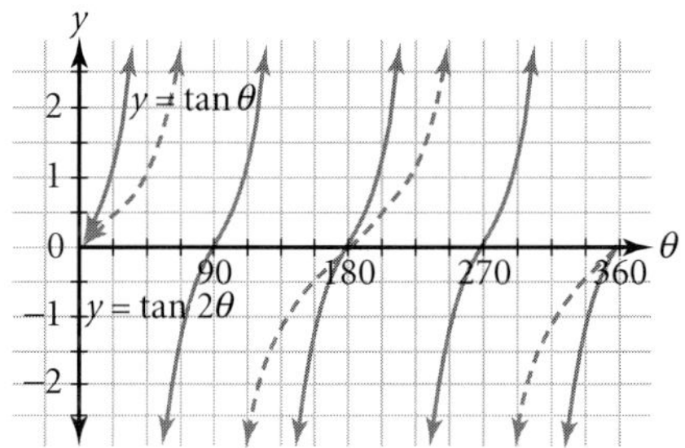

Lesson 13.6

1. 60° + n360° and 120° + n360°
3. 135° + n360° and 225° + n360°
5. 135° + n360° and 315° + n360° **7.** 90° **9.** 30°
11. –45° **13.** $\sqrt{3}$ **15.** $\frac{\sqrt{2}}{2}$ **17.** 0° **19.** 38°

CHAPTER 14

Note: Throughout Chapter 14, answers may vary slightly due to rounding, method of calculation, or order in which solutions were found.

Lesson 14.1

1. 144.5 sq. in. **3.** 94.0 cm² **5.** 8.7 **7.** 7.6
9. $B = 95°$, $a = 8.2$, $c = 3.1$ **11.** $B = 55°$, $a = 4.4$, $c = 11.8$
13. $B = 86°$, $b = 15.6$, $c = 10.9$ **15.** 0 **17.** 7875.8 sq ft

Lesson 14.2

1. SAS, $a = 93.4$ **3.** SAS, $b = 12.3$ **5.** SAS, $a = 100.6$
7. $A = 59.5°$, $B = 83.9°$, $C = 36.6°$
9. $A = 38.6°$, $B = 48.5°$, $C = 92.9°$
11. $A \approx 24.1°$, $B = 30.8°$, $C \approx 125.1°$
13. SSS, $A = 48.5°$, $B = 55.8°$, $C = 75.7°$
15. SSA, $A = 51.2°$, $C = 56.8°$, $c \approx 8.8$
17. SSA, not possible **19.** 24.6°, 24.6°, and 130.8°

Lesson 14.3

1. $(\sec\theta)(\sin\theta) = \frac{r}{x} \cdot \frac{y}{r} = \frac{y}{x} = \tan\theta$
3. $\tan\theta = \frac{y}{x} = \frac{1}{\frac{x}{y}} = \frac{1}{\cot\theta}$
5. $\sin^2\theta$ **7.** 1 **9.** $\cot^2\theta$ **11.** $\dfrac{\frac{1}{\cos\theta} - \cos\theta}{\frac{\sin\theta}{\cos\theta}} = (\sin\theta)$
13. $\frac{\cos\theta}{\sin\theta}(1 - \sin\theta) + \cos\theta = \frac{\cos\theta}{\sin\theta} = \cot\theta$
15. $\dfrac{\sin\theta + \frac{\sin\theta}{\cos\theta}}{1 + \frac{1}{\cos\theta}} = \sin\theta$

Lesson 14.4

1. $\frac{\sqrt{6}}{4} - \frac{\sqrt{2}}{4}$ **3.** $-\frac{\sqrt{2}}{4} - \frac{\sqrt{6}}{4}$ **5.** $-\frac{1}{2}$ **7.** $-\frac{1}{2}$ **9.** $-\frac{\sqrt{6}}{4} - \frac{\sqrt{2}}{4}$
11. $\frac{\sqrt{6}}{4} + \frac{\sqrt{2}}{4}$ **13.** $\begin{bmatrix} 0.87 & -0.5 \\ 0.5 & 0.87 \end{bmatrix}$ **15.** $\begin{bmatrix} 0.17 & -0.98 \\ 0.98 & 0.17 \end{bmatrix}$

Lesson 14.5

1. $8\cos^4\theta - 8\cos^2\theta + 1$ *or* $1 - 8\sin^2\theta\cos^2\theta$
3. $\cos^2\theta$ **5.** $\cos\theta$ **7.** $\frac{24}{25}, \frac{7}{25}$ **9.** $\frac{1}{\sqrt{5}}$ *or* $\frac{\sqrt{5}}{5}$, $\frac{2}{\sqrt{5}}$ *or* $\frac{2\sqrt{5}}{5}$

Lesson 14.6

1. 225° + n360° and 315° + n360°
3. 60° + n360° and 120° + n360° **5.** 0°, 60°, 180°, and 300° **7.** 120° and 240° **9.** 0°, 45°,135°, 180°, 225°, and 315° **11.** 90.0°, 199.5°, 340.5°

Index

INDEX

Definitions of bold face entries can be found in the glossary.

Index

T

Credits

PHOTOS

Abbreviated as follows: (t), top, (b), bottom, (l), left, (r), right, (c), center, (bckgd) background.

COVER: Tom Paiva/FPG International. TABLE OF CONTENTS: Page vi (tl), Peter Van Steen/HRW Photo, location courtesy Strait Music Co.; vi (bl), Mark M. Lawrence/The Stock Market; vii (tl), (cl), Sam Dudgeon/HRW Photo; vii (bl), John Langford/HRW Photo; vii (br), Warren Faidley/International Stock Photo; viii (bl), Blair Seitz/Photo Researchers; viii (tl), L.D. Gordon/The Image Bank; ix (br), UPI/Corbis-Bettmann; ix (cl), Sam Dudgeon/HRW Photo; x (b), VCG/FPG International; x (cl), G.A. Plimpton Collection, Rare Book & Manuscript Library, Columbia University; xi (br), Patrick Cocklin/Tony Stone Images; xi (l), Telegraph Colour Library/Masterfile; xii (b), Bill Losh/FPG International; xii (tl), Miwako Ikeda/International Stock Photo; xiii (b), Andrew Freeman/ SportsChrome-USA; xiii (cl), NASA; xiv (bl), Image Copyright © 2001 PhotoDisc, Inc.; xiv (cl), Mark C. Burnett/Science Source/Photo Researchers; xv (br), eStudios/HRW Photo; xv (cl), Superstock; xvi (bl), David Seelig/Allsport; xvii (br), Image Copyright © 2001 PhotoDisc, Inc.; xvii (cl), Ralph H. Wetmore/Tony Stone Images; xviii (b), Stephen Durke/Washington-Artists' Represents; xviii (cl), Mark E. Gibson; xix (l), Superstock. **CHAPTER ONE:** Page 2 (bc), Superstock; 2 (bl), George Lepp/ Tony Stone Images; 2–3 (bckgd), George Lepp/Tony Stone Images; 2–3 (t), Image Copyright © 2001 PhotoDisc, Inc.; 4 (t), Peter Van Steen/HRW Photo, location courtesy Strait Music Co.; 5 (tl), Ron Chapple/FPG International; 8 (tl), David De Lossy/The Image Bank; 10 (br), 1994 Burke/Triolo Productions/FoodPix; 10 (tl), Uniphoto; 12 (t), John Langford/HRW Photo; 19 (b), Jan Becker; 19 (cl), Ron Tanaka; 20 (tl), Renee Lynn/Photo Researchers; 21 (t), Luis Castaneda/The Image Bank; 25 (br), Michelle Bridwell/HRW Photo; 27 (b), Pascal Rondeau/Tony Stone Images; 29 (t), Uniphoto; 32 (cl), NASA/Science Photo Library/ Photo Researchers; 35 (tl), (tr), Courtesy of the Oriental Institute of the University of Chicago; 36 (tl), Mark M. Lawrence/The Stock Market; 37 (tr), Navaswan/FPG International; 41 (bl), (cl), Photo Courtesy Indianapolis Motor Speedway; 41 (tl), Ron McQueeney/Photo Courtesy Indianapolis Motor Speedway; 43 (tl), UPI/Corbis-Bettmann; 44 (tl), Uniphoto; 45 (tr), Ron Tanaka; 46 (cl), Randal Alhadeff/HRW Photo; 48 (tl), D. Young-Wolff/ PhotoEdit; 50 (b), Aaron Haupt/Photo Researchers; 51 (tr), Roy Morsch/The Stock Market; 52 (cl), 53 (tc), (tr), Maryland Historical Society, Baltimore; 54 (tc), Myrleen Ferguson/PhotoEdit; 56 (tr), Maratea/International Stock Photo; 59 (bl), Margerin Studios Inc./FPG International; 59 (br), Lou Manna/International Stock Photo; 59 (cr), Uniphoto; 61 (c), VCG/FPG International; 67 (br), Mark Gamba/The Stock Market; 68 (br), Uniphoto; 69 (tr), Christian Grzimek/OKAPIA/Photo Researchers; 70 (bl), Image Copyright © 2001 PhotoDisc, Inc.; 70–71 Rob Waymen Photography; 70–71 (c), Ron Tanaka. **CHAPTER TWO:** Page 84 (bl), Paolo Curto/The Image Bank; 84 (c), Janice Travia/Tony Stone Images; 85 (cr), Image Copyright © 2001 PhotoDisc, Inc.; 85 (t), Michael J. Howell/International Stock Photo; 86 (tc), Michael Newman/ PhotoEdit; 86 (tr), John Langford/HRW Photo; 88 (cr), Randal Alhadeff/HRW Photo; 90 (cl), David R. Frazier/Photo Researchers; 91 (br), The Granger Collection; 92 (cr), Lori Adamski Peek/Tony Stone Images; 93 (c), Corbis, photo manipulation by Morgan-Cain & Associates; 94 (tr), 97 (br), Michael Newman/PhotoEdit; 98 (cr), Sam Dudgeon/HRW Photo, prop courtesy Custom Model Products; 100 (tr), Uniphoto; 101 (br), NASA; 102 (t), Uniphoto; 106 (br), Spencer Grant/PhotoEdit; 107 (tl), Randal Alhadeff/HRW Photo; 108 (tr), Rob Waymen Photography; 109 (br), Randal Alhadeff/HRW Photo; 111 (t), Sanford/Agliolo/ International Stock Photo; 114 (tr), Peter Van Steen/HRW Photo, location courtesy Dyer Electronics; 116 (br), Sam Dudgeon/HRW Photo; 116 (tr), Don Smetzer/Tony Stone Images; 124 (truck driver), Dana White/PhotoEdit; 124 (truck), Larry Grant/FPG International; 126 (cl), Sam Dudgeon/HRW Photo; 129 (tr), Robert Brenner/PhotoEdit; 131 (br), Steve Lacey/ Uniphoto, photo manipulation by Morgan-Cain & Associates; 131 (tr), Randal Alhadeff/ HRW Photo; 133 (t), Jeff Kaufman/FPG International; 141 (tl), Alan D. Carey/Vireo; 142 (br), 143 (tr), Corbis; 146 (br), Eric Bouvet/ The Image Bank.
CHAPTER THREE: Page 154 (b), Don Couch/HRW Photo; 155 (cl), Lucien Clergue/Tony Stone Images; 155 (cr), Bob Daemmrich Photo; 155 (tl), Uniphoto; 155 (tr), David Waldorf/FPG International; 156 (t), Blair Seitz/Photo Researchers; 161 (tl), Judy Unger/FoodPix; 162 (br), Allsport USA/Tony Duffy; 163 (tr), L.D. Gordon/ The Image Bank; 164 (inset), (t), Peter Van Steen/HRW Photo, location courtesy Make-A-Frame; 165 (cl), Randal Alhadeff/HRW Photo; 170 (br), Uniphoto; 170 (tr), Noboru Komine/Photo Researchers; 171 (bl), Peter Van Steen/HRW Photo; 172 (bckgd), Map © by Rand McNally, R.L. #99-S-64; 172 (bl), Photos provided courtesy of Daimler Chrysler; 172 (br), Courtesy Ford Motor Company; 172 (tr), ©1996 GM Corp. Used with permission GM Media Archives; 177 (bl), Peter Van Steen/HRW Photo; 178 (tl), Steve Payne/Uniphoto; 179 (tr), Image Copyright © 2001 PhotoDisc, Inc.; 184 (bc), (bl), Peter Van Steen/HRW Photo; 184 (cr), Ron Tanaka; 185 (l), Ladew Topiary Gardens, Monkton MD, Photography by Runk/Schoenberger from Grant Heilman Photography; 185 (r), Ron Tanaka; 186 (c), Peter Van Steen/HRW Photo; 187(tr), G. Ryan & S. Beyer/Tony Stone Images; 191 (cl), Mark E. Gibson; 192 (br), Randal Alhadeff/HRW Photo; 193 (bl), Image Copyright © 2001 PhotoDisc, Inc.; 195 (tr), George Hall/Check Six; 199 (bl), Tomasso Derosa/Allsport USA; 200 (bl), Rob Waymen Photography; 201 (tl), Lisa Valder/Tony Stone Images; 202 (bl), Runk/ Schoenberger from Grant Heilman; 202 (cl), Peter Beck/The Stock Market; 203 (tiles left to right): (1), Pascal Perret/The Image Bank; (2), Siqui Sanchez/The Image Bank; (3), & (4), John Foxx Images; 203 (bl), Michael Rosenfeld/Tony Stone Images; 203 (tl), Stephen Simpson/FPG International; 206 (bc), (br), Mark E. Gibson.
CHAPTER FOUR: Page 214 (bl), Scott Barrow/International Stock Photo; 214 (cr), Elliot Smith/International Stock Photo; 214–215 (t), Chip Henderson/Tony Stone Images; 216 (t), Uniphoto; 218 (cr), Peter Van Steen/HRW Photo; 218 (tr), Randal Alhadeff/HRW Photo, props courtesy of Home Quarters; 222 (bl), 223 (tr), Ron Tanaka; 223 (tr), Jan Becker; 225 (tr), Jerry Wachter/Photo Researchers; 227 (cl), Ron Tanaka; 228 (cl), Sam Dudgeon/HRW Photo; 229 (cl), Michael Newman/PhotoEdit; 231 (br), Jan Becker; 234 (tr), UPI/Corbis-Bettmann; 237 (c), Courtesy of NSA; 238 (br), Sam Dudgeon/HRW Photo; 242 (br), Randal Alhadeff/HRW Photo; 242 (c), Steve Grohe/ Thinking Machines Corporation 1991; 242 (tr), Image Copyright © 2001 PhotoDisc, Inc.; 243 (cl), Courtesy of NSA; 244 (tr), Bruce Ayres/Tony Stone Images; 245 (cr), Nick Dolding/Tony Stone Images; 251 (tr), 253 (tl), Michelle Bridwell/HRW Photo; 256 (bl), 258 (b), (br), (c), (t), Ron Tanaka; 259 (tr), Wayne Aldridge/International Stock Photo; 261 (br), John Langford/HRW Photo. **CHAPTER FIVE:** Page 272 (b), Superstock; 272 (c), Jim Cummins/FPG International; 272 (cl), Globus Brothers/The Stock Market; 272–273 (t), Image Copyright © 2001 PhotoDisc, Inc.; 274 (t), Clint Clemons/ International Stock Photo; 279 (cr), Jan Becker; 281 (tr), Chuck Mason/ International Stock Photo; 284 (tl), The Bettmann Archive; 284 (tr), G.A. Plimpton Collection, Rare Book & Manuscript Library, Columbia University; 288 (cl), Rob Waymen Photography; 297 (br), Yellow Dog Productions/The Image Bank; 298 (br), Frank Cezus/FPG International; 299 (t), 303 (tr), Mark E. Gibson; 304 (cl), John Michael/ International Stock Photo; 305 (c), David K. Crow/PhotoEdit; 307 (t), Peter Van Steen/ HRW Photo; 312 (tr), Matt Lambert/Tony Stone Images; 313 (br), Frank Cezus/FPG International; 314 (tc), Photos courtesy of Daimler Chrysler; 315 (bl), Science Photo Library/Photo Researchers; 315 (br), Dr. Jeremy Burgess/Science Photo Library/Photo Researchers; 321 (bl), Andy Christiansen/HRW Photo; 322 (t), 325 (tr), Bill Losh/FPG International; 327 (tl), Vincent Graziani/ International Stock Photo; 328 (cl), VCG/FPG International; 330 (t), Robert Waymen Photography; 335 (br), VCG/FPG International; 336 (bl), Randal Alhadeff/HRW Photo; 337 (tr), Peter Van Steen/HRW Photo, location courtesy Austin Shoe Hospital; 338 (basketball), Frank Cezus/FPG International; 338 (cl), 338–339 (b), Image Copyright © 2001 PhotoDisc, Inc.; 339 (br), Corbis; 339 (tl), Image Copyright © 2001 PhotoDisc, Inc.
CHAPTER SIX: Page 352 (bl), Jerry Jacka; 352 (cl), Patrick Aventurier/Gamma Liaison; 352 (cr), Richard Price/FPG International; 353 (cr), Arizona State Museum/University of Arizona; 353 (t), Mark Newman/International Stock Photo; 354 (cl), Lloyd Sutton/Masterfile; 354 (cr), David Scharf/Peter Arnold Inc.; 355 (cl), Randal Alhadeff/HRW Photo; 356 (tr), Paolo Negri/ Tony Stone Images; 357 (cr), Michelle Bridwell/HRW Photo; 359 (br), Superstock; 360 (br), Telegraph Colour Library/Masterfile; 361 (cr), David Starrett; 362 (t), Richard Ustinich/The Image Bank; 365 (cr), Vincent Graziani/International Stock Photo; 366 (tr), FPG International; 369 (br), David Starrett; 370 (t), Greg Pease/Tony Stone Images; 373 (br), David Starrett; 376 (tl), Stewart Cohen/Tony Stone Images; 376 (tr), Jeff Greenberg/Photo Researchers, Inc.; 377 (cl), (cr), The Granger Collection; 377 (tr), UPI/Corbis-Bettmann; 383 (tr), Doug Martin/Photo Researchers; 384 (cr), David Starrett; 385 (tl), Chris Baker/Tony Stone Images; 385 (tr), David Starrett; 386 (c), (cl), The Bettmann Archive; 389 (cl), David Starrett; 389 (cr), Paul Shambroom/Science Source/Photo Researchers; 390 (c), Patrick Cocklin/Tony Stone Images; 392 (t), Louis Psihoyos/Matrix; 396 (tl), The Granger Collection; 399 (cl), FPG International; 399 (cr), Ed Lallo/Tony Stone Images; 400 (bl), Jefferson National Expansion Memorial/National Park Service; 401 (tr), Alan Nyiri/FPG International; 402 (tl), Allan Seiden/The Image Bank; 402 (tr), Ulf E. Wallin/ The Image Bank; 403 (tr), Dan McCoy/First Light; 409 (br), 410–411 (all), David Starrett; 414 (br), Corbis. **CHAPTER SEVEN:** Page 422 (bl), Thomas Friedmann/ Photo Researchers; 422 (cr), Rohan/Tony Stone Images; 423 (br), Don Couch/HRW Photo; 423 (t), 424 (t), Uniphoto; 430 (bl), Mark Joseph/Tony Stone Images; 431 (br), (cl), (cr), Randal Alhadeff/HRW Photo; 432 (t), Bill Losh/FPG International; 437 (tl), Image Copyright © 2001 PhotoDisc, Inc.; 439 (tl), Camille Tokerud/Photo Researchers; 440 (t), Peter Van Steen/HRW Photo; 447 (cl), Randal Alhadeff/HRW Photo; 454 (bl), Sam Dudgeon/HRW Photo; 454 (c), Ron Tanaka; 454 (tr), The Bettmann Archive; 455 (cr), Randal Alhadeff/HRW Photo; 456 (bl), (c), Cedar Point Photos by Dan Feicht; 456 (popcorn), Richard Hutchings/PhotoEdit; 457 (r), Doug Armand/Tony Stone Images; 458 (tr), John Langford/HRW Photo; 462 (cr), Artbase Inc.; 462 (tr), The Bettmann Archive; 464 (bl), Larry Ulrich/Tony Stone Images; 465 (tr), Miwako Ikeda/ International Stock Photo; 466 (cl), 466–467 (b), Randal Alhadeff/HRW Photo. **CHAPTER EIGHT:** Page 478 (bl), Ellen Martorelli/Tony Stone Images; 478 (br), Uniphoto; 479 (t), D. Young-Wolff/PhotoEdit; 479 (t), Photo by Stuart Bowey/Adlibitum from *Discoveries: Great Inventions* © Weldon Owen Pty Ltd; 480 (t), Jerry Wachter/Photo Researchers; 484 (cr), Bob Thomason/Tony Stone Images; 487 (bl), Stan Osolinski/FPG International; 487 (br), Dan Sudia/Photo Researchers; 487 (cl), Mark Joseph/Tony Stone Images; 489 (t), Uniphoto; 495 (cr), Astrid & Hanns-Frieder Michler/Science Photo Library/Photo Researchers; 496 (br), Ken Cavanagh/ Photo Researchers; 498 (tc), Christine Galida/HRW Photo; 498 (tr), 501 (tr), 503 (bl), Randal Alhadeff/HRW Photo; 505 (t), Ed Pritchard/Tony Stone Images; 508 (cl), Leonard Lessio/Peter Arnold Inc.; 510 (cr), Scott Barrow/International Stock Photo; 512 (t), Andrew Freeman/SportsChrome-USA; 518 (br), VGC/FPG International; 519 (br), Brian Bailey/Tony Stone Images; 520 (t), Phil Degginger/Tony Stone Images; 525 (cr), Randal Alhadeff/HRW Photo; 526 (br), Mark Wagner/Tony Stone Images; 527 (c), Tom & Pat Leeson/Photo Researchers; 528 (t), 530 (br), Peter Van Steen/HRW Photo; 535 (tr), Tony Freeman/PhotoEdit; 536 (t), 541 (bl), John Neubauer/PhotoEdit; 543 (tr), Audrey Gibson; 544–545 (from left to right), (1), Chuck Szymanski/ International Stock Photo; (2), E.J. West/Index Stock; (3), Wayne Aldridge/International Stock Photo; (4), Michael Lichter/International Stock Photo; (5), S.I. Swartz/Index Stock; (6), Lester Lefkowitz/The Stock Market; (7), S.I. DeYoung/Index Stock; 550 (br), NASA. **CHAPTER NINE:** Page 560 (bl), David Nunuk/Science Photo Library/Photo Researchers; 560–561 (t), NASA; 560–561 (all), photo manipulation by Uhl Studio Incorporated; 561 (br), David Ducros/Science Photo Library/Photo Researchers; 565 (tl), SIU/Peter Arnold, Inc.; 567 (tr), Bill Stormont/The Stock Market; 570 (t), 573 (tl), Bob Daemmrich Photos; 578 (cr), Don Couch/HRW Photo; 579 (t), Bob Firth/International Stock Photo; 581 (bl), Lonnie Duka/Tony Stone Images; 582 (br), Mark C. Burnett/Science Source/Photo Researchers; 585 (cr), Jeff Zaruba/Tony Stone Images; 586 (cr), John Langford/HRW Photo; 586 (t), David A. Hardy/Science Photo; 588 (bl), United States Geological Survey, Flagstaff, Arizona; NASA; 591 (cr), Antonio Rosario/The Image Bank; 593 (cr), NASA/Science Source/Photo Researchers; 594 (cr), Don Couch/HRW Photo; 595 (t), Bryn Campbell/Tony Stone Images; 600 (bl), Sam Dudgeon/HRW Photo; 602 (br), Cliff Hollenbeck/International Stock Photo; 603 (cr), Don Couch/HRW Photo; 604 (br), Brett Froomer/The Image Bank; 605 (tr), Sam Dudgeon/HRW Photo; 606 (t), Alan Oddie/PhotoEdit; 608 (cr), Ron Tanaka, photo manipulation by Jun Park; 614 (t), Image Copyright © 2001 PhotoDisc, Inc.; 615 (br), Image Copyright © 2001 PhotoDisc, Inc.; 618 (br), Art Wolfe/Tony Stone Images. **CHAPTER TEN:** Page 626 (bl), Alison Wright/Photo Researchers; 626 (cr), Ken Hawkins/Uniphoto; 627 (cr), Sam Dudgeon/HRW Photo; 627 (tr), Roslan Rahman/AFP Photo; 628 (t), 629 (br), 630 (cr), 630 (tr), eStudios/HRW Photo; 631 (bl), Matt Bowman/Foodpix; 632 (cl), Roy Morsch/The Stock Market; 633 (tl), eStudios/HRW Photo; 636 (t), Arnold Schönberg Center; 637 (br), Randal Alhadeff/HRW Photo; 638 (br), Steve Satushek/The Image Bank; 639 (br), Ron Tanaka; 640 (cr), Sam Dudgeon/HRW Photo; 641 (br), Superstock; 644 (br), Christel Rosenfeld/Tony Stone Images; 648 (b), Rudi Von Briel/PhotoEdit; 650 (tr), 651 (b), ABC Productions; 651 (c), Image Copyright © 2001 PhotoDisc, Inc.; 652 (t), Peter Van Steen/HRW Photo; 654 (cr), Marty Granger/Edge Video Productions/ HRW; 658 (tr), David Young-Wolff/ PhotoEdit; 659 (t), VCG/FPG International; 660 (br), Digital Stock Corp.;

663 (tr), Llewellyn/Uniphoto; 664 (t), Bob Daemmrich Photo; 667 (tr), Don Couch/HRW Photo; 669 (br), Chip Simons/FPG International; 671 (tl), (tr), Superstock; 672 (cr), Alan Schein/The Stock Market; 673 (tc), Peter Gridley/FPG International; 678 (bl), (tr), Image Copyright © 2001 PhotoDisc, Inc.; 679 (br), Stockman/International Stock Photo. **CHAPTER ELEVEN:** Page 688 (br), Image Copyright © 2001 PhotoDisc, Inc.; 688 (cr), Arizona State Museum/University of Arizona; 689 (t), James Randklev/Tony Stone Images; 690 (t), Mehau Kulyk/Science Photo Library/Photo Researchers; 693 (c), Runk/Schoenberger from Grant Heilman; 697 (br), Dr. Tony Brain/Science Photo Library/Photo Researchers; 698 (t), Randal Alhadeff/HRW Photo; 699 (t), Courtesy of Rainbird; 703 (tr), Mark Bolster/International Stock Photo; 705 (cr), Stephen Simpson/FPG International; 706 (br), John Langford/HRW Photo; 707 (t), 712 (tr), Don Couch/HRW Photo; 713 (t), John Langford/HRW Photo; 718 (br), Walter Bibikow/FPG International; 720 (t), John Langford/HRW Photo; 726 (cl), Globus, Holway & Lobel/The Stock Market; 727 (tr), Bob Daemmrich/Uniphoto; 728 (t), *Fractals Everywhere* ©1988 Academic Press; 735 (bl) frame, Image Copyright © 2001 PhotoDisc, Inc.; 735 (t), Stanley Meltzoff; 740 (cr), reprinted with permission of Cambridge University Press, 1959; 741 (t), David Seelig/Allsport; 743 (tl), Courtesy of The Topps Company, Inc.; 746 (bc), (br), Image Copyright © 2001 PhotoDisc, Inc.; 747 (tr), Stephen Simpson/FPG International; 748 (tr), Christine Galida/HRW Photo; 749 (bl), Sam Dudgeon/HRW Photo.
CHAPTER TWELVE: Page 762 (bl), David Young-Wolff/Tony Stone Images; 762 (c), Mark Scott/FPG International; 762 (tr), Novastock/PhotoEdit; 763 (tl), Janeart/The Image Bank; 764 (t), John Langford/HRW Photo; 765 (br), Robert E. Daemmrich/Tony Stone Images; 766 (bl), E.R. Degginger/Science Source/Photo Researchers; 768 (cl), Billy Hustace/Tony Stone Images; 769 (cl), David De Lossy/The Image Bank; 770 (bl), Sam Dudgeon/HRW Photo; 772 (tr), Loren Santow/Tony Stone Images; 773 (frame), Image Copyright © 2001 PhotoDisc, Inc.; 773 (tr), Rob Lewine/The Stock Market; 774 (tr), Andre Jenny/International Stock Photo; 776 (br), Charles D. Winters/Science Source/Photo Researchers; 778 (tl), Uniphoto; 779 (bl), Robert Ginn/PhotoEdit; 781 (tl), Jeff Hunter/The Image Bank; 781 (tr), John Livzey/Tony Stone Images; 784 (bl), National Baseball Hall of Fame Library & Archive; 784 (br), Milo Stewart Jr./Baseball Hall of Fame Library; 786 (bl), Grandadam/Tony Stone Images; 787 (tl), Michael Newman/PhotoEdit; 788 (tl), UPI/Corbis-Bettmann; 790 (bl), VCG/FPG International; 790 (br), Image Copyright © 2001 PhotoDisc, Inc.; 791 (br), Ron Tanaka, photo manipulation by Jun Park; 792 (tl), John Terence Turner/ FPG International; 792 (tr), David Pollack/The Stock Market; 793 (tr), Superstock; 795 (cl), Peter Pearson/Tony Stone Images; 797 (bl), William Sallaz/The Image Bank; 798 (b), Scott Barrow/International Stock Photo; 799 (t), Yoav Levy/Phototake NYC; 801 (cr), Gabe Palmer/The Stock Market; 801 (tr), Helmut Gritscher/Peter Arnold, Inc.; 803 (cr), Renee Lynn/Science Source/Photo Researchers; 804 (bc), Randal Alhadeff/HRW Photo; 804 (bl), Corbis; 805 (tr), Matt Bradley/Uniphoto; 806 (t), Ralph H. Wetmore/Tony Stone Images; 809 (tr), Robert Essel/The Stock Market; 810 (tr), David Frazier/Tony Stone Images; 811 (cl), Gerhard Gscheidle/Peter Arnold, Inc.; 812 (bl), Sigrid Owen/International Stock Photo; 812 (cr), Tony Freeman/PhotoEdit; 814 (bl), Scott Barrow/International Stock Photo; 814 (tc), Image Copyright © 2001 PhotoDisc, Inc.; 814 (tl), Michael Young/HRW Photo; 815 (br), (tr), Image Copyright © 2001 PhotoDisc, Inc. **CHAPTER THIRTEEN:** Page 826 (bl), F. Hidalgo/The Image Bank; 827 (bl), Superstock; 827 (C), Image Copyright © 2001 PhotoDisc, Inc.; 827 (tr), Stephen Studd/Tony Stone Images; 828 (t), S.J. Krasemann/Peter Arnold, Inc.; 833 (cl), Mark E. Gibson; 834 (br), Grant Heilman Photography; 836 (t), Joe McBride/Tony Stone Images; 841 (tl), Neville Dawson/Check Six; 843 (tc), Tom Tracy/FPG International; 851 (t), Daily Telegraph Colour Library/International Stock Photo; 853 (bl), Roger Tully/Tony Stone Images; 854 (cr), Warren Faidley/International Stock Photo; 855 (tl), Matt Brown/Uniphoto; 858 (tr), D. Roundtree/The Image Bank; 862 (tr), Ron Scherl/Stage Image; 865 (cl), Marc Romanelli/The Image Bank; 872 (cr), Merritt Vincent/PhotoEdit; 874 (br), Peter Pearson/Tony Stone Images; 874–875 (bckgd), UPI/Corbis Bettmann; 875 (tr), Carnegie Library, Pittsburgh.
CHAPTER FOURTEEN: Page 884 (bc), David Parker/Science Photo Library/Photo Researchers; 884 (br), Spencer Jones/FPG International; 885 (t), Tony Stone Images; 886 (t), Superstock; 892 (cl), VCG/FPG International; 893 (tl), Joe Towers/The Stock Market; 894 (t), Grant V. Faint/The Image Bank; 900 (br), Walter Bibicow/The Image Bank; 901 (tl), Uniphoto; 902 (t), Superstock, photo manipulation by Morgan-Cain & Associates; 905 (cr), Ben Osborne/Tony Stone Images; 906 (c), Image Copyright © 2001 PhotoDisc, Inc.; 907 (br), Superstock; 908 (cl), Francois Gohier/Photo Researchers; 909 (t), Adam Peiperl/The Stock Market; 915 (br), Warren Bolster/Tony Stone Images; 915 (cl), Dennis Hallinan/FPG International; 916 (br), Will Ryan/The Stock Market; 917 (t), Superstock; 920 (frame), Image Copyright © 2001 PhotoDisc, Inc.; 920 (tr), Erich Lessing/Art Resource, NY; 921 (tr), Rich Kane/SportsChrome USA, 922 (tl), Uniphoto; 922 (tr), David Madison/Tony Stone Images; 925 (bl), Henry T. Kaiser/ Uniphoto; 927 (bl), Bill Beatty/Visuals Unlimited; 928 (bl), Corbis; 928 (l), T. Shinoda/Photonica; 929 (br), Randal Alhadeff/HRW Photo; 929 (r), T. Simabukuro/Photonica; 929 (tr), Corbis.

ILLUSTRATIONS

All technical and line art by Morgan-Cain & Associates. Other art, unless otherwise noted, by Holt, Rinehart & Winston.

Abbreviated as follows: (t) top, (b) bottom, (l) left, (r) right, (c) center.
CHAPTER ONE: Page 3 (cr), Morgan-Cain & Associates; 9 (bl), Stephen Durke/Washington-Artists' Represents; 22 (bl), Michael Morrow Design; 42 (c), Visual Sense Illustration/Margo Davies Leclair; 43 (t), Ian Phillips; 50 (cr), Leslie Kell; 51 (tl), Leslie Kell; 54 (tr), Stephen Durke/Washington-Artists' Represents; 66 (t), Michael Morrow Design. **CHAPTER TWO:** Page 88 (c), Leslie Kell; 90 (cr), Stephen Durke/Washington-Artists' Represents; 92 (cl), Stephen Durke/Washington-Artists' Represents; 100 (bl), Stephen Durke/Washington-Artists' Represents; 107 (bl), Stephen Durke/Washington-Artists' Represents; 113 (tc), Stephen Durke/Washington-Artists' Represents; 118 (t), Stephen Durke/Washington-Artists' Represents; 123 (c), Stephen Durke/Washington-Artists' Represents; 124 (tr), Leslie Kell. **CHAPTER THREE:** Page 154 (c), Morgan-Cain & Associates; 158 (br), Stephen Durke/Washington-Artists' Represents; 172 (c), Leslie Kell; 182 (tr), Leslie Kell. **CHAPTER FOUR:** Page 214 (c), Morgan-Cain & Associates; 232 (tc), Stephen Durke/Washington-Artists' Represents; 244 (tr), Leslie Kell; 249 (br), Leslie Kell; 250 (tc), Jun Park. **CHAPTER FIVE:** Page 274 (c), Stephen Durke/Washington-Artists' Represents; 279 (cl), Stephen Durke/Washington-Artists' Represents; 283 (cr), Stephen Durke/ Washington-Artists' Represents; 289 (tr), Stephen Durke/Washington-Artists' Represents; 290 (t), Uhl Studio Incorporated; 295 (tr), Uhl Studio Incorporated; 307 (cr), Stephen Durke/Washington-Artists' Represents; 312 (cl), Uhl Studio Incorporated; 314 (tc), Stephen Durke/Washington-Artists' Represents. **CHAPTER SIX:** Page 360 (tl), Leslie Kell; 368 (cr), Martha Newbigging; 374 (cr), Stephen Durke/Washington-Artists' Represents; 383 (cr), Stephen Durke/Washington-Artists' Represents; 391 (cr), Stephen Durke/Washington-Artists' Represents; 398 (br), Nenad Jakesevic; 405 (bl), Stephen Durke/Washington-Artists' Represents; 407 (br), Leslie Kell; 408 (t), Jun Park. **CHAPTER SEVEN:** Page 424 (tr), Stephen Durke/Washington-Artists' Represents; 448 (tr), Uhl Studio Incorporated; 453 (tr), Stephen Durke/Washington-Artists' Represents; 458 (tc), Leslie Kell.
CHAPTER EIGHT: Page 478 (c), Uhl Studio Incorporated; 484 (tr), Uhl Studio Incorporated; 504 (t), Stephen Durke/Washington-Artists' Represents; 510 (b), Stephen Durke/Washington-Artists' Represents; 533 (tr), Stephen Durke/Washington-Artists' Represents; 544 (c), Leslie Kell. **CHAPTER NINE:** Page 560–1 (all), Uhl Studio Incorporated; 562 (tr), Stephen Durke/Washington-Artists' Represents; 564 (br), Ortelius Design; 577 (bl), Jun Park; 586, (br), Jun Park; 593 (bl), Leslie Kell; 610 (bl), Uhl Studio Incorporated; 613 (t), Stephen Durke/Washington-Artists' Represents.
CHAPTER TEN: Page 634 (br), Michael Herman; 643 (t), Stephen Durke/ Washington-Artists' Represents; 643 (t), Stephen Durke/Washington-Artists' Represents; 645 (cr), Leslie Kell; 647 (cl), Stephen Durke/Washington-Artists' Represents; 650 (bc), Leslie Kell; 657 (br), Leslie Kell; 662 (br), Stephen Durke/Washington-Artists' Represents; 675 (tr), Leslie Kell; 677 (tr), Leslie Kell. **CHAPTER ELEVEN:** Page 711 (br), Stephen Durke/Washington-Artists' Represents; 719 (t), Uhl Studio Incorporated; 722 (b), Uhl Studio Incorporated; 725 (br), Michael Herman; 727 (bl), Leslie Kell; 728 (cr), Michael Herman; 744 (bl), Pronk & Associates. **CHAPTER TWELVE:** Page 762 (b), Morgan-Cain & Associates; 763 (tr), Stephen Durke/ Washington-Artists' Represents; 782 (cr), Leslie Kell; 785 (cl), Bernadette Lau. **CHAPTER THIRTEEN:** Page 828 (cl), Morgan-Cain & Associates; 831 (cr), Morgan-Cain & Associates; 831 (bl), Nenad Jakesevic; 833 (tr), Terry Guyer; 834 (cr), Nenad Jakesevic; 835 (cr), Terry Guyer; 837 (tr), Leslie Kell; 849 (cl), Uhl Studio Incorporated; 850 (cr), Terry Guyer; 856 (cr), Uhl Studio Incorporated; 856 (br) David Puckett; 867 (t), Stephen Durke/Washington-Artists' Represents; 872 (bl), Morgan-Cain & Associates; 873 (tr), Terry Guyer; 873 (cr), Stephen Durke/Washington-Artists' Represents. **CHAPTER FOURTEEN:** Page 892 (cr), Morgan-Cain & Associates; 892 (b), Morgan-Cain & Associates; 893 (tr), Morgan-Cain & Associates; 896 (tr), Morgan-Cain & Associates; 901 (br), Leslie Kell; 927 (c), Morgan-Cain & Associates; 932 (all), Morgan-Cain & Associates.

PERMISSIONS

For permission to reprint copyrighted material, grateful acknowledgment is made to the following sources:

The New York Times Company: From "The Quest for True Randomness Finally Appears Successful" by James Gleick from *The New York Times*, April 19, 1988. Copyright © 1988 by The New York Times Company. From "Biggest Division a Giant Leap in Math" by Gina Kolata and "Factoring a 155-Digit Number: The Problem Solved" from *The New York Times*, June 20, 1990. Copyright © 1990 by The New York Times Company.

Sandusky Register, Ohio: From "Coasting to Records" from *Sandusky Register*, July 27, 1989. Copyright © 1989 by Sandusky Register.

St. Louis Mercantile Library Association: Photo caption "St. Louis Can Now Boast of the Nation's Highest Memorial" from "Arch Completed but Fight for Funds to Finish Memorial Still Goes On" from *St. Louis Globe-Democrat*, October 29, 1965. From the collections of the St. Louis Mercantile Library at the University of Missouri, St. Louis.

Time Inc.: From "Time for Some Fuzzy Thinking" by Philip Elmer-Dewitt from *Time*, September 25, 1989. Copyright © 1989 by Time Inc.

Marilyn vos Savant and Parade: From column "Ask Marilyn™" by Marilyn vos Savant from *PARADE*, September 9, 1990. Copyright © 1990 by Parade.